# PSYCHOLOGY

# PSYCHOLOGY

## An International Perspective

### MICHAEL W. EYSENCK

Ψ Psychology Press
Taylor & Francis Group

HOVE AND NEW YORK

Published in 2004 by Psychology Press Ltd, 27 Church Road, Hove, East Sussex, BN3 2FA

www.psypress.co.uk

Simultaneously published in the USA and Canada by Psychology Press Inc, 29 West 35th Street, New York, NY 10001

*Psychology Press is part of the Taylor & Francis Group*

*British Library Cataloguing in Publication Data*

A catalogue record for this book is available from the British Library

*Library of Congress Cataloging-in-Publication Data*
Eysenck, Michael W.
 Psychology: an international perspective/Michael W. Eysenck.
   p. cm.
 Includes bibliographical references and index.
 ISBN 1-84169-360-X (hardcover)—ISBN 1-84169-361-8 (pbk.)
 1. Psychology–Textbooks. I. Title.

 BF121.E954 2004
 150—dc22

                                        2004004644

 ISBN 1-84169-360-X (Hbk)
 ISBN 1-84169-361-8  (Pbk)

Typeset in India by Newgen Imaging Systems (P) Ltd
Printed and bound in Spain by Book Print SL

*To William with love*

Learning without thought is labour lost;
thought without learning is perilous

CONFUCIUS (c. 551–479 BC)

# Acknowledgements

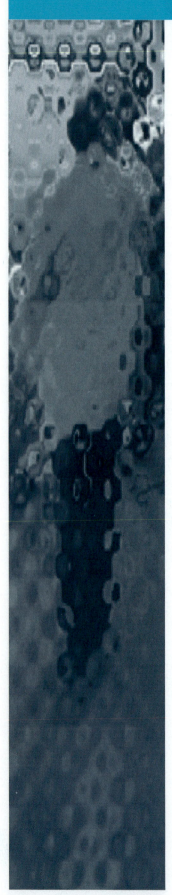

| | |
|---|---|
| Consultants | Evie Bentley, Hans-Werner Bierhoff, Roz Brody, Alan Carr, David Carey, Jo-Anne Cartwright, John Cartwright, Tony Cassidy, Susan Cave, Colin Cooper, Richard Dafters, Dmitry Davydov, Terry Dowdall, George Erdos, Philip Erwin, Eamon Fulcher, Usha Goswami, Ruth Green, Trevor Harley, Peter Hayes, Paul Hibbard, Casper Hulshof, Barbara Krahe, Daniel Lagace-Seguin, Nick Lund, John Pearce, Donald Pennington, Rosey Phillips, Ken Richardson, S. Ian Robertson, Mark Rogers, Curtis Samuels, Kevin Silber, John Stirling, Rolf Ulrich, Nick Wade, Wim Waterink, Robyn Young |
| Editor | Lucy Farr |
| Production manager | Mandy Collison |
| Production editor | Sarah Webb |
| Copy editor | Liz Quarterman |
| Proofreader | Lesley Edwards |
| Cold readers | Frances Auty, Dawn Booth, Katherine Carson, Eleanor Flood, Annette Musker, Lesley Winchester |
| Author index | Ingrid Lock |
| Subject index | Lewis Derrick |
| Typesetting | Newgen Imaging Systems (P) Ltd |
| Cartoons | Sean Longcroft, Foghorn Studio, Brighton |
| Cover design | Terry Foley, anú design |
| Printer | Book Print SL, Spain |

# Contents

# About the Author

Michael W. Eysenck is one of the best-known British psychologists. He is Professor of Psychology and head of the psychology department at Royal Holloway University of London, which is one of the leading departments in the United Kingdom. His academic interests lie mainly in cognitive psychology, with much of his research focusing on the role of cognitive factors in anxiety in normal and clinical populations.

He has written nearly 30 books over the years. His previous textbooks published by Psychology Press include *Simply Psychology* (1996, 2002), *Cognitive Psychology: A Student's Handbook* (2000, 2005, with Mark Keane), *Psychology for AS Level* (2000 with Cara Flanagan, 2003), *Principles of Cognitive Psychology* (1993, 2001), *Psychology for A2 Level* (2001, with Cara Flanagan), *Key Topics in A2 Psychology* (2003), and *Psychology: A Student's Handbook* (2000). He has also written the research monographs *Anxiety and Cognition: A Unified Theory* (1997) and *Anxiety: The Cognitive Perspective* (1992), along with the popular title *Happiness: Facts and Myths* (1990). He has lived with his wife Christine in Wimbledon, south-west London, for the past 30 years. He supports Crystal Palace football club.

# Preface

One of the rewards of writing a book covering most of psychology is that you learn a lot in the process. There has been an explosion in psychological research in recent years, and it has been gratifying to me to see how fruitful all this research has been. We now have an excellent understanding of the complexities of human behaviour from several different perspectives, including the cognitive, social, developmental, and biopsychological. In addition, we have great knowledge of key dimensions of individual differences, and the factors responsible for individual differences in personality and intelligence. Finally, and in practical terms most importantly, psychologists have discovered so much about mental disorders that we have a range of very effective forms of therapy to relieve the misery previously experienced by tens of millions of individuals. All in all, the key message of this book is that psychology has come of age as a fully developed and successful science.

One of the themes running through the book is the importance of the cross-cultural approach to psychology. There was a time in the not-too-distant past in which it was implicitly (or even explicitly) assumed that the behaviour of American college students was representative of the behaviour of people of all ages living in amazingly diverse cultures! This assumption was convincingly disproved many years ago, and psychologists are now moving on to the task of understanding the reasons behind the similarities and differences we observe in different cultures.

I would like to express my great thanks to all those who so kindly agreed to read a first draft of the manuscript or of parts of it, particularly Evie Bentley, Roz Brody, and Susan Cave. Their comments have helped considerably to improve the final manuscript by correcting some of my errors and by identifying major omissions. As authors always feel duty-bound to say (but it is absolutely true in my case), I accept total responsibility for any errors that remain. I would also like to thank Mike Forster, Lucy Farr, and Mandy Collison, and everyone else at Psychology Press who provided help and encouragement as the book was being written, and gently coaxed me as and when necessary. Mike Forster, who is in charge of Psychology Press, has an uncanny knack of coming up with a seemingly endless stream of good ideas for books that I might write. More importantly, he has been very supportive of my book-writing activities for 20 years so far, and this has encouraged me to keep going.

Finally, I want to thank my family for their total support throughout the writing of this book. Without that support, my life would be poorer and this book would have remained unwritten. This book is dedicated to my son William, in spite of the fact that he has decided that medicine is a lot more interesting and important than psychology.

Michael W. Eysenck
SYDNEY, AUSTRALIA

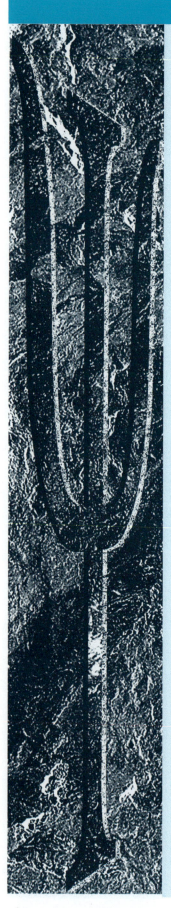

# Introduction

## WHAT IS PSYCHOLOGY?

We will make a start by considering the meaning of the term "psychology". The commonest definition is that it is the scientific study of behaviour, with most psychologists accepting the importance of observing and measuring behaviour. However, this definition is too limited. The reason is that the main interest of psychologists is usually in trying to understand *why* people or members of other species behave in certain ways. To achieve that understanding, we must consider internal processes and motives. Thus, we arrive at the following definition:

*Psychology is a science in which behavioural and other evidence is used to understand the internal processes leading people (and members of other species) to behave as they do.*

## Diversity of psychology

As you read this book, you may be bewildered by the numerous approaches psychologists have adopted in their attempts to understand human behaviour. These approaches exist because our behaviour is jointly determined by several factors, such as the following:

- The specific stimuli presented to us.
- Our recent experiences (e.g., being stuck in a traffic jam).
- Our genetic endowment.
- Our physiological system.
- Our cognitive system (our perceptions, thoughts, and memories).
- The social environment.
- The cultural environment.
- Our previous life experiences (including those of childhood).
- Our personal characteristics (including intelligence, personality, and mental health).

The notion that there are various levels of explanation can be illustrated by taking a concrete example. Suppose one man attacks another man very aggressively by punching him repeatedly on the head and body. How can we understand this behaviour? It may depend in part on the genes that the man has inherited from his parents. It may also depend on the attacker's childhood experiences, for example, the presence of violence within the family. It may also depend in part on a recent stressful experience such as being caught in heavy traffic. The attacker's clinical history may also be relevant. For example, he may have a history of psychopathic or anti-social behaviour. It may depend on his thoughts and feelings (e.g., the other person upset him). It may depend on social factors. For example, the man behaving aggressively may believe that the other man has insulted members of his family. It may depend on the physiological state of the man behaving aggressively: his internal bodily state may be highly aroused and agitated. Finally, it may depend on cultural factors, in that expressing one's aggression by punching is regarded as more acceptable (or less unacceptable) in some cultures than others.

The key point of the above example is that there is no *single* "correct" interpretation of the aggressive man's behaviour. Indeed, it is likely that several of the factors discussed above contributed to his behaviour. Thus, the scope of psychology needs to be very broad if we are to understand human behaviour. Eysenck (1994b, p. 15) argued that psychology is a multi-disciplinary science, pointing out that "psychology has been enriched by physiologists, neurologists, sociologists, zoologists, anthropologists, biologists, and others".

Some of the main approaches within psychology are as follows: biological psychology, cognitive psychology, individual differences, developmental psychology, social psychology, and abnormal psychology. We will consider below *what* each approach is concerned with, and *why* that approach is important. When we consider any given approach, some indication will be given of the topics discussed within that approach. However, most topics are relevant to several approaches, and so allocating topics to approaches has its limitations. For example, personality is dealt with within the individual differences approach. However, individual differences in personality depend in part on genetic factors (biological approach), on cognitive processes (cognitive approach), on developmental factors (developmental approach), and on social processes (social approach). Thus, the various approaches are not as separate from each other as might be imagined.

## Biological psychology

It is hard to imagine the enormous impact that *Origin of Species* by Charles Darwin (1809–1882) had on the way people think about themselves. Before its publication in 1859, most people assumed that only human beings have souls, and so we are radically different from other species. The notion that human beings had evolved from other species suggested this view of the importance of the human species needed reassessment. However, many people found it very hard to accept that human beings should be regarded simply as members of the animal kingdom.

Darwin was a biologist rather than a psychologist, but his views on evolution had several major implications for psychology. First, psychologists realised it was worth considering human psychology from the biological perspective. Second, Darwin emphasised the importance of heredity, and the notion that offspring tend to resemble their parents. This suggested to psychologists that the role of heredity in influencing human behaviour should be explored. Third, Darwin focused on variations among the members of a species, with evolution selectively favouring some members rather than others (i.e., survival of the fittest). This led to an interest in the role of genetic factors in explaining individual differences in intelligence and personality.

What is the scope of biological psychology (sometimes known as biopsychology)? It is concerned with the attempt to understand human behaviour from the biological perspective. It involves studying physiological processes within the body, the detailed functioning of the brain, and so on. Biological psychology is dealt with in Chapters 2–5 of this book, and a wide range of topics is covered. For example, we consider heredity, emotion, stress, hunger, sex, sleep, the effects of drugs, and the role played by hormones and neurotransmitters.

Why is this approach to psychology of importance? First, everyone (apart from identical or monozygotic twins) has their own unique set of genes, and genes influence our intelligence, personality, and behaviour. Second, our motivational systems (e.g., hunger, sex) were developed originally as a result of the biological imperative to survive and to pass on our genes to successive generations. Third, the processes studied by biological psychologists are involved in virtually all human behaviour.

## Cognitive psychology

The study of human cognition, with its focus on thinking and other mental processes, originated with Plato and Aristotle. It remained the dominant area within psychology for 2000 years. However, it was relatively ignored during the first half of the twentieth century because of the influence of **behaviourism**, an approach to psychology in which the emphasis was on behaviour rather than internal processes. In contrast, cognitive psychologists focus mainly on the internal processes and structures involved in cognition (defined as "the mental act or process by which knowledge is acquired" in *Collins English Dictionary*), and so are interested in observable responses mainly to the extent that they provide information about these underlying processes and structures.

Charles Darwin, 1809–1882.

KEY TERM

**Behaviourism:** an American school of psychology with an emphasis on measuring observable behaviour.

Cognitive psychology became of great importance in the mid-1950s. At about this time, several major cognitive psychologists (e.g., Donald Broadbent, Jerome Bruner, George Miller, Herb Simon) began to explore cognitive processes and structures in detail. However, even they probably didn't fully realise the extent to which cognitive psychology would become the dominant approach within the whole of psychology, strongly influencing the social, developmental, and abnormal approaches.

There are several main areas of research within cognitive psychology, including attention, perception, learning, memory, problem solving, and language. Taken together, these areas of research allow us to understand the complex processes intervening between presenting an individual with some stimulus (e.g., a question on the *Who Wants to be a Millionaire?* TV programme) and his/her response (e.g., correct or incorrect answer). All the main areas of cognitive psychology are discussed at some point in Chapters 6–11.

Why is this approach to psychology so important? First, as mentioned earlier, the understanding of human cognition developed by cognitive psychologists has had a great impact on social, developmental, and abnormal psychology. Second, the insights obtained by cognitive psychologists have had real-life application in the design of computer and other systems to make them relatively easy for us to use. Third, it is becoming increasingly possible to assist brain-damaged patients to regain some of their lost cognitive skills by using our accumulating knowledge of human cognition.

Cognitive explanations are in part inspired by information-processing concepts, using terms like "input", "processing", and "networks".

## Individual differences

The systematic study of individual differences started with the work of Sir Francis Galton (1822–1911), a cousin of Charles Darwin. The publication of Galton's book *Hereditary Genius* in 1869 was a landmark in the study of individual differences, with the previous lack of interest in the subject being rather surprising. As Murphy and Kovach (1972) pointed out, "Individual differences had not been seriously treated before as part of the subject matter of psychology. Perhaps their neglect had been the most extraordinary blind spot in previous formal psychology. It was Darwinism, rather than the previous history of psychology, which brought about an interest in the problem."

In principle, the study of individual differences includes comparisons between children of different ages, between normal and abnormal populations, between healthy and brain-damaged individuals, and so on. In practice, however, researchers on individual differences have focused mainly on intelligence and personality (discussed in Chapters 12 and 13 of this book). One of the key issues with respect to both intelligence and personality is to try to understand the factors responsible for individual differences in those characteristics. As mentioned above, the evidence suggests that our intelligence and personality are influenced by genetic factors, by developmental factors, by cognitive factors, and by social factors.

Why is this approach to psychology important? First, individual differences in intelligence and personality influence most forms of behaviour, and the magnitude of their influence is often as great as that of the situation in which the behaviour is performed. Second, if our educational system is to be effective, account needs to be taken of the particular skills and abilities possessed by individual children. Third, it is necessary in many real-life situations to use information about individuals' intelligence and personality. For example, it is very important in personnel selection to select the applicant whose personal characteristics are most suitable for the job in question.

Sir Francis Galton, 1822–1911.

## Developmental psychology

It is generally accepted nowadays that it is important to study the psychology of childhood both for its own sake and because it helps us to understand adult thinking and behaviour. However, it was only when Sigmund Freud's psychoanalytic theories became widely known in the early part of the twentieth century that serious attention was paid to developmental psychology. Thereafter, the greatest impetus to developmental psychology came from the work of Jean Piaget (1896–1980), who spent several decades studying the childhood development of thinking and intelligence.

The experiences we have during childhood have a great impact on our adult lives.

Social psychology looks at our relationships with other people and society.

Developmental psychology is concerned mainly with the changes occurring during the course of childhood, and with the impact of childhood experiences on adult behaviour. At the risk of over-simplification, two main areas of development are of fundamental importance. First, there is cognitive development, which involves the child developing skills of dealing with increasingly complex tasks. Second, there is social development, which involves the child developing social skills, and so interacting effectively with other people. Cognitive and social development are discussed in considerable detail in Chapters 14–17 of this book.

Why is this approach to psychology of importance? First, we can obtain some understanding of adult behaviour by considering the kinds of experiences adults had during the years of childhood. Second, if we could understand the factors promoting good cognitive development, we would be in a strong position to improve the educational system so as to realise the potential of children more fully than happens at present. Third, if we begin to understand more clearly the factors underlying social development, this can help to ensure that as many children as possible develop good social skills.

## Social psychology

Social psychology was one of the last areas of psychology to be fully accepted. As Thomson (1968, p. 370) says in his historical review, "Social psychology did not become sufficiently coherent and technically advanced to receive much recognition until after the Second World War."

Social psychology covers numerous topics, several of which are discussed in Chapters 18–21 of this book. Some social psychologists are concerned with processes within individuals (e.g., their attitudes and beliefs). Other social psychologists focus on networks of friendships and relationships that characterise the social interactions of everyday life. Still other social psychologists consider broader issues concerned with intergroup relations, including important issues such as prejudice and discrimination.

Why is this approach to psychology of importance? First, it takes full account of the fact that we are social animals, who continually interact with other people. Even when we are alone, we use social knowledge to make sense of our lives, and we reflect on social events in which we have been involved. Second, social psychologists have discovered that there are numerous distortions and biases in our perceptions of ourselves and other people. It is desirable that we develop a fuller understanding of the strengths and limitations of our social perceptions. Third, our behaviour is often influenced by other people to a much greater extent than we realise. Once again, it is desirable that we become more fully aware of the powerful impact of social influence on our everyday behaviour.

## Abnormal psychology

For many centuries, the treatment applied to those suffering from mental disorders was positively barbaric. It was believed that mental disorders were caused by demons or other supernatural forces. Popular "cures" for mental illness were based on the idea of making things as unpleasant as possible for the demon, and included immersing the patient in boiling hot water, flogging, starvation, and torture. As is well-known, Sigmund Freud (1856–1939) was the first psychologist to argue strongly that psychological approaches to treatment were needed *and* to provide such an approach by developing psychoanalysis.

Abnormal psychology is not only concerned with producing effective forms of therapy for patients suffering from mental disorders. It also deals with issues such as developing satisfactory systems for diagnosing and classifying mental disorders and understanding the numerous factors causing mental disorders. These key issues are all considered in detail in Chapters 22 and 23 of this book.

Why is this approach to psychology important? First, one of the main long-term goals of abnormal psychology is to develop a detailed understanding of the factors underlying mental disorders in order to try to prevent their occurrence. Second, as our ability to diagnose and classify mental disorders increases, so does the ability of clinical psychologists and psychiatrists to identify appropriate forms of treatment for individuals with mental disorders. Third, the study of abnormal psychology has led to substantial improvements in therapy, thereby dramatically reducing human misery.

## Methods in psychology

As we have seen, psychologists have used several approaches to arrive at a detailed understanding of human behaviour. They also differ among themselves as to the best method or methods to use to achieve that understanding. Many argue that psychology is like other sciences, in that understanding is most likely to result from detailed and well-controlled experiments carried out under laboratory conditions. Most of the research discussed in this book is of that type. However, there is a potential limitation with such research. It is important for psychological studies to possess **ecological validity** (meaning that the findings are applicable to everyday life), but this is lacking in some laboratory studies.

Some psychologists argue that the best way to ensure ecological validity is to use a range of non-experimental methods. For example, people can be observed going about their everyday lives, they can be interviewed, or they can be studied over time in great detail by means of a case study. Thus, there is a very wide range of techniques available to psychologists. The various methods (together with their strengths and limitations) are discussed in much more detail by Eysenck (2000) and by Gravetter and Forzano (2002).

What is the best way of studying people? There is no clear answer to that question. Each method has its own strengths and limitations, and each method is more appropriately used in some situations than in others. However, the **experimental method** is of particular importance. It involves controlling some aspect of the environment (the independent variable) in order to assess its impact on participants' behaviour (the dependent variable). Philosophers of science tell us that it is impossible to establish causality with certainty. However, the experimental method has the great advantage over other methods in that it allows us to have some confidence that the independent variable has influenced the dependent variable.

Psychologists hope that by combining information from all methods we will finally achieve the goals of psychology. As you will discover as you read this book, considerable progress has been made. However, we are still some way from reaching those goals!

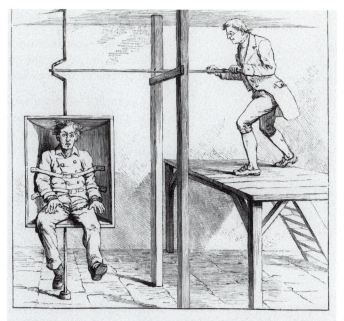

THE DOCTOR THINKS THAT "NO WELL-REGULATED INSTITUTION SHOULD BE UNPROVIDED WITH THE CIRCULATING SWING." 1818.

This illustration from 1818 shows a "Swing to Treat Depression". The circulating swing was supposed to bring the depressive back to "sound reasoning".

*The Rake's Progress: Scene in Bedlam* by William Hogarth. A group of mentally disturbed patients sits in Bethlehem Hospital, known as Bedlam, in London. Thankfully, substantial improvements in therapy have been made since this scene was sketched in the eighteenth century.

**KEY TERMS**
**Ecological validity:** the extent to which the findings of a study are applicable to the real world.
**Experimental method:** an approach to research involving manipulation of some aspect of the environment (independent variable) in order to observe its effects on some aspect of the participants' behaviour (dependent variable).

## Is psychology a science?

There is no consensus on the answer to this question. However, we will try to make progress in answering the question by seeing the extent to which psychology possesses the main criteria of science. Accordingly, we will start by identifying those criteria:

1. *Controlled observations.* In most sciences (except astronomy and a few others), it is typical for experiments to involve observing the effects of some specific manipulation (e.g., mixing two chemicals together). As applied to psychology, this generally involves observing the effects of some manipulation of the environment on participants' behaviour.

2. *Objectivity.* It has often been argued that science requires the collection of data in an objective way. However, it is more realistic to claim that scientists should be as objective as possible. Popper (1969, 1972) pointed out that scientific observations are theory driven rather than objective. The famous demonstration he used in his lectures involved telling his audience, "Observe!" Their obvious and immediate retort was, "Observe what?" This demonstration makes the point that no-one observes without some idea of what they are looking for. Thus, what you observe depends in part on what you expect to see.

3. *Testing theoretical predictions.* Scientific experiments are typically carried out to test the predictions of some theory. This makes sense, because there is in principle an infinite number of experiments that could be carried out, and scientific theories assist in the task of identifying which experiments are worthwhile.

4. *Falsifiability.* According to Popper (1969), the hallmark of science is **falsifiability**, which is the notion that scientific theories can potentially be disproved by evidence. You may think that this sounds odd, and that the focus should be on proving theories correct. However, they can never be proved to be correct. Even if a theory has been supported by the findings from hundreds of experiments, it is still possible it may be disproved in the future, perhaps in some culture in which the theory has not been tested so far.

5. *Replicability.* It is important for scientific research to possess **replicability**, meaning that many (or most) of its findings can be replicated or repeated. If we obtained different findings every time we carried out an experiment, we would be unable to make any real progress.

6. *Use of a paradigm.* According to Kuhn (1962, 1977), the most essential ingredient in a science is a **paradigm**, which is a general theoretical orientation accepted by the great majority of workers in any given field of study. Kuhn argued that there are three distinct stages in the development of a science. First, there is pre-science, in which there is no paradigm and a wide range of opinion about the best theoretical approach to adopt. Second, there is normal science, in which there is a generally accepted paradigm. Third, there is revolutionary science, in which the problems with the current paradigm become so great that it is eventually overthrown and replaced by a different paradigm (this is known as paradigm shift).

How many of the above criteria for a science are satisfied by psychology? Some research in psychology satisfies all (or nearly all) of them. As we will see in the rest of this book, participants' behaviour has been observed under controlled conditions in huge numbers of studies using the experimental method. Data are often collected in a relatively objective way (e.g., by having the participants' responses recorded by a computer), and most experiments are designed to test various predictions from pre-existing theories. In addition, most theories in psychology are falsifiable, although this is certainly not true of all of them. For example, it is hard (or impossible) to imagine any findings which would disprove Freud's notion that the mind consists of three parts (id, ego, and superego; see Chapter 13). Furthermore, many of the findings in psychology have proved to be replicable.

Kuhn (1962) argued that psychology has failed to develop a paradigm, and so remains at the pre-science stage. In support of this argument is the fact that psychology is an unusually fragmented discipline. It has connections with several other disciplines, including biology, physiology, biochemistry, neurology, and sociology. This fragmentation and diversity make it unlikely that agreement can be reached on a common paradigm or general theoretical orientation.

Valentine (1982, 1992) argued for a different position. She claimed that behaviourism could be regarded as coming close to being a paradigm. As she pointed out, behaviourism has had a massive influence on psychology through its insistence that psychology is the study of behaviour, and that behaviour should be observed in controlled experiments. However, behaviourism's greatest impact on psychology has been at the methodological level, with its emphasis on research methods focusing on the measurement of behaviour. In contrast, a paradigm in Kuhn's sense is more concerned with a general theoretical orientation. Thus, behaviourism does not seem to be a paradigm, and Kuhn (1962) may well be right to place psychology at the pre-science stage.

In my opinion, the main problem with much of psychology relates to the criterion that observations should be made under controlled conditions. It is true that we can manipulate certain variables under controlled conditions when use is made of the experimental method. However, it is certainly not true that we can manipulate *all* variables of interest. More specifically, the experimental method can most easily be used when we want to study the effects of the immediate situation on behaviour. However, our behaviour is also determined by numerous factors in addition to the immediate situation, and most of these factors cannot be manipulated. These factors include recent events (e.g., row with boyfriend), our physical health, our personality, childhood events (e.g., parents divorcing), genetic factors, cultural expectations, and so on. The fact that we cannot control these factors (or can only control them with difficulty) limits the development of psychology as a fully scientific discipline.

Before Copernicus showed that the planets, including the earth, revolved around the sun, all astronomical theories had been based on the paradigm that the earth was the centre of the universe. The complete change in science post-Copernicus is an example of a paradigm shift.

## "PSYCHOLOGY IS JUST COMMON SENSE"

An unusual feature of psychology is the way that everyone is to some extent a psychologist. We all observe the behaviour of other people and of ourselves, and everyone has access to their own conscious thoughts and feelings. One of the main tasks of psychologists is to predict behaviour, and the prediction of behaviour is important in everyday life. The better we are able to anticipate how people will react in any given situation, the more contented and rewarding our social interactions are likely to be.

The fact that everyone is a psychologist has led many people to under-estimate the achievements of scientific psychology. If the findings of scientific psychology are in line with common sense, then it can be argued that they tell us nothing we did not already know. On the other hand, if the findings do not accord with common sense, then people often respond, "I don't believe it!"

There are several problems with the view that psychology is no better than common sense. It is misleading to assume that common sense forms a coherent set of assumptions about behaviour. This can be seen if we regard proverbs as providers of commonsensical views. A girl parted from her lover may be saddened if she thinks of the proverb, "Out of sight, out of mind." However, she may cheer up if she tells herself that "Absence makes the heart grow fonder."

"Look before you leap" vs "He who hesitates is lost".

There are several other pairs of proverbs expressing opposite meanings. For example, "Look before you leap" can be contrasted with "He who hesitates is lost", and "Many hands make light labour" is the opposite of "Too many cooks spoil the broth." As common sense involves such inconsistent views of human behaviour, it cannot be used as the basis for explaining that behaviour.

The notion that psychology is just common sense can also be disproved by considering psychological studies in which the findings were very unexpected. A famous example is the work of Stanley Milgram (1974), discussed more fully in Chapter 20. The experimenter divided his participants into pairs to play the roles of teacher and pupil in a simple learning task. The "teacher" was asked to give electric shocks to the "pupil" every time the wrong answer was given, and to increase the shock intensity each time. At 180 volts, the "pupil" yelled, "I can't stand the pain", and by 270 volts the response had become an agonised scream. If the "teacher" showed a reluctance to give the shocks, the experimenter (a professor of psychology) urged him/her to continue.

Do you think you would be willing to give the maximum (and potentially deadly) 450-volt shock in this experiment? What percentage of people do you think would be willing to do it? Milgram (1974) found that everyone denied they personally would do any such thing. Psychiatrists at a leading medical school predicted that only one person in a thousand would go on to the 450-volt stage. In fact, about 60% of Milgram's participants gave the maximum shock, which is 600 times as many people as the expert psychiatrists had predicted! Thus, people are much more conformist and obedient to authority than they realise. There is a strong tendency to go along with the decisions of someone (e.g., a professor of psychology) who seems to be a competent authority figure.

In sum, common sense is of little use in understanding and predicting human behaviour. According to most psychologists, the best way of achieving these goals is via the experimental and other methods available to the psychological researcher. The fruits of psychological research fill the pages of this book.

Hindsight bias

## Hindsight bias

We have seen that it is wrong to assume that the findings in psychology merely confirm common sense. Why is it, then, that so many people claim that most psychological findings are not surprising and contain nothing new? In other words, why do they argue, "I knew it all along?" An important part of the answer was identified by Fischhoff and Beyth (1975). They asked American students to estimate the probability of various possible outcomes on the eve of President Nixon's trips to China and Russia. After the trips were over, the students were asked to do the same task, but without taking into account their knowledge of what had actually happened. In spite of these instructions, participants with the benefit of hindsight gave events that had actually happened a much higher probability than they had done before the events had occurred. The participants had added their knowledge of what had happened to what they already knew in such a way that they could not remember how uncertain things had looked before the trips. This tendency to be wise after the event is known as **hindsight bias**.

Slovic and Fischhoff (1977) carried out a similar study involving predictions about the results of a series of scientific experiments. Some participants were told what had happened in the first experiment of the series, but were told *not* to use this information when making their predictions. However, participants thought a given outcome was much more likely to occur in future experiments if it had already been obtained. This is another example of hindsight bias.

Hindsight bias is very strong, and is hard to eliminate. In another study, Fischhoff (1977) told his participants about hindsight bias, and encouraged them to avoid it. However, this had little or no effect on the size of the hindsight bias. Hindsight bias poses a problem for teachers of psychology, because it can produce students who are unimpressed by almost everything in psychology!

## PSYCHOLOGY AROUND THE WORLD

Most research in psychology is carried out in the Western world, especially the United States. According to Rosenzweig (1992), 64% of the world's 56,000 researchers in psychology are Americans. Their impact on textbooks in psychology is often even greater. For example, consider Baron and Byrne's (1991) textbook on social psychology. In that book, 94% of the studies referred to were from North America, compared to 2% from Europe, 1% from Australasia, and 3% from the rest of the world. Smith and Bond (1998, p. 3) considered several textbooks in social and organisational psychology, and concluded as follows: "Among these English-language texts, the universe of social and organisational behaviours that is being sampled is almost entirely restricted to studies done within less than a dozen of the more than 200 countries in the world, constituting little more than 10 per cent of the world's population."

In spite of what has just been said, North American psychologists do *not* carry all before them. Haggbloom et al. (2002) identified the 100 most eminent psychologists of the twentieth century. They used information such as citations of an individual's work in journals, citations in introductory textbooks, and mentions in a survey in which psychologists were asked to identify the greatest psychologists of the twentieth century. Just under 20% of the 100 most eminent psychologists were non-American, nearly all of them European. The non-American psychologists included the following: Jean Piaget, Sigmund Freud, H.J. Eysenck, Carl Jung, Ivan Pavlov, Wolfgang Kohler, Joseph Wolpe, Donald Broadbent, Konrad Lorenz, Alfred Adler, Michael Rutter, Alexander Luria, Lev Vygotsky, Amos Tversky, Wilhelm Wundt, and Anna Freud. The 50 most eminent psychologists in order are shown in the box below. The research of most of these psychologists (but by no means all!) is discussed at some point in this book.

| Rank | Name | Rank | Name | Rank | Name |
|------|------|------|------|------|------|
| 1. | B.F. Skinner | 18. | Kurt Lewin | 35. | R.B. Zajonc |
| 2. | Jean Piaget | 19. | Donald Hebb | 36. | Endel Tulving |
| 3. | Sigmund Freud | 20. | George Miller | 37. | Herbert Simon |
| 4. | Albert Bandura | 21. | Clark Hull | 38. | Noam Chomsky |
| 5. | Leon Festinger | 22. | Jerome Kagan | 39. | Edward Jones |
| 6. | Carl Rogers | 23. | Carl Jung | 40. | Charles Osgood |
| 7. | Stanley Schachter | 24. | Ivan Pavlov | 41. | Solomon Asch |
| 8. | Neal Miller | 25. | Walter Mischel | 42. | Gordon Bower |
| 9. | Edward Thorndike | 26. | Harry Harlow | 43. | Harold Kelley |
| 10. | A.H. Maslow | 27. | J.P. Guilford | 44. | Roger Sperry |
| 11. | Gordon Allport | 28. | Jerome Bruner | 45. | Edward Tolman |
| 12. | Erik Erikson | 29. | Ernest Hilgard | 46. | Stanley Milgram |
| 13. | H.J. Eysenck | 30. | Lawrence Kohlberg | 47. | Arthur Jensen |
| 14. | William James | 31. | Martin Seligman | 48. | Lee Cronbach |
| 15. | David McClelland | 32. | Ulric Neiser | 49. | John Bowlby |
| 16. | Raymond Cattell | 33. | Donald Campbell | 50. | Wolfgang Kohler |
| 17. | John Watson | 34. | Roger Brown | | |

Psychoanalyst Sigmund Freud and his daughter and fellow psychoanalyst Anna Freud arrive in Paris in 1938, after fleeing the Nazi occupation of their home country, Austria. They went on to London, where Sigmund died the next year. Anna did major work in the field of child psychology until her death in 1982.

There is a tendency for one culture to judge another as being "undeveloped" or "primitive".

Words can have different meanings in different cultures. For example, the Japanese understanding of "work" is different to many other cultures because it includes the requirement to socialise with colleagues.

# Cross-cultural psychology

A central theme of this book is that psychology needs to take full account of the richness and diversity of human experience and behaviour throughout the entire world. However, note that relatively little psychological research has been carried out in many parts of the world (e.g., most of Africa). The above theme is discussed in several chapters, but a general introduction to it will be provided here. What we will be discussing is generally known as **cross-cultural psychology**, which is concerned with similarities and differences among the world's cultures. What is a culture? According to Smith and Bond (1998, p. 39), a culture "is a *relatively organised* system of shared meanings". For example, the word "work" has a rather different meaning in the Japanese culture than in others. In Japan, it typically includes going drinking after normal working hours, and sharing in other recreational activities with one's work colleagues. A broader definition was offered by Fiske (2002, p. 85):

*A culture is a socially transmitted or socially constructed constellation consisting of such things as practices, competencies, ideas, schemas, symbols, values, norms, institutions, goals, constitutive rules, artefacts, and modifications of the physical environment.*

Why is it important to study a wide range of cultures? First, most theories in psychology are based mainly (or exclusively) on findings from people living in Western societies. If there are important cultural differences, then our theories will have limited applicability. This can only be discovered by carrying out cross-cultural studies. Second, cultural influences have a significant impact on people's behaviour. As a result, we must study cultural factors to develop a full understanding of human behaviour. Third, cross-cultural research can allow us to decide which of various competing theories provides the most accurate overall account. Fourth, cross-cultural research indicates which aspects of human functioning and behaviour are universal and which vary across cultures. In general terms, we would expect basic psychological processes (e.g., detection of movement, limited capacity of attention, colour perception) to be very similar in every culture. In contrast, most social behaviour is likely to be influenced by the cultural context.

# Emic vs. etic constructs

Berry (1969) emphasised the distinction between emic constructs and etic constructs, a distinction initially made by the linguist Kenneth Pike. **Emic constructs** are specific to a given culture, and so vary from one culture to another. In contrast, **etic constructs** refer to universal factors which hold across all cultures. The notion of the "family" is an example of an etic construct. According to Berry, the history of psychology is full of examples of what are actually emic constructs mistakenly being regarded as etic constructs. The study of intelligence (discussed next) can be used to illustrate this point.

It has often been argued that the same abilities of problem solving, reasoning, memory, and so on define intelligence in every culture. Berry (1974) disagreed strongly with that view. He favoured a viewpoint known as cultural relativism, according to which the meaning of intelligence differs in each culture. For example, as Sternberg (1985, p. 53) pointed out, "Co-ordination skills that may be essential to life in a preliterate society (e.g., those motor skills required for shooting a bow and arrow) may be all but irrelevant to intelligent behaviour for most people in a literate and more 'developed' society." In Western cultures, intelligence is typically regarded as an individual's ability to think effectively and to solve complex problems. In many non-Western cultures, on the other hand, intelligence is defined in much more social terms. It is regarded as involving social responsibilities, co-operating with other people, and showing various interpersonal skills (see Chapter 12).

Most studies in cross-cultural psychology have involved comparisons between different countries. However, a country is generally *not* the same as a culture. As Smith and Bond (1998, p. 41) pointed out, "When we compare national cultures, we risk losing track of the enormous diversity found within many of the major nations of the world." For example, consider the distinction between collectivism (group-centred approach to life) and individualism (self-centred approach to life). As is discussed below, most of the evidence indicates that the American culture is individualistic rather than collectivistic. Vandello and Cohen (1999) found that that was clearly the case in the Mountain West and the Great Plains. However, collectivistic tendencies were prevalent in the Deep South, and so there is no single American culture.

It has often been assumed that most phenomena found in American research could also be observed in nearly all other cultures. This assumption is probably incorrect. For example, Smith and Bond (1998) considered several well-known phenomena in social psychology found in American research. They concluded as follows: "The only topic on which there is much evidence for consistently successful replication are the studies on obedience" (p. 31). Research on obedience to authority (see earlier in chapter) has revealed that most participants are surprisingly willing to administer potentially lethal electric shocks to another person (Milgram, 1963, 1974).

Amir and Sharon (1987) tried to repeat the findings of six American studies on two different groups within Israel. There were 64 significant findings in the American studies, only 24 of which were repeated among the Israeli participants. Thus, 40 of the American findings were not repeated. In addition, there were six new Israeli findings that had not been obtained in the American studies. Overall, this research suggested there are reasonably strong cultural differences in social behaviour.

What are the main differences between cultures? Westen (1996, p. 679) expressed some of them in vivid terms:

*By twentieth century Western standards, nearly every human who has ever lived outside the contemporary West is lazy, passive, and lacking in industriousness. In contrast, by the standards of most cultures in human history, most Westerners are self-centred and frenetic [frenzied].*

## Biases

It has often been claimed that Western psychologists show an insensitivity to cultural differences. For example, Howitt and Owusu-Bempah (1990) argued that there is clear evidence of racial bias in much of psychology. They considered every issue of the *British Journal of Social and Clinical Psychology* between 1962 and 1980. They were dismayed at the way in which Western personality tests were used inappropriately in non-Western cultures. As they pointed out (p. 399), "There were no studies which attempted to explore, for example, the Ghanaian or Chinese personality structures in their own terms rather than through Western eyes."

Owusu-Bempah and Howitt (1994) claimed to have found evidence of racism in the well-known textbook by Atkinson, Atkinson, Smith, and Bem (1993). They pointed out that Atkinson et al. tended to categorise Western cultures together, and to do the same for non-Western ones. They also identified the tendency to refer to studies on African tribes without bothering to specify which tribe or tribes had been studied. Owusu-Bempah and Howitt (p. 165) argued as follows: "The *cumulative* effect of this is the 'naturalness' of white people and their ways of life, and the resultant exclusion ... of black people and their cultures."

!Kung hunters (above) and Masai men performing a traditional dance (below). There has been a tendency for Western scientists to categorise all African tribes together, whereas, in reality, different tribes may have very different cultures.

The ability to wrestle with a mammoth went down well with the ladies.

**KEY TERM**

**Evolutionary psychology:** the view that human behaviour and the functioning of the human mind depend in part on natural selection.

The central point made by Owusu-Bempah and Howitt (1994) was that Atkinson et al. (1993) evaluated other cultures in relation to the technological and cultural achievements of the United States and Europe. In Owusu-Bempah and Howitt's words (p. 163), "Cultures which fall short of this arbitrary Euro-centric standard are frequently described as 'primitive', 'undeveloped' or, at best, 'developing'. Religion, morality, community spirit, etc., are ignored in this racist ideological league table."

In sum, many Western psychologists have written insensitively about cross-cultural differences. Sometimes the mistaken impression may have been given that some cultures are "better" than others rather than simply different. There are certainly grounds for concern, but thankfully any explicit or implicit racism is in decline.

## Origins of sex differences

As mentioned earlier, the findings from cross-cultural research can be used to adjudicate between competing theories. For example, Wood and Eagly (2002) addressed two important questions concerning the origins of sex differences. First, why are some activities (e.g., hunting) nearly always carried out by men, whereas others (e.g., cooking) are carried out mainly by women? Second, why do men often have greater status and power than women?

We will consider two theoretical approaches providing answers to these questions. First, there is **evolutionary psychology**, which assumes that human behaviour and the functioning of the human mind depend on natural selection (this approach is discussed fully in Chapter 2). According to Wood and Eagly (2002, p. 704):

> *Evolutionary psychologists assume that the activities of men across societies reflect competitive acquisition of resources in order to attract women ..., given women's evolved preference for mates who can provide resources to support them and their children ... men's desire to be certain about paternity and to acquire defensible resources should emerge in an overall cross-cultural tendency for them to control women's sexuality ... men's evolved dispositions to acquire resources and to control women's sexuality should be expressed in gender hierarchies of power, status, and resources that are universal.*

According to this theory, men should be mainly responsible for acquiring resources (e.g., food) and should have power and status in all cultures.

Second, there is the biosocial theory proposed by Wood and Eagly (2002). According to this theory:

> *The cross-cultural pattern of each sex's activities should reflect women's reproductive roles and men's size and strength ... To the extent that men and women are biologically specialised to efficiently perform different activities, the sex that can more readily perform the activities that yield status and power is advantaged in a gender hierarchy (p. 704).*

According to this theory, there should be substantial cross-cultural differences. In some societies, obtaining resources (e.g., food) requires size and strength, and in addition women's reproductive roles make it hard for them to be involved in obtaining resources. In such societies, men will engage in obtaining resources and will have power and status. In contrast, there are other societies in which obtaining resources does *not* require size and strength, and women's reproductive roles are *not* an obstacle to being involved in resource gathering. In such societies, there should be more equality of the sexes in obtaining resources and in power and status.

## Evidence

According to the biosocial theory, men should be more involved than women in obtaining food resources when hunting and/or fishing is involved, but this should be less so when food gathering is involved. Ember (1978) analysed 181 non-industrialised societies. Men contributed more than women to obtaining food in 99% of societies reliant on hunting and/or fishing. In contrast, women had the main involvement in obtaining food when gathering was involved.

Why don't women's reproductive roles prevent them from having a major involvement in obtaining food in gathering societies? Schlegel and Barry (1986) found that there were longer sex taboos after childbirth in such societies. This has the effect of reducing the number of children, thereby freeing women for food gathering.

The prediction from the evolutionary approach that men should have more power and status than women in *all* cultures or societies has not been supported. Whyte (1978) considered 93 non-industrialised societies, and found that men dominated their wives in 67% of them. In 30% of the societies there was equality of the sexes, and women dominated their husbands in 3%. According to the biosocial theory, men should be dominant in societies in which they are better equipped than women to perform vital tasks. The clearest support comes from the finding that men are particularly dominant in non-industrialised societies engaging in very frequent warfare (Goldstein, 2001). In addition, men are typically dominant in non-industrialised societies in which the economic contributions of men are much greater than those of women (Schlegel & Barry, 1986).

## Evaluation

- ⊕ Cross-cultural research has greatly increased our understanding of sex differences in behaviour.
- ⊕ The research has disproved simple evolutionary explanations and provided support for the biosocial theory.
- ⊕ The biosocial theory also provides an explanation for the substantial changes over recent decades in the status of women in most industrialised societies. As Wood and Eagly (2002, p. 721) pointed out, "Weakening both the traditional division of labour and patriarchy [male dominance] are women's increased control over reproduction through contraception and relatively safe abortions, the marked decline in birth rates, and the decrease in the proportion of productive activities that favour male size and strength."
- ⊖ Research has focused mainly on non-industrialised cultures, and so is somewhat limited.
- ⊖ The direction of causality is not always clear. For example, engaging frequently in warfare may cause male dominance in a society, but having male dominance may play a part in causing a society to be warlike.

## Individualism vs. collectivism

Many psychologists argue there is a crucial difference between cultures emphasising **individualism** and those emphasising **collectivism**. These terms were defined as follows by Oyserman, Coon, and Kemmelmeier (2002, p. 5): "[We may] conceptualise individualism as a worldview that centralises the personal—personal goals, personal uniqueness, and personal control—and peripheralises the social … the core element of collectivism is the assumption that groups bind and mutually obligate individuals."

Oyserman et al. (2002) considered the components of individualism and collectivism as assessed by 27 different questionnaires. They identified six components of individualism and eight components of collectivism:

---

### Individualism

1. Independent (free; control over one's life).
2. Goals (striving for one's own goals and achievements).
3. Compete (personal competition and success).
4. Unique (focus on one's unique characteristics).
5. Private self-know (keeping one's thoughts private from others).
6. Direct communicate (stating clearly what one wants and needs).

### Collectivism

1. Related (considering close others as part of the self).
2. Belong (enjoying belonging to groups).
3. Duty (being willing to make sacrifices as a group member).
4. Harmony (concern for group harmony).
5. Advice (turning to close others for help with decisions).
6. Context (self alters across situations).
7. Hierarchy (emphasis on status issues).
8. Group (preference for working in groups).

---

The first theoretical account of individualism and collectivism was proposed by Hofstede (1980, 1983). He argued that individualism and collectivism are opposites. Individualistic cultures are those with an emphasis on *independence* and individual responsibility, whereas collectivistic cultures are those with an emphasis on *interdependence* and group membership.

## Evidence

The first convincing evidence that cultures differ in terms of individualism–collectivism was reported by Hofstede (1980). He surveyed work-related values among workers from 40 countries belonging to a large multi-national company (IBM). Hofstede (1983) subsequently enlarged his sample to cover other countries. The countries scoring highest on individualism were the United States (Rank 1), Australia (Rank 2), Great Britain (Rank 3), and Canada and the Netherlands (joint Rank 4). Hofstede (1980, 1983) assumed that countries scoring lowest on individualism were the highest on collectivism. Those scoring lowest on individualism were Guatemala (Rank 53), Ecuador (Rank 52), Panama (Rank 51), and Venezuela (Rank 50). Several countries in the Far East (e.g., Indonesia, South Korea, Taiwan, and Thailand) also scored low on individualism.

One of Hofstede's (1980) key findings was that individualism correlated +.82 with modernity as measured by national wealth. This suggests that wealthier countries are generally individualistic, presumably because there is less need to be reliant on other people in such countries. The finding of a strong positive association between individualism and national wealth was also obtained by Kashima and Kashima (2003).

It is often assumed in Western cultures that individuals' level of life satisfaction depends mainly on their inner experience of positive and negative emotional states. In other words, those with the greatest life satisfaction have many positive emotional experiences and few negative ones. However, Suh et al. (1998) found in a study of 40 countries that this is much more true of individualistic than of collectivistic cultures. Indeed, life satisfaction was influenced much more by cultural norms relating to the desirability of life satisfaction in collectivistic cultures than in individualistic ones. These findings make sense: Life satisfaction depends on personal feelings and experiences in individualistic cultures, but it depends on the broader social context (e.g., cultural norms) in collectivistic cultures.

There has been increasing criticism of theory and research on individualism–collectivism. For example, Hofstede's (1980) research is clearly flawed even though it has been very influential. As Smith and Bond (1998, p. 49) pointed out, "His sample was predominantly male, it was drawn only from the marketing and servicing divisions and the data were all collected at least twenty-five years ago."

We have already seen that the concepts of individualism and collectivism are both very general, with Oyserman et al. (2002) identifying six components of individualism and eight components of collectivism. As Fiske (2002, p. 83) pointed out, "IND [individualism] amalgamates Thomas Paine, Vincent van Gogh, Mahatma Gandhi, Michael Jordan, Hugh Hefner, and Adolf Hitler into one category!" So far as collectivism is concerned, it combines "social bonds with all kinds of groups and networks. There are many kinds of sociality, and there is no reason to believe that cultural emphasis on one kind of relationship, membership, or obligation is positively correlated with emphases on other kinds" (p. 82).

In spite of the breadth of the categories of individualism and collectivisim, cultures can easily be categorised in additional ways. For example, Smith and Schwartz (1997) argued that there are *two* key dimensions in terms of which cultures differ. First, there is the cultural view of relations between the individual and the group. In their terminology, some cultures are characterised by autonomy (closely related to individualism), whereas others are characterised by embeddedness (similar to collectivism). Second, there is the cultural view of how to motivate responsible behaviour and to allocate resources. Some cultures believe in equality, whereas others believe in a hierarchy (with an acceptance of inequality).

Smith and Schwartz's (1997) theoretical approach produces four culture types:

1. *Particularism* (individualism + hierarchy). This type of culture is found in several countries in Central and Eastern Europe (e.g., Russia, Czech Republic, Romania).
2. *Universalism* (individualism + equality). This type of culture is dominant in Northern and Western Europe, the United States, Australia, and New Zealand.
3. *Vertical collectivism* (collectivism + hierarchy). This cultural type is most common in Pacific Asian countries (e.g., Indonesia, South Korea, Japan).
4. *Horizontal collectivism* (collectivism + equality). This type of culture is dominant in Southern European countries (e.g., Greece, Turkey, Spain).

A more devastating attack on Hofstede's (1980, 1983) theoretical position was mounted by Triandis et al. (1993) and by Gelfand, Triandis, and Chan (1996). Triandis et al. obtained various measures of individualism and collectivism across several cultures. Their key finding was that individualism and collectivism were essentially independent or uncorrelated with each other. This contrasts with Hofstede's assumption that they should be strongly negatively correlated. Gelfand et al. presented American students with concepts relating to individualism (e.g., choosing own goals, broad-minded), to collectivism (e.g., family security, reciprocate favours), and to authoritarianism (e.g., submissiveness, punish deviates). There were two key findings. First, individualism and collectivism were unrelated to each other. Second, there was a strong negative relationship between individualism and authoritarianism, suggesting that authoritarianism rather than collectivism is the opposite of individualism. In general terms, individualists want to control their own lives, whereas authoritarians want to control other people's lives.

It has often been assumed that what is true at the level of a culture is also true at the level of individuals within that culture. In other words, individuals within an individualistic

Although both are in Western Europe, Smith and Schwartz's (1997) approach suggests that France (above) and Spain (below) have different culture types. France falls into their "Universalism" category (individualism + equality), and Spain falls into their "Horizontal collectivism" category (collectivism + equality).

culture will nearly all be individualistic (idiocentric), whereas those in collectivistic cultures will be collectivistic (allocentric). However, this is not strictly correct. Triandis et al. (2001) studied several cultures. About 60% of those living in individualistic cultures are idiocentrics, and about 60% of those living in collectivistic cultures are allocentrics. Thus, there is only a moderate tendency for matching between individuals and the culture in which they find themselves.

## Evaluation

⊕ There is an important distinction between individualism and collectivism.

⊕ The distinction between individualism and collectivism has been very influential, and has led to more cross-cultural research than any other distinction.

⊕ Life satisfaction depends much more on inner emotional feelings in individualistic cultures than in collectivistic ones, whereas it depends much more on cultural norms concerning the desirability of life satisfaction in collectivistic cultures (Suh et al., 1998).

⊖ Much cross-cultural research has been based on the mistaken assumption that what is true at the level of a culture is also true at the level of individuals within that culture.

⊖ The assumption that individualism and collectivism are strongly negatively correlated with each other is dubious, because they have often been found to be uncorrelated (Gelfand et al., 1996; Triandis et al., 1993).

⊖ The categories of "individualism" and "collectivism" are very broad and vague.

⊖ There is some overlap between individualism and collectivism. For example, as Oyserman et al. (2002, p. 20) pointed out, "Perhaps for Americans, sense of belonging and seeking advice [two components of collectivism] tap into feelings of *choice* about membership in the group and *pleasure* in relating to others—concepts more commensurate [in line] with conceptualisations of relationships developed within an individualistic value frame."

⊖ The heavy reliance on questionnaires to assess individualism and collectivism is adequate only if people have conscious access to *all* relevant information about themselves and their culture. However, "Most contemporary theories posit [assume], and fieldwork confirms, that culture consists of diverse, loosely connected constituents, only a few of which are articulable [capable of being expressed]" (Oyserman et al., 2002, p. 20).

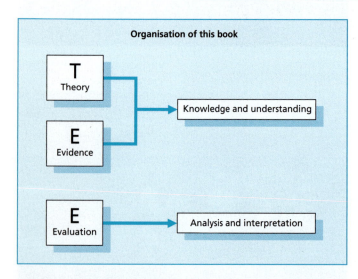

Organisation of this book

## STUDYING PSYCHOLOGY

This book is designed to provide a detailed (but accessible) account of psychology. As a result, it should be of value to all students starting to study psychology, and who want a readable introduction to the subject. In order to study psychology successfully, you will need to develop a good level of knowledge and understanding of psychological theories, studies, methods, and concepts. In addition, you will need to analyse and interpret your knowledge effectively.

The structure of the book is designed to help you to achieve the above goals. What I call the **TEE approach** has been used throughout the book. The discussion of most topics starts with theory (T), moves on to evidence (E), and then concludes with evaluation (E). Evaluation mostly involves considering the strengths and limitations of the theories or ideas that have been discussed. The strengths or positive features are indicated by the symbol "+", whereas the limitations or negative features are indicated by the symbol "−". Occasionally an evaluative point has positive *and* negative features, so things are not always neat and tidy!

# Study skills

Students of psychology should find it easier than other students (at least in theory!) to develop good study skills. This is because psychological principles are at the heart of study skills. For example, study skills are designed to promote effective learning and remembering, and learning and memory are key areas within psychology. Study skills are also concerned with motivation and developing good work habits, and these also fall very much within psychology. In what follows, I will try to focus on detailed pieces of advice rather than on vague generalities (e.g., "Work hard", "Get focused").

## Motivation

Most people find it hard to maintain a high level of motivation over long periods of time (e.g., a college or degree course). How can you make yourself well motivated? As is discussed in Chapter 3, human motivation generally depends on how we think about the future, and about the kinds of goals we set ourselves. Edwin Locke (1968) put forward an influential goal-setting theory. According to the original version of this theory, our work performance depends mainly on goal difficulty: The harder the goals we set ourselves, the better our performance is likely to be. Wood, Mento, and Locke (1987) reviewed 192 studies that had examined this hypothesis, and concluded that it was supported in 175 of them.

As you might imagine, motivation involves more than goal difficulty. For example, it also involves goal commitment. There is little point in setting yourself the goal of obtaining an excellent examination result in psychology if you do not fully commit and dedicate yourself to the achievement of that goal. Research on goal-setting theory (reviewed by Locke & Latham, 1990) indicates that goal setting is most effective in the following seven circumstances:

1. You must set yourself a goal that is hard but achievable.
2. You need to commit yourself as fully as possible to attaining the goal, perhaps by telling other people about it.
3. You should focus on goals that can be achieved within a reasonable period of time (e.g., no more than a few weeks). A long-term goal (e.g., obtaining an Upper Second class degree in psychology) needs to be broken down into a series of short-term goals (e.g., obtaining an excellent mark on your next essay).
4. You should set yourself clear goals, and avoid very vague goals such as simply "doing well".
5. You should obtain feedback on how well you are moving towards your goal (e.g., checking your progress with a teacher or friend).
6. You should feel pleased whenever you achieve a goal. However, avoid complacency and set yourself a slightly harder goal for the future.
7. You should try to learn from failure by being very honest about the reasons why you failed: Was it really "just bad luck"?

Your attempts to motivate yourself are only likely to be successful if you make use of all seven points. If you set yourself a very clear, medium-term goal, and obtain feedback, but the goal is impossible to achieve, then you are more likely to *reduce* rather than *increase* your level of motivation.

There is one further important aspect of motivating yourself to perform well academically that Locke overlooked. If you are going to achieve your goals of doing well academically, you must resist distractions from friends and other people. This can probably best be done by forming what are known as implementation intentions (see Chapter 3). **Implementation intentions** are detailed plans for achieving some goal or other, and typically include

> **KEY TERM**
> **Implementation intentions:** intentions specifying in detail how individuals are going to achieve the goals they have set themselves.

**Goals or aims**
- Must be realistic and achievable.
- Must stretch our abilities.
- Must be broken into smaller, short-term goals.
- Must be clear, unambiguous, and specific.

**Achievements**
- Must be measurable.
- Must be given feedback.
- Must be rewarded when achieved.
- Must be honestly evaluated when not achieved.

information about *where* and *when* the necessary work is going to be done. Implementation intentions often go beyond this, and can include planning in advance what to do if there is a distraction. For example, suppose you have a very important examination in a week's time, and are concerned that your friends will distract you from your studies. Part of your implementation intentions might include the rule that you will study during the main part of the day, and socialise in the evening after you have made satisfactory progress with your studies.

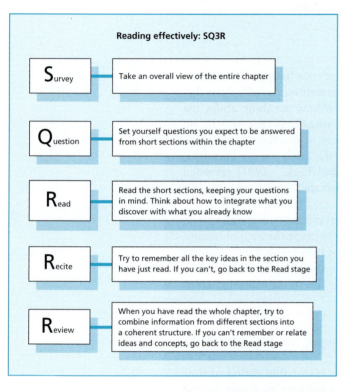

**Reading effectively: SQ3R**

**S**urvey — Take an overall view of the entire chapter

**Q**uestion — Set yourself questions you expect to be answered from short sections within the chapter

**R**ead — Read the short sections, keeping your questions in mind. Think about how to integrate what you discover with what you already know

**R**ecite — Try to remember all the key ideas in the section you have just read. If you can't, go back to the Read stage

**R**eview — When you have read the whole chapter, try to combine information from different sections into a coherent structure. If you can't remember or relate ideas and concepts, go back to the Read stage

## Reading skills: Books

You probably spend some of your time reading psychology books, and it is obviously important to read them in as effective a way as possible. Morris (1979) described the SQ3R approach, which has proved to be very useful. SQ3R stands for Survey, Question, Read, Recite, Review, and these represent the five stages in effective reading. We will consider these five stages with respect to the task of reading a chapter of this book.

The Survey stage involves getting an overall view of the way in which the information in the chapter is organised. If there is a chapter summary, this will probably be the easiest way to achieve that goal. Otherwise, you could look through the chapter to find out what topics are discussed and how they are linked to each other.

The Question stage should be applied to fairly short sections of the chapter of no more than 3000 words or so. The essence of this stage is that you should think of relevant questions to which you expect this section to provide answers.

The Read stage involves reading through each section identified at the Question stage. There are two main goals at this stage. First, you should try to answer the questions you thought of during the previous stage. Second, you should try to integrate the information provided in the section of the chapter to your pre-existing knowledge of the topic.

The Recite stage involves you in trying to remember all the key ideas contained in the section of the chapter you have been reading. If you cannot remember some of them, then you should go back to the Read stage.

The Review stage occurs when you have read the entire chapter. If all has gone well, you should remember the key ideas from the chapter, and you should be able to combine information from different sections into a coherent structure. If you cannot do these things, then go back to earlier stages in the reading process.

The key reason why the SQ3R approach works so well is because it ensures that you do not simply read in a passive and mindless way. Instead, it encourages you to engage with the reading material in a very *active* and *proactive* way. As Eysenck (1998) pointed out, there is another important reason why the SQ3R approach is effective. If you read a chapter in a book in a passive way, you may convince yourself that all is well when the material in it seems familiar. However, there is a big difference between *recognising* information as familiar and being able to produce it at will during an anxiety-inducing examination. In order to succeed in examinations, you must be able to *recall* the information you need. The Recite and Review stages of the SQ3R approach are designed to achieve precisely that.

## Reading skills: Research articles

One of the most important skills which students of psychology need to acquire is the ability to evaluate or provide a critical analysis of psychological research. Indeed, the Quality Assurance Agency (QAA) in the United Kingdom has identified "critical thinking" as one of the skills developed by psychology students (see Barber, 2002). It typically takes several years for students to develop skills of critical analysis, but it is important to start developing these skills as soon as possible. Hopefully, you will find that the numerous Evaluation sections contained in every chapter of this book will prove helpful in this respect.

Barber (2002) argued that critical thinking about research can be developed by working through four successive stages with research articles:

1. *Establishing the facts*. The article is read through carefully to determine what was done and what was found. It is important at this stage for you to identify the main findings that have emerged from the research.
2. *Thematic focus*. This stage consists of evaluating the specific themes explored in the research, the specific contributions to knowledge claimed by those who conducted the research, the specific issues allegedly resolved, and the researchers' specific recommendations and conclusions. At this stage, you need to decide whether the specific claims made by the researchers are correct and supported by the evidence.
3. *Generic commentary*. This involves identifying the strengths and weaknesses of the article with respect to its rationale, logic, presentation, statistical analyses, theoretical importance, and so on. At this stage, you need to consider whether the research seems to have made an important contribution to our understanding.
4. *Research proposal*. According to Barber (2002, p. 98), this stage "includes a consideration of what might be done as an alternative to what was done, and what improvements might be made (ranging from the reasoning around the issues addressed to the way in which the results were analysed)". If you are a first-year student, you can probably safely forget about this stage for the time being!

## Time management

What do you do with the 100 or so hours a week during which you are awake? I would guess that the honest answer is that you have only a vague idea where most of your time goes. Since time is such a valuable commodity (in terms of having fun as well as studying), it is an excellent idea to use it efficiently. Here are some suggestions on how to achieve that goal:

- Create a timetable of the time available for work over, say, a whole week after taking account of other commitments and social activities. Indicate on it also times that are *not* available for work. You will probably be surprised at how much time is available for work. Now indicate on your timetable those subjects that are going to be given study time on a different days, and how much time within each day you are going to spend on any subject.
- Decide what is, for you, a reasonable span of attention (possibly 30–40 minutes). Set aside a number of periods of time during the week for study. Make a commitment to yourself to use these periods for study.
- Note that the more of a habit studying becomes, the less effortful it will be, and the less resistant you will be to making a start.
- No-one has limitless concentration. After initially high levels of concentration, the level decreases until the end is in sight. Regular breaks are needed to bring you to a fresh peak of concentration. So make sure that the time you commit to studying is realistic. You can probably improve your level of concentration by including short (10 minute) rest periods. Remember to avoid distractions (e.g., television) in your study area.
- During these study times, there will be a tendency to find other things to do (e.g., watch the end of a television programme, have a drink). This is where the hard bit comes. You must try to be firm and say to yourself that this is time you have committed to studying, and that is what you are going to do. However, you will have time available later for other things. It is hard to do on the first occasion, but it gets easier.

## Planning fallacy

Most people are familiar with the planning fallacy, even though they may never have heard it called that. It was first systematically studied by Kahneman and Tversky (1979).

They defined the **planning fallacy** as, "a tendency to hold a confident belief that one's own project will proceed as planned, even while knowing that the vast majority of similar projects have run late".

Why are we subject to the planning fallacy? Kahneman and Tversky (1979) distinguished between *singular information* (focusing on the current task) and *distributional information* (focusing on similar tasks completed in the past). When we are deciding how long a current work task will take to finish, we typically make use of singular information but ignore distributional information. According to Kahneman and Tversky, it is this failure to take account of our previous failures to keep to schedule that produces the planning fallacy.

Buehler, Griffin, and Ross (1994) also found evidence for the planning fallacy. On average, students submitted a major piece of work 22 days later than they had predicted. The tendency to under-estimate the time to completion was just as great among those students who were specifically told that the purpose of the study was to examine the accuracy of people's predictions. Buehler et al. also found that students were much more accurate at predicting completion times for other students than for themselves. The reason for this is that they were more likely to use distributional information when making predictions about other students.

It is important for you to avoid the planning fallacy, because you will probably find yourself losing marks if you hand in essays late. There are three main ways of avoiding the planning fallacy. First, simply being aware of the existence of the planning fallacy may make you more accurate in predicting completion times. Second, make use of information about the length of time taken to complete previous essays or assignments. Third, focus on the kinds of difficulties that might occur during the preparation of a piece of work: problems in finding the right books, problems in organising your essay, minor illnesses, and so on. Such a focus should correct the tendency to under-estimate completion times.

## How to succeed at psychology

- Set yourself hard, clear, short- and medium-term goals, and commit yourself to them.
- Be an active participant in the learning process: Have clear aims in mind when you read a textbook, and avoid being passive and uninvolved.
- Follow the TEE strategy: Make sure you know the key theories and ideas, the relevant evidence, and that you know how to evaluate them.
- Remember that every theory and study in psychology is limited in some ways: Do not be afraid to point this out!
- Try to master the key skills.
- Avoid the planning fallacy.

> **KEY TERM**
>
> **Planning fallacy:** the tendency to under-estimate how long a work task will take to complete in spite of evidence from similar tasks completed in the past.

## SUMMARY

*What is psychology?*

Psychology is the science which makes use of behavioural and other evidence to understand the internal processes underlying behaviour. Several different kinds of factors jointly determine most human behaviour. Some of the main approaches to psychology are the biological, cognitive, individual differences, developmental, social, and abnormal approaches. Each of these focuses on particular topics, and has proved its usefulness and real-world applicability. Understanding human behaviour is a complex task, and so psychologists have devised several experimental and non-experimental methods to shed light on human behaviour. The criteria for a discipline to be regarded as a science include controlled observations, objectivity, testing theoretical predictions, falsifiability, replicability, and use of a paradigm. Some psychological research satisfies most (or all) of these criteria. However, several factors influencing human behaviour cannot be manipulated experimentally, which inhibits the development of psychology as a fully scientific discipline.

It is misleading to assume that common sense forms a coherent set of assumptions about behaviour, as can be seen from a study of proverbs. Many psychological findings (e.g., those of Milgram) are very different to what most people would have predicted. In spite of this, hindsight bias leads many people to under-estimate the achievements of psychology.

*"Psychology is just common sense"*

Almost 20% of the 100 most eminent psychologists of the twentieth century were non-American, nearly all of them European. It is important to distinguish between emic constructs (specific to a given culture) and etic constructs (universal across cultures). Historically, Western psychologists often ignored cultural differences, but the situation is improving rapidly. Cross-cultural studies are not only interesting in themselves, but can also be used to adjudicate between competing theories. For example, cross-cultural research on sex differences in behaviour supports biosocial theories over evolutionary theories. Cultures can be categorised as individualistic or collectivistic. Individualism and collectivism are frequently regarded as being opposite to each other, but often seem to be unrelated. The two categories (individualism and collectivism) are very broad, and what is true at the level of an entire culture is not necessarily true at the level of individuals within that culture.

*Psychology around the world*

To succeed at psychology, you need to acquire detailed knowledge of theory and research in psychology. As importantly, you need to be able to evaluate this knowledge, and criticise it effectively. This book uses the TEE approach, in which theory, evidence, and evaluation are clearly identified. For maximal motivation, you should set yourself hard, clear, medium-term goals to which you are committed. You should obtain feedback, praise yourself for success, analyse failure honestly, and form clear implementation intentions. Effective reading of textbooks involves the five stages of Survey, Question, Read, Recite, and Review. This is an active and focused approach. It is important to develop critical thinking by evaluating the strengths and weaknesses of psychological research. Effective time management involves setting and keeping to a timetable, allowing short breaks when studying, and avoiding the planning fallacy.

*Studying psychology*

## FURTHER READING

- Eysenck, M.W. (2000). *Psychology: A student's handbook*. Hove, UK: Psychology Press. Chapters 30–32 provide a gentle introduction to research methods in psychology.
- Eysenck, M.W. (2002). *Simply psychology* (2nd ed.). Hove, UK: Psychology Press. The author of this book was attempting to present psychology in a very accessible way to new students of the subject. Only you can decide whether he achieved this goal.
- Gravetter, F.J., & Forzano, L.-A.B. (2002). *Research methods for the behavioural sciences*. New York: Thomson/Wadsworth. This book discusses in detail the main research methods available to researchers in psychology.
- Gravetter, F.J., & Wallnau, L.B. (1998). *Essentials of statistics for the behavioural sciences*. New York: Thomson/Wadsworth. Numerous statistical tests used to analyse data obtained from psychological studies are discussed fully in this textbook.
- McBride, P. (1994). *Study skills for success*. Cambridge, UK: Hobsons Publishing. This book provides simple and effective strategies to help students to enhance their study skills and achieve their academic goals.
- Smith, P.B., & Bond, M.H. (1998). *Social psychology across cultures* (2nd ed.). London: Prentice Hall. The major findings from cross-cultural research are discussed in a well-informed and critical fashion.

# Biological Psychology

**Biological psychology** (often shortened to biopsychology) can be defined as "the study of behaviour and experience in terms of genetics, evolution, and physiology, especially the physiology of the nervous system" (Kalat, 1998, p. 1). More generally, biological psychology involves using a biological approach to study psychology and to obtain an understanding of human (and animal) behaviour.

Within the field of biological psychology, we can identify several approaches. According to Pinel (1997), there are five main approaches, and we will briefly consider each one. First, there is **physiological psychology**. The key aspect of this approach is that there is direct manipulation of the nervous system of non-human animals to observe the effects of such manipulation on the neural mechanisms of behaviour. This direct manipulation can take various forms, including surgery, electrical stimulation, or the use of chemicals. Such manipulations are not always as informative as might be imagined. We can consider an analogy with trying to discover the workings of a television set (something I have never managed to do!). If we destroy its plug, the television set will not work. However, it would be ludicrous to argue that the plug is the most important reason why we see clear coloured moving images on our television screens!

For obvious ethical reasons, most of the interventions discussed above simply cannot be used with human participants. Note there is some controversy as to the relevance of research on non-human species for an understanding of human functioning. In general terms, we can only be confident that findings from non-human animals are applicable to humans when there is clear supporting evidence from human research.

Second, there is psychopharmacology. **Psychopharmacology** resembles physiological psychology, but is more specifically focused on the effects of various drugs on neural activity and on behaviour. In general terms, research in psychopharmacology is more applied than research in physiological psychology, with the emphasis being on the development of drugs having beneficial effects and minimal adverse side effects. In addition, psychopharmacologists consider the damaging effects of various illegal drugs on the brain and on behaviour. Other pharmacologists are more interested in basic research. They argue that studying the effects of drugs sheds light on the detailed chemical processes occurring in the brain.

Third, there is **psychophysiology**, which involves studying the relationship between physiological activity on the one hand and psychological processes on the other hand. Most psychophysiological research is carried out on humans. Psychophysiologists make use of a wide range of measures, including heart rate, electrical conductance of the skin, pupil dilation, and the electroencephalogram (EEG; based on recordings of electrical brain activity measured at the surface of the scalp). In the past 20 years, event-related potentials (ERPs) have become one of the most popular EEG-based techniques for studying cognitive processes

**KEY TERMS**

**Biological psychology:** an approach to animal and human psychology that emphasises the role of biological factors.

**Physiological psychology:** an approach to biological psychology in which neural mechanisms of behaviour are studied via surgical and other interventions.

**Psychopharmacology:** an approach to biological psychology focusing on the effects of drugs on neural activity and on behaviour.

**Psychophysiology:** an approach to biological psychology based on the study of relationships between physiological activity and psychological processes in human participants.

(e.g., attention). In essence, the same stimulus is presented several times. After that, the segment of EEG following each stimulus is extracted and lined up with respect to the time of stimulus onset. These EEG segments are then averaged together to produce a single waveform otherwise known as the event-related potential or ERP. ERPs provide detailed information about the time course of brain activity following stimulus presentation.

Several neuroimaging techniques have been developed in recent years, and more are still in the process of development. These techniques (e.g., PET scans, functional MRI) provide information concerning the activity of different brain areas when an individual is engaged in some task. For detailed information on neuroimaging techniques, see the Introduction to the Cognitive Psychology part of this book.

Fourth, there is **neuropsychology**, which is mainly concerned with assessing the effects of brain damage in humans on their psychological functioning and behaviour. Neuropsychologists often try to determine which part or parts of the brain have been damaged, using a variety of techniques including magnetic resonance imaging (MRI; see the Introduction to Cognitive Psychology). There are a number of similarities between neuropsychology and cognitive neuropsychology (see the Introduction to Cognitive Psychology). Other neuropsychologists study neurologically intact individuals with a view to understanding brain mechanisms of behaviour. For example, Annett (e.g., 1999) has carried out much research on differences in cognition between people who are left-handed and those who are right-handed.

Fifth, there is **comparative psychology**, in which similarities and differences in behaviour across various species are considered. Comparative psychologists also compare different species with respect to their evolutionary history and the current adaptiveness of their behaviour, although their underlying interest is often in trying to use information about other species to try to explain human behaviour. In practice, there will be relatively little discussion of non-human species in this book.

Which of the five major approaches within biological psychology offers the greatest potential for understanding human behaviour? There is no simple answer to that question. As Pinel (1997, pp. 11–12) pointed out, "Because none of the five biopsychological approaches to research is without its shortcomings, major biopsychological issues are rarely resolved by a single experiment or even by a single series of experiments taking the same general approach. Progress is most rapid when different approaches are focused on a single problem in such a way that the strengths of one approach compensate for the weaknesses of the others".

Another approach within biological psychology is somewhat distinct from those discussed so far. The approach is known as **evolutionary psychology**, and it has fairly strong links with comparative psychology. It differs from comparative psychology in that there is less emphasis on comparing the human species with other species. The key theoretical assumption of this approach is that the functioning of our brains and our behaviour both depend in part on the evolutionary forces to which the human race has been exposed over the millennia.

Central topics within biological psychology are discussed in Chapters 2–5. Chapter 2 focuses mainly on the structure of the nervous system, and considers how it influences behaviour. There is a discussion of the effects of drugs on behaviour, because many drugs have a direct influence on brain functioning. There is also an account of evolutionary psychology, and the influence of genetic factors on behaviour. Chapter 3 is devoted to motivation and homeostasis. Among the topics discussed are the regulatory mechanisms underlying the control of body temperature and eating behaviour, the ever-interesting topic of sex and sexual behaviour, and theories of work motivation.

Chapter 4 is concerned with states of awareness. At the start of the chapter, there is a discussion of the complex topic of consciousness. After that, the topics discussed include bodily rhythms, sleep, dreaming, and the controversies surrounding hypnosis. There have been recent advances in our understanding of all of these topics. Chapter 5 is the final chapter devoted to biological psychology. It is concerned with emotion and stress. Several issues relating to emotion are examined, such as the number and nature of emotions, theories of emotion, and physiological systems underlying emotional experience. The subsequent discussion of stress focuses on the physiological systems involved in stress, the relationship between stress and illness, and various methods of coping with stress.

**KEY TERMS**

**Neuropsychology:** an approach to biological psychology in which the emphasis is on relating areas of brain damage to cognition and to behaviour.

**Comparative psychology:** an approach to biological psychology in which the biological and behavioural differences among species are studied.

**Evolutionary psychology:** the view that human behaviour and the functioning of the human mind depend in part on natural selection.

Note that biological psychology is relevant to topics other than those dealt with in Chapters 2–5. For example, we will be considering aspects of biological psychology when discussing vision (Chapter 7), intelligence (Chapter 12), personality (Chapter 13), altruism (Chapter 19), and mental disorders (Chapter 22). In addition, neuropsychological and brain-imaging findings are discussed in connection with learning (Chapter 8), memory (Chapter 9), and language (Chapter 11).

In summary, there are five main approaches within biological psychology. Physiological psychology involves direct manipulation of the nervous system of non-human animals. Psychopharmacology is concerned with the effects of drugs on neural activity and on behaviour. Psychophysiology is concerned with the relationship between physiological activity and psychological processes. Neuropsychology is concerned with the effects of brain damage in humans on their psychological functioning and behaviour. Comparative psychology focuses on similarities and differences in behaviour across various species. In addition to the above five approaches, there is an increasingly influential approach known as evolutionary psychology.

- **Evolutionary perspective and genetics**
  Genetic factors.

  Darwin's evolutionary approach: variation, inheritance, competition, natural selection, adaptation
  Selective breeding
  The role of genetics: dominant and recessive genes
  Chromosomes
  Nature–nurture controversy
  Evolution and behaviour
  Individual differences
  Wason selection task
  The impact of culture

- **Nervous system**
  Its structure and how it works.

  Structure
  Neurons
  Central nervous system: hind-, mid-, and forebrain, spinal cord
  Peripheral nervous system: somatic and autonomic nervous systems

- **Synapses and neurotransmitters**
  Electrical impulses in detail.

  Synapses and neurotransmitters
  Action potential processes
  The mechanism of synaptic transmission
  Six classes of neurotransmitter: neuropeptides, amino acids, monoamines, acetylcholine, purines, soluble gases
  Practical applications: agonists and antagonists

- **Drugs and behaviour**
  How drugs can influence behaviour.

  Psychoactive drugs: depressants, stimulants, hallucinogens
  Depressants, e.g., alcohol
  Opiates, e.g., heroin
  Stimulants, e.g., cocaine, amphetamine
  Hallucinogens, e.g., LSD
  Cannabinoids, e.g., marijuana
  Addiction: tolerance, dependence, and detoxification
  Positive reward theory

- **Endocrine system and hormones**
  The effects of hormones on behaviour.

  Description of the endocrine system
  Definition of hormones
  Differences between hormones and neurotransmitters
  Hormones secreted by the hypothalamus, pituitary, gonad, adrenal, thyroid and parathyroid, pancreas, and pineal glands
  The importance of hormones

# Biological bases of behaviour

The nervous system (especially the brain) has enormous influence on our behaviour, and so is of central importance within biological psychology. As a result, most of this chapter is devoted to the functioning of the nervous system. However, before embarking on a discussion of the nervous system, we consider the contribution of evolutionary psychology and genetics to an understanding of human behaviour. The importance of this approach was captured by Dobzhansky (1973), who wrote an article entitled, "Nothing in biology makes sense except in the light of evolution." The **nature–nurture controversy** is an important issue within biological psychology. It concerns the extent to which our behaviour is determined by heredity (nature) or by learning and environment (nurture). For example, how much of your personality has been pre-determined by your genetic make-up as opposed to your lifelong experiences in the world? The approach based on evolutionary psychology (which originated with Darwin, 1859) has made major contributions to this controversy. Some of the main ways in which the evolutionary approach has influenced psychology are considered in this chapter.

Any serious application of a biological approach to psychology must involve a systematic focus on the brain and how it works. That is a central concern of this chapter. Our coverage of the brain starts with a consideration of the nervous system. Some of the nervous system (the central nervous system) is located within the brain and the spinal cord, with the rest of it (the peripheral nervous system) being located outside those parts of the body (the peripheral nervous system). We will deal with the processes involved in the transmission of neural impulses within the nervous system. We will also discuss the relationships between the nervous system and hormonal processes in the endocrine system.

Towards the end of the chapter we focus on psychopharmacology. Why is this of relevance in a chapter on basic neural and hormonal processes? The answer is that drugs have their effects on behaviour because they influence basic neural processes. Indeed, it is as a result of our enhanced understanding of neural transmission that drug companies have been able to develop increasingly sophisticated drugs having fairly precise effects on behaviour.

## EVOLUTIONARY PERSPECTIVE AND GENETICS

The evolutionary approach is mainly associated with Charles Darwin (1859), although very similar ideas were put forward independently by Alfred Russel Wallace. Darwin wanted to obtain answers to several questions, such as why some species die out, and why new species appear. He was struck by the fact that most species seemed well-designed for the environment in which they found themselves, arguing that other theories, "could [not] account for the innumerable cases in which organisms of every kind are beautifully adapted to their habits of life—for instance, a woodpecker or tree-frog to climb trees, or a seed for dispersal by hooks and plumes. I had always been struck by such adaptations" (from Darwin's autobiography; see Ridley, 1996, p. 9).

Several kinds of evidence indicate that most species have changed or evolved over long periods of time. For example, examination of the fossil record reveals there have been progressive changes over time in the size and shape of many species. However, fossil records are of limited value, because there are often gaps in the record and they provide information only about the hard parts of an animal. Additional evidence that species change over

KEY TERM

**Nature–nurture controversy:** the issue of the extent to which human behaviour is determined by heredity versus environmental factors.

MR. BERGH TO THE RESCUE.

The Defrauded Gorilla. "That *Man* wants to claim my Pedigree. He says he is one of my Descendants."

Mr. Bergh. "Now, Mr. Darwin, how could you insult him so?"

A cartoon about evolution, circa 1871. Charles Darwin is rebuked for slighting a gorilla by claiming man may be descended from apes.

*Can you think of any animals that have evolved to adapt to very specific environments?*

time can be obtained by studying the members of any given species in different parts of the world. It is typically found that there are several differences from region to region, with these differences making adaptive sense in view of variations in climate, food, and predator densities, and other environmental pressures on survival and reproduction.

Darwin (1859) addressed the issues mentioned above by providing an explanation of the processes involved in producing changes in a species over time in his theory of natural selection. This theory was based on five major ideas:

1. *Variation.* Individuals within a species differ from each other in their physical characteristics (e.g., height) and in their behaviour.
2. *Inheritance.* At least some of the variation among members of a species is inherited. As a result, offspring tend to resemble their parents more than other members of the species.
3. *Competition.* The members of most species produce far more offspring than can survive. Darwin (1859) worked out that a pair of elephants could have about 19 million descendants alive 750 years after their birth if there were no problems of survival, given the expected reproductive productivity of any pair of mating elephants. In fact, however, there is competition for mates, food, and places to live.
4. *Natural selection.* Those members of a species who survive the process of competition and go on to breed will tend to have characteristics better suited to the environment than those who do not. Thus, there is natural selection or survival of the fittest (in the sense of survival or reproductive success rather than physical fitness!).
5. *Adaptation.* As a result of natural selection, successive generations will tend to be better adapted to their environment. They will possess characteristics allowing them to obtain food and to reproduce.

In sum, the key to evolution by natural selection is differential reproductive success. Thus, those members of a species well adapted to their environment are more likely to reproduce than those poorly adapted. Over hundreds or thousands of generations, this gradual process of natural selection can produce substantial changes within any given species. However, changes sometimes occur relatively rapidly. This happens when there is a **mutation** or change in a single gene during reproduction.

Why is the theory of natural selection of importance to psychology? According to Darwin (1859), the theory applies as much to behaviour as to physical characteristics. Since psychology focuses very much on trying to understand behaviour, Darwinian theory is of direct relevance. In addition, regardless of your stance on the nature–nurture controversy, it is indisputable that natural selection has had a great impact on the human brain, and that is the organ most involved in processing environmental stimulation.

**KEY TERM**

**Mutation:** a change in a given gene, which occurs during reproduction.

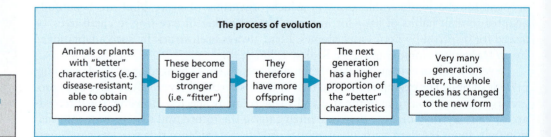

**The process of evolution**

Animals or plants with "better" characteristics (e.g. disease-resistant; able to obtain more food) → These become bigger and stronger (i.e. "fitter") → They therefore have more offspring → The next generation has a higher proportion of the "better" characteristics → Very many generations later, the whole species has changed to the new form

## Evidence

Darwin's (1859) theory of natural selection is difficult to test directly. Why is that? It can take hundreds of thousands or even millions of years for natural selection to produce significant changes in the physical appearance and/or behaviour of the members of a species, and human experimenters cannot wait that long to obtain their findings. However, Darwin argued we can obtain relevant evidence within much shorter periods of time by carrying out studies on selective breeding. The essence of **selective breeding** is that animals showing a high level of some characteristic or trait are mated together, as are those showing a low level of that characteristic. If the characteristic in question is heritable, then the groups high and low on that characteristic should become increasingly different from each other.

Darwin himself carried out some limited research on selective breeding. He bred pigeons, and observed changes in them from one generation to the next. He claimed the changes produced artificially by selective breeding resembled those occurring under natural conditions. Since Darwin's time, there have been numerous studies on selective breeding (see Plomin, De Fries, & McClearn, 1997). As we will see, these studies have provided strong support for Darwin's theory.

Tryon (e.g., 1940) carried out classic studies on selective breeding of maze-bright and maze-dull rats. First of all, rats ran a complex maze. Those who least often went down incorrect alleys during training were called maze-bright, and were bred with each other. In similar fashion, maze-dull rats who entered several incorrect alleys were also bred with each other. This procedure was continued through 21 generations of rats. The findings were fairly striking. By the time Tryon reached the eighth generation, there was practically no overlap in the maze-learning performance of the two groups of rats: All but the very worst of the so-called maze-bright rats outperformed the best of the maze-dull rats.

Tryon's (1940) findings indicated clearly that variations in some characteristics are inherited. However, what was inherited was *not* simply differences in learning ability. Searle (1949) compared maze-dull and maze-bright rats on 30 different tests. The two groups differed on motivational tests as well as on learning ones. This pattern of findings led Searle to conclude that maze-bright rats had greater food motivation than maze-dull rats, and were also less distracted by alternatives in the maze.

Tryon's (1940) research should not be taken to show that environmental factors are unimportant. Cooper and Zubek (1958) reared maze-bright and maze-dull rats in wire-mesh cages providing either an enriched environment (e.g., visual displays, ramps) or an impoverished environment (a bare cage). The maze-learning performance of maze-bright rats was significantly better than that of maze-dull rats among those rats raised in the impoverished environment. However, the key finding was that there was no difference in

All dogs have the same distant ancestors, but selective breeding has resulted in major variations. Above right is a Great Dane and left is a Miniature Schnauzer. Great Danes originated in Germany in the sixteenth century and were originally used to hunt wild boar, however, they are now used mainly as pets. The Miniature Schnauzer was developed for use as a farm dog in the nineteenth century. Its small size makes it an ideal pet to keep in a house.

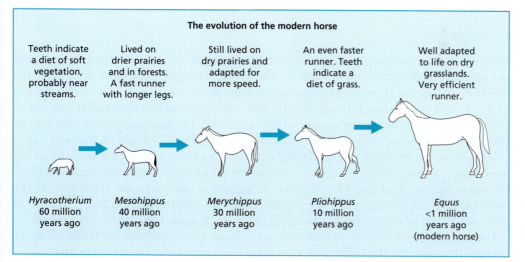

**The evolution of the modern horse**

| Teeth indicate a diet of soft vegetation, probably near streams. | Lived on drier prairies and in forests. A fast runner with longer legs. | Still lived on dry prairies and adapted for more speed. | An even faster runner. Teeth indicate a diet of grass. | Well adapted to life on dry grasslands. Very efficient runner. |
|---|---|---|---|---|
| *Hyracotherium* 60 million years ago | *Mesohippus* 40 million years ago | *Merychippus* 30 million years ago | *Pliohippus* 10 million years ago | *Equus* <1 million years ago (modern horse) |

**KEY TERM**

**Selective breeding:** animals high on a given trait are mated together, as are animals low on that trait, in order to show that the trait is heritable.

Colour variants of the peppered moth.

---

**CASE STUDY: *The Peppered Moth***

What has often been regarded as fairly direct support for some of the assumptions of Darwin's theory was obtained by Kettlewell (1955). He studied two variants of the peppered moth, one of which was darker than the other. The difference in colour is inherited, with the offspring of the darker type being on average darker than those of the lighter type. Both types of peppered moth are eaten by birds such as robins and redstarts that rely on sight to detect them. Kettlewell observed the moths when they were on relatively light lichen-covered trees and when they were on dark, lichenless trees in industrially polluted areas. The lighter coloured moths survived better on the lighter trees and the darker coloured moths survived better on the darker trees.

According to Darwin's theory, the number of darker moths should increase if there is an increase in the proportion of dark trees. Precisely this happened in England due to the industrial revolution, when pollution killed the lichen and coated the trees with sooty deposits. The proportion of peppered moths that were dark apparently went from being almost nil to over half the resident population in a period of about 50 years. However, the evidence that there were few dark peppered moths in the late nineteenth century comes from moth collections. As Hailman (1992, p. 126) pointed out, "Those collections were not scientific samples but were made by amateurs … Perhaps they did not like ugly black moths."

---

maze-learning performance by maze-bright and maze-dull rats raised in the enriched environment. Thus, the genetic disadvantages of the maze-dull rats were overcome provided that the environment was an enriched one.

## Genetics

One of the great limitations of Darwin's (1859) theory of natural selection was that it did not specify the *mechanisms* involved in inheritance. Thus, Darwin failed to answer the question, "How are characteristics passed on from one generation to the next?" By one of those quirks of history, Darwin actually had in his possession a manuscript (unread or unappreciated) containing the answer to that question! The manuscript had been sent to Darwin by an obscure monk called Gregor Mendel (see the Key Study on the next page).

We focus on the work of Mendel for two reasons. First, it is of enormous historical importance. Second, it shows clearly some of the basic aspects of genetic transmission. However, bear in mind that what happens in humans is often far more complicated. The great majority of human traits (e.g., intelligence) are controlled by a large number of different genes rather than being determined by a single gene. In addition, many genes do not function in a dominant or recessive way. Some genes are additive (with all genes contributing towards the offspring's phenotype), whereas others have interactive effects

Austrian botanist Gregor J. Mendel (1822–1884), photographed circa 1880.

# Mendel: The mechanics of inheritance

Mendel (1822–1884) studied inheritance in pea plants, the seeds of which were either green or yellow. He started by cross-breeding the offspring of pea plants that produced only green seeds with the offspring of pea plants that produced only yellow seeds. He found that all of the first-generation offspring had green seeds. However, when the first-generation offspring were bred with each other, about three-quarters of the second-generation offspring had green seeds and one-quarter had yellow seeds. He obtained similar findings with other characteristics of pea plants. The characteristic or trait found in all of the first-generation offspring and three-quarters of the second-generation offspring is called a dominant trait, and depends on a **dominant gene**. The trait found in one-quarter of the second-generation offspring is called a recessive trait, and depends on a **recessive gene**. In humans, for example, brown eyes are dominant and blue eyes are recessive.

How did Mendel explain his findings? He argued there are two kinds of factors (e.g., green-seed factor and yellow-seed factor) for simple traits that can occur only in one of two forms, but that cannot occur in mixed form. Such inherited factors are now called genes, with a **gene** being defined as "the smallest discrete unit that is inherited by offspring intact, without being broken up or blended" (Buss, 1999, p. 10). Each organism possesses two inherited factors or genes for each simple trait. In the case of pea plants, they can have two yellow-seed genes, two green-seed genes, or one gene of each type.

Mendel then assumed the offspring receive one gene at random from each of their "parents". When the two genes are identical (e.g., both yellow-seed genes), then the offspring will have the trait associated with those genes (e.g., yellow seeds). When the two genes differ (e.g., one yellow-seed gene and one green-seed gene), then the offspring will have the trait associated with the dominant gene.

Mendel's findings challenged the conventional wisdom that offspring simply inherit the traits of their parents. The findings suggested there is an important distinction between the **genotype** (underlying genetic potential) and the **phenotype** (observable traits or characteristics). For example, as we have seen, Mendel found that one-quarter of the offspring resulting from breeding with green seeds had yellow seeds. What we have here is an important difference between the phenotype and the genotype of the initial green seeds: At the level of the phenotype they had green seeds, but at the level of the genotype they had one green-seed gene and one yellow-seed gene.

## Discussion points

1. *How might Darwin have incorporated Mendel's findings into his theory?*
2. *Why are the Mendel's findings important for psychology?*

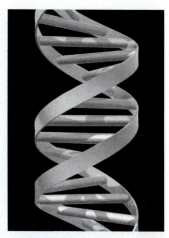

Computer artwork of part of a strand of DNA. The DNA molecule carries genetic information in all cellular organisms. It consists of two strands wound around each other in a double helix.

### KEY TERMS

**Dominant gene:** the gene that determines the observable characteristic when paired with a recessive gene.

**Recessive gene:** the gene that does not determine the observable characteristic when paired with a dominant gene.

**Gene:** the unit of hereditary transmission.

**Genotype:** an individual's potential in the form of genes.

**Phenotype:** an individual's observable characteristics, depending in part on his/her genotype.

**Partial penetrance:** a characteristic of certain genes, in which they influence behaviour only in certain circumstances.

**Chromosomes:** strands of DNA bearing the genes.

**Deoxyribonucleic acid (DNA):** double-stranded coils of molecules of genetic material forming chromosomes.

**Meiosis:** the process of forming gametes (sex cells); the chromosomes divide, with one chromosome in each pair forming a separate gamete.

**Gametes:** sperm cells and egg cells formed by the process of meiosis.

**Zygote:** a fertilised egg cell.

on each other. In addition, some genes have **partial penetrance**, meaning that they influence an individual's life only in certain circumstances. For example, genes increasing the risk of alcoholism will not influence someone living in a culture in which alcohol is not available.

What is the nature of genes? In essence, **chromosomes** are strands of **deoxyribonucleic acid (DNA)** bearing the genes. Chromosomes occur in matched pairs, with humans having 23 pairs of chromosomes in each of their body cells. Each strand of DNA consists of a sequence of four nucleotide bases (adenine, thymine, guanine, and cytosine) arranged in a particular order, and these strands essentially form the genetic code. The two strands of DNA forming each chromosome are coiled around each other in a double helix (i.e., spiral) pattern. These strands are bonded together, with guanine on one strand binding with cytosine on the other strand, and with adenine binding with thymine.

What happens during sexual reproduction? There is **meiosis**, which is a process of forming sperm cells and egg cells (known as **gametes**). More specifically, the chromosomes divide, with one chromosome of each pair forming a separate gamete. When fertilisation occurs, a sperm cell and an egg cell combine to form a **zygote**, which is a fertilised egg cell. Meiosis is very important, because it plays a major role in human genetic diversity.

The discoverers of the structure of DNA, James Watson (left) and Francis Crick (right), with their model of part of a DNA molecule in 1953.

What happens after the formation of a zygote is **mitosis**, which is a process in which the number of chromosomes doubles, followed by a division of the cell to create two cells, each of which has 23 pairs of chromosomes. Mitosis occurs repeatedly during the entire course of development, and involves re-creating huge numbers of copies of the original zygote.

Of particular importance are the two sex chromosomes, X and Y. Female mammals have two X chromosomes, whereas male mammals have an X and a Y. During reproduction, the male contributes either an X or a Y chromosome, and the female always contributes an X chromosome. If the male contributes a Y chromosome, the offspring will be male, whereas it will be female if the male contributes an X chromosome.

When we compare ourselves with other species, we discover some fairly uncomfortable similarities. As is well known, human beings and chimpanzees share more than 98% of their DNA! What is even more disturbing is that some human genes are very similar in chemical structure to those found in a transparent worm called *Caenorhabditis elegans*. An implication of this finding is that humans and worms evolved from a common ancestor at some point in the past (Wade, 1997).

## Behavioural genetics

Our knowledge of genetic transmission allows us to understand the extent of genetic similarity (or degree of relatedness) between members of a family. We know that children share 50% of their genetic material with each of their parents, that siblings also share 50% of their genetic material, that the figure is 25% for grandparents and grandchildren, and that it is 12.5% for first cousins. Of particular importance, **monozygotic twins** (identical twins) have the same genetic make-up, whereas **dizygotic twins** (fraternal twins) share only 50% of their genetic make-up. This is because identical twins come from the same zygote which splits post-fertilisation, whereas fraternal twins come from two different eggs.

*What are the limitations of using twin studies to investigate the nature–nurture debate?*

Why is knowledge of genetic relatedness within families of value to psychology? The answer is very straightforward: It allows us to shed some light on the nature–nurture controversy. Suppose we want to know whether individual differences in a given trait (e.g., assertiveness) are influenced by genetic factors. We could carry out a study assessing assertiveness within a large number of families. If genetic factors are of importance, then we can make various predictions. For example, identical twins should resemble each other more in assertiveness than fraternal twins. More generally, the greater the similarity in genetic make-up between members of a family, the more similar they should be with respect to assertiveness. In contrast, genetic relatedness should not matter if environmental factors are all-important. Of particular significance, identical twins brought up apart should be very similar in assertiveness if only genetic factors are important, whereas they should generally not resemble each other in assertiveness if only environmental factors determine assertiveness (see Chapter 13).

Researchers in this area who want to be more specific about the contributions of heredity and environment use the notion of heritability. **Heritability** refers to the proportion of the variance in a given characteristic or trait within a particular population which is accounted for by genetic factors. You may be surprised to discover that most forms of human behaviour possess some heritability. For example, there is significant heritability for television watching (Plomin, Corley, DeFries, & Fulker, 1990), even though we presumably do not have a television-watching gene! How does this happen? There is obviously no *direct* influence of genes on television watching, so the effects must be *indirect*. For example, those who watch the most television may be genetically predisposed to be overweight and low in physical fitness.

As has been mentioned already heritability is a measure of the impact of genetic factors on individual differences in any given characteristic, but it is *not* a measure of genetic determination. We can see the distinction by considering an example given by Block (1995a; see also Chapter 12). What is the heritability for the number of fingers individuals have on their right hand? Since heritability relates *only* to individual differences (i.e., who your parents are is irrelevant for the number of fingers you have, unless you are Bart Simpson), we need to consider the factors causing some people to have more or fewer than five fingers on each hand. Nearly all of these factors are environmental (e.g., car or industrial accidents), and so heritability is low. However, we know that the number of fingers that human beings have on each hand is determined very largely by genetic factors. Thus, the genetic determination of the number of fingers is extremely high, whereas heritability is very low.

There is another important limitation of heritability. It is a population measure, and it can vary greatly from one population to another. For example, there are some cultures where the environmental conditions in which different children live vary enormously (e.g., some children have 10–20 years of education while others have no education at all). In such cultures, environmental factors are likely to have a greater impact on individual differences in intelligence than in most Western cultures. As a result, heritability would be lower in such cultures (see discussion in Chapters 12 and 13).

It is sometimes assumed that anything having high heritability is impossible to change. However, that is not correct. Consider, for example, **phenylketonuria** or PKU. It is a genetically caused form of mental disorder, which is found in individuals who lack the ability to metabolise the amino acid phenylalanine. PKU has very high heritability in most circumstances. However, adherence to a strict diet which minimises the levels of phenylalanine is effective in preventing mental retardation

The approach we have described in this section is known as **behavioural genetics**. As we will see elsewhere in this book, it has been applied successfully to explore the role of genetic factors in intelligence and personality (see Chapters 12 and 13). It has also been applied in abnormal psychology to assess which mental disorders are determined in part by genetic factors (see Chapter 22). There is convincing evidence that genetic factors are important in all of these areas, even if the precise importance of such factors remains controversial.

# Evolutionary psychology

Many of the ideas discussed earlier have been incorporated into a new theoretical approach known as **evolutionary psychology**. What is the essence of evolutionary psychology? According to Buss (1999, p. 3):

> *Evolutionary psychology focuses on four key questions: (1) Why is the mind designed the way it is? ... (2) How is the human mind designed—what are its mechanisms or component parts, and how are they organised? (3) What are the functions of the component parts and their organised structure—that is, what is the mind designed to do? (4) How does input from the current environment, especially the social environment, interact with the design of the human mind to produce observable behaviour?*

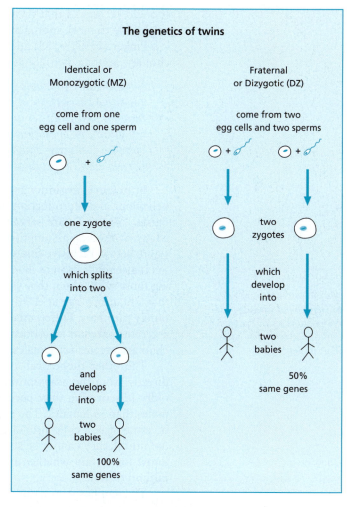

**The genetics of twins**

Identical or Monozygotic (MZ)

come from one egg cell and one sperm

one zygote

which splits into two

and develops into

two babies

100% same genes

Fraternal or Dizygotic (DZ)

come from two egg cells and two sperms

two zygotes

which develop into

two babies

50% same genes

It could be argued that Buss's definition of evolutionary psychology is too broad, and is applicable to most approaches to psychology (David Carey, personal communication).

Pinker (1997, p. 23) addressed the issue of the historical origins of evolutionary psychology, arguing as follows:

> *Evolutionary psychology brings together two scientific revolutions. One is the cognitive revolution of the 1950s and 1960s, which explains the mechanics of thought and emotion in terms of information and computation. The other is the revolution in evolutionary biology of the 1960s and 1970s, which explains the complex adaptive design of living things in terms of selection among replicators [animals that reproduce].*

In practice, evolutionary psychology has focused mainly on issues related to sexual behaviour and reproduction (see Chapters 3 and 19). According to evolutionary psychologists, "Brains ... are servants of the gonads [sexual organs]" (Kenrick, 2001, p. 15). Many of the key assumptions made by evolutionary psychologists are contained in the figure below. **Inclusive fitness** is the notion that natural selection favours organisms which maximise replication of their genes whether directly by reproduction or indirectly by helping those with whom they share genes (e.g., immediate family). **Kin selection** is the notion that organisms are selected to favour their own offspring and other genetically-related family members. **Differential parental investment** is the notion that females typically have a greater parental investment than males. That means that the consequences of having a child are greater for females, and so they are more selective in their choice of mates.

The other theoretical assumptions shown in the figure below follow more or less directly from the assumptions already discussed. For example, it is assumed that cuckoldry (discovering their partner has had sex with someone else) causes more jealousy in males than in females. The explanation is as follows. Men can only justify their parental investment in a child provided the child was actually fathered by them. If their partner is unfaithful, they cannot be sure that any child is actually theirs. In contrast, women always know for certain whether any given child is theirs regardless of whether their partner is faithful or not.

The emphasis on natural selection and on adaptation to the environment might lead us to assume that evolutionary psychologists believe humans are well-adapted in most

*In what ways are the consequences of having children greater for females than males?*

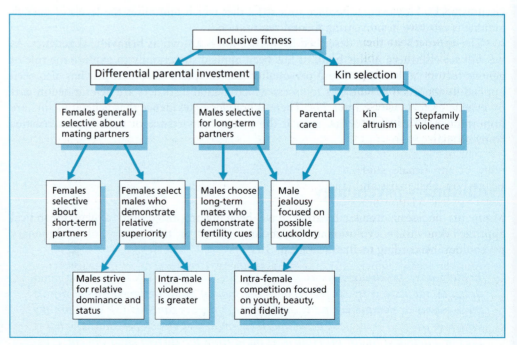

The theoretical approach adopted by evolutionary psychologists, with the most general assumptions at the top and the most specific assumptions at the bottom. From Kenrick (2001).

respects to their environment. This assumption is false, because it can take thousands of generations for natural selection to produce substantial genetic changes. As Buss (1999, p. 20) pointed out, "We carry around a Stone-Aged brain in a modern environment. A strong desire for fat, adaptive in a past environment of scarce food resources, now leads to clogged arteries and heart attacks." More generally, some of the most convincing support for evolutionary psychology comes from cases in which our functioning and behaviour are clearly *not* well-adapted, even though they were in the distant past.

Another misunderstanding about evolutionary psychology is that it assumes that behaviour is genetically determined in a very direct way. Pinker (1997, p. 42) clarified the situation:

*Natural selection ... acts by designing the generator of behaviour: the package of information-processing and goal-pursuing mechanisms called the mind. Our minds are designed to generate behaviour that would have been adaptive, on average, in our ancestral environment, but any particular deed done today is the effect of dozens of causes.*

A final common misunderstanding about evolutionary psychology is that people are highly motivated to maximise the replication of their genes in the next generation (i.e., they consciously make decisions about their genetic transmission in some direct way). According to Pinker (1997, p. 44), "By making us enjoy life, health, sex, friends, and children, the genes buy a lottery ticket for representation in the next generation, with odds that were favourable in the environment in which we evolved. Our goals are subgoals of the ultimate goal of the genes, replicating themselves ... As far as *we* are concerned, our goals ... are not about genes at all, but about health and lovers and children and friends." Thus, the success most of us have in spreading our genes often occurs as a by-product of our goals in life rather than in a direct way.

## Evidence

Mate selection, altruism, and jealousy are all relevant to the assumptions contained in the figure on the previous page. Since all of these topics are discussed at some length elsewhere in the book (see Chapters 3 and 19), we will only refer to them briefly here. The central prediction from evolutionary psychology so far as mate selection is concerned is that people should try to select a mate who will maximise their chances of having offspring. Buss (1989) obtained findings from 37 cultures around the world which he claimed provided support for that prediction. Men in all 37 cultures said they would prefer a mate who was younger than they were, whereas women in 36 cultures (Spain was the exception) preferred men older than themselves. This can be explained by assuming that younger women are more likely to be able to have children, and older men are more likely to have the resources to provide adequately for children.

According to evolutionary psychologists, females should be more selective than males in their choice of mates. Much evidence supports this assumption (see Chapter 3). For example, in a study by Clark and Hatfield (1989), male and female students were approached by an attractive stranger of the opposite sex who offered to have sex with them. Seventy-five per cent of the male students agreed to the suggestion but none of the female students. Buss and Schmidt (1993) focused on what males and females would accept in a temporary sexual relationship. Males were much more willing to tolerate undesirable characteristics in a potential mate, such as being disliked by others, lacking humour, being violent, and being ignorant.

Another area in which evolutionary psychology is relevant is unselfish or altruistic behaviour. So far as altruism is concerned, the central problem is to explain why people often behave in an altruistic or selfless way, which might appear to be contrary to their own genetic or reproductive interests. According to the notions of inclusive fitness and kin selection, individuals can help to ensure the survival of

### Parental care and altruism

"Bringing up baby" involves heavy costs to many animal parents: in mammals this includes biological investment in egg production, growth and development of the foetus in the womb, milk production after birth, time and effort spent in care and defence, etc. In birds there is a similar amount of investment in nest building, egg production, incubation, feeding, etc. These behaviours could be argued to be of no benefit to the parents directly, and so could come under the heading of altruism. This altruism is even more marked if the parents are assisted by other family members, i.e. others who share the same genes. Mumme (1992) observed a type of Florida jay whose older broods acted as helpers with younger offspring, with the result that the younger brood had a greatly increased survival rate.

*How could altruism towards strangers be explained by evolutionary principles?*

their genes not only by reproducing themselves, but also by helping to ensure close relatives (with whom they share genes) are able to reproduce. The main prediction following from this theoretical approach is that we should be more willing to behave altruistically towards close relatives than towards distant relatives or strangers. Burnstein, Crandall, and Kitayama (1994) presented their participants with various scenarios in which individuals had problems, and asked them whether they would be willing to help. The key finding (in line with prediction) was that the participants were much more willing to help close relatives than other people, and this was especially so with a serious emergency (a house was burning rapidly, and only one of the three people in the house could be saved).

Burnstein et al. (1994) considered hypothetical situations, and it is possible the participants responded in socially desirable ways rather than in line with what they would actually do in real life. However, Essock-Vitale and McGuire (1985) obtained similar findings based on real-life data. Female participants described occasions on which they had received or given help. They were five or six times more likely to help their close kin (e.g., children) than less close kin (e.g., nephews or nieces). In addition, older people were much more likely to help younger people than vice versa. Evolutionary psychologists argue that this occurs because of the greater future reproductive potential of younger people. There are some problems of interpretation with this study. For example, most women spend much more time with their own children than with their nephews or nieces, and so there is a confounding between closeness of kin and familiarity.

So far as jealousy is concerned, some of the evidence supports the assumption that unfaithfulness in a partner should create more jealousy in males than in females (see Chapter 3). However, most of the studies have involved hypothetical situations. Harris (2002) considered actual infidelity, and found that males and females were equally distressed by it.

Evolutionary psychology has also been applied to the issue of explaining human fears. Many evolutionary psychologists argue that the costs of assuming that an object is safe when it is actually dangerous are typically much higher than the costs of assuming that a safe object is dangerous. Accordingly, we may still have a predisposition to fear certain objects (e.g., snakes) that posed much greater dangers in our evolutionary past than now. This predisposition is known as **preparedness**. Relevant evidence was reported by Tomarken, Mineka, and Cook (1989). They showed female participants slides of a feared object (e.g., snake, spider) and of a neutral object (e.g., flower, mushroom). After each slide, the participants received an electric shock, a tone, or nothing, with equal frequency. There was evidence for **covariation bias**: The participants estimated shock had followed the feared stimulus between 42% and 52% of the time (compared to the actual figure of 33%), with the over-estimate being greater in females having the strongest fear of the stimulus.

In another study, Tomarken et al. (1989) found no covariation bias when electric shock followed slides showing a damaged electrical outlet. Thus, people are much more likely to associate the fear associated with an electric shock with objects that were dangerous in our evolutionary past than with dangerous objects that have only recently come into existence. So, the findings seem more consistent with evolutionary psychology than with a purely environmental explanation based on our actual experiences.

We can contrast cognitive psychology with evolutionary psychology. Cognitive psychologists have often assumed that the human information-processing system can readily be used to tackle almost any problem. For example, cognitive psychologists have sometimes made use of the computer metaphor, arguing that human information processing resembles that found in computers. In contrast, evolutionary psychologists assume our cognitive system is specialised for solving problems that have been important for adaptation during human history.

The two approaches described above make different predictions on certain versions of the Wason selection task (Wason, 1968; see Chapter 10). Before considering these different predictions, we need to consider the original version of the task. In this version, participants were presented with four cards: R, G, 2, and 7, together with a rule: "If there is an R on one side of the card, then there is a 2 on the other side of the card." They had to decide which cards needed to be selected to establish whether the rule was correct or incorrect. The most popular choices were the R and 2 cards. The correct answer (chosen by only about 10% of participants) is actually the R and 7 cards: If the 7 card has an R on the other side, then it falsifies the rule. People tend not to focus enough on trying to *falsify* the rule.

Cognitive psychologists have sometimes interpreted the above findings as indicating that people find it hard to think in terms of falsifying or breaking rules. Evolutionary psychologists (e.g., Cosmides & Tooby, 1992) argue that it has been important throughout human history to detect cheats, because we need to identify those who take benefits from us without helping us in return. Cosmides and Tooby argued that people would do very well on the Wason selection task if the task were phrased in such a way that showing that the rule was false involved detecting cheats. They tested this prediction by varying the Wason selection task. The participants had to imagine they were at the counter in a bar, and had to test the following rule: "If a person is drinking alcohol, then he or she must be 21 years old or older." There were four people: someone drinking beer, someone drinking soda, a 16-year-old, and a 25-year-old. Nearly everyone solved this correctly, choosing the beer drinker and the 16-year-old. The reason for this was the participants knew a 16-year-old might try to cheat by drinking alcohol when below the legal age limit.

## Evaluation

➕ "Evolutionary theory may serve as the umbrella idea (i.e., an overarching scheme) so desperately needed in the social sciences" (de Waal, 2002, p. 187).
➕ Evolutionary psychology has produced several original theoretical insights on topics such as altruism and mate selection.
➕ There is reasonable support for the notion that natural selection has influenced how we think and behave.
➖ Any type of behaviour can be explained by claiming it is adaptive in an evolutionary sense if it is desirable (e.g., parenting) or maladaptive due to evolutionary time lag if undesirable (e.g., male violence). In this way, evolutionary psychologists can "explain" everything, but not in a convincing way.
➖ Evolutionary psychology predicts there will be gender differences in mate preference across cultures, but tends to de-emphasise cross-cultural differences. In Buss's (1989) data, culture was about six times more important than gender in accounting for variation in the factors regarded as important in mate preference (Smith & Bond, 1998).
➖ Evolutionary psychology needs to, "put a little less evolution and a little more psychology into its explanations" (de Waal, 2002, p. 189). In other words, the direct relevance of evolution to psychology is not always clear.

> **KEY TERMS**
> **Central nervous system:** the part of the body consisting of the brain and the spinal cord.
> **Peripheral nervous system:** the part of the body consisting of the nerve cells in the body other than those found in the central nervous system.

## NERVOUS SYSTEM

The nervous system contains all the nerve cells in the body. As we will see, the various parts of the nervous system are specialised for different functions. The nervous system itself is made up of between 15 and 20 billion neurons and a much larger number of glia. The nervous system is divided into two main sub-systems:

● **Central nervous system.** This consists of the brain and the spinal cord; it is protected by bone and by fluid circulating around it.
● **Peripheral nervous system.** This consists of all the other nerve cells in the body. It is divided into the somatic nervous system, which is concerned with voluntary movements of skeletal muscles (those attached to our

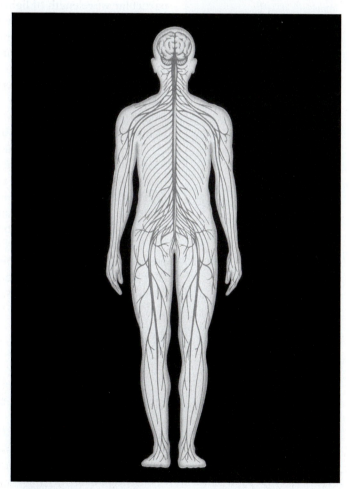

The nervous system within a human male figure. The brain and spinal cord constitute the central nervous system. The CNS integrates all nervous activities. There are 31 pairs of nerves that branch off the spinal cord into a network; they carry nerve impulses from the CNS to various structures of the body and back from these structures to the CNS. Nerves outside the CNS are part of the peripheral nervous system.

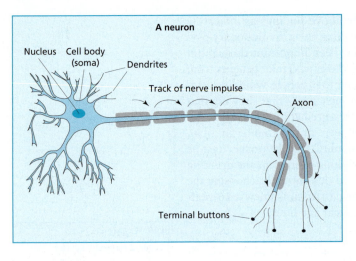

**A neuron**

Nucleus  Cell body (soma)  Dendrites

Track of nerve impulse

Axon

Terminal buttons

bones), and the autonomic nervous system, which is concerned with involuntary movements of non-skeletal muscles (e.g., those of the heart).

**Neurons** are cells that are specialised to conduct electrical impulses, and they form the basic units of the nervous system. There are various kinds of neurons, but most possess certain key features:

- A cell body or **soma** which contains a nucleus. It is in the soma that most of the metabolic work of each neuron occurs.
- At one end of the cell body are **dendrites**, which receive input from other neurons and conduct nerve impulses towards the soma.
- At the other end of the cell body is the **axon**, which conducts nerve impulses away from the soma and towards other neurons.

The average neuron sends impulses to about one thousand other neurons. Neurons differ considerably in terms of their size and specific function. For example, some large neurons transmit information over large distances, whereas small neurons transmit information over short distances. Neurons can be divided into sensory neurons, motor neurons, and interneurons. Sensory neurons respond to a given type of stimulation (e.g., particular wavelength of light), whereas motor neurons conduct impulses towards muscle or gland cells. Most of the neurons in the human nervous system are interneurons, which receive input from sensory neurons or from other interneurons, and send impulses to motor neurons or to other interneurons.

In order to understand how neurons work, we will consider the membrane potential, which is the difference in electrical charge between the inside and the outside of a neuron. The membrane potential can be assessed by inserting one electrode inside a neuron and a second electrode in the extracellular fluid. The **resting potential** is about –70 mV (millivolts). In other words, the potential inside the neuron is 70 mV less than outside it.

There are **ions** inside and outside the neuron. These are particles, some of which are positively charged and the remainder of which are negatively charged. The fact that a neuron's resting potential is –70 mV is due to a higher proportion of negative ions inside the neuron compared to outside it. There are complex reasons why this should be so. Part of what is involved is the sodium–potassium pump, which pumps potassium ions into the neuron and pumps sodium ions out.

**Glia** are cells in the nervous system, only about one-tenth the size of neurons, which probably do not conduct impulses to other cells. We know less about glia than about neurons. However, some glia remove waste material when neurons die, whereas others absorb chemicals released by neurons.

## KEY TERMS

**Neurons:** cells that are specialised to conduct electrical impulses.

**Soma:** a cell body containing a nucleus.

**Dendrites:** parts of the neuron that conduct nerve impulses towards the soma or cell body.

**Axon:** a part of the neuron that conducts nerve impulses away from the cell body or soma.

**Resting potential:** the condition in which the neuron is not firing, when the electrical charge inside it is about –70 mV.

**Ions:** particles that are either positively or negatively charged.

**Glia:** small cells in the nervous system that fulfil various functions (e.g., absorb chemicals released by neurons; remove waste material from dead neurons).

## Central nervous system

We will start our coverage of the central nervous system with the brain, and then consider the spinal cord. The first point that needs to be made about the brain is its complexity. In order to understand the brain, we must learn about its structure and about the functions of the various parts. It has proved rather easier to study *structure* than *function*. Only recently have technological advances allowed us to identify the functions of different brain areas by observing the brain in action (see the Introduction to the Cognitive Psychology part of this book).

In view of the importance of the brain, it is not surprising that it is the most protected part of the body. Both the

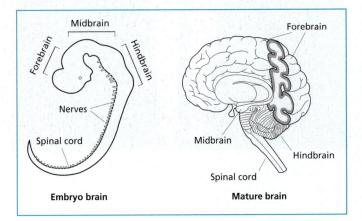

Midbrain

Forebrain

Forebrain  Hindbrain

Nerves

Spinal cord

**Embryo brain**

Midbrain

Hindbrain

Spinal cord

**Mature brain**

brain and the spinal cord are encased in bone and covered by protective membranes. In addition, there is the **blood–brain barrier**. This is a protective mechanism permitting blood to flow freely to the brain, but ensuring that most substances in the bloodstream do not reach the brain tissue.

The brain is divided into three main regions: hindbrain, midbrain, and forebrain. These terms refer to their locations in the embryo's nervous system, and do *not* indicate clearly the relative position of the different brain regions in an adult. We will consider each of these regions in turn.

## Hindbrain

The hindbrain is at the back of the brain. It consists of the medulla, the pons, and the cerebellum. The **medulla** is located immediately above the spinal cord. It is involved in the control of various crucial functions such as breathing, vomiting, salivation, and the regulation of the cardiovascular system. The **pons** is in front of the medulla, and the two structures together contain the **reticular formation**, which is involved in controlling levels of arousal and is also of relevance to consciousness (see Chapter 4).

Finally, there is the cerebellum, which is a large structure within the hindbrain. The **cerebellum** is involved in the control of balance and movement. It is possible the cerebellum is actually more involved in using sensory information needed to guide movements than in controlling the actual movements themselves. Canavan et al. (1994) found that individuals who had suffered damage to the cerebellum found it hard to shift their attention between visual and auditory stimuli.

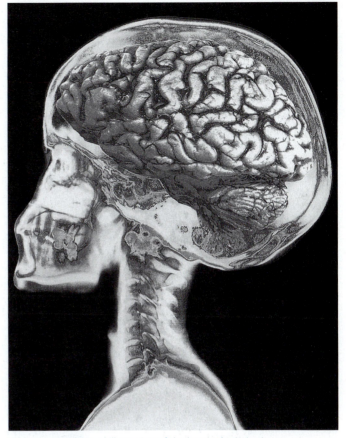

A computer enhanced illustration of the human brain in situ.

## Midbrain

The midbrain, which starts in the middle of the brain, is relatively smaller in mammals (including humans) than it is in reptiles, birds, and fish. It is divided into the tectum or roof and the tegmentum, which is the middle part of the midbrain. The tectum consists of

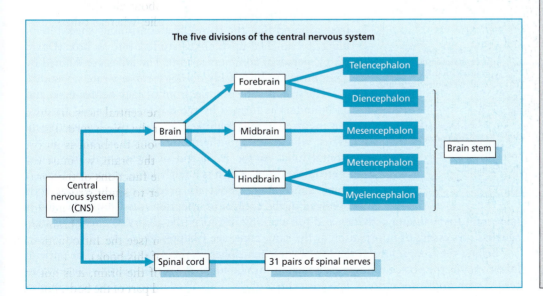

**The five divisions of the central nervous system**

Central nervous system (CNS) → Brain → Forebrain → Telencephalon / Diencephalon
Brain → Midbrain → Mesencephalon
Brain → Hindbrain → Metencephalon / Myelencephalon
Diencephalon, Mesencephalon, Metencephalon, Myelencephalon → Brain stem
Central nervous system (CNS) → Spinal cord → 31 pairs of spinal nerves

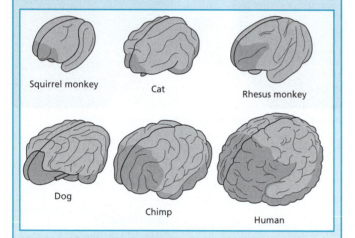
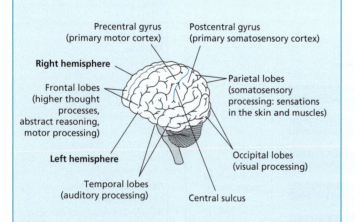

Precentral gyrus (primary motor cortex)

Postcentral gyrus (primary somatosensory cortex)

**Right hemisphere**

Frontal lobes (higher thought processes, abstract reasoning, motor processing)

Parietal lobes (somatosensory processing: sensations in the skin and muscles)

**Left hemisphere**

Occipital lobes (visual processing)

Temporal lobes (auditory processing)

Central sulcus

the superior colliculus and the inferior colliculus, both of which are used as routes for sensory information. The tegmentum contains parts of the reticular formation (other parts lying within the hindbrain). It also contains the substantia nigra. The **substantia nigra** is a brain structure, and damage to it can lead to depletion of dopaminergic cells and the onset of Parkinson's disease.

## Forebrain

This is easily the largest and the most important division of the human brain. The outer area of the forebrain is the cerebral cortex. About 90% of the human cerebral cortex is neocortex (literally new cortex), which consists of six layers. The neurons in the neocortex are mainly linked to other neurons within the same layer or within an adjacent layer. As a result, the neocortex is organised in columns, with each column running vertically through the six layers. There are various other structures under the cerebral cortex, and these other structures will be discussed shortly.

The cerebral cortex plays a crucial role in thinking, the use of language, perception, and numerous other cognitive abilities. It is deeply furrowed or grooved. The ridges between these furrows are known as gyri. Far and away the largest furrow is the longitudinal fissure running between the cerebral hemispheres. The two hemispheres are almost separate from each other, but are connected directly by a bridge known as the corpus callosum.

Two of the most obvious features of each hemisphere are the central sulcus and the lateral (or Sylvian) fissure ("fissure" means "furrow"). These features help to define the four lobes or areas of each hemisphere: the frontal lobe, the parietal lobe, the temporal lobe, and the occipital lobe. We will discuss these four lobes in turn. Much of our knowledge about the functions of each lobe has come from various brain-imaging techniques (discussed in the Introduction to the Cognitive Psychology part of this book). However, bear in mind that for most purposes all lobes work together in an integrated way to process information and produce appropriate forms of behaviour. Also bear in mind that the cortex is a continuous sheet resembling a crunched-up blanket stuffed into a box (David Carey, personal communication). The lobes are defined by anatomists, and probably do not form separate structures.

The frontal lobe is at the front of each hemisphere, and its boundary is formed by the central and lateral fissures. It is involved in the planning of movements. The precentral gyrus, which contains the motor cortex, is located in the frontal lobe. At the front end of the frontal lobe is the prefrontal cortex, which is a fairly large structure. There is some controversy about its precise functions, but it is involved in the control of attention (see Chapter 6) and is important for planning activities and for working memory (the ability to engage in storage and processing of information at the same time; see Chapter 9).

Behind the frontal lobe at the top of each hemisphere is the parietal lobe. The parietal lobe contains the postcentral gyrus, which in turn contains the somatosensory cortex concerned with bodily sensations. The postcentral gyrus is involved in processing information about touch sensations and information from the muscles. It appears that the parietal lobe monitors information concerning the positions of the head, the eye, and the body, and then passes this information on to other areas of the brain involved in the control of movement (Gross & Graziano, 1995).

The temporal lobe is behind the frontal lobes and underneath the parietal lobe. The superior temporal gyrus, which contains the auditory cortex, is located in the temporal lobe. In the great majority of humans, the left temporal lobe plays a crucial role in language processing (see Chapter 11). In addition, the temporal lobe is involved in some forms of emotional and motivational behaviour. Damage to the temporal lobe sometimes produces what is known as the Klüver–Bucy syndrome, in which animals are no longer fearful in the presence of dangerous objects and animals.

The occipital lobe is at the back of the cortex. It is of major importance in the processing of information from visual stimuli. At the back of the occipital lobe is the primary visual cortex, damage to which causes partial or total blindness (see Chapter 7). The various areas within the occipital lobe involved in visual processing are discussed in detail in Chapter 7.

We turn now to those parts of the forebrain that are underneath the cerebral cortex. Two series of interconnected structures in this part of the brain are the **limbic system** and the basal ganglia motor system. The limbic system consists of various structures including the amygdala, the septum, the **hippocampus**, the hypothalamus, the cingulate cortex, the fornix, and the mammillary body. The main functions of the limbic system are to regulate several kinds of motivated behaviour, including eating, aggression, avoidance behaviour, and sexual behaviour, and associated emotions such as anger and anxiety (see Chapter 5). The basal ganglia consist of the striatum, globus pallidus, and the amygdala (which is often regarded as part of this system as well as the limbic system). The basal ganglia assist in the production of voluntary motor responses.

*What problem might result from damage to the hippocampus?*

The thalamus and the hypothalamus are two important structures. The **hypothalamus** is much smaller than the thalamus. It is situated below the thalamus. The hypothalamus is involved in the control of several functions such as body temperature, hunger, and thirst. It is also involved in the control of sexual behaviour. Finally, the hypothalamus plays an important role in the control of the endocrine (hormonal) system. For example, the hypothalamus is directly connected to the anterior pituitary gland, which has been described as the body's "master gland".

What about the **thalamus**? It acts as a relay station passing signals on to higher brain centres. For example, the medial geniculate nucleus receives signals from the inner ear and sends them to the primary auditory cortex. In similar fashion, the lateral geniculate nucleus receives information from the eye and sends it to the primary visual cortex, and the ventral posterior nucleus receives somatosensory (bodily sensation) information and sends it to the primary somatosensory cortex. In addition, there are projections in the opposite direction, for example, proceeding from the primary visual cortex down to the thalamus.

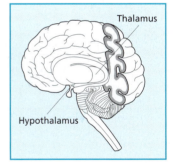

## Spinal cord

The only part of the central nervous system we have not discussed is the spinal cord. It is a thin structure going from the base of the brain all the way down to the coccyx bone at the lower end of the back. The spinal cord is protected by 24 vertebrae or bony segments running from the neck to the lower back regions. There are holes in these vertebrae, and the spinal cord passes through these holes.

The spinal cord consists of an inner area of grey matter and an outer area of white matter. White matter consists mainly of myelinated or sheathed axons, whereas grey matter consists of cell bodies and unmyelinated axons. The spinal cord contains 31 pairs of spinal nerves, with each nerve dividing into two roots as it approaches the spinal cord. The dorsal root, which is at the back, contains sensory neurons which assist in the transmission of sensory signals to the brain. The ventral root, which is at the front, contains motor neurons. These neurons are involved in the transmission of motor signals to skeletal muscles and to the internal organs (e.g., stomach, heart).

## Peripheral nervous system

The peripheral nervous system consists of all the nerve cells in the body not contained within the central nervous system. It consists of two parts: the somatic nervous system and the autonomic nervous system. The somatic nervous system is concerned with interactions with the external environment, whereas the autonomic nervous system is concerned with the body's internal environment.

The first issue to be discussed is the relationship between the peripheral nervous system and the central nervous system. Most of the nerves of the peripheral nervous system project from the spinal cord. Some spinal nerves are involved in receiving signals from (and sending them to) skeletal muscles within the somatic nervous system, whereas others receive signals from (and send them to) the internal organs within the autonomic nervous system. In addition, there are connections between the central nervous system and the peripheral nervous system via 12 pairs of cranial nerves. Most of them contain both sensory and motor fibres, and nearly all transmit signals to and from the head or neck. The major exception is the tenth or vagus nerve, which regulates the functioning of the abdominal and thoracic organs.

The somatic nervous system consists of afferent nerves that carry signals from the eyes, ear, skeletal muscles, and the skin to the central nervous system, and efferent nerves that carry signals that have come from the central nervous system to the skeletal muscles, skin, and so on.

The autonomic nervous system is concerned with regulating the functioning of the internal environment, including the heart, stomach, lungs, intestines, and various glands (e.g., pancreas, salivary glands, and adrenal medulla). It is called the autonomic nervous system because many of the activities it controls are autonomous or self-regulating (e.g., digestion). These activities do not require conscious effort on our part, and continue even when we are asleep.

As is the case with the somatic nervous system, the autonomic nervous system consists of afferent nerves and efferent nerves. The afferent nerves carry sensory signals from the internal organs to the central nervous system, whereas the efferent nerves carry motor signals from the central nervous system to the internal organs.

The autonomic nervous system is divided into the sympathetic nervous system and the parasympathetic nervous system. Nearly all the internal organs of the body receive signals

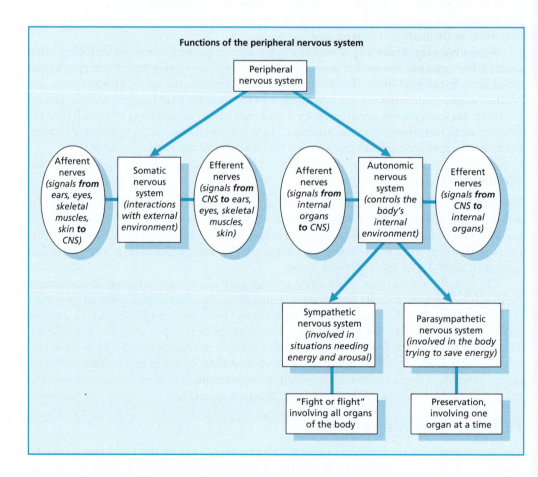

from both sympathetic and parasympathetic nerves. In general terms, the effects of activation of the sympathetic and parasympathetic nervous systems are opposite. The sympathetic nervous system is called into play in situations needing energy and arousal (e.g., fight or flight). For example, the body's initial response to a stressor involves the sympathetic adrenal medullary system (see Chapter 5). In essence, what happens is that adrenaline and noradrenaline are secreted, which causes increased arousal of the sympathetic nervous system. The sympathetic nervous system produces increased heart rate, reduced activity within the stomach, pupil dilation or expansion, and relaxation of the bronchi of the lungs.

In contrast, the parasympathetic nervous system is involved when the body is trying to save energy. The parasympathetic nervous system produces decreased heart rate, increased activity within the stomach, pupil contraction, and constriction of the bronchi of the lungs. In general terms, the sympathetic nervous system tends to act as a whole, whereas the parasympathetic nervous system often affects only one organ at a time.

The level of activity in any of the internal organs depends on the relative levels of activity within the sympathetic and parasympathetic nervous systems. For example, heart rate will tend to be high if there is more sympathetic than parasympathetic nervous system activity, whereas it will be low if parasympathetic activity is greater.

The sympathetic and parasympathetic nervous systems often operate in opposition to each other. However, as Atkinson, Atkinson, Smith, and Bem (1993) pointed out, there are some exceptions. For example, the sympathetic nervous system is very active in states of fear or excitement, and yet parasympathetic activity can cause people who are fearful or excited to have an involuntary discharge of their bladder or bowels. Another example is sex in the male. Parasympathetic activity is required to obtain an erection, whereas sympathetic activity is needed for ejaculation.

*Can you think of some situations in which the "fight or flight" response might be activated?*

# SYNAPSES AND NEUROTRANSMITTERS

As discussed earlier, neurons are cells specialised to conduct electrical impulses. **Synapses** are the very small gaps that exist between adjacent neurons. When neurons fire, they release chemicals or **neurotransmitters** which cross the synapses and affect the receptors on the adjacent neurons. These neurotransmitters either *increase* or *decrease* the membrane potential of the adjacent neurons. If they increase the membrane potential, they reduce the likelihood (or frequency) of the receptor neuron firing. If they decrease the membrane potential, they increase the likelihood (or frequency) of the receptor neuron firing.

So far we have been talking as if the receptor area of each neuron only has a single synapse. In fact, there are generally thousands of synapses associated with the receptor area of each neuron. What determines whether or not any given neuron fires? If its membrane potential is reduced to –65 mV or less, then the neuron fires. This consists of an **action potential** which is generated at the axon hillock. It is a brief electrical and chemical event, and it is always the same size and duration. More specifically, an action potential lasts for about 1 ms, and it reverses the membrane potential from about –65 mV to about +50 mV.

Pinel (1997) compared the firing of a neuron to the firing of a gun. In both cases, there is a threshold that has to be reached: sufficient stimulation by other neurons or sufficient pressure on the trigger. In both cases, exceeding the threshold does not increase the size of the effect. If the action potential is always the same, how can we tell the difference between a strong and a weak stimulus? When a strong stimulus is presented, far more neurons fire, and they fire more frequently, than is the case when a weak stimulus is presented.

We will now discuss in a little more detail the processes occurring during an action potential. Initially, the sodium and potassium ion channels open. This causes sodium ions to enter the neuron, followed very shortly by potassium

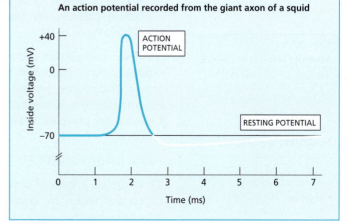

An action potential recorded from the giant axon of a squid

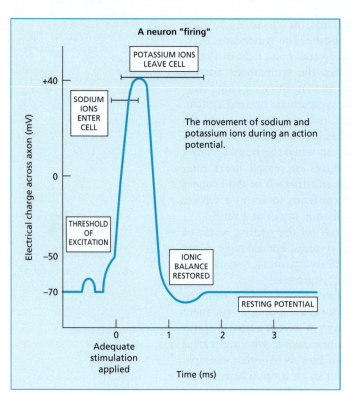

**A neuron "firing"**

POTASSIUM IONS LEAVE CELL

SODIUM IONS ENTER CELL

The movement of sodium and potassium ions during an action potential.

THRESHOLD OF EXCITATION

IONIC BALANCE RESTORED

RESTING POTENTIAL

Electrical charge across axon (mV)

+40

0

−50

−70

0    1    2    3

Adequate stimulation applied

Time (ms)

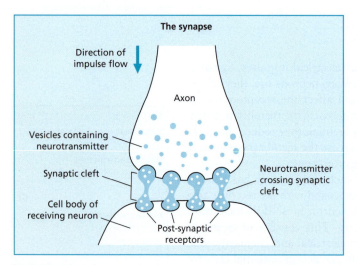

**The synapse**

Direction of impulse flow

Axon

Vesicles containing neurotransmitter

Synaptic cleft

Cell body of receiving neuron

Neurotransmitter crossing synaptic cleft

Post-synaptic receptors

ions being driven out of the neuron. After about 1 ms, the sodium ion channels close, followed by the potassium channels. The closure of these channels causes the action potential to come to an end. However, there is a very short period after the start of an action potential before a neuron can fire again; this is known as the **absolute refractory period**. The absolute refractory period in most neurons ends within 2 ms of the start of an action potential, and so such neurons can fire with a frequency of about 500 times per second. However, there are other neurons which can sometimes fire with a frequency of 1000 times per second.

Many neurons in the nervous system have axons covered in a fatty sheath known as myelin, whereas other neurons do not. In addition, there are numerous neurons that do not have axons and so do not produce action potentials. Myelinated axons have gaps in the myelin sheath known as the nodes of Ranvier, and action potentials jump from node to node along the axon. Action potentials travel much faster along myelinated axons than along unmyelinated axons, with respective speeds of 80–100 metres per second versus only 2 or 3.

## Synaptic transmission

Most synapses are directed synapses, meaning the site of neurotransmitter release from one neuron is very close to the site of neurotransmitter reception at another neuron. It used to be thought that each neuron only released *one* neurotransmitter. However, it has been known for some time that many neurons release *two or more* neurotransmitters.

Neurotransmitters initiate reactions in the postsynaptic neuron by binding to its receptors. Most neurotransmitters can bind to various types of receptors (e.g., dopamine has at least five types of receptors and serotonin has at least ten), and the nature of the receptor response varies from one type to another. We can think of neurotransmitters as keys and of receptors as locks: There has to be a fit between the two for anything to happen.

There are two basic types of receptor:

1. *Ion-channel linked receptors*. These receptors are activated *directly* by neurotransmitters.

2. *G-protein linked receptors*. These receptors are activated *indirectly* in a rather complex way. The effects of neurotransmitters on these receptors (compared to ion-channel linked receptors) are "slower to develop, longer-lasting, more diffuse, and more varied" (Pinel, 1997, p. 95).

Two mechanisms prevent a neurotransmitter from having a long-lasting effect on synapses. First, there is **re-uptake**, in which neurotransmitters are drawn back into the presynaptic neuron. Second, there is enzymatic degradation. What happens here is that the neurotransmitter is degraded or broken apart in the synapse by the action of enzymes. **Enzymes** are proteins that control the rate of various chemical reactions.

## Neurotransmitters

There are six classes of neurotransmitters. One class of neurotransmitters consists of neuropeptides, which are large-molecule transmitters. Some neuropeptides are neuromodulators, meaning they affect the sensitivity of neurons to signals but do not themselves send signals to other neurons. Endorphins are among the most important neuropeptides. They play a significant role in activating the systems involved in pleasure and in pain suppression. Drugs such as heroin, morphine, and opium affect the same receptors as the endorphins.

The other five classes of neurotransmitters are as follows: the amino acids, the monoamines, acetylcholine, purines, and the soluble gases. Two of the most commonly found amino acids in the central nervous systems of mammals are gamma-aminobutyric acid (GABA) and glutamate. GABA is the main inhibitory neurotransmitter in the central nervous system, whereas glutamate is the main excitatory neurotransmitter.

There are four monoamine neurotransmitters: dopamine, serotonin, adrenaline, and noradrenaline. Dopamine acts as a neurotransmitter primarily in the midbrain. In contrast, adrenaline and noradrenaline function as neurotransmitters mainly in the peripheral nervous system, and serotonin acts mainly close to the mid-line of the brainstem. All these neurotransmitters are important. For example, it has been argued that dopamine and serotonin are both involved in schizophrenia (see Chapter 22). Degeneration of the dopamine-releasing neurons in the substantia nigra plays a part in causing Parkinson's disease, a disorder involving poor muscular control. Serotonin is involved in the regulation of arousal, sleep, and mood. Adrenaline and noradrenaline are involved in emotion and stress (see Chapter 5) and in the workings of the endocrine system.

Acetylcholine is the only neurotransmitter in its class. It is found at numerous synapses within the nervous system, including those in the central nervous system and the autonomic nervous system. Acetylcholine is the most important chemical messenger for motor neurons in the peripheral nervous system, including the autonomic nervous system. Within the central nervous system, it excites skeletal muscles and inhibits cardiac muscle. In addition, acetylcholine is involved in learning and memory.

Adenosine and adenosine triphosphate (ATP) are both purine transmitters. Adenosine acts to inhibit the release of several neurotransmitters such as acetylcholine and serotonin. ATP is a neurotransmitter that is used to deliver energy to various parts of the body.

The soluble gas transmitters were discovered more recently than most of the other neurotransmitters. They include carbon monoxide and nitric oxide. These neurotransmitters exist for a very short period of time, because they are rapidly broken down and produce other chemicals or second messengers.

You may have been surprised to discover that there are numerous neurotransmitters and that most neurotransmitters have several types of receptors associated with them. Why are matters so complicated? The answer is that they need to be in order to permit the complexities of human thought and behaviour.

## Practical applications

What are the practical applications of discovering the detailed processes involved in synaptic transmission? Probably the greatest benefit has come from the development of drugs designed to have certain effects on synaptic transmission. In this section, we will consider some of the various ways in which drugs affect synaptic transmission. Their effects on behaviour are discussed in the following section.

Drugs affect synaptic transmission by changing the effects of neurotransmitters. Some drugs (**agonists**) increase the effects of a given neurotransmitter on synaptic transmission. In contrast, other drugs (**antagonists** or blockers) reduce the effects of a neurotransmitter. Agonists and antagonists can be divided into those acting directly and those that act indirectly. Drugs acting directly are typically very similar in chemical structure to the neurotransmitter, and like the neurotransmitter they affect synaptic receptors. Direct-acting agonists stimulate synaptic receptors, whereas direct-acting antagonists prevent the neurotransmitter from stimulating synaptic receptors. Heroin is an example of a direct-acting agonist, and the depressant drug chlorpromazine is an example of a direct-acting antagonist.

Indirect-acting drugs also change the effects of neurotransmitters, but do not do so by affecting synaptic receptors. The stimulant drug amphetamine is an indirect-acting agonist which increases the release of neurotransmitter substance from the presynaptic terminal. *Para*-Chlorophenylalanine (PCPA) is an indirect antagonist. It produces a large reduction in

*Why is it so important to prevent neurotransmitters from having a long-term effect on the synapse?*

*Why might it be useful to have excitatory and inhibitory transmitters?*

**KEY TERMS**

**Agonists:** drugs that increase the effects of a given neurotransmitter on synaptic transmission; see antagonists.

**Antagonists:** drugs that decrease the effects of a given neurotransmitter on synaptic transmission; see agonists.

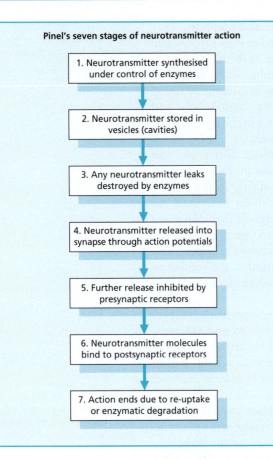

**Pinel's seven stages of neurotransmitter action**

1. Neurotransmitter synthesised under control of enzymes

2. Neurotransmitter stored in vesicles (cavities)

3. Any neurotransmitter leaks destroyed by enzymes

4. Neurotransmitter released into synapse through action potentials

5. Further release inhibited by presynaptic receptors

6. Neurotransmitter molecules bind to postsynaptic receptors

7. Action ends due to re-uptake or enzymatic degradation

the production of the neurotransmitter serotonin by inhibiting one of the enzymes needed to synthesise serotonin.

The effects of neurotransmitters and of drugs on synaptic transmission are much more complex than has been indicated so far. Pinel (1997) argued that neurotransmitter action often involves seven distinct stages or processes (some of which we have discussed already):

1. Neurotransmitter molecules are synthesised under enzymal control.
2. Neurotransmitter molecules are stored in vesicles (cavities).
3. Molecules that leak from vesicles are destroyed by enzymes (proteins that control the rate of chemical reactions).
4. Action potentials cause vesicles to release the neurotransmitter molecules into the synapse.
5. Neurotransmitter molecules bind with presynaptic receptors and inhibit additional neurotransmitter release.
6. Neurotransmitter molecules bind to postsynaptic receptors.
7. Neurotransmitter molecules cease to affect postsynaptic receptors via re-uptake or enzymatic degradation.

As you can imagine, the fact that several processes are involved in neurotransmitter action means there are several ways in which drugs can change neurotransmitter action. Pinel (1997) identified six mechanisms of agonistic drug action and five mechanisms of antagonistic drug action. Some agonists increase the synthesis of neurotransmitter molecules (Stage 1), whereas others destroy degrading enzymes (Stage 3), or block the inhibition of neurotransmitter release (Stage 5), or block the processes of re-uptake or enzymatic degradation (Stage 7). Some antagonists destroy synthesising enzymes (Stage 1), and others increase the leakage of neurotransmitter molecules from vesicles or cavities (Stage 3), or increase the inhibition of neurotransmitter release (Stage 5), or block the binding of neurotransmitter molecules to postsynaptic receptors (Stage 6).

# DRUGS AND BEHAVIOUR

There are hundreds (or possibly thousands) of different drugs. The media have tended to focus on illegal drugs (e.g., ecstasy, heroin, cocaine), but numerous legal drugs are taken every day by millions of people. These include alcohol, nicotine, and caffeine (found in drinks such as tea, coffee, and cola). The emphasis in this section is on drugs that can have very damaging effects on the central nervous system, which can tell us something about the workings of the brain (e.g., underlying neurotransmitter function), and which alter psychological processes. However, many drugs have positive effects on behaviour. These include drugs used in therapy (e.g., anti-anxiety drugs, anti-depressant drugs, and drugs used to control the symptoms of schizophrenia) (see Chapter 22).

Psychologists have been particularly interested in **psychoactive drugs**, which alter psychological or mental processes. There are many different ways to categorise psychoactive drugs, but all tend to exaggerate the similarities among drugs within the same category. According to Hamilton and Timmons (1995), three of the main categories are as follows:

1. *Depressants.* These drugs (e.g., alcohol, barbiturates) produce feelings of relaxation and drowsiness; they have what is known as a sedative effect.
2. *Stimulants.* These drugs (e.g., amphetamine, caffeine, nicotine) produce a state of alertness, and can increase feelings of confidence.

**KEY TERM**

**Psychoactive drugs:** drugs that have a significant effect on one or more psychological or mental processes.

3.  *Hallucinogens*. These drugs (e.g., LSD) produce mental distortions and hallucinations, and can cause psychotic symptoms.

The above list is by no means exhaustive. For example, it leaves out several kinds of dangerous drugs, such as the opiates (e.g., heroin, morphine) or marijuana, which are discussed below.

Drugs affect our behaviour by influencing neurotransmitters (see detailed discussion above). There is a crucial distinction between two types of drugs: (1) agonists, which *increase* the effects of a given neurotransmitter; and (2) antagonists, which *reduce* the effects of a neurotransmitter. Some drugs act *directly* on neurotransmitters at the synapse, whereas others act *indirectly* (see above).

Most drugs have several effects on brain functioning. We can see this very clearly in the case of drugs (e.g., anti-anxiety drugs, anti-depressant drugs) designed to reduce the symptoms of mental disorder (see Chapter 22). Nearly all such drugs have a range of unwanted side effects, and this happens because it has not proved possible to devise drugs that have very precise and specific modes of action.

## Depressants

There are several depressant drugs including alcohol and the barbiturates. We will focus on alcohol, which is used by hundreds of millions of people around the world. It is regarded as a depressant drug, because it reduces neural firing at moderate doses and above. How does alcohol do this? It has various effects on the nervous system:

> *It reduces the flow of calcium into neurons by acting on calcium channels, increases the action of the inhibitory neurotransmitter GABA by acting on the GABA receptor complex, increases the number of binding sites for the excitatory neurotransmitter glutamate, reduces the effects of glutamate at some of its receptor subtypes, and interferes with second messenger systems inside neurons (Pinel, 1997, p. 332).*

Small amounts of alcohol typically make people feel less anxious, more relaxed, and less inhibited (Gray, 1982). This occurs in part because alcohol leads to increased GABA transmission. Small amounts of alcohol stimulate dopamine pathways, with the increased levels of dopamine probably playing a role in producing the pleasurable effects of alcohol (Rosenzweig, Breedlove, & Leiman, 2002). In large quantities, alcohol has a sedative effect on many people, but it makes others argumentative and aggressive. Very large amounts of alcohol cause loss of co-ordination, socially unacceptable behaviour, and even unconsciousness. People who consume a large amount of alcohol over a short period of time subsequently experience alcohol withdrawal syndrome consisting of three stages. First, they experience headaches, nausea, sweating, and abdominal cramps about 5 hours after drinking has stopped. Second, they experience convulsions which can last for several hours about 1 day after drinking has stopped. Third, there is **delirium tremens**, which involves hallucinations, agitation, delusions, and high temperature.

High doses of alcohol can make people aggressive and violent. For example, most murders are committed by people who have been drinking (Bushman & Cooper, 1990). Alcohol probably makes people aggressive because it reduces their tendency to focus on the social and other constraints that prevent sober individuals from behaving aggressively (see Chapter 19).

The effects of alcohol on driving performance are of special importance to society. Drew, Colquhoun, and Long (1958) found surprisingly small doses of alcohol disrupted driving performance by slowing reaction times, reducing steering efficiency, and lowering attention to speedometer readings. Sabey and Codling (1975) considered the effects of the introduction of legislation in Great Britain putting a legal limit on the level of alcohol in the blood. In the year after the legislation was introduced, there was a 36% decrease in the number of people killed on the roads during the main drink hours of 10 pm to 4 am. There was a reduction of only 7% in fatalities for the hours 4 am to 10 pm.

Hockey (1983) summarised the negative effects of alcohol on performance. Alcohol reduces alertness, decreases speed of performance, reduces accuracy of performance, and reduces short-term memory capacity. As a result, alcohol impairs performance on nearly all tasks.

**KEY TERM**
**Delirium tremens:** a state produced by excessive alcohol intake that involves hallucinations, agitation, delusions, and high temperature.

What is another name for experiencing effects after taking a "dummy drug"?

We must distinguish between the effects of alcohol directly on the nervous system and those due to *expectations* about its effects. This has been addressed by giving people non-alcoholic drinks they are led to believe are alcoholic. The expectations within any given culture have a strong impact on behaviour (see Hull & Bond, 1986). For example, male participants who thought mistakenly they had drunk alcohol reported higher sexual arousal and less guilt when exposed to sexually arousing stimuli regardless of whether or not they had actually consumed any alcohol.

## Alcoholism

Some people (especially men) become alcoholics as a result of their addiction to alcohol. Cloninger (1987) argued there are two kinds of alcoholics: (1) steady drinkers, who drink virtually every day and find it very hard to abstain from drinking; and (2) binge drinkers, who drink only occasionally, but cannot stop drinking when they have started.

Why do people become alcoholics? Cloninger, Bohmann, Sigvardsson, and von Knorring (1985) carried out an adoption study to assess the relative importance of heredity and environment. There was a major effect of heredity on steady drinking in men but not in women: Men tended to become steady drinkers if their biological father was a steady drinker, but the drinking behaviour of members of their adoptive family had no effect. Binge drinking in males and females depended on both heredity and environment. Binge drinkers tended to have a biological parent who was a binge drinker *and* one or more heavy drinkers in their adoptive family.

More direct evidence of the importance of genetic factors in alcoholism was reported by Smith et al. (1992), who focused on a gene associated with a visible marker in one of the chromosomes. This particular gene was found in 69% of alcoholics compared to only 20% of non-alcoholics.

Other genes are also involved. After someone has consumed alcohol, enzymes in the liver metabolise it to acetaldehyde, which is a poisonous substance. Another enzyme (acetaldehyde dehydrogenase) converts acetaldehyde into acetic acid, which is a source of energy. Approximately 50% of Asians have rather low amounts of acetaldehyde dehydrogenase. As a result, many Asians feel unwell or have severe face flushing after drinking alcohol. This helps to explain why Chinese and Japanese people drink less alcohol than those in the Western world. It is of relevance here to mention the drug Antabuse, which is used to treat alcoholism. Antabuse produces a decrease in the level of acetaldehyde dehydrogenase, so anyone consuming alcohol within the following 2 days can become seriously ill.

What are the consequences of alcoholism? It can cause cirrhosis of the liver. It can also cause severe damage by preventing the liver from metabolising the vitamin thiamine. Thiamine deficiency leads to the loss of brain neurons, eventually producing amnesia or memory loss in the form of **Korsakoff's syndrome**. Patients suffering from this syndrome have great difficulties in acquiring new knowledge about the world and their experiences, and so they have poor long-term memory in those areas (see Chapter 9).

## Opiates

The opiates are drugs having effects similar to those of opium, and among the opiates are to be found some of the most dangerous and addictive drugs. The opiates are based on opium, which is a sticky resin produced by the opium poppy. Morphine is the main active ingredient of opium, and heroin and codeine can both be produced from morphine. Heroin (technically, diacetylmorphine) was developed because soldiers given morphine to relieve pain often became addicted to it. This led the Bayer drug company to develop heroin as a substitute drug at the end of the nineteenth century. However, heroin turned out to be as addictive as morphine.

What are the effects of the opiates on the brain? Opiates such as heroin stimulate specialised opiate receptors in different parts of the brain. Why do these opiate receptors exist? There are various naturally occurring or endogenous opiates. Two examples of opiates occurring naturally in the body are **encephalin** and **β-endorphin**.

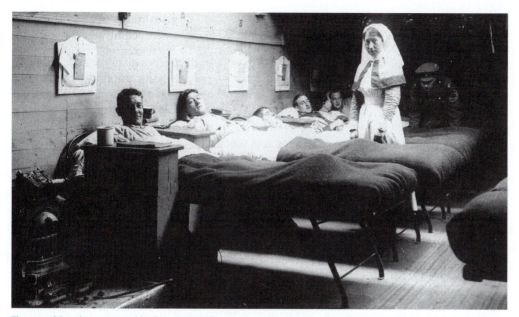

The morphine that was used in the nineteenth century in war hospitals sometimes resulted in addiction.

Four major effects of repeated use of heroin are as follows: analgesia or absence of pain, reinforcement or reward, sedation, and hypothermia or reduction of body temperature. There appear to be separate opiate receptors associated with each of these effects:

1. *Analgesia.* This is produced via opiate receptors in a part of the midbrain known as the periaqueductal grey matter.
2. *Reinforcement.* The reinforcing effects of opiates occur via opiate receptors in a part of the basal forebrain known as the nucleus accumbens and in the ventral tegmental area. The neurotransmitter dopamine is involved in the brain's reward system (see below), and opiates activate dopamine synapses indirectly. More specifically, the opiates cause inhibitory effects on neurons releasing GABA, which is a neurotransmitter inhibiting dopamine release. As a result, opiates increase dopamine release.
3. *Sedation.* There are relevant opiate receptors in the mesencephalic reticular formation.
4. *Hypothermia.* There are opiate receptors for hypothermia (low body temperature) in the preoptic area.

What are the effects of the opiates on people's psychological states? Heroin (the most commonly used opiate) produces an almost immediate feeling of euphoria and extreme well-being, followed by feelings of relaxation and contentment. Morphine produces similar effects, and is also very effective as an **analgesic** or painkiller. However, there are very serious consequences of repeated use of these drugs (e.g., a general increase in aggression, a reduced ability to get on with other people). Those taking heroin on a regular basis develop tolerance to it, with a given amount of the drug having decreasing effect. Not surprisingly, this growing tolerance leads most users of heroin to take increasingly large amounts of it to experience feelings of euphoria.

Heroin users rapidly become dependent on it. As a result, they find it very difficult to stop taking heroin, even though they recognise it is a dangerous drug. If heroin users do manage to stop, they experience several withdrawal symptoms. These include agitated behaviour, increased heart rate, sweating, insomnia, and uncontrollable leg movements. However, the withdrawal symptoms are typically nothing like as dramatic as they appear in films. Indeed, they have been likened to suffering from flu (Carlson, 1994).

## Stimulant drugs

Numerous stimulant drugs increase activity within the sympathetic nervous system. Cocaine, amphetamine, ecstasy, nicotine, and caffeine are just some examples of stimulant drugs. We will focus on two of the most important ones: cocaine and amphetamine.

KEY TERM

**Analgesic:** a drug that provides relief from pain.

A Bolivian miner chewing coca leaves. Chewing coca leaves serves as a stimulant and alleviates tiredness, hunger, and thirst. The leaves of the coca shrub have been used for medicinal and religious purposes in Bolivia for thousands of years.

## Cocaine

Cocaine comes from the leaves of the coca shrub, which is found in several countries including Peru, Colombia, and Bolivia. It is a powerful drug having very strong reinforcing properties. Cocaine can be used in the form of powder, with the drug entering the bloodstream rapidly. Crack cocaine can be smoked, and enters the bloodstream and the brain even more rapidly than cocaine powder. As a result, crack cocaine is more addictive than cocaine powder.

Some evidence of the power of cocaine was reported by Bozarth and Wise (1985). Rats could press a lever to administer cocaine to themselves. After 25 days of unlimited access to cocaine, over 90% of the rats had died because they had taken so much of it. In contrast, only 40% of rats who had unlimited access to heroin died over the same period of time.

What are the effects of cocaine on brain functioning? Cocaine blocks the re-uptake of noradrenaline, dopamine, and serotonin. The effect of this blocking is to prolong their effects.

People who have taken cocaine say it makes them feel euphoric, very wide-awake, and powerful. It also influences their behaviour, typically making people more talkative and energetic. Sigmund Freud often took cocaine. In 1885, he described "the exhilaration and lasting euphoria ... You perceive an increase of self-control and possess more vitality and capacity for work" (1885/1950 p. 9).

The positive effects wear off within about 30 minutes or so, producing feelings of depression and extreme tiredness. These negative after-effects of taking cocaine are sometimes known as "crashing". People taking cocaine on a regular basis often experience psychotic symptoms such as hallucinations, paranoid delusions, and mood disturbances.

Repeated use of cocaine leads to addiction, but this does not seem be due to physical dependence. Cocaine users who stop taking cocaine do not generally show any withdrawal symptoms, nor do they develop tolerance for cocaine while they are taking it.

### Change over time

Attitudes to drugs of all types have changed and will continue to change over time. When Freud first tried cocaine he was enthusiastic about its use as a therapeutic drug, and recommended it to many people, including his friends and family. His close friend Fleischl became severely addicted to cocaine, which eventually contributed to his death (Stevens, 1989). Nowadays cocaine would not be seen as therapeutically useful.

In the 1960s and 1970s, amphetamines were prescribed to suppress appetite and help in weight loss. However, once the dramatic side-effects of amphetamine use became known, this practice waned, and is now regarded as very dangerous.

## Amphetamine

Amphetamine is an artificial substance whose effects resemble those of cocaine. Amphetamine makes people feel very alert, aroused, and full of energy. One difference from cocaine is that these effects typically last for several hours rather than 30 minutes or so. When the effects of the amphetamine wear off, there is a similar crashing to that found with cocaine. Persistent use of amphetamines can produce psychotic symptoms and high levels of anger and aggression.

What are the effects of amphetamine on brain functioning? One of its molecules has a structure similar to that of the neurotransmitters noradrenaline, adrenaline, and dopamine. Amphetamine leads to increased release of all three neurotransmitters from the presynaptic terminals. Amphetamine also increases the length of time during which the catecholamine neurotransmitters remain in the synaptic cleft, which enhances their effects. This happens in part because amphetamine blocks the re-uptake of catecholamines into the presynaptic terminal.

The effects of amphetamine on behaviour were summarised by Hockey (1983). Amphetamine in moderate doses increases the speed of performance, but this is sometimes achieved at the cost of more errors. There is increased attentional selectivity, with less important environmental stimuli being ignored. Finally, there is a reduction in the capacity of short-term memory.

*Natural forms of many of these drugs have been used by other cultures for centuries. Can you think of any examples?*

## Hallucinogens

Hallucinogens are drugs producing visual hallucinations, illusions, and other distortions of thinking. Some hallucinogens are naturally occurring, whereas others are synthetic or

**KEY TERM**

**Hallucinogens:** drugs that produce visual hallucinations and distorted thoughts.

manufactured substances. Naturally occurring hallucinogens include psilocybin, which is found in magic mushrooms, and mescaline, which comes from the peyote cactus. Manufactured hallucinogens include lysergic acid diethylamide or LSD, dimethyltryptamine or DMT, and phencyclidine or phenylcyclohexylpiperidine (PCP).

Hallucinogenic drugs have numerous effects on those who take them. Halgin and Whitbourne (1997, p. 441) concluded these drugs:

*cause anxiety, depression, ideas of reference [misinterpreting trivial remarks as having personal significance], fear of losing one's mind, paranoid thinking, and generally impaired functioning. Also prominent are perceptual changes such as the intensification of perceptions, feelings of depersonalisation, hallucinations, and illusions. Physiological responses may include dilation of the pupils, increased heart rate, sweating, heart palpitations, blurred vision, tremors, and uncoordination.*

Repeated use of hallucinogens leads to hallucinogen persisting perception disorder, which is typically found when no hallucinogens have been taken for some weeks. It involves flashbacks, hallucinations, delusions, and mood changes, many of them resembling the effects of hallucinogenic intoxication.

Of the various hallucinogens, most is known about LSD or acid. It was discovered towards the end of the 1943 by a scientist called Albert Hoffmann. He swallowed the drug extract of a fungus which he thought might help people with breathing difficulties. Unfortunately, the drug gave him vivid hallucinations on his way home. According to Hoffmann, "It was so unusual that I really got afraid that I had become insane." In the 1960s, LSD played an important role in the drug culture that started with a Harvard University Professor, Timothy Leary, in the United States.

When someone has taken LSD, the resultant "trip" typically lasts for between 4 and 12 hours. The distorted thought processes produced by LSD can delude people into thinking

During the 1960s Timothy Leary, a professor at Harvard University, described drugs such as LSD as "mind-expanding", and advocated their use. He advised people to "tune in, turn on, and drop out", much to the consternation of the establishment.

they can fly or jump safely from the top of a tall building. If such delusions are acted on, they can cause death. Repeated use of LSD does not seem to lead to physical dependence, and when people stop taking it there are few if any withdrawal symptoms. It is not altogether clear whether LSD can cause **psychological dependence.**

Some of the effects of PCP or "angel dust" resemble those of LSD, but it is a more dangerous drug. PCP can make people aggressive, agitated, and violent, and it can produce some of the symptoms of schizophrenia. It can also cause confusion and stereotyped behaviour. Worst of all, it can produce high blood pressure, convulsions, and even coma.

What are the effects of hallucinogenic drugs on the brain? The structure of LSD is similar to that of serotonin, and as a result has effects on the serotonin system. More specifically, LSD is a serotonin agonist, and it stimulates serotonin receptors. It is also known that serotonin is involved in the control of dreaming (Carlson, 1994). If we put these facts together, it seems likely that some of the effects of LSD on the brain produce dream-like activity even though the individual is awake. PCP stimulates the release of the neurotransmitter dopamine (Gorelick & Balster, 1995). However, "Research continues to attempt to find the brain circuits specifically affected by PCP" (Rosenzweig, Leiman, & Breedlove, 1999, p. 97).

## Marijuana or cannabis

Marijuana is the name given to the dried leaves of the cannabis sativa or hemp plant, which is grown mainly in warm climates. The main active ingredient in this plant is delta-9-tetrahydrocannabinol or THC. However, marijuana contains dozens of other chemicals resembling THC, some of which may also have effects on the brain. Hashish or hash also contains THC. It is more powerful than marijuana or cannabis, because it contains THC taken from the resin of the plant. THC binds to receptors located in various regions of the brain, including the hippocampus, cerebellum, the caudate nucleus, and the neocortex (Matsuda, Lolait, Brownstein, Young, & Bonner, 1990). THC, marijuana, hashish, and some related substances are known as cannabinoids. One of the effects of THC is to stimulate the release of dopamine. Chen et al. (1990) found dopamine was released in the nucleus accumbens and medial frontal cortex after rats were injected with THC. Di Tomaso, Beltramo, and Plomelli (1996) found that chocolate contains very small amounts of cannabinoids. This may help to explain why so many people enjoy eating it!

*Given the parts of the brain that are affected by cannabis, what effects do you expect it to have on behaviour?*

Marijuana or cannabis has been taken for its effects on the mind for at least 6000 years according to Chinese records. It is usually smoked in a cigarette-like joint, but can also be eaten or injected. The effects of the drug last for about 2 hours, but THC remains in the body for several days.

What are the effects of marijuana or cannabis on mental processes and behaviour? Its psychological effects are surprisingly varied, and depend in part on the expectations of the person taking it. The effects of small doses tend to be rather subtle. According to the National Commission on Marijuana and Drug Abuse (1972, p. 68), someone who has had a small dose of marijuana:

> *may experience an increased sense of well-being: initial restlessness and hilarity followed by a dreamy, carefree state of relaxation; alteration of sensory perceptions including expansion of space and time; and a more vivid sense of touch, sight, smell, taste, and sound; a feeling of hunger, especially a craving for sweets; and subtle changes in thought formation and expression.*

High doses of marijuana or cannabis have more negative effects. There is poor co-ordination, an inability to concentrate, social withdrawal, impaired short-term memory, sensory distortion, watery eyes, and slurred speech. Some of these effects influence an individual's ability to drive a car. In a study of fatal car accidents in Alabama, it was found that 17% of drivers had taken cannabis (Fortenberry, Brown, & Shevlin, 1986). Cannabis use causes drivers to be relatively slow to realise that they should stop, but has little or no effect on their reaction time once they have decided to stop (Moskowitz, Hulbert, & McGlothin, 1976).

Marijuana or cannabis is typically not very addictive, and any withdrawal symptoms (e.g., nausea, sleep disturbance) tend to be mild and short-lived. However, many people do use cannabis regularly over long time periods, and there are various possible negative effects of such long-term use. First, it can impair respiratory functioning by causing coughs, asthma, and bronchitis. Second, it has been claimed that cannabis reduces the level of motivation, and prevents people from working effectively. However, there is little evidence to support this claim. Brill and Christie (1974) found the academic performance of college cannabis users and non-users was the same. However, prolonged heavy use of cannabis may lead to lethargy.

> **Cannabis and psychosis**
>
> In recent years, cases of cannabis psychosis have been reported in many countries. This is a condition that can produce uncharacteristic outbursts of aggression in between periods of lethargy, as well as schizophrenia and/or depressive symptoms (Rey & Tennant, 2002). The cause could be higher strength cannabis, i.e., a higher concentration of THC, and/or a genetic vulnerability to the drug. Longitudinal studies in Sweden, the Netherlands, New Zealand, and the USA all support a causal link between cannabis use and psychosis, which increases proportionally with the amount of the drug used. The research now focuses on whether use triggers an underlying predisposition, or actually causes the psychosis.

Third, it has been suggested that long-term use of cannabis in males reduces the level of the male sex hormone testosterone, and thus impairs sexual functioning. However, most of the evidence does not support these suggestions (see Pinel, 1997). Fourth, it has been argued that cannabis use can lead to physical disease, because it causes impaired functioning of the immune system and because it produces increased heart rate. However, once again the evidence is unconvincing.

# Drug addiction

Millions of people around the world are said to suffer from some form of drug addiction. However, it is not easy to provide a good definition of addiction. The *Diagnostic and Statistical Manual of Mental Disorders* (4th ed.; DSM-IV; American Psychiatric Association, 1994) refers to substance-related disorders. Those suffering from such a disorder often exhibit dependence, which consists of "a cluster of cognitive, behavioural, and physiological symptoms indicating that the individual continues use of the substance despite significant substance-related problems" (p. 176). Some of the criteria used within DSM-IV to identify dependence are as follows: tolerance (e.g., much larger doses are needed to achieve a given effect); efforts to reduce or control substance use are unsuccessful; the substance is often taken in larger amounts or over a longer period than the individual intended; the individual devotes a lot of time to making sure he/she has access to the substance; and important social, occupational, or recreational activities are reduced or given up as a result of substance use.

*Why might it be difficult to carry out research into drug addiction?*

Most drug users develop **drug tolerance**, meaning the effects of any given amount of a drug tend to decrease with repeated use. For example, a small alcoholic drink can have an intoxicating effect on someone who has never had alcohol before, but will have little or no effect on a seasoned drinker. Not surprisingly, drug tolerance often leads drug users to take progressively larger amounts of the drug in question.

What causes drug tolerance? Several factors are involved. First, the rate at which the drug is broken down or metabolised within the body may increase. For example, in the case of alcohol, the liver increases the rate of production of various enzymes, and this speeds up the metabolism of alcohol. Second, neurons may become less sensitive to the effects of a drug with repeated use.

Third, situational factors are surprisingly important. For example, Le et al. (1979) looked at the reduction of body temperature in rats after they had been administered alcohol. When it was administered on several days in the same room, there was increased drug tolerance (i.e., body temperature reduced progressively less). However, when the rats who had developed this tolerance were administered alcohol in a new situation, there was no evidence of tolerance (i.e., there was as great a reduction in body temperature as at the start of the experiment).

Textbook discussions of drug addiction sometimes convey the impression that individuals are typically addicted to or dependent on only one drug. In fact, that is *not* the case. Most drug abusers are heavy users of two or more drugs (Gossop, 1995, p. 440).

There are two main theoretical approaches to drug addiction or dependence. According to one approach (the physical dependence theory), people become addicted

> **KEY TERM**
>
> **Drug tolerance:** the reduced effects of a given amount of a drug as a result of frequent use.

because doing without drugs is so unpleasant. According to the other approach (positive reward theory), addiction occurs because drugs are perceived to be so pleasant and rewarding. We will now consider the evidence relating to these two theoretical approaches.

## Physical dependence theory

It has often been argued that addiction involves **physical dependence**, which occurs when the body needs a given drug and there are severe withdrawal symptoms if the drug is no longer available. More specifically, it is assumed that, "physical dependence traps addicts in a vicious circle of drug taking and withdrawal symptoms. The idea was that drug users whose intake has reached a level sufficient to induce physical dependence are driven by their withdrawal symptoms to self-administer the drug each time they attempt to curtail their intake" (Pinel, 1997, p. 340). This type of theory is adhered to by many non-experts, but is seriously flawed.

## Evidence

Many addicts are put through a process of **detoxification**. What happens is that the drug to which they are addicted is gradually withdrawn until it has disappeared from their bodies and they suffer no withdrawal symptoms. According to physical-dependence theories, this should stop the addiction. The reality is very different. In fact, the great majority of detoxified addicts soon start taking their drug of choice again.

According to physical-dependence theories, there should be withdrawal effects when someone stops taking drugs on which they have become dependent. This is frequently the case, but there are numerous exceptions. For example, drugs such as cocaine and amphetamine are rarely associated with severe withdrawal symptoms (Kalat, 2000).

As we have seen, it is hard for physical-dependence theories to explain why addicts often relapse even after all traces of the drug have been eliminated from their bodies. Koob et al. (1993) argued that what may be involved is a process of conditioning. Suppose an addict returns to a situation in which he/she has had considerable past experience with the drug. Exposure to this situation produces conditioned withdrawal effects, which may persuade the addict to resume taking the drug in question. In fact, however, addicts put back into an environment in which they have taken drugs are more likely to experience positive effects than negative withdrawal effects. For example, some heroin addicts are known as "needle freaks", because they seem to enjoy sticking empty needles into themselves.

## Evaluation

➕ The theory may help to explain dependence on alcohol.
➕ The predicted withdrawal symptoms are often found.
➖ The typical failure of detoxification is contrary to theoretical expectations.
➖ The strong withdrawal effects predicted by the theory are typically not found with some drugs (e.g., cocaine, amphetamine).
➖ Advocates of physical dependence theory de-emphasise the role played by the reward value of drugs in addiction or dependence.

## Positive reward theory

The key assumption of the positive reward theory was expressed succinctly by Wise (1996, p. 319): "The pharmacological rewards of addictive drugs are habit forming because they act in the brain circuits that subserve more natural and biologically significant rewards." More specifically, it is assumed that some of the main brain areas associated with reward are located along the medial forebrain bundle (parts of which pass through the hypothalamus), the ventral tegmental area, the nucleus accumbens, and the pons. What is also assumed to be important is that, "several of the more addictive substances ... elevate ... dopamine concentrations in the nucleus accumbens and other dopamine terminal fields" (Wise, 1996, p. 333). **Dopamine** is a neurotransmitter found in several parts of the brain including the medial forebrain bundle and the nucleus accumbens.

Many addicts continue to take drugs even though the drugs themselves do not seem to create much pleasure, in large part because of increased tolerance for the drugs. According to Robinson and Berridge (1993), this can be explained by distinguishing between the pleasurable effects of drugs and the *anticipated* pleasure of taking them. Initially, drugs are taken because of their pleasurable effects, but in addicts they are taken mostly because of the anticipated pleasure.

## Evidence

One of the first attempts to locate a reward system in the brain was reported by Olds and Milner (1954). They found rats could be trained to press a lever to receive stimulation in the septal area of the brain. Subsequent research (e.g., Olds & Olds, 1963) indicated that stimulation of a wide range of limbic and diencephalic structures was also rewarding, and showed the medial forebrain bundle was of particular importance. In many of these studies, rats worked very hard to receive self-stimulation of the brain, sometimes pressing the lever up to 2000 times per hour. Such findings suggest the self-stimulation was very rewarding. A final key finding from these self-stimulation studies is that brain stimulation is mostly rewarding in tracts of axons that release dopamine, indicating that dopamine plays an important role within the brain's reward system.

*What are the advantages and disadvantages of carrying out brain research on rats?*

Most of the areas in which self-stimulation is rewarding are within what is known as the mesotelencephalic dopamine system. This is a system of dopaminergic neurons projecting from the midbrain into various regions within the forebrain. However, as can be seen in the figure on the right, there are numerous brain areas (at least in the rat!) which have shown rewarding effects of brain stimulation.

Another way of assessing the role of the mesotelencephalic dopamine system is by lesion studies, in which parts of that system are damaged or destroyed. Several studies have confirmed the importance of this region. Fibiger et al. (1987) found that lesions to the ventral tegmental area produced a substantial reduction in self-stimulation.

Evidence of the role of dopamine in the reward system and in addiction has been obtained by administering dopaminergic antagonists that selectively block dopamine. Such antagonists have been found to reduce self-stimulation in animals (see Rosenzweig et al., 2002). In addition, studies on humans have revealed that dopaminergic antagonists eliminate cocaine craving (e.g., Berger et al., 1996). They also eliminate the euphoric feelings associated with the use of amphetamines (e.g., Wise & Bozarth, 1984).

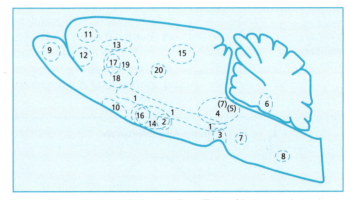

Areas of the rat brain in which rewarding effects of brain stimulation have been recorded. Some of the key areas are the medial forebrain bundle (1 in figure), the substantia nigra and ventral segmental area (3 in figure), and the nucleus accumbens (18 in figure). From Wise (1996).

It is important to establish that natural and biologically significant rewards (e.g., food, drink, sex) involve the same reward system as the one identified from studies of self-stimulation. In general terms, that is the case (see Wise, 1996). In addition, it has been found that sexual excitement is associated with the release of dopamine (Kalat, 2000), and that the presentation of fruit juice to monkeys leads to increased levels of dopamine (Mirenowicz & Schultz, 1996).

Do most of the addictive drugs discussed above have their effects via the reward system described above? There are various lines of research indicating that the answer is "Yes". First, one clear prediction is that drugs of abuse should increase the effects of self-stimulation on the rate of bar pressing. This prediction has been confirmed with several drugs, including amphetamine, morphine, cocaine, nicotine, and cannabis (see Wise, 1996, for a review).

Second, dopamine plays a central role within the reward system. As we have seen, several drugs increase dopamine activity whether directly or indirectly. These drugs include opiates (e.g., heroin, morphine), stimulants (e.g., cocaine, amphetamine), marijuana, and PCP. It is not clear that other addictive drugs increase dopamine activity. However, there is some evidence that the habit-forming effects of alcohol depend in part on the dopamine system (Samson et al., 1993).

Third, more evidence on the importance of dopamine was reported by Kuhar et al. (1991). They carried out a study on animals in which they observed the effects of drugs which selectively blocked dopaminergic receptors. As predicted by the theory, these drugs abolished the rewarding properties of cocaine.

We must avoid overstating the importance of the above reward system and dopamine in drug addiction. For example, Carlezon and Wise (1996) found that heroin continued to have some rewarding effects after dopamine synapses had been blocked. LSD attaches to (and stimulates) serotonin receptors rather than dopamine receptors. The drug methylenedioxymethamphetamine (commonly known as ecstasy) stimulates the release of dopamine at low doses. At high doses, however, it has progressively larger effects on serotonin synapses.

What conclusions can we draw? Wise (1996, p. 332) reviewed the literature, which he summarised as follows:

> *Several of the more addictive substances—the psychomotor stimulants, the opiates, nicotine, phencyclidine, and cannabis—synergise [work together] with rewarding medial forebrain bundle stimulation, and elevate—as does the stimulation itself ... —dopamine concentrations in the nucleus accumbens and other dopamine terminal fields.*

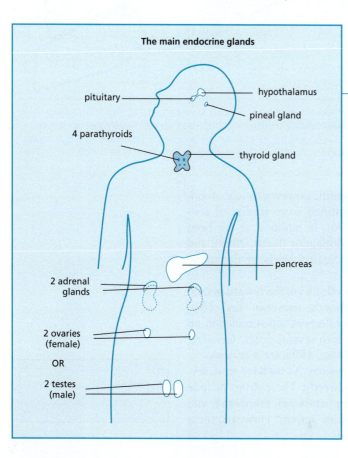

**The main endocrine glands**

pituitary

4 parathyroids

2 adrenal glands

2 ovaries (female)

OR

2 testes (male)

hypothalamus

pineal gland

thyroid gland

pancreas

## KEY TERMS

**Endocrine system:** this system consists of a number of glands that release hormones into the bloodstream.

**Hormones:** chemical substances released into the bloodstream.

## Evaluation

➕ The positive reward model helps to explain dependence on numerous drugs, including the opiates, stimulants, marijuana, and PCP.

➕ The main brain areas associated with reward have been identified, and the key role of dopamine has been established for several drugs.

➖ "Not all habit-forming drugs cause reliable reductions in reward thresholds or elevate extracellular dopamine levels" (Wise, 1996). Drugs to which the model does *not* apply well include alcohol, caffeine, the barbiturates, and the benzodiazepines.

➖ Stimulation in numerous brain areas is rewarding or reinforcing, and it remains unclear whether there is a single reward system or a number of partially connected systems.

## ENDOCRINE SYSTEM AND HORMONES

The **endocrine system** consists of various glands, including the following: the pituitary gland, the thyroid gland, the parathyroid gland, the adrenal gland, the pancreas, and the gonads. The endocrine system is not part of the nervous system, but there are numerous interactions between the endocrine system and the peripheral nervous system. More specifically, the endocrine glands secrete hormones (a term that comes from the Greek "hormon" meaning to excite). **Hormones** are chemical substances released into the bloodstream, and are so important they have been described as "the messengers of life". Dozens of hormones have already been identified, and additional ones are still being discovered from time to time.

There are various classes of hormones. One class is formed by protein hormones (e.g., insulin) and peptide hormones, both of which consist of chains of amino acids.

In general, the chains of amino acids are longer with proteins than with peptides. Another class of hormones consists of the steroid hormones, each of which contain four carbon rings. Examples of steroid hormones (most of which are discussed further below) are progesterone, testosterone, estradiol, corticosterone, and cortisol. In general, protein hormones produce their effects within a relatively short period of time (seconds or minutes), whereas steroid hormones typically take several hours to have an effect.

Hormones can have dramatic effects on our feelings and behaviour. However, they take some time to produce these effects because most hormones are transmitted fairly slowly by the bloodstream. Endocrine glands are ductless glands. They can be compared with glands having ducts or passages along which substances such as sweat or tears travel to the surface of the body.

According to Rosenzweig et al. (1999), there are 10 general principles of hormone action:

- Most hormones act fairly gradually.
- Hormones typically change the intensity or the probability of some form of behaviour, but do not have more dramatic effects.
- Hormones can be released either by environmental factors or by internal factors.
- Most hormones have several different effects, which can include effects on organs, tissues, and behaviour.
- Hormones are generally produced in fairly small amounts, and tend to be secreted or released in bursts.
- Several hormonal systems are strongly influenced by circadian systems, as a result of which hormonal levels tend to vary across the day (see Chapter 4).
- Hormones mostly have effects on other hormones.
- Hormones produce various metabolic changes, and can be involved in the breakdown of proteins, lipids, and carbohydrates.
- Any given hormone may have different functions from one species to another.
- Hormones only have effects on certain cells, namely, those having a protein that "recognises" the particular hormone.

*Can you think of any environmental factors that contribute to hormone release?*

## Hormonal vs. neural communication

There are various similarities between hormonal and neural communication via neurotransmitters (discussed earlier). First, endocrine glands store their hormones for later release, and neurons store chemicals for later release. Second, several chemicals (e.g., adrenaline, noradrenaline, cholecystokinin) act as both hormones and as neurotransmitters.

What are the main differences between hormonal and neural communication? Some key ones are as follows:

- Neural messages are distributed rapidly (within milliseconds), whereas hormonal messages are distributed fairly slowly (seconds, minutes, or hours).
- Neural messages control the activities of the body *directly* by activating muscles and glands, whereas the endocrine system exerts control *indirectly* via hormones circulating in the bloodstream.
- Neurotransmitters in the nervous system have specific and highly localised effects, whereas hormones typically spread around the body.
- Neurotransmitters in the nervous system generally have short-lived effects, whereas hormones can remain in the bloodstream for long periods of time.

Westen (1996, p. 84) neatly summarised the differences between the two systems. He argued that, "the difference between the communication that takes place through the two systems is analogous to the difference between word of mouth [nervous system] and mass media [endocrine system] (which can communicate information to hundreds of millions of people at once)".

We will shortly move to a discussion of the *main* glands and the hormones associated with them (the coverage is not exhaustive). The various parts of the endocrine system will be discussed separately, which may suggest these parts operate in many ways independently of each other. In fact, this is *not* the case. There is a reasonable amount of *interdependence* between the constituent parts of the endocrine system. Furthermore, the entire endocrine system should be regarded as forming part of a larger, integrated system.

| Nervous system | Endocrine system |
|---|---|
| ● Consists of nerve cells | ● Consists of ductless glands |
| ● Acts by transmitting nerve impulses | ● Acts by release of hormones |
| ● Acts rapidly | ● Acts slowly |
| ● Direct control | ● Indirect control |
| ● Specific localised effects of neurotransmitters | ● Hormones spread around the body |
| ● Short-lived effects | ● Hormones remain in the blood for some time |

## Hypothalamus

The parts of the endocrine system are distributed in various areas of the body. However, most of the endocrine system is controlled by the **hypothalamus**, which is a small structure at the base of the brain. There are direct connections between the hypothalamus and the anterior pituitary gland. Hypothalamic hormones (e.g., corticotropin-release factor) stimulate the anterior pituitary gland to secrete its hormones. After that, the hormones secreted by the anterior pituitary gland control the functioning of the other endocrine glands. However, what happens is not simply that the hypothalamus controls the anterior pituitary gland, and the anterior pituitary gland controls the other endocrine glands. In addition, hormones released by the endocrine glands often influence the hypothalamus and the anterior pituitary gland. More specifically, there is a negative-feedback system (Wickens, 2000): Increases in hormone levels are detected by the pituitary gland, and this leads to a decrease in the release of the hormones it controls.

## Pituitary gland

In view of its importance, the pituitary gland is often referred to as the "master gland" of the body. The anterior pituitary gland synthesises several hormones, with their release being controlled by the hypothalamus. These hormones are as follows:

- Growth hormone (also called somatotropin), which promotes growth throughout the body.
- Prolactin, which controls the secretions of the mammary glands.
- Adrenocorticotrophic hormone (ACTH), which controls the secretions of the adrenal cortex.
- Follicle-stimulating hormone, which helps to control the secretions of the gonads (sex organs).
- Luteinising hormone, which also plays a part in controlling the secretions of the gonads.
- Thyroid-stimulating hormone, which controls secretions of the thyroid gland.

The posterior pituitary gland is an outgrowth of the hypothalamus. It releases the following hormones: vasopressin (also known as antidiuretic hormone), which stimulates the kidneys to retain water in the body, and oxytocin, which produces contractions of the smooth tissues of the uterus during labour. There is evidence that oxytocin can help to reduce stress (see Chapter 5). In addition, the posterior pituitary gland releases very small amounts of various other peptides.

## Gonads

The gonads are the sexual glands of the body (see Chapter 3). The male gonads are known as testes and the female gonads as ovaries. Activity in the gonads is stimulated by luteinising hormone from the anterior pituitary gland. The male gonads produce sperm, and the female gonads produce ova or eggs. The gonads also secrete various hormones:

- **Androgens**. These are (slightly misleadingly) known as male sex steroid hormones, being found in greater quantities in male gonads; the main androgen is testosterone, which affects sex drive to some extent.

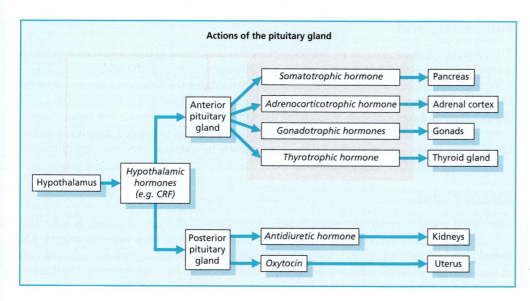

**Actions of the pituitary gland**

- **Oestrogens**. A range of sex hormones produced primarily in the ovaries, the main one being oestradiol; they influence the growth of breasts, the development of the female genitals, and may affect sex drive.
- **Gestagens**. A range of hormones produced by the ovaries; these hormones (of which progesterone is the main one) help to facilitate and to maintain pregnancy

Female primates have a reproductive cycle known as the menstrual cycle, whereas the females of other mammalian species have oestrous cycles. Both kinds of reproductive cycle start with the anterior pituitary gland secreting gonadotropic hormones. These hormones stimulate the growth of ovarian follicles which surround the ovum or egg. Oestradiol is secreted as the ovarian follicles develop, producing growth in the lining of the uterus. After that, luteinising hormone is secreted by the anterior pituitary gland, and this causes ovulation.

## Adrenal glands

There are two adrenal glands located just above the kidneys. Each gland consists of a central part known as the adrenal medulla, and an outer covering known as the adrenal cortex. When the adrenal glands are stimulated by ACTH from the anterior pituitary gland, they secrete various hormones including adrenaline and noradrenaline, both of which play a role in arousal (e.g., increased heart rate and blood pressure) and influence the sympathetic nervous system. High levels of adrenaline and noradrenaline are sometimes used as measures of stress (see Chapter 5).

The adrenal cortex releases the glucocorticoids including cortisone, hydrocortisone, and corticosterone, and cortisol. The glucocorticoids help to convert stored protein and fat into more usable forms of energy. They also serve to suppress the immune system. In addition, cortisol has powerful anti-inflammatory effects, and is released by the adrenal glands in response to injury.

## Thyroid and parathyroid glands

The thyroid gland is situated just underneath the larynx, which contains the vocal cords. The thyroid gland produces the hormone thyroxin, which increases the body's metabolic rate. Someone whose thyroid gland produces too much thyroxin suffers weight loss and insomnia. In contrast, under-production of that hormone causes obesity and general sluggishness.

The parathyroid gland is close to the thyroid gland. It has rather limited functions. It releases the hormone calcitonin. This hormone reduces the release of calcium from the skeleton, and by so doing prevents the level of calcium in the blood from becoming too high.

*Which psychological problems have been attributed to hormonal changes in women?*

**KEY TERMS**
**Oestrogens:** a class of hormones found in greater quantities in females than in males.
**Gestagens:** a class of hormones produced by the ovaries and of use during pregnancy.

## Pancreas gland

The pancreas is in the middle of the body close to the adrenal glands and the stomach. It secretes two important hormones: insulin and glucagon. Insulin influences the concentration of glucose in the blood, whereas glucagon stimulates the release of glucose into the blood. If insufficient insulin is produced, this leads to high blood-sugar levels and to a condition called **diabetes mellitus**. This condition is potentially fatal, but it can be kept under control by means of insulin injections. If too much insulin is produced, this leads to low blood-sugar levels, and to a condition characterised by extreme tiredness and dizziness. Insulin levels influence eating behaviour (see Chapter 3).

## Pineal gland

The pineal gland is relatively small, being approximately the size of a pea. It is located atop the brain stem, and receives neural input from the sympathetic nervous system. The pineal gland releases a hormone called melatonin. This hormone is typically released only at night, which explains why it is sometimes known as the Dracula hormone. Melatonin is an important hormone, because it plays a major role in inducing sleep (see Chapter 4).

## How important are hormones?

As we have seen, hormones have numerous different kinds of effects on our bodies, feelings, and behaviour. Thus, we need to study hormones and how they work to achieve a full understanding of human behaviour. However, the clearest evidence of the vital importance of hormones can be seen by considering what happens if the levels of various hormones become either deficient or excessive. For example, consider individuals with abnormal levels of thyroid release. Those with excessive levels are typically very anxious and agitated. In contrast, individuals with low levels of thyroid release are often depressed and show evidence of cognitive impairments.

There are several other negative consequences of abnormal hormone levels, but we will consider only two more. Some individuals with excessive release of glucocorticoids by the adrenal cortex suffer from Cushing's syndrome. This syndrome is characterised by depression, fatigue, and an abnormal distribution of hair. Parathyroid deficiency can cause the build-up of a calcium deposit in the basal ganglia, which in turn leads to a range of symptoms similar to those found in schizophrenia. In sum, inadequate or excessive levels of hormones can produce diverse behavioural, anatomical, and physiological disorders.

> **KEY TERM**
> **Diabetes mellitus:** a condition in which the failure of insulin to produce glucose absorption by the body causes large quantities of glucose in urine.

## SUMMARY

*Evolutionary perspective and genetics*

According to Darwin, species change via a process of natural selection. Studies of selective breeding support this view. Characteristics are passed on from one generation to the next via genes. Of crucial importance is fertilisation, in which genetic material in an egg cell and a sperm cell combines to form a zygote. Genetic factors influence individual differences in intelligence, personality, and mental disorder. Evolutionary psychology has shed light on mate selection, altruism, jealousy, and detection of cheating. However, evolutionary psychology is often speculative, and does not account well for the impact of culture on behaviour.

*Nervous system*

The nervous system contains neurons and glia. The nervous system is divided into the central nervous system (brain and spinal cord) and the peripheral nervous system. The brain has three major regions (hindbrain, midbrain, and forebrain). The hindbrain contains the cerebellum, which is involved in the control of balance and movement. It also contains the medulla, which helps to control breathing, salivation, and the cardiovascular system. The midbrain consists of the tectum and the tegmentum. There are routes for sensory information in the midbrain, and parts of the reticular formation are contained within it. In addition, the midbrain contains the substantia nigra, damage to which can lead to Parkinson's disease. The outer area of the forebrain is the cerebral cortex, mostly consisting of neocortex in humans. There are four lobes in the cerebral cortex: the frontal lobe (involved in the control of attention and working memory), the parietal lobe (involved in processing bodily sensations and touch information), the temporal lobe (involved in language processing and some aspects of emotion and motivation), and the occipital lobe (specialised for visual processing). The forebrain also contains the hypothalamus and the thalamus. The hypothalamus is involved in the control of body temperature, hunger, and thirst, and the thalamus is a relay station for sensory signals. The peripheral nervous system consists of the somatic nervous system (concerned with interactions with the external environment) and the autonomic nervous system (concerned with the body's internal environment). The autonomic nervous system is divided into the sympathetic nervous system and the peripheral nervous system. The former is involved when energy and arousal are needed (e.g., stressful situations), whereas the latter is involved when energy conservation is required.

When neurons fire, they release chemicals or neurotransmitters which cross the synapses and affect the receptors on adjacent neurons. Neurotransmitters alter the membrane potential of adjacent neurons, decreasing or increasing the chances (and frequency) of receptor neurons firing and producing an action potential. At the start of an action potential, sodium ions enter the neuron, followed by potassium ions being driven out. There are six classes of neurotransmitters. They have only short-lived effects on synapses because of re-uptake and enzymatic degradation. Knowledge of synapses and neurotransmitters is important to understand drug effects.

*Synapses and neurotransmitters*

Alcohol is a depressant drug reducing feelings of anxiety. Opiates (e.g., heroin, morphine) produce feelings of euphoria followed by contentment. Prolonged use can lead to aggression and an inability to get on with others. Cocaine makes people feel euphoric, powerful, and very wide-awake, but repeated use produces psychotic symptoms. The effects of amphetamine are similar. Cocaine and amphetamine are **dopamine agonists**, and dopamine affects the brain's reward system. Hallucinogens such as LSD and PCP produce hallucinations, illusions, and other distortions of thinking. Prolonged use of hallucinogens can produce anxiety, paranoid thinking, and aggression. The hallucinogens affect the serotonin system. Cannabis contains THC, which can produce relaxation, good humour, and increased sexual interest. Prolonged use can lead to reduced reproductive functioning and extreme lethargy. Many addictive drugs (e.g., opiates, stimulant drugs) increase dopamine secretion and increase activity in a reward system including the medial forebrain bundle. However, this system does not account for the effects of alcohol, caffeine, and the barbiturates.

*Drugs and behaviour*

The endocrine system consists of various glands including the pituitary, thyroid, parathyroid, adrenal, and pineal glands, and the pancreas and gonads. The endocrine glands secrete or release hormones. Hormones act gradually and typically have several effects across large areas. Most of the endocrine system is controlled by the hypothalamus. It is connected to the anterior pituitary gland, which is the "master gland" of the body, and releases numerous hormones. The gonads are the sexual glands of the body; they secrete androgens, oestrogens, and gestagens. The adrenal glands secrete various hormones (e.g., adrenaline, noradrenaline, and cortisol). The thyroid gland produces the hormone thyroxin, which increases the body's metabolic rate. The pancreas secretes insulin (which controls blood glucose levels) and glucagon (which stimulates the release of glucose into the blood).

*Endocrine system and hormones*

> **KEY TERM**
> **Dopamine agonists:** drugs that stimulate activity of the neurotransmitter dopamine.

# FURTHER READING

- Buss, D.M. (1999). *Evolutionary psychology: The new science of the mind*. Boston: Allyn & Bacon. This was the first textbook on evolutionary psychology, and it describes clearly the successes (and failures) of this approach.
- Kalat, J.W. (2000). *Biological psychology* (7th ed.). Belmont, CA: Wadsworth. This textbook contains accessible accounts of the nervous system and its effects on behaviour.
- Rosenzweig, M.R., Breedlove, S.M., & Leiman, A.L. (2002). *Biological psychology: An introduction to behavioural, cognitive, and clinical neuroscience* (3rd ed.). Sunderland, MA: Sinauer Associates. The biological bases of behaviour are discussed in detail in this textbook.

- **Need theories**
  Theories of motivation.

  *Maslow's hierarchy of needs;*
  *self-actualisation*
  *Alderfer's ERG theory*

- **Homeostasis: temperature and hunger**
  Regulating the body's internal environment.

  *Body temperature*
  *Regulatory mechanisms*
  *Systems of temperature regulation*
  *Hunger and eating behaviour*
  *What food is for*
  *Systems of weight regulation:*
  *  chemicals, hypothalamus, satiety*
  *Dietary variety*
  *Obesity*

- **Sex and sexual behaviour**
  The physiological processes and evolutionary history.

  *Genetic diversity*
  *Female reproductive system*
  *Male reproductive system*
  *Masters & Johnson's sexual*
  *  behaviour study*
  *Sex hormones*
  *Sexual orientation*
  *Wilson and sociobiology*
  *Trivers' theory of parental investment*
  *Baumeister—gender differences*
  *  in sexuality*

- **Work motivation and performance**
  Factors influencing success at work.

  *Personality: Type A behaviour pattern,*
  *  locus of control*
  *Adams' equity theory*
  *Locke's goal-setting theory*

# Motivation and homeostasis

The study of motivation is of major importance to developing a full understanding of human behaviour. Motivation helps to determine how well we do academically, the kind of job we have, how successfully we perform that job, and how we spend our leisure time. Motivation is highly relevant to the following:

- *Direction of behaviour*. The goal or goals being pursued.
- *Intensity of behaviour*. The amount of effort, concentration, and so on, invested in behaviour.
- *Persistence of behaviour*. The extent to which a goal is pursued until reached.

A definition including the above ingredients was put forward by Taylor, Sluckin, Davies, Reason, Thomson, and Colman (1982): "Motivation ... is generally conceived of by psychologists in terms of a process, or a series of processes, which somehow starts, steers, sustains and finally stops a goal-directed sequence of behaviour" (p. 160). For example, if someone is very hungry, we would expect their behaviour to be directed towards the goals of finding and eating food, we would expect them to put in much effort, and we would expect them to continue looking for food until they found some.

It is difficult to achieve a good understanding of human motivation. There are two main reasons for this. First, human beings are motivated by a bewildering range of goals. Most of us are motivated to eat and drink, to find an attractive sexual partner, to have a high level of self-esteem, to be liked by other people, to earn money, and to enjoy life. Some of us are motivated to become a great athlete, to write books, to sail around the world, or to appear on television.

Second, motivation involves processes operating at several different levels. For example, consider hunger drive and eating behaviour. Eating behaviour depends in part on basic physiological processes. However, it also depends on various psychological factors, such as the habit of eating at certain times of day (e.g., around midday) and the desire to lose weight.

We will start our coverage with need theories of motivation. Most need theories make two key assumptions:

1. Humans have a wide range of needs which motivate them.
2. The particular needs of greatest importance to a given individual vary over time.

Need theories are comprehensive theories of motivation, and so they will serve to illustrate the wide range of human needs. After that, we will consider more specific types of motivation, including the processes involved in regulation of the body, hunger and eating behaviour, and sexual behaviour. Finally, we will turn our attention to motivation at work, including a consideration of some of the reasons why there are large individual differences in work motivation. Biological approaches have had little impact on our understanding of work motivation. However, this topic is considered here because of its general importance to an understanding of human motivation.

## NEED THEORIES

Probably the best-known need theory is the hierarchical theory put forward by Maslow (1954), and so it is with that theory that we will begin. After that, we consider Alderfer's

(1969) existence, relatedness, growth (ERG) theory, which was an attempt to overcome weaknesses within Maslow's theory.

## Maslow's hierarchical theory

According to Abraham Maslow (1954, 1970), most theories of motivation are very limited. They deal with basic physiological needs such as hunger and thirst, or with the need to avoid anxiety. However, such theories generally omit many important needs relating to personal growth. Maslow addressed these issues by putting forward a theory based on a **hierarchy of needs**. Physiological needs or requirements (e.g., those for food, drink, air, and sleep) are at the bottom level of the hierarchy. Safety needs are at the next level of the hierarchy, and include the need for security, freedom from fear, for protection, and for structure and order.

*Do you think that this theory would be equally applicable to all cultures?*

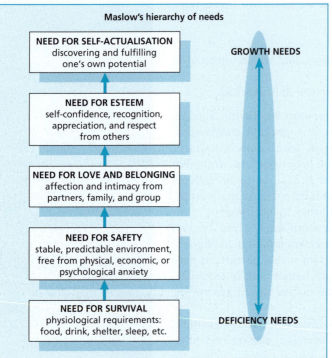

In the middle of the hierarchy are needs for affection and intimacy. Maslow argued there are two types of love: D-love and B-love. D-love is based on deficiency, and is selfish in that it involves taking rather than giving. However, we need to experience D-love before moving on to B-love, which is a "love for the Being of another person". B-love is unselfish, and is based on a growth need rather than on deficiency. Above that level, there is the need for esteem. There are two aspects to the need for esteem: (1) the need for admiration and respect; and (2) the need to regard oneself as competent and successful. Finally, the need for **self-actualisation** (or fulfilling one's potential) is at the top of the hierarchy. Rogers (e.g., 1951) made use of the notion of self-actualisation in his theory of personality (see Chapter 13).

Maslow regarded all the needs towards the bottom of the hierarchy as deficiency needs, because they are designed to reduce inadequacies or deficiencies. Needs towards the top of the hierarchy (e.g., self-actualisation) represent growth needs, and are designed to promote personal growth. The key notion of self-actualisation was described as follows by Maslow (1954): "A musician must make music, an artist must paint, a poet must write, if he [sic] is to be ultimately at peace with himself. What a man can be, he must be. This need we may call self-actualisation."

Self-actualised individuals are characterised by an acceptance of themselves, spontaneity, the need for privacy, resistance to cultural influences, empathy, profound interpersonal relationships, a democratic character structure, creativeness, and a philosophical sense of humour. Maslow (1954) identified Abraham Lincoln and Albert Einstein as famous people who were self-actualised.

How can we measure self-actualisation? Maslow (1962) focused on **peak experiences**, in which the world is experienced totally for what it is, and there are feelings of euphoria, wonder, and awe. Peak experiences occur most often during sexual intercourse or when listening to music, and sometimes when doing both at the same time. Maslow found self-actualised individuals reported more peak experiences than other people. It is also possible to assess self-actualisation by means of self-report questionnaires (e.g., the Index of Self-Actualisation).

Maslow's hierarchical theory of motivation is more complex than is sometimes appreciated. He believed most individuals work upwards through the hierarchy of needs, but accepted that is not always the case. Some individuals have to satisfy their need for self-esteem before they can satisfy their needs for love. Maslow accepted we do not have to satisfy our physiological or safety needs totally before we focus on higher-level needs. Finally, Maslow recognised we are often motivated by a number of needs at the same time. For example, he claimed sex is often motivated by the need for sexual release, but can also

**KEY TERMS**

**Hierarchy of needs:** in Maslow's theory, a range of needs from physiological ones at the bottom of the hierarchy to self-actualisation at the top.

**Self-actualisation:** the need to discover and fulfil one's potential.

**Peak experiences:** heightened experiences associated with feelings of joy and wonder.

"be motivated by a need to win or express affection, a sense of conquest or mastery, or a desire to feel masculine or feminine. People have sex to satisfy any one of these needs or to satisfy all of them" (Burger, 1993, p. 337).

## Evidence

According to Maslow (1954, 1970), people generally only focus on their growth needs after their deficiency needs have been met. An implication of this view is that fewer people manage to satisfy their growth needs than to satisfy their deficiency needs. Maslow (1970) estimated that Americans satisfy about 85% of their physiological needs, 70% of their safety needs, 50% of their belongingness and love needs, 40% of their self-esteem needs, and only 10% of their self-actualisation needs. However, these estimates were based on very limited data, and the percentage figures should not be taken too seriously.

Aronoff (1967) tested the prediction that higher needs will only emerge when lower needs are satisfied. He compared fishermen and cane cutters in the British West Indies. Fishermen worked on their own, generally earning more than cane cutters, who worked in groups. Cane cutting was a more secure job, because the rewards fluctuated much less than for fishermen, and because cane cutters were paid even when unwell. According to Maslow's theory, it should be mainly those whose security and esteem needs were met who chose the more challenging and responsible job of fisherman. This prediction was confirmed by Aronoff.

Further support for Maslow's assumption that we generally move up the hierarchy of needs only when needs at lower levels are largely satisfied was reported by Graham and Balloun (1973). They asked 37 participants to describe the most important things in their lives. As predicted, individuals at any given level of the needs hierarchy were more satisfied with needs below that level than with those above it.

There has been a fair amount of research concerned with peak experiences. In general, descriptions of peak experiences correspond to those expected by Maslow. For example, Ravizza (1977) asked athletes in various sports to describe their "greatest moments" as athletes. They reported experiencing a God-like feeling of control, feeling at one with the universe, feeling totally involved in what they were doing, and feeling wonder and ecstasy. Mathes et al. (1982) produced a Peak Scale to assess individual differences in the tendency to have peak experiences. High scorers on the Peak Scale were more likely than low scorers to emphasise higher-level values (e.g., beauty, truth, justice) in their everyday lives, and less likely to focus on lower-level deficiency values (e.g., taking from others rather than giving).

In spite of supporting evidence for Maslow's views on peak experiences, he was wrong in at least one respect. More specifically, he suggested that all peak experiences are positive. In fact, however, it has been reported several times (e.g., Wilson & Spencer, 1990) that some peak experiences are negative and occur in threatening circumstances.

Aronoff (1967) found that most West Indian fishermen had their security and esteem needs met, and this enabled them to handle an income and lifestyle that was less predictable than cane cutting.

**Motivation and tourism**

Cameron and Gatewood (2003) suggest that the motivation for the increasing popularity of heritage-site tourism is spiritual, which fits in with Maslow's concept of self-actualisation. Surveys show that actual historical knowledge is not an important factor, and suggest that people's imaginations, feelings, empathy, and memories are more important motivators in making these visits. Typical statements that bring agreement include:

- I like to use my mind to go back in time while visiting historic sites and museums.
- I am sometimes able to connect deeply with the objects displayed in exhibits.
- I enjoy reflecting on a site or museum after visiting it.
- I enjoy imagining the day-to-day life of people who lived in the past.
- Some sites and museums provoke an almost "spiritual" response in me.

## Evaluation

- ⊕ Maslow's approach to motivation is more comprehensive than other approaches. For example, the needs for self-actualisation and for esteem seem very important, but were excluded from earlier theories of motivation.
- ⊕ Maslow emphasised the more positive and uplifting aspects of human motivation, whereas many previous theorists (e.g., Freud) had focused more on the negative side of human nature.
- ⊖ The notion of self-actualisation is vague, and it has proved hard to measure it accurately.
- ⊖ It is very hard to carry out research into the theory, in part because of the somewhat anti-scientific approach favoured by Maslow. As Maslow (1968, p. 13) put it, "The uniqueness of the individual does not fit into what we know of the science. Then so much the worse for that conception of science."
- ⊖ Maslow was too optimistic in his assumption that everyone has the potential to become a self-actualiser. The fact that the average British person spends 25 hours a week watching television suggests there are many people whose motivation for personal growth is not enormous!
- ⊖ The influence of the environment in facilitating the development of self-actualisation is not emphasised enough. In fact, individuals who become self-actualised usually owe much to environmental factors (e.g., schooling, training, supportive parents).
- ⊖ Maslow's approach seems more relevant to individualistic cultures than to collectivistic ones (see Chapter 1). He focused on self-esteem and personal achievement, whereas the emphasis in collectivistic cultures (e.g., China) is on co-operation and working for the benefit of the group rather than of the individual.

*In what way does uniqueness present a problem for science?*

## Existence, relatedness, growth theory

Alderfer (1969) believed Maslow's hierarchical theory was broadly correct. However, he also believed that Maslow's theory was unduly complex, which led him to put forward his existence, relatedness, growth (ERG) theory. According to this theory, there are *three* major needs rather than the *five* identified by Maslow:

1. *Existence needs*. The desire for material (e.g., money) and physiological (e.g., food, water) well-being.
2. *Relatedness needs*. The desire for fulfilling personal relationships with family, friends, and fellow workers.
3. *Growth needs*. The desire for personal growth and development.

These needs are arranged along a horizontal line or continuum, with existence needs at the left end and growth needs at the right end. They are organised in terms of their concreteness. Existence needs involve physical objects and so are the most concrete, whereas growth needs are the least concrete because they may not involve physical objects at all.

Maslow argued that individuals typically move up the need hierarchy. In contrast, Alderfer (1969) argued that the reality is more complex. If one of an individual's needs is satisfied (e.g., existence needs), then he/she will have an increased desire for less concrete needs (growth needs). However, when one of an individual's needs cannot be satisfied, he/she will experience frustration-regression, redirecting his/her focus to needs at a more concrete level. Thus, for example, people thwarted in their attempts to satisfy growth needs may devote more time and effort to social interactions.

### Motivation and children's behaviour

A study in Beijing has shown that high motivation links to a reduction in non-compliant behaviour. In this study 216 preschool children were videotaped as they played with a familiar toy. A novel toy was available, but the children had to wait before being allowed to play with it. The most compliant, and perhaps the most motivated, children were the girls. According to Alderfer (1969), this could mean that the boys found the wait more frustrating, and redirected their focus elsewhere in a non-compliant way.

## Evidence

Wanous and Zwany (1977) obtained some support for ERG theory. They asked workers to rate the importance of

23 work needs, and the extent to which their needs were satisfied. Their analysis of work need fulfilment indicated strong support for the notion of growth needs, moderate support for existence needs, but somewhat weak support for relatedness needs. As predicted by ERG theory, Wanous and Zwany found workers with high satisfaction of their relatedness needs had the greatest need for growth.

Two findings reported by Wanous and Zwany (1977) failed to support ERG theory. First, the level of satisfaction with existence needs was *unrelated* to relatedness needs, whereas those whose existence needs were most satisfied should have had the greatest relatedness needs. Second, individuals with the greatest relatedness satisfaction rated relatedness needs as more important than did those with lower relatedness satisfaction, which is the opposite of the theoretical prediction.

As Schermerhorn, Hunt, and Osborn (2000, p. 112) pointed out, the theory "may help to explain why ... workers' complaints focus on wages, benefits, and working conditions—things relating to existence needs. Although these needs are important, their importance may be exaggerated because the workers' jobs cannot satisfy relatedness and growth needs."

## Evaluation

⊕ ERG theory is a simpler and more readily testable theory than Maslow's hierarchical theory.
⊕ The notion that failure to satisfy needs at one level can lead the individual to emphasise more concrete needs is a valuable one.
⊖ The three major types of needs (especially growth needs) are defined vaguely, making it hard to assess the extent to which needs have been satisfied.
⊖ Numerous strategies can be used to satisfy any of the major needs, and it is not possible to predict which strategy any given person will select.

# HOMEOSTASIS: TEMPERATURE AND HUNGER

The French physiologist Claude Bernard noticed that the body's internal environment generally remains almost constant in spite of large changes in the external environment. This observation led to much work into the phenomenon of **homeostasis**, which is the tendency for an individual's internal environment to remain fairly constant. The word "homeostasis" comes from two Greek words: "homos" meaning "same" and "therme" meaning "heat".

One of the most obvious examples of homeostasis is body temperature, which in humans is normally very close to 98.6 °F or 37 °C. This is the case in spite of the fact that the external temperature in the United Kingdom can vary by as much as about 54 °F or 30 °C between winter and summer. There are numerous other forms of homeostasis, including regulation of the body's water supply, its oxygen concentration, and its concentration of nutrient substances such as glucose. The concentration of glucose in the bloodstream needs to be between 60 and 90 milligrams per 100 cubic centimetres of blood. If it falls below this range, then coma and death can result. If it consistently exceeds this range, then diabetes or some other disease is likely to follow. In similar fashion, death can occur if our body temperature remains considerably above or below its normal level for several hours, or if we are totally deprived of water for 4 or 5 days.

The French physiologist Claude Bernard (1813–1878) performing vivisection in his laboratory at the Collegé de France. Bernard famously said *"La fixité du milieu interieur est la condition de la vie libre"* [To have a free life, independent of the external environment, requires a constant internal environment].

**KEY TERM**

**Homeostasis:** the tendency for individuals to keep their internal environment (e.g., body temperature) fairly constant.

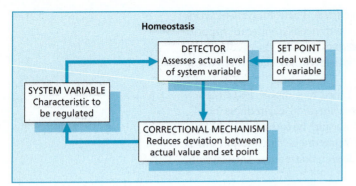

Homeostasis

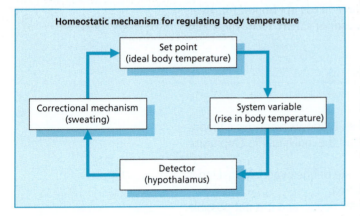

Homeostatic mechanism for regulating body temperature

*Can you try to map out the homeostatic mechanism for hunger in the same way as that given above for temperature regulation?*

In view of the crucial importance to us of maintaining appropriate levels of food, water, and warmth, it is not surprising that we have complex systems which monitor and regulate each of these factors. As Carlson (1994) pointed out, the regulatory mechanisms within the body allowing homeostasis to occur all involve four key features:

1. *A system variable.* This is the characteristic (e.g., temperature) that needs to be regulated.
2. *A set point.* The ideal or most appropriate value of the system variable.
3. *A detector.* The actual or current value of the system variable needs to be assessed.
4. *A correctional mechanism.* This serves to reduce or eliminate the discrepancy between the actual value and the ideal value.

All these regulatory mechanisms are present in central heating systems, which are designed to regulate temperature. The thermostat is set to the chosen temperature, and it detects deviations between the actual and chosen temperatures. When the temperature falls too low, the boiler of the central heating system is activated to restore the chosen temperature.

Two key general points need to be made before we consider in detail the homeostatic mechanisms involved in temperature regulation and hunger. First, what we find in humans are typically only approximations to homeostatic processes. As Kalat (1998, p. 270) pointed out, these processes, "are not *exactly* homeostatic, because they anticipate future needs as well as react to current needs … For example, in a frightening situation that might call for vigorous activity, you begin to experience a cold sweat even before you start to move." In addition, as many of us have found to our cost, it can be hard to maintain a given body weight. Accordingly, it may make more sense to think in terms of a set zone rather than a highly specific set point.

Second, homeostatic systems for regulation of warmth, food, and water are all characterised by *redundancy*, meaning that destruction of part of the system can be compensated for by other parts of the system. In other words, most homeostatic systems contain several mechanisms which are jointly responsible for preserving homeostasis. This makes complete evolutionary sense, because failures of homeostatic systems are often followed by death.

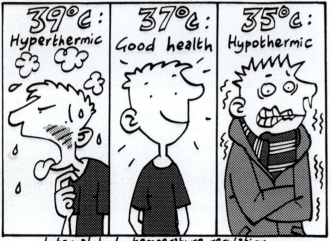

Internal body temperature regulation is very important to humans.

## Temperature regulation

Temperature regulation is of very great importance to humans. For example, consider what happens if someone suffers from a high fever over a long period of time. That person is at risk of dying, because the brain centres involving in regulating heart rate and breathing are sensitive to high temperatures. Exposure to very low temperatures can cause extensive damage to the layers forming cellular membranes, so that they cannot recover even after thawing has taken place. However, regulation of our body temperature is not absolutely precise. For example, our body temperature varies slightly during the course of the day, tending to be highest in the late afternoon and lowest in the middle of the night (see Chapter 4).

*Why* do humans typically have a body temperature of 37 °C? There would be some advantages if we had a higher

Natural selection has helped the human race to cope with extremes of temperature. Humans who have a high surface-to-volume ratio are better at losing heat through the skin than are humans of the same weight having a low surface-to-volume ratio. That means that it would be advantageous for humans living in the Tropics (such as the Masai warriors on the right) to be taller and slimmer than those living in very cold areas (such as the Eskimo family on the left). This is generally speaking the case.

body temperature, in that it would increase our potential activity level. However, the disadvantage is that more fuel would be needed to maintain a higher body temperature. According to Long (1996), we would have to increase our metabolic rate by 13% if our body temperature went up by only 1°C. If we had a lower body temperature, then our activity levels would decrease. In addition, we would need to sweat much more to keep our body temperature low. All in all, it appears that our actual body temperature is just about right!

As would be expected, our *internal* temperature is influenced by the *external* temperature. Van Marken-Lichtenbelt, Westerterp-Plantenga, and van Hoydonck (2001) found that 48-hour exposure to a temperature of 27 °C caused a significant increase in body temperature. Exposure to high or low external temperatures often has adverse effects on our ability to perform moderately complex tasks. Pilcher, Nadler, and Busch (2002) carried out a meta-analysis of studies of the effects of temperature on performance. Temperatures in excess of 90 °F (32.2 °C) produced an average performance decrement of 15%, and temperatures below 50 °F (10 °C) produced a decrement of 14%. These findings indicate it is hard for our homeostatic mechanisms to cope fully with extremes of external temperature.

## Multiple systems

At a very general level, body temperature can be regulated in two ways. First, it can be regulated by internal mechanisms. Second, it can be regulated by means of appropriate forms of behaviour (e.g., moving into the shade, putting on a coat). Animals that use internal mechanisms to maintain the correct body temperature are known as **endotherms**. In contrast, animals using behavioural means are known as **ectotherms**. Such animals obtain much of their body heat from the environment. Humans (and other mammals) are basically endotherms. However, we obviously use numerous forms of behaviour to maintain our body temperature, especially when exposed to unusually hot or cold external temperatures.

Rosenzweig, Breedlove, and Leiman (2002) identified the advantages and disadvantages of being an endotherm. The advantages include being able to cope reasonably well with extreme temperatures and being able to maintain high levels of muscular activity over long periods of time. The disadvantages include the need for large quantities of food to provide energy, the need for elaborate internal systems to maintain body temperature, and the potential damage caused if body temperature deviates much from its optimal level.

**KEY TERMS**

**Endotherms:** animals that regulate their body temperature mainly by means of various internal mechanisms.

**Ectotherms:** animals whose body temperature depends on environmental heat, and that regulate body temperature mainly by altering their behaviour.

*What effect would electrical stimulation of a) the lateral hypothalamus, and b) the preoptic area have on temperature regulation?*

What internal regulatory mechanisms are involved in the control of temperature? At least *three* thermostats control body temperature in humans, but the hypothalamus is of particular importance. Parts of the hypothalamus detect the current value of blood temperature, which is usually closely related to body temperature. In addition, the hypothalamus is also involved in initiating corrective action.

How does the hypothalamus regulate body temperature? It contains receptor cells responding to the temperature of the fluids surrounding the brain. Evidence for this was obtained by Magoun, Harrison, Brobeck, and Ranson (1938). Cats whose anterior hypothalamus was heated artificially reacted as if they were too hot by panting and by vasodilation (widening of the skin's capillaries), even though the rest of their bodies were below normal temperature.

The anterior hypothalamus (and adjacent preoptic area) plays a role in cooling the body down, whereas the posterior hypothalamus is involved in heating the body up. For example, Andersson, Grant, and Larsson (1956) found in goats that electrical stimulation of the anterior hypothalamus caused vasodilation and panting. In contrast, destruction of that area caused death by overheating.

The hypothalamus influences the autonomic nervous system in the regulation of body temperature. The parasympathetic nervous system is activated when the body temperature is too high: This produces sweating or panting causing heat loss by evaporation. It also produces vasodilation, which sends warm blood to the skin and causes heat loss by radiation. The sympathetic nervous system is activated when the body temperature is too low. There is vasoconstriction, in which there is a narrowing of the skin's capillaries. This conserves heat by removing blood from the cold periphery of the body. The sympathetic nervous system is also involved in producing shivering. In addition, cold temperatures cause the sympathetic nervous system to stimulate metabolism in brown-fat cells (e.g., those around vital organs in the trunk and spinal cord), which leads to an increase in body temperature. In some species, the sympathetic nervous system also causes the fur to stand out and so create additional protection against the cold. The goose pimples we experience in cold weather are the human equivalent, but are useless because we are no longer covered in fur!

According to Satinoff (1978), the regulatory system based on the hypothalamus is of greatest importance, in that it helps to co-ordinate activity within the other systems. This system is also the most sensitive, in that it responds to very small deviations in temperature. Satinoff argued there are two further systems, one based in the brain stem and the other based in the spinal cord. Both of these are less sensitive to temperature change than the hypothalamic system, with the spinal cord system being less sensitive than the brain-stem system. We can regard these systems as forming a hierarchy, with the hypothalamus system at the top.

Support for Satinoff's (1978) views comes from studies on spinal animals in which the brain is disconnected from the spinal cord. If there were only a hypothalamic system for temperature regulation, the spinal animals would be unable to control their body temperature at all. In fact, they show some ability to regulate their body temperature, indicating the existence of a non-hypothalamic system. These spinal animals do not try to regulate their body temperature until it has altered by about 2 or 3 °C from normal, showing that non-hypothalamic systems are relatively insensitive to changes in body temperature (Rosenzweig et al., 2002).

So far we have focused on the ways in which the hypothalamic and other systems regulate temperature via autonomic responses (e.g., vasodilation, sweating). However, body temperature is also influenced by behavioural responses. For example, if we are too cold, we put on extra clothes such as a sweater or coat, or we become more active. On the other hand, if we are too hot, we may take off some of our clothes, have a cold drink, or go for a swim. Van Zoren and Stricker (1977) found different brain regions regulate autonomic and behavioural responses. Lesions in the lateral hypothalamus of rats stopped them from regulating their temperature via behaviour, but did not reduce autonomic regulation of temperature (e.g., shivering, vasoconstriction). In contrast, lesions in rats' preoptic area disrupted autonomic temperature regulation but had no effect on behavioural regulation of temperature.

Sweating is part of the parasympathetic nervous system's response to high body temperature. The evaporation of sweat from the skin helps to cool the body down.

There is evidence for the existence of more than one brain region controlling the behavioural responses involved in the regulation of body temperature. Consider a study by Roberts and Mooney (1974), who studied rats' reactions to heat. In normal circumstances, rats exposed to increasing heat initially groom themselves, then they move about looking for somewhere cooler, and finally they sprawl out and keep still. Roberts and Mooney obtained different findings when they warmed small areas in the diencephalon and the mesencephalon of rats. Each area tended to produce only *one* of these behaviours rather than the typical sequence just described.

In sum, it has become increasingly clear that several mechanisms are involved in maintaining a relatively constant body temperature in humans and other mammals. Most of these mechanisms influence autonomic responses, but some influence behavioural responses designed to increase or reduce body temperature. Satinoff's (1978) theory that there is a hierarchy of mechanisms or systems (with the hypothalamus being the site of the most important system) seems to be broadly correct. However, as yet we do not have a detailed understanding of the *interactions* among these various systems.

## Hunger

You may feel it is easy to understand hunger and eating behaviour. We start eating when our stomach and other parts of the body signal the level of nutrients is too low, and we stop eating when our stomach is full. It is certainly true that physiological and biological factors are of great importance in determining hunger and eating behaviour. However, that is not the whole story. As Wickens (2000, p. 106) pointed out:

*Hunger and eating behaviour are the end points of a hugely complex biological system that involves all levels of the brain, and doesn't appear to be linked to simple physiological responses in any direct way … we typically eat not in response to hunger, but in anticipation of it.*

*How may eating disorders such as anorexia and obesity support the idea that eating behaviour is not just biologically determined?*

Much evidence supports Wickens' viewpoint, with social and cultural factors being especially important in relatively affluent parts of the world. For example, we often eat because it is the normal time for lunch or dinner. As Bolles (1990) pointed out, our wristwatch is one of the most important determinants of whether we feel hungry.

De Castro and de Castro (1989) found social factors are important influences on eating behaviour. Participants kept a diary record of all the food they ate and the number of other people present while they were eating. There were two key findings. First, the more people present, the more food that was consumed. Second, the amount of food eaten was influenced by the time since the last meal for participants eating on their own, but not for those eating with other people. Thus, social factors were more powerful than the body's energy needs in determining how much was eaten.

Below we consider physiological processes involved in hunger and weight regulation. Three points should be borne in mind as you read about these processes. First, several homeostatic mechanisms are involved. Second, the various processes and mechanisms typically *interact* with each other, but we have as yet little understanding of the precise nature of these interactions. Third, much of the research has used mammalian species other than the human. It is generally assumed that the basic processes involved in eating behaviour and weight regulation are very similar across most mammals, but we often lack definitive evidence to support this assumption.

Standardised eating times are the norm, with work and social schedules being planned around them.

## Why do we need food?

We need food for two main purposes: (1) to supply nutrients, which are needed for the nourishment of the body; and (2) to supply energy. We require nutrients to assist in the growth, maintenance, and repair of bodily structures. For example, there are nine essential **amino acids** (the breakdown products of proteins) that we find very hard or impossible to manufacture ourselves. As a consequence, it is only through an appropriate diet we can ensure having adequate levels of these amino acids. In addition to essential amino acids, it is crucially important that our diet contains various minerals and vitamins.

What about the role played by food in energy regulation? We start with three fundamental points. First, the amount of energy we use is calculated in calories. Most adults use between 2000 and 3000 calories per day, although some (e.g., lumberjacks) use many more. Second, energy is needed for *all* our activities, not just motor activities such as walking and running. Thus, for example, we need energy to breathe, to think, and even to watch television. Third, as Rosenzweig, Leiman, and Breedlove (1999, p. 366) pointed out, "No animal can afford to run out of energy or nutrients; there must be a reserve on hand at all times. If the reserves are too large, though, mobility (for avoiding predators or securing prey) will be compromised."

According to Rosenzweig et al. (2002), the energy created by food consumption is used for three main purposes. First, it is used to process ingested food. As evidence of this, you may have noticed you sometimes feel warmer after eating a meal than beforehand. Second, the energy

Tour de France riders consume between 6000 and 10,000 calories a day. They cycle 3500 km over a period of 22 stages so need to eat almost constantly to provide enough energy to cope with this gruelling schedule.

created within the body allows us to move around and use our brains effectively. Third, energy is needed so we can maintain our body temperature and other basic functions (e.g., breathing). The energy required for this purpose is known as basal metabolism. Our basal metabolism decreases when we are deprived of food, and increases when we have overeaten. The former finding helps to explain why people find it so hard to lose much weight on a diet. Bray (1969) found obese people on a very low calorie diet showed a reduction of 15% in their basal metabolism. This meant their energy expenditure went down, and thus reduced the effectiveness of the diet.

It is now time to consider how the body turns food into energy. Glucose is a sugar playing a key role in energy utilisation. One way in which the body obtains glucose is by breaking down large carbohydrate molecules into simple carbohydrates, including glucose. Glucose is the main source of energy used by the brain. The body can also make use of glucose as an energy source, but additionally uses fatty acids. It would be very dangerous if no glucose were readily available at any time. This danger is avoided, because there is a storage system in the liver for excess glucose. More specifically, glucose molecules are combined to form a carbohydrate known as **glycogen**. When the need arises, the liver simply converts glycogen back into glucose molecules, and releases them into circulation.

How is glucose turned into glycogen, and glycogen into glucose? A protein hormone in the pancreas known as insulin assists in the breakdown of glucose into glycogen. Another protein hormone in the pancreas (glucagon) assists in the breakdown of glycogen into glucose.

So far we have not considered long-term energy storage. That is provided in the form of fat cells, which form what is called **adipose tissue**. Some fat is present in the food we eat, but fat is also manufactured in the body from various nutrients including glucose. As overweight people know to their cost, when we eat more than is needed for current energy demands, some of the surplus is stored away in fat cells.

Our discussion so far has minimised the fundamental significance of the protein hormone insulin in energy utilisation. We have already seen that insulin is involved in

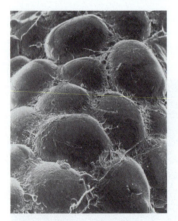

Scanning electron micrograph of the adipocytes (fat cells) that make up adipose connective tissue. Adipose connective tissue forms a thick layer under the skin, which insulates the body and acts as a reserve energy store.

converting glucose into glycogen. In addition, insulin is needed for the body to make use of glucose. If insulin is not available, our bodies are reliant on fatty acids to provide energy.

The importance of insulin is especially clear in the case of patients suffering from Type 1 diabetes mellitus, a disease in which the pancreas stops producing insulin. As a result, the body has to make use of energy from fatty acids and cannot use energy from glucose. This has three consequences. First, in spite of the fact that untreated individuals with diabetes mellitus eat large meals, they tend to lose weight. The reason is that their bodies can only use fatty acids, which provide a less efficient source of energy than glucose. Second, patients with Type 1 diabetes mellitus produce large quantities of urine, because this is a way of disposing of the excess glucose that accumulates in the kidneys. As a result, untreated diabetics tend to experience great thirst. Third, the excess glucose circulating through the body can cause damage (e.g., to the retina).

The severe problems experienced by Type 1 diabetics indicate that insulin plays a key role in energy utilisation. More specifically, insulin is involved at three stages of during eating and energy utilisation. First, when we see or smell food, there is an anticipatory release of insulin to prepare for increased glucose levels in the blood. Second, the pancreas releases insulin in response to food entering the stomach and the intestines. Third, glucostats (cells within the liver) detect the increased levels of glucose in the blood, and signal the pancreas to release insulin.

A technician prepares an insulin injection for an obese laboratory rat as part of medical research into obesity.

## Hunger and satiety: chemicals

We turn now to a consideration of factors involved in hunger and satiety. Evidence that blood-borne chemicals are involved in producing satiety was reported by Davis et al. (1969). They gave blood transfusions from well-fed rats to rats that had been food-deprived. These transfusions caused the food-deprived rats to eat much less than they would have done otherwise. Davis et al. also found the transfusions had their greatest effect when the blood came from animals that had eaten 45 minutes before donating blood. This is significant, because it takes about that length of time after eating for the levels of various chemicals in the blood to increase substantially.

The study by Davis et al. (1969) does not tell us *what* causes hunger and satiety. Insulin is of major importance, with low levels causing hunger and higher levels causing a cessation of eating (see below). When steps are taken to ensure that an animal's blood insulin levels are low, it will typically eat a large meal (Rosenzweig et al., 2002). Injections of moderate levels of insulin cause animals to eat much less than usual (Rosenzweig et al., 2002).

Glucose levels influence hunger and satiety. For example, evidence that low glucose levels can produce hunger was reported by Smith and Campfield (1993). They used drugs to produce reductions in the level of blood glucose. As a result, food consumption increased. Glucose can also affect satiety. Lavin et al. (1996) found that human participants who had glucose infused into the duodenum or small intestine rapidly reported experiencing satiety. In similar fashion, Campfield, Brandon, and Smith (1985) found they could delay eating in rats by infusing glucose into their blood as soon as there were signs of a reduction in blood glucose levels.

There are various sites throughout the body at which glucose levels are detected. However, the liver seems to be of special importance. It is the first organ of the body to receive nutrients from the small intestine, which means it is well placed to monitor food intake. Evidence consistent with the notion that the liver contains key glucose detectors was reported by Russek (1971). When glucose was injected in the hepatic portal vein (which is connected to the liver), animals stopped eating. However, different results were

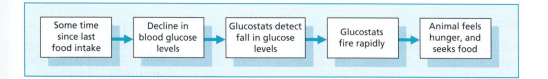

| Some time since last food intake | → | Decline in blood glucose levels | → | Glucostats detect fall in glucose levels | → | Glucostats fire rapidly | → | Animal feels hunger, and seeks food |

obtained when glucose was injected into the jugular vein, which is a considerable distance from the liver. In this condition, glucose injections had little effect on eating behaviour.

Levels of the peptide hormone **cholecystokinin (CCK)** increase immediately after a meal, and there is evidence that CCK released by part of the intestine acts as a satiety signal. Pi-Sunyer et al. (1982) found injections of CCK decreased food consumption, even though they did not lead to a delay in eating. These rats ate much less than usual, probably because increased CCK levels indicate there are sufficient amounts of food in the gastro-intestinal tract. Additional evidence pointing to the importance of CCK was reported by Cooper and Dourish (1990). Antagonists of CCK receptors led the affected animals to eat much more than usual.

We need to be a little wary of accepting the view that CCK plays a major role in curbing eating behaviour. CCK can produce nausea in humans, and it is at least possible that injections of CCK in animals reduce eating because of nausea rather than because it signals satiety (Chen et al., 1993). In addition, West, Fey, and Woods (1984) found rats given CCK-8 at the start of every meal ate smaller quantities than normal. However, they ate more meals, and so they maintained their body weight.

You probably feel there are so many factors underlying eating behaviour that it is hard to keep track of all of them. In fact, we have not discussed several chemicals (e.g., bombesin, corticotropin-releasing hormone, orexins, melanocortin) that may well play important roles in hunger and eating.

> ### Hunger and cannabis
>
> Anecdotal evidence, backed up by some empirical studies, suggests that cannabis stimulates the hunger centres in the brain. Recent studies (e.g., Rogers, 2001) show that cannabis-like chemicals are naturally present in the brain and produce "hunger pangs". French research is seeking a drug that will block the action of these natural cannabis-type molecules and help obese people control their food intake and subsequently lose weight.

## Regulation of body weight

It is important to distinguish between *short-term* and *long-term* factors influencing eating behaviour. For example, we may eat several chocolate biscuits in rapid succession because the level of glucose is reduced shortly after eating a biscuit, which prompts us to eat another one. In contrast, we need to address long-term factors when considering why most people's body weight remains fairly constant over long periods of time.

Woods et al. (1998) proposed a theory focusing on long-term factors underlying regulation of body weight. According to them, such regulation depends crucially on maintaining a relatively constant amount of adipose or fat tissue in the body. In order for this to happen, information about levels of adipose tissue must be transmitted to the brain and other regions having a direct influence on eating behaviour and satiety. Woods et al. argued that two hormones (insulin and leptin) play a crucial role. We have discussed insulin already, but **leptin** is a protein secreted by fat cells. Leptin comes from the Greek word "leptos" meaning "thin", and is associated with reduced levels of eating.

*What does this suggest about leptin levels in obese people?*

It is claimed that insulin and leptin are both secreted in large amounts when the fat stores are larger than usual, but are secreted in small amounts when the fat stores are smaller than usual. This forms a very important homeostatic mechanism, because large amounts of insulin and leptin inhibit eating behaviour.

The essential features of the theory proposed by Woods et al. (1998, p. 1381) are as follows:

> *The size of the fat stores can influence daily feeding behaviour ... An underweight individual who has reduced leptin and insulin concentrations is less sensitive to single-meal satiety signals; hence, larger meals are consumed ... Likewise, an animal that has recently overeaten and gained excess weight will be more sensitive to meal-generated signals and tend to eat smaller meals.*

## Evidence

According to the theory, individuals with larger fat stores should generally have higher levels of leptin and insulin. Woods et al. (1998) discussed evidence supporting this assumption. For example, Considine et al. (1996) found leptin levels were *four* times

> **KEY TERMS**
>
> **Cholecystokinin (CCK):** a peptide hormone released by the duodenum that is believed to act as a satiety signal.
>
> **Leptin:** a protein secreted by fat cells which decreases feeding behaviour.

higher in obese people than in those of normal weight. Why don't such high levels of leptin lead obese people to reduce their food intake and thus lose weight? Many obese individuals are relatively insensitive to leptin, which does not reduce their hunger in the way that it does with individuals of normal weight.

As predicted, insulin and leptin both act to reduce food intake. For example, Woods et al. (1996) found the more insulin that was injected into animals' brains, the greater the reduction in food intake and body weight. In similar fashion, Campfield et al. (1995) found there was a decrease in hunger when the levels of leptin injected into the hypothalamus were high. Halaas et al. (1995) found that injections of leptin into genetically obese mice caused a 30% reduction in their body weight in only two weeks.

How does leptin reduce hunger? Leptin and insulin both activate receptors in the hypothalamus, which is an area of great importance in eating behaviour and satiety (see below). When leptin activates receptors in the hypothalamus, this serves to inhibit the release of neuropeptide Y (Stephens et al., 1995). **Neuropeptide Y** is a neurotransmitter stimulating hunger and eating behaviour. It has been found that injections of neuropeptide Y into the hypothalamus cause satiated rats to start eating again immediately (Wickens, 2000). Repeated injections of neuropeptide Y into the paraventricular nucleus of the hypothalamus produce obesity within several days (Stanley et al., 1986). Thus, we have a somewhat complicated situation: Neuropeptide Y *increase*s eating behaviour, but this increase is prevented by leptin. As a result, leptin leads to a *reduction* in eating behaviour and to loss of body weight.

It is not entirely clear how leptin and insulin interact with the other chemicals influencing eating behaviour and satiety. However, we know that leptin and insulin both influence the effectiveness of satiety peptides such as cholecystokinin (CCK). For example, Matson et al. (1997) found that CCK reduced meal size, but did so to a greater extent when insulin or leptin was administered at the same time.

## Evaluation

● Individuals who are overweight typically have higher levels of leptin and insulin than those who are not.
● The evidence supports the view that regulation of body weight depends crucially on levels of insulin and leptin in most people.
● Obese individuals are often relatively insensitive to the effects of leptin, but in most cases we do not know why that is the case.
● It is not known in detail how the system described in the theory interacts with other physiological processes underlying satiety.

## Brain centre: hunger

Hunger levels depend in part on the levels of various chemicals. However, to achieve a full understanding of the basic systems involved in hunger, we need to identify the control centres in the brain that co-ordinate information about levels of chemicals. The hypothalamus is of major importance in regulating hunger. However, it would be an over-simplification to assume there is a *single* brain centre for hunger.

Early research on animals suggested the hypothalamus plays a major role in regulating eating behaviour. It was claimed (e.g., Anand & Brobeck, 1951) that the lateral hypothalamus is a feeding centre responsible for initiating food intake. The basic notion was that factors such as glucose and insulin levels influenced eating behaviour through their effects on the lateral hypothalamus.

According to the above hypothesis, a lesion (small cut) in the lateral hypothalamus should lead to a refusal to eat (known as aphagia). Anand and Brobeck (1951) found lesions to the lateral nucleus stopped rats from eating, so they lost weight rapidly.

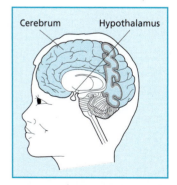

**KEY TERM**
**Neuropeptide Y:** a neurotransmitter that increases feeding behaviour.

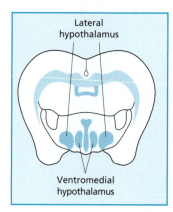

Lateral hypothalamus

Ventromedial hypothalamus

*Think about your own eating habits. What other factors might be involved in eating behaviour?*

A potential problem with this study (and many others) is that the lesions damaged dopamine-containing axons passing through the lateral hypothalamus as well as the lateral hypothalamus itself. However, when damage to the lateral hypothalamus is produced by an acid sparing axons passing through it, there is a long-term reduction in eating (Dunnett, Lane, & Winn, 1985). We can also clarify what is happening by injections of 6-hydroxydopamine (6-OHDA), which damages the dopamine-containing axons but has little effect on the lateral hypothalamus. Animals given such injections become very inactive, but they eat normally when they have food in their mouth (Berridge, Venier, & Robinson, 1989).

Teitelbaum and Stellar (1954) found lesions of the lateral hypothalamus in rats caused substantial reductions in eating. However, some of the rats began to eat again about a week after the operation, suggesting other areas of the brain can be involved in the initiation of eating behaviour. What are those other areas? According to Rosenzweig et al. (1999, p. 374), "Among the regions whose destruction impairs the regulation of feeding are the amygdaloid nuclei, the frontal cortex, and the substantia region … Peripheral structures, notably the liver, also play a crucial role in signalling the brain to activate or inhibit eating."

Keesey and Boyle (1973) considered long-term effects of lesions of the lateral hypothalamus. The lesioned rats maintained a lower body weight than normal rats. However, they responded in similar ways to manipulations of their diet. For example, lesioned and normal rats both showed a substantial increase in body weight when only very rich food (eggnog) was available.

The evidence we have considered so far has been obtained from rats. What about the effects of damage to the lateral hypothalamus on hunger in humans? Lesions or tumours of the lateral hypothalamus have variable effects on humans. However, as predicted by the hypothalamic theory of hunger, such lesions sometimes lead to considerable weight loss (e.g., White & Hain, 1959).

How does the lateral hypothalamus influence feeding behaviour? Kalat (2000) identified four ways. First, signals from the lateral hypothalamus influence cells within the nucleus tractus solitarius, increasing taste sensations and/or increasing the salivary response. Second, activation of the lateral hypothalamus leads to excitation in dopamine-containing cells, which influences learned behaviours related to feeding. Third, axons from the lateral hypothalamus facilitate both ingestion and swallowing, and lead cortical cells to respond more to seeing and tasting food (Critchley & Rolls, 1996). Fourth, activity in the lateral hypothalamus causes the release of insulin by the pancreas, and also leads to increased stomach digestive juices (Morley et al., 1985).

## Evaluation

➕ There is convincing evidence that the lateral hypothalamus plays an important role in triggering eating behaviour.
➖ Animals with lesions to the lateral hypothalamus often recover and start to feed in the normal way.
➖ Several regions in addition to the lateral hypothalamus are involved in feeding behaviour, including the frontal cortex and the amygdaloid nuclei.
➖ The hypothalamic theory of hunger exaggerates the role of the brain in controlling hunger.

## Brain centre: satiety

Hetherington and Ranson (1940) argued the hypothalamus plays a central role in satiety (cessation of feeding). More specifically, they claimed the ventromedial hypothalamus is the satiety centre, which causes animals to stop eating. According to this hypothesis, the ventromedial hypothalamus controls the cessation of eating, in part by using information about the levels of various chemicals in the bloodstream.

## Evidence

There is much support for the notion that the ventromedial hypothalamus and surrounding areas are involved in satiety. In the original study, Hetherington and Ranson (1940) found that lesions of the ventromedial hypothalamus caused rats to become obese. Humans with a tumour in the ventromedial hypothalamus sometimes put on weight at the rate of over 10 kilograms a month (e.g., Al-Rashid, 1971). However, their weight eventually reaches a plateau at a high level.

In spite of the above findings, there are several reasons for rejecting the hypothesis that the ventromedial hypothalamus is the satiety centre. First, rats with lesions in the ventromedial hypothalamus become obese, but do not seem very hungry in some ways. For example, lesioned rats given food that tastes bitter because it contains quinine typically do not eat very much (Sclafani et al., 1976). Indeed, their body weight sometimes becomes lower than that of normal rats exposed to the same bitter food.

Second, Hoebel and Teitelbaum (1966) found lesions to the ventromedial nucleus produced complex effects in two phases: the dynamic and the static. Rats ate two or three times the normal amount of food during the dynamic phase, which usually lasted between 4 and 12 weeks. During the subsequent static phase, however, there was no further increase in body weight, with food consumption being regulated to maintain the weight reached at the end of the dynamic phase.

Third, marked increases in feeding are mainly found when there is damage to areas close to the ventromedial hypothalamus as well as to the ventromedial hypothalamus itself. For example, large increases in body weight are found when there is damage to the ventral noradrenergic bundle which runs through the hypothalamus (Ahlskog, Randall, & Hoebel, 1975). The paraventricular nucleus of the hypothalamus also seems to be important. Rats with damage in this area eat larger meals than other rats, and so put on weight (Leibowitz, Hammer, & Chang, 1981).

Fourth, the pattern of feeding shown by rats with lesions in and around the ventromedial hypothalamus is not precisely as predicted. According to the theory, we would expect such rats to eat much larger meals than normal because they have lost their satiety centre. In fact, however, their meals are typically of normal size, but they have more meals (Hoebel & Hernandez, 1993). Why is this? King, Smith, and Frohman (1984) found that damage to the ventromedial hypothalamus produces a long-lasting increase in insulin production. As a result, a high proportion of each meal is stored as fat. This opens up the possibility that lesioned rats overeat because they have little fuel available to provide for their daily needs.

## Evaluation

⊕ The ventromedial hypothalamus has some involvement in producing satiety.
⊖ Animals with ventromedial hypothalamus lesions are "finicky, lazy and show exaggerated reactions to palatability ... these findings do not square very well with the theory that the ventromedial hypothalamus is the brain's satiety centre" (Wickens, 2000, p. 118).
⊖ Satiety depends on other areas of the brain (e.g., the paraventricular nucleus, the ventral noradrenergic bundle) as well as the ventromedial hypothalamus.
⊖ Animals with lesions of the ventromedial hypothalamus still typically show some ability to regulate their weight at a higher level than normal.
⊖ Animals with damage to the ventromedial hypothalamus eat more meals rather than larger ones, perhaps because such damage increases insulin production rather than because it eliminates the satiety centre.

# Dietary variety

One very important factor influencing eating behaviour in animals and in humans has been largely ignored in biological theories: dietary variety. The basic idea is that we

A number of studies have concluded that increased dietary variety leads to increased consumption of food. The availability of a wide variety of high-calorie foods may have contributed to the increase in obesity in Western societies.

consume more food when a meal contains variety (e.g., in taste) than when it does not. This helps to explain why large meals typically contain a mixture of savoury (salty or spicy) and sweet dishes. According to McCrory et al. (1999), the substantial increase in the number of overweight people in Western societies in recent years has occurred in part because of the ready availability of a much greater variety of energy-dense sweets and snack foods than used to be the case.

Why might increased dietary variety lead to greater food consumption? According to Rolls (1981), the main reason is **sensory-specific satiety**: the pleasantness of any given taste or flavour decreases progressively with continued exposure to it. The effects are specific, because there is generally no reduction in the perceived pleasantness of other tastes or flavours. Sensory-specific satiety encourages us to consume a varied diet, which helps to ensure we have the full range of nutrients we need, and thus that we avoid malnutrition.

## Evidence

It has often been found that dietary variety leads to increased food consumption (see Raynor & Epstein, 2001, for a review). For example, Rolls, van Duijvenvoorde, and Rolls (1984) provided human participants with a meal consisting of four courses. In the dietary variety condition, one course consisted of sausages, one of bread and butter, one of chocolate dessert, and one of bananas. In the other conditions, the participants were given four courses consisting of only one of these foods presented four times. Those participants exposed to dietary variety consumed 44% more food and 60% more calories than those receiving the same food throughout.

Dietary variety in terms of a range of tastes is not always sufficient to produce increased food consumption. Rolls, Rolls, and Rowe (1982a) provided participants with three flavours of yoghurt (raspberry, strawberry, and cherry) that were similar in both colour and texture. These participants ate no more than did participants presented with only one flavour of yoghurt.

Rolls (1981) assumed the key mechanism producing the effects of dietary variety is **sensory-specific satiety**, involving a steady decrease in the pleasantness of any given food as more of it is consumed. This assumption was tested by Rolls et al. (1984). They classified sausages, bread and butter, potato chips, and cheese and crackers as savoury foods, and chocolate whipped dessert, yoghurt, bananas, and oranges as sweet foods. When *one* of the sweet foods was eaten, this decreased pleasantness ratings of *all* the sweet foods, but had no effect on pleasantness ratings of savoury foods. In similar fashion, eating one of the savoury foods reduced the pleasantness ratings of the other savoury foods but not of the sweet ones.

Sensory-specific satiety is not limited to taste. Rolls, Rowe, and Rolls (1982b) found the rated pleasantness of chocolate sweets that had been consumed decreased more than that of chocolate sweets not consumed. This occurred even though the sweets differed only in colour and not in taste. Rolls et al. (1982b) also found that decreased pleasantness ratings for pasta that had been consumed did not extend to other pasta differing only in shape. Thus, sensory-specific satiety can extend to colour and shape in addition to taste. More recently, Rolls and Rolls (1997) found sensory-specific satiety also applies to smell.

It has generally been assumed that consumption of any given food reduces the pleasantness of its taste rather than reducing the pleasantness of eating it. Mela and Rogers (1998) obtained both types of ratings from participants eating a meal of cheese sandwiches. There were much larger reductions in rated pleasantness of eating the sandwiches than in pleasantness of the taste of the sandwiches.

**KEY TERM**

**Sensory-specific satiety:**
reduced pleasantness ratings for foods that have been consumed coupled with no reduction in ratings for unconsumed foods.

Most studies on dietary variety in humans have been short term, and thus tell us little or nothing about the effects of dietary variety (or its opposite) on long-term eating patterns. However, the limited evidence suggests the longer-term effects resemble the short-term effects. For example, Cabanac and Rabe (1976) persuaded participants to consume only a vanilla-flavoured diet for 3 weeks. There was an average weight loss of 3.13 kilos over the three-week period.

*How might this be relevant to many commercial diet plans?*

## Evaluation

⊕ Dietary variety typically has fairly large effects on food consumption.
⊕ Sensory-specific satiety covering the taste, smell, shape, and colour of food underlies the effects of dietary variety and its opposite.
⊖ It is not clear whether sensory-specific satiety is associated with reduced pleasantness of the taste of a consumed food or reduced pleasantness of eating the food.
⊖ More research is needed to discover whether the long-term effects of dietary variety (and lack of variety) are similar to the short-term ones.

## Obesity

There are two main eating disorders: bulimia nervosa and anorexia nervosa (discussed in Chapter 22). Obesity is not regarded as an eating disorder, but it can cause reduced mobility, and misery. **Obesity** is normally defined as a body mass index (BMI) of more than 30, calculated by dividing an individual's weight in kilograms by their height in metres squared. Individuals with a BMI of between 25 and 30 are said to be overweight, which is bad news for me because my weight is typically just over a BMI of 25!

You have probably heard experts saying that there is an epidemic of obesity in the Western world. It is certainly true that there have been dramatic increases in the percentage of obese individuals in numerous countries. In the United States, 22% of adults are obese and 54% are overweight (Hill & Peters, 1998), and the picture is similar elsewhere. In Australia, the percentage of obesity increased between 1980 and 1989 from 8.0% to 13.2% in women and from 9.3% to 11.5% in men (Taubes, 1998). In the United Kingdom, obesity increased between 1980 and 1994 from 6% to 15% in men and from 8% to 16.5% in women (Taubes, 1998). In Brazil, the percentage of obesity increased between 1976 and 1989 from 3.1% to 5.9% in men and from 8.2% to 13.3% in women (Taubes, 1998).

How big a problem is the increase in obesity? Obesity is certainly associated with several health problems (e.g., high blood pressure, heart attacks, various cancers) (see Wickelgren, 1998). However, we are talking about an *association*, which does not prove that obesity is the causal factor. For example, individuals who are obese typically take less exercise than those who are not, and their lack of physical fitness may be important. Wickelgren discussed an American study in which it was found that unfit men of normal weight had twice the mortality than did physically fit men who were obese or nearly so. The most reasonable conclusion is that being obese and being physically unfit both contribute to physical ill-health and reduced longevity.

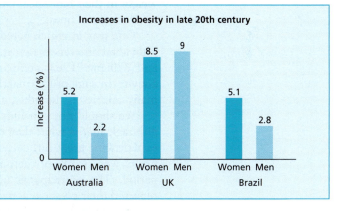

## Causes

If we are to reduce the incidence of obesity (or at least stop it increasing), it is important to understand the factors causing obesity. As we will see, numerous factors are involved.

**KEY TERM**
**Obesity:** a body mass index (BMI) exceeding 30, measured by dividing weight in kilograms by height in metres squared.

*How could this be linked to recent increases in obesity in children?*

Increased levels of obesity occur in part because people in most Western countries have greater access to food than ever before. The importance of this factor can be seen if we adopt an evolutionary perspective. As Pinel, Assanand, and Lehman (2000, p. 1105) pointed out:

*Because of the scarcity and unpredictability of food in nature, humans and other animals have evolved to eat to their physiological limits when food is readily available, so that excess energy can be stored in the body as a buffer against future food shortages. The discrepancy between the environment in which the hunger and eating system evolved and the food-replete environments in which many people now live has led to the current problem of over-consumption existing in many countries.*

Increased dietary variety is probably of relevance in accounting for increasing levels of obesity in numerous countries. McCrory et al. (1999) considered individual differences in dietary variety for 10 different types of food (e.g., snacks, vegetables). Individuals who had a varied diet with respect to high-energy-dense foods (sweets, snacks, seasonings, main courses, carbohydrates) had increased energy intake and body fatness. However, individuals who consumed a great variety of fruits and vegetables weighed *less* than those who did not.

Genetic factors help to determine who will (and will not) become obese. Grilo and Pogue-Geile (1991) reviewed evidence from thousands of twin pairs. Monozygotic or identical twins were much more similar to each other in weight and body mass than were dizygotic or fraternal twins. Similar findings were reported by Plomin, DeFries, and McClearn (1997). They found that 60–70% of identical twins were very similar in weight, compared to only 30–40% of fraternal twins. The much greater genetic similarity of identical twins than fraternal twins (100% vs. 50%; see Chapter 2) probably accounts for their much greater similarity in weight.

The notion that genetic factors are of prime importance in determining body weight would receive support if family environment has little or no effect. Stunkard et al. (1986) considered the weight of adults adopted as infants. Their body weight was not correlated with that of their adoptive parents. However, it was highly correlated with the body weight of their biological parents, suggesting that genetic factors are more important than environmental ones.

One way in which heredity might influence body weight would be via metabolic rate. Individual differences in metabolic rate exist and can certainly influence body weight. Rose and Williams (1961) compared people matched for body weight, height, age, and level of activity. In spite of this matching, there were pairs in which one person consumed twice as many calories as the other, and thus presumably had a much higher metabolic rate.

We should not conclude that all obese individuals simply have a low metabolic rate, although that is what they often claim. Lichtman et al. (1992) studied obese individuals experiencing great difficulty in losing weight on reduced-calorie diets. Accurate measurements were made of their food intake and amount of physical activity over a 2-week period. The participants under-reported their actual food intake by 47% and over-reported their physical activity by 51%!

In spite of the importance of genetic factors, dramatic environmental changes can also have powerful effects on weight. The inhabitants of the island of Nauru used to have a very low standard of living. However, their island has rich supplies of seabird excrement, which now provides a source of phosphates used by fertiliser companies. The Nauru islanders now have one of highest standards of living in the world, and buy a wide range of expensive imported foods. As a result, large numbers of them became obese within a single generation (Gibbs, 1996).

Reduced amounts of exercise help to account for the steep increase in obesity. Over the past 20 years, the average daily calorie intake in several Western countries has actually *decreased* (Hill & Peters, 1998), in part because most people walk less and use cars more. Exercise uses up energy (and therefore calories), and anyone will put on weight if the calories he/she consumes are greater than the ones used in energy expenditure. Thus, reduced usage of calories each day could easily lead to obesity in the long run.

Obese individuals typically have problems with **adipocytes**, which are body cells that store fat. Most people have about 25 billion adipocytes, but some obese individuals have a substantially larger number (hyperplastic obesity). There is another form of obesity in which the main problem is that the fat cells are enlarged rather than unduly numerous (hypertropic obesity).

## Evaluation

⊕ Genetic factors are of major importance in the determination of body weight and obesity.

⊕ Various environmental factors (e.g., greater access to food, increased dietary variety, reduced exercise) have all been shown to increase obesity.

⊕ Dietary variety and metabolic rate both play a role in influencing body weight.

⊖ There are various kinds of obesity, and the factors responsible vary from one kind to another.

⊖ Our understanding of obesity is as yet insufficient to permit the development of consistently effective programmes producing long-term weight loss.

# SEX AND SEXUAL BEHAVIOUR

No-one doubts the human sex drive involves various biological factors (e.g., sex hormones). However, that is only part of the story. As Westen (1996, p. 387) remarked, "The primary sexual organ in humans is arguably not the genitals but the brain." Since this is a chapter on biological psychology, we will address issues such as the physiological processes involved in sexual intercourse, and the impact of our evolutionary history on reproductive behaviour. Psychological factors determining sexual attractiveness are discussed in Chapter 19.

## Sexual reproduction

Why does sexual reproduction exist? That may seem like an odd question, and you may feel the answer is obvious. However, biologists have focused on this question, because of the various disadvantages associated with sex. In the words of Grier and Burk (1992, p. 319):

> *Sexual behaviour involves the expenditure of large amounts of time and energy, and its conspicuousness often increases the risk of predation (not to mention the danger from sexually transmitted parasites and pathogens). Worst of all, from an evolutionary standpoint, sexual reproduction is a particularly inefficient method of passing on one's particular alleles [genes].*

We all know about some of the main processes involved in sexual reproduction. However, biologists focus on rather different processes (see also Chapter 2). According to the definition offered by Krebs and Davies (1993, p. 175), "Sexual reproduction entails gamete formation by meiosis and the fusion of genetic material from two individuals." Some of the terms in this definition need to be considered. First, a gamete is a reproductive cell (e.g., a spermatozoon or sperm; an ovum or egg) that can undergo fertilisation. Second, meiosis is a type of cell division in which a nucleus divides into four nuclei, each containing half of the chromosome number of the original nucleus. Third, the two individuals involved are a male and a female. In the human

> **KEY TERM**
> **Adipocytes:** body cells that store fat.

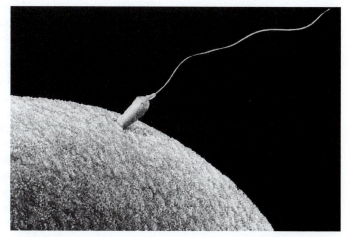

Fertilisation of a human egg by a sperm, an example of anisogamy, where the gametes of the two sexes are dissimilar.

species, males produce gametes or sperm that are very tiny, numerous, and mobile, whereas females produce gametes or eggs that are large and immobile.

What are the evolutionary advantages of sexual reproduction? The most important is that sexual reproduction produces genetic diversity. As can be seen in large human families, two parents typically produce offspring differing significantly in height, shape, intelligence, and personality. This occurs mainly because the precise genetic make-up of each child is different, except in the case of monozygotic or identical twins (see Chapter 2). Environmental conditions often change in unpredictable ways, and genetic diversity maximises the chances of the members of a species coping with such changes.

In order for an individual's genes to be passed on to the next generation, his/her gametes need to survive long enough for them to be involved in sexual reproduction. One strategy for achieving this is to produce a few large gametes designed to survive in an unfriendly environment. This strategy is used by females with their eggs. Another strategy is to produce large numbers of very mobile gametes so that one or more of them may fertilise the female's eggs before this is done by another individual. This strategy is used by males with their sperm.

Human females produce relatively few eggs, whereas males produce very large numbers of sperm. Indeed, there are enough sperm in a typical male ejaculation to fertilise about 500 million females! Thus, each female gamete is much more valuable than each male gamete or sperm. Females can usually maximise their reproductive success by providing food and care for their offspring. In contrast, males can often maximise their reproductive success by fertilising several females rather than by caring for their offspring.

*Monogamy is the normal mating strategy in our culture. How well does it permit both sexes to maximise their reproductive success? Can you think of any alternative systems found in other cultures that fulfil evolutionary requirements for reproductive success more fully?*

## Female reproductive system

The probability of sexual intercourse leading to conception depends on the woman's menstrual cycle, which typically lasts about 28 days. The key phases of the menstrual cycle are as follows:

- *Follicular phase*. Increased levels of follicle-stimulating hormone cause ovarian follicles to grow around egg cells or ova; then the ovarian follicles start to release oestrogens (sex hormones), which reach a peak 1–2 days before ovulation.
- *Ovulation phase*. The oestrogens stimulate the hypothalamus to increase the release of luteinising hormone and follicle-stimulating hormone from the anterior pituitary. The increased level of luteinising hormone causes one of the follicles to rupture and so release its ovum.
- *Luteal phase*. The ruptured follicle starts to release progesterone (a hormone). As a result, the lining of the uterus is prepared for the implantation of a fertilised ovum or egg. More specifically, progesterone leads to the production of nourishing substances for the implantation of the egg if it is fertilised.
- *Premenstrual and menstrual phases*. The ovum or egg moves into the Fallopian tube. If it is not fertilised, progesterone and oestrogen levels decrease.

There has been some controversy as to whether or not women living in close proximity to each other show menstrual synchrony, i.e., go through the various stages of the menstrual cycle at about the same time. Most of the evidence supports the notion of menstrual synchrony (see Weller & Weller, 1993). It is not clear how this comes about. However, Stern and McClintock (1998) carried out an interesting (if rather unsavoury) study in which women had the sweat of other women applied to their upper lip. This led to menstrual synchrony, indicating that the effect depends at least in part on **pheromones**, chemicals released by one individual that influence someone else.

Sexual intercourse must occur around the time of ovulation to maximise the probability of conception. Much evidence suggests that women are *not* more likely to have sex around the time of ovulation than at other points in the menstrual cycle, which seems counter to what would be predicted by many evolutionary psychologists. However, we must distinguish between sexual behaviour and sexual motivation. As Wallen (2001, p. 354) pointed out,

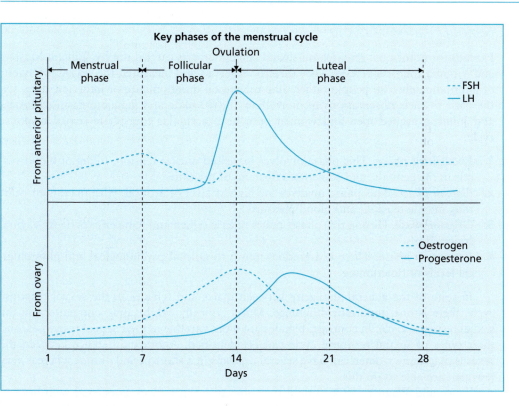

*The specific patterns of sexual behaviour engaged in by women reflect an inter-action between their level of sexual desire, which is affected by their hormonal state, the level of their partner's sexual desire, and the women's or the couple's desire to avoid, or achieve, pregnancy.*

There is much evidence that women's sexual desire peaks around the time of ovulation. Harvey (1987) found women's sexual activity was greater around ovulation than at any other point in the cycle. This was *not* due to an increase in sexual intercourse, but resulted entirely from an increase in auto-sexual activity (i.e., masturbation). Stanislaw and Rice (1988) asked married women to keep a daily record of their sexual desire over a 2-year period. The women expressed sexual desire much more frequently around the time of ovulation, with a steady increase in the days beforehand and a steady decrease afterwards. Van Goozen et al. (1997) found that sexual activity initiated by the female was more than three times greater shortly before ovulation than during the luteal phase. However, there were no changes in sexual activity initiated by the male across the female cycle.

## Male reproductive system

In men, sperm are produced in the testis (plural is testes), and then mature in the adjacent epididymis. There is a small tube (known as the vas deferens) attached to the epididymis. Muscles lining the vas deferens contract to send sperm to the urethra, a tube running the length of the penis. There are various glands around the area in which the vas deferens from each testis connects with the urethra. For example, the seminal vesicles contain a cloudy, sticky fluid, and the prostate produces a clear fluid. At the point of ejaculation, a mixture of sperm and various fluids (including those from the seminal vesicles and the prostate) is expelled from the penis.

During erection, the penis fills with blood. This happens because pro-erectile neurotransmitters (e.g., nitric oxide, acetylcholine) signal the muscles of the penile arteries to relax, which causes additional blood to flow into the penis. Blood is trapped within spongy chambers inside the penis, causing an erection. Viagra, a drug often used to treat erection problems, helps to hold blood in the penis by reducing the rate of breakdown of one of the chemicals keeping the muscles of the penile arteries relaxed (Goldstein, 2000).

## Sexual response cycle

Famous (or notorious) research on sexual behaviour was carried out by William Masters and Virginia Johnson (1966). They directly observed and measured the sexual behaviour of approximately 700 people rather than relying on questionnaire or interview data. On the basis of their observations of more than 10,000 male and female orgasms, Masters and Johnson argued men and women both have a similar four-phase **sexual response cycle**:

1. *Excitement phase.* This phase involves increased muscle tension, filling of blood vessels in the genitals, and sometimes flushing of the skin.
2. *Plateau phase.* This phase involves the highest level of arousal, with maximum heart rate, muscle tension, and blood pressure.
3. *Orgasm phase.* During this phase, males release semen and females experience vaginal contractions.
4. *Resolution phase.* There is a gradual return to normal psychological and physiological levels of functioning.

*What difficulties might arise when carrying out research in this area using a) observation, and b) questionnaires?*

In spite of the general similarity between males and females in the sexual response cycle, there is one important difference. Males typically exhibit only one pattern in the sexual response cycle. In contrast, females are more variable in their sexual responses, and three types of sexual response cycle can be identified. Another difference between the sexes is that many women can have several orgasms in a short period of time whereas very few men are able to do this.

Vance and Wagner (1976) found the subjective experiences associated with orgasm were very similar in males and females. Indeed, psychologists and gynaecologists could not distinguish between men's and women's descriptions of their orgasms. Here are two of the descriptions obtained by Vance and Wagner:

> *The feeling of orgasm in my opinion is a feeling of utmost relief of any type of tension. It is the most fulfilling experience I have ever had of enjoyment. The feeling is exuberant and the most enjoyable feeling I have ever experienced.*

> *An orgasm feels like heaven in the heat of hell; a tremendous build-up of pleasure that makes the tremendous work of releasing that pleasure worthwhile.*

One of those descriptions was written by a man and the other by a woman. Can you work out which is which? In fact, the first one was written by a woman and the second by a man.

## Hormonal factors

There are two major classes of sex hormones: **androgens** and **oestrogens**. The most common androgen is testosterone, and the most common oestrogen is oestradiol. Males have higher levels of androgens than oestrogens, whereas the opposite is the case for females. In non-pregnant females, oestrogens (mostly oestradiol but also some oestrone and oestriol) are secreted primarily by the ovaries. This gender difference has led some people to describe androgens as "male hormones" and oestrogens as "female hormones". This is misleading, because males and females produce both types of hormones. However, it is true that the level of androgens is about 10 times higher in men than in women, whereas the level of oestrogens is about 10 times higher in women than in men.

What processes are involved in the release of sex hormones? First, the hypothalamus secretes a substance known as gonadotropin-releasing hormone. In males, the medial pre-optic area of the hypothalamus is especially important, whereas the ventromedial hypothalamus is of central importance in females (Wickens, 2000). Second, gonadotropin-releasing hormone then controls the secretion of two hormones from the anterior pituitary gland called luteinising hormone and follicle-stimulating hormone. Third, both of these hormones are released into the bloodstream, causing them to be transported to the testes (in males) and to the ovaries (in females). In males, the release of luteinising hormone stimulates the Leydig cells in the testes to produce the sex hormone testosterone. In females, on the other hand, the release of luteinising hormone triggers ovulation, as we saw earlier.

Follicle-stimulating hormone stimulates the production of sperm in males, whereas it prepares the ovaries for ovulation in females.

How important are sex hormones in influencing human sexual behaviour? They are clearly of some importance, but less so than in many other species. For example, oestrogen levels in females are highest around the time of ovulation. As we have seen, women's sexual desire often peaks at around that time, but the effects on sexual behaviour are more inconsistent. Note that female oestrogen levels are about 10 times higher around the time of ovulation than early in the follicular phase, whereas the increase in sexual desire is relatively modest.

Evidence that sex hormones matter comes from studying castrated men, most of whom report decreased sexual activity over time. The typical sequence is that the ability to ejaculate is lost, followed by the ability to have an erection, and then finally sexual interest disappears. However, there are large individual differences. Bremer (1959) considered 157 castrated men, many of whom had been castrated to reduce the amount of time they would need to spend in prison for sex-related offences. About 50% of these men became asexual and had little sexual interest within a few weeks. However, a few of the men continued to have sex, but did so with less enjoyment than previously.

The evidence generally suggests men do not need high levels of testosterone and other sex hormones to be sexually active. As Pinel (1997, p. 286) pointed out, "Sex drive and testosterone levels are uncorrelated in healthy men, and testosterone injections do not increase their sex drive. It seems that each healthy male has far more testosterone than is required to activate the neural circuits that produce his sexual behaviour."

What about the role of sex hormones in female sexual behaviour? Various kinds of evidence suggest that female sex drive may be determined more by androgens such as testosterone than by oestrogens (e.g., oestradiol). First, women who have their ovaries removed, and who thus show a marked reduction in oestradiol level, generally have a normal level of sex drive (Sherwin, 1988). Second, surgically menopausal women receiving oestrogen and androgen had higher levels of sexual desire and sexual satisfaction than did those receiving only oestrogen (Sherwin et al., 1985). Third, Shifren et al. (2000) studied 65 surgically menopausal women who had low sexual desire and sexual satisfaction, all of whom were given oestrogen. Those who also received a large dose of the androgen testosterone showed the greatest increase in sexual functioning. Fourth, Morris, Udry, Khan-Dawood, and Dawood (1987) found that frequency of intercourse in married women was associated much more with their testosterone levels than with their oestradiol levels.

Ovulation in humans is hidden but in many other species there is a visual manifestation of ovulation. For example, in the female chacma baboon (above) a swelling and reddening of the rump occurs around the time of ovulation. This indicates to the males that the female is sexually receptive.

### Hormones and attractiveness

A small study in Texas (Davis, 2001) showed physiological and psychological changes when a woman is most fertile, but these changes relate to her attractiveness or sexiness. The female curvy shape becomes accentuated around ovulation as the breasts are more symmetrical and the waist shrinks by a centimetre or so. Figure-hugging clothing is chosen, which also reveals more skin, and more make-up is worn. The participants' diaries also showed increased thoughts about love and sex, decreased stress levels, more positive moods, and fewer headaches. Presumably all these effects are down to the balance of sex hormones at ovulation.

KEY TERM

**Sexual orientation:** the extent of one's sexual attraction to men and women, which may or may not be closely associated with sexual behaviour.

## Sexual orientation

It is important to distinguish between sexual orientation and sexual behaviour. According to Bailey, Dunne, and Martin (2000, p. 524), "**Sexual orientation** is one's degree of sexual attraction to men or women." There is generally a fairly close relationship between sexual orientation and sexual behaviour, but social and cultural pressures sometimes produce a clear difference between them.

### CASE STUDY: *Testosterone replacement therapy*

Additional evidence that sex hormones are important to male sexuality comes from studies of testosterone replacement therapy. For example, consider the case of a 38-year-old World War I veteran whose testes had been destroyed by a shell fragment. Testosterone replacement therapy had a dramatic effect on him: "Testosterone had resurrected a broken man to a manhood he had believed lost forever" (de Knuif, 1945, p. 100).

About 5–10% of the adult population in most countries are homosexual in sexual orientation, and men and women are equally likely to be homosexual. However, Bailey et al. (2000) identified an interesting difference between the sexes, even though the same percentage (92%) of men and women in their sample were exclusively heterosexual. Of the remaining 8%, women were more likely than men to have slight or moderate homosexual feelings, whereas men were more likely to be nearly exclusively homosexual.

Several theories of the origins of sexual orientation have been proposed. One approach has been to argue that genetic factors play an important role. Another theoretical approach assumes that homosexuality results from being subject to atypical levels of certain hormones in the course of development, with these atypical levels having effects on neural development (e.g., LeVay, 1993).

*Why do the principles of natural selection make it unlikely that homosexuality would have a significant genetic component?*

## Evidence

The issue of the involvement of genetic factors in sexual orientation has been considered in several twin studies. Such studies indicate that sexual orientation depends in part on heredity. For example, Bailey and Pillard (1991) studied male homosexuals having twin brothers. They found that the concordance rate (level of agreement) was 52% for identical twins compared to 22% for fraternal twins. In a study on female homosexuals, Bailey et al. (1993) found the concordance rate was 48% for identical twins and 16% for fraternal twins. These figures suggest that homosexuality in both men and women is moderately influenced by genetic factors.

The involvement of genetic factors in homosexuality may be less than appears to be the case in most reported twin studies. As Bailey et al. (2000) pointed out, volunteers in previous twin studies knew they were taking part in a study on homosexuality. As a result, they may have taken account of the sexual orientation of their co-twins before agreeing to participate. Another issue is that many volunteers were recruited via advertisements in homosexual publications, and so individuals with only moderate homosexual feelings may have been excluded.

Bailey et al. (2000) largely avoided the above problems in their study. Among male twins, the concordance rate was 20% for identical twins and 0% for fraternal twins. Among female twins, the concordance rates were 24% (identical twins) and 10.5% (fraternal twins). These figures are markedly lower than those obtained in previous studies, and suggest sexual orientation may be only modestly influenced by heredity.

## Theories of sexual behaviour

In most societies, there are gender differences in sexual attitudes and behaviour. Accordingly, various theorists have tried to explain *why* these differences occur. Many of these differences are probably due to social and cultural influences. However, some theorists claim at least some gender differences occur as a result of the evolutionary history of the human species. Some of the main theories in this area are discussed below.

## Evolutionary psychology

Wilson (1975) put forward a version of Darwin's evolutionary theory designed to explain human sexual behaviour. By so doing, he established sociobiology. The key assumption of **sociobiology** is that, "individuals should act to maximise their inclusive fitness. Inclusive fitness refers to the number of descendants left in future generations, including those of relations as well as direct descendants" (Smith, 1983, p. 224). In other words, there have been pressures on humans to ensure their genes survive. This can be achieved *directly* by reproduction. In addition, however, parents who care for their children and ensure their children survive and reproduce are *indirectly* assisting in the survival of their own genes. The reason is that each child has 50% of its genes from its father and 50% from its mother (see Chapter 2).

Wilson (1975, p. 156) attached enormous significance to the role of genetic factors in determining human behaviour: "Only small parts of the brain represent a *tabula rasa*

**KEY TERM**

**Sociobiology:** the notion that human social behaviour is strongly influenced by the goal of survival of one's genes.

[clean slate]; this is true even for human beings. The remainder is more like an exposed negative, waiting to be dipped into developer fluid."

In recent years, sociobiology has increasingly been replaced by evolutionary psychology. There is a substantial overlap between the two approaches. However, **evolutionary psychology** is a broader approach (see Chapter 2). It is concerned with the effects of evolutionary history on the psychological mechanisms underlying human cognition as well as on social behaviour. In general terms, evolutionary psychologists have been more willing than sociobiologists to acknowledge that the effects of evolutionary processes are nearly always modified by social and cultural factors.

Sociobiology and evolutionary psychology have both been greatly influenced by Trivers' (1972) theory of parental investment. Trivers defined **parental investment** as, "any investment by the parent in an individual offspring that increases the offspring's chance of surviving (and hence reproductive success) at the cost of the parent's ability to invest in other offspring". In most cultures, female parental investment has always been much greater than male parental investment. As Buss (1999, p. 102) pointed out:

Trivers (1972) defined parental investment as "any investment by the parent in an individual offspring that increases the offspring's chance of surviving (and hence reproductive success) at the cost of the parent's ability to invest in other offspring." In most cultures the parental investment by females is greater than it is for males.

*A man in human evolutionary history could walk away from a casual coupling having lost only a few hours or even a few minutes. A woman in evolutionary history risked getting pregnant as a result, and therefore could have incurred the cost of that decision for years.*

What are the implications of the female's greater parental investment in her offspring? According to Trivers (1972), "Where one sex invests considerably more than the other, members of the latter will compete among themselves to mate with members of the former." Thus, women will typically be more discriminating than men in their choice of sex partners, because the consequences of mating with an unsuitable partner are potentially much greater for women than for men. If males have to compete for the right to have sex with females, then natural selection would have favoured those characteristics making it easier to compete. For example, it might have led to men being larger than women, and also more aggressive (see Chapter 19).

When a child is born, there is no doubt about the identity of the mother, but that of the father may be uncertain. According to evolutionary theory, men should be unwilling to invest resources (e.g., money, time) in a child not possessing any of their genes. It follows that men should be very concerned that their partner is faithful to them. Many men are right to have such concerns, because it has been estimated that about 14% of the offspring of married couples have a father other than the husband! In contrast, a woman is reliant on the resources her partner can provide, and so is especially concerned if he becomes emotionally involved with another woman. The predictions following from this analysis are as follows: Men should experience most jealousy when their partner has sex with another man, whereas women should experience most jealousy when their partner forms an emotional bond with another woman.

Another issue addressed by evolutionary psychologists is the almost complete absence of incest between brothers and sisters. As Pinker (1997, p. 455) argued, "People have sex with and marry those with whom they interact the most—their co-workers, the girl or boy next door—and the people most like themselves—those of the same class, religion, race, and appearance. The forces of sexual attraction should pull siblings together like magnets." According to evolutionary psychologists, this does not happen for powerful evolutionary reasons: The offspring of parents who are closely related genetically are far more likely than other offspring to be genetically defective.

Evolutionary psychology has often been criticised because it allegedly assumes that much human behaviour is determined fairly directly by the processes of natural selection

## Women are promiscuous, naturally

"So many men, so little time!" The actress Mae West jested about it, but scientists—male ones anyway—are convinced they have proved it. Women—far from being naturally monogamous—are, like men, naturally promiscuous. Biologists believe that women are genetically programmed to have sex with several different men in order to increase their chances of healthy children.

This theory helps to explain the high incidence of mistaken paternity. One study suggested that as many as one in seven people may not be the biological child of the man he or she thinks is the father.

Two recent reports have added to a growing body of evidence that females from across the animal kingdom—including birds, bees, fish, scorpions, crabs, reptiles, and mammals—are promiscuous. Promiscuity is suggested by the "good gene" theory, as shown in the great weed warbler. The female warbler may nest with a male with a small song repertoire but she will seek "extra-pair copulation" with males with big song repertoires, which tend to live longer. This way she gets the best offspring (from mate 2) and they are looked after (by mate 1).

"We don't all get the exact partner we want, we make some kind of compromise. That's true of humans as well. A woman might find a man who is good at providing food and looking after children, but she doesn't necessarily want him to be the father of her kids," says Tim Birkhead, professor of evolutionary psychology.

The only comfort that men can take from the animal world is that females have an incentive not to have all their offspring from adulterous liaisons.

"If they are totally unfaithful to their social partner, they might just be abandoned," said Birkhead.

Adapted from A. Brown (2000) "Women are promiscuous, naturally." The *Observer*, 3 September.

that have made us the way we are (see Chapter 2). If evolutionary psychology made that assumption, it would clearly be wrong. However, what evolutionary psychologists actually believe is that human behaviour is determined by numerous factors, most of which are socially and/or culturally based. In addition, adaptations produced by natural selection influence at least some aspects of human behaviour.

## Evidence

One way of testing the theory of human sexual selection proposed by evolutionary psychologists is by carrying out a cross-cultural study of preferred characteristics in mates. If the theory is correct, there should be clear differences in the characteristics preferred by men and by women, and these differences should be consistent across cultures. Some support for these predictions was reported by Buss (1989)— see Key Study below and Chapter 2, page 37.

What about men's strong preference for physically attractive mates? Convincing evidence that female physical attractiveness influences marital choice was reported by Elder (1969). Physical attractiveness ratings of adolescent unmarried women were obtained, and these women were then followed up 10 years later. Among women from working-class backgrounds, there was a correlation of +.46 between their physical attractiveness in adolescence and their husband's occupational status. The correlation was +.35 among women from middle-class backgrounds.

Evidence supporting the prediction from sociobiological theory that females are more selective than males in their choice of sexual partners was reported by Clark and Hatfield (1989). Attractive male and female students approached students of the opposite sex, and said, "Hi, I've been noticing you around town lately, and I find

### KEY STUDY EVALUATION—Buss

The findings of Buss (1989) are of key importance, but they are less clear cut than they seem for two main reasons. First, they do not actually show that sex differences in mate preference are consistent across cultures. In fact, there were much smaller sex differences in more developed cultures than in less developed ones on most measures, including preferred age differences, importance of financial prospects, and the value of chastity in a mate. Second, the sociobiological approach is more concerned with behaviour than with the preferences assessed by Buss. In fact, the actual average age difference between husband and wife across cultures was 2.99 years, which is similar to the preferred age differences for males (2.66 years) and for females (3.42 years). However, it is by no means clear that there would be this level of agreement between preferences and behaviour for the other measures obtained by Buss.

## Buss: Cross-cultural support for the evolutionary account of mate choice

Buss (1989) obtained data from 37 cultures in 33 countries (see Chapter 2). Males in virtually every culture preferred females younger than them, and so likely to have good reproductive potential. In contrast, females in all cultures preferred males who were older, and thus more likely to have good resources. As predicted, females rated good financial prospects in a potential mate as more important than did males. It could be argued that males should value physical attractiveness in their mates more highly than females, because of its association with reproductive potential. In 36 out of 37 cultures, males valued physical attractiveness in mates more than did females. Finally, males tended to value chastity in a potential mate more than did females, but the difference between the sexes was not significant in 38% of the cultures sampled.

*In all cultures, both sexes wanted intelligence and personality in a mate. How can evolutionary principles explain this?*

## Discussion points

1. Does this research provide strong support for the evolutionary approach?
2. Why do you think that sex differences in mate preference vary between Western and non-Western cultures?

you very attractive. Would you have sex with me?" As you have probably guessed, this offer was received much more eagerly by male students than by female ones. None of the female students accepted the invitation, whereas 75% of the male students did. Some of the men who refused offered their humble apologies (e.g., "My fiancée is in town at the moment").

Additional evidence that women are more discriminating than men was reported by Buss and Schmitt (1993). They asked men and women about required standards in a partner for a temporary sexual relationship. Men required a lower level of several characteristics including the following: charming, honest, generous, sociable, kind, intellectual, sense of humour, and emotionally stable. More strikingly, men had fewer objections than women to undesirable characteristics in a short-term partner such as violent, bisexual, disliked by others, selfish, excessive drinker, ignorant, promiscuous, and lacking humour.

According to evolutionary psychologists, it makes evolutionary sense for men to desire more sex partners than do women. This issue was addressed by Buss and Schmitt (1993), who asked unmarried American college students how many sex partners they would ideally like to have over various time periods. On average, men wanted more than six sex partners over the next year, and eighteen over their lifetime. In contrast, women wanted only one sex partner over the next year, and a modest four or five over their lifetime.

Buunk et al. (1996) investigated factors responsible for jealousy in males and females in the United States, Germany, and The Netherlands. Their participants indicated whether they would be more distressed if their partner enjoyed passionate sex with another person or if their partner formed a close emotional bond with someone of the opposite sex. In all three countries, men showed a greater tendency than women to be more distressed by the thought of their partner having sex with someone else, whereas women were more distressed by the thought of their partner forming a close emotional bond. In addition, Buunk et al. found that thoughts of their partner's sexual unfaithfulness caused greater physiological arousal in men than in women in all three countries.

Buunk et al.'s (1996) findings are precisely in line with the predictions of evolutionary psychology. However, DeSteno, Bartlett, Salovey, and Braverman (2002) argued these findings are misleading, because the participants' decisions may well have been influenced by the belief that the existence of one type of infidelity implies the existence of the other. Many women believe that a man's emotional infidelity implies sexual infidelity as well, whereas a man can be sexually unfaithful without any real emotional involvement with the other woman. Thus, women may have decided that emotional infidelity was more distressing because of the high probability that sexual infidelity would also be involved ("double shot" of infidelity).

DeSteno et al. (2002) arranged a situation in which the participants decided whether sexual or emotional infidelity was more important while carrying out another task at the same time. The argument was this would prevent them from drawing any complex inferences about the implications of either type of infidelity. As can be seen in the figure on the right, men and women both chose sexual infidelity as more distressing when not having the processing resources to work out the implications of each form of infidelity.

**Monogamy and health**

Promiscuous species of monkeys and apes have a large number of white blood cells—cells of the immune system that protect us from disease—compared to species with few partners or only one (Nunn, 2000). It has been suggested that this is a sign of powerful immune systems that have evolved to cope with the increased health risks of having many sexual partners.

Does this research relate to us? Apparently not, as human white blood cell counts are lower and support the idea that we evolved to have fewer, rather than more, sexual relationships.

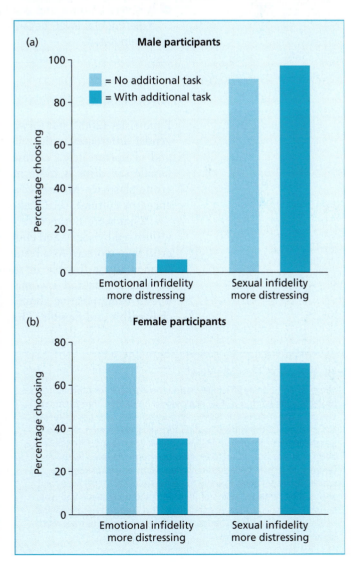

*Do you think that the research of evolutionary psychologists has sampled an adequate range of cultures?*

However, the findings of Buunk et al. (1996) were replicated when there were no constraints on processing resources. As DeSteno et al. (p. 1114) concluded, "In direct contradiction to the evolutionary view, both men and women appear to experience more distress in response to extra-dyadic [non-partnership] sexual encounters than to emotional infidelities."

There is more bad news for evolutionary psychologists. Harris (2002) pointed out most previous studies had examined reactions to *hypothetical* rather than *actual* infidelity. When she examined participants' reactions to actual infidelity by their partner, there were no differences between men and women. Members of both sexes focused more on emotional than on sexual infidelity. These findings are totally inconsistent with the notion that evolutionary pressures have led men and women to respond very differently to sexual and emotional infidelity.

## Evaluation

⊕ Some aspects of sexual attitudes and sexual behaviour are as predicted by evolutionary psychology.

⊕ Evolutionary psychology helps to explain some gender differences in sexual attitudes and behaviour.

⊖ Evolutionary psychology is not well placed to account for *changes* in human sexual behaviour from one generation to the next (e.g., the enormous changes in sexual attitudes and behaviour within many Western cultures during the course of the twentieth century).

⊖ It is very hard (or impossible) to test the assumptions of evolutionary psychology at an experimental level, because the key variables (e.g., natural selection) cannot readily be manipulated.

## Baumeister's theory of erotic plasticity

Baumeister (2000) put forward a theory of human sexuality based on the notion there are gender differences in the relative influence of nature (biological and evolutionary factors) and of nurture (e.g., culture). The key assumptions of the theory are as follows: "The female sex drive is more malleable [flexible] than the male, indicating higher average erotic plasticity. More precisely, female sexual responses and sexual behaviours are influenced by cultural, social, and situational factors to a greater extent than male" (p. 348).

What were Baumeister's (2000) reasons for assuming that female sexuality is more influenced by social and cultural factors? First, men are generally stronger and more powerful than women. As a result, during the course of evolution men have had less need than women to be flexible in their approach to sexual behaviour. Second, sexual activity between a man and a woman typically starts when the woman changes from being negative to being positive about having sex with the man. This requires her to be somewhat changeable and flexible. Third, according to Baumeister, women generally have a weaker sex drive than men. As a result, "Women could … be more easily be persuaded to accept substitutes or alternate forms of satisfaction, as compared with men."

### Women's sexual orientations

Veniegas and Conley (2000) evaluated the available scientific evidence on factors influencing female homosexual behaviour. They point out that only gay male brains have been studied. Only one pair of female twins raised apart has been studied for sexual orientation, and no genetic markers for lesbian behaviour have been found. The public belief that exposure in utero to abnormal hormone levels leads, in females, to lesbian behaviour is challenged by empirical research, which shows the great majority to be heterosexual in behaviour and also in their fantasies. Levels of hormones and body shape and type are also unrelated to sexual orientation. This seems to mean that we know quite a lot about what does not affect sexuality, but not much about what does!

## Evidence

A clear prediction from Baumeister's (2000) theory is that women's sexual behaviour should vary more than men's across cultures. Evidence in line with this prediction was reported by Barry and Schlegel (1984), who reviewed findings on adolescent sexual behaviour in 186 cultures. Females showed greater cross-cultural variation than males on all their measures of sexual behaviour.

Another prediction from the theory is that genetic factors should influence male sexuality more than female sexuality. Evidence relevant to this prediction was reported by Dunne et al. (1997). They studied age at first intercourse among people who had grown up after the "sexual revolution" of the 1960s. Genetic factors accounted for 72% of individual differences among males in age at first intercourse, but accounted for only 40% in females.

It might also be predicted from Baumeister's theory of erotic plasticity that females would be more influenced than males by the sexual behaviour of their best friend. Billy and Udry (1985) found female virgins were six times more likely to lose their virginity over the following 2 years if their best friend was not a virgin. In contrast, the sexual status of their best friend was not related to the probability of male virgins losing their virginity over a 2-year period.

Other evidence suggests male and female sexuality may differ less than is implied by Baumeister (2000). For example, Oliver and Hyde (1993) carried out a meta-analysis of data on gender differences in eight aspects of attitudes about sexuality (e.g., premarital sex, masturbation) and nine aspects of sexual behaviour (e.g., oral sex, incidence of masturbation). There were small (or non-existent) gender differences for most aspects of sexual attitudes and behaviour. However, there were large gender differences with respect to casual sex and incidence of masturbation.

## Evaluation

- ➕ The notions that nature is more important in male sexuality than in female sexuality, but that nurture is more important in female sexuality, are potentially important.
- ➕ Female sexuality seems to be more influenced than male sexuality by social and cultural factors.
- ➖ The reasons for gender differences in erotic plasticity remain unclear. However, Hyde and Durik (2000, p. 375) proposed a possible explanation: "Groups with less power (in this case, women) pay more attention and adapt their behaviour more to those with power (men) than the reverse." Thus, women show more flexibility than men in their sexuality because their behaviour is more under the control of other people.

# WORK MOTIVATION AND PERFORMANCE

It is generally accepted that a high level of motivation is essential for success in academic courses and in a career. In this section, we will consider the relationship between work motivation and performance. Any given individual's level of work motivation depends on several factors. For example, his/her personality may well make a difference. Workers' motivation also depends on whether they feel fairly treated, on the amount of support and encouragement provided by their employers, the work goals they set for themselves, and so on. We will briefly consider some of these factors before discussing the role of goal setting at greater length. We focus on goal setting because Locke's goal-setting theory is the most influential theory of work motivation, and has received the strongest empirical support.

## Personality

Work motivation and performance have been related to various dimensions of personality. For example, conscientiousness (e.g., dependable, hard-working) is one of the so-called Big Five personality factors (see Chapter 13), and is consistently related to work performance. Indeed, Barrick and Mount (1991) found in a meta-analysis that job performance was predicted better by conscientiousness than by any of the other Big Five dimensions (agreeableness, extraversion, neuroticism, openness). Here, however, we consider two personality dimensions that have attracted the most research: Type A behaviour pattern, and locus of control. Effects of self-efficacy on performance are discussed in Chapter 13.

In order to succeed in an academic course a high level of motivation is needed!

The stock exchange is the ideal environment for individuals with a Type A behaviour pattern.

## Type A behaviour pattern

The **Type A behaviour pattern** consists of, "extremes of competitive achievement striving, hostility, aggressiveness, and a sense of time urgency, evidenced by vigorous voice and psychomotor mannerisms" (Matthews, 1988, p. 373). It was originally proposed by Friedman and Rosenman (1959), and is discussed in Chapter 5. They contrasted it with the Type B behaviour pattern, which involves a more relaxed approach to life and a lack of the central features of Type A.

As we have seen, the Type A behaviour pattern consists of a diverse set of characteristics. Martin, Kuiper, and Westra (1989, p. 781) shed light on how these characteristics are inter-related:

*Type A individuals attempt to maintain a positive view of self by fulfilling unrealistic performance demands through hard-driven, work-directed behaviours; and to engage in aggressive and hostile behaviour when they perceive themselves as being thwarted in such attempts.*

It is clear that Type A individuals are highly motivated. However, it does not necessarily follow that their work performance should be superior to that of Type Bs. For example, their hostility and aggressiveness may often be counterproductive, and actually impair the quality of their work.

## Evidence

Taylor, Locke, Lee, and Gist (1984) considered the performance of Type As and Type Bs carrying out research in a university setting. Type As produced more research publications than Type Bs. In addition, the research publications of Type As were of significantly higher quality than those of Type Bs as measured by the number of times the publications were cited by other scientists. These performance differences occurred because Type As set themselves higher performance goals, they were more likely to be working on several projects at the same time, and they perceived themselves as higher in self-efficacy.

Byrne and Reinhart (1989) studied 432 workers in managerial and professional roles. There was a correlation of +.15 between Type A and occupational level, indicating that Type As tended to be in higher positions than Type Bs within their work organisation. Why did this happen? Byrne and Reinhart also found that Type A correlated +.32 with total hours of work per week, and +.31 with amount of weekend work. Further statistical analyses indicated that the higher occupational level of Type As occurred almost entirely because of their higher level of motivation as reflected in the hours they worked.

*Think about the people you mix with regularly. Can you categorise all of them as being either Type A or Type B?*

## Evaluation

- ✚ Type A is reliably related to higher levels of work motivation and effort.
- ✚ Type A is often (but by no means always) related to higher levels of work performance.
- ➖ It is a substantial over-simplification to assign everyone to the two categories of Type A and Type B.
- ➖ Work motivation and work performance depend on the type of work, the extent to which workers can use their skills, and so on, as well as on their personality.

## Locus of control

Rotter (1966) argued there are important individual differences in **locus of control**, a dimension of personality concerned with perceptions about the factors influencing what happens to us. In essence, people with an internal locus of control have the general expectation that rewards or outcomes will depend mainly on their own efforts. In contrast, people with an external locus of control have the general expectation that outcomes will depend mainly on fate, chance, or other external factors. Rotter devised the Internal–External Locus of Control Scale to assess whether any given individual had an internal or external locus of control.

It is predicted that internals will exhibit superior work performance to externals. Why should this be so? Internals argue that exerting a high level of effort at work is more worthwhile than do externals, because they believe there is a closer link between their efforts and the rewards they receive.

## Evidence

Workers with an internal locus of control are typically more successful than those with an external locus of control (see Spector, 1982, for a review). For example, Heisler (1974), in a study of government employees considered the relationship between locus of control and an index of effectiveness based on the number of promotions, salary increases, awards received, and current salary. The correlation was −.25, indicating that internals were more effective at work than were externals.

*What is the alternative explanation for this finding? (Clue: remember that it is a correlation.)*

Lied and Pritchard (1976) argued internals have higher levels of work performance than externals because they are more likely to have two expectancies: (1) they expect effort will produce good performance; and (2) they expect good performance will produce rewards. The first expectancy correlated −.40 with locus of control, and the second expectancy correlated −.20 with locus of control. Thus, internals were more likely than externals to have each of these expectancies.

It is typically assumed that the positive association between internal locus of control and occupational status occurs because internal locus of control helps to produce higher occupational status. However, it is also possible that when individuals achieve higher occupational status, this influences their locus of control. Supporting evidence was reported by Andrisani and Nestel (1976), who carried out a longitudinal study on male workers between 1969 and 1971. Those workers having an internal locus of control in 1969 had increased their occupational status and salary by 1971 more than those who were externals in 1969. In addition, however, workers improving their occupational status over those 2 years became more internal, whereas those whose occupational status declined became more external. Thus, locus of control influences work success, *and* work success influences locus of control.

## Evaluation

⊕ Internals typically perform better at work than do externals.

⊕ One of the main reasons why internals have better work performance is because they believe more strongly than externals that exerting hard effort improves performance and rewards.

⊖ Rotter's (1966) original scale is very general, and does not refer specifically to work expectancies. However, more specific questionnaires have been developed (e.g., Spector's, 1988, Work Locus of Control Scale).

⊖ Some of the apparent effects of locus of control on work performance are due to the effects of work performance on locus of control.

⊖ The effects of locus of control on work motivation and performance probably depend on various situational factors (e.g., nature of the job).

## Equity theory

Equity theory was originally proposed by Adams (1965) to account for certain aspects of personal relationships. However, it has been applied to work motivation by various

**Extrinsic motivators**

These are things like pay, rewards, awards, and conditions of work. They can also be regarded as positive reinforcers in operant conditioning. The power of these motivators can be seen in many workplaces in the resentment shown if one worker or group of workers gets an extra or better reward when they have done nothing extra to gain it. This resentment is predicted by equity theory.

theorists, including Huseman, Hatfield, and Miles (1987). According to equity theory, individuals are motivated to achieve what they perceive as fairness or equity. They do this by comparing themselves against other people, who may be fellow workers, workers doing similar work elsewhere, or some other group. They work out the ratio between their inputs (e.g., effort at work, experience, ability) and outcomes (e.g., pay, fringe benefits, status, interest level of the work) and those of other people.

What is the relevance of equity theory to motivation? According to the theory, work motivation will be highest when workers perceive their input–outcome ratio is similar to those of comparison workers. In other words, what they receive from their employer is similar to what is received by other workers having similar levels of ability and work effort. Motivation will be relatively low when workers perceive there is underpayment inequity, meaning they believe that other people are receiving more outcomes for their inputs. Thus, for example, a worker will experience underpayment inequity if he/she knows most other people doing similar work are paid 25% more than him/her. This will produce anger, and can lead to various attempts to improve equity or fairness, such as increasing outcomes (e.g., asking for a pay rise), reducing inputs (e.g., putting in less effort), or changing jobs.

According to the theory, work motivation will also be low if there is overpayment inequity, meaning workers think they are receiving more pay and other outcomes for their ability and work effort than are other people. You might think that workers in such a situation would be very pleased (it sounds pretty good to me!), but it is assumed within equity theory that they experience guilt. As a result, they may take various forms of corrective action, such as the following: increasing inputs by working harder; distorting the situation (e.g., "I am actually better than most people doing my kind of job"); or changing the workers against whom they compare themselves to workers having higher status and ability.

## Evidence

Most research on equity theory has been carried out under laboratory conditions. This research was reviewed by Locke and Henne (1986). They found underpayment inequity generally led to a lower level of performance as predicted by the theory. However, overpayment inequity rarely led to the predicted improvement in performance.

There have been attempts to apply the theory to work settings. Greenberg and Ornstein (1983) studied the effects on work performance of workers receiving a high-status job title without increased pay. As predicted, workers who felt that the new job title had been earned responded by increasing their work effort. Iverson and Roy (1994) carried out a study on Australian blue-collar workers. Those experiencing underpayment inequity were more likely than other workers to have the intention of leaving their job and also exhibited more job-search behaviour.

Equity theory apparently assumes everyone is equally affected by perceptions of inequity or unfairness. In fact, however, there is evidence (e.g., King, Miles, & Day, 1993) that individuals differ greatly in what has been called equity sensitivity. Individuals high in equity sensitivity are very concerned if their input–outcome ratio differs from that of other workers, whereas those low in equity sensitivity are not.

## Evaluation

⊕ Perceived fairness in the workplace influences workers' motivation (e.g., underpayment inequity can reduce motivation).

⊖ It is not clear within the theory precisely how individual workers select other workers for comparison.

⊖ Overpayment inequity does not typically lead workers to correct the inequity by working harder.

⊖ The theory ignores individual differences in equity sensitivity.

# Goal-setting theory

Goal-setting theory was originally put forward by Locke (1968), and subsequently modified (e.g., Locke, Shaw, Saari, & Latham, 1981). It has been a very influential approach to work motivation. Indeed, Arnold, Cooper, and Robertson (1995, p. 220) claimed that, "by the early 1990s, well over half the research on motivation published in leading academic journals reported tests, extensions or refinements of goal-setting theory."

What are the key ingredients in goal-setting theory? First, it is assumed the main factor in motivation is the goal, which can be defined as "what the individual is consciously trying to do" (Locke, 1968, p. 159). The goal that someone has set him/herself can be assessed by direct questioning.

Second, there is predicted to be a straightforward relationship between goal difficulty and performance. According to Locke (1968, p. 162), "the harder the goal the higher the level of performance." The reason is that individuals try harder when difficult goals are set.

Third, Locke (1968) argued task performance also depends on goal commitment, which is the determination to reach a goal. According to the theory, high performance occurs only when goal difficulty and goal commitment are both high. As can be seen in the figure on the right, the relationship between goal difficulty and performance should be stronger when commitment is high than when it is low.

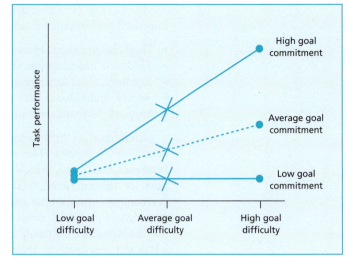

The effects of goal difficulty and goal commitment on task performance according to Locke's goal-setting theory. From Klein et al. (1999).

*Are all of our goals conscious ones?*

## Evidence

Latham and Yukl (1975) carried out a study using workers whose job involved cutting and transporting wood. These workers were divided into three kinds of groups:

1. Workers simply instructed to "do your best" (do-your-best groups).
2. Groups assigned to a specific hard goal in terms of hundreds of cubic feet of wood per week (assigned groups).
3. Groups in which everyone participated in setting a specific hard production goal (participative groups).

Latham and Yukl (1975) found the do-your-best groups set the easiest goals, and so were predicted to have the poorest work performance. In contrast, the participative groups set the hardest goals, and so should have performed the best. In line with prediction, the do-your-best groups averaged 46 cubic feet of wood per hour; the assigned groups averaged 53 cubic feet; and the participative groups averaged 56 cubic feet. These differences may not seem large. However, the work performance of the participative groups was almost 22% greater than that of the do-your-best groups, and any company would be delighted to increase the productivity of its workers by 22%!

Goal-setting theory has also been applied to the effects of incentive on performance. According to Locke et al. (1968, p. 1104), "Incentives such as money should affect action only if and to the extent that they affect the individual's goals and intentions." Support for this hypothesis was obtained by Farr (1976) in a study on speed of card sorting. The provision of financial incentives led to the setting of much higher goals and to increased sorting speed.

Earley, Connolly, and Ekegren (1989) argued goal setting can have adverse effects on performance when people are performing a novel task and there are numerous possible strategies that could be applied to it. Their participants carried out a task involving making stock-market predictions. Those who were assigned specific, hard goals actually performed worse than those given a "do-your-best" goal. The participants with the specific, hard goals changed their strategies more often than did the "do-your-best" participants, and so they may have focused too much on task strategy and not enough on task performance.

Locke et al. (1981) reviewed the evidence on goal-setting theory. Goal setting had led to improved performance in about 90% of studies, especially under the following conditions:

- *Goal commitment*. Individuals accept the goal that has been set.
- *Feedback*. Information about progress towards the goal is provided.
- *Rewards*. Goal attainment is rewarded.
- *Ability*. Individuals have enough ability to attain the goal.
- *Support*. Management or others provide encouragement.

Klein et al. (1999) carried out a meta-analysis on goal commitment and goal setting based on 74 studies. The average correlation between goal commitment and task performance was +.20, which was highly significant. The meta-analysis also provided support for the predicted relationship between goal difficulty and goal commitment: The correlation between goal commitment and performance was greater when goal difficulty was high (+.31) than when goal difficulty was low (+.16).

What factors influence an individual's level of goal commitment? Klein et al. (1999) addressed this issue in their meta-analysis. Two key factors were attractiveness of goal attainment and expectancy of goal attainment if reasonable effort were applied. Klein et al. (p. 890) also identified various other factors: "Higher levels of commitment resulted from having high ability, a voice in the determination of the goal, task or job satisfaction, specific goals, task experience, receiving feedback on one's performance, and the form of that feedback."

Most studies investigating goal-setting theory have been laboratory based. An exception was a study by Yearta, Maitlis, and Briner (1995), who studied scientists and professional staff working at the research centre of a large multi-national company. Their findings were not in line with the theory:

> *Three of the four relevant correlations indicated moderate but significant relationships between difficulty and performance, with higher levels of perceived difficulty associated with lower levels of perceived performance. Thus the direction of this relationship was the reverse of that predicted by goal setting theory. (p. 246)*

Why might studies in work organisations produce different findings from laboratory studies? First, it is often much harder to define goals clearly in work settings than in the laboratory. Second, the best way to achieve a goal is generally much less clear in work settings than in the laboratory. It follows that goal-setting theory might receive more support in work settings if the work goals were clearly defined and the workers knew the appropriate strategy to achieve the goal.

Support for the above predictions were reported by Doerr, Mitchell, Klastorin, and Brown (1996), in a study carried out in a fish-processing plant in the northwestern United States. The workers had to clean and dress salmon as rapidly as possible, and did so under one of three conditions: individual goal; group goal (i.e., total output of all group members had to reach a certain level); and control (no specific goal). The average time to process 50 fish was 702 seconds in the no-goal control group, compared to 570 seconds (group goal), and 538 seconds (individual goal). Thus, goal setting led to improved performance in this work setting, perhaps because of the straightforward nature of the goals and the task.

There are other important differences between the work environment and most laboratory studies of goal-setting theory. As Yearta et al. (1995, p. 239) pointed out:

> *Goals set in controlled studies are typically single specific tasks that can be completed in a short, strictly limited, time period. In contrast, employees in organisations are often trying to achieve multiple goals simultaneously, in the midst of many other distractions, and over an extended period of time. In a recent Institute of Personnel Management ... report, 54 per cent of organisations surveyed set performance requirements over a six- to 12-month period.*

Gollwitzer (1999) has addressed directly the issue of how people can move from goal setting to goal attainment in a world full of complications and distractions, an issue de-emphasised within goal-setting theory. His key concept is that of **implementation intentions**, which "specify the when, where, and how of responses leading to goal attainment" (p. 494). In order to see the value of implementation intentions, we will consider a concrete example. Suppose a student called Rita has set herself the goal of spending 4 hours on a given Saturday revising for a forthcoming examination. However, there are obstacles in the way. Rita normally chats for several hours a day with her flatmates, and she also enjoys watching television. Thus, there is a real danger that Rita will be distracted from her studies, and finish up doing little or no revision.

How can Rita try to ensure the revision gets done? According to Gollwitzer (1999), this is where implementation intentions come in. Two possible implementation intentions are as follows: (1) "When one of my flatmates knocks on the door, I will tell her that I will see her in the pub at 8 o'clock"; (2) "If I discover there is something interesting on television, I will ask my flatmates to video it so I can watch it later." As you have probably guessed, the crucial prediction made by Gollwitzer is that goals are much more likely to be attained if individuals form implementation intentions than if they do not.

Evidence that implementation intentions make it more likely that goals will be achieved was reported by Gollwitzer and Brandstatter (1997). Their participants were given the goal of writing a report on how they spent Christmas Eve within the following 2 days. Half the participants were told to form implementation intentions by indicating when and where they intended to write the report, whereas the other half did not indicate a specific time and place. The goal was achieved by 75% of those who formed implementation intentions, but by only 33% of those who did not.

## Evaluation

⊕ Goal setting and goal commitment are often important in determining the level of work performance, as predicted by goal-setting theory.
⊕ Goal-setting theory helps to explain individual differences in motivation and performance: Highly motivated workers set themselves higher goals and are more committed to them than are poorly motivated workers.
⊖ Goal-setting theory may be less applicable within work organisations than in the laboratory (Yearta et al., 1995).
⊖ An individual's goal level is seen as corresponding to his/her conscious intentions. However, people's motivational forces are not always open to conscious awareness.
⊖ Goal-setting theory does not emphasise enough the processes (e.g., implementation intentions) intervening between goal setting and goal attainment.
⊖ Goal setting can actually impair performance when people are in the process of learning how to perform a task. As Kanfer and Ackerman (1989, p. 687) pointed out, "Interventions [such as goal setting] designed to engage motivational processes may impede task learning when presented prior to an understanding what the task is about. In these instances, cognitive resources necessary for task understanding are diverted towards self-regulatory activities (e.g., self-evaluation)."

> **KEY TERM**
> **Implementation intentions:** intentions specifying in detail how individuals are going to achieve the goals they have set themselves.

## SUMMARY

Maslow put forward a theory of motivation based on a hierarchy of needs ranging from physiological needs at the bottom to the need for self-actualisation at the top. Individuals tend to satisfy lower-level needs before considering higher-level needs. Self-actualised people have more peak experiences than other people. The theory has the advantage of being unusually comprehensive. However, some of the concepts (e.g., self-actualisation) are imprecise, and self-actualisation depends on environmental support more than is assumed within the theory. Alderfer (1969) proposed a simplified version of Maslow's

*Need theories*

hierarchical theory based on existence, relatedness, and growth needs. According to this theory, when one of an individual's needs cannot be satisfied, he/she will refocus on needs at a more concrete level (e.g., existence needs). A limitation with this theory is that it does not specify what strategies a given individual will use when trying to satisfy a need.

## Homeostasis: temperature and hunger

Homeostatic systems have a system variable, a set point, a detector, and a correctional mechanism. The hypothalamus is involved in detecting changes in body temperature and in initiating corrective action. The parasympathetic nervous system is activated when body temperature is too high, and the sympathetic nervous system is activated when body temperature is too low. In addition to the hypothalamic system, there are less sensitive systems for temperature regulation based in the brain stem and in the spinal cord. Eating behaviour cannot be accounted for by a simple homeostatic model based on the maintenance of energy levels. We need food to supply nutrients and energy. Energy allows us to process the food we have ingested, to think and move around, and to maintain our basal metabolism. Glucose is the main source of energy used by the brain, whereas the body can use fatty acids as well as glucose. Patients with Type 1 diabetes, whose pancreas has stopped producing insulin, cannot make efficient use of the energy derived from food. Glucose, insulin, and CCK all play a role in hunger and satiety. Regulation of body weight depends on levels of leptin and insulin, which are secreted in proportion to the amount of fat tissue. The lateral hypothalamus is involved in the control of hunger, and the ventromedial hypothalamus is involved in the control of satiety, but other brain regions are also involved. People eat more when there is more dietary variety than when there is less variety; this is due mainly to sensory-specific satiety. Obesity depends on genetic factors, and probably also depends in part on dietary variety and on individual differences in metabolic rate.

## Sex and sexual behaviour

The evolutionary advantage of sexual reproduction is that it produces genetic diversity, which maximises the chances of members of a species coping with environmental changes. The menstrual cycle consists of successive follicular, ovulation, luteal, and premenstrual and menstrual phases. The sexual response cycle consists of excitement, plateau, orgasm, and resolution phases. The two main classes of sex hormones are androgens and oestrogens, with the former being found in greater quantities in men and the latter in women. Sex motivation in both sexes depends more on androgen levels than on oestrogen levels. Genetic factors influence childhood gender non-conformity and adult

sexual orientation. According to evolutionary psychologists, the greater parental investment of women than of men means that women are more discriminating than men in their choice of sex partners, and men are more competitive than women for sexual access to members of the opposite sex. As predicted by evolutionary psychology, there are clear differences in the characteristics preferred by men and by women (e.g., men want their wife to be younger than them, whereas women want their husband to be older). There is some support for Baumeister's theory of erotic plasticity, according to which female sexuality is influenced more than male sexuality by social and cultural factors.

Work motivation and performance depend in part on the individual worker's personality, with conscientiousness, Type A, and internal locus of control all having beneficial effects. However, the effects of personality depend in part on situational factors such as the nature of the work. According to equity theory, workers are motivated to achieve fairness or equity. They do this by comparing their inputs and outcomes with those of others. Underpayment inequity often reduces motivation, but workers typically do not try to correct overpayment inequity. According to goal-setting theory, task performance depends on goal difficulty and goal commitment. There is less support for goal-setting theory in studies carried out in work organisations than in laboratories, presumably because work goals are often less clearly defined and it is harder to determine the best strategy to achieve the goal. Goal-setting theory de-emphasises processes (e.g., implementation intentions) intervening between goal setting and goal attainment.

*Work motivation and performance*

## FURTHER READING

- Kalat, J.W. (2000). *Biological psychology* (7th ed.). Pacific Grove, CA: Brooks/Cole Publishing Co. Reasonably detailed accounts of most of the topics discussed in this chapter are contained in this well-written textbook.
- Riggio, R.E. (2000). *Introduction to industrial/organisational psychology* (3rd ed.). Upper Saddle River, NJ: Prentice Hall. Several theories of work motivation are considered in Chapter 7 of this textbook.
- Rosenzweig, M.R., Breedlove, S.M., & Leiman, A.L. (2002). *Biological psychology: An introduction to behavioural, cognitive, and clinical neuroscience* (3rd ed.). Sunderland, MA: Sinauer Associates. There are readable accounts of biological approaches to motivation in this textbook.

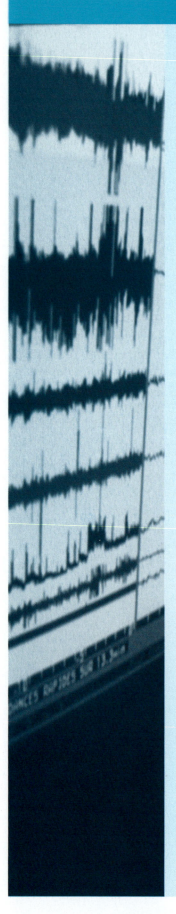

- **Consciousness**
  The study of consciousness.

  Definition of consciousness
  Features of conscious experience
  The role of the brain
  Phenomenal vs. access consciousness
  Theories of the function of
      consciousness: functionalism,
      dual-aspect
  The argument against unitary
      consciousness: split-brain,
      dissociative identity

- **Bodily rhythms**
  Rhythms and cycles affecting
  the body.

  Biological rhythms: circadian,
      infradian, ultradian
  Sleep–wake cycle
  Physiological changes in the
      sleep–wake cycle
  Disruption of the natural light–dark
      cycle: jet lag, shiftwork
  Psychological circadian cycle
  Infradian cycle; pre-menstrual
      syndrome
  Circannual cycle: seasonal affective
      disorder

- **Sleep**
  Aspects of the sleep cycle.

  Measuring brain-wave activity
  Five stages of sleep
  The regulation of sleep
  Sleep-deprivation studies:
      psychological and performance
      effects
  Theories: recovery/restoration;
      adaptive/evolutionary

- **Dreaming**
  Looking at dreams.

  Definitions of dreaming
  When dreaming occurs
  Problems with studying dreams
  Freud's wish fulfilment theory
  Hobson's activation–synthesis theory
  Revonsuo's evolutionary hypothesis

- **Hypnosis**
  The phenomenon of hypnosis.

  Definition of hypnosis
  How the hypnotic state is produced
  Individual differences
  The hypnotic state
  Four phenomena: hypnotic amnesia,
      hypnotic analgesia, trance logic,
      attentional narrowing
  Altered states theories:
      neo-dissociation
  Non-state theories
  Applications of hypnosis

# States of awareness

4

Every day, we all experience several states of awareness, some of which form the focus of this chapter. For example, there is clearly an important difference between the waking and sleeping states, and within the sleeping state we must distinguish between dreaming and non-dreaming. There are also changes in our state of alertness during the course of the day, with many of them depending on various bodily rhythms. Before discussing such states of awareness, we will consider the central issue of consciousness, including what it is and what functions it serves.

There are various ways in which our state of awareness can be altered. For example, people use numerous drugs, some of which are legal (e.g., alcohol) and some of which are illegal (e.g., ecstasy). Effects of drugs on our states of awareness are considered in detail in Chapter 2. Another way of influencing our internal state is by hypnosis. In the United Kingdom, much interest has been created in the hypnotic state by the television demonstrations of Paul McKenna and others. Perhaps the key question about hypnosis is the following: Does hypnosis produce a special state of awareness? Some psychologists answer that question "No", whereas others answer it "Yes". Towards the end of the chapter, we will consider both sides of the argument in the light of the relevant evidence.

## CONSCIOUSNESS

The only issue relating to consciousness on which there is a high level of agreement is that it is one of the most difficult topics to study in the whole of psychology. What is **consciousness**? According to Velmans (2000, p. 6), "A person is conscious if they experience *something*; conversely, if a person or entity experiences nothing, they are not conscious. Elaborating slightly, we can say that when consciousness is present, phenomenal content is present. Conversely when *phenomenal content* is absent, consciousness is absent."

Valentine (1992) identified several features of conscious experience:

- It is private.
- It can consist of information combined across different sensory modalities (e.g., vision, hearing).
- It contains information about the *products* or outcomes of thought processes rather than the *processes* themselves. For example, if you are asked to name the capital of France, you think of the answer without any awareness of the processes involved.
- It is constantly changing like a river or a stream.

Which parts of the brain are most involved in consciousness? Surprisingly, most patients with widespread brain damage retain conscious awareness (Velmans, 2000). More precisely, brain damage rarely leads to a *general* loss of conscious awareness, but it often leads to the loss of *specific* forms of awareness. For example, some patients with damage to the primary visual cortex suffer from blindsight, a condition in which there is no conscious awareness of objects presented to certain parts of the visual field (see Chapter 7). However, patients with blindsight have intact conscious experience of themselves and of other events.

In spite of what has just been said, there *can* be profound general effects on conscious experience when there is damage to the reticular activating system. This system is located in the hindbrain and the midbrain, and influences states of arousal and sleep (see Chapter 2 and later in this chapter). Karen Ann Quinlan was a 21-year-old woman who sustained extensive damage to the reticular activating system because she took a minor tranquilliser and had a few drinks. As a result, she went into a coma (a state of deep unconsciousness) in which she remained for the rest of her short life (Quinlan & Quinlan, 1977).

A key role in conscious experience is played by the thalamus, located just below the cortex in the diencephalon (see Chapter 2). The thalamus acts as a gateway for information going to the cerebral cortex, and may also be a gateway to consciousness. According to Baars and McGovern (1996, p. 80):

> The importance of the thalamus in the neuropsychology of consciousness is highlighted by the long-known fact that lesioning the reticular and/or intraliminar nucleus of the thalamus uniquely abolishes consciousness and produces coma. On the other hand, cortical lesions, even as large as hemispherectomies [loss of one hemisphere of the brain], only abolish some contents of consciousness, not consciousness itself.

In what follows we will address three key issues relating to consciousness. First, we consider the nature of conscious experience. Second, we deal with the issue of the function or functions served by consciousness. Third, we consider whether everyone possesses a single, unitary consciousness, or whether some people have two or more rather separate consciousnesses.

## Nature of conscious experience

As we all know, the contents of conscious experience vary dramatically over time. We can be consciously aware of rain falling on a roof, of our behaviour, of our last summer holiday, of our secret thoughts, or of a spectacular sunset. This variety suggests the value of distinguishing between different forms of consciousness. For example, we can distinguish between direct experience or consciousness (e.g., perception of the environment) and reflexive consciousness. In terms of an example used by Marcel (1993), seeing a pink elephant involves direct experience or consciousness, but knowing it is *you* who is seeing a pink elephant involves reflexive consciousness. In more general terms, reflexive consciousness can be regarded as an important part of self-consciousness.

Block (1995b) drew a different distinction between two types of consciousness:

1. **Phenomenal consciousness**. This involves the experience of seeing, hearing, touching, and so on, and corresponds to direct consciousness.
2. **Access consciousness**. This involves becoming aware of information stored in long-term memory (e.g., remembering the events of the day).

*Assuming that animals are capable of conscious experience, what does this suggest about the phenomenal consciousness of animals (such as bats) that have very different sensory capabilities to our own?*

Velmans (2000) considered direct or phenomenal consciousness in detail. He argued convincingly that much of our conscious awareness consists of a partial but workable representation of the world around us. This representation depends largely on our various sensory systems (e.g., visual, auditory), and is influenced by the limitations of those systems. For example, the range of electromagnetic frequencies our eyes can detect is surprisingly limited: We cannot see radio waves, radar waves, gamma rays, X-rays, microwaves, or infrared and ultra-violet radiation.

### Evidence

If the distinction between phenomenal consciousness and access consciousness is important, we might expect to find brain-damaged patients having good phenomenal consciousness but very poor access consciousness. One such case is that of CW, who became amnesic as a result of developing herpes simplex encephalitis. His phenomenal consciousness was intact, but his ability to remember what had happened to him was extremely poor. According to his wife, "He [CW] sees what is right in front of him but as soon as that information hits the brain it fades. Everything goes in perfectly well … he perceives his world as you or I do, but as soon as he's perceived it and looked away it's gone for him. So it's a moment to moment consciousness" (Wilson & Wearing, 1995, p. 15). Indeed, his access consciousness for personal experiences was so poor he kept having the impression he had just woken up after his illness. His access consciousness was also poor for general knowledge. Even though he had been a professional musician, he could only think of the names of four composers in 1 minute.

Are there brain-damaged patients with good access consciousness but poor phenomenal consciousness? According to Block (1995b), such individuals would resemble "zombies", because they would typically behave like normal human beings, but would lack subjective experience of the environment. Bogen (1997) suggested speculatively that the right hemispheres of split-brain patients come close to fitting that description. So far as we can tell, the right hemispheres of most split-brain patients have little phenomenal consciousness (see below). Their right hemispheres may have more access consciousness, but it is hard to judge.

Convincing evidence that conscious experience depends on our sensory systems comes from studies on individuals with severe visual or auditory impairments. For example, Sheila Hocken had very poor vision from birth, eventually becoming blind in her late teens. Her conscious recollections of her childhood did not contain visual information. She recalled the house she lived in as a child, "by the smell of bread baking and pies cooking, and the warmth and sound of a coal fire crackling and hissing in the grate. But no more" (Hocken, 1977). In similar fashion, profoundly deaf children typically do not experience their thoughts as inner speech like other children. Their thoughts are mostly in the form of hand signs and symbols, or bodily and facial expressions (Conrad, 1979).

We seem to be skilful at producing effective conscious representations of the visual environment even when psychologists try to make things difficult for us. Kohler (1962) carried out studies in which participants wore distorting goggles. One set of goggles made objects seem narrower when the head turned to the left, but they seemed broader when the head turned to the right. When the head moved up and down, objects appeared to slant one way and then the other way. The overall effect was to make the world appear to be made of rubber. In spite of these distortions, visual perception returned to normal over a period of weeks for the person wearing these goggles. When he removed the goggles, he experienced the reverse distortions to those created by the goggles, but again his visual perception adapted gradually.

# Functions of consciousness

There are more theoretical views about the functions of consciousness than you can shake a stick at. At one extreme was the position adopted by the behaviourists. The behaviourists were American psychologists who established psychology as a scientific discipline in the early part of the twentieth century, and who denied that consciousness served any useful purpose. According to the founder of behaviourism, John Watson (1913, p. 163), "The time seems to have come when psychology must discard all reference to consciousness … its sole task is the prediction and control of behaviour and introspection can form no part of its method." Thankfully, most psychologists in recent times have ignored Watson.

## *Functionalism*

Functionalism is one of the most influential approaches to consciousness. The essence of this approach (which originated with Aristotle) is that consciousness and the mind are functions of the brain. This is basically a reductionist approach, in which the complexities of consciousness can be explained in simple physical terms. As Velmans (1996b, p. 4) pointed out, "Reductionists maintain that science will eventually show consciousness to be just a state of the brain … Alternatively, they maintain that consciousness is nothing more than a set of … brain functions that may be found not just in brains but also in 'thinking' machines."

Numerous psychologists (e.g., Baars, 1997; William James, 1890; Mandler, 1997) have developed the functionalist approach by specifying the functions of consciousness in information-processing or neural network terms. For example, Baars (1997) related attention and consciousness by considering sentences such as, "We look in order to see", and, "We listen in order to hear." He argued that, "The distinction is between selecting an

Historical portrait of the Greek philosopher Aristotle (384–322 BC). Aristotle is one of the most important figures in the history of Western thought. He produced a huge output in many areas of knowledge, heavily influencing later thinkers. The idea that consciousness and the mind are functions of the brain originated with Aristotle.

experience and being conscious of the selected event. In everyday language, the first word of each pair involves attention; the second word involves consciousness" (p. 389). Thus, the contents of consciousness are often determined by attentional processes. According to Baars, attentional processes resemble selecting a given television channel, and consciousness resembles what then appears on the television screen (see Chapter 6).

Baars and McGovern (1996) proposed a functional theory of consciousness. They argued that the brain has numerous specialised processors (e.g., detectors for line orientation, detectors for faces) operating very efficiently below the level of consciousness. These specialised processors transmit information to a limited-capacity global workspace, which integrates information from these diverse sources. According to Baars and McGovern (p. 92), "Information in the global workspace corresponds to conscious contents … Consciousness appears to be the major way in which the central nervous system adapts to novel, challenging and informative events in the world."

The notion that there are important links between selective attention and consciousness has received much empirical support (see Velmans, 2000). However, the functionalist approach suffers from an important limitation. As Velmans pointed out, consciousness is indisputably a "first-person" phenomenon: We have detailed knowledge of our own conscious experience, but cannot observe directly anyone else's conscious experience. However, accounts of consciousness by functionalist theorists are "third-person" accounts describing various processes of relevance to consciousness. Why is this a problem? According to Velmans (p. 66):

> [Functionalist] theories typically move, without blinking, from relatively well-justified claims about the forms of information processing with which consciousness is associated, to entirely unjustified claims about what consciousness is or what it does. Baars and McGovern (1996), for example, move without any discussion … to the claim that consciousness actually carries out the functions of the global workspace.

We can see clearly the limitations of the functionalist approach if we consider the views of computational functionalists such as Sloman and Logan (1998). According to such theorists, "There is nothing to prevent mind and consciousness in non-human systems, for the reason that mental operations are nothing more than computations" (Velmans, 2000, p. 73). Thus, a computer programmed carefully to mimic the attentional and other processes of human beings would have conscious experiences! That seems wildly improbable to me (and to you?), and certainly has not been shown to be the case. However, it follows from the functionalist position. Sloman (1997) has gone a step further, and argued it should be possible to design a machine that could fall in love. Pleeeeeeeease! How could this be done? According to Sloman, what we would need to do is the following: "Read what poets and novelists and playwrights say about love, and ask yourself: what kinds of information processing mechanisms are presupposed." For example, if X is in love with Y, we would expect X to find it hard to think of anything except Y. Personally, I will be amazed if anyone ever succeeds in devising a machine that can fall in love.

## Conscious experience and autism

While we can have detailed knowledge of only our own conscious experience, we learn when very young that others' conscious experience is often different, and we also learn to interpret cues or clues as to their different experiences. This learning is something that autistic people do achieve, and current research suggests this is due to a fault in the hard-wiring of the brain (see Chapter 14).

*If a biological replica of a human being were built, do you think that it would inevitably have consciousness?*

## Dual-aspect theory

The central limitation of the functionalist approach is that it considers consciousness almost exclusively from the third-person perspective and ignores the first-person perspective. A broader approach was favoured by the philosopher Baruch Spinoza (1632–1677). In his double aspect theory, Spinoza (1677/1955, p. 131) argued that mind and body are simply different aspects of a single underlying reality: "Mind and body are one and the same thing … the order of states of activity or passivity in our bodies is simultaneous in nature with the order of states of activity and passivity in the mind." Velmans (e.g., 2000) developed the above approach in his dual-aspect theory by claiming that consciousness and aspects of brain activity are *one* process with *two* sides. What are the practical implications of this position? Velmans (p. 247) considered a situation in which he has access to your brain activity (e.g., via neuroimaging): "I know something about your mental states that you do not know (their physical embodiment). But you know something about them that I do not know (their manifestation in experience). Such first- and third-person information is *complementary*. We need your first-person story and my third-person story for a complete account of what is going on."

What functions are served by consciousness according to dual-aspect theory? First, as Velmans (2000, p. 257) pointed out, "Conscious representations of inner, body and external events … generally represent those events and their causal interactions sufficiently well to allow a fairly accurate understanding of what is happening in our lives. Although they are only *representations* of events and their causal interactions, for everyday purposes we can take them to *be* those events and their causal interactions." That is likely to be of great importance when it comes to making decisions about what we should do in the immediate future. Second, "From a first-person view, it is obvious how this [consciousness] affects our life and survival. Without it, life would be like nothing. So without it, there would be no point to survival" (p. 278).

## Evidence

According to the functionalist approach, consciousness plays an important role in information processing, especially in the integration and dissemination (distribution) of information. However, as we will see, conscious awareness typically occurs only *after* the crucial processing has already occurred. Consider, for example, Velmans' (2000, p. 209) account of what happens when you read: "You are conscious of what is written, but not conscious of the complex input analysis involved. Nor are you aware of *consciously* carrying out any system-wide integration and dissemination of information … Rather, information that enters consciousness has *already been integrated*."

Evidence that conscious awareness can occur surprisingly late in processing was reported by Frith, Perry, and Lumer (1999). There were three rods near the participants, and they had to grasp the illuminated one. On some trials, the rod which was illuminated changed *after* participants had started to move their hand. They were asked to make a vocal response to indicate their conscious awareness of the target switch. The key finding was that the participants often grasped the new target rod about 300 ms *before* making the vocal response.

> **Conscious awareness of pain**
>
> If you have ever stepped on a sharp object, or mistakenly picked up a very hot plate, you will know that first of all you leap off the nail or drop the plate. Only then does the pain kick in, after we are "safe". This is so because the nerves (known as the reflex arc) organising the reception of and response to the threat are fast, and those transmitting pain are slow. It's obvious that it is more important to retreat from the harmful stimulus and that feeling the pain and learning from it can wait a second.

More dramatic findings were reported by Libet (1989), who instructed participants to perform a rapid flexion (bending) of their wrist and fingers at a time of their choosing. Three key measures were obtained:

1. **Event-related potentials**, which revealed a consistent pattern (the readiness potential) occurring prior to the movement of the wrist and fingers.
2. The time at which participants were consciously aware of the intention to move their wrist and fingers.
3. The moment at which the hand muscles were activated using an electromyogram.

The main findings are somewhat surprising (but consistent with other findings obtained by Libet, 1989). The readiness potential in the brain occurred about 350 ms *before* there was conscious awareness of the intention to bend the wrist and fingers. This means that, "Initiation of the voluntary process is developed unconsciously, well before there is any awareness of the intention to act" (Libet, 1996, p. 112). The fact that conscious awareness occurred about 200 ms before the actual hand movement started, "provides time in which the conscious process could interfere with or 'veto' the consummation of the voluntary act" (p. 112).

According to dual-aspect theory, the mental state of consciousness and physical brain activity form two sides of a single underlying process. If there is a single underlying process, then we might expect that physical states can cause mental states, and that mental states

> **KEY TERM**
> **Event-related potentials:** regularities produced in the brain-wave or electroencephalograph record produced by repeated presentations of a stimulus.

*Can you think of any other examples of a) physical states causing mental states, and b) mental states causing physical states? (Clue: see Chapter 5.)*

can cause physical states. There is plentiful evidence (e.g., from the use of drugs in therapy; see Chapter 23) that physical states can cause mental states. However, the notion that mental states can cause physical states remains controversial in spite of much supporting evidence. For example, consider what happens when patients are given a salt tablet but told that it contains active ingredients. This often improves the physical health of the patients (this is known as a placebo effect; see Rosenzweig, Breedlove, & Leiman, 2002). Hashish, Finman, and Harvey (1988) provided evidence of a placebo effect. They found that there was less jaw swelling and tightness after the removal of wisdom teeth when an ultrasound machine was used. Of relevance here, the beneficial effects were obtained when the patients were misleadingly told they were exposed to ultrasound. Thus, as predicted by dual-aspect theory, mental states can influence subsequent physical states.

## Is consciousness unitary?

Most people believe they have a single, unitary consciousness. However, that belief has been challenged. For example, Young (1996, p. 122) argued as follows:

> *Why should we assume that consciousness is a unitary phenomenon, requiring a unitary explanation? It seems more reasonable to begin by supposing that, like many complex biological phenomena, consciousness also involves different aspects which will need to be accounted for in different ways … there is no reason to seek the solution to the problem of consciousness, instead it is essential to be clear about which aspect of consciousness is being discussed.*

There are groups of people who may lack a single, unitary consciousness. For example, consider **split-brain patients** who have very few connections between the two brain hemi-

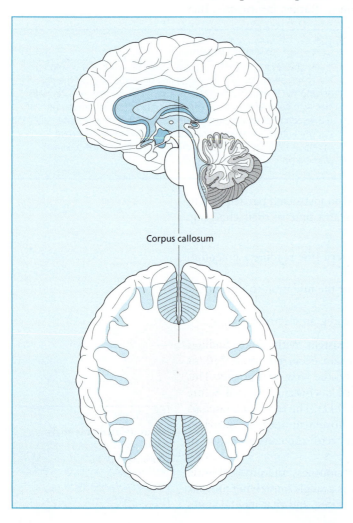

Corpus callosum

spheres as a result of surgery. In the great majority of cases, the corpus callosum (bridge) between the two brain hemispheres was cut surgically to contain epileptic seizures within one hemisphere. The corpus callosum is a collection of 250 million axons connecting sites in one hemisphere with those in the other. There are two other pathways connecting the two hemispheres, but the corpus callosum is far more important in terms of the rapid transmission of information between the two hemispheres. Thus, split-brain patients potentially provide an exciting opportunity to decide whether it is possible to have two minds or consciousnesses, one based in each hemisphere.

Another group consists of patients suffering from **dissociative identity disorder**. The key feature of this disorder (also known as multiple personality disorder) is that the individual has two or more personalities, but is only aware of one of these personalities at any given time. On the face of it, such individuals possess more than one consciousness, one associated with each of their identities or personalities. If so, they may have conscious awareness of events and knowledge relating only to the particular identity they are currently adopting.

Perhaps the best-known case of dissociative identity disorder is Chris Sizemore, whose life formed the basis of the film, *The Three Faces of Eve*. One of her identities was Eve Black, who was impulsive and promiscuous. A second identity was Eve White. She was very different, being inhibited and conformist in her behaviour. Her third identity was Jane, who had the most stable character. Eve Black knew of the existence of Eve White, but Eve White did not know about Eve Black. Jane knew about both Eves, but tended to prefer Eve Black.

The actress Joanne Woodward used different expressions, make-up and clothes to portray the different "personalities" of Chris Sizemore in the film *The Three Faces of Eve*.

According to the post-traumatic model (Gleaves, 1996), dissociative identity disorder occurs as a result of childhood abuse and other traumatic events, with the formation of multiple personalities helping the individual to separate off the traumatic experiences of childhood from conscious awareness. As predicted, many of those with dissociative identity disorder suffered sexual abuse in childhood (Ross, Miller, Reagor, Bjornson, Fraser, & Anderson, 1990). However, Lilienfeld et al. (1999) argued there is little direct evidence of causal links between child abuse and dissociative identity disorder.

Some experts claim dissociative identity disorder is an **iatrogenic disorder**, meaning it is unintentionally caused or produced by therapists. However, contrary evidence was reported by Gleaves, Hernandez, and Warner (1999). They found supporting evidence (e.g., medical records, family) for at least some symptoms being present prior to therapy in 67% of patients with dissociative identity disorder.

## Evidence

It is often thought that split-brain patients have great difficulty in functioning effectively. This is *not* the case. Indeed, it was not realised initially that cutting the corpus callosum caused any problems for split-brain patients, leading the neurophysiologist Karl Lashley to wonder jokingly whether the function of the corpus callosum was to stop the brain hemispheres from sagging! In fact, split-brain patients ensure environmental stimulation reaches both hemispheres simply by moving their eyes around. Researchers who have found impaired performance in split-brain patients have typically done so by presenting visual stimuli briefly to only one hemisphere.

The language abilities of most people (including split-brain patients) are located mainly in the left hemisphere. The lack of language ability in the right hemisphere makes it hard to decide whether the right hemispheres of most split-brain patients have conscious experiences. Accordingly, it is important to study split-brain patients with reasonable language abilities in the right hemisphere.

Gazzaniga and LeDoux (1978) reported findings from PS, a split-brain patient with unusually well-developed right-hemisphere language abilities. The left hand is connected to the right hemisphere, and PS showed evidence of consciousness in his right hemisphere by responding appropriately to questions using his left hand. For example,

> **KEY TERM**
> **Iatrogenic disorder:** a disorder caused unintentionally by a therapist during the course of treatment.

PS could spell out his own name, that of his girlfriend, his hobbies, his current mood, and so on.

Gazzaniga, Ivry, and Mangum (1998) argued that PS and other split-brain patients with reasonable right-hemisphere skills have very limited right-hemisphere consciousness. For example, these patients find it hard to make inferences. Consider the task of deciding which of six possible answers best describes the causal relationship between two words (e.g., "bleed" describes the relation between "pin" and "finger"). The split-brain patients understood the meanings of the words, but their task performance was poor. Gazzaniga et al. (p. 549) concluded as follows: "It is hard to imagine that the left and right hemispheres have similar conscious experiences. The right cannot make inferences; consequently, it is extremely limited in what it can have feelings about. It deals mainly with raw experience in an unembellished [unadorned] way."

Some split-brain patients may possess limited dual consciousness. If they have two minds, then it might be possible to produce a dialogue between these minds. However, MacKay (1987) argued this has not happened: "Despite all encouragements we found no sign at all of recognition of the other 'half' as a separate person." One of the patients even asked MacKay, "Are you guys trying to make two people out of me?"

Subsequent research has produced somewhat more promising findings. Baynes and Gazzaniga (2000) discussed the case of VJ, whose writing and speech are controlled by different hemispheres. According to Baynes and Gazzaniga (p. 1362), "[VJ] is the first split ... who is frequently dismayed by the independent performance of her right and left hands. She is discomfited by the fluent writing of her left hand to unseen stimuli and distressed by the inability of her right hand to write out words she can read out loud and spell." Speculatively, we could interpret the evidence from VJ as suggesting limited dual consciousness.

We turn now to patients with dissociative identity disorder. If they really have two or more separate identities, it follows that when adopting one identity they should have amnesia for their other identities. The evidence is mixed. When relatively direct tests of memory (e.g., recall, recognition) are used, there is generally little or no memory for the non-current identities (see Allen & Iacono, 2001, for a review). However, there is more evidence of memory for non-current identities when indirect tests of implicit memory (not involving conscious recollection) are used (Allen & Iacono, 2001). The findings from direct memory tests may differ from those of indirect tests because it is easier to feign amnesia for other identities when direct tests are used. Allen and Iacono (p. 311) concluded as follows: "Empirical research fails to unequivocally [unambiguously] substantiate patients' claims of amnesia between identities, and reports of such amnesia should not be regarded as conclusive."

Another way of trying to decide whether patients with dissociative identity disorder really have two or more separate identities is to record psychophysiological responses (e.g., heart rate, event-related potentials) when patients are adopting different identities. For example, Putnam (1984) found each identity within a given individual was associated with its own pattern of event-related potentials. Normal individuals pretending to adopt various identities did not produce distinctive patterns associated with their fake identities, suggesting the findings with patients may be genuine.

*If dissociative identity disorder patients genuinely have more than one consciousness, what would be the legal implications in terms of their responsibility for criminal behaviour?*

## BODILY RHYTHMS

There are numerous bodily rhythms, most of which can conveniently be divided into biological or physiological rhythms and psychological rhythms. One of the most important bodily rhythms is the sleep–wake cycle, but several other bodily rhythms have a significant impact on human behaviour.

## Biological rhythms

Many biological rhythms possessed by human beings repeat themselves every 24 hours, and are known as **circadian rhythms** (from two Latin words meaning "about" and

**KEY TERM**
**Circadian rhythms:** biological rhythms that repeat every 24 hours or so.

"day"). Mammals possess about 100 different biological circadian rhythms. For example, temperature in humans varies over the course of the 24-hour day, reaching a peak of about 37.4°C in the late afternoon and a low point of about 36.5°C in the early hours of the morning. Other examples of human circadian rhythms are the sleep–wake cycle and the release of hormones from the pituitary gland.

Humans possess other bodily rhythms involving cyclical variations in various physiological or psychological processes. Apart from circadian rhythms, there are infradian and ultradian rhythms. **Infradian rhythms** involve repeating cycles lasting more than a day. A well-known example of an infradian rhythm in humans is the menstrual cycle, which typically lasts about 28 days. The phases of the human menstrual cycle are determined by hormonal changes. The key phases are as follows (see Chapter 3 for more details):

- *Follicular phase*. Follicle-stimulating hormone causes ovarian follicles to grow around egg cells or ova, followed by the ovarian follicles releasing oestrogens (sex hormones).
- *Ovulation phase*. Oestrogens lead to increased release of luteinising hormone and follicle-stimulating hormone from the anterior pituitary, causing a ruptured follicle to release its ovum.
- *Luteal phase*. The ruptured follicle releases progesterone, so preparing the lining of the uterus for the implantation of a fertilised ovum or egg.
- *Pre-menstrual and menstrual phases*. The ovum or egg moves into the fallopian tube; if unfertilised, progesterone and oestradiol levels decrease.

**Ultradian rhythms** involve cycles lasting less than a day. A good example of an ultradian rhythm is to be found within sleep. As is discussed later in the chapter, there is a characteristic sleep cycle lasting about 90 minutes, and most sleepers work through a number of sleep cycles.

## Sleep–wake cycle

The 24-hour sleep–wake cycle is of particular importance, and is associated with other circadian rhythms. For example, as we have seen, bodily temperature is at its highest about halfway through the waking day (early to late afternoon) and at its lowest halfway through the sleeping part of the day (about three in the morning). Why is the sleep–wake cycle 24 hours long? Perhaps it is strongly influenced by external events such as the light–dark cycle, and the fact that each dawn follows almost exactly 24 hours after the preceding one. Another possibility is that the sleep–wake cycle is **endogenous**, i.e., based on internal biological mechanisms or pacemakers.

How can we decide whether the sleep–wake cycle depends mainly on external or on internal factors? One approach is to study individuals removed from the normal light–dark cycle, e.g., by being kept in the dark. Michel Siffre spent 7 months in a dark cave. At first, there was no very clear pattern in his sleep–wake cycle. Later on, however, he developed a sleep–wake cycle of about 25 hours rather than the standard one of 24 hours (Green, 1994). Wever (1979) discussed studies on people who spent weeks or months in a bunker or isolation suite. Most of them settled down to a sleep–wake cycle of about 25 hours.

The above evidence suggests there is an endogenous circadian pacemaker having a period of about 25 hours.

### Did you know?

The fact that there are circadian rhythms for many hormones has important applications in medicine. When a doctor takes a sample of blood or urine it is important to record the time of day at which the sample was taken in order to properly assess it. For example, the stress hormone cortisol is at its highest level in the morning. If an early morning sample of urine was tested for cortisol but thought to have been taken later in the day, it might be assumed that the person was highly stressed.

Recent research has also suggested that biorhythms should be considered when prescribing medicines. It seems that the standard practice of taking a drug at regular intervals throughout the day may not only be ineffective, but can also be counterproductive or even harmful. Evidence shows that certain medical illnesses whose symptoms show a circadian rhythm respond better when drugs are co-ordinated with that rhythm (Moore-Ede et al., 1982).

### KEY TERMS

**Infradian rhythms:** biological rhythms with a cycle of more than 1 day.
**Ultradian rhythms:** biological rhythms with a cycle of less than 1 day.
**Endogenous:** based on internal biological mechanisms.

### CASE STUDY: *The sleep–wake cycle*

Michel Siffre was studied for 7 months in 1972 when he volunteered to live underground in caves out of any contact with daylight and without any other clues about what time of day it was, that is no watch or clocks or TV. He was safe and well fed, and the caves were warm and dry. He was always monitored via computers and video cameras, he had a 24-hour phone-link to the surface and was well catered for in mind and body with books and exercise equipment. In this isolated environment he quickly settled into a regular cycle of sleeping and waking. The surprise was that his cycle was of almost 25 hours, not 24! It was a very regular 24.9-hour rhythm, so that each "day" he was waking up nearly an hour later. The effect of this was that by the end of his months underground he had "lost" a considerable number of days and thought he had been underground for much less time than had actually passed (Bentley, 2000).

This is somewhat odd, because it is not clear *why* we would have an endogenous rhythm discrepant from the 24-hour day we normally experience. In fact, however, there is a significant limitation in the above studies. There was relatively little control over the participants' behaviour, and they were able to control their own lighting conditions. Czeisler et al. (1999) compared what happened with the traditional approach (known as the free-running paradigm) with the forced desynchrony paradigm, in which artificial 20- or 28-hour days were imposed on the participants, i.e., they did not control the lighting conditions. There was evidence for a 25-hour circadian rhythm in temperature with the free-running paradigm. However, with the more rigorous forced desynchrony approach, the temperature circadian rhythm averaged 24 hours and 10 minutes with both the 20- and 28-hour days. Thus, the endogenous circadian pacemaker has a period of 24 hours, but this can be lengthened in artificial environments.

*What problem does this pose for shift workers?*

The free-running paradigm led to over-estimation of the duration of the circadian pacemaker because participants could turn the lights on whenever they wanted. This matters because light is a **zeitgeber** (literally, "time giver"), which partially controls biological rhythms. You probably wake up earlier in the summer than in the winter, which provides some evidence that you are responsive to the zeitgeber of light. Convincing evidence that light is an important zeitgeber was shown by Czeisler et al. (1989). When participants were exposed to bright light in the early morning, there was an advance in the circadian temperature rhythm. In contrast, there was a delay in the circadian temperature rhythm when bright light was presented in the late evening.

In sum, there is an endogenous circadian pacemaker with a 24-hour cycle, which is generally appropriate in view of the fact that we all experience a 24-hour day. In addition, this endogenous pacemaker has the flexibility that it can be reset when required (e.g., after flying across several time zones). Without that flexibility, visitors to Europe from Asia would find themselves going to sleep in mid-afternoon throughout their visit!

## Physiological systems

There are substantial changes in many brain areas during the course of the sleep–wake cycle. These changes were shown by Braun et al. (1997) in a study in which they obtained PET scans throughout the sleep–wake cycle. Among their discoveries was the following: "Shifts in the level of activity of the striatum [consisting of the caudate nucleus and putamen] suggested that the basal ganglia might be more integrally involved in the orchestration of the sleep–wake cycle than previously thought" (p. 1173). The basal ganglia are involved in movement, which is obviously of greater importance in the waking than the sleeping state.

The **suprachiasmatic nucleus (SCN)**, which is located within the hypothalamus, is an internal mechanism of special importance in influencing the sleep–wake cycle. We know the suprachiasmatic nucleus (there are actually two nuclei very close together) forms the main circadian clock. For example, while lesions of the SCN do not reduce how much of their time mammals spend sleeping, they do eliminate the normal sleep–wake cycle (Stephan & Nunez, 1977). Additional evidence comes from studies in which the SCN is isolated surgically from the rest of the brain. Even in these extreme circumstances, the SCN still exhibits circadian cycles of electrical and biochemical activity (e.g., Groos & Hendricks, 1982).

The most compelling evidence that the SCN controls the sleep–wake cycle comes in research by Ralph, Foster, Davis, and Menaker (1990). They transplanted the suprachiasmatic nuclei from the foetuses of hamsters belonging to a strain having a 20-hour sleep–wake cycle into adult hamsters belonging to a strain having a sleep–wake cycle lasting 25 hours. These adult hamsters rapidly adopted a 20-hour sleep–wake cycle.

**KEY TERMS**

**Zeitgeber:** external events that partially determine biological rhythms.

**Suprachiasmatic nucleus (SCN):** the structure within the hypothalamus that is involved in controlling various circadian rhythms, including the sleep–wake cycle.

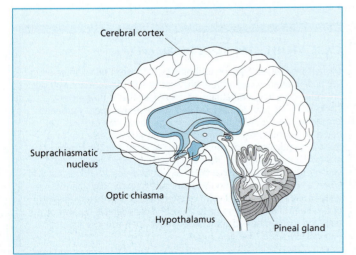

Cerebral cortex

Suprachiasmatic nucleus

Optic chiasma

Hypothalamus

Pineal gland

As Wickens (2000) pointed out, a brain area has to possess *three* characteristics to fulfil the function of a circadian pacemaker. So far we have discussed only one, namely, that the brain area in question should possess its own intrinsic rhythm. Another vital characteristic is that the brain area should receive visual information from the eyes to permit resetting of circadian rhythms in response to changing patterns of light and dark. The SCN is very close to the optic chiasma, which is where the nerve fibres from each eye cross to the other side of the brain. There is a pathway (the retinohypothalamic tract) which branches off from the optic nerve and projects to the SCN. When this tract was cut in hamsters, they could not reset their circadian clocks even though they could still see (Rusak, 1977).

It has always been assumed that light information only reaches the brain via the eyes. However, in a study suggestive of science fiction, Campbell and Murphy (1998) found that light applied to the back of the knees could shift the circadian rhythms for body temperature and melatonin

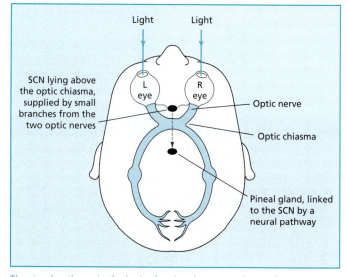

secretion in humans. When you next go on holiday, you might find that sunbathing face down may help to keep you awake during the long hours of clubbing!

The visual pathway in the brain showing the connection to the suprachiasmatic nucleus (SCN) and onward to the pineal gland.

The third characteristic of a circadian pacemaker is that it should have output to other brain areas involved in circadian behaviour (e.g., the sleep–wake cycle). The SCN has connections with the pituitary gland and other areas of the hypothalamus. However, its most important projection is to the pineal gland (an endocrine gland) via the superior cervical ganglion. What happens is that darkness causes the superior cervical ganglion to release noradrenaline into pineal cells, which is followed by the transformation of serotonin into melatonin. The key role played by melatonin in the sleep–wake cycle is discussed below.

In spite of the importance of the SCN, other systems can play a part in producing circadian rhythms. For example, studies on hamsters with SCN lesions show that circadian rhythms can still be determined by the pattern of availability of food throughout the day (e.g., Stephan, 1992).

Activity in the SCN leads to the release of the hormone **melatonin** from the pineal gland, with more melatonin being released when light levels are low. Melatonin influences the brainstem mechanisms involved in sleep regulation, and so plays a part in controlling the timing of sleep and waking periods. Individuals with a tumour in the pineal gland reducing melatonin secretion often find it very difficult to get to sleep (Haimov & Lavie, 1996). People flying across several time zones often take melatonin, because it makes them feel sleepy two hours afterwards (Haimov & Lavie, 1996).

It is often assumed that the need for sleep increases progressively during the course of the waking day. This is not, in fact, the case. As mentioned in the Key Study overleaf, Shochat et al. (1997) found the pressure to sleep showed a paradoxical *drop* in the early evening before rising again later in the evening. Consistent findings were reported by Aeschbach, Matthews, Postolache, Jackson, Giesen, and Wehr (1997), who found several aspects of the EEG record (e.g., alpha, delta, theta) indicated *reduced* sleep pressure in the early evening

How can we explain this surprisingly low pressure to sleep in the early evening? According to Lavie (2001, p. 293), the evidence "points to the existence of a powerful

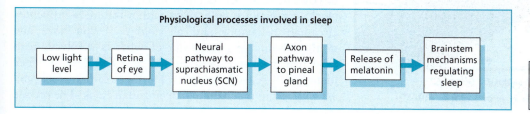

**KEY TERM**
**Melatonin:** a hormone that influences the onset of sleep.

## Shochat et al.: Melatonin and the sleep–wake cycle

Convincing evidence of the involvement of melatonin in the sleep–wake cycle was reported by Shochat, Luboshitzky, and Lavie (1997). They used the ultra-short sleep–wake paradigm, with six male participants spending 29 hours between 7 a.m. one day and noon the following day in the sleep laboratory. Throughout that time the participants spent 7 minutes in every 20 lying down in bed in a completely darkened room trying to sleep. This method allowed the experimenters to measure sleep propensity (the tendency to sleep) at different times of day. The period of greatest sleep propensity is known as the "sleep gate", and starts in the late evening. Surprisingly, the period of lowest sleep propensity (the "wake maintenance zone") occurs in the early evening shortly before the sleep gate.

Shochat et al. (1997) measured the levels of melatonin by taking blood samples up to three times an hour during the 29-hour session. The key finding was as follows: "We demonstrated a close and precise temporal relationship between the circadian rhythms of sleep propensity and melatonin; the noctural [night] onset of melatonin secretion consistently precedes the noctural sleep gate by 100–120 min" (p. R367). This close relationship between increased melatonin levels and increased sleep propensity doesn't prove they are causally related. However, Shochat et al. (1997) discussed other studies strengthening the argument that melatonin is important in determining sleep propensity. For example, individuals suffering from insomnia find it much easier to get to sleep when given melatonin about two hours before bedtime (Rosenzweig et al., 2002).

### KEY STUDY EVALUATION—Shochat et al.

Shochat et al.'s results were important in demonstrating that melatonin plays a role in sleep–wake cycles. However, it could be argued that trying to sleep in a laboratory situation is a task that does not have a great deal of ecological validity. The demand characteristics of the experiment and evaluation apprehension may have affected the participants, possibly even at a hormonal level. The sample used by Shochat et al. was also very small, consisting of only six male volunteers, and was not really representative. However, the study, like many others, provides a strong basis for future work.

### Discussion points

1. What are some of the good features of the study carried out by Shochat et al.?
2. What are the limitations of their approach?

---

drive for wakefulness at the end of the 'wakeful' day … Such an active drive for wakefulness has never been considered in any of the models or theories proposed to explain sleep–wake regulation." In order to understand the sleep–wake cycle fully, we need to consider the drive for wakefulness as well as the drive for sleep.

From what has been said, it might be thought there is a *single* endogenous mechanism or internal clock. In fact, matters may be more complex than that. Nearly all participants in long-term bunker studies lasting for more than a month showed different patterns in the sleep–wake cycle and the temperature cycle (Wever, 1979). Similar results were obtained from a study in which young adults lived on a 30- or 28-hour sleep–wake cycle (Boivin et al., 1997). Both schedules produced a discrepancy between the participants' sleep–wake cycle and their endogenous circadian pacemaker. These findings suggest there may be more than one internal circadian clock, but it is hard to be sure.

Finally, it should be noted that much remains to be discovered about the detailed functioning of the circadian clock, especially how activity within the SCN influences circadian behaviour and physiology. If you have any doubts about the complexity of what is involved, read an article by Panda, Hogenesch, and Kay (2002). They identified 8 genes involved in the fly circadian clock and 10 involved in the mammalian circadian clock. The precise

Can you think of anyone whose melatonin cycle differs from the norm?

ways in which these various genes interact and combine to produce circadian behaviour are largely unknown.

## Effects of jet lag and shiftwork

In our everyday lives, there is usually no conflict between our endogenous sleep–wake cycle and external events or zeitgebers. However, there are situations in which there is a real conflict (e.g., jet lag, shiftwork).

*Are the problems with shiftwork likely to be entirely caused by biological factors?*

It is sometimes thought that jet lag occurs because travelling by plane can be time-consuming and tiring. In fact, jet lag occurs only when flying from east to west or from west to east. It depends on a discrepancy between internal and external time. For example, suppose you fly from Scotland to the east coast of the United States. You leave at eleven in the morning British time, and arrive in Boston at five in the afternoon British time. However, the time in Boston is probably midday. As a result of the 5-hour difference, you are likely to feel very tired by about eight o'clock in the evening Boston time.

Klein, Wegman, and Hunt (1972) found adjustment of the sleep–wake cycle was much faster for westbound flights than for eastbound ones, regardless of which direction was homeward. For eastbound flights, readjustment of the sleep–wake cycle took about 1 day per time zone crossed. Thus, for example, it would take about 6 days to recover completely from a flight to England from Boston.

Why is it easier to adapt to jet lag when flying in a westerly direction? The day of travel is effectively lengthened when travelling west, whereas it is shortened when travelling east. It used to be argued the endogenous sleep–wake cycle is about 25 hours, which would make it easier to adapt to a day of more than 24 hours than to one of fewer than 24 hours. However, the endogenous circadian rhythm is 24 hours rather than 25 (Czeisler et al., 1999), which makes it harder to explain why jet lag is less pronounced when we fly from east to west.

What about shiftwork? As they say, there are only two problems with shiftwork: You have to work when you want to be asleep, and you have to sleep when you want to be awake. There are several different types of shift system. Monk and Folkard (1983) identified two major types: (1) rapidly rotating shifts, in which workers only do one or two shifts at a given time before shifting to a different work time; and (2) slowly rotating shifts, in which workers shift work time much less often (e.g., every week or month). There are problems with both shift systems. However, rapidly rotating shifts are preferable. They allow workers to maintain fairly constant circadian rhythms, whereas slowly rotating shifts can cause harmful effects through major changes to individuals' circadian rhythms.

Jet lag can be a problem for airline staff who frequently cross time zones in the course of their work.

## CASE STUDY: *Melatonin and aircrew*

Melatonin is now available in US chemists and some claim it is the cure for jet lag. Jet lag can lead to fatigue, headache, sleep disturbances, irritability, and gastrointestinal disturbances—all with a potentially negative impact on flight safety. Interestingly, reported side effects of melatonin use include many similar symptoms. Although some researchers claim melatonin is among the safest known substances, no large clinical evaluations have been performed to evaluate long-term effects.

Scientists believe melatonin is crucial for the functioning of our body clock. Studies suggest that treating jet lag with melatonin can not only resolve sleeping problems but also increase the body clock's ability to adjust to a new time zone. However, those in the medical community advise caution. Melatonin is not a universal remedy for everyone who must travel over many time zones. It is thought by some that it should not be used unless the user intends to spend more than 3 days in the new time zone. International aircrews will often cover several time zones, typically flying overnight west to east,

spending 24 hours on the ground, then returning during the day (east to west). This cycle is likely to be repeated several times before an extended period of sleep is possible. Melatonin usage to adjust the body clock in these circumstances is viewed by many scientists as inappropriate.

Timing the dose of melatonin is very important. Studies show that resynchronisation of the sleep–waking cycle only occurred if the subjects were allowed to sleep after taking the medication. In those participants unable to sleep after taking melatonin, the circadian rhythm was actually prolonged. More worryingly, melatonin's effect on fine motor and cognitive tasks is unknown and the nature of melatonin's sedative effects are uncertain.

Unfortunately, there are no published clinical studies evaluating flying performance while taking melatonin. The US Armed Forces are actively evaluating melatonin's aeromedical usefulness. Despite ongoing research, no US military service permits the routine use of melatonin by aviators. Significantly, aircrew participating in experimental study groups are not allowed to perform flying duties within 36 hours of using melatonin.

# Psychological circadian rhythms

So far we have focused mainly on circadian rhythms depending directly on underlying biological or physiological processes. There are also psychological rhythms influenced by basic circadian rhythms. For example, there are fairly consistent patterns of performance on many tasks throughout the day, with a variation of about 10% between the best and worst levels of performance. Peak performance on most tasks is reached at around midday (Eysenck, 1982).

Why do people perform at their best at midday rather than earlier or later in the day? Relevant evidence was obtained by Akerstedt (1977). Self-reported alertness (assessed by questionnaire) was greatest at about noon, as was the level of adrenaline. Adrenaline is a hormone associated with states of high physiological arousal within the autonomic nervous system (see Chapter 2). However, the notion of physiological arousal is rather vague and imprecise. Psychological and physiological activation are both high at midday, which may account for the peak performance shown at that time. However, these are correlational data, and it is hard to be sure that the high level of midday performance *depends* on activation.

Blake (1967) found most of his participants showed a clear reduction in performance at 13.00 compared to their performance at 10.30. This reduction in performance occurred shortly after lunch, and is commonly known as the "post-lunch dip". What seems to happen is that the physiological processes involved in digestion make us feel sluggish and reduce our ability to work efficiently.

*How could you test whether the change in performance was due to the time of day or to digesting lunch?*

# Infradian rhythms

Infradian rhythms are bodily rhythms for which the cycle time is greater than 1 day but less than 1 year. One of the clearest examples of an infradian rhythm is the menstrual cycle in women. In evolutionary terms, we might expect that women would be most sexually active around the time of ovulation, when they are most fertile. This pattern has been found in newly married African women (Hedricks, Piccinino, Udry, & Chimbia, 1987), and there is some evidence of increased sexual desire in ovulating women in Western societies (see Chapter 3).

Pre-menstrual syndrome or PMS is an important aspect of the menstrual cycle. It refers to the fact that many women experience tension, depression, headaches, and so on in the last few days prior to menstruation. However, about 30–40% of women show little or no evidence of pre-menstrual syndrome. Women are more likely to commit crimes shortly before menstruation than at other times of the month (Dalton, 1964). This is presumably due to pre-menstrual syndrome.

**Pre-menstrual syndrome**

It has been pointed out (e.g. Bunker-Rohrbaugh, 1980) that the definition of a "pre-menstrual syndrome" presents some difficulties. Studies of the syndrome tend to use questionnaires with a negative bias, asking women how "depressed" and "anxious" they feel, as opposed to how "happy". In addition, the attitudes of many Western women to menstruation in general are often negative, as opposed to some non-Western cultures in which it is celebrated. This too may bias research in this area.

There is reasonable evidence for pre-menstrual syndrome in most cultures (McIlveen & Gross, 1996), suggesting the importance of physiological factors (e.g., changing hormone levels) rather than environmental ones. However, the menstrual cycle itself can be influenced by environmental factors. Reinberg (1967) reported the case of a woman who lived in a dimly lit cave for a period of 3 months. During that time her menstrual cycle was reduced to just under 26 days.

# Circannual rhythms

**Circannual rhythms** are biological rhythms lasting for about 1 year before repeating. They are more common in some animal species than in humans, and this is especially true of species hibernating during the winter. Convincing evidence of a circannual rhythm in the gold-mantled ground squirrel was reported by Pengelley and Fisher (1957). They put a squirrel in a highly controlled environment with artificial light on for 12 hours every day, and a constant temperature of 0 °C. The squirrel hibernated from October through to the following April, with its body temperature dropping dramatically from 37 °C before hibernation to 1 °C during hibernation. The circannual rhythm for this squirrel was somewhat less than a year, having about 300 days duration.

Some people suffer from **seasonal affective disorder**, which resembles a circannual rhythm. The great majority of sufferers from this disorder experience severe depression during the winter months, but a few seem to experience depression in the summer instead. Seasonal affective disorder can involve serious symptoms. However, individuals with seasonal affective disorder suffer less than those with major depression from hopelessness, weight loss, and cognitive impairments (Michalak, Wilkinson, Hood, & Dowrick, 2002).

Seasonal affective disorder is related to seasonal variations in the production of melatonin (Comer, 2001). Melatonin (associated with increased sleepiness) is produced primarily at night, and so more is produced during the dark winter months. As would be expected, seasonal affective disorder is more common in northern latitudes where the winter days are very short. Terman (1988) found that nearly 10% of those living in New Hampshire (a northern part of the United States) suffered from seasonal affective disorder, compared to only 2% in the southern state of Florida.

Phototherapy is recommended for the treatment of seasonal affective disorder. This involves exposing sufferers to about 2 hours of intense light shortly after they wake up in the morning. This has been found to reduce or even eliminate depression (Lam et al., 2000). Natural light can also be effective. Wirz-Justice et al. (1996) found that patients with seasonal affective disorder were helped by taking morning walks.

A young seasonal affective disorder sufferer receiving phototherapy from a light box on the right of the picture.

There is evidence for a circannual rhythm for suicide. Altamura, VanGastel, Pioli, Mannu, and Maes (1999) reviewed numerous studies carried out in Europe, North America, and South Africa. The peak months for suicides were May and June and the fewest suicides occurred in November, December, and January. Altamura et al. obtained similar findings in Cagliari in Italy. It is by no means clear *why* suicide rates show this pattern. However, Maes et al. (1994) found in Belgium that the suicide rate was greatest a few weeks after a rise in outside temperature, suggesting that rising temperature activates internal biological mechanisms triggering suicide. Altamura et al. (1999) also found that suicide was more common at some times of day than others. Suicides occurred most often between 8:30 and 12:30, and were least likely to occur between 20:30 and 0:30.

Palinkas et al. (2001) studied circannual rhythms in men and women who spent the winter at McMurdo Station in Antarctica. They found there were circannual rhythms in thryotropin-stimulating hormone and mood, with both peaking in November and July and having their lowest levels during March and April. These findings suggested that "winter-over syndrome" (which involves negative moods, anxiety, and confusion) is due in part to a low level of thyroid function.

## SLEEP

Sleep is an important part of all our lives. Indeed, it may well be the commonest form of human behaviour (apart from breathing!). Sleep generally occupies about one-third of our time, although the proportion decreases as we get older. There are various ways of trying to understand sleep. However, the electroencephalograph or EEG is of particular value. In essence, scalp electrodes are used to obtain a continuous measure of brain-wave activity, which is recorded as a trace. Other useful physiological measures include

**KEY TERM**
**Seasonal affective disorder:**
a disorder that nearly always involves the sufferer experiencing severe depression during the winter months only.

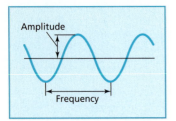

eye-movement data from an electro-oculogram or EOG, and muscle movements from an electromyogram or EMG.

There are two main aspects to EEG activity: frequency and amplitude. Frequency is defined as the number of oscillations of EEG activity per second, whereas amplitude is defined as half the distance between the high and low points of an oscillation. Frequency is used more often than amplitude to describe the essence of EEG activity.

The most important finding from physiological studies such as those of Dement and Kleitman (1957) is that there are five different stages of sleep:

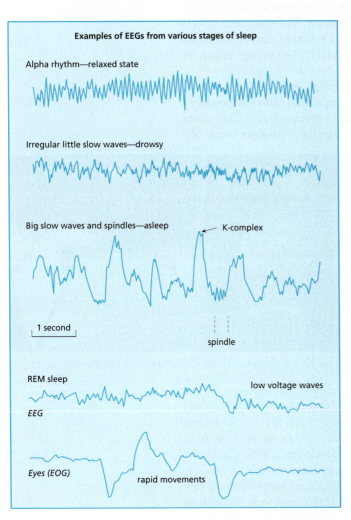

- *Stage 1*. There are alpha waves in the EEG, there is slow eye rolling, and reductions in heart rate, muscle tension, and temperature; this stage can be regarded as a state of drowsiness.
- *Stage 2*. The EEG waves become slower and larger, but with short bursts of high-frequency sleep spindles; there is little activity in the EOG.
- *Stage 3*. The EOG and EMG records are similar to Stage 2, but there are many long, slow delta waves with some sleep spindles; this is a deeper stage of sleep than either of the first two stages.
- *Stage 4*. There is a majority of the long, slow delta waves present in smaller amounts in the previous stage, and very little activity in the EOG or the EMG. This is a deeper stage of sleep than any of the first three stages.
- *Stage 5*. Rapid eye movement or **REM sleep**, in which there are rapid eye movements and a very low level of EMG activity, while the EEG record is like that of Stage 1 (small amplitude fast EEG waves). REM sleep has been called paradoxical sleep, because it is harder to awaken someone from REM sleep than from any of the other stages, even though the EEG indicates the brain is very active.

In spite of the clear differences among Stages 1, 2, 3, and 4, they are often referred to collectively as **slow-wave sleep**.

After the sleeper has worked through the first four stages of progressively deeper sleep, he/she reverses the process. Stage 4 sleep is followed by Stage 3, and then by Stage 2. However, Stage 2 is followed by REM sleep (Stage 5). After REM sleep, the sleeper starts another sleep cycle, working his/her way through Stages 2, 3, and 4, followed by Stage 3, then Stage 2, and then REM sleep again. A complete sleep cycle or ultradian cycle lasts about 90 minutes. Most sleepers complete about five ultradian cycles during a normal night's sleep. The proportion of the cycle devoted to REM sleep *increases* from one cycle to the next, whereas the time spent in Stage 4 sleep *decreases*.

REM sleep is the most interesting stage of sleep. Aserinsky and Kleitman (1953) discovered it is associated with dreaming. They woke up their participants when in REM sleep, and most of them reported they had just been dreaming. However, dreaming does *not* only occur in REM sleep. Foulkes and Vogel (1965) found up to 50% of awakenings from non-REM sleep produce dream reports. About 20% of these non-REM dream reports cannot be distinguished from REM dream reports. However, dreams during REM sleep tend to be vivid and detailed, whereas non-REM dreams contain much less detail and tend to be more "thought-like" (Solms, 2000a).

Other evidence indicates we should not equate REM sleep with dreaming. For example, damage to the REM-generating parts of the brainstem does not stop people from dreaming (Solms, 1997). Which is the crucial part of the brain for dreaming? According to evidence discussed by Solms (1997), individuals with damage to higher forebrain structures do not dream. However, they do continue to show REM sleep (see later in chapter). Solms (2000b, p. 618) reviewed the evidence on dreaming, and came to the following conclusion: "The bold equation 'REM = dreaming' should be replaced by a more prosaic formula: 'brain activation during sleep (regardless of sleep stage) triggers dreaming'."

*How could this be useful when carrying out research on dreaming?*

## Sleep regulation

We saw earlier that the suprachiasmatic nuclei and the hormone melatonin both play a role in sleep regulation. In addition, we need to consider the reticular activating system. Moruzzi and Magoun found sleeping cats woke up when their reticular formation was electrically stimulated, and there was a long period of EEG desynchronisation indicative of a state of arousal. They also reported that lesions of the reticular formation produced persistent sleep in animals. These findings led Moruzzi and Magoun to argue the reticular formation is involved in wakefulness, implying that sleep occurs as a result of low levels of activity in the reticular formation. However, as Kolb and Whishaw (2001, p. 477) pointed out, "Despite substantial evidence that the RAS [reticular activating system] has a role in sleep–wake behaviour, attempts to localise sleep to a particular structure or group of neurons within the RAS have not been successful."

Many sleep researchers have tried to identify the areas involved in producing REM and slow-wave sleep. Some progress has been made, but the complexity of neural systems means that we still have nothing like a complete understanding of what is involved. So far as REM sleep is concerned, the pons is of particular importance. Humans with naturally occurring lesions of the pons have little or no REM sleep (Solms, 2000a). Electrical stimulation of the pons produces (or prolongs) REM sleep (Rosenzweig, Leiman, & Breedlove, 1999), and there are neurons within the pons which only seem to be active during REM sleep (Siegel, 1994). In addition, it is only in REM sleep that EEG records reveal PGO waves, which involve activity going from the pons to the lateral geniculate and on to the occipital cortex.

The pons is also important in sending signals to the spinal cord leading to inhibition of the motor neurons controlling the large muscles of the body. Morrison et al. (1995) found that cats with lesions in the pons still had some REM sleep, but unlike intact cats they moved around as if acting out their dreams.

The transmitters serotonin and acetycholine also play a role in REM sleep (Benington & Heller, 1995). Drugs blocking serotonin receptors in the forebrain stop the onset of REM sleep, and drugs blocking acetylcholine synapses inhibit the continuation of REM sleep (Rosenzweig et al., 1999). Baghdoyan, Spotts, and Snyder (1993) found that stimulation of acetylcholine synapses using the drug carbachol led to an increase in REM sleep.

What about slow-wave sleep? Various areas seem to be involved in producing this form of sleep. For example, there is the basal forebrain region very close to the hypothalamus. Lesions in that area often eliminate slow-wave sleep. In addition, slow-wave sleep can be produced by means of electrical stimulation of the basal forebrain (Sterman & Clemente, 1962). More specifically, there is the nucleus of the solitary tract, lying just below the raphe nuclei. Stimulation of this area produces an EEG pattern similar to that found in short-wave sleep. However, lesions to the nucleus of the solitary tract do not disrupt sleep (Wickens, 2000), suggesting that it has a limited role.

## Sleep deprivation

We spend about one-third of our lives asleep. That adds up to almost 200,000 hours of sleep in the course of a lifetime! It is reasonable to assume that sleep must serve one or more key functions, but it has proved hard to discover these functions. One way of trying to work out *why* we sleep is to deprive people of sleep and see what happens. The kinds of problems and impairments experienced by sleep-deprived individuals may be those sleep is designed to prevent.

People often cope surprisingly well when deprived of sleep. Consider, for example, the case of Peter Tripp. He was a New York disc jockey who took part in a "wakeathon"

Peter Tripp is shown yawning after completing 200 hours without sleep.

*What are the limitations of these case studies of sleep-deprived individuals?*

for charity. He managed to stay awake for 8 days or about 200 hours. He suffered from delusions and hallucinations (e.g., that his desk drawer was on fire, that he was being drugged). These delusions were so severe it was hard to test his precise level of psychological functioning. However, he showed no long-term effects from having stayed awake for more than a week. It should be noted that he was not studied under well-controlled conditions.

Horne (1988) discussed the case of Randy Gardner, a 17-year-old student who remained awake for 264 hours or 11 days in 1964. Towards the end of the 11-day period, he suffered from disorganised speech, blurred vision, and some paranoia (e.g., thinking that other people regarded him as stupid because of his impaired functioning). In view of the fact that Randy Gardner missed out on about 80–90 hours of sleep, he had remarkably few problems. He was clearly less affected than Tripp by sleep deprivation, even though he remained awake for 3 extra days. For example, on the last night of his period of sleep deprivation, Randy Gardner went to an amusement arcade with the psychologist William Dement. They competed several times on a basketball game, and Randy Gardner won every time!

After his ordeal was over, Randy Gardner slept for 15 hours. However, over several nights thereafter, he never recovered more than 25% of the sleep he had missed. In spite of that, he recovered almost 70% of Stage 4 deep sleep and 50% of REM sleep, with very small recovery percentages for the other stages of sleep. This suggests Stage 4 and REM sleep are of special importance.

Everson et al. (1989) studied rats deprived of sleep over long periods of time. Sleep deprivation led to increased metabolic rate and to weight loss, and it eventually led to death after an average of about 19 days. Everson (1993) found that rats who were deprived of sleep for several days developed body sores relatively early on, followed by infections from numerous bacteria. The rats had no inflammatory response to the infections, which is important because inflammation allows additional immune cells to attack any infection.

It is hard to be sure whether findings on rats also apply to humans. However, Lugaressi et al. (1986) studied a 52-year-old man who could hardly sleep at all because of damage to parts of his brain involved in sleep regulation. Not surprisingly, he became absolutely exhausted, and could not function normally. Some individuals inherit a defect in the gene for the prion protein, leading to degeneration of the thalamus and to **fatal familial insomnia**. They sleep normally for many years, but then stop sleeping when about 35 or 40 years old. Individuals with fatal familial insomnia typically die within 2 years of the onset of the insomnia (Medori et al., 1992). Evidence based on autopsies of people who have died from fatal familial insomnia indicates that there is degeneration of the thalamus (Manetto et al., 1992). This may be responsible for the insomnia, given that electrical stimulation of the thalamus produces sleep in animals (Rosenzweig et al., 2002).

We should not conclude that sleep deprivation always has serious consequences. Indeed, provided that it is not too prolonged, sleep deprivation can even have positive effects! For example, Renegar et al. (2000) found that sleep deprivation was associated with *reduced* influenza in humans, and Bergman et al. (1996) found it was associated with *reduced* tumour growth in rats.

## REM sleep deprivation

We saw in the case of Randy Gardner that he recovered more of his lost REM sleep than most other stages of sleep after 11 days without sleep. Dement (1960) carried out

**KEY TERM**

**Fatal familial insomnia:** an inherited disorder in which the ability to sleep disappears in middle age and is typically followed by death several months later.

a systematic study of REM and non-REM sleep. Some participants were deprived of REM sleep over a period of several days, whereas others were deprived of non-REM sleep. The effects of REM sleep deprivation were more severe, including increased aggression and poor concentration. Those deprived of REM sleep tried to catch up on the REM sleep they had missed. They started on REM sleep 12 times on average during the first night in the laboratory, but this rose to 26 times on the seventh night. When they were free to sleep undisturbed, most of them spent much longer than usual in REM sleep; this is known as a rebound effect.

Slow-wave sleep (especially Stage 4 sleep) is also very important. For example, remember that Randy Gardner recovered most of his Stage 4 sleep after 11 days without sleep. The notion that short-wave sleep is important is suggested by the fact that virtually all mammals have short-wave sleep but not all have REM sleep. For example, the spiny anteater and the dolphin both lack REM sleep.

> **CASE STUDY:** *Sleep problems on a space station*
>
> Back in 1997 Jerry Linenger lived on space station Mir for 5 months. He had real sleep problems because the station lights, which were meant to mimic a 24-hour light–dark cycle, were so dim. The best light cues came in through the windows, and the sun's light was very, very bright. But as Mir orbited the earth every 90 or so minutes this produced 15 day–night, i.e., light–dark cycles every 24 hours. Jerry says he tried to cope, but couldn't, and that he'd see his Russian colleagues suddenly nod off and float around the cabin. Monk (2001) monitored Jerry during his time in space and reported findings that after 90 days the astronaut's quality of sleep deteriorated very rapidly. Monk thinks the brain's endogenous pacemaker had become disrupted by the abnormal light rhythm.

## Psychological effects

Impaired performance on boring tasks is the main problem caused by sleep deprivation over the first 3 nights of sleep loss (see below). During the fourth night of sleep deprivation, there are very short (2–3 second) periods of micro-sleep during which the individual is unresponsive (Hüber-Weidman, 1976). In addition, there is the "hat phenomenon", in which the sleep-deprived person feels as if he/she were wearing a rather small hat that fits very tightly. From the fifth night on, there are delusions as reported by Peter Tripp. From the sixth night on, there are more severe problems (e.g., partial loss of a sense of identity, increased difficulty in dealing with other people and the environment). Some of these symptoms were experienced by Randy Gardner.

## Task performance

The performance of sleep-deprived individuals has been studied systematically in controlled laboratory studies (see Eysenck, 1982, for a review). Sleep deprivation over the first 3 days or so has few adverse effects on tasks which are complex and interesting. However, sleep-deprived individuals perform poorly on monotonous and lengthy tasks, especially in the early hours of the morning. A good example is the vigilance task, in which participants have to detect signals (e.g., faint lights) which are only presented occasionally. A real-world example is motorway driving at night, where the evidence indicates that sleepiness plays a role in many fatal accidents (Horne & Reyner, 1999).

Harrison and Horne (2000) reviewed studies of the effects of sleep deprivation on performance. They found that sleep deprivation impairs decision making and effective responding to unexpected events, particularly when alertness is low in the early morning. For example, they noted that serious disasters or near-disasters at four nuclear power plants (Chernobyl, Three Mile Island, Rancho Seco in Sacramento, Davis-Beese in Ohio) all occurred in the early morning.

The effects of sleep deprivation on task performance are often surprisingly small or even non-existent. For example, Drummond et al. (2000) found that sleep deprivation had no effect on recognition memory, although it impaired recall. The use of brain imaging indicated what was happening. Those participants showing the least impairment on recall memory tended to have the greatest activity within the prefrontal cortex. Indeed, they had more activity in this area than participants who had not been sleep deprived. This suggests that sleep-deprived individuals can *compensate* for the adverse effects of sleep deprivation by greater use of the prefrontal cortex, which plays an important role in cognitive functioning.

There is another factor which accounts for many failures to find adverse effects of sleep deprivation on performance. According to Wilkinson (1969), it is "difficult for us to assess

### Overview of sleep-deprivation studies

| Nights without sleep | Effects |
|---|---|
| 1 | People do not feel comfortable, but can tolerate one night's sleep loss |
| 2 | People feel a much greater urge to sleep, especially when the body-temperature rhythm is lowest at 3–5 a.m. |
| 3 | Cognitive tasks are much more difficult, especially giving attention to boring ones. This is worst in the very early hours. |
| 4 | Micro-sleep periods start to occur, lasting about 3 seconds, during which the person stares blankly into space and temporarily loses awareness. They become irritable and confused. |
| 5 | As well as what is described above, the person may start to experience delusions, though cognitive ability (for example problem-solving) is all right. |
| 6 | The person starts to lose their sense of identity, to be depersonalised. This is known as sleep-deprivation psychosis. |

Source: Bentley (2000), p. 47.

the 'real' effect of lost sleep upon subjects' *capacity* as opposed to their *willingness* to perform" (p. 39). Wilkinson found most adverse effects of sleep loss on performance could be eliminated if attempts were made to motivate the participants (e.g., by providing knowledge of results). Thus, poor performance by sleep-deprived individuals is usually due to low motivation rather than reduced capacity, as the leading British psychologist, the late Donald Broadbent, discovered to his cost. He was employed by a television company as a consultant on a programme designed to show the adverse effects of sleep deprivation on performance. Those taking part were deprived of all sleep for 3 or 4 nights before the show. However, the bright lights and excitement of appearing on national television meant an embarrassed Broadbent was unable to show any negative effects of sleep deprivation at all!

## Theories of sleep

Several theories of sleep function have been proposed. However, most belong to two broad classes or categories:

1. Recovery or restoration theories.
2. Adaptive or evolutionary theories.

Pinel (1997, p. 301) provided a brief description of some of the key aspects of these two types of theories: "Recuperation [recovery] theories view sleep as a nightly repairman [sic] who fixes damage caused by wakefulness, while circadian [adaptive] theories regard sleep as a strict parent who demands inactivity because it keeps us out of trouble."

### Recovery or restoration theories

Important functions of sleep are probably to save energy and to permit the restoration of tissue. These notions are central to various recovery or restoration theories, such as those of Horne (1988) and Oswald (1980). These theories focus on the benefits of sleep for the physiological system. According to Oswald's recovery theory, slow-wave sleep is useful for recovery processes in the body. There is a substantial release of growth hormone from the pituitary gland during slow-wave sleep (Takahashi, 1979), and this seems to provide strong support for the theory. This may stimulate protein synthesis, and so contribute to the repair of tissues within the body. However, protein synthesis requires insulin and the release of amino acids into the blood, and the levels of insulin and amino acids are typically low during the night. Oswald also argued that important recovery processes occur in the brain during REM sleep.

Horne (1988) put forward a recovery theory resembling that of Oswald (1980). However, he emphasised the fact that members of the human species have periods of relaxed wakefulness during which there are rather low levels of energy expenditure. According to Horne (1988), the repair of bodily tissues occurs during periods of relaxed wakefulness rather than during sleep itself. However, what is common to all recovery theories is the crucial assumption that sleep is essential for well-being and ultimately for survival. The disagreements concern the precise mechanisms involved in recovery and/or restoration.

Horne (2001) argued that sleep is important for the recovery of cerebral function, especially that of the pre-frontal cortex. The pre-frontal cortex plays an important role in decision making and dealing with unexpected events, and we have seen that sleep

*How could this theory be put to the test?*

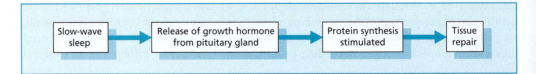

deprivation has strongly negative effects on those abilities (Harrison & Horne, 2000). As Horne pointed out, the notion that sleep serves to permit recovery of cerebral function is likely to be most applicable to advanced mammalian species.

## Evidence

Support for physiologically based recovery or restoration theories was discussed by Allison and Cicchetti (1976). They surveyed 39 mammalian species to work out the amount of time spent in slow-wave sleep and in REM sleep. Body weight was the best predictor of short-wave sleep, with smaller mammals having more such sleep. Metabolic rate, which is highly correlated with body weight, was also very predictive of short-wave sleep. However, other factors unrelated to recovery or restoration predict species differences in the amount of REM sleep. Vulnerability to danger (e.g., danger of being preyed upon) was the best predictor of the amount of REM sleep, with those most vulnerable having least REM sleep.

A key finding from the perspective of recovery theories is the association between metabolic rate and the duration of slow-wave sleep. We can interpret this association in various ways. However, it seems likely that small mammals are in particular need of the energy conservation function of sleep because of their high metabolic rate.

Oswald (1980) claimed important recovery processes occur in the brain during REM sleep. There is some support for this proposal. Newborn infants (who experience enormous brain growth) spend a very high percentage of their time asleep devoted to REM sleep (Green, 1994). More generally, growth processes of all kinds are much more important in newborn infants and young children. Their greater need for the release of growth hormone during sleep may help to explain why neonates sleep for about 16 hours a day reducing to 12 hours a day by the age of 2.

What should happen to the sleep pattern of humans who are extremely active during the day or who are sleep deprived? According to recovery theories, such individuals should be in great need of recovery or restoration processes. There are two likely consequences of that great need. First, they should tend to sleep longer than usual. Second, a higher proportion of their sleeping time should be devoted to the most important stages of sleep (Stage 4 slow-wave sleep, REM sleep).

There is support for both of those predictions. Evidence relevant to the first prediction was reported by Shapiro, Bortz, Mitchell, Bartel, and Jooste (1981), who studied runners taking part in an ultra marathon covering 57 miles. These runners slept about an hour and a half longer than normal on the 2 nights after the ultra marathon. As we saw earlier, Randy Gardner slept for 15 hours after his extremely long period of sleep deprivation.

The second prediction has also received support from the study of Randy Gardner. After his long period of sleep deprivation, there was much greater recovery of REM sleep and Stage 4 slow-wave sleep than of the other stages of sleep. In another study discussed earlier (Dement, 1960), individuals deprived of REM sleep showed a strong tendency to catch up on their REM sleep when the opportunity presented itself. More generally, sleep-deprived individuals have been found to regain much (or most) of their lost Stage 4 and REM sleep. In addition, runners who have completed an ultra marathon show an especially large increase in the amount of time devoted to Stage 4 sleep (Shapiro et al., 1981).

One key difference between recovery and adaptive theories is that the former claim sleep is essential, whereas the latter sometimes claim merely that it is highly desirable. On that argument, the finding that individuals suffering from fatal familial insomnia die within 2 years of the start of insomnia (Medori et al., 1992) supports recovery theories over adaptive theories.

One possible function of sleep is to permit restoration of psychological functions. There are various studies in which associations have been found between quality of sleep and

Although studies show that people need extra sleep following extreme exertion, there is no evidence that people who take little or no exercise reduce their sleeping time.

mood. Insomniacs (who have persistent problems with sleeping) tend to be more worried and anxious than people who sleep normally. Such evidence is hard to interpret, but may be more a question of people's worries and concerns disrupting sleep than of disrupted sleep causing worries. However, the causality probably goes both ways. Berry and Webb (1983) assessed self-reported anxiety. When people slept well during a given night, their level of anxiety on the following day was lower than when they had slept poorly. Naitoh (1975) discussed various studies concerned with the effects of 1 night's sleep deprivation on mood. The effects were consistently negative. Sleep-deprived individuals described themselves as less friendly, relaxed, good-natured, and cheerful than those who had not been sleep deprived.

What about Horne's (2001) notion that sleep permits recovery of cerebral function, and especially that of the pre-frontal cortex? Brain-imaging studies indicate that sleep deprivation has especially great effects on the prefrontal cortex (Drummond et al., 2000; Thomas et al., 2000). More supporting evidence comes in a study by Maquet (2000). PET scans revealed that there was a considerable amount of cerebral shutdown during slow-wave sleep (especially Stage 4), and that this shutdown was very pronounced in the prefrontal cortex.

*Do you think that all of the stages of sleep have to serve the same purpose?*

## Evaluation

- ⊕ Recovery theories provide several reasons why sleep is important and essential.
- ⊕ The fact that sleep is found in all species is consistent with the notion that it is essential.
- ⊕ The fact that total sleep deprivation in fatal familial insomnia leads to death within 2 years supports the view that sleep is essential.
- ⊕ Findings indicating that individuals who are sleep deprived or excessively active respond by sleeping for an unusually long time and/or by having a high proportion of Stage 4 slow-wave and REM sleep support recovery theories.
- ⊖ As Wickens (2000, p. 172) pointed out, "This theory [recovery theory] flounders on the simple fact that no-one has yet clearly identified a specific physiological process that is restored by sleep."
- ⊖ Recovery theories do not provide an explanation for why species vary in terms of *when* during the 24-hour day they sleep.

## Adaptive or evolutionary theories

According to various theorists (e.g., Meddis, 1979; Webb, 1968), sleep is adaptive behaviour favoured by evolution. More specifically, the sleep behaviour shown by any species depends on the need to adapt to environmental threats and dangers. Thus, for example, sleep serves the function of keeping animals fairly immobile and safe from predators during periods of time when they cannot engage in feeding and other kinds of behaviour. In the case of those species depending on vision, it is adaptive for them to sleep during the hours of darkness. Finally, sleep fulfils the useful function of conserving energy.

It seems to follow that species in danger from predators should sleep more of the time than those species that are predators. In fact, however, predators tend to sleep more than those preyed upon (Allison & Cicchetti, 1976). This might seem inconsistent with adaptive theories of sleep. However, species in danger from predators might well benefit from remaining vigilant most of the time and sleeping relatively little. This seems like an example of having your cake and eating it, in that any pattern of findings can be explained by the adaptive or evolutionary approach! However, the basic assumption that each species' pattern of sleep has been influenced by evolutionary pressures seems reasonable, even if it is difficult to prove.

## Evidence

Support for the notion that the pattern of sleep is often dictated by the environmental threats faced by animals was reported by Pilleri (1979). Dolphins living in the river Indus are in constant danger from debris floating down the river. As a consequence, these dolphins sleep for only a few seconds at a time to protect themselves from the debris. More generally, as we have seen, species vulnerable to attack by other species sleep less than those under little or no threat (Allison & Cicchetti, 1976).

There is reasonable evidence that sleep patterns within most species are adaptive. Several species of mammal that are unlikely to be attacked and that eat food rich in nutrition sleep most of the time. For example, cats sleep 14.5 hours per day, and armadillos sleep 18.5 hours a day. In contrast, species that are herbivores (plant eaters) need to graze most of the time and be on their guard against predators, and so sleep relatively little. For example, sheep sleep on average 3.8 hours per day, and cows 3.9 hours a day.

Another example of an adaptive sleep pattern is found in dolphins, who have to go up to the surface of the water very often in order to breathe. They do not have REM sleep, and they only have slow-wave sleep on one side of the brain at a time (Mukhametov, 1984).

What evidence indicates that sleep is useful in conserving energy, as is predicted by adaptive theories? In the first place, the body temperature of most mammals is slightly lower during sleep, suggesting sleep is helpful for energy conservation. Stronger evidence was reported by Berger and Phillips (1995), who considered the effects of food shortages. Animals responded to food shortages by increasing the amount of time they spent asleep or by decreasing their body temperature more than usual in the sleeping state. However, sleep in humans is of little value in energy conservation. As Horne (2001, p. 302) pointed out, "The energy saved by being asleep throughout the night rather than sitting relaxed but awake is trivial—the energy equivalent to a slice of bread."

Sleep is regarded as less essential within adaptive theories than within recovery theories. Modest support for adaptive theories comes from a few reports of individuals leading normal healthy lives in spite of regularly sleeping for very short periods of time each day (e.g., Meddis, Pearson, & Langford, 1973). One especially impressive case was Miss M, a cheerful 70-year-old retired nurse who typically only slept for 1 hour per day. She generally sat on her bed reading or writing until about 2 in the morning, after which she would sleep for about 1 hour. When she was studied under laboratory conditions, she slept an average of 67 minutes per night.

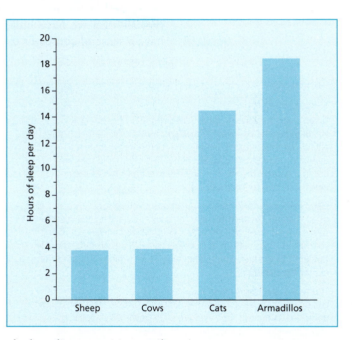

Herbivores, such as these springboks, need to graze most of the time and be on their guard against predators, so sleep relatively little.

## Evaluation

⊕ Adaptive theories provide plausible explanations of why species vary in their sleeping patterns.

⊕ Adaptive theorists have identified factors (e.g., vulnerability to attack, feeding patterns, breathing patterns) helping to determine species differences in amount and timing of sleep.

⊕ The notion that sleep serves to conserve energy is supported by the evidence from numerous species.

⊖ The theoretical assumption that sleep is very useful but not essential seems inconsistent with the fact that sleep is found in all species.

⊖ Adaptive theories provide no obvious explanation for the existence of fatal familial insomnia, in which prolonged sleep deprivation causes death.

## *Conclusions*

You may be wondering at this point which of the two theories concerned with the functions of sleep provides the better account. Recovery/restoration theories and adaptive/evolutionary theories have both contributed much to our understanding of the functions of sleep. It is preferable to regard the two theories as complementary rather than in direct conflict with each other. Recovery/restoration theories focus mainly on the issue of *why* we need to sleep. In contrast, adaptive/evolutionary theories concentrate on the issues of *when* we sleep and *how long* we sleep each day. If we combine the insights from the two theories, we have promising answers to the main questions concerning the functions of sleep in humans and other species.

## DREAMING

What is dreaming? According to Solms (2000a, p. 849), it is "the subjective experience of a complex hallucinatory episode during sleep". According to Empson (1989), there are several important differences between dreaming and waking consciousness. First, we typically feel we have little or no control over our dreams, whereas we nearly always have a sense of conscious control in our waking lives. However, people occasionally have

### Sleepwalking

Dreams don't always occur in REM sleep. REM dreaming is accompanied by paralysis, probably to protect the sleeper from acting out their dreams and injuring themselves. People also dream in non-REM (NREM) sleep, but less often, and they are not in a paralysed state. It is possible to act out NREM dreams, which can lead to sleepwalking.

Sleepwalking is more common than one might guess. Thirty per cent of all children between the ages of 5 and 12 have walked in their sleep at least once, and persistent sleepwalking occurs in 1–6% of youngsters. Boys walk in their sleep more often than girls, and the tendency to wander during deep sleep is sometimes inherited from one of the parents.

The typical sleepwalking episode begins about 2 hours after the person goes to sleep, when they suddenly "wake" and abruptly sit up in bed. Although their eyes are wide open, they appear glassy and staring. When asked, sleepwalkers respond with mumbled and slurred single-word speech. The person may perform common acts such as dressing and undressing, opening and closing doors, or turning lights on and off. Sleepwalkers seem to see where they are going since they avoid most objects in their way, but they are unaware of their surroundings. Unfortunately, this means that they cannot tell the difference between their bedroom door and the front door, or the toilet and the wastebasket. The sleepwalker is usually impossible to awaken and does not remember the episode in the morning. The episode typically lasts 5 to 15 minutes and may occur more than once in the same night.

Although sleepwalkers avoid bumping into walls and tripping over furniture, they lack judgement. A sleepwalking child might do something like going to the garage and getting in the car, ready to go to school at 4 o'clock in the morning. Sometimes their lack of judgement can be dangerous. One sleepwalking child climbed a tree and another was found by the police walking down the street in the middle of the night. Therefore, sleepwalkers are in danger of hurting themselves and must be protected from self-injury.

Most children outgrow sleepwalking by the time they are teenagers, but for a small number of individuals the pattern continues into adulthood.

Christian Murphy escaped with cuts and bruises when he fell from his first-floor bedroom window while sleepwalking. His mother's Mercedes that was parked below broke his fall. Once he had landed he got up, still sleepwalking, and set off down the road.

lucid dreams, in which they know they are dreaming and can sometimes control the dream content. For example, LaBerge, Greenleaf, and Kedzierski (1983) studied a woman who could create lucid sex dreams producing orgasms.

Second, dreams often contain elements that would seem illogical or nonsensical in our waking consciousness. For example, dreams sometimes include impossible events or actions (e.g., someone floating above the ground), and they can also include various hallucinations and delusions.

Third, we are often totally absorbed by our dream imagery, reflecting what Empson (1989) described as "the single-mindedness of dreams". In contrast, when we are awake, we can usually stand back from our conscious thoughts and avoid being dominated by them.

Most dreams take place during REM (rapid eye movement) sleep. However, the common views that dreaming *only* occurs during REM sleep and that REM sleep is always associated with dreaming are profoundly mistaken. According to Solms (2000b, p. 618), "As many as 50 per cent of awakenings from non-REM sleep elicit dream reports, and 20 per cent of these are indistinguishable by any criterion from REM reports (by blind raters)." Nielsen (1999) reviewed studies in this area. On average, individuals woken up during REM sleep recalled dream-like material on only 82% of occasions, compared to 42.5% during non-REM sleep. What was recalled from REM sleep was typically more vivid, more animated, more emotionally loaded, and of less relevance to waking life than recall from non-REM sleep.

Adults spend about 2 hours a day in REM sleep. Thus, they probably devote well over 700 hours a year to dreaming. This suggests that dreams are likely to fulfil some important function or functions. As we will see shortly, various theorists have tried to identify those functions.

*Keep a record of your dreams (a dream diary) over a week. How many could you remember? What kinds of things did you dream about?*

## Methodological issues

It may not seem as if we spend over 2 hours a night dreaming. The explanation is that we forget more than 95% of our dreams. What are these forgotten dreams about? Researchers have answered this question by using sleep laboratories, in which sleepers are woken up during REM sleep. The dreams normally forgotten tend to be much more ordinary and less bizarre than the dreams we remember in everyday life (Empson, 1989).

The above finding is important. It shows the dreams we normally remember in our everyday lives are not *representative* or typical of our dreams in general. It would thus

*not* be appropriate to produce a theory of dreaming purely on the basis of the 5% of dreams we normally remember. However, the use of sleep laboratories may also be limited. According to Hobson, Pace-Schott, and Stickgold (2000, p. 803), "Anyone who has ever slept in a sleep laboratory ... knows that it is an inhospitable and unnatural setting that makes sleep more difficult and less deep than is possible in more naturalistic settings." As a result, the kinds of dreams experienced in the laboratory may differ from those in everyday life.

There is another potential problem associated with the study of dreams, whether in the laboratory or in normal life. As Coenen (2000, p. 923) pointed out, "A dream is what someone describes upon awakening and researchers infer a one-to-one relationship between the dream and the way it is reported. It is therefore impossible to exclude such confounding factors as poor memory, overestimation, suppression or the effects of psycho-emotional factors on recall."

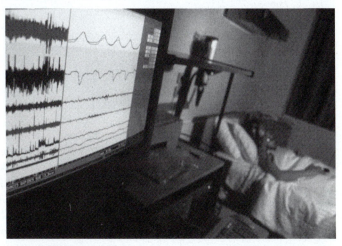

Electroencephalogram (EEG) traces of a patient's brain activity as she sleeps. The EEG traces show the electrical activity of the brain, which can be measured by placing electrodes on the patient's scalp.

# Freud's wish fulfilment theory

Probably the best-known theory of dreaming was put forward by Sigmund Freud (1900). He claimed all dreams represent wish fulfilment, mainly of repressed desires (e.g., sexual). These wish fulfilments are often unacceptable to the dreamer, leading Freud to describe dreams as "the insanity of the night". As a result of the unacceptable desires expressed in dreams, the actual dream and its meaning (the **latent content**) are generally distorted into a more acceptable form (the **manifest content**) by the time the dreamer is consciously aware of his/her dream. What Freud called dream-work is involved in transforming the original unconscious wishes into the manifest content of the reported dream. Some of the mechanisms involved in dream-work are as follows:

1. *Displacement.* One element in the dream is substituted by something else (e.g., having sex is represented by riding a horse).
2. *Regression.* Thoughts are transformed into perceptions (e.g., the sizes of individuals in a dream reflect their significance to you).
3. *Condensation.* Several elements in the dream are combined into a single image (e.g., failure and sadness are transformed into a descending escalator).

*What problems might arise when trying to work out what dreams really mean?*

How can we identify the original latent content of a dream on the basis of its manifest content as reported by the dreamer? In essence, this involves some of the techniques of psychoanalysis. The dreamer provides associations to the various aspects of the manifest content, and the psychoanalyst then identifies the main underlying themes. An important piece of dream analysis involves working out the meaning of various dream symbols. For example, licking a lollipop might be a symbol for oral sex, or a cigar might be a symbol for a penis. However, as Freud himself admitted, "Sometimes a cigar is only a cigar."

Why is wish fulfilment the main goal of dreams? According to Freud, when we are asleep, our minds are not influenced by the external environment and by the constraints it imposes on our behaviour. However, we are influenced by internal factors (e.g., basic sexual and other motivational forces). We imagine acting in accordance with these motivational forces when we dream, and this defers our need to act on them in real life. This line of argument led Freud to conclude that, "dreams are the guardians of sleep".

## *Evidence*

Studies on brain-damaged patients have shed light on those parts of the brain of crucial importance in dreaming. According to Solms (2000b), dreaming is eliminated when there is damage to the so-called "seeking system", which connects the midbrain to the limbic system and to the frontal lobes. This system "instigates goal-seeking behaviours and an organism's appetitive interactions with the world" (Panksepp, 1985, p. 273). According to Solms (p. 619), "No single brain system comes closer in its functional properties than this one to the 'libido' [sexual instinct] of Freudian dream theory."

> ### Politics and dream content
> The Association for the Study of Dreams (2001) found that political views could influence dream content. People with right-wing views report having more violent and scary dreams than people with left-wing views. If this is true, it could support the Freudian view that dreams have a hidden content or message.

The transformation of the latent content into the manifest content complicates the task of predicting the nature of the dreams we might expect from Freud's theory. However, it seems reasonable to predict that most dreams involving wish fulfilment should be associated with positive emotional states. In fact, Hall and van de Castle (1966) found that 80% out of a total of 1000 dream reports involved negative emotions. It could be argued that recurrent dreams (in which the same events recur in several different dreams) would be most likely to show clear evidence of the fulfilment of powerful wishes. Zadra (1996) examined recurrent dreams in adults and in children. About 85% of these dreams contained negative or unpleasant emotions, and only 10% contained exclusively pleasant emotions.

**KEY TERMS**

**Latent content:** in Freud's theory, the underlying meaning of a dream that is hard to recollect consciously.

**Manifest content:** in Freud's theory, the surface or remembered meaning of a dream.

## *Evaluation*

⊕ Freud put forward the first systematic theory of dream function, and provided an explanation for the puzzling finding that dreams often seem rather incoherent or even meaningless.

⊕ As Freud claimed, dreams reveal something about the thoughts and feelings of the dreamer, although probably rather less than he imagined.

⊕ Some brain areas of crucial importance in dreaming are of relevance in sexual and other motivation.

⊖ It is improbable there is much repression of unacceptable desires in today's liberal and permissive society.

⊖ Many dreams (e.g., nightmares) are very frightening or evoke various negative emotional states, and it is hard to regard them as wish fulfilling even in a distorted way.

⊖ The latent content of a dream as identified through psychoanalysis generally seems open to question, because the interpretation of the manifest content of a dream may be heavily influenced by the biases of the person providing the interpretation.

⊖ Freud focused only on the unrepresentative 5% of dreams that are spontaneously remembered, and his theory is less applicable to the remaining 95% of dreams.

## Activation–synthesis theory

Hobson and McCarley (1977) were impressed by the fact that the brain is as physiologically active during rapid eye movement (REM) sleep as during normal waking. This led them to put forward the activation–synthesis theory of dreaming. According to this theory, the state of activation during REM sleep depends mainly on the pontine brain stem, which is also responsible for triggering dreaming. Activity in the pontine brain stem produces high levels of activation in several parts of the brain, including those involved in perception, action, and emotional reactions. This activation is essentially random. Dreamers react to the high level of random brain activation by synthesising or combining the information contained in the bursts of neural activity. This synthesis occurs in the forebrain, which makes "the best of a bad job in producing even partially coherent dream imagery from the relatively noisy signals sent up from the brain stem" (p. 1347). How is this possible? According to Hobson (1988), "The brain is so inexorably bent upon the quest for meaning that it attributes and even creates meaning when there is little or none in the data it is asked to process."

In sum, the original version of activation–synthesis theory made three key assumptions:

1. A high level of activation in pontine brainstem mechanisms is needed for dreaming to occur.
2. Activation in pontine brainstem mechanisms produces REM sleep as well as dreaming, and all dreams occur during REM sleep.
3. The forebrain tries to impose meaning on the more-or-less random activation from the brain stem to produce partially coherent dreams.

Assumption 2 has been abandoned in more recent versions of the theory (e.g., Hobson et al., 2000), which is now known as the AIM (activation–input–modulation) model. It is still claimed that activation in the pontine brain stem is needed for dreaming, but it is accepted such activation (and dreaming) can occur in non-REM sleep as well as in REM sleep.

Some additional aspects of activation–synthesis theory should be mentioned before we consider the relevant evidence. Those parts of the cortex responsible for producing actions are inhibited during REM sleep. The reason for this is the existence of an *output* blockade at the top of the spinal column preventing commands for action being acted upon. In addition, there is inhibited processing of environmental stimuli via an *input* blockade. However, signals resembling those normally coming from the eyes and ears are generated within the hindbrain and midbrain structures. Dreamers generally interpret these internally generated signals as if produced by external stimuli.

Hobson (1994) developed the activation–synthesis theory. He noted that cortical levels of the neurotransmitters noradrenaline and serotonin are lower during REM sleep than during non-REM sleep or waking life. According to Hobson, these reduced levels of noradrenaline and serotonin prevent the effective use of attentional processes and of processing capacity. This makes it easier for the brain to misinterpret internally generated signals as if they came from external stimuli or from responses. Hobson argued the problems of attention caused by low levels of noradrenaline and serotonin may explain why we fail to remember our dreams.

## Evidence

As assumed within action–synthesis theory, there is typically high activation within the pontine brain stem during REM sleep. Hobson et al. (2000) reviewed four PET studies in which brain activity during REM sleep was assessed. There was consistent evidence of activation in the pontine brain stem. In addition, parts of the forebrain were generally activated during REM sleep.

According to the theory, brainstem lesions should eliminate REM sleep. As predicted, large lesions of the pontine brain stem in cats completely eliminate REM sleep (Jones, 1979). There is additional evidence from various studies that naturally occurring brainstem lesions in humans also eliminate (or nearly eliminate) REM sleep (see Solms, 2000a, for a review).

Do lesions of the pontine brain stem also eliminate dreaming as predicted by the theory? It is hard to say, in part because lesions that eliminate REM sleep typically render patients unconscious. However, Solms (2000a) concluded there was clear evidence of cessation of dreaming in only one out of 26 such patients.

More convincing evidence that there are real problems with activation–synthesis theory comes from studies of brain-damaged patients who dream either rarely or never. Solms (2000a, p. 846) reviewed 111 such cases, and concluded as follows:

> **PET scans reveal the dreaming brain's activity**
>
> Maquet et al.'s (1996) research supports the idea that the thalamus is involved in dreaming. His seven male volunteers were first slightly sleep-deprived to ensure they would sleep well. They then slept, immobilised in a PET scanner. They were wakened at various intervals to see if they were dreaming. What Maquet found was that dreaming coincided with greater blood flow, meaning greater activity in the thalamus, part of the limbic system. This area of the brain is also involved in memory and emotion. Reduced blood flow was seen in the frontal cortex, responsible for complex thought. All this could explain the mix of memories and emotions, plus the distorted sense of time and a reduction or loss of self-awareness which we experience in dreams. It might also explain the rapid loss of memories of dreaming once we wake.

*The lesion was localised to the forebrain—and the pontine brain stem was completely spared—in all but one case ... Critically, the REM state was entirely preserved in all of the forebrain cases in which the sleep cycle was evaluated.*

Thus, activation of the pontine brain stem and the presence of REM sleep do *not* ensure dreaming will occur.

Another major prediction of activation–synthesis theory is that dreams are rather incoherent and even bizarre. *Some* dreams are certainly bizarre, but that is not true of the great majority. For example, Hall (1966) examined 815 reports of dreams occurring at home or in the laboratory. Only about 10% of these dream reports contained at least one "unusual element". Why did Hobson and McCarley (1977) claim dreams are bizarre and incoherent? According to Vogel (2000, p. 1014), this view, "is based mostly upon reported dreams that are spontaneously recalled upon waking in the morning. These dreams are likely the most dramatic, bizarre dreams and are not representative of dream life in general. The collection of large dream samples from throughout the night from ordinary people ... has shown that dreams are mundane, organised, everydayish stories."

## Evaluation

⊕ The theory is based on detailed information about the physiological activity of the brain during sleep and dreaming. For example, smells and tastes rarely or never appear in our dreams, because "the neurons responsible are not activated during REM sleep" (McIlveen & Gross, 1996, p. 108).

- Dreams are often triggered by activation of the pontine brain stem, but such stimulation is not essential (Solms, 2000a).
- Random activity in the brain and attentional processes not functioning effectively may make some dreams hard to understand.
- The original notion that dreaming occurs only during REM sleep has been convincingly disproved, and has had to be abandoned. As Solms (2000a, p. 843) pointed out, "REM is controlled by cholinergic brainstem mechanisms whereas dreaming seems to be controlled by dopaminergic forebrain mechanisms."
- The role of the pontine brain stem in producing dreams is exaggerated in the theory, but the role of the forebrain is minimised (see Solms, 2000a, 2000b).
- "Dreams are more coherent, consistent over time for both individuals and groups, and continuous with the past than Hobson et al.'s emphasis on brainstem-driven bizarreness can accommodate" (Domhoff, 2000, p. 928).

## Evolutionary hypothesis

Revonsuo (2000) argued we can understand the function served by dreams by adopting an evolutionary perspective. Until relatively recently, human life was typically short, and the environment was often threatening and dangerous. As a result, "A dream-production mechanism that tends to select threatening waking events and simulate them over and over again in various combinations would have been valuable for the development and maintenance of threat-avoidance skills" (p. 793). According to Revonsuo, our dreams continue to show evidence of being influenced by such concerns, even though the environment is now less threatening than hundreds or thousands of years ago. This led Revonsuo (p. 877) to produce his evolutionary hypothesis, according to which, "the psychological function of dreaming is to simulate threatening events and to rehearse threat perception and threat avoidance".

*How could cross-cultural studies provide useful information related to this claim?*

The key assumptions of the evolutionary hypothesis have already been stated. It follows from these assumptions that dreams should provide a simulation of the external environment and should not be disorganised or bizarre. It also follows that our dreams should be greatly affected by severe environmental threats encountered in our everyday lives. Finally, the threatening events found in dreams should be realistic to prepare the dreamer to perceive and avoid threat in future.

### Evidence

There is general support for the prediction that many dreams should incorporate threatening themes. For example, in a study already mentioned, Zadra (1996) analysed recurrent dreams from childhood and from adulthood. In 40% of these dreams, the dreamer found him/herself in a dangerous situation. This most often involved chase and pursuit (42% of childhood dreams and just under 15% of adulthood dreams). In similar fashion, Gregor (1981) found that 60% of the dreams reported by Mehinaku Indian men in Central Brazil had a threatening situation as a theme. Germain, Nielsen, Zadra, and Montplaisir (2000) administered the Typical Dreams Questionnaire to about 2000 participants. The most frequent typical theme involved the threatening situation of being chased or pursued.

Other findings reported by Germain et al. (2000) were less consistent with the evolutionary hypothesis. Dreams of sexual experiences and of falling were among the most common themes, but neither theme relates directly to the kinds of threatening experiences emphasised by Revonsuo (2000). The same is the case for the ninth most common theme (flying or soaring through the air), which was generally associated with positive emotion.

There was mixed support for the evolutionary hypothesis from a study of 1000 dreams by Hall and van de Castle (1966). There were seven times as many dreams involving misfortune (e.g., mishaps, dangers) as good fortune (411 dreams vs. 58, respectively). The much greater incidence of negative dreams than positive ones follows from the hypothesis, but the existence of dozens of positive dreams is hard to explain.

Many dreams are relevant to current concerns. Hajek and Belcher (1991) studied the dreams of smokers involved in a programme to help them stop smoking, who would be expected to find the prospect of resuming smoking threatening. Most of the participants reported dreams of absent-minded transgressions during the course of treatment and for a year afterwards. In these dreams, engaging in smoking was followed by feelings of panic or guilt. Hajek and Belcher also found dreaming about smoking (and feeling bad about it) seemed to help the ex-smokers. Those having the most such dreams were less likely to start smoking again than those having few such dreams. This suggests dreams can have real survival value! However, these are correlational findings, and do not prove the dreams reduced smoking behaviour.

*Studies of dream content rely on self-report. Think about your own dream diary to identify the potential problems with this technique.*

Nader (1996) reported findings relevant to the prediction that people should have nightmares about threatening experiences they had had. Of children who had been kidnapped and buried in a truck trailer, 100% had nightmares about their experiences, as did 83% of children who underwent a life-threatening operation, and 40% of children exposed to radioactivity after a major accident at a nuclear power plant.

## Evaluation

⊕ Revonsuo's evolutionary hypothesis is based on a serious attempt to understand the main kinds of content found in dreams.

⊕ The hypothesis accurately predicts that many dreams focus on realistic threatening events and on the dreamer's current concerns.

⊖ It is not clear from the hypothesis why there are so many dreams about sexual experiences or falling.

⊖ It is doubtful whether dreaming about frightening events allows us to cope more successfully with them. As Montangero (2000, p. 73) pointed out, "No experimental data have shown that people's threat avoidance skills are improved after having nightmares … Nobody needs numerous rehearsals in order to know how to run away, to hide behind a rock, or to lie flat in the grass in the presence of a danger."

⊖ The evolutionary hypothesis is limited, in that it does not provide a ready explanation for the existence of dreams involving good fortune (e.g., Hall & van de Castle, 1966).

### KEY TERM

**Hypnosis:** a state of heightened suggestibility that may or may not represent an altered state of consciousness.

# HYPNOSIS

What is hypnosis? The word comes from the Greek word *hypnoun* meaning to put to sleep, but a hypnotised person is not actually asleep. Westen (1996, p. 354) defined hypnosis as "an altered state characterised by deep relaxation and suggestibility (proneness to follow the suggestions of the hypnotist)". As we will see, there is controversy as to whether **hypnosis** is a genuine phenomenon, or whether it merely involves the hypnotised person co-operating with the wishes of the hypnotist. Hypnosis has often been regarded as an inexplicable state, and is linked in the popular mind to trickery and show business. In fact, as we will see, researchers have started to unravel some of the mysteries of hypnosis, and interesting links are being formed between hypnosis and cognitive neuroscience (see Raz & Shapiro, 2002).

How can we produce the hypnotic state? It is generally achieved by induction procedures based on suggestions for sleep and relaxation. Initially, the participant may be asked by the hypnotist to focus on a given target (e.g., a swinging watch chain, a spot of light). When the participant's

A photograph from the 1940s of hypnotist W.J. Ousby catching a woman who has fallen into a trance after being hypnotised. Ousby used hypnotism before psychoanalysing his patients in order to cure them of psychological complexes.

attention is directed fully at the target, the hypnotist suggests to the participant that he/she is feeling relaxed and sleepy. The suggestion is also made that the participant's arms and legs are feeling heavy and relaxed. Typically, about 10 or 15 minutes are spent producing the passive and sleep-like hypnotic state. After that, more time is spent in assessing the depth or strength of the hypnotic state created.

There are large individual differences in susceptibility to hypnosis. These individual differences can be assessed by scales such as the Stanford Hypnotic Susceptibility Scale or the Harvard Group Scale of Hypnotic Susceptibility. These scales consist of various suggestions (e.g., "Your hand is heavy, and you can't hold it up", "You will forget what I have just said"). The number of these suggestions followed by the individual provides a measure of his or her susceptibility to hypnosis.

We will consider the Stanford Hypnotic Susceptibility Scale as a concrete example. It consists of 12 items or suggestions, some of which are fairly easy and are followed by many people (e.g., imagine a mosquito is buzzing around your head, and try to brush it away). Other suggestions are more difficult and are only followed by a small percentage of people (e.g., negative visual hallucination, in which the individual can no longer see a small box following the hypnotist's suggestion). About 5% of people come out as highly susceptible to hypnosis on the Stanford Hypnotic Susceptibility Scale, and about one in ten show practically no signs of susceptibility.

What kinds of people are particularly susceptible to hypnosis? They tend to be fantasy prone, meaning that they report having a large number of vivid fantasies (McIlveen, 1995). They also tend to score highly on absorption, which McIlveen defines as "the tendency to become deeply involved in sensory and imaginative experiences" (p. 11). However, according to McIlveen, absorption only predicts hypnotic susceptibility among people expecting to undergo hypnosis. Another characteristic of those having high hypnotic susceptibility is that they are more willing than most to take orders from others. Finally, age is important, with the peak age for susceptibility to hypnosis being about 10, with a progressive reduction in susceptibility during adolescence and early adulthood.

---

**The Stanford Hypnotic Susceptibility Scale**

1  *Arm lowering*: A participant is told that their outstretched arm is getting increasingly heavier, the arm starts to fall.

2  *Moving hands apart*: When a participant's arms are stretched out straight in front and told that the hands repel each other, the two hands start to move apart.

3  *Mosquito hallucination*: The participant responds to a suggestion of an annoying mosquito buzzing around by trying to swat it away.

4  *Taste hallucination*: The participant agrees with suggestions of sweet and then sour tastes in their mouth.

5  *Arm rigidity*: After being told that an outstretched arm is getting more and more stiff the participant is unable to bend it.

6  *Dream*: The hypnotised participant is told they will dream about hypnosis, and then reports this happening.

7  *Age regression*: The participant acts in accordance with whatever younger age they are told, including suitable handwriting being produced.

8  *Arm immobilisation*: after being told that the arm cannot be lifted, the participant finds it is so.

9  *Anosmia (loss of smell)*: The participant becomes unable to smell household ammonia after being told it is odourless.

10  *Hallucinated voice*: The participant answers to a hallucinated voice.

11  *Negative visual hallucination*: After being told there are only two coloured boxes when there are three, the participant says only two are seen.

12  *Post-hypnotic amnesia*: Until a pre-arranged sign or signal is made, the "awakened" participant cannot recall certain information given when hypnotised.

From Bentley (2000).

---

# Hypnotic state

What brain areas are affected by the hypnotic state? Rainville, Hofbauer, Bushnell, Duncan, and Price (2001) addressed this issue using PET scans (see the introduction to the Cognitive Psychology part of the book) before and after the induction of hypnosis. There was evidence that hypnosis is an altered state of consciousness, because areas involved in the regulation of consciousness (e.g., the thalamus, the anterior cingulate cortex, the ponto-mesencephalic brainstem) were all affected by the hypnotic state. In addition, hypnosis produced increased activity in a network of cortical and sub-cortical structures involved in attention, suggesting that the hypnotic state is associated with increased attention.

Various phenomena have been reported in the hypnotic state. Some (e.g., active reliving of past lives) are highly improbable, but others deserve careful consideration. We will consider four such phenomena:

1.  Hypnotic amnesia.
2.  Hypnotic analgesia.
3.  Trance logic.
4.  Attentional narrowing.

## Hypnotic amnesia

Hypnotised individuals are sometimes instructed to forget what they have just learned or done. They generally show a high level of forgetting in those circumstances; this forgetting is known as **hypnotic amnesia**. It is not forgetting in the ordinary sense, because the "forgotten" information is usually remembered when the hypnotised person is given a release signal (e.g., "Now you can remember"). The most striking example of such forgetting is known as post-hypnotic amnesia. Hypnotised individuals are told they will forget the entire hypnotic session when they come out of the hypnotic state. Post-hypnotic amnesia is shown by most individuals. It is not permanent forgetting, because the events of the hypnotic session can usually be recalled when the individuals are hypnotised again and instructed to remember what happened the last time they were hypnotised.

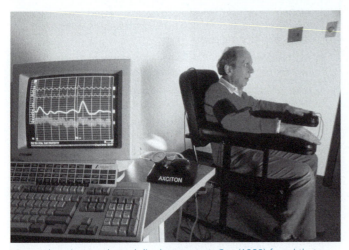

Man undergoing a polygraph lie-detector test. Coe (1989) found that when hypnotised individuals were questioned using a lie detector, they remembered whatever they had been told to forget under hypnosis.

A phenomenon related to post-hypnotic amnesia is known as **post-hypnotic suggestion**. The hypnotist gives an instruction to a hypnotised individual to carry out some action when the signal is given (e.g., start sneezing when the hypnotist says "Hay fever"). The hypnotist tells the hypnotised person he/she will not remember the instruction. The signal is given when the person is back in the normal waking state. He/she carries out the specified action, but does not remember the post-hypnotic suggestion.

The simplest explanation of hypnotic amnesia is that hypnotised individuals either do not try to remember or that they distract themselves from the memory task. Evidence consistent with these explanations was reported by Coe (1989). He found hypnotic amnesia usually disappeared when the participants were instructed to be honest, attached to a lie detector, and shown a videotape of their own performance. Wagstaff (1977) found participants allowed to indicate they were role playing rather than in a hypnotic trance usually showed no evidence of hypnotic amnesia.

### KEY TERMS

**Hypnotic amnesia:** temporary forgetting in hypnosis caused by suggestion.

**Post-hypnotic suggestion:** this involves an individual who has received an instruction while hypnotised carrying it out when in the normal waking state without consciously remembering the instruction.

**Hypnotic analgesia:** reduced experience of pain in hypnosis.

## Hypnotic analgesia

The phenomenon of **hypnotic analgesia** is shown when a hypnotised individual experiences little or no pain when exposed to a very painful situation. As early as the 1840s, a British surgeon called Ward reported a striking example of hypnotic analgesia. He claimed to have amputated a man's leg without causing him any pain simply by using hypnosis!

In a typical laboratory study on hypnotic analgesia, the painful situation involves the participants putting their hand into ice-cold water or having a pressure stimulus applied to them. Suggestions that pain will not be experienced are usually more effective when given in the hypnotic state than in the normal state (Hilgard & Hilgard, 1983). Patterson and Jensen (2003) reviewed clinical studies in which hypnosis was used to reduce either acute pain (e.g., produced by surgery or by burns) or chronic pain (e.g., migraine). Hypnosis was generally effective in reducing pain, and it was often more effective than other treatments such as cognitive-behaviour therapy, relaxation training, emotional support, and distraction. According to Patterson and Jensen (p. 507), "Treatments described as hypnosis by investigators ... are at least as, and about half the time even more, effective than other treatments for reducing the pain associated with invasive medical procedures in both children

The cold pressor test—most people can only keep their arm in ice-cold water for 25 seconds, but hypnotised individuals who have been told that they will not feel any pain can keep their arm in the water for about 40 seconds.

and adults." Hypnosis was moderately effective in reducing chronic pain, but was typically no more effective than other treatments. For both acute and chronic pain, individuals high in hypnotic suggestibility generally showed the greatest reduction in pain under hypnosis.

The findings on hypnotic analgesia are impressive, but compliance or faking may sometimes be involved. Spanos, Perlini, Patrick, Bell, and Gwynn (1990) administered a painful stimulus to their participants. Those led to believe subsequently that they were hypnotised at the time reported less pain than those who believed they were not hypnotised, and this difference was found regardless of whether or not they were actually hypnotised when receiving the painful stimulus.

More evidence that hypnotic analgesia may be a suspect phenomenon was reported by Pattie (1937), who told hypnotised individuals they would feel nothing in one hand. Then he asked them to interlock the fingers on their two hands. They were next told to twist their arms around so it would be hard for them to know which hand any given finger was on. Finally, Pattie touched some of their fingers, and asked the participants to indicate how many times their fingers had been touched. They included touches to fingers on both hands, indicating they still had feeling in the allegedly "anaesthetised" hand.

Other evidence suggests hypnotic analgesia may involve real (rather than merely reported) reductions in the experience of pain. Price and Barrell (2000) reviewed several studies on the effects of hypnotic analgesia on activity within the brain. Hypnotic analgesia produced inhibited processing of pain-related stimuli arriving at the somatosensory cortex. It also produced changes in activation of the limbic system which may reduce the experience of pain.

*What ethical issues need to be considered when carrying out research of this nature?*

## Trance logic

Another phenomenon associated with the hypnotic state is that of **trance logic**. This refers to the finding that hypnotised individuals do not display logical consistency in their thinking. For example, there is what Orne (1959) called the "double hallucination" response: When hypnotised individuals look at someone, and are told to hallucinate that person standing somewhere else, they typically report seeing the person and the hallucinated image at the same time. Another example of trance logic occurs when hypnotised individuals imagine someone is sitting on an empty chair. They usually report seeing the chair through the person. In contrast, non-hypnotised individuals told to act as if they were hypnotised (simulators) do not show trance logic.

There has been some dispute about the existence and significance of trance logic. In some studies, there was no difference between hypnotised participants and simulators on the double hallucination response (de Groot & Gwynn, 1989). What do hypnotised individuals mean when they say they can see someone and their hallucinated image at the same time? If hypnotised individuals are given the choice, they usually prefer to claim they "imagined" rather than "saw" the hallucinated image (Spanos, 1982). This suggests the double hallucination effect is less dramatic than is often supposed.

## Attentional narrowing

The next phenomenon we will consider is **attentional narrowing**, which involves a reduction in the processing of environmental information. For example, hypnotised individuals instructed to pay attention only to the hypnotist will often report being unaware of other people. Does this attentional narrowing mean hypnotised individuals are *actually* processing less environmental information? Interesting evidence was reported by Miller, Hennessy, and Leibowitz (1973), who presented hypnotised participants with the Ponzo illusion. People in the normal waking state report the top horizontal rectangle is longer than the bottom one, in spite of the fact that they are actually the same length. Miller et al. made use of hypnotic suggestion so that the hypnotised individuals reported they could no longer see the slanting lines. However, they still reported the normal Ponzo illusion. Thus, they processed information about the slanting lines even though they were not aware of doing so.

> **KEY TERMS**
> **Trance logic:** a form of illogical thinking found in hypnotised individuals.
> **Attentional narrowing:** an apparent reduction in the amount of environmental information being processed during hypnosis.

The Ponzo illusion

The Ponzo illusion—as rectangles A and B are the same size on the retinal image, the more distant rectangle (A) must actually be larger than the nearer one (B).

Neo-dissociation theory suggests that hypnosis reveals more than one stream of consciousness.

# Altered state approaches: Neo-dissociation theory

The crucial question about hypnosis is whether it represents a special, altered state of consciousness. The most prominent advocate of that view is Ernest Hilgard (1986), who put forward a **neo-dissociation theory**. According to this theory, in hypnosis there is "a dissociation (or division) of consciousness into separate channels of mental activity. This division allows us to focus our attention on the hypnotist and, simultaneously, enables us to perceive other events peripherally (or 'subconsciously')" (McIlveen, 1996, p. 24).

Hilgard (1986) argued that what we say and do in the normal state is under conscious control, but most of this conscious control disappears in the hypnotic state. Hypnotic phenomena occur because there is a dissociation (separating off) of one part of the body's system from the rest by means of amnesic barriers. For example, hypnotised individuals exposed to painful stimuli may exhibit the normal physiological responses associated with pain, even though they report experiencing little or no pain. This suggests the part of the brain registering conscious awareness of pain is separated off from those parts registering basic physiological responses.

Hypnotised individuals often report their experiences as involving an absence of conscious control. For example, they describe their obedience to the hypnotist's instructions as involving involuntary actions rather than planned and deliberate ones. According to Hilgard (1986), more direct evidence for his neo-dissociation theory comes from the **hidden observer phenomenon** that can be observed in hypnotised individuals. This involves taking a hypnotised person and giving him/her the following instructions: "When I place my hand on your shoulder, I shall be able to talk to a hidden part of you that knows things are going on in your body, things that are unknown to the part of you to which I am now talking … You will remember that there is a part of you that knows many things that are going on that may be hidden from either your normal consciousness or the hypnotised part of you" (Knox, Morgan, & Hilgard, 1974, p. 842).

A good example of the hidden observer phenomenon was discussed by Hilgard (1986). He used the cold pressor test, in which the participant's arms are kept in ice-cold water for as long as possible. Most people can only tolerate this for about 25 seconds. However, hypnotised individuals told that they will not experience any pain keep their arms in the water for about 40 seconds, and report much less pain than non-hypnotised individuals. The hidden observer, who was told to "remain out of consciousness", reported a very intense experience of pain. Thus, the consciousness of these hypnotised individuals seemed to divide into two parts.

Hilgard (1986) has used the neo-dissociation theory to explain various hypnotic phenomena. Hypnotic amnesia may occur because the "forgotten" memories are dissociated or separated from conscious control, and so cannot be retrieved voluntarily. There is also evidence of dissociation with hypnotic analgesia, in which suggestions that pain will not be experienced are often effective when given in the hypnotic state. As we have seen, Hilgard used the hidden observer technique with the cold pressor test. He found the "hidden part" reported higher levels of pain than were reported for other parts of

## Processes in hypnosis

Gruzelier's team at Imperial College London has been researching the processes in hypnosis (Gruzelier, 2002). They used detailed EEG traces from electrodes on the surface of the head (electro-dermal) and from others actually in the brain (electro-cortical). Marked changes during hypnosis were seen in the limbic system, particularly the inhibition of the amygdala and the excitation of the hippocampus. Interestingly, these changes were only seen in participants susceptible to hypnosis, and seemed to relate to reduced processing in the auditory cortex. This explains how hypnotised people can ignore their surroundings and just attend to what the hypnotist says.

The researchers went on to study a specific process, an error detection system in the limbic system and frontal lobes. This monitors existing activities and changes behaviour as a response to new stimuli, for example when the brain receives conflicting information—as can happen in hypnosis. This system of error-detection operates early on in processing, perhaps pre-consciously; and it continues to work even when the participant is hypnotised. Really interestingly, this system is able to dissociate from other cognitive processing, for example it operates when the hypnotised person behaves in an irrational or non-logical way. This could be because, cognitively, the hypnotist is in control. However, this error-detection part of the brain *is* aware of the mismatch between what it knows and what it is being told. Hilgard's hidden observer has been found!

the body. According to Hilgard, only the hidden part is not protected from awareness of pain by an amnesic barrier. Spanos (1989) argued that hypnotised individuals simply report what they think they should report. He found that "hidden observers" can be led to report high or low levels of pain depending on the expectations they have been given.

On the face of it, the illogical responses given by hypnotised participants in trance logic can easily be explained by the neo-dissociation theory. All that needs to be assumed is that different parts of consciousness are being accessed separately during hypnosis, so hypnotised individuals do not notice the inconsistencies in what they report. Do the reported hallucinations in trance logic really indicate what hypnotised individuals think they are seeing? Some supporting evidence was obtained by Bowers (1983), who found that hypnotised individuals instructed to be honest reported hallucinations which were more vivid than those of non-hypnotised individuals.

*What are the implications of this theory for theories about the nature of consciousness, outlined earlier (see page 104)?*

## Evaluation

➕ Hilgard's (1986) neo-dissociation theory accounts for many hypnotic phenomena, and the notion that hypnosis involves an altered state has received support.
➕ On the face of it, the existence of the hidden observer phenomenon seems to provide good support for the theory, as does the recent research of Gruzelier (2002).
➖ Many demonstrations of the hidden observer phenomenon can be explained on the basis that hypnotised individuals report what they think they are expected to say.
➖ Many other phenomena found in hypnotised individuals can be explained in simple terms not involving the notions of dissociation and amnesic barriers.

## Non-state theories

Several theorists (e.g., Wagstaff, 1991) have argued the hypnotic state is not substantially different from the normal waking state. Their theories can be regarded as non-state theories. As Wagstaff (1994) pointed out, "Non-state theorists argue that hypnotic phenomena are readily explicable in terms of more mundane psychological concepts, mainly from the areas of social and cognitive psychology, such as attitudes, expectancies, beliefs, compliance, imagination, attention, concentration, distraction, and relaxation" (p. 993).

Wagstaff (1991) argued the behaviour of hypnotised individuals can be explained by assuming there are three stages in their response to the hypnotic situation:

| The hypnotised person makes assumptions about expected behaviour on the basis of the hypnotist's instructions | ➡ | The hypnotised person uses various strategies so as to behave in the expected ways | ➡ | If the strategies prove ineffective, he or she makes use of compliance or faking |
|---|---|---|---|---|

## Evidence

There are two types of findings supporting the non-state approach to hypnosis. First, most phenomena associated with hypnosis have also been observed in non-hypnotised individuals. What has generally been used is the "real–simulator" design, in which hypnotised individuals are compared with those instructed to pretend to be hypnotised. Another approach is to use a task-motivated control group, in which the participants are told to do their best to experience hypnotic suggestions even though they have not been hypnotised. With either design, those pretending to be hypnotised can mimic most of the behaviour of hypnotised individuals (see Wagstaff, 1991).

There are some exceptions to the general rule that the behaviour of hypnotised individuals is found in non-hypnotised controls. McIlveen (1995) discussed a study in which the participants were either hypnotised or told to behave as if they had been hypnotised.

*Individual differences in hypnotic suggestibility are associated with variation in other characteristics, such as willingness to follow orders (see page 133). What are the implications of this for non-state theories?*

Both groups were told to touch their forehead with their hand whenever they heard the word "experiment". The hypnotised participants responded appropriately 70% of the time when a secretary said the word "experiment" three times. In contrast, the participants who only pretended to have been hypnotised responded appropriately only 8% of the time.

If the hypnotic state differs little from the normal waking state, then we might expect to find measures of brain activity would typically not differ in the two states. As we saw earlier, that is *not* the case. Rainville et al. (2001) found using PET scans that hypnosis seems to produce an altered state of consciousness in the brain, and also increases activity in those parts of the brain involved in attentional processes.

Do hypnotised individuals deliberately distort their reports of their experiences as suggested by non-state theorists? Evidence against this possibility was reported by Kinnunen, Zamanky, and Block (1995). They compared hypnotised individuals and those pretending to be hypnotised (simulators), measuring skin conductance to assess the level of deception or lying when participants were asked about their conscious experiences. There was more evidence of deception among the simulators than among the hypnotised participants, presumably because the simulators knew they were only pretending to have certain experiences. Of key importance, the hypnotised individuals did not seem to be lying about their experiences.

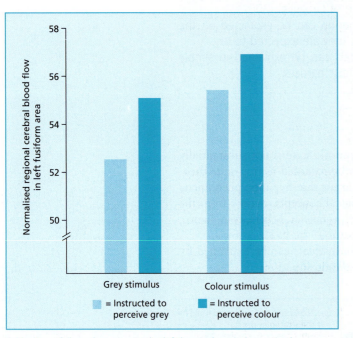

Activation of the colour area in the left hemisphere in hypnotised individuals as a function of the stimulus (grey vs. colour) and instructions (perceive grey vs. perceive colour). Data from Kosslyn et al. (2000).

We have seen the reported experiences of hypnotised individuals differ from those of non-hypnotised individuals. However, it is generally hard to know whether these differences indicate that hypnosis is a psychological state distinctively different from the normal waking state rather than simply deliberate distortion by hypnotised individuals. We might obtain stronger evidence by considering the neural mechanisms underlying specific experiences, on the assumption that neural mechanisms are less susceptible than reported experiences to deliberate distortion. Kosslyn, Thompson, Costantini-Ferrando, Alpert, and Spiegel (2000) presented highly hypnotisable participants (sometimes hypnotised and sometimes not) with stimuli in colour or in various shades of grey. The participants were told to visualise each stimulus either in shades of grey or in colour, and PET scans were taken to assess activity in the colour areas of the left hemisphere.

What did Kosslyn et al. (2000) find? When the participants were hypnotised, the colour area in the left hemisphere was more activated when they were asked to perceive colour, regardless of whether the stimulus itself was coloured. In contrast, when they were not hypnotised, instructions to perceive colour had no effect on activation of the colour area. These findings provide convincing evidence that hypnosis is a distinct state, because it is hard to see how hypnotised individuals could "fake" activity in the colour areas of the left hemisphere. As Kosslyn et al. concluded (p. 1283), "People who are highly hypnotisable can modulate the neural responses underlying colour perception by both enhancing those responses and diminishing them. The left hemisphere colour area registered what they were told to see only when subjects were formally hypnotised."

## Evaluation

● The fact that many phenomena associated with hypnotic states can also be found in individuals pretending to be hypnotised provides support for non-state theories.

● There are moderately strong similarities between the hypnotic state and the states associated with relaxation or meditation.

➕ Non-state theories provide simple explanations of hypnotic phenomena requiring none of the complex mechanisms identified within neo-dissociation theory.
➖ Some differences in behaviour and in brain activity have been found between waking and hypnotic states, and it is hard to account for such differences on non-state theories.
➖ There is evidence from brain-imaging studies (e.g., Kosslyn et al., 2000) that hypnosis produces a psychological state differing from the normal waking state.

# Applications

As we have seen, hypnosis has been used extensively in the treatment of pain. It has also been used to treat various other conditions, including stress. For example, Whitehouse et al. (1996) studied the effects of self-hypnosis training on medical students during their first semester at medical school. The self-hypnosis group reported significantly less distress than did controls who did not hypnotise themselves.

Kiecolt-Glaser et al. (2001) studied the effects of hypnotic-relaxation training in medical and dental students high in hypnotic susceptibility who faced an important examination. Those students receiving hypnotic-relaxation training reported less stress than those not receiving it. Of particular importance, examination-related stress had less serious effects on the functioning of the immune system in students receiving training than in those who did not.

Another area in which hypnosis has been applied is that of criminal justice. The media have reported numerous cases in which hypnosis seems to have been remarkably effective in bringing forgotten memories to light. For example, the Israeli National Police Force and many other police forces have used hypnosis to collect relevant evidence from eyewitnesses about matters such as car number plates and the physical features of wanted criminals. The term **hypermnesia** has been used to refer to the enhanced memory of the kind claimed to be characteristic of hypnosis.

What does the evidence suggest? Hypnosis is often effective in increasing the amount of information which eyewitnesses can recall. For example, Geiselman, Fisher, MacKinnon, and Holland (1985) found that eyewitnesses given a standard interview produced an average of 29.4 correct statements, whereas eyewitnesses under hypnosis produced 38.0 correct statements. However, the downside was that they also made significantly more errors.

> **KEY TERM**
>
> **Hypermnesia:** enhanced ability to remember events (e.g., under hypnosis).

---

### CASE STUDY: *Stage Hypnosis*

In recent years, shows featuring hypnosis have become more common, both on television and on stage. On 12 December 1994 the UK's House of Commons held a debate on the alleged harm suffered by some participants in public performances of stage hypnotism, which led to a full review of the current Hypnotism Act (1952) and subsequent tightening of legislation in the UK.

The panel of experts placed advertisements in five journals requesting clinicians to submit any relevant medical evidence. There were 25 reported cases of harm related to performances of stage hypnotism over the previous 25 years. In four of these cases the problems complained of were physical ailments linked to accidents on the stage; two participants fell from the stage while under hypnosis, and two others fractured bones in their hands while acting out hypnotic suggestions. In the remaining cases, identifying whether there was a link between an ailment and previous participation in stage hypnosis was not straightforward. Frequent complaints were of headaches, dizziness and persistent tiredness, resulting in feelings of lethargy. Some participants reported difficulty in sleeping or disturbed sleep, and feelings of depression were mentioned in half the cases.

In seven of the cases serious psychological problems such as severe depression, post-traumatic stress disorder, and chronic paranoid schizophrenia were diagnosed. Some cases received considerable press coverage. However, it was decided that the evidence suggests there is not a significant problem directly associated with stage hypnotism. Although a number of individuals have suffered following participation in stage hypnosis, most people who choose to attend or participate in demonstrations of stage hypnotism find them enjoyable and suffer no ill-effects.

Apart from obeying the authority of the hypnotist, other social factors are present in stage hypnosis such as audience pressure and pressure from other volunteers. Studies indicate that these factors play a part in the undesirable effects experienced by some individuals. It seems that some participants will find the process of performing frivolous acts on stage in front of a large crowd, and the feeling of loss of control over their own actions, disturbing. In addition, the intermittent bouts of physical exertion and relaxation that form part of many shows may themselves cause some participants to feel tired and experience headaches or dizziness. However, as these side-effects might equally be experienced following a variety of other activities, it is difficult to say that they are a direct result of stage hypnosis.

The law now recommends that all individuals should be aware that some people, particularly those with a history of emotional problems and vulnerable mental health, can find the experience of being hypnotised and then asked to perform actions in front of an audience unpleasant or distressing.

The tendency of hypnosis to make eyewitnesses less cautious in what they report was studied by Putnam (1979). He showed people a videotape of an accident involving a car and a bicycle. They were then asked several questions, some of which contained misleading information. Some of the participants were asked these questions while hypnotised, whereas others were not hypnotised. The hypnotised participants made more errors in their answers than did the non-hypnotised ones, and this was especially the case with the misleading questions. These findings led Putnam to conclude that participants are "more suggestible in the hypnotic state and are, therefore, more easily influenced by the leading questions" (p. 444).

# SUMMARY

### Consciousness

It is difficult to study consciousness, because we have no direct knowledge of anyone else's conscious experience. Consciousness does not seem to be a unitary phenomenon, and there is an important distinction between phenomenal consciousness and access consciousness. Some amnesic patients have good phenomenal consciousness but very poor access consciousness. Some split-brain patients provide suggestive evidence of a dual consciousness. It is important to distinguish between direct experience and reflexive consciousness. There is some evidence that patients with dissociative identity disorder have amnesia for those identities not currently active, suggesting that they lack access consciousness to those identities.

### Bodily rhythms

The sleep–wake cycle is largely endogenous, with the main pacemaker being the suprachiasmatic nucleus, which triggers the release of the hormone melatonin. The sleep–wake cycle is also influenced by external cues (e.g., changes in light and dark). Disturbances of the sleep–wake cycle (e.g., jet lag, shiftwork) can create tiredness and inefficiency, especially when motivation is poor. Performance is best around midday, when alertness is at a peak. There are infradian rhythms (e.g., the menstrual cycle) and some species have circannual rhythms. There is some evidence of circannual rhythms in humans (e.g., seasonal affective disorder, pattern of suicides, winter-over syndrome).

### Sleep

There are five stages of sleep, with a complete sleep cycle lasting about 90 minutes. The reticular formation and the basal forebrain are involved in sleep regulation. Sleep deprivation for a few days has little effect on task performance if the participants are motivated. It has been claimed that a major function of sleep is to permit the restoration of tissue via the release of growth hormone. It may also permit the restoration of psychological functions. Sleep-deprived individuals tend to sleep longer than usual afterwards, with increased slow-wave sleep (associated with the release of growth hormone) An alternative view is that sleep fulfils an adaptive function. For example, sleep keeps animals immobile and safe from predators at night. According to adaptive theories, sleep is very useful but not essential. This seems inconsistent with evidence that sleep is found in all species, and that sleep deprivation can have fatal consequences.

### Dreaming

We remember less than 5% of our dreams, and those we remember are more intense and bizarre than those we forget. Dreams differ from waking consciousness in that we have less control over dreams. Freud argued all dreams represent wish fulfilment, and that the unconscious wishes expressed in the latent content of dreams are transformed by dreamwork into the more acceptable form of the manifest content. Many dreams are threatening and do not seem to represent wish fulfilment. The task of using the manifest content of a dream to infer the latent content is subjective and arbitrary. According to synthesis–activation theory, activation in the pontine brain stem triggers dreams, with the forebrain trying to impose meaning on this activation. The role of the brain stem is exaggerated in the theory, and dreams are generally more coherent than is assumed within the theory. According to the evolutionary hypothesis, dreaming has functional value because it simulates (and so prepares the dreamer for) threatening events. This hypothesis is too narrow, and it fails to explain how dreamers selectively dream about threatening experiences.

Those most susceptible to hypnosis tend to be fantasy prone, high on absorption, and relatively young. There is evidence for hypnotic amnesia, but it may occur simply because hypnotised individuals do not try to remember. Another common phenomenon is hypnotic analgesia, which has been shown in clinical situations as well as in the laboratory. A further phenomenon is trance logic (e.g., seeing someone and their hallucinated image at the same time). However, hypnotised individuals generally claim only that they "imagined" the hallucinated image rather than that they "saw" it. According to neo-dissociation theory, consciousness is divided into separate channels of activity in hypnosis. Many phenomena associated with hypnotic states have been found in individuals pretending to be hypnotised, suggesting the hypnotic state may differ little from the normal waking state. However, recent brain-imaging research suggests the hypnotic state represents a distinct form of consciousness. Hypnosis has been used to treat stress and to enhance the memory of eyewitnesses.

*Hypnosis*

# FURTHER READING

- Hobson, J.A., Pace-Schott, E.F., & Stickgold, R. (2000). Dreaming and the brain: Toward a cognitive neuroscience of conscious states. *Behavioral and Brain Sciences, 23*, 793–1121. This article and the ones following it in this issue of *Behavioral and Brain Sciences* give a very complete and up-to-date account of theory and research on the psychology of dreaming.
- Horne, J. (2001). State of the art: Sleep. *The Psychologist, 14*, 302–306. This article provides interesting insights into the nature of sleep.
- Kalat, J.W. (2001). *Biological psychology* (7th ed.). Belmont, CA: Wadsworth Thomson Learning. This reader-friendly textbook provides accessible accounts of topics such as sleep and biological rhythms.
- Rosenzweig, M.R., Breedlove, S.M., & Leiman, A.L. (2002). *Biological psychology: An introduction to behavioural, cognitive, and clinical neuroscience* (3rd ed.). Sunderland, MA: Sinauer Associates. There is good coverage of biological rhythms and sleep in this textbook.
- Velmans, M. (2000). *Understanding consciousness*. London: Routledge. The complexities of consciousness are discussed in a very coherent way in this excellent book.

# Emotion, stress, and coping

**5**

Most (or even all!) of the really important events in our lives are associated with high levels of emotion. When we pass major examinations we feel elated, when we embark on a new relationship we feel excited, when we fail to achieve something we had set our hearts on we feel depressed, and when someone close to us dies we experience overpowering grief. Thus, emotions play a central role in our lives. The first part of this chapter is devoted to a consideration of emotion and the main theories in this area of psychology. After that, the focus shifts to stress. Among the issues considered are an assessment of the effects of stress on our physical health, and various ways of coping with stress.

## WHAT IS EMOTION?

What is emotion? A representative definition was offered by Watson and Clark (1994, p. 89):

> [Emotions] we can define as distinct, integrated psychophysiological response systems ... An emotion contains three differentiable response systems: (1) a prototypic form of expression (typically facial), (2) a pattern of consistent autonomic changes, and (3) a distinct subjective feeling state.

We will consider Watson and Clark's (1994) application of the above definition to fear. When someone is fearful, they typically have a particular expression on their face: The eyebrows are raised and close together, the eyes are opened wider than usual, the lips are pulled back, and there is evidence of tension in the lower lip. So far as the second component of emotion is concerned, fear is associated with a substantial increase in autonomic nervous system activity (e.g., faster heart rate, sweating). Finally, fearful individuals use adjectives such as "nervous", "frightened", and "scared to death" to describe their subjective feeling state.

## Response systems

Lang (1971, 1985) also proposed three response systems, which are similar (but not identical) to those of Watson and Clark (1994): (1) behavioural; (2) physiological; and (3) verbal or cognitive (self-report).

Do these various response systems all respond similarly when an individual is in an emotional situation? According to the notion of concordance, there should be agreement or concordance among different emotional responses. Thus, for example, pianists performing in public who experience the highest levels of self-reported anxiety should have the greatest level of autonomic activity and the poorest level of performance. In fact, the concordance assumption doesn't seem to apply to pianists. Craske and Craig (1984) found that measures of anxiety belonging to different response systems generally failed to correlate significantly with each other.

There are numerous cases of failures of concordance. For example, Beidel, Turner, and Dancu (1985) considered anxious responses in participants with anxious and non-anxious personalities placed in various situations (e.g., giving a talk). The two groups differed considerably in self-reported anxiety in stressful situations. However, the difference was much smaller with respect to behavioural anxiety as assessed by judges.

Why are there so many failures of concordance? One reason is because many of the response measures are of limited validity. For example, heart rate and skin conductance both reflect autonomic activity, but they typically correlate only modestly (about +.3) with each other (Lacey, 1967). An additional complicating factor is **individual response stereotypy**, meaning that individuals vary in terms of which physiological measures are most sensitive. Self-report measures can be influenced by **social desirability bias**, in which individuals deliberately distort their responses in the socially desirable direction (e.g., pretending they are less anxious or depressed than is actually the case).

There is a more interesting reason why measures of the various emotional response systems are often weakly correlated. Each response system fulfils a somewhat different function, and this leads each response system to operate in partial independence. Thus, autonomic activity serves to support the performance of specific action tendencies (e.g., approach or avoidance behaviour); non-verbal behaviour (e.g., facial expression) communicates information to other people; and the subjective experience of emotions leads the individual to continue pursuing the current goal or to change goals.

> **An unconscious subjective emotional response**
>
> Murphy and Zajonc (1996) have found that subliminal viewing of smiling faces produces a measurable rise in positive frame of mind—a 4 millisecond presentation is too short-lived to reach the conscious mind, and yet it makes the viewer happier. This positive emotion then influences the viewer's response to other things, i.e., their mood.

## Emotions and moods

What are the main differences between emotions and moods? First, they differ in duration: **Moods** tend to last for a long time, whereas **emotions** are typically much shorter lasting. Watson and Clark (1994, p. 90) provided a good example: "The full emotion of anger may last for only a few seconds or minutes, an annoyed or irritable mood may last for several hours or even for a few days."

Second, emotions are typically more intense than moods. As a consequence, while moods resemble emotions in having a subjective feeling state, they generally lack the pronounced facial expressions and large changes in autonomic activity associated with emotions. Emotional states are often so intense they become the individual's major focus of attention. In contrast, moods provide a background to our everyday activities, and we generally do not attend directly to our own mood states.

Third, emotions differ from moods in the factors causing them. Emotions are typically caused by a specific event (e.g., being shouted at), whereas the reason for being in a particular mood is often unclear. Frijda (1994, p. 60) considered how emotions revolve around events or objects: "Emotions imply and involve relationships of the subject with a particular object. One is afraid of something, angry at someone, happy about something, fearful behaviour is directed away from something." Moods lack these characteristics, and so are not object-related.

The reader may be forgiven for feeling bewildered, because I have implied that emotions and moods are strikingly different. In fact, however, there are dynamic links between emotions and moods. According to Frijda (1994, p. 63), "Every emotion tends to prolong itself into a mood ... every emotion ... tends to entail a mood change." The direction can also run in the opposite direction: "Moods may give rise to emotions, since they often imply a lowering of threshold for particular emotions" (p. 67).

The fact that emotions can create moods, and that moods can turn into emotions, means we cannot draw a sharp distinction between them. The imprecise boundary between emotion and mood is reflected in much of the literature, in which the two terms are sometimes used almost interchangeably.

## How useful are emotions?

It is popularly believed that most emotions (especially negative ones) are useless and undesirable. That belief is understandable for various reasons. First, practically no-one wants to become anxious or depressed. Second, emotions often disrupt our current activities and behaviour. Third, as Keltner and Gross (1999, pp. 467–468) pointed out, emotions "generally lack the logic, rationality, and principled orderliness of reason and other cognitive processes".

**KEY TERMS**

**Individual response stereotypy:** the finding that individuals differ in terms of the physiological responses showing greatest sensitivity in emotional situations.

**Social desirability bias:** the tendency to provide socially desirable but inaccurate responses on self-report questionnaires.

**Moods:** emotional experiences that are typically longer lasting and less intense than emotions.

**Emotions:** emotional experiences that are usually more intense and shorter lasting than moods.

The notion that emotions benefit us little was advanced by Skinner (1948, p. 92), in his novel (*Walden Two*) about an ideal society: "We all know that emotions are useless and bad for our peace of mind and our blood pressure." Other psychologists (e.g., Hebb, 1949) argue that emotions produce disorganised behaviour. Everyday experience indicates that emotions can cause us to stop what we were doing before becoming emotional. For example, seeing a car approaching rapidly as we cross the road thinking about our plans for the evening causes us to feel anxious and to take evasive action.

## Functional approaches

In spite of the arguments discussed above, the dominant view nowadays (dating back to Aristotle) is that emotions are useful, and serve valuable functions. For example, Eysenck (1992, p. 4) considered possible functions of anxiety:

*It is clear that rapid detection of the early warning signs of danger possesses considerable survival value … The key purpose or function of anxiety is probably to facilitate the detection of danger or threat in potentially threatening environments.*

In line with that analysis, there is a considerable amount of evidence that anxious individuals selectively attend to threat-related stimuli to a greater extent than do non-anxious ones (see Eysenck, 1997, for a review).

The physiological activity associated with emotional states can also be regarded as functional. As Levenson (1999, p. 492) argued, "Anger and fear can increase cardiovascular levels far beyond those thought to be optimal for the organism's long-term survival, but which are optimal for the short-term needs of actively dealing with threatening environmental challenges." Relevant evidence concerning the usefulness of the physiological stress response is discussed later in the chapter.

Oatley and Johnson-Laird (1987) put forward an influential functional theory, according to which there are five basic emotions. Each of these emotions occurs at a key juncture with respect to a current goal or plan:

1. *Happiness.* Progress has been made on a current goal.
2. *Anxiety.* The goal of self-preservation is threatened.
3. *Sadness.* The current goal cannot be achieved.
4. *Anger.* The current goal is frustrated or blocked.
5. *Disgust.* A gustatory [taste] goal is violated.

According to Oatley and Johnson-Laird (1987), emotions serve the crucial function of influencing individuals to pursue whatever goal has the greatest survival or other value in the current situation. Thus, for example, happiness encourages the individual to continue with the current goal. In contrast, sadness leads people to abandon their current (unachievable) goal, and to conserve their energy so that they can subsequently pursue an alternative goal. Anxiety motivates individuals to deal with threats to the achievement of some important goal.

What are the limitations of the above theoretical account? Levenson (1999, p. 493) pointed out, "Most theoretical accounts of emotion take a 'one-size-fits-all' approach, providing an overarching model that, by implication, accounts for all emotions. However, this often leads to models that fit some emotions well and others quite poorly." Most functional theories of emotion fit negative emotions better than positive ones. Negative emotions lead individuals to change goals, and are accompanied by bodily changes making it easier to attain those new goals. In contrast, positive emotions such as happiness or

Frank Sinatra in *Tony Rome*. Danger causes anxiety, which produces an adrenaline rush. This is adaptive as it enables the person to react quickly to avoid the danger.

*Why might increased cardiovascular activity be a) useful in the short-term, and b) problematic in the long-term?*

**Idleness**

Clough and Sewell's (2000) research supports the Fredrickson and Levenson argument, as they found that inactivity promotes positive emotions in a study comparing people who chose to exercise or play sport regularly with others who chose physically inactive pastimes such as chess or other board games. The latter group were in a more positive mood than the former, and unlike the former this did not depend on how well they had performed. This was a self-report diary study of 50 students.

contentment do not lead to a change of goal, and often fail to produce changes in autonomic activity (see Levenson, 1999).

What functions, then, are served by positive emotions? Positive emotions are often associated with high levels of arousal, but Fredrickson and Levenson (1998) argued that such emotions sometimes reduce the high levels of arousal associated with negative emotions. In their study, they measured how long it took for participants' cardiovascular arousal to return to normal after exposure to a threatening stimulus. As predicted, this happened fastest when the threatening stimulus was followed by a stimulus producing contentment or amusement.

## Summary

In spite of strong reasons for assuming that most (or all) emotions serve a useful function, emotions can be disruptive and unpleasant. Is it possible to reconcile these apparently conflicting facts? Levenson (1999, p. 496) made an interesting attempt to do precisely that: "Viewed from the perspective of what we were trying to accomplish prior to the emotion taking hold, the subsequent emotional behaviour may appear chaotic and *disorganised*. But, viewed from the perspective of the survival of the organism, the emotional behaviour represents an elegant, adaptive, and highly *organised* state of affairs."

## HOW MANY EMOTIONS ARE THERE?

The question, "How many emotions are there?", sounds easy. Unfortunately, there is little agreement on the answer, partly because the question is ambiguous and can be interpreted in two ways. First, it invites us to consider the number and nature of basic or fundamental emotions. Second, it suggests a focus on the total number of emotions that can be identified, even though many of them may be complex emotions derived from the basic emotions. In either case, a complicating factor is that the boundary between one emotion and another is often fuzzy: There are occasions when we find it hard to decide precisely which emotion we are experiencing!

We will consider only the basic emotions, and will do so initially from the perspective of research on facial expressions and on self-report questionnaires (research based on brain mechanisms is discussed later). Why are we starting with facial expressions? The main reason is that we all display numerous facial expressions, and it is a reasonable assumption that each of our basic emotions is associated with its own distinctive expression. Another reason is that it provides a manageable way of discussing a complex and confusing topic. Note that emotions revolving around sexual behaviour (e.g., jealousy) are discussed in Chapter 2.

## Facial expressions

*Before reading on, think about the facial expressions that you would associate with particular emotions in other people. How many different ones can you distinguish?*

The American psychologist, Paul Ekman, has probably carried out the most research into the psychological significance of facial expressions. His research (coupled with that of other investigators) indicates that a small number of emotions can be identified from facial expressions. Ekman, Friesen, and Ellsworth (1972) reviewed the literature, and concluded that observers can detect the following six emotions in faces: happiness, surprise, anger, sadness, fear, and disgust combined with contempt.

Nearly all the studies reviewed by Ekman et al. (1972) were carried out in Western societies. It was thus unclear whether the relationships between facial expressions and the emotions they conveyed were universal and would be found in all cultures. If the findings are universal, this would strengthen the argument that happiness, surprise, anger, sadness, fear, and disgust are basic emotions. The required study was carried out by Ekman et al. (1987) in cross-cultural research involving participants from 10 countries (Estonia, Germany,

Facial expressions associated with emotion are generally recognised across cultures, suggesting that the expressive aspect of emotion is innate.

Greece, Hong Kong, Italy, Japan, Scotland, Sumatra, Turkey, and the United States). These participants judged 18 photographs of faces in terms of the emotion displayed. The findings were clearcut. As Ekman et al. (p. 712) concluded, "Agreement was very high across cultures about which emotion was the most intense. The 10 cultures also agreed about the second most intense emotion signalled by an expression."

It could be argued that the high level of cross-cultural agreement on the emotions associated with facial expressions occurs because nearly all cultures are exposed to Western ideas. However, Ekman and Friesen (1971) reported some evidence against that argument in a study on the South Fore in Papua New Guinea. This group used stone tools, and had had no exposure at all to Western media. In spite of that, the South Fore identified the same emotions on faces as had members of numerous Western cultures.

Much research on facial expressions is rather narrow and artificial. What often happens in such research is that people follow instructions about which muscles to contract to produce the facial expressions characteristic of various emotions. When they have succeeded, photographs are taken and presented to observers. Apart from its artificiality, this type of research is limited because it ignores two of the three main components of emotion (i.e., autonomic changes, subjective feeling state).

*What are the limitations of using photographs in studies of emotional expression?*

The above issues were addressed by Levenson, Ekman, and Friesen (1990). Their participants moved their facial muscles to produce certain expressions without being told what emotion was supposed to be associated with each expression. Various psychophysiological measures (e.g., heart rate, skin conductance, finger temperature) were recorded. There were three key findings. First, participants generally reported experiencing the predicted emotional states associated with the various facial expressions. Second, the facial expressions produced significant changes in autonomic activity. Third, the pattern of autonomic changes varied from emotion to emotion. For example, disgust and surprise produced smaller increases in heart rate than did anger, fear, sadness, or happiness, and fear was the only emotion associated with a reduction in finger temperature. Overall, the findings indicated that voluntarily producing various facial expressions generates genuine emotions in which all three emotion components (expression, autonomic changes, subjective feeling state) are present.

There is a final issue concerning facial expressions. It would be unwise to assume there is a *direct* relationship between emotional experience and facial expression. This is so in part because facial expressions are designed to communicate in social situations as well as to reflect underlying emotional states. For example, Gilbert et al. (1987) considered facial responses to odours. There were many more facial responses when the participants were in a social setting than when they were on their own.

## Evaluation

⊕ Facial expressions provide valuable observable information concerning the emotional experience of other people.

⊕ There is good consistency in interpretation of facial expressions across several cultures.

⊖ Most research has involved the use of posed facial expressions. It is actually surprisingly difficult to identify emotions other than happiness from spontaneous facial expressions of emotion (Wagner, MacDonald, & Manstead, 1986).

⊖ Some cross-cultural differences are not apparent when participants indicate the emotions shown on faces by choosing from a list provided by the experimenter. For example, Boucher and Carlson (1980) allowed their participants to describe facial emotions in their own words. Individuals from the United States, Malaysia, and the Temuans (an aboriginal Malaysian group) didn't describe the expressions in identical ways.

⊖ As Ekman (1993) admitted, there seem to be emotions lacking clear corresponding facial expressions (e.g., guilt, shame, awe), and the same facial expression can underlie various emotions (e.g., smile underlying different positive emotions).

## Self-report approach

We have seen that there is good evidence for the existence of six basic emotions from studies on facial expression. Another major approach to assessing emotions or moods is via self-report inventories. Such inventories typically consist of numerous adjectives (e.g., sad, lonely, happy, nervous, irritable), and the participants indicate which of the adjectives describe their feelings "right now" or "at this moment".

What happens when we try to identify basic emotions or moods in the way described above? There are numerous self-report inventories designed to assess several emotional states. For example, consider the Positive and Negative Affect Schedule (PANAS-X; Watson & Clark, 1994). This inventory contains 11 different scales (fear, sadness, hostility, guilt, shyness, fatigue, surprise, joviality, self-assurance, attentiveness, and serenity). Another well-known self-report inventory is the Profile of Mood States (POMS; McNair, Lorr, & Droppelman, 1971). This inventory provides measures of six different mood states.

One of the problems with most of these self-report inventories is that the scales assessing the various mood states correlate highly with each other. For example, many of the scales of the POMS correlate +.60 or more with other scales. Thus, some scales are measuring rather similar mood states, even though different names have been attached to them.

Watson and Tellegen (1985) and Watson and Clark (1992) argued that the evidence was consistent with a hierarchical model. In this model, there are several correlated (but distinguishable) emotional states at the lower level. At the upper level, there are two broad and independent factors called Negative Affect and Positive Affect. All emotional or mood states can be related to the two-dimensional structure formed by Negative and Positive Affect. Watson and Clark (p. 490) described the hierarchical model as follows: "The lower level reflects the specific *content* of the mood descriptors (i.e., the distinctive qualities of the individual discrete affects), whereas the upper level reflects their *valence* (i.e., whether they represent negative or positive states)."

It is possible to obtain a clearer idea of what the higher level of the model is like by reference to the figure on page 149. The dimension of Negative Affect is characterised by adjectives such as "fearful" and "nervous" at high levels and by "calm" and "relaxed" at low levels. In contrast, Positive Affect is characterised by "elated" and "excited" at high levels and by "dull" and "drowsy" at low levels. Then there are more specific emotions or mood states at the lower level of the hierarchy.

### Self-report research

The greatest problem with self-report data is obvious—it is probably impossible to know how accurate or truthful these data are. We are all influenced by social norms and expectations, we don't want to be seen as socially undesirable, and we all have personal secrets. However, for some research, such as the study of emotions, self-reported data are unavoidable.

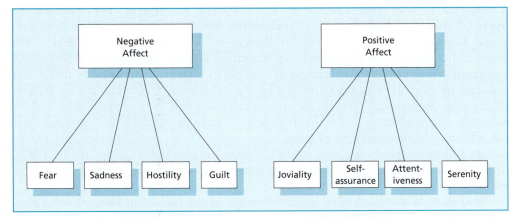

A two-level hierarchical model of emotion. Based on Watson and Clark (1992).

You probably find it hard to think of positive and negative affect as being *independent* of each other rather than as simple *opposites*. Russell (e.g., Feldman Barrett & Russell, 1998) proposed a two-dimensional model of emotion, which seems more in line with our intuitions. According to this model, there are two independent dimensions: (1) pleasure–misery; and (2) arousal–sleep. The first dimension concerns the type of emotional experience (i.e., pleasurable or displeasurable) and the second dimension concerns the intensity of the experience. While this model seems rather different from the one put forward by Watson and Tellegen (1985), it is actually remarkably similar. The similarities can be seen in the figure on the right. In addition, detailed analyses of findings using emotion questionnaires have indicated clearly that these two theoretical models are alternative descriptions of the same two-dimensional space (Russell & Feldman Barrett, 1999).

The two-dimensional framework for emotion showing the two dimensions of pleasure–misery and arousal–sleep (Feldman Barrett & Russell, 1998) and the two dimensions of Positive Affect and Negative Affect (Watson & Tellegen, 1985). Based on Feldman Barrett and Russell (1998).

## Evidence

Is it possible to fit emotional or mood states into a hierarchical structure? Positive evidence was reported by Watson and Tellegen (1985). What they did was to work out the extent to which the data from several major self-report inventories could be accounted for in terms of the unrelated or independent dimensions of Negative Affect and Positive Affect. Factor analyses revealed that all the inventories studied measured these two broad dimensions. About 50–65% of the variance in the data from these inventories could be accounted for in terms of Negative Affect and Positive Affect.

Watson and Clark (1992) tested the hierarchical model more systematically. They considered the higher-level dimension of Negative Affect and four of the lower-level emotions or moods associated with Negative Affect: fear, sadness, hostility, and guilt. According to the model, scales for each of the four negative emotions should be measuring two things: (1) the specific mood in question; (2) the broader dimension of Negative Affect. The findings of Watson and Clark confirmed this prediction. Each scale was in part assessing the specific mood it was designed to measure. In addition, all four scales correlated moderately (about +.60) with each other, because they all contributed to the higher-order Negative Affect dimension.

Watson, Wiese, Vaidya, and Tellegen (1999) discussed other kinds of evidence supporting the notion that Positive and Negative Affect are independent of each other. First, there are separate physiological systems associated with approach and withdrawal.

Various names have been attached to these systems, but Fowles (1987) termed the approach system the behavioural activation system and the withdrawal system the behavioural inhibition system. According to Watson et al. (1999), Positive Affect is the emotional component of the behavioural activation system, and Negative Affect is the emotional component of the behavioural inhibition system. Supporting evidence was reported by Gray (1982), who argued that the behavioural inhibition system consists of the septo-hippocampal system, its neocortical projection in the frontal lobe, and its monoaminergic afferents from the brainstem. Extensive research has revealed that the effects of lesions (removal of parts of the brain) to the septo-hippocampal system in rats and other species are very similar to those of anti-anxiety drugs (Gray, 1982). This indicates that the septo-hippocampal system is crucial to the negative emotion of anxiety.

*Why is it difficult to carry out research on emotions using animals?*

Second, as is discussed later, the involvement of the two brain hemispheres differs between Positive Affect and Negative Affect. More specifically, "happy ... individuals tend to show relatively greater resting activity in the left prefrontal cortex than in the right prefrontal area; conversely, ... dissatisfied individuals display relatively greater right anterior activity" (Watson et al., 1999, p. 830).

Third, the daily or circadian rhythms for Positive Affect and for Negative Affect are very different (Watson et al., 1999). The level of Positive Affect typically rises during the morning, remains at a fairly high level until the evening, and then decreases during the evening. In contrast, Negative Affect shows practically no consistent changes throughout the day. This probably happens because we experience Negative Affect mainly in response to threats, and threats can occur unpredictably at any point during the day.

Are the dimensions of Positive Affect and Negative Affect independent of each other (as is implied by the model) when individuals complete self-report inventories? This issue is more complicated than might be imagined (see Russell & Carroll, 1999), because the size of the correlation depends on *what* is measured and *how* it is measured. However, many reported correlations between the two dimensions are fairly similar. Green, Goldman, and Salovey (1993) reported a correlation of –.58, whereas Tellegen, Watson, and Clark (1999) reported a correlation of –.43. These fairly strong negative correlations have sometimes been regarded as showing the limitations of Watson and Tellegen's (1985) two-dimensional model.

In sum, Negative Affect and Positive Affect probably involve separate physiological systems. However, most situations produce mainly Positive Affect or Negative Affect (e.g., a party or an examination failure, respectively). As a result, Positive and Negative Affect tend to be negatively related to each other at any given moment in time.

## Evaluation

⊕ Self-report evidence suggests that most affects or moods are closely related either to Positive Affect or to Negative Affect.

⊕ The two-level hierarchical model accounts for most of the relevant self-report data.

⊕ There is reasonable evidence for separate brain systems underlying Positive and Negative Affect.

⊖ The typical finding that the level of Positive Affect is moderately negatively correlated with the level of Negative Affect has not been fully explained by those arguing that Positive and Negative Affect are independent dimensions.

⊖ The entire self-report approach is limited because of its reliance on language. For example, there are more than 500 categories describing emotions in English, about 50 in Ifaluk, and about 7 in Chewong (Russell & Feldman Barrett, 1999). Thus, there are likely to be important (but almost unexplored) differences in emotion categories across different languages and cultures.

⊖ The model relies heavily on self-report data, and has not been shown to account for other kinds of data (e.g., facial expressions, physiological measures of emotion).

## Cultural differences

We have seen there is some evidence that the main emotions are rather similar across diverse cultures (e.g., Ekman et al., 1987). However, there are nevertheless important differences between individualistic (emphasis on individual responsibility) and collectivistic cultures (emphasis on the group) in the area of emotion (see Chapter 1 for a discussion of individualism–collectivism). For example, Eid and Diener (2001) studied participants from two individualistic cultures (Australia, United States) and two collectivistic cultures (China, Taiwan). With respect to positive emotions, 83% of Australian and American participants regarded them as desirable and appropriate, compared to only 9% of Chinese and 32% of Taiwanese participants. With respect to negative emotions, about 40% of Australian, American, and Taiwanese participants regarded them as desirable and appropriate, compared to only 14% of Chinese participants.

Eid and Diener (2001) found their Chinese participants reported the lowest frequency and intensity of both positive and negative emotional states. This is consistent with the typical Chinese view that emotions are dangerous and irrelevant, and can cause illness. However, these findings seem inconsistent with my own experience. In 1994, I went to a conference in Xian, and was surprised to hear almost continuous gales of laughter during meals. Perhaps the most important findings obtained by Eid and Diener related to the emotions of pride and guilt. People typically experience pride as a result of personal achievement, whereas guilt is associated with failure to conform to social norms. Thus, pride should be regarded as more desirable than guilt in individualistic cultures, but guilt should be deemed more desirable than pride in collectivistic cultures. That is precisely what Eid and Diener found.

Mesquita (2001) obtained further information on differences in emotions between individualistic (Dutch) and collectivistic (Turkish and Surinamese) cultures. Individualistic participants generally regarded their emotions as reflecting their own inner world, whereas collectivistic participants were more likely to regard their emotions as reflecting a social reality. The content of emotions also differed between the two groups: "Collectivist emotions emerged as relational phenomena, embedded in relationships with others and perceived to reflect the state of those relationships. Individualist emotions … refer much less to the social environment" (p. 72).

*What do these cultural differences imply about the nature/origins of emotional expression?*

## THEORIES OF EMOTION

Numerous theories of emotion have been put forward over the years. They differ considerably from one another, in part because of the different aims of the various theorists. Some have viewed emotion mainly from a physiological perspective, whereas others emphasise the cognitive processes associated with emotion. Still other theorists have tried to provide an overall account of the relationships among the cognitive, physiological, and behavioural systems. Our coverage starts with a consideration of some theories of historical importance, followed by more contemporary theories.

## James–Lange theory

The first major theory of emotion was put forward independently by William James in the United States and by Carl Lange in Denmark in the mid-1880s. For obvious reasons, it came to be known as the James–Lange theory. According to this theory, the following successive stages are involved in producing emotion:

1. There is an emotional stimulus (e.g., a car comes rapidly towards you as you are crossing the road).
2. This produces bodily changes (e.g., arousal in the autonomic nervous system).
3. Feedback from the bodily changes leads to the experience of emotion (e.g., fear or anxiety).

The essence of this approach was expressed by James (1890, p. 451): "If we fancy some strong emotion, and then try to abstract from our consciousness of it all the feelings

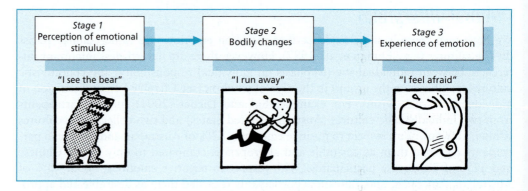

| Stage 1 Perception of emotional stimulus | Stage 2 Bodily changes | Stage 3 Experience of emotion |
| "I see the bear" | "I run away" | "I feel afraid" |

of its bodily symptoms, we find we have nothing left behind." In other words, our emotions are essentially our experience of our bodily symptoms. James gave the following example of the predicted sequence of events according to the theory: "I see a bear, I run away, I feel afraid." This runs counter to the more commonsensical sequence: "I see a bear, I feel afraid, I run away."

## Evidence

Hohmann (1966) reported findings supporting the James–Lange theory. He studied 25 paralysed patients who had suffered damage to the spinal cord, and who as a consequence had greatly restricted awareness of their own physiological arousal. Those patients with the least ability to experience arousal showed a large reduction in their emotional experiences of anger, grief, and sexual excitement. In the words of one patient, "Sometimes I act angry when I see some injustice. I yell and cuss and raise hell … but it just doesn't have the heat to it that it used to. It's a kind of mental anger."

Subsequent research has generally *not* confirmed the findings of Hohmann (1966). For example, Bermond, Nieuwenhuyse, Fasotti, and Schwerman (1991) found most of their patients with spinal damage reported *increased* intensity of emotions. They even reported that the bodily symptoms of emotion were as great as before they were injured. These findings suggest feedback from bodily changes is *not* needed for emotion to be experienced.

One of the main assumptions within the James–Lange theory is that every emotion is associated with its own specific pattern of physiological activity. As we saw earlier, there is some evidence that various emotions do differ from each other in the pattern of autonomic activity (e.g., Levenson et al., 1990). However, as Dalgleish (1998, pp. 466–467) pointed out, "although some emotions may be distinguished on the basis of their physiological characteristics, it is clearly not the case that every nuance of emotion is physiologically distinct from every other".

## Evaluation

⊕ Physiological changes often influence the subjective experience of emotion.
⊖ Feedback from bodily changes is *not* necessary in order for emotions to be experienced (e.g., Bermond et al., 1991).
⊖ Physiological changes do not differ sufficiently from one emotion to another to provide the sole basis for experiencing a wide range of emotions.
⊖ The James–Lange theory provides a very limited account of emotion. It is uninformative about the cognitive processes intervening between the presentation of an emotional stimulus and the onset of physiological changes.

# Arousal–interpretation theory

One of the best-known approaches to emotion is the arousal–interpretation theory of Schachter and Singer (1962). It can be said to have started the modern era in emotion research with its emphasis on cognitive factors. Schachter and Singer's main assumption was that there are two factors, both of which are essential for emotions to be experienced:

1. High physiological arousal.
2. An emotional interpretation of that arousal.

They argued that very similar states of physiological arousal are associated with each of the emotions. We experience fear, anger, or whatever other emotion because of the specific way in which the arousal is interpreted.

## *Evidence*

One of the main predictions of arousal–interpretation theory is that no emotion will be experienced if *either* high physiological arousal *or* an emotional interpretation is absent. A study by Marañón (1924) supports that prediction. The participants were injected with adrenaline, a drug whose effects resemble those of a naturally occurring state of arousal. When asked how they felt, 71% simply reported their physical symptoms with no emotional experience. Most of the remaining participants reported "as if" emotions, i.e., emotions lacking their normal intensity. Why did almost none of the participants report true emotions? They perceived their state of arousal as having been produced by the drug, and so did not interpret it as indicating an emotional state.

Schachter and Singer (1962) carried out an expanded version of Marañón's (1924) study—see the Key Study below.

## Schachter and Singer: Suproxin

All of Schachter and Singer's participants were told the study was designed to test the effects of the vitamin compound "Suproxin" on vision. In fact, they were injected with adrenaline (to produce arousal) or a salt-based solution having no effect on arousal. Some of those given adrenaline were correctly informed about the effects of the drug. Others were misinformed or uninformed (being told simply that the injection was mild and would have no side effects). After the injection, the participants were put in a situation designed to produce either euphoria (joy) or anger. This was done by putting them in the same room as someone who acted joyfully (making paper planes and playing paper basketball) or angrily (reacting to a very personal questionnaire).

Which groups were the most emotional? It should have been those groups that were given adrenaline (and so were very aroused), but would not interpret the arousal as having been produced by the drug. Thus, it was predicted that the misinformed and uninformed groups given adrenaline should have been the most emotional. The participants' emotional states were assessed by judges and by self-reports. The findings broadly supported the predictions, but some effects were rather small and non-significant.

### Discussion points

1. How does the approach adopted by Schachter and Singer differ from those of previous theorists?
2. What are the weaknesses with this research and this theoretical approach?

### KEY STUDY EVALUATION—Schachter and Singer

For such a classic study, it is surprising how inadequately it was carried out. Here are just a few of the problems. First, physiological arousal was assessed only by means of pulse rate, which is a poor single measure to use. Second, the judges who rated emotion knew which condition the participants were in, and this may have biased their ratings. Third, the judges didn't use a standardised coding system for recording the participants' behaviour.

One of the reasons why the study by Schachter and Singer (1962) didn't produce convincing findings may have been because those given the salt-based solution became physiologically aroused by being put into an emotional situation. If so, they would have had the high arousal *and* emotional interpretation, which together produce a strong emotional state. Schachter and Wheeler (1962) argued that the way to stop people becoming aroused was to give them a depressant drug to reduce arousal. The participants were given a depressant, or adrenaline, or a substance having no effects, and were told in each case that the drug had no side effects. They then watched a slapstick film called *The Good Humour Man*. As predicted, those given adrenaline (and thus aroused) found the film the funniest, whereas those given the depressant (and thus de-aroused) found it least funny.

*Schachter and Singer also failed to take baseline measures of participants' mood before they gave them injections. How might this have affected results?*

It has proved difficult to repeat the findings of Schachter and Singer (1962). For example, Marshall and Zimbardo (1979) found large doses of adrenaline reduced (rather than increased) their participants' happiness in the euphoria or joy condition. They suggested that people may interpret high levels of unexpected arousal as signalling a negative state of affairs. Similar findings were reported by Mezzacappa, Katkin, and Palmer (1999), in a study in which participants watched film clips known to produce anger, fear, or amusement. Participants given adrenaline (but misinformed about its effects) expressed increased fear to the fear films. More importantly, they did not show increased anger to the anger films or increased amusement to the amusement films. The failure of high physiological arousal created by adrenaline to increase either anger or amusement is inconsistent with Schachter and Singer's (1962) theory. According to that theory, adrenaline produces a neutral arousal state, and thus will enhance *any* emotional state created by external stimuli.

## Evaluation

⊕ The two factors emphasised within arousal–interpretation theory (arousal, emotional interpretation) both influence the nature and intensity of emotional experience.
⊕ The theory was one of the first in which the role of cognitive processes was properly recognised.
⊖ Different emotions are often associated with different patterns of physiological arousal (e.g., Levenson et al., 1990), which is contrary to the theory.
⊖ The theory has received only weak support from the studies designed to test it. High arousal tends to be interpreted negatively regardless of the situation, which should not be the case.
⊖ Schachter and Singer (1962) focused on very artificial situations in which high levels of arousal are hard to interpret. The relevance of such situations to typical everyday situations is unclear.

## Cognitive theories

Suppose a stimulus (e.g., a spider) is presented to someone, as a result of which his/her affective response to that stimulus changes. Is it essential for the stimulus to be processed cognitively for the changed affective response to occur? This issue is of theoretical importance. If affective responses to all stimuli depend on cognitive processing, theories of emotion should have a distinctly cognitive flavour. In contrast, if cognitive processing is *not* necessary in the development of affective responses to stimuli, then a specifically cognitive approach to emotion may be less necessary.

Zajonc (1980, 1984) argued that the affective evaluation of stimuli can occur independently of cognitive processes. According to Zajonc (1984, p. 117), "affect and cognition are separate and partially independent systems and … although they ordinarily function conjointly, affect could be generated without a prior cognitive process." In contrast, Lazarus (1982, p. 1021) claimed some cognitive processing is an essential prerequisite for an affective reaction to a stimulus to occur: "Cognitive appraisal (of meaning or significance) underlies and is an integral feature of all emotional states."

Zajonc (1980) claimed in his affective primacy hypothesis that we often make affective judgements about people and objects even though we have processed very little information about them. He discussed several studies supporting the notion of affective primacy. In these studies, stimuli such as melodies or pictures were presented either very briefly below the level of conscious awareness or while the participant was involved in a task. Even though these stimuli could not subsequently be recognised, participants were still more likely to choose previously presented stimuli than comparable new ones when asked to select the ones they preferred. Thus, there was a positive affective reaction to the previously presented stimuli (as assessed by their preference judgements), but no evidence of cognitive processing (as assessed by recognition-memory performance). This phenomenon is known as the **mere exposure effect.**

Studies on the mere exposure effect have little obvious relevance to ordinary emotional states. Participants make superficial preference judgements about fairly meaningless stimuli unrelated to their lives, and so only minimal affect is involved. Another major limitation is that the conclusion the stimuli are not processed cognitively is based on a failure of recognition memory. This may make sense if one equates cognition with conscious awareness, but the data do not rule out the possibility that there was extensive preconscious processing involving automatic and other processes. Murphy and Zajonc (1993, p. 724) have accepted the term "cognitive" can be used to refer to non-conscious processes: "We do not require either affect or cognition to be accessible to consciousness."

According to the affective primacy hypothesis, simple affective qualities of stimuli can be processed much faster than more cognitive ones. Murphy and Zajonc (1993) provided some support for this hypothesis in a series of priming studies. In these studies, a priming stimulus was presented for either 4 milliseconds or 1 second, and was followed by a second stimulus. In one study, the priming stimuli consisted of happy and angry faces, and there was a no-priming control condition. The priming stimuli were followed by Chinese ideographs which were given liking ratings. The liking ratings were influenced by the affective primes when presented for only 4 milliseconds, but not when presented for 1 second. Presumably participants in the latter condition realised their affective reaction was produced by the priming stimulus, and so that reaction did not influence their rating of the second stimulus.

In another study, Murphy and Zajonc required participants to make a cognitive judgement. Male or female priming faces were followed by Chinese ideographs, which were rated for femininity. These ratings were influenced by the priming faces when presented for 1 second, but not when presented for 4 milliseconds. The various findings obtained by Murphy and Zajonc suggest the following conclusions:

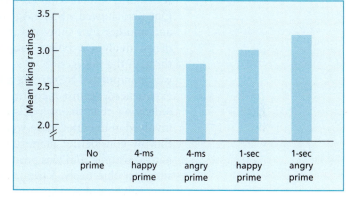

Liking ratings for Chinese ideographs following the presentation of a happy or angry priming stimulus for 4 ms or 1 second. Based on data in Murphy and Zajonc (1993).

1. Affective processing can sometimes occur faster than cognitive processing;
2. The initial affective processing of a stimulus is very different from the later cognitive processing.

## Conclusions

Zajonc (1980) and others have provided evidence that affective responses can occur in the absence of any conscious awareness of cognitive processing, and Lazarus (1982) does not dispute this. As Williams et al. (1997, p. 3) pointed out, "There would ... be fairly wide support for a reformulated version of Zajonc's thesis that emotion can be independent of *conscious* cognitive processes."

Several theorists have argued that this dispute between Zajonc and Lazarus is based on a false assumption. According to Power and Dalgleish (1997, p. 67), "The distinction presupposed in the Zajonc–Lazarus debate between cognition and emotion is a false one ... The 'emotion' and the 'cognition' are integral and inseparable parts of each other and though it is useful to use different names for different aspects of the generation of emotion, the parts are no more separable than are waves from the water on which they occur." This view may exaggerate the similarities between emotion and cognition.

### *Lazarus's appraisal theory*

Lazarus (1982, 1991) argued that **cognitive appraisal** plays a crucial role in emotional experience. Cognitive appraisal can be subdivided into three more specific forms of appraisal:

- *Primary appraisal.* An environmental situation is regarded as being positive, stressful, or irrelevant to well-being.

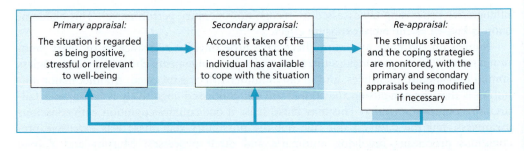

- *Secondary appraisal*. Account is taken of the resources that the individual has available to cope with the situation.
- *Re-appraisal*. The stimulus situation and coping strategies are monitored, with the primary and secondary appraisals being modified if necessary.

The importance of cognitive appraisal in determining emotional experience has been shown in several studies by Lazarus and his associates. For example, Speisman, Lazarus, Mordkoff, and Davison (1964) presented anxiety-evoking films under various conditions. One film showed a Stone Age ritual in which adolescent boys had their penises deeply cut, and another film showed various workshop accidents. The most dramatic of these accidents involves a board caught in a circular saw which rams with tremendous force through the midsection of a worker, who dies writhing on the floor. Cognitive appraisal was manipulated by varying the accompanying soundtrack, and then comparing the stress experienced against a control condition without a soundtrack. Denial was produced by indicating that the subincision film did not show a painful operation, or that those involved in the safety film were actors. Intellectualisation was produced in the subincision film by considering matters from the perspective of an anthropologist viewing strange native customs, and was produced in the workshop film by telling the viewer to consider the situation objectively. Various psychophysiological measures of arousal or stress (e.g., heart rate, galvanic skin response) were taken continuously during the viewing of the film.

Denial and intellectualisation both produced substantial reductions in stress as indexed by the psychophysiological measures. Thus, manipulating an individual's cognitive appraisal when confronted by a stressful event can have a significant impact on physiological stress reactions. However, it has not always proved easy to replicate these findings (e.g., Steptoe & Vogele, 1986).

Smith and Lazarus (1993) adopted a rather different approach. They argued there are six appraisal components, two of which involve primary appraisal and four of which involve secondary appraisal:

- *Primary*. Motivational relevance. (Related to personal commitments?)
- *Primary*. Motivational congruence. (Consistent with the individual's goals?)
- *Secondary*. Accountability. (Who deserves the credit or blame?)
- *Secondary*. Problem-focused coping potential. (Can the situation be resolved?)
- *Secondary*. Emotion-focused coping potential. (Can the situation be handled psychologically?)
- *Secondary*. Future expectancy. (How likely is it that the situation will change?)

Smith and Lazarus (1993) argued that different emotional states can be distinguished on the basis of which appraisal components are involved. Thus, for example, anger, guilt, anxiety, and sadness all possess the primary appraisal components of motivational relevance and motivational incongruence (these emotions only occur when goals are blocked), but differ in terms of secondary appraisal components. Guilt involves self-accountability, anxiety involves low or uncertain emotion-focused coping potential, and sadness involves low future expectancy for change.

Smith and Lazarus (1993) used scenarios in which the participants were told to identify with the central character. In one scenario, the central character has performed poorly in an important course, and he appraises the situation. Other-accountability was produced by having him put the blame on the unhelpful teaching assistants; self-accountability was produced by having him accept he made a lot of mistakes (e.g., doing work at the last minute); low emotion-focused coping potential was produced by thinking there was a great danger he would finish with a poor academic record; and low future expectancy for change was produced by having him think it was impossible to succeed with his chosen academic path. The appraisal manipulations generally had the predicted effects on the emotional states reported by the participants, indicating there are close links between appraisal on the one hand and experienced emotion on the other hand.

Lazarus (e.g., 1982) has argued consistently that cognitive appraisal always precedes any affective reaction, but that such appraisal may not be at the conscious level. There is convincing evidence (e.g., Ohman & Soares, 1994, discussed later in the chapter) that emotional reactions can be produced without the intervention of conscious processing. However, there are doubts whether such automatic processing can plausibly be said to involve appraisal processes.

*Can you write another scenario that shows different aspects of the six appraisal components?*

## Evaluation

⊕ Appraisal processes are important in determining our emotional reactions to stimuli.
⊕ Individual differences in cognitive appraisal of a given situation help to explain why individuals differ in their emotional reactions.
⊖ The notion of appraisal is rather broad and vague, making it hard to assess an individual's appraisals. For example, Lazarus (1991, p. 169) referred to two kinds of appraisal processes—"one that operates automatically without awareness or volitional control, and another that is conscious, deliberate, and volitional".
⊖ There are several problems of interpretation with studies such as the one by Speisman et al. (1964). In essence, the soundtrack manipulations may not have had a direct impact on the appraisal process (Parkinson & Manstead, 1992). Changing the soundtrack changed the stimulus information presented to the participants, and different soundtracks may have influenced the direction of attention rather than the interpretive process itself.
⊖ Lazarus's approach represents a rather limited view of emotion: "Appraisal theory has taken the paradigm [model] of emotional experience as an individual passive subject confronting a survival-threatening stimulus" (Parkinson & Manstead, 1992, p. 146). Thus, Lazarus's approach de-emphasises the social context in which emotion is normally experienced.

## Parkinson: Four-factor theory

The major theories of emotion we have considered are often thought of as being in competition with each other. However, it is probably preferable to combine elements of previous theories to produce a synthesis, as was done by Parkinson (1994) in his four-factor theory (subsequently developed by Eysenck, 1997). According to this theory, emotional experience depends on four separate factors:

1. *Appraisal of some external stimulus or situation*. This is the most important factor, and was the one emphasised by Lazarus (1982, 1991).
2. *Reactions of the body (e.g., arousal)*. This is the factor emphasised in the James–Lange theory.
3. *Facial expression*. The importance of this factor was shown in a study by Strack, Martin, and Stepper (1988) in which participants were more amused by cartoons when adopting a facial expression close to a smile than when having an expression resembling a frown.
4. *Action tendencies*. For example, preparing to advance in a threatening way is associated with anger, whereas preparing to retreat is associated with fear (Frijda, Kuipers, & ter Schure, 1989).

These four factors are not independent of each other. Cognitive appraisal of the situation affects bodily reactions, facial expression, and action tendencies, as well as having a direct

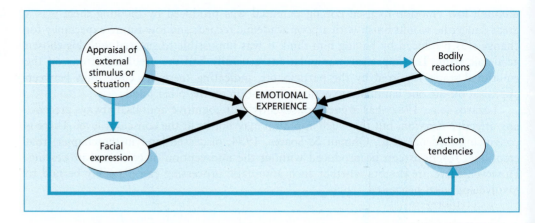

effect on emotional experience. Thus, cognitive appraisal is probably the most important of the four factors.

## Power and Dalgleish: SPAARS

There is growing support for the notion that emotions can be created in various ways involving different processes. Theories based on this notion are sometimes called multi-level theories. Why are multi-level theories preferable to single-level theories such as those we have been discussing? As Teasdale (1999, p. 667) pointed out, "Within mainstream cognitive psychology, a multi-level approach is normative [standard]. Accordingly, it is prudent to assume a multi-level approach if we wish to integrate cognition–emotion relations into any more comprehensive view." Thus, the cognitive system is so complex it is unlikely that a single-level approach can do justice to its complexity.

One of the most interesting multi-level theories was put forward by Power and Dalgleish (1997) in their Schematic Propositional Associative and Analogical Representational Systems (SPAARS) approach. The various components of the model are as follows (see also figure on p. 159):

- *Analogical system.* This is involved in basic sensory processing of environmental stimuli.
- *Propositional system.* This is an essentially emotion-free system that contains information about the world and about the self.
- *Schematic system.* Within this system, facts from the propositional system are combined with information about the individual's current goals to produce an internal model of the situation. This will lead to an emotional response if the current goals are being thwarted.
- *Associative system.* Its workings were described by Dalgleish (1998, p. 492): "If the same event is repeatedly processed in the same way at the schematic level, then an associative representation will be formed such that, on future encounters of the same event, the relevant emotion will be *automatically* elicited."

The SPAARS approach has some relevance to the Zajonc–Lazarus debate. According to Power and Dalgleish (1997), there are two main ways in which emotion can occur. First, it can occur as a result of thorough cognitive processing when the schematic system is involved. Second, it occurs automatically and without the involvement of conscious processing when the associative system is involved.

How does the schematic system decide on the appropriate emotion in a given situation? Power and Dalgleish (1997) relied on an earlier theory of Oatley and Johnson-Laird (1987), discussed earlier in the chapter. According to this theory, there are five basic emotions, each of which occurs at a key juncture with respect to a current goal or plan. Within the SPAARS model, information about an individual's current goals is processed within the schematic system, and this helps to determine the emotion experienced.

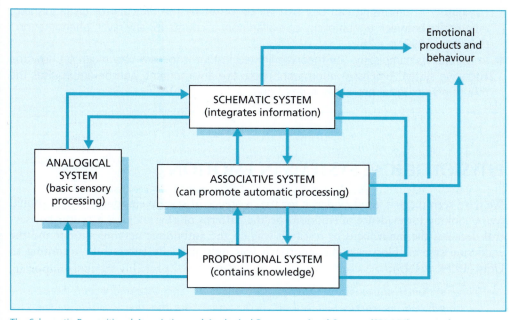

*Which type of processes are not mentioned by this model?*

The Schematic Propositional Associative and Analogical Representational Systems (SPAARS) approach put forward by Power and Dalgleish (1997).

## Evidence

There is a considerable body of research indicating that multi-level theories such as that of Power and Dalgleish (1997) are on the right lines. A key prediction is that there can be emotional processing at one level of the cognitive system combined with a lack of such processing at other levels. For example, individuals with spider phobia become very frightened when they see a spider even though they may "know" that most spiders are harmless (Dalgleish, 1998). This can be explained by assuming that fear is generated automatically by the associative system, whereas conflicting knowledge that the great majority of spiders are harmless comes from the propositional system.

   Is it possible for emotions to be produced automatically and below the level of conscious awareness? According to the SPAARS model, the answer is "Yes", because stimuli could be processed automatically at the associative level without involving the propositional or schematic model levels. Supporting evidence was reported by Ohman and Soares (1994). They presented snake and spider phobics with pictures of snakes, spiders, flowers, and mushrooms; the pictures were presented very rapidly so they could not be identified. In spite of this fact the spider phobics reacted emotionally to the spider pictures, as did the snake phobics to the snake pictures. There were greater physiological responses (in the form of skin conductance responses) to the phobia-relevant pictures. In addition, the participants experienced more arousal and felt more negative when exposed to those pictures rather than to the other pictures.

## Evaluation

⊕ Multi-level theories of emotion such as that of Power and Dalgleish (1997) provide explanations for emotional conflict.
⊕ There is good evidence (e.g., Ohman & Soares, 1994) that emotions can be produced automatically at the associative level without involving conscious processing. Some of the mechanisms involved in rapid, automatic emotional processing have been identified by LeDoux (1992, 1996), and are discussed shortly.
⊖ "The richness of multi-level theories … allows us to do justice to the observed variations in the ways that emotion can be elicited … However, … the advantages that such

complexity in theorising can buy us may be offset by the difficulty of distinguishing, empirically, between a multiplicity of explanatory accounts for any given phenomenon" (Teasdale, 1999, p. 675).

● In spite of its complexity, the theory is limited in that it focuses very much on how the cognitive system processes information from the environment, and de-emphasises the role of physiological processes in emotion.

## PHYSIOLOGICAL SYSTEMS IN EMOTION

We have seen there is good evidence for the existence of several emotions. Where should we be looking for evidence of emotion-specific patterns of physiological activity? For several decades, the main focus of research was on the autonomic nervous system and the endocrine system. However, this approach was only partially successful. According to Gray (1994, p. 243):

> These systems [autonomic and endocrine] are concerned essentially with house-keeping functions, energy metabolism, tissue repair, and the like. It would be surprising if these functions bore any specific relation to particular emotional states, since energy requirements, for example, are likely to be the same whenever an animal undertakes vigorous action, whatever the emotional significance of the action.

Nevertheless, a full understanding of emotion clearly requires consideration of the role played by the autonomic nervous system and the endocrine system (see Chapter 2).

Researchers focused on the autonomic and endocrine systems because it was relatively easy to study them, and to observe the changes in them during various emotional states. They also focused on these systems because they are involved in emotion. However, the brain is of particular importance in understanding emotion. As Panksepp (1994, p. 258) argued, "The clearest physiological distinctions between emotions will be found among the circuits of the brain." Researchers in the past did not devote much attention to the brain, because it was extremely hard to do so. However, the situation is changing rapidly.

*Why was it previously difficult to carry out research on the brain? Which currently available techniques have changed this?*

Panksepp (2000, p. 143) pursued the notion that the brain is of crucial importance in distinguishing among emotions. He argued that our main emotions are based on "a set of circuits situated in intermediate areas of the brain linking higher limbic zones for cingulate, frontal, and temporal cortices with midbrain emotion integrator zones such as the periaqueductal gray". Panksepp identified seven basic emotional systems centred on the brain:

- Seeking/expectancy.
- Rage/anger.
- Fear/anxiety.
- Lust/sexuality.
- Care/nurturance.
- Panic/separation.
- Play/joy.

We can compare the above list to the one proposed by Ekman et al. (1972; discussed above) on the basis of facial expressions. The good news is that three of the emotions identified by Ekman et al., namely, anger, fear, and happiness, are very similar to those identified by Panksepp (2000). The bad news is that there is otherwise practically no overlap! Ekman et al. also identified surprise, sadness, and disgust, which are simply missing from Panksepp's list.

## Approaches

Three main approaches have been taken to understanding the role of the brain in emotion. First, there is the lesion method, in which the effects of brain damage on emotion are considered. For example, Damasio (1999) discussed a patient, EVR, who had brain damage in the orbito-frontal cortex caused by a tumour. EVR could make effective decisions when asking about hypothetical moral dilemmas, but he made irrational and poor decisions about his own life. According to Damasio's somatic marker hypothesis, we typically use "marker" signals from our emotions to guide our decision making (e.g., "It feels right"). EVR's frontal-lobe damage prevented him from using emotional information, and this impaired his personal decision making.

Second, there is the imaging method for examining the brain's involvement in emotion. Several imaging techniques can be used for this purpose (see the Introduction to the Cognitive Psychology part of this book). These techniques are being used increasingly to indicate the brain areas most active when individuals experience any given emotion.

Third, we can use drugs to stimulate (or reduce) activity in parts of the brain. The effects of these drugs on self-reported emotion and on behaviour can then be assessed. This approach has the disadvantage that many drugs increase (or decrease) activity levels in several regions of the brain. As a result, it can be hard to identify precisely the role of any brain area in changing the individual's emotional state.

> **CASE STUDY: *Phineas Gage***
>
> The link between brain damage and emotions was famously demonstrated in the case of Phineas Gage, who was working on the construction of a railway. On 13 September 1848, he had a terrible accident, in which an explosion caused a large iron rod to enter his skull close to his left eyebrow and to exit through the top of his head. The force of the explosion was such that the iron rod landed 30 metres away! Gage survived this accident, and eventually showed good physical recovery. However, the accident changed his personality, making him much more aggressive and irritable than before, and unable to make long-term plans. After his death, Gage's skull was kept in a museum at Harvard Medical School, and was re-examined by Damasio, Grabowski, Frank, Galaburda, and Damasio (1994) using neuroimaging techniques involving computer simulation. They concluded the brain damage Gage suffered was in both frontal lobes, especially the left orbito-frontal cortex.

## Papez–MacLean limbic model

One of the first systematic attempts to identify key brain systems involved in emotion was made by Papez (1937). He studied cases of rabies, a disease that typically produces high levels of aggression in those suffering from it. This increased aggression seemed to be associated with damage to the hippocampus. Papez combined this information with findings from studies of brain-damaged individuals to propose the **Papez circuit** as the basis of emotion. This circuit "forms a closed loop running from the hippocampus to the hypothalamus and from there to the anterior thalamus. The circuit continues via the cingulate gyrus and the entorhinal cortex back to the hippocampus" (McIlveen & Gross, 1996, p. 153).

MacLean (1949) emphasised the importance of the limbic system, which consists of various structures including the amygdala, the hippocampus, the septum, and the cingulate cortex. He developed the ideas of Papez into what became known as the Papez–MacLean

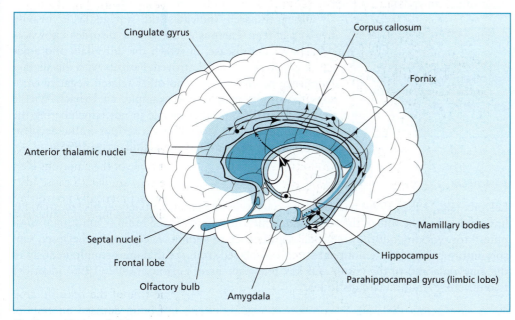

The Papez–MacLean limbic system.

> **KEY TERM**
>
> **Papez circuit:** a brain circuit or loop involved in emotion, based on the hypothalamus, hippocampus, and thalamus.

limbic model. This model differed from the original Papez circuit in that the role of the cingulate gyrus was reduced, and there was increased emphasis on the amygdala and the hippocampus. Part of the reason for this emphasis on the amygdala came from the work of Kluver and Bucy (1939). Monkeys with the anterior temporal lobe removed became less aggressive, showed little fear, tended to put objects in their mouths, and engaged in more sexual activity. This pattern of behaviour is known as the **Kluver–Bucy syndrome**. It depends mostly on damage to the amygdala, which lies within the temporal lobe. In humans, damage to the amygdala can occur through tumours or head injuries. Surprisingly, removal of the amygdala sometimes leads to increased rage (Bard & Mountcastle, 1948). The reasons for the different findings are unclear, but it should be noted that the amygdala is a very complex structure.

Other kinds of evidence indicate the limbic system (including the amygdala) is important in emotion. Servan-Schreiber and Perlstein (1998) administered the drug procaine hydrochloride, and used PET scans to show it produced activation in parts of the limbic system. The drug produced various intense emotional states, including anxiety, euphoria or joy, and depression. These emotional states were free-floating, i.e., they were not attached to any external events or to conscious thoughts.

---

### Amygdalotomies

As a result of work such as that of Kluver and Bucy (1939), "psychosurgeons" in the United States carried out numerous operations on criminals serving jail sentences. Many of these operations were amygdalotomies, in which parts of the amygdala were destroyed. This was done by putting fine wire electrodes into the amygdala through a small hole drilled in the skull, and then passing strong electric currents through the electrodes. These amygdalotomies reduced fear and anger in those operated on, but they often had very unfortunate side-effects. For example, Thomas R was a 34-year-old engineer who suffered delusions and could not work after surgery. He was found on one occasion walking about with his head covered by bags, rags, and newspapers. He justified his behaviour by saying he was frightened other bits of his brain might be destroyed. Thankfully, amygdalotomy is very rarely carried out nowadays.

---

## Amygdala

Only certain parts of the limbic system play a major role in emotion. The amygdala is of special importance. Interesting evidence on the role played by the amygdala in emotion was reported by Calder, Young, Rowland, Perrett, Hodges, and Etcoff (1996) and by Scott, Young, Calder, Hellawell, Aggleton, and Johnson (1997). They studied a woman (DR), who had an operation for epilepsy involving lesions to the amygdala. When DR described the emotions revealed by various emotional expressions in other people, she was particularly poor at identifying fearful expressions. In another study, DR listened to neutral words spoken in different emotional tones, and tried to identify the relevant emotion. She was very poor at recognising fear and anger.

What do these findings tell us about emotion? As Scott et al. (1997, p. 256) concluded, "Impaired recognition of fear and anger after amygdala damage reflects involvement of the amygdala in the appraisal of danger and the emotion of fear."

Other research indicates the amygdala is heavily involved in fear. There is a rare genetic disorder known as **Urbach–Wiethe disease**, in which the amygdala and adjacent areas are gradually destroyed. Patients with this disease experience much less fear and other related negative emotions than most people. For example, an Urbach–Wiethe patient differed from other people in not remembering the distressing parts of a story about a serious traffic accident better than the rest of the story (Cahill et al., 1995).

---

### The amygdala and brain imaging

Davidson's (1996) brain-imaging research shows that the amygdala lights up as soon as people see disturbing images. And he thinks that a predisposition to anxiety or depression could be linked to unusually high amygdala activity. The stoics among us are the ones with a quieter amygdala.

---

### LeDoux

LeDoux (e.g., 1992, 1996) has focused exclusively on fear and anxiety in his research. He has emphasised the role of the amygdala, which he regards as the brain's "emotional computer" for working out the emotional significance of stimuli. According to LeDoux, sensory information about emotional stimuli is relayed from the thalamus simultaneously to the amygdala and to the cortex. Of key relevance here, LeDoux (1992, 1996) identifies two different emotion circuits in fear:

1.  A slow-acting thalamus-to-cortex-to-amygdala circuit involving detailed analysis of sensory information.

2. A fast-acting thalamus–amygdala circuit based on simple stimulus features (e.g., intensity); this circuit bypasses the cortex.

LeDoux's theory is of relevance to the debate about whether cognitive processes always precede emotional experience (see earlier). According to LeDoux (1992, p. 275), "The activation of the amygdala by inputs from the neocortex is … consistent with the classic notion that emotional processing is postcognitive, whereas the activation of the amygdala by thalamic inputs is consistent with the hypothesis, advanced by Zajonc (1980), that emotional processing can be preconscious and precognitive."

Why do we have two emotion circuits? The thalamus–amygdala circuit allows us to respond rapidly in threatening situations, and thus can be valuable in ensuring our survival. In contrast, the cortical circuit produces a detailed evaluation of the emotional significance of the situation, and so allows us to respond appropriately.

> **Emotion: Is it a physiological or a cognitive experience?**
>
> Some kinds of emotional experience are more physiological, others are more cognitive.
>
> - *A physiological experience.* A jet screams over your head, you duck and experience a tightness in your chest. Past experience and individual differences will determine the emotion you might report feeling—fear, surprise, elation. For each of us it will be different, but the basis will be arousal. Such responses are more related to emotion as an adaptive response.
> - *A cognitive experience.* You hear that you have passed an exam and feel ecstatic, which may lead to physiological sensations.
>
> This might explain why emotion can sometimes occur with arousal and sometimes without it. It also fits in with LeDoux's suggestion that there are two pathways in the brain, one more physiological and the other more related to higher-order processing.

## Hemispheric differences

The two hemispheres of the brain play somewhat different roles in emotion. In general terms, the right hemisphere is more involved than the left hemisphere in the processing of emotional expressions and other emotional stimuli. Spence, Shapiro, and Zaidel (1996) presented emotionally disturbing information to only one hemisphere. Presentation of this information to the right hemisphere produced greater changes in heart rate and in blood pressure than presentation to the right hemisphere.

There is also evidence from **split-brain patients** (see Chapter 4). These patients have had an operation to sever the corpus callosum, a bridge between the two hemispheres. As a result of this operation (normally carried out to reduce epilepsy), the two sides of the cortex function fairly independently. It appears that split-brain patients are only able to recognise or identify emotional stimuli and events accurately when the information goes to the right side of the cortex.

The role of the two hemispheres in emotion depends on the type of emotion involved. Pleasant emotions are associated mainly with activation of the left frontal cortex, whereas unpleasant emotions are associated more with activation of the right frontal lobe. Tomarken et al. (1992) identified some individuals having more activation in the left hemisphere than in the right one, and others showing the opposite pattern. Those with a bias towards left-hemisphere activation experienced more positive affect than those with a right-hemisphere bias, whereas those with a right-hemisphere bias experienced more negative affect.

Further evidence of hemispheric differences related to positive and negative emotional states was reported by Schiff and Lamon (1994). Their participants contracted muscles on each side of the face in turn. When those on the left side of the face were contracted, the participants generally experienced positive emotions. In contrast, contraction of facial muscles on the right side led to negative emotional states.

*Who would you expect to be more indifferent to the effects of their injuries—patients with left or right hemisphere damage?*

## Neurotransmitters

In order to understand the role of the brain in emotion, it is not enough to identify the main areas of the brain involved. It is also necessary to focus on communication among these various areas. This is a complicated issue, and we will consider only a small part of the relevant evidence based on the role of neurotransmitters (see Chapter 2). **Neurotransmitters** are chemicals transmitting electrical impulses from one neuron to another. More than 50 neurotransmitters have been discovered, some of which are involved in emotion. One of the most important neurotransmitters is **serotonin**, which plays a part in the regulation of emotion, sleep, and eating.

> **KEY TERMS**
>
> **Split-brain patients:** individuals in whom the corpus callosum connecting the two hemispheres of the brain has been destroyed.
>
> **Neurotransmitters:** chemicals that cross synapses and affect the receptors on adjacent neurons.
>
> **Serotonin:** a neurotransmitter that influences emotional states.

What effects does serotonin have on emotion? Serotonin plays an inhibitory role within the nervous system, with moderate levels of serotonin inhibiting both anger and depression. Individuals with low levels of serotonin find it harder to inhibit these negative emotional states. The evidence on anger and aggression was reviewed by Bernhardt (1997, p. 48), who concluded that, "Low serotonin levels have been found in the hypothalamus and the amygdala in aggressive animals." He argued that this happens because low levels of serotonin make animals and humans more sensitive to frustrating stimuli.

So far as depression is concerned, a review by McNeal and Cimbolic (1986) concluded that serotonin levels are generally low in depressed patients. Delgado et al. (1990) gave a special diet designed to reduce serotonin level to patients who had recovered from depression. As predicted, this lowering of serotonin levels caused the symptoms of depression to return in about two-thirds of the patients.

In sum, neurotransmitters play an important role in emotion. As we have seen, serotonin levels influence various emotions such as depression and anger. Other neurotransmitters are also involved in emotion, but there is insufficient space to consider them here (see Kolb & Whishaw, 2001).

## STRESS

*Why might people be more prepared to report that they are stressed these days?*

It is often said that this is the "age of stress", and it is certainly true that more people than ever report that they are highly stressed. However, it is not clear that most people are more stressed than was the case previously. Of course, we have many things to be stressed about. However, our ancestors had to contend with major epidemics, poor life expectancy, poverty, and an almost complete absence of holidays. Taking all that into account, my hunch is that stress levels nowadays are much the same as in the past.

What is stress? Selye (1950) defined stress as "the nonspecific response of the body to any demand". He subsequently (Selye, 1956) defined stress as, "the rate of all the wear and tear caused by life". These definitions are not very useful because the nature of the stress response depends on the situation, and the factors causing stress are not included. It makes sense to use the term "stressor" to refer to any situation that creates stress, reserving the term "stress" to refer to our reactions to a stressor.

According to the transactional model (Cox, 1978), stress depends on the interaction between an individual and his/her environment. This approach leads to Steptoe's (1997, p. 175) definition: "Stress responses ... arise when demands exceed the personal and social resources that the individual is able to mobilise." Thus, for example, driving is stressful to a learner driver, because he/she has limited ability to meet the demands of handling a car in traffic. Driving is not stressful to experienced drivers, because they are confident that their driving ability will allow them to cope with most driving situations.

What are the effects of being exposed to stress? Many effects are physiological in nature, and so stress is considered within biological psychology. However, other changes also occur inside stressed individuals. There are four major kinds of effects associated with

*Emotional effects:*
- Feelings of anxiety and depression
- Increased physical tension
- Increased psychological tension

*Cognitive effects:*
- Poor concentration
- Increased distractibility
- Reduced short-term memory capacity

*Physiological effects:*
- Release of adrenaline and noradrenaline
- Shut-down of digestive system
- Expansion of air passages in lungs
- Increased heart rate
- Constriction of blood vessels

*Behavioural effects:*
- Increased absenteeism
- Disrupted sleep patterns
- Reduced work performance

stress: emotional, physiological, cognitive, and behavioural. Some specific examples are shown in the figure on page 164.

We will start by considering physiological or bodily effects. It is of key importance to understand that stress involves an immediate shock response, which is followed by a countershock response. The first (shock) response depends mainly on the sympathetic adrenal medullary system (SAM), whereas the second or countershock response involves the hypothalamic pituitary–adrenocortical axis (HPA). These two response systems (which are discussed below) are shown in the figure on the right.

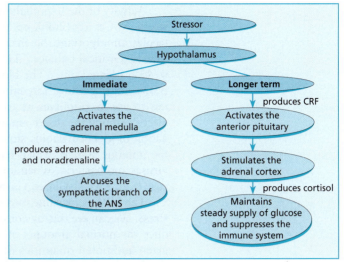

## Sympathetic adrenal medullary system

The initial shock response involves the sympathetic adrenal medullary system (SAM). In essence, activity in the sympathetic branch of the autonomic nervous system stimulates the adrenal medulla, which forms part of the adrenal glands. The adrenal medulla secretes the hormones adrenaline and noradrenaline (Americans call these epinephrine and norepinephrine, respectively). These hormones lead to increased arousal of the sympathetic nervous system and reduced activity in the parasympathetic nervous system.

Heightened activity of the sympathetic adrenal medullary system prepares us for "fight or flight". More specifically, there are the following effects: an increase in energy, increased alertness, increased blood flow to the muscles, increased heart and respiration rate, reduced activity in the digestive system, and increased release of clotting factors into the bloodstream to reduce blood loss in the event of injury. Adrenaline and noradrenaline increase the output of the heart, which can cause an increase in blood pressure.

SAM activity forms an important part of the stress response. It is an appropriate reaction of the body, because it prepares us for fight or flight. However, SAM activity is not *only* associated with stress. We also have elevated levels of adrenaline and noradrenaline when we are concentrating hard on a task. There is also the issue of how we perceive our internal physiological state. Sometimes we perceive heightened activity in SAM as indicating that we are stressed, but sometimes we interpret such activity as meaning that we are excited or stimulated.

*In what ways are bodily resources being used up by the SAM system?*

## Hypothalamic pituitary–adrenocortical axis

If someone is exposed to any given stressor for several hours or more, activity within the SAM system increasingly uses up bodily resources. As a result, there is a countershock response designed to minimise any damage that might be caused. As mentioned earlier, this countershock response involves the hypothalamic pituitary–adrenocortical axis (HPA), the details of which are discussed below.

The glands of the endocrine system are distributed throughout the body. Most of the system is controlled by the hypothalamus. This is a small structure at the base of the brain producing hormones (e.g., corticotropin-releasing factor or CRF) which stimulate the anterior pituitary gland. The anterior pituitary gland releases several hormones, of which the most important is adrenocorticotrophic hormone (ACTH). ACTH stimulates the adrenal cortex, which forms part of the adrenal glands. The adrenal cortex produces various glucocorticoids, which are hormones having effects on glucose metabolism. The key glucocorticoid with respect to stress is cortisol, which is sometimes called the "stress hormone" because excess amounts are found in the urine of individuals experiencing stress.

Cortisol is important for coping with long-term stress, because it permits maintenance of a steady supply of fuel. More generally, the secretion of cortisol and other glucocorticoids during the countershock response has various effects. First, the glucocorticoids help to conserve glucose for neural tissues. Second, they elevate or stabilise blood glucose concentrations. Third, they mobilise protein reserves. Fourth, they conserve salts and water.

Activity of the hypothalamic–pituitary–adenocortical axis is very useful in coping with stress. As Gevirtz (2000, pp. 61–62) pointed out, "Adrenal steroids [such as cortisol] seem to play an important role in countering many of the body's initial responses to stress, maintaining a critical balance." However, there is a price to be paid for this. As Westen (1996, p. 427) pointed out, "The blood still has elevated levels of glucose (for energy) and some hormones (including adrenaline and the pituitary hormone ACTH), and the body continues to use its resources at an accelerating rate. Essentially, the organism remains on red alert." Among the disadvantages of continuing HPA activity is that the anti-inflammatory action of glucocorticoids slows wound healing. More generally, glucocorticoids suppress the immune system, which has the task of protecting the body against intruders such as viruses and bacteria. When immune responses are low, we are more likely to develop a disease (e.g., Kiecolt-Glaser, Garner, Speicher, Penn, Holliday, & Glaser, 1984).

The HPA is of value in reducing many of the effects of the first or shock response to stress. We can see this by considering individuals without adrenal glands who cannot produce the normal amounts of glucocorticoids. When exposed to a stressor, they must be given additional quantities of glucorticoid to survive (Tyrell & Baxter, 1981). However, the beneficial effects of HPA activity are achieved at considerable cost, and the HPA cannot continue indefinitely at an elevated level of activity. If the adrenal cortex stops producing glucocorticoids, this eliminates the ability to maintain blood glucose concentrations at the appropriate level.

We have discussed the SAM and the HPA as if they were different systems. This is basically correct, but the two systems do not operate in complete independence of each other. As Evans (1998, p. 60) pointed out, "At the level of the central nervous system, the crucially important SAM and HPA systems can be considered as one complex: they are as it were the lower limbs of one body."

## General adaptation syndrome

Historically, the work of Selye was very important. He first popularised the term "stress", which had not been used previously as a psychological concept. Selye (1950) studied

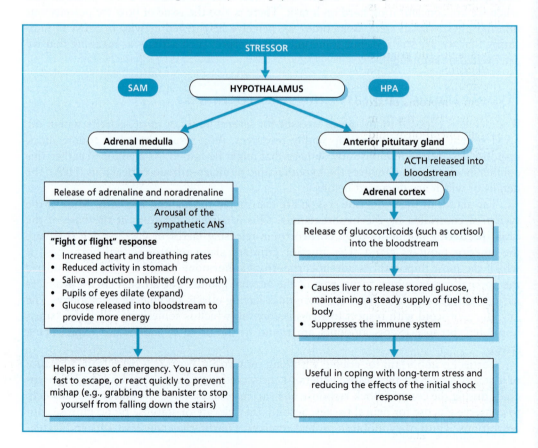

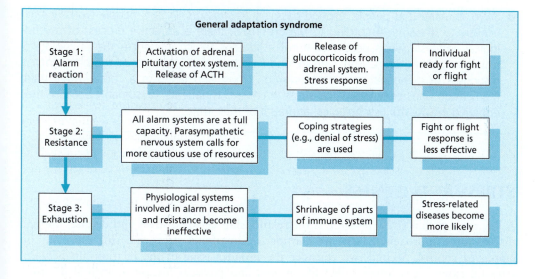

hospital patients with various injuries and illnesses. He noticed they all seemed to show a similar pattern of bodily response, which he called the **general adaptation syndrome**. He argued that it consisted of three stages:

1. *Alarm reaction stage*. This involves increased activity in the SAM and HPA systems, although Selye emphasised the role of the HPA in his account. According to Selye, the alarm reaction develops 6–48 hours after stress (e.g., injury), and includes loss of muscle tone, drop in body temperature, and decrease in size of the spleen and liver.
2. *Resistance stage*. This is the stage of adaptation, and also involves activity in the HPA. The body is adapting or fitting in with environmental demands. As this stage proceeds, the parasympathetic nervous system (which is involved in energy-storing processes) requires more careful use of the body's resources to cope. The system is being taxed to its limits. This stage is initially marked by an increase in the size of the adrenal glands and a decrease in some pituitary activity (e.g., production of growth hormone). If the stress is not too great (e.g., slight injuries), the body returns to a near-normal state.
3. *Exhaustion stage*. When stress is very prolonged, the physiological systems used in the previous two stages eventually become ineffective. The initial autonomic nervous system symptoms of arousal reappear (increasing heart rate, sweating, and so on). In extreme cases, the damaged adrenal cortex leads to failure of the parasympathetic system (metabolism and storage of energy) and collapse of the body's immune system. Stress-related diseases (e.g., high blood pressure, asthma, heart disease) become more likely.

## Evaluation

- ➕ Selye carried out pioneering research to identify some of the major components of the stress response.
- ➕ Selye correctly focused on what is now called the HPA system.
- ➕ Selye correctly emphasised the importance of the glucocorticoids.
- ➖ In his research, Selye paid little attention to the SAM system, and he did not fully understand the relationship between the HPA and SAM systems.
- ➖ Selye over-simplified when he claimed that stress always produces the same physiological pattern. For example, Mason (1975) compared the reactions to stressors varying in the degree of how much fear, anger, or uncertainty they created. The various stressors produced different patterns of adrenaline, noradrenaline, and corticosteroid secretion.
- ➖ Selye's model exaggerates the role of physiological factors at the expense of emotional and cognitive factors.

**KEY TERM**
**General adaptation syndrome:** the bodily response to stress, consisting of alarm reaction, resistance, and then exhaustion.

● Selye assumed that people respond *passively* to stressors. In fact, people typically react *actively* to stressors. According to Mason (1975) there is an active process of psychological appraisal when people confront a stressor, which influences the physiological response. Symington, Currie, Curran, and Davidson (1955) compared the physiological responses of dying patients remaining conscious, and being in a coma. There were many more signs of physiological stress in conscious patients, presumably because they engaged in stressful psychological appraisal of their state.

## STRESS AND ILLNESS

A key topic within stress research is the relationship between stress and disease. We will discuss three approaches. First, we consider occupational stress, focusing especially on employee control. Second, we consider the broader issue of the relationship between stressful experiences (often called **life events**) and physical disease or mental disorder. Third, we address the assumption that there are individual differences in vulnerability to stress. According to this approach, some individuals are especially susceptible to stress, and so are more likely than other people to develop physical or mental illnesses. Note that stress has been linked with numerous physical illnesses, including headaches, infectious illness (e.g., influenza), cardiovascular disease, diabetes, asthma, and rheumatoid arthritis (Curtis, 2000).

## Occupational stress

Millions of adults attribute their highly stressed state mainly to occupational stress. This makes sense given that most of them spend about 2000 hours a year at work. It has been estimated (Cartwright & Cooper, 1997) that occupational stress costs American businesses more than 150 billion euros per year. What is it about the work environment that creates stress? There are many factors, but Karasek (1979) argued persuasively that lack of perceived control is of key importance. He claimed that workers can cope successfully with highly demanding jobs provided that they have perceived control over their work.

*Can you think of any other factors that might be implicated in stress at work?*

### Evidence

Spector, Dwyer, and Jex (1988) assessed perceived control in workers. Low levels of perceived control were associated with frustration, anxiety, headaches, stomach upsets, and visits to the doctor. Ganster, Fox, and Dwyer (2001) studied occupational stress in a 5-year study on nurses. High perceived control at the start of the study predicted less use of medical services and better mental health over the course of the study.

Findings from a 5-year longitudinal study on more than 9000 British civil servants were reported by Marmot et al. (1997) and by Bosma, Stansfeld, and Marmot (1998). Workers on the lowest employment grades were about *four* times more likely to die of a heart attack than those on the most senior grade. They were also more likely to suffer from cancer, strokes, and gastrointestinal disorders. These differences apparently occurred because those in the lower positions had much less control over their work than those in the higher positions. Perceived control was assessed by a self-report survey, and "objective" control was assessed by supervisors. Both measures of control predicted subsequent levels of coronary heart disease.

> **KEY TERM**
> **Life events:** experiences (predominantly negative) that can increase stress levels.

> **Occupational stress in Sweden**
> Frankenhaeuser (1975) found a link between perceived lack of control at work and high levels of stress. Some sawmill workers were given jobs where they fed logs into the mill machines, continually, all day. This repetitive and monotonous task also isolated them as it was extremely noisy, and the machine speeds dictated how fast the workers fed in the logs. The workers felt isolated, with a minimum of control. And, compared to the other mill workers who had more control and were not similarly isolated, these workers suffered far more from headaches, digestive disorders such as ulcers, and high blood pressure.

## Evaluation

⊕ "There is mounting evidence that perceived control at work is an important element in employees' health and well-being" (Spector, 2002, p. 136).

⊕ Perceived control is probably strongly related to stress in other areas of life (e.g., relationships).

⊖ Several other work factors influence psychological well-being. For example, Warr (1996) identified the following: availability of money, opportunity for skills use, work demands, variety, physical security, opportunity for interpersonal contact, environmental clarity, and valued social position.

⊖ There is some danger of a circular argument: stress is often defined as demands exceeding resources, and perceived control implies that demands do not exceed resources!

## Life events and hassles

It is generally believed that stress plays a part in causing various illnesses, and much of the available evidence supports this belief. Cohen, Tyrrell, and Smith (1991) carried out a well-controlled study in which the participants were given nasal drops containing cold viruses. Those with the highest level of stress (they had experienced many negative life events and felt out of control) were almost twice as likely to develop colds as those with the lowest level of stress. There is also evidence that stress can help to cause gastric ulcers. Stress often increases the secretion of hydrochloric acid, and also weakens the defences of the gastrointestinal tract against it. As a result, gastric ulcers can develop (Pinel, 1997).

Early work on life events was carried out by Holmes and Rahe (1967), who noted that patients often experienced several life events in the months before the onset of illness. This led them to develop the Social Readjustment Rating Scale, on which people indicate which out of 43 life events have happened to them over a period of time (usually 6 or 12 months). These life events are assigned a value in terms of their likely impact. Here are various life events taken from this scale, with their associated life change units in brackets:

death of a spouse (100)
divorce (73)
marital separation (65)
gaol (63)
death of a close family member (63)
change in eating habits (15)
holiday (13)
minor violations of the law (11)

Why are holidays treated as stressful life events? According to Holmes and Rahe, any change (whether desirable or undesirable) can be stressful.

You have probably sometimes felt very stressed even in the absence of any of the life events contained in measures such as the Social Readjustment Rating Scale. This suggests the possible importance of **hassles**, which are "the irritating, frustrating, distressing demands that ... characterise everyday transactions with the environment" (Kanner, Coyne, Schaefer, & Lazarus, 1981, p. 3). Hassles include being stuck in traffic jams, losing an essay that needs to be handed in, and being unable to make a computer do what you want it to do. Several researchers (e.g., Stone et al., 1987) have argued that our daily experiences can (and do) influence our health.

> **KEY TERM**
> **Hassles:** the irritating demands of everyday life; they can increase stress levels.

Changes can be stressful, even the usually pleasant ones associated with going on holiday.

## Evidence

Rahe (1968) used the Social Readjustment Rating Scale to divide naval personnel into high-risk and low-risk groups on the basis of their life events over the previous 6 months. Members of the high-risk group were twice as likely to develop illnesses during their first month at sea. It has been found in numerous studies using the Social Readjustment Rating Scale that people experiencing events totalling more than 300 life change units over a period of 1 year are more at risk for numerous physical and mental illnesses. These illnesses include heart attacks, diabetes, TB, asthma, anxiety, and depression (Martin, 1989). However, the correlations between life change units and susceptibility to any particular illness are rather low, indicating a weak association between life events and illness.

Indirect evidence that stressful life events can play a role in life-threatening diseases was reported by Tache, Selye, and Day (1979). Cancer was more common among adults who were divorced, widowed, or separated than among married people. The most likely explanation is that those who were not married were more stressed because of a lack of social support. However, it is hard to establish causal relationships from such data. Perhaps those who were divorced or separated were initially more vulnerable to stress than those who were married, and this stress vulnerability played a role in the collapse of their marriages.

There are individual and group differences in the reactions to many stressful life events. For example, consider a study by Miller and Rahe (1997), who compared the reactions of men and women to several life events. In general, women experienced more stress than men following the death of a close family member, a major injury or illness, loss of a job, reduced income, or moving home.

The effects of hassles on health were studied by Stone et al. (1987). They considered the hassles and desirable events experienced by participants developing a respiratory illness during the 10 days before its onset. They had experienced more hassles and fewer desirable events during that period than had control participants who did not develop a respiratory illness.

*How might some of these events be directly linked to illness, without stress necessarily being involved?*

## Evaluation

- ⊕ The Social Readjustment Rating Scale and other measures of life events have generated valuable research.
- ⊕ The notion that life events influence stress-related illnesses is a reasonable one.
- ⊖ It is often not clear whether life events have caused some stress-related illness, or whether stress caused the life events. For example, stress may cause a change in eating habits rather than a change in eating habits causing stress.
- ⊖ The impact of life events varies from person to person and from group to group. For example, marital separation may be less stressful for someone who has already established an intimate relationship with another person. Some measures take account of the *context* in which people experience life events (e.g., the Life Events and Difficulties Schedule or LEDS; see Harris, 1997).
- ⊖ It has often been assumed that almost any serious life event can help to produce almost any type of illness. This has led to a relative ignoring of more *specific* effects. For example, Finlay-Jones and Brown (1981) found that anxious patients were more likely than depressed patients to have experienced danger events (involving future threats), whereas depressed patients were more likely to have experienced loss events (involving past losses).

## Vulnerability to stress

Numerous researchers have argued there are important individual differences in vulnerability to stress. Various personality dimensions have been implicated, but here we will focus on only two of the major ones: negative affectivity and Type A behaviour pattern.

## Negative affectivity

Watson and Clark (1984) identified a personality dimension called **negative affectivity**. Those high in negative affectivity experience frequent unpleasant emotional states (e.g., anxiety, depression). The dimension of negative affectivity is essentially the same as neuroticism or trait anxiety (see Chapter 13). It seems reasonable to argue that negative affectivity is closely related to stress vulnerability. Indeed, individuals high in negative affectivity typically report they are more stressed and distressed than those low in negative affectivity (see Watson & Clark, 1984, for a review).

## Evidence

Watson and Pennebaker (1989) considered the evidence linking negative affectivity with health. Individuals high in negative affectivity complain of many more physical ailments than those low in negative affectivity. For example, they are more likely to report having colds, coughing, sore throats, dizziness, stomach pains, irritable bowel syndrome, and so on.

*What alternative explanation could you offer for this finding?*

The above findings suggest that those high in negative affectivity may suffer worse health than those low in negative affectivity, presumably because of their greater vulnerability to stress. However, the evidence is much weaker when actual physical disease and mortality are considered rather than merely reports of health complaints. For example, there is generally no relationship between negative affectivity and mortality. Keehn et al. (1974) reported the findings of a 25-year follow-up of approximately 9000 army veterans discharged from the army because of neurosis. This group did not differ in overall mortality from a control group of people who had not suffered from neurosis. Shekelle et al. (1981) discussed the findings from their 17-year study on 2020 middle-aged men. Measures related to negative affectivity were not associated with overall mortality.

Is there an association between negative affectivity and death from heart disease? Booth-Kewley and Friedman (1987) carried out a meta-analysis of the relevant studies, and found an overall correlation of +.14 between anxiety (closely related to negative affectivity) and heart disease. However, that low correlation indicates anxiety accounts for only 1.96% of the variance in heart disease.

Strong evidence that negative affectivity is more strongly linked to health complaints than to physical illness can be illustrated with coronary heart disease. As we have seen, there is very little relationship between negative affectivity and death from coronary heart disease. Supporting evidence comes from objective measures predictive of heart disease. If anything, individuals high in negative affectivity have slightly lower blood pressure and serum cholesterol levels than those low in negativity (Watson & Pennebaker, 1989). However, those high in negative affectivity report more chest pain and angina pectoris (sudden intense pains in the chest) than other people (see Watson & Pennebaker, 1989).

Watson and Pennebaker (1989, p. 244) concluded as follows:

*They [individuals high in negative affectivity] complain of angina but show no evidence of greater coronary risk or pathology. They complain of headaches but do not report any increased use of aspirin. They report all kinds of physical problems but are not especially likely to visit their doctor or to miss work or school. In general, they complain about their health but show no hard evidence of poor health or increased mortality.*

### CASE STUDY: *Don't let it get you down*

"Comfort always, cure rarely" is an old medical motto. And it may be nearer the truth than modern medicine would like to admit. Perhaps if patients were less depressed and more optimistic they might be more likely to recover from stressful operations.

In one study of 100 patients about to undergo bone marrow transplants for leukaemia it was found that 13 of the patients were severely depressed. Of these patients 12 had died within a year of the operation (92%) whereas only 61% of the not-depressed died within 2 years of the study.

Other research has looked at the effects of pessimism and found this to be the biggest single predictor of death from a heart attack. For example, 122 men were evaluated for pessimism or optimism at the time they had a heart attack. Eight years later their state of mind was found to correlate with death more highly than any of the other standard risk factors such as damage to the heart, raised blood pressure, or high cholesterol levels. Of the 25 men who were most pessimistic, 21 had died whereas only 6 of the most optimistic 25 had died.

Peterson, Seligman, and Valliant (1988) studied optimists and pessimists. They suggested that pessimists tended to explain setbacks in their lives as the result of things within their personality that were unchangeable. In contrast, optimists tended to explain setbacks as the result of things arising from situations within their control, but which were not their own fault. Peterson et al. rated a number of Harvard undergraduates for pessimism and optimism on the basis of essays they wrote about their wartime experiences. After an interval of more than 20 years, the pessimists (aged 45) were more likely to be suffering from some chronic disease. However, smaller effects of personality on disease have been reported in other research (see main text).

Adapted from Goleman (1991).

Why is negative affectivity related to physical health complaints but not to physical disease? Individuals high in negative affectivity or trait anxiety have an **interpretive bias**: They are more likely than other people to interpret ambiguous stimuli and situations as being threatening (Eysenck, 1997). For example, Eysenck, MacLeod, and Mathews (1987) used a tape recorder to present homophones (i.e., two or more words sounding the same but spelled differently) having a threat-related and a neutral interpretation (e.g., die, dye; pain, pane). Those high in trait anxiety or negative affectivity produced a larger number of threatening interpretations of these homophones. Thus, negative affectivity is associated with a tendency to exaggerate the threateningness of stimuli, and this could explain why those high in negative affectivity report so many physical health complaints.

## Type A behaviour pattern

Two cardiologists, Meyer Friedman and Ray Rosenman (1959) argued that individuals with the Type A behaviour pattern are more stressed than Type B individuals, and so are more likely to suffer from coronary heart disease. The **Type A behaviour pattern** was defined by Matthews (1988) as including "extremes of competitive achievement striving, hostility, aggressiveness, and a sense of time urgency, evidenced by vigorous voice and psychomotor mannerisms" (p. 373). In contrast, Type B behaviour is more relaxed, and lacks the features found in Type A behaviour.

The Type A behaviour pattern was initially assessed by means of the Structured Interview. This assessment procedure involves two main kinds of information: (1) the answers given to the questions asked during the interview; and (2) the individual's behaviour, including aspects of his/her way of speaking (e.g., loudness, speed of talking). The individual's tendencies towards impatience and hostility are assessed by the interviewer deliberately interrupting the person being interviewed. The Type A behaviour pattern has also been assessed by various self-report questionnaires (e.g., the Jenkins Activity Survey).

## Evidence

The notion that Type A individuals are more likely than Type B individuals to suffer from coronary heart disease was tested in the Western Collaborative Group Study (Rosenman, Brand, Jenkins, Friedman, Straus, & Wurm, 1975). The findings were striking. Of nearly 3200 men having no symptoms of coronary heart disease at the outset of the study, Type As were nearly twice as likely as Type Bs to have developed coronary heart disease over the following 8½ years. This remained so, even when account was taken of various other factors (e.g., blood pressure, smoking, obesity) known to be associated with heart disease.

In the Western Collaborative Group Study as reported by Rosenman et al. (1975), it was unclear which aspect of the Type A behaviour pattern was most closely associated with heart disease. Matthews, Glass, Rosenman, and Bortner (1977) reanalysed the data from the Western Collaborative Group Study, and found that coronary heart disease was most associated with the hostility component of Type A.

Why is Type A (or its hostility component) associated with heart disease? As Ganster, Schaubroeck, Sime, and Mayes (1991) pointed out, it has often been assumed that "chronic elevations of the sympathetic nervous system [in Type As] lead to deterioration of the cardiovascular system" (p. 145). Ganster et al. put their participants into stressful situations and recorded various physiological measures (e.g., blood pressure, heart rate). Only the hostility component of Type A was associated with high levels of physiological reactivity. These findings (when combined with those of Matthews et al., 1977) suggest that high levels of hostility produce increased activity within the sympathetic nervous system, and this influences the development of coronary heart disease.

Some researchers have failed to find any relationship between Type A and coronary heart disease. This has led many psychologists to doubt the importance of the Type A behaviour pattern as a factor in causing heart disease. However, Miller, Turner, Tindale, Posavac, and Dugoni (1991) reviewed the literature, and found many of the negative findings were obtained in studies using self-report measures of Type A. Studies using the

KEY TERMS
**Interpretive bias:** the tendency to interpret ambiguous situations in a negative or threatening way.
**Type A behaviour pattern:** a personality type characterised by impatience, competitiveness, time pressure, and hostility.

Structured Interview with initially healthy populations reported a mean correlation of +.32 between Type A behaviour and coronary heart disease, indicating a moderate relationship between the two variables. Significant findings have probably been more common when Type A is assessed by the Structured Interview because it provides information about people's actual behaviour in a stressful situation.

Myrtek (1995) carried out a **meta-analysis** based on combining the findings from 16 studies including 46,789 individuals. The average correlation between Type A and coronary heart disease was only +.009, meaning there is practically no relationship between Type A and heart disease. The correlation was only very slightly larger when the hostility component of Type A was correlated with heart disease.

## Evaluation

- It seems plausible the personality characteristics of Type A individuals would lead to stress and possibly to physical illness.
- Type A includes several components (e.g., time urgency, hostility, competitiveness), and these components don't really form a coherent personality type.
- Different measures of Type A (e.g., Structured Interview and the Jenkins Activity Survey) correlate poorly with each other (Mayes, Sime, & Ganster, 1984), and so are clearly not measuring the same personality dimension.
- If we consider all the evidence, there is at best a rather small relationship between Type A and coronary heart disease.

## Mechanisms: How does stress cause illness?

There is good evidence that stress can increase the chances of someone becoming ill. There are two major ways in which stress can cause illness:

1. *Directly*, by reducing the body's ability to fight illness.
2. *Indirectly*, by leading the stressed individual to adopt an unhealthy lifestyle (e.g., increased smoking and drinking).

## Immune system

Stress may cause illness by impairing the workings of the **immune system**. The organs of the body containing most of the immune system's cells are the bone marrow, lymph nodes, thymus, tonsils, spleen, appendix, and small intestines. The term **psychoneuroimmunology** refers to the study of the effects of stress and other psychological factors on the immune system. Stress can affect the immune system fairly directly. Alternatively, it can affect the immune system indirectly via an unhealthy lifestyle. Cells in the immune system have receptors for various hormones and neurotransmitters involved in the stress response, so it is easy to see how the physiological stress response could influence the functioning of the immune system.

How does the immune system work? The cells within the immune system are known as white blood cells (**leucocytes**). These cells identify and destroy foreign bodies (**antigens**) such as viruses. In addition, the presence of antigens leads to the production of antibodies. **Antibodies** are produced in the blood. They are protein molecules attaching themselves to antigens, and marking them out for later destruction.

**KEY TERMS**
**Meta-analysis:** an analysis in which the findings from several similar studies are combined to provide an overall picture.
**Immune system:** a system of cells within the body that is involved in fighting disease.
**Psychoneuroimmunology:** the study of the effects of stress and other psychological factors on the immune system.
**Leucocytes:** white blood cells that find and destroy antigens.
**Antigens:** foreign bodies such as viruses.
**Antibodies:** protein molecules that attach themselves to invaders, marking them out for subsequent destruction.

Like some monster in a movie, the white blood cells of the immune system kill "invaders" by engulfing them. In the photograph a white blood cell is engulfing *M. Tuberculosis* bacteria.

There are several kinds of white blood cells or leucocytes within the immune system, including T cells, B cells, and natural killer cells. T cells destroy invaders, and T-helper cells increase immunological activity. These T-helper cells are attacked by HIV, the virus causing AIDS. B cells produce antibodies. Natural killer cells are involved in the fight against both viruses and tumours.

How can we assess the functioning of the immune system? It is very difficult to gain direct access to the cells of the immune system. However, circulating blood carries immune components between organs of the immune system and areas of inflammation, and so analysis of such blood provides indirect evidence of the functioning of the immune system. Three measures of intact immune system functioning are as follows:

- The increase in lymphocyte cells in response to mitogens, which are lymphocyte activators.
- The level of activity of natural killer cells.
- The production of antibodies, especially secretory immunoglobulin A (sIgA).

It is tempting (but wrong!) to assume that high levels of the above measures indicate the immune system is functioning well, whereas low levels mean the immune system is impaired. As Evans, Clow, and Hucklebridge (1997, p. 303) pointed out, we should, "think of the immune system as striving to maintain a state of delicate balance". Thus, it is hard to interpret changes in immune system functioning. In discussing the evidence, I will sometimes refer to impaired functioning of the immune system, but this should be regarded as shorthand for reduced levels of one or more measures of immune system functioning.

## Evidence

Schliefer, Keller, Camerino, Thornton, and Stein (1983) found stress can alter the functioning of the immune system. They compared the functioning of the immune system in the husbands of women with breast cancer. The husbands' immune system seemed to function less well after their wives had died than before, showing the impact of bereavement on the immune system.

Stress can affect natural killer cell cytotoxicity, which is of major importance in the defence against various infections and cancer. Reduced levels of natural killer cell cytotoxicity have been found in people who are highly stressed, including students facing important examinations, bereaved individuals, and those who are severely depressed (Ogden, 1996). Goodkin et al. (1992) studied natural killer cell cytotoxicity in HIV-positive homosexual men having no physical symptoms when tested. The level of natural killer cell cytotoxicity was higher among those men having plenty of vitamin A in their diet and who drank little alcohol. These findings may reflect an indirect effect of stress on the immune system, with the most stressed men adopting a less healthy lifestyle than the others in terms of diet and alcohol use. In addition, those HIV men with an active coping style focusing on (and expressing) their emotions had higher levels of natural killer cell cytotoxicity than those with other coping styles. This suggests a direct effect of stress on the immune system.

Herbert and Cohen (1993) reported a meta-analysis based on the findings from 38 studies. They reported that long-term stressors of several kinds reduced various aspects of immune system functioning. As Herbert and Cohen (p. 372) concluded, "We find substantial evidence for a relation between stress and … immune measures in humans."

So far we have considered the effects of long-term stress on the immune system, and we have seen that its functioning is often reduced by such stress. However, the effects are rather different with short-term stress, which can produce an improvement in at least some aspects of immune system functioning. For example, Zeier, Brauchli, and Joller-Jemelka (1996) studied air traffic controllers on a work shift. During this shift, they showed an increase in secretory immunoglobulin A (sIgA), suggesting there was enhanced immune system functioning. Delahanty et al. (1996) looked at the effects of short-term stress under laboratory conditions. Their participants performed a mental arithmetic task with harassment, immersed their hand in

*Why might taking blood samples not be a very good way of assessing the effects of stress in some people?*

### Exam stress and illness
Kiecolt-Glaser et al. (1986) assessed stress levels and also took blood samples from medical students twice; 6 weeks before their exams and again actually during their exams. Stress levels increased during exams, and their circulating killer T lymphocytes, part of the immune system in the blood, significantly reduced in number.

cold water at 3 °C, or read magazines. There was greater natural killer cell activity during the two stressful tasks than during the control task of reading magazines, suggesting enhanced functioning of the immune system.

## Evaluation

➕ Stress can produce changes in the immune system, and can increase the probability of individuals developing various physical diseases. This is likely to be mainly the case among individuals whose immune system is already weakened (Bachen, Cohen, & Marsland, 1997).

➖ The functioning of the immune system in most stressed individuals remains within the normal range. This led Bachen et al. (1997, p. 38) to conclude as follows: "It is not yet clear that either the nature or magnitude of immunological change found in PNI [psychoneuroimmunology] research bears any relevance to increased disease susceptibility" (p. 38).

➖ Long-term stressors may impair the functioning of the immune system, whereas short-term stressors do not.

➖ The immune system is very complex, and so the quality of an individual's immune system is hard to assess.

➖ "What is missing in the literature … is strong evidence that the associations between psychological factors and disease that do exist are attributable to immune changes" (Cohen & Herbert, 1996, p. 113).

## Lifestyle

There is reasonably convincing evidence that lifestyle has a major impact on illness and longevity. In a well-known study, Belloc and Breslow (1972) asked residents of Alameda County in California to indicate which of the following seven health behaviours they practised on a regular basis:

- Not smoking.
- Having breakfast each day.
- Having no more than one or two alcoholic drinks per day.
- Taking regular exercise.
- Sleeping 7 to 8 hours per night.
- Not eating between meals.
- Being no more than 10% overweight.

Belloc and Breslow found that adults who practised most of the above health behaviours reported that they were healthier than did those practising few or none of them. More striking findings emerged in a follow-up study 9½ years later. Breslow and Enstrom (1980) found that individuals practising all seven health behaviours had only 23% of the mortality rate found among those practising fewer than three of them. My personal score is five, which is modestly encouraging!

Stress can cause illness *indirectly* via changes to lifestyle. Stressed individuals are more likely to expose themselves to **pathogens**, agents causing physical illness. Stressed individuals tend to smoke more, to drink more alcohol, to take less exercise, and to sleep less than non-stressed individuals (Cohen & Williamson, 1991). For example, adolescents experiencing high levels of stress are more likely to start smoking than those whose lives are less stressful (Wills, 1985). Adults are more likely to resume smoking after having given up when experiencing much

> **KEY TERM**
> **Pathogens:** agents that cause physical illness.

*Stress can lead to an unhealthy lifestyle.*

stress in their lives (Carey, Kalra, Carey, Halperin, & Richard, 1993). So far as alcohol is concerned, there is much support for tension reduction theory (Ogden, 1996). According to this theory, tension in the form of anxiety, fear, or depression leads to an increase in alcohol consumption to reduce the level of tension.

Evidence that illness depends on lifestyle as well as on stress was reported by Brown (1991). The effects of stress in the form of negative life events were compared in students who were high or low in physical fitness. Stress almost trebled the number of visits to the health clinic made by unfit students, but had little effect on visits made by those physically fit.

## COPING WITH STRESS

There has been much interest in the ways in which individuals handle and resolve stress. The emphasis has been especially on **coping**, defined as "efforts, both action-oriented and intrapsychic [within the mind], to manage (that is, to master, tolerate, reduce, minimise) environmental and internal demands and conflicts among them which tax or exceed a person's resources" (Lazarus & Launier, 1978, p. 311). Thus, coping can involve behavioural or cognitive strategies (or both).

First of all, we will consider gender differences in coping with stress. After that, we will consider the main coping strategies that people use in their everyday lives. Finally, we consider various intervention techniques that have been used to provide help to individuals exposed to severe stress.

## Gender differences

According to Cannon (1932), our physiological stress response equips us for fight or flight. If we can overcome someone attacking us, we are likely to fight. If the threat is greater, then we resort to flight. This view remains popular. However, Taylor, Klein, Lewis, Gruenewald, Gurung, and Updegraff (2000) argued there are important differences between men and women in their reactions to stress. Men are much more likely than women to respond to stressful situations with a "fight-or-flight" response, whereas women generally respond with a "tend-and-befriend" response. Thus, women respond to stressors by protecting and looking after their children (the tend response) and by actively seeking social support from others (the befriend response). Some of these effects are found across cultures. Edwards (1993) found in 12 cultures that girls were much more likely than boys to provide help and support to infants.

*What gender differences would you expect to find and why?*

Taylor et al. (2000) emphasised the role of **oxytocin**, which is a hormone secreted by men and women as part of the stress response. Oxytocin makes people less anxious and more sociable, and so is associated with the tend-and-befriend response. Its effects are reduced by male sex hormones but increased by the female hormone oestrogen.

### Evidence

One assumption of the theory is that males are more likely than females to respond to stressful situations with the fight-or-flight response. There is some support for this assumption in studies of aggression. Eagly and Steffen (1986) carried out a meta-analysis. They found that males are on average somewhat more aggressive than females, especially with respect to physical aggression.

There is much evidence that females are more likely than males to respond to stressful situations with tending and/or befriending. For example, Schachter (1959) found that women had a much greater desire than men to affiliate or be close to others when under stress. Indeed, he found so little evidence for affiliative behaviour in stressed men that he used only females in all his subsequent research! Luckow, Reifman, and McIntosh (1998) reviewed 26 studies on gender differences in seeking and using social support. Women sought social support more than men in 25 of these studies, and there was no gender difference in the other study.

Most of the evidence that oxytocin is associated with the tend-and-befriend response comes from research on other species. However, there is some relevant human research.

Uvnäs-Moberg (1996) found that oxytocin in breastfeeding women was associated with level of calm and self-reported sociability. Turner et al. (1999) found that oxytocin levels in women increased in response to relaxation massage but decreased in response to sadness. Sociable women had greater increases in oxytocin during massage than did unsociable women. In a study on older women, Taylor et al. (1999) reported that higher levels of oxytocin were associated with smaller cortisol stress responses and with faster recovery of the hypothalamic–pituitary–adrenocortical axis (HPA) after being exposed to a stressful situation.

> **Behaviour, gender, and stress**
> Frankenhaeuser (1983) monitored adrenaline levels (a measure of stress) in male and female engineering students and bus drivers in response to stressors. He found no significant difference between the male and female results, suggesting that in some cases the supposed gender difference in stress responses had been eroded by women's adoption of male-type jobs and behaviour patterns.

Most of the research on oxytocin has involved other species, and so may not be of direct relevance to humans. However, it is interesting that there are strong effects of oxytocin in rats. Rats who are calmed by means of oxytocin often remain calm for several weeks thereafter, suggesting that oxytocin may play a key role in reducing stress.

## Evaluation

⊕ The theory is an ambitious attempt to understand gender differences in coping with stress.

⊕ The theory may help us to understand why women in many cultures live on average 5–7 years longer than men.

⊖ As Taylor et al. (2000, p. 422) admitted, "We have suggested that oxytocin and endogenous opioids may play important roles in female responses to stress, and it remains to be seen if these are as significant players as we have suggested."

⊖ Neuroendocrine responses under stress vary from stressor to stressor (Sapolsky, 1992), but the theory has little to say about the ways in which stress responses depend on the nature of the stressor.

## Coping strategies

Psychologists have devised numerous questionnaires to assess the main types of coping strategies that are used in stressful situations. These questionnaires differ from each other in many ways. However, there is reasonable agreement there are only a few major coping strategies, and we will consider one illustrative measure based on that assumption.

Endler and Parker (1990) devised the Multidimensional Coping Inventory to assess three major coping strategies:

- *Task-oriented strategy*. This involves obtaining information about the stressful situation and about alternative courses of action and their probable outcome; it also involves deciding on priorities and acting so as to deal directly with the stressful situation.
- *Emotion-oriented strategy*. This can involve efforts to maintain hope and to control one's emotions; it can also involve venting feelings of anger and frustration, or deciding that nothing can be done to change things.
- *Avoidance-oriented strategy*. This involves denying or minimising the seriousness of the situation; it also involves conscious suppression of stressful thoughts and their replacement by self-protective thoughts.

Individuals high in the personality dimension of trait anxiety, and who thus experience much stress and anxiety, tend to use the emotion-oriented and avoidance-oriented strategies rather than the task-oriented strategy (Endler & Parker, 1990). In contrast, individuals low in trait anxiety tend to use the task-oriented strategy.

Stevan Hobfoll (e.g., Monnier, Hobfoll, & Stone, 1996) has argued that most approaches to coping have de-emphasised the social context. Three dimensions are identified in their multi-axial model of coping: (1) active vs. passive; (2) pro-social vs. anti-social: social joining and seeking social support vs. anti-social action, instinctive action, and

*Avoidance-oriented strategy*

aggressive action; and (3) direct vs. indirect: actions directly or indirectly applied to the problem. The pro-social vs. anti-social dimension is regarded as being of central importance. Individuals coping best with stress ensure that they invest time and energy to construct strong social support networks when they are not stressed.

## Evidence

*Do you think that other cultures would take the same view of these coping strategies?*

Which kind of coping strategy is most effective in reducing stress? As Lazarus (1993, p. 238) pointed out, "Of the two functions of coping, problem-focused [task-oriented] and emotion-focused, there is a strong tendency in western values to venerate the former and distrust the latter. Taking action against problems rather than reappraising the relational meaning seems more desirable." There is some support for this point of view. Folkman et al. (1986) asked people to report on the coping strategies they had used to handle stressful events, and also asked them to rate the extent to which the outcome had been satisfactory or unsatisfactory. Planned problem-solving tended to be associated with satisfactory outcomes, whereas confrontative coping (e.g., expressing anger) and distancing (trying to forget about the problem) were associated with unsatisfactory outcomes.

There is additional evidence the avoidance-oriented strategy is often ineffective. Carver et al. (1993) studied women diagnosed with breast cancer. Those women who used avoidant coping strategies such as denial or simply refusing to try to cope had higher levels of distress than those who accepted the diagnosis and retained a sense of humour. Epping-Jordan, Compas, and Howell (1994) studied young men and women suffering from various types of cancer. The disease had progressed further over a 1-year period among those who used avoidant coping (e.g., "I try not to think about it") than among those who did not.

In spite of the above evidence discussed, it would be very mistaken to conclude that any given type of coping is always useful and another type is useless. The effectiveness of any coping strategy depends on the individual, on the context, and on the nature of the stressful situation. The task- or problem-oriented coping strategy is generally effective, except when there is little or nothing that the individual can do to improve matters. For example, Collins et al. (1983) considered people living in the area around Three Mile Island shortly after a major nuclear incident. Individuals using problem-oriented coping strategies were more distressed than those using emotion-oriented coping.

The avoidance-oriented coping strategy is also effective in some circumstances. For example, Cohen and Lazarus (1973) considered the coping strategies used by patients during hospitalisation after surgery. Patients using denial showed improved rate of healing (and had fewer minor complications) than those who did not.

An important point is that many stressful situations change over time, and the best coping strategy may also change over time. For example, Folkman and Lazarus (1985) found students faced by a stressful examination sought information and social support before the examination. Afterwards, while waiting to hear the results, they typically made use of the avoidance-oriented strategy (e.g., forgetting all about the examination). In a different context, the avoidance-oriented strategy of denial is dangerous when an individual has just suffered a heart attack, but is useful during the subsequent period of hospitalisation (Levine et al., 1987). Denial becomes dangerous again if it continues for a long period after discharge from hospital (Levine et al., 1987).

## Evaluation

⊕ Coping strategies play an important role in determining the effects of stressful events on an individual's physical and mental state.
⊕ There is reasonable agreement on the nature of some of the major coping strategies (e.g., task-oriented, avoidance-oriented).
⊖ Coping strategies as manifested in actual behaviour often differ from coping strategies as assessed by self-report questionnaire.

● What often happens is that individuals' preferred coping strategies in general are assessed. As Lazarus (1993, p. 241) pointed out, "Broad coping styles do not adequately explain or predict intraindividual [within the individual] variations in the way given sources of stress are dealt with in specific contexts."

● According to Lazarus (1993, p. 242), "Coping process measures would be far more meaningful and useful if we knew more about the persons whose coping thoughts and actions are being studied. Now they tend to be disembodied, as it were, from that person." For example, responding to possible examination failure by using an avoidance-oriented coping strategy makes more sense if the individual is not motivated to achieve success than if he/she is very ambitious.

## Social support

It has often been claimed that social support can help to provide protection against stress (e.g., Monnier et al., 1996). Before discussing the evidence, however, we need to consider definitions of social support. We can distinguish between structural social support, which is an individual's basic network of social relationships, and functional social support, which is concerned with the quality of social support.

According to Schaefer, Coyne, and Lazarus (1981), there are important differences in the effects of these types of social support on health and well-being. Functional social support is positively related to health and well-being, whereas structural social support is unrelated related to well-being. Social network can even be negatively related to well-being, because it is very time-consuming and demanding to maintain a large social network.

*How might social support help with the different types of coping outlined on page 177?*

### Evidence

The importance of social support was shown by Brown and Harris (1978). They found that 61% of severely depressed women had experienced a very stressful life event in the previous 9 months, compared with only 25% of non-depressed women. However, many women managed to cope with severe life events without becoming depressed. Of those women who experienced a serious life event, 37% of those without an intimate friend became depressed, against only 10% of those who did have a very close friend.

Convincing evidence of the value of good social support was discussed by House et al. (1988), who reviewed several large prospective studies. Individuals who had high levels of social support had much lower mortality rates than those with poor social support.

How does social support protect people from various causes of mortality? One way that it does so is by having beneficial effects on cardiovascular functioning. This was supported by Uchino, Cacioppo, and Kiecolt-Glaser (1996), who reviewed over 50 studies. Blood pressure was lower in individuals having high levels of social support than in those without good social support. Uchino et al. also reviewed 19 studies in which the effects of social support on immune functioning were addressed. Individuals with good social support tended to have stronger functioning of the immune system (e.g., greater natural killer cell responses).

Uchino, Uno, and Holt-Lunstad (1999) discussed the evidence considered here. They came to the following conclusion: "Social support may influence mortality via changes in the cardiovascular, endocrine, and immune systems" (p. 145).

We must avoid exaggerating the value of social support, especially when an individual is facing a very severe stressor. For example, Bolger et al. (1996) found that high levels of social support for patients suffering from breast cancer did not reduce their distress or the progression of the disease.

Social support is one of the psychological approaches to reducing stress levels.

## Intervention techniques

Numerous intervention techniques have been devised to reduce the high levels of stress experienced by many people. It would be impossible to do justice to all of them here. Accordingly, we will focus on three of the main techniques. We start with a cognitive intervention technique (stress inoculation training). After that, we will consider biofeedback, which is a technique combining physiological and psychological ingredients. Finally, we consider various drug treatments for stress.

### Stress inoculation training

Several forms of cognitive therapy have been devised for the treatment of clinical anxiety and depression (see Chapter 23). The essence of this approach to therapy is to replace negative and irrational thoughts (e.g., "I am totally incompetent") with positive and rational ones (e.g., "I can achieve many things if I try hard enough"). Cognitive therapy is used with patients who are already suffering from high levels of anxiety and/or depression. Meichenbaum (1977, 1985) argued that we should use cognitive therapy *before* people become very anxious or depressed rather than afterwards. This led him to develop stress inoculation training.

There are three main phases in stress inoculation training:

1. *Assessment*. The therapist discusses the nature of the problem with the individual, together with the individual's perception of how to eliminate it.
2. *Stress reduction techniques*. The individual learns various techniques for reducing stress, such as relaxation and self-instruction. The essence of self-instruction is that the individual practises several coping self-statements. The self-statements vary across stages of a stressful situation:
   (a) Preparing for a stressor (e.g., "What do I have to do?").
   (b) Confronting and handling a stressor (e.g., "Relax and take a slow, deep breath").
   (c) Coping with the feeling of being overwhelmed (e.g., "Just try to keep fear at a manageable level").
3. *Application and follow-through*. The individual imagines using the stress reduction techniques learned in the second phase in difficult situations, and/or engages in role play of such situations with the therapist. Finally, the techniques are used in real-life situations.

Meichenbaum (1985, 1993) developed some of his earlier ideas on stress inoculation training. In particular, he put more emphasis on some of the cognitive processes involved. For example, he argued it is important to consider how individuals think about the situations they find especially stressful.

### Evidence

Meichenbaum (1977) compared his stress inoculation technique against a form of behaviour therapy known as desensitisation (see Chapter 23). These methods were applied to

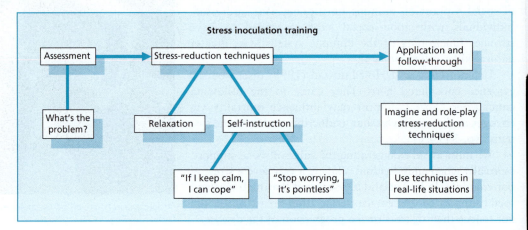

individuals who suffered from both snake phobia and rat phobia, but treatment was only provided for one phobia. Both forms of treatment were effective in reducing or eliminating the treated phobia. However, stress inoculation also greatly reduced the non-treated phobia, whereas desensitisation did not. The implication is that self-instruction easily generalises to new situations, which makes it more useful than very specific forms of treatment.

Stress inoculation training has proved effective in the treatment of individuals experiencing stress for a variety of reasons. For example, it is "moderately helpful to people who suffer from test-taking and performance anxiety, stress associated with life change, and mild forms of anxiety" (Comer, 2001, p. 133). Stress inoculation training was also found to be helpful for stressed families in which there were step-children (Fausel, 1995).

> ## Examples of coping self-statements used in Meichenbaum's stress inoculation training
>
> Preparing for a stressful situation:
> What is it you have to do?
> You can develop a plan to deal with it.
> Just think about what you can do. That's better than getting anxious.
> Maybe what you think is anxiety is in fact eagerness to confront it.
>
> Confronting and handling a stressful situation:
> Just "psych" yourself up—you can meet this challenge.
> One step at a time, you can handle the situation.
> This tenseness can be an ally, a cue to cope.
> Relax; you're in control. Take a slow deep breath. Ah, good.
>
> Coping with the feeling of being overwhelmed:
> When fear comes, just pause.
> Keep the focus on the present; what is it you have to do?
> You should expect your fear to rise.
> It's not the worst thing that can happen.
>
> Reinforcing self-statements:
> It wasn't as bad as you expected.
> Wait until you tell your therapist about this.
> You made more out of the fear than it was worth.
> You did it!

## Evaluation

- ⊕ Stress inoculation training has proved effective in treating stress stemming from various causes.
- ⊖ Stress inoculation training is of relatively little value when treating individuals who are highly stressed or exposed to very stressful situations.
- ⊖ Some individuals find it hard to use coping self-statements in stressful situations.

## Biofeedback

Biofeedback is often used to reduce stress. In essence, **biofeedback** is a technique that provides the individual with detailed information about some aspect of his/her physical functioning. For example, an electromyograph can be attached to an individual's forehead muscles to provide visual or auditory feedback about the level of muscular tension. The individual is also trained in techniques known to reduce physiological aspects of stress. For example, there is relaxation training, part of which involves breathing in a regular and calm way.

Biofeedback training involves three stages:

1. Developing an awareness of the particular physiological response (e.g., heart rate, muscular tension).
2. Learning ways of controlling that physiological response in quiet conditions; this can include providing rewards for successful control in addition to feedback.
3. Transferring that control into the conditions of everyday life.

It seems unlikely we would be able to exert voluntary control over apparently involuntary processes such as blood pressure. Consider, however, the escapologist Harry Houdini. He escaped from dangerous situations when securely shackled and having had his clothes and body searched thoroughly to ensure he was not hiding any keys. How did he do it? He held a key suspended in his throat, and regurgitated it when no-one was looking. The natural reaction to having an object stuck in your throat is to gag.

> **KEY TERM**
> **Biofeedback:** a technique in which individuals are provided with information or feedback about their current physiological activity in order to facilitate the reduction of stress.

People learn to use biofeedback techniques to control normally involuntary bodily functions such as heart rate. The technique may involve a machine that monitors relevant bodily functions and produces visual or auditory signals. Through relaxation, the individual learns to alter the rate of these signals and thus to control the involuntary functions.

This is a picture of the world famous American escapologist Harry Houdini, who carried out many apparently miraculous escapes from dangerous or even potentially fatal situations. One of his favourite tricks (discussed in the text) involved using a form of biofeedback to suspend a key hidden in his throat.

However, Houdini had spent hours practising with a small piece of potato on a string until he could control his gag reflex.

Biofeedback can produce short-term reductions in heart rate, blood pressure, skin temperature, and brain-wave rhythms. This happens in spite of the fact that we cannot control *directly* our heart rate and blood pressure, because they are controlled automatically by the autonomic nervous system. However, it is possible to exert control *indirectly*. For example, breathing deeply, using methods of relaxation, or simply moving around can produce changes in various physiological measures.

## Evidence

We can distinguish between laboratory and clinical studies of biofeedback, both of which have reported beneficial effects. Victor, Mainardi, and Shapiro (1978) carried out a laboratory study using the cold pressor test, in which participants have to keep their hand immersed in freezing water and ice for about 30 seconds. Exposure to the cold pressor test typically leads to increased heart rate and to high levels of pain. Victor et al. found that participants who had been given biofeedback training managed to reduce their heart rate during the cold pressor test, and also reported less pain than participants who had not received training.

Newton, Spence, and Schotte (1995) reported the findings from a clinical study. They found that biofeedback was effective in the treatment of back pain. Biofeedback has also been used in the treatment of essential hypertension, and is associated with a reduction in blood pressure (see Blanchard, 1994, for a review). However, biofeedback is often accompanied by relaxation training, and some of the evidence suggests that relaxation training plays a larger role than biofeedback in reducing blood pressure in sufferers from essential hypertension (Blanchard, 1994).

Holroyd and French (1994) reported on the findings from several clinical studies on sufferers from tension headaches. Electromyograph biofeedback led to an average reduction of 46% in the number of headaches reported. However, there is controversy about *how* these effects are produced. Holroyd et al. (1984) found that electromyograph biofeedback was associated with a reduction in tension headaches. However, participants who believed *falsely* they were reducing muscular tension through biofeedback experienced fewer headaches. Thus, the beneficial effects of biofeedback may work through perceptions of control rather than through direct effects on physiological processes.

## Evaluation

⊕ Several laboratory studies have reported beneficial effects of biofeedback on stress.
⊕ In clinical studies, use of biofeedback has been found to be associated with reductions in conditions such as essential hypertension, tension headaches, and back pain.
⊖ The precise reasons why biofeedback has beneficial effects are not clearly understood.
⊖ Some of the effects of biofeedback may be due to relaxation training or perceived control (e.g., Holroyd et al., 1984).
⊖ Biofeedback is unlikely to achieve long-term reductions in stress among individuals who have a tense and driven lifestyle.

People who practise yoga have been reported to be able to slow their heartbeat down sufficiently for them to survive in a sealed booth long after most people would have suffocated to death. They use relaxation to control their bodily systems.

## Drug treatment

One way of reducing stress is by giving people anti-anxiety drugs (see also Chapter 23). The most used anti-anxiety drugs are the **benzodiazepines** (e.g., Valium, Librium). There are benzodiazepine receptors in the brain forming part of the GABA receptor complex. The benzodiazepines increase the activity of the neurotransmitter GABA, which inhibits activation throughout the nervous system. The benzodiazepines are very effective at reducing anxiety, and are used by tens of millions of people around the world.

**KEY TERM**

**Benzodiazepines:** a class of drugs (e.g., Valium) that serve to reduce anxiety levels.

In spite of their effectiveness, benzodiazepines have several unwanted side effects. They often have sedative effects, and can make people feel drowsy. In addition, the benzodiazepines can cause cognitive and memory impairments, they sometimes lead to feelings of depression, and they can interact unpredictably with alcohol (Ashton, 1997). As a result, individuals taking benzodiazepines are more likely to be involved in accidents. Finally, many people become dependent on benzodiazepines, and experience severe withdrawal symptoms after long periods of taking them (Wickens, 2000). Among individuals who had taken benzodiazepines for at least 1 year before stopping, only 43% managed to stop for at least 1 week (Rickels et al., 1990).

**Buspirone** offers advantages over benzodiazepines. It is a serotonin agonist, meaning it facilitates the effects of the neurotransmitter serotonin. It doesn't have the sedative effects of benzodiazepines, and there are no marked withdrawal symptoms. However, buspirone produces side effects such as headaches and depression (Goa & Ward, 1986). In addition, buspirone is less effective than the benzodiazepines in dealing with acute stress, because its onset of action can be up to 2 weeks (Wickens, 2000).

**Beta blockers** are drugs that lower stress and anxiety by reducing activity in the sympathetic nervous system. They have a direct action on the heart and circulatory system, thereby decreasing heart rate and lowering peripheral blood pressure. Their effects are on the body, and they do not have direct effects on brain activity. Beta blockers have proved useful in reducing blood pressure and in treating patients with heart disease. For example, Lau et al. (1992) considered the findings from numerous studies in a meta-analysis, and found that beta blockers reduced the risk of death by about 20% in patients with heart disease. An advantage of beta blockers is that there are no problems of dependence. However, beta blockers can produce various unwanted side effects, including cold extremities, fatigue, nightmares, and hallucinations.

Anti-anxiety drugs can be very effective at reducing intense feelings of stress. However, they do not address the problems causing the stress, and can have unfortunate side effects. The benzodiazepines should generally be limited to short-term use of no more than 4 weeks (Ashton, 1997). In addition, they should only be given to individuals with severe anxiety symptoms, and the drugs should be given in the minimal effective doses. Individuals who have become dependent on benzodiazepines should have their dosage reduced gradually. The good news is that about 70% of dependent users of benzodiazepines who are motivated to give them up manage to do this for periods of several years or more (Ashton, 1997).

There are a number of types of anti-anxiety drugs, the most commonly used of which are benzodiazepines such as Valium and Librium.

**KEY TERMS**
**Buspirone:** a serotonin agonist that is used as an anti-anxiety drug.
**Beta blockers:** drugs reducing stress by reducing activity in the sympathetic nervous system.

# SUMMARY

Emotions consist of various response systems, including facial and other expressions, changes in physiological activity, subjective feeling states, and patterns of behaviour. There is typically relatively little agreement or concordance among the various emotional response systems. This occurs because response measures are imperfect, and because each response system has its own function. Emotions are short-lasting and more intense than moods, and are more often caused by a specific event. Emotions serve various functions (e.g., anxiety facilitates the detection of threat). The physiological changes associated with anger and fear help the individual to cope with environmental challenges. Emotions influence individuals to pursue the goal having greatest survival value. Emotion often disrupts what we were doing beforehand, but leads to highly organised behaviour designed to achieve a more important goal than the one we had been pursuing.

*What is emotion?*

Research by Ekman suggests six basic emotions can reliably be identified from facial expressions: happiness, surprise, anger, sadness, fear, and disgust combined with contempt. There is much cross-cultural agreement on the emotions associated with facial expressions, but much research is based on posed photographs. Self-report evidence is consistent with a hierarchical model with Negative Affect and Positive Affect at the top level, and more specific emotions at the bottom level. There is controversy as to whether Positive and Negative Affect are independent as proposed within the model.

*How many emotions are there?*

**Theories of emotion**

According to the James–Lange theory, our emotions are determined by our experience of our bodily symptoms. However, feedback from physiological changes is not necessary for emotions to be experienced, and physiological patterns vary less from one emotion to another than predicted. According to arousal–interpretation theory, high physiological arousal and an emotional interpretation of that arousal are both needed for emotion to be experienced. This cognitive theory has received only weak support, and cannot account for the finding that high arousal is generally interpreted negatively. Lazarus's appraisal theory claims that cognitive appraisal helps to determine emotional experience. The theory de-emphasises the social context in which emotion is usually experienced, and automatic processing of emotional stimuli is not considered. Parkinson's four-factor theory provides a reasonable synthesis of several previous theories. According to the SPAARS model, emotion can occur as a result of either thorough cognitive processing or automatic processing. The model often fails to make clear predictions, and the role of physiological processes is not considered sufficiently.

**Physiological systems in emotion**

The role of the brain in emotion has been studied by the lesion method, by imaging techniques, and by using drugs. According to the Papez–MacLean limbic model, the limbic system plays a key role in emotion. Part of the limbic system (the amygdala) is of special importance for fear and anger. According to LeDoux, there are two brain routes involved in anxiety: a slow-acting route between the thalamus and the amygdala going via the cortex, and a fast-acting route that bypasses the cortex. Pleasant emotions mainly involve the left cortex, whereas unpleasant ones mostly involve the right cortex. Serotonin plays an inhibitory role, with moderate levels of serotonin inhibiting both anger and depression.

Viewing a smiling face can increase your positive frame of mind.

Physiologically, stress consists of an immediate shock response involving the sympathetic adrenal medullary system, followed by a countershock response involving the hypothalamic–pituitary–adrenocortical axis. Selye in his general adaptation syndrome focused on the latter response and de-emphasised the initial shock response. He also paid insufficient attention to the fact that different stressors produce somewhat different patterns of physiological responding.

*Stress*

Life events and hassles are associated with numerous physical and mental illnesses. It is often hard to decide whether life events have caused some stress-related illness, or vice versa. Many factors at work cause stress and ill health, but a lack of perceived control seems to be of special importance. The impact of most life events varies from person to person, and from group to group. Individuals high in negative affectivity report high levels of stress and physical symptoms, but these reports are often exaggerated. Type A behaviour (and especially its hostility component) is associated with coronary heart disease, but the association is a modest one. Long-term stress (but not short-term stress) often has an adverse effect on the immune system. However, the effects are typically small and complex, and it is not clear that the immune system is affected sufficiently to produce physical illness.

*Stress and illness*

People use various coping strategies (e.g., task-oriented, emotion-oriented, avoidance-oriented) when confronted by stressful situations. Males are more likely to respond to stress with the fight-or-flight response, whereas females often use the tend-and-befriend response. The task- or problem-oriented coping strategy is generally effective, except when there is little the individual can do to improve matters. Many stressful situations change over time, and this can mean the best coping strategy also changes. Social support can protect people from various causes of mortality. This may happen because social support produces changes in the cardiovascular, endocrine, and immune systems. Stress inoculation training involves successive phases of assessment, stress reduction techniques, and application and follow-through. Biofeedback can produce significant long-term reductions in heart rate and blood pressure, but it is hard to explain how these beneficial effects occur. Anti-anxiety drugs can reduce stress, but often have unwanted side effects.

*Coping with stress*

# FURTHER READING

- Dalgleish, T. (1998). Emotion. In M.W. Eysenck (Ed.), *Psychology: An integrated approach*. Harlow, UK: Longman. This chapter contains a fairly detailed account of major issues in the field of emotion.
- Lewis, M., & Howland-Jones, J.M. (2000). *Handbook of emotions* (2nd. ed.). New York: Guilford Press. The chapters of this edited book contain comprehensive accounts of emotion written by leading experts.
- Pitts M., & Phillips, K. (1998). *The psychology of health: An introduction* (2nd. ed.). London: Routledge. The effects of stress on physical health are discussed in an accessible way in various chapters of this book.
- Wickens, A. (2000). *Foundations of biopsychology*. Harlow, UK: Prentice Hall. Chapter 5 in this book deals with the biological aspects of emotion.

# Cognitive Psychology

Cognitive psychology is concerned with the main internal psychological processes that are involved in making sense of the environment and in deciding what action might be appropriate. These processes include attention, perception, learning, memory, language, problem solving, reasoning, and thinking.

Cognitive psychology has become progressively more important in several other areas of psychology. For example, consider the areas of developmental psychology, social psychology, and abnormal psychology. In order to understand how infants develop into adolescents and adults, it is essential to consider the massive cognitive changes that occur during childhood. In order to understand how individuals interact with each other in social situations, we need to take account of the knowledge of themselves and of each other they have stored in memory, their interpretations of the current social situation, and so on. In order to understand patients suffering from anxiety disorders or depression, it is important to focus on their biased interpretations of themselves and of their current and future prospects.

## FOUR MAJOR APPROACHES

Cognitive processes typically occur very rapidly, and they occur inside the head where they cannot be observed directly. As a result, such processes are not easy to study. The responses people make when given some task to perform tell us something about the internal cognitive processes that have occurred, but most of the time they provide only an indirect reflection of those processes.

How have cognitive psychologists responded to the challenge of understanding human cognition? They have developed four major approaches to the study of human cognition (discussed below), and have assumed that combining information from all of them is the best way to proceed. This makes sense, given that each approach has its own strengths and weaknesses. When similar findings are obtained from two or more approaches, we can have some confidence that the findings are genuine and of importance.

The four major approaches are as follows:

- **Experimental cognitive psychology**. This involves carrying out experiments on normal individuals, typically under laboratory conditions.
- **Cognitive neuropsychology**. This involves studying the patterns of cognitive impairment shown by brain-damaged patients to understand normal human cognition.
- **Cognitive science**. This involves developing computational models to simulate (and to understand) human cognition.

- **Cognitive neuroscience.** This involves using several techniques for studying brain functioning (e.g., brain scans) to identify the processes and structures used in cognition.

The actual distinctions are less neat and tidy than has been implied. Terms such as "cognitive science" and "cognitive neuroscience" are fairly often used in a much broader way to cover most (or even all) of the four approaches we have identified. In addition, many studies combine elements from more than one approach. For example, there is what we could call "connectionist neuropsychology", in which computer networks are "lesioned" or damaged to see whether the resulting pattern of performance looks like that of brain-damaged patients. This approach combines cognitive science and cognitive neuropsychology.

## Experimental cognitive psychology

Experiments carried out on normals under laboratory conditions tend to be tightly controlled and "scientific". However, people may behave differently in the laboratory to the ways in which they behave in everyday life. As Heather (1976, p. 33) pointed out, "The main kind of knowledge gleaned from years of experimentation with human subjects is information about how strangers interact in the highly artificial and unusual social setting of the psychological experiment."

Problems about the artificiality of laboratory research have often been expressed by claiming that such research lacks ecological validity. According to Kvavilashvili and Ellis (in press), **ecological validity** has two aspects: (1) representativeness; and (2) generalisability. Representativeness refers to the naturalness of the experimental situation, stimuli, and task. In contrast, generalisability refers to the extent to which the findings of a study are applicable to the real world. Generalisability is more important than representativeness, and so we need to reassure ourselves that experimental studies possess generalisability.

## Cognitive neuropsychology

Cognitive neuropsychologists assume that the cognitive system consists of several **modules** or cognitive processors within the brain. These modules operate fairly independently of each other, so that brain damage can impair the functioning of some modules while leaving others intact. Thus, for example, the modules or processors involved in understanding speech are presumably rather different from those involved in actually speaking. As a result, there are some brain-damaged patients who are good at language comprehension but poor at speaking, whereas others have the opposite pattern.

Cognitive neuropsychologists look for dissociations. A dissociation occurs when a patient performs at a normal level on one task, but is severely impaired on a second task. For example, amnesic patients perform well on tasks involving short-term memory but have very poor performance on most long-term memory tasks (see Chapter 9). Such findings suggest that short-term memory and long-term memory involve separate modules. However, it could be argued that brain damage simply reduces the ability to perform hard (but not easy) tasks, and that long-term memory tasks are harder than short-term memory tasks. In fact, this explanation is incorrect, because other brain-damaged patients have good long-term memory but poor short-term memory.

The memory research discussed above illustrates a double dissociation. A **double dissociation** between two tasks occurs when some patients perform task A normally but are impaired on task B, whereas other patients perform task B normally but are impaired on task A. Double dissociations provide strong evidence for the existence of separate modules. As we will see, the cognitive neuropsychological approach has provided a wealth of important information about the workings of human cognition, perhaps especially in the area of language. Research on brain-damaged patients has greatly increased our understanding of the complex processes underlying apparently simple activities such as reading visually presented words aloud (see Chapter 11).

In spite of its many successes, there are some potential interpretive problems with research in cognitive neuropsychology. First, we may not observe the full effects of brain

**KEY TERMS**

**Cognitive neuroscience:** an approach to cognitive psychology based on the use of various techniques (e.g., brain scans) to study the brain in a fairly direct way.

**Ecological validity:** the extent to which the findings of laboratory studies are applicable to everyday settings.

**Modules:** independent or separate processors within the cognitive system.

**Double dissociation:** the finding that some individuals (often brain damaged) perform normally on task A and poorly on task B, whereas others show the opposite pattern.

damage on cognitive functioning, because brain-damaged patients may develop compensatory strategies to cope with the damage. However, in practice this is rarely a serious problem. Second, it is important not to exaggerate the extent to which cognitive functions are localised within the brain. As Banich (1997, p. 52) noted, "the brain is comprised of about 50 billion *interconnected* neurons. Therefore, even complex cognitive functions for which a modular description seems apt rely on a number of interconnected brain regions or systems."

Third, the cognitive neuropsychological approach is complex because there are individual differences among individuals having broadly similar brain damage. As Banich (1997, p. 55) pointed out, such individuals, "typically vary widely in age, socioeconomic status, and educational background. Prior to brain damage, these individuals may have had diverse life experiences. Afterward, their life experiences likely vary too."

# Cognitive science

The computational models developed by cognitive scientists can show us how a given theory can be specified in detail. This is a definite advantage over many previous theories in cognitive psychology, which were expressed so vaguely that it was not clear exactly what predictions were supposed to follow from them.

In recent years, connectionist networks have become very popular. **Connectionist networks** typically consist of elementary or neuron-like units or nodes connected together. Most networks have different structures of layers, often consisting of a layer of input links, intermediate layers (of so-called "hidden units"), and a layer of output units. Within such networks, memories are distributed over the network rather than being in a single location.

Why are connectionist networks so popular? One reason is because the numerous elementary units within a connectionist network seem superficially to resemble the neurons within the brain. Another reason is that connectionist networks can to some extent programme themselves, and so can "learn" to produce specific outputs when certain inputs are given to them. Finally, most previous models were based on **serial processing**, in which only one process happens at a time. In contrast, connectionist models engage in **parallel processing** (two or more cognitive processes occurring at the same time). This is an advantage, because parallel processing is very common in human cognition.

In spite of many promising developments in cognitive science, there are various limitations with this approach. First, as Gazzaniga, Ivry, and Mangun (1998, p. 102) pointed out, "Modelling research tends to occur in isolation. There may be lots of ways to model a particular phenomenon, but [little] effort has been devoted to devising critical tests that pit one theory against another." Second, connectionist models fail to resemble the human brain. They typically use thousands or tens of thousands of connected units to model a cognitive task that might be performed by tens of millions of neurons in the brain. Third, a given set of findings can sometimes be "explained" by several models. As Carey and Milner (1994, p. 66) pointed out, "any neural net which produces a desired output from a specified input is hugely under-constrained; an infinitely large number of solutions can be found for each problem addressed".

# Cognitive neuroscience

Technological advances have produced several methods for studying the brain in a fairly direct way. As you have probably noticed, there has been considerable media coverage of these new techniques. Newspapers and magazines have printed numerous multi-coloured pictures of the brain, with the various colours indicating the relative activation of different parts of the brain during the performance of some task. In principle, these new techniques allow us to establish *where* and *when* certain cognitive processes occur. Such information can also allow us to determine the order in which different parts of the brain become active when someone is performing a task.

The various techniques for studying the brain differ in their spatial resolution (the precision with which they identify which areas of the brain are active when a task is being

**Techniques used by cognitive neuroscientists**

| Method | Strengths | Weaknesses |
|---|---|---|
| Single-unit recording | Fine-grain detail. Information obtained over a wide range of time periods. | Invasive. Only neuronal-level information is obtained. |
| ERPs | Detailed information about the time course of brain activity. | Lack precision in identifying specific areas of the brain. Can only be used to study basic cognitive processes. |
| PET | Active areas can be located to within 3–4 mm. Can identify a wide range of cognitive activities. | Cannot reveal rapid changes in brain activity. Provides only an indirect measure of neural activity. Findings from a subtraction technique can be hard to interpret. |
| MRI and fMRI | No known biological risk. Obtains accurate anatomical information. fMRI provides good information about timing. | Indirect measure of neural activity. Cannot track the time course of most cognitive processes. |
| MEG | Provides a reasonably direct measure of neural activity. Gives detailed information about the time course of cognitive processes. | Irrelevant sources of magnetism may interfere with measurement. Does not give accurate information about brain areas active at a given time. |

performed). They also differ in their temporal resolution (the precision with which the time course of such activation is measured). Some techniques provide information about brain activity on a millisecond-by-millisecond basis, whereas others only indicate brain activity over much longer periods of time (e.g., minutes, hours). In similar fashion, some techniques provide information at the level of the single cell, whereas others only reveal activity over large areas of the brain. We now consider some of the main techniques in current use.

- **Event-related potentials** (ERPs). Electroencephalograms (EEGs) based on recordings of electrical brain activity measured at the scalp are obtained several times to repeated presentations of a stimulus, and then averaged. ERPs have excellent temporal resolution but very poor spatial resolution.
- **Positron emission tomography** (PET). This technique is based on the detection of positrons, which are the atomic particles emitted by some radioactive substances. PET has reasonable spatial resolution but poor temporal resolution.
- **Magnetic resonance imaging** (MRI and fMRI). Radio waves are used to excite atoms in the brain, and this produces magnetic changes detected by an 11-ton magnet surrounding the individual. MRI provides information about brain structure, and can detect very small brain tumours. Functional MRI (fMRI) detects brain activity. It is more useful than PET, because it provides more precise spatial information, and it shows changes over much shorter periods of time.
- **Magneto-encephalography** (MEG). This involves using a super-conducting quantum interference device (SQUID), which measures the magnetic fields produced by electrical brain activity. MEG assesses neural activity fairly directly, and supplies detailed information at the millisecond level about the time course of cognitive processes.

The techniques used within cognitive neuroscience are most useful when applied to aspects of cognition involving only a few easily identifiable areas of the brain (S. Anderson, personal comm.). This seems to be the case with various aspects of perception (see Chapter 7). Most higher order cognitive functions (e.g., reasoning, decision) are probably not organised so clearly. As a result, numerous areas of the brain become activated, and it is hard to obtain a clear picture of what is happening in the brain.

Cognitive neuroscience typically provides information about *where* in the brain certain cognitive functions occur. However, it generally tells us relatively little about *how* those cognitive functions are accomplished, i.e., the detailed processes involved. This has become less of a problem in recent years as we develop an increasingly detailed theoretical understanding of the functioning of the main areas of the brain.

## Conclusions

Everyone agrees that understanding fully how the brain works is one of the crucial scientific challenges of the twenty-first century. What is really exciting is that scientists finally have access to the technology and approaches needed to meet that challenge successfully. Scientists are making increasingly effective use of all four approaches described in this introduction (experimental cognitive psychology, cognitive neuropsychology, cognitive science, and cognitive neuroscience). Indeed, in my opinion, there has probably been more progress in understanding human cognition in the past decade than ever before, and the omens look very favourable for the future.

Our current understanding of the major areas in cognitive psychology is discussed over the next six chapters. We start in Chapter 6 with a consideration of the processes involved in attention (e.g., do we attend to objects or to a given region in space?). This chapter is also concerned with some of the factors which determine how well (or badly!) we cope with trying to do two tasks at the same time. Chapter 7 deals with visual perception. In this chapter, we consider visual processes all the way from the retina to our three-dimensional perception of the world around us. Chapter 8 deals with learning, which is of fundamental importance to the human species. We start by considering traditional approaches to learning based on conditioning and move on to more cognitive approaches involved in accounting for complex learning (e.g., acquisition of expertise).

Chapter 9 deals with human memory, and considers both short-term and long-term memory. It focuses on the processes involved in the storage and subsequent retrieval of information ranging from individual words to entire texts. Chapter 10 deals with some of the higher mental processes, namely those involved in problem solving and reasoning. There is an emphasis on the issue of what the findings obtained from laboratory studies tell us about everyday problem solving and reasoning. Finally, Chapter 11 deals with language. Our possession of language is one of the greatest advantages we have over most other species, and this chapter is devoted to understanding the surprisingly complex processes involved in the comprehension and production of language.

- **Attention**
  The nature and meaning of attention.

  *Attention and consciousness*
  *Focused and divided attention*
  *Action slips*

- **Focused auditory attention**
  Theories of selective auditory attention.

  *Cherry's "cocktail party" problem*
  *The shadowing and dichotic listening tasks*
  *Broadbent's filter theory*
  *Alternative theories: Treisman; Deutsch and Deutsch*

- **Focused visual attention**
  Theories of selective visual attention.

  *Eriksen and St. James' zoom-lens model*
  *Unattended visual stimuli; unilateral neglect*
  *Visual search*
  *Treisman's feature integration theory*
  *Wolfe's guided search theory*

- **Divided attention**
  Theoretical approaches to divided attention.

  *Exploration of dual-task studies*
  *Dual-task performance—task similarity, practice, task difficulty*
  *Proactive and retroactive interference in stimuli–response process*
  *Theories of central capacity*
  *Welford's bottleneck theory and the psychological refractory period effect*
  *Wickens' multiple-resource model*

- **Automatic processing**
  The role of attention in automatic processes.

  *Shiffrin and Schneider's distinction between controlled and automatic processes*
  *Norman and Shallice's schema-activation model*
  *The supervisory attentional system*

- **Action slips**
  Examination of unintended actions.

  *Reason's diary studies—five categories of attention failure*
  *Hay and Jacoby's findings in laboratory studies*
  *Sellen and Norman's schema theory*

# Attention and performance limitations

**6**

## ATTENTION

That part of cognitive psychology concerned with attention is the main focus of this chapter. The concept of attention has been used in several senses. It sometimes means the same as concentration, but can also refer to our ability to select some aspect of incoming stimulation for further analysis. It has also been argued that there are close links between attention and arousal, with aroused individuals being more attentive than drowsy individuals to the environment. However, attention is most often used to refer to selectivity of processing.

What is the relationship between attention and consciousness? Baars (1997) argued that access to consciousness is controlled by attentional mechanisms. Consider, for example, sentences such as, "We look in order to see", or "We listen in order to hear." According to Baars (p. 364), "The distinction is between selecting an experience and being conscious of the selected event. In everyday language, the first word of each pair ['look', 'listen'] involves attention; the second word ['see', 'hear'] involves consciousness." Thus, attention resembles choosing a television channel and consciousness resembles the picture seen on the screen.

We need to distinguish between focused attention and divided attention. **Focused attention** is studied by presenting people with two or more stimulus inputs at the same time, and instructing them to respond to only one. Such studies tell us how well people can *select* certain inputs rather than others. It also allows us to study the nature of the selection process and the fate of unattended stimuli. Focused attention is involved when students taking examinations try to avoid being distracted by other students, noises outside the room, and so on.

**Divided attention** is studied by presenting two stimulus inputs at the same time, with the instructions indicating that both inputs should be attended to and responded to. Studies of divided attention (**dual-task studies**) provide useful information about an individual's processing limitations. They may also tell us something about attentional mechanisms and their capacity. For example, can students do their homework effectively while listening to music?

We can also learn about the workings of attention by studying **action slips** (actions not carried out as intended). The most important reason for action slips is a failure to attend sufficiently to what we are doing. An example of an action slip is feeding baked beans to the cat, because the tin looks very similar to the tin of cat food.

As we will see, much of value has been learned about human attention. However, most laboratory research differs from everyday life in that what participants attend to in the laboratory is determined by the experimental instructions. In contrast, what we attend to in the real world is largely determined by our current goals. As Allport (1989, p. 664) pointed out, "What is important to recognise ... is not the location of some imaginary boundary between the provinces of attention and motivation, but, to the contrary, their essential interdependence."

## FOCUSED AUDITORY ATTENTION

In the early 1950s, the British scientist Colin Cherry became interested in the "cocktail party" problem: How do we follow only *one* conversation when several people are talking at once? (see Key Study on the next page).

(see Key Study on the next page).

**KEY TERMS**

**Focused attention:** a situation in which people try to attend to only one source of stimulation while ignoring other stimuli.

**Divided attention:** a situation in which people try to perform two tasks at the same time; see dual-task studies.

**Dual-task studies:** studies in which participants perform two tasks at the same time; see divided attention.

**Action slips:** actions that are not carried out as intended.

## KEY STUDY EVALUATION—Cherry

The research by Colin Cherry is a very good example of how a psychologist, noticing a real-life situation, is able to devise a hypothesis and carry out research in order to explain a phenomenon, in this case the "cocktail party" effect. Cherry tested his ideas in a laboratory using a shadowing technique and found that participants were really only able to give information about the physical qualities of the non-attended message (whether the message was read by a male or a female, or if a tone was used instead of speech). Cherry's research could be criticised for having moved the real-life phenomenon into an artificial laboratory setting. However, this work opened avenues for other researchers, beginning with Broadbent, to elaborate theories about focused auditory attention.

# Cherry: The cocktail party problem

Cherry (1953) found that we use physical differences between the various auditory messages to select the one of interest. These physical differences include differences in the sex of the speaker, in voice intensity, and in the location of the speaker. When Cherry presented two messages in the same voice to both ears at once (thereby removing these physical differences), the participants found it very hard to separate out the two messages purely on the basis of meaning.

Cherry (1953) also carried out studies using a **shadowing task**, in which one auditory message had to be shadowed (repeated back out aloud) while a second auditory message was presented to the other ear. Very little information seemed to be obtained from the second or non-attended message. Listeners rarely noticed even when that message was spoken in a foreign language or in reversed speech. In contrast, physical changes (e.g., the insertion of a pure tone) were usually detected, and listeners noticed the sex of the speaker and the intensity of sound of unattended messages. The suggestion that unattended auditory information receives very little processing is supported by other evidence. For example, there is very little memory for words on the unattended message even when presented 35 times each (Moray, 1959).

## Discussion points

1. Are you surprised by any of Cherry's findings?
2. Why do you think that Broadbent found Cherry's findings of great interest?

How do we distinguish and follow one conversation out of many in situations like this?

### KEY TERMS

**Shadowing task:** a task in which there are two auditory messages, one of which has to be repeated back aloud or shadowed.

**Dichotic listening task:** a task in which pairs of items are presented one to each ear, followed by recall of all items.

**Sensory buffer:** a mechanism that maintains information for a short period of time before it is processed.

Broadbent (1958) discussed findings from what is known as the **dichotic listening task**. What usually happens is that three digits are presented one after the other to one ear, while at the same time three different digits are presented to the other ear. After the three pairs of digits have been presented, the participants recall them in whatever order they prefer. Recall is typically ear by ear rather than pair by pair. Thus, for example, if 496 were presented to one ear and 852 to the other ear, recall would be 496852 rather than 489562. Note that various kinds of stimuli (e.g., letters, words) can be used with the dichotic listening task.

## Broadbent's filter theory

The British psychologist Donald Broadbent (1958) put forward the first detailed theory of attention. His filter theory was based on findings from the shadowing and dichotic listening tasks. The key assumptions in this theory were as follows:

- Two stimuli or messages presented at the same time gain access in parallel (at the same time) to a **sensory buffer**. This holds information for a short period before it is attended to or disappears from the processing system.
- One of the inputs is then allowed through a filter on the basis of its physical characteristics, with the other input only briefly in the buffer for later processing.
- This filter prevents overloading of the limited-capacity mechanism beyond the filter; this mechanism processes the input thoroughly.

This theory handles Cherry's basic findings, with unattended messages being rejected by the filter and thus receiving very little processing. It also accounts for performance on Broadbent's original dichotic listening task, since it is assumed that the filter selects one

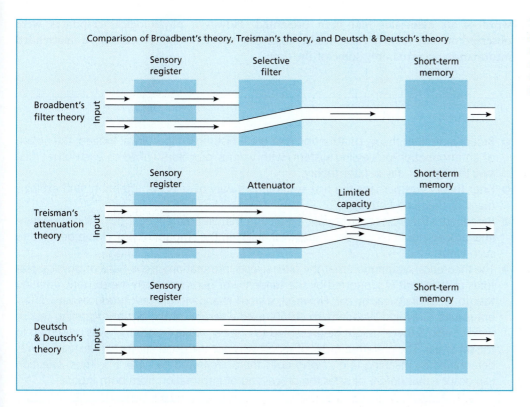

Comparison of Broadbent's theory, Treisman's theory, and Deutsch & Deutsch's theory

*These models use an information processing metaphor for modelling attention. Do you think this is a useful way of explaining human attention?*

input on the basis of the most obvious physical characteristic distinguishing the two inputs (i.e., the ear of arrival). However, the theory does not explain other findings. For example, it is assumed incorrectly that the unattended message is *always* rejected early in processing. The original shadowing studies involved participants with no previous experience of shadowing messages, who had to devote nearly all their processing resources to the shadowing task. Underwood (1974) asked participants to detect digits presented on either the shadowed or the non-shadowed message. Participants who had not done the task before detected only 8% of the digits on the non-shadowed message. In contrast, a participant with extensive practice of shadowing detected 67% of the non-shadowed digits.

The two messages were very similar (i.e., both auditorily presented verbal messages) in early studies on the shadowing task. Allport, Antonis, and Reynolds (1972) found that the *similarity* between the two messages had a major impact on memory for the non-shadowed message. When shadowing of auditorily presented passages was combined with auditory presentation of words the participants were asked to learn, memory for the words was very poor. However, when shadowing was combined with picture presentation, memory for the pictures was very good (90% correct). If two inputs differ clearly from each other, they can both be processed more thoroughly than was allowed for on Broadbent's filter theory.

The findings of Allport et al. (1972) helped to clarify why Broadbent (1958) came to the mistaken conclusion that there is very little processing of unattended auditory messages. The experimental evidence prior to 1958 nearly all involved two very similar auditory inputs. These are the very conditions in which there is minimal processing of the unattended input.

Broadbent (1958) assumed there was no processing of the meaning of unattended messages, because the participants had no conscious awareness of their meaning. However, meaning may be processed without awareness. Von Wright, Anderson, and Stenman (1975) gave participants two auditorily presented lists of words. They told them to shadow one list and ignore the other. When a word previously associated with electric shock was presented on the non-attended list, there was sometimes a physiological response. There was the same effect when a word very similar in sound or meaning to the shocked word was presented. Thus, some information on the unattended message was processed in terms of both sound and meaning. These physiological reactions occurred even though the participants were not consciously aware that the previously shocked

*Do you think recall would be different for dichotic listening tasks if different stimuli were used?*

word or its associates had been presented. However, physiological responses were observed on only relatively few trials, suggesting that thorough processing of unattended information occurred only some of the time.

## Evaluation

⊕ Broadbent's filter theory of attention is of great historical importance. Indeed, the notion of an information-processing system, with various processes linked to each other, first saw the light of day in filter theory.

⊕ Filter theory was perhaps the first systematic theory of selective attention, and explains many of the main findings.

⊖ Broadbent's theory is too *inflexible*, predicting that an unattended input will receive minimal processing. In fact, there is great variability in the amount of processing devoted to such input.

⊖ The theoretical assumption that the filter selects information on the basis of physical features of the input is supported by the tendency of participants on the dichotic listening task to recall digits ear by ear. However, a small change in the task produces very different results. Gray and Wedderburn (1960) used a version of the dichotic listening task in which "who 6 there" might be presented to one ear, while "4 goes 1" was presented to the other ear. The preferred order of report was *not* the usual ear by ear; instead, it was determined by meaning (e.g., "who goes there" followed by "4 6 1"). Thus, selection can occur either *before* or *after* the processing of information from both inputs.

## Alternative theories

*What kind of information do you think would be most likely to "breakthrough" from an unattended message to attention?*

Treisman (1960) found that selective attention was more flexible than was assumed by Broadbent (1958). She found with the shadowing task that the participants sometimes said a word that had been presented on the unattended message. This is known as "breakthrough", and mostly occurs when the word on the unattended message is highly probable in the context of the message on the attended channel. Findings such as the discovery of "breakthrough" led Treisman (1964) to propose an attenuation theory of attention, in which the processing of unattended information is attenuated or reduced. In Broadbent's filter theory, it was proposed that there is a bottleneck early in processing. In Treisman's theory, the location of the bottleneck is more flexible. It is as if people possess a "leaky" filter, making selective attention less efficient than was assumed by Broadbent.

According to Treisman (1964), stimulus processing proceeds systematically, starting with analyses based on physical cues, and then moving on to analyses based on meaning. If there is insufficient processing capacity to allow full stimulus analysis, then some later analyses are omitted with "unattended" stimuli. This theory neatly predicts Cherry's (1953) finding that it is usually the physical characteristics of unattended inputs (e.g., sex of the speaker) that are noticed rather than their meaning.

The extensive processing of unattended sources of information that was embarrassing for filter theory can be accounted for by Treisman's attenuation theory. However, the same findings were also explained by Deutsch and Deutsch (1963). They claimed that all stimuli are analysed for at least some aspects of meaning, with the most important or relevant stimulus determining the response. This theory differs from filter theory and attenuation theory in placing the bottleneck closer to the response end of the processing system.

Treisman's (1964) theory is more plausible than that of Deutsch and Deutsch (1963). The assumption made by Deutsch and Deutsch that all stimuli are analysed for meaning, but that most of the analysed information is lost very rapidly seems rather wasteful. In fact, studies by Treisman and Geffen (1967) and by Treisman and Riley (1969) provided support for attenuation theory rather than the theory of Deutsch and Deutsch.

Treisman and Geffen (1967) told participants to shadow one of two auditory messages, having been told to tap whenever they detected a target word in either message.

According to attenuation theory, there should be reduced analysis of the non-shadowed message, and so fewer targets should be detected on that message than on the shadowed one. According to Deutsch and Deutsch (1963), there is reasonably thorough processing of all stimuli, and so it might be predicted that there would be no difference in detection rates between the two messages. In fact, the detection rate on the shadowed or attended message was much higher.

Deutsch and Deutsch (1967) pointed out that their theory assumes that only *important* inputs lead to responses. As the task used by Treisman and Geffen (1967) required their participants to make two responses (i.e., shadow and tap) to shadowed target words, but only one response (i.e., tap) to non-shadowed targets, the shadowed targets were more important than the non-shadowed ones. Thus, their theory could account for the findings.

Treisman and Riley (1969) responded by carrying out a study in which exactly the same response was made to targets in either message. Their participants were told to stop shadowing and to tap whenever they detected a target in either message. Many more target words were detected on the shadowed message than on the non-shadowed one, a finding which is inconsistent with Deutsch and Deutsch's (1963) theory.

Neurophysiological studies provide support for early selection theories (see Luck, 1998, for a review). Woldorff et al. (1993) used the task of detecting auditory targets presented to the attended ear, with fast trains of non-targets being presented to each ear. **Event-related potentials** (ERPs; regularities in the brain-wave responses to repeated stimuli) were recorded from attended and unattended stimuli. There were greater event-related potentials to attended than unattended stimuli 20–50 milliseconds after stimulus onset. This suggests that there was attenuated or reduced processing of unattended stimuli compared with attended ones.

Only important input leads to responses...

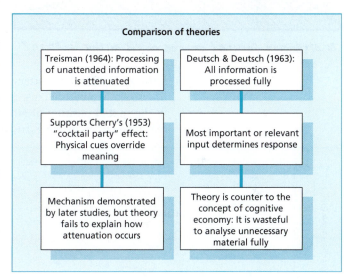

Comparison of theories

| | |
|---|---|
| Treisman (1964): Processing of unattended information is attenuated | Deutsch & Deutsch (1963): All information is processed fully |
| Supports Cherry's (1953) "cocktail party" effect: Physical cues override meaning | Most important or relevant input determines response |
| Mechanism demonstrated by later studies, but theory fails to explain how attenuation occurs | Theory is counter to the concept of cognitive economy: It is wasteful to analyse unnecessary material fully |

## Evaluation

● The analysis of unattended auditory inputs can be greater than was originally believed by Broadbent (1958).

● The most reasonable account of focused auditory attention is probably along the lines suggested by Treisman (1964), with reduced or attenuated processing of sources of information outside focal attention.

● "Discovering precisely where selection occurs is only one small part of the issues surrounding attention, and finding *where* selection takes place may not help us to understand *why* or *how* this happens" (Styles, 1997, p. 28).

## FOCUSED VISUAL ATTENTION

Over the past 25 years, far more researchers have studied visual than auditory attention. Why is this? One reason is because it is easier to control the presentation times of visual stimuli than of auditory stimuli: It can be surprisingly difficult to decide exactly when a

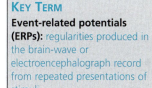

**KEY TERM**

**Event-related potentials (ERPs):** regularities produced in the brain-wave or electroencephalograph record from repeated presentations of stimuli.

spoken word begins and ends. Another reason is that most early research on focused attention had been concerned with auditory attention, and so there was much to be discovered about focused visual attention.

There are more studies on focused visual attention than you can shake a stick at. Accordingly, we will consider only two key issues. First, what is selected in selective or focused attention? Second, what happens to unattended stimuli?

Is attention focused on the object or the location?

## What is selected?

The most popular answer to above question is that we select a given area or region of space, such as when we look behind us to identify the source of a sound. In some ways, focused visual attention resembles a spotlight: Everything within a fairly small region of the visual field can be seen clearly, but it is much harder to see anything not falling within the beam of the attentional spotlight. Attention can be shifted by moving the spotlight. A similar (but more complex) view of focused visual attention was put forward by Eriksen and St. James (1986). According to their zoom-lens model, attention is directed to a given region of the visual field. The area of focal attention can be increased or decreased in line with task demands (e.g., we can decide whether to attend to part of an object or to the whole object).

### Evidence

Findings favouring the zoom-lens model were reported by LaBerge (1983). Five-letter words were presented. A probe requiring rapid response was occasionally presented instead of (or immediately after) the word. The probe could appear in the spatial position of any of the five letters of the word. In one condition, an attempt was made to focus the participants' attention on the *middle letter* of the five-letter word by asking them to categorise that letter. In another condition, the participants were required to categorise the *entire word*. It was expected that this would lead the participants to adopt a broader attentional beam.

LaBerge (1983) assumed that the attentional spotlight would have a very narrow beam on the letter task, but would have a broader beam on the word task. He also assumed that the probe would be responded to faster when it fell within the central attentional beam than when it did not. LaBerge's findings were as predicted on these assumptions, with the width of the attentional beam being affected by the task.

The zoom-lens model fits our intuitions about how we use our visual attentional system. However, there is increasing evidence that it is wrong (or at least greatly oversimplified)! According to the model, we should be unable to show **split attention**, in which attention is directed to two regions of space not adjacent to each other. Awh and Pashler (2000) carried out a study on split attention. The participants were presented with a 5 × 5 visual array containing 23 letters and 2 digits, having been told to report the identity of the two digits. Immediately before the display was presented, the participants were given two cues indicating the likely locations of the two digits. However, these cues were misleading or invalid on 20% of trials. Part of what was involved can be seen in the figure on the next page. The crucial condition was one in which the cues were invalid, with one of the digits being presented in between the cued

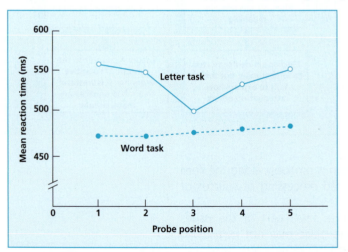

Mean reaction time to the probe as a function of probe position. The probe was presented at the time that a letter string would have been presented. Data from LaBerge.

locations. If attention is directed to a *single* area of space, performance should have been high for this digit. In contrast, if split attention is possible, performance should have been low. In fact, performance was much lower than for digits presented to cued locations, indicating that split attention is possible.

There is a second problem with the zoom-lens model, namely, that visual attention is often directed to *objects* rather than to a particular *region* of space. For example, consider a study by O'Craven, Downing, and Kanwisher (1999). They presented their participants with two stimuli (a face and a house) transparently overlapping at the same location, with one of the objects moving slightly. The participants were told to attend either to the direction of motion of the moving stimulus or to the position of the stationary stimulus.

Suppose that attention is location based. In that case, the participants would have to attend to both stimuli, because they were both in the same location. In contrast, suppose that attention is object based. In that case, processing of the attended stimulus should be more thorough than processing of the unattended stimulus. Evidence obtained from fMRI (functional magnetic resonance imaging) indicated that visual attention was object based rather than location based.

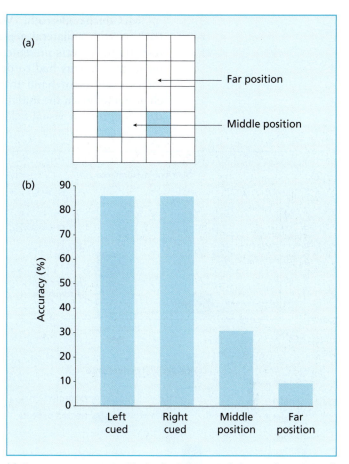

(a) One cue arrangement with the shaded squares being cued. On 80% of trials the targets were presented to the cued squares; on 20% of trials the targets were presented to the middle and far positions. Adapted from Awh and Pashler (2000).
(b) Target detection as a function of whether target was cued (left or right) or not (middle and far positions). Data from Awh and Pashler (2000).

## Evaluation

● Visual attention resembles a spotlight or zoom lens in some ways. It is more like a zoom lens, because the size of the visual field within focal attention can vary considerably (e.g., LaBerge, 1983).
● Visual attention is often directed to a single region of space as is predicted by the spotlight and zoom-lens models.
● Both the spotlight and zoom-lens models assume that visual attention is directed towards a single region of the visual field. However, the phenomenon of split attention indicates that visual attention can be directed to two non-adjacent regions at the same time.
● Visual attention is often directed to *objects* rather than to a particular *region* of space (O'Craven et al., 1999).

## What happens to unattended stimuli?

What happens to unattended visual stimuli? Cognitive psychologists used to argue that there is very little processing of such stimuli. However, the general view nowadays is that unattended visual stimuli typically receive a reasonable amount of processing, but less than attended stimuli. For example, Wojciulik, Kanwisher, and Driver (1998) presented their participants with displays containing two faces and two houses, and the task required them to attend either to the faces or to the houses. The area of the brain which responds strongly to faces was more active (as assessed by fMRI or functional magnetic resonance imaging) when the faces needed to be attended to than when they did not, indicating that they received less processing when unattended. However, there was significant activity in the face-specific area of the brain even with unattended faces, indicating that the faces were processed to some extent.

*Do you think that there is implicit learning of unattended stimuli even in the absence of explicit learning?*

McGlinchey-Berroth, Milber, Verfaellie, Alexander, and Kilduff (1993) studied patients with **unilateral neglect**, a condition in which patients do not notice (or fail to respond to) objects presented to one side of them (typically the left side). In one experiment, the patients had to decide which of two drawings matched a drawing presented immediately beforehand to the left or the right visual field. Neglect patients were at chance level when the initial drawing was presented to the left visual field, suggesting that stimuli in the left visual field were not processed (see the figure below).

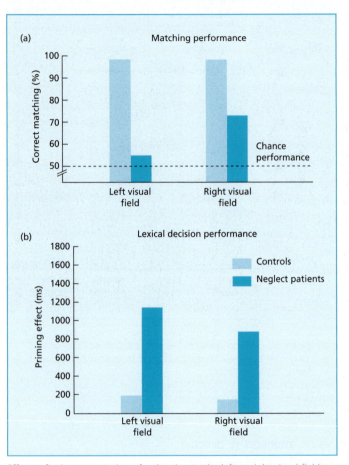

Effects of prior presentation of a drawing to the left or right visual field on matching performance and lexical decision in neglect patients. Data from McGlinchey-Berroth et al. (1993).

A very different conclusion emerged from a second experiment, in which patients with unilateral neglect had to decide whether letter strings formed words. Decision times were faster on "yes" trials when the letter string was preceded by a semantically related object rather than an unrelated object (the difference is known as the priming effect). This effect was the same size regardless of whether the object was presented to the left or the right visual field (see the figure on the left). These findings indicate that there was some processing of the meaning of left-field stimuli by neglect patients.

Why did the findings differ in the two experiments of McGlinchey-Berroth et al. (1993)? The simplest explanation is that patients with unilateral neglect processed the meaning of stimuli presented to the left visual field, but had no conscious awareness of that processing. When conscious awareness of such processing was needed to perform the task (first experiment), performance was at chance level. When conscious awareness of such processing was *not* needed for task performance (second experiment), performance benefited from the processing of stimuli presented to the left visual field.

## Visual search

One of the main ways we use focused visual attention in our everyday lives is in **visual search**, in which a target stimulus presented in the context of other stimuli has to be detected. As Peterson, Kramer, Wang, Irwin, and McCarley (2001, p. 287) pointed out, "From the time we wake in the morning until we go to bed at night, we spend a good deal of each day searching the environment ... in the office, we may look for a coffee cup, the manuscript we were working on several days ago, or a phone number of a colleague that we wrote down on a scrap of paper."

How can we study the processes involved in visual search? Typically, participants are presented with a visual display containing a variable number of items (the set or display size). A target (e.g., a red G) is presented on half the trials, and the task is to decide as rapidly as possible whether the target is in the display. Factors determining the speed and accuracy of visual search are discussed below.

### Feature integration theory

Treisman (e.g., 1988, 1992) distinguished between the features of objects (e.g., colour, size, lines of particular orientation) and the objects themselves. Her feature integration theory includes the following assumptions:

- There is a rapid initial *parallel* process in which the visual features of objects in the environment are processed at the same time; this is *not* dependent on attention.

- There is then a serial process in which features are combined to form objects.
- The serial process is slower than the initial parallel process, especially when the set size is large.
- Features can be combined by focused attending to the location of the object, in which case focused attention provides the "glue" forming unitary objects from the available features.
- Feature combination can be influenced by stored knowledge (e.g., bananas are usually yellow).
- In the absence of focused attention or relevant stored knowledge, features from different objects will be combined randomly, producing "illusory conjunctions".

## Evidence

Treisman and Gelade (1980) had previously obtained support for this theory. Their participants searched for a target in a visual display having a set or display size of between 1 and 30 items. The target was either an object (a green letter T), or consisted of a single feature (a blue letter or an S). When the target was a green letter T, all the non-targets shared one feature with the target (i.e., they were either brown letter Ts or green letter Xs). It was predicted that focused attention would be needed to detect the object target (because it was defined by a combination of features), but would not be needed with the single-feature targets.

Set or display size had a large effect on detection speed when the target was defined by a combination or conjunction of features (i.e., a green letter T), presumably because focused attention was required (see the figure below). However, there was very little effect of display size when the target was defined by a single feature (i.e., a blue letter or an S). The explanation of this finding is that *only* the fast initial parallel process was needed to perform this task.

Illusory conjunctions occur when features from two different objects are incorrectly perceived as belonging to the same object. For example, someone might mistakenly claim to see a red letter X in a display containing numerous red objects and numerous letter Xs. According to feature integration theory, lack of focused attention can produce illusory conjunctions. Treisman and Schmidt (1982) confirmed this prediction. There were numerous illusory conjunctions when attention was widely distributed, but not when the stimuli were presented to focal attention.

Treisman and Sato (1990) argued that the degree of *similarity* between the target and the distractors influences visual search time. They found that visual search for an

Picking out one unfamiliar face from all these children might take some time, but how quickly would you locate your own face if you were in the picture?

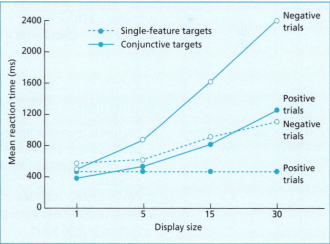

Performance speed on a detection task as a function of target definition (conjunctive vs. single feature) and display size. Adapted from Treisman and Gelade (1980).

object target defined by more than one feature was typically limited to those distractors having at least one of the target's features. For example, if you were looking for a blue circle in a display containing blue triangles, black circles, and black triangles, you would ignore black triangles. This contrasts with the views of Treisman and Gelade (1980), who argued that none of the stimuli would be ignored.

## Guided search theory

Guided search theory was put forward by Wolfe (1998). It represents a substantial refinement and development of feature integration theory. Wolfe replaced Treisman and Gelade's (1980) assumption that the initial processing is necessarily parallel and subsequent processing is serial with the notion that processes are more or less efficient. Why did he do this? As Wolfe pointed out, there should be no effect of set or display size on detection times if parallel processing is used, but a substantial effect of set size if serial processing is used. In fact, most findings fall between these two extremes, suggesting that processing is rarely purely parallel or purely serial.

According to guided search theory, the initial processing of basic features produces an activation map, in which each of the items in the visual display has its own level of activation. Suppose you were searching for red, horizontal targets. Feature processing would activate all red objects and all horizontal objects. Attention is then directed towards items on the basis of their level of activation, starting with those with the highest level of activation. It follows that distractors sharing at least one feature with the target are activated and slow down visual search, which is what was found by Treisman and Sato (1990).

A problem with the original version of feature integration theory was that targets in large displays are typically found faster than predicted. The activation-map notion provides a plausible way in which visual search can be made more efficient: Stimuli not sharing any features with the target stimulus are ignored because they receive little or no activation.

## *Evaluation*

*How might you apply feature integration theory to real-life experiences of visual search?*

- ⊕ Feature integration theory has been very influential. The assumption that two successive processes are involved in visual search is generally accepted, as is the assumption that the first process is fast and efficient, whereas the second process is slower and less efficient.
- ⊕ Feature integration theory provides a reasonable account of illusory conjunctions.
- ⊕ Subsequent theories (e.g., guided search theory) have developed Treisman's ideas in various fruitful ways.
- ⊖ The assumption in the original version of feature integration theory that visual search is either entirely parallel or entirely serial is too strong, and is inconsistent with the evidence (Wolfe, 1998).
- ⊖ The original version of feature integration theory ignored the effect of similarity between non-target and target stimuli in influencing speed of visual search. However, this omission has been rectified in subsequent theories (e.g., guided search theory).
- ⊖ We need to find out more about the relevance of laboratory research to visual search in the real world. Laboratory studies typically use relatively simple stimuli of similar size to each other, but this is fairly unusual in our everyday lives.

# DIVIDED ATTENTION

What happens when people try to do two things at once? The answer clearly depends on the nature of the two "things". Sometimes the attempt is successful, such as when an experienced motorist drives a car while holding a conversation. At other times, such as when someone tries to rub their stomach with one hand while patting their head with the other, there can be a complete disruption of performance.

Dual-task studies (studies in which two tasks must be performed at the same time) indicate that there are frequent performance impairments. Some theorists (e.g., Baddeley, 1986; Norman & Shallice, 1986) argue that such impairments often reflect the limited capacity of a single multi-purpose central processor or central executive sometimes described as "attention" (see Chapter 9). Other theorists (e.g., Allport, 1989; Wickens, 1984) are more impressed by our apparent ability to perform two fairly complex tasks at the same time without disruption or interference. Such theorists favour the notion of several specific processing resources, arguing that there will be no interference between two tasks if they make use of different processing resources.

We can predict fairly accurately whether or not two tasks can be combined successfully, even though the accounts offered by different theorists are very diverse. Accordingly, we will discuss some of the factual evidence before moving on to the more complex issue of how the data are to be explained.

## Dual-task performance

Dual-task performance depends on several factors. We will focus on what are perhaps the three most important ones: task similarity, practice, and task difficulty.

### Task similarity

When we think of pairs of activities that are performed well together in everyday life, the examples that come to mind usually involve two rather dissimilar activities (e.g., driving and talking; reading and listening to music). As we have seen, when people shadow or repeat back prose passages while learning auditorily presented words (two similar activities), their subsequent recognition-memory performance for the words is at chance level (Allport et al., 1972). However, memory is excellent when the to-be-remembered material consists of pictures.

There are various kinds of similarity. For example, two tasks can be presented in the same sense modality (e.g., visually or auditorily). Two tasks can also be similar because they require the same type of response. McLeod (1977) asked participants to perform a continuous tracking task with manual responding at the same time as a tone-identification task. Some participants responded vocally to the tones, whereas others responded manually with the hand not involved in the tracking task. Performance on the tracking task was worse with high response similarity (manual responses on both tasks) than with low response similarity (manual responses on one task and vocal ones on the other).

Similarity of stimulus modality was studied by Treisman and Davies (1973). Two monitoring tasks interfered with each much more when the stimuli on both tasks were in the same sense modality (visual or auditory) than when they were in different modalities.

It is often hard to measure similarity. How similar are piano playing and poetry writing, or driving a car and watching a football match? Only when there is a better understanding of the processes involved in the performance of such tasks will sensible answers be forthcoming.

*What factors do you think might affect our ability to perform two tasks simultaneously?*

**Switch off your mobile!**

Believe it or not, some students feel that cognitive psychology has little relevance to everyday life. However, research on divided attention is of direct relevance to a practical issue that has been much debated in recent years, namely whether motorists should be allowed to use mobile phones while driving. As someone who has nearly been hit by two mobile-using motorists who were driving on the wrong side of the road, I have my own personal views on the matter. What about the scientific evidence? Strayer and Johnston (2001) found that the chances of missing a red light more than doubled when the participants were engaged in conversation on a hand-held mobile phone, and the effects were almost as great when using a hands-free mobile phone. In addition, using a mobile phone greatly reduced the speed of responding to those traffic signals that were detected. These various adverse effects were greater when the participants were talking than when they were listening, but both effects were significant.

The above findings led Strayer and Johnston (2001, p. 462) to conclude that, "[Mobile]-phone use disrupts performance by diverting attention to an engaging cognitive context other than the one immediately associated with driving." That conclusion strongly suggests that the use of mobile phones while driving should be restricted or banned, as is already the case in more than a dozen countries.

## Practice

The old saying, "Practice makes perfect", is very applicable to dual-task performance. For example, learner drivers find it almost impossible to drive and hold a conversation, whereas expert drivers find it fairly easy (unless they are using a mobile phone!). Evidence for the importance of practice was obtained by Spelke, Hirst, and Neisser (1976) in a study on two students called Diane and John. These students received extensive training on various tasks. Their first task was to read short stories for comprehension while writing down words to dictation. They found this very hard initially, and their reading speed and handwriting both suffered considerably. After 6 weeks of training, however, they could read as rapidly and with as much comprehension when taking dictation as when only reading, and the quality of their handwriting had also improved.

*Can you think of a way to test Spelke et al.'s claim that with practice, two complex tasks can be performed together without disruption?*

Spelke et al. (1976, p. 229) doubted whether the popular notion that we have limited processing capacity is accurate, basing themselves on the dramatic findings with John and Diane: "People's ability to develop skills in specialised situations is so great that it may never be possible to define general limits on cognitive capacity." However, there are other ways of interpreting their findings. Perhaps the dictation task was performed rather automatically, and so placed few demands on cognitive capacity, or there might have been a rapid alternation of attention between reading and writing.

Hirst et al. (1980) claimed that writing to dictation was *not* done automatically, because the students understood what they were writing. They also claimed that reading and dictation could only be performed together with success by alternation of attention if the reading material were simple and highly redundant. However, they found that most participants could still read and take dictation effectively when less redundant reading matter was used.

Do the studies by Hirst et al. (1980) and Spelke et al. (1976) show that two complex tasks can be performed together without disruption? Not really. One of the participants used by Hirst et al. was tested at dictation *without* reading, and made fewer than half the number of errors that occurred when reading at the same time.

Skilled touch typists can hold a conversation and attend to other stimuli with very little effect on their typing speed or accuracy.

There are other cases of apparently successful performance of two complex tasks, but the requisite skills were always highly practised. For example, expert pianists can play from seen music while repeating back or shadowing heard speech (Allport et al., 1972), and an expert typist can type and shadow at the same time (Shaffer, 1975). These studies are often regarded as providing evidence of completely successful task combination. However, there are some signs of interference (Broadbent, 1982).

Why does practice help dual-task performance? First, people may develop new strategies for performing the tasks to minimise task interference. Second, the demands that a task makes on attentional or other central resources may be reduced by practice. Third, although a task initially requires the use of several specific processing resources, practice may reduce the number of resources required. These possibilities are discussed in more detail later.

## Task difficulty

The ability to perform two tasks together depends on their difficulty. For example Sullivan (1976) used the tasks of shadowing (repeating back) an auditory message and detecting target words on a non-shadowed message at the same time. When the shadowing task was made harder by using a less redundant message, fewer targets were detected on the non-shadowed message. However, it is hard to define task difficulty.

The demands for resources of two tasks performed together might be thought to equal the sums of the demands of the two tasks when performed separately. However, the necessity to perform two tasks together often introduces new demands of co-ordination and avoidance of interference. Duncan (1979) asked his participants to respond to closely successive stimuli, one requiring a left-hand response and the other a right-hand response.

The relationship between each stimulus and response was either corresponding (e.g., right-most stimulus calling for response of the right-most finger) or crossed (e.g., left-most stimulus calling for response of the right-most finger). Performance was poor when the relationship was corresponding for one stimulus but crossed for the other. In these circumstances, the participants were sometimes confused, with their errors being largely those expected if the inappropriate stimulus–response relationship had been selected.

## Summary

The extent to which two tasks can be performed successfully together depends on various factors. As a rule of thumb, two dissimilar, highly practised, and simple tasks can typically be performed well together, whereas two similar, novel, and complex tasks cannot. In addition, having to perform two tasks together rather than separately often produces entirely new problems of co-ordination. We now consider some of the theoretical accounts that have been offered of these (and other) findings.

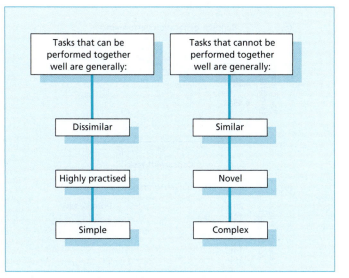

## Central capacity theories

A simple way of accounting for many dual-task findings is to assume there is some central capacity or resources, which can be used flexibly across numerous activities. Capacity theories were proposed by Kahneman (1973) and Norman and Bobrow (1975). Two crucial

### Bourke et al.: Support for central capacity

Evidence supporting central capacity theories was reported by Bourke, Duncan, and Nimmo-Smith (1996). First of all, they selected four tasks designed to differ as much as possible from each other:

1. *Random generation*. Generating letters in a random order.
2. *Prototype learning*. Working out the features of two patterns or prototypes from seeing various exemplars.
3. *Manual task*. Screwing a nut down to the bottom of a bolt and back up to the top, and then down to the bottom of a second bolt and back up, and so on.
4. *Tone task*. Detecting the occurrence of a target tone.

The participants were given two of these tasks to perform together, with one task being identified as more important than the other. The basic argument was as follows: If there is a central or general capacity, then the task making most demands on this capacity will interfere most with all three of the other tasks. In contrast, the task making fewest demands on this capacity will interfere least with all the other tasks.

What did Bourke et al. (1996) find? First, these very different tasks did interfere with each other. Second, the random generation task interfered the most overall with the performance of the other tasks, and the tone task interfered the least. Third, and of greatest importance, the random generation task consistently interfered most with the prototype, manual, and tone tasks, and it did so whether it was the primary or the secondary task. The tone task consistently interfered least with each of the other three tasks. Thus, the findings accorded with the predictions of a general capacity theory (see the figure on the next page).

### KEY STUDY EVALUATION—Bourke et al.

As we have seen, the four tasks used by Bourke et al. are very different from each other. If performance depended only on very specific processes, then there would presumably have been little or no interference between tasks. The fact that there was considerable interference is strong evidence for a general central processing capacity. It may have occurred to you that participants with special expertise might have found it easier to combine some of the tasks; for example, a mechanic might be very good at handling nuts and bolts. However, the participants were recent university students, and lacked special expertise for any of the tasks.

### Discussion points

1. Is it surprising that these very different tasks interfered with each other?
2. Why do you think that the random generation task interfered the most with other tasks, whereas the tone task interfered the least?

*Do you think these four tasks would be of equal difficulty for all people?*

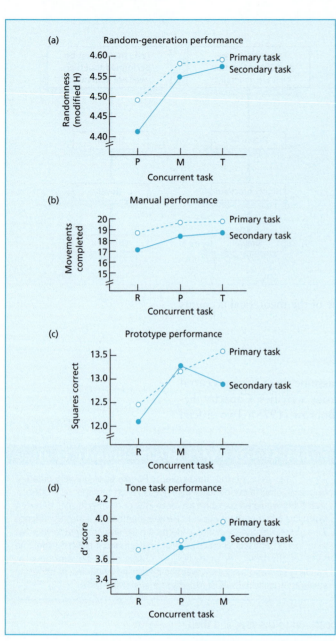

Performance on random generation (R), prototype learning (P), manual (M), and tone (T) tasks as a function of concurrent task. Adapted from Bourke et al. (1996).

*Hegarty, Shah, and Miyake's findings suggest that dual-task performance is affected by factors other than demands on central capacity. Can you think what these factors might be?*

assumptions are made by such theories:

- There is some central capacity (attention or effort) with limited resources.
- The ability to perform two tasks together depends on the demands placed on those resources by the two tasks.

It follows that dual-task performance will be poor if the two tasks require more resources than are available. However, the two tasks will be performed successfully if their combined demands for resources are less than the total resources of the central capacity. The beneficial effects of practice might occur because it reduces the resources needed to perform each task.

In the interests of fairness, it must be pointed out that some other studies using the same general approach as Bourke et al. (1996) have reported less support for central capacity theories. For example, consider a study by Hegarty, Shah, and Miyake (2000). They had evidence from previous research that an identical-pictures task (the participants viewed a target figure and decided which test figure was identical to it) made few demands on central capacity. Theoretically, that task should have been little affected by the necessity to perform another task at the same time. In fact, however, the evidence indicated that the identical-pictures task was severely disrupted by the other task, suggesting that factors other than demands on central capacity are important in determining dual-task performance. More specifically, Hegarty et al. argued that the identical-pictures task involves frequent response selection, which inhibits the ability to perform another task at the same time.

A well-known capacity theory was put forward by Kahneman (1973). In addition to the assumptions that people have limited capacity, and that the ability to perform two tasks together depends on the total demand on resources, Kahneman made the following assumptions:

1. The greater the level of arousal, the greater the pool of resources or capacity available; this relationship may break down at high levels of arousal. (Please note that terms such as "arousal" and "pool of resources" are rather vague.)
2. Decisions about how to make use of the available capacity are made by the allocation policy.
3. The allocation policy is determined by four factors:
   (i) Enduring dispositions (e.g., attend to intense or novel stimuli).
   (ii) Momentary intentions (e.g., attend to your psychology textbook and ignore the television).
   (iii) Evaluation of demands: If there is insufficient capacity to perform two activities at the same time, then one is carried through to completion.
   (iv) The level of arousal produced by external stressors: High arousal produces a narrowing of attention and a reduced ability to discriminate between relevant and irrelevant cues (this is known as Easterbrook's hypothesis).
4. Individuals evaluate the demands on their available capacity, and this can lead to an increase in effort and in the available capacity.

What predictions follow from Kahneman's theory? First, dual-task performance should depend on the demands of each task on the total available capacity. The findings of Bourke et al. (1996) support that prediction, but those of Hegarty et al. (2000) do not. Second, there will be an increase in effort as task demands increase. Supporting evidence was reported by Kahneman et al. (1969) using pupillary dilation as a measure of effort. There was a digit-transformation task, in which the participants were presented with four digits and added one to each digit (e.g., 4826 became 5937). Pupil dilation increased steadily during digit presentation, suggesting (but not proving) that the participants were increasing their level of effort in response to increasing task demands.

Third, the amount of spare processing (the difference between total capacity and capacity supplied to the primary task) decreases as primary task demands increase. This prediction was also tested by Kahneman et al. (1969). Digit transformation was the primary task, and there was a subsidiary task of monitoring a display for a specified letter. As predicted, performance on the subsidiary task became steadily worse throughout digit presentation as the amount of capacity allocated to the primary task increased.

According to central capacity theories, the main determinant of dual-task performance is the difficulty level of the two tasks. In fact, however, the effects of task difficulty are often swamped by those of task similarity. For example, Segal and Fusella (1970) asked their participants to detect a weak visual or auditory signal while maintaining a visual or an auditory image. The auditory image task impaired detection of auditory signals more than the visual task did suggesting that the auditory image task was more demanding than the visual image task. However, the auditory image task was *less* disruptive than the visual image task when each task was combined with a task requiring detection of visual signals, suggesting the opposite conclusion. In this study, task similarity was clearly a much more important factor than task difficulty: Performance was much worse when both tasks were in the same modality (visual or auditory).

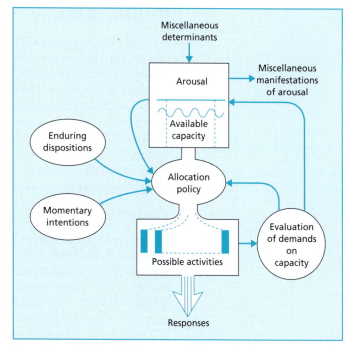

A capacity model for attention. From Kahneman (1973).

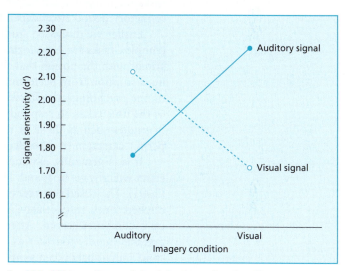

Sensitivity (d') to auditory and visual signals as a function of concurrent imagery modality (auditory vs. visual). Adapted from Segal and Fusella (1970).

## Evaluation

⊕ There is some support for the key assumption of central capacity theories that task difficulty helps to predict dual-task performance (e.g., Bourke et al., 1996).

⊕ Kahneman's assumption that the available processing capacity varies as a function of effort expenditure is plausible, and has received experimental support.

⊖ Kahneman (1973) did not define his key terms clearly, referring to "a nonspecific input, which can be variously labelled 'effort', 'capacity', or 'attention.'" Instead of equating the concepts of "effort" and "attentional capacity", it may be preferable to argue that effort can cause increased attention.

⊖ Central capacity theories are embarrassed by the finding that task similarity often has large effects on dual-task performance (e.g., Segal & Fusella, 1970).

⊖ Central capacity theories are not very explanatory. As Allport (1989, p. 647) pointed out, "It is possible to 'explain' dual-task performance by assuming that the resources of some central capacity have been exceeded, and to account for a lack of interference by assuming that the two tasks did not exceed those resources. However, ... this is simply a re-description of the findings rather than an explanation."

## Bottleneck theory

Welford (1952) argued that there is a processing bottleneck making it hard (or impossible) for two decisions about the appropriate responses to two different stimuli to be made at the same time. His views influenced the development of Broadbent's (1958) filter theory discussed earlier in the chapter. Much of the supporting evidence comes from studies of the **psychological refractory period**. There are two stimuli (e.g., two lights) and two responses (e.g., button presses), and the task is to respond rapidly to each stimulus. When the second stimulus is presented very shortly after the first one, there is generally a clear slowing of the response to the second stimulus: This is the psychological refractory period effect (see Welford, 1952). According to the theory, the psychological refractory period effect should *always* be present even when the two stimuli and responses differ greatly.

*Can you think of a way to test the theory that the psychological refractory effect should always be present?*

### Evidence

The psychological refractory period effect has been obtained in dozens of studies (see Pashler, Johnston, & Ruthruff, 2001, for a review). However, in most of these studies, the two tasks both involved manual responses, and it may simply be that people find it very hard to control their two hands separately. This issue was investigated by van Selst, Ruthruff, and Johnston (1999). They used two tasks, one of which required a vocal response and the other of which required a manual response. The initial psychological refractory period effect was 353 ms but this reduced to only 50 ms after extended practice. The psychological refractory period effect was much greater after practice when the experiment was repeated with both tasks requiring manual responses. This suggests that most (but not all) of the psychological refractory period effect depends on manual responses being required on both tasks.

Earlier we discussed studies (e.g., Hirst et al, 1980; Spelke et al., 1976) in which two complex tasks were performed remarkably well together. Such findings may seem inconsistent with the notion that there is a bottleneck in processing, because there was little or no disruption from performing the tasks together compared with singly. However, studies on the psychological refractory period effect have the advantage of very precise assessment of the time taken to respond to any given stimulus. The coarse-grained measures obtained in studies such as those of Hirst et al. and Spelke et al. may simply be too insensitive to permit detection of a bottleneck.

It was generally assumed until fairly recently that a psychological refractory period effect will always be found. However, contrary evidence was reported by Schumacher et al. (2001). They used two tasks: (1) say "one", "two", or "three" to low-, medium-, and high-pitched tones, respectively; (2) press response keys corresponding to the position of a disc on a computer screen. After 2064 trials, some of the participants performed these two tasks as rapidly together as singly. Thus, the bottleneck in processing may disappear for some individuals when simple tasks are highly practised.

### Evaluation

⊕ Numerous studies indicate that there is generally a bottleneck in dual-task processing. This suggests that at least some central processing is serial in nature, dealing with one task at a time.
⊕ Studies of the psychological refractory period provide precise assessment of the time taken to process (and respond to) stimuli in dual-task conditions.
⊖ The magnitude of the psychological refractory period effect is typically fairly small. It is thus entirely possible that many (or most) of the processes involved in dual-task performance occur in parallel.
⊖ Some evidence (e.g., Schumacher et al., 2001) suggests that there is not always a bottleneck in processing when two tasks need to be performed together.

## Multiple resources

Wickens (1984, 1992) argued that people possess multiple resources. He proposed a three-dimensional structure of human processing resources. According to his model, there are *three* successive stages of processing (encoding, central processing, and responding). Encoding involves the perceptual processing of stimuli, and typically involves the visual or auditory modalities. Encoding and central processing can involve spatial or verbal codes. Finally, responding involves manual or vocal responses. Any given task makes use of some of the processing resources shown in the figure on the right. More specifically, most tasks involve some form of encoding (visual or auditory), followed by central processing (spatial or verbal), concluding with responding (manual or vocal).

There are two key assumptions in this model:

1. There are several pools of resources based on the distinctions among stages of processing, modalities, codes, and responses.
2. If two tasks make use of different pools of resources, then people should be able to perform both tasks without disruption.

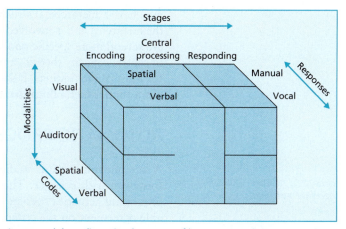

A proposed three-dimensional structure of human processing resources. From Wickens (1984).

## Evidence

There is much support for this type of multiple-resource model, and its prediction that several kinds of task similarity influence dual-task performance. For example, as we have seen, there is more interference when the stimuli on the two tasks are from the same modality (e.g., Allport et al., 1972; Treisman & Davies, 1973). As we have also seen, there is also more interference when two tasks share the same type of response (e.g., McLeod, 1977; van Selst et al., 1999).

In general terms, evidence supporting central capacity theories poses problems for a model emphasising the importance of multiple resources. According to Wickens' model, two tasks not sharing any common pools of resources should be performed as well together as individually. Consider the study by Bourke et al. (1996), discussed above, in which four very different tasks (random generation, prototype learning, manual task, tone task) had to be performed. The prediction from Wickens' model would seem to be that these tasks should not interfere with each other. In fact, however, all of the tasks interfered significantly with each other. In similar fashion, it is not clear from Wickens' model why conversing on a mobile phone should disrupt the very different activity of car driving (Strayer & Johnston, 2001).

## Evaluation

⊕ There is reasonable evidence for the existence of multiple resources as proposed by Wickens (1984, 1992).
⊕ There is support for the notion that the amount of dual-task interference depends on the extent to which two tasks share common processing resources.
⊖ The model focuses only on visual and auditory inputs, but tasks could be presented in other modalities (e.g., touch).
⊖ There is often some disruption to performance even when two tasks make use of separate pools of resources (e.g., Bourke et al., 1996; Strayer & Johnston, 2001). This may occur when two tasks make demands on some central capacity which is more general than the processing resources identified by Wickens (1984).
⊖ The model minimises the problems associated with the higher-level processes of co-ordinating and organising the demands of different tasks (e.g., Duncan, 1979).

## Conclusions

There appears to be a grain of truth associated with all of the theoretical approaches (central capacity theories, bottleneck theory, multiple-resource model). This suggests that it might be useful to combine elements of these theories. For example, the processing system may have a hierarchical structure. The central processor or central executive is at the top of the hierarchy, and is involved in the co-ordination and control of behaviour. Below this level are several more specific pools of processing resources. This suggestion incorporates aspects of central capacity theories and of the multiple-resource model, and may potentially account for most of the findings. It should be noted that Baddeley's (1986) working memory model has a similar hierarchical structure to the one proposed here (see Chapter 9).

# AUTOMATIC PROCESSING

*Try to think of real-life examples of tasks that have become automatic as a result of practice.*

A key phenomenon in studies of divided attention is the dramatic improvement of performance with practice. The commonest explanation for this phenomenon is that some processing activities become automatic as a result of prolonged practice. There is reasonable agreement on the criteria for automatic processes:

- They are fast.
- They do not reduce the capacity for performing other tasks (i.e., they demand zero attention).
- They are unavailable to consciousness.
- They are unavoidable (i.e., they always occur when an appropriate stimulus is presented).

These criteria are generally hard to satisfy. For example, the requirement that automatic processes do not need attention means they should have no influence on the concurrent performance of an attention-demanding task. This is rarely the case (see Pashler, 1998). There are also problems with the unavoidability criterion. The **Stroop effect**, in which the naming of the colours in which words are printed is slowed down by using colour words (e.g., the word YELLOW printed in red), has often been regarded as involving unavoidable and automatic processing of the colour words. However, Kahneman and Henik (1979) found that the Stroop effect was much larger when the distracting information (i.e., the colour name) was in the same location as the to-be-named colour rather than in an adjacent location. Thus, the processes producing the Stroop effect are *not* entirely unavoidable.

Few processes are fully automatic in the sense of conforming to all the criteria. Later in this section we consider a theoretical approach (that of Norman & Shallice, 1986) which distinguishes between fully automatic and partially automatic processes.

## Controlled vs. automatic processes

Schneider and Shiffrin (1977) and Shiffrin and Schneider (1977) distinguished between controlled and automatic processes. According to their theory, controlled processes are of limited capacity, require attention, and can be used flexibly in changing circumstances. Automatic processes suffer no capacity limitations, do not require attention, and are very hard to modify once learned. Schneider and Shiffrin (1977) tested these ideas in a series of studies (see Key Study below).

## Schneider and Shiffrin: Controlled vs. automatic processes

In Schneider and Shiffrin's (1977) study the basic situation was one in which the participants memorised one, two, three, or four items (consonants or numbers); this was called the memory set. They were then shown a visual display containing one, two, three, or four items (consonants or numbers). Finally, they had to decide rapidly whether any item was present in both the memory set and the visual display.

Of crucial importance is the distinction between *consistent mapping* and *varied mapping*. With consistent mapping, *only* consonants were used as members of the memory set, and *only* numbers were used as distractors in the visual display (or vice versa). Consider someone who was given only numbers as members of each memory set. If a number was seen in the visual display, it had to be member of the current memory set. According to Shiffrin and Schneider (1977), the participants' years of practice at distinguishing between letters and numbers allowed them to perform the consistent-mapping task automatically. With varied mapping, the memory set consisted of a mixture of consonants and numbers, and so did the visual display. In this condition, automatic processes cannot be used.

In order to clarify this key difference between consistent mapping and varied mapping, we will consider a few examples of each:

*Consistent mapping*

| Memory set | Visual display | Response |
| --- | --- | --- |
| H B K D | 4 3 B 7 | Yes |
| H B K D | 9 2 5 3 | No |
| 5 2 7 3 | J 5 D C | Yes |
| 5 2 7 3 | B J G H | No |

*Varied mapping*

| Memory set | Visual display | Response |
| --- | --- | --- |
| H 4 B 3 | 5 C G B | Yes |
| H 4 B 3 | 2 J 7 C | No |
| 5 8 F 2 | G 5 B J | Yes |
| 5 8 F 2 | 6 D 1 C | No |

*Looking at the experimental stimuli used by Shiffrin and Schneider, do you think Cheng's (1985) argument was correct?*

There was a large difference in performance between the consistent and varied mapping conditions. The number of items in the memory set and the visual display had very little effect on decision time with consistent mapping, but had a large effect with varied mapping. According to Shiffrin and Schneider (1977), performance in the consistent-mapping condition reflected the use of automatic processes operating in parallel. On the other hand, performance in the varied mapping condition reflects the use of attentionally demanding controlled processes operating in a serial fashion. The more items that have to be considered, the slower is the decision time.

The notion that automatic processes develop as the result of prolonged practice was studied by Shiffrin and Schneider (1977). They used consistent mapping, with the memory set items always being drawn from the consonants B to L, and the distractors in the visual display always being drawn from the consonants Q to Z, or vice versa. There were 2100 trials, and the dramatic improvement in performance over these trials presumably reflected the development of automatic processes.

After automatic processes had developed, there were a further 2400 trials with the reverse consistent mapping. Thus, for example, if the memory set items had been drawn from the first half of the alphabet during the initial 2100 trials, they were taken from the second half of the alphabet during the subsequent 2400 trials. It took almost 1000 trials with reverse consistent mapping for performance to recover to its level at the very start of the experiment! This shows that it is hard to change automatic processes.

The greatest advantages of automatic over attentional processes are that they operate much more rapidly, and that many automatic processes can take place at the same time. However, automatic processes are at a disadvantage when there is a change in the environment or in the task, because they lack the adaptability and flexibility of controlled processes.

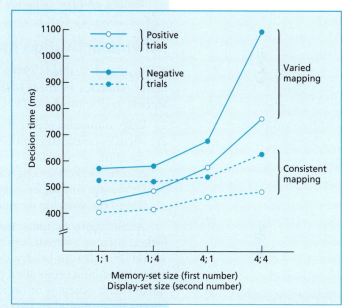

Response times on a decision task as a function of memory-set size, display-set size, and consistent versus varied mapping. Data from Shiffrin and Schneider (1977).

## Discussion points

1. How useful is this research by Shiffrin and Schneider (see next for some pointers)?
2. Think of some examples of automatic and controlled processes in your everyday life.

## Evaluation

⊕ Shiffrin and Schneider (1977) drew a clear distinction between automatic and controlled processes, and provided evidence to support the distinction.

⊕ Shiffrin and Schneider (1977) showed clearly the key role of practice in the development of automatic processes.

⊖ The theoretical assumption that automatic processes operate in parallel and place no demands on capacity means there should be a slope of zero (i.e., a horizontal line) in the line relating decision speed to the number of items in the memory set and/or in the visual display when automatic processes are used. However, this is not the case.

⊖ It is not clear whether the participants in the consistent mapping condition searched through the memory set and visual display looking for a match. Cheng (1985) argued that participants who knew that any consonant in the visual display had to be an item from the memory set simply scanned the visual display looking for a consonant.

⊖ The theoretical approach is descriptive rather than explanatory. For example, the claim that some processes become automatic with practice does not tell us *how* this happens. Logan (1988) offered some relevant suggestions. According to him, practice leads to the storage of detailed information about the stimulus and about what to do with it. With sufficient practice, the correct response can be accessed directly from long-term memory, and performance becomes automatic.

## Schema-activation model

Norman and Shallice (1986) distinguished between fully automatic and partially automatic processes in their schema-activation model, which represents a development of Shiffrin and Schneider's (1977) theory. They identified three levels of functioning:

1. Fully automatic processing controlled by schemas (organised plans).
2. Partially automatic processing involving contention scheduling without deliberate direction or conscious control; contention scheduling is used when it is necessary to resolve conflicts among schemas.
3. Deliberate control by a supervisory attentional system resembling the central executive of the working memory system (see Chapter 9).

According to Norman and Shallice (1986), fully automatic processes occur with very little conscious awareness of the processes involved. However, such automatic processes would often disrupt behaviour if left entirely to their own devices. As a result, there is an automatic conflict resolution process known as contention scheduling. This selects one of the available schemas or organised plans on the basis of environmental information and current priorities when two competing schemas are activated at the same time. There is generally more conscious awareness of the partially automatic processes involving contention scheduling than of fully automatic processes. Finally, the higher level attentional supervisory system is involved in decision making and trouble-shooting, and it permits flexible responding in novel situations. This system may well be located in the frontal lobes.

Shallice and Burgess (1996) identified some of the processes carried out by the supervisory attentional system. For example, consider how we cope with a novel situation. According to Shallice and Burgess, three processes are involved:

1. We *construct* a new schema to control behaviour.
2. We *implement* or make use of the new schema.
3. We *monitor* for errors to check that the appropriate schema is being used.

*According to Norman and Shallice, the supervisory attentional system is located in the frontal lobes. If this is correct, how might you expect patients with frontal lobe damage to perform on tests of attention?*

## Evidence

As discussed earlier, it has proved hard to find examples of automatic processes that satisfy all the criteria of automaticity. Such evidence suggests the value of assuming that many processes are only partially automatic. Shallice and Burgess (1993) studied patients with frontal lobe damage who had severe problems with their supervisory attentional system. The behaviour of these patients often seemed to be under the control of contention scheduling. For example, when they saw a pack of cards, they would deal the cards for no obvious reason.

Evidence supporting the distinction between construction and implementation of schemas was reported by Burgess and Shallice (1996). Patients with frontal lesions predicted which of various circles would be filled on each one of a series of cards that were presented to them. The circle that was filled was determined by various rules, and so successful performance of the task involved constructing a schema corresponding to the current rule. The errors made by the frontal patients indicated that some of them had problems with schema construction, whereas others had problems mainly with schema implementation. This pattern is known as a **double dissociation**. It suggests that construction and implementation are separate processes within the supervisory attentional system.

## Evaluation

⊕ The notion that there are two separate control systems (contention scheduling, supervisory system) explains why some processes are fully automatic, but many others are only partially automatic.

⊕ Some of the main processes associated with the supervisory attentional system have now been identified.

⊖ The detailed functioning of the supervisory system remains unclear, and it is not known whether it forms a single unitary system.

⊖ Much of the evidence supporting the schema-activation model comes from brain-damaged patients, and it would be useful to test the model more thoroughly with healthy participants.

## ACTION SLIPS

**Action slips** involve the performance of actions that were not intended. My most devastating action slip occurred when I was word processing a book. I had two icons on the computer screen, one of which contained 25,000 words and the other of which contained nothing. What I intended to do was to copy the 25,000 words into the empty icon. Instead what I did was to copy nothing into the icon containing the 25,000 words, meaning that one-quarter of the book disappeared!

Attentional failures are usually involved in action slips, and this is recognised in the notion of "absent-mindedness". There are two main ways of investigating action slips: (1) diary studies, and (2) laboratory studies. We will consider these two approaches in turn.

*Can you think of your own experiences of action slips? Do you think there are different types of action slip?*

## Diary studies

Reason (1979) asked 35 people to keep diaries of their action slips over a 2-week period. Over 400 action slips were reported, most belonging to five major categories. Forty per cent of the slips involved *storage failures*, in which intentions and actions were forgotten or recalled incorrectly. Here is one of Reason's (p. 74) examples of a storage failure: "I started to pour a second kettle of boiling water into a teapot of freshly made tea."

A further 20% of the errors were *test failures*, in which the progress of a planned sequence was not monitored adequately at crucial junctures or choice points. Here is an example from Reason (1979, p. 73): "I meant to get my car out, but as I passed through the back porch on my way to the garage I stopped to put on my Wellington boots and gardening jacket as if to work in the garden." *Subroutine failures* accounted for another 18% of the errors; these involved insertions, omissions, or reorderings of the various stages in an action sequence. Reason (p. 73) gave this example: "I sat down to do some work and before starting to write I put my hand up to my face to take my glasses off, but my fingers snapped together rather abruptly because I hadn't been wearing them in the first place."

**KEY TERMS**

**Double dissociation:** the finding that some individuals (often brain damaged) perform normally on task A and poorly on task B, whereas others show the opposite pattern.

**Action slips:** actions that are not carried out as intended.

*How generalisable do you think findings from diary studies are?*

The remaining two categories occurred only rarely in the diary study. *Discrimination failures* (11%) consisted of failures to discriminate between objects (e.g., mistaking shaving cream for toothpaste). *Programme assembly failures* (5%) involved inappropriate combinations of actions. For example, "I unwrapped a sweet, put the paper in my mouth, and threw the sweet into the waste bucket" (Reason, 1979, p. 72).

## Evaluation

➕ Diary studies provide valuable information about the action slips of everyday life.
➖ The percentage figures in diary studies are based only on action slips that were detected, and we simply do not know how many action slips went undetected.
➖ In order to interpret the figures, we need to know the number of occasions on which each kind of slip might have occurred but did not. Thus, the small number of discrimination failures may reflect either good discrimination or a relative lack of situations requiring fine discrimination.

## Laboratory studies

In view of the problems with diary studies, we might argue that laboratory studies are preferable. However, potential disadvantages with the laboratory approach were identified by Sellen and Norman (1992). They pointed out that many naturally occurring action slips happen,

> *when a person is internally preoccupied or distracted, when both the intended actions and the wrong actions are automatic, and when one is doing familiar tasks in familiar surroundings. Laboratory situations offer completely the opposite conditions. Typically, subjects are given an unfamiliar, highly contrived task to accomplish in a strange environment. Most subjects arrive motivated to perform well and ... are not given to internal preoccupation. (p. 334)*

Robertson et al. (1997) devised a task in which a long sequence of random digits was presented, with participants responding with a key press to every digit except 3. Failures to withhold responses to 3s were regarded as action slips. Patients with damage to the frontal lobes produced many more such action slips than did healthy participants (30% vs. 12%, respectively). This suggests that attention and action slips both depend in part on the frontal lobes.

## Theories of action slips

Several theories of action slips have been proposed, including those of Reason (1992) and Sellen and Norman (1992). In spite of differences between these theories, Reason and Sellen and Norman agree that there are two modes of control:

- *An automatic mode.* Motor performance is controlled by schemas or organised plans; the schema determining performance is the strongest one available.
- *A conscious control mode.* This involves some central processor or attentional system; this mode of control can override the automatic control mode.

The advantages of automatic control are that it is fast and permits attentional resources to be devoted to other processing activities. However, it is inflexible, and action slips occur when there is too much reliance on this mode of control. Conscious control has the advantages that it is less prone to error than automatic control, and that it responds flexibly to environmental changes. However, it operates fairly slowly, and is an effortful process.

Action slips occur when someone is in the automatic mode of control and the strongest available schema or motor programme is the wrong one. The involvement of the automatic mode of control can be seen in many of Reason's (1979) action slips. One common type of action slip involves repeating an action because the first action has been forgotten

*Do you think all well practised tasks rely on the automatic mode? What factors, other than practice, do you think might determine which control mode we use to perform a task?*

# Hay and Jacoby: Action slips

In spite of the problems, some interesting findings have been obtained from laboratory studies. For example, Hay and Jacoby (1996) argued that action slips are most likely to occur when two conditions are satisfied:

1. The correct response is *not* the strongest or most habitual one.
2. Attention is not fully applied to the task of selecting the correct response.

For example, suppose you are looking for your house key. If it is not in its usual place, you are nevertheless likely to waste time by looking there first of all. If you are late for an important appointment as well, you may find it hard to focus your attention on thinking about other places in which the key might have been put. As a result, you look in several wrong places.

Hay and Jacoby (1996) gave participants a memory test on which they had to complete paired associates (e.g., knee: b _ n _) on the basis of a previous learning task. Sometimes the correct response from the learning task was also the strongest response (e.g., bend), and sometimes it was not (e.g., bone). The participants had either 1 second or 3 seconds to respond. Hay and Jacoby argued that action slips would be most likely when the correct response was not the strongest one, and when the response had to be made rapidly. As predicted, the error rate in that condition was 45% against a mean of only 30% in the other conditions.

Why is the research by Hay and Jacoby (1996) important? As they themselves pointed out, "Very little has been done to examine action ... slips by directly manipulating the likelihood of their occurrence in experimental situations ... we not only manipulated action slips, but also teased apart the roles played by automatic and intentional responding in their production" (p. 1332).

> ### KEY STUDY EVALUATION—Hay and Jacoby
>
> Hay and Jacoby's research looked at action slips in a laboratory setting. There has been little experimental research in this area. Action slips can be seen to be important in real-life settings. For example, consider a technician on a battleship who has to decide whether an approaching target is hostile or not. Hay and Jacoby found that action slips were most likely to occur when the correct response was not the strongest and had to be made rapidly. This would suggest that for the battleship technician the necessity for speed and previous practice in responding to mainly hostile targets may make an action slip (attacking a non-hostile target) more likely.

## Discussion points

1. Does the approach of Hay and Jacoby seem to explain any action slips you have had lately?
2. Are there limitations of the laboratory-based approach used by Hay and Jacoby?

(e.g., brushing one's teeth twice in quick succession, trying to start a car engine that has already been started). As we saw earlier in the chapter, unattended information is held very briefly and then forgotten. When brushing one's teeth or starting a car occurs in the automatic mode of control, it would be predicted that later memory for what has been done should be very poor. As a result, the action would often be repeated.

## *Schema theory*

Sellen and Norman (1992) proposed a schema theory, according to which actions are determined by hierarchically arranged schemas or organised plans. Note that the term schemas is being used in a different way from that typically found in theories of memory (see Chapter 9). The highest-level schema represents the overall intention or goal (e.g., buying a present), and the lower-level schemas correspond to the actions involved in achieving that goal (e.g., taking

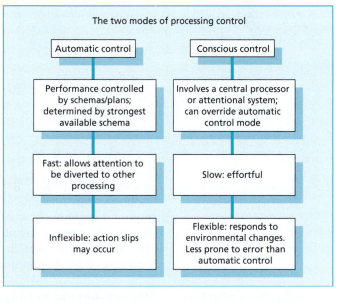

money out of the bank, taking the train to the shopping centre). Any given schema determines action when its level of activation is high enough, and when the appropriate triggering conditions exist (e.g., getting into the train when it stops at the station). The activation level of the schemas is determined by current intentions and by the immediate situation.

Although these acrobats have practised these actions thousands of times, the consequences of any action slips are too serious for the actions to become purely automatic.

Why do action slips occur according to schema theory? There are various possible reasons. First, there may be errors in the formation of an intention. Second, there may be faulty activation of a schema, leading to activation of the wrong schema, or to loss of activation in the right schema. Third, the situation may result in faulty triggering of active schemas, leading to action being determined by the wrong schema.

Many of the action slips recorded by Reason (1979) can be related to schema theory. For example, discrimination failures can lead to errors in the formation of an intention. In addition, storage failures for intentions can produce faulty triggering of active schemas.

## Evaluation

⊕ It seems reasonable to argue (as is done within schema theory) that action slips are "the normal by-products of the design of the human action system" (Sellen & Norman, 1992, p. 318). Thus, there is a single action system which normally functions well, but occasionally produces action slips.

⊕ The theories predict correctly that action slips should occur most often with highly practised activities, because automatic processes are most likely to be used with such activities.

⊖ Action slips are much more common with actions of minor importance than those regarded as very important. For example, many circus performers carry out well-practised actions, but the element of danger ensures that they do not make use of the automatic mode of control. Most theories do not provide an adequate account of such phenomena.

⊖ We know relatively little about the attentional system associated with the conscious control mode, and it is not clear that only a single attentional system is involved.

⊖ The distinction between automatic and controlled processes is probably a substantial over-simplification of a complex reality.

# SUMMARY

Cognitive psychologists have developed four major approaches to the study of human cognition: experimental cognitive psychology, cognitive neuropsychology, cognitive science, and cognitive neuroscience. Each of these approaches has its own strengths and weaknesses, and so cognitive psychologists increasingly make use of more than one approach in their research. The development of these four approaches means that there is now rapid progress in understanding human cognition and the brain.

**Focused auditory attention**    We can follow one auditory message and ignore another message by making use of physical differences (e.g., sex of speaker) between them. According to Broadbent's filter theory, a filter allows one auditory message at a time through to a limited-capacity mechanism beyond the filter on the basis of its physical characteristics. There is more processing of unattended messages than predicted by Broadbent. According to Treisman's attenuation theory, the processing of unattended information is attenuated or reduced.

According to Deutsch and Deutsch, all stimuli are analysed for meaning. The evidence indicates there is fuller processing of attended than of unattended auditory stimuli, which is most consistent with attenuation theory.

Focused visual attention resembles a spotlight or zoom lens. According to the spotlight and zoom-lens models, visual attention is directed towards a given region in the visual field. Two findings are inconsistent with these models: (1) the existence of split attention, and (2) visual attention is often directed to objects rather than a particular region. Unattended visual stimuli are processed less thoroughly than attended ones, but healthy participants and patients with unilateral neglect often process the meaning of such stimuli. Visual search involves two processes. The first process is fast and efficient, whereas the second process is slower and less efficient. Speed of visual search depends on the similarity between the target and the distractors.

*Focused visual attention*

Dual-task performance is typically best when the two tasks are dissimilar, highly practised, and easy. Many findings from dual-task studies can be accounted for by central capacity theories (e.g., Kahneman, 1973). However, the nature of the central capacity is usually poorly specified, and such theories cannot readily explain effects of task similarity on performance. The existence of a psychological refractory period effect provides evidence of a central bottleneck in processing. However, this bottleneck is not always found when well-practised participants perform simple tasks. Some findings from dual-task studies can be explained by Wickens' multiple-resource model, but it does not account for interference between two tasks requiring different resources.

*Divided attention*

In principle, automatic processes are fast, demand zero attention, and are unavoidable. However, these criteria are rarely satisfied. Shiffrin and Schneider (1977) distinguished between automatic and controlled processes, and showed that automatic processes develop with practice. They also showed that automatic processes lack the adaptability and flexibility of controlled processes. According to Logan, increased information is stored in long-term memory as a result of practice, and this permits rapid access to the appropriate responses to stimuli and the development of automatic processes. Norman and Shallice distinguished between fully and partially automatic processes. The notion that many processes are only partially automatic is consistent with the finding that relatively few processes satisfy all the criteria for automaticity.

*Automatic processing*

Diary studies indicate that many action slips involve storage failures, test failures, or subroutine failures, but we do not know how many action slips were undetected. Action slips are most likely to occur when the correct response is not the strongest one, and attention is not fully applied to the task of selecting the correct response. Theoretically, it has been argued that there are two modes of control: (1) an automatic, schema-driven mode, and (2) a conscious control mode. According to schema theory, action slips can occur because of errors in the formation of an intention or faulty activation of a schema. There is limited understanding of the processes involved in automatic and controlled processing, and the distinction between automatic and controlled processes is probably an over-simplification.

*Action slips*

# FURTHER READING

- Driver, J. (2001). A selective review of selective attention research from the past century. *British Journal of Psychology, 92*, 53–78. This article contains interesting accounts of British contributions to several key topics in attention.
- Eysenck, M.W. (2001). *Principles of cognitive psychology* (2nd ed.). Hove, UK: Psychology Press. Chapter 4 of this textbook provides detailed coverage of the main topics within the field of attention.
- Pashler, H., Johnston, J.C., & Ruthroff, E. (2001). Attention and performance. *Annual Review of Psychology, 52*, 629–651. Issues relating to automatic processes and the effects of practice are discussed thoroughly.

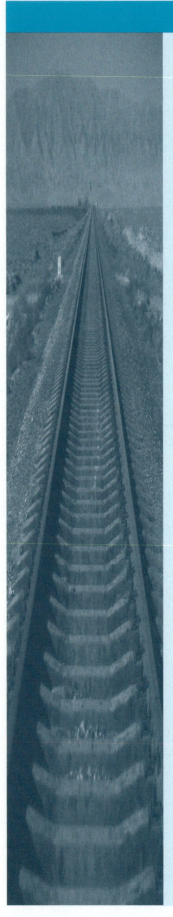

# Visual perception

Visual perception is of enormous importance in our everyday lives. For example, it allows us to move around freely, to see people with whom we are interacting, to read magazines and books, to admire the wonders of nature, and to watch films and television. Therefore, it is no surprise that far more of the cortex is devoted to vision than to any other sensory modality (e.g., hearing).

This chapter is concerned with key issues in visual perception. The first part of the chapter deals with the visual system and the ways in which visual perception is organised. In addition, it deals with issues relating to the accuracy (or inaccuracy) of perception. After that, there are discussions of the processes involved in colour perception, movement perception, and depth perception. The final part of the chapter focuses on the processes involved in object and face recognition. More specifically, how do we recognise or identify the three-dimensional stimuli we encounter? If you want to know more about the development of visual perception in infants and young children, this topic is covered in Chapter 14.

Of course, there are several sense modalities other than vision. Some aspects of auditory perception (i.e., speech perception) are covered in Chapter 11. We know less about the other sense modalities (e.g., taste, smell, touch), but what is known is discussed in various specialist textbooks (e.g., Sekuler & Blake, 2002).

## THE VISUAL SYSTEM

What happens when a visual stimulus reaches receptors in the retina of the eye? At a very general level, there are *three* major consequences (Kalat, 2000). First, there is *reception*, which involves absorption of physical energy by the receptors. Second, there is *transduction*, in which the physical energy is converted into an electrochemical pattern in the neurons. Third, there is *coding*, meaning there is a direct or one-to-one correspondence between aspects of the physical stimulus on the one hand and aspects of the resultant nervous system activity on the other hand.

The human visual system carries out numerous complex processing activities. In the words of Pinel (1997, p. 151), "From the tiny, distorted, upside-down, two-dimensional retinal images projected upon the visual receptors lining the backs of our eyes, the visual system creates an accurate, richly detailed, three-dimensional perception."

Light waves from objects in the environment pass through the transparent cornea at the front of the eye and proceed to the iris. This is just behind the cornea and it gives the eye its distinctive colour. The amount of light entering the eye is determined by the pupil, which is an opening in the iris. This is achieved by the pupil becoming smaller when the lighting is very bright, and larger when there is relatively little light. The lens focuses light onto the retina at the back of the eye. Each lens adjusts in shape by a process of accommodation to bring images into focus on the retina.

The retina itself is complex. It consists of five different layers of cells: receptors, horizontal cells, bipolar cells, amacrine cells, and retinal ganglion cells. The arrangement of these cells is slightly odd. Light from the lens goes through all the layers of cells until it reaches the receptor cells at the back, after which the neural message goes back through the layers. Impulses from the retina leave the eye via the optic nerve, which is at the front of the retina.

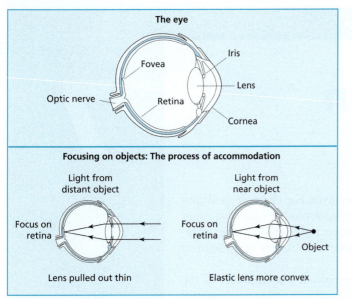

**The eye**

Fovea
Iris
Lens
Optic nerve
Retina
Cornea

**Focusing on objects: The process of accommodation**

Light from distant object
Light from near object

Focus on retina
Focus on retina

Object

Lens pulled out thin
Elastic lens more convex

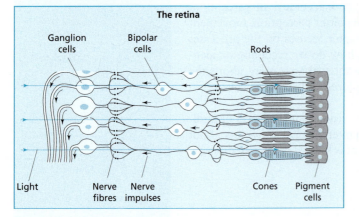

**The retina**

Ganglion cells
Bipolar cells
Rods

Light
Nerve fibres
Nerve impulses
Cones
Pigment cells

**Binocular disparity**

You can demonstrate this easily by shutting your left eye and then holding a pencil or pen up and, using your right eye, lining the pencil up with another object, e.g., the edge of a window. Hold the pencil steady but now close your right eye and open your left eye. The pencil appears to jump from side to side! This is called parallax error, and happens because of binocular disparity, i.e., we have a slightly different image on each retina.

**KEY TERM**

**Binocular disparity:** the slightly different images of a visual scene that are present on the retinas of the two eyes.

There are two types of visual receptor cells in the retina: cones and rods. There are about six million cones, mostly in the fovea or central part of the retina. The cones are specialised for colour vision and for sharpness of vision (see later section on colour perception). There are about 125 million rods concentrated in the outer regions of the retina. Rods are specialised for vision in dim light and for the detection of movement. Many of these differences between cones and roads stem from the fact that a retinal ganglion cell receives input from only a few cones but from hundreds of rods. Thus, only rods produce much activity in retinal ganglion cells in poor lighting conditions.

Why do we have two eyes? A key reason is because this produces **binocular disparity**, meaning the image of any given object is slightly different on the two retinas. Binocular disparity provides useful information for the task of constructing a three-dimensional world out of two-dimensional retinal images (see later in chapter).

## From eye to cortex

The main pathway between the eye and the cortex is the retina-geniculate-striate pathway. This transmits information from the retina to the primary visual cortex or striate cortex via the lateral geniculate nuclei of the thalamus. The entire retina-geniculate-striate system is organised in a similar way to the retinal information. Thus, for example, two stimuli adjacent to each other in the retinal image will also be adjacent to each other at higher levels within that system.

Each eye has its own optic nerve, and the two optic nerves meet at the optic chiasma. At this point, the axons from the outer halves of each retina proceed to the hemisphere on the same side, whereas the axons from the inner halves cross over and go to the other hemisphere. Signals then proceed along two optic tracts within the brain. One tract contains signals from the left half of each eye, and the other signals from the right half.

After the optic chiasma, the optic tract proceeds to the lateral geniculate nucleus, which is part of the thalamus. Nerve impulses finally reach the primary visual cortex within the occipital lobe before spreading out to nearby secondary visual cortical areas. In what follows, you may find it useful to bear in mind Goldstein's (1996, p. 97) overview of the visual system: "As we travel farther from the retina, neurons require more specific stimuli to fire ... this specialisation increases even further as we move into visual areas of the cortex."

There is another important feature of the retina-geniculate-striate system. There are two relatively independent channels or pathways within this system:

1. *The parvocellular (or P) pathway*. This pathway is most sensitive to colour and to fine detail; most of its input comes from cones.
2. *The magnocellular (or M) pathway*. This pathway is most sensitive to information about movement; most of its input comes from rods.

However, as Sawatari and Callaway (1996) found, there are parts of the visual cortex in which the P and M pathways are not strictly segregated from each other. We will discuss these two major pathways in more detail in a little while.

# Brain areas and systems

As Preuss, Qi, and Kaas (1999, p. 11601) pointed out, "Our current understanding of the structure and function of the human visual system [in the cortex] depends critically on experimental studies of non-human primates, especially macaque monkeys." The common assumption that the visual systems of humans and non-humans are basically similar is broadly correct, but is not entirely so. For example, Preuss et al. discovered various important differences between humans and apes in the organisation of primary visual cortex.

You might imagine that one part of the brain would be responsible for all aspects of visual processing. In fact, however, the situation is very different, with different parts of the cortex tending to be specialised for different visual functions; not surprisingly, the term "functional specialisation" is used to describe this state of affairs. Some of the main areas of the visual cortex in the macaque monkey are shown below. The various areas (V1, V2, and so on) are discussed below. Note that some caution may be needed when applying the same terms to the human visual system.

- *V1 and V2.* These areas (V1 is known as primary visual cortex and V2 as secondary visual cortex) are involved at an early stage of visual perception. They contain different groups of cells, some of which are responsive mainly to colour and form, whereas others respond to motion.
- *V3 and V3A.* Cells in these areas are responsive to form (especially the shapes of objects in motion) but not to colour.
- *V4.* The overwhelming majority of cells in this area are responsive to colour; many are also responsive to line orientation.
- *V5.* This area is specialised for visual motion. Studies with macaque monkeys revealed that cells in this area are responsive to motion but not to colour (see Zeki, 1993).

There are cells specialised for the processing of colour, form, and motion, and these cells tend to be found in anatomically separate parts of the visual cortex. However, we must not exaggerate the extent to which this happens. For example, consider a study by Leventhal, Thompson, Liu, Zhou, and Ault (1995), who studied cells in layers 2, 3, and 4 of the primary visual cortex (V1) in monkeys. They discovered little support for the notion of specialised cells: "Our findings are difficult to reconcile with the hypothesis that there is a strict segregation of cells sensitive to orientation, direction, and colour in layers 2 and 3 [of the primary visual cortex]. In fact, the present results suggest the opposite since most cells in these layers are selective for a number of stimulus attributes" (p. 1808).

So far we have produced a kind of sketch-map of the main visual areas in the cortex. We turn now to a more detailed consideration of these areas (and the functions they fulfil). Relatively little will be said about V3. As Lennie (1998, p. 914) pointed out, "V3 is the most enigmatic of the occipital areas, because its cells generally lack distinctive visual characteristics."

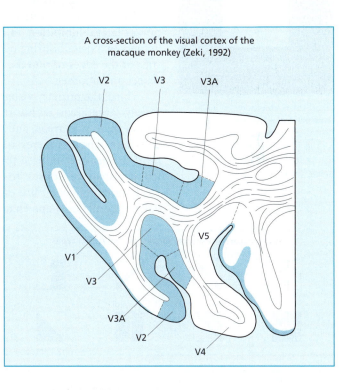

**Route of visual signals**
Note that all light from the fields left of centre of both eyes (blue) falls on the right sides of the two retinas; and information about these fields goes to the right visual cortex. Information about the right fields of vision (grey) goes to the left cortex. Data about the binocular vision go to both cortices.

A cross-section of the visual cortex of the macaque monkey (Zeki, 1992)

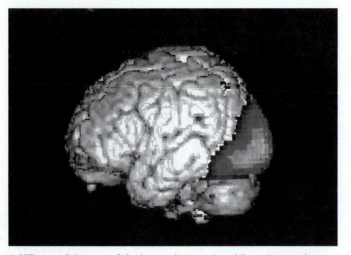

A PET scan of the area of the human brain active while seeing words or pictures. The left side of the brain is seen, with the front at left. Active parts of the cerebral hemisphere are tinted. The visual stimuli have activated the visual area in the occipital cortex.

Form perception will not be discussed in detail, because it involves several areas of the cortex. Areas V1 and V2 are important in form perception, as are areas IT (inferotemporal cortex), V3, and V4 (see Lennie, 1998, for a review). However, IT seems to be of particular importance. For example, Rolls and Tovée (1995) carried out a study on monkeys in which 23 faces and 45 other stimuli were presented. Any one cell in IT showed strong responses to a few faces, coupled with little responding to the other faces or to the non-faces. There is much additional evidence that many neurons in IT respond in a highly selective way to only certain stimuli (see Gross, 1998). Sugase et al. (1999) found that the pattern of activity in some neurons in IT showed an interesting time course. The initial neural activity was determined by the type of object (e.g., a human face, a monkey face, a geometric object). However, the subsequent neural activity was determined by more specific aspects of the stimulus presented to the neuron's receptive field (e.g., the facial expression).

## Primary and secondary visual cortex

The process of lateral inhibition results in the edges of the square being emphasised. Edge detection is especially important in perception because it helps to define objects.

We will start with three important general points. First, in order to understand visual processing in the primary and secondary visual cortex, it is important to consider the notion of receptive field. The **receptive field** for any given neuron is that region of the retina in which light affects its activity.

Second, neurons often have effects on each other. For example, there is the phenomenon of **lateral inhibition**, in which there is a reduction of activity in one neuron caused by activity in a neighbouring neuron. Lateral inhibition is useful, because it increases the contrast at the edges of objects, thus making it easier to identify the dividing line between one object and another.

Third, the primary visual cortex (V1) and the secondary visual cortex (V2) occupy relatively large areas within the cortex. A substantial amount of visual processing occurs within these two areas, and only some of the types of processing involved will be considered here. There is increasing evidence that early visual processing in areas V1 and V2 is more extensive than used to be thought. For example, Hegde and van Essen (2000) studied neuronal responses to complex shapes in macaque monkeys. They found that, "approximately one-third of the V2 cells showed significant differential responsiveness to various complex shape characteristics, and many were also selective for the orientation, size, and/or spatial frequency of the preferred shape. These results indicate that V2 cells explicitly represent complex shape information" (p. RC61).

Much of our knowledge of neurons (and their receptive fields) in primary and secondary visual cortex comes from the Nobel Prize winning research of Hubel and Wiesel. They used single-unit recordings to study individual neurons, and found that many cells responded in two different ways to a spot of light depending on which part of the cell was affected:

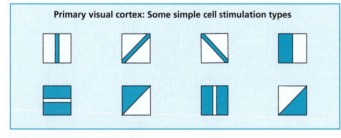

**Primary visual cortex: Some simple cell stimulation types**

**KEY TERMS**

**Receptive field:** the region of the retina within which light influences the activity of a particular neuron.

**Lateral inhibition:** reduction of activity in one neuron caused by activity in a neighbouring neuron.

1. An "on" response, with an increased rate of firing while the light was on.
2. An "off" response, with the light causing a decreased rate of firing.

On-centre cells produce the on-response to a light in the centre of their receptive field and an off-response to a light in the periphery; the opposite is the case with off-centre cells.

Hubel and Wiesel (e.g., 1979) discovered the existence of two types of neurons in the receptive fields of the primary visual cortex: simple cells and complex cells. Simple cells have "on" and "off" regions, with each region being rectangular in shape. These cells play

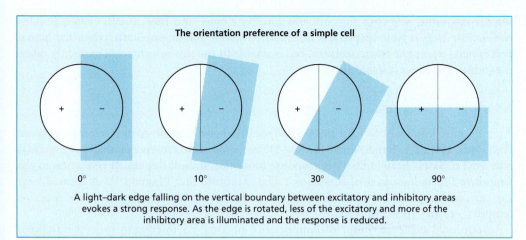

**The orientation preference of a simple cell**

0°          10°          30°          90°

A light–dark edge falling on the vertical boundary between excitatory and inhibitory areas evokes a strong response. As the edge is rotated, less of the excitatory and more of the inhibitory area is illuminated and the response is reduced.

an important role in detection. They respond most to dark bars in a light field, light bars in a dark field, or to straight edges between areas of light and dark. Any given simple cell only responds strongly to stimuli of a particular orientation, and so the responses of these cells could be relevant to feature detection.

Complex cells resemble simple cells in that they respond maximally to straight-line stimuli in a particular orientation. However, complex cells have large receptive fields, and they respond more to moving contours. There is also evidence for the existence of hyper-complex cells. These cells respond most to rather more complex patterns than do simple or complex cells. For example, some respond maximally to corners, whereas others respond to other various specific angles.

*Try to think of a way of remembering the difference between simple and complex cells.*

Cortical cells provide *ambiguous* information, because they respond in the same way to different stimuli. For example, a cell responding maximally to a horizontal line moving slowly may respond moderately to a horizontal line moving rapidly and to a nearly horizontal line moving slowly. We need to combine information from numerous neurons in order to remove ambiguities.

## Colour processing

The notion that colour and motion processing involve different areas of the cortex received support in a study by Cavanagh, Tyler, and Favreau (1984). They presented a moving grating consisting of alternating red and green bars of equal brightness. The observers reported either that the bars did not seem to be moving, or there was only a modest impression of movement. Cavanagh et al. argued that the moving display only affected the colour processing system. It did not stimulate the motion processing system, because that system responds only to differences in brightness.

Evidence that area V4 is specialised for colour processing was reported by Lueck et al. (1989). They presented coloured or grey squares and rectangles to observers. PET scans indicated that there was about 13% more blood flow within area V4 with the coloured stimuli, but other areas were not more affected by colour. However, area V4 is not the only one involved in colour processing. Wade, Brewer, Rieger, and Wandell (2002) used fMRI, and found that areas V1 and V2 were actively involved in colour processing in addition to the involvement of area V4.

If area V4 is specialised for colour processing, then patients with damage mostly limited to that area should show little or no colour perception, combined with fairly normal form and motion perception. This is the case in some patients with **achromatopsia**. However, many of them do have problems with object recognition as well as an inability to identify colours by name. In spite of the fact that patients with achromatopsia complain the world seems devoid of colour, some aspects of colour processing are preserved. Heywood, Cowey, and Newcombe (1994) studied MS, a patient with achromatopsia. He performed well on a task on which he had to select the odd form out of a set of stimuli. This task could only be performed accurately by using colour information, but did not require conscious access to that information. As Köhler and Moscovitch (1997, p. 326) concluded, "MS is able to process information about colour implicitly when the actual perceptual judgement concerns form, but is unable to use this information explicitly when the judgement concerns colour."

## Motion processing

Area V5 (also known as MT for medial temporal) is heavily involved in motion processing. Anderson, Holliday, Singh, and Harding (1996) used magneto-encephalography (MEG) and MRI to assess brain activity in response to motion stimuli (see the introduction to the Cognitive Psychology part of this book). They reported that "human V5 is located near the occipito-temporal border in a minor sulcus [groove] immediately below the superior temporal sulcus" (p. 428).

Additional evidence about the importance of area V5 in motion processing comes from studies on brain-damaged patients with **akinetopsia**. In this condition, stationary objects can generally be perceived fairly normally, but objects in motion become invisible. Zihl, von Cramon, and Mai (1983) studied LM, a woman with akinetopsia who had suffered brain damage in both hemispheres. A subsequent high-resolution MRI scan revealed that LM had bilateral damage to V5 (Shipp, de Jong, Zihl, Frackowiak, & Zeki, 1994). She was good at locating stationary objects by sight, she had good colour discrimination, and her binocular visual functions (e.g., stereoscopic depth perception) were normal. However, her motion perception was grossly deficient. According to Zihl et al.:

> She had difficulty ... in pouring tea or coffee into a cup because the fluid appeared to be frozen, like a glacier. In addition, she could not stop pouring at the right time since she was unable to perceive the movement in the cup (or a pot) when the fluid rose.

LM's condition did not improve over time. However, she developed various ways of coping with her lack of motion perception. For example, she stopped looking at people who were talking to her, because she found it disturbing that their lips did not seem to move (Zihl et al., 1991).

Striking evidence of the involvement of V5 in motion perception was reported by Beckers and Zeki (1995). They produced temporary inactivation of V5, which led to a short-lasting (but complete) akinetopsia. However, other brain areas are also involved in motion perception. For example, Vaina (1998) reported findings from two patients who had suffered damage to area MST (medial superior temporal), which is adjacent to and just above V5 or MT. Both patients had problems relating to motion perception. For example, one of the patients (RR), "frequently bumped into people, corners and things in his way, particularly into moving targets (e.g., people walking)" (p. 498).

## Overview

Earlier I mentioned the existence of the important M and P pathways when discussing the retina-geniculate-striate system. An over-simplified view of the P and M pathways with respect to the main cortical areas involved in visual processing is shown on the next page. There are three main ways in which the illustration is over-simplified. First, there are numerous interconnections between the two pathways. Second, there are probably at least 30 or 40 visual areas in the human brain. Third, there is evidence that the two pathways become three within the cortex (van Essen & DeYoe, 1995):

1. Part of the P pathway continues to be involved in form processing.
2. The main part of the M pathway continues to be heavily involved in motion processing.
3. The third pathway combines parts of the P and M pathways, and is involved in the processing of colour and brightness.

What is the significance of the M and P pathways? Several theorists (e.g., Mishkin & Ungerleider, 1982) have argued that vision is used for two crucial functions. First, there is object perception (*what* is it?). Second, there is spatial perception (*where* is it?). There is

*What kind of problems do you think patients with akinetopsia would experience in their everyday lives?*

**KEY TERM**

**Akinetopsia:** a brain-damaged condition, in which objects in motion cannot be perceived, whereas stationary objects are perceived fairly normally.

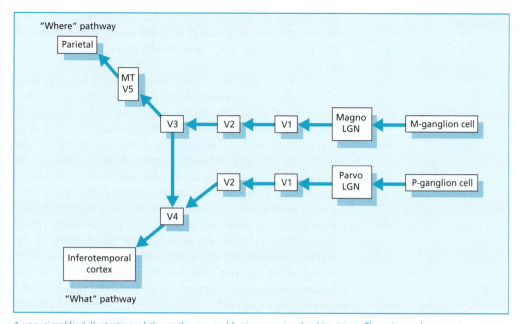

"Where" pathway

Parietal

MT V5

V3 ← V2 ← V1 ← Magno LGN ← M-ganglion cell

V2 ← V1 ← Parvo LGN ← P-ganglion cell

V4

Inferotemporal cortex

"What" pathway

A very simplified illustration of the pathways and brain areas involved in vision. There is much more interconnectivity within the brain (V1 onwards) than is shown, and there are additional unshown brain areas involved in vision. Adapted from Goldstein (1996).

reasonable evidence (at least in macaque monkeys) that these two functions map reasonably well onto the two major pathways:

1. *The P or ventral (front) pathway* running from the primary visual area in the cortex to the inferior temporal cortex is specialised for object perception (i.e., what is it?).
2. *The M or dorsal (back) pathway* running from the primary visual area in the cortex to the posterior parietal cortex is specialised for spatial perception (i.e., where is it?).

There is much support for the general views expressed by Mishkin and Ungerleider (1982). For example, Haxby et al. (1994) obtained PET scans from participants while they carried out an object-recognition task and a spatial task. As predicted, the object-recognition task produced heightened activity in the inferior and medial temporal cortex, whereas the spatial task led to increased activation in the parietal cortex.

The ideas of Mishkin and Ungerleider (1982) have been developed by Milner and Goodale (1995, 1998), and their theoretical views are considered later. These theories (and others we have considered) assume that certain areas of the cortex are specialised for certain kinds of visual processing. At some point, information about colour, form, and motion has to be combined or integrated in order for full object recognition to occur. The issues this raises are known as the **binding problem**, and as yet we know little of how the brain solves this problem.

*Try to think of some everyday tasks that use either the ventral or the dorsal pathway.*

## PERCEPTUAL ORGANISATION

It is important to account for perceptual segregation, i.e., our ability to work out which parts of the visual information available to us belong together and thus form separate objects. We generally have no problem in doing this, but it is more of an achievement than you might imagine. For example, consider what happens when you look at a car parked behind a telephone pole (Palmer, 2002). Why do we perceive a single complete car rather than seeing two disconnected parts of cars?

The first systematic attempt to study perceptual segregation and the perceptual organisation to which it gives rise was made by the Gestaltists. They were a group of German psychologists (including Koffka, Köhler, and Wertheimer) who emigrated to the United States between the two World Wars. Their fundamental principle of perceptual organisation was

KEY TERM
**Binding problem:** issues arising when different kinds of information need to be integrated to produce object recognition.

**Examples of the law of Prägnanz**

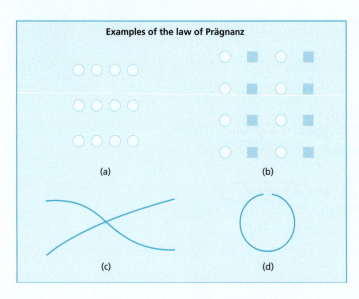

(a)          (b)

(c)          (d)

The faces–goblet ambiguous figure is an example of figure and ground—which is figure and which is ground?

the law of Prägnanz: "Of several geometrically possible organisations that one will actually occur which possesses the best, simplest and most stable shape" (Koffka, 1935, p. 138).

Although the law of Prägnanz was their key organisational principle, the Gestaltists put forward several other laws, most of which can be subsumed under the law of Prägnanz. The fact that three horizontal arrays of dots rather than vertical groups are perceived in (a) of the figure on the left indicates visual elements tend to be grouped together if they are close to each other (the law of proximity). Part (b) of the figure illustrates the law of similarity, which states that elements will be grouped together perceptually if they are similar. Vertical columns rather than horizontal rows are seen because the elements in the vertical columns are the same, whereas those in the horizontal rows are not. We see two crossing lines in (c), because we group together those elements requiring the fewest changes or interruptions in straight or smoothly curving lines (law of good continuation). Part (d) of the figure illustrates the law of closure, according to which missing parts of a figure are filled in to complete the figure. Thus, a circle is seen even though it is actually incomplete.

The Gestaltists emphasised the importance of **figure–ground organisation** in perceptual organisation. The key object or part of the visual field is identified as the figure, whereas the rest of the visual field is of less significance and so forms the ground. The laws of perceptual organisation permit this segregation into figure and ground to happen. The figure is perceived as having a distinct form or shape, whereas the ground lacks form. In addition, the figure is perceived as being in *front* of the ground.

You can check the validity of these claims about figure and ground by looking at reversible figures such as the faces–goblet figure. When the goblet is the figure, it seems to be in front of a black background; the faces are in front of a white background when they form the figure.

The Gestaltists explained their laws of perceptual organisation by their doctrine of **isomorphism**. According to this doctrine, the experience of visual organisation is mirrored by a precisely corresponding process in the brain. It was assumed that there are electrical "field forces" in the brain which help to produce the experience of a stable perceptual organisation.

## Evidence

Weisstein and Wong (1986) found more attention is paid to the figure than to the ground. They flashed vertical and slightly tilted lines onto the faces–goblet figure (see above), and gave their participants the task of deciding whether the line was vertical. Performance was much better when the line was presented to what the participants perceived as the figure than to the ground.

The Gestaltists' pseudo-physiological ideas (i.e., the doctrine of isomorphism) have not survived. Much damage was done to the theory by Lashley, Chow, and Semmes (1951) in a study on two chimpanzees. They placed four gold foil "conductors" in the visual area of one of the chimpanzees, and twenty-three gold pins vertically through the cortex of the other chimpanzee. Lashley et al. argued persuasively that this would have severely disrupted any electrical field forces. In fact, the perceptual abilities of their chimpanzees were hardly affected, suggesting electrical field forces are of much less significance than the Gestaltists claimed.

According to the Gestaltists, the various laws of grouping operate in a bottom-up way to produce segmentation and perceptual organisation. Thus, knowledge about objects in the visual field is *not* used to determine how the visual field is segmented. Evidence inconsistent with the Gestaltist position was reported by Vecera and Farah (1997). Their participants found it easier to achieve segmentation between two overlapping transparent letters when they were presented *upright* rather than *upside down*. Information about the nature of the letters was more accessible when they were presented upright, and this object-related information influenced the segmentation process.

When does perceptual grouping occur? The Gestaltists assumed that grouping of perceptual elements occurs *early* in visual processing, but there is increasing evidence that it often happens *late* in processing (see Palmer, 2002). For example, Rock and Palmer (1990) discussed an experiment in which luminous beads on parallel strings were presented in the dark. The beads were closer to each in the vertical direction than the horizontal one. As the law of proximity predicts, the beads were perceived as forming columns. When the display was slanted backwards, the beads were closer to each other horizontally than vertically in the two-dimensional retinal image, but remained closer to each other vertically in three-dimensional space. The observers saw the beads organised in vertical columns. As Rock and Palmer (p. 51) concluded, "Grouping was based on perceived proximity in three-dimensional space rather than on actual proximity on the retina. Grouping by proximity must therefore occur after depth perception."

*Are the Gestaltists explaining visual perception?*

What happens when two or more laws of grouping are in conflict? This important issue was de-emphasised by the Gestaltists, but was subsequently addressed by Quinlan and Wilton (1998). They found the visual elements in a display were initially grouped or clustered on the basis of proximity. However, when there was a conflict between the laws of proximity and of similarity (see part (a) of the figure on the right), some observers grouped by proximity and some by similarity. With complicated displays such as those shown in parts (b) and (c) proximity was ignored, with grouping tending to occur on the basis of colour rather than shape.

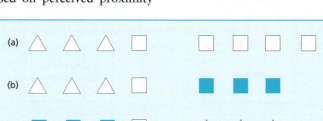

Laws of grouping: (a) display involving a conflict between proximity and similarity; (b) display with a conflict between shape and colour; (c) a different display with a conflict between shape and colour.

## Evaluation

● "The laws of grouping have withstood the test of time. In fact, not one of them has been refuted" (Rock & Palmer, 1990, p. 50).
● The Gestaltists' account of the figure–ground organisation is essentially accurate.
● The Gestaltists produced *descriptions* of interesting perceptual phenomena rather than adequate *explanations*.
● The assumption that observers use the laws of grouping in a bottom-up way to achieve perceptual organisation is over-simplified (Vecera & Farah, 1997).
● Grouping often occurs later in perceptual processing than was assumed by the Gestaltists.
● The Gestaltists did not consider fully the complexities of what happens when there are conflicts among the laws of grouping.

## PERCEPTION: ACCURATE OR INACCURATE?

One of the factors influencing *what* we see and the *accuracy* of visual perception is context. A simple example is shown on the right. The stimulus in the middle of each column is the same in each case, but is seen as a "B" or as "13" depending on context.

Additional evidence concerning the importance of contextual information was provided by Palmer (1975). He presented a scene (e.g., a kitchen) in pictorial form, followed by the very brief presentation of the picture of an object. This object was appropriate to the context (e.g., loaf) or inappropriate (e.g., mailbox). There was also a further condition in which no contextual scene was presented. The probability of identifying the object

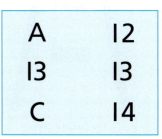

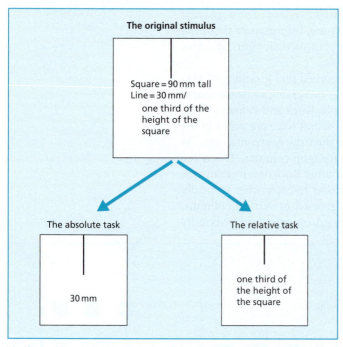

The framed-line test with examples of the absolute and the relative tasks. From Kitayama et al. (2003).

correctly was greatest when appropriate to the context, intermediate when there was no context, and lowest when inappropriate.

Kitayama, Duffy, Kawamura, and Larsen (2003) found interesting cultural differences in the tendency to take account of contextual information. Japanese and American participants were given the framed-line test. On each trial, a square frame containing a vertical line was presented, followed by the presentation of another square frame of the same or different size. The task was *either* to draw a line identical in length to the first line (absolute task) *or* to draw a line in proportion to the height of the surrounding frame (relative task).

What did Kitayama et al. (2003) find? They argued the American culture is individualistic, meaning there is an emphasis on the individual rather than the social context (see Chapter 1). In contrast, the Japanese culture is a collectivistic one, meaning that the social and other context is of prime importance. Successful performance on the relative task involves taking account of context, whereas successful performance on the absolute task involves ignoring context. Thus, it was predicted that American participants would perform better on the absolute task than on the relative one, whereas Japanese participants would show the opposite pattern. That is precisely what Kitayama et al. found.

As we have seen, contextual information can make perception more or less accurate. In more general terms, however, it seems reasonable to argue that visual perception must be accurate most of the time. If that were not the case, then we might find ourselves falling down flights of stairs, falling over cliffs, and so on. However, visual perception is by no means always accurate, as is clear from the existence of numerous visual illusions. We will make a start by discussing some of the major visual illusions, in most of which contextual information plays a crucial role. After that, we will consider theoretical approaches to understanding the conditions in which perception is accurate and inaccurate.

## Visual illusions

One of the best-known visual illusions is the Ponzo illusion. The long lines look like railway lines or the edges of a road receding into the distance. Thus, the top horizontal line can be seen as further away from us than the bottom horizontal line. As rectangles A and B are the same size in the retinal image, the more distant rectangle (A) must actually be larger.

Evidence consistent with Gregory's theory (see Key Study on the next page) was reported by Segall, Campbell, and Herskovits (1963). They argued that the Müller–Lyer illusion would only be perceived by those with experience of a "carpentered environment" containing numerous rectangles, straight lines, and regular corners. People in Western cultures live in carpentered environments, but Zulus living in tribal communities do not. Rural Zulus did not show the Müller–Lyer illusion. However, this finding might simply mean that rural Zulus cannot interpret two-dimensional drawings. This is unlikely in view of another of Segall et al.'s findings. They studied the horizontal–vertical illusion, which involves overestimating vertical extents relative to horizontal ones in a two-dimensional drawing. Rural Zulus showed the horizontal–vertical illusion to a greater extent than

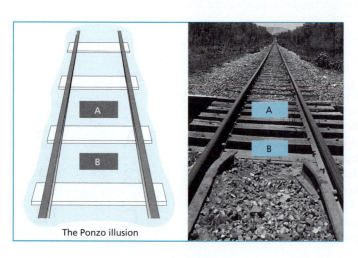

The Ponzo illusion

# Gregory: Size constancy

Gregory (1972, 1980) developed the explanation given above for the Ponzo illusion into a general theory of visual illusions. He assumed that rules derived from the perception of three-dimensional objects are applied inappropriately to the perception of two-dimensional figures. For example, people typically see a given object as having a constant size by taking account of its apparent distance. **Size constancy** means an object is perceived as having the same size whether it is looked at from a short or a long distance away (see later in the chapter). Size constancy contrasts with the size of the retinal image, which becomes progressively smaller as an object recedes into the distance. According to this misapplied size-constancy theory, this kind of perceptual processing is applied wrongly to produce several illusions.

We will see how Gregory's theory accounts for the Müller–Lyer illusion. The vertical fins in the two figures are the same length. However, the vertical line on the left looks longer than the one in the figure on the right. According to Gregory (1970), the Müller–Lyer figures can be regarded as simple perspective drawings of three-dimensional objects. The left figure looks like the inside corners of a room, whereas the right figure is like the outside corners of a building. Thus, the vertical line in the right figure is closer to us than its fins. Since the size of the retinal image is the same for both vertical lines, the principle of size constancy tells us that the line that is further away (i.e., the one in the left figure) must be longer. This is precisely the Müller–Lyer illusion.

Gregory argued that figures such as the Ponzo and the Müller–Lyer are treated in many ways as three-dimensional objects. Why, then, do they seem flat and two-dimensional? According to Gregory, cues to depth are used *automatically* whether or not the figures are seen to be lying on a flat surface. As Gregory predicted, the two-dimensional Müller–Lyer figures appear three-dimensional when presented as luminous models in a darkened room. However, they are not seen three-dimensionally by everyone.

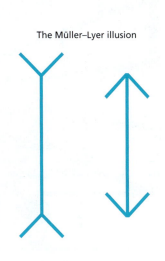

The Müller–Lyer illusion

## Discussion points

**1.** Is it likely that any single theory of visual illusions will explain them all?
**2.** What grounds are there for doubting Gregory's misapplied size-constancy theory?

Europeans, presumably because of their greater familiarity with large open spaces.

Other researchers have produced different findings. Gregor and McPherson (1965) compared two groups of Australian Aborigines. One group lived in a carpentered environment, but the other group lived in the open air and had very basic housing. The two groups did not differ on either the Müller–Lyer or the horizontal–vertical illusion. Cross-cultural differences in visual illusions may depend more on training and education than on whether or not a given group lives in a carpentered environment.

DeLucia and Hochberg (1991) obtained convincing evidence that Gregory's theory is incomplete. They used a three-dimensional display consisting of three 2-foot high fins on the floor. It was obvious all the fins were at the same distance from the viewer, but the typical Müller–Lyer effect was obtained. You can check this out for yourself by placing three open books in a line so that the ones on the left and the right are open to the right and the one in the middle is open to the left. The spine of the book in the middle should be the same distance from the spines of each of the other two books. In spite of this, the distance between the spine of the middle book and the spine of the book on the right should look longer.

Matlin and Foley (1997) proposed the incorrect comparison theory, according to which our perception of visual illusions is influenced by parts of the figure not being

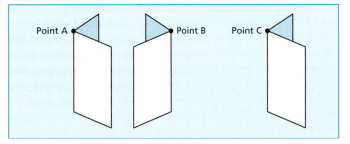

In DeLucia and Hochberg's study, three fins that were 2 feet high were positioned on the floor and participants asked to say whether point A was closer to point B than B was to C. The Müller–Lyer illusion persists even though depth is obvious in this three-dimensional situation; a fact that does not fit Gregory's misapplied size-constancy theory.

**KEY TERM**

**Size constancy:** objects are perceived as having a given size regardless of the size of the retinal image.

These creatures are identical in size, although the one in the background appears to be larger than the creature in the foreground due to the depth cues that indicate they are running down a passageway.

*How would you go about testing Milner and Goodale's model?*

judged. Evidence in line with this theory was reported by Coren and Gingus (1972). The Müller–Lyer illusion was greatly reduced when the fins were in a different colour to the vertical lines, because this made it easier to ignore the fins.

We have now considered various possible explanations for visual illusions. However, what remains puzzling is the contrast between the numerous perceptual errors and biases revealed by visual illusions and our generally excellent ability to move successfully around the environment. Attempts to solve this puzzle are considered below.

## Perception–action model

Milner and Goodale (1995, 1998) proposed a theoretical model containing a key distinction between *perception for recognition* (in which objects are recognised and identified) and *perception for action* (in which the precise location of visual stimuli is determined). The distinction between perception for recognition and perception for action is supported by evidence from cognitive neuroscience and from cognitive neuropsychology. There appears to be a ventral [front] stream of processing more involved in perception for recognition. This is the P pathway shown in the figure on p. 225. There is also a dorsal (back) stream more involved in perception for action, which is the M pathway (also see the figure on p. 221). In fact, however, perception for most purposes is typically based on both processing streams.

Why do we have these two systems? According to Milner and Goodale (1998, p. 12), the dorsal system, "is designed to guide actions purely in the here and now, and its products are consequently useless for later reference ... it is only through knowledge gained via the ventral stream that we can exercise insight, hindsight and foresight about the visual world".

Milner and Goodale's (1995, 1998) perception–action model can explain why we are subject to various visual illusions but can move around the environment without knocking into things. In essence, we use the perception-for-recognition system when looking at visual illusions, whereas we use the perception-for-action system when moving around. It is assumed that the perception-for-action system typically functions very efficiently and without significant error.

## *Evidence*

Suppose we found some patients having intact perception-for-recognition but impaired perception-for-action and some patients showing the opposite pattern. That would form what is known as a **double dissociation**, and would provide support for the notion that there are two separate systems underlying perception. As we will see, there is evidence for this double dissociation.

Patients with **visual agnosia** have severe difficulties in recognising objects, but often have reasonably good perception-for-action abilities. Goodale et al. (1991) studied a visual agnosic, DF, who could not recognise objects or even describe their shape, size, or orientation. However, when DF was asked to pick up a block, she adjusted her grasping movements so they were appropriate to the size of the block. In a second study by Goodale et al., DF was asked to place a card in a slot. She was as accurate as normal individuals in her ability to orientate her hand to match the slot. However, DF's ability to use visual information to control action was limited. Carey, Harvey, and Milner (1996) found DF did *not* show normal grasping behaviour when trying to pick up complex objects (e.g., crosses) in which two different orientations were present together. It may be that the perception-for-recognition system is needed to assist in the control of action with relatively complex stimuli.

What about patients with good perception-for-recognition but impaired perception-for-action? Patients with **optic ataxia** show this pattern. According to Georgopoulos (1997, p. 142), such patients "do not usually have impaired vision or impaired hand or arm movements, but show a severe impairment in visually guided reaching in the absence of perceptual disturbance in estimating distance". For example, Perenin and Vighetto (1988) found patients with optic ataxia experienced great difficulty in rotating their hands appropriately when given the task of reaching towards and into a large orientated slot in front of them. Pisella et al. (2000) found that normal individuals rapidly corrected reaching movements of the hand when a target jumped from one place to another. In contrast, reaching movements could only be corrected slowly in a patient with optic ataxia.

It is now time to return to the visual illusions. We know there is strong evidence for illusions when the perception-for-recognition system is used, but what happens when the perception-for-action system is used? Surprisingly (but consistent with the perception–action model), many illusions are either reduced or disappear altogether! For example, Gentilucci et al. (1996) carried out a study with the Müller–Lyer illusion. The participants were asked to point to various parts of the figures. There were small effects of the illusion on hand movements, but these effects were much smaller than those obtained using perceptual judgements.

Similar findings were reported by Aglioti, Goodale, and DeSouza (1995) with the Ebbinghaus illusion. In this illusion, the central circle surrounded by smaller circles looks larger than a central circle of the same size surrounded by larger circles. Aglioti et al. constructed a three-dimensional version of this illusion, and obtained the usual illusion effect. More interestingly, when the participants reached to pick up one of the central discs, the maximum grip aperture of their reaching hand was almost entirely determined by the actual size of the disc. Thus, no illusion was apparent in the size of the hand grip. Haffenden and Goodale (1998) obtained similar findings even when the participants could not compare their hand opening with the disc as they reached for it. However, Glover and Dixon (2002a) found the Ebbinghaus illusion influenced initial grip aperture, although this influence decreased as the hand approached the target.

Most of the findings on visual illusions we have considered so far fit the perception–action model, because they suggest that various visual illusions have little or no effect on perception-for-action. However, there are several exceptions. In many cases, hand and/or arm movements are susceptible to visual illusions (see Glover, in press, for a review; see also below). Accordingly, it is not possible to account for all findings on visual illusions within the perception–action model.

The spine of the middle book is closer to the spine of which other book? Now check your answer with a ruler.

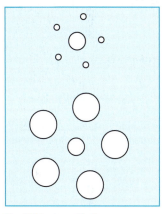

The Ebbinghaus illusion.

*Do you think the same visual illusions "fool" people in all cultures?*

## Evaluation

⊕ The assumption that separate systems underlie perception for action and perception for recognition is a powerful one, and has received much support.

⊕ The perception–action model played a key role in the recent upsurge of interest in the extent to which illusion effects are found with body movements.

⊖ The theoretical assumptions about the processing occurring within the dorsal and ventral streams are over-simplified.

⊖ As Milner and Goodale (1998, p. 12) admitted, "One of the important questions that remains to be answered is how the two streams interact with each other and with other brain regions in the production of purposive behaviour."

⊖ The model cannot easily explain why perception for action is sometimes influenced by visual illusions.

**KEY TERM**

**Optic ataxia:** a condition in which there are problems with making visually guided limb movement.

## Planning–control model

Glover (in press) was interested in explaining how visual information is used in the production of human action (e.g., reaching for a pint of beer). In his planning–control model, he argued we initially use a planning system followed by a control system, but with the two systems overlapping somewhat in time. This model is in some ways a development of Milner and Goodale's perception–action model, but it does make some different predictions. Here are the key characteristics of the planning and control systems identified within the model:

*Planning system*
- This system is used mostly *before* the initiation of movement, but is also used early during the movement.
- The functions of this system include selecting an appropriate target (e.g., pint of beer), deciding how it should be grasped, and the timing of the movement.
- This system is influenced by several factors (e.g., the individual's goals, the nature of the target object, visual context, various cognitive processes).
- This system is relatively slow because it makes use of a wide range of information, and is susceptible to conscious influence.

*Control system*
- This system is used after the planning system and operates during the carrying out of a movement.
- The functions of this system are to ensure that movements are accurate and to make adjustments if required.
- This system is influenced *only* by the target object's spatial characteristics (e.g., size, shape, orientation).
- This system is relatively fast because it makes use of little information and is not susceptible to conscious influence.

*Can you think which visual illusions depend on the planning system and which depend on the control system?*

Glover's planning–control model is of relevance to an understanding of the factors determining whether perception is accurate or inaccurate. Of crucial importance, most errors and inaccuracies in perception and action stem from the planning system, whereas the control system typically ensures that human action is accurate and achieves its goal. So far as visual illusions are concerned, many of them occur because of the influence of the surrounding visual context. According to the planning–control model, information about visual context is used by the planning system but not by the control system. Accordingly, responses to visual illusions should typically be inaccurate if they depend on the planning system but should be accurate if they depend on the control system.

## Evidence

There is much support for the planning–control model from studies of visual illusions. Glover and Dixon (2002a), in a study discussed above, found the Ebbinghaus illusion as assessed by grip aperture decreased as the hand approached the target. According to the model, this happened because the initial planning process is influenced by the illusion but the subsequent control process is not.

Jackson and Shaw (2000) used the Ponzo illusion, and asked participants to grasp an object and lift it into the air. The illusion had no effect on the grip aperture between index finger and thumb as the participants moved to pick it up. However, the illusion did influence the perceived weight of the object as assessed by the force of the grip used to pick it up. What do these findings mean? Theoretically, grip aperture close to the object is based on perception of object size, and depends on the control system. In contrast, perceived weight involves taking account of additional kinds of information (e.g., density of the object), and thus involves the planning system.

Glover and Dixon (2001) presented a small bar on a background grating which caused the bar's orientation to be misperceived. The participants were instructed to pick up the bar. What Glover and Dixon found was that the effects of the illusion on hand orientation were relatively large early in the reaching movement, but almost disappeared as the hand approached the bar. This is predicted by the model: Initially the movement is influenced by the error-prone planning system, but it is influenced by the control system as the movement continues.

Glover and Dixon (2002b) used a task in which participants reached for an object that had either the word "LARGE" or the word "SMALL" written on it. According to the planning–control model, the cognitive processes involved in understanding word meaning are associated with the planning system rather than the control system. Early in the reach (when movement was directed by the planning system), the participants showed an illusion effect in that their grip aperture was greater for objects with the word "LARGE" on them. Later in the reach (when movement was directed by the control system), the illusion effect decreased.

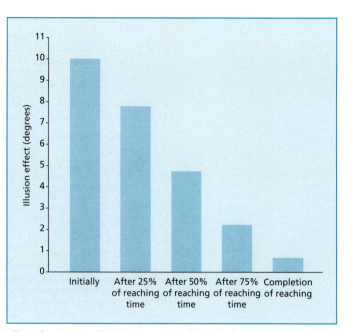

Effect of orientation illusion on accuracy of hand orientation at different points in reaching for a bar. Data from Glover and Dixon (2001).

## Evaluation

➕ There is much support for the notion that separate planning and control systems are involved in reaching for and grasping objects.
➕ The errors involved in starting to reach for objects seem to be due primarily to the planning system rather than to the control system.
➖ The precise number and nature of the processing activities carried out within the planning system are unclear.
➖ The planning–control model considers body movements but not eye movements, in spite of the fact that co-ordination of eye and body movements is important.

# COLOUR PERCEPTION

Why has colour vision developed? After all, if you see an old black-and-white film on television, you can easily make sense of the moving images presented to your eyes. There are two main reasons why colour vision is of value to us (Sekuler & Blake, 2002):

• *Detection.* Colour vision helps us to distinguish between an object and its background.
• *Discrimination.* Colour vision makes it easier for us to make fine discriminations among objects (e.g., between ripe and unripe fruit).

There are three qualities associated with colour. First, there is *hue*, which is what distinguishes red from yellow or blue. Second, there is *brightness*, which is the perceived intensity of light. Third, there is *saturation*, which allows us to determine whether a colour is vivid or pale.

## Young–Helmholtz theory

Cone receptors (discussed earlier) contain light-sensitive photopigment allowing them to respond to light. According to the component or trichromatic theory put forward by Thomas Young (1773–1829) and developed by Hermann von Helmholtz (1821–1894), there are "three distinct sets of nervous fibres" differing in the light wavelengths to which they respond most strongly. Subsequent research led to these sets of fibres becoming identified with cone receptors. One type of cone receptor is most sensitive to short-wavelength light, and has the greatest response to stimuli perceived as blue. A second type of cone

*Can you remember the characteristics of cones and rods, discussed earlier?*

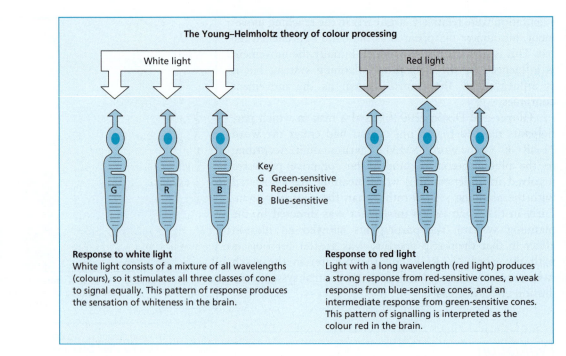

The Young–Helmholtz theory of colour processing

White light

Red light

Key
G  Green-sensitive
R  Red-sensitive
B  Blue-sensitive

**Response to white light**
White light consists of a mixture of all wavelengths (colours), so it stimulates all three classes of cone to signal equally. This pattern of response produces the sensation of whiteness in the brain.

**Response to red light**
Light with a long wavelength (red light) produces a strong response from red-sensitive cones, a weak response from blue-sensitive cones, and an intermediate response from green-sensitive cones. This pattern of signalling is interpreted as the colour red in the brain.

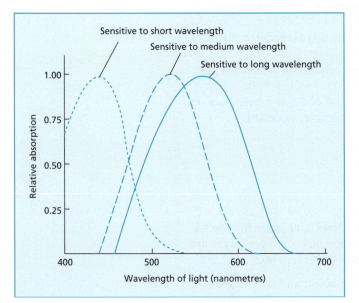

Three types of colour receptors or cones identified by microspectrophotometry. From Dartnall et al. (1983).

receptor is most sensitive to medium-wavelength light, and responds greatly to stimuli that are seen as green. The third type of cone receptor responds most to long-wavelength light such as that coming from stimuli distinguished as red.

How do we see other colours? According to the theory, many stimuli activate two or even all three cone types. The perception of yellow is based on the second and third cone types, and white light involves the activation of all three cone types.

Dartnall, Bowmaker, and Mollon (1983) obtained support for this theory using a technique known as **microspectrophotometry** (a technique allowing measurement of the amount of light absorbed at various wavelengths by individual cone receptors). This revealed there are three types of cones or receptors responding maximally to different wavelengths of light. Each cone type absorbs a wide range of wavelengths, and so we must not equate one cone type with perception of blue, one with green, and one with red. There are four million long-wavelength cones, over two million medium-wavelength cones, and under one million short-wavelength cones (Cicerone & Nerger, 1989).

Most individuals with colour deficiency are not completely colour blind. The most common type of colour blindness is *red–green deficiency*, in which blue and yellow can be seen but not red and green. There are rarer forms of colour deficiency, such as an inability to perceive blue or yellow, combined with the ability to see red and green. According to the Young–Helmholtz theory, we can explain why red–green deficiency is the commonest form of colour blindness by arguing the medium- and long-wavelength cone types are more likely to be damaged or missing than the short-wavelength cones. That is the case (Sekuler & Blake, 2002). There are rarer cases in which the short-wavelength cones are missing, and this disrupts perception of blue and yellow. However, the Young–Helmholtz theory fails to explain what is known as the **negative afterimage**. If you stare at a square of a given colour for several seconds, and then shift your gaze to a white surface, you will see a negative afterimage in the complementary colour. For example, a green square produces a red afterimage, whereas a blue square produces a yellow afterimage.

## Opponent-process theory

Ewald Hering (1878) put forward an opponent-process theory handling findings that cannot be explained by the Young–Helmholtz theory. Hering's key assumption was that there are three types of opponent processes in the visual system. One type of process produces perception of green when responding one way and of red when responding in the opposite way. A second type of process produces perception of blue or yellow in the same fashion. The third type of process produces the perception of white at one extreme and of black at the other.

Supporting evidence was reported by Abramov and Gordon (1994). They presented observers with single wavelengths, who indicated the percentage of blue, green, yellow, and red they perceived. According to Hering's theory, we cannot see blue and yellow together or red and green together, but the other colour combinations are possible. That is what Abramov and Gordon found.

Opponent-process theory helps to explain colour deficiency and negative afterimages. Red–green deficiency occurs when the high- or medium-wavelength cones are damaged or missing, and so the red–green channel cannot be used. Individuals lacking the short-wavelength cones cannot make effective use of the yellow–blue channel, and so their perception of these colours is disrupted. Negative afterimages can be explained by assuming that prolonged viewing of a given colour (e.g., red) produces one extreme of activity in the relevant opponent processes. When attention is then directed to a white surface, the opponent process moves to its other extreme, producing the negative afterimage.

DeValois and DeValois (1975) discovered opponent cells in monkeys. These cells are located in the lateral geniculate nucleus and show increased activity to some wavelengths of light but decreased activity to others. For some cells, the transition point between increased and decreased activity occurred between the green and the red parts of the spectrum. As a result, they were called red–green cells. Other cells had a transition point between the yellow and blue parts of the spectrum, and were called blue–yellow cells.

## Synthesis

The Young–Helmholtz and Hering theories are both partially correct, and have been combined into a two-stage theory (Sekuler & Blake, 2002). According to this theory, signals from the three cones types identified by the Young–Helmholtz theory are sent to the opponent cells described within the opponent-process theory (see figure over the page). The short-wavelength cones send excitatory signals to the blue–yellow opponent cells, and the long-wavelength cones send inhibitory signals. If the strength of the excitatory signals is greater than that of the inhibitory ones, blue is seen; if the opposite is the case, then yellow is seen.

The medium-wavelength cones send excitatory signals to the green–red opponent cells, and the long-wavelength cones send inhibitory signals. Green is seen if the excitatory signals are stronger than the inhibitory ones, and red is seen otherwise. There is support for the theory from individuals suffering from the various forms of deficient colour perception discussed earlier.

## Colour constancy

**Colour constancy** is the tendency for a surface or object to appear to have the same colour when the illumination varies. Colour constancy indicates that colour vision does not depend *only* on the wavelengths of the light reflected from objects. If that were the case, then the same object would appear redder in artificial light than in natural light. In fact, we generally show reasonable colour constancy in such circumstances.

Why do we show colour constancy? One factor is **chromatic adaptation**, in which sensitivity to light of any given colour decreases over time. For example, if you stand outside after dark, you may be struck by the yellowness of the artificial lights in people's houses.

**KEY TERMS**

**Colour constancy:** the tendency for any given object to be perceived as having the same colour under widely varying viewing conditions.

**Chromatic adaptation:** reduced sensitivity to light of a given colour after lengthy exposure.

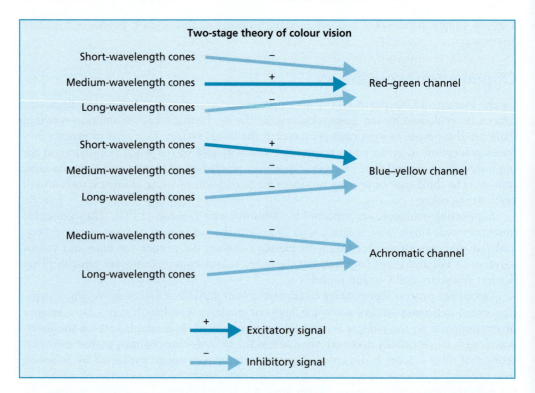

## Land: How can we explain colour constancy for unfamiliar objects?

Land (1977) presented participants with two displays (known as Mondrians) consisting of rectangular shapes of different colours. He then adjusted the lighting of the displays so that two differently coloured rectangles (one from each display) reflected exactly the same wavelengths of light. The two rectangles were seen in their actual colours, showing strong evidence of colour constancy in the absence of familiarity. Finally, Land found the two rectangles looked exactly the same (and so colour constancy broke down) when everything else in the two displays was blocked out.

What was happening in Land's study? According to Land's (1977, 1986) retinex theory, we decide the colour of a surface by *comparing* its ability to reflect short, medium, and long wavelengths against that of adjacent surfaces. Colour constancy breaks down when such comparisons cannot be made.

### Discussion points

1. Why is colour constancy important?
2. How convincing is the evidence for retinex theory provided by Land (1977)?

*How else might you account for the colour constancy effect for familiar objects?*

However, if you have been in a room illuminated by artificial light for some time, the light does *not* seem yellow. Chromatic adaptation reduces the distorting effects of any given illumination on colour constancy.

Familiarity is another factor in colour constancy. British people know pillar boxes are bright red, and so they look the same colour whether they are illuminated by the sun or by artificial street lighting. Delk and Fillenbaum (1965) presented various shapes cut out of the same orange-red cardboard. The shapes of objects that are typically red (e.g., heart, apple) were perceived as slightly redder than the shapes of other objects (e.g., mushrooms). However, it is hard with such evidence to distinguish between genuine perceptual effects and response or reporting bias.

The Mondrian stimuli used by Land (1977) are very artificial. Kraft and Brainard (1999) constructed a more natural visual environment including a tube wrapped in tin foil, a pyramid, and a cube in addition to a Mondrian stimulus. They obtained some support for retinex theory. The most important factor determining colour constancy was local contrast, which involved comparing the light reflected from the target surface with that from the immediate background. When local contrast could not be used, colour constancy dropped from 83% to 53%. Global contrast was also important. Global contrast involved comparing light reflected from the target surface with the average light reflected from the whole visual scene. When neither global contrast nor local contrast could be used, colour constancy dropped to 39%.

The fact that there was still some evidence of colour constancy even when global and local contrast were eliminated runs counter to retinex theory. What information were observers using under these conditions? The most useful information was in the form of reflected highlights from glossy surfaces (e.g., tube wrapped in tin foil). When all of the non-target objects were removed, this information could not be used and colour constancy dropped to only 11%.

Bloj, Kersten, and Hurlbert (1999) identified another factor influencing colour constancy. Suppose there is an artificial light shining on three three-dimensional objects (A, B, and C). Light is likely to be reflected from each of these objects on to the other objects. As a result, some of the light reflected into the eye from object A consists of indirect reflections (inter-reflections) from the other objects. Can we ignore the effects of these inter-reflections when deciding on the colour of an object? Bloj et al. set up a situation in which an object painted magenta (purplish red) reflected light on to an object painted white. The observers reported that the white object looked slightly pinkish, indicating that they were largely successful in preserving colour constancy and ignoring inter-reflections.

## Evaluation

- ⊕ As predicted by retinex theory, the perception of an object's colour depends on a *comparison* of the wavelengths of light reflected from that object and from adjacent objects in the visual field.
- ⊖ According to retinex theory, colour constancy should be complete, provided observers can see the surroundings of a shape or object. However, the amount of colour constancy varies across studies from about 20% to 130% (Bramwell & Hurlbert, 1996).
- ⊖ Retinex theory does not consider directly the role of familiar colours of objects in colour constancy.
- ⊖ Colour constancy is influenced by factors (e.g., reflected highlights from glossy surfaces, inter-reflections) not considered within retinex theory.

# MOVEMENT PERCEPTION

Historically, most research on visual perception involved a motionless observer viewing one or more static objects. Such research lacked ecological validity or relevance to our everyday experiences. We reach for objects, and we walk, run, or drive through the environment. At other times, we are stationary, but other living creatures or objects in the environment are in movement relative to us. Some of these important everyday issues are discussed below.

## Time to contact

Imagine an object (e.g., a car) is approaching you at constant velocity or speed. How do you work out the time to contact? Perhaps you estimate the speed of the object and its distance from you, and combine information from the two estimates. According to various theorists (e.g., Lee, 1980), time to contact can be calculated using only *one* variable, namely, the rate of expansion of the object's retinal image: The faster the image is expanding, the less time there is to contact. Lee (1980) proposed a measure of time to contact called T or tau, defined as the inverse of the rate of expansion of the retinal image of the object: T = 1/(rate of expansion of object's retinal image). Lee assumed that information about time to contact is directly available and requires minimal calculation.

In order to test Lee's (1980) theory, it would be valuable to manipulate the rate of expansion of an object's retinal image as directly as possible. Savelsbergh, Pijpers, and van Santvoord (1993) achieved this by asking participants to catch a deflating or non-deflating ball swinging towards them on a pendulum. The rate of expansion of the retinal image is less for a deflating than for a non-deflating ball. According to Lee's theory, participants should assume the deflating ball would take longer to reach them than was actually the case. The peak grasp closure was 30 ms later with the deflating ball than the non-deflating one, which is in line with prediction.

Wann (1996) argued that strict application of the tau hypothesis to the findings of Savelsbergh et al. (1993) indicates that the peak grasp closure should have occurred about 230 ms later with the deflating ball than the non-deflating ball, rather than the actual 30 ms. As Wann (p. 1043) concluded, "The results of Savelsbergh et al. point to it [tau] being only one component in a multiple-source evaluation process."

Wann and Rushton (1995) used a virtual reality set-up, which allowed them to manipulate both tau and binocular disparity (slight differences in the images projected on the two retinas). The participants' task was to grasp a moving virtual ball with their hand. Tau and binocular disparity were both used to determine the timing of the participants' grasping movements. Whichever variable predicted an earlier arrival of the ball had more influence on grasping behaviour.

Additional evidence that tau is not the only source of information used by observers was reported by Peper et al. (1994). Observers judged whether a ball had passed within arm's reach, and their judgements were generally accurate. However, they systematically misjudged the distance between themselves and the ball when it was larger or smaller than expected. Thus, familiar size can influence judgements of object motion relative to an individual observer.

### Evaluation

⊕ Tau is often taken into account when deciding on the time to contact.
⊖ Tau is *not* the only source of information used to estimate time to contact. Familiar size, binocular disparity, angular position, and velocity of the object relative to the observer are other important variables (Tresilian, 1995).

## Biological movement

Most people are very good at interpreting the movements of other people. How successful would we be at interpreting biological movement if the visual information available to us were greatly reduced? Johansson (1975) addressed this issue by attaching lights to actors' joints (e.g., wrists, knees, ankles). The actors were dressed entirely in black so only the lights were visible, and they were then filmed moving around. Reasonably accurate perception of a moving person was achieved even with only six lights and a short segment of film.

Runeson and Frykholm (1983) filmed actors as they carried out a sequence of actions naturally or as if they were a member of the opposite sex. Observers guessed the gender of the actor correctly 85.5% of the time when he or she acted naturally, and there was only a modest reduction to 75.5% correct in the deception condition.

*What cues do you think helped Runeson and Frykholm's participants to determine the actors' gender?*

### Theoretical accounts

Does our ability to perceive biological motion accurately involve complex cognitive processes? Much of the evidence suggests it does not. For example, Fox and McDaniel

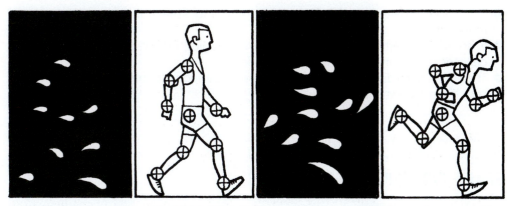

Johansson attached lights to an actor's joints. While the actor stood still in a darkened room, observers could not make sense of the arrangement of the lights. However, as soon as he started to move around, they were able to perceive the lights as defining a human figure. They could even distinguish men from women.

(1982) presented two different motion displays side by side to infants. One display consisted of dots representing someone running on the spot, and the other showed the same activity but presented upside down. Infants 4 months of age spent most of their time looking at the display that was the right way up, suggesting they could detect biological motion. The findings of Fox and McDaniel are consistent with Johansson's (1975) view that the ability to perceive biological motion is innate. However, 4-month-old infants may have learned to perceive biological motion.

What cues do observers use to make accurate sex judgements? Cutting, Proffitt, and Kozlowski (1978) pointed out that most men show relatively greater side to side motion (or swing) of the shoulders than of the hips, whereas women show the opposite. This occurs because men typically have broad shoulders and narrow hips in comparison to women. The shoulders and hips move in opposition to each other, that is, when the right shoulder is forward, the left hip is forward. One can identify the **centre of moment** in the upper body, which is the neutral reference point around which the shoulders and hips swing. The position of the centre of moment is determined by the relative sizes of the shoulders and hips, and is typically lower in men than in women. Cutting et al. found the centre of moment correlated well with the sex judgements made by observers.

Mather and Murdoch (1994) used artificial point-light displays (i.e., the lights were *not* attached to people). Most previous studies had involved movement across the line of sight, but the "walkers" in their displays appeared to be walking either towards or away from the camera. There are two correlated cues which may be used by observers to decide whether they are looking at a man or a woman in point-light displays:

1. Structural cues based on the tendency of men to have broad shoulders and narrow hips, whereas women have the opposite tendency; these structural cues form the basis of the centre of moment.
2. Dynamic cues based on the tendency for men to show relatively greater body sway with the upper body than with the hips when walking, whereas women show the opposite.

Sex judgements were based much more on dynamic cues than on structural ones when the two cues were in conflict. Thus, the centre of moment may be less important than assumed by Cutting (e.g., 1978).

*Why is it useful to use young infants in experiments on perception?*

## Evaluation

➕ We are very good at detecting and interpreting biological movement even when the available visual information seems fairly impoverished.

This dried-out lake bed is an example of a real-life texture gradient. As the earth slants away from the viewer, the pattern seems to get smaller and less distinct.

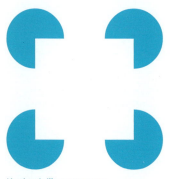

Kanizsa's illusory square.

**KEY TERMS**

**Monocular cues:** cues to depth that can be used with one eye, but can also be used with both eyes.

**Binocular cues:** cues to depth that require both eyes to be used together.

**Oculomotor cues:** kinaesthetic cues to depth based on sensations produced by contractions of the muscles around the eye.

**Linear perspective:** a cue to depth based on the convergence of parallel lines in two-dimensional representations.

**Interposition:** a cue to depth based on a closer object hiding part of a more distant one.

**Motion parallax:** a cue to depth based on the tendency of images of closer objects to move faster across the retina than images of more distant objects.

⊕ The ability to detect biological movement seems to depend in part on the centre of movement.
⊖ It is unclear whether our ability to perceive biological motion is innate or whether it depends on certain kinds of learning experiences.
⊖ There have been disagreements about the relative importance of structural and dynamic cues in sex judgements.

## SPACE OR DEPTH PERCEPTION

In visual perception, the two-dimensional retinal image is transformed into perception of a three-dimensional world. In everyday life, cues to depth are often provided by movement either of the observer or of objects in the visual environment. However, the emphasis here will be on depth cues available even if the observer and the objects in the environment are static. **Monocular cues** require the use of only one eye, but can also be used when someone has both eyes open. Such cues clearly exist, because the world still retains a sense of depth with one eye closed. **Binocular cues** involve both eyes being used together. Finally, **oculomotor cues** are kinaesthetic, depending on sensations of muscular contraction of the muscles around the eye.

## Monocular cues

There are various monocular cues to depth. They are sometimes known as pictorial cues, because they are used by artists trying to create the impression of three-dimensional scenes. One such cue is **linear perspective**. Parallel lines pointing directly away from us seem closer together as they recede into the distance (e.g., railway tracks). This convergence of lines can create a powerful impression of depth in a two-dimensional drawing.

Another cue related to perspective is texture. Most objects possess texture, and textured objects slanting away from us have a texture gradient (Gibson, 1979). This is an increased gradient (rate of change) of texture density from the front to the back of a slanting object. For example, if you look at a large patterned carpet, the details towards its far end are less clear than those towards its near end.

A further cue is **interposition**, in which a nearer object hides part of a more distant object. Evidence of the power of interposition is provided by Kanizsa's (1976) illusory square. There is a strong subjective impression of a white square in front of four black circles. We make sense of the four sectored black discs by perceiving an illusory interposed white square.

Another cue to depth is provided by shading, or the pattern of light and dark on and around an object. Flat, two-dimensional surfaces do not cause shadows, and so shading provides good evidence for the presence of a three-dimensional object.

Another cue to depth is familiar size. If we know an object's actual size, then we can use its retinal image size to provide an estimate of its distance. When participants looked at playing cards through a peephole, unusually large ones looked closer than they actually were, whereas under-sized playing cards looked further away than was the case (Ittelson, 1951).

Another aspect of perspective is known as aerial perspective. Light is scattered as it travels through the atmosphere, especially if the atmosphere is dusty. As a result, more distant objects lose contrast and seem somewhat hazy.

The final monocular cue is **motion parallax**. This is based on the movement of an object's image over the retina. Consider, for example, two objects moving left to right across the line of vision at the same speed, but one object is much further away from the observer than is the other. The image cast by the nearer object would move much faster across the retina.

# Binocular and oculomotor cues

There are three other depth cues. However, the first two cues (itemised below) lose any effectiveness they may have when objects are more than a short distance away. The third cue (while more powerful) is also less effective at longer distances.

1. **Convergence**. The eyes turn inwards to focus on an object to a greater extent when the object is very close; this is an oculomotor cue.
2. **Accommodation**. The thickening of the lens of the eye when focusing on a close object; this is an oculomotor cue.
3. **Stereopsis**. Stereoscopic vision depends on the disparity in the images projected on the retinas of the two eyes; this is the only true binocular cue.

There has been controversy about the value of convergence as a cue to distance, with negative findings often obtained when real objects are used. Accommodation is also of modest usefulness. Its potential value as a depth cue is limited to the region of space immediately in front of you. However, distance judgements based on accommodation are inaccurate, even when the object is at close range (Künnapas, 1968).

The importance of stereopsis was shown by Wheatstone (1838), who was the inventor of the stereoscope. In a stereoscope, separate pictures or drawings are presented to the observer so that each eye receives the information it would receive if the objects depicted were actually presented.

Stereoscopic vision involves two stages. First, matched features in the input to the two eyes need to be identified. Second, the retinal disparities between these sets of features need to be calculated. There are many binocular neurons which receive input from both eyes, and which typically respond maximally when the two eyes view matched features. These binocular neurons are of use in calculating retinal disparities or differences. Some of them respond most to features giving rise to zero disparity, whereas others respond most to features imaged on different areas of the two eyes. By the way, stereoscopic vision is involved when you look at a "magic eye" picture and a hidden figure suddenly emerges from the background.

*Try to apply what you now know about stereoscopic vision to your experiences with "magic eye" pictures.*

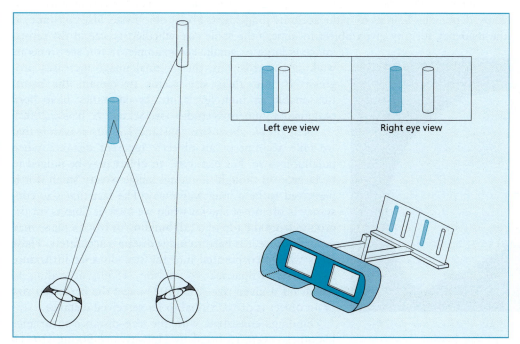

Left eye view        Right eye view

As the eyes are set a short distance apart, each eye receives a slightly different image from the same scene. The difference in the retinal images, at identical places on each eye, is called binocular disparity. The brain makes use of these slight differences as one way of registering spatial depth. This is the principle of the stereoscope, where photographs taken from slightly different angles, corresponding to the position of each eye, appear to the viewer to fuse as a single three-dimensional image.

## Combining information from cues

*Do you think it is possible to reproduce the real world experience of visual perception in a laboratory experiment?*

So far, we have considered depth cues one at a time. In the real world, however, we generally have access to several depth cues at the same time, and so we need to know how information from various cues is combined and integrated. Bruno and Cutting (1988) identified three strategies that might be used by observers who had information available from two or more depth cues:

1. *Additivity*. All the information from different cues is simply added together.
2. *Selection*. Information from one cue is used, with information from the other cue or cues being ignored.
3. *Multiplication*. Information from different cues interacts in a multiplicative way.

Bruno and Cutting (1988) presented three untextured parallel flat surfaces in depth. The observers viewed the displays monocularly, and there were four sources of depth information: relative size, height in the projection plane, interposition, and motion parallax. The findings supported the additivity notion. However, the visual system probably often makes use of *weighted* addition: Information from different depth cues is combined, but more weight is attached to some cues than to others.

It often makes sense to combine information from depth cues. Most depth cues sometimes provide inaccurate information, and so relying totally on one cue would often lead to error. In contrast, taking account of *all* the available information can help to ensure depth perception is accurate.

What happens when cues are in direct conflict with each other? According to Sekuler and Blake (2002, p. 347), "Depth perception is degraded when cues conflict, implying that no single source of information dominates." For example, Rogers and Collett (1989) set up a complex display in which binocular disparity and motion parallax cues provided conflicting information about depth. They found that the conflict was resolved by taking both cues into account.

## Size constancy

Judgements of the size of an object depend in part on judgements of its distance from us. Thus, depth cues help us to make accurate judgements about object size. **Size constancy** is the tendency for any given object to appear the same size whether its size in the retinal image is large or small. For example, if you see someone walking towards you, their retinal image increases progressively, but their size seems to remain the same. Reasonable or high levels of size constancy have been obtained in numerous studies (see Sekuler & Blake, 2002).

Why do we show size constancy? A key reason is that we take account of an object's apparent distance when judging its size. For example, an object may be judged to be large even though its retinal image is very small if it is perceived to be a long way away. The fact that size constancy is often not shown when we look at objects on the ground from the top of a tall building or from a plane may occur because it is hard to judge distance accurately. These ideas were incorporated into the size–distance invariance hypothesis (Kilpatrick & Ittelson, 1953), according to which for a given size of retinal image, the perceived size of an object is proportional to its perceived distance.

Findings consistent with the size–distance invariance hypothesis were reported by Holway and Boring (1941). Participants sat at the intersection of two hallways. The test circle was presented in one hallway, and the comparison circle was presented in the other one. The test circle could be of various sizes and at various distances, and the

The moon illusion shows a breakdown of size constancy. If you see the moon just as it is rising, you may be staggered by its apparent hugeness. The explanation is that when the moon is overhead, there is nothing else to relate it to except the vastness of the sky. Compared with this vastness, the moon appears small. Near the horizon, there are many familiar objects, such as trees and buildings that provide a sense of scale for judging apparent distance and size.

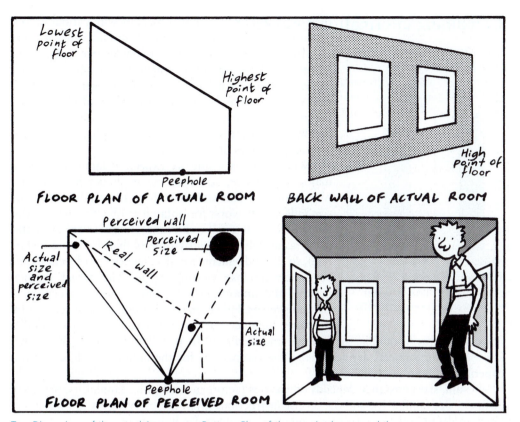

Top: Dimensions of the actual Ames room. Bottom: Plan of the perceived room and the room as seen through the peephole.

participants' task was to adjust the comparison circle so it was the same size as the test circle. Their performance was very good when depth cues were available. However, it became poor when depth cues were removed by placing curtains in the hallway and requiring the participants to look through a peephole.

If size judgements depend on perceived distance, then size constancy should not be found when the perceived distance of an object is very different from its actual distance. The Ames room provides a good example. It has a peculiar shape: The floor slopes, and the rear wall is not at right angles to the adjoining walls. In spite of this, the Ames room creates the same retinal image as a normal rectangular room when viewed through a peephole. The fact that one end of the rear wall is much further from the viewer is disguised by making it much higher. The cues suggesting that the rear wall is at right angles to the viewer are so strong that observers mistakenly assume that two adults standing in the corners by the rear wall are at the same distance from them. This leads them to estimate the size of the nearer adult as being much greater than that of the adult who is further away.

*What does the Ames Room experiment tell us about the importance of perceived distance and familiar size?*

The relationship between perceived distance and perceived size is influenced by the kind of size judgements that observers are asked to make. Kaneko and Uchikawa (1997) argued the instructions given to observers in previous studies were not always clear. They distinguished between perceived linear size (what the *actual* size of the object seems to be) and perceived angular size (the *apparent* retinal size of the object). Kaneko and Uchikawa manipulated various depth cues, and found more evidence for size constancy with linear-size instructions than with angular-size instructions. Thus, the size–distance invariance hypothesis is more applicable to judgements of linear size than of angular size.

Haber and Levin (2001) argued that size perception of objects typically depends on memory of their familiar size rather than on perceptual information concerning their distance from the observer. In their first experiment, participants estimated the sizes of common objects with great accuracy purely on the basis of memory. Haber and Levin then tested

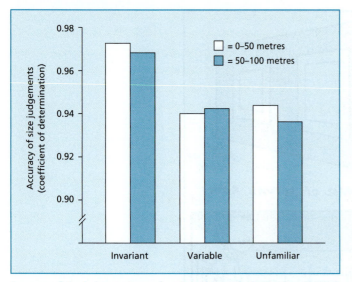

Accuracy of size judgements as a function of type of stimulus (invariant size; variable size; unfamiliar) and viewing distance (0–50 metres; 50–100 metres). Adapted from Haber and Levin (2001).

their argument by presenting observers with various objects at close viewing range (0–50 m) or distant viewing range (50–100 m), and asking them to make size judgements. Some stimuli belonged to categories of objects almost invariant in size or height (e.g., tennis racquet, guitar, bicycle), whereas others belonged to categories of objects varying in size (e.g., house plant, television set, Christmas tree). Finally, there were some unfamiliar stimuli (ovals, rectangles, and triangles of various sizes).

What findings would we expect? If familiar size is of major importance, size judgements should be better for objects of invariant size than those of variable size, with size judgements worst for unfamiliar objects. Suppose distance perception is all-important. Distances are estimated more accurately for nearby objects than for more distant ones, so size judgements for all categories of objects should be better at close viewing range. The actual findings indicate the importance of familiar size to accuracy of size judgements. However, we obviously cannot account for the fairly high accuracy of size judgements of unfamiliar objects in terms of familiar size. Haber and Levin (2001, p. 1150) admitted, "We do not know how the subjects arrived at the size estimations for the unfamiliar objects in this experiment."

In sum, size constancy depends on various factors including size familiarity, perceived distance, size familiarity, and the precise instructions given to observers. As yet, we do not know in detail how these factors combine to produce size judgements.

## Evaluation

⊕ As predicted by the size–distance invariance hypothesis, the perceived size of an object is often related to its perceived distance.

⊖ There is less support for the size–distance invariance hypothesis when observers judge angular size rather than linear size (Kaneko & Uchikawa, 1997).

⊖ Familiar size is a very important factor in determining size judgements (Haber & Levin, 2001), but it is de-emphasised within the size–distance invariance hypothesis.

## PERCEPTION WITHOUT AWARENESS

When we think about visual perception, we typically regard it as a *conscious* process, meaning we are consciously aware of the objects or objects at which we are looking. However, there have been numerous attempts to demonstrate **subliminal perception**, which is perception occurring below the level of conscious awareness. We will consider evidence on subliminal perception in normals. After that, we will discuss evidence from brain-damaged patients with **blindsight**, who can apparently respond appropriately to visual stimuli in the absence of conscious awareness of those stimuli.

## Subliminal perception

Americans first became interested in subliminal perception in 1957. James Vicary, whose marketing business was failing, claimed to have flashed the words EAT POPCORN and DRINK COCA-COLA for 1/300th of a second numerous times during the showing of a film in a cinema. This subliminal advertising continued for 6 weeks, and allegedly led to an 18% increase in the cinema sales of Coca-Cola and a 58% increase in the sales of popcorn.

**KEY TERMS**

**Subliminal perception:** perceptual processes occurring below the level of conscious awareness.

**Blindsight:** the ability to respond appropriately to visual stimuli in the absence of conscious vision in patients with damage to the primary visual cortex.

However, the film that was showing (*Picnic*) contained scenes of eating and drinking, and it is unclear whether it was the subliminal advertising or the film itself that caused the increased sales. In fact, James Vicary probably made up the whole study to prop up his business (Weir, 1984), and there is practically no evidence that subliminal advertising changes *behaviour* (Pratkanis & Aronson, 1992). However, that does not mean that subliminal perception does not exist.

In laboratory research, a key issue concerns the threshold or criterion used to define conscious awareness of visual stimuli. Merikle, Smilek, and Eastwood (2001) distinguished between two thresholds:

1. *Subjective threshold*. This is defined by an individual's ability to report conscious awareness of a stimulus.
2. *Objective threshold*. This is defined by an individual's ability to make accurate forced-choice decisions about stimuli (e.g., guess at above chance level whether they are words).

People often show "awareness" of a stimulus as assessed by the objective threshold, even though the stimulus is below the subjective threshold (Merikle et al.). Thus, what appears to be subliminal perception using the subjective threshold is often no longer subliminal when the objective threshold is used. Which threshold is preferable? It is hard to say. However, as Merikle et al. (p. 120) pointed out, "A widely held view is that objective measures of perceptual discriminations provide a more accurate method for determining whether or not perception is accompanied by an awareness of perceiving than is provided by subjective measures of conscious experiences."

## Evidence

There is still controversy as to whether or not subliminal perception has been demonstrated in the laboratory. Many of the early studies were poorly carried out (see Holender, 1986). For example, objective and/or subjective thresholds need to be assessed several times during the experiment, because they may change over time. More recent studies are harder to criticise, and seem to have provided reasonably convincing evidence for the existence of subliminal perception. For example, Dehaene et al. (1998) found that participants could not distinguish between trials on which a masked digit was or was not presented very briefly (objective threshold). After that, participants were presented with a masked digit followed by a clearly visible target digit, and had to decide whether this target digit was larger or smaller than 5. The masked digit was either congruent with the target (both digits either larger or smaller than 5) or it was incongruent. The key finding was that performance was slower on incongruent trials than on congruent ones, indicating that information from the masked digit had been perceived.

Suppose that information perceived with awareness allows us to control our actions, whereas information perceived without awareness does not. If that is the case, then there should be situations in which perceiving with or without awareness should have very different effects on behaviour. Debner and Jacoby (1994) presented words either very briefly or sufficiently long for them to be consciously perceived. Immediately after each word was presented, the first three letters of the word were presented again. The participants' task was to think of the first word that came to mind starting with those letters except for the word that had just been presented. When the masked word was presented long enough to be consciously perceived, the participants followed instructions to avoid using that word on the word-completion task. In contrast, when the word was presented very briefly, participants often used it to complete the word. This suggests that there was subliminal perception of the word, with the absence of conscious awareness meaning that its use in the word-completion task was not inhibited.

## Blindsight

Area V1 (the primary visual cortex) plays a central role in visual perception. Nearly all signals from the retina pass through this area before proceeding to the other areas

*Why do you think subliminal advertising was made illegal?*

specialised for different aspects of visual processing. Patients with partial or total damage to this area have a loss of vision in part or all of the visual field. However, some of these patients can make accurate judgements and discriminations about visual stimuli presented to the "blind" area. Such patients are said to show blindsight.

The most thoroughly studied patient with blindsight was DB, who was tested by Weiskrantz (e.g., 1986). Following an operation, DB was left with an area of blindness in the lower left quadrant of the visual field. However, he guessed with above-chance accuracy whether or not a visual stimulus had been presented to the blind area, and he could also identify its location.

In spite of DB's performance, he seemed to have no conscious visual experience. According to Weiskrantz, Warrington, Sanders, and Marshall (1974, p. 721), "When he was shown a video film of his reaching and judging orientation of lines, he was openly astonished." However, it is hard to be sure that DB had *no* conscious visual experience.

DB has been tested again more recently (see Weiskrantz, 2002). It was found that DB could guess correctly the facial expressions of static faces presented in the blind field, and he could also discriminate different emotional expressions for faces. He also showed intriguing evidence of conscious after-images. For example, suppose you stared at a red square for several seconds. Immediately afterwards, you would experience an after-image of a green square. DB had such conscious after-images in spite of the fact that he had no conscious awareness at all of the original red square!

Evidence that blindsight does not depend on conscious visual experience was reported by Rafal et al. (1990). Blindsight patients performed at chance level when given the task of detecting a light presented to the blind area of the visual field. However, their speed of reaction to a light presented to the intact part of the visual field was slowed down when a light was presented to the blind area at the same time. Thus, a light not producing any conscious awareness nevertheless received sufficient processing to disrupt visual performance on another task.

*Can you think of a way of determining whether or not DB had no conscious visual experience?*

## Brain systems

What brain systems underlie blindsight? There is no single answer to this question, because the residual visual abilities of blindsight patients vary. Köhler and Moscovitch (1997) discussed findings from several patients who had had an entire cerebral hemisphere removed. These patients showed evidence of blindsight for stimulus detection, stimulus localisation, form discrimination, and motion detection. These findings led Köhler and Moscovitch (p. 322) to conclude: "The results ... suggest that subcortical rather than cortical regions may mediate blindsight on tasks that involve these visual functions."

Another possibility is that there is a "fast" pathway proceeding directly to V5 (motion processing) without passing through V1 (primary visual cortex). Ffytche, Guy, and Zeki (1995) obtained visual event-related potentials when moving stimuli were presented, and found V5 became active before, or at the same time as, V1. Blindsight patients may use this pathway even if V1 is totally destroyed.

## Evaluation

⊕ There is reasonable evidence for subliminal perception from studies of subliminal perception in normals.

⊕ There is good evidence of subliminal perception from studies of blindsight in brain-damaged patients.

⊕ Research on subliminal perception has suggested that the unconscious is less complicated than was proposed by Freud and others. As Greenwald (1992) pointed out, the main achievement of subliminal perception is probably the partial processing of the meaning of individual words.

⊖ There is less evidence for subliminal perception when conscious awareness is defined by an objective threshold rather than by a subjective threshold.

● Some blindsight patients may have residual conscious vision, which is characterised by "a contentless kind of awareness, a feeling of something happening" (Weiskrantz et al., 1995, p. 6122).

# OBJECT RECOGNITION

It is now time to turn our attention to the recognition of three-dimensional stimuli. This is a topic of great importance, because a key function of perception is to identify the objects in the visual environment. Numerous theories have been put forward to account for object recognition. However, we will focus mainly on those proposed by Marr (1982), Biederman (1987), and Tarr and Bülthoff (1995, 1998).

## Marr's computational approach

Marr's (1982) key assumption was that three visual representations of increasing complexity are formed during visual perception. The first representation is the **primal sketch**, which consists largely of information about features such as edges, contours, and blobs. There are two versions of the primal sketch. First, there is the raw primal sketch containing information about light-intensity changes in the visual scene. Second, there is the full primal sketch, which uses information from the raw primal sketch to identify the number and outline shapes of visual objects.

The primal sketch is used to form a second representation, the **2½-D sketch**. This representation is more detailed than the primal sketch, and includes information about the

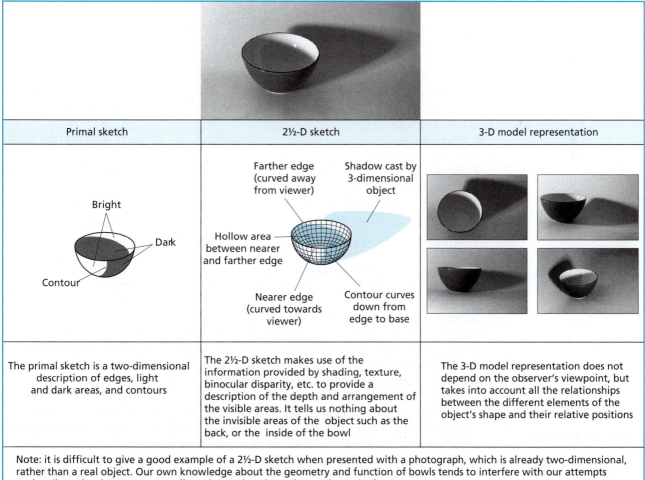

| Primal sketch | 2½-D sketch | 3-D model representation |
|---|---|---|
| The primal sketch is a two-dimensional description of edges, light and dark areas, and contours | The 2½-D sketch makes use of the information provided by shading, texture, binocular disparity, etc. to provide a description of the depth and arrangement of the visible areas. It tells us nothing about the invisible areas of the object such as the back, or the inside of the bowl | The 3-D model representation does not depend on the observer's viewpoint, but takes into account all the relationships between the different elements of the object's shape and their relative positions |

Note: it is difficult to give a good example of a 2½-D sketch when presented with a photograph, which is already two-dimensional, rather than a real object. Our own knowledge about the geometry and function of bowls tends to interfere with our attempts to describe only what we are actually seeing, rather than what we know is also present!

*Do you think Marr's Computational Approach can account for all the information provided by an object?*

depth and orientation of visible surfaces. It is a viewer-centred representation, meaning the visual information in it depends on the precise angle from which an object is viewed. What information is used in changing the primal sketch into the 2½-D sketch? The main kinds of information are those relating to shading, motion, texture, shape, and binocular disparity.

Finally, there is the **3-D model representation**, which is a complete representation free of the limitations of the 2½-D sketch. This representation incorporates a three-dimensional representation that is independent of the viewer's viewpoint (this is known as viewpoint-independent). Thus, this representation remains the same regardless of the viewing angle.

According to Marr and Nishihara (1978), object recognition involves matching the 3-D model representation against a set of 3-D model representations stored in memory. They argued that concavities (area where the contour points into the object) are identified first. With the human form, for example, there is a concave area in each armpit. These concavities are used to divide the visual image into segments (e.g., arms, legs, torso, head). Finally, the main axis of each segment is found.

Why is there this emphasis on axes? One reason is that it is possible to calculate the lengths and arrangement of axes of most visual objects regardless of the viewing angle. Another reason is that information about the axes of an object can assist in the process of object recognition. As Humphreys and Bruce (1989) pointed out, it is easy to distinguish humans from gorillas on the basis of the relative lengths of the axes of the segments corresponding to arms and legs: Our legs are longer than our arms, whereas the opposite is true of gorillas.

## Evaluation

⊕ Marr (1982) argued correctly that object recognition depends on very complex processes, and provided a more detailed and systematic account of those processes than any previous theorist.

⊖ Marr's theory is mostly a bottom-up theory, and the role of top-down processes (e.g., expectations) in perception is neglected.

⊖ The theory accounts for unsubtle perceptual discriminations (e.g., that object is a cup), but not for more precise discriminations *within* a class of objects (e.g., that object is my favourite cup).

⊖ Marr's account of the 3-D model representation is less complete than his description of the primal sketch.

⊖ As we will see later, the notion that object recognition is viewpoint-independent has proved highly controversial.

## Biederman's recognition-by-components theory

Biederman (1987, 1990) proposed a theory of object recognition, which built on the foundations of Marr's (1982) theoretical approach. The central assumption of his recognition-by-components theory is that objects consist of basic shapes or components known as "geons" (geometric ions). Examples of geons are blocks, cylinders, spheres, arcs, and wedges. According to Biederman (1987), there are about 36 different geons, which can be arranged in almost endless different ways. For example, a cup can be described by an arc connected to the side of a cylinder, and a pail can be described by the same two geons, but with the arc connected to the top of the cylinder.

The stage we have discussed so far is that of the determination of the components or geons of a visual object and their relationships. When this information is available, it is matched with stored object representations or structural models containing information about the nature of the relevant geons, their orientations, sizes, and so on. The identification of any given visual object is determined by whichever stored object representation fits best with the component- or geon-based information obtained from the visual object.

Only part of Biederman's theory has been presented so far. What has been omitted is any analysis of how an object's components or geons are determined. The first step is edge extraction: "An early edge extraction stage, responsive to differences in surface characteristics namely, luminance, texture, or colour, provides a line drawing description of the object" (Biederman, 1987, p. 117).

The next step is to decide how a visual object should be segmented to establish the number of its parts. Biederman (1987) argued that the concave (i.e., curving inwards) parts of an object's contour are of particular value in accomplishing this task.

Which edge information from an object remains invariant across different viewing angles? According to Biederman (1987), there are five invariant properties of edges:

- *Curvature.* Points on a curve.
- *Parallel.* Sets of points in parallel.
- *Cotermination.* Edges terminating at a common point.
- *Symmetry.* Versus asymmetry.
- *Co-linearity.* Points in a straight line.

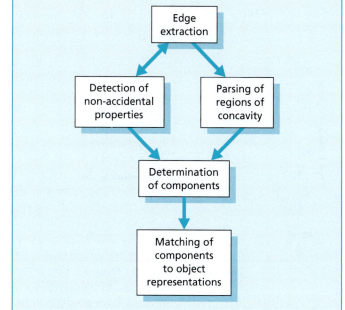

An outline of Biederman's recognition-by-components theory. Adapted from Biederman (1987).

The components or geons of a visual object are constructed from these invariant properties. Thus, for example, a cylinder has curved edges and two parallel edges connecting the curved edges, whereas a brick has three parallel edges and no curved edges.

According to Biederman (1987), there are various reasons why we can achieve object recognition when the viewing conditions are poor:

- The invariant properties (e.g., curvature, parallel lines) can be detected even when only parts of edges can be seen.
- Provided that the concavities of a contour are visible, there are mechanisms allowing the missing parts of a contour to be restored.
- There is normally much redundant information available for recognising complex objects (e.g., a giraffe could be identified from its neck alone).

*Does Biederman's theory overcome the problems associated with Marr's Computational Approach?*

Where does Biederman's recognition-by-components theory stand on the key issue of whether object recognition is viewpoint-dependent or viewpoint-independent? It is assumed that object recognition is typically viewpoint-independent: Provided that an object's geons are visible to observers, their viewpoint will not influence ease of object recognition.

## Evidence

Biederman, Ju, and Clapper (1985) tested the notion that complex objects can be detected even when some of the geons are missing. Line drawings of complex objects having six or nine components were presented briefly. Even when only three or four of the components were present, participants identified the objects 90% of the time.

Biederman (1987) discussed a study in which degraded line drawings of objects were presented. Object recognition was much harder to achieve when parts of the contour providing information about concavities were omitted than when other parts of the contour were deleted. Thus, information about concavities is important for object recognition, as is predicted by the theory.

Biederman (1987) argued that edge-based extraction processes provide enough information to permit object recognition. Sanocki et al. (1998) obtained strong support

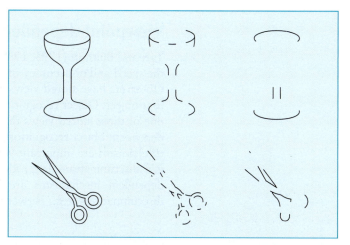

Intact figures (left-hand side), with degraded line drawings either preserving (middle column) or not preserving (far-right column) parts of the contour providing information about concavities.

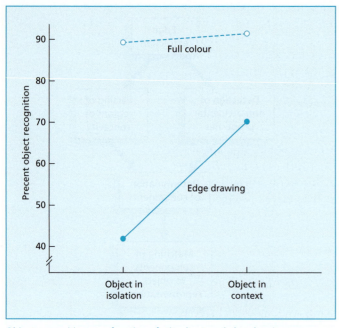

Object recognition as a function of stimulus type (edge drawings vs. colour photographs) and presence vs. absence of context. Data from Sanocki et al. (1998).

for the view that edge information is often insufficient to allow object recognition. Their participants were presented briefly with objects presented in the form of edge drawings or full-colour photographs, and these objects were presented in isolation or in context. Object recognition was much worse with the edge drawings, especially when objects were presented in isolation.

According to the theory, ease of object recognition is generally unaffected by the observer's viewpoint. This viewpoint-independent approach resembles Marr's (1982) viewpoint-invariant 3-D model representation. Evidence against the viewpoint-independent approach was discussed by Tarr and Bülthoff (1995). Participants were given extensive practice at recognising novel objects from certain specified viewpoints. The objects were then presented from various novel viewpoints. The findings across several studies were very consistent: "Response times and error rates for naming a familiar object in an unfamiliar viewpoint increased with rotation distance between the unfamiliar viewpoint and the nearest familiar viewpoint" (p. 1500). Such findings support viewpoint-dependent theories (see below).

## Evaluation

⊕ Biederman (1987) provided a more detailed account than Marr (1982) of some of the processes involved in object recognition.
⊕ The concavities of a contour are of particular importance in object recognition.
⊕ Viewpoint-invariant mechanisms often seem to be found with simple categorical discriminations.
⊖ In contrast to the theory, edge-based extraction processes sometimes do *not* provide sufficient information for object recognition.
⊖ Object recognition is often viewpoint-dependent (Tarr & Bülthoff, 1995).
⊖ Recognition-by-components theory only accounts for fairly unsubtle perceptual discriminations. Thus, it allows us to decide whether the animal in front of us is a dog or not, but not whether it is our pet dog or cat.
⊖ Biederman's theory de-emphasises the role played by context in object recognition.

## Viewpoint-dependence or viewpoint-independence?

Tarr and Bülthoff (1995, 1998) proposed a theory of object recognition, according to which the speed and/or accuracy of object recognition often depends on the observer's viewpoint. Observers have stored views of any given object as a result of their previous experience of that object. Object recognition is easier when the current view of an object corresponds to one of those stored views than when it does not. In spite of their emphasis on viewpoint-dependent object recognition, Tarr and Bülthoff (1995) argued that viewpoint-independent mechanisms are important when an object-recognition task involves making easy categorical discriminations (e.g., identifying stimuli as cars or bicycles). In contrast, viewpoint-dependent mechanisms are important when a task involves difficult within-category discriminations (e.g., between makes of car).

## Evidence

Research by Tarr and Bülthoff (1995), discussed above, provided evidence for viewpoint-dependent object recognition. There is also evidence that the relative importance of viewpoint-dependent and viewpoint-independent mechanisms depends on the difficulty of the discriminations involved in object recognition. Tarr, Williams, Hayward, and Gauthier (1998) considered recognition of the same three-dimensional objects under various conditions. Performance was close to viewpoint-independent when the recognition task was easy (e.g., detailed feedback was provided on each trial). However, it was viewpoint-dependent when the task was difficult (e.g., no feedback was provided).

Vanrie, Béatse, Wagemans, Sunaert, and van Hecke (2002) made use of tasks designed to involve either extreme viewpoint-dependency or viewpoint-independency. The pattern of brain activity as revealed by fMRI was rather different on the two tasks. There was more activity in parietal areas than in occipito-temporal areas on the viewpoint-dependent task, whereas the opposite was the case on the viewpoint-independent task. The fact that the pattern of brain activity differed in the two cases strengthens the notion that there are somewhat separate viewpoint-dependent and viewpoint-independent mechanisms.

## Evaluation

● There is increasing evidence that object recognition is sometimes viewpoint-dependent and sometimes viewpoint-independent.
● Some of the factors (e.g., stimulus discriminability) determining whether object recognition is viewpoint-dependent or viewpoint-independent have been identified.
● Much remains to be done to clarify the circumstances in which object recognition is primarily viewpoint-dependent or viewpoint-independent.

## Visual agnosia

So far we have only considered object recognition based on findings from individuals with normal visual processes. However, we can also reach an understanding of the processes involved in object recognition by considering brain-damaged patients whose object recognition is impaired. **Visual agnosia** is "the impairment of visual object recognition in people who possess sufficiently preserved visual fields, acuity and other elementary forms of visual ability to enable object recognition, and in whom the object recognition impairment cannot be attributed to ... loss of knowledge about objects ... [Agnosics'] impairment is one of visual recognition rather than naming, and is therefore manifest on naming and non-verbal tasks alike" (Farah, 1999, p. 181). Historically, a distinction was often made between two forms of visual agnosia:

1. **Apperceptive agnosia.** Object recognition is impaired because of deficits in perceptual processing.
2. **Associative agnosia.** Perceptual processes are essentially intact, but object recognition is impaired partly or mainly because of difficulties in accessing relevant knowledge about objects from memory.

How can we distinguish between patients with apperceptive agnosia and those with associative agnosia? As Humphreys (1999) pointed out, a common practice has been to assess patients' ability to copy objects that cannot be recognised. Patients who can copy objects are said to have associative agnosia, and those who cannot have apperceptive agnosia. Note that it is hard to show that any given patient satisfies the criterion for associative agnosia that perceptual processes should be intact (Parkin, 1996). As a result, the term is used less now than it used to be.

There is some evidence that different brain areas are damaged in apperceptive agnosia and associative agnosia. Jankowiak and Albert (1994) considered findings from studies in which scanning had been used to work out the brain areas affected. They concluded that, "Lesion location in apperceptive visual agnosia tends to be posterior in the cerebral hemispheres, involving occipital, parietal, or posterior temporal regions bilaterally. Small focal or unilateral [one-sided] lesions rarely, if ever, produce this syndrome" (p. 436). In

**KEY TERMS**

**Visual agnosia:** an impairment of visual object recognition in brain-damaged individuals who possess basic visual abilities and reasonable knowledge about objects.

**Apperceptive agnosia:** a form of visual agnosia in which there is impaired perceptual analysis of familiar objects.

**Associative agnosia:** a form of visual agnosia in which perceptual processing is fairly normal, but there is an impaired ability to derive the meaning of objects.

---

### CASE STUDY: *The man who mistook his wife for a hat*

Mr P was "a musician of distinction, well-known for many years as a singer, and then at the local School of Music, as a teacher. It was here, in relation to his students, that certain strange problems were first observed. Sometimes a student would present himself, and Mr P would not recognise him; or specifically, would not recognise his face. The moment the student spoke, he would be recognised by his voice. Such incidents multiplied, causing embarrassment, perplexity, fear—and, sometimes, comedy."

"At first these odd mistakes were laughed off as jokes, not least by Mr P himself ... His musical powers were as dazzling as ever; he did not feel ill ... The notion of there being 'something the matter' did not emerge until some three years later, when diabetes developed. Well aware that diabetes could affect his eyes, Mr P consulted an ophthalmologist, who took a careful history, and examined his eyes closely. 'There's nothing the matter with your eyes,' the doctor concluded. 'But there is trouble with the visual parts of your brain. You don't need my help, you must see a neurologist.' "

And so Mr P went to see Oliver Sacks who found him quite normal except for the fact that, when they talked, Mr P faced him with his *ears* rather than his *eyes*. Another episode alerted Sacks to the problem. He asked Mr P to put his shoe back on.

" 'Ach,' he said, 'I had forgotten the shoe', adding *sotto voce*, 'The shoe? The shoe?' He seemed baffled."

He continued to look downwards, though not at the shoe, with an intense but misplaced concentration. Finally his gaze settled on his foot: 'That is my shoe, yes?'

Did he mis-hear? Did he mis-see?

'My eyes,' he explained, and put his hand to his foot. '*This* is my shoe, no'

'No that is not. That is your foot. *There* is your shoe.'

'Ah! I thought it was my foot.'

Was he joking? Was he mad? Was he blind?"

Oliver Sacks helped Mr P put on his shoe and gave him some further tests. His eyesight was fine, for example he had no difficulty seeing a pin on the floor. But when he was shown a picture of the Sahara desert and asked to describe it, he invented guesthouses, terraces, and tables with parasols. Sacks must have looked aghast but Mr P seemed to think he had done rather well and decided it was time to end the examination. He reached out for his hat, and took hold of his wife's head, and tried to lift it off. He apparently had mistaken his wife's head for his hat.

The condition Mr P suffered from is called visual agnosia and results from brain damage of some kind.

From Oliver Sacks (1985). *The man who mistook his wife for a hat*, Picador.

---

contrast, associative agnosics typically have bilateral (i.e., two-sided) posterior lesions in those parts of the posterior cerebral artery supplying blood to the temporal lobe and to parts of the visual cortex. How does this cause brain damage? According to Jankowiak and Albert, such damage may disrupt pathways sending visual information to brain areas containing stored visual information about objects.

The distinction between apperceptive and associative agnosia has various limitations. First, while the perceptual abilities of associative agnosics are greatly superior to those of apperceptive agnosics, these abilities are typically not at normal level. For example, associative agnosics produce normal copies of objects, but "the process by which [they] produce their good copies is invariably characterised as slow, slavish, and line-by-line" (Farah, 1999, p. 191).

Second, the distinction between apperceptive and associative agnosia is over-simplified. As we will see, patients suffering from various different problems can all be categorised as having apperceptive agnosia.

Third, patients with apperceptive agnosia and associative agnosia have fairly *general* deficits in object recognition. However, many patients with visual agnosia have relatively *specific* deficits. For example, later in the chapter we discuss prosopagnosia, which is a condition in which there are specific problems with recognising faces rather than objects in general. Other patients suffer from category-specific agnosia, in which there is impaired recognition of objects from a given category (e.g., living things).

Several theorists (e.g., Biederman, 1987; Marr, 1982) have proposed theories in which various successive processes are involved in object recognition. In general terms, initial processes are concerned with the identification of features such as edges and contours. After that, there are processes concerned with shape or object components such as geons. Finally, the representation constructed from the stimulus is matched against stored representations to find the best fit. It follows from this theoretical approach that there are several reasons why object recognition might be impaired by brain damage. Research on brain-damaged patients provides general support for this approach, because patients with visual agnosia have widely differing patterns of impairment.

*How can studying patients with visual agnosia help us to understand normal visual perception?*

## Apperceptive agnosia

Warrington and Taylor (1978) argued the key problem in apperceptive agnosia is an inability to achieve object constancy, which involves identifying objects regardless of viewing conditions. They used pairs of photographs, one of which was a conventional or usual view and the other of which was an unusual view. For example, the usual view of a flat-iron was photographed from above, whereas the unusual view showed only the base of the iron and part of the handle. The patients were much better at identifying the objects when they were shown one at a time in the usual or conventional view than when shown from an unusual angle.

Humphreys and Riddoch (1984, 1985) argued the view of an object can be unusual in at least two ways:

1. The object is foreshortened, thus making it hard to determine its principal axis of elongation.
2. A distinctive feature of the object is hidden from view.

They found in four patients that poor object recognition was produced by foreshortening rather than by the absence of a distinctive feature.

Warrington and James (1988) studied three patients with right-hemisphere damage and apperceptive agnosia. Their findings confirmed previous ones, in that all three patients had severe problems on *perceptual categorisation* tasks (e.g. tasks on which they had to categorise different versions of the same object as equivalent). However, the patients performed surprisingly well on various tasks involving *semantic categorisation*. For example, they knew which object in a display is found in the kitchen, and they could match pairs of drawings having the same function and names (e.g., two types of boat).

The patients studied by Warrington and James (1988) had no significant problems in everyday life, in spite of having seriously deficient perceptual categorisation ability. Thus, perceptual categorisation is of less importance in visual perception than might have been supposed. Rudge and Warrington (1991) proposed there is a perceptual categorisation system in the right hemisphere and a semantic categorisation system in the left hemisphere. There is a route from basic visual analysis to semantic categorisation that does not involve the perceptual categorisation system.

In sum, "the apperceptive impairment can be considered as one in which the patient has lost an ability to categorise different versions of the same object as equivalent" (Davidoff & Warrington, 1999, p. 75). This impairment has relatively little impact on access to semantic knowledge in some (but not all) patients. In some ways, we could argue that a central problem of patients with apperceptive agnosia is that they find it very hard to move from viewpoint-dependent representations to viewpoint-independent ones.

## Integrative agnosia

Humphreys (1999a) discussed what he termed **integrative agnosia**, a condition in which the patient has great difficulties in combining or integrating visual information about the parts of objects to identify them. Since patients with integrative agnosia have perceptual difficulties, the condition can be regarded as a form of apperceptive agnosia. Humphreys and Riddoch (1987) studied HJA, who produced accurate drawings of objects he could not recognise, and who could draw objects from memory. However, he found it very hard to *integrate* visual information. In HJA's own words: "I have come to cope with recognising many common objects, if they are standing alone. When objects are placed together, though, I have more difficulties. To recognise one sausage on its own is far from picking one out from a dish of cold foods in a salad".

Evidence that HJA had a serious problem in grouping or organising visual information was obtained by Humphreys et al. (1992). The task of searching for an inverted T target among a set of upright Ts is easy for most people. However, HJA's performance was very slow and error-prone, presumably because he found it very hard to group the distractors together.

Humphreys (1999a, p. 555) concluded his discussion of patients with integrative agnosia as follows: "The deficit appears to affect a stage of visual processing intermediate

> **KEY TERM**
> **Integrative agnosia:** impaired object recognition due to problems in integrating or combining elements of objects.

```
TTTTTTTTT
TTTTTTTTT
TTTTTTTTT
TTTTTT⊥TT
TTTTTTTTT
```

*What kind of problems do you think HJA might experience in his everyday life?*

between basic shape coding and visual access to memory representations, concerned with parallel perceptual grouping and the integration of perceptual parts into wholes."

More recent evidence is broadly consistent with Humphreys' views. Behrmann and Kimchi (2003) studied two patients (RN and SM), both of whom suffered from integrative agnosia. Both patients had severe problems with object recognition, since they failed to identify more than one-third of simple objects presented to them. Behrmann and Kimchi focused on the following question: Which aspects of perceptual organisation are intact in the two patients and which ones are not? The patients could group objects by proximity or by similarity (see earlier in the chapter). However, they were poor at shape formation or configuring the elements of a stimulus into a coherent whole. The implication of these findings is that the processes underlying shape formation are crucial for object recognition.

## Overview

According to Humphreys and Riddoch (1993), visual object recognition involves a series of stages: feature coding, feature integration, accessing stored structural object descriptions, and accessing semantic knowledge about objects. Problems with visual object recognition can occur because of impairments at *any* of these stages, and the study of patients with visual agnosia can help to identify the major processes involved in normal object recognition. For example, Behrmann and Kimchi (2003, p. 38) have shown that, "simple grouping [e.g., by proximity or similarity] is not sufficient for object recognition, whereas shape formation and configuring are critical for it".

# FACE RECOGNITION

Why should we study face recognition? Face recognition is the most common way we identify people, and so the ability to recognise faces is of great significance. In addition, face recognition differs from other forms of object recognition. For example, consider **prosopagnosia**. Prosopagnosic patients cannot recognise familiar faces, and this can even extend to their own faces in a mirror. However, they generally have few problems in recognising other familiar objects.

## Prosopagnosia

Why do patients with prosopagnosia have specific problems with recognition of faces? Perhaps more precise discriminations are required to distinguish between faces than to distinguish between other kinds of objects (e.g., a chair and a table). Alternatively, there may be specific processing mechanisms used only for face recognition. Before we discuss such evidence, note that prosopagnosics often retain some aspects of face recognition. For example, Bauer and Verfaellie (1988) asked a prosopagnosic patient to select the names corresponding to presented famous faces. The patient had no explicit knowledge about the faces, and so his performance was at chance level. However, there were greater electrodermal responses when the names matched the faces than when they did not. This means that there was some relevant processing of the famous faces, even though this was not sufficient to allow conscious recognition of the appropriate names.

## Evidence

Farah (1994) found prosopagnosic patients can be good at making precise discriminations for stimuli other than faces. She studied LH, who developed prosopagnosia as a result of a car crash. LH and controls were presented with various faces and pairs of spectacles, and were then given a recognition-memory test. LH performed at about the same level as the normal controls in recognising pairs of spectacles, but was at a great disadvantage on face recognition.

The notion that face processing involves specific mechanisms would be strengthened if we could show a double dissociation, with some patients having normal face recognition but poor recognition or visual agnosia for objects. Such patients have been identified (e.g., Moscovitch, Winocur, & Behrmann, 1997). If face processing involves specific mechanisms, we might also expect to find somewhat separate brain regions associated with face and object recognition. Kanwisher, McDermott, and Chun (1997) used fMRI to compare brain activity to faces, scrambled faces, houses, and hands. Parts of the right fusiform gyrus were only active when faces were being processed. In similar fashion, Hadjikhani and de Gelder (2002) found with fMRI that normal individuals showed more activity to faces than to objects in the mid-fusiform gyrus and the inferior occipital gyrus. However, patients with prosopagnosia had the same levels of activity in those areas to faces and objects, suggesting that damage to these areas played a role in their problems with face processing.

There are two complications with respect to the picture of prosopagnosia presented so far. First, there is evidence that prosopagnosia can take more than one form. Sergent and Poncet (1990) asked prosopagnosic patients to rate the similarity between pairs of faces. Some patients based their ratings on the overall similarity of the faces, which is what is found in normal individuals. However, other patients based their ratings on very specific features (e.g., hairline). Such findings suggest that no theory will apply equally well to all prosopagnosics.

Second, the notion that all prosopagnosics have *selective* problems with face recognition has been challenged. Gauthier, Behrmann, and Tarr (1999) presented faces and non-face objects (e.g., synthetic snowflakes), and found that prosopagnosic patients showed inferior recognition to normals with both kinds of objects. The patients had greater problems when they had to recognise objects as belonging to a specific category (e.g., "my son William") rather than to a more general category ("a male face"). This is clearly a serious problem in everyday life, because we nearly always need to identify specific faces. Overall, these findings suggest at least some prosopagnosics have general problems with complex object recognition regardless of whether faces are involved.

## Farah's two-process model

Farah (1990, 1994) proposed a two-process model of object recognition distinguishing between two processes or forms of analysis:

1. *Holistic analysis*, in which the configuration or overall structure of an object is processed.
2. *Analysis by parts*, in which processing focuses on the constituent parts of an object.

Farah (1990) argued both forms of analysis are involved in the recognition of most objects. However, face recognition depends mainly on holistic analysis, and reading words or text mostly involves analytic processing.

*Try to think of your own experiences of face recognition. Do you think it depends mainly on holistic analysis or analysis by parts?*

## Evidence

Support for the view that face recognition depends more than object recognition on holistic analysis was reported by Farah (1994). The participants were presented with drawings of faces or houses, and associated a name with each face and each house. Then the participants were presented with whole faces and houses or with only a single feature (e.g., mouth, front door), and decided whether a given feature belonged to the individual whose name they had been given previously.

Recognition performance for facial features was much better when the whole face was presented. In contrast, recognition for house features was very similar in whole and single-feature conditions. These findings suggest holistic analysis is much more important for face recognition than for object recognition.

Several other studies indicate that face processing is often holistic or configural, but this is not always the case.

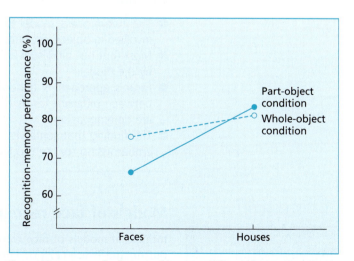

Recognition memory for features of houses and faces when presented with whole houses or faces or with only features. Data from Farah (1994).

Searcy and Bartlett (1996) produced facial distortions in photographs in two ways:

1. *Configural distortions* (e.g., moving the eyes up and the mouth down).
2. *Component distortions* (e.g., blackening the teeth, blurring the pupils of the eyes).

The faces were then presented either upright or inverted, and the participants provided grotesqueness ratings. What was found was that component distortions were nearly always detected regardless of whether the faces were presented upright or inverted. In contrast, configural or holistic distortions were often *not* detected with inverted faces.

Farah (1990) discussed evidence based on patients suffering from one or more of the following: prosopagnosia, visual agnosia, and **alexia** (problems with reading in spite of good ability to comprehend spoken language and good object recognition). According to the theory, prosopagnosia involves impaired holistic or configurational processing, alexia involves impaired analytic processing, and visual agnosia (apperceptive agnosia and associative agnosia) involves impaired holistic *and* analytic processing.

Farah (1990) considered the co-occurrence of the above three conditions in 87 patients. What would we expect to find? First, patients with visual agnosia (having impaired holistic and analytic processing) should also suffer from prosopagnosia or alexia, or both. This prediction was confirmed. There were 21 patients with all three conditions, 15 patients with visual agnosia and alexia, 14 patients with visual agnosia and prosopagnosia, but only 1 patient who may have had visual agnosia on its own.

Second, there was a double dissociation between prosopagnosia and alexia. There were 35 patients suffering from prosopagnosia without alexia, and there are numerous patients having alexia without prosopagnosia. Thus, the processes and brain systems underlying face recognition seem to differ from those underlying word recognition.

Third, it is assumed within the model that reading and object recognition both involve analytic processing. Thus, patients with alexia (who have problems with analytic processing) should be impaired in their object recognition. This contrasts with the conventional view that patients with "pure" alexia have impairments only to reading abilities. Behrmann, Nelson, and Sekuler (1998) studied six patients who seemed to have "pure" alexia. Five of them were significantly slower than normal participants to name visually complex pictures, which is as predicted from Farah's theory.

Some evidence does not fit Farah's (1990) model. For example, Rumiati et al. (1994) studied a patient, Mr W, who suffered from visual agnosia for real objects and for pictures. However, he showed no signs of either prosopagnosia or alexia. According to Farah's model, the existence of visual agnosia means that Mr W must have a deficit in holistic and/or analytic processing, and thus would suffer from prosopagnosia and/or alexia.

## Evaluation

⊕ The two-process model describes major similarities and differences in the processes involved in object recognition, face recognition, and reading.
⊕ Most (but not all) visual agnosics also suffer from alexia or prosopagnosia as predicted by the model.
⊖ Farah's approach is general and over-simplified. For example, important differences between different forms of visual agnosia (e.g., apperceptive and associative agnosia) are de-emphasised.
⊖ The finding that some visual agnosics do not have alexia (e.g., Rumiati et al., 1994) is embarrassing for the model.

## Models of face recognition

Influential models of face recognition were put forward by Bruce and Young (1986) and Burton and Bruce (1993). There are eight components in the Bruce and Young model:

• *Structural encoding.* This produces various representations or descriptions of faces.
• *Expression analysis.* People's emotional states can be inferred from their facial features.

- *Facial speech analysis.* Speech perception can be aided by observation of a speaker's lip movements.
- *Directed visual processing.* Specific facial information may be processed selectively.
- *Face recognition units.* They contain structural information about known faces.
- *Person identity nodes.* They provide information about individuals (e.g., their occupation, interests).
- *Name generation.* A person's name is stored separately.
- *Cognitive system.* This contains additional information (e.g., that actors and actresses tend to have attractive faces); this system also influences attentional processes.

The recognition of familiar faces depends mainly on structural encoding, face recognition units, person identity nodes, and name generation. In contrast, the processing of unfamiliar faces involves structural encoding, expression analysis, facial speech analysis, and directed visual processing.

Burton and Bruce (1993) subsequently developed and extended the above theoretical approach in their interactive activation and competition model developed from the theory of Valentine et al. (1991). This model accounts for many of the basic phenomena of face recognition, and has also been applied to prosopagnosia. Information about this model can be found in Eysenck (2001).

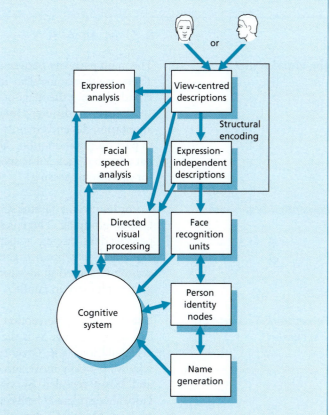

The model of face recognition proposed by Bruce and Young (1986).

## Evidence

According to the Bruce and Young (1986) model, the name generation component can be accessed only via the appropriate person identity node. Thus, we should be unable to put a name to a face in the absence of other information about that person (e.g., his/her occupation). Young, Hay, and Ellis (1985) asked participants to keep a diary record of problems in face recognition. Participants never reported putting a name to a face while knowing nothing else about that person. In contrast, there were numerous occasions on which a participant could remember a fair amount of information about a person, but not their name.

According to the model, another kind of problem should be fairly common. If the appropriate face recognition unit is activated, but the person identity node is not, there should be a feeling of familiarity coupled with an inability to think of any relevant information about the person. This was also reported on occasions.

Reference back to the figure above suggests further predictions. When we look at a familiar face, familiarity information from the face recognition unit should be accessed first, followed by information about that person (e.g., occupation) from the person identity node, followed by that person's name from the name generation component. As predicted, familiarity decisions about a face were made faster than decisions based on person identity nodes (Young et al., 1986b). The prediction that decisions based on person identity nodes should be made faster than those based on the name generation component has also been supported (Young et al., 1986a).

## Evaluation

- ⊕ The model provides a detailed and coherent account of the processes involved in face recognition.
- ⊕ Some of the differences in the processing of familiar and unfamiliar faces are spelled out.
- ⊖ According to the model, names can be accessed only via relevant autobiographical information stored at the person identity node. However, an amnesic patient, ME, matched

*Can Bruce and Young's model account for the face recognition impairments experienced by prosopagnosic patients?*

the faces and names of 88% of famous people for whom she could not recall any auto-biographical information (de Haan, Young, & Newcombe, 1991).

● A prediction from the model is that some patients should have better recognition of familiar than unfamiliar faces, with others showing the opposite pattern. However, Young, Newcombe, de Haan, Small, and Hay (1993) obtained only very weak supporting evidence in a study on 34 brain-damaged men.

# SUMMARY

**The visual system**

The main pathway between the eye and the cortex is the retina-geniculate-striate system. There are two somewhat independent channels within this system: the parvocellular or P pathway and the magnocellular or M pathway. Different parts of the visual cortex are specialised for different functions. Lateral inhibition is involved in edge perception. Dark adaptation depends mainly on changes in the sensitivity of the rods and cones, but also in part on pupil dilation. There is evidence from neuroimaging and from brain-damaged patients that area V4 is specialised for colour processing, whereas area V5 is specialised for motion processing.

**Perceptual organisation**

According to the Gestaltists, perceptual segregation and organisation depend on several laws of grouping. There is segregation into figure and ground, with only the figure being perceived as having a distinct form or shape. The Gestaltists described rather than explained perceptual organisation, and they de-emphasised the role of top-down processing in such organisation. They also minimised the complexities involved when laws of grouping are in conflict.

**Perception: Accurate or inaccurate?**

The accuracy of perception depends in part on contextual information. Such information can be misleading, as is the case with many visual illusions. There are several theories of visual illusions (e.g., Gregory's misapplied size-constancy theory). A key puzzle is to explain why we typically move successfully about the environment in spite of the numerous errors and biases revealed by visual illusions. In their perception–action model, Milner and Goodale distinguish between separate perception-for-recognition and perception-for-action systems. There is evidence that the perception-for-action system is generally less error-prone than the perception-for-recognition system even with visual illusions. Glover has proposed a planning–control model resembling the perception–action model. However, one difference is that Glover argues that the initial movements involved in reaching are more error-prone than the later movements, and this is generally supported by the evidence.

**Colour perception**

The Young–Helmholtz theory led to the assumption that there are three types of cone receptors differing in the wavelengths of light to which they are most sensitive. This theory cannot explain negative afterimages. According to Hering's opponent-process theory, there are three types of opponent processes. This theory helps to explain the patterns of colour deficiency and of negative afterimages. According to a combined theory, signals from the three cone types of the Young–Helmholtz theory are sent to the opponent cells of Hering's theory. Colour constancy depends on chromatic adaptation, object familiarity, and comparisons of the light reflected from adjacent surfaces. Retinex theory explains many of the findings on colour constancy. However, it ignores various factors (e.g., reflected highlights from glossy surfaces, inter-reflections) that influence colour constancy.

**Movement perception**

Judgements of the time to contact of an object depend in part on the rate of expansion of the retinal image of the object. However, other factors (e.g., binocular disparity) are also important. Judgements of biological movement are very accurate even when only minimal visual information is available. Observers' ability to make accurate sex judgements when viewing point-light displays may depend on the centre of moment and on more dynamic cues.

There are monocular, binocular, and oculomotor cues to depth. The monocular cues include linear perspective, aerial perspective, texture, interposition, shading, familiar size, and motion parallax. The binocular and oculomotor cues are convergence, accommodation, and stereopsis, and are only effective with close objects. Information from different cues is generally combined in an additive way. Size constancy depends very much on familiar size, on the apparent distance of the object, and on the precise instructions given to observers.

*Space or depth perception*

Studies of subliminal advertising have not produced convincing evidence of its effectiveness. However, there is evidence of subliminal perception in numerous laboratory studies, especially when the subjective threshold is used rather than the objective threshold. Patients with blindsight provide good evidence for perception without awareness, although it is hard to be sure no conscious awareness is involved. Blindsight may depend on subcortical processes and/or a direct pathway to Area V5.

*Perception without awareness*

Marr (1982) argued three successive representations are formed during visual perception: a primal sketch, a 2½-D sketch, and a 3-D model representation. Marr's theory does not account for subtle perceptual discriminations, and the role of top-down processes was de-emphasised. According to Biederman's (1987) theory, information about the components or geons of a visual object is matched with stored object representations. Biederman attached too much weight to edge-based extraction processes in object recognition. Biederman put forward a viewpoint-independent theory, but viewpoint-dependent mechanisms are important when observers make difficult within-category discriminations. Different patterns of brain activity are associated with the use of viewpoint-dependent and viewpoint-independent mechanisms. Some patients with visual agnosia find it hard to recognise objects when they are foreshortened, perhaps because this makes it hard to attain a 3-D model representation. Some patients with associative agnosia have much greater problems in recognising living than non-living things, probably because living things are more visually similar to each other. Many patients with visual agnosia cannot readily integrate visual features into a coherent whole. Evidence from visual agnosics can potentially assist in the development of theories of object recognition in normals.

*Object recognition*

Most patients with prosopagnosia have selective problems with face recognition, suggesting that there are important differences between face and object recognition. There is also evidence that certain brain regions are of more importance in face recognition than in object recognition. Farah (1990) argued that face recognition depends mainly on holistic processing, object recognition on holistic and analytic processing, and reading on analytic processing. The theory is over-simplified, and cannot explain cases of visual agnosia without alexia or prosopagnosia. Bruce and Young (1986) proposed an eight-component model, according to which familiar and unfamiliar faces are processed differently, and the name of a face cannot be retrieved in the absence of other information about that person. This model, which has been developed and expanded by Burton and Bruce (1993), has attracted much empirical support.

*Face recognition*

# FURTHER READING

- Eysenck, M.W. (2001). *Principles of cognitive psychology* (2nd ed.). Hove, UK: Psychology Press. There is more extensive coverage of the topics discussed here in Chapters 2 and 3 of this book.
- Sekuler, R., & Blake, R. (2002). *Perception* (4th ed.). New York: McGraw-Hill. There is good introductory coverage of perception in all the main sense modalities in this American textbook.
- Wade, N.J., & Swanston, M.T. (2001). *Visual perception* (2nd. ed.). Hove, UK: Psychology Press. This book contains fascinating accounts of many visual phenomena, and is unusual in that the historical perspective is fully covered.

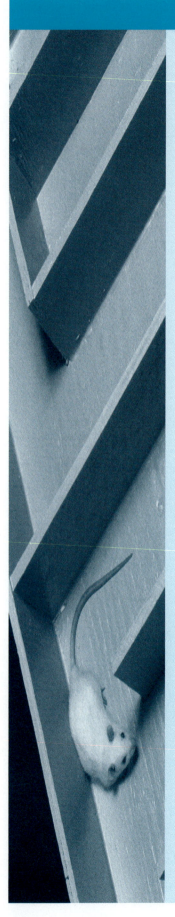

- **Classical conditioning**
  The importance of associations.

  *Pavlov's findings: conditioned and unconditioned stimulus, reflex and response*
  *Explanation of Pavlov's theory*
  *Rescorla & Wagner's model*
  *The ecological perspective*
  *The importance of conscious awareness*

- **Operant conditioning**
  The effect of reward or reinforcement.

  *Skinner's studies with rats*
  *Primary and secondary reinforcers*
  *Schedules of reinforcement*
  *Learning through shaping*
  *Chaining*
  *Studies into the impact of punishment*
  *Avoidance learning*
  *Seligman and learned helplessness*
  *Exploration of what is learned*

- **Observational learning**
  The importance of learning through observation in humans.

  *The efficiency of observational learning*
  *Observation vs. learning*
  *The power of observational learning*
  *The effectiveness of observational learning*

- **Implicit learning**
  Learning without the processes of learning.

  *Why implicit learning and implicit memory are researched separately*
  *Implicit vs. explicit learning and memory*
  *Studies: artificial grammar learning, serial reaction time task, amnesic patients,*
  *Theoretical issues*

- **Skill acquisition and expertise**
  Long-term learning.

  *Cognitive vs. perceptual motor skills*
  *Knowledge-rich learning*
  *How skills are learned*
  *Fitts' phases of skill acquisition: cognitive, associative, autonomous*
  *Studies in chess: template theory and synthesis*
  *Anderson's ACT theory: chunking and knowledge compilation*
  *Ericsson's studies of deliberate practice*

# Conditioning and learning

Compared to most other species, we are extremely good at learning. Learning is clearly of the utmost importance to us in our everyday lives. Adults are much better equipped than children to deal with the complexities of life, because they have spent several years acquiring knowledge and skills. Not surprisingly, the study of learning was *the* major focus of research when psychology emerged as a scientific discipline around the start of the twentieth century. This can be seen in the work of Pavlov and the early behaviourists such as John Watson.

The **behaviourists** assumed that learning was of fundamental importance. However, they mostly considered very simple forms of learning, such as learning to salivate when a bell sounds or learning to press a lever for food reward. More complex forms of learning (e.g., becoming a grandmaster at chess, obtaining a degree in psychology) certainly involve very different processes to those emphasised by the behaviourists.

The psychology of learning is a vast and fascinating area. The complexity of what is being learned varies from the very simple (e.g., lever pressing) to the very complex (e.g., mastering physics). In addition, we can focus on the early stages of learning or on the effects of prolonged practice on learning and performance. We can also distinguish between intellectual (or cognitive) skills and perceptual-motor skills. Playing chess effectively or understanding complex legal documents are examples of intellectual skills, whereas playing tennis skilfully or excelling on a musical instrument are examples of perceptual-motor skills.

## CLASSICAL CONDITIONING

Imagine you have to go to the dentist. As you lie down on the reclining chair, you may feel frightened. Why are you frightened *before* the dentist has caused you any pain? The sights and sounds of the dentist's surgery lead you to expect or predict that you are shortly going to be in pain. Thus, you have formed an *association* between the neutral stimuli of the surgery and the painful stimuli involved in drilling. Such associations are of central importance in classical conditioning. In essence, the fear created by the drilling is now triggered by the neutral stimuli of the surgery.

Textbook writers nearly always focus on unpleasant everyday examples of **classical conditioning** (I've just been guilty of that myself!). However, there are also pleasant examples. Most middle-aged people have especially positive feelings for the music that was popular when they were in their teens and early twenties. Associations are formed between the music and various exciting kinds of stimuli encountered during adolescence (Marc Brysbaert, personal communication).

Classical conditioning may be relevant to the development of some phobias, which involve an extreme fear of certain objects (e.g., snakes, spiders). It has been argued that phobias develop when neutral stimuli become associated with stimuli causing fear (see Chapter 22), causing the neutral stimuli to produce a fear response.

## Basic findings

The best-known example of classical conditioning comes from the work of Ivan Pavlov (1849–1936). Dogs (and other animals) salivate when food is put in their mouths. In technical terms, what we have here is an unlearned or **unconditioned reflex** involving a connection between the **unconditioned stimulus** of the food in the mouth and the **unconditioned response** of salivation. Pavlov found he could train a dog to salivate to other stimuli. In some of his studies, he presented a tone (a neutral stimulus which became the **conditioned stimulus**) just before food several times, so that the tone signalled that food would arrive soon. Finally, he presented the same tone (the test stimulus) on its own without any food following, and found the dog salivated to the tone. In technical terms, the dog had learned a **conditioned reflex**, in which the conditioned stimulus (the tone) was associated with the unconditioned stimulus (sight of food), and the learned or **conditioned response** was salivation. Note that it is essential for the food to follow very shortly after the tone in order for a conditioned reflex to be formed. There is a progressive increase in salivation (the conditioned response) over the course of learning.

Similar findings have been obtained in numerous studies on human participants. In eyeblink conditioning, for example, a tone (conditioned stimulus) is presented shortly before a puff of air (unconditioned stimulus) is administered to the eye. After a series of trials, participants react to the tone with an eyeblink (the conditioned response).

Pavlov discovered several features of classical conditioning in his research on dogs. One of these was generalisation. The conditioned response of salivation was greatest when the tone presented on its own was the same as the tone that had previously been presented just before food. A smaller amount of salivation was obtained when a different tone was used. **Generalisation** refers to the fact that the strength of the conditioned response (e.g., salivation) depends on the *similarity* between the test stimulus and the previous training stimulus.

Pavlov also identified the phenomenon of **discrimination**. Suppose a given tone is paired several times with the sight of food. The dog will learn to salivate to the tone. Then another tone is presented on its own. It produces a smaller amount of salivation than the first tone through generalisation. Next the first tone is paired with food several more times, but the second tone is never paired with food. Salivation to the first tone increases, whereas that to the second tone decreases. In other words, the dog has discriminated between the two tones.

Another key feature of classical conditioning is **experimental extinction**. When Pavlov presented the tone on its own several times, there was less and less salivation. Thus, the repeated presentation of the conditioned stimulus in the absence of the unconditioned stimulus removes the conditioned response. This finding is known as experimental extinction.

Extinction does *not* mean the dog or other animal has lost the relevant conditioned reflex. Animals brought back into the experimental situation after extinction has occurred produce some salivation in response to the tone. This is known as **spontaneous recovery**. It shows that the salivary response to the tone was inhibited rather than lost during extinction.

## Simple theory

What is going on in the classical conditioning situation? It might seem as if two factors are of special importance. First, the conditioned and the unconditioned stimuli need to be presented very close together in time. This is sometimes known as the law of association by contiguity (contiguity means closeness in time or space). Second, there is a process of stimulus substitution: The conditioned stimulus simply acting as a substitute for the unconditioned stimulus. For example, the sight of the dentist's surgery evokes the fear originally associated with the dentist's drilling.

The above account is incorrect. So far as the first factor is concerned, it is true that conditioning is usually greatest when the conditioned stimulus is presented a short time (about half a second) before the unconditioned stimulus, and stays on while the unconditioned stimulus is presented. However, there is little or no conditioning if the unconditioned

**KEY TERMS**

**Unconditioned reflex**: an association between the unconditioned stimulus and the unconditioned response.

**Unconditioned stimulus**: a stimulus that produces an unconditioned response in the absence of learning.

**Unconditioned response**: an unlearned response to an unconditioned stimulus.

**Conditioned stimulus**: a stimulus that becomes associated through learning with the unconditioned stimulus.

**Conditioned reflex**: the new association between a stimulus and response formed in classical conditioning.

**Conditioned response**: a response which is produced by the conditioned stimulus after a learning process in which the conditioned stimulus has been paired several times with the unconditioned stimulus.

**Generalisation**: the tendency of a conditioned response to occur in a weaker form to stimuli similar to the conditioned stimulus.

**Discrimination**: the strength of the conditioned response to one conditioned stimulus is strengthened at the same time as that to a second conditioned stimulus is weakened.

**Experimental extinction**: the elimination of a response when it is not followed by reward (operant conditioning) or by the unconditioned stimulus (classical conditioning).

**Spontaneous recovery**: the re-emergence of responses over time following experimental extinction.

stimulus is presented shortly before the conditioned stimulus. This situation is known as **backward conditioning**. Thus, contiguity alone is not enough.

Kamin (1969) showed that classical conditioning does *not* always occur when a conditioned stimulus is followed closely by an unconditioned stimulus. The animals in the experimental group received light (conditioned stimulus 1) paired with electric shock, and learned to react with fear and avoidance when the light came on. The animals in the contrast group had no training. Then both groups received a series of trials with a light–tone combination followed by shock. Finally, both groups received only the tone (conditioned stimulus 2). The contrast group responded with fear to the tone on its own, but the experimental group did not.

What is going on here? The experimental animals learned that light (conditioned stimulus 1) predicted shock, and so they ignored the fact that the tone (conditioned stimulus 2) also predicted shock. The contrast animals learned that the tone predicted shock, because they had not previously learned something different. The term **blocking** is used to refer to what happened with the experimental animals: A second conditioned stimulus (e.g., tone) does not lead to conditioned responses if another conditioned stimulus (e.g., light) already predicts the onset of the unconditioned stimulus.

What about the notion that the conditioned stimulus acts as a substitute for the unconditioned stimulus? Let us go back to Pavlov's research. When food is presented to a dog, it typically engages in chewing and swallowing as well as salivating (unconditioned response). However, the conditioned stimulus (e.g., tone) produces salivation but not chewing and swallowing. In addition, the tone often produces conditioned responses (e.g., tail wagging, looking at the place where food is usually presented) that do not occur at all in response to the food itself (Jenkins et al., 1978). The clear differences between the conditioned and unconditioned responses indicate that the conditioned stimulus is *not* simply a substitute for the unconditioned stimulus.

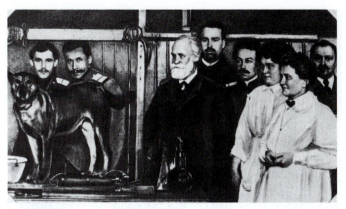

Russian psychologist Ivan Pavlov, a dog, and his staff, photographed ca. 1925–1936.

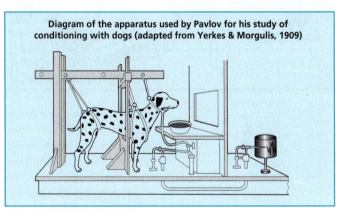

**Diagram of the apparatus used by Pavlov for his study of conditioning with dogs (adapted from Yerkes & Morgulis, 1909)**

*Do you think that Pavlov's theory of conditioning can account for human learning and behaviour?*

## Rescorla–Wagner model

Rescorla and Wagner (1972) proposed a very influential theoretical approach to classical conditioning, which represented a considerable advance on the simple theory described above. The Rescorla–Wagner model is complex, but its central assumption is that associative learning between a conditioned stimulus and an unconditioned stimulus occurs when a conditioned stimulus is found to *predict* the arrival of the unconditioned stimulus. Several predictions (all of which have received strong empirical support) follow from this assumption, and are discussed below.

- The theory explains why backward conditioning is so ineffective. If the conditioned stimulus is only presented after the unconditioned stimulus, then it cannot predict the arrival of the unconditioned stimulus.
- The theory accounts for blocking. If one conditioned stimulus already predicts the arrival of the unconditioned stimulus, then the addition of a second conditioned stimulus does not improve the animal's or human's ability to predict the arrival of the unconditioned stimulus. As a result, the second conditioned stimulus is redundant and blocking occurs.
- We can make sense of the finding that dogs in the Pavlov situation respond to a tone by wagging their tails and looking at the place where food is normally presented. These are precisely the forms of behaviour that would be exhibited by a dog who expected food to be presented.

**KEY TERMS**

**Backward conditioning:** the unconditioned stimulus is presented just before the conditioned stimulus in classical conditioning.

**Blocking:** the failure of a conditioned stimulus to produce a conditioned response because another conditioned stimulus already predicts the presentation of the unconditioned stimulus.

- There is the unconditioned stimulus pre-exposure effect: When an unconditioned stimulus is presented on its own several times before being paired with a conditioned stimulus, there is reduced conditioning (Randich & LoLordo, 1979). According to the model, when the unconditioned stimulus is pre-exposed in the experimental context, an association develops between the stimulus and the context. This makes the presence of the unconditioned stimulus less surprising during conditioning trials, and thus slows down conditioning.

### Evidence

We have already considered evidence supporting the Rescorla–Wagner model. However, other findings fail to support it (see Miller, Barnet, & Grahame, 1995, for a review). Some of these failures stem from the incorrect assumption that there is a direct relationship between the strength of the association between conditioned and unconditioned stimuli on the one hand and strength of conditioned responses on the other hand. For example, it is assumed within the model that experimental extinction occurs because there is an unlearning of the association between the conditioned and unconditioned stimuli. However, the existence of spontaneous recovery means that the association has *not* been unlearned.

The model encounters similar problems when trying to account for blocking. According to the model, no association is formed between the second or blocked conditioned stimulus and the unconditioned stimulus. This has been disproved. For example, the blocked conditioned stimulus produces the conditioned response when presented on its own outside the experimental context (Balaz et al., 1982).

### Evaluation

➕ The notion that associative learning occurs when a conditioned stimulus predicts the arrival of an unconditioned stimulus accounts for numerous findings in classical conditioning.

➕ The Rescorla–Wagner model led to the development of several other cognitive theories of conditioning (see Gray, 2002).

➖ Classical conditioning has turned out to be surprisingly complex, and the model fails to account for many of these complexities (Miller et al., 1995).

➖ The assumption that there is a direct relationship between learning (association between conditioned and unconditioned stimuli) and performance (conditioned responses) is incorrect.

## Ecological perspective

Can we produce conditioned reflexes equally well with almost any combination of conditioned stimulus and unconditioned stimulus? Those psychologists favouring the ecological perspective (e.g., Hollis, 1997) argue that the answer is, "No". According to them, animals and humans have various inherited behavioural tendencies that help them to survive in their natural environment. These behavioural tendencies are often modified through learning to equip animals and humans to cope successfully with the particular environmental conditions they face. From this perspective, certain forms of learning are more useful than others, and tend to be acquired more easily.

*What forms of learning do you think ethologists regard as being more useful than others?*

It is vitally important for the members of all species to avoid poisonous foods, and so the ecological perspective is especially relevant to food-aversion learning. Consider, for example, the very influential research of Garcia and Koelling (1966). They studied classical conditioning using three conditioned stimuli at the same time: saccharin-flavoured water, light, and sound. Some rats had these stimuli paired with the unconditioned stimulus of X-rays, which caused nausea. Other rats had these stimuli paired with a different unconditioned stimulus, electric shock. After that, Garcia and Koelling presented each conditioned stimulus on its own. Rats that had experienced nausea showed an aversion to the flavoured water but not to the light or sound cues. In contrast, the rats exposed to electric shock avoided the light and sound stimuli but not the flavoured water. Thus, the animals learned to associate being sick with taste, and they learned to associate shock with light and sound stimuli.

What do these findings mean? They indicate there is a biological readiness to associate some stimuli together, but not others. For example, there is obvious survival value in learning rapidly to develop a taste aversion to any food followed by illness. This is an example of the phenomenon known as **preparedness**.

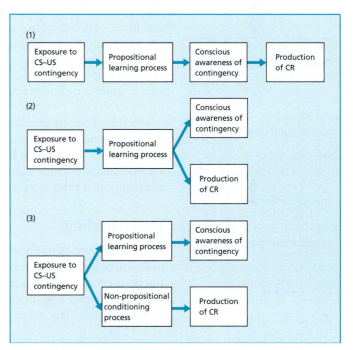

Many caterpillars are poisonous and can be deadly, therefore potential predators must quickly learn not to eat them. If too many are eaten before the predators learn to avoid them, then the brightly coloured signalling strategy is not working.

## Is awareness necessary?

It is important to understand the mechanisms underlying conditioning. A key issue here is to consider the role of conscious awareness of the relationship between the conditioned stimulus and the unconditioned stimulus. Some experts claim that conditioning is totally dependent on such conscious awareness, whereas others argue that conditioning is independent of awareness. Lovibond and Shanks (2002) identified three models of conditioning and awareness. In the first model, conscious awareness of the relationship between the conditioned and unconditioned stimuli is essential for production of the conditioned response. In the second model, there is a single learning process giving rise to conscious awareness and to the production of conditioned responses, but conscious awareness is not needed to elicit the conditioned response. In the third model, one type of learning leads to conscious awareness, and a second, lower-level, type of learning is totally responsible for the production of conditioned responses. Some of the relevant evidence is discussed briefly below.

Three models of conditioning and awareness. CS = conditioned stimulus; US = unconditioned stimulus; CR = conditioned response. From Lovibond and Shanks (2002).

## Evidence

There have been numerous experiments in which conditioned responses and conscious awareness of the relationship between conditioned and unconditioned stimuli were both assessed. According to the first model, there should be a very close correspondence between the two measures, because the production of conditioned responses is dependent on conscious awareness. According to the second model, there should be a fairly close correspondence, because both measures depend on the same learning process. According to the third model, awareness and conditioned responses are produced by independent learning processes, and so there is no necessary correspondence between awareness and conditioned responses.

Lovibond and Shanks (2002) have reviewed the relevant evidence. They came to the following conclusions: "The results are more supportive of the single-process models [first and second models]. Not only were examples of conditioning in the absence of awareness relatively rare, but they were often obtained with measures of awareness that may have underestimated conscious knowledge" (p. 22). In addition, they found that the correspondence

*Think of your own experiences of learning. Do you think you need to have conscious awareness to acquire knowledge?*

B.F. Skinner, 1904–1990.

between conscious awareness and conditioned responses was often weaker than would be expected on the first model, suggesting that the second model is the most valid.

Other evidence is also inconsistent with the third model. For example, McNally (1981) initially used a series of conditioning trials on which a given conditioned stimulus was followed by an unconditioned stimulus. The participants were then told that the conditioned stimulus would no longer be followed by the unconditioned stimulus, which led to an immediate substantial reduction in conditioned responses to the conditioned stimulus. The finding that propositional knowledge in the form of verbal instructions influenced conditioned responses is hard to reconcile with the notion that propositional learning is irrelevant to the production of conditioned responses.

## OPERANT CONDITIONING

In everyday life, people are often persuaded to behave in certain ways by the offer of reward or reinforcement. For example, young people deliver the morning papers because they are paid, and amateur athletes take part in competitions because they find it rewarding to do so. These are merely two examples of what is known in psychology as operant conditioning or instrumental conditioning. Much of **operant conditioning** is based on the **law of reinforcement**: The probability of a given response occurring increases if that response is followed by a reward or positive reinforcer such as food or praise.

According to B.F. Skinner (1904–1990), operant conditioning is of enormous importance. Indeed, Skinner believed that what we learn and how we behave in everyday life are both very heavily influenced by the conditioning experiences we have had throughout our lives.

Operant conditioning has several practical applications, three of which we will mention here. First, it is used extensively in the training of circus animals. Second, operant conditioning is used in the treatment of patients suffering from various mental disorders (see Chapter 23). For example, there are token economies, in which patients who behave in desirable ways receive tokens which can be exchanged for various rewards (e.g., sweets). Token economies have proved useful in the treatment of patients with schizophrenia or anti-social personalities. Third, there is biofeedback, which is used in the treatment of conditions such as high blood pressure and migraine (see Chapter 5). What happens in biofeedback is that the individual receives a signal whenever a given physiological measure (e.g., heart rate) moves in the desired direction.

## Basic findings

The best-known example of operant conditioning is provided by the work of Skinner. He placed a hungry rat in a small box (often called a Skinner box) containing a lever. When the rat pressed the lever, a food pellet appeared. The rat slowly learned that food could be obtained by lever pressing, and so pressed the lever more and more often. This is a clear example of the law of reinforcement. The effects of a reward or positive reinforcer are greater if it follows shortly after the response has been produced than if it is delayed.

The probability of a response has been found to decrease if it is not followed by a positive reinforcer. This phenomenon is known as experimental extinction. As with classical conditioning, there is usually some spontaneous recovery after extinction has occurred.

There are two major types of positive reinforcers or rewards: primary reinforcers and secondary reinforcers. **Primary reinforcers** are stimuli that are needed for survival (e.g., food, water, sleep, air). **Secondary reinforcers** are rewarding because we have learned to associate them with primary reinforcers. Secondary reinforcers include money, praise, and attention.

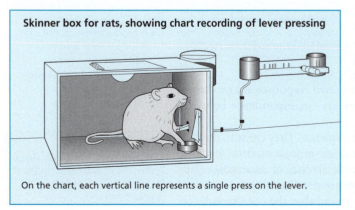

**Skinner box for rats, showing chart recording of lever pressing**

On the chart, each vertical line represents a single press on the lever.

# Skinner: Schedules of reinforcement

We tend to keep doing things that are rewarded and to stop doing things that are not rewarded. However, Skinner (1938, 1953) found some complexities in operant conditioning. We have looked so far at *continuous reinforcement*, in which the reinforcer or reward is given after every response. However, it is rare in everyday life for our actions to be continuously reinforced. Consider what happens with partial reinforcement, in which only some of the responses are rewarded. Skinner (1938) discovered four main schedules of partial reinforcement:

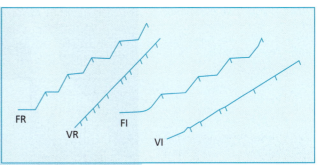

Typical pattern of responding over time on the four main schedules of partial reinforcement: FR (fixed ratio); VR (variable ratio); FI (fixed interval); and VI (variable interval). From Atkinson et al. (1996).

- **fixed ratio schedule**. Every nth (e.g., fifth, tenth) response is rewarded; workers who receive extra money for achieving certain targets are on this schedule.
- **variable ratio schedule**. Every nth response is rewarded on average, but the gap between two rewarded responses may be very small or fairly large; this schedule is found in fishing and gambling.
- **fixed interval schedule**. The first response produced after a given interval of time (e.g., 60 seconds) is rewarded; workers who are paid regularly every week are on this schedule—they receive reward after a given interval of time, but do not need to produce a specific response.
- **variable interval schedule**. On average, the first response produced after a given interval of time (e.g., 60 seconds) is rewarded; however, the actual interval is sometimes shorter than this and sometimes longer; as Gross (1996) noted, self-employed workers whose customers make payments at irregular times are rewarded at variable intervals, but they do not need to produce a specific response.

Although these gamblers have no idea when or if they will receive a payout, they continue to play. This is an example of the most successful reinforcement schedule—variable ratio reinforcement.

It might be thought that continuous reinforcement (with reward available after every response) would lead to better conditioning than partial reinforcement. In fact, the opposite is the case. Continuous reinforcement leads to the lowest rate of responding, with the variable schedules (especially variable ratio) leading to very fast rates of responding. This helps to explain why gamblers often find it hard to stop their addiction.

What about extinction? Those schedules of reinforcement associated with the best conditioning also show the most resistance to extinction. Thus, rats who have been trained on the variable ratio schedule will keep responding in extinction (in the absence of reward) longer than rats on any other schedule. Rats trained with continuous reinforcement stop responding the soonest. One reason why continuous reinforcement leads to rapid extinction is that there is a very obvious shift from reward being provided on every trial to reward not being provided at all. Animals trained on the variable schedules are used to reward being provided infrequently and irregularly, and so it takes much longer for them to realise that they are no longer going to be rewarded for their responses.

## Discussion points

1. Can you think of some examples of situations in everyday life involving the various schedules of reinforcement?
2. What are the limitations of Skinner's operant conditioning approach?

# Shaping

One of the features of operant conditioning is that the required response has to be made before it can be reinforced. How can we condition an animal to produce a complex response that it would not produce naturally? The answer is by means of **shaping**, in

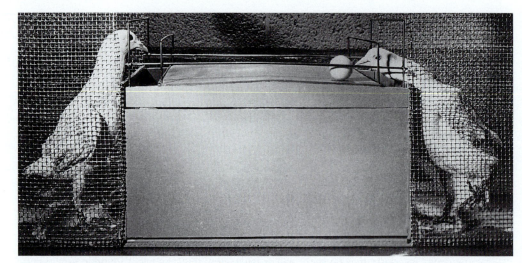

Skinner taught pigeons to play a basic form of table tennis by rewarding them every time they made contact with a table-tennis ball.

"Well, I simply trained them to give me fish by pressing this over and over again."

which the animal's behaviour moves slowly towards the desired response through successive approximations. Suppose we wanted to teach pigeons to play table tennis. To start with, they would be rewarded for making any contact with the table-tennis ball. Over time, their actions would need to become more and more like those involved in playing table tennis for them to be rewarded. In this way, Skinner actually persuaded pigeons to play a basic form of table tennis!

## Chaining

Operant conditioning can be used to produce complex sequences of behaviour. For example, suppose a rat learns that lever pressing produces food when a tone is on but does not produce food when the tone is absent. The tone becomes a **discriminative stimulus**, meaning that its presence is a cue that reinforcement is available. Discriminative stimuli acquire reinforcing value, and so animals can learn to produce a given response (e.g., climbing a step) to obtain the discriminative stimulus. Thus, a rat could learn to climb a step to hear a tone which would lead to lever pressing. This learned sequence of responses is known as **chaining**.

Pierrel and Sherman (1963) described an impressive case of chaining. A rat called Barnabus learned via operant conditioning to produce the following sequence of nine responses: climbing a ramp, pushing down a drawbridge, crossing a moat, climbing a staircase, crawling through a tunnel, entering an elevator, operating the elevator, raising a tiny flag, and pressing a lever for food.

## Punishment: Positive and negative

So far we have considered the effects of positive reinforcers or rewards on performance. However, operant conditioning can also involve unpleasant or *aversive stimuli* such as electric shocks or failure feedback. Humans and other species learn to behave in ways that reduce their exposure to aversive stimuli just as they learn to increase their exposure to positive reinforcers or rewards. As we will see, they also learn to avoid making responses that are followed by the removal of positive reinforcers or rewards.

Operant conditioning in which a response is followed by an aversive stimulus is known as **positive punishment** (sometimes simply called punishment). If the aversive stimulus occurs shortly after the response, then it has the effect of reducing the likelihood the response will be produced in future.

Skinner argued that punishment can suppress certain responses for a while, but it does not produce new learning. Estes (1944) reported findings supporting this view. Two groups of rats learned to press a lever for food, and were then given a series of extinction trials. One group was given a strong electric shock for every lever press during the early stages of extinction, but the other group was not. The punishment reduced the rate of responding for a while (suppression). However, in the long run the two groups produced the same number of responses. This suggested that the effects of punishment are short-lived.

Punishment doesn't always have temporary effects on behaviour. One of the features of the study by Estes (1944) was that the only way in which the rats could obtain positive reinforcement was by pressing the lever. Punishment usually has a more lasting effect when it is possible to obtain positive reinforcement with some response other than the one punished. For example, a child who is punished for putting his or her elbows on the table at mealtimes is most likely to stop doing this if he/she is also rewarded for sitting properly.

Baron (1977) reviewed the effects of punishment on children's aggressive behaviour. He identified the following requirements for punishment to reduce aggressive behaviour:

1. There should be a very short time interval between the aggressive action and the punishment.
2. Punishment should be relatively strong.
3. Punishment should be applied consistently and predictably.
4. The person giving the punishment should not be seen as an aggressive model.
5. The person receiving punishment should understand clearly why he/she is being punished.

It has often been argued that punishment applied to children has various unfortunate effects and is thus undesirable. Gershoff (2002) carried out several meta-analyses to identify the main effects on children of being physically punished by parents. Punishment typically produced immediate compliance to the wishes of the parent, but is associated with several undesirable outcomes, including the following: aggressive behaviour in childhood and adulthood, criminal and anti-social behaviour in childhood and adulthood, impaired mental health (e.g., depression) in childhood and adulthood, and a tendency to abuse their own children or spouse in adulthood. However, most of the evidence is correlational, and so we cannot be sure that these outcomes were actually caused by physical punishment.

There is another form of punishment known as negative punishment. What happens in **negative punishment** is that a positive reinforcer or reward is removed following the production of a particular response. For example, a child who refuses to eat properly and starts throwing food on the floor may have the food removed from him/her. The typical effect of negative punishment is to reduce the probability that the punished response will be produced thereafter.

Negative punishment is used in what is known as the time-out technique. For example, a child who behaves aggressively is prevented from continuing with such behaviour by being sent to his/her room. Negative punishment is involved, because the child is removed from pleasurable activities. The evidence suggests that the time-out technique often improves children's behaviour while avoiding the negative effects associated with positive punishment (Rortvedt & Miltenberger, 1994). This is especially the case if parents are firm and relatively unemotional.

*Try to think of some real-life examples of positive and negative punishment.*

## Avoidance learning

Nearly all drivers stop at red traffic lights because of the possibility of aversive stimuli in the form of an accident or trouble with the police if they do not. This is a situation in which no aversive stimulus is presented if suitable action is taken, and it is an example of **avoidance learning**. Many aversive stimuli strengthen any responses that stop the aversive stimuli being presented; they are known as *negative reinforcers*.

**KEY TERMS**

**Positive punishment:** a form of operant conditioning in which the probability of a response is reduced by following it with an unpleasant or aversive stimulus; sometimes simply known as punishment.

**Negative punishment:** a form of operant conditioning in which the probability of a response being produced is reduced by following it with the removal of a positive reinforcer or reward.

**Avoidance learning:** a form of operant conditioning in which an appropriate avoidance response prevents presentation of an unpleasant or aversive stimulus.

Avoidance learning can be very effective, as was shown by Solomon and Wynne (1953). Dogs were placed in a two-compartment apparatus. A change in the lighting served as a warning that a strong electric shock was about to be presented. The dogs could avoid being shocked by jumping into the other compartment. Most dogs received a few shocks at the start of the experiment. After that, however, they generally avoided the shock for the remaining 50 or more trials.

Mowrer (1947) put forward two-process learning theory to account for avoidance learning. According to this theory, the first process involves classical conditioning. The pairing of neutral (e.g., walls of the compartment) and aversive stimuli (electric shock) produces conditioned fear. The second process involves operant conditioning. The avoidance response of jumping into the other compartment is rewarded or reinforced by fear reduction.

Two-process theory provides a plausible account of avoidance learning. However, there are some problems with the notion that the avoidance response occurs to reduce fear. Dogs in the Solomon and Wynne (1953) study typically responded to the warning signal in about 1.5 seconds, which is probably too little time for the fear response to have developed. After the avoidance response occurred regularly, the dogs did not behave as if they were anxious. Thus, it is hard to argue that their avoidance behaviour was motivated *only* by fear reduction.

## Learned helplessness

Seligman (1975) studied another form of learning based on aversive stimuli. Dogs were exposed to electric shocks they could not avoid. After that, they were put in a box with a barrier in the middle. The dogs were given shocks after a warning signal, but they could escape by jumping over the barrier into the other part of the box. In fact, most of the dogs passively accepted the shocks, and did not learn to avoid or escape them. Seligman used the term **learned helplessness** to refer to passive behaviour in situations in which unpleasant stimuli could be escaped or avoided by appropriate action. Seligman also found that dogs who had *not* previously received unavoidable shocks rapidly learned to avoid the shocks by jumping over the barrier as soon as the warning signal was presented. These dogs were simply showing avoidance learning.

*Can you think of situations in which humans might display learned helplessness?*

Seligman (1975) argued that the learned helplessness seen in dogs is very similar to the passive helplessness shown by humans suffering from clinical depression (see Chapter 22). A cognitive account of the processes involved in learned helplessness was offered by Abramson, Seligman, and Teasdale (1978). In their attribution theory, they argued that people might attribute failure to an internal cause (themselves) or to an external cause (other people, the situation). In addition, they might attribute failure to a stable cause that was likely to continue in the future or to an unstable cause that might change soon. Finally, people might attribute failure to a global cause (relevant to many situations) or to a specific cause (relevant only to one situation).

Abramson et al. (1978) argued that people suffering from learned helplessness tend to attribute failure to internal, stable, and global causes. Thus, they feel personally responsible for failure, they think the factors leading to the current failure will continue in the future, and they think those factors will influence other situations. What we have just described is what Abramson et al. referred to as "personal helplessness". They contrasted that with "universal helplessness", in which the individual attributes failure to the beliefs that everyone would fail in solving the problem, and that the failure results from external causes.

It is now recognised that individuals can respond in various ways to uncontrollable failure. Abramson et al.'s (1978) cognitive theory was modified by Abramson, Metalsky, and Alloy (1989) and by Abramson et al. (1999), and it is now argued that experiencing personal helplessness is often insufficient to produce depressive symptoms. Additional feelings of hopelessness are required if symptoms of depression are to be triggered.

Bodner and Mikulincer (1998) argued that experience of uncontrollable failure sometimes produces paranoid-like responses rather than depressive responses. For example, a student who always fails on class tests set by a particular teacher may attribute his/her persistent failure to the teacher picking on him/her. Bodner and Mikulincer found that what was important was attentional focus. When people experiencing personal failure focused attention on themselves, they had depressive responses. However, when they focused attention on the threatening agent (the experimenter), then they reacted to persistent personal failure with paranoid-like responses.

## Theoretical perspectives

What is learned in operant conditioning? We will start with the simplest explanation, which was proposed by several early behaviourists (e.g., Guthrie, 1952) and supported in general terms by Skinner. According to this explanation, reinforcement or reward strengthens the association between the discriminative stimulus (e.g., the inside of the Skinner box) and the reinforced response (e.g., lever press). We can contrast that view with a more cognitive theory (e.g., Tolman, 1959), according to which animals learn much more than is implied by Guthrie's theory. Tolman argued that operant conditioning involves the learning of means–end relationships. A **means–end relationship** is the knowledge that the production of a given response in a given situation will have a specific effect. For example, it might be the knowledge that pressing a lever in the Skinner box will lead to the presentation of a food pellet.

The evidence indicates that animals *do* learn means–end relationships. For example, Dickinson and Dawson (1987) trained some rats to press a lever to receive sugar water, whereas others were trained to press a lever for dry food pellets. Some of the rats were then deprived of food, whereas others were deprived of water. Finally, all of them were tested under extinction conditions, in which no reward was provided. The key findings involved the rats who were thirsty. Those who had been reinforced previously with sugar water produced far more lever presses in extinction than did those who had been reinforced with dry food pellets. Why was there this difference? The rats used their knowledge of the expected reinforcer to decide how worthwhile it was to press the lever. Thirsty rats wanted something to drink, and so the expectation of dry food pellets did not encourage them to engage in much lever pressing.

The existence of reward contrast effects also indicates that animals acquire knowledge about the reinforcer to which they have been exposed. For example, suppose that animals have become accustomed to a certain amount of reinforcement, but then start receiving less reinforcement. This produces a **negative contrast effect**, in which animals show a marked decrease in response rate; indeed, their response rate is less than that of animals who receive the smaller reinforcement throughout (Pecoraro et al., 1999).

How important is reinforcement for learning? Skinner argued that it was of fundamental importance, whereas Tolman claimed that it was not. According to Tolman, reinforcement may be of vital importance for *performance* or behaviour, but it is not essential for *learning*. The phenomenon of learning occurring without any obvious effects on performance is known as **latent learning**.

Several studies of latent learning have focused on rats running in mazes. Rats who explore a maze but receive no food reward for doing so seem from their behaviour to have learned very little. However, when food is provided in the goal box at the end or centre of the maze, the rats run rapidly to it, thus indicating that latent learning has occurred. In one study, Tolman and Honzik (1930) compared maze running in rats who had received no reward over the first 10 days with rats who had been rewarded every day. When the former group started to receive food

*How does this theory relate to Abramson et al.'s (1978) theory of internal vs. external attributional styles?*

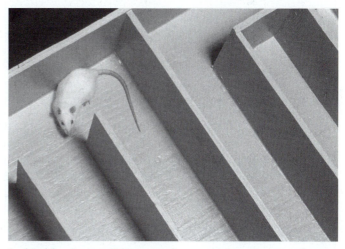

A white laboratory rat, *Rattus norvegicus*, moves through a maze. Apart from laboratory mice, the white rat is the commonest mammal used in animal experimentation.

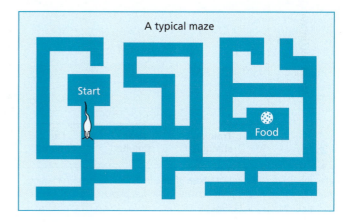

A typical maze

Start

Food

reward, their performance rapidly improved to the level of the latter group. Thus, latent learning can be as good as learning based on operant conditioning. However, it is hard to be sure that participants in the no-reward conditioning have actually received no reward or reinforcement.

Are there any limitations on operant conditioning? According to Skinner, the answer is, "No". He claimed that virtually any response can be conditioned in any stimulus situation; this is known as **equipotentiality**. In fact, some forms of operant conditioning are much more difficult to produce than others. Breland and Breland (1961) tried to train a pig to insert a wooden token into a piggy bank for reward. The pig picked up the token, but then repeatedly dropped it on the floor. In the words of Breland and Breland, the pig would "root it, drop it again, root it along the way, pick it up, toss it in the air, drop it, root it some more, and so on". They argued that their findings showed evidence of instinctive drift, meaning that what animals learn tends to resemble their instinctive behaviour.

Additional evidence that instinctive behaviour plays a much larger role in operant conditioning than Skinner believed was provided by Moore (1973). He took films of pigeons pecking at keys for either food or water reward. Students were then asked to decide what the reward was by looking at the films of the pigeons' pecking behaviour. They were correct 87% of the time. Birds pecking for food usually struck the key with an open beak, and made sharp, vigorous pecks. When pecking for water, the pigeons had their bill closed and there was a more sustained contact with the key.

The experiments we have just discussed suggest that it may be useful to look at operant conditioning from the ecological perspective. That is to say, animals find it easier to learn forms of behaviour which enable them to cope with their natural environment. Evidence supporting that point of view was reported by Gaffan et al. (1983). Rats in a T-shaped maze had to decide whether to turn left or right. Suppose that a rat turns left and finds food at the end of that arm of the maze. According to conditioning principles, the rat has been rewarded for turning left, and so should turn left on the following trial. However, in the rat's natural environment, it is not sensible to return to a place from which all the food has just been removed. Gaffan et al. found that rats early in training tended to avoid the arm of the T-shaped maze in which they had previously found food, which is as predicted from the ecological perspective.

Does operant conditioning involve the same mechanisms in humans as in other species? Nearly all the phenomena of operant conditioning have been found in humans as well as other species (see Gray, 2002). However, differences have sometimes been found. For example, Wills and Mackintosh (1998) compared humans and pigeons on a task involving learning to discriminate between two stimuli varying in brightness (e.g., the brighter stimulus was positive and the darker stimulus was negative). After the training phase, the pigeons and humans were tested with a range of stimuli including some not used during the learning phase. The pigeons responded most strongly on the test to stimuli that were similar to (but somewhat more extreme than) the positive training stimulus. This is known as a **peak shift**. However, they did not respond strongly to test stimuli that were much more extreme than the positive training stimulus. This pattern of results is typically thought to reflect associative learning. In contrast, the human participants responded most strongly to test stimuli that were much more extreme

> **KEY TERMS**
>
> **Equipotentiality:** the notion that any response can be conditioned in any stimulus situation.
>
> **Peak shift:** a phenomenon found in discrimination learning, in which there is maximal responding during the test phase to stimuli that are somewhat more extreme than the positive training stimulus.

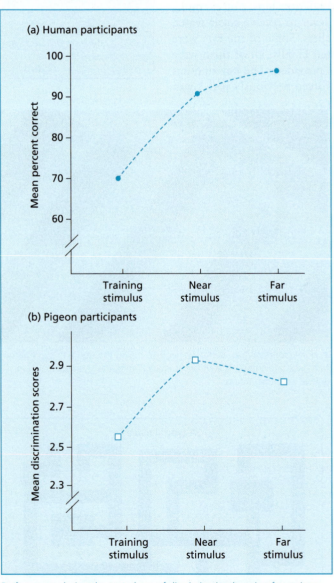

Performance during the test phase of discrimination learning for various stimuli (training, near, far) in humans (a) and in pigeons (b). Data from Wills and Mackintosh (1998).

than the positive training stimulus. Why did they do this? They made use of a rule such as, "Press one key for the brighter stimulus, the other for the darker."

In sum, operant conditioning is more complex than used to be thought. Animals and humans learn a considerable amount in most conditioning situations, far more than simply associating a discriminative stimulus with the rewarded response. There is clearly some validity in the ecological perspective on operant conditioning. Finally, it seems likely that much human learning differs from that of other species in that it is rule based.

*Do you think operant conditioning can account for human learning and behaviour?*

## Overall evaluation

⊕ Operant conditioning is often very effective. The behaviour of humans and other species can be controlled by clever use of reinforcement (e.g., the training of circus animals).

⊕ Operant conditioning has been used successfully in the treatment of various mental disorders (see Chapter 23).

⊕ Operant conditioning has been shown in numerous species (see Grier & Burk, 1992).

⊖ In real life, it is simply not the case that we learn things mainly by performing responses that are rewarded. What happens instead is that we learn an enormous amount simply by observing the behaviour of other people (Bandura, 1977a; see next section). More generally, operant conditioning only accounts for some forms of learning, most of which are relatively simple.

⊖ Skinner exaggerated the importance of *external* or environmental factors as influences on behaviour and minimised the role of *internal* factors (e.g., goals). As Bandura (1977a, p. 27) pointed out, "If actions were determined solely by external rewards and punishments, people would behave like weather vanes, constantly shifting in radically different directions to conform to the whims of others." This criticism probably applies less to non-human species, because other species are much less likely than humans to act in line with long-term goals.

⊖ Operant conditioning often has more effect on performance than on learning. Suppose you were offered a reward of £1 every time you said, "The earth is flat." You might (especially if short of money!) say that sentence hundreds of times, so that the reinforcement or reward would have influenced your performance or behaviour. However, it is very unlikely that it would affect your knowledge or learning so that you really believed that the earth was flat.

⊖ The evidence strongly suggests that Skinner's notion of equipotentiality is incorrect, as is his assumption that operant conditioning is uninfluenced by instinctive behaviour.

## OBSERVATIONAL LEARNING

As we have seen, Bandura (e.g., 1977a, 1986) has made pertinent criticisms of the conditioning approach to learning. Skinner and other advocates of operant conditioning argued that most human learning requires us to produce responses that are then rewarded or punished by some external agency. In contrast, Bandura (1977a, 1986, 1999) emphasised the importance of **observational learning**, which is learning occurring as a result of observing the behaviour of some other person or model. According to Bandura (1999, p. 170):

*Humans have evolved an advanced capacity for observational learning that enables them to expand their knowledge and competencies rapidly through the information conveyed by the rich variety of models. Virtually all behavioural, cognitive, and affective learning from direct experience can be achieved vicariously [second-hand] by observing people's actions and the consequences for them.*

Why is observational learning so important to humans? One key reason is because it is typically much more efficient than learning (e.g., operant conditioning) which involves actually experiencing a given situation. In the course of a single day, you can readily

**KEY TERM**
**Observational learning:**
learning that occurs as a consequence of watching the behaviour of some other person (often called a model).

observe the behaviour of numerous people in hundreds of situations. In contrast, it would be very difficult (or impossible) to put yourself in all of those situations in a short period of time. It can also be safer to observe the fate of others who engage in dangerous actions rather than performing the same actions yourself!

Bandura has consistently argued that there is an important difference between learning and performance. More specifically, observational learning will only manifest itself in performance in certain circumstances. Suppose, for example, that someone observes a model, who behaves in a given way and is then punished. Even though observational learning may occur, the observer will probably be reluctant to imitate the behaviour of the model.

*What other factors do you think might determine whether or not we imitate observed behaviour?*

### Evidence

There is a substantial body of research indicating that observational learning is effective. Much of that research has been carried out on children, and has shown that children's aggressive and prosocial behaviour are influenced by observational learning (see Chapter 16). The power of observational learning in children was shown clearly by Rushton (1975). Children observed a model who won some tokens in a bowling game. The model then argued in favour of generosity ("Give half to charity") or in favour of selfishness ("Keep the lot yourself"), but sometimes their actual behaviour was in conflict with what they said. In those conflict situations, the children usually imitated what the model did rather than what she said. Thus, observing the behaviour of a model can have effects even when his/her words belie their behaviour.

A study by Meltzoff (1988) seemed to provide strong evidence for observational learning. Infants of 14 months watched while an adult model turned on a table-mounted pressure-sensitive light using her forehead. This led to good observational learning: One week later, two-thirds of the babies used their forehead to turn on the light. This is an impressive finding, given that babies rapidly discover the value of using their hands to change the environment.

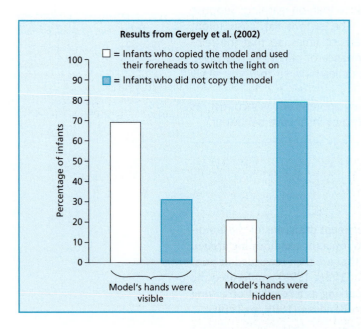

Gergely, Bekkering, and Kiraly (2002) argued that the findings from the study by Meltzoff (1988) were less conclusive than they appeared. In that study, the model's hands were on the table, and so the infants could see she had deliberately preferred to use her forehead rather than her hands to turn the light on. Accordingly, Gergely et al. included a second condition, in which the adult model pretended to be cold and so had her hands under the table wrapped in a blanket. This had a dramatic effect on the results. When the model's hands were free, 69% of the infants (who were 14 months old) copied her behaviour by using their forehead to put on the light. In contrast, when the model's hands were *not* free, only 21% of the babies copied her behaviour.

What should we conclude from Gergely et al.'s (2002) study? First, the findings indicate that observational learning is more complex than suggested by Bandura. According to Bandura, children who observe a model performing an action that is successful or rewarded should imitate that action. However, this simply did not happen in the condition in which the model's hands were under the blanket.

Second, the findings suggest that even infants are capable of fairly complex processing. The infants had already learned from experience that hands are very useful for touching objects and altering the environment. As a result, observational learning only influenced their behaviour when they believed that the model had deliberately preferred to use her forehead rather than her hands to turn on the light. According to Gergely et al. (2002, p. 755), "Imitation by 14-month-olds goes beyond emulation [imitation]. We conclude that the early imitation of goal-direct actions is a selective, inferential process that involves evaluation of the rationality of the means in relation to the constraints of the situation."

# Bandura: Observational learning and the Bobo doll

Bandura (1965) explored the issue of the relationship between observational learning and performance (see also Chapter 16). Young children watched a film in which an adult model behaved aggressively towards an inflatable Bobo doll. In one condition, a second adult appeared towards the end of the film and gave the model some sweets and a soft drink for having put up a "championship performance" (reward condition). In a second condition, a second adult scolded and spanked the model for behaving aggressively (punishment condition). In a third condition, the model did not receive reward or punishment (control condition).

Bandura (1965) then observed the behaviour of the children in the presence of the Bobo doll. Children in the reward and control conditions imitated more of the aggressive actions of the model than did the children in the punishment condition. What about the children in the punishment condition? It had not been clear from the findings whether or not they had achieved much observational learning. Accordingly, Bandura then offered all of the children some fruit juice and toys for showing what they had learned from the adult model. This revealed that the amount of observational learning was as great for children in the punishment condition as for children in the other two conditions.

Imitation of aggressive behaviour by children as a function of the way an aggressive adult was treated (reward, control, punishment) and whether the children were or were not rewarded at the test for imitating the adult's aggressive behaviour. Data from Bandura (1965).

## Discussion points

1. What are some of the limitations of this famous research by Bandura?
2. How important do you think observational learning is with respect to producing aggressive behaviour?

### KEY STUDY EVALUATION —Bandura

In his classic Bobo doll study, Bandura controlled the behaviour of his adult models. They used novel actions such as hitting the doll with a hammer, or throwing it in the air and saying "Pow! Boom!". These actions were chosen because the children would be unlikely to behave like this spontaneously, so that if the actions were produced, the researchers could be fairly confident that the children were imitating the adult model.

Adult "models" and children attack the Bobo doll.

*What are the implications of such findings for media violence? What do you think the relationship is between observing aggression in the media and behaving aggressively oneself?*

Third, it needs to be borne in mind that the participants in the study by Gergely et al. (2002) were only 14 months of age. If their tendency to imitate (or not to imitate) a model depends on complex thought processes, then it is surely the case that this will be even more true of older children. Thus, it is necessary to consider cognitive processes at all ages in order to understand something as apparently straightforward as observational learning and imitation.

We have seen that there is compelling evidence that observational learning influences behaviour in numerous situations. However, the evidence we have discussed still leaves open various questions. For example, is observational learning as effective as learning based on actually performing the behaviour in question? Are the same or different mechanisms involved in observational learning and learning through practice? As we will see, provisional answers to these questions were provided by Blandin and Proteau (2000).

In their first experiment, Blandin and Proteau (2000) had participants perform a four-segment timing task under one of three conditions: (1) prior observational learning, (2) prior physical practice, and (3) no prior experience. The key findings on an immediate retention test were as follows: "Observation allowed the observers to perform as well and to develop error detection mechanisms as efficient as those acquired during physical practice ... In addition, the observers had ... more efficient mechanisms for the detection and correction of errors than did the control group."

In their second experiment, Blandin and Proteau (2000) used a different timing task. Half the models were provided with biased knowledge of results, which produced systematic errors on their performance both at the time and on a subsequent test. Half the observers watched a model performing under conditions of biased knowledge of results. When these observers subsequently performed the timing task, they made very similar errors to the models they had watched.

What can we conclude from the above findings? First, observational learning can produce as much learning of a task as occurs through physical practice. Second, as Blandin and Proteau (2000, p. 846) concluded, "These results suggest that observation engages one in cognitive processes similar to those occurring during physical practice."

## Evaluation

⊕ Observational learning occurs very frequently in children and in adults.

⊕ Observational learning can have powerful effects on subsequent behaviour that are comparable in size to actual behaviour.

⊖ Bandura (1999, p. 173) pointed out that, "Modelling is not simply a process of response mimicry as commonly believed." Instead, he argued that the observer's behaviour should "embody the same rule" as the model's behaviour. The difficulty with this is that it can be very hard to decide whether the observer's behaviour does, in fact, embody the same rule.

⊖ There is only modest evidence for observational learning in children's acquisition of language. They initially produce much shorter utterances than adults, and rapidly move on to producing novel utterances. Neither of these aspects of children's language would be predicted on the basis of observational learning.

⊖ The processes underlying observational learning and imitation can be much more complex than was assumed by Bandura (e.g., Gergely et al., 2002).

## IMPLICIT LEARNING

The levels-of-processing approach was concerned with the processes involved in the conscious acquisition and retrieval of information (see Chapter 9). However, some learning is not like that, and the term "implicit learning" has been used to refer to such learning. According to Frensch and Runger (2003, p. 14), **implicit learning** is "the capacity to learn without awareness of the products of learning". There are clear similarities between implicit learning and **implicit memory**, which is memory that does not depend on conscious recollection (see Chapter 9).

The reader may wonder why implicit learning and implicit memory are not discussed together. After all, there can be no memory without prior learning, and learning necessitates the involvement of a memory system. Researchers tend to study either implicit learning or implicit memory, and have developed different kinds of tasks. Implicit learning researchers often use relatively complex, novel stimulus materials, whereas those studying implicit memory use simple, familiar stimulus materials. It is hard to compare the findings from such different tasks.

How do the systems involved in implicit learning and memory differ from the systems involved in explicit learning and memory? Reber (1993) proposed five such characteristics:

1. *Robustness*. Implicit systems should be relatively unaffected by disorders (e.g., amnesia) affecting explicit systems.
2. *Age independence*. Implicit learning is little influenced by age or developmental level.
3. *Low variability*. There are smaller individual differences in implicit learning and memory than in explicit learning and memory.
4. *IQ independence*. Performance on implicit tasks is relatively unaffected by IQ (see Chapter 12).
5. *Commonality of process*. Implicit systems are common to most species.

Reber (1997, p. 139) argued that there is very clear evidence for the existence of implicit learning, citing the case of language development: "Formal instruction is essentially irrelevant, explicit processes are absent, individual differences in the basic skill are minimal, [and] language users have virtually no access to the rules of their language." However, it is clearly useful to consider more experimental attempts to demonstrate implicit learning, and that is precisely what is done in the next section.

## Evidence

Much research on implicit learning has involved artificial grammar learning. The participants initially memorise various letter strings (e.g., XXRTRXV, QQWMWTR), all of which conform to the rules of a grammar. After that, they are presented with new letter strings, and have to decide whether they are grammatical or ungrammatical. Most participants show implicit learning by discriminating fairly well between grammatical and ungrammatical strings, even though they cannot verbalise the rules of the grammar (see Reber, 1993).

There has been much controversy as to exactly what participants are learning on artificial grammar learning tasks. One key issue is that most artificial grammars only permit certain letter pairs (e.g., TR but not RT). Accordingly, participants may show reasonable levels of performance because they recognise familiar letter pairs rather than because they have learned the artificial grammar. This issue can be addressed by ensuring that grammatical and ungrammatical strings consist of equally familiar letter pairs. What happens when this is done? Much of the evidence suggests that participants do *not* learn the abstract rules of the artificial grammar, but instead indicate that letter strings are grammatical if they contain familiar letter pairs (Channon, Shanks, Johnstone, Vakili, Chin, & Sinclair, 2002).

Another issue which is important in studies on artificial grammar learning is whether the learning involved is implicit or explicit. Most participants who perform the task well cannot describe the underlying grammatical rules, which suggests their performance is based on implicit learning. However, the same participants often show some ability to

| Reber's (1993) characteristics of implicit and explicit memory | | |
| --- | --- | --- |
| Characteristic | Implicit | Explicit |
| Robustness | Unaffected by disorders (e.g., amnesia) | Affected by disorders (e.g., amnesia) |
| Age independence | Little affected by age or developmental level | Much affected by age or developmental level |
| Variability | Small individual differences | Larger individual differences |
| IQ | Performance relatively unaffected by IQ | Performance affected by IQ |
| Commonality of process | Implicit systems are common to most species | Explicit systems are mainly (exclusively) found in humans |

*Do you think such tasks reflect implicit learning in everyday life?*

**KEY TERM**
**Implicit memory:** memory that does not depend on conscious recollection.

recognise which letters are important in determining whether a letter string is grammatical or ungrammatical (see Frensch & Runger, 2003). Such findings suggest that at least some of what the participants have learned is explicit.

A different task often used in studies of implicit learning is the serial reaction time task. A stimulus appears at various locations in a fixed sequence, and the participants have to press keys matching these locations. For example, Howard and Howard (1992) used a task in which an asterisk appeared in one of four positions on a screen, under each of which was a key. The task was to press the key corresponding to the position of the asterisk as rapidly as possible. The position of the asterisk over trials conformed to a complex pattern. The participants showed clear evidence of learning the pattern by responding faster and faster to the asterisk. However, when asked to predict where the asterisk would appear next, their performance was at chance level. Thus, the participants apparently showed implicit learning of the pattern, but no explicit learning.

The strongest evidence that there is a valid distinction between explicit memory (involving conscious recollection) and implicit memory (not based on conscious recollection) has come from the study of amnesic patients (see Chapter 9). More specifically, amnesic patients have severely impaired explicit memory but essentially intact implicit memory. In similar fashion, the distinction between explicit and implicit learning would be strengthened if it were found that amnesic patients have intact implicit learning but impaired explicit learning. That pattern has been found in some studies. For example, Knowlton, Ramus, and Squire (1992) found that amnesic patients performed as well as normal individuals in learning to distinguish between grammatical and ungrammatical strings of letters. Thus, amnesic patients showed intact implicit learning.

*How would you go about testing the implicit and explicit learning abilities of amnesic patients?*

Knowlton et al. (1992) obtained different findings when the participants recalled the specific strings used during learning, and tried to use these strings to aid task performance. The amnesics performed much worse than the normal participants in this condition, presumably because performance depended more on explicit learning.

In spite of the findings of Knowlton et al. (1992), amnesic patients often have inferior implicit learning to healthy individuals. For example, Channon et al. (2002) used the artificial grammar learning task, and found amnesic patients and healthy controls failed to learn the rules of the grammar. However, the healthy controls were significantly better than the amnesic patients at distinguishing between familiar and unfamiliar strings.

Gooding et al. (2000) reported a meta-analysis of studies on implicit learning involving amnesic patients. Their key conclusion was that amnesics typically have normal implicit learning for familiar material. However, amnesic patients perform worse than normals when the implicit learning involves novel or unfamiliar material.

Much of the evidence for implicit learning is controversial and open to more than one interpretation. However, fairly convincing evidence that implicit learning can occur in the absence of consciously accessible knowledge was reported by Shea, Wulf, Whitacre, and Park (2001), in a study discussed next.

The participants in the study by Shea et al. (2001) were given the task of standing on a platform, and trying to move it to mimic the movements of a line displayed on a computer screen. The participants performed the task several times. On each occasion, the middle segment was identical, but the first and third segments varied. The participants were not told that the middle segment would remain the same. Performance on the middle segment improved more than did performance on the other segments, providing clear evidence the participants had benefited from having that segment repeated. It appeared that this learning was implicit. Two-thirds of the participants said they did not think that part of the pattern had been repeated, and they performed at chance level when trying to identify the repeated segment on a subsequent recognition test.

In a second experiment, two of the three segments were repeated, and the participants were told explicitly about one of the repeated segments. Performance was significantly worse on this segment than on the repeated segment about which the participants had not been told. This finding suggests that implicit learning was superior to explicit learning on this task.

The notion that implicit learning is separate from explicit learning would receive support if different brain regions were found to underlie the two types of learning. Grafton, Hazeltine, and Ivry (1995) obtained PET scans from participants engaged in learning motor sequences under implicit learning conditions or under conditions making it easier for them to become consciously aware of the sequence. The motor cortex and the supplementary motor area were activated during implicit learning. In contrast:

> *Explicit learning and awareness of the sequences required more activations in the right premotor cortex, the dorsolateral cingulate, areas in the parietal cortex associated with working memory, the anterior cingulate, areas in the parietal cortex concerned with voluntary attention, and the lateral temporal cortical areas that store explicit memories. (Gazzaniga, Ivry, & Mangun 1998, p. 279)*

Thus, there seem to be differences between the systems involved in explicit and implicit learning.

## Theoretical considerations

A key theoretical issue is whether learning is possible with little or no conscious awareness of what has been learned. Shanks and St. John (1994) proposed two criteria for learning to be regarded as unconscious:

1. *Information criterion.* The information that the participants are asked to provide on the awareness test must be the information responsible for their improved level of performance.
2. *Sensitivity criterion.* "We must be able to show that our test of awareness is sensitive to all of the relevant knowledge" (p. 11). People may be consciously aware of more task-relevant knowledge than appears on an insensitive awareness test, which may lead us to under-estimate their consciously accessible knowledge.

*Do the studies previously discussed in this section meet these criteria?*

The two criteria proposed by Shanks and St. John (1994) are hard to use in practice. However, Shanks and St. John argued that the sensitivity criterion could be replaced provided that the performance and awareness tests resemble each other as closely as possible. If you look back over the studies discussed in this section, you can see that there is generally little similarity between the performance and awareness tests. However, in the study by Howard and Howard (1992), the ability to predict the next location of the asterisk was of central importance to both the performance and the awareness tests.

Another important theoretical issue concerns the relationship between explicit and implicit learning. One view was expressed by Anderson (e.g., 1983, 1996) in his Adaptive Control of Thought (ACT) model (see later in chapter). According to ACT, during the development of automatic skills, conscious representations are gradually transformed into unconscious ones. Thus, there is an initial process of explicit learning followed by implicit learning. A different view was expressed by Willingham and Goedert-Eschmann (1999), who argued that explicit and implicit learning develop together in parallel rather than one preceding the other. According to this theoretical position, performance is initially supported by explicit processes. After sufficient practice, implicit processes acquired at the same time as the explicit processes become strong enough to support performance on their own.

Willingham and Goedert-Eschmann (1999) obtained evidence supporting the hypothesis that explicit and implicit learning develop together. They used a serial reaction time task in which participants had to respond rapidly with the appropriate responses to four different stimuli over a long series of trials, with the stimuli being arranged in a given sequence. Participants in the explicit learning condition were told there was a repeating sequence, and were encouraged to memorise it. In contrast, participants in the implicit learning condition were not informed about the sequencing.

The participants were then given a further series of transfer trials designed to assess implicit knowledge. The stimuli on these trials were mostly presented in a random order, and participants who had engaged in explicit learning were told that the purpose of these trials was to see how rapidly they could respond when the stimuli were random. However, the previously learned sequence or a novel sequence was introduced during the course of the trials without the awareness of the participants. What happened on this test of implicit knowledge? According to Willingham and Goedert-Eschmann (1999), "Participants with explicit training showed sequence knowledge equivalent to those with implicit training, implying that implicit knowledge had been acquired in parallel with explicit knowledge."

Much more evidence is needed to clarify the relationship between explicit and implicit learning. It is possible that the two forms of learning develop together on simple motor tasks such as the one used by Willingham and Goedert-Eschmann (1999), but that explicit learning precedes implicit learning on more complex or non-motor tasks.

## Evaluation

⊕ Evidence that there are important differences between implicit and explicit learning has been obtained in well-controlled studies (e.g., Howard & Howard, 1992; Shea et al., 2001).

⊕ It seems increasingly likely that most implicit learning involves simple fragments of information (e.g., letter pairs) rather than complex information (e.g., abstract grammatical knowledge).

⊕ PET studies (e.g., Grafton et al., 1995) suggest that different parts of the brain are activated during explicit and implicit learning, but the evidence is not clear-cut.

⊖ It is hard (or even impossible) to devise tests of awareness able to detect all of the task-relevant knowledge of which participants have conscious awareness.

⊖ Evidence from amnesic patients is inconsistent. However, it is often the case that their implicit learning is inferior to that of normal individuals.

⊖ It is sometimes not clear whether explicit learning is followed by implicit learning, or whether explicit and implicit learning develop together.

## SKILL ACQUISITION AND EXPERTISE

So far in this chapter we have focused mainly on studies in which the time available for learning has been short and the tasks involved relatively limited. In the real world, however, people sometimes spend several years acquiring knowledge and skills in a given area (e.g., law, medicine). The end point of such long-term learning is the development of **expertise**, which can be defined as "highly skilled, competent performance in one or more task domains [areas]" (Sternberg & Ben-Zeev, 2001, p. 365). We can, of course, study the processes involved on the road to achieving expertise. This involves the investigation of **skill acquisition**, which was defined by Rosenbaum, Carlson, and Gilmore (2001, p. 454):

> *When we speak of a 'skill' we mean an ability that allows a goal to be achieved within some domain with increasing likelihood as a result of practice. When we speak of 'acquisition of skill' we refer to the attainment of those practice-related capabilities that contribute to the increased likelihood of goal achievement.*

As we saw earlier, it has been customary to distinguish between intellectual or cognitive skills and perceptual-motor skills. Cognitive skills are involved in mastering most academic subjects at school and university (e.g., history, psychology, medicine), whereas perceptual-motor skills are involved in becoming proficient at sports such as hockey or tennis.

The development of expertise resembles problem solving, in that experts are extremely efficient at solving a wide range of problems in their area of expertise. However, most traditional research on problem solving made use of "knowledge-lean" problems, meaning that no special training or knowledge is required to solve them (see Chapter 10). In contrast, studies on expertise have typically used "knowledge-rich" problems, requiring the use of much knowledge beyond that presented in the problem itself. "Knowledge-rich" problems resemble the problems of everyday life more closely than do "knowledge-lean" problems. In addition, comparisons between the performance of experts and novices are likely to tell us much about the processes involved in problem solving.

# Skill acquisition

It seems reasonable to assume that cognitive skills and perceptual-motor skills are very different. As Rosenbaum et al. (2001) pointed out, the two types of skills seem to differ substantially in several ways:

- Perceptual-motor skills seem more basic and primitive than cognitive skills. Those parts of the brain involved in cognitive skills (e.g., association areas of the cerebral cortex) tend to be more developed in humans than in other species.
- Perceptual-motor skills seem narrower than cognitive skills in terms of the ways in which they are expressed. For example, even if you have become an excellent tennis player using your right hand, you would probably play very poorly if you had to use your left hand. However, skill at tennis might help you to learn how to play badminton. In contrast, if you have developed great skill as a poet, your poetry will be good whether you use a biro, a word processor, or a tape recorder when producing a new poem.
- It is generally more difficult to verbalise the knowledge we possess about perceptual-motor skills than cognitive skills. As Rosenbaum et al. (2001, p. 455) pointed out, "No one has ever managed to write the instructions for riding a bicycle or bouncing on a trampoline and then find the reader successfully engaging in these tasks based on reading alone."
- Those who possess excellent cognitive skills (e.g., accountants) are often clumsy and have poor perceptual-motor skills, and many gifted sportspeople are poor at communication.

*Excellent perceptual-motor skills are required to be an expert at tennis.*

Although Rosenbaum et al. (2001) listed the differences described above, they concluded that there are important similarities in the acquisition of intellectual and perceptual-motor skills. We can see why they came to that conclusion by considering evidence inconsistent with the above claimed differences. First, there is the notion that different (and more powerful) brain areas underlie cognitive skills than underlie perceptual-motor skills. It is known that the cerebellum and the motor cortex are both involved in the co-ordination and control of movement. However, accumulating evidence indicates that these brain regions (especially the cerebellum) are also involved in cognitive skills (e.g., prediction, planning). Nevertheless, large areas of the cortex seem to be primarily involved in cognitive skills rather than perceptual-motor skills.

One way of deciding whether perceptual-motor skills are more specific than cognitive skills is to study transfer specificity. **Transfer specificity** refers to the extent to which skills developed on one task transfer or carry over to other tasks. In general terms, it would be expected that there would be less transfer for perceptual-motor skills than for cognitive skills. The evidence does not provide clear support for those expectations. For example, most people can learn to write fluently with their non-preferred hand (Newell & van Emmerik, 1989), and they can eventually learn to write with a pen between their toes or teeth. Transfer is often very limited for cognitive skills. As students have found to their cost, there is generally very little transfer from learning one foreign language to learning another. Ericsson and Chase (1982) studied a student whose **digit span** (immediate recall of random digits) increased from 7 to 80 (see later in the chapter). There was no transfer at all, because his word and letter span did not increase at all.

What about the notion that we find it much easier to verbalise our knowledge of cognitive skills than of perceptual-motor ones? As we saw earlier, there is reasonable (although controversial) evidence that implicit learning can occur with cognitive skills as well as with perceptual-motor ones. In addition, very few adults can express the rules for producing grammatical sentences. Thus, we do not have conscious access to the cognitive skills underlying something as fundamentally important as language.

What about the view that most people find it easier to develop perceptual-motor skills rather than cognitive skills? There are two main counterarguments. First, many people may have superior skills in one area rather than the other due to personal preference and interest, rather than because they have more natural ability in that area. Second, it would be misleading to assume that perceptual-motor skills form a coherent set of abilities. When people are given several perceptual-motor tasks to learn, the correlations among the tasks rarely exceed +.40 (Schmidt & Lee, 1999). Thus, individuals who rapidly develop skills on one perceptual-motor task often fail to do so on other perceptual-motor tasks.

One reason why we have failed to appreciate the important similarities between different types of skills is because we have under-estimated the complexity of perceptual-motor skills.

*What do such findings tell us about our understanding of perceptual-motor skills?*

> **KEY TERMS**
>
> **Transfer specificity:** the extent to which skills acquired on one task transfer or carry over on to other tasks.
>
> **Digit span:** number of random digits that can be recalled immediately after presentation.

Computers may be programmed to surpass human abilities in specific tasks, but they cannot possess the full range of human skills.

As Rosenbaum et al. (2001, pp. 465–466) pointed out:

> *The fact that modern technology has enabled computers to beat the world's greatest chess master ..., but has not yet enabled robots to climb trees as well as five-year-olds or pick strawberries as well as farm workers attests to the fact that our understanding of the psychological substrates of perceptual-motor skill is still primitive compared to what we know about intellectual skills.*

What conclusions can we draw? Most skills may be performatory, meaning they are grounded in (and supported by) perceptual-motor activity. Thus, for example, many cognitive skills require precise co-ordination and timing, with mental activity being co-ordinated with information available in the external environment (Cary & Carlson, 1999).

## Phases of skill acquisition

Fitts (1964) argued that the acquisition of perceptual-motor skills goes through three phases. As might be expected from our discussion above, it has turned out that his theoretical views also help to account for the acquisition of cognitive skills.

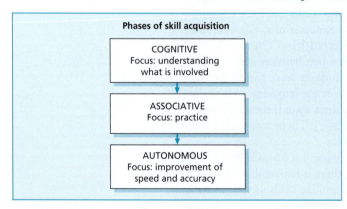

**Phases of skill acquisition**

COGNITIVE
Focus: understanding
what is involved

↓

ASSOCIATIVE
Focus: practice

↓

AUTONOMOUS
Focus: improvement of
speed and accuracy

According to Fitts (1964), what comes first is the cognitive phase. During this phase, the individual's main focus is on understanding what is involved, but without as yet trying to apply his/her increasing knowledge. This phase of learning is effortful, with the learner memorising a considerable amount of knowledge relevant to the skill in question. According to Fitts and Posner (1967, p. 12), the learner's behaviour during the cognitive phase is, "truly a patchwork of old habits ready to be put together into new patterns and supplemented by a few new habits". At this stage, the learner selects those skills he/she already possesses which seem relevant to the new task.

After the cognitive phase, there is the associative phase. During this phase, the learner engages in extensive practice, trying to assemble patterns of behaviour appropriate for the task in question. Practice has various effects, such as "chunking [grouping] of information, the integration of the components of the skill, and their appropriate tuning to the specific task" (Hampson & Morris, 1996, p. 136). As a result, performance gradually becomes more precise, and fewer errors are made. The amount of practice required during the associative stage varies considerably from task to task, but often takes only a few hours. For example, trainee pilots are sometimes in a position to make their first solo flight after about 10 hours of training (Fitts & Posner, 1967).

The third phase is the autonomous phase. During this phase, the speed and accuracy of performance continue to improve, even though the basic approach to performing the task remains essentially unchanged. A crucial aspect of the autonomous phase is that many (or most) components of skilled performance become automatic (see Chapter 5). As a result, skilled performers in the autonomous phase often cannot describe how they are carrying out the task. For example, when my son was learning to drive, he asked me various questions about changing gear, use of the foot pedals, and so on. I realised with embarrassment that I couldn't answer most of these questions, because my driving skills became automatic many years ago.

## Evidence

Reasonable support for the distinction between the associative and autonomous phases of skill acquisition was reported by Zbrodoff (1995). Their participants had to solve alphabet arithmetic problems. A sample problem is S + 3 = ?, which involves working three letters through the alphabet and working out that the answer is V. The number of letters that needed to be added on (the addendum) varied between two and four. Initially, performance was fastest when the addendum was 2 and slowest when it was 4, because the participants were working through the alphabet letter by letter. During the course of the associative phase, performance became progressively faster. Eventually, the participants were able to produce the answers automatically based on their past experience, and there was then no effect of the size of the addendum. Thus, extensive practice allowed the participants to reach the autonomous phase.

## Evaluation

● The three phases of skill acquisition seem appropriate to the development of cognitive skills as well as perceptual-motor skills.

● The general approach put forward by Fitts (1964) has been developed into a currently influential theory (Anderson's ACT theory), mentioned earlier and discussed later in the chapter.

● "The three-phase chronology [sequence] is an idealisation. The boundaries between phases are not as sharp as the description suggests" (VanLehn, 1996, p. 516).

● It is hard to know precisely which component skills are being used by a learner, and it is also hard to decide when performance has become automatic (see Chapter 5).

During the autonomous phase, people skilled in tasks such as driving find that the processes involved are automatic.

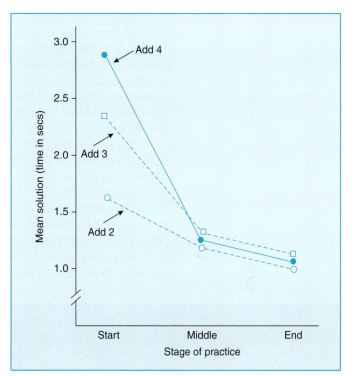

Speed of solution of alphabet arithmetic problems as a function of stage of practice and size of addendum (add 2, 3, or 4). Data from Zbrodoff (1995).

## Chess expertise

Why are some people much better than others at playing chess? Solso (1994) provided the obvious answer in the form of an anecdote: "Several years ago the late Bill Chase gave a talk on experts in which he promised to tell the audience what it would take to become a grandmaster chess player. His answer: "Practice." After the talk, I asked Chase how much practice. "Did I forget to say how much?" he asked quizzically. "Ten thousand hours."

What benefits occur as a result of practice? Expert chess players have very detailed information about chess positions stored in long-term memory, and this allows them to relate the position in the current game to previous games. This notion was first tested by De Groot (1965), and then more thoroughly by Chase and Simon (1973).

Chase and Simon (1973) argued that chess players who were asked to memorise board positions would break them down into about seven chunks or units. Their key assumption was that the chunks formed by expert players contain more information than those

*Why is it interesting for psychologists to study experts and novices?*

of other players, because they can bring more chess knowledge to bear on the memory task. They asked three chess players to look at the position of the pieces on one board, and to reconstruct that board position on a second board with the first board still visible. Chase and Simon calculated the size of the chunks being formed by taking account of the number of pieces placed on the second board after each glance at the first board. The most expert player (a master) had chunks averaging 2.5 pieces, whereas the novice had chunks averaging only 1.9 pieces. Recent evidence from Gobet and Simon (1998) suggests that Chase and Simon under-estimated the chunk size of masters.

We should not assume that the *only* advantage that chess experts have over novices is that they have stored information about tens of thousands of chess pieces. That would be like arguing that the only advantage that Shakespeare had over other writers was that he had a larger vocabulary! Holding and Reynolds (1982) asked chess players to think of the best move from various random board positions, chosen so that even expert players would be unable to make use of their detailed stored knowledge of board positions. The expert players produced moves of superior quality to those of non-expert players, suggesting they possessed better strategic processing skills.

## Template theory

Various theories of chess expertise have been produced. According to template theory (Gobet & Simon, 1996), outstanding chess players owe much of their success to the relevant knowledge they have stored. Much of this knowledge is in the form of templates, which are schematic structures more general than actual board positions. Each template consists of a core (fixed information concerning about 12 chess pieces) and slots (variable information about other pieces). When a template is retrieved from long-term memory during a game of chess, it can serve to suggest the next move and a plan of action.

According to template theory, outstanding players owe their excellence mostly to their superior template-based knowledge of chess. This knowledge can be accessed rapidly, and allows them to narrow down the possible moves they need to consider. This approach can be contrasted with that of Holding and Reynolds (1982), who emphasised the importance of strategic thinking and considering numerous possible moves. These theories can be tested by comparing the performance of an outstanding player when playing a single opponent and when playing simultaneously against up to eight opponents with very little time to make each move. According to template theory, the greatly reduced time to search for future moves in the multiple-opponent situation should have little effect on an outstanding player's performance. Precisely this was reported by Gobet and Simon (1996) based on the chess games of Garry Kasparov, the ex-World Champion.

Lassiter (2000) disputed Gobet and Simon's (1996) arguments. He pointed out that Kasparov's playing strength was reduced significantly (about 100 Elo points) when he was engaged in simultaneous chess rather than playing a single opponent. This reduction is most plausibly attributed to reduced opportunities to search for, and to evaluate, future moves.

Lassiter (2000) also discussed matches in which expert players competed against chess-playing computers. When the game must be completed in 25 minutes, computers gain about 100 Elo points (a measure of playing strength) relative to their human opponents. More strikingly, computers gain 200 or more Elo points when the game is limited to 5 minutes. According to Lassiter (p. 172), "The tendency for chess-playing computers to become relatively stronger at shorter time controls is most likely due to the fact that a human's ability to engage in search-evaluation is more hampered by increasingly higher time constraints than is a computer's."

Template theory (Gobet & Simon, 1996) states that expert chess players have a superior template-based knowledge of chess, which they can draw upon to make their next move. This contrasts with theories focusing on strategic thinking and consideration of all possible next moves (Holding & Reynolds, 1982). Gobet and Simon (1996) demonstrated template theory by studying the games of Garry Kasparov under timed conditions. The reduced time had little effect on his performance.

## Synthesis

Outstanding chess players possess various kinds of expertise. These can be subdivided into routine and adaptive expertise (Hatano & Inagaki, 1986). Routine expertise is involved when someone can solve familiar problems rapidly and efficiently. This is the kind of expertise involved when chess players make use of standard board-position knowledge. Adaptive expertise is involved when a board position is relatively unknown, and so the chess player has to develop strategies for evaluating the situation and deciding what to do next. Early research (e.g., Chase & Simon, 1973; De Groot, 1965) focused on routine expertise, whereas Holding and Reynolds (1982) emphasised the importance of evaluation and of adaptive expertise. The templates emphasised within template theory provide much of the knowledge needed to demonstrate both kinds of expertise.

## Anderson's ACT theory

Anderson (e.g., 1983, 1993, 1996) has produced a series of models deriving in part from the work of Fitts (1964), and designed to account for the development of expertise. All these models are based on a rather similar cognitive architecture known as the Adaptive Control of Thought (ACT), and so they are called ACTE, ACT*, and ACT-R. At the heart of this approach there are three interconnected systems:

1. *Declarative memory*. This consists of a semantic network of interconnected concepts.
2. *Procedural or production memory*. This consists of production rules (e.g., if someone hits you, then you hit them).
3. *Working memory*. This contains information that is currently active (see Chapter 9).

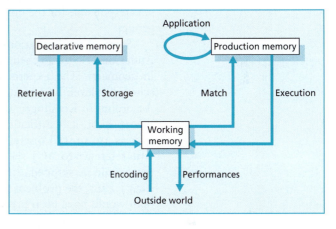

There are important differences between declarative and procedural knowledge. Declarative knowledge is stored in **chunks** or small packets of knowledge, and is consciously accessible. It can be used across a wide range of situations. For example, suppose you have acquired a considerable amount of declarative knowledge about attention. You can use this information flexibly in a seminar group, in an essay, or in an examination essay. In contrast, it is often not possible to gain conscious access to procedural knowledge, which is used automatically whenever a production rule matches the current contents of working memory. The use of procedural knowledge is tied to specific situations (e.g., we only use procedural knowledge about subtraction when given a suitable mathematical problem), which makes it less flexible.

*Try to apply this theory to your own experiences of knowledge acquisition. Can the theory account for these experiences?*

Anderson's crucial assumption is that skill acquisition typically involves knowledge compilation. What happens with **knowledge compilation** is a progressive shift from the use of declarative knowledge to that of procedural knowledge, and an increase in automaticity. This resembles progress from the cognitive and associative phases to the autonomous phase in Fitts' (1964) theory. A clear example of knowledge compilation is the development of touch-typing skills. Typing speed increases greatly with practice, with a fairly skilled typist able to make one keystroke every 60 milliseconds. The *nature* as well as the *speed* of the processes involved change with practice. As Fitts and Posner (1967) pointed out, typists initially rely on rules of which they are consciously aware (e.g., move the index finger of the left hand to the right to type the letter g). These rules are stored in what we would now call declarative memory. Eventually, typing becomes fast, accurate, and automatic, and depends only on procedural memory. For example, I have typed about four million words in my life, but find it very hard to tell anyone where any given letter is on the keyboard!

What processes are involved in knowledge compilation? First, there is **proceduralisation**, which involves the creation of specific procedural rules to reduce or eliminate the necessity to search through long-term memory during skilled performance. For example, as a result of proceduralisation, typists do not need to ask themselves where the letters are on the keyboard. Second, there is **composition**, which improves performance by reducing a repeated sequence of actions to a more efficient single sequence.

**KEY TERMS**

**Chunks:** integrated units of information.

**Knowledge compilation:** this involves a shift from the use of declarative knowledge to the use of procedural knowledge as a result of prolonged practice.

**Proceduralisation:** this involves the creation of specific condition-action rules to produce.

**Composition:** a process by which a frequently repeated sequence of actions is reduced to a more efficient single sequence.

## Evidence

Much research suggests that extended practice on most tasks leads to increased use of automatic processes (see Chapter 6). In addition, most studies reporting findings supporting Fitts's three-phase model (e.g., Zbrodoff, 1995) are consistent with the predictions of ACT theory. A different prediction seems to follow from ACT theory, according to which skilled performance depends on procedural rather than declarative knowledge. An implication is that skilled performance might be disrupted more in individuals who access declarative knowledge than in those who do not. This prediction was tested by Masters (1992) in a study discussed below.

Masters (1992) gave participants considerable practice in putting (400 putts). Some of them (explicit learning) were encouraged to acquire much declarative knowledge about putting by being asked to read detailed instructions on how to putt before starting to practise. In contrast, other participants (implicit learning) were given no special instructions. They were also asked to generate letters in a random way while practising so they would not have conscious thoughts about the skills involved in putting. Both groups were then put under pressure by being told that the money they received would depend on their performance in a final test session. As predicted, the performance of the explicit learning group was worse than it had been, whereas that of the implicit learning group improved. Presumably declarative knowledge from an earlier stage of skill acquisition was responsible for the much poorer performance of the explicit group than of the implicit group.

Some of the limitations of the ACT approach emerged in a study by Koedinger and Anderson (1990). In their study, they focused on experts given the task of solving proofs in geometry. The experts spent much of their time planning at a rather abstract or schematic level, and tended to skip the same steps on the way to solving the proofs. According to Koedinger and Anderson, these findings produce some problems for ACT theory. First, it is difficult within the theory to understand *why* the schemas formed by experts are so well organised. Second, as Koedinger and Anderson (p. 545) pointed out with reference to ACT theory, "We would not expect any regularity in the kinds of steps that would be skipped ... However, such a regularity is exactly what we observed of subjects." Thus, the problem solving of the experts was more systematic and better organised than would have been predicted by ACT theory.

## Evaluation

⊕ Anderson's ACT approach has been applied to several kinds of skill acquisition, including the learning of geometry, computer text-editing, and computer programming (see Eysenck & Keane, 2000).

⊕ The development of expertise often involves a progressive shift from use of declarative knowledge to use of procedural knowledge.

⊖ The ACT approach is most applicable to the development of routine expertise requiring unvarying procedures (e.g., touch-typing), and is less relevant when *flexibility* of approach is important. Thus, the model has little to say about expertise that is creative and/or adaptive (e.g., constructing scientific theories).

⊖ The problem solving of experts is sometimes more systematic and organised than predicted by the theory.

⊖ The notion that we use production rules may be no more than a convenient fiction. As Copeland (1993, p. 101) argued, "My actions [when making an omelette] can be described by means of if–then sentences: if the mixture sticks then I flick the pan, and so on. But it doesn't follow from this that my actions are produced by some device in my brain scanning through lists of if–then rules of this sort."

⊖ Explicit or declarative learning may not always occur before implicit or procedural learning (Willingham & Goedert-Eschmann, 1999, discussed in the earlier section on implicit learning).

# Ericsson: Deliberate practice

Nearly everyone would accept that prolonged and carefully structured practice plays an essential role in the development of expertise. However, Ericsson (e.g., 1996) went further. He claimed that practice of the right sort is not only necessary but also sufficient for expertise to develop. He emphasised the importance of **deliberate practice**, which has four aspects:

1. The task is at an appropriate level of difficulty (not too easy or too hard).
2. The learner is provided with informative feedback about his/her performance.
3. The learner has sufficient opportunities for repetition.
4. It is possible for the learner to correct his/her errors.

What is controversial about Ericsson's position is the notion that innate talent or ability has almost *no* influence on expert performance. According to Ericsson, Krampe, and Tesch-Romer (1993) it is only for height that innate characteristics have convincingly been shown to matter: Being tall is an advantage for some sports (e.g., basketball) and a disadvantage for others (e.g., gymnastics).

## *Evidence*

Deliberate practice has been shown to be of crucial importance in the development of expertise. Ericsson et al. (1993) reported a study on violinists in a German music academy. The key difference between 18-year-old students having varying levels of expertise on the violin was the amount of deliberate practice they had had over the years. The most expert violinists had spent on average nearly 7500 hours engaged in deliberate practice, compared to the 5300 hours clocked up by the good violinists.

What we have in the above study is essentially a correlation or association between amount of deliberate practice and level of performance. One possible interpretation of that correlation is that those musicians with the greatest innate talent and/or musical success decide to spend more time practising than do those with less talent or previous success. Evidence tending to go against that interpretation was reported by Sloboda, Davidson, Howe, and Moore (1996). They compared highly successful young musicians with less successful ones. The two groups did not differ in terms of the amount of practice time they required to achieve a given level of performance, suggesting the advantage possessed by the very successful musicians was not due to their greater level of natural musical ability.

Evidence from a very different task that deliberate practice can have massive effects was reported by Ericsson and Chase (1982). SF was a young man, who was a student at Carnegie-Mellon University in the United States. He was given extensive practice on the digit-span task, on which random digits have to be recalled immediately in the correct order. Initially, his digit span was about seven digits, which is an average level of performance. He was then paid to practise the digit-span task for 1 hour a day for 2 years. At the end of that time, he reached a digit span of 80 digits. This is very impressive, because hardly anyone in the normal population has a digit span or more than about 10 or 11 items. The beneficial effects of practice were very limited, because his letter and word spans at the end of the study were no greater than those of most other people.

How did SF do it? He reached a digit span of about 18 items by using his extensive knowledge of running times. For example, if the first few digits presented were "3594", he would note that this was Banister's world-record time for the mile, and so those four digits would be stored as a single unit or chunk. He then increased his digit span by organising these chunks into a hierarchical structure.

What about the notion that talent plays little or no role in the development of expertise? Howe (1999) considered biographical information about great writers such as H.G. Wells and John Stuart Mill. Nearly all of them took many years to acquire expert writing skills, and their early attempts at writing were often poor. Howe concluded that deliberate practice rather than innate talent was responsible for the success of these writers.

Hulin, Henry, and Noon (1990) considered the relationship between IQ and performance. The key findings were as follows: (1) the correlation between IQ and performance decreased steadily over time, and (2) the correlation was only slightly greater than zero among individuals with more than 5 years of professional experience. Thus, innate talent in the form of intelligence was relatively unimportant at high levels of expertise.

*Do you think that anyone can become an expert at a task if they practise enough, or do you think they must first possess an innate talent?*

> **KEY TERM**
>
> **Deliberate practice:** this is practice in which the learner is provided with informative feedback and has the opportunity to correct his/her errors.

Relatively few studies have assessed both the amount of deliberate practice *and* innate talent or genetically determined ability. One such study was reported by Horgan and Morgan (1990), who focused on the progress made by elite child chess players. Improvement in chess-playing performance was determined mainly by deliberate practice, motivation, and the degree of parental support. However, individual differences in non-verbal intelligence were of some importance as well, accounting for 12% of the variation in performance.

## Evaluation

⊕ Deliberate practice is necessary for the achievement of an outstanding level of expertise.
⊕ There is some support for the notion that deliberate practice may be sufficient for the development of expertise.
⊖ Innate talent (at least as assessed by IQ) predicts long-term career success in many occupations (see Chapter 12).
⊖ As Sternberg and Ben-Zeev (2001, p. 302) pointed out, the notion that innate talent is unimportant seems implausible: "Is one to believe that anyone could become a Mozart if only he or she put in the time? ... Or that becoming an Einstein is just a matter of deliberate practice?"
⊖ Perhaps it is mainly those individuals possessing high levels of talent who are willing to put in thousands of hours of deliberate practice. If that is the case, then the amount of deliberate practice reflects talent as well as practice itself. This would make it very hard to interpret most of the evidence.
⊖ If nearly all experts in a given field have enormous talent, then it is not surprising that individual differences in talent do not predict levels of expertise. This resembles the situation in professional basketball, in which virtually all players are so tall that height does not predict performance (Detterman, Gabriel, and Ruthsatz, 1998).
⊖ Much more remains to be discovered about the precise ways in which deliberate practice translates into expert performance. It is probable that the processes involved vary as a function of the task or domain in which the expertise is developed.

## SUMMARY

*Classical conditioning*

Classical conditioning involves the formation of an association between a conditioned stimulus and an unconditioned stimulus. The phenomena of classical conditioning include discrimination, generalisation, experimental extinction, and spontaneous recovery. According to the Rescorla–Wagner model, associative learning between a conditioned stimulus and an unconditioned stimulus occurs when the conditioned stimulus predicts the arrival of the unconditioned stimulus. The model explains phenomena such as blocking and the unconditioned stimulus pre-exposure effect, but does not distinguish adequately between learning and performance. As a result of evolution, it is much easier to produce classical conditioning with some pairings of conditioned stimulus and unconditioned stimulus than with others. Classical conditioning is usually accompanied by conscious awareness of the relationship between the conditioned stimulus and the unconditioned stimulus, but this does not seem necessary for conditioning to occur.

*Operant conditioning*

The most important assumption of operant conditioning is that the probability of a given response occurring is increased when it is followed by reward. Partial reinforcement typically leads to more conditioning than does continuous reinforcement. Positive punishment (aversive stimulus follows response) and negative punishment (reward removal follows response) both reduce the likelihood of the punished response being produced in future. Avoidance learning occurs when someone learns to produce a response that avoids the presentation of an aversive stimulus. Learned helplessness refers to passive behaviour in a situation in which unpleasant stimuli could be escaped or avoided by appropriate action. During operant conditioning, the participants acquire knowledge that the production of a given response in a given situation will have a specific effect. The operant conditioning approach exaggerates the importance of behaviour and of environmental factors in learning. Skinner mistakenly believed in equipotentiality. Operant conditioning often influences performance more than learning. Associative learning is of relevance to humans, but people also make much use of rules and hypotheses.

*Observational learning*

According to Bandura, much human learning is based on observing the behaviour of some other person or model. Such observational learning is typically more efficient than learning based on actually experiencing a given situation. According to Bandura, observational learning leads to imitation when the model is rewarded, but not when the model is punished. In fact, complex cognitive processes can also determine whether imitation occurs. Observational learning can produce as much learning of a task as occurs through physical practice, and seems to involve similar cognitive processes. Observational learning is limited in scope. For example, it does not account for most language learning by children.

*Implicit learning*

It has been claimed that implicit learning differs from explicit learning in the following ways: greater robustness, smaller influence of age, smaller individual differences, less affected by IQ, and more common processes across species. Several complex tasks (e.g., artificial grammar learning) have provided evidence of implicit learning, as have studies showing that amnesic patients have intact implicit learning but impaired explicit learning. In order to demonstrate implicit learning, we need to show that participants do not have conscious access to relevant information. However, it is hard to ensure that tests of awareness assess all the task-relevant knowledge possessed by participants. It has been argued that skill acquisition often proceeds from explicit learning to implicit learning, but some evidence suggests that explicit and implicit learning occur together.

*Skill acquisition and expertise*

It has often been assumed that perceptual-motor skills are more primitive and narrow than cognitive skills, and that we have more conscious access to knowledge about cognitive skills than perceptual-motor ones. The differences between these two types of skills are actually less clear-cut than has been assumed, and it is possible that most or all skills are performatory in nature. Fitts (1964) claimed that skill acqustion proceeds through successive cognitive, associative, and autonomous phases, but the reality is less neat and tidy. Chess expertise depends in part on stored knowledge of chess positions, possibly in the form of templates. It also depends on search and evaluation processes. According to Anderson's ACT theory, the development of expertise involves reduced reliance on consciously accessible knowledge and increased reliance on less accessible procedural knowledge. This theory is more applicable to the development of routine expertise than to creative and/or adaptive expertise. Deliberate practice is necessary for the achievement of outstanding expertise, but it is probably generally not sufficient.

## FURTHER READING

- Bandura, A. (1999). Social cognitive theory of personality. In L.A. Pervin & O.P. John (Eds.), *Handbook of personality: Theory and research* (2nd ed.). New York: Guilford Press. This chapter provides a thorough and up-to-date account of Bandura's theoretical ideas.
- Eysenck, M.W. (2001). *Principles of cognitive psychology* (2nd ed.). Hove, UK: Psychology Press. There is introductory coverage of implicit learning and expertise in this textbook.
- Gray, P. (2002). *Psychology* (4th ed.). New York: Worth. There are very clear accounts of classical and operant conditioning in Chapter 4 of this textbook.
- Robertson, S.I. (2001). *Problem solving*. Hove, UK: Psychology Press. Chapters 8 and 9 of this book contain good coverage of theory and research on expertise.
- Sternberg, R.J., & Ben-Zeev, T. (2001). *Complex cognition: The psychology of human thought*. Oxford, UK: Oxford University Press. Several chapters in this book (especially Chapter 13) provide up-to-date coverage of complex learning.

- **Multi-store model**
  The structure of the memory system.

  *Modality-specific sensory stores*
  *Limited capacity of the short-term store, leading to forgetting*
  *Long-term memory*
  *Evidence for and against separate memory stores*

- **Working memory**
  The role of conscious awareness in thinking and problem solving.

  *The role of the phonological loop in learning new words*
  *The idea of the visuo-spatial sketchpad as working memory storage*
  *The function of the central executive as an attentional system*

- **Levels of processing**
  Craik and Lockhart's theoretical approach to the processes of learning.

  *The importance of depths of processing and analysis*
  *The importance of elaboration and distinctiveness*
  *Morris et al.'s transfer-appropriate processing theory*
  *Explicit and implicit memory*
  *Recent theoretical updates*

- **Theories of forgetting**
  Research into the deterioration of memories over time.

  *Freud and repression*
  *Proactive and retroactive interference in stimuli–response process*
  *Cue-dependent forgetting*

- **Theories of long-term memory**
  Theoretical approaches to the complexity of long-term memory systems.

  *Tulving's distinction between episodic and semantic memory*
  *The interconnections and separateness of perceptual and procedural memory systems*

- **Amnesia**
  Research into those with problematic long-term memory.

  *Anterograde and retrograde amnesia*
  *The importance of residual memories: short-term memory, skill learning, repetition priming, and conditioning*
  *Theories of amnesia*

- **Schema theories**
  Information is packaged in schemas, allowing us to form expectations.

  *Bartlett's schema theory*
  *Schank and Abelson's script-pointer-plus-tag hypothesis*

- **Everyday memory**
  The difficulties of studying memory in the real world.

  *Flashbulb memories*
  *Eyewitness testimony*
  *Autobiographical memory*

# Human memory

How important is memory? Imagine if we were without it. We would not recognise anyone or anything as familiar. We would be unable to talk, read, or write, because we would remember nothing about language. We would have extremely limited personalities, because we would have no recollection of the events of our own lives and, therefore, no sense of self. In sum, we would have the same lack of knowledge as newborn babies.

We use memory for numerous purposes. It allows us to keep track of conversations, to remember telephone numbers while we dial them, to write essays in examinations, to make sense of what we read, and to recognise people's faces. The richness of memory suggests that we have several memory systems. This chapter explores in detail some of the proposed subdivisions of human memory.

There are close links between learning and memory (see Chapter 8). The existence of memory depends on previous learning, and learning can most clearly be demonstrated by good performance on a memory test. Learning and memory involve three stages:

1. *Encoding*, which involves the processes occurring during presentation of the learning material.
2. *Storage*, in which, as a result of encoding, some information is stored within the memory system.
3. *Retrieval*, which involves recovering or extracting stored information from the memory system.

Those interested in learning focus on encoding and storage, whereas those interested in memory concentrate on retrieval. However, all these processes depend on each other.

There is an important distinction between *structure* and *processes*. Structure refers to the organisation of the memory system, whereas processes are the activities taking place within the memory system. Structure and processes are both important. However, theorists differ in the emphasis they put on these two aspects of the memory system.

The main focus in the first half of the chapter is on short-term memory. After that, the emphasis shifts to a detailed consideration of long-term memory.

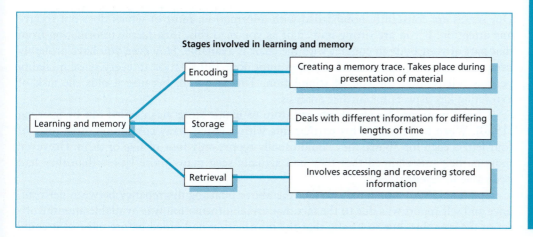

**Stages involved in learning and memory**

Encoding — Creating a memory trace. Takes place during presentation of material

Learning and memory — Storage — Deals with different information for differing lengths of time

Retrieval — Involves accessing and recovering stored information

As with storage of books in a library, information is stored in an organised way in the memory system. Imagine how difficult it would be to find a book if the library organised them by colour or size!

# MULTI-STORE MODEL

Several memory theorists (e.g., Atkinson & Shiffrin, 1968) have described the basic architecture of the memory system. We can identify a multi-store model on the basis of the common features of their approaches. Three types of memory store were proposed:

- *Sensory stores*, each of which holds information very briefly and is modality specific (limited to one sensory modality).
- *Short-term store* of very limited capacity.
- *Long-term store* of essentially unlimited capacity, which can hold information over extremely long periods of time.

Environmental information is initially received by the sensory stores. These stores are modality specific (e.g., vision, hearing). Information is held very briefly in the sensory stores, with some being attended to and processed further by the short-term store. Some information processed in the short-term store is transferred to the long-term store. Long-term storage of information often depends on rehearsal (according to Atkinson and Shiffrin), with a direct relationship between the amount of rehearsal in the short-term store and the strength of the stored memory trace.

The distinction between short-term and long-term memory has a long history. For example, William James (1890) emphasised the importance of the distinction. More improbably, Sigmund Freud did the same. He drew an analogy between memory and a children's toy known as a Magic Marker. The child writes on a pad, pulls it out and pushes it back. What was written can no longer be seen, but there is a permanent record on the carbon paper underneath. According to Freud, the fragile top copy corresponds to short-term memory, whereas the permanent underlying record corresponds to long-term memory.

There is much overlap between the areas of attention and memory. Broadbent's (1958) theory of attention (see Chapter 6) was an important influence on the multi-store approach to memory. For example, there is a clear resemblance between the notion of a sensory store and his "buffer" store, and both theories emphasise the severe limitations on processing capacity.

Within the multi-store approach, the memory stores form the basic structure, and processes such as attention and rehearsal control the flow of information between them. However, the main emphasis within this approach was on structure.

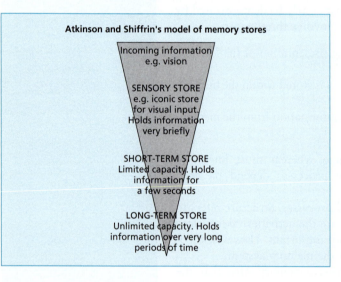

**Atkinson and Shiffrin's model of memory stores**

Incoming information e.g. vision

SENSORY STORE e.g. iconic store for visual input. Holds information very briefly

SHORT-TERM STORE Limited capacity. Holds information for a few seconds

LONG-TERM STORE Unlimited capacity. Holds information over very long periods of time

## Sensory stores

Our senses are constantly bombarded with information, most of which does not receive any attention. If you are sitting in a chair as you read this, then tactile information from that part of your body in contact with the chair is available. However, you have probably been unaware of that tactile information until now. Information in every sense modality persists briefly after the end of stimulation. This is useful, because it aids the task of extracting key aspects for further analysis.

Classic work on the visual sensory store or **iconic store** was carried out by Sperling (1960). When he presented his participants with a visual array containing three rows of four letters each for 50 ms, they could usually report only four or five of them. However, most participants claimed that they had actually seen many more letters than they had been able to report.

Sperling (1960) wondered whether the above puzzling discrepancy between performance and self-report was due to the fact that visual information was available after the offset of the stimulus, but so briefly that the information had faded before most of it could be reported. He explored this hypothesis by asking participants to report only one-third of the presented information, using a cueing tone to signal which row was to be reported. The tone was presented either 0.1 s before the onset of the visual display (which lasted 50 ms) or at intervals of up to 1 s after stimulus offset. Since the three rows were tested at random, Sperling could estimate the total amount of information available to each participant by multiplying the number of items recalled by three. When the tone was presented immediately before or after the onset of the display, about nine letters seemed to be available, but this dropped to six letters when the tone was heard 0.3 s after the presentation of the display, and it fell to only four and a half letters with an interval of 1 s. Thus, there is a form of visual storage which fades rapidly (within about 0.5 s according to most estimates).

Sperling (1960) argued that information in iconic storage is held in a relatively raw and uninterpreted form. However, Butler (1974) found that participants do better when the letters in non-cued rows resemble English words than when they do not, suggesting that iconic information is not necessarily unanalysed. In similar fashion, the Canadian researcher Merikle (1980) found that category cues were as effective as location cues in enhancing recall from iconic storage, indicating that categorical information is available in iconic storage.

How useful is iconic storage? Haber (1983) claimed it is irrelevant to normal perception, except when trying to read in a lightning storm! His argument was that the icon formed from one visual fixation is rapidly masked by the next fixation. Haber was mistaken. He assumed that the icon is created at the *offset* of a visual stimulus, but it is actually created at its *onset* (Coltheart, 1983). Thus, even with a continuously changing visual world, iconic information can still be used. The mechanisms responsible for visual perception always operate on the icon rather than directly on the visual environment.

The sensory store in the auditory modality is known as the **echoic store**. The echoic store is a transient store holding relatively unprocessed input. For example, suppose someone reading a newspaper is asked a question. The person addressed will sometimes ask, "What did you say?", but then realise that he/she does know what has been said. This "playback" facility depends on the echoic store.

Treisman (1964) asked people to shadow (repeat back aloud) the message presented to one ear while ignoring a second message presented to the other ear. They were not told that the two messages were identical. When the second or non-shadowed message preceded the shadowed message, the two messages were only recognised as the same when within 2 seconds of each other. This suggests the temporal duration of unattended auditory information in echoic storage is about 2 seconds. However, Darwin, Turvey, and Crowder (1972) obtained evidence that some information remains within the echoic store for at least 4 seconds.

## Short- and long-term stores

Trying to remember a telephone number for a few seconds is an everyday example of the use of the **short-term store**. It shows two key characteristics of this store:

- Very limited capacity (only about seven digits can be remembered).
- Fragility of storage, as any distraction usually causes forgetting.

The capacity of short-term memory has been assessed by span measures and by the recency effect in free recall. Digit span is a span measure, in which participants repeat back a series of random digits in the correct order after hearing them. The span of immediate memory is usually "seven plus or minus two" whether the units are numbers, letters, or words (Miller, 1956). Miller claimed that about seven chunks (integrated pieces or units of information) could be held in short-term memory. For example, "IBM" is one chunk for those familiar with the company name International Business Machines, but three chunks for everyone else. However, the span in chunks is less with larger chunks (e.g., eight-word phrases) than with smaller chunks (e.g., one-syllable words; Simon, 1974).

The **recency effect** in **free recall** (recalling the items in any order) refers to the finding that the last few items in a list are usually much better remembered in immediate recall

**KEY TERMS**

**Echoic store:** a sensory store in the auditory modality that can hold information for about 2 seconds.

**Short-term store:** a memory store of very limited capacity that holds information for a few seconds.

**Recency effect:** the finding that recall is much higher for the last few list items in immediate free recall than for other items.

**Free recall:** a form of memory test in which the participants retrieve the to-be-remembered items in any order.

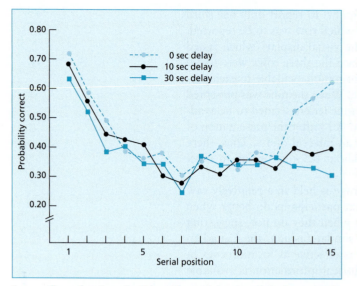

Free recall as a function of serial position and duration of the interpolated task. Adapted from Glanzer and Cunitz (1966).

than are the items from the middle of the list. Counting backwards for only 10 seconds between the end of list presentation and the start of recall mainly affects the recency effect (Glanzer & Cunitz, 1966). The two or three words (sometimes more) forming the recency effect may be in the short-term store at the end of list presentation, and thus especially vulnerable to forgetting. However, Bjork and Whitten (1974) found there was still a recency effect in free recall when the participants counted backwards for 12 seconds after each item in the list was presented. According to Atkinson and Shiffrin (1968), this should have eliminated the recency effect.

How can we understand the two types of recency effect discussed above? According to Glenberg (1987), it is useful to compare the recency effect to what happens when we look along a row of telephone poles. The closer poles are more distinct than the ones further away, just as the more recent list words are more discriminable than the others (Glenberg, 1987). This enhanced discriminability presumably makes the last items easier to identify and to recall than those in the middle of the list.

Recall was better for the first few items than for those in the middle of the list. This is known as the **primacy effect**. According to Atkinson and Shiffrin (1968), rehearsal plays a key role in determining long-term memory, and so the primacy effect could be explained by assuming that the first few list items receive more rehearsal than do later ones. Evidence for this was obtained by Rundus and Atkinson (1970). Their overt rehearsal technique allowed the participants to rehearse any of the list items, but required them to rehearse aloud. They obtained the usual primacy effect in free recall, and also found that the first few items received a disproportionately large amount of rehearsal. This suggests that the primacy effect is due to extra rehearsal. However, other factors are also involved. When the amount of rehearsal given to each list item was the same, the primacy effect was reduced but not eliminated (Fischler, Rundus, & Atkinson, 1970).

*Do you think there would be a difference in recall between consonants presented at the beginning of the list and those presented at the end (i.e., primacy–recency effect)?*

## Forgetting

How is information forgotten or lost from short-term memory? One possibility is that forgetting is due to *displacement*. If we think of the short-term store as resembling a box of limited capacity, then it could be argued that new items can only be entered into the box by displacing or removing items currently in it. This approach assumes we have very limited short-term memory capacity because of structural limitations. In fact, however, short-term memory capacity is probably limited because of processing limitations, especially attentional ones.

Peterson and Peterson (1959) carried out a classic study on forgetting from short-term memory. Three consonants (e.g., F B M) were presented, followed immediately by a three-digit number. The participants' task was to count backwards by threes from the number until the signal was given to recall the consonants. Consonant recall was almost 100% with no retention interval, but fell to only 10–20% with a retention interval of 18 seconds. These findings can be explained by assuming that counting backwards prevented rehearsal of the consonants, with information about the consonants decaying rapidly as a result.

There are reasons for doubting that forgetting from short-term memory depends mainly on decay. For example, Keppel and Underwood (1962) used the same task as

> **KEY TERM**
>
> **Primacy effect:** the finding that free recall for the first few items in a word list is better than for items in the middle of the list.

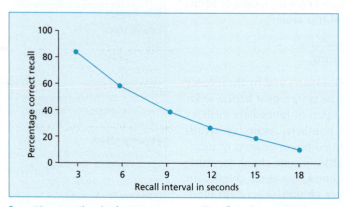

Forgetting over time in short-term memory. Data from Peterson and Peterson (1959).

Peterson and Peterson (1959). There was *no* forgetting over time on the very first trial, but thereafter forgetting resembled that observed by Peterson and Peterson. The most plausible explanation for these findings is that only the items presented on the first trial avoided proactive interference (the disruption of current learning and memory by previous learning; see later in chapter).

Nairne, Whiteman, and Kelley (1999) found that rapid decay of information is *not* inevitable in the absence of rehearsal. They presented their participants with five-item word lists, and took two steps to reduce the forgetting rate. First, memory was tested *only* for order information and not for the words themselves. This was done by re-presenting the five words at test, and asking participants to arrange them in the correct order. Second, the words on each trial differed in order to reduce proactive interference. There was a rehearsal-prevention task during the retention interval (reading aloud digits presented on a screen). There was remarkably little forgetting even over 96 seconds. Thus, rapid decay of information is not inevitable provided there is little proactive interference and the memory task is relatively simple.

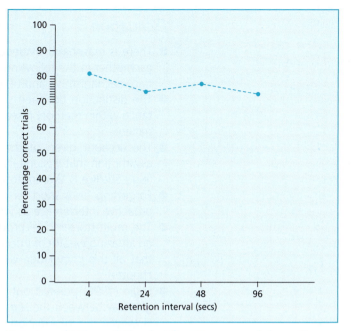

Percentage of trials on which order information was recalled correctly as a function of retention interval. Data from Nairne et al. (1999).

## Long-term memory

During the 1960s, rehearsal was regarded as the main way in which information enters long-term memory. In contrast to the short-term memory store, the capacity of the long-term memory store is essentially infinite. Most information stored in the long-term memory store remains there. However, it may become inaccessible over time because of interference from other information that has been learned.

## Separate stores

How do we know that there are separate short-term and long-term memory stores? Convincing evidence comes from studies of brain-damaged patients. The logic is as follows. Suppose there are separate short-term and long-term memory stores in somewhat different areas of the brain. We might then expect to find some brain-damaged patients with damage to brain areas involved in short-term memory but not long-term memory, and vice versa. Thus, there might be some patients with good short-term memory but poor long-term memory, and others with good long-term memory but poor short-term memory. This pattern is known as a **double dissociation**, and it has been found. Amnesic patients have fairly intact short-term memory but impaired long-term memory (see later in the chapter). The reverse problem is rare, but some cases have been reported. For example, KF had no problem with long-term learning and recall. However, his digit span was greatly impaired, and he had a recency effect of only one item under some circumstances (Shallice & Warrington, 1970).

Findings *not* fitting the multi-store model were reported by Shallice and Warrington (1974). They found that KF's short-term memory deficit was limited to verbal materials such as letters, words, and digits, and did not extend to other meaningful sounds (e.g., telephones ringing). Thus, only part of short-term memory was impaired.

There is another problem for the multi-store model, according to which information in long-term memory has previously been processed in the short-term store (look back at the figure on p. 292). That means that damage to the short-term store should have negative effects on long-term memory. However, as we have just seen, such negative effects are sometimes not found.

*Why do Shallice and Warrington's findings relating to KF not fit the multi-store model?*

### KEY TERM

**Double dissociation:** the finding that some individuals (often brain damaged) perform well on task A and poorly on task B, whereas others show the opposite pattern.

## Evaluation

⊕ There is reasonable evidence for three different types of memory store, differing from each other in the following ways: (1) temporal duration, (2) storage capacity, (3) forgetting mechanism(s), and (4) effects of brain damage.

⊕ The distinction between short-term and long-term memory remains of central importance within memory research, and is strongly supported by research on brain-damaged patients.

⊖ The account given of the short-term store is very over-simplified. For example, the assumption that it is unitary (and so always operates in a single, uniform way) is incorrect (e.g., Shallice & Warrington, 1974).

⊖ Forgetting from short-term memory is still not well understood, but seems to involve proactive interference as well as decay.

⊖ The multi-store model provides an over-simplified view of long-term memory. There is an amazing wealth of information stored in long-term memory, and it is simply incorrect that all this knowledge is stored within a single long-term memory store (see later in chapter).

⊖ Logie (1999) pointed out that the model assumes that the short-term store acts as a gateway between the sensory stores and long-term memory (see the figure on p. 292). However, the information processed in the short-term store has already made contact with information stored in long-term memory. For example, our ability to engage in verbal rehearsal of visually presented words depends on prior contact with stored information about pronunciation. Thus, access to long-term memory occurs *before* information is processed in short-term memory.

⊖ The role of rehearsal in enhancing long-term memory was exaggerated by multi-store theorists. Rehearsal often has surprisingly small effects on long-term memory (e.g., Glenberg, Smith, & Green, 1977; see later in the chapter).

## WORKING MEMORY

The concept of the short-term store within the multi-store model is very limited, in spite of the fact that it has often been assumed that the short-term store consists of "the contents of consciousness". We can see some of the limitations by considering what can be found in our own conscious awareness. It is certainly true that the rehearsal of words can occur in consciousness, as predicted within the multi-store model. However, conscious awareness can also involve visual or spatial information (e.g., when we think about a famous film star). Thus, the range of information we can consider in conscious awareness is greater than is implied within the multi-store memory.

There is another major limitation associated with the concept of the short-term store. Conscious awareness seems to be important when we are thinking or trying to solve a problem. In contrast, it is assumed within the multi-store theory that the short-term memory store is only of relevance to memory.

Baddeley (1986) and Baddeley and Hitch (1974) were aware of the above limitations with the concept of the short-term store. Accordingly, they argued that it should be replaced with the much broader notion of working memory, with the working memory system consisting of three components:

1. **Central executive.** A modality-free component of limited capacity resembling attention.
2. **Phonological loop.** This holds information briefly in a phonological (i.e., speech-based) form.
3. **Visuo-spatial sketchpad.** This is specialised for spatial and/or visual coding.

The most important component is the central executive. It has limited capacity, and is used when dealing with most cognitive tasks. The phonological loop and the visuo-spatial

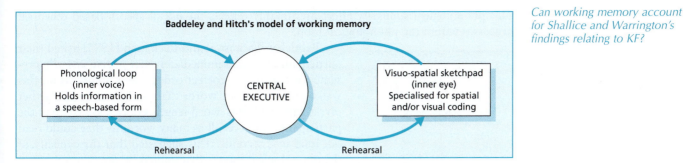

**Baddeley and Hitch's model of working memory**

Phonological loop (inner voice) Holds information in a speech-based form

CENTRAL EXECUTIVE

Visuo-spatial sketchpad (inner eye) Specialised for spatial and/or visual coding

Rehearsal                    Rehearsal

*Can working memory account for Shallice and Warrington's findings relating to KF?*

sketchpad are slave systems used by the central executive for specific purposes. The phonological loop preserves the order in which words are presented, and the visuo-spatial sketchpad stores and manipulates spatial and visual information.

The working memory model can be used to predict whether or not two tasks can be performed successfully at the same time. Each component of the working memory system has limited capacity, and is relatively independent of the other components. Two predictions follow:

1. If two tasks make use of the same component, they cannot be performed successfully together.
2. If two tasks make use of different components, it should be possible to perform them as well together as separately.

*Think of real-life examples of tasks making use of the same or different components of working memory. How well can you perform them together?*

Numerous dual-task studies have been carried out on the basis of these assumptions (see also Chapter 6). For example, Robbins, Anderson, Barker, Bradley, Fearnyhough, Henson et al. (1996) considered the involvement of the three components of working memory in the selection of chess moves by weaker and stronger players. The main task was to select continuation moves from various chess positions while performing one of the following concurrent tasks:

- Repetitive tapping: this was the control condition.
- Random number generation: this involved the central executive.
- Pressing keys on a keypad in a clockwise fashion: this used the visuo-spatial sketchpad.
- Rapid repetition of the word "see-saw": this used the phonological loop.

Random number generation and pressing keys in a clockwise fashion both reduced the quality of the chess moves selected. Thus, selecting chess moves involves the central executive and the visuo-spatial sketchpad. However, rapid word repetition did *not* affect the quality of chess moves, and so the phonological loop is not involved in selecting chess moves. The effects of the various concurrent tasks were similar on stronger and weaker players, suggesting that both groups use the working memory system in the same way.

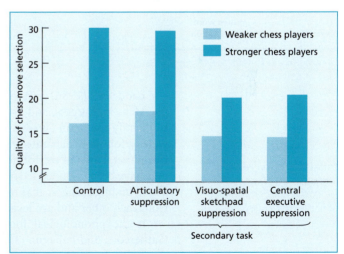

Effects of secondary tasks on quality of chess-move selection in stronger and weaker players. Adapted from Robbins et al. (1996).

# Phonological loop

Reasonable evidence that we use the phonological loop on short-term memory tasks comes from the **phonological similarity effect**, in which serial recall of a short list of *visually* presented words is worse when the words are phonologically similar than when they are phonologically dissimilar. For example, FEE, HE, KNEE, LEE, ME, SHE form a list of phonologically similar words, whereas BAY, HOE, IT, ODD, SHY, and UP form a list of phonologically dissimilar words. Larsen, Baddeley, and Andrade (2000) used those lists, and found that serial recall was 25% worse with the phonologically similar list.

This phonological similarity effect presumably reflects the use of speech-based rehearsal processes within the phonological loop.

Baddeley, Thomson, and Buchanan (1975) asked their participants to recall immediately sets of five *visually* presented words in the correct order. Their ability to do this was better with short words than with long ones. Further investigation of this **word-length effect** showed that the participants could recall as many words as they could read out loud in 2 seconds. This suggested that the capacity of the phonological loop is determined by time duration.

The phonological loop is more complex than assumed by Baddeley and Hitch (1974). For example, although Baddeley et al. (1975) found that articulatory suppression eliminated the word-length effect with *visual* presentation, it did not do so with *auditory* presentation. Baddeley (1986, 1990) developed his theory by drawing a distinction between a phonological or speech-based store and an articulatory control process. According to Baddeley, the phonological loop consists of:

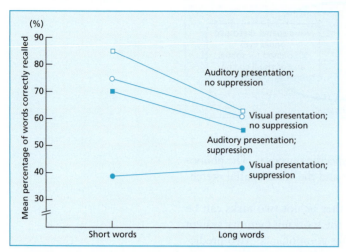

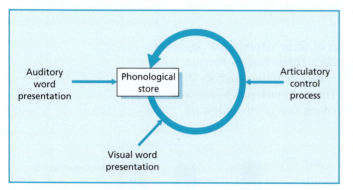

Immediate word recall as a function of modality of presentation (visual vs. auditory), presence versus absence of articulatory suppression, and word length. Adapted from Baddeley et al. (1975).

- A passive phonological store directly concerned with speech perception.
- An articulatory process linked to speech production that gives access to the phonological store.

According to this revised account, words presented auditorily are processed differently from those presented visually. Auditory presentation of words produces *direct* access to the phonological store regardless of whether the articulatory control process is used. As a result, the word-length effect remains even with articulatory suppression (see figure above). In contrast, visual presentation of words only permits *indirect* access to the phonological store through subvocal articulation. Articulatory suppression eliminates the word-length effect here because access to the phonological store is prevented (see figure above).

Phonological loop system as envisaged by Baddeley (1990).

Baddeley's (1986) revised account is also supported by neuroimaging studies. For example, Henson, Burgess, and Frith (2000) used fMRI (functional magnetic resonance imaging) to identify the brain areas associated with use of the phonological loop. Their key findings were as follows: "Separate areas were implicated in storage and rehearsal, namely a left inferior parietal area in the former and left prefrontal areas in the latter" (p. 439). Similar findings have been obtained in studies on brain-damaged patients (see Eysenck & Keane, 2000). These findings suggest that the phonological store and the articulatory process are separate from each other and are located in different parts of the brain.

*Both storage and retrieval of language information make use of the* left *hemisphere. Why might this be?*

Is the phonological loop of much use in everyday life? According to Baddeley, Gathercole, and Papagno (1998, p. 158), "the function of the phonological loop is not to remember familiar words but to learn new words". Evidence supporting the above viewpoint was reported by Papagno, Valentine, and Baddeley (1991). Native Italian speakers learned pairs of Italian words and pairs of Italian-Russian words. Articulatory suppression (which reduces use of the phonological loop) greatly slowed the learning of foreign vocabulary, but had little effect on the learning of pairs of Italian words.

## Visuo-spatial sketchpad

The visuo-spatial sketchpad is used in the temporary storage and manipulation of spatial and visual information. As such, it is very useful in everyday life, as was emphasised by Baddeley (1997, p. 82): "The spatial system is important for geographical orientation, and for planning spatial tasks. Indeed, tasks involving visuo-spatial manipulation ...

**KEY TERM**

**Word-length effect:** the finding that word span is greater for short words than for long words.

have tended to be used as selection tools for professions ... such as engineering and architecture."

The most developed ideas about the visuo-spatial sketchpad were proposed by Logie (1995). He argued that visuo-spatial working memory can be subdivided into *two* components:

- The **visual cache**, which stores information about visual form and colour.
- The **inner scribe**, which deals with spatial and movement information. It rehearses information in the visual cache and transfers information from the visual cache to the central executive.

## Evidence

Support for the notion that there is a visuo-spatial sketchpad separate from the phonological loop was reported by Quinn and McConnell (1996a). They told their participants to learn a list of words using either visual imagery or rote rehearsal. This learning task was performed either on its own or in the presence of dynamic visual noise (a meaningless display of dots that changed randomly) or irrelevant speech in a foreign language. It was assumed that dynamic visual noise would gain access to the visuo-spatial sketchpad, whereas irrelevant speech would gain access to the phonological loop.

The findings were clear: "Words processed under mnemonic (imagery) instructions are not affected by the presence of a concurrent verbal task but are affected by the presence of a concurrent visual task. With rote instructions, the interference pattern is reversed" (Quinn & McConnell, 1996a, p. 213). Thus, imaginal processing used the visuo-spatial sketchpad, whereas rote rehearsal used the phonological loop.

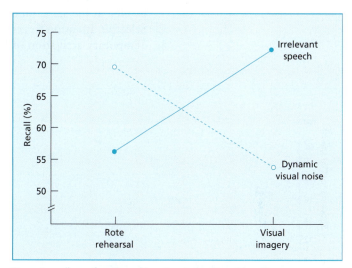

Percent recall as a function of learning instructions (visual imagery vs. rote rehearsal) and of interference (dynamic visual noise or irrelevant speech). Data from Quinn and McConnell (1996a).

Is there is a *single* visuo-spatial sketchpad or are there *separate* visual and spatial systems? Evidence suggesting there are separate systems was reported by Smith and Jonides (1997). Two visual stimuli were presented together, followed by a probe stimulus. The participants had to decide either whether the probe was in the same location as one of the initial stimuli (spatial task) or had the same form (visual task). The stimuli were identical in the two tasks, but there were clear differences in brain activity as revealed by PET (positron emission tomography). Regions in the right hemisphere (prefrontal cortex, premotor cortex, occipital cortex, and parietal cortex) became active during the spatial task. In contrast, the visual task produced activation in the left hemisphere, especially the parietal cortex and the inferotemporal cortex. However, it is likely that the visual and spatial systems are closely linked.

Quinn and McConnell (1996b) obtained evidence consistent with Logie's (1995) division of visuo-spatial working memory into a visual cache and an inner scribe. Their participants learned word lists in two different ways: (1) the method of loci with each word being associated with a different familiar location; and (2) the pegword technique, in which each word was associated to easily memorised items or pegs based on the rhyme, "one is a bun, two is a shoe, three is a tree, four is a door, ...". Mental images were formed by associating the first list word with a bun, the second word with a shoe, and so on.

It was assumed that the method of loci mainly requires visual processing, whereas the pegword technique requires both visual *and* spatial processing. These assumptions were tested by using either a spatial or a visual interference task. As predicted, memory performance based on the method of loci was disrupted by the visual task but not by the spatial task, suggesting that learning depended mainly on the visual cache rather than the inner scribe. In contrast, memory performance based on the pegword technique was adversely affected by both interference tasks, suggesting that learning with this technique required the visual cache and the inner scribe.

**KEY TERMS**

**Visual cache:** according to Logie, the part of the visuo-spatial sketchpad that stores information about visual form and colour.

**Inner scribe:** according to Logie, the part of the visuo-spatial sketchpad that deals with spatial and movement information.

# Central executive

The central executive (which resembles an attentional system) is the most important and versatile component of the working memory system. Baddeley (1996) argued that damage to the frontal lobes of the cortex can cause impairments to the central executive. It follows that patients with damage to the frontal system should behave as if they lack a control system allowing them to direct, and to redirect, their processing resources appropriately. Such patients are said to suffer from **dysexecutive syndrome** (Baddeley, 1996).

Baddeley (1996) identified the following major functions of the central executive:

1. Switching of retrieval plans.
2. Timesharing in dual-task studies (dividing attention between two tasks being performed at the same time).
3. Selective attention to certain stimuli while ignoring others.
4. Temporary activation of long-term memory.

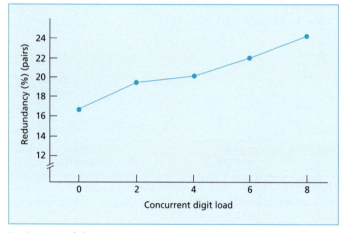

Randomness of digit generation (greater redundancy means reduced randomness) as a function of concurrent digit memory load. Data from Baddeley (1996).

## Evidence

One task Baddeley has used to study the workings of the central executive is random generation of digits or letters. It is assumed that close attention is needed on this task to avoid producing stereotyped (and non-random) sequences. Baddeley (1996) reported a study in which the participants held between one and eight digits in short-term memory while trying to generate a random sequence of digits. It was assumed that demands on the central executive would be greater as the number of digits to be remembered increased. As predicted, the randomness of the sequence produced on the generation task decreased as the digit memory load increased.

Baddeley (1996) argued that performance on the random generation task might depend on the ability to switch retrieval plans rapidly and so avoid stereotyped responses. This hypothesis was tested as follows. The random digit generation task involved pressing numbered keys. This task was done on its own, or in combination with reciting the alphabet, counting from 1, or alternating numbers and letters (A 1 B 2 C 3 D 4 ...). Randomness on the random generation task was reduced by the alternation task, presumably because it required constant switching of retrieval plans. This suggests that rapid switching of retrieval plans is one of the functions of the central executive.

The notion that the central executive may play an important part in timesharing or distributing attention across two tasks was considered in various studies discussed by Baddeley (1996). One study involved patients with **Alzheimer's disease**, a disease involving progressive loss of mental powers and reduced central executive functioning. First of all, each participant's digit span was established. Then they were given several digit-span trials with that number of digits. Finally, they were given more digit-span trials combined with the task of placing a cross in each of a series of boxes arranged in an irregular pattern (dual-task condition). All the Alzheimer's patients showed a marked reduction in digit-span performance in the dual-task condition, but none of the normal controls did. These findings are consistent with the view that Alzheimer's patients have particular problems with the central executive function of distributing attention between two tasks.

The central executive may consist of partially separate components rather than forming a single unitary system. Eslinger and Damasio (1985) studied a former accountant, EVR, who had had a large cerebral tumour removed. He had a high IQ, and performed well on tests requiring reasoning, flexible hypothesis testing, and resistance to distraction and memory interference, suggesting that his central executive was essentially intact. However, he had very poor decision making and judgements (e.g., he would often take

*Can you think of examples of non-random, stereotyped sequences of digits/letters?*

hours to decide where to eat). As a result, he was dismissed from various jobs. Presumably EVR's central executive was partially intact and partially damaged. This implies that the central executive consists of two or more component systems.

Shah and Miyake (1996) presented students with tests of verbal and spatial working memory. The verbal task was the reading span task (Daneman & Carpenter, 1980; see Chapter 11). In this task, the participants read a series of sentences for comprehension, and then recall the final word of each sentence. The reading span is the maximum number of sentences for which they can do this. There was also a spatial span task. The participants had to decide whether each of a set of letters was in normal or mirror-image orientation. After that, they had to indicate the direction in which the top of each letter had been pointing. The spatial span was the maximum number of letters for which they were able to do this.

The correlation between reading span and spatial span was a non-significant +.23, suggesting that verbal and spatial working memory are rather separate. The other findings of Shah and Miyake (1996) supported this conclusion. Reading span correlated +.45 with verbal IQ, but only +.12 with spatial IQ. In contrast, spatial span correlated +.66 with spatial IQ, and only +.07 with verbal IQ. On the basis of these findings, Shah and Miyake put forward a multiple-resource model, in which verbal and spatial working memory were regarded as independent of each other. This is a more complex view than the one favoured by Baddeley (1996).

## Evaluation

⊕ The working memory system has the advantage over previous views on short-term memory that it is concerned with both active processing and the brief storage of information. Thus, it is relevant to activities such as mental arithmetic, verbal reasoning, and comprehension.

⊕ The working memory model accounts for many findings which are hard to explain within the multi-store approach, especially our ability to perform some tasks together without disruption.

⊕ The theory accounts well for the word-length effect, the effects of articulatory suppression, and the performance of various brain-damaged patients.

⊕ The phonological loop is useful in the learning of new words.

⊕ The working memory model views verbal rehearsal as an *optional* process occurring within the phonological loop. This is more realistic than the central importance of verbal rehearsal in the multi-store model.

⊕ There is reasonable support for the notion that there is a visuo-spatial sketchpad consisting of a visual cache and an inner scribe.

⊕ Several theorists (e.g., Conway, Cowan, Bunting, Therriault, & Minkoff, 2002; Engle, 2002) have argued that individual differences in intelligence depend in part on working memory capacity (see Chapter 12). The evidence generally supports that argument.

⊖ According to Andrade (2001, pp. 286–287), "Although simplicity is a strength of the WM [working memory] model, it is also its downfall, because the simple model fails to reflect the complexity of 'real' cognition, and is hard to apply to phenomena outside the domain of laboratory short-term memory tasks."

⊖ Little is known about the central executive. Its capacity has not been measured accurately, and precise details of its functioning are not known. Most importantly, we do not know whether the central executive forms a unitary system.

## LEVELS OF PROCESSING

The notion that long-term memory depends on processes occurring at the time of learning sounds obvious. However, Craik and Lockhart (1972) were among the first memory theorists to construct a theoretical approach based on this notion. In their levels-of-processing theory, they assumed that attentional and perceptual processes during learning determine what information is stored in long-term memory. Their approach was strongly influenced by the earlier theorising of Treisman (e.g., 1964; see Chapter 6). There are various levels of processing, ranging from shallow or perceptual analysis of a stimulus (e.g., detecting specific letters in words) to deep or semantic analysis. Craik (1973, p. 48) defined depth as "the meaningfulness extracted from the stimulus rather than ... the number of analyses performed upon it."

The key theoretical assumptions made by Craik and Lockhart (1972) were as follows:

- The level or depth of processing of a stimulus has a large effect on its memorability.
- Deeper levels of analysis produce more elaborate, longer lasting, and stronger memory traces than do shallow levels of analysis.

Craik and Lockhart (1972) distinguished between maintenance and elaborative rehearsal. **Maintenance rehearsal** involves repeating analyses previously carried out, whereas **elaborative rehearsal** involves deeper or more semantic analysis of the learning material. According to levels-of-processing theory, only elaborative rehearsal improves long-term memory. This contrasts with the view of Atkinson and Shiffrin (1968) that rehearsal *always* enhances long-term memory.

*Can you think of an effective way of remembering the difference between maintenance and elaborative rehearsal?*

## Evidence

Levels-of-processing theory can be tested by presenting the same word list to different groups of participants, with each group processing the words differently. The effects of these various processing or orienting tasks on long-term memory are then assessed. For example, Hyde and Jenkins (1973) used the following orienting tasks: rating the words for pleasantness; estimating the frequency with which each word is used in the English language; detecting the occurrence of the letters "e" and "g" in the list words; deciding on the part of speech of each word; and deciding whether the words fitted sentence frames. It was assumed (perhaps dubiously) that only the tasks of rating pleasantness and rating frequency of usage involved processing of meaning.

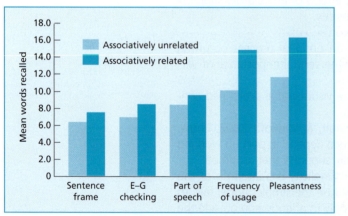

Mean words recalled as a function of list type (associatively related or unrelated) and orienting task. Data from Hyde and Jenkins (1973).

Free recall for lists containing words either associatively related or unrelated in meaning in the Hyde and Jenkins (1973) study is shown in the figure on the left. Recall was 51% higher after the semantic tasks than the non-semantic tasks with associatively unrelated words, and it was 83% higher with associatively related words.

As predicted by Craik and Lockhart (1972), rehearsal generally leads to better long-term memory than maintenance rehearsal. However, maintenance rehearsal usually has some beneficial effect on memory, which is contrary to prediction. Glenberg et al. (1977) found that a nine-fold increase in the time devoted to maintenance rehearsal only increased recall by 1.5%, but increased recognition memory by 9%. Maintenance rehearsal may have prevented the formation of associations among the items in the list, and such associations benefit recall more than recognition.

Long-term memory does not depend *only* on the depth or level of processing. For example, elaboration of processing (i.e., the amount of processing of a particular kind) and the distinctiveness or uniqueness of processing are also important. Craik and Tulving (1975) showed the value of elaboration of processing in a study in which the participants decided whether list words fitted the blanks in sentences. Some of the sentences were high in elaboration (e.g., "The great bird swooped down and carried off the struggling ___"), whereas others were low in elaboration (e.g., "She cooked the ___ "). Subsequent cued recall for the list words was twice as great when they occurred in high-elaboration sentences.

Bransford, Franks, Morris, and Stein (1979) showed that distinctiveness or uniqueness of processing can be more effective than elaboration of processing. They presented

### KEY TERMS

**Maintenance rehearsal:** rehearsal in which analyses previously performed are repeated; see elaborative rehearsal.

**Elaborative rehearsal:** rehearsal in which there is deeper or more semantic analysis of the learning material; see maintenance rehearsal.

participants with distinctive but not elaborate similes (e.g., "A mosquito is like a doctor because they both draw blood") and with non-distinctive but elaborate similes (e.g., "A mosquito is like a racoon because they both have heads, legs, jaws"). Recall was much better for the distinctive similes than for the non-distinctive ones.

Morris, Bransford, and Franks (1977) argued that information is remembered only if it is of *relevance* to the memory test. Their participants answered semantic or shallow (rhyme) questions for lists of words. After that, two kinds of memory test were used: (1) a standard recognition test (list and non-list words presented); and (2) a rhyming recognition test, on which the list words themselves were not presented, and the task was to select words that rhymed with list words. For example, if the word FABLE appeared on the test and TABLE was a list word, then the participants should have selected it.

*Why do you think distinctive similes were better recalled than elaborate ones?*

There was the typical superiority of deep over shallow processing with the standard recognition test, but the *opposite* finding was obtained with the rhyme test. This latter finding disproves the notion that deep processing always enhances long-term memory. Morris et al. proposed a transfer-appropriate processing theory to explain their findings. According to this theory, whether the information stored due to processing at acquisition is remembered later depends on the *relevance* of that information to the memory test. For example, stored semantic information is essentially irrelevant when the memory test requires the selection of words rhyming with list words. What is required for this kind of test is shallow rhyme information.

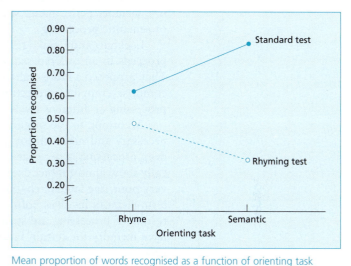

The levels-of-processing approach was designed to account for performance on tests of **explicit memory** (e.g., recall, recognition), on which there is conscious and deliberate retrieval of past events. However, there is also **implicit memory** (memory not involving conscious recollection). This can be assessed by asking participants to write down the first word they think of which completes a word fragment (e.g., _en_i_ is a fragment for "tennis"). Participants who have seen or heard the word "tennis" shortly beforehand are more likely to complete the word fragment successfully, thereby showing implicit memory. Levels-of-processing theory does not work well with tests of implicit memory. There is typically only a small (and often non-significant) levels-of-processing effect on such tests (Challis & Brodbeck, 1992).

Mean proportion of words recognised as a function of orienting task (semantic or rhyme) and of the type of recognition task (standard or rhyming). Data are from Morris et al. (1977), and are from positive trials only.

*Can you think of some of the problems associated with designing an experiment looking at levels of processing in implicit memory?*

## Evaluation

- The original article by Craik and Tulving (1975) has been enormously influential, and has been referred to thousands of times in the world's research literature.
- "One of the main contributions of the levels-of-processing (LOP) article was to reinforce the idea of remembering as processing, as an activity of mind, as opposed to structural ideas of memory traces as entities that must be searched for" (Craik, 2002, p. 306).
- Craik and Lockhart (1972) de-emphasised the role of the particular memory test used in influencing the magnitude of the levels-of-processing effect (Morris et al., 1977).
- The levels-of-processing approach provides a better account of explicit memory than of implicit memory (Challis & Brodbeck, 1992).
- It is hard to be sure of the level of processing used by learners, because there is generally no independent measure of processing depth. However, neuroimaging studies indicate that semantic processing is associated with more activity in left prefrontal regions of the cortex than is the case with shallow processing (see Nyberg, 2002, for a review).
- The levels-of-processing approach is descriptive rather than explanatory. Craik and Lockhart (1972) failed to explain *why* deep or semantic processing is so effective.

**KEY TERMS**

**Explicit memory:** memory that depends on conscious recollection, see implicit memory.

**Implicit memory:** memory that does not depend on conscious recollection; see explicit memory.

## Update

Lockhart and Craik (1990) and Craik (2002) accepted that their levels-of-processing approach was greatly over-simplified. They also accepted the notion of transfer-appropriate processing proposed by Morris et al. (1977). However, they argued that the two approaches are compatible. According to Lockhart and Craik, transfer-appropriate theory predicts that there will be interactions between the type of processing at learning and the type of processing at retrieval (see figure on p. 302), and levels-of-processing theory predicts a main effect of processing depth when transfer appropriateness is held constant. There is supporting evidence in the findings of Morris et al. Transfer appropriateness was high with semantic processing followed by a standard recognition test and with rhyme processing followed by a rhyming test. However, as predicted by levels-of-processing theory, memory performance was much higher in the former condition, which involves deep or semantic processing.

Lockhart and Craik (1990) accepted that their original theory implied that processing proceeds in an ordered sequence from shallow sensory levels to deeper semantic levels. They proposed a more realistic (but vaguer) view: "It is likely that an adequate model will comprise complex interactions between top-down and bottom-up processes, and that processing at different levels will be temporally parallel or partially overlapping" (p. 95).

According to the original levels-of-processing theory, deep or semantic processing is necessary and sufficient for good long-term memory. However, Craik (2002) argued that deep processing is necessary but *not* sufficient. As he pointed out, amnesic patients typically show almost intact deep or semantic processing, but their long-term memory is often very poor (see later in chapter). Craik argued that such findings suggest that good long-term memory involves both deep processing *and* a process of consolidation, in which the results of processing are stored securely in the brain. Amnesic patients have poor long-term memory for certain kinds of information because they have deficient consolidation processes.

## THEORIES OF FORGETTING

As we all know to our cost, memory for information generally becomes worse as the time since learning increases. The first systematic attempt to establish the forgetting function over time was made by Hermann Ebbinghaus (1885/1913). He carried out numerous studies using himself as the only participant. Forgetting of lists of nonsense syllables was very rapid over the first hour or so after learning, with the rate of forgetting slowing considerably thereafter.

Ebbinghaus's findings suggested that the forgetting function is approximately logarithmic. This was confirmed by Rubin and Wenzel (1996), who analysed the forgetting functions from numerous data sets. The main exception to a logarithmic-loss function was found in studies of autobiographical memory, where the rate of forgetting was relatively slow. This may have happened because participants in studies on autobiographical memory are typically free to produce any memory they want from their lives, and the retention interval can be decades rather than minutes or hours.

Most studies of forgetting have focused on explicit memory, in which there is conscious recollection of information. However, a few studies have considered implicit memory, in which memory performance does not involve conscious recollection. Comparisons of forgetting rates in explicit and implicit memory have produced somewhat inconsistent findings. However, McBride, Dosher, and Gage (2001) found that the forgetting rates for explicit and implicit memory were essentially the same over 45 minutes.

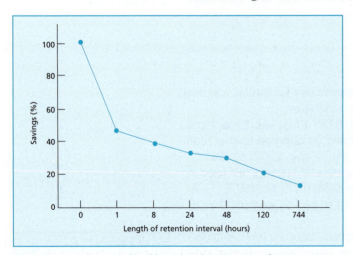

Forgetting over time as indexed by reduced savings. Data from Ebbinghaus (1885/1913).

It is often believed that forgetting is always a bad thing, and that we should do everything we can to reduce it. This belief is not altogether correct. We often need to update our knowledge, and it is helpful to forget the previous state of affairs. For example, when driving you might find it hard to remember the speed limit applying to the area through which you are driving if you had a clear recollection of different speed limits during earlier parts of the drive.

Major theories of forgetting are discussed below. As we will see, it has proved very difficult to clarify the processes underlying forgetting. It is possible that the various theories are all partially correct, with each one explaining forgetting in some circumstances.

## Repression

Sigmund Freud (1915, 1943) emphasised the importance of emotional factors in forgetting. He argued that very threatening or anxiety-provoking material (e.g., experiences of childhood abuse) is often unable to gain access to conscious awareness, using the term **repression** to refer to this phenomenon. According to Freud (1915, p. 86), "The essence of repression lies simply in the function of rejecting and keeping something out of consciousness." However, Freud sometimes used the concept to refer merely to the inhibition of the capacity for emotional experience (Madison, 1956). Thus, threatening material could be said to be repressed even when available to consciousness, provided it did not produce an emotional reaction.

Freud's ideas on repression emerged from his clinical experiences with patients having great difficulty in remembering traumatic events that had happened to them. The central problem in testing Freud's theory is that there are obvious ethical reasons why repression cannot be produced under laboratory conditions. As a result, most relevant evidence comes from non-laboratory studies. Large numbers of adults claim to have recovered repressed memories of childhood physical and/or sexual abuse. There has been a fierce controversy about the genuineness of these recovered memories. In general, clinical psychologists tend to be more convinced than experimental psychologists that at least some recovered memories are genuine.

*What problems might there be in generalising from Freud's theories?*

### Evidence

Andrews et al. (1999) obtained detailed information from 108 therapists about recovered memories from a total of 236 patients. Their evidence suggested that some recovered memories may be genuine. For example, 41% of the patients reported that there was supporting evidence (e.g., someone else had also reported being abused by the alleged abuser). Those who believe that most recovered memories are false assume that such false memories often involve direct pressure from the therapist. However, only 28% of the patients studied by Andrews et al. claimed that the trigger for the first recovered memory occurred during the course of a therapeutic session. In 22% of cases, the trigger occurred *before* therapy had even started, and so could not have been influenced by the therapist. However, it is possible that these patients falsely believed they had been abused because of media reporting of abuse or the reading of books suggesting that adult problems often stem from repressed memories of abuse.

In contrast to the above findings, Lief and Fetkewicz (1995) studied 40 patients who had retracted their "memories" of childhood abuse. In about 80% of these cases, the therapist had made direct suggestions that the patient was the victim of sexual abuse. In 68% of cases, hypnosis (known to produce mistaken memories; see Chapter 4) had been used to recover memories. In 40% of cases, the patient had read numerous books about sexual abuse.

Clancy, Schacter, McNally, and Pitman (2000) used a situation known to produce false memories in most individuals: Participants are given a list of semantically associated words, and are then found to falsely "recognise"

> **KEY TERM**
> **Repression:** motivated forgetting of traumatic or other threatening events.

> **CASE STUDY: *What happened to Susan?***
> Zimbardo reports the case of Susan, an 8-year-old who vanished when playing with her friend. Twenty years later, when looking into her own daughter's eyes, this friend started to remember what had happened. She recalled her own father sexually assaulting Susan before killing her. He then threatened his own daughter with the same fate if she revealed what she had seen. As a result of the recovered memory there was a police investigation and the man concerned was convicted and imprisoned. This could be an example of a recovered repressed memory, and the memory would certainly fulfil Freud's concept of very threatening material. However, there is no way of testing whether this memory was truly repressed, or whether it was suppressed until the friend was adult enough to feel safe in remembering it.

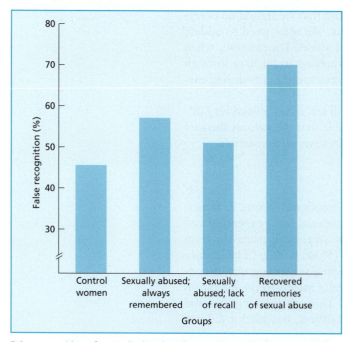

False recognition of a word related to those presented in four groups of women (controls; sexually abused, always remembered; sexually abused, lack of recall; and women with recovered memories of sexual abuse). Data from Clancy et al. (2000).

other semantically related words not actually presented. They compared women with recovered memories of childhood sexual abuse with women who believed they had been sexually abused but could not recall the abuse, women who had always remembered being abused, and control women. Their key findings were as follows: "Women who reported recovered memories of CSA [childhood sexual abuse] were more prone than other subjects to exhibit false recognition of semantic associates ... women who report recovered memories of sexual abuse are more prone than others to develop certain types of illusory memories" (pp. 29–30).

There is experimental evidence that people can be misled into believing in the existence of events that never happened. For example, Ceci (1995) asked preschool children to think about real and fictitious (but plausible) events. The children found it hard to distinguish between the real and fictitious events, with 58% of them providing detailed stories about fictitious events which they falsely believed had occurred. Experienced psychologists could not tell from videotapes which events were real and which were false.

## Evaluation

➕ Some recovered memories may be genuine, but many experts remain sceptical about this.

➖ Some reports of recovered memories are definitely false, often being produced in response to pressure from therapists (e.g., Lief & Fetkewicz, 1995).

➖ Women with recovered memories are susceptible to illusory memories (Clancy et al., 2000).

➖ It is relatively easy to persuade people to believe that memories for events which never happened are genuine.

➖ Repression theory is limited, in that most of the information we forget does not relate to anxious or traumatic events.

## Interference theory

Interference theory can be traced back to Hugo Munsterberg in the nineteenth century. For many years, he kept his pocket watch in one particular pocket. When he started keeping it in a different pocket, he often fumbled about in confusion when asked for the time. He had learned an association between the stimulus, "What time is it, Hugo?", and the response of removing the watch from his pocket. Later on, the stimulus remained the same but a different response was now associated with it.

According to interference theory, our ability to remember what we are currently learning can be disrupted (or interfered with) either by what we have previously learned or by subsequent learning. When previous learning interferes with our memory of later learning, we have **proactive interference** (as shown in the case of Munsterberg and his pocket watch). When later learning disrupts memory for earlier learning, there is **retroactive interference**. Proactive and retroactive interference are both maximal when two different responses have been associated with the *same* stimulus; intermediate when two similar responses have been associated with the same stimulus; and minimal when two *different* stimuli are involved (Underwood & Postman, 1960).

**KEY TERMS**

**Proactive interference:**
disruption of memory by previous learning, often of similar material; see retroactive interference.

**Retroactive interference:**
disruption of memory by learning of other material during the retention interval; see proactive interference.

Strong evidence for retroactive interference has been obtained in studies of eyewitness testimony, in which memory of an event is interfered with by post-event questioning (see later in the chapter). However, most of the evidence for retroactive interference has come from studies using lists of paired associates (see figure on the right).

An example of proactive interference you may have encountered is when a woman marries and changes her surname. It is easy to fall into the error of continuing to use her maiden name, because the stimulus (the woman) has remained the same, but the response (surname) has changed. There are numerous other examples in everyday life. For example, it can be hard to remember new computer passwords if they are changed regularly, or to remember where we have put our keys if for some reason they are not in their usual place.

The importance of proactive interference was shown by Underwood (1957), who reviewed studies on forgetting over a 24-hour retention interval. About 80% of what had been learned was forgotten in one day if the participants had previously learned 15 or more lists in the same experiment, against only 20% or so if no earlier lists had been learned. These findings suggested that proactive interference can produce a massive amount of forgetting. However, there is a problem with these studies. The learning of each list was equated in that all lists were learned to the same criterion (e.g., all items recalled correctly on an immediate test). However, the participants reached the criterion more rapidly with the later lists. Thus, they had less exposure to the later lists, and perhaps learned them less thoroughly. When the amount of exposure to all lists was equated (Warr, 1964), the amount of proactive interference was much less than reported by Underwood.

Jacoby, Debner, and Hay (2001) argued that proactive interference might occur for two different reasons. First, it might be due to the great strength of the incorrect response learned initially. Second, it might be due to problems in retrieving the correct response. In other words, participants might show proactive interference because the correct response is very weak or because the incorrect response is very strong. Jacoby et al. found that proactive interference was due mainly to the strength of the incorrect response.

Most interference studies have focused on explicit memory, in which the participants engage in conscious recollection of previously learned material. Is implicit memory (not involving conscious recollection) also vulnerable to interference? According to Lustig and Hasher (2001, p. 624), who reviewed the relevant evidence, the answer is clearly "Yes": "For both implicit and explicit memory, interference occurs when similar non-targets compete with the target as potential responses to the memory cue ... the degree of interference on both implicit and explicit tests is influenced by the number of competing items and their relative strength."

| Proactive interference | | | |
|---|---|---|---|
| Group | Learn | Learn | Test |
| Experimental | A–B (e.g. Cat–Tree) | A–C (e.g. Cat–Dirt) | A–C (e.g. Cat–Dirt) |
| Control | – | A–C (e.g. Cat–Dirt) | A–C (e.g. Cat–Dirt) |

| Retroactive interference | | | |
|---|---|---|---|
| Group | Learn | Learn | Test |
| Experimental | A–B (e.g. Cat–Tree) | A–C (e.g. Cat–Dirt) | A–B (e.g. Cat–Tree) |
| Control | A–B (e.g. Cat–Tree) | – | A–B (e.g. Cat–Tree) |

Note: for both proactive and retroactive interference, the experimental group exhibits interference. On the test, only the first word is supplied, and the subjects must provide the second word.

Methods of testing for proactive and retroactive interference.

*How might you apply the concept of rehearsal to this finding?*

## Evaluation

- ⊕ Hundreds of studies show the existence of proactive and retroactive interference.
- ⊕ Proactive and retroactive interference have been found in implicit memory as well as explicit memory.
- ⊕ Proactive and retroactive interference both seem to be important in everyday life.
- ⊖ Interference theory is uninformative about the internal processes involved in forgetting.
- ⊖ It requires special conditions for substantial interference effects to occur (i.e., the same stimulus paired with two different responses), suggesting that much forgetting involves factors other than interference.
- ⊖ Associations learned *outside* the laboratory seem less susceptible to interference than those learned *inside* the laboratory (Slamecka, 1966).

After reorganising the contents of kitchen cupboards, you may find yourself looking for something in its old location, even weeks after everything has been moved. This is an example of interference— memory for the old location is interfering with memory for the new one.

## Cue-dependent forgetting or retrieval failure

According to Tulving (1974), there are two main reasons for forgetting. First, there is trace-dependent forgetting, in which the information is no longer stored in memory. Second, there is cue-dependent forgetting, in which the information is in memory, but cannot be accessed. Such information is available (i.e., it is still stored) but not accessible (i.e., it cannot be retrieved). In other words, forgetting is based on retrieval failure. It is often argued that most forgetting is cue-dependent (dependent on retrieval failure). Evidence of cue-dependent forgetting will be discussed in this section.

Tulving and Psotka (1971) compared the cue-dependent approach with interference theory. There were between one and six word lists, with four words in six different categories in each list. After each list had been presented, the participants recalled as many words as possible. That was the original learning. After all the lists had been presented, the participants recalled the words from *all* of them. That was total free recall. Finally, all the category names were presented, and the participants tried again to recall all the words from all the lists. That was total free cued recall.

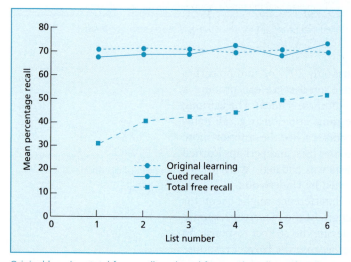

Original learning, total free recall, and total free cued recall as a function of the number of interpolated lists. Data from Tulving and Psotka (1971).

Retroactive interference appeared in total free recall, with word recall from any list decreasing as the number of other lists intervening between learning and recall increased. This finding would be interpreted within interference theory by assuming there had been unlearning of the earlier lists. However, this interpretation does not fit with the findings from total cued recall. There was essentially *no* retroactive interference or forgetting when the category names were available to the participants. Thus, the forgetting observed in total free recall was basically cue dependent and involved retrieval failure.

We can obtain some theoretical understanding of what is involved in cue-dependent forgetting by considering the **encoding specificity principle**, proposed by Tulving (1979). According to this principle, there is information in the memory trace and information is also available on the memory test (e.g., retrieval cue). The greater the *overlap* between these two sources of information, the greater the probability that memory will occur. Of crucial importance, Tulving assumed that the information stored in memory would typically include contextual information. This contextual information can include information about the external learning environment, current mood state, and so on.

The major prediction from the encoding specificity principle is as follows: Memory performance will be worse (and so forgetting will be greater) when the contextual information present at retrieval *differs* from the contextual information stored in memory. According to this view, memory should be better when an individual's state (e.g., mood state) at the time of testing matches his/her state at the time of learning. This phenomenon was shown amusingly in the film, *City Lights*, in which Charlie Chaplin saves a drunken millionaire from attempted suicide, and is befriended in return. When the millionaire sees Charlie again, he is sober, and fails to recognise him. However, when the millionaire becomes drunk again, he catches sight of Charlie, treats him like a long-lost friend, and takes him home with him. The next morning, when the millionaire is sober again, he forgets that Charlie is his invited guest, and gets his butler to throw him out.

Kenealy (1997) provided experimental evidence of state-dependent memory. In one study, the participants looked at a map and learned a set of instructions concerning a particular route until their learning performance exceeded 80%. The following day they were given tests of free recall and cued recall (the visual outline of the map). Context was manipulated by using music to create happy or sad mood states at learning and at retrieval. As predicted, free recall was better when the context (mood state) was the same at learning and retrieval than when it differed. However, there was no context effect with cued recall. Thus, context in the form of mood state can affect memory, but does so only when no other powerful retrieval cues are available.

*Can you think of applications for this research (e.g., for advertising)?*

**KEY TERM**

**Encoding specificity principle:** the notion that remembering depends on the amount of overlap between the information in the memory trace and in the retrieval environment.

The film *City Lights* illustrates the concept of mood-state-dependent memory.

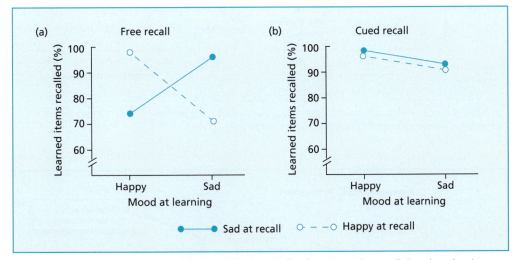

Free and cued recall as a function of mood state (happy or sad) at learning and at recall. Based on data in Kenealy (1997).

A further (more unexpected) prediction follows from the encoding specificity principle. As you would expect, recognition memory is generally much better than recall (e.g., it is easier to recognise an acquaintance's name than to recall it). According to Tulving, however, recall in the presence of much relevant context could be better than recognition in the absence of contextual information, because the overlap between information in the memory trace and in the retrieval environment would be greater for recall. Relevant evidence was reported by Muter (1978). Participants were presented with names of people (e.g., DOYLE, FERGUSON, THOMAS) and asked to circle those they "recognised as a person who was famous before 1950". They were then given recall cues in the form of brief descriptions plus first names of the famous people whose surnames had appeared on the recognition test (e.g., author of the Sherlock Holmes stories: Sir Arthur Conan _____; Welsh poet: Dylan _____ ). Participants recognised only 29% of the names but recalled 42%.

Tulving assumed that context affects recall and recognition in the same way. However, that is not the case according to Baddeley (1982). He proposed a distinction between intrinsic context and extrinsic context. **Intrinsic context** has a direct impact on the meaning or significance of a to-be-remembered item (e.g., strawberry versus traffic as intrinsic context for the word "jam"), whereas **extrinsic context** (e.g., the room in which learning takes place) does not. According to Baddeley, recall is affected by both intrinsic and extrinsic context, but recognition memory is affected only by intrinsic context.

Relevant evidence was obtained by Godden and Baddeley (1975, 1980). Godden and Baddeley (1975) asked participants to learn a list of words either on land or 20 feet underwater, and they were then given a test of free recall on land or underwater. Those who had learned on land recalled more on land, and those who learned underwater did better when tested underwater. Retention was about 50% higher when learning and recall took place in the same extrinsic context. Godden and Baddeley (1980) carried out a very similar study, but using recognition instead of recall. Recognition memory was *not* affected by extrinsic context.

*Can you apply such findings to your own learning? How might you use these findings to improve your performance?*

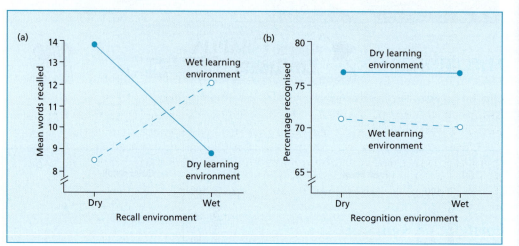

(a) Recall in the same versus different contexts. Data from Godden and Baddeley (1975); (b) Recognition in the same versus different contexts. Data from Godden and Baddeley (1980).

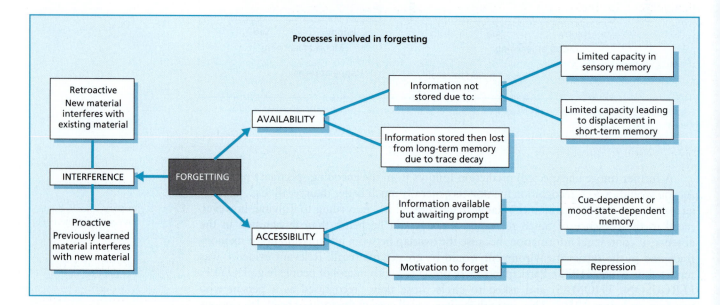

## Evaluation

- ➕ As is assumed by the encoding specificity principle, memory and forgetting often depend on the *relationship* between the information contained in the memory trace and the information available on the memory test.
- ➕ As Tulving argued, we need to take account of context effects to explain memory and forgetting.
- ➖ There is a danger of circularity in applying the encoding specificity principle. Memory is said to depend on "informational overlap", but there is seldom any direct measure of that overlap. If we infer the amount of informational overlap from the level of memory performance, this produces completely circular reasoning.
- ➖ Tulving assumed that the information available at the time of retrieval is compared in a simple and direct fashion with the information stored in memory to ascertain the amount of informational overlap. This is often implausible if one considers what happens if memory is tested by asking the question, "What did you do 6 days ago?" Most people answer such a question by engaging in a complex problem-solving strategy to reconstruct the relevant events. Thus, retrieval is often more complex than was assumed by Tulving.
- ➖ It is not clear within Tulving's approach why extrinsic context has different effects on recall and recognition memory.

# THEORIES OF LONG-TERM MEMORY

Our long-term memories contain an amazing variety of different kinds of information. As a result, it is tempting to assume there are various long-term memory systems, each specialised for certain types of information. There have been several attempts to identify these memory systems. In this section, we focus on two of the most important theoretical approaches in this area. In the following section of the chapter, these approaches are considered in terms of their ability to explain the findings from brain-damaged patients suffering from amnesia, which involves a substantial impairment of long-term memory.

## Episodic vs. semantic memory

Tulving (1972) argued for a distinction between **episodic memory** and **semantic memory**. According to Tulving episodic memory refers to the storage (and retrieval) of specific events or episodes occurring in a particular place at a particular time. Thus, memory for what you had for breakfast this morning is an example of episodic memory. In contrast, semantic memory contains information about our stock of knowledge about the world. Tulving (p. 386) defined semantic memory as follows:

> It is a mental thesaurus, organised knowledge a person possesses about words and other verbal symbols, their meanings and referents, about relations among them, and about rules, formulas, and algorithms for the manipulation of these symbols, concepts, and relations.

Wheeler, Stuss, and Tulving (1997, p. 333) defined episodic memory rather differently, arguing that it depends on "the type of awareness experienced when one thinks back to a specific moment in one's personal past and consciously recollects some prior episode or state as it was previously experienced". In contrast, retrieval of semantic memories lacks this sense of conscious recollection of the past. It involves instead thinking objectively about something one knows.

How has the distinction between episodic and semantic memory changed? According to Wheeler et al. (1997, pp. 348–349), "The major distinction between episodic and semantic memory is no longer best described in terms of the type of information they work with. The distinction is now made in terms of the nature of subjective experience that accompanies the operations of the systems at encoding and retrieval."

Tulving (2002, p. 5) clarified the relationship between episodic and semantic memory: "Episodic memory ... shares many features with semantic memory, out of which it grew, ... but it also possesses features that semantic memory does not ... Episodic memory is a recently evolved, late-developing, and early-deteriorating past-oriented memory system, more vulnerable than other memory systems to neuronal dysfunction."

In spite of the major differences between episodic and semantic memory, there are also important similarities and overlaps. When we store information in episodic memory, information is typically also stored in semantic memory, and vice versa. Something similar applies at retrieval. If we recall with fondness an event from our last summer holiday, our subjective experience typically indicates that the event is being recalled from episodic memory. However, many of the concepts in the recalled event (e.g., beach, hotel) depend on information stored in semantic memory.

Some memory researchers (e.g., Parkin, 2001) doubt that the distinction between episodic and semantic memory is of major importance. Accordingly, we will focus on evidence suggesting that there are important differences between the two types of memory.

## Evidence

If there are separate episodic and semantic memory systems, then it seems reasonable to assume that they would involve different parts of the brain. We can consider brain activity during the original learning or *encoding* of episodic and semantic memories as well as brain activity during *retrieval* of these memories. Wheeler et al. (1997) reviewed the evidence. In 20 PET (positron emission tomography) studies, attempts were made to identify brain regions involved in episodic encoding but not in semantic encoding. In 18 of these studies, the left prefrontal cortex was more active during episodic than semantic encoding.

What about brain activation during retrieval? Wheeler et al. (1997) reported that the right prefrontal cortex was more active during episodic memory retrieval than during semantic memory retrieval in 25 out of 26 PET studies. A more detailed picture was revealed by Lepage, Ghaffar, Nyberg, and Tulving (2000). Six brain regions were more active during episodic retrieval than during semantic retrieval. All these regions were in the frontal lobes, and five of them were in the prefrontal cortex (three strong ones in the right hemisphere and two weaker ones in the left hemisphere).

Research on amnesic patients having problems with long-term memory are discussed later in the chapter. Most amnesic patients have severely impaired episodic and semantic memory. However, some amnesic patients are much more impaired with respect to episodic than semantic memory (e.g., Vargha-Khadem et al., 1997). This is consistent with Tulving's (2002) view that episodic memory is more vulnerable or fragile than semantic memory.

## Evaluation

- ⊕ The evidence from neuroimaging studies suggests that there is an important distinction between episodic and semantic memory.
- ⊕ As we will see, some evidence from amnesic patients suggests that episodic memory is more vulnerable than semantic memory, and can be impaired even when semantic memory is not.
- ⊖ The fact that the great majority of amnesic patients have severe impairments for both episodic and semantic memories suggests the need to be cautious before concluding that episodic and semantic memory form separate memory systems.
- ⊖ Research so far has focused on the differences between episodic and semantic memory. As a result, we know relatively little about the similarities and interconnections between them.

# Implicit vs. explicit memory

Traditional measures of memory (e.g., free recall, cued recall, and recognition) involve the use of direct instructions to retrieve specific information. Thus, they can all be regarded as measures of explicit memory (Graf & Schacter, 1985, p. 501): "Explicit memory is revealed when performance on a task requires conscious recollection of previous experiences." It is generally assumed that episodic and semantic memory are both forms of explicit memory, with the term **declarative memory** often being used to cover both episodic and semantic memory. In contrast, "Implicit memory is revealed when performance on a task is facilitated in the absence of conscious recollection" (p. 501).

In order to understand what is involved in implicit memory, we will consider a study by Tulving, Schacter, and Stark (1982). Their participants learned a list of multi-syllabled and relatively rare words (e.g., "toboggan"). One hour or one week later, they were simply asked to fill in the blanks in word fragments to make a word (e.g., _ O _ O _ G A _). The solutions to half of the fragments were words from the list that had been learned, but the participants were not told this. As conscious recollection was not required on the word-fragment completion test, it can be regarded as a test of implicit memory.

There was evidence for implicit memory, with the participants completing more of the fragments correctly when the solutions matched list words. This is an example of a **repetition-priming effect**, in which the processing of a stimulus is faster and/or easier when it is presented on more than one occasion. You might imagine that repetition priming occurred because the participants deliberately searched through the previously learned list, so that the test actually involved explicit memory. However, Tulving et al. (1982) reported an additional finding going against that possibility. Repetition priming was no greater for target words that were recognised than for those that were not. Thus, the repetition priming effect was *unrelated* to explicit memory performance as assessed by recognition memory. This suggests that repetition priming and recognition memory involve different forms of memory.

If explicit and implicit memory really are separate forms of memory, then they probably involve different brain regions. This issue was explored by Schacter et al. (1996) in a study using PET scans. When the participants performed an explicit memory task (recall of semantically processed words), there was much activation of the hippocampus. In contrast, when they performed an implicit memory task (word-stem completion), there was reduced blood flow in the bilateral occipital cortex, but the task did not affect hippocampal activation.

The most convincing evidence that the distinction between explicit and implicit memory is important comes from research on amnesic patients (see next section in chapter). Amnesic patients generally have greatly impaired explicit memory (episodic + semantic memory) but largely intact implicit memory.

Does implicit memory form a *single* memory system? The fact that there are numerous kinds of implicit memory tasks ranging from motor skills to word completion suggests that various memory systems and brain areas may be involved. Schacter, Wagner, and Buckner (2000) argued that there are *two* memory systems involving implicit memory: the perceptual representation system and procedural memory. In our coverage so far, we have focused on the **perceptual representation system**, which underlies the repetition-priming effect. Thus, the perceptual representation system is involved when a stimulus is processed faster or more easily on successive presentations. In contrast, **procedural memory** is involved in the learning of motor and cognitive skills (e.g., learning to ride a bicycle, acquiring reading skills).

The jury is still out on the issue of whether there really are separate perceptual and procedural memory systems. However, suggestive evidence that they may not be truly separate was reported by Poldrack and Gabrieli (2001), who studied skill learning and repetition priming on a mirror-reading task. They used fMRI to assess brain activity, and concluded as follows: "All of the regions identified ... as exhibiting skill-related changes in activation also exhibited long-term repetition priming effects, and a number of them also exhibited short-term priming effects as well ... These data are plainly inconsistent with the notion that skills learning and repetition priming are independent" (p. 80).

*Why might there be a difference between amnesic patients' explicit and implicit memory?*

**KEY TERMS**

**Declarative memory:** a form of memory resembling explicit memory often believed to consist of episodic memory and semantic memory.

**Repetition-priming effect:** more efficient processing of a stimulus when it has been presented and processed previously.

**Perceptual representation system:** an implicit memory system involved in the repetition priming effect.

**Procedural memory:** a form of memory resembling implicit memory, and based on memory for skills.

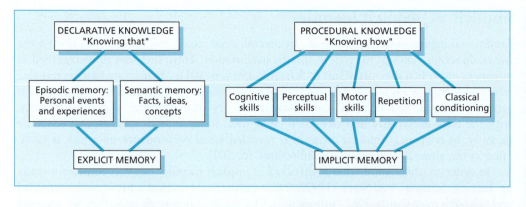

## Evaluation

⊕ The finding that different brain regions are involved in explicit and implicit memory suggests that there is an important difference between these two forms of memory.

⊕ The distinction between explicit and implicit memory has received strong support from studies on amnesic patients having poor explicit memory but intact implicit memory.

⊖ The distinction between explicit and implicit memory *describes* different forms of memory, but does not *explain* adequately what is happening.

⊖ The crucial difference between explicit and implicit memory is in terms of the involvement of conscious recollection, and it is often hard to decide whether someone's memory performance depends on conscious recollection.

⊖ It is not clear whether implicit memory involves a single memory system or whether it involves a number of memory systems (e.g., perceptual representation system, procedural memory).

## AMNESIA

Memory researchers have carried out numerous studies on brain-damaged patients suffering from a range of memory problems. Of particular interest have been patients with **amnesia,** a condition involving severe problems with long-term memory. Why have amnesic patients been the focus of research? One reason is that the study of such patients provides a good *test-bed* for existing theories of normal memory. Another important reason is that research on amnesia has suggested theoretical distinctions relevant to our understanding of memory in normal individuals. Some examples are discussed later in the chapter.

Patients become amnesic for various reasons. Closed head injury is the most common cause of amnesia, and other causes include bilateral stroke and chronic alcoholism. Most research has involved sufferers from **Korsakoff's syndrome**, which occurs through chronic alcohol abuse. There has been less research on patients with closed head injury. Such patients often have a range of cognitive impairments, making it hard to interpret their memory deficit.

Two major symptoms are exhibited by most amnesic patients. First, there is **anterograde amnesia**, consisting of a marked impairment in the ability to remember new information learned after the onset of the amnesia. Second, there is **retrograde amnesia**, consisting of great difficulty in remembering events from *before* the onset of amnesia, especially those occurring shortly beforehand. Most research has focused on anterograde amnesia, the devastating effects of which were described by Korsakoff (1889):

> *He does not remember whether he had his dinner, whether he was out of bed. On occasion the patient forgets what happened to him just an instant ago: you came in, conversed with him, and stepped out for one minute; then you come in again and the patient has absolutely no recollection that you had already been with him.*

Amnesia can be produced by damage to brain structures in two areas of the brain: a sub-cortical region called the diencephalon, and a cortical region known as the medial temporal lobe. Patients with Korsakoff's syndrome have brain damage in the diencephalon, especially the medial thalamus and the mamillary nuclei, but typically the frontal cortex is also damaged. Other patients have damage in the medial-temporal region. This can happen as a result of herpes simplex encephalitis, anoxia (due to lack of oxygen), infarction, or sclerosis (involving a hardening of tissue or organs).

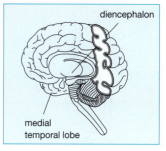

Recent developments in neuroimaging techniques have allowed accurate assessment of the damaged areas while the patient is alive. Aggleton and Brown (1999, p. 426) used evidence from neuroimaging studies to propose a new theory: "The traditional distinction between temporal lobe and diencephalic amnesics is misleading: both groups have damage to the same functional system ... The proposed hippocampal-diencephalic system is required for the encoding of episodic information, permitting the information to be set in its spatial and temporal context."

Are different parts of the brain involved in anterograde and retrograde amnesia? Evidence that this may be the case was reported by Reed and Squire (1998) in a study of four amnesic patients. Magnetic resonance imaging (MRI) examinations revealed that all four had hippocampal damage, but only two also had temporal lobe damage. The two patients with temporal lobe damage had much more severe retrograde amnesia than the other two, suggesting that retrograde amnesia involves the temporal lobe.

## Residual learning ability

Amnesics are generally poor at remembering information learned after the onset of amnesia. However, it is important to discover those aspects of learning and memory which remain fairly intact in amnesic patients. A comparison of the lists of those memory abilities impaired and not impaired in amnesia might facilitate the task of identifying the processes and/or memory structures affected in amnesic patients. Some of the main memory abilities that remain in amnesic patients are as follows (see Spiers, Maguire, & Burgess, 2001, for a review):

1. *Short-term memory*. Amnesic patients perform almost as well as normals on digit span (immediate ordered recall of random digits; Butters & Cermak, 1980).
2. *Skill learning*. Amnesic patients have normal rates of learning for serial reaction time, mirror tracing, and the pursuit rotor (Gabrieli, 1998). Mirror tracing involves tracing with a stylus a figure seen reflected in a mirror. The pursuit rotor involves manual tracking of a moving target.

3. *Repetition priming.* Amnesics show normal or nearly normal repetition priming effects across a range of tasks (see earlier in the chapter). For example, Cermak, Talbot, Chandler, and Wolbarst (1985) used a perceptual identification task, which involved presenting words at the minimal exposure time needed to identify them correctly. Some of these words were primed, in the sense that they had previously been presented in a list of words to be learned. Amnesic patients showed a similar priming effect to controls, i.e., primed words were detected at shorter presentation times than non-primed words.

4. *Conditioning.* Many amnesic patients show normal eyeblink conditioning (see Gabrieli, 1998). This is a form of classical conditioning in which individuals learn to blink to a tone previously paired with a puff of air delivered to the eyes.

It is hard to detect much similarity among these different memory abilities. However, a common theme is that most do not necessarily require conscious recollection of previous stimuli or events. More specifically, the assessment of skill learning, repetition learning, and conditioning is based on behavioural measures of performance rather than on the ability to bring previously acquired knowledge into consciousness.

## Theories of amnesia

### Episodic vs. semantic memory

As we saw earlier, Tulving (1972, 2002) distinguished between episodic memory (concerned with a sense of conscious recollection of events or episodes happening at a given time in a given place) and semantic memory (concerned with general knowledge about the world). He argued that amnesic patients often have more anterograde amnesia for episodic memory than for semantic memory, suggesting there is an important difference between these two types of memory. Some support for this viewpoint was reported by Spiers et al. (2001), who reviewed 147 cases of amnesia. There was evidence of impairment on tests of episodic memory in all patients, but several of them had reasonable ability to form new semantic memories.

Some of the most convincing evidence that episodic and semantic memory are separate was reported by Vargha-Khadem et al. (1997). They studied two patients (Beth and Jon) who had suffered bilateral hippocampal damage at an early age before they had had the opportunity to develop semantic memories. Both patients had very poor episodic memory for the day's activities, television programmes, and so on. However, they both attended ordinary schools, and their levels of speech and language development, literacy, and factual knowledge (e.g., vocabulary) were within the normal range. Vargha-Khadem, Gadian, and Mishkin (2002) carried out a follow-up study on Jon at the age of 20. As a young adult, he had a high level of intelligence (IQ = 114), and his semantic memory continued to be markedly better than his episodic memory.

Vargha-Khadem et al. (1997) explained their findings by arguing that episodic and semantic memory depend on different brain regions. Why, then, do so many amnesics have great problems with both episodic and semantic memory? According to Vargha-Khadem et al. the brain regions underlying episodic and semantic memory are very close to each other in the area in and around the hippocampus. As a result, brain damage sufficient to impair episodic memory generally affects the part of the brain involved in semantic memory as well.

The distinction between episodic and semantic memory has also been supported in studies on retrograde amnesia (impaired memory for events before the onset of amnesia). The relevant evidence was reviewed by Kapur (1999). She found that some patients had retrograde amnesia for episodic memory but not for semantic memory, whereas others showed the opposite pattern. These findings suggest that episodic and semantic memories are stored in different parts of the brain.

*Do these findings fit with the intact memory abilities of amnesic patients, as described above?*

### Evaluation

➕ Research on anterograde amnesia suggests that episodic memory is more vulnerable to disruption by brain damage than is semantic memory.

➕ Research on retrograde amnesia supports the distinction between episodic and semantic memory, in that often only one or the other type of memory is affected.
➖ The distinction between episodic and semantic memory sheds no light on the finding that most amnesic patients have intact repetition-priming effects and skill learning.
➖ The fact that most amnesic patients have impaired episodic and semantic memory casts some doubts on the value of the distinction.

## Explicit vs. implicit memory

Schacter (1987) argued that amnesic patients are at a severe disadvantage when tests of explicit memory (requiring conscious recollection) are used, but that they perform at normal levels on tests of implicit memory (not requiring conscious recollection). As predicted by this theory, most (but no means all) amnesic patients display impaired performance on tests of recently acquired episodic and semantic memories. Most studies on motor skills and on various repetition-priming effects are also consistent with Schacter's theoretical perspective, in that they are basically implicit memory tasks on which amnesic patients perform normally or nearly so.

*Can explicit and implicit memory explain amnesic patients' memory impairments?*

A hackneyed anecdote related by Claparède (1911) is consistent with Schacter's (1987) position. He hid a pin in his hand before shaking hands with one of his amnesic patients. After that, she was understandably reluctant to shake hands with him, but was embarrassed because she was unable to explain why. The patient's behaviour revealed clearly that there was long-term memory for what had happened, but this occurred without any conscious recollection of the incident. Thus, there was implicit memory but no explicit memory.

Striking findings were reported by Graf, Squire, and Mandler (1984). Word lists were presented, with each list being followed by one of four memory tests. Three of the tests were conventional explicit memory tests (free recall, recognition memory, cued recall), but the fourth test (word completion) involved implicit memory. On this last test, participants were given three-letter word stems (e.g., STR___) and simply wrote down the first word they thought of starting with those letters (e.g., STRAP, STRIP). Implicit memory was assessed by the extent to which the word completions corresponded to words from the previous list. The amnesic patients did much worse than normals on all three explicit memory tests, but performed as well as normals on the implicit memory test.

Amnesic patients do *not* always perform well on tests of implicit memory. For example, Ryan, Althoff, Whitlow, and Cohen (2000) presented amnesic and healthy participants with colour images of real-world scenes in three conditions:

1. Novel scenes not presented previously.
2. Repeated old scenes.
3. Manipulated old scenes, in which the positions of some of the objects had been changed.

The crucial measure was the proportion of eye fixations in the critical region (i.e., the part of the scene systematically altered in the manipulation condition). The healthy controls had significantly more fixations in the critical region in the manipulation condition than in the other two conditions.

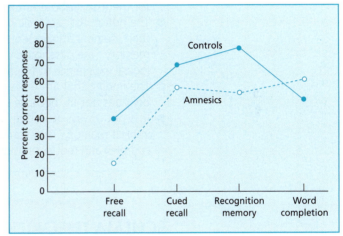

Free recall, cued recall, recognition memory, and word completion in amnesic patients and controls. Data from different experiments reported by Graf et al. (1984).

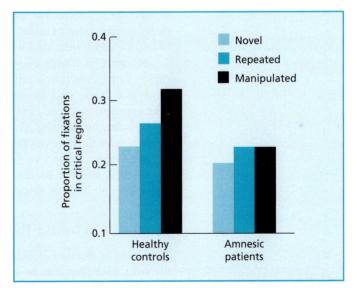

Proportion of eye fixations in the critical region as a function of condition (novel, repeated, manipulated) and group (healthy controls vs. amnesic patients). From Ryan et al. (2000).

This occurred because these participants had implicit memory for the relations among the objects in the original scene. In contrast, the amnesic patients did not devote more fixations to the critical region in the manipulation condition, because they had no implicit memory for the relations among the elements of previously presented scenes.

The evidence suggests that amnesic patients have intact implicit memory for *simple* information (e.g., single actions or words; Claparède, 1911; Graf et al., 1984). However, amnesic patients have impaired implicit memory for *complex* information (e.g., relations among objects; Ryan et al., 2000). As yet, we do not have a theory providing an adequate explanation of these findings.

## Evaluation

- ⊕ The distinction between explicit and implicit memory is of great value in categorising tests of long-term memory on which amnesic patients typically do and do not perform poorly.
- ⊕ The finding that amnesic patients generally perform well on tests involving implicit memory and poorly on tests involving explicit memory provides a useful starting point for theorising about amnesia.
- ⊖ The notion that amnesic patients have deficient explicit memory is not an *explanation* of their memory impairments. As Schacter (1987, p. 501) pointed out, implicit and explicit memory "are descriptive concepts that are primarily concerned with a person's psychological experience at the time of retrieval".
- ⊖ The finding that amnesics have nearly normal performance on tests of short-term memory does not fit, because such tests involve explicit memory.
- ⊖ It is not always true that amnesic patients perform at normal levels on tests involving implicit memory. They can show impaired implicit memory performance when the task is complex and requires remembering the relations among objects (e.g., Ryan et al., 2000).

## SCHEMA THEORIES

Most of the research considered so far has been concerned with words, pictures, or sentences. However, it is also important to consider our long-term memory for stories, events, and so on. Theories in this area have focused on **schemas** (well-integrated packages of information about the world, events, people, and actions). Scripts and frames are relatively specific kinds of schemas. Scripts deal with knowledge about events and consequences of events, and frames deal with knowledge about the properties of objects and locations.

Schemas or scripts allow us to form *expectations*. In a restaurant, for example, we expect to be shown to a table, to be given a menu by the waiter or waitress, to order the food and drink, and so on. If any of these expectations is violated, then we usually take appropriate action. For example, if no menu is forthcoming, we try to catch the eye of the waiter or waitress. As our expectations are generally confirmed, schemas make the world a reasonably predictable place.

We will consider two schema or script theories here. First, and of great historical importance, there is Bartlett's (1932) schema theory. Second, there is the script-pointer-plus-tag hypothesis of Schank and Abelson (1977).

### Bartlett's schema theory

According to Bartlett (1932), what we remember from stories is determined not only by the story itself, but also by our store of relevant prior knowledge in the form of schemas. He tested this notion by presenting his participants (mostly Cambridge University students) with stories producing a *conflict* between what was presented to them and their prior knowledge. The prediction was that people reading a story from a different culture (e.g., North American Indian culture) would have a distorted memory of the story,

**KEY TERM**

**Schemas:** integrated chunks of knowledge stored in long-term memory.

making it more conventional and acceptable from the standpoint of their own cultural background.

Bartlett's (1932) findings supported the above prediction. In particular, a substantial proportion of the recall errors were in the direction of making the story read more like a typical English story. He used the term **rationalisation** to refer to this type of error. Bartlett reported findings supporting this prediction. He also found other kinds of errors, including flattening (failure to recall unfamiliar details) and sharpening (elaboration of certain details).

Bartlett (1932) assumed that memory for the precise material presented is forgotten over time, whereas memory for the underlying schemas is not. Thus, rationalisation errors (which depend on schematic knowledge) should increase in number at longer retention intervals. Supporting evidence was reported by Sulin and Dooling (1974). They presented some of their participants with a story about Gerald Martin: "Gerald Martin strove to undermine the existing government to satisfy his political ambitions ... He became a ruthless, uncontrollable dictator. The ultimate effect of his rule was the downfall of his country" (p. 256).

*What findings might you expect if the same experiment were to be carried out with North American Indian participants?*

## Bartlett: The War of the Ghosts

In his 1932 study Bartlett asked his English participants to read a North American Indian folk tale called "The War of the Ghosts", after which they tried to recall the story. Part of the story was as follows:

> One night two young men from Edulac went down the river to hunt seals, and while they were there it became foggy and calm. Then they heard war-cries, and they thought: "Maybe this is a war-party." They escaped to the shore, and hid behind a log. Now canoes came up, and they heard the noise of paddles, and saw one canoe coming up to them. There were five men in the canoe, and they said: "What do you think? We wish to take you along. We are going up the river to make war on the people."

> ... one of the young men went but the other returned home ... [it turns out that the five men in the boat were ghosts and after accompanying them in a fight, the young man returned to his village to tell his tale] ... and said: "Behold I accompanied the ghosts, and we went to fight. Many of our fellows were killed, and many of those who attacked us were killed. They said I was hit, and I did not feel sick."

> He told it all and then he became quiet. When the sun rose he fell down. Something black came out of his mouth. His face became contorted ... He was dead. (p. 65)

One of the subject's recall of the story (two weeks later):

> There were two ghosts. They were on a river. There was a canoe on the river with five men in it. There occurred a war of ghosts ... They started the war and several were wounded and some killed. One ghost was wounded but did not feel sick. He went back to the village in the canoe. The next morning he was sick and something black came out of his mouth, and they cried: "He is dead." (p. 76)

Bartlett found that the participants' recall distorted the content and style of the original story. The story was shortened, and the phrases, and often words, were changed to be similar to the English language and concepts (e.g., "boat" instead of "canoe"). He also found other kinds of errors, including flattening (failure to recall unfamiliar details) and sharpening (elaboration of certain details).

### KEY STUDY EVALUATION—Bartlett

Bartlett's research is important because it provided some of the first evidence that what we remember depends in an important way on our prior knowledge, in the form of schemas.

However, Bartlett's studies are open to criticism. He did not give very specific instructions to his participants (Bartlett, 1932, p. 78: "I thought it best, for the purposes of these experiments, to try to influence the subjects' procedure as little as possible.") As a result, some distortions observed by Bartlett were due to conscious guessing rather than deficient memory. Gauld and Stephenson (1967) found that instructions stressing the need for accurate recall eliminated almost half the errors usually obtained.

Another criticism of Bartlett's work was that his approach to research lacked objectivity. Some psychologists believe that well-controlled experiments are the only way to produce objective data. Bartlett's methods were somewhat casual. He simply asked his group of participants to recall the story at various intervals and there were no special conditions for this recall. It is possible that other factors affected their performance, such as the conditions around them at the time they were recalling the story, or it could be that the distortions were simply guesses by participants who were trying to make their recall seem coherent and complete rather than genuine distortions in recall.

On the other hand, one could argue that his research is more ecologically valid than those studies that involve the recall of syllables or lists of words. In recent years there has been an increase in the kind of research conducted by Bartlett, looking more at "everyday memory".

## Discussion points

1. Why do you think that Bartlett's research has been so influential?
2. Do you think that the kinds of errors and distortions observed by Bartlett would be found with other kinds of material?

### KEY TERM

**Rationalisation:** in Bartlett's theory, the tendency for story recall to be distorted to conform to the cultural conventions of the rememberer.

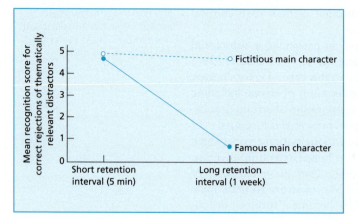

Correct rejection of thematic distractor as a function of main actor (Gerald Martin or Adolf Hitler) and retention interval. Data from Sulin and Dooling (1974).

Other participants were given the same story, but the name of the main actor was given as Adolf Hitler. Those participants told the story was about Adolf Hitler were much more likely than the other participants to believe incorrectly that they had read the sentence, "He hated the Jews particularly and so persecuted them." Their schematic knowledge about Hitler distorted their recollections of what they had read. As Bartlett predicted, this type of distortion was more frequent at a long than a short retention interval.

Bartlett (1932) assumed that memorial distortions occur mainly because of schema-driven reconstructive processes operating at the time of *retrieval*. However, schemas can also influence story *comprehension*. For example, Bransford and Johnson (1972, p. 722) presented a passage in which it was hard to work out which schemas were relevant. Part of it was as follows:

*The procedure is quite simple. First, you arrange items into different groups. Of course one pile may be sufficient depending on how much there is to do. If you have to go somewhere else due to lack of facilities that is the next step; otherwise, you are pretty well set.*

*What do Bartlett's findings tell us about the reliability of human memory?*

Participants hearing the passage in the absence of a title rated it as incomprehensible, and recalled an average of only 2.8 idea units. In contrast, those supplied beforehand with the title "Washing clothes" found it easy to understand and recalled 5.8 idea units on average. This effect of relevant schema knowledge occurred because it helped comprehension of the passage. Bransford and Johnson favoured a constructive theory, according to which schematic knowledge affects the way in which stories and other material are interpreted and comprehended.

Evidence more supportive of Bartlett (1932) was reported by Anderson and Pichert (1978). Participants read a story from the perspective of either a burglar or someone interested in buying a home. After they had recalled as much as they could of the story from the perspective they had been given, they shifted to the alternative perspective, and recalled the story again. On the second recall, participants recalled more information that was important only to the second perspective or schema than they had done on the first recall.

There are doubts as to whether Bartlett's main findings can be replicated under more naturalistic conditions. Wynn and Logie (1998) tested students' recall of "real-life" events experienced during their first week at university at various intervals of time ranging from 2 weeks to 6 months. What they found was as follows: "The initial accuracy sustained throughout the time period, together with the relative lack of change over time, suggests very limited use of reconstructive processes" (p. 1). This failure may have occurred in part because the students had not had time to develop many relevant schemas.

If we are trying to explain text comprehension and memory in terms of the activation of certain schemas, then we really require independent evidence of the characteristics of those schemas. Such evidence is generally not available, but was provided in a study by Bower, Black, and Turner (1979). Students listed 20 actions or events associated with various events (e.g., eating at a restaurant, attending a lecture). There was considerable agreement across participants, suggesting that different people have similar schemas. When Bower et al. presented stories eliciting specific underlying schemas or scripts, they found that unstated schema-relevant actions were often recalled or falsely recognised.

According to schema theory, top-down processes lead to the generation of numerous inferences during story

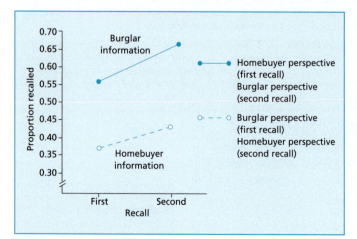

Recall as a function of perspective at the time of retrieval. Based on data from Anderson and Pichert (1978).

comprehension. Most early research provided support for this assumption. For example, Bransford, Barclay, and Franks (1972) presented sentences such as, "Three turtles rested on a floating log, and a fish swam beneath them." They argued that the inference would be drawn that the fish swam under the log. To test this, some participants on a subsequent recognition-memory test were given the sentence, "Three turtles rested on a floating log, and a fish swam beneath it." Most participants were confident that this inference was the original sentence. Indeed, their level of confidence was as high as it was when the original sentence was re-presented on the memory test!

Graesser, Singer, and Trabasso (1994) argued that most schema theories fail to specify *which* inferences are drawn when people read a story. They remedied this omission in their search-after-meaning theory based on the following assumptions:

- *The reader goal assumption.* Readers construct a meaning for the text that addresses their goals.
- *The coherence assumption.* Readers try to construct a coherent meaning for the text.
- *The explanation assumption.* Readers try to explain the actions, events, and states referred to in the text.

Readers will draw few inferences if their goals do not require them to understand the meaning of the text (e.g., in proofreading), if the text appears to lack coherence, or if they lack the necessary background knowledge to make sense of the text. Even if readers do search after meaning, several kinds of inference are not normally drawn: ones about future developments (causal consequence); the precise way in which actions are accomplished (subordinate goal-actions); and the author's intent (see Graesser et al., 1994). Schema theories do not make it clear why such inferences are not drawn (see Chapter 11).

## Evaluation

- ➕ Our organised knowledge of the world in the form of schemas influences text comprehension and recall.
- ➕ The inferences we draw when reading or listening to a story are determined in part by our schematic knowledge.
- ➕ As predicted by Bartlett, memory distortions produced by schemas are often more prevalent at a long retention interval than at a short one.
- ➖ Bartlett exaggerated the number of memory distortions produced by schematic knowledge.
- ➖ Schema-induced memory distortions may be less common in naturalistic conditions than in the laboratory (e.g., Wynn & Logie, 1998).
- ➖ There is generally no independent evidence of the characteristics of schemas. As a result, most schema theories are rather lacking in testability.
- ➖ Schema theories generally predict that readers will draw more inferences when reading a text than is actually the case.

## Script-pointer-plus-tag hypothesis

The script-pointer-plus-tag hypothesis was put forward by Schank and Abelson (1977). It consists of various assumptions about memory for script- or schema-based stories:

- Information from the story is combined with information from the underlying script or schema in memory.
- Actions in a story are either typical (consistent with the underlying script or schema) or atypical (inconsistent with the underlying script).
- Information about atypical actions is tagged individually to the underlying script.
- Recognition memory will be worse for typical than for atypical actions, because typical actions *present* in the story are hard to discriminate from typical actions *absent* from the story.

- Initial recall for atypical actions should be better than for typical actions, because they are tagged individually in memory.
- Recall for atypical actions at long retention intervals should be worse than for typical actions, because recall increasingly relies on the underlying script or schema.

## Evidence

Most studies support the prediction that recognition memory for atypical actions is better than for typical ones at all retention intervals (Davidson, 1994). However, the findings with respect to recall are more inconsistent. Davidson shed light on these inconsistencies. She used routine atypical actions that were irrelevant to the story and atypical actions that interrupted the story. For example, in a story about going to the cinema, "Sarah mentions to Sam that the screen is big" belongs to the former category and "Another couple, both of whom are very tall, sits in front of them and blocks their view" belongs to the latter category. Both kinds of atypical actions were better recalled than typical ones at a relatively short retention interval (1 hour), which is in line with prediction. After 1 week, the routine atypical actions were worse recalled than typical or script actions, but the interruptive atypical actions were better recalled than typical actions.

What is going on here? Presumably, interruptive atypical actions are well recalled at the longer retention interval because they remain clearly differentiated from the underlying script or schema. As Davidson (1994, p. 772) concluded, "Part of the problem with existing schema theories is that they do not specify how different types of atypical actions will be recalled."

# EVERYDAY MEMORY

Most research on human memory has been carried out in the laboratory, and may appear to have little relevance to real life. This state of affairs has led many researchers to study everyday memory. As Koriat and Goldsmith (1996) pointed out, many everyday memory researchers differ from other memory researchers in their answers to three questions:

1. *What memory phenomena should be studied?* According to everyday memory researchers, the kinds of phenomena people experience everyday should be the main focus.
2. *How should memory be studied?* Everyday memory researchers emphasise the importance of the ecological validity of memory research. **Ecological validity** consists of two aspects: (a) *representativeness*, and (b) *generalisability* (Kvavilashvili & Ellis, in press). Representativeness refers to the naturalness of the experimental situation, stimuli, and task, whereas generalisability refers to the extent to which the findings of a study are applicable to the real world. Generalisability is more important than representativeness.
3. *Where should memory phenomena be studied?* Some everyday memory researchers argue in favour of naturalistic settings.

In fact, matters are not as neat and tidy as suggested so far. As Koriat and Goldsmith (1996) pointed out, "Although the three dimensions—the what, how, and where dimensions—are correlated in the reality of memory research, they are not logically interdependent. For instance, many everyday memory topics can be studied in the laboratory, and memory research in naturalistic settings may be amenable to strict experimental control" (p. 168).

Neisser (1996) identified a crucial difference between memory as studied traditionally and memory in everyday life. The participants in traditional memory studies are generally motivated to be as *accurate* as possible in their memory performance. In contrast, everyday memory research should be based on the notion that "remembering is a form of purposeful action" (p. 204). This approach involves three assumptions about everyday memory:

1. It is purposeful.
2. It has a personal quality about it, meaning that it is influenced by the individual's personality and other characteristics.

*How might you go about testing everyday memory?*

**3.** It is influenced by situational demands (e.g., the wish to impress one's audience) rather than by the need to be accurate.

For example, when you tell someone about what happened at a recent party, you may deliberately exaggerate your positive contributions to its success while leaving out some of the things you did after having had too much to drink!

We will focus on three important topics within everyday memory research: flashbulb memories, eyewitness testimony, and autobiographical memory. The study of flashbulb memories for major world events is intrinsically interesting. Research on eyewitness testimony has possibly been of more practical benefit than any other research in memory. Autobiographical memory is of direct relevance to our everyday lives, and has been studied intensively in recent years.

## Flashbulb memories

Some world events (the destruction of the twin towers of the World Trade Centre on September 11; death of Princess Diana) are so dramatic that they leave us with very vivid and detailed memories. Brown and Kulik (1977) used the term **flashbulb memories** to describe such memories. They argued that a special neural mechanism may be activated by such events, provided they are seen by the individual as surprising and having real consequences for that person's life. This mechanism "prints" the details of such events permanently in the memory system. Flashbulb memories are claimed to be accurate and very long lasting, and they often include the following categories of information: informant (person who supplied the information), place where the news was heard, ongoing event, individual's own emotional state, emotional state of others, and consequences of the event for the individual.

Conway et al. (1994) studied flashbulb memories for the resignation of Mrs Thatcher in 1990. Memory for this event was regarded as surprising and consequential by most British people, and so should theoretically have produced flashbulb memories. Flashbulb memories were found in 86% of British participants after 11 months, compared to 29% in other countries. The British participants were students, and Wright, Gaskell, and Muircheartaigh (1998) wondered whether these findings could be replicated in a more representative sample. They found that only 12% of English people sampled remembered Mrs Thatcher's resignation vividly 18 months afterwards.

Many experts (e.g., Neisser, 1982) are sceptical about flashbulb memories for various reasons. First, flashbulb memories may be remembered clearly because they have been rehearsed frequently rather than because of the processing that occurred when learning about the dramatic event. Second, it is generally hard to check on the accuracy of reported flashbulb memories, and many may be mistaken.

Third, Winningham, Hyman, and Dinnel (2000) argued that memories for dramatic events often change and develop in the first few days thereafter, and so flashbulb memories are *not* formed in their entirety at the moment when individuals learn about such events. They tested their ideas by studying American people's memory for hearing about the acquittal of O.J. Simpson. He had been an American football star, and was accused of murdering his ex-wife Nicole Brown Simpson and her friend Ron Goodman in 1994. The key findings of Winningham et al. came from participants who were initially questioned 5 hours after the acquittal verdict and who were then retested 8 weeks later. If these participants had genuine flashbulb memories, their recollections at the two testing times should have been very similar. In fact, however, there were significant changes in what they remembered on the two testing occasions for 77% of the participants, in part because they had learned more about the dramatic event in the first few days after the acquittal.

What were you doing when you heard about Princes Diana's fatal accident? Why do so many people have a vivid memory for this and other extremely emotional and important events?

*What individual and cultural factors might affect how an event is remembered?*

**KEY TERM**

**Flashbulb memories:** vivid and detailed memories of dramatic events.

In sum, evidence for flashbulb memories has been obtained in several studies (see Eysenck, 2001), and it is clear that many people strongly believe that they have flashbulb memories for certain events. For example, I remember very clearly discussing a forthcoming trip to Spain with two colleagues (Martyn Barrett and Duncan Harris) when I heard that Mrs Thatcher had resigned. However, it has proved difficult to show that flashbulb memories differ in any important way from ordinary memories.

## Eyewitness testimony

Thousands of people have been put in prison purely on the basis of eyewitness testimony. Even if the rate of mistaken identification is low, it would still follow that many innocent individuals languish in prison because of the fallibility of eyewitness testimony. Eyewitness testimony is often inaccurate because eyewitnesses often do not realise initially that a crime or other event is happening, and so do not attend fully to it. In addition, the memory that an eyewitness has of an event is fragile, and can easily be distorted by questioning or information occurring after the event (post-event information). We will start by considering evidence for this fragility.

Eyewitness testimony has been found by psychologists to be extremely unreliable, yet jurors tend to find such testimony highly believable.

### Post-event information

In their well-known study Loftus and Palmer (1974) demonstrated that eyewitness memory is very fragile and easily distorted by post-event information (see Key Study below).

Even apparently trivial differences in the way in which a question is asked can have a marked effect on the answers produced. Loftus and Zanni (1975) showed people a short

## Loftus and Palmer: Leading questions

Loftus and Palmer (1974) showed their participants projected slides of a multiple car accident. After that, the participants described what had happened, and answered specific questions. Some were asked, "About how fast were the cars going when they smashed into each other?", whereas for other participants the verb "hit" was substituted for "smashed into". Control participants were not asked a question about car speed. The estimated speed was affected by the verb used in the question, averaging 41 mph when the verb "smashed" was used versus 34 mph when "hit" was used. Thus, the information implicit in the question affected the way in which the accident was remembered.

One week later, all the participants were asked, "Did you see any broken glass?" There was actually no broken glass in the accident, but 32% of the participants who had been asked previously about speed using the verb "smashed" said they had seen broken glass. Only 14% of the participants asked using the verb "hit" said they had seen broken glass, and the figure was 12% for the control participants. Thus, our memory for events is fragile and susceptible to distortion.

### KEY STUDY EVALUATION—Loftus and Palmer

Methodologically, this study was well controlled, although, as is common, students were used as participants and it could be argued that students are not necessarily representative of the general population. However, the experiment lacks ecological validity, in that the participants were not real-life witnesses, and it could be said that the emotional effects of being a real-life witness could affect recall. On the one hand film clips may not contain as much information as you would get in real life, but on the other hand the participants knew that something interesting was being shown to them and therefore they were paying full attention to it. In real life, eyewitnesses are typically taken by surprise and often fail to pay close attention to the event or incident, therefore this research lacks mundane realism. The study has real-life applications, particularly in respect of the credence given to eyewitness testimony in court, and the use of taped interviews in police stations.

### Discussion points

1. How confident can we be that such laboratory-based findings resemble what would be found in the real world?
2. What are some of the practical implications of this research?

film of a car accident, and then asked them various questions. Some eyewitnesses were asked, "Did you see a broken headlight?", whereas others were asked, "Did you see the broken headlight?" In fact, there was no broken headlight in the film, but the latter question implied there was (this is known as a leading question). Only 7% of those asked about *a* broken headlight said they had seen it, compared to 17% of those asked about *the* broken headlight.

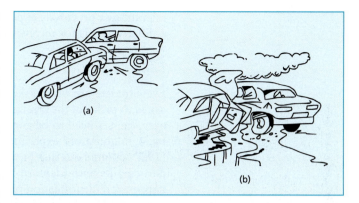

Post-event information does *not* always distort eyewitness reports. Yuille and Cutshall (1986) found that real-life recall can be very accurate. They analysed interviews from people who had witnessed a crime in which one person was shot dead and another was seriously injured. There were interviews with the police immediately after the crime and several months later with the researchers. Yuille and Cutshall found that the accuracy and amount of information recalled did not decrease over time. Of special importance, the eyewitnesses' accounts were *not* distorted by leading questions posed by the police. These findings suggest that post-event information may distort memory less in real life than in the laboratory.

Most studies have *only* provided evidence that eyewitness memory for peripheral details is distorted by post-event information. In fact, there is typically much less memory distortion for central details than for peripheral ones (e.g., Heath & Erickson, 1998). This reduces somewhat the practical importance of research on post-event information.

*What do such findings suggest about the reliability of human memory?*

Why does post-event information often distort what eyewitnesses report? In general, what we have here is simply retroactive interference (see earlier in the chapter). Some understanding of what is involved can be obtained with reference to the source monitoring framework (Johnson, Hashtroudi, & Lindsay, 1993). A memory probe (e.g., question) activates memory traces having informational overlap with it. The individual decides on the source of any activated memory on the basis of the information it contains. If the memories from one source resemble those from another source, this increases the chances of source misattribution. If eyewitnesses falsely attribute the source of misinformation to the original event, then the misinformation will form part of their recall of the event.

A key prediction from the source monitoring framework is as follows: Any manipulation that increases the extent to which memories from one source resemble those from another source increases the likelihood of source misattribution. Allen and Lindsay (1998) presented two narrative slide shows 48 hours apart describing two different events with different people in different settings. Thus, the participants knew that the post-event information contained in the second slide show was not relevant to the event described in the first slide show. However, some of the details in the two events were rather similar (e.g., a can of Pepsi vs. a can of Coca-Cola). This caused source misattribution, and led the participants to substitute details from the post-event information for details of the event itself.

Loftus (1979) argued that information from the misleading questions permanently alters memory for an incident: The previously formed memory trace is "overwritten" and destroyed. In one study, she offered participants $25 for accurate recall. Their recollections were still distorted by the misleading information they had heard, suggesting that the information might have been destroyed. However, the views of Loftus are *not* generally accepted. Dodson and Reisberg (1991) used an implicit memory test to show that misinformation had *not* destroyed the original memories of an event. They concluded that misinformation simply makes these memories inaccessible.

Loftus (1992) emphasised the notion of *misinformation acceptance*: The participants "accept" misleading information presented to them after an event, and subsequently regard it as forming part of their memory of that event. There is a greater tendency to accept post-event information in this way as time passes.

Much research in this area can be interpreted within Bartlett's (1932) schema theory (discussed earlier in the chapter). According to Bartlett, retrieval involves a process of *reconstruction*, in which all available information about an event is used to reconstruct its details on the basis of "what must have been true". On that account, new information relevant to a previously experienced event can affect recollection of that event by providing a different basis for reconstruction.

## Face recognition

Eyewitnesses are often asked to describe the facial features of the criminal, and may be asked to pick out the criminal from among other people at an identification parade. Thus, eyewitnesses need to be good at face recognition. There is generally accurate memory for faces in laboratory experiments, but face recognition is often poor in everyday life. Bruce (1982) pointed out that face recognition in the laboratory typically involves presenting the participants with *identical* pictures at study and at test, which differs greatly from what happens on identification parades. She found in a laboratory study that recognition memory was 90% correct when identical pictures of faces were used at study and test, but it dropped to 60% when the viewpoint and expression changed.

Beales and Parkin (1984) studied the effects of the context in which someone is seen. Face recognition from photographs was better when the face was in the same context at study and at test than when a different context was used. An important limitation on these studies was identified by Groeger (1997, p. 182): "Even though recognition judgements can be unreliable when the individual is portrayed in a different location, or where their physical appearance is different, these difficulties probably only apply to people who are not known to the witness."

The probability of mistakes being made on identification parades is influenced by whether or not the eyewitness is warned that the culprit may not be in the line-up (Wells, 1993). This is especially important with real-life line-ups, since eyewitnesses may feel the police would not have set up an identification parade unless they were fairly certain the actual culprit was present.

*Can you think of any other ways of improving the reliability of police line-ups?*

Wells (1993, p. 560) argued that eyewitnesses use *relative judgements* with identification parades: "The eyewitness chooses the line-up member who most resembles the culprit relative to the other members of the line-up." One way of reducing eyewitnesses' reliance on relative judgements is to use sequential line-ups, in which members of the line-up or identification parade are presented one at a time.

"Well I know he was wearing tights."

## CASE STUDY: *The antique shop murder*

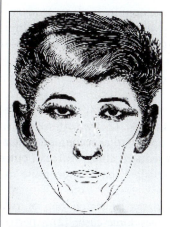

In March 1961 Edwin Bush went into an antique shop in London, owned by Louis Meier, and took an interest in a dress sword and some daggers. Bush returned to the shop shortly afterwards and spoke to Elsie Batten, who worked for Mr Meier.

The next day Meier discovered the dead body of Elsie Batten. She had been stabbed and an ivory handled dagger remained in the chest wound. The police interviewed Mr Meier and from his recollections were able to compile a facial picture of the suspect using the 'Identikit'. Another facial likeness of the suspect was built up from the recollections of another witness, Paul Roberts. (Bush had tried to sell the sword to him.) The similarity of the two witnesses' recollections was outstanding so the police photographed the pictures side by side, circulated them to all police forces and released them to the media in the hope that the man could be identified.

A few days later PC Cole was on duty when he saw a man answering the description of the suspect. The man was detained—it was Edwin Bush. An identification parade was arranged but Louis Meier could not make a positive identification. However, Paul Roberts immediately identified Bush. Bush wrote a full statement admitting the murder.

The detective in charge of the investigation said:

*This case is of particular interest because the arrest of the murderer was achieved as a direct result of the use of an American system, known as "Identikit". This was the first time this equipment had ever been used in this country, but so skilfully was it operated and so effective was the resultant "picture", that a Police Constable was able to recognise the wanted man and detain him ...*

Unfortunately facial recognition in everyday life is not usually this good!

based on www.met.police.uk/history/bush.htm

## Confidence

Most people assume that an eyewitness's confidence is a good predictor of his/her identification accuracy. This assumption is often false. For example, Perfect and Hollins (1996) gave their participants recognition memory tests for the information contained in a film about a girl who was kidnapped, and for general knowledge questions. Accuracy of memory was *not* associated with confidence for questions about the film, but it was with general knowledge questions. Perfect and Hollins (p. 379) explained the above difference as follows: "Individuals have insight into their strengths and weaknesses in general knowledge ... So, for example, individuals will know whether they tend to be better or worse than others at sports questions. However, eyewitnessed events are not amenable to such insight: subjects are unlikely to know whether they are better or worse ... than others at remembering the hair colour of a participant in an event, for example."

Perfect and Hollins (1996) found that eyewitnesses typically had more confidence in their accurate answers than in their inaccurate ones. Thus, they could decide on the quality of their own memories to some extent, even though they did not know whether they were better or worse than others at remembering details of an event.

There is not always a poor relationship between eyewitness confidence and accuracy. Sporer, Penrod, Read, and Cutler (1995) carried out a meta-analysis of several studies in which they distinguished between choosers (eyewitnesses making a positive identification) and non-choosers. There was practically no correlation between confidence and accuracy among non-choosers. However, the average correlation was +.41 among choosers, which indicates a moderate association between confidence and accuracy.

## Confirmation bias

Eyewitness testimony can be distorted by **confirmation bias**. This occurs when what is remembered is influenced by the observer's expectations. For example, students from two universities in the United States (Princeton and Dartmouth) were shown a film of a football game involving both universities. The students showed a strong tendency to report that their opponents had committed many more fouls than their own team.

## Weapon focus

Another factor involved in eyewitness testimony is **weapon focus**. This was described in the following way by Loftus (1979, p. 75): "The weapon appears to capture a good deal of the victim's attention, resulting in, among other things, a reduced ability to recall other details from the environment, to recall details about the assailant, and to recognise the assailant at a later time."

Loftus, Loftus, and Messo (1987) asked their participants to watch one of two sequences: (1) a person points a gun at a cashier and receives some cash; (2) a person hands a cheque to the cashier and receives some cash. Loftus et al. recorded the participants' eye movements, and found they looked more at the gun than at the cheque. In addition, memory for details unrelated to the gun/cheque was poorer in the weapon condition.

## Evaluation

- ➕ The memories of eyewitnesses are fragile, and are susceptible to retroactive interference.
- ➕ The evidence that post-event information can easily distort an eyewitness's recollections of an incident indicates the necessity of being very careful when questioning eyewitnesses.
- ➕ Another important finding is that eyewitness confidence is often not a good predictor of accuracy of identification.
- ➖ Post-event information is less likely to distort witnesses' memory for key details (e.g., the murder weapon) than for minor or peripheral details.
- ➖ Post-event information may distort eyewitness recall less in real life than in the laboratory (Yuille & Cutshall, 1986).

# Autobiographical memory

According to Conway and Rubin (1993), "**Autobiographical memory** is memory for the events of one's life" (p. 103). As such, it relates to our major life goals. There is much overlap between autobiographical memory and episodic memory (discussed earlier), in that the recollection of personal events and episodes occurs with both types of memory. However, there are two differences: (1) trivial events are more likely to be found in episodic memory than in autobiographical memory; (2) there is always a feeling of re-experiencing with episodic memory but not necessarily with autobiographical memory.

## Memories across the lifetime

Suppose we ask 70-year-olds to think of personal memories suggested by cue words (e.g., nouns referring to common objects). From which parts of their lives would most of the memories come? Rubin, Wetzler, and Nebes (1986) answered this question. There are various features about the findings:

- **Infantile amnesia,** shown by the almost total lack of memories from the first 3 years of life.
- A **reminiscence bump,** consisting of a surprisingly large number of memories coming from the years between 10 and 30 (especially 15–25).

- A *retention function* for memories up to 20 years old, with the older memories being less likely to be recalled than more recent ones.

The reminiscence bump has not generally been found in people younger than 30 years of age, and has not often been observed in 40-year-olds. However, it is nearly always found among older people. Rubin, Rahhal, and Poon (1998) found that 70-year-olds show the reminiscence bump for the following: particularly memorable books, vivid memories, memories the participants would want included in a book about their lives, names of winners of Academy Awards, and memory for current events.

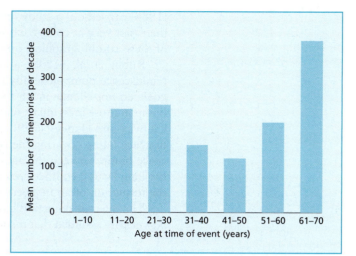

Memory for past events in the elderly as a function of the decade in which the events occurred. Based on Rubin et al. (1986).

## Theoretical perspectives

Howe and Courage (1997) related infantile amnesia to the emergence of the *cognitive self* towards the end of the second year of life (see Chapter 16). The crucial theoretical assumption made by Howe and Courage (p. 499) was as follows: "The development of the cognitive self late in the second year of life ... provides a new framework around which memories can be organised." It follows that the lower limit for people's earliest autobiographical memories should be about 2 years of age. That is approximately in line with the findings in the literature (Rubin, 2000). However, it is hard to show that the emergence of a sense of self is the causal factor.

Howe and Courage (1997) also assumed that the processes (e.g., rehearsal) used in learning and memory develop during the years of childhood. As a result, relatively few autobiographical memories should come from the years 2 to 5. In Rubin's (2000) literature review, only 22% of memories from the first 10 years of life came from the years 2 to 5.

According to social interactionist theory, "The primary functions of autobiographical memory are to develop a life history and to tell others what one is like through relating one's past experiences" (Harley & Reese, 1999, p. 1338). It follows from this theory that the way in which parents talk to their children about the past should influence the children's autobiographical memories. More specifically, they distinguished between two maternal reminiscing styles: high elaborative (in which past events are discussed in detail) and low elaborative. Children between the ages of 19 and 32 months reported more autobiographical memories if their mother had a high-elaborative reminiscing style. In addition, as predicted by Howe and Courage (1997), children with early self-recognition reported more autobiographical memories than those with later self-recognition.

## Reminiscence bump

We turn now to the reminiscence bump. Rubin et al. (1998, pp. 13–14) argued that, "the best situation for memory is the beginning of a period of stability that lasts until retrieval". Most adults have a period of stability starting in early adulthood, because it is then that a sense of adult identity develops. Memories from early adulthood also tend to have the advantage of novelty, in that they are formed shortly after the onset of adult identity. These two factors of novelty and stability produce strong memories for the following reasons:

- *Stability*
  Events from a stable period of life are more likely to serve as models for future events. This provides a cognitive structure serving as a stable organisation to cue events.
- *Novelty*
  This causes more effort to find meaning.
  There is a relative lack of **proactive interference** (interference from previous learning). This produces distinctive memories (see earlier in chapter).

Novelty (e.g., first-time experiences) is an important factor in increasing the accessibility of autobiographical memories. For example, Pillemer, Goldsmith, Panter, and White

*What period of your life do most of your autobiographical memories come from? Briefly make a list—do you have a reminiscence bump?*

**KEY TERM**

**Proactive interference:** disruption of memory by previous learning, often of similar material; see retroactive interference.

(1988) carried out a study on middle-aged participants who recalled four memories from their first year at college more than 20 years previously. Their key finding was that 41% of these autobiographical memories came from the first month of the course.

Rubin et al. (1998) and Conway and Pleydell-Pearce (2000) assumed that the reminscence bump generally extends only to about the age of 30 because the self and its goals do not change much thereafter. It follows that there should be a later reminscence bump in those individuals whose self and/or goals change dramatically after the age of 30. Conway and Haque (1999) found that older Bangladeshi individuals had a second reminiscence bump covering the period 35–55 years of age in addition to the typical reminiscence bump between the ages of 10 and 30. This second reminiscence bump was due to the long-lasting conflict between Pakistan and the Bengalee people that ultimately led to the formation of an independent Bangladesh.

The retention function has attracted relatively little empirical or theoretical interest. It is generally assumed that it simply reflects the typical phenomenon of forgetting over time.

## Diary studies

It is generally hard to assess the accuracy of an individual's recollections of the events of his/her own life. Wagenaar (1986) resolved this problem by carrying out a diary study, recording more than 2000 events over a 6-year period. For each event, he noted down information about who, what, where, and when, together with the rated pleasantness, saliency or rarity, and emotionality of each event. He then tested his memory by using the who, what, where, and when information cues one at a time or in combination. "What" information provided the most useful retrieval cue, perhaps because autobiographical memories are organised in categories. "What" information was followed in order of declining usefulness by "where", "who", and "when" information. "When" information on its own was almost totally ineffective. The more cues that were presented, the higher was the resultant probability of recall (see figure on the left). However, even with three cues almost half the events were forgotten within 5 years. When these forgotten events involved another person, that person provided further information about the event. In nearly every case, this proved sufficient for Wagenaar to remember the event. Thus, the great majority of life events may be stored away in long-term memory. High levels of salience, emotional involvement, and pleasantness were all associated with high levels of recall, especially high salience or rarity. The effects of salience and emotional involvement remained strong over retention intervals ranging from 1 to 5 years, whereas the effects of pleasantness decreased over time.

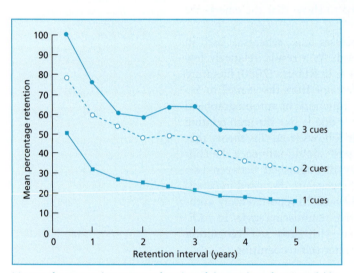

Memory for personal events as a function of the number of cues available and the length of the retention interval. Adapted from Wagenaar (1986).

A more complex picture emerged when Wagenaar (1994) carried out a detailed analysis of 120 very pleasant and unpleasant memories from his 1986 study. When someone else played the major role in an event, pleasant events were much better remembered than unpleasant ones. However, the opposite was the case for events in which Wagenaar himself played the major role, perhaps because he tends to be self-critical (Groeger, 1997).

*How generalisable do you think the results of diary studies are?*

## Self-memory system

According to Conway and Pleydell-Pearce (2000), we possess a self-memory system consisting of an autobiographical knowledge base and the current goals of the working self. There are three levels within the autobiographical knowledge base:

1. *Lifetime periods.* These typically cover substantial periods of time defined by major ongoing situations (e.g., time as an undergraduate student). According to Conway and Pleydell-Pearce (2000, p. 262), "The content of a lifetime period represents *thematic* knowledge about common features of that period ..., as well as *temporal* knowledge about the duration of a period."

2.  *General events.* These include repeated events (e.g., visits to a sports club) and single events (e.g., a holiday in Australia).
3.  *Event-specific knowledge.* This knowledge consists of images, feelings, and other details relating to general events and spanning time periods from seconds to hours.

How do we access information contained in the autobiographical knowledge base? According to the theory, we have a working self, which is concerned with the self and what it may become in future. The currently active goals of this working self determine which autobiographical memories we retrieve. In addition, the goals of the working self influence the kinds of memories *stored* in the autobiographical knowledge base. Thus, "autobiographical memories are primary records of success or failure in goal attainment" (Conway & Pleydell-Pearce, 2000, p. 266), and reflect the kind of person we are.

According to the theory, autobiographical memories are usually accessed by generative retrieval, in which "memories are actively and intentionally constructed through an interaction between the working self goal structure and the autobiographical memory knowledge base" (Conway, Pleydell-Pearce, & Whitecross, 2001, p. 495). There is also direct retrieval, in which autobiographical memories seem to come spontaneously to mind.

## Evidence

Studies of brain-damaged patients have provided evidence for the notion that there are three types of autobiographical knowledge. Of particular interest are cases of **retrograde amnesia**, in which there is widespread forgetting of events preceding the brain injury. Conway and Pleydell-Pearce (2000, p. 263) discussed several studies of patients with severe retrograde amnesia in which there was, "an inability to retrieve specific memories, whereas access to knowledge of lifetime periods and general knowledge from the period covered by their amnesias remained intact". Thus, event-specific knowledge is more vulnerable to loss or disruption than knowledge about lifetime periods or general events.

A key assumption made by Conway and Pleydell-Pearce (2000) was that autobiographical memory and the self are very closely related. There is support for this assumption. For example, Woike, Gershkovich, Piorkowski, and Polo (1999) considered individuals having two personality types: (1) agentic personality type, with an emphasis on independence, achievement, and personal power; and (2) communal personality type, with an emphasis on interdependence and similarity to others. Agentic individuals recalled emotional autobiographical memories relating to mastery and humiliation, whereas communal individuals recalled emotional memories relating to friendship and love. Such findings suggest that the recall of autobiographical memories is influenced by the goals of the working self.

Conway and Pleydell-Pearce (2000) assumed that autobiographical memories produced via generative retrieval are constructed rather than simply reproduced. Two supporting findings were reported by Conway (1996). First, he found that it took people much longer to retrieve autobiographical memories than other kinds of information. For example, they took about 4 seconds to retrieve autobiographical memories, compared to about 1 second to verify personal information (e.g., name of their bank). It seems likely that it would take longer to retrieve constructed memories than reproduced ones. Second, Conway found that the information contained in autobiographical memories produced on two occasions differed considerably. If autobiographical memories were reproduced, they would presumably be highly similar from one retrieval to another.

The distinction between generative and direct retrieval was studied by Berntsen (1998). Generative retrieval was assessed by presenting cues to elicit autobiographical memories, whereas direct retrieval was assessed by asking the participants to keep a record of autobiographical memories that came to mind without any deliberate attempt to retrieve them. More autobiographical memories produced by direct retrieval than by generative retrieval were of specific events (89% vs. 63%, respectively). According to Berntsen (p. 136), "We maintain a considerable amount of specific episodes in memory which may often be inaccessible for voluntary [generative] retrieval but highly accessible for involuntary [direct] retrieval."

*Can you think of any reasons why event-specific knowledge may be more vulnerable to loss than knowledge about lifetime periods or general events?*

**KEY TERM**

**Retrograde amnesia:** impaired memory for events occurring before the onset of amnesia; see anterograde amnesia.

## Evaluation

⊕ Conway and Pleydell-Pearce (2000) have put forward the most comprehensive theory of autobiographical memory currently available.

⊕ Several key assumptions of the theory (e.g., the hierarchical structure of autobiographical memory; the intimate relationship between autobiographical memory and the self) are well supported by the evidence.

⊖ The precise ways in which the working self interacts with the autobiographical knowledge base to produce recall of specific autobiographical memories are unspecified.

⊖ Some evidence supports the distinction between generative and direct retrieval (e.g., Berntsen, 1998), but more research is needed.

## SUMMARY

**Multi-store model**

There are three types of memory store within the multi-store model: sensory stores, short-term store, and long-term store. The sensory stores are modality specific, and hold information very briefly. The short-term store has very limited capacity. Information is lost from this store because of interference, diversion of attention, and decay. Evidence from brain-damaged patients supports the distinction between short-term and long-term memory stores. The memory stores differ with respect to temporal duration, storage capacity, and forgetting mechanisms. The multi-store model is very over-simplified, and the role of rehearsal is exaggerated.

**Working memory**

The working memory system consists of a central executive, a phonological loop, and a visuo-spatial sketchpad. Two tasks can be performed successfully together only when they use different components of the working memory system. The phonological loop consists of a passive phonological store and an articulatory process. Its primary function is to assist in the learning of new words. The visuo-spatial sketchpad consists of a visual cache and an inner scribe, and there may be separate visual and spatial systems. The central executive is involved in various functions such as switching of retrieval plans, time-sharing, selective attention, and temporary activation of long-term memory. There may be relatively separate verbal and spatial working memory systems.

**Levels of processing**

According to levels-of-processing theory, long-term memory is better for information that is processed deeply or semantically at the time of learning. In addition, elaborative rehearsal improves long-term memory but maintenance rehearsal does not. Some evidence supports these theoretical assumptions. However, long-term memory depends on elaboration and distinctiveness of processing as well as on depth of processing. Long-term memory depends on the relevance of the stored information to the requirements of the memory test (transfer-appropriate processing). The theory is more applicable to tests of explicit memory than to those of implicit memory. Finally, the theory provides a description rather than an explanation of certain memory phenomena.

**Theories of forgetting**

The forgetting function is generally logarithmic with a few exceptions (e.g., autobiographical memory). There is controversial evidence concerning recovered memories of childhood abuse. There is convincing evidence of the existence of proactive and retroactive interference. However, special conditions are required for substantial interference effects to occur, and interference theory says little about the processes involved in forgetting. Most forgetting is cue-dependent, and is greater when the contextual information present at retrieval differs from that stored in memory.

**Theories of long-term memory**

There is an important distinction between episodic and semantic memory, and the pre-frontal cortex is much more involved in episodic memory than in semantic memory. However, there are several similarities and inter-connections between them. There is a major distinction between explicit and implicit memory. PET studies have revealed that rather different areas of the brain are activated in explicit and implicit memory tasks. There are different types of implicit memory (e.g., perceptual and conceptual).

Most amnesic patients suffer from anterograde and retrograde amnesia. Amnesics have fairly intact short-term memory, skill learning, repetition priming, and conditioning. Amnesics typically have great difficulties in acquiring new episodic and semantic memories, but are more likely to have impaired episodic memories. Amnesic patients generally have relatively intact implicit memory but severely impaired explicit memory. However, amnesic patients have impaired implicit memory for information that needs to be integrated.

*Amnesia*

Schemas are well-integrated packages of information that allow us to form expectations and to draw inferences. Bartlett found that systematic schema-based distortions (e.g., rationalisations) increased over time. Schemas can influence both comprehension and retrieval processes. According to the script-pointer-plus-tag hypothesis, recognition memory should always be better for atypical actions than for typical ones, whereas recall for atypical actions should be worse than for typical ones at long retention intervals. However, interruptive atypical actions are better recalled than typical ones at all retention intervals. Most schema theories are low in testability. The range of inferences drawn during story comprehension is less than predicted by most schema theories.

*Schema theories*

Flashbulb memories are vivid and detailed. It has been claimed that they involve special neural mechanisms, but there is little clear evidence that flashbulb memories differ in any important way from ordinary memories. Eyewitness memory for an event is easily distorted by post-event information. This is an example of retroactive interference, and can be partially understood within the source monitoring framework. Face recognition is reduced when there are changes in the appearance of a face between study and test or the context changes. Eyewitness confidence is often a poor predictor of identification accuracy. Other problems with eyewitness testimony stem from confirmation bias and weapon focus. Autobiographical memory is organised into lifetime periods, general events, and event-specific knowledge. The self and major life goals help to determine which autobiographical information is stored and retrieved. Autobiographical memories are mostly accessed by generative retrieval, but can also be accessed spontaneously by direct retrieval. Autobiographical memories produced by generative retrieval are constructed rather than reproduced.

*Everyday memory*

## FURTHER READING

- Eysenck, M.W. (2000). *Principles of cognitive psychology*. Hove, UK: Psychology Press. The topics discussed in this chapter are dealt with in more detail in Chapters 5 and 6 of this book.
- Haberlandt, K. (1999). *Human memory: Exploration and applications*. Boston: Allyn and Bacon. Several chapters in this book (e.g., 4, 5, and 10) provide readable accounts of major topics within long-term memory.
- Tulving, E., & Craik, F.I.M. (2000). *The Oxford handbook of memory*. New York: Oxford University Press. This excellent book contains numerous chapters dealing with the topics discussed in this chapter.

- **Problem solving**
  Moving from recognition of a problem to its solution.

  *Definition*
  *Distinction between well- and ill-defined problems*
  *Thorndike's trial-and-error learning*
  *Studies on insight and functional fixedness*
  *Information-processing theory*
  *Newell & Simon's computational approach*

- **Judgement research**
  Calculating the likelihood of various possibilities.

  *Bayes' theorem*
  *Base-rate information*
  *Representativeness heuristic*
  *Availability heuristic*
  *Subjective probability*
  *The value of heuristics*

- **Decision making**
  Selecting one out of two or more possibilities.

  *Prospect theory: objective and subjective values*
  *Loss aversion studies*
  *Risk seeking and risk aversion; framing effects*
  *Tetlock's social functionalist approach*
  *Omission bias*

- **Deductive reasoning**
  The conclusions necessarily following assumptions.

  *Rules of conditional reasoning: modus ponens, modus tollens*
  *Wason selection task*
  *Social contract theory*
  *Syllogistic reasoning: premises and biases*
  *Cross-cultural differences*

- **Theories of deductive reasoning**
  Explanations of mental logic errors.

  *Braine's abstract-rule theories*
  *Johnson-Laird's mental model approach*

- **Inductive reasoning**
  Decisions about truth.

  *Wason's relational rule; confirmation bias*
  *Simulated research environment studies*
  *Analogical reasoning*

- **How flawed is human thinking?**
  Everyday thinking vs. laboratory situations.

  *Differences in rationality*
  *Bounded rationality*

334

# Thinking

This chapter is concerned with the higher-level cognitive processes involved in thinking. It is divided into sections on problem solving, decision making, judgement, deductive reasoning, and inductive reasoning, with the related topic of expertise being discussed in detail in Chapter 8. Bear in mind that we use the *same* cognitive system to deal with all of these types of task. As a result, many distinctions among different forms of thinking are rather arbitrary and camouflage underlying similarities in cognitive processes. However, some distinctions *are* worth making. For example, problem solving involves generating various possibilities and then choosing among them in order to make progress to a goal. In contrast, in decision making the possibilities are presented, and the task only involves choosing one of them. Judgement is that part of decision making concerned with working out the probability of occurrence of one or more events. Finally, reasoning involves calculating which inferences or conclusions follow from a given set of information.

Many of the cognitive processes discussed in this chapter closely resemble those assessed by traditional intelligence tests (see Chapter 11). The reader could be forgiven for being puzzled that there seems to be very little cross-fertilisation between these two research areas. Why is this? The initial work on intelligence was motivated by the attempt to provide an accurate *description* of individuals' intellectual ability for practical purposes (e.g., identifying mentally retarded children, personnel selection). In contrast, cognitive psychologists focus on the detailed processes underlying performance on cognitive tasks, and so their emphasis is more on providing an *explanation* of that performance. However, some cognitive psychologists (e.g., Stanovich & West, 2000; Sternberg, 1985) are starting to bridge the gap between intelligence research and cognitive psychology.

## PROBLEM SOLVING

According to Mayer (1990, p. 284), problem solving is, "cognitive processing directed at transforming a given situation into a goal situation when no obvious method of solution is available to the problem solver." This definition suggests that there are three major

| Forms of thinking | |
|---|---|
| Problem solving: | Cognitive activity that involves moving from the recognition that there is a problem through a series of steps to the solution or goal state. Most other forms of thinking involve some problem solving. |
| Decision making: | Selecting one out of a number of presented options or possibilities. |
| Judgement: | The component of decision making that involves calculating the likelihood of various possible events. |
| Deductive reasoning: | Deciding what conclusions follow necessarily provided that various statements are assumed to be true; the form of thinking most closely associated with logic. |
| Inductive reasoning: | Deciding whether certain statements or hypotheses are true on the basis of the available information; a form of thinking used by scientists and detectives. |

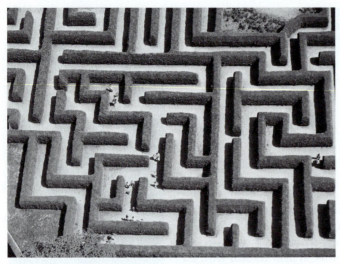

Escaping from, or reaching the middle of, a maze is an example of a well-defined problem. It is clear when a solution is reached.

How to retrieve your car keys from a locked car is an ill-defined problem. It can be very hard to identify the best solution.

**KEY TERM**

**Trial-and-error learning:** a type of problem solving in which the solution is reached by producing fairly random responses rather than by a process of thought.

aspects to problem solving:

- It is purposeful (i.e., goal directed).
- It involves cognitive rather than automatic processes.
- A problem only exists when someone lacks the relevant knowledge to produce an immediate solution. Thus, a problem for most people (e.g., a mathematical calculation) may not be so for someone with relevant expertise (e.g., a professional mathematician).

There is an important distinction between well-defined and ill-defined problems. Well-defined problems are ones in which all aspects of the problem are clearly specified: These include the initial state or situation, the range of possible moves or strategies, and the goal or solution. The goal is well specified in the sense that it is clear when the goal has been reached. For example, a maze is a well-defined problem, in which escape from it (or reaching the centre as in the Hampton Court maze) is the goal.

In contrast, ill-defined problems are under-specified. Suppose you have locked your keys inside your car, and want to get into it without causing any damage. However, you have urgent business to attend to elsewhere, and there is no-one around to help you. In such circumstances, it may be very hard to identify the best solution to the problem.

Most everyday problems are ill-defined problems. In contrast, psychologists have focused mainly on well-defined problems. Why is this? One important reason is that well-defined problems have a best strategy for their solution. As a result, we can identify the errors and deficiencies in the strategies adopted by human problem solvers.

There is a further important distinction between knowledge-rich and knowledge-lean problems. Knowledge-rich problems can only be solved by individuals possessing a considerable amount of specific knowledge, whereas knowledge-lean problems do not require the possession of such knowledge. In approximate terms, most traditional research on problem solving has involved the use of knowledge-lean problems, whereas research on expertise (e.g., chess grandmasters; see Chapter 8) has involved knowledge-rich problems.

## Gestalt approach

Some of the earliest research on problem solving was carried out by Thorndike (1898). He placed hungry cats in closed cages within sight of a dish of food outside the cages. The cage doors could be opened when a pole inside the cage was hit. Initially, the cats thrashed about and clawed the sides of the cages. However, after some time, the cats hit the pole inside the cage and opened the door. On repeated trials, the cats gradually learned what was required of them. Eventually they would hit the pole almost immediately, and so gain access to the food. Thorndike was unimpressed by the cats' performance, referring to their apparently almost random behaviour as **trial-and-error learning**.

There was a reaction against the above view by German psychologists known as the Gestaltists during the 1920s and 1930s. They argued that Thorndike's (1898) problem situation was unfair, because there was a purely arbitrary relationship between the cats' behaviour (hitting the pole) and the desired consequence (the opening of the cage door).

A key difference between Thorndike's (1898) approach and that of the Gestaltists is captured in the distinction between reproductive and productive problem solving. **Reproductive problem solving** involves the re-use of previous experiences, and was the focus of Thorndike's research. In contrast, **productive problem solving** involves a novel restructuring of the problem. It is more complex than reproductive problem solving, but the Gestaltists argued that several species are capable of this higher-level form of problem solving.

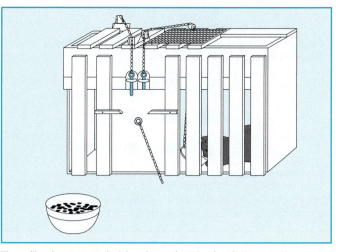

Thorndike demonstrated trial-and-error learning by placing a cat in a puzzle box. The cat eventually discovered how to get out and on subsequent trials did this immediately, an example of instrumental learning.

## Insight

Köhler (1925) showed that animals can engage in productive problem solving. In one of his studies, an ape called Sultan was inside a cage, and could only reach a banana outside the cage by joining two sticks together. The ape seemed lost at first. However, it then seemed to realise how to solve the problem, and rapidly joined the sticks together. According to Köhler, the ape had suddenly restructured the problem. By so doing, it had shown **insight** (which is often accompanied by the "ah-ha experience").

There is at least one potential difficulty with Köhler's (1925) claimed demonstrations of insight in apes. The apes had spent the early months of their lives in the wild, and so could have acquired useful information about sticks and how they can be combined. Birch (1945) found that apes raised in captivity showed little evidence of the kind of insightful problem solving observed by Köhler (1925).

What about studies on problem solving in humans? Maier (1931) carried out a famous study of restructuring in which people were given the "two-string" or "pendulum problem". The participants were brought into a room containing various objects (e.g., poles, pliers, extension cords), plus two strings hanging from the ceiling. The task was to tie together the two strings hanging from the ceiling, but the strings were too far apart for the participants to reach one string while holding the other. The most "insightful" (but rarely produced) solution was the pendulum solution. This involved taking the pliers, tying them to one of the strings, and then swinging the string like a pendulum. In this way, it was possible to hold one string and to catch the other on its upswing.

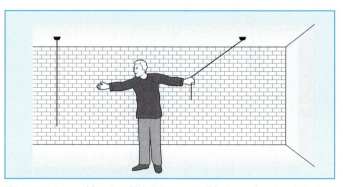

The two-string problem in which it is not possible to reach one string while holding the other.

Maier (1931) also found that it was possible to facilitate problem restructuring or insight by having the experimenter apparently accidentally brush against the string to set it swinging. Soon afterwards, many participants produced the pendulum solution, but few reported having noticed the experimenter brush against the string. This finding is sometimes known as the unconscious cue effect.

In spite of its fame, Maier's (1931) study was fairly slipshod. Of particular importance, the *unconscious* cue effect does not seem to have been replicated (J. Evans, personal communication). However, there is evidence for a *conscious* cue effect. Battersby et al. (1953) found the experimenter could greatly speed up solution times on the pendulum problem by highlighting objects that might be relevant to the problem.

The Gestaltists claimed that insight involves special processes, and is thus quite different from normal problem solving (see Gilhooly, 1996). Relevant findings were reported by Metcalfe and Weibe (1987). They recorded participants' feelings of "warmth" (closeness to solution) while engaged in solving insight and non-insight problems. There was a progressive increase in warmth during non-insight problems. With insight problems, in contrast, the warmth ratings remained at the same low level until suddenly increasing dramatically shortly before the solution was reached. These findings suggest (but do not prove) that insight *is* special, and occurs in an all-or-none fashion.

*Do you think it is possible to define the cognitive processes involved in insight? How might you go about discovering what these might be?*

**Trial-and-error or insight learning?**

The problem here is to turn this square grid of nine boxes into a triangle by moving only two of the boxes.

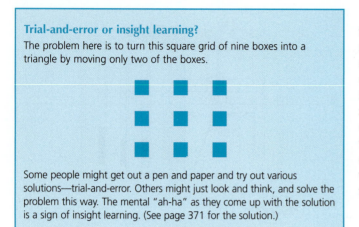

Some people might get out a pen and paper and try out various solutions—trial-and-error. Others might just look and think, and solve the problem this way. The mental "ah-ha" as they come up with the solution is a sign of insight learning. (See page 371 for the solution.)

Additional evidence that there is an important distinction between insight and non-insight problems was reported by Schooler, Ohlsson, and Brooks (1993). They asked participants to verbalise the steps they were taking on the way to problem solution. Such verbalisation interfered with the participants' ability to solve insight but not non-insight problems. Non-insight problems involve a series of steps that can be self-monitored and easily verbalised. In contrast, insight problems involve a sudden restructuring, and the processes involved conflict with the requirement to verbalise the problem solver's thoughts.

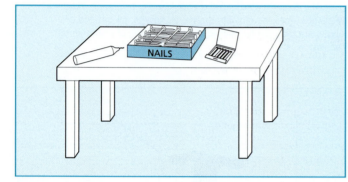

The objects presented to participants in the candle problem.

## Functional fixedness

Past experience usually benefits our ability to solve problems. However, Duncker (1945) argued this is not always the case. He studied **functional fixedness**, in which we fail to solve problems because we assume from past experience that any given object only has a limited number of uses. Duncker gave his participants a candle, a box of nails, and several other objects. Their task was to attach the candle to a wall by a table so it did not drip onto the table below.

Most participants tried to nail the candle directly to the wall or to glue it to the wall by melting it. Only a few decided to use the inside of the nail-box as a candle holder, and then nail it to the wall. According to Duncker, the participants "fixated" on the box's function as a container rather than as a platform. More correct solutions were produced when the nail-box was empty at the start of the experiment, presumably because that made the box appear less like a container.

Weisberg and Suls (1973) argued that many participants given Duncker's candle problem failed to solve it because they hardly noticed that the box had been present. When non-solvers of the problem were asked to recall all the objects which had been available to solve the problem, 54% of them did not recall the box.

Duncker (1945) assumed that functional fixedness occurred in his study because of the participants' past experience with boxes. However, he had no direct evidence. Luchins (1942) adopted the superior approach of *controlling* participants' relevant past experience by providing it within the experiment. He used water-jar problems involving three water jars of varying capacity. The participants' task was to imagine pouring water from one jar to another to finish up with a specified amount of water in one of the jars.

*Why do you think there was such a large difference in success rate between Luchins' two groups of participants?*

The most striking finding obtained by Luchins (1942) can be illustrated by considering one of his studies in detail. One problem was as follows: Jar A can hold 28 quarts of water, jar B 76 quarts, and jar C 3 quarts. The task is to end up with exactly 25 quarts in one of the jars. The solution is not difficult: Jar A is filled, and then jar C is filled from it, leaving 25 quarts in jar A. Ninety-five per cent of participants who had previously been given similar problems solved it. Other participants were trained on a series of problems, all having the same complex three-jar solution. Of these participants, only 36% managed to solve this relatively simple problem. These findings led Luchins (p. 15) to conclude: "Einstellung—habituation—creates a mechanised state of mind, a blind attitude towards problems; one does not look at the problem on its own merits but is led by a mechanical application of a used method."

**KEY TERM**

**Functional fixedness:** a limitation in problem solving in which individuals focus on likely functions or uses of objects while ignoring other, more unusual, uses.

## Evaluation

➕ The Gestaltists showed that problem solving could involve productive processes as well as reproductive ones.

➕ Past experience can disrupt (rather than benefit) current problem solving (e.g., functional fixedness). Thus, some problems cannot be solved by simply making use of well-learned responses.

➕ The Gestaltists' research revealed the importance of restructuring, and provided suggestive evidence of insight.

➖ Many Gestalt concepts (e.g., "insight", "restructuring") are rather vague and hard to measure.

➖ The Gestaltists did not clarify the processes underlying insight.

## Post-Gestalt approach

There have been various attempts to incorporate key aspects of the Gestalt approach into an information-processing theory of problem solving. According to Ohlsson (1992, p. 4), "insight occurs in the context of an impasse [block], which is unmerited in the sense that the thinker is, in fact, competent to solve the problem." The key assumptions of Ohlsson's theory are as follows:

• The way in which a problem is currently represented or structured in the problem solver's mind serves as a memory probe to retrieve related knowledge from long-term memory (e.g., operators or possible actions).

• The retrieval process is based on spreading activation among concepts or items of knowledge in long-term memory (see Chapter 9).

• An impasse or block occurs when the way a problem is represented does not permit retrieval of the necessary operators or possible actions.

• The impasse is broken when the problem representation is changed, thus permitting the problem solver to access the necessary knowledge in long-term memory.

• Changing the representation of a problem can occur in various ways:
  • Elaboration or addition of new problem information;
  • Constraint relaxation, in which inhibitions on what is regarded as permissible are removed;
  • Re-encoding, in which some aspect of the problem representation is reinterpreted (e.g., a pair of pliers is reinterpreted as a weight in the pendulum problem).

• Insight occurs when an impasse is broken, and the retrieved knowledge operators are sufficient to solve the problem.

## Evidence

Changing the representation of a problem often leads to a solution. For example, consider the mutilated draughtboard problem. Initially the board is completely covered by 32 dominoes which occupy two squares each. Then two squares from diagonally opposite corners are removed. Can the remaining 62 squares be filled by 31 dominoes? Kaplan and Simon (1990) asked participants to think aloud while trying to solve the problem. They all started by mentally covering squares with dominoes. However, this strategy is ineffective, because there are 758, 148 permutations of the dominoes!

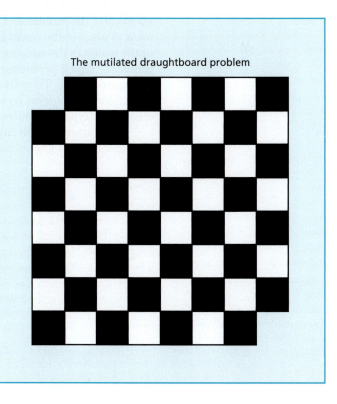

The mutilated draughtboard problem

In order to solve the mutilated draughtboard problem, you have to form a new representation of the problem involving elaboration and re-encoding. If you represent each domino as an object covering one white and one black square (re-encoding), and represent the draughtboard as having lost two white (or two black) squares (elaboration), then it becomes clear that the 31 dominoes cannot cover the mutilated board.

Yaniv and Meyer (1987) found their participants' initial efforts to access relevant stored information were often unsuccessful. However, these unsuccessful efforts produced spreading activation to other concepts stored in long-term memory. As a result, the participants were more likely to recognise relevant information when it was presented to them.

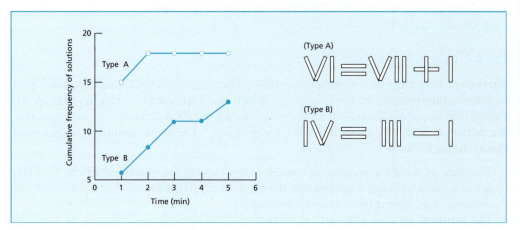

Two of the matchstick problems used by Knoblich et al. (1999), and the cumulative solution rates produced for these types of problems in their study.

Knoblich, Ohlsson, Haider, and Rhenius (1999) showed the importance of constraints in reducing the likelihood of insight. They presented their participants with problems such as those shown above. As you can see, you would need to know all about Roman numerals to solve the problems! The task involved moving a *single* stick to produce a true statement in place of the initial false one. Some problems (type A) only required changing two of the values in the equation (e.g., VI = VII + I becomes VII = VI + I). In contrast, other problems (type B problems) involved a more fundamental change in the representation of the equation (e.g., IV = III − I becomes IV − III = I). Knoblich et al. found it was much harder for participants to relax the normal constraints of arithmetic (and thus to show insight) for type A problems than for type B ones.

What factors lead to constraint relaxation and problem solution on insight problems? Consider the well-known nine dots problem, in which you have to draw four straight lines connecting all nine dots without taking your pen or pencil from the paper. According to Scheerer (1963), the difficulty most people have with this problem is that they mistakenly assume that they have to stay within the square formed by the dots. It follows that providing visual cues showing lines outside the square should lead to a substantial improvement in performance on the nine dots problem. However, MacGregor, Ormerod, and Chronicle (2001) found that such cues were only modestly useful. They argued that most people draw lines within the square, because that approach initially allows several dots to be cancelled with each line. It is only when failure is experienced repeatedly that participants relax the constraint of remaining within the square and move to an insightful solution.

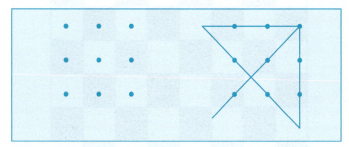

Scheerer's (1963) nine-dot problem requires you to draw four continuous straight lines, connecting all dots without lifting your pen off the paper. Most people find it difficult to solve this because they assume all lines have to stay within the square formed by the dots. In Gestalt terms, participants have "fixated" on the shape, which results in a state of functional fixedness.

## Evaluation

⊕ Ohlsson's view that insight occurs when there is restructuring of a problem (i.e., changing the representation) is a useful one.
⊕ Constraint relaxation is of major importance in solving insight problems.
⊕ Ohlsson's theory is an improvement on the Gestalt approach because the mechanisms underlying insight are specified more precisely.
⊖ Ohlsson paid little attention to individual differences in problem-solving skills.
⊖ It is often not possible to predict when (or in what way) the representation of a problem will change.

## Computational approach: Newell and Simon

Allen Newell and Herb Simon (1972) argued that it is possible to produce systematic computer simulations of human problem solving. They achieved this with their General Problem Solver, which is a computer program designed to solve a fairly wide range of well-defined problems. Newell and Simon's starting assumptions in the construction of the General Problem Solver were that information processing is serial (one process at a time), that people possess limited short-term memory capacity, and that they can retrieve relevant information from long-term memory.

*Do you think a computer program can completely capture and model human problem solving?*

Newell and Simon (1972) started by asking people to solve problems while thinking aloud. They then used these verbal reports to decide what general strategy was used on each problem. Finally, Newell and Simon specified the problem-solving strategy in sufficient detail for it to be programmed in their General Problem Solver. In the General Problem Solver, problems are represented as a problem space. This problem space consists of the initial state of the problem, the goal state, all of the possible mental operators (e.g., moves) that can be applied to any state to change it into a different state, and all of the intermediate states of the problem. Thus, the process of problem solving involves a sequence of different knowledge states. These knowledge states intervene between the initial state and the goal state, with mental operators producing the shift from one knowledge state to the next.

The above notions can be illustrated by considering the Tower of Hanoi problem. The initial state of the problem consists of three discs piled in decreasing size on the first of three pegs. When all the discs are piled in the same order on the last peg, the goal state has been reached. The rules specify that only one disc can be moved at a time, and a larger disc cannot be placed on top of a smaller disc. These rules restrict the possible mental operators on each move.

How do people select mental operators or moves as they proceed through a problem? According to Newell and Simon (1972), the complexity of most problems means that we rely heavily on **heuristics** or rules of thumb. Heuristics can be contrasted with **algorithms**, which are generally complex methods or procedures guaranteed to lead to problem solution. The most important of the various heuristic methods is **means–ends analysis**:

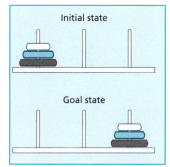

The initial state and goal state in the Tower of Hanoi problem.

1. Note the difference between the current state of the problem and the goal state.
2. Form a sub-goal that will reduce the difference between the current and goals states.
3. Select a mental operator that will permit attainment of the sub-goal.

Means–ends analysis is a heuristic rather than an algorithm because (while useful), it is not guaranteed to lead to problem solution.

The way in which means–ends analysis is used can be illustrated with the Tower of Hanoi problem. A reasonable sub-goal in the early stages of the problem is to try to place the largest disc on the last peg. If a situation arises in which the largest disc must be placed on either the middle or the last peg, then means–ends analysis will lead to that disc being placed on the last peg.

Newell and Simon (1972) applied the General Problem Solver to 11 rather different problems (e.g., letter-series completions, missionaries and cannibals, the Tower of Hanoi).

> **KEY TERMS**
> **Heuristics:** rules of thumb or approximate methods that are used in problem solving.
> **Algorithms:** methods or procedures that will definitely solve a problem.
> **Means–ends analysis:** an approach to problem solving in which the difference between the current position and the goal position is reduced.

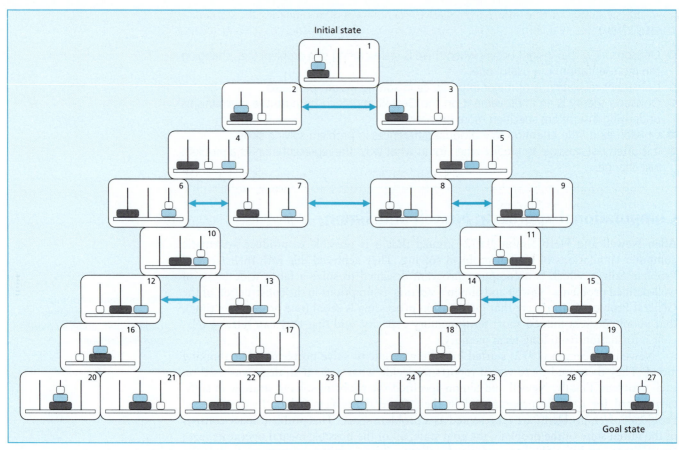

Using means–ends analysis, the diagram above shows the problem space of legal moves in the Tower of Hanoi problem. If boxes touch each other, or are joined by arrows, this indicates that one can move from one state to the other using a legal operator.

The General Problem Solver could solve all the problems, but it did not always do so in the same way as people.

## Evidence

Thomas (1974) argued that people should experience difficulties in solving a problem at those points at which it is necessary to make a move that temporarily *increases* the distance between the current state and the goal state. In other words, problem solvers should struggle when means–ends analysis is inadequate. He used a variant of the missionaries and cannibals problem based on hobbits and orcs. In the standard form of this problem, three missionaries and three cannibals need to be transported across a river in a boat which can hold only two people. The number of cannibals on either bank of the river must never exceed the number of missionaries, because then the cannibals would eat the missionaries. One move involves transferring one cannibal and one missionary back to the starting point, and thus seems to be moving away from the solution. As predicted, it was at this point that the participants experienced severe difficulties. However, the General Problem Solver did *not* find this move especially difficult.

*Why do you think the General Problem Solver did not find this move especially difficult?*

Thomas (1974) also obtained evidence that participants set up sub-goals. They would often carry out a block of several moves at increasing speed, followed by a long pause before embarking on another rapid sequence of moves. This suggested that participants were dividing the problem up into three or four major sub-goals.

Simon and Reed (1976) studied a more complex version of the missionaries and cannibals problem. It can be solved in 11 moves, but on average participants took 30 moves to solve it. There was evidence that the participants initially adopted a *balancing strategy*, in which they simply tried to ensure there were equal numbers of missionaries and cannibals on each side of the river. After a while, the participants shifted to the *means–ends strategy*, in which the focus was on moving more people to the goal side of the river. Finally, the participants used an *anti-looping heuristic* designed to avoid any moves reversing the immediately preceding move.

## Evaluation

⊕  The Newell and Simon approach works well with several well-defined problems.

⊕  The theory allows us to specify the shortest sequence of moves from the initial state to the goal state. Thus, we can see exactly when and how an individual participant's performance deviates from the ideal.

⊕  The theoretical approach is consistent with our knowledge of human information processing. For example, we have limited working memory capacity, and that helps to explain why we typically use heuristics or rules of thumb rather than algorithms.

⊖  The General Problem Solver is better than humans at remembering what has happened on a problem. However, it is inferior to humans at planning future moves: It focuses on only a single move, whereas humans often plan small sequences of moves (Greeno, 1974).

⊖  Most problems in everyday life are ill-defined, and so are very different from the problems studied by Newell and Simon. Solving the ill-defined problems of real life typically depends much more on possessing relevant specific knowledge and expertise.

## JUDGEMENT RESEARCH

We often change our opinion of the likelihood of something being the case in the light of new information or evidence. Suppose you are 90% confident that someone has lied to you. However, their version of events is subsequently confirmed by another person, and this leads you to believe that there is only a 60% probability that you have been lied to. Everyday life is full of cases in which the strength of our belief is increased or decreased by fresh information.

The Rev. Thomas Bayes provided a more precise way of thinking about such cases. He produced a mathematical formula allowing us to work out the impact of new evidence on a pre-existing probability. Bayes focused on situations in which there are two possible beliefs or hypotheses (e.g., X is lying vs. X is not lying), and he showed how new information or data can change the probabilities of the two hypotheses. Of key importance in Bayes' theorem was the notion that we need to take account of the relative probabilities of the two hypotheses *before* the data are obtained. These probabilities form the **base-rate information**, defined by Koehler (1996, p. 16) as "the relative frequency with which an event occurs or an attribute is present in the population".

Consider the taxi-cab problem used by Tversky and Kahneman (1980). In this problem, a taxi-cab was involved in a hit-and-run accident one night. Of the taxi-cabs in the city, 85% belong to the Green company and 15% to the Blue company. An eyewitness identified the cab as a Blue cab. However, when her ability to identify cabs under appropriate visibility conditions was tested, she was wrong 20% of the time. What is the probability that the cab involved in the accident was Blue? If your views coincide with those of most of the participants in this study, your answer is that there is an 80% probability that the cab was Blue.

The above answer is wrong, because it ignores the base-rate information that 85% of the cabs belong to the Green company and only 15% to the Blue company. If you had been asked to indicate the probability that the cab was blue without knowing what the eyewitness said, you would probably have said the probability was 15%. What we need to do is to follow Bayes' theorem, taking account of the eyewitness *and* the base-rate information. When that is done, we emerge with the correct answer of 41%. Thus, the base-rate information tips the balance in favour of the taxi-cab involved in the accident being green in spite of the fact that the eyewitness said it was blue.

**KEY TERM**
**Base-rate information:**
the relative frequency of an event within a population.

# Neglecting or using base rates

Could we change the taxi-cab problem so that people would take account of the base-rate information? Tversky and Kahneman (1980) reworded the problem to emphasise that green cabs were responsible for 85% of cab accidents in the city. This rewording drew a clear *causal* relationship between the accident record of a cab company and the likelihood of it being responsible for any given accident. Participants given the reworded version of the problem indicated on average there was about a 60% probability that the cab responsible for the accident was blue.

There have been numerous other studies designed to look at the conditions in which base-rate information is used. We will consider in some detail the related studies of Casscells, Schoenberger, and Graboys (1978) and of Cosmides and Tooby (1996). The problem used by Casscells et al. was as follows:

> *If a test to detect a disease whose prevalence is 1/1000 has a false positive rate of 5%, what is the chance that a person found to have a positive result actually has the disease, assuming that you know nothing about the person's symptoms or signs?*

Forty-five per cent of staff and students at Harvard Medical School ignored the base-rate information, and so produced the wrong answer of 95%. The correct answer (which is 2%) was given by only 18% of the participants. Why is 2% correct? According to the base-rate information, 999 people out of 1000 do not suffer from the disease. The fact that the false positive rate is 5% means that 50 out of every 1000 people tested would give a misleading positive finding. Thus, 50 times as many people give a false positive result as give a true positive result (the 1 person in 1000 who actually has the disease), and so there is only a 2% chance that a person testing positive has the disease.

*Why do you think so many people got the answer wrong?*

Cosmides and Tooby (1996) emphasised the *frequencies* of individuals in the various categories relevant to the problem. Part of their instructions were worded as follows: "One out of 1000 Americans has disease X ... out of every 1000 people who are perfectly healthy, 50 of them test positive for the disease ... How many people who test positive for the disease will actually have the disease? (—out of—)".

Cosmides and Tooby (1996) found 76% of the participants produced the correct answer when the problem was presented in frequency terms, compared with 12% with the original form. The most plausible explanation of this difference is that the numerical calculations are simpler when dealing with frequencies rather than probabilities (Johnson-Laird et al., 1999).

## Conclusions

Koehler (1996, p. 1) reviewed findings on the use of base-rate information, and concluded that this literature, "does not support the conventional wisdom that people routinely ignore base rates. Quite the contrary, the literature shows that base rates are almost always used." There is reasonable support for that viewpoint. However, what is of more practical importance is the extent to which people use base-rate information in everyday life. As Koehler (p. 14) admitted, "When base rates in the natural environment are ambiguous, unreliable, or unstable, simple normative rules for their use do not exist. In such cases, the diagnostic value of base rates may be substantially less than that associated with many laboratory experiments."

Base-rate information is often not used effectively in the real world even by experts. Hoffrage et al. (2000) gave advanced medical students four realistic diagnostic tasks containing base-rate information presented in either a probability or a frequency version. These experts paid little attention to base-rate information in the probability versions, but performed much better when given the frequency versions.

## Representativeness heuristic

Why do we fail to make proper use of base-rate information? According to Tversky and Kahneman (1973), we often use a simple heuristic or rule of thumb known as the representativeness heuristic. When people use this heuristic, "events that are representative or typical of a class are assigned a high probability of occurrence. If an event is highly similar to most of the others in a population or class of events, then it is considered representative" (Kellogg, 1995, p. 385). The representativeness heuristic is studied in situations in which people judge the probability that an object or event A belongs to a class or process B. Suppose you are given the description of an individual, and are asked to estimate the probability that he/she has a certain occupation. What you would probably do is to estimate the probability in terms of the *similarity* between that individual's description and your stereotype of that occupation.

Kahneman and Tversky (1973) studied people's use of the representativeness heuristic. Their participants were given a description such as the following: "Jack is a 45-year-old man. He is married and has four children. He is generally conservative, careful, and ambitious. He shows no interest in political and social issues and spends most of his free time on his many hobbies which include home carpentry, sailing, and mathematical puzzles" (p. 241). The participants decided the probability that Jack was an engineer or a lawyer. They were all told the description had been selected at random from a total of 100 descriptions. Half the participants were told there were descriptions of 70 engineers and 30 lawyers, whereas the other half were told there were descriptions of 70 lawyers and 30 engineers.

What did Kahneman and Tversky (1973) find? The participants decided on average there was a .90 probability Jack was an engineer, and they did so regardless of whether most of the 100 descriptions were of lawyers or engineers. Thus, the participants ignored the base-rate information (i.e., the 70:30 split of the 100 descriptions).

The representativeness heuristic is used more strikingly to produce the **conjunction fallacy**. This is the mistaken belief that the conjunction or combination of two events (A and B) is more likely than one of the two events. Tversky and Kahneman (1983) obtained evidence of the conjunction fallacy based on the following description:

*Linda is 31 years old, single, outspoken, and very bright. She majored in philosophy. As a student, she was deeply concerned with issues of discrimination and social justice, and also participated in anti-nuclear demonstrations.*

They were then asked to rank order eight possible categories in terms of the probability that Linda belonged to each one. Three of the categories were bank teller, feminist, and feminist bank teller. Most participants ranked feminist bank teller as more probable than either bank teller or feminist. This is incorrect, because *all* feminist bank tellers belong to the larger categories of bank tellers and feminists!

Fiedler (1988) compared performance on the original version of the Linda problem with that on a frequency version, in which the participants indicated how many of 100 people fitting Linda's description were bank tellers, and how many were bank tellers and active feminists. The percentage of participants showing the conjunction fallacy was dramatically lower with the frequency version. Performance may have been better with the frequency version because people are more used to dealing with frequencies than with probabilities.

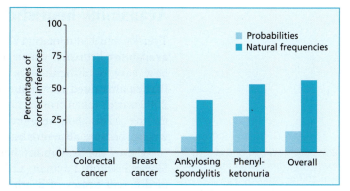

Percentage of correct inferences by medical students in four realistic diagnostic tasks presented in a probability or a frequency version. From Hoffrage et al. (2000).

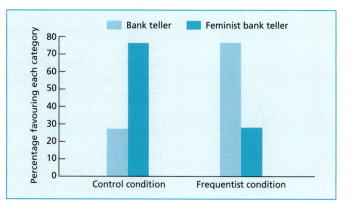

Performance on the Linda problem in the frequentist and control conditions. Data from Fiedler (1988).

**CASE STUDY: *Picking lottery numbers***

In general, people have a very poor understanding of randomness and probability, as evidenced by the types of numbers commonly selected in national lotteries. Even people who claim to understand that any given number is as likely to come up as any other will be heard to despair: "Oh, I'll never win with that—four numbers in a row!", or "All my numbers are bunched up under 20—I'd better spread them out a bit to get a better pattern." In fact, statistics suggest that you're actually better off picking numbers with a skewed or bunched appearance: you're no more likely to win, but in the unlikely event that you do, you'll be less likely to have to share your prize with anyone else!

## Availability heuristic

Tversky and Kahneman (1983) studied another heuristic or rule of thumb. This was the **availability heuristic**, which involves estimating the frequencies of events on the basis of how easy or difficult it is to retrieve relevant information from long-term memory. Participants rated the frequency of seven-letter words ending in "ing" and "-n-" out of 2000 words taken from a novel. Most claimed there would be many more words ending in "ing". This claim resulted from use of the availability heuristic. However, it is entirely wrong, because all words ending in "ing" also end in "-n-"!

Use of the availability heuristic often produces errors in everyday life. Lichtenstein, Slovic, Fischoff, Layman, and Combs (1978) asked people to judge the relative likelihood of different causes of death. Those causes of death which attract considerable publicity (e.g., murder) were judged more likely than those that do not (e.g., suicide), even when the opposite is actually the case.

People do *not* always use the availability heuristic when judging the frequency of events. For example, Brown (1995) presented category–exemplar pairs (e.g., Country–France), with each category being presented several times. The category name was always accompanied by the same exemplar (same context) or a different exemplar (different context). The task was to decide how frequently each category name had been presented. In the different-context condition, about 60% of the participants reported using the availability heuristic. However, very few used the availability heuristic in the same-context condition, and almost 70% of the participants in that condition reported that they had not used any coherent strategy on the task.

*How might you go about testing the strength of the availability heuristic in determining how people make judgements?*

## Support theory

Tversky and Koehler (1994) put forward a support theory of subjective probability, which can be seen in part as extending the notion of an availability heuristic. The crucial theoretical assumption is that any given event will appear more or less likely depending on the way it is described. Thus, we need to distinguish between events themselves and the descriptions of those events. For example, you would almost certainly assume that the probability that you will die on your next summer holiday is extremely low. However, it might seem more likely if you were asked the following question: "What is the probability that you will die on your next summer holiday from a disease, a sudden heart attack, an earthquake, terrorist activity, a civil war, a car accident, a plane crash, or from any other cause?"

Why would the subjective probability of death on holiday be greater in the second case that the first? According to support theory, a more explicit description of an event has greater subjective probability than the same event described in less explicit terms. There are two main reasons for this theoretical prediction:

- An explicit description may draw attention to aspects of the event not obvious in the non-explicit description.
- Memory limitations may mean that people do not remember all of the relevant information if it is not supplied.

### Evidence

Most of the evidence is consistent with support theory (see Tversky & Koehler, 1994). For example, Johnson, Hashtroudi, and Lindsay (1993) offered some participants hypothetical health insurance covering hospitalisation for any reason, whereas others were offered health insurance for any disease or accident. These offers are the same, but participants were willing to pay a higher premium in the latter case. The explicit references to disease and accident made it seem more likely that hospitalisation would be required, and so increased the value of being insured.

Surprisingly, the finding that subjective probability is higher for an event when it is explicitly described has been obtained even with experts who could presumably fill in all the missing details of a non-explicit description from their own knowledge and experience.

According to support theory any event can seem more likely depending on how it is described.

For example, Redelmeier et al. (1995) presented doctors at Stanford University with a description of a woman suffering from abdominal pain. Half the doctors estimated the probabilities of two specified diagnoses (gastroenteritis and ectopic pregnancy) and of a residual category of everything else. The remaining doctors estimated the probabilities of each of five specified diagnoses (two of which were gastoenteritis and ectopic pregnancy) and of a residual category of everything else. The former group of doctors produced a mean subjective probability of .50 for the residual category. The appropriate comparison figure for the latter group consists of the three additional diagnoses (excluding gastroenteritis and ectopic pregnancy) plus the residual category. The mean subjective probability was .69, indicating that subjective probabilities are higher for explicit descriptions even among experts.

## Evaluation

⊕ People make use of various heuristics or rules of thumb in numerous situations.

⊕ People often show a partial or complete neglect of base-rate information even when it is appropriate.

⊖ Kahneman and Tversky have not provided process models specifying *when* and *how* the various heuristics are used (Gigerenzer, 1996).

⊖ Some errors of judgement occur simply because participants misunderstand parts of the problem. For example, between 20% and 50% of participants given the Linda problem interpret, "Linda is a bank teller", as implying she is not active in the feminist movement (see Gigerenzer, 1996).

⊖ Small differences in the wording of problems can produce large effects which are hard to explain. For example, performance is often much better when problems are expressed in frequencies rather than probabilities (e.g., Cosmides & Tooby, 1996; Fiedler, 1988).

⊖ There are large individual differences on many of the problems that have been studied (see Stanovich & West, 2000). Highly intelligent individuals often use fewer misleading heuristics than do less intelligent ones.

## Are heuristics valuable?

It would appear from the research discussed so far that heuristics or rules of thumb often lead us to make errors of judgement or thinking. Gigerenzer, Todd, and the ABC Research Group (1999) and Goldstein and Gigerenzer (2002) argued that heuristics are valuable in

Which of these animals sleeps the longest? If you don't recognise the sloth, you might say the cat, relying on the recognition heuristic. (Two-toed sloths sleep for 20 hours a day; cats for around 14.5.)

many circumstances; indeed, their 1999 book was entitled *Simple Heuristics That Make Us Smart*. In these books the central focus was on fast and frugal heuristics, which are, "simple rules in the mind's adaptive toolbox for making decisions with realistic mental resources" (Todd & Gigerenzer, 2000, p. 727). Such heuristics are used in one-reason decision making: "Stop looking for cues as soon as one is found that differentiates between the two options being considered" (p. 733).

Gigerenzer and his colleagues have focused mainly on the **recognition heuristic**, which is defined as choosing between two objects on the basis that one is recognised whereas the other is not. For example, suppose you are asked to decide whether Hamburg or Cologne has the larger population. If you recognise the name Hamburg but not Cologne, you might use the recognition heuristic and guess that Hamburg is the larger city. The recognition heuristic can be used in many other situations (e.g., to predict the results of football matches or to decide which of two companies to invest in).

The recognition heuristic is limited, because it cannot be used when someone recognises both objects (e.g., cities). In those circumstances, it is assumed that individuals will adopt the "take the best" strategy, which involves "take the best, ignore the rest." More specifically, cues (e.g., Is the city recognised? Does the city have a football club? Does the city have a university?) are searched in decreasing order of validity. As soon as a cue is found which differentiates between the two options (e.g., one city has a football club but the other does not), a judgement is made.

*Why do you think people so often rely on the recognition heuristic?*

### Evidence

When participants were given the task of deciding which was the larger of two cities, 90% of them used the recognition heuristic when one city was recognised and the other was not (Goldstein & Gigerenzer, 2002). You could argue that this finding is trivial, because many participants may have had no other useful knowledge to guide their judgement. However, 90% of participants used the recognition heuristic even when informed which German cities had football teams, and told that the German cities with football teams tend to be larger than those without (Goldstein & Gigerenzer, 2002).

Why do people use the recognition heuristic? First, it can be used very rapidly and imposes practically no cognitive demands on the person using it. Second, it is moderately valid: Goldstein and Gigerenzer (2002) reported correlations of +.60 and +.66 between the number of people recognising a city and its population.

Goldstein and Gigerenzer (2002) presented American and German students with pairs of American cities and pairs of German cities, and asked them to select the larger

**KEY TERM**

**Recognition heuristic:** choosing the one of two objects or options that is recognised as familiar.

city in each pair. Common sense would suggest that performance would be better when participants judged cities in their own country, because they would obviously have much more knowledge about them. However, the disadvantage is that you cannot apply the recognition heuristic (which is moderately valid) when you recognise both of the cities in a pair. The findings were impressive: American and German students performed worse on their own cities than on those of the other country.

Todd and Gigerenzer (2000) compared the effectiveness of various strategies, including the following:

1. *Minimalist*. Cues are selected at random.
2. *Take the best*. Described above.
3. *Dawes's rule*. The difference between the number of cues for and against a given choice determines the choice.
4. *Multiple regression*. All the cues are weighted and summed in an optimal way.

Three measures of the effectiveness of these strategies were then calculated. First, there was frugality, which is the mean number of cues used. Second, there was fitting, which was the percentage success rate when each strategy was used. Third, there was generalisation, which was the percentage success rate when the strategies were applied to parts of the data sets not seen in training.

The findings are shown in the figure below. The simple heuristic (take the best) was more effective than the minimalist strategy. It was of comparable effectiveness to Dawes's rule and multiple regression, even though it made use of far fewer cues. In addition, the simple heuristic showed better generalisation than the other strategies, leading Todd and Gigerenzer (2000, p. 736) to conclude that the simplicity of simple heuristics, "allows them to be robust when confronted by environmental changes and enables them to generalise well to other situations".

Broder (2000) found that the extent to which people use the take-the-best heuristic depends on the costs involved in obtaining information. In one of his studies, the participants pretended they were stockbrokers, and had to decide between two share options on each trial. There was a low or a high cost associated with obtaining each piece of information about the shares. When the cost was high, 65% of the participants used the take-the-best heuristic, compared to only 15% when the cost was low. Thus, most people do not restrict themselves to the limited information required to use the take-the-best heuristic when it is relatively easy and inexpensive to obtain further information.

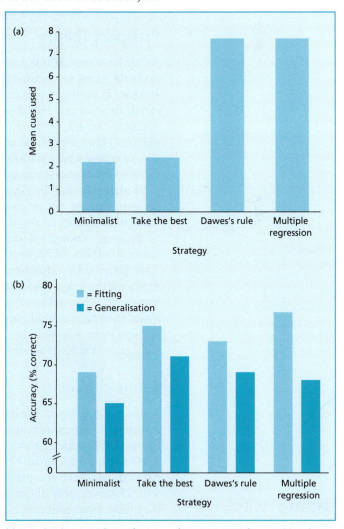

(a) Frugality (cues used) as a function of strategy. Data from Todd and Gigerenzer (2000).
(b) Fitting (correct answers) and generalisation (correct on new data) as a function of strategy. Data from Todd and Gigerenzer (2000).

## Evaluation

⊕ Simple heuristics can be surprisingly effective and accurate in certain situations.
⊕ Simple heuristics are of particular usefulness when decisions have to be made rapidly.
⊖ Simple heuristics are typically not used when it is easy to obtain additional information (e.g., Broder, 2000).
⊖ "It may be that it is not that simple heuristics make us smart ...; rather, it may be that we resort to simple heuristics to do the very thing we are *not* smart at" (Chater, 2000, p. 745).
⊖ In many situations, several heuristics could be used, and the theory often does not allow us to predict *which* will be selected (Newstead, 2000).

# DECISION MAKING

As mentioned before, there are clear similarities between decision making and problem solving. Decision making requires an element of problem solving, in that individuals are typically trying to make the best possible choice from a range of options. However, all the options are present in decision making, whereas they need to be generated in problem solving.

*How would you describe your own decision-making processes? Are these different for different decisions?*

Life is full of decisions (e.g., choice of holiday destination, choice of partner, choice of career). Typically, there are various benefits and costs associated with each option, and that often makes decision making rather difficult. How do we decide what to do? At one time, it was assumed that most people behave rationally, and so will select the best option. This assumption formed an important part of normative theories, which focused on how people *should* make decisions rather than on how they actually *do* make decisions. For example, according to the utility theory put forward by von Neumann and Morgenstern (1947), we try to maximise *utility*, which is the subjective value we attach to an outcome. When we have to choose between simple options, we assess the expected utility or expected value of each one by means of the following formula:

Expected utility = (probability of a given outcome) × (utility of the outcome)

As we will see shortly, there is precious little support for normative theories of decision making. The decisions we make are often influenced by a range of emotional, social, and other factors, and thus do not conform neatly to the predictions of such theories.

## Prospect theory

As we have seen, it follows from normative theories that rational decision makers should make decisions to maximise expected value or utility. This is often difficult to do for two reasons. First, the objective probabilities of different outcomes are often unknown. As a result, we must rely on subjective probabilities based on our belief in the likelihood of each outcome. Second, we need to distinguish between the *objective* and *subjective* value of any outcome. For example, when deciding whether to take a highly paid job with no job security, or a less well paid job with complete job security, some people would attach more value to the financial rewards than to job security, whereas others would do the opposite.

Kahneman and Tversky (1984) argued that the problems with normative theories of decision making are much greater than simply working out the predictions they would make with respect to any decision. According to their prospect theory, important aspects of decision making are simply not rational. More specifically, our decision making is strongly influenced by whether the decision in question concerns possible gains or losses. They proposed a value function relating value to gains and losses. As can be seen in the figure on the left, losses cause much greater changes in subjective value than do equivalent gains. What follows from the notion that people are much more sensitive to potential losses than to potential gains? The most direct prediction is that people will make decisions so as to minimise the chance of any loss occurring, even if that means forgoing possible gains. Evidence relating to prospect theory is discussed below.

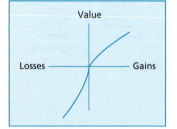

A hypothetical value function. From Kahneman and Tversky (1984).

### Gains and losses

Support for prospect theory has come from studies of a phenomenon known as **loss aversion**, in which individuals show greater sensitivity to loss than to gain. Tversky and Shafir (1992) offered participants a gamble in which there was a 50% chance of gaining $200 and a 50% chance of losing $100. According to normative theories, all the participants should have accepted this gamble, because it provided an average expected gain of $50. However, only about one-third of the participants agreed to accept the bet, because they were more concerned about possible losses than possible gains.

Most people find the thought of losing money so aversive that they are willing to engage in **risk seeking** to try to avoid losses. Kahneman and Tversky (1984) offered participants the choice between a sure loss of $800 or an 85% probability of losing $1000 with a 15%

probability of not incurring any loss. Most decided to take a chance on avoiding loss, even though this decision increased the average expected loss from $800 to $850!

A phenomenon resembling risk seeking is the **sunk-cost effect**, in which additional resources are expended to justify some previous investment. Dawes (1988) discussed a study in which participants were told that two people had paid a $100 non-refundable deposit for a weekend at a resort. On the way to the resort, both of them became slightly unwell, and felt they would probably have a more pleasurable time at home than at the resort. Should they drive on or turn back? Many participants argued that the two people should drive on to avoid wasting the $100: This is the sunk-cost effect. This decision seems perverse in some ways: It involves extra expenditure (money spent at the resort vs. staying at home), even though it is less preferred than being at home!

You'll have to drop her to catch me, so are you feeling lucky, punk?

What happens when the decision only concerns gains rather than losses? Kahneman and Tversky (1984) found most people preferred a sure gain of $800 to an 85% probability of gaining $1000 and a 15% probability of gaining nothing. This is known as **risk aversion**, and occurs even though the expected value of the risky decision is greater than that of the sure gain ($850 vs. $800, respectively). According to prospect theory, the subjective value of a large gain is not much greater than that of a small gain, and so there is little incentive for people to gamble in order to try to increase the size of a gain.

Some people are much more willing than others to engage in risky decision making, but these individual differences have rarely been studied. An exception was a study by Lopes (1987), who used a short questionnaire to identify risk-averse and risk-seeking participants. The participants had to choose among several lotteries varying in terms of risk. As predicted, risk-averse participants tended to avoid the riskier lotteries, but that was not the case for the risk-seeking ones. Lopes (pp. 274–275) came to the following conclusion: "Risk-averse people appear to be motivated by a desire for *security*, whereas risk-seeking people appear to be motivated by a desire for *potential*."

## Framing effects

Risky decision making is often influenced by irrelevant aspects of the situation, such as the precise way in which an issue is presented. This phenomenon is known as **framing**. Some framing effects can be accounted for in terms of loss aversion. For example, Tversky and Kahneman (1981) studied framing effects in the Asian disease problem. Participants were told there was likely to be an outbreak of an Asian disease in the United States, and it was expected to kill 600 people. Two programmes of action had been proposed: Programme A would allow 200 people to be saved; programme B would have a one-third probability that all 600 people would be saved, and a two-thirds probability that no-one would be saved. When the choices were expressed in this form (with an emphasis on the number of lives saved), 72% of the participants favoured programme A. This occurred even though the two programmes (if implemented several times) would on average both lead to the saving of 200 lives. This illustrates the phenomenon of risk aversion when the focus is on gains.

Tversky and Kahneman (1981) also used the Asian disease problem in a negatively framed version. In this version, the participants were told programme A would lead to 400 dying, whereas programme B carried a one-third probability that nobody would die, and a two-thirds probability that 600 people would die. The problem is actually the same as in the positively framed version, but there was a marked difference in the participants' decisions. With the negatively framed version, 78% of the participants chose programme B. Thus, they showed risk-seeking behaviour when the focus was on losses.

Wang (1996) showed that considerations of fairness can influence decision making in the Asian disease problem. Participants chose between definite survival of two-thirds

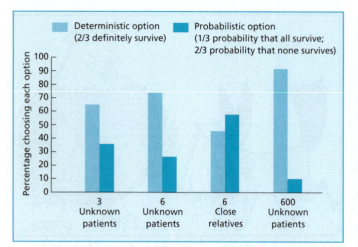

Effects of fairness manipulation on choice of the option with selected or with non-selected survivors. Data from Wang (1996).

*Do you think prospect theory can account for all decisions that we make in our everyday lives?*

of the patients (deterministic option) or a one-third probability of all the patients surviving and a two-thirds probability of none surviving (probabilistic option). The patient group consisted of 3, 6, or 600 patients unknown to the participants, or 6 patients who were close relatives. On average, the deterministic option would lead to survival of twice as many patients as the probabilistic option, but the probabilistic option seems fairer. The preferred option was greatly influenced by group size and by the relationship between the group members and the participants. Presumably the increased percentage of participants choosing the probabilistic option with small group size (especially for relatives) occurred because the social context and psychological factors relating to fairness were regarded as more important in those conditions.

Framing effects have been found in real-world decision making. Banks et al. (1995) studied the effectiveness of two videotapes in persuading women to undergo a mammogram or breast examination. Both videotapes contained the same medical facts, but one emphasised the gains of mammography whereas the other focused on the risks of not undergoing a mammogram. As predicted by prospect theory, more of the women who watched the risk-focused videotape had a mammogram within the following 12 months.

## Evaluation

⊕ The key assumption of prospect theory, that people attach more weight to losses than to gains, has been supported in numerous studies in the laboratory and in the real world.

⊕ The research generated by prospect theory has been important in revealing some of the limitations of normative theories of decision making.

⊖ As Hardman and Harries (2002, p. 76) pointed out, "There is no apparent rationale for ... the value function ... The value function is descriptive of behaviour but does not go beyond this."

⊖ Individual differences in willingness to make risky decisions are de-emphasised in the theory (e.g., Lopes, 1987).

⊖ Perhaps the greatest limitation of prospect theory is that it minimises the effects of emotional and social factors on decision making (cf., Wang, 1996). These factors are considered in the next section.

## Social functionalist approach

In the laboratory, people typically make decisions about hypothetical situations, and their families and friends neither know nor care about those decisions. In contrast, other people generally know about the decisions we make in everyday life, and so we feel the need to be able to justify our decisions to other people. Such considerations led Tetlock (2002) to put forward a social functionalist approach, in which the social context of decision making is taken fully into account. According to this approach, people often behave like intuitive politicians, in that an important part of their focus in decision making involves, "anticipating objections that others are likely to raise to alternative courses of action and crafting accounts that pre-empt those objections" (p. 454). It follows from Tetlock's approach that there should be strong evidence for decisions being influenced by a range of social and emotional factors.

## Evidence

Shafir, Simonson, and Tversky (1993) showed how the need to be able to justify oneself influences decision making. Participants imagined they had the chance to buy a very cheap holiday in Hawaii, but the special offer expired the next day. They had three choices: (1) buy the holiday; (2) decide not to buy the holiday; (3) pay a $5 non-refundable fee to retain the opportunity to buy the holiday in 2 days' time. All the participants were asked to assume they had just taken a difficult examination. In one version of the problem, they knew they had passed the examination. In a second version, they knew they had failed. In the third version, they would find out the next day whether they had passed or failed.

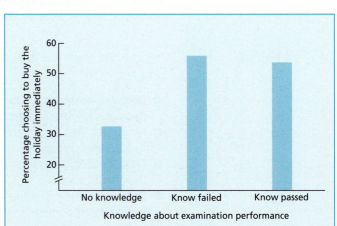

What do you these three groups decided to do? Of those who had passed or failed, a majority decided to buy the holiday immediately. However, only 32% of those who did not know their examination result decided to buy the holiday immediately. Those who had passed could justify the holiday as a reward, and those who had failed could justify it as a consolation. However, for those who did not know their examination result, there was no clear justification for taking a holiday.

Percentage choosing to buy a holiday immediately as a function of having passed an examination, failed an examination, or not knowing whether the examination has been passed or failed. Data from Tversky and Shafir (1992).

Tetlock's (2002) theoretical approach accounts well for various findings on the sunk-cost effect, which involves putting in additional resources to justify some previous investment. Simonson and Staw (1992) told participants to decide whether a light beer or a non-alcoholic beer should receive an additional $3 million in marketing support (e.g., advertising). They were then told that the president of the company making both beers had made the same decision as the participant, but that the marketing support had proved ineffective. They then had to decide how to allocate $10 million of additional marketing support between the two beers. In the high-accountability condition, participants were told that information about their decisions might be shared with other students and instructors, and they were asked to give permission to record an interview about their decisions. In the low-accountability condition, participants were told their decisions would be confidential, and that there was no connection between participants' performance on the task and their managerial effectiveness or intelligence.

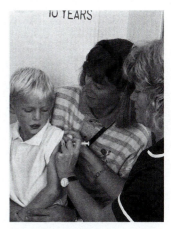

What do you think the participants decided to do? The tendency towards a sunk-cost effect (i.e., putting most of the extra money into marketing the same beer as before) was significantly stronger in the high-accountability condition than in the low-accountability condition. Participants in the high-accountability condition experienced a greater need to justify their previously ineffective course of action (i.e., fruitless investment in one type of beer) by increasing their commitment to it.

Human adults almost certainly experience more need to justify themselves than do children or the members of other species. It follows that we would expect to find a smaller sunk-cost effect in children and other species than in human adults. This is precisely what has been found (see Arkes & Ayton, 1999, for a review). These are striking findings, because adults do not typically commit more errors than children or members of other species.

Ritov and Baron (1990) found that omission bias was shown when participants were asked if they would vaccinate their children against a disease. Many would put their children at risk by selecting the option not to vaccinate even if the odds were higher for the child catching the disease than from the danger of the vaccine.

The need which people have to justify their actions to themselves and to others lies behind **omission bias**, which is the tendency to prefer inaction to action. Ritov and Baron (1990) asked participants to assume their child had 10 chances in 10,000 of dying from flu during an epidemic if he/she were not vaccinated. The vaccine was certain to prevent the child from catching flu, but had potentially fatal side effects. The participants indicated the maximum death rate from the vaccine itself they were willing to tolerate to have their child vaccinated. The average maximum acceptable risk was 5 deaths per 10,000. Thus, people would avoid having their child vaccinated when the likelihood of the vaccine causing death was much lower than the death rate from the disease against which the vaccine protects!

> **KEY TERM**
> **Omission bias:** the tendency to prefer inaction to action when engaged in risky decision making.

*Do you think the social functionalist approach can explain decision making across all cultures?*

What was going on in the above study? The participants argued they would feel more responsible for the death of their child if it resulted from their own actions rather than from their inaction. This is an example of omission bias. An important factor in omission bias is anticipated regret, which is often greater when an unwanted outcome has been caused by an individual's own actions. Omission bias and anticipated regret influence many real-life decisions, including those involving choices between consumer products, sexual practices, and medical decisions (see Mellers, Schwartz, & Cooke, 1998).

## Evaluation

⊕ Decision making is typically influenced by social factors, and by our need to justify our decisions to ourselves and to other people.

⊕ Many so-called errors and biases (e.g., omission bias) can be explained within a social functionalist approach.

⊖ Tetlock's (2002) social functionalist approach does not make detailed predictions, and is thus hard to test.

⊖ Decision making is influenced by numerous social factors, and we are a long way from having a comprehensive theory within which to account for these social influences.

# DEDUCTIVE REASONING

Reasoning is related to problem solving, because people trying to solve a reasoning task have a definite goal and the solution is not obvious. However, problem solving and reasoning are typically treated separately. Reasoning problems differ from other kinds of problems in that they often owe their origins to systems of formal logic. However, there are clear overlaps between the two areas. Of particular importance, the fact that some reasoning problems can be solved by the application of the rules of logic does not necessarily mean that that is how people normally solve them.

There is an important distinction between deductive reasoning and inductive reasoning. **Deductive reasoning** (discussed in this section) allows us to draw conclusions which are certain provided that other statements are assumed to be true. For example, if we assume that

Tom is taller than Dick, and Dick is taller than Harry, the conclusion that Tom is taller than Harry is necessarily true. In contrast, **inductive reasoning** (discussed in the next section) involves drawing general conclusions from specific information, but the conclusions are *not* necessarily true. For example, dozens of experiments may all provide support for a given theory, and we may conclude that the theory is correct. However, we cannot rule out the possibility that future experiments may show that the theory is incorrect.

Researchers have studied various types of deductive reasoning. However, we will focus on conditional reasoning and syllogistic reasoning. After we have discussed the relevant research, theoretical explanations of the findings will be considered.

## Conditional reasoning

Conditional reasoning has been studied to decide whether human reasoning is logical. It has its origins in propositional calculus, in which logical operators such as not; as ... if; not; if and only if are included in propositions. Consider, for example, the following problem in conditional reasoning:

> *Premises*
> If it is raining, then Fred gets wet.
> It is raining.
> *Conclusion*
> Fred gets wet.

This conclusion is valid. It illustrates an important rule of inference known as *modus ponens*: "If A, then B", and also given A, we can validly infer B.

Another major rule of inference is *modus tollens*: from the premise, "If A, then B", and the premise, "B is false", the conclusion "A is false" necessarily follows. This rule of

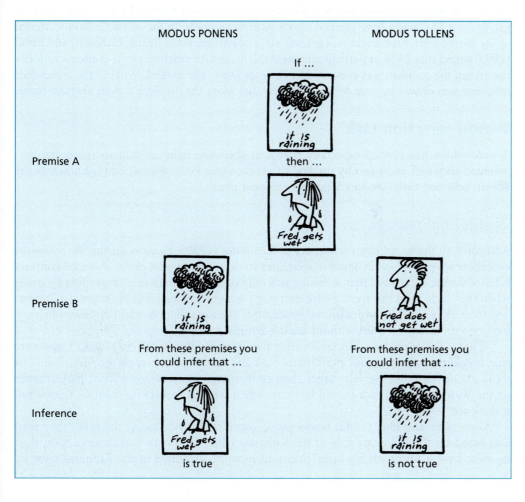

**KEY TERM**

**Inductive reasoning:** a form of reasoning in which a generalised conclusion is drawn from specific information.

inference is shown in the following example:

> *Premises*
> If it is raining, then Fred gets wet.
> Fred does not get wet.
> *Conclusion*
> It is not raining.

*Why do you think people make more errors with "modus tollens" than with "modus ponens"?*

People consistently perform much better with *modus ponens* than *modus tollens*. Evans (1989) reviewed the literature, and concluded that very few errors are made with *modus ponens*, but the error rate often exceeds 30% with *modus tollens*.

Two other inferences are worth considering at this stage. The first is called *affirmation of the consequent*, and the second is called *denial of the antecedent*. Here is an example of affirmation of the consequent:

> *Premises*
> If it is raining, then Fred gets wet.
> Fred gets wet.
> *Conclusion*
> Therefore, it is raining.

Here is an example of denial of the antecedent:

> *Premises*
> If it is raining, then Fred gets wet.
> It is not raining.
> *Conclusion*
> Therefore, Fred does not get wet.

Most people argue that the above conclusions are both valid, but they are both invalid. In the first example (affirmation of the consequent), it does not have to be raining for Fred to get wet (e.g., he might have jumped into a swimming pool). In the second example (denial of the antecedent), Fred might still get wet via a swimming pool. Evans, Clibbens, and Rood (1995) found that 21% of participants drew the invalid affirmation of the consequent inference when the problem was presented in abstract form. The invalid denial of the antecedent inference was drawn by over 60% of participants when the problem was in abstract form.

## Wason selection task

A task which has proved especially useful in shedding light on human reasoning was invented about 45 years ago by the British psychologist Peter Wason, and is known as the Wason selection task (see Key Study on the next page).

### Theoretical perspectives

According to the social contract theory of Cosmides (1989), humans during the course of evolution have developed cognitive strategies to detect those who cheat. A social contract is based on the agreement that someone will only receive a benefit (e.g., travelling by train) when they have paid the appropriate cost (e.g., bought a ticket). People possess a "cheat-detecting algorithm" (computational procedure) allowing them to identify cases of cheating (e.g., travelling by train without having bought a ticket).

What is the relevance of social contract theory to the Wason selection task? Cheats are rule breakers, and successful performance on the selection task requires participants to think about falsifying the rule rather than confirming its correctness. Thus, performance on the Wason selection task should be better when the task focuses on cheating than when it does not.

Gigerenzer and Hug (1992) tested social contract theory. One of the tasks they used was based on the following rule of the Kulumae tribe: "If a man eats cassava root, then he must have a tattoo on his face." Married men are identified in the Kulumae tribe by

# Wason: A selection task to study deductive reasoning

In the standard version of the Wason selection task there are four cards lying on a table. Each card has a letter on one side and a number on the other. The participant is told that there is a rule which applies to the four cards (e.g., "If there is an R on one side of the card, then there is a 2 on the other side of the card"). The task is to select only those cards that would need to be turned over to decide whether or not the rule is correct.

In one of the most used versions of this selection task, the four cards have the following symbols visible: R, G, 2, and 7, and the rule is the one just given. What answer would you give to this problem? Most people select either the R card or the R and 2 cards. If you did the same, then you got the answer wrong! You need to see whether any of the cards *fail* to obey the rule. From this perspective, the 2 card is irrelevant. If there is an R on the other side of it, then all this tells us is that the rule might be true. If there is any other letter on the other side, then we have also discovered nothing at all about the validity of the rule.

The correct answer is to select the cards with R and 7 on them, an answer given by only about 10% of university students. The 7 is necessary because it would definitely disprove the rule if it had an R on the other side. There are striking similarities between Wason's selection task and syllogistic reasoning. The selection of the 7 card follows from the *modus tollens* rule of inference: From the premises "If there is an R on one side of the card, then there is a 2 on the other side" and "The 7 card does not have a 2 on it", it follows logically that the 7 card should not have an R on the other side. If it does, then the premise specifying the rule must be incorrect. Thus, incorrect performance on the Wason selection reflects the general difficulty people have with making the *modus tollens* inference.

Several researchers have argued that the abstract nature of the Wason task makes it hard to solve. Wason and Shapiro (1971) used four cards (Manchester, Leeds, car, and train) and the rule, "Every time I go to Manchester I travel by car". The task was to select only those cards that need to be turned over to prove or disprove the rule. The correct answer that the Manchester and train cards need to be turned over was given by 62% of the participants, against only 12% when the Wason selection task was given in its abstract form.

The findings of Wason and Shapiro (1971) suggest that the use of concrete and meaningful material facilitates performance on the Wason task. However, Griggs and Cox (1982) used the same tasks as Wason and Shapiro with American students in Florida. They failed to find a greater success rate for the meaningful task, presumably because most American students have no direct experience of Manchester or Leeds.

*Which cards do you need to turn over (selecting as few as possible) in order to decide if the rule is correct?*

Rule: If there is an R on one side of the card, then there is a 2 on the other.

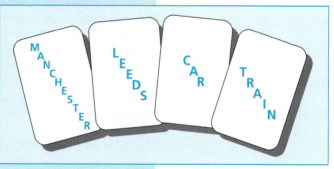

A more concrete version of the Wason selection task.

## Discussion points

1. Why do you think most people find the original version of the Wason selection task so difficult?
2. How can the Wason selection task be made easier?

having a tattoo on their faces. The four cards used in the selection task were "has a tattoo", "has no tattoo", "eats cassava root", and "eats molo nuts". In the cheating version of the task, the cassava root was described as a rare aphrodisiac. The participants were told the rule was designed to provide the rare cassava root for married men, and so reduce pre-marital sex. In the non-cheating version, the instructions told the participants to adopt the perspective of an anthropologist.

There was clear support for social contract theory. About 85% of the participants turned over the correct cards with cheating versions of the task, compared to only 40% when the task was presented in a non-cheating version.

Oaksford (1997) and Chater and Oaksford (1999) put forward the information gain model. According to this model, most people have developed reasoning processes that are effective and useful in everyday life. These processes serve the purpose of maximising the amount of information gain, and are often used on the Wason selection task.

Oaksford (1997) gave the example of testing the rule, "All swans are white". According to formal logic, people should try to find swans and non-white birds. However, there is a problem with formal logic when applied to the real world: Only a few birds are swans, and the overwhelming majority of birds are non-white, and so the pursuit of non-white swans may take up enormous amounts of time and effort. Thus, it makes more sense in the real world to look for white birds to see whether they are swans.

Kirby (1994) obtained evidence that people follow the goal of maximising information gain on the Wason selection task. At an abstract level, we can regard the rule on the Wason selection task as being of the following form: "If a card has p on one side, then it has q on the other side." In order to maximise information gain, the participants should show an increased tendency to select the not-q card (the one Wason said should be selected) and a decreased tendency to select the q card as the probability of p increases. That is precisely what Kirby (1994) found.

## Evaluation

➕ There is reasonable support for social contract theory, with performance on the Wason selection task being very good when the problem focuses on breaking social contracts.

➕ There is reasonable support for the information-gain model, which has the advantage of relating performance on the Wason selection task to rule testing in everyday life.

➖ Some participants provide the right answer on the Wason selection task even when the problem is unrelated to social contracts. Thus, social contract theory provides a limited account of performance on that task.

➖ Social contract theory has little relevance to other kinds of reasoning task.

➖ The information gain model fails to provide an account of the cognitive processes involved in calculating the expected gain in information from selecting a card (Johnson-Laird, 1999).

## Syllogistic reasoning

Syllogistic reasoning has been studied for over 2000 years. A syllogism consists of two premises or statements followed by a conclusion, and you have to decide whether the conclusion is valid in the light of the premises. The validity (or otherwise) of the conclusion depends *only* on whether it follows logically from the premises. Thus, the validity of the conclusion in the real world is irrelevant. Consider the following example:

*Premises*
All children are obedient.
Juliet and William are children.
*Conclusion*
Therefore, Juliet and William are obedient.

The conclusion follows logically from the premises. Thus, it is valid regardless of your views about the obedience of children.

The premises in the above example are both universal affirmative premises having the form "All A are B". However, the premises in syllogistic reasoning can have various other forms: particular affirmative premises ("Some A are B"), universal negative premises ("No A are B"), and particular negative premises ("Some A are not B").

## Biases

People often make errors in syllogistic reasoning, in part because of the existence of various biases. For example, there is the **belief bias**, in which people accept believable conclusions and reject unbelievable conclusions irrespective of their logical validity or invalidity. For example, Oakhill, Garnham, and Johnson-Laird (1990) presented syllogisms such as the following:

*Can this theory explain* human *reasoning?*

> All of the Frenchmen are wine drinkers.
> Some of the wine drinkers are gourmets.
> Therefore, some of the Frenchmen are gourmets.

The conclusion is very believable, and is endorsed by many people. However, the conclusion is actually invalid, and does *not* follow logically from the premises.

Another factor in producing poor performance on reasoning tasks is the **atmosphere effect** (Woodworth & Sells, 1935), in which the form of the premises of a syllogism influences our expectations about the form of the conclusion. For example, if both premises include the word "all", then we expect the conclusion to include it as well. There is modest support for the atmosphere effect (see Gilhooly, 1996), but it predicts far more errors than actually occur.

Another factor leading to poor performance is **conversion error**, in which a statement in one form is mistakenly converted into a statement with a different form. As Chapman and Chapman (1959) found, participants often assume that "All As are Bs" means that "All Bs are As", and that "Some As are not Bs" means that "Some Bs are not As". Ceraso and Provitera (1971) tried to prevent conversion errors from occurring by spelling out the premises more unambiguously (e.g., "All As are Bs" was stated as "All As are Bs, but some Bs are not As"). This produced a substantial improvement in performance.

## Evaluation

- ⊕ Many people are prone to biases in their syllogistic reasoning.
- ⊖ Accounts focusing on biases and errors provide a *description* rather than an *explanation*. For example, a proper explanation would indicate *why* people convert statements or are influenced by the "atmosphere" created by the premises.
- ⊖ Most bias-based approaches do not explain why some individuals manage to avoid biases and errors in their syllogistic reasoning.

> **KEY TERMS**
> **Belief bias:** the tendency to decide whether the conclusion of a syllogism is valid on the basis of whether or not it is believable.
> **Atmosphere effect:** the tendency to accept a conclusion if its form is consistent with the form of the premises.
> **Conversion error:** a mistake in syllogistic reasoning occurring because a statement is invalidly converted from one form into another.

---

### Cross-cultural differences in deductive reasoning

Most people in the Western world are willing to try to solve reasoning problems referring to hypothetical individuals placed in hypothetical situations. However, there are important cross-cultural differences, with members of some cultures preferring to rely on concrete evidence rather than hypothetical statements. Consider, for example, the following discussion between a man belonging to the Kpelle tribe in Africa and a Western experimenter (Scribner, 1975, p. 155, cited in Sternberg & Ben-Zeev, 2001):

Experimenter: All Kpelle men are rice farmers. Mr Smith (this is a Western name) is not a rice farmer. Is he a Kpelle man?

Participant: I don't know the man in person. I have not laid eyes on the man himself.

Experimenter: Just think about the statement.

Participant: If I know him in person then I can answer the question, but since I do not know him in person I cannot answer that question.

Experimenter: Try and answer from your Kpelle sense.

Participant: If you know a person, if a question comes up about him you are able to answer. But if you do not know the person, if a question comes up about him, it's hard for you to answer it.

The above discussion shows clearly that forms of reasoning vary from culture to culture. The Kpelle man adopted the reasonable position that he was unwilling to accept the validity of the experimenter's hypothetical statements, and was much happier to rely on his own experiences and knowledge of the world. There is a great need for more systematic investigation of cross-cultural differences in approaches to deductive reasoning.

# THEORIES OF DEDUCTIVE REASONING

We have seen that people are prone to making errors across a wide range of reasoning tasks. Several theories of reasoning have been put forward to account for these errors, but here we will focus on two of the major ones. First, there are abstract-rule theories (e.g., Braine, 1994, 1998), according to which people are basically logical, but can be led into error if they misunderstand the reasoning task. Second, there is the mental model approach (e.g., Johnson-Laird, 1983, 1999). According to this approach, people form mental models or representations of the premises, and use these mental models (rather than rules) to draw conclusions.

## Abstract-rule theories

According to abstract-rule theories, people use a mental logic when confronted by a reasoning task. Invalid inferences are made when people misunderstand or misrepresent the reasoning task. However, after their initial misunderstanding, people engage in a logical reasoning process.

We will focus on the abstract-rule theory originally proposed by Braine (1978), and subsequently developed and extended by various theorists (e.g., Braine, Reiser, & Rumain, 1984; Braine, 1994, 1998). According to the theory, people comprehend the premises of an argument. After that, they turn them into abstract rules (e.g., a *modus ponens* rule) from which they make inferences.

Braine et al. (1984) argued that there are three main reasons why people make errors in reasoning:

1. *Comprehension errors.* The premises of a reasoning problem are interpreted incorrectly (e.g., conversion error).
2. *Heuristic inadequacy.* The participant's reasoning process fails to locate the correct line of reasoning.
3. *Processing errors.* The participant fails to attend fully to the task in hand or suffers from memory overload.

## *Evidence*

We can see how this theory works in practice by considering its account of a reasoning error known as affirmation of the consequent. Earlier in the chapter, we considered an example of this error, in which it is mistakenly assumed that the premises, "If it is raining, then Fred gets wet" and "Fred gets wet", lead to the valid conclusion, "Therefore, it is raining". According to Braine et al. (1984), this error occurs because of a conversion error: "If it is raining, then Fred gets wet" is interpreted to mean, "If Fred gets wet, then it has been raining." Why should this be so? According to Braine et al., we assume other people will provide us with the information we need to know. If someone says, "If it is raining, then Fred gets wet", it is reasonable to assume that rain is the *only* event likely to make Fred wet.

*Do you think there are any other factors that might determine whether or not we draw valid conclusions when reasoning?*

Braine et al. (1984) obtained evidence supporting their theory. For example, they tried to prevent participants from misinterpreting the premises in affirmation of the consequent syllogisms by providing an additional, clarifying premise:

> *Premises*
> If it is raining, then Fred gets wet.
> If it is snowing, then Fred gets wet.
> Fred gets wet.
> *Conclusion*
> ?

Participants were much more likely to argue correctly there is no valid conclusion when the additional premise was used.

According to Braine et al. (1984) people have a mental rule corresponding to modus ponens. Thus, syllogisms based on modus ponens are easy to handle, and pose no comprehension problems. However, Byrne (1989) showed this is not always true. She presented syllogisms of the following type with the starred premise either present or absent:

*Premises*
If she has an essay to write, then she will study late in the library.
*If the library stays open, then she will study late in the library.
She has an essay to write.
*Conclusion*
?

The participants were much less likely to draw the valid *modus ponens* conclusion (e.g., "She will study late in the library") when the additional (starred) premise was presented; this is known as a context effect. Thus, the processes involved in reasoning can be more complex (and less logical) than is assumed by the theory.

## Evaluation

- ⊕ The abstract-rule approach accounts for many experimental findings with only relatively few reasoning rules.
- ⊕ Comprehension errors and heuristic inadequacy undoubtedly cause many problems in deductive reasoning.
- ⊖ The comprehension component of the model is under-specified, and so it is not always clear what predictions should be made from the model.
- ⊖ The abstract-rule approach has mainly been applied to propositional reasoning, and it is not known whether it can be applied successfully to other forms of reasoning.
- ⊖ The theory does not provide an adequate account of context effects (e.g., Byrne, 1989).

## Mental models

One of the most influential approaches to deductive reasoning is the mental model theory of Johnson-Laird (e.g., 1983, 1999). According to Johnson-Laird (1999, p. 130), "Reasoning is just the continuation of comprehension by other means." This view has important implications, because we do not normally use logical processes when understanding sentences. It follows that we should stop arguing that thinking is logical when it succeeds and illogical when it fails. Instead, successful thinking results from the use of appropriate mental models and unsuccessful thinking occurs when we use inappropriate mental models.

What is a **mental model**? According to Johnson-Laird (1999, p. 116), "Each mental model represents a *possibility*, and its structure and content capture what is common to the different ways in which the possibility might occur." That definition may obscure rather than clarify, so we will consider a concrete example:

*Premises*
The lamp is on the right of the pad.
The book is on the left of the pad.
The clock is in front of the book.
The vase is in front of the lamp.
*Conclusion*
The clock is to the left of the vase.

According to Johnson-Laird (1983), people use the information contained in the premises to construct a mental model like this:

book     pad     lamp

clock             vase

**KEY TERM**
**Mental model:** a representation of a possible state of affairs; used especially with reference to deductive reasoning.

*Do you think different people's mental models are based on the same strategy? Other than constructing a mental image, how else might you come to a valid conclusion?*

It is easy to see that the conclusion that the clock is to the left of the vase follows from the mental model. The fact that we cannot construct a mental model consistent with the premises but inconsistent with the conclusion indicates that it is valid.

It is tempting (but wrong) to assume that mental models always give rise to images. Sometimes they do, but there are numerous exceptions. For example, negation can be represented in a mental model but cannot be visualised.

It is assumed that the construction of mental models involves the limited processing resources of working memory (see Chapter 9). Thus, people should find it harder to reason accurately when a problem requires the construction of several mental models rather than just one. A more specific prediction follows from another assumption of the model known as the principle of truth: "Individuals minimise the load on working memory by tending to construct mental models that represent explicitly only what is true, and not what is false" (Johnson-Laird, 1999, p. 116). Thus, people will make more errors in reasoning when a problem requires the representation of what is false.

## Evidence

The notion that people's ability to construct mental models is constrained by the limited capacity of working memory was tested by Johnson-Laird (1983). Participants indicated what conclusions followed validly from sets of premises. The demands on working memory were varied by manipulating the number of mental models consistent with the premises. Seventy-eight per cent of participants drew the valid conclusion when the premises only allowed the generation of one mental model. This figure dropped to 29% when two mental models were possible, and to 13% with three mental models.

According to the theory, it takes time to construct a mental model. Thus, reasoning problems requiring the generation of several mental models should take longer than those requiring the generation of only one model. Bell and Johnson-Laird (1998) argued that a single mental model can establish that something is possible, but *all* models must be constructed to show something is not possible. In contrast, all mental models must be constructed to show that something is necessary, but *one* model can show that something is not necessary. Bell and Johnson-Laird used reasoning problems consisting of premises followed by a question about a possibility (e.g., "Can Betsy be in the game?") or a question about a necessity (e.g., "Must Betsy be in the game?).

According to the theory, people should respond faster to *possibility* questions when the correct answer is "Yes" rather than "No". However, they should respond faster to *necessity* questions when the answer is "No" rather than "Yes". That is precisely what Bell and Johnson-Laird (1998) found.

Johnson-Laird et al. (1999) discussed the principle of truth, according to which most mental models represent what is true and ignore what is false. It follows from this principle that most people should make systematic and predictable errors when given a reasoning problem requiring active consideration of falsity. This prediction was tested by Johnson-Laird and Goldvarg (1997). The participants received the following problem:

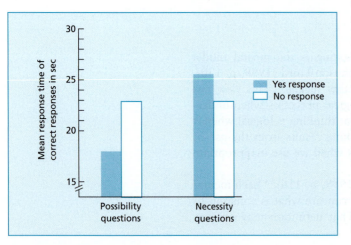

Mean response times (in seconds) for correct responses (yes and no) to possibility and necessity questions. Based on data in Bell and Johnson-Laird (1998).

Only one of the following premises is true about a particular hand of cards:

(1) There is a king in the hand or there is an ace, or both.
(2) There is a queen in the hand or there is an ace, or both.
(3) There is a jack in the hand or there is a 10, or both.

Is it possible that there is an ace in the hand?

What do you think is the correct answer? Johnson-Laird and Goldvarg found that 99% of their participants gave the answer, "Yes", which is amazingly high given that the correct answer is, "No". According to Johnson-Laird and Goldvarg the participants formed mental models of the premises. Thus, for example, the first premise generates the following mental models:

King

        Ace

King   Ace

These mental models suggest that an ace is possible, as do the mental models formed from the second premise. However, this is the wrong answer, because it ignores issues of falsity revolving around the fact that only *one* of the premises is true. If there were an ace in the hand, then premises (1) and (2) would both be true, which is inconsistent with the requirement that only one premise is true. Thus, the participants' over-emphasis on the principle of truth caused nearly all of them to produce faulty reasoning. According to Johnson-Laird (1999), the faulty reasoning shown on this problem cannot be predicted within the abstract-rule approach.

## Evaluation

- ⊕ The theory accounts for reasoning performance across a very wide range of problems.
- ⊕ Most of the predictions of the theory have been confirmed experimentally.
- ⊕ The notion that reasoning involves very similar processes to normal comprehension is powerful, and is a convincing alternative to the view that we possess a mental logic. An important implication is that the artificial problems used in most reasoning studies may be more relevant to everyday life than is generally supposed.
- ⊖ The processes involved in forming mental models are under-specified. Johnson-Laird and Byrne (1991) argued that people make use of background knowledge when forming mental models. However, the theory does not spell out how we decide which pieces of information should be included in a mental model.
- ⊖ The number of mental models people will construct when solving a reasoning problem is often hard to work out (Bonatti, 1994).
- ⊖ The theory tends to ignore individual differences. For example, Sternberg and Weil (1980) found that some participants on a reasoning task used a mental model strategy based on imagery or spatial relationships, others used a deduction rule strategy based on verbal or linguistic processing, and a majority used a mixture of both strategies.
- ⊖ The mental model approach predicts that deductions depending on numerous models should be hard to make. However, people often fail to construct all of the possible mental models (O'Brien, Braine, & Yang, 1994).

## INDUCTIVE REASONING

As we saw earlier in the chapter, inductive reasoning involves making a generalised conclusion from premises that refer to particular instances. One of the key features of inductive reasoning is that the conclusions of inductively valid arguments are probably (but not necessarily) true. Consider, for example, the premise, "Every relevant experiment has found that learning depends on reward or reinforcement". We might use that information to draw the general conclusion, "Learning always depends on reward or reinforcement". This conclusion may seem reasonable. However, it is possible that future experiments might reveal circumstances in which learning can occur in the absence of reward.

We often use categories in inductive reasoning. For example, we know that bats belong to the category of mammal, and that mammals feed their offspring. Accordingly, we may well be willing to infer that bats feed their offspring even if we are not certain.

*Why do you think there should be these cultural differences in reasoning?*

Choi, Nisbett, and Smith (1997) argued that East Asians use categories less often than Americans in their everyday lives. In support of their argument, they found Americans were more likely than Koreans to make spontaneous use of various categories in inductive reasoning. They also argued that there should be an exception: Members of collectivistic cultures (e.g., the Korean) use social categories (e.g., age, occupations, status) to describe people more than do members of individualistic cultures (see Chapter 1). As predicted, Koreans used social categories more often than Americans on inductive reasoning problems. Thus, cultural factors can have systematic effects on inductive reasoning.

## Hypothesis testing: Relational rule

An inductive reasoning task that has attracted much interest was devised by Peter Wason (1960). He told his participants that the three numbers 2 4 6 conformed to a simple relational rule. Their task was to generate sets of three numbers, and to provide reasons for each choice. After each choice, the experimenter indicated whether or not the set of numbers conformed to the rule the experimenter had in mind. The task was simply to discover the nature of the rule. The rule was apparently very simple: "Three numbers in ascending order of magnitude." However, it took most participants a long time to produce the rule, and only 21% of them were correct with their first attempt to state the rule.

Why was performance so poor on Wason's relational rule problem? According to Wason (1960), the participants showed **confirmation bias**, i.e., they tried to generate sets of numbers confirming their original hypothesis. For example, participants whose original hypothesis or rule was that the second number is twice the first, and the third number is three times the first number tended to generate sets of numbers consistent with that hypothesis (e.g., 6 12 18; 50 100 150). Confirmation bias and failure to try hypothesis disconfirmation prevented the participants from replacing their initial hypothesis, which was too narrow and specific, with the correct general rule.

Tweney et al. (1980) found a way of reducing people's reliance on confirmation bias with the relational rule problem. Their participants were told that the experimenter had two rules in mind, and it was their task to identify these rules. One of these rules generated DAX triples, whereas the other rule generated MED triples. They were also told that 2 4 6 was a DAX triple. Whenever the participants generated a set of three numbers, they were informed whether the set fitted the DAX rule or the MED rule. The correct answer was that the DAX rule was any three numbers in ascending order, and the MED rule covered any other set of numbers.

What did Tweney et al. (1980) find? Over 50% of the participants produced the correct answer on their first attempt. The reason for this high level of success was that the participants did not have to focus on disconfirmation of hypotheses. They could identify the DAX rule by confirming the MED rule, and so they did not have to try to disconfirm the DAX rule.

### Application of Popper's argument

The hypothesis, "Learning always depends on reward or reinforcement" cannot be proved correct but can potentially be falsified. Accordingly, researchers who want to test this hypothesis should focus on trying to identify situations or types of participants who might disprove it. For example, research in other cultures might show that people living in some non-Western cultures are relatively uninfluenced by reward.

## Conclusions

Wason (1968) argued that there were important similarities between the behaviour of participants on his task and that of scientists engaged in testing a hypothesis. More specifically, he claimed that scientists generally design experiments to confirm an existing hypothesis. He then went on to argue that this is not a good strategy, because scientific hypotheses cannot be confirmed conclusively. Karl Popper (1972), the philosopher of science, proposed that the distinguishing characteristic of a scientific theory is *falsifiability*, meaning that such a theory can potentially be falsified or disconfirmed.

*I wish I'd decided to check that it wouldn't explode if it wasn't heated, rather than the other way round!*

Klayman and Ha (1987) argued that the participants in Wason's studies were trying to produce positive tests of their hypotheses rather than trying to confirm their hypotheses as Wason had claimed. Positive tests involve seeing whether sets of numbers consistent with their hypothesis conform or fail to conform to the relational rule. In contrast, negative tests involve seeing whether sets of numbers inconsistent with their hypothesis conform to the relational rule. Klayman and Ha showed that the positive test strategy can be more effective than the negative test strategy. For example, it is more likely to produce falsifying results when relatively few number sequences match the relational rule. However, in the unusual conditions used by Wason (1968), numerous number sequences match the rule, and so negative testing is needed to produce falsifying results.

## Hypothesis testing: Simulated research environments

Mynatt, Doherty, and Tweney (1977) studied some of the issues raised by Wason's (1968) research in a set-up designed to simulate a real research environment. The participants were presented with computer-generated displays containing several shapes varying in brightness. There was a particle that could be fired across the screen, and which was stopped when it came close to some objects but not others. The participants' task was to think of a hypothesis to explain the behaviour of the particle. The correct hypothesis was that the particle was stopped when it came close to dim objects. However, the participants' initial experience of the task led most of them to form the hypothesis that object shape played a part in determining whether the particle stopped.

*Can such laboratory studies of simulated research provide a complete view of the processes involved in real-life hypothesis testing? What other factors might be involved in a real-life situation?*

The key part of the Mynatt et al. (1977) study was to see which of two environments the participants chose following their initial experience:

1. An environment in which their observations would probably confirm their initial incorrect hypothesis.
2. An environment in which other hypotheses could be tested.

Mynatt et al. found that most participants chose the first environment, thus providing evidence for a confirmation bias. However, those participants who obtained information that falsified their original hypothesis tended to reject it rather than stubbornly sticking to it.

Dunbar (1993) also made use of a simulated research environment. The participants were given the difficult task of providing an explanation for the ways in which genes are controlled by other genes using a computer-based molecular genetics laboratory. The difficulty of the task can be seen in the fact that solving this problem in real life had led to the award of the Nobel prize! The participants were led to focus on the hypothesis that the gene control was by activation, whereas it was actually by inhibition.

Dunbar (1993) found that those participants who simply tried to find data consistent with their activation hypothesis failed to solve the problem. In contrast, the 20% of the participants who did solve the problem set themselves the goal of trying to explain the discrepant findings. According to the participants' own reports, most of them started with the general hypothesis that activation was the key controlling process. They then applied this hypothesis in specific ways, focusing on one gene after another as the potential activator. It was typically only when all the various specific activation hypotheses had been disconfirmed that some participants focused on explaining the data that did not fit the general activation hypothesis.

How closely do the findings in simulated research environments resemble those in real research environments? Mitroff (1974) studied geologists involved in the Apollo space programme as experts in lunar geology. They devoted most of their time to trying to confirm rather than

Mitroff (1974) found that real scientists, such as lunar geologists, were more reluctant than participants in simulated research studies to abandon their hypotheses.

falsify their hypotheses, but they were not opposed to the notion of falsifying the hypotheses of other scientists. Their focus on confirmation rather than falsification resembles that found in participants in simulated research environments. However, the real scientists seemed more reluctant than the participants in simulated research studies to abandon their hypotheses. There are probably two main reasons for this:

- The real scientists emphasised the value of commitment to a given position as a motivating factor.
- Real scientists are more likely than participants in an experiment to attribute contrary findings to deficiencies in the measuring instruments.

## Analogical reasoning

*Can you think of any drawbacks to relying on analogical reasoning to solve problems?*

Many problems can be solved by making use of **analogical reasoning**, in which the solver notices important similarities between the current problem and one or more problems solved in the past. Analogical reasoning is a form of inductive reasoning involving problem solving. Analogical reasoning has proved important in the history of science. Examples include the computer model of human information processing, the billiard-ball model of gases, and the hydraulic model of the blood circulation system.

Spearman (1927) carried out studies using analogical problems having the form, "A is to B as C is to D" (e.g., "North is to south as top is to bottom"). The participants were either given the task of deciding whether the analogy was correct, or the final (D) term was missing and had to be supplied. Spearman obtained a correlation of +.8 between analogical reasoning and IQ, indicating that there is a close association between success at analogical reasoning and intelligence.

In what circumstances do people make successful use of previous problems in order to solve a current problem? Everyone agrees that successful analogical reasoning depends on similarities between the current problem and a previous one. According to Chen (2002), there are three main types of similarity between problems:

1. *Superficial similarity*. Solution-irrelevant details (e.g., specific objects) are common to both problems;
2. *Structural similarity*. Causal relations among some of the main components are shared by both problems.
3. *Procedural similarity*. Procedures for turning the solution principle into concrete operations are common to both problems.

As we will see, these forms of similarity all influence analogical reasoning.

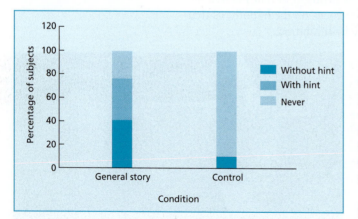

Some of the results from Gick and Holyoak (1980, experiment 4) showing the percentage of participants who solved the radiation problem when they were given an analogy (general-story condition) or were just asked to solve the problem (control condition). Note that just under half of the participants in the general-story condition had to be given a hint to use the story analogue before they solved the problem.

### Evidence

Gick and Holyoak (1980) used Duncker's radiation problem (Duncker, 1945), in which a patient with a malignant tumour in his stomach can only be saved by a special kind of ray. However, a ray of sufficient strength to destroy the tumour will also destroy the healthy tissue, whereas a ray that will not harm healthy tissue will be too weak to destroy the tumour.

Only about 10% of the participants given the problem managed to solve it. The answer is to direct several low-intensity rays at the tumour from different directions. However, other participants were given three stories to memorise, one of which was structurally similar to the radiation problem. This story was about a general capturing a fortress by having his army converge at the same time on the fortress along several different roads. When the participants were told that one of the three stories might be relevant to solving the radiation problem, about 80% of them solved it. When the hint was not offered, however, only about 40% of those given the stories to memorise solved the problem. Thus, the fact that relevant information is stored in long-term memory is no guarantee that it will be used.

Why did most participants in the Gick and Holyoak (1980) study fail to make spontaneous use of the relevant story they had memorised? Keane (1987) hypothesised that it might be because of the lack of superficial similarities between the story and the problem. He presented participants with either a semantically close story (about a surgeon using rays on a cancer) or a semantically remote story (the general-and-fortress story). They were given this story during a lecture, and were then asked to take part in an experiment several days later. Of those participants who had been given the close analogy, 88% spontaneously retried it when given the radiation problem. In contrast, only 12% of those who had been given the remote analogy spontaneously retried it.

It has often been assumed that problem solvers who realise that a current problem has important similarities with a previous problem are almost bound to solve it. However, Chen (2002) disputed that assumption. He argued that people may use a previous problem to gain insight into the type of solution needed on a current problem, but may still be unable to solve it if the two problems do not share procedural similarity.

Chen (2002) supported the above argument by studying the weigh-the-elephant problem: A boy needs to weigh an elephant, but only has access to scales weighing objects up to 200 pounds. The general solution is based on weight equivalence, and involves using smaller objects to equal the weight of the elephant, and then weighing the smaller objects separately on the scales. This solution can be implemented by using two different sets of procedures or concrete operations:

- Put the elephant into a boat and mark the water level on the boat; replace the elephant with smaller objects until the water level is the same; weigh the smaller objects separately.
- Harness the elephant with one end of a length of rope which is thrown over the branch of a tree; attach a container to the other end of the rope and balance the rope by placing several objects in the container; weigh the smaller objects separately.

Participants provided with an initial story resembling the weigh-the-elephant problem in both structural and procedural similarity performed much better on the problem than did those provided with an initial story containing only structural similarity to the problem. Many participants in the latter condition grasped the general solution based on weight equivalence, but could not find appropriate procedures to solve the problem. Thus, effective analogies often need to possess procedural as well as structural similarity to a current problem.

## Evaluation

- ⊕ Several factors determining whether problem solvers will use relevant past knowledge on analogical reasoning problems have been identified.
- ⊕ Superficial, structural, and procedural similarity between past problems and a current problem are all important.
- ⊖ In the laboratory, analogical problems can often be solved simply by using an appropriate analogy provided earlier in the experiment. In everyday life, in contrast, the fit or match between previous knowledge and the current problem is typically imprecise.
- ⊖ Little research has focused on individual differences in performance on analogical reasoning problems.

# HOW FLAWED IS HUMAN THINKING?

*Do you think that laboratory studies of human reasoning can explain how we reason in our everyday lives or are there differences between these situations?*

People often make mistakes when engaged in reasoning or decision making under laboratory conditions. However, there is something paradoxical about these findings, because most people cope well or very well with their everyday problems. Why do we often fail miserably to solve reasoning and other problems in the laboratory?

Evans and Over (1997) answered the above question by distinguishing between two types of rationality: rationality$_1$ and rationality$_2$. According to Evans and Over (p. 403), people have personal rationality or rationality$_1$ "when they are generally successful in achieving their basic goals, keeping themselves alive, finding their way in the world, and communicating with each other". This form of rationality depends on an implicit cognitive system operating at an unconscious level. Rationality$_1$ permits us to cope effectively with everyday life.

In contrast, people display impersonal rationality or rationality$_2$ when "they act with good reasons sanctioned by a normative theory such as formal logic or probability theory" (Evans & Over, 1997, p. 403). This form of rationality depends on an explicit cognitive system operating at a conscious level; it also differs from rationality$_1$ in that it allows us to think in a hypothetical way about the future. Evans (2000) clarified the essence of rationality$_2$: "Rationality$_2$ involves individual differences in g [general factor of intelligence] ... Hence intelligence—in the sense of g—depends upon the effective use of the explicitly thinking system." Laboratory research has focused on rationality$_2$, which can be error-prone even when rationality$_1$ is not.

The distinction between rationality$_1$ and rationality$_2$ appears useful. However, it can be argued that Evans and Over (1997) have described two forms of rationality, but have not provided an explanatory account of human rationality.

Oaksford (1997) also argued that people's reasoning powers are more rational than might initially appear to be the case. He pointed out there are important differences between reasoning in the real world and in the laboratory. People often make everyday decisions on the basis of very incomplete information, but this is not typically the case in laboratory studies. There are other situations in the real world in which people are exposed to much redundant or unnecessary information, and this is also not true of most laboratory studies. People's reasoning strategies work reasonably well in everyday life, but may not do so in the laboratory. As Oaksford (p. 260) argued, "Many of the errors and biases seen in people's reasoning are likely to be the result of importing their everyday probabilistic strategies into the lab."

---

**How might your actions differ if you reason using rationality$_1$ rather than rationality$_2$ in this situation?**

| | | |
|---|---|---|
| Goals | • to leave college and catch the train from the station<br>• to post a letter in the letterbox on the way<br>• to collect some heavy shopping at the supermarket on the way | |
| Information | • the supermarket is closer to the college than the station<br>• the letterbox is closer to the station than the college<br>• the walk from the supermarket to the station is slightly longer if you go via the letterbox | |
| Plan of action | **Rationality$_1$**<br><br>• first post the letter<br>• double back to the supermarket<br>• then to the station | **Rationality$_2$**<br><br>• go to the nearest destination first (the supermarket)<br>• then to the letterbox<br>• then to the station |
| Reasoning | If I get rid of the letter first, I won't have to carry the shopping as far, even though I walk further overall. | This is the shortest overall route, and involves no backtracking. |

Similar arguments apply to our use of heuristics or rules of thumb. As Maule and Hodgkinson (2002, p. 71) pointed out:

*Often ... people have to judge situations or objects that change over time, making it inappropriate to expend a good deal of effort to make a precise judgement at any particular point in time. Under these circumstances, an approximate judgement based on a simpler, less effortful heuristic may be much more appropriate.*

Johnson-Laird's mental model theory (Johnson-Laird, 1983) is an example of an approach based on the assumption that processes used in everyday life are applied to laboratory reasoning problems. More specifically, Johnson-Laird assumed that the processes typically involved in language comprehension are used on reasoning problems, and that these processes often fail to provide a complete representation of such problems. The success of this theoretical approach suggests that people often import their everyday thinking and reasoning strategies into the laboratory.

Not everyone agrees with the views expressed so far. Some experts (e.g., Shafir & LeBoeuf, 2002) argue there are grounds for concern about human decision making and reasoning. They point out that there is a substantial weight of experimental evidence from well-conducted studies showing serious flaws, distortions, and errors in human thinking. That is true, but it is important not to exaggerate the limitations of human thinking. For example, Stanovich and West (1998) found that individuals of high cognitive ability showed more evidence of rational thought and produced fewer errors and biases than did those of lower cognitive ability on a wide range of tasks.

In sum, most people can be regarded as showing **bounded rationality** (Simon, 1955), which means that they behave rationally within their processing limitations, and thereby produce workable (but not ideal) solutions to problems. According to Simon (1990, p. 7), bounded rationality is the norm, because "Human rational behaviour is shaped by a scissors whose two blades are the structure of task environments and the computational capabilities of the actor."

> **KEY TERM**
> **Bounded rationality:** the notion that people are as rational as their processing limitations permit.

# SUMMARY

Psychologists typically study well-defined problems, but most everyday problems are ill-defined. Gestalt psychologists emphasised productive problem solving. Insight can be thwarted by functional fixedness. Many of the concepts used by the Gestalt theorists are vague. Newell and Simon produced computer simulations of human problem solving based on heuristic methods such as means–ends analysis. The problems they used were ones for which the participants had little relevant specific knowledge, which is quite unlike most real-life problems.

*Problem solving*

We often fail to make full use of base-rate information when deciding on the likelihood of an event, in part because of reliance on the representativeness heuristic. The conjunction fallacy illustrates use of the representativeness heuristic, but sometimes occurs because of misunderstanding of the problem. Another heuristic often used in judgement research is the availability heuristic. According to support theory, any given event will appear more likely when described in explicit terms. Heuristics (e.g., recognition heuristic, the take-the-best heuristic) are sometimes very effective. We lack process models specifying in detail when and how the various heuristics are used.

*Judgement research*

The notion that decision makers are more sensitive to potential losses than to potential gains receives support from the phenomenon of loss aversion. Framing effects and breakdowns of the dominance principle provide evidence against normative decision theory. Decision makers are often influenced by emotional, social, and political factors. For example, a key reason for omission bias is that the level of anticipated regret is greater when an unwanted outcome is caused by an individual's own actions.

*Decision making*

**Deductive reasoning**

Many errors are made in conditional reasoning, especially on the Wason selection task. According to social contract theory, performance on the Wason task should be better when it focuses on cheating than when it does not. According to the information gain model, people's apparently faulty reasoning on the Wason task may be effective and useful in everyday life. There is some evidence that people try to maximise the information gain from each choice. Syllogistic reasoning is often faulty because of belief bias and conversion errors. However, accounts focusing on biases and errors provide a description rather than an explanation.

**Theories of deductive reasoning**

According to abstract-rule theories, people use a mental logic when dealing with a reasoning task. Invalid inferences occur when people misunderstand or misrepresent a reasoning task. According to the mental model theory, reasoning uses very similar processes to those involved in language comprehension. People construct mental models of the premises of a reasoning task, and use these mental models to decide whether the conclusion is valid or invalid. There are two main reasons why the full set of possible mental models is often not formed: (1) the construction of mental models involves the limited processing resources of working memory, and (2) there is a tendency to construct mental models that represent what is true but not what is false. The mental model approach accounts for performance on numerous reasoning problems, and it predicts the very poor performance found when falsity needs to be considered.

**Inductive reasoning**

Wason devised an inductive reasoning task based on a simple relational rule. Performance was surprisingly poor on this task, and Wason argued that this was due to a confirmation bias. He also argued that scientists often mistakenly use the same bias in their research. There is evidence that participants use a positive test strategy rather than confirmation bias, and that a positive test strategy is often more effective than a negative test strategy. Findings resembling those with Wason's relational rule task have been obtained in simulated research environments, and there is evidence that real scientists focus on confirmation rather than falsification of hypotheses. Research on analogical reasoning indicates that the probability of using a previous problem to solve a current problem depends on the superficial, structural, and procedural similarity between the two problems.

There is an apparent contradiction between our ability to deal effectively with our every-day environment, and our failure to perform well on many laboratory reasoning tasks. One possible explanation is that there are two types of rationality: personal rationality or rationality$_1$ and impersonal rationality or rationality$_2$. An alternative position, exemplified by the mental model approach, is that people use their everyday thinking and reasoning strategies when confronted by reasoning problems in the laboratory. Most people show bounded rationality in their approach to problems in the laboratory and in everyday life.

*How flawed is human thinking?*

# FURTHER READING

- Eysenck, M.W. (2001). *Principles of cognitive psychology* (2nd ed.). Hove, UK: Psychology Press. This book contains a detailed introduction to problem solving and reasoning.
- Eysenck, M.W., & Keane, M.T. (2000). *Cognitive psychology: A student's handbook* (4th ed.). Hove, UK: Psychology Press. Nearly all the topics discussed in this chapter are discussed more fully in this book.
- Johnson-Laird, P.N. (1999). Deductive reasoning. *Annual Review of Psychology, 50,* 109–135. This article contains a good account of major theoretical approaches to deductive reasoning.
- Robertson, S.I. (2001). *Problem solving.* Hove, UK: Psychology Press. The area of problem solving is covered thoroughly in this well-written textbook.
- Sternberg, R.J., & Ben-Zeev, T. (2001). *Complex cognition: The psychology of human thought.* Oxford, UK: Oxford University Press. Chapters 5–8 provide useful introductory coverage of reasoning, problem solving, and decision making.

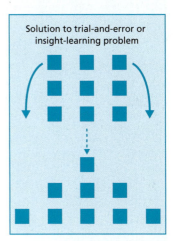

Solution to trial-and-error or insight-learning problem

- **Speech perception**
  The problems of understanding speech.

  *Recognising spoken words*
  *Prosodic features*
  *Lip-reading*
  *Theories of word recognition*
  *Auditory analysis system*
  *Deep dysphasia*

- **Basic reading processes**
  How we read words and sentences.

  *Research methods*
  *Identifying words*
  *Interactive activation model*
  *Reading aloud*
  *Dual route cascaded model*
  *Reading disorders*
  *How the eyes move in reading*
  *Sentence parsing*

- **Discourse processing**
  Looking at sentences in context.

  *Drawing inferences*
  *Minimalist hypothesis*
  *Search-after-meaning theory*

- **Story processing**
  Selective comprehension and remembering.

  *Construction–integration model*
  *Event-indexing model*

- **Speech production**
  Making conversation.

  *Grice's Co-operative Principle*
  *Grice's four maxims: quantity, quality,*
    *relation, manner*
  *Discourse markers and prosodic cues*
  *Speech errors*
  *Production processes:*
    *conceptualisation, formulation,*
    *articulation*
  *Planning utterances*
  *Spreading-activation theory*
  *Levelt et al.'s WEAVER++ model*

- **Speech disorders**
  Research into language disorders.

  *Broca's aphasia*
  *Wernicke's aphasia*
  *Anomia*
  *Agrammatism*
  *Jargon aphasia*

- **Language and thought**
  Exploring the relationship between language and thought.

  *Whorf's hypothesis—language*
    *determines thinking*
  *Cross-language research*

# Language

Our lives would be totally different without language. Our social interactions with other people rely very heavily on language, and a good command of language is vital for all students. We are much more knowledgeable than people of previous generations, and the main reason is because knowledge is passed on from one generation to the next in the form of language.

According to Harley (2001, p. 5), language can be defined as, "a system of symbols and rules that enable us to communicate". Parrots may say certain words. However, they are not really using language, because they do not use rules and are not trying to communicate. As Harley pointed out, it is sometimes very difficult to decide whether language is being used. For example, there has been much controversy as to whether attempts to teach language to apes have proved successful (see Chapter 14).

The fascinating issue of how children acquire language is discussed in detail in Chapter 14. In this chapter, we will deal with five main areas of language research based mainly on adults. First, speech perception will be discussed. Second, we will focus on the basic processes involved in reading. Third, there is the comprehension of connected **discourse** (written text or speech), which deals with larger units of language than are usually considered in studies on speech perception or reading. Fourth, there is speech production, which is concerned with the complex processes involved in speaking fluently. Fifth, there is the relationship between language and thought. Our focus will be mainly on whether language influences or determines thought.

## SPEECH PERCEPTION

Listeners are confronted by several problems when trying to understand speech:

- *Speed*. Language is spoken at a rate of up to 12 **phonemes** (basic speech sounds) per second, and so requires rapid processing. Amazingly, we can understand speech artificially speeded up to 50–60 sounds or phonemes per second.
- *The segmentation problem*. Speech typically consists of a continuous pattern of sound, which has to be divided up into words.
- **Co-articulation**. In normal speech, the way in which a phoneme is produced is influenced by the phonemes preceding and following it. The existence of co-articulation means that the pronunciation of any given phoneme is not invariant, which can create problems for the listener.
- *Individual differences*. Listeners have to contend with significant individual differences from one speaker to another, including differences in dialect (Sussman, Hoemeke, & Ahmed, 1993).

## Word recognition

A key issue is to identify the processes involved in recognising spoken words. We will first consider some of the major processes involved, and will then turn to a discussion of relevant theories. Spoken word recognition is generally achieved by a mixture of bottom-up processes triggered by the acoustic signal, and top-down processes generated from the

Knowledge is passed on from one generation to the next in the form of language.

linguistic context. However, there are disagreements about precisely how these processes combine to produce word recognition.

Spoken language consists of sounds or phonemes incorporating various features. Among the features for phonemes are the following:

- *Manner of production* (oral vs. nasal vs. fricative, involving a partial blockage of the airstream).
- *Place of articulation.*
- *Voicing.* The larynx vibrates for a voiced but not for a voiceless phoneme.

The notion that bottom-up processes in word recognition use feature information was supported by Miller and Nicely (1955). They gave participants the task of recognising consonants presented auditorily against a background of noise. The most frequently confused consonants were those differing on the basis of only one feature.

Evidence that top-down processing based on context is involved in speech perception was obtained by Warren and Warren (1970), who studied the **phonemic restoration effect**. Participants heard one of the following sentences in which a small portion had been replaced with a meaningless sound (indicated by an asterisk):

- It was found that the *eel was on the axle.
- It was found that the *eel was on the shoe.
- It was found that the *eel was on the table.
- It was found that the *eel was on the orange.

The perception of the crucial element in the sentence (i.e., *eel) was influenced by sentence context. Participants listening to the first sentence heard "wheel", those listening to the second sentence heard "heel", and those exposed to the third and fourth sentences heard "meal" and "peel", respectively. The auditory stimulus was identical in all cases, so all that differed was the contextual information.

What causes the phonemic restoration effect? Samuel (1997) argued that there are two main possible explanations. First, listeners may simply be guessing at the missing phoneme ("a matter of not really noticing that the lexical item is missing"; p. 98). Second, listeners may restore the missing phoneme perceptually ("a true top-down creation of the missing phonemic information"; p. 98). Samuel carried out a complex experiment supporting the second explanation rather than the first one.

## Prosodic patterns

Spoken speech contains **prosodic cues** (e.g., stress, intonation). These cues can be used by the listener to work out syntactic or grammatical structure. For example, in the ambiguous sentence, "The old men and women sat on the bench", the women may or may not be old. If the women are not old, then the spoken duration of the word "men" will be relatively long, and the stressed syllable in "women" will have a steep rise in pitch contour. Neither of these prosodic features will be present if the sentence means that the women are old. Beach (1990) found that listeners generally interpret prosodic information correctly, and that this information is used rapidly.

## Lip-reading

Many people (especially the hard of hearing) are aware of using lip-reading to understand speech. However, this happens far more than is generally believed among those whose hearing is normal. McGurk and MacDonald (1976) provided a striking demonstration of the importance of lip-reading. They prepared a videotape of someone repeating "ba" over and over again. The sound channel then changed so there was a voice saying "ga" repeatedly in

*People interpret prosadic cues to make sense of an ambiguous sentence.*

synchronisation with lip movements indicating "ba". Participants heard "da", representing a blend of the visual and the auditory information.

The so-called **McGurk effect** is surprisingly robust. Green, Kuhl, Meltzoff, and Stevens (1991) found the effect even with a female face and a male voice. They suggested that information about pitch becomes irrelevant early in speech processing, and this is why the McGurk effect is found even with a gender mismatch between vision and hearing.

*Are you aware of using lip-reading in your everyday life?*

## Theories of word recognition

There are several theories of spoken word recognition. However, two theories (cohort theory and the TRACE model) have been very influential, and our discussion will focus on them.

### Cohort theory

Marslen-Wilson and Tyler (1980) proposed cohort theory based on the following assumptions:

- Early in the auditory presentation of a word, those words known to the listener conforming to the sound sequence heard so far become active; this collection of words is the "word-initial cohort".
- Words in this cohort are then eliminated if they cease to match further information from the presented word, or if they are inconsistent with the semantic or other context.
- Processing of the presented word continues only until contextual information and information from the word itself leave only one word in the word-initial cohort; this is the "recognition point" of the word.

> **KEY TERM**
>
> **McGurk effect:** the finding that the sound that is heard is influenced by the speaker's lip movements.

According to cohort theory, various knowledge sources (e.g., lexical, syntactic, semantic) *interact* and combine with each other in complex ways to produce an efficient analysis of spoken language.

Marslen-Wilson and Tyler (1980) tested their theoretical notions in a word-monitoring task, in which participants had to identify pre-specified target words presented in spoken sentences as rapidly as possible. There were normal sentences, syntactic sentences (grammatically correct but meaningless), and random sentences (unrelated words). The target was a member of a given category, a word that rhymed with a given word, or a word identical to a given word.

> **A word-cohort**
>
> This idea suggests that our brains process a word in sections, as it is said, gradually identifying it.
>
> | gen- | gener- | generous |
> |---|---|---|
> | gendarme | general | |
> | gender | generate | |
> | general | generous | |
> | generate | | |
> | generous | | |
> | gentleman | | |
> | gentian | | |
> | gentile | | |

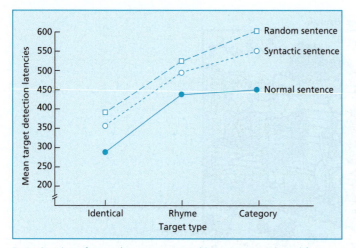

Detection times for word targets presented in sentences. Adapted from Marslen-Wilson and Tyler (1980).

According to cohort theory, sensory information from the target word and contextual information from the rest of the sentence are both used at the same time. As expected, complete sensory analysis of the longer words was not needed when there was adequate contextual information. It was only necessary to listen to the entire word when the sentence context contained no useful syntactic or semantic information (i.e., random condition).

It was assumed in the original theory that a spoken word will generally not be recognised if its initial phoneme is ambiguous. However, Connine, Blasko, and Titone (1993) referred to a study in which a spoken word ending in "ent" had an ambiguous initial phoneme between "d" and "t". The words "dent" and "tent" were both activated when the target word was presented. This finding was inconsistent with the original theory.

Marslen-Wilson (1990) and Marslen-Wilson and Warren (1994) revised cohort theory. In the original version, words were either in or out of the word cohort. In the revised version, candidate words vary in activation level, and so membership of the word cohort is a matter of degree. Marslen-Wilson assumed the word-initial cohort contains words having similar initial phonemes, rather than being limited to words having the initial phoneme of the presented word. This revised version accounts for the findings of Connine et al. (1993).

There is a second major difference between the original and revised versions of cohort theory. In the original version, context influenced word recognition very early in processing. In the revised version, the effects of context occur later. The evidence supports the revised theory. For example, Zwitserlood (1989) found that context exerted its influence only *after* the point at which a spoken word could be uniquely identified.

## Evaluation

➕ Cohort theory is an influential approach to spoken word recognition.
➕ The assumption in the revised version of the theory that membership of the word cohort is flexible appears essentially correct.
➕ The assumption in the revised version of the theory that contextual effects typically occur late in processing has received support (e.g., Zwitserlood, 1989).
➖ The revised version of cohort theory is less precise than the original version. As Massaro (1994, p. 244) pointed out, "These modifications are necessary to bring the model in line with empirical results, but they … make it more difficult to test against alternative models."

## TRACE model

McClelland and Elman (1986) and McClelland (1991) produced a network model of speech perception. Their TRACE model of speech perception resembles the original version of cohort theory. For example, it is argued within both theories that several sources of information combine interactively in word recognition.

The TRACE model is based on the following theoretical assumptions:

- There are individual processing units or nodes at three different levels: features (e.g., voicing, manner of production), phonemes, and words.
- Feature nodes are connected to phoneme nodes, and phoneme nodes are connected to word nodes.
- Connections *between* levels operate in both directions, and are only facilitatory.

- There are connections among units or nodes *within* the same level; these connections are inhibitory.
- Nodes influence each other in proportion to their activation levels and the strengths of their interconnections.
- As excitation and inhibition spread among nodes, a pattern of activation develops.
- The word that is recognised is determined by the activation level of the possible candidate words.

The TRACE model assumes bottom-up and top-down processing interact during speech perception. Bottom-up activation proceeds upwards from the feature level to the phoneme level and on to the word level. Top-down activation proceeds in the opposite direction from the word level to the phoneme level and on to the feature level. Evidence that top-down processes are involved in spoken word recognition was discussed earlier in the chapter (e.g., Marslen-Wilson & Tyler, 1980; Warren & Warren, 1970).

Cutler, Mehler, Norris, and Segui (1987) studied a phenomenon lending itself to explanation by the TRACE model. They used a phoneme monitoring task, in which participants detected a target phoneme. There was a word superiority effect, with phonemes detected faster when presented in words than in non-words. According to the TRACE model, this phenomenon occurs because of top-down activation from the word level to the phoneme level.

Marslen-Wilson, Moss, and van Halen (1996) presented their participants with "words" such as p/blank, in which the initial phoneme was halfway between a /p/ and a /b/. They wanted to see whether this "word" would facilitate lexical decision for words related to plank (e.g., wood) or to blank (e.g., page). The TRACE model predicts a significant facilitation or priming effect because of spreading activation. In contrast, the original cohort theory assumed that only words *matching* the initial phoneme of the presented word are activated. Thus, there should be no priming effect. The findings supported the cohort theory over the TRACE model.

*Does the TRACE model allow for learning new words?*

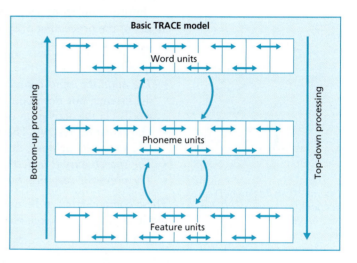

The model predicts that speech perception depends *interactively* on top-down and bottom-up processes. However, this was not confirmed by Massaro (1989) using a phoneme-discrimination task. Bottom-up effects stemming from stimulus discriminability and top-down effects stemming from phonological context both influenced performance. However, they did so in an *independent* rather than interactive way.

## Evaluation

⊕ The TRACE model accounts for various phenomena (e.g., the word superiority effect).
⊕ The model's assumption that spoken word recognition depends on bottom-up *and* top-down processes is correct.
⊖ The TRACE model predicts that speech perception depends *interactively* on bottom-up and top-down processes. This is probably incorrect (e.g., Massaro, 1989).
⊖ The TRACE model predicts that words phonologically similar to a presented word will be activated immediately even though they do not match the presented word in the initial phoneme. This prediction has not been supported (e.g., Marslen-Wilson et al., 1996).
⊖ As Protopapas (1999, p. 420) pointed out, TRACE "does not learn anything. It is prewired to achieve all its remarkable results".

## Section summary

Theories of spoken word recognition are becoming increasingly similar. Most theorists agree that activation of several candidate words occurs early in word recognition. It is also agreed that the speed of word recognition indicates that most of the processes involved proceed in parallel (at the same time) rather than serially. There is also general agreement that the activation levels of candidate words vary in degree rather than being either very high or very low. Finally, nearly all theorists agree that bottom-up and top-down processes combine to produce word recognition. The revised version of cohort theory and the TRACE model both incorporate all these assumptions.

It is hard to know precisely *when* contextual information is used in spoken word recognition. More specifically, it is unclear whether context influences processing *before* or *after* listeners have focused their search down to a single candidate word.

## Cognitive neuropsychology

Repeating a spoken word immediately after hearing it is apparently simple. However, many brain-damaged patients experience difficulties with this task, even though they are not deaf. Detailed analysis of these patients suggests various processes that can be used to permit repetition of a spoken word.

Information from such patients was used by Ellis and Young (1988) to propose a model of the processing of spoken words (see the figure below for a modified version):

- *The auditory analysis system*. This extracts phonemes or other sounds from the speech wave.
- *The auditory input lexicon*. This contains information about spoken words known to the listener, but not about their meaning. The lexicon permits recognition of familiar words via the activation of the appropriate word units.
- *The semantic system*. The meanings of words are stored within the semantic system (cf., **semantic memory**, discussed in Chapter 9).
- *The speech output lexicon*. This provides the spoken forms of words.
- *The phoneme response buffer*. This provides distinctive speech sounds.

*Do you think this model can account for a range of different neurological impairments?*

These components can be used in various combinations, producing three different routes between hearing a spoken word and saying it. The key assumption is that saying a spoken

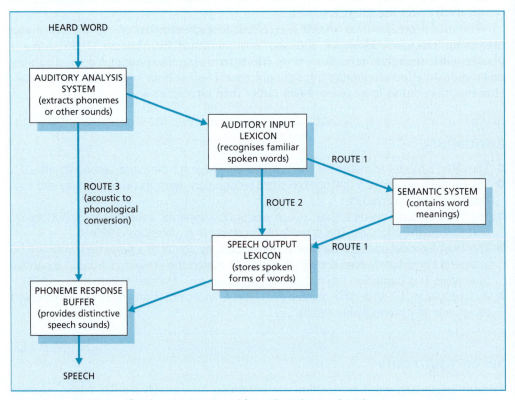

Processing and repetition of spoken words. Adapted from Ellis and Young (1988).

**KEY TERM**

**Semantic memory:** general knowledge about the world stored in long-term memory.

word can be achieved in three different ways, and it is this assumption to which we will devote the most attention. Before doing so, however, we consider the role of the auditory analysis system in speech perception.

## Auditory analysis system

Suppose a patient had damage only to the auditory analysis system, thereby producing a deficit in phonemic processing. Such a patient would have impaired speech perception for words and non-words, especially for words containing phonemes that are hard to discriminate. However, such a patient would have generally intact speech production, reading, and writing, would have normal perception of non-verbal environmental sounds (e.g., coughs, whistles), and unimpaired hearing. Patients conforming to this pattern suffer from **pure word deafness**.

If patients with pure word deafness only have a severe deficit in phonemic processing, their speech perception should improve when they have access to other kinds of information. Okada, Hanada, Hattori, and Shoyama (1963) studied a patient with pure word deafness who could use contextual information. The patient understood spoken questions much better when they all referred to the same topic than when they did not.

A crucial aspect of pure word deafness is that auditory perception problems are highly *selective*, and do not apply to non-speech sounds. Saffran, Marin, and Yeni-Komshian (1976) studied a patient with pure word deafness who could not repeat speech and who had very poor auditory comprehension. However, this patient could identify non-speech sounds and musical instruments.

- *Route 1.* This route uses the auditory input lexicon, the semantic system, and the speech output lexicon. It is how familiar words are identified and comprehended by those with no brain damage. If a brain-damaged patient could use only this route (plus perhaps Route 2), then familiar words would be said correctly. However, there would be severe problems with saying unfamiliar words and non-words, because they have no entries in the auditory input lexicon, and so use of Route 3 would be required. McCarthy and Warrington (1984) described a patient, O.R.F., fitting the bill. O.R.F. repeated words much more accurately than non-words (85% vs. 39%, respectively), indicating that Route 3 was severely impaired.
- *Route 2.* If patients could use Route 2, but Routes 1 and 3 were severely impaired, they would repeat familiar words without understanding their meaning. In addition, they would have problems with non-words, because non-words cannot be handled through Route 2. Finally, since such patients would make use of the input lexicon, they would distinguish between words and non-words.

Patients suffering from **word meaning deafness** (an extremely rare condition) fit the above description. One of the clearest cases, Dr O., was studied by Franklin, Turner, Ralph, Morris, and Bailey (1996). Dr O. showed "no evidence of any impairment in written word comprehension, but auditory comprehension was impaired, particularly for abstract or low-imageability words" (p. 1144). His ability to repeat words was dramatically better than his ability to repeat non-words (80% vs. 7%, respectively). Finally, Dr O. was almost perfect at distinguishing between words and non-words.

- *Route 3.* A patient with damage to Route 3 only would show good ability to perceive and understand spoken familiar words, but would be impaired at perceiving and repeating unfamiliar words and non-words. This is the case in patients with **auditory phonological agnosia**. Such a patient was studied by Beauvois, Dérouesné, and Bastard (1980). Their patient, J.L., had almost perfect repetition and writing to dictation of spoken familiar words, but his repetition and writing of non-words were very poor. However, he was very good at *reading* non-words. J.L. had an intact ability to distinguish between words and non-words, indicating he had no problems with access to the input lexicon.

## Deep dysphasia

Some brain-damaged patients have extensive problems with speech perception, suggesting that several parts of the speech perception system are damaged. For example, patients

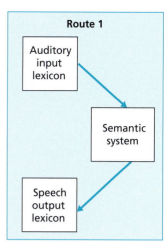

Route 1

Auditory input lexicon → Semantic system → Speech output lexicon

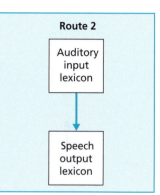

Route 2

Auditory input lexicon → Speech output lexicon

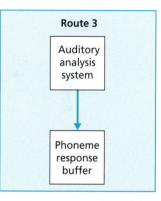

Route 3

Auditory analysis system → Phoneme response buffer

with **deep dysphasia** make semantic errors when repeating spoken words (i.e., saying words related in meaning to those spoken). They also find it harder to repeat abstract words than concrete ones, and have very poor ability to repeat non-words. Perhaps none of the three routes between heard words and speech is intact (see figure on page 378). The presence of semantic errors suggests some impairment involving the semantic system.

Valdois, Carbonnel, David, Rousset, and Pellat (1995) studied E.A., a 72-year-old man who had suffered a stroke. He showed all the symptoms of deep dysphasia, including numerous semantic errors when repeating spoken words having a synonym (word of very similar meaning). In addition, E.A. had very poor short-term memory for auditory and visual verbal material. Valdois et al. discussed six more deep dysphasics who had a very severe deficit in short-term memory (memory span of one or two items). These findings led them to propose that damage to part of the processing system (perhaps the phoneme response buffer) can cause deep dysphasia and impaired short-term memory. However, three other deep dysphasics had only slightly impaired short-term memory, so the factors responsible for deep dysphasia vary from patient to patient.

## Evaluation

➕ Brain-damaged patients show different patterns of impairment in the ability to repeat and to understand spoken words, suggesting there are various routes between hearing a word and saying it.
➕ In general terms, the types of impairment predicted by the three-route model have been identified.
➖ The three-route model is relatively complex, and its validity will become clear only after much further research.
➖ The three-route model is a limited approach, because it focuses on speech perception of individual words.

# BASIC READING PROCESSES

Reading is very important, because adults without effective reading are at a great disadvantage in most societies. As a result, we need to discover enough about reading processes to sort out the problems of poor readers.

Some reading processes are concerned with identifying and extracting meaning from individual words and sentences, whereas others deal with the overall understanding of an entire text or story. In this section, we will focus on individual words and sentences, leaving a discussion of text comprehension for later in the chapter.

## Research methods

Several methods are available for studying reading. For example, various techniques have been used to assess the time taken for word identification. There is the **lexical decision task** (deciding whether a string of letters forms a word) and the **naming task** (saying a word as rapidly as possible). These techniques ensure certain processing has occurred within a given time. However, normal reading processes are disrupted by the additional task, and the detailed processes involved in lexical decision or naming are unclear.

Balota, Paul, and Spieler (1999) argued that reading involves several kinds of processing, including **orthography** (the spelling of words), **phonology** (the sound of words), and word meaning. The naming task emphasises the links between orthography and phonology, whereas the lexical decision task emphasises the links between orthography and meaning. Thus, the naming and lexical decision tasks are limited in terms of the processing they require.

The method of recording eye movements during reading has three particular strengths: (1) it provides a detailed moment-by-moment record; (2) it is unobtrusive; and

(3) it can be used to study the processing of words, sentences, and entire texts. However, it is hard to know *what* processing occurs during each eye fixation (e.g., has the reader identified the word he/she is fixating?).

# Word identification

College students typically read at about 300 words per minute, thus averaging only 200 milliseconds to identify each word. However, it has proved hard to decide exactly how long word identification normally takes, in part because of imprecision about the meaning of "word identification". The term can refer to accessing either the name of a word or its meaning. However, reading rate is slowed by only about 15% when a mask appears 50 milliseconds after the start of each eye fixation (Rayner, Inhoff, Morrison, Slowiaczek, & Bertera, 1981). This suggests that word identification in both senses occurs very rapidly.

## Automatic processing

Rayner and Sereno (1994) argued that word identification is generally fairly automatic. This makes intuitive sense if you consider that most college students have already read between 20 and 70 million words. It has been argued that automatic processes are unavoidable and unavailable to consciousness (see Chapter 6). Evidence that word identification may be unavoidable comes from the **Stroop effect** (Stroop, 1935). The colours in which words are printed are named as rapidly as possible, and naming speed is slowed when the words are conflicting colour names (e.g., the word BLUE printed in black). The Stroop effect suggests that word meaning is extracted even when people try not to process it.

| | | |
|---|---|---|
| BLACK | BLUE | BLACK |
| BLUE | BLUE | BLACK |
| BLACK | BLUE | BLUE |
| BLUE | BLACK | BLACK |

*Try the Stroop task above for yourself. Does it take you longer to articulate the word when it is written in a different colour?*

Cheesman and Merikle (1984) replicated the Stroop effect. They also found the effect could be obtained even when the colour name was presented below the level of conscious awareness, suggesting that word identification does not require conscious awareness.

## Context effects

Is word identification influenced by context? Lucas (1999) carried out a **meta-analysis** (statistical analysis based on combining data across studies) focusing on context effects in lexical access. In these studies, the context sentences contained an ambiguous word (e.g., "The man spent the entire day fishing on the *bank*"). The ambiguous word was immediately followed by a target word on which a naming or lexical decision task was performed. The target word was either appropriate (e.g., "river") or inappropriate (e.g., "money") to the meaning of the ambiguous word in the sentence context. Overall, Lucas found that there was a small effect of context, with word identification occurring faster when the target word was related to the appropriate meaning of the ambiguous word from the sentence.

## Letter vs. word identification

Common sense suggests that the recognition of a word on the printed page involves two successive stages:

1. Identification of its individual letters.
2. Word identification.

However, the notion that letter identification must be complete before word identification can begin is wrong. Consider the **word superiority effect** (Reicher, 1969). A letter string is presented very briefly followed by a pattern mask. The task is to decide which of two letters was presented in a particular position (e.g., the third letter). The word superiority effect is defined by better performance when the letter string forms a word than when it does not.

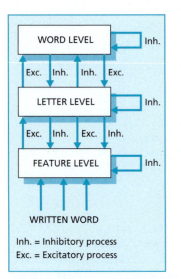

Inh. = Inhibitory process
Exc. = Excitatory process

McClelland and Rumelhart's (1981) interactive activation model of visual word recognition. Adapted from Ellis (1984).

*Can McClelland and Rumelhart's model account for recognition of all words?*

## Interactive activation model

McClelland and Rumelhart (1981) put forward an influential interactive activation model. According to this model, visual word recognition involves bottom-up and top-down processes. Some of the main theoretical assumptions made by McClelland and Rumelhart are as follows:

- There are recognition units at three levels: the feature level, the letter level, and the word level.
- When a feature in a letter is detected (e.g., vertical line at the right-hand side of a letter), activation goes to all letter units containing that feature (e.g., H, M, N), and inhibition to all other letter units.
- When a letter in a particular position within a word is identified, activation is sent to the word level for all four-letter word units containing that letter in that position, and inhibition is sent to all other word units.
- Activated word units increase the level of activation in the letter-level units for the letters forming that word (e.g., activation of the word SEAT would increase activation for the four letters S, E, A, and T at the letter level) and inhibit activity of all other letter units.
- At each level in the system, activation of one particular unit leads to suppression or inhibition of competing units.

## Evidence

It follows from the above assumptions that visual word recognition depends on bottom-up processes stemming directly from the written word proceeding from the feature level through the letter level to the word level by means of activation and inhibition. Top-down processing is involved in the activation and inhibition processes going from the word level to the letter level. The word superiority effect occurs because of top-down influences of the word level on the letter level. Suppose the word SEAT is presented, and the participants are asked whether the third letter is an A or an N. If the word unit for SEAT is activated at the word level, this will increase the activation of the letter A at the letter level, and inhibit the activation of the letter N.

The finding that common or high-frequency words are easier to recognise than rare or low-frequency words can be explained by assuming either that stronger connections are formed between the letter and word units of high-frequency words, or that high-frequency words have a higher resting level of activation. It follows from either explanation that there should be a greater word superiority effect for high-frequency words than for low-frequency words, because they produce more activation from the word level to the letter level. In fact, however, the word superiority effect is the same for common and rare words (e.g., Gunther, Gfoerer, & Weiss, 1984).

## Evaluation

- ⊕ The interactive activation model has been very influential.
- ⊕ The model accounts for various phenomena (e.g., the word superiority effect).
- ⊖ The model is very limited, being designed only to account for word recognition on four-letter words written in capital letters.
- ⊖ The model cannot easily account for the finding that the word superiority effect is the same for high-frequency and low-frequency words (Gunther et al., 1984).
- ⊖ It follows from the original model that human performance on word-recognition tasks should not be variable, which is contrary to the available evidence (see Ellis & Humphreys, 1999). Accordingly, McClelland (1993) developed the model to include variable or stochastic processes.

# Word naming

Suppose you were asked to read out the following:

CAT FOG COMB PINT MANTINESS FASS

It seems simple, but actually involves some hidden complexities. For example, how do you know that "b" in "comb" is silent, and that "pint" does not rhyme with "hint"? Presumably you have specific information stored away in long-term memory about how to pronounce these words. However, this does not explain how you are able to pronounce non-words such as "mantiness" and "fass". Perhaps non-words are pronounced by analogy with real words (e.g., "fass" is pronounced to rhyme with "mass"). Another possibility is that people use rules to translate letter strings into sounds.

The study of brain-damaged patients with impaired reading skills has proved useful in understanding the processes and structures involved in reading. It suggests there are several reading disorders, depending on which parts of the cognitive system involved in reading are damaged. We turn now to theories that have considered reading aloud in unimpaired and brain-damaged individuals.

*Why is it useful for psychologists to study brain-damaged patients?*

## *Dual route cascaded model*

One of the most influential theories of reading is the dual route cascaded model (Coltheart, Rastle, Perry, Ziegler, & Langdon, 2001). The basic assumptions of their model are shown in the figure on the right. The key message is that there are three routes between the printed word and speech, all of which start with orthographic analysis (used for identifying and grouping letters in printed words). You may be puzzled as to why a model with three routes is called a dual route model. The explanation is that the crucial distinction is between a lexical or dictionary look-up route (Routes 2 and 3) and a non-lexical route (Route 1).

- *Route 1* (grapheme–phoneme conversion). Route 1 differs from the other routes in making use of grapheme–phoneme conversion. This may involve working out pronunciations for unfamiliar words and non-words by translating letters or letter groups (graphemes) into phonemes (sounds) by the application of rules. However, Kay and Marcel (1981) argued that unfamiliar words and non-words are actually pronounced by analogy with familiar words. They found that the pronunciations of non-words by normal readers were sometimes altered to rhyme with real words that had just been presented. For example, a non-word such as "raste" is generally pronounced to rhyme with "taste", but is more likely to be pronounced to rhyme with "mast" if preceded by the word "caste".

If a brain-damaged patient could use only Route 1, what would we expect to find? The use of grapheme–phoneme conversion rules should permit accurate pronunciation of words having regular spelling–sound correspondences, but not of irregular words. If an irregular word such as "pint" has grapheme–phoneme conversion rules applied to it, it should be pronounced to rhyme with "hint". Finally, the grapheme–phoneme conversion rules can be used to provide pronunciations of non-words.

Patients adhering fairly closely to exclusive use of Route 1 are surface dyslexics (Marshall & Newcombe, 1973). **Surface dyslexia** is a condition in which patients have

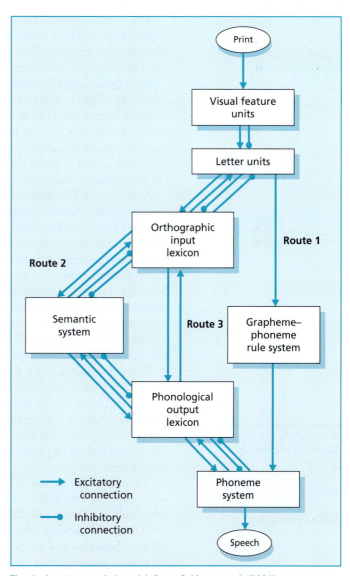

The dual route cascaded model. From Coltheart et al. (2001).

particular problems in reading irregular words. For example, the surface dyslexic patient, M.P., read non-words well, and had a reading accuracy of over 90% with common and rare regular words. In contrast, although common irregular words were read with an accuracy of about 80%, only 40% of rare irregular words were read accurately (Bub, Cancelliere, & Kertesz, 1985).

● *Route 2* (lexicon plus semantic system). Route 2 is the route generally used by adult readers. The basic idea is that representations of thousands of familiar words are stored in an orthographic input lexicon. Visual presentation of a word leads to activation in the orthographic input lexicon. This is followed by obtaining its meaning from the semantic system after which its sound pattern is generated in the phonological output lexicon.

How could we identify patients using Route 2 but not Route 1? Their intact orthographic input lexicon means they should experience little difficulty in pronouncing *familiar* words (regular and irregular). However, their inability to use grapheme–phoneme conversion should make it very hard to pronounce relatively *unfamiliar words* and non-words.

Phonological dyslexics fit this predicted pattern fairly well. **Phonological dyslexia** is a condition in which there are particular problems with reading unfamiliar words and non-words. The first case of phonological dyslexia reported systematically was R.G. (Beauvois & Dérouesné, 1979). R.G. successfully read 100% of 40 real words but only 10% of 40 non-words. Funnell (1983) reported similar findings with patient W.B. He read 85% of words correctly. However, he was totally unable to read non-words, suggesting he could not use Route 2 at all.

There are various theories of phonological dyslexia. According to Harm and Seidenberg (2001), a general problem with phonological (sound) processing underlies phonological dyslexia. This is consistent with the evidence, since virtually all phonological dyslexics have widespread difficulties with phonological processing (Harley, 2001).

**Deep dyslexia** is a condition in which there are particular problems in reading unfamiliar words. In addition, there are semantic reading errors, in which a word related in meaning to the printed word is read (e.g., "ship" read as "boat"). Deep dyslexics resemble phonological dyslexics in finding it very hard to read unfamiliar words and non-words, suggesting they cannot use grapheme–phoneme conversion effectively. Deep dyslexics may mainly use Route 2, but damage within the semantic system itself (or in the connections between the orthographic input lexicon and the semantic system) makes this route error-prone.

According to Coltheart et al. (2001), "Deep dyslexics are reading, not with a damaged version of the normal reading system, but with a completely different reading system located in the right hemisphere." This hypothesis is controversial and appears inconsistent with some of the evidence. For example, we can compare deep dyslexics against split-brain patients when able to use only their right hemisphere (see Chapter 4). According to the hypothesis, the two groups should have comparable reading performance. In fact, however, most deep dyslexics have much better reading performance than split-brain patients. Additional evidence against Coltheart et al.'s hypothesis was reported by Laine, Salmelin, Helenius, and Marttila (2000). They used magneto-encephalography (MEG; see introduction to Cognitive Psychology section), and found that a 46-year-old deep dyslexic had activation mainly in the *left* hemisphere when performing various reading tasks.

● *Route 3* (lexicon only). Route 3 resembles Route 2 in that the orthographic input lexicon and the phonological output lexicon are involved in reading (see figure on the previous page). However, the semantic system is bypassed in Route 3, so printed words that are pronounced are not understood. Otherwise, the expectations about reading performance for users of Route 3 are the same as those for users of Route 2: Familiar regular and irregular words should be pronounced correctly, whereas most unfamiliar words and non-words should not.

Schwartz, Saffran, and Marin (1980) reported the case of W.L.P., a 62-year-old woman with senile dementia. She could read most familiar words whether regular or irregular, but often indicated these words meant nothing to her. She could not relate the written names of animals to pictures of them, although she was fairly good at reading animal names aloud. These findings are consistent with the view that W.L.P. was bypassing the semantic system when reading words. In similar fashion, Coslett (1991) found a patient, W.T., who was reasonably good at reading irregular words, but had no understanding of them.

*Why is it important to distinguish between different types of dyslexia?*

**KEY TERMS**

**Phonological dyslexia:** a condition in which familiar words can be read but there is impaired ability to read unfamiliar words and non-words.

**Deep dyslexia:** a condition in which reading of unfamiliar words is impaired, and there are semantic reading errors (e.g., reading "missile" as "rocket").

She was extremely poor at reading non-words, indicating that she could hardly use Route 1 at all.

## Computational model

Coltheart et al. (2001) produced a detailed computational model to provide a thorough test of their approach. They tested this model with 7981 one-syllable words based on the assumption that the pronunciation which was most activated by processing in the lexical and non-lexical routes would determine the naming response. The model is cascaded, because any activation at one level in the system is passed on immediately to other levels.

Coltheart et al. (2001) found in simulations that the model pronounced 7898 (99%) of the 7981 words correctly. In addition, it read 98.9% of 7000 one-syllable non-words correctly. According to the model, the lexical and non-lexical routes are both involved in the naming task, and so the two routes do not operate independently. Evidence reported by Glushko (1979) is consistent with this assumption. He compared naming times of two kinds of non-words: (1) those having irregular word neighbours (e.g., "have" is an irregular word neighbour of "mave", whereas "gave" and "save" are regular word neighbours); and (2) non-words having only regular word neighbours. Non-words of the former type were named more slowly, suggesting that the lexical route can influence the non-lexical route in the reading of non-words.

*Do you think the models discussed here can account for reading in all languages?*

## Evaluation

➕ The dual route cascaded model identifies clearly the main routes involved in reading.
➕ The model provides an excellent account of disorders such as surface dyslexia and phonological dyslexia, and can account for the reading performance of unimpaired individuals. The model has successfully simulated 18 effects with reading aloud or naming (Coltheart et al., 2001).
➖ The model contains 31 variables, which means that almost any set of data could be fitted by the model.
➖ As Coltheart et al. (2001, p. 236) admitted, "The Chinese, Japanese, and Korean writing systems are structurally so different from the English writing system that a model like the DRC [dual route cascaded] model would simply not be applicable: for example, monosyllable non-words cannot even be written in the Chinese script or in Japanese kanji, so the distinction between a lexical and non-lexical route for reading aloud cannot even arise."
➖ The model provides a very limited account of reading, because its emphasis is on the pronunciation of individual one-syllable words rather than on the understanding of text.

## Connectionist approach

Within the dual-route approach, it is assumed that separate mechanisms are required to pronounce irregular words and non-words. This contrasts with the connectionist approach of Plaut, McClelland, Seidernberg, and Patterson (1996), according to which, "All of the system's knowledge of spelling-sound correspondences is brought to bear in pronouncing all types of letters strings [words *and* non-words]. Conflicts among possible alternative pronunciations of a letter string are resolved ... by co-operative and competitive interactions based on how the letter string relates to all known words and their pronunciations." Thus, Plaut et al. assumed that pronunciation of words and non-words is based on a highly *interactive* system.

The two approaches can be contrasted by considering the distinction between regularity and consistency. Dual-route theorists divide words into two categories: *regular*, meaning their pronunciation can be generated by applying rules; and *irregular*, meaning their pronunciation is not rule based. Regular words can generally be pronounced more rapidly. In contrast, Plaut et al. (1996) argued that words vary in *consistency* (the extent

| Regular words | Irregular words |
|---|---|
| fantasy | chemistry |
| meet | hierarchy |
| passenger | sapphire |
| Swiss | Worcester |

**Inconsistent words**

through, cough, sought, thorough, rough

to which their pronunciation agrees with those of similarly spelled words). Highly consistent words are pronounced faster and more accurately than inconsistent words, because more of the available knowledge supports the correct pronunciation of such words. Word naming is generally predicted better by consistency than by regularity (e.g., Glushko, 1979), as is predicted by the connectionist model.

Plaut et al. (1996) tried various computer simulations based on two crucial notions:

1. The pronunciation of a word or non-word is influenced strongly by consistency based on the pronunciations of all those words similar to it.
2. Pronunciation of a word is more influenced by high-frequency or common words than by low-frequency or rare words.

The network in the simulations learned to pronounce words accurately as connections developed between the visual forms of letters and combinations of letters (grapheme units) and their corresponding phonemes (phoneme units). The network received prolonged training with a set of 2998 words, after which the performance of the network closely resembled that of adult readers in several ways:

- Inconsistent words took longer to name than consistent ones.
- Rare words took longer to name than common ones.
- The effects of consistency were much greater for rare words than for common ones.
- The network pronounced over 90% of non-words "correctly", as do most adult readers.

*Can the connectionist approach account for the impairments found in different types of dyslexia?*

The above simulation did not take semantic information into account. However, Plaut et al. (1996) expanded their network model to include semantic information. Such a network learned to read regular and irregular words much faster than a network lacking semantic information.

## Surface dyslexia and phonological dyslexia

Plaut et al. (1996, p. 95) advanced the following theory of surface dyslexia: "Partial semantic support for word pronunciations alleviates the need for the phonological pathway to

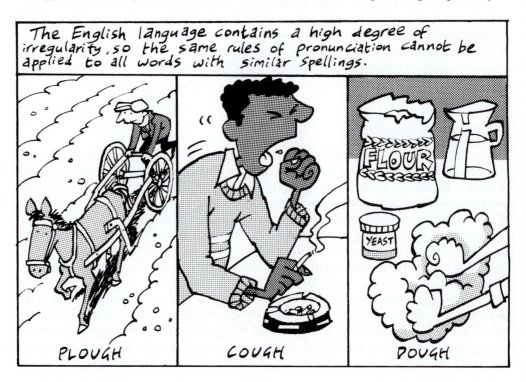

The English language contains a high degree of irregularity, so the same rules of pronunciation cannot be applied to all words with similar spellings.

PLOUGH          COUGH          DOUGH

master all words such that, when the support is eliminated by brain damage, the surface dyslexic reading pattern emerges." Plaut et al. tested this theory by making "lesions" to the network to reduce or eliminate the contribution from semantics. The network's reading performance was very good on regular high- and low-frequency words and on non-words, worse on irregular high-frequency words, and worst on irregular low-frequency words. This is the same pattern of reading performance found in surface dyslexics.

What about phonological dyslexia? Plaut et al. (1996, p. 99) only considered this disorder in general terms: "A lesion to the network that severely impaired the phonological pathway while leaving the contribution of semantics to phonology (relatively) intact would replicate the basic characteristics of phonological dyslexia."

## Evaluation

⊕ The evidence supports the key assumption that the reading of words and of non-words involves an interactive system.
⊕ The connectionist approach avoids the sharp distinction between regular and irregular words within the dual-route approach. This is preferable, because the evidence does not support the notion of a rigid distinction.
⊕ As predicted by the connectionist approach, speed and accuracy of word and non-word pronunciation depend more on consistency than on regularity.
⊖ As Plaut et al. (1996, p. 108) admitted, "the nature of processing within the semantic pathway has been characterised in only the coarsest way".
⊖ The connectionist approach provides only a sketchy account of various key issues, such as the nature of the impairment in phonological dyslexia.
⊖ The simulations carried out by Plaut et al. (1996) to test the theory only used one-syllable words, and so its applicability to multi-syllable words is unclear.

## Eye movements

Our eyes seem to move smoothly across the page while reading. In fact, they actually move in rapid jerks (**saccades**). Saccades are ballistic (once initiated their direction cannot

A saccadic eye movement: the next saccade is planned during processing of the current fixation via covert attention.

be changed). There are regressions, in which the eyes move backwards in the text, accounting for about 10% of all saccades. Saccades take 10–20 milliseconds to complete, and are separated by fixations lasting about 200–250 milliseconds. The length of each saccade is about eight letters or spaces. Information is extracted from the text only during each fixation, and not during the intervening saccades.

The perceptual span is defined as the amount of text from which useful information is obtained on each fixation. It is affected by the difficulty of the text, the size of the print, and so on. However, it usually extends to no more than about three or four letters to the left of fixation and 15 letters to the right.

## E-Z Reader model

Reichle, Pollatsek, Fisher, and Rayner (1998) explained the pattern of eye movements during reading in their E-Z Reader model (the name makes more sense in American English, where Z is pronounced "zee"!). About 80% of content words (nouns, verbs, and adjectives) are fixated. However, only about 20% of function words (articles, conjunctions, prepositions, and pronouns) are fixated, and we need to identify the factors leading such words to be "skipped" or not fixated.

The E-Z Reader model was designed to explain the following findings (see Reichle et al., 1998):

- Rare words are fixated for longer than common words.
- Words more predictable in the sentence context are fixated for less time.
- Words not fixated tend to be common, short, or predictable.
- The fixation time on a word is longer when preceded by a rare word: the "spillover" effect.

*Are these the kind of findings you would expect, i.e., do they make intuitive sense to you?*

What would be the most obvious kind of model? Perhaps readers fixate on one word until they have processed it, after which they fixate the next word. However, there are two major problems with this approach:

1. It takes about 150–200 milliseconds to execute an eye-movement programme. If readers behaved according to this simple model, they would waste time waiting for their eyes to move.
2. Readers could not safely skip words, because they would know nothing about the next word until they fixated it.

How can we get round these problems? Reichle et al. (1998) argued that the next eye movement is programmed after only *part* of the processing of the currently fixated word has occurred. This greatly reduces the time between completion of processing on the current word and movement of the eyes to the next word. Any spare time is used to start processing the next word. If the processing of the next word is completed rapidly enough, it is skipped.

Reichle et al. (1998) emphasised several general assumptions in their E-Z Reader model:

1. Readers check the frequency of the word they are currently fixating.
2. Completion of frequency checking of a word initiates an eye-movement programme.
3. Readers also engage in **lexical access**, in which stored information (e.g., semantic) about the word is retrieved from the **lexicon**. This takes longer to complete than does frequency checking.
4. Completion of lexical access to one word is the signal to shift covert (internal) attention to the next word.
5. Frequency checking and lexical access are completed faster for common words than for rare ones, especially lexical access.
6. Frequency checking and lexical access are completed faster for predictable than for unpredictable words.

Assumptions 2 and 5 together predict that the time spent fixating common words will be less than the time fixating rare words, which is consistent with the evidence. According

**KEY TERMS**

**Lexical access:** processes involved in entering the lexicon.

**Lexicon:** the range of knowledge possessed about words, including their meaning, spelling, pronunciation, and grammatical rules.

to the model, readers spend the time between completion of lexical access to a word and the next eye movement in processing the next word outside the central or foveal part of the retina. The amount of time spent in such parafoveal processing is less when the fixated word is rare than when it is common. Thus, the word following a rare word is generally fixated for longer than the word following a common word (the spillover effect described earlier).

Why are words that are common, predictable, or short more likely than other words to be skipped or not fixated? According to the model, a word is skipped when its lexical access is completed while the previous word is still fixated. This is most likely to happen for common, predictable, or short words, because lexical access is faster for these words than for others (assumptions 5 and 6).

According to the model, readers detect word frequency at an early stage of processing. Support for this prediction was reported by Sereno, Rayner, and Posner (1998). They found that there were effects of word frequency on event-related potentials (see introduction to Cognitive Psychology section) 150 milliseconds into word processing.

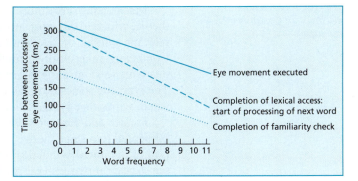

The effects of word frequency on eye movements according to the E-Z Reader model. Adapted from Reichle et al. (1998).

## Evaluation

● The E-Z Reader model specifies the main factors determining eye movements in reading.
● The predictions of the model are generally in good agreement with actual eye-movement data, suggesting that reading occurs on a word-by-word basis with a certain amount of parafoveal processing outside the central or foveal area of the eye.
● The model de-emphasises the involvement of higher-level cognitive processes in reading. For example, readers have a long fixation on the word "seems" in the confusing sentence, "Since Jay always jogs a mile seems like a short distance" (Frazier & Rayner, 1982), but the model does not explain this.
● It is not clear how the motor programming system translates the signal to move to the next word into a saccade of the appropriate length.

## Parsing

**Parsing** involves an analysis of the syntactical (grammatical) structure of sentences. What is grammar? In essence, it is concerned with the ways in which words in a sentence are combined, since the meaning of a sentence depends importantly on the order of the words within it. The relationship between syntactic (grammatical) and semantic (meaning) analysis is a matter of controversy. There are at least four major possibilities:

1. Syntactic analysis generally precedes (and influences) semantic analysis.
2. Semantic analysis usually occurs *prior* to syntactic analysis.
3. Syntactic and semantic analysis occur at the same time.
4. Syntax and semantics are very closely associated, and have a hand-in-glove relationship (Altmann, personal communication).

*Which of these four possibilities do you think is most likely to be correct?*

### Theoretical approaches

Most theoretical approaches to parsing can be divided into one-stage or two-stage models (Harley, 2001). According to one-stage models, all sources of information (syntactic and semantic) are used at the same time to form a syntactic construction of sentences. In contrast, the first stage of processing in two-stage models uses *only* syntactic information, with semantic information being used during the second stage.

**KEY TERM**

**Parsing:** analysing the syntactical (grammatical) structure of sentences.

*Do you think theories of parsing can be applied to all languages?*

MacDonald, Pearlmutter, and Seidenberg (1994) put forward the constraint-based theory, which is the most influential one-stage model. According to MacDonald et al. all relevant sources of information or constraints are available immediately to the parser. Competing analyses of a sentence are activated at the same time (especially with ambiguous sentences), and the analyses are ranked according to the strength of their activation. The syntactic structure receiving most support from the various constraints is highly activated, with other syntactic structures being less activated.

Frazier and Rayner (1982) put forward the garden-path model, which is the most influential two-stage model. According to this model, meaning is not involved in the selection of the initial syntactical structure. The simplest possible syntactical structure is chosen, based on two general principles:

1. *The principle of minimal attachment.* The grammatical structure producing the fewest nodes (constituent parts of a sentence such as noun phrase and verb phrase) is preferred.
2. *The principle of late closure.* New words encountered in a sentence are attached to the current phrase or clause if that is grammatically permissible.

## Evidence

Much research on parsing has focused on sentences that are ambiguous. Why is this the case? Parsing generally occurs very rapidly, and this makes it hard to study the processes involved. However, observing the problems encountered by readers struggling with ambiguous sentences can provide revealing information about parsing processes.

There is considerable evidence that readers typically follow the principles of minimal attachment and late closure as predicted by the garden-path model (see Harley, 2001). However, the most important difference between the theories is whether or not semantic factors influence the construction of the initial syntactic structure, and much of the relevant evidence does not favour the garden-path model. According to that model, prior context should not influence the initial parsing of an ambiguous sentence. Contrary evidence was reported by Tanenhaus, Spivey-Knowlton, Eberhard, and Sedivy (1995), who presented their participants with the sentence, "Put the apple on the towel in the box." According to the garden-path model, "on the towel" should initially be understood as the place where the apple should be put, because that is the simplest syntactic structure. That did

PARSING AND AMBIGUITY: "She bit into the doughnut with relish".

"she bit into the doughnut, with relish"

"She bit into, the doughnut with relish"

*not* happen when the visual context consisted of two apples, one on a towel and the other on a napkin. With that context, the participants interpreted "on the towel" as a way of identifying which apple was to be moved. Thus, context influenced parsing.

Findings consistent with constraint-based theory were reported by Pickering and Traxler (1998). Participants were presented with sentences such as the following:

1. As the woman edited the magazine amused all the reporters.
2. As the woman sailed the magazine amused all the reporters.

These two sentences are identical syntactically, and thus should be processed in the same way according to the garden-path model. However, the semantic constraints favouring the wrong syntactic structure are greater in sentence (1) than in sentence (2). These constraints should make it much harder for readers of sentence (1) to change their incorrect syntactic analysis when it needs to be abandoned (i.e., when the verb "amused" is reached). As predicted, eye-movement data indicated that eye fixations in the verb and post-verb regions were longer for those reading sentence (1).

Evidence against constraint-based theory was obtained by Boland and Blodgett (2001), who studied the effects of misleading context as in the following example:

> As they walked around, Kate looked at all of Jimmy's pets.
> She saw her duck and stumble near the barn.

Reading time was slowed down when the context was misleading, which fits constraint-based theory more than the garden-path theory. However, the crucial finding was that misleading context influenced syntactic processing later than predicted by constraint-based theory. Thus, the notion that all relevant sources of information are used immediately to influence syntactic processing was not correct so far as previous context was concerned.

## Evaluation

➕ There is reasonable experimental support for many of the main theoretical assumptions of both theories.

➕ There is evidence that semantic factors (e.g., context) influence initial parsing as predicted by constraint-based theory (but not by the garden-path model).

➖ Constraint-based theory may be incorrect in assuming that all sources of information are used immediately to construct a syntactic structure (e.g., Boland & Blodgett, 2001).

➖ It is assumed within constraint-based theory that several syntactic structures are formed by the language processor. However, there is little direct evidence supporting this assumption.

➖ Most of the evidence has failed to distinguish clearly between the two theories. As Harley (2001, p. 264) noted, "Proponents of the garden path model argue that the effects that are claimed to support constraint-based models arise because the second stage of parsing begins very quickly, and that many experiments that are supposed to be looking at the first stage are in fact looking at the second stage of parsing."

## DISCOURSE PROCESSING

So far in this chapter we have focused on the basic processes involved in identifying and pronouncing spoken and written words. We normally encounter spoken and written words in the form of discourse, which consists of a connected sequence of sentences (e.g., a story, newspaper article). What are the important differences between sentence processing and discourse processing? According to Graesser, Millis, and Zwaan (1997, p. 164), "A sentence out of context is nearly always ambiguous, whereas a sentence in a discourse context is rarely ambiguous ... Both stories and everyday experiences include people

performing actions in pursuit of goals, events that present obstacles to these goals, conflicts between people, and emotional reactions."

## Inference drawing

In order to comprehend discourse, we need to gain access to relevant stored knowledge. This is especially obvious when we use such knowledge to draw inferences to fill in the frequent gaps in what we listen to or read. Some idea of how readily we make inferences can be formed by reading the following story (Rumelhart & Ortony, 1977):

1.  Mary heard the ice-cream van coming.
2.  She remembered the pocket money.
3.  She rushed into the house.

You probably made various inferences while reading the story. Possible inferences include the following: Mary wanted to buy some ice-cream; buying ice-cream costs money; and Mary had only a limited amount of time to get hold of some money before the ice-cream van arrived. None of these assumptions is explicitly stated. It is so natural for us to draw inferences that we are often unaware of doing so.

We can distinguish among logical inferences, bridging inferences and elaborative inferences. **Logical inferences** depend only on the meanings of the words. For example, we can infer that someone who is a widow is female. **Bridging inferences** establish coherence between the current part of the text and the preceding text, whereas **elaborative inferences** simply add details to the text.

Most theorists accept that readers generally draw logical and bridging inferences, both of which are essential for full understanding. What is more controversial is the extent to which non-essential or elaborative inferences are drawn automatically. Singer (1994) compared the time taken to verify a test sentence (e.g., "A dentist pulled a tooth") following one of three contexts: (1) the information had already been explicitly presented; (2) a bridging inference was needed to understand the test sentence; and (3) an elaborative inference was needed. Verification times in conditions (1) and (2) were fast and the same, suggesting that the bridging inference was drawn automatically during comprehension. However, verification times were significantly slower in condition (3) because the elaborative inference was *not* drawn automatically.

The simplest form of bridging inference is involved in **anaphora**, in which a pronoun or noun has to be identified with a previously mentioned noun or noun phrase (e.g., "Fred sold John his lawn mower, and then he sold him his garden hose"). It requires a bridging inference to realise that "he" refers to Fred.

The ease of establishing the appropriate anaphoric inference often depends on the distance between the pronoun and the noun to which it refers: This is the distance effect. However, Clifton and Ferreira (1987) showed that distance is not always important. The reading time for a critical phrase containing a pronoun was faster if the relevant noun was still the topic of discourse, but distance as such had no effect.

## Minimalist hypothesis

Various inferences are made while people read text or listen to speech. *Why* are inferences made, and *which* inferences are likely to be made in any given situation? McKoon and Ratcliff (1992, p. 440) proposed the *minimalist hypothesis*, according to which strategic inferences are formed in pursuit of the reader's goals. In addition, some inferences are formed automatically:

- Some automatic inferences rely on information that is readily available, because it forms part of the reader's general knowledge or because it is explicitly stated in the text.

---

"Sam had been in pain all night. In the morning the dentist drilled and filled his tooth."

Logical inference: Sam is male.

Bridging inference: The dentist treated Sam's tooth.

Elaborative inference: Sam phoned the dentist early to get an emergency appointment. The treatment cured the pain.

---

*Try to think of a way of remembering the difference between logical, bridging, and elaborative inferences.*

---

**KEY TERMS**

**Logical inferences:** inferences that depend only on the meanings of words.

**Bridging inferences:** inferences that are drawn to increase the coherence between the current and preceding parts of a text.

**Elaborative inferences:** inferences that add details to a text that is being read.

**Anaphora:** the use of a pronoun or noun to represent some previously mentioned noun or noun phrase.

● Some automatic inferences allow the reader to make sense of the part of the text currently being read.

Those favouring the minimalist hypothesis claim there are very definite constraints on the number of inferences generated automatically. In contrast, those supporting the constructionist viewpoint (e.g., Bransford, 1979) argue that numerous automatic inferences are drawn in reading. According to constructionist theorists, these automatic inferences facilitate full comprehension of what is being listened to or read.

## Evidence

McKoon and Ratcliff (1986) compared the above two theories. They argued that a sentence such as, "The actress fell from the fourteenth storey", would automatically lead to the inference that she died from the constructionist (but not the minimalist) viewpoint. Participants read several short texts containing such sentences, followed by a recognition memory test containing critical test words representing inferences from a presented sentence (e.g., "dead" for the sentence about the actress). The correct response to these critical test words was "No". However, if participants had formed the inference, they might make errors. There were very few errors as predicted by the minimalist hypothesis.

More evidence consistent with the minimalist position was reported by Dosher and Corbett (1982). They used instrumental inferences (e.g., a sentence such as, "Mary stirred her coffee", has "spoon" as its instrumental inference). In order to decide whether participants generated these instrumental inferences during reading, Dosher and Corbett used an unusual procedure. The time taken to name the colour in which a word is printed is slowed down if the word has recently been activated. Thus, if presentation of the sentence, "Mary stirred her coffee", activates the word "spoon", this should slow the time taken to name the colour in which the word "spoon" is printed. In a control condition, the words presented bore no relationship to the preceding sentences.

*Do you think such studies reflect the inferences we make when reading in normal as opposed to laboratory conditions?*

What did Dosher and Corbett (1982) find? With normal reading instructions, there was no evidence that instrumental inferences had been formed. However, when the participants were instructed to guess the instrument in each sentence, the instrumental inferences were made. The above findings indicate clearly that whether an inference is drawn depends on the reader's intentions or goals, as assumed by McKoon and Ratcliff (1992). These findings are in line with the minimalist hypothesis, but at variance with the constructionist position. It is necessary to infer the instrument used in stirring coffee to attain full understanding, but such instrumental inferences are not normally drawn.

McKoon and Ratcliff (1992) assumed that local inferences are drawn automatically to assist understanding the current part of the text, but global inferences (inferences connecting widely separated pieces of textual information) are not drawn automatically. They tested these assumptions with short texts containing a global goal (e.g., assassinating a president) and one or two local or subordinate goals (e.g., using a rifle). Local inferences were drawn automatically, but global ones were not. These findings are more consistent with the minimalist hypothesis than with the constructionist position, in which no distinction is drawn between local and global inferences.

## Evaluation

⊕ The minimalist hypothesis clarifies which inferences are drawn automatically.
⊕ The minimalist hypothesis emphasises the distinction between automatic and strategic inferences. The notion that many inferences will be drawn only if consistent with the reader's goals is important.
⊖ The minimalist hypothesis under-estimates the number of inferences drawn when the reader is reading a text slowly for enjoyment (Graesser et al., 1997).
⊖ We cannot always predict accurately from the hypothesis which inferences will be drawn. For example, automatic inferences are drawn if the necessary information is "readily available", but this can be hard to establish.

## Search-after-meaning theory

Graesser, Singer, and Trabasso (1994) put forward a search-after-meaning theory resembling the minimalist hypothesis. According to this theory, readers engage in a search after meaning based on the following:

- *The reader goal assumption.* The reader constructs a meaning for the text addressing his/her goals.
- *The coherence assumption.* The reader tries to construct a meaning for the text that is coherent locally and globally.
- *The explanation assumption.* The reader tries to explain the actions and events described in the text.

According to the theory, the reader will not search after meaning if his/her goals do not require the construction of a meaning representation of the text (e.g., in proofreading); if the text seems to lack coherence; or if the reader lacks the necessary background knowledge to make sense of the text. Even if readers do search after meaning, several kinds of inferences are not generally drawn according to the theory, including ones about future developments (causal consequences); the precise way in which actions are accomplished (subordinate goal-actions); and the author's intent.

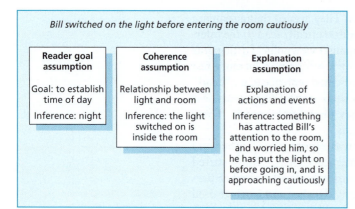

*Bill switched on the light before entering the room cautiously*

**Reader goal assumption**

Goal: to establish time of day

Inference: night

**Coherence assumption**

Relationship between light and room

Inference: the light switched on is inside the room

**Explanation assumption**

Explanation of actions and events

Inference: something has attracted Bill's attention to the room, and worried him, so he has put the light on before going in, and is approaching cautiously

## *Evidence*

Most findings supporting the minimalist hypothesis are also consistent with search-after-meaning theory (see earlier discussion). However, there are some important differences between the two theories. For example, only search-after-meaning theory predicts that various global inferences will be drawn. These include inferences relating to the supraordinate or main goal of the text and those relating to the emotional reactions of the characters in a story.

*Study this text box. Which theory is supported by the most evidence?*

| | Type of inference | Answers query | Predicted by search-after-meaning theory | Predicted by minimalists | Normally found |
|---|---|---|---|---|---|
| 1. | Referential | To what previous word does this apply? (e.g., anaphora) | ✓ | ✓ | ✓ |
| 2. | Case structure role assignment | What is the role (e.g., agent, object) of this noun? | ✓ | ✓ | ✓ |
| 3. | Causal antecedent | What caused this? | ✓ | ✓ | ✓ |
| 4. | Supraordinate goal | What is the main goal? | ✓ | | ✓ |
| 5. | Thematic | What is the overall theme? | ✓ | | ? |
| 6. | Character emotional reaction | How does the character feel? | ✓ | | ✓ |
| 7. | Causal consequence | What happens next? | | | ✗ |
| 8. | Instrument | What was used to do this? | | | ✗ |
| 9. | Subordinate goal-action | How was the action achieved? | | | ✗ |

The types of inferences normally drawn, together with the predictions from the search-after-meaning and minimalist perspectives. Adapted from Graesser et al. (1994).

Nine different types of inference are described in the figure on the previous page. According to Graesser et al. (1994), it is assumed within search-after-meaning theory that six of these types of inference are generally drawn, whereas only three are drawn on the minimalist hypothesis. The evidence seems to be more in line with the predictions of the search-after-meaning theory than those of the minimalist hypothesis.

## Evaluation

- ➕ Search-after-meaning theory provides a clear account of the types of inferences generally drawn.
- ➕ The theory predicts more inferences will be drawn than does the minimalist hypothesis, but fewer than does the constructionist approach. The evidence supports the predictions of the search-after-meaning theory better than those of the competing theories (see Graesser et al., 1994).
- ➖ Search-after-meaning theory is probably less correct than the minimalist hypothesis when the reader lacks much background knowledge and is reading rapidly (Graesser et al., 1997).
- ➖ The theory does not consider fully individual differences. For example, it has been found that individuals with high working memory capacity (ability to process and store information at the same time) find it easier than those with low working memory capacity to draw elaborative inferences (Calvo, 2001).

## STORY PROCESSING

If someone asks us to tell them about a story or book we have read recently, we discuss its major events and themes, and omit the minor details. Thus, our description of the story is highly *selective*, and determined by its meaning. Indeed, imagine the questioner's reaction if we simply recalled sentences taken at random from the story!

Gomulicki (1956) showed the selective way in which stories are comprehended and remembered. One group of participants wrote a précis (summary) of a story visible in front of them, and a second group recalled the story from memory. A third group of participants who were given each précis and recall found it very hard to tell them apart. Thus, story memory resembles a précis with people focusing mainly on important information.

How we process and remember stories depends in part on the relevant knowledge we possess in the form of **schemas** (well-integrated packets of information about the world, events, people, and actions). Two of the main

*The Parisian Novels (The Yellow Books)* by Vincent van Gogh. Our recall of stories or books is selective, i.e., we are likely to remember the theme, characters and plot, but not individual sentences.

schema theories (Bartlett's theory and the script-pointer-plus-tag hypothesis) are discussed in detail in Chapter 9. Schema theories are of most relevance to an understanding of what is remembered from stories, and that is why they are discussed in the chapter on memory. Below we consider major theories in which the focus is more on the processes involved in story comprehension.

## Kintsch's construction–integration model

Kintsch (1988, 1994) put forward a construction–integration model. According to the model, the following stages occur during comprehension:

1. Sentences in the text are turned into propositions representing its meaning.

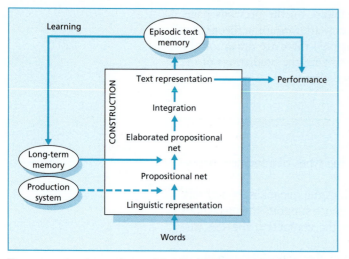

The construction–integration model. Adapted from Kintsch (1994).

*Do you think Kintsch is correct in proposing three levels of representation, or can you think of any others?*

2. These propositions are entered into a short-term buffer and form a *propositional net*.

3. Each proposition constructed from the text retrieves associatively related propositions (including inferences) from long-term memory.

4. The propositions constructed from the text plus those retrieved from *long-term memory* jointly form the *elaborated propositional net*; this net contains many irrelevant propositions.

5. A spreading activation process is then used to select propositions for the text representation; clusters of highly interconnected propositions attract most of the activation and are most likely to be included in the text representation: this is the *integration process*.

6. The *text representation* is an organised structure stored in *episodic text memory*; information about the relationship between any two propositions is included if the two propositions were processed together in the short-term buffer.

7. Three levels of representation can be constructed:
   • Surface representation (the text itself).
   • Propositional representation or textbase (propositions formed from the text).
   • Situational representation (a mental model describing the situation referred to in the text). Schemas can help the construction of situational representations or models.

According to the model, the processes involved in the construction of the elaborated propositional net are *inefficient*, with many irrelevant propositions being included. This is basically a bottom-up approach, in that the elaborated propositional net is constructed ignoring the context provided by the overall theme of the text. In contrast, "most other models of comprehension attempt to specify strong, 'smart' rules which, guided by schemata, arrive at just the right interpretations, activate just the right knowledge, and generate just the right inferences" (Kintsch, Welsch, Schmalhofer, & Zimny, 1990, p. 136). Such strong rules are very complex and lack flexibility. The weak rules incorporated into the construction–integration model are much more robust, and can be used in virtually all situations.

### Evidence

Kintsch et al. (1990) tested the theoretical assumption that text processing produces three levels of representation (surface, propositional, and situational). Participants were presented with texts, and then their recognition memory was tested immediately or at times ranging up to 4 days. There was rapid and complete forgetting of the surface representation, whereas information from the situational representation showed no forgetting over 4 days. Propositional information differed from situational information in that there was forgetting over time, and differed from surface information in that there was only partial forgetting. As Kintsch et al. had predicted, the most complete representation of the meaning of the text (i.e., the situational representation) was best remembered, and the least complete representation (i.e., the surface representation) was worst remembered.

Zwaan (1994) argued that the reader's goals influence the extent to which different representational levels are constructed. For example, someone reading an excerpt from a novel might focus on the text itself (e.g., the wording, stylistic devices), and so form a strong surface representation.

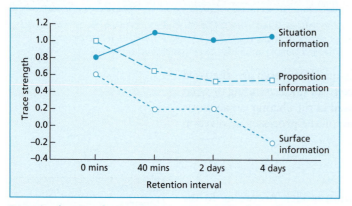

Forgetting functions for situation, proposition, and surface information over a 4-day period. Adapted from Kintsch et al. (1990).

In contrast, someone reading a newspaper article may focus on updating his/her representation of a real-world situation, and so form a strong situation representation. Zwaan devised texts described as either literary extracts or news stories. As predicted, memory for surface representations was better for stories described as literary, whereas memory for situation representations was better for stories described as newspaper reports.

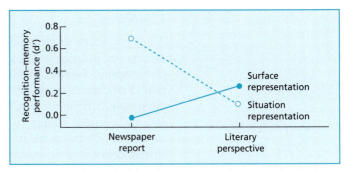

Memory for surface and situation representations for stories described as literary or as newspaper reports. Data from Zwaan (1994).

According to the model, people having much relevant knowledge should find it easier than others to construct the propositional and situational levels of representation when reading a text. In contrast, those with minimal relevant knowledge may focus mainly on forming a surface representation. Caillies, Denhiere, and Kintsch (1992) presented texts describing the use of software packages to participants whose knowledge ranged from non-existent to advanced, and found evidence supporting the various predictions of the model.

## Evaluation

⊕ The ways in which text information combines with the reader's knowledge are spelled out in detail in the construction–integration model.
⊕ There is good support for the notion that three levels of representation are constructed, and that relevant knowledge and the reader's goals influence which levels are constructed.
⊕ The emphasis on spreading activation points to important similarities between story processing and the processing of individual words.
⊖ Situational representations are not always constructed, even by individuals having enough relevant knowledge to be able to do so. Limited processing capacity often restricts the formation of situational representations (e.g., Zwaan & van Oostendorp, 1993).
⊖ According to the model, numerous inferences are considered initially, with most of them being discarded before the reader becomes aware of them. This key theoretical assumption has not been tested properly.
⊖ There may be more levels of representation than the three identified by Kintsch (1988, 1994). For example, Graesser et al. (1997) identified the genre level, which is concerned with the nature of the text (e.g., narration, description).

## Event-indexing model

Kintsch's (1988, 1994) construction–integration model is not specific about the processes involved in the construction of situation models. However, Zwaan, Langston, and Graesser (1995a) put forward an event-indexing model to remedy this omission. According to this model, readers monitor five aspects or indexes of the evolving situation model when they read stories:

1. *The protagonist.* The central character or actor in the present event compared to the previous event.
2. *Temporality.* The relationship between the times at which the present and previous events occurred.
3. *Causality.* The causal relationship of the current event to the previous event.
4. *Spatiality.* The relationship between the spatial setting of the current event and that of the previous event.
5. *Intentionality.* The relationship between the character's goals and the present event.

## Evidence

A key prediction of the model is that *discontinuity* (unexpected change) in any of the five aspects or indexes (e.g., a flashback in time) creates difficulties in situation-model construction. Zwaan, Magliano, and Graesser (1995b) reported support for this prediction. Participants took 297 milliseconds longer to read a sentence involving temporal discontinuity than one involving temporal continuity. In addition, they found that it took 201 milliseconds longer to read a sentence involving causal discontinuity rather than continuity. Zwaan et al. found in another experiment that reading times for events in a story increased as a function of the number out of the five aspects on which there was discontinuity with the previous event. They also showed that each of the five aspects had its own influence on reading time.

According to the model, readers typically update their situational model to take account of changes in the situations described in a text. It follows that previous information which is not relevant to the current situational model should be less accessible than information which is relevant. Radvansky and Copeland (2001) tested this prediction by presenting people with short stories such as the following, with either "picked up" or "set down" in the second sentence:

> *Warren spent the afternoon shopping at the store. He picked up/set down his bag and went over to look at some scarves. He had been shopping all day. He thought it was getting too heavy to carry.*

*Does this finding support the event-indexing model?*

The above story was followed by the word "bag", with the participants having to decide whether it had appeared in the story. According to Radvansky and Copeland (2001), the bag still formed part of the current situational model at the end of the story when the words "picked up" were used in the second sentence, but not when the words "set down" were used. As predicted, the participants given "set down" were less likely to recognise the word "bag" as having been in the story.

## Evaluation

⊕ The emphasis within the event-indexing model on the construction of situation models is probably warranted.

⊕ The event-indexing model identifies key processes involved in creating and updating situation models.

⊖ The model explicitly focuses on only a few of the processes involved in text comprehension.

⊖ According to the model, readers make inferences when there are discontinuities in a text. Such inferences are more likely to be drawn when readers have the goal of understanding the text thoroughly (see discussion of the minimalist hypothesis earlier in the chapter), but the model does not consider the reader's goals.

⊖ The five situational aspects are regarded as independent of each other within the model. However, the reality is rather different: Text comprehension typically involves combining and integrating information from the five aspects.

## SPEECH PRODUCTION

For most people (unless there is something seriously wrong with them!), speech nearly always occurs as conversation in a social context. Grice (1967) argued that the key to successful communication is the Co-operative Principle, according to which speakers and listeners should try to be co-operative.

In addition to the Co-operative Principle, Grice (1967) proposed four maxims speakers should heed:

- *Maxim of quantity*. Speakers should be as informative as necessary, but not more so.
- *Maxim of quality*. Speakers should be truthful.

- *Maxim of relation.* Speakers should say things relevant to the situation.
- *Maxim of manner.* Speakers should make their contributions easy to understand.

What needs to be said (maxim of quantity) depends on what the speaker wishes to describe (often called the referent). It is also necessary to know the objects from which the referent must be differentiated. It is sufficient to say, "The boy is good at football", if the other players are all men, but not if some of them are also boys. In the latter case, it is necessary to be more specific (e.g., "The boy with red hair is good at football").

If you have ever had to give a prepared speech, you probably noticed that it differed in various ways from your spontaneous conversational speech. For example, several words and phrases (e.g., "well", "you know", "oh") are far more common in spontaneous than in prepared speech. Such **discourse markers** do not contribute directly to the content of utterances, but are still useful. Flowerdew and Tauroza (1995) found listeners understood a videotaped lecture better when the discourse markers were left in compared to the same lecture with markers removed. Why do we use discourse markers? According to Fox Tree (2000, pp. 392–393), they are used, "to show politeness ... to play down interpersonal difficulty, and to identify with a social group ... Discourse markers like *oh, then, now*, and *well* can help listeners deal with speakers' shifts of topics and focus by indicating when a topic shift will occur ... *Anyway* and *anyway be that as it may* can be used to mark the end of a digression and the return to the prior topic."

Another aspect of speech production is the use of prosodic cues. These cues include rhythm, stress, and intonation, and they make it easier for listeners to understand what the speaker is trying to say. Lea (1973) analysed hundreds of naturally occurring spoken sentences, and syntactic boundaries (e.g., ends of sentences) were generally signalled by prosodic cues. However, most people make little use of prosodic cues. Keysar and Henly (2002) asked participants to read ambiguous sentences to convey a specific meaning, with listeners deciding which of two meanings was intended. The speakers didn't use prosodic cues (or used them ineffectively), because the listeners only guessed correctly 61% of the time (chance = 50%). Part of the problem was that speakers over-estimated their performance. They believed the listeners understood the intended meaning 72% of the time, which was significantly higher than the actual figure.

*Can you think of any other ways in which prepared speech differs from spontaneous speech?*

## Speech errors

It is hard to identify the processes involved in speech production, partly because they normally occur so rapidly (we produce two or three words per second on average). One approach is to focus on the errors in spoken language. As Dell (1986, p. 284) pointed out, "The inner workings of a highly complex system are often revealed by the way in which the system breaks down."

There are various collections of speech errors (e.g., Garrett, 1975; Stemberger, 1982), consisting of those personally heard by the researchers concerned. This approach is imprecise, because some kinds of error are more readily detectable than others. Thus, we should be sceptical about percentage figures for the different kinds of speech errors.

We will consider some of the main types of speech errors here, and then discuss their theoretical significance. Many speech errors involve problems with selecting the correct word (lexical selection). A simple kind of lexical selection error is *semantic substitution* (the correct word is replaced by a word of similar meaning, e.g., "Where is my tennis bat?" instead of "Where is my tennis racquet?"). The substituted word is nearly always of the same form class as the correct word (e.g., nouns substitute for nouns).

*Blending* is another kind of lexical selection error (e.g., "The sky is shining" instead of "The sky is blue" or "The sun is shining"). A further kind of lexical selection error is the *word-exchange error*, in which two words switch places (e.g., "I must let the house out of the cat" instead of "I must let the cat out of the house"). The two words involved in a word-exchange error are typically further apart in the sentence than the two words involved in *sound-exchange errors* (two sounds switching places) (Garrett, 1980).

*Morpheme-exchange errors* involve inflections or suffixes remaining in place but attached to the wrong words (e.g., "He has already trunked two packs"). Such errors

*Try to think of speech errors you have made or have heard recently. Which category do they fall into?*

> **KEY TERM**
> **Discourse markers:** spoken words and phrases that do not contribute directly to the content of what is being said but still serve various functions (e.g., clarify the speaker's intentions).

suggest the positioning of inflections or suffixes is dealt with by a rather separate process from the one responsible for positioning word stems (e.g., "trunk", "pack"). The word stems seem to be worked out *before* the inflections are added. Inflections are generally altered to fit in with the new word stems to which they are linked. For example, the "s" sound in the phrase, "the forks of a prong", is pronounced in a way that is appropriate within the word "forks", but this is different to the "s" sound in the original word "prongs".

One of the best-known speech errors is the spoonerism, in which the initial letter or letters of two or more words are switched. The Rev. William Archibald Spooner is credited with several memorable examples, including "You have hissed all my mystery lectures" and "The Lord is a shoving leopard to his flock." Alas, most of his gems were the result of much painstaking effort. Consonants always exchange with consonants and vowels with vowels in spoonerisms, and the exchanging phonemes are generally similar in sound (see Fromkin, 1993).

## Speech production processes

All theorists agree that speech production involves various processes which typically occur in a given order. For example, Levelt (1989) identified three main processes:

1. *Conceptualisation.* The speaker plans the message he/she wishes to communicate.
2. *Formulation.* The speaker transforms the intended message into a specific sentence, and works out the sounds of the words to be spoken.
3. *Articulation.* The speaker turns the words of the sentence into speech.

We will start by considering the conceptualisation or planning stage. After that, we will consider the two most important theories of speech production.

### Speech planning

According to Clark and Carlson (1981), speakers must take account of what they called the "common ground". The common ground between two people consists of their mutual beliefs, expectations, and knowledge. If you overhear a conversation between two friends, it can be very hard to follow, because you lack the common ground they share.

Horton and Keysar (1996) distinguished between two theoretical positions:

1. *The initial design model.* The speaker's initial plan for an utterance takes full account of the common ground with the listener.
2. *The monitoring and adjustment model.* Speakers plan their utterances initially on the basis of information available to them *without* considering the listener's perspective. Then they monitor and correct their plans to take account of the common ground.

The importance of common ground is clear if you overhear a conversation between two people who are friends. Because you lack the common ground that they share, it can be very hard to understand what they are saying to each other.

Horton and Keysar (1996) tested these models. Participants' descriptions were in line with the initial design model when they had enough time to plan their utterances in detail. However, their descriptions were more in accord with the monitoring and adjustment model when they had little time available, presumably because there was insufficient time for the monitoring and adjustment to occur. In general, we communicate more effectively when operating on the basis of the initial design model. However, the processing demands in always taking account of the listener's knowledge when planning utterances are often excessive.

The task of producing fluent speech often makes heavy demands on our processing system, especially when speaking a foreign language. For example, I find that talking in

French for even a few minutes leaves me absolutely exhausted! Smith (2000) identified two ways we reduce processing demands when planning an utterance. First, there is preformulation, which involves producing phrases used before. According to Altenberg (1990), 70% of our speech consists of word combinations we use repeatedly. Second, there is under-specification, which involves using simplified expressions. Smith gave this example: "Wash and core six cooking apples. Put them in an oven." In this example, the word "them" under-specifies "six cooking apples". As Smith (p. 342) concluded, "Speakers try to ... shift as much of the processing burden onto the listener as possible."

Do we engage in planning while we are speaking, or is planning complete before we start to speak? Ferreira and Swets (2002) found that speakers planned fully what they were going to say when there was no time pressure. However, some planning took place while speaking when speakers were under time pressure. Thus, we do as much advance planning as is possible in the circumstances.

## Spreading-activation theory

Spreading-activation theory was put forward by Dell (1986) and Dell and O'Seaghdha (1991). The key assumptions of the theory (including the notion that speech production involves four levels) are as follows:

- *Semantic level.* The meaning of what is to be said; this level is not considered in detail within the theory.
- *Syntactic level.* The grammatical structure of the words in the planned utterance.
- *Morphological level.* The morphemes (basic units of meaning or word forms) in the planned sentence.
- *Phonological level.* The phonemes or basic units of sound within the sentence.
- A *representation* is formed at each level.
- *Processing* during speech planning occurs at the same time at all four levels, and is both parallel and interactive; however, it typically proceeds more rapidly at higher levels (e.g., semantic and syntactic).
- There are *categorical rules* at each level. These rules are constraints on the acceptable categories of items and the combinations of categories.
- There is a *lexicon* (dictionary). It contains nodes for concepts, words, morphemes, and phonemes. When a node is activated, it sends activation to all the nodes connected to it.
- *Insertion rules* select the items for inclusion in the representation at each level according to the following criterion: *The most highly activated node belonging to the appropriate category is chosen.* For example, if the categorical rules at the syntactic level dictate that a verb is required at a particular point within the syntactic representation, then the verb whose node is most activated will be selected. The activation level of a selected word immediately reduces to zero, preventing it from being selected repeatedly.
- *Speech errors* occur when an incorrect item has a higher level of activation than the correct item.

*How well do you think spreading-activation theory can explain speech errors? Can you think of any problems with it?*

| Spreading-activation level | Explanation | Example | | | |
|---|---|---|---|---|---|
| Semantic | Abstract representation of idea(s) | | | | |
| Syntactic | Outline, including grammar | Subject | Verb | Article | Object |
| Morphological | Vocabulary in position | I | want | a | biscuit |
| Phonological | Information about pronunciation | aɪ | wɒnt | eɪ | bɪskɪt |

The sentence "I want a biscuit" broken down into spreading-activation levels.

## Evidence

What kinds of errors are predicted by the theory? First, errors should belong to the appropriate category (e.g., an incorrect noun replacing the correct noun), because of the operation of the categorical rules. As expected, most errors do belong to the appropriate category (Dell, 1986).

Second, many errors should be anticipation errors, in which a word is spoken too early in the sentence (e.g., "The sky is in the sky"). This happens because all words in a sentence tend to become activated during the planning for speech. As predicted, speakers make several anticipation errors.

Third, anticipation errors should often turn into exchange errors, in which two words within a sentence are swapped (e.g., "I must write a wife to my letter"). Remember that the activation level of a selected item immediately reduces to zero. Therefore, if "wife" has been selected too early, it is unlikely to compete successfully to be selected in its correct place in the sentence. This allows a previously unselected and highly activated item such as "letter" to appear in the wrong place. Many speech errors are of the exchange variety.

Fourth, anticipation and exchange errors generally involve words moving only a relatively short distance within the sentence. Those words relevant to the part of the sentence under current consideration will generally be more activated than those relevant to more distant parts of the sentence.

Fifth, speech errors should tend to consist of actual words (the **lexical bias effect**). Baars, Motley, and MacKay (1975) presented word pairs briefly, and asked participants to say both words as rapidly as possible. The error rate was twice as great when the word pair could be re-formed to create two new words (e.g., "lewd rip" can be turned into "rude lip") than when it could not (e.g., "Luke risk" turns into "ruke lisk").

Sixth, the notion that the various levels of processing interact flexibly with each other means speech errors can have more than one cause. Dell (1986) quoted the example of someone saying "Let's stop" instead of "Let's start". The error is certainly semantic. However, it is also phonological, because the substitute word ("stop") shares a common sound with the appropriate word ("start"). With word-substitution errors, the spoken word and the intended word are more similar in sound than would be expected by chance alone (Dell & O'Seaghdha, 1991).

Seventh, according to the theory, speech errors occur when the wrong word is more highly activated than the correct one. Thus, there should be many errors when incorrect words are readily available. This prediction was tested by Glaser (1992) in a study in which participants had to name pictures (e.g., of a table). There should have been a large increase in the number of errors made when each picture was accompanied by a related distractor word (e.g., chair). In fact, this produced only a small increase in the error rate. With reference to this study, Roelofs (2000, p. 82) concluded as follows: "When multiple words are activated under experimental conditions ... almost no errors are made. Yet, the Dell model predicts massive amounts of errors."

Dell, Burger, and Svec (1997) developed spreading-activation theory, arguing that most speech errors belong to two categories:

1. *Anticipatory*. Sounds or words are spoken too early (e.g., "cuff of coffee" instead of "cup of coffee").
2. *Perseverated*. Sounds or words are spoken too late (e.g., "beef needle" instead of "beef noodle").

Note that their theory was concerned *only* with these speech errors.

The key assumption is that expert speakers are better than non-expert speakers at planning ahead when speaking, and so more of their speech errors should be anticipatory: "Practice enhances the activation of the present and future at the expense of the past. So, as performance gets better, perseverations become relatively less common" (Dell et al., 1997, p. 140). Thus, the increasing activation levels of present and future sounds and words increasingly prevent the past from intruding into present speech.

Dell et al. (1997) gave participants extensive practice at saying several tongue twisters (e.g., five frantic fat frogs; thirty-three throbbing thumbs). As the participants developed expertise at this task, the number of errors went down. However, the key finding was that (as predicted) the proportion of anticipatory errors increased.

## Evaluation

⊕ The four levels assumed to be involved in speech production are consistent with the evidence.

⊕ Spreading-activation theory makes precise (and reasonably accurate) predictions about the kinds of errors occurring most often in speech production.

⊕ The emphasis on spreading activation provides links between speech production and other cognitive activities (e.g., word recognition, McClelland & Rumelhart, 1981).

⊕ In principle, our tendency to produce novel sentences should be facilitated by the widespread activation assumed to occur during speech production.

⊖ Spreading-activation theory focuses on individual words rather than broader issues relating to message construction.

⊖ The theory predicts the nature and number of errors produced in speech. However, it cannot predict the *time* taken to produce spoken words.

⊖ The theory predicts too many errors when irrelevant words are activated at the same time as relevant ones (e.g., Glaser, 1992).

Dell et al.'s (1997) study confirmed that, because expert speakers are better than non-expert speakers at planning ahead when speaking, more of their speech errors are anticipatory, rather than perseverated.

## Levelt's theoretical approach

Levelt, Roelofs, and Meyer (1999a) put forward a computational model called WEAVER++ (Word-form Encoding by Activation and VERification). According to this model, speech production involves activation proceeding forwards through a network. There are three main levels within the network. At the highest level of the network, there are nodes representing lexical concepts. At the second level, there are nodes representing lemmas or abstract words from the mental lexicon or dictionary. At the lowest level, there are nodes representing word forms in terms of morphemes (basic units of meaning) and their phonemic (sound-based) segments.

The model shows how word production proceeds from meaning (lexical concepts and lemmas or abstract words) to sound. Levelt et al. (1999a, p. 2) referred to "the major rift" between a word's *meaning* and its *sound*, and argued that crossing this rift is of major importance in speech production. The early stages of spoken word production involve deciding which word is to be produced, and the later stages involve working out the details of its word form, phonological representation, and pronunciation. Levelt et al. argued that **lemma selection** or selection of an abstract word is *completed* before phonological information about the word is accessed. Thus, speech production involves a series of processing stages following each other in serial fashion.

## Evidence

**Lexicalisation** is "the process in speech production whereby we turn the thoughts underlying words into sounds: we translate a semantic representation (the meaning) of a content word into its phonological representation or form (its sound)" (Harley, 2001, p. 359). According to Levelt et al. (1999a), lexicalisation is an important process occurring when the lemma or abstract word is translated into its word form.

The "tip-of-the-tongue" state supports the views of Levelt et al. (1999a). We have all had the experience of having a concept or idea in mind, but searching in vain for the right word to describe it. This frustrating (and even embarrassing) situation defines the tip-of-the-tongue state. Brown and McNeill (1966) stated that a participant in this state, "would appear to be in a mild torment, something like the brink of a sneeze" (p. 325). They presented their participants with dictionary definitions of rare words, and asked them to identify the words defined. For example, "a navigational instrument used in measuring

**KEY TERMS**

**Lemma selection:** selection of an abstract word at an early stage of speech production.

**Lexicalisation:** the process of translating the meaning of a word into its sound representation during speech production.

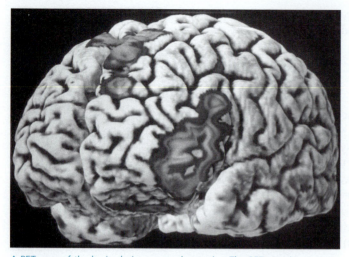

A PET scan of the brain during a speech exercise. The PET scan is superimposed onto a black and white three-dimensional magnetic resonance imaging (MRI) scan. The front of the brain is at left. The scan shows the areas of brain activity (darker areas) associated with speech. These areas are in the speech cortex of the brain's frontal lobe.

angular distances, especially the altitude of the sun, moon and stars at sea" defines the word "sextant". The tip-of-the-tongue state occurs when the lemma or abstract word has been activated, but the actual word cannot be accessed.

Additional support for the general approach contained within WEAVER++ comes from neuroimaging studies. Indefrey and Levelt (2000) considered 58 brain-imaging studies in which the participants had to name pictures or objects. They found that the processes involved in speech production occurred mainly in the left hemisphere. There was activity in the left middle temporal gyrus within 275 milliseconds of a picture or object being presented, which was interpreted as reflecting the processes involved in lemma retrieval. After that, brain activity occurred in nearby brain areas, reflecting the processing of phonological information about the name of the object.

Levelt et al. (1999a) argued in their serial processing model that phonological information about a word is only accessed *after* the abstract word or lemma selection is completed. In contrast, other theorists (e.g., Dell et al., 1997) have argued that phonological processing can start before word selection is completed, and so the two stages are *not* totally independent of each other. Theoretical approaches based on that assumption are often termed cascade models.

How can we test these models? According to the cascade model, phonological processing can start *before* lemma selection is completed, whereas this is impossible on Levelt et al.'s (1999a) model. An attempt to test these two models was reported by Morsella and Miozzo (2002). Participants were presented with two coloured pictures, with one superimposed on the other. The participants' task was to name the pictures of a given colour (target pictures) and to ignore the pictures in a different colour (distractor pictures). Some of the distractor pictures were phonologically related (related in sound) to the target pictures (e.g., "bell" as a distractor presented with "bed"), whereas others were not phonologically related (e.g., "hat" as a distractor presented with "bed").

According to Levelt et al.'s (1999a) model, the phonological features of the names for distractor pictures should not be activated. Thus, speed of naming target pictures should not be influenced by whether or not the names of the two pictures are phonologically related. In contrast, cascade models (e.g., Dell, 1986) predict that the phonological features of distractors are often activated. As a result, target pictures should be named more rapidly when accompanied by phonologically related distractors rather than by unrelated distractors. The findings were as predicted by cascade models, but directly opposed to the predictions of Levelt et al.'s model.

*Think of your own experiences of the tip-of-the-tongue state. How well does Levelt et al.'s theory account for these?*

## Evaluation

● WEAVER++ makes detailed predictions about the speed with which words are produced in various situations.

● WEAVER++ is an elegant model, and it is probably correct that the processes involved in speech production often occur in a serial fashion.

● Speech production is normally relatively error-free, and so the fact that Levelt et al. (1999a) focused much more than Dell (1986) on error-free speech makes sense.

● WEAVER++ cannot account readily for the finding that there can be phonological processing of more than one word at a time (e.g., Morsella & Miozzo, 2002).

● As Levelt, Roelofs, and Meyer (1999b, p. 63) admitted, "WEAVER++ has been designed to account primarily for latency [time] data, not for speech errors." For example, Levelt et al. (1999a) found that WEAVER++ predicted far fewer word-exchange errors than were actually produced by participants.

● WEAVER++ is of most relevance to the production of single words, and is relatively uninformative about the complex processes involved in generating entire sentences.

## SPEECH DISORDERS

We can learn much about the processes involved in speech production by studying brain-damaged patients with language disorders. Why is the cognitive neuropsychological approach of value? The main reason is that it allows us to see the extent to which different aspects of speech production (e.g., lemma selection, syntactic processing, word naming) are separate from each other. If they are genuinely separate, then we might expect to find brain-damaged patients showing impairments primarily for one aspect of speech production but not for others.

For convenience, we will categorise patients in terms of syndromes or labels. However, please note that these syndromes over-simplify matters, because patients with any given syndrome rarely have precisely the same symptoms.

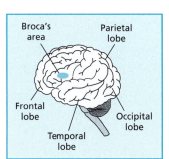

### Broca's and Wernicke's aphasia

As long ago as the nineteenth century, researchers made a distinction between Broca's aphasia and Wernicke's aphasia. Patients with **Broca's aphasia** have slow, non-fluent speech. In addition, they have a poor ability to produce syntactically (grammatically) correct sentences, even though their speech comprehension is relatively intact. In contrast, patients with **Wernicke's aphasia** have fluent and apparently grammatical speech which often lacks meaning. In addition, they have severe problems with speech comprehension.

According to the classical view, these two forms of **aphasia** involve different brain regions within the left hemisphere. Broca's aphasia was claimed to stem from damage within the frontal lobe (the so-called Broca's area), whereas Wernicke's aphasia stemmed from damage within the posterior temporal lobe (Wernicke's area).

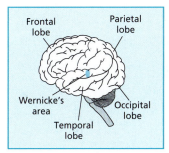

### *Evidence*

Research has provided only limited support for the classical view. De Bleser (1988) studied six very clear cases of fluent or Wernicke's aphasia and seven very clear cases of non-fluent or Broca's aphasia. The brain-damaged areas were assessed by computerised tomography (CT) scans. Four of the six patients with fluent aphasia had damage only to Wernicke's area, but the other two had lesions in Broca's area as well as in Wernicke's area. Of the seven non-fluent aphasic patients, four had damage to Broca's area, but the others had damage to Wernicke's area.

PET studies have provided clearer evidence of the involvement of Wernicke's area in speech comprehension. For example, Howard et al. (1992) compared two conditions in which normal participants either repeated real words or listened to reversed words and said the same word to each stimulus. There was greater activation of Wernicke's area in the former condition.

According to the classical view, patients with Broca's aphasia have much greater problems in speaking grammatically than do patients with Wernicke's aphasia. However, Dick, Bates, Wulfeck, Utman, Dronkers, and Gernsbacher (2001) argued that patients with Wernicke's aphasia have severe problems with speaking grammatically, but these problems are obscured among speakers of English because of the nature of the English language. They compared findings obtained from speakers of several languages, and came to the following conclusion: "Studies of speech production in richly inflected languages [e.g., Italian, German, Hungarian] show that Wernicke's aphasic patients make grammatical errors similar in quantity and severity to the errors produced by Broca's aphasic patients ... The English system of

*Do you think it is useful to categorise such disorders?*

## CASE STUDY: *"Tan"*

Paul Broca's first and most famous neurological patient was "Tan": so-called because the only syllables he could utter were "tan-tan". For years Tan was also paralysed on his right side, and became a patient of the surgeon Broca because of an infected bedsore. Broca found that Tan's understanding of speech seemed relatively intact. Broca was curious about why this should be, and when Tan died, Broca performed a post-mortem and found damage in what is now known as Broca's area of the brain. Tan's brain is embalmed and preserved in a museum in Paris, and the damaged area is clearly visible.

grammatical morphology [building up of words from basic units of meaning] is so impoverished that it offers few opportunities for grammatical substitution errors" (p. 764).

## Evaluation

⊕ There is some evidence for the distinction between Broca's and Wernicke's aphasia.

⊖ The brain areas damaged in Broca's and Wernicke's aphasia are much more variable than was traditionally assumed.

⊖ The usefulness of syndromes such as Broca's aphasia or Wernicke's aphasia is undermined by the fact that patients with the same syndrome nevertheless exhibit a wide range of different symptoms.

⊖ The finding that patients with Wernicke's aphasia often make as many grammatical errors as those with Broca's aphasia blurs the distinction between the two types of aphasia.

## Anomia

Some patients suffer from **anomia**, which is an impaired ability to name objects. There are two main reasons why such patients have difficulties in naming (Levelt et al., 1999a). First, there can be a problem in lemma selection (thinking of the appropriate word concept), in which case errors in naming are similar in meaning to the correct word. Second, there can be a problem in finding the appropriate phonological form of the word after the correct lemma has been selected.

A case of anomia involving a semantic impairment (deficient lemma selection) was reported by Howard and Orchard-Lisle (1984). The patient, J.C.U., was very poor at naming the objects shown in pictures unless given the first phoneme or sound as a cue. If the cue was the first phoneme of a word closely related to the object shown in the picture, then J.C.U. would often produce the wrong answer. J.C.U. had access to *some* semantic information, but this was often insufficient to specify precisely what she was looking at.

Kay and Ellis (1987) studied a patient, E.S.T., who had problems retrieving the phonological forms of words. His overall performance on a range of tasks was very good, indicating he had no real problem with lemma or abstract word selection. However, he had a very definite anomia, as can be seen from his attempt to describe a picture:

> *Er ... two children, one girl one male ... the ... the girl, they're in a ... and their, their mother was behind them in in, they're in the kitchen ... the boy is trying to get ... a ... er, a part of a cooking ... jar ... He's standing on ... the lad, the boy is standing on a ... standing on a ... standing on a ... I'm calling it a seat.*

E.S.T.'s speech is reasonably grammatical, and his greatest problem lies in finding words other than very common ones. What are we to make of E.S.T.'s anomia? Kay and Ellis (1987) argued that his condition resembles in greatly magnified form the "tip-of-the-tongue" state.

Some patients with anomia have problems with both lemma selection *and* finding the correct phonological form of words. For example, Lambon Ralph, Sage, and Roberts (2000) studied G.M. When a related word was presented just before a picture that had to be named (e.g., the word "ladder" before a picture of stilts), G.M.'s naming performance became much worse. This happened because the presence of the related word disrupted lemma selection. When only a picture was presented, G.M. was sometimes unable to name it. However, he nearly always guessed correctly the number of syllables in the word, indicating that he generally accessed the right word. Thus, some of his word-naming problems occurred because he could not identify detailed phonological information about the word.

In sum, most of the evidence on anomia is consistent with the assumption contained within WEAVER++ that lemma selection is complete before processing of the phonological or sound features of the selected word. However, Lambon Ralph et al. (2000) found that G.M. often gained access to relevant phonological information even though lemma selection was not complete. This suggests that the processes involved in naming performance overlap in time rather than occurring purely in a serial fashion.

How do you think the impairments experienced by the patients previously discussed might manifest themselves in their everyday lives?

# Agrammatism

According to most theories of speech production, there are rather separate stages of working out the syntax or grammatical structure of utterances and producing the content words to fit that grammatical structure (e.g., Dell, 1986). Thus, there should be some brain-damaged patients who can find the appropriate words, but cannot order them grammatically. Such patients are said to suffer from **agrammatism** or non-fluent aphasia. Patients with agrammatism typically produce short sentences containing content words (e.g., nouns, verbs) but lacking function words (e.g., the, in, and) and word endings. This makes sense, because function words help to provide a grammatical structure for sentences. Finally, it has often been assumed that patients with agrammatism cannot comprehend sentences which are syntactically complex.

## Evidence

Saffran, Schwartz, and Marin (1980a, 1980b) studied patients suffering from grammatical impairments. For example, one patient was asked to describe a picture of a woman kissing a man, and produced the following: "The kiss ... the lady kissed ... the lady is ... the lady and the man and the lady ... kissing." Saffran et al. also found that agrammatic aphasics had great difficulty in putting the two nouns in the correct order when asked to describe pictures containing two living creatures in interaction.

There is support for the notion that patients with agrammatism have particular problems in processing function words. Biassou et al. (1997) gave such patients the task of reading words. The patients made substantially more errors on function words than on content words.

Do the syntactic deficiencies of agrammatic aphasics extend to language comprehension? Berndt, Mitchum, and Haendiges (1996) did a meta-analysis of studies of comprehension of active and passive sentences by agrammatic aphasics. They concluded that some (but by no means all) agrammatic aphasics have major problems with language comprehension.

## Evaluation

⊕ Research on agrammatism provides general support for the notion (e.g., Dell, 1986) that speech production involves a syntactic level at which the grammatical structure of an utterance is formed. Most of the problems of agrammatic patients (including their problems with function words) seem to involve this level of processing.

⊖ Patients with agrammatism differ considerably in their symptoms. For example, Miceli, Silveri, Romani, and Caramazza (1989) found that some patients omitted many more prepositions than definite articles from their speech, whereas others showed the opposite pattern.

⊖ Some patients with agrammatism have only minor problems with language comprehension (e.g., Berndt et al., 1996).

⊖ The considerable differences in symptoms among agrammatic patients shed real doubt on the value of identifying a syndrome of agrammatism.

# Jargon aphasia

Agrammatic aphasics possess reasonable ability to find the words they want to say, but cannot produce grammatically correct sentences. We might expect to find other patients showing the opposite pattern: They speak fairly grammatically but have great difficulty in

**KEY TERM**

**Agrammatism:** a condition in which speech lacks grammatical structure and many function words and word endings are omitted.

finding the right words. This is approximately the case with patients suffering from **jargon aphasia** or fluent aphasia, a condition in which word-finding problems are so great that patients often produce neologisms (made-up words).

Ellis, Miller, and Sin (1983) studied a jargon aphasic, R.D. He produced the following description of a picture of a scout camp (the words he tried to say are in brackets): "A b-boy is swi'ing (SWINGING) on the bank with his hand (FEET) in the stringt (STREAM). A table with orstrum (SAUCEPAN?) and ... I don't know ... and a three-legged stroe (STOOL) and a strane (PAIL)—table, table ... near the water." R.D., in common with most jargon aphasics, produced more made-up words when the word he wanted was not a common one.

Most jargon aphasics (even those who have good speech comprehension ability) are largely unaware of the fact that they are producing neologisms and so do not try to correct them. Why is this? There are basically two possible reasons: (1) They do not possess sufficient word knowledge to detect neologisms; (2) they have sufficient knowledge, but are often unable to use it effectively. The evidence generally supports the latter reason (see below).

Maher, Rothi, and Heilman (1994) studied A.S., a jargon aphasic with reasonable auditory word comprehension. A.S. was better at detecting his own speech errors when they were played back to him than at the time he made them. A.S. was probably poor at detecting his own speech errors at the time because he had insufficient processing resources to speak and to monitor his speech at the same time. In similar fashion, Marshall et al. (1998) studied a jargon aphasic, C.M., who had reasonable comprehension ability. He was given two tasks: naming pictures; and repeating words he had produced on the naming task. C.M. was much better at detecting neologisms or made-up words on the repetition task than on the naming task. He detected 95% of neologisms on the repetition task, indicating that he possessed considerable word knowledge.

## Overall evaluation

➕ Cognitive neuropsychological evidence provides some support for major theories of speech production. For example, some findings from anomic patients suggest the value of two-stage theories of lexicalisation (e.g., Levelt et al., 1999a).

➕ Agrammatic aphasics and jargon aphasics provide evidence there are separate stages of syntactic planning and content-word retrieval in speech production. What we have here is a **double dissociation**; one group has good syntactic planning but poor word retrieval, whereas the other group has the opposite pattern.

➖ The patients assigned to any given syndrome (e.g., agrammatism) are so variable in their symptoms that few generalisations can be made which apply to all of them.

➖ The evidence from brain-damaged patients is generally not detailed enough to allow us to choose between the main theories.

## LANGUAGE AND THOUGHT

The major language processes discussed in this chapter and the two previous ones raise the issue of the relationship between language and thought. For example, speaking and writing are both activities in which thinking about what one wants to say or write (the intended message) is translated into language. More generally, language is the medium which we use most often to communicate our thoughts to other people.

## Whorfian hypothesis

The best-known theory about the inter-relationship between language and thought was put forward by Benjamin Lee Whorf (1956). He was a fire prevention officer for an insurance company, but spent his spare time working in linguistics. According to his hypothesis of linguistic relativity (known as the **Whorfian hypothesis**), language determines or influences thinking. It is useful to distinguish between three versions of this hypothesis (Miller & McNeill, 1969). According to the strong hypothesis, language *determines* thinking. Our thought processes are limited by the language in which we think. This hypothesis implies that some thoughts expressible in one language cannot be expressed in a second language. This is the issue of *translatability*: Can all sentences in one language be translated accurately into sentences in a second language? There is reasonable evidence for translatability, which goes against the strong hypothesis.

According to the weak form of the Whorfian hypothesis, language *influences* perception. Finally, the weakest hypothesis claims only that language *influences* memory. Hunt and Agnoli (1991, p. 379) proposed a cognitive account of the Whorfian hypothesis: "Different languages lend themselves to the transmission of different types of messages. People consider the costs of computation when they reason about a topic. The language that they will use will partly determine those costs. In this sense, language does influence cognition." Thus, our native language helps to determine the computational costs of different cognitive processes, and this may influence our ways of thinking.

*What implications does the Whorfian hypothesis have for languages of different cultures?*

## Evidence

Casual inspection of the world's languages reveals significant differences among them. For example, the Hanuxoo people in the Philippines have 92 different names for different varieties of rice, and there are hundreds of camel-related words in Arabic. It is possible that these differences among languages influence thought. However, it is more likely that different environmental conditions affect the things people think about, and this in turn affects their linguistic usage. Thus, these differences occur because thought affects language.

There has been a fair amount of research concerned with possible cultural differences in colour categorisation and memory. According to the Whorfian hypothesis, colour categorisation and memory should vary as a function of the participants' native language. In contrast, Heider (1972) argued that colour categorisation and memory are universal, and thus do *not* vary from language to language. She was influenced by the work of Berlin and Kay (1969), who argued that that there are 11 basic colour terms (white, black, red, yellow, blue, green, brown, purple, pink, orange, and grey), although some languages do not have words for all 11 colours. Such languages always have words corresponding to "black" and "white", but typically do not have words corresponding to "purple", "pink", "orange", and "grey".

Heider (1972) made use of the fact that all 11 basic colour terms are found in the English language, and each has a generally agreed best or focal colour. English speakers find it easier to remember focal than non-focal colours, and Heider wondered whether the same would be true of the Dani. The Dani are a Stone-Age agricultural people living in Indonesian New Guinea, and their language has only two basic colour terms: "mola" for bright, warm hues, and "mili" for dark, cold hues.

What findings would we expect? If memory for colours is universal, then the Dani should be similar to English speakers in remembering focal colours better than non-focal colours. On the other hand, if language plays a part in colour memory, then the performance of the Dani might be very different from that of English speakers. In fact, Heider (1972) found the Dani resembled English-speaking Americans in showing better recognition memory for focal than for non-focal colours. These findings go against the Whorfian hypothesis, because they suggest that language has little or no influence on colour memory.

Roberson, Davies, and Davidoff (2000) argued that Heider (1972) had not really proved that colour categories are universal and so do not depend on language. They pointed out that there was a problem with Heider's choice of stimuli, namely, that the focal colours she used were more perceptually discriminable than the non-focal colours. Accordingly, the focal colours they used were carefully equated for discriminability with the non-focal colours. They had two groups: English participants and members of the Berinmo. The Berinmo belong to a Stone-age culture in Papua New Guinea, and their language contains

**Basic colour words in English**

WHITE
RED
GREEN
BLACK
YELLOW
BLUE
BROWN
PURPLE
PINK
ORANGE
GREY

**KEY TERM**
**Whorfian hypothesis:** the notion that language determines or influences the ways in which we think.

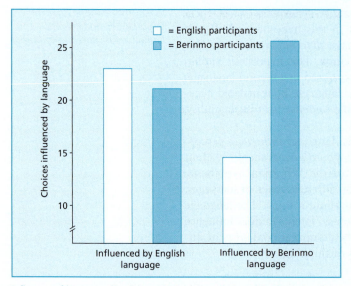

Influence of language (English vs. Berinmo) on choice of similar pairs of stimuli by English and Berinmo participants. Data from Roberson et al. (2000).

*Does the Whorfian hypothesis explain how language influences thought?*

**KEY TERM**

**Categorical perception:** assigning stimuli to categories, as a result of which it is easier to discriminate between stimuli belonging to different categories than stimuli belonging to the same category.

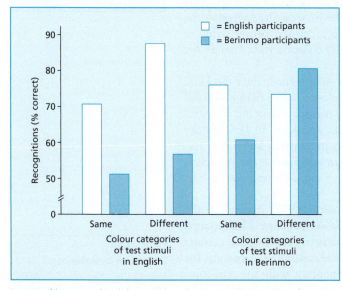

Impact of language (English vs. Berinmo) on recognition memory for English and Berinmo participants. Data from Roberson et al. (2000).

only five basic colour terms. Roberson et al. (p. 382) totally failed to replicate Heider's findings: "When … the discriminability advantage for focal colours is removed, the advantage for focal colours in recognition memory disappears for both English and Berinmo speakers."

Roberson et al. (2000) went on to show that language can have a significant impact on colour perception and memory. In one experiment, they studied **categorical perception:** When people assign stimuli to categories, they typically find it easier to discriminate between stimuli belonging to *different* categories than stimuli belonging to the *same* category. In the English language, we have colour categories of "green" and "blue", whereas Berinmo has categories of "nol" (roughly similar to green) and "wor" (roughly similar to yellow). Roberson et al. presented English and Berinmo participants with three coloured stimuli, and asked them to select the two most similar ones.

What findings would we expect to see? Suppose two of the stimuli would normally be described as "green" in English and the third one as "blue". According to the notion of categorical perception, English speakers should regard the two green stimuli as being most similar. However, there is no reason why Berinmo speakers should do the same, given that their language does not distinguish between blue and green. In similar fashion, Berinmo speakers presented with two "nol" stimuli and one "wor" stimulus should select the two "nol" stimuli, but we would not expect English speakers to do the same.

What did Roberson et al. (2000) find? As predicted on the Whorfian hypothesis, language determined performance. As can seen in the figure above, English participants and Berinmo ones showed clear evidence of categorical perception based on their own language.

Roberson et al. (2000) then turned their attention to the effects of categorical perception on memory. The participants were first shown a target stimulus followed by two test stimuli presented together. They had to decide which of the two test stimuli matched the target stimulus. Categorical perception would be demonstrated if the participants found it easier to perform this recognition-memory task when the two test stimuli belong to different colour categories than when they belong to the same colour category. Thus, English speakers should have good recognition memory when the test stimuli cross the green–blue colour boundary, but this should be irrelevant to the Berinmo. In contrast, Berinmo speakers should perform well when the test stimuli cross the nol–wor boundary, but this should be irrelevant to the English participants. That is exactly what was found (see the figure to the left).

We have spent some time discussing the findings of Roberson et al. (2000) because they provide convincing support for the Whorfian hypothesis. As Roberson et al. (p. 396) concluded, "The driving force behind the similarity judgements of colour is language … we conclude that there is an extensive influence of language on colour categorisation. The influence is deep rather than superficial, applying both to perceptual and memorial processes."

An interesting demonstration of how language can influence thinking was provided by Hoffman, Lau, and Johnson (1986). Bilingual English-Chinese speakers read descriptions of individuals, and were later asked to provide free interpretations of the individuals described using either the English or the Chinese language. The initial descriptions conformed to either Chinese or English stereotypes of personality. For example, there is a stereotype of the artistic type in English, consisting of a mixture of artistic skills, moody and intense temperament, and bohemian lifestyle, but this stereotype does not exist in Chinese. Bilinguals thinking in Chinese made use of Chinese stereotypes in their free impressions, whereas bilinguals thinking in English used English stereotypes. Thus, the kinds of inferences we draw about other people can be much influenced by the language in which we are thinking.

More evidence consistent with Whorf (1956) and with Hunt and Agnoli (1991) was reported by Pederson, Danziger, Wilkins, Levinson, Kita, and Senft (1998). They pointed out that space can be coded in either a *relative* system (e.g., left, right, up, down) or an *absolute* system (e.g., north, south). In the English language, of course, we can make use of either system. However, many languages do not have words conveying notions such as "left", "right", "front" and "back". Speakers of such languages typically express all directions in terms of points of the compass, i.e., they rely only an absolute system for coding space (see Levinson, Kita, Haun, & Rasch, 2002).

Pederson et al. (1998) gave speakers of 13 languages various spatial reasoning tasks that could be solved using either system. For example, there was the animals-in-a-row task, in which three animals were presented in a row. After that, the participants rotated 180 degrees, and then reconstructed the array so that it matched the original one. The key finding was that participants' choice of system was determined largely by the dominant system of spatial coding in their native language, presumably because it was easier for them to do this.

## Evaluation

● The Whorfian hypothesis has attracted increased support in recent years. As Harley (2001, p. 87) concluded, "There is now a considerable amount of evidence suggesting that linguistic factors can affect cognitive processes. Even colour perception and memory ... show some influence of language." Thus, the evidence supports the weakest versions of the Whorfian hypothesis.

● When tasks are used giving participants *flexibility* in the approach they adopt (e.g., Hoffman et al., 1986; Pederson et al., 1998), there is even some support for the strong version of the Whorfian hypothesis.

● We still lack a detailed account of *how* language influences cognitive processes. For example, Hunt and Agnoli (1991) argued that an estimate of computational costs helps to determine whether language influences cognition, but these costs have rarely been measured.

● Whorf (1956) assumed it would be hard to change the effects of language on cognition, whereas Hunt and Agnoli (1991) assumed it would be easy. We do not really know who is right.

# SUMMARY

Listeners to speech confront the linearity, non-invariance, and segmentation problems. Studies on the phonemic restoration effect suggest that contextual information influences speech perception in a top-down way. Prosodic cues are often used by listeners. The role played by lip-reading is shown by the McGurk effect. According to the original version of cohort theory, the initial sound of a word is used to construct a word-initial cohort, which is reduced to only one word by using additional information from the presented word and from the context. Cohort theory is now more flexible. According to the TRACE model, bottom-up and top-down processes interact during speech perception. This assumption is probably incorrect, and the importance of top-down processes is exaggerated. Evidence from brain-damaged patients suggests that saying a spoken word can be achieved using three different routes. Patients with pure word deafness have problems with speech

*Speech perception*

perception because of impaired phonemic processing in the auditory analysis system. Patients with word meaning deafness can repeat familiar words without understanding their meaning, but have problems with non-words. Patients with auditory phonological agnosia have damage within Route 3. Deep dysphasia may reflect damage to all three routes, or to a system underlying short-term memory.

**Basic reading processes**

Word identification is affected by context. According to the interactive activation model, word recognition depends on top-down as well as bottom-up processes. The word superiority effect occurs because of top-down influences of the word level on the letter level of processing. The model cannot account for the finding that the size of the word superiority effect is uninfluenced by word frequency, and it only predicts word recognition on four-letter words. According to the dual route cascaded theory, there are two main routes between the printed word and speech, one used mainly for familiar words and the other used for unfamiliar words and non-words. This theory is supported by evidence from surface dyslexics and phonological dyslexics. However, the model cannot account for naming performance in languages such as Chinese, Japanese, and Korean. Plaut et al. (1996) argued that the pronunciation of words and non-words is based on a highly interactive system. They provided a sketchy account of phonological dyslexia, and had little to say about the role of semantic processing in reading. According to the E-Z Reader model, the next eye movement in reading is programmed after only part of the processing of the currently fixated word has occurred. Completion of lexical access to the currently fixated word produces a shift of covert attention to the next word. The model de-emphasises the impact of higher-level cognitive processes on fixation times. There are several theories of parsing. According to one-stage models, all sources of information are used together to form a syntactic construction of sentences. In contrast, the first stage of processing in two-stage models uses *only* syntactic information, with semantic information being used during the second stage. The evidence tends to favour one-stage models.

**Discourse processing**

There is an important distinction between bridging and elaborative inferences, with the simplest form of bridging inference being involved in anaphora. According to the minimalist hypothesis, relatively few inferences are drawn automatically. In addition, strategic or goal-directed inferences may also be drawn. According to the constructionist approach, numerous automatic inferences are drawn in order to facilitate full comprehension. According to search-after-meaning theory, readers engage in a search after meaning based on the reader's goals. The evidence is most consistent with the search-after-meaning theory.

**Story processing**

Story memory resembles a précis. It has been claimed that the structure of all stories is consistent with a story grammar, but there is no agreement on its main features. According to Kintsch's construction–integration model, three levels of text representation are formed: surface, propositional, and situational. The evidence supports this hypothesis, but a situational representation is sometimes not formed because of limited processing capacity. There may be other levels of representation (e.g., the genre level). According to the event-indexing model, readers monitor five aspects or indexes of the evolving situational model. The model focuses on only a few of the processes involved in text comprehension, and fails to consider adequately the reader's goals.

**Speech production**

Speakers take full account of the common ground they share with the listener only when they have adequate processing time. According to Dell's spreading-activation theory, four levels of representation are involved in speech production: semantic, syntactic, morphological, and phonological. Insertion rules select the items for inclusion in the representation at each level on the basis of the level of activation of the competing items. Speech errors occur when an incorrect item has a higher level of activation than the correct item. Spreading-activation theory does not predict the time taken to produce spoken words. According to Levelt's WEAVER++ model, abstract word or lemma selection is completed before phonological information about the word is accessed. The model is supported by research on the tip-of-the-tongue state, but has little to say about speech errors. Neither spreading-activation theory nor WEAVER++ addresses issues relating to message construction by speakers.

Some patients with anomia have problems in thinking of the appropriate word concept, whereas others have difficulties in finding the appropriate phonological word form. Patients with agrammatism can find the appropriate words, but cannot order them grammatically. In contrast, patients with jargon aphasia speak fairly grammatically but cannot find the right words. They produce neologisms, which they often fail to detect due to a limited ability to speak and monitor their own speech at the same time. Evidence from agrammatic aphasics and jargon aphasics suggests there are separate stages of syntactic planning and content-word retrieval in speech production. However, the evidence from brain-damaged patients is not detailed enough to advance theoretical development.

*Speech disorders*

According to the weak form of the Whorfian hypothesis, language influences thought. In support, there is evidence that language can affect perceptual processes and memory for colours. Hunt and Agnoli (1991) put forward a cognitive account of the Whorfian hypothesis, according to which any given language makes it easier to think in some ways than in others. This theory has been supported on tasks giving participants flexibility in their approach.

*Language and thought*

# FURTHER READING

- Eysenck, M.W. (2001). *Principles of cognitive psychology* (2nd ed.). Hove, UK: Psychology Press. Chapters 7 and 8 of this book provide more detailed coverage of the topics discussed here.
- Harley, T. (2001). *The psychology of language: From data to theory* (2nd ed.). Hove, UK: Psychology Press. This is an excellent book covering the main topics in the psychology of language in a detailed but accessible way.
- Sternberg, R.J., & Ben-Zeev, T. (2001). *Complex cognition: The psychology of human thought*. Oxford, UK: Oxford University Press. Issues relating to language and the relationship between language and thought are discussed in an introductory way in Chapters 9 and 10 of this textbook.

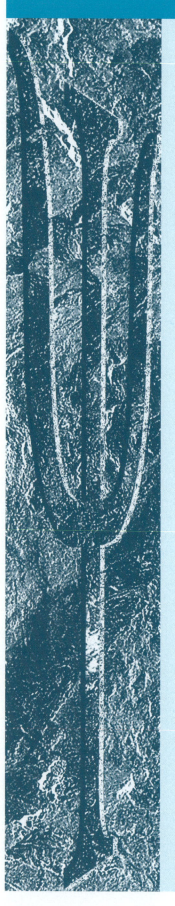

# Individual Differences

Most of psychology (and this book) is devoted to the search for broad generalisations and laws of behaviour which are applicable to virtually everyone. For example, consider cognitive psychology, which was covered in Chapters 6–11. Cognitive psychologists have generally assumed that everyone (apart from brain-damaged patients) makes use of the same attentional and perceptual processes, has a working memory system, adopts the same learning strategies, forgets information over time, makes certain inferences when reading text, and so on. The situation is similar in social psychology (Chapters 18–21). It is assumed that people tend to be obedient to authority, to conform to the views of other group members, to fall in love with people who are similar to them, to show prejudice in certain circumstances, and so on.

The above approach has proved very successful, and numerous very important generalisations have emerged as a result. However, as we will see in this section of the book, an approach that focuses on generalisations that are universally applicable omits much that is of importance. What is missing is the extraordinary diversity of human behaviour, which is obvious to us nearly all the time in the course of our everyday lives. For example, some people are much better than others at remembering information over long periods of time, some people can control their attentional processes much better than others, some people refuse to obey the orders of authority figures whereas others are highly conformist, and some people are completely lacking in prejudice whereas others are bigoted and biased in their views of minority groups.

As mentioned already, we are constantly aware of individual differences, which form the subject matter of Chapters 12 and 13. These individual differences have a great influence on our behaviour. For example, if you need advice when writing a coursework essay, you probably find it easier to approach some people rather than others, maybe because they are friendlier or more knowledgeable. In similar fashion, we take full account of individual differences when choosing friends. Thus, we are more likely to become friends with other people who seem similar to us, who are warm and sociable, and who we feel can be trusted with secrets.

It is relevant at this point to mention an important article by Cronbach (1957). He argued that there are two scientific disciplines within psychology, one devoted to the search for general laws and the other devoted to the study of individual differences. Cronbach's most important point was that what was needed in order for psychology to realise its potential were wholehearted attempts to combine these two scientific disciplines into one. According to him, there is no necessary conflict between the two scientific disciplines. As a result, it should be possible to consider general laws and individual differences within a single approach. It is disappointing (and somewhat surprising) that more has not been done along the lines suggested by Cronbach in the 50 years or so since he wrote his thought-provoking article.

## ASPECTS OF INDIVIDUAL DIFFERENCES

It is now time to return to issues relating to individual differences. Which aspects of individual differences are of most consequence? It is hard to answer that question, given that people differ from each other in a bewilderingly large number of ways. Indeed, if you sat down to draw up a list, you could probably identify literally dozens of interesting and important ways in which the people you know differ from each other. However, academic and occupational psychologists have (rightly or wrongly) tended to focus mainly on individual differences in intelligence and personality, although some research on other aspects of individual differences (e.g., social attitudes) has also been carried out.

There has been much emphasis on individual differences within occupational psychology. So far as this branch of psychology is concerned (e.g., Arnold, Cooper, & Robertson, 1995), it is common for the intelligence and personality of job applicants to be assessed in personnel selection. As we will see, there are sound reasons for focusing on these aspects of individual differences, in part because highly intelligent individuals on average have superior work performance and career development than those who are less intelligent, especially when the job concerned is relatively complex (see Gottfredson, 1997).

Individual differences in intelligence are of great importance in the real world. For example, academic performance and occupational success are predicted more successfully by individual differences in intelligence than by any other aspect of individual differences. In general terms, individuals high in intelligence perform almost any cognitively demanding task faster and more accurately than those of lower intelligence.

You may feel that it is fairly obvious that individual differences in intelligence predict the ability to perform complex tasks and jobs. However, individual differences in intelligence are also relevant to a wide range of other life outcomes. For example, individuals who are highly intelligent have a much smaller probability than those who are unintelligent of being divorced within 5 years or marriage (9% vs. 21% based on American data; see Gottfredson, 1997). In addition, highly intelligent women have only one-quarter the probability of unintelligent women of having an illegitimate child, and one-seventh the probability of finding themselves in prison (Gottfredson, 1997).

It is also the case that individual differences in personality are important in predicting individuals' behaviour in numerous real-world situations. For example, as we will see in Chapter 13, the personality we have helps to determine how happy we are, and how many friends we have. In addition, there are interesting associations between certain types of personality on the one hand and various mental disorders on the other hand. It is hard to be sure that the personality you have actually influences the probability that you will develop any given mental disorder, but the evidence suggests that it is likely.

When we think of individual differences, we almost certainly think initially of personality. We know that Kate is always cheerful and friendly, whereas Sue is reserved and unsure of herself. If we like Kate and Sue, we may well have asked ourselves why their personalities are so different. Did Kate have a happier and more secure childhood than Sue? Do the differences lie in the genes? Is it some kind of mixture or interaction of genetic factors and environment that is responsible for the personality differences between Kate and Sue? As we will see in Chapter 13, psychologists have identified the major dimensions of personality and are having increasing success in accounting for the factors responsible for individual differences in personality.

There are three issues that are of central importance to researchers who study individual differences. First, it is important to consider the *nature* of individual differences, including the structure of intelligence and personality. More specifically, what are the main components of human intelligence, and what are the main dimensions of personality? These are important questions, because we can observe individual differences in ability on hundreds or thousands of demanding tasks, and the English language has in excess of 1500 adjectives describing various aspects of personality.

Second, when we have worked out the structure of intelligence and personality, we then need to establish the *origins* of these individual differences. For example, are some individuals more intelligent or more extraverted than others because of their genetic make-up, because of their experiences in life, or because of some combination of the two?

Third, we also need to understand the underlying *mechanisms* that are directly responsible for individual differences in behaviour and personality. Several very different kinds of mechanisms (e.g., physiological; cognitive) may be involved. For example, one of the reasons why some individuals have an anxious personality may be because they tend to interpret the environment as being more threatening than it appears to other people.

In general terms, the first issue is concerned with *description* and the second and third issues are concerned with *explanation*. As is so often the case in psychology and science generally, it has proved relatively easier to provide answers at the descriptive level than at the explanatory level.

- **Intelligence testing**
  The nature of intelligence and the various methods developed to test it.

  *The definition and scope of the concept of "intelligence"*
  *Intelligence tests, e.g., IQ*
  *The importance of reliability and the various types of validity*

- **Factor theories**
  Attempts to measure intelligence using factor analysis.

  *Spearman's two-factor theory*
  *Thurstone's seven-factor theory*
  *Cattell's distinction between fluid and crystallised ability*
  *The hierarchical approach, combining all these theories*

- **Heredity and environment**
  The nature–nurture debate relating to intelligence.

  *The interdependence of heredity and environment as factors in intelligence*
  *The problem of measuring intelligence: genotype and phenotype*
  *Twin and family studies*
  *Adoption studies—biased by selective placement*
  *Heritability*
  *Research into possible genetic differences between groups and cultures*

- **Environmental influences**
  The influence of environmental factors.

  *The distinction between shared and non-shared environment*
  *The Flynn effect—rising Western IQ*
  *Sameroff et al.'s 10 environmental factors*
  *The difficulties of comparison across cultures*
  *Attempts to enrich environments to enhance intelligence: Operation Headstart and the Carolina Abecedarian project*

- **Theories of intelligence**
  Other theoretical approaches to the testing of intelligence.

  *Duncan et al.'s concept of "general intelligence"*
  *Gardner's multiple intelligences approach*
  *Definitions of an "intelligence"*
  *A discussion of emotional intelligence*
  *Mayer et al.'s Multi-Factor Emotional Intelligence Scale*
  *Relating intelligence to working memory, e.g., by measuring reading span*

# Intelligence

There has been more controversy about research in intelligence than almost any other area within psychology. Some researchers think individual differences in intelligence are of great importance in understanding why people behave in different ways from each other, whereas others argue that intelligence is an almost valueless concept. Some researchers (e.g., H.J. Eysenck, 1981) believe that individual differences in intelligence are almost entirely due to heredity, but others (e.g., Kamin, 1981) claim that only environmental factors are of importance. It is highly regrettable that many psychologists have allowed their views on intelligence to be influenced by ideological concerns rather than by the relevant evidence. As a result, it is especially important to focus on the evidence itself.

Before proceeding any further, we should consider the meaning of the term "intelligence". It is generally agreed that those who are good at abstract reasoning, problem solving, and decision making are more intelligent than those who are poor at these mental activities. A reasonable definition of **intelligence** was offered by Sternberg and Ben-Zeev (2001, p. 368): "the ability to learn from experience and to adapt to the surrounding environment".

The greatest issue surrounding the definition of "intelligence" is the range of abilities to be included. Are "street-wise" individuals, who are very skilful at furthering their own ends, necessarily highly intelligent? Should someone who is sensitive to the needs of others be said to possess emotional intelligence? There are no definite answers to these questions. However, most psychologists now accept that the definition of intelligence should include skills (e.g., street-wisdom) valued by the culture or society in which one lives. Sternberg and Detterman (1986) asked 24 experts in intelligence to provide definitions of intelligence. These experts emphasised the role of culture, arguing that behaviour which is regarded as intelligent in one culture may not be so regarded in another culture.

Sternberg and Kaufman (1998) provide an interesting discussion of cultural differences in the meaning of "intelligence". In general terms, we can distinguish between individualistic cultures and collectivistic ones (see Chapter 1). In individualistic cultures (e.g., the United States, northern Europe) there is a focus on individuals being independent and accepting responsibility for their own behaviour. In collectivistic cultures (e.g., many Asian and African cultures), the focus is on the group rather than the individual. As might be guessed, definitions of "intelligence" in collectivistic cultures tend to emphasise social considerations. For example, Chewa adults in Zambia emphasise social responsibilities, obedience, and co-operativeness as key ingredients in intelligence (Serpell, 1982). In Zimbabwe, the word for intelligence is *ngware*, which means to be careful and prudent in social relationships. Yang and Sternberg (1997) considered the conceptions of intelligence held by Taiwanese Chinese people. One of the factors regarded as important was interpersonal intelligence, i.e., an ability to understand (and to get on well with) other people.

Cultural differences in conceptions of intelligence do exist, but they are not typically very great. Sternberg, Conway, Ketron, and Bernstein (1981) found that there were three ingredients to Americans' conceptions of intelligence: verbal ability, practical problem solving, and social competence. The emphasis on social competence means that the views of Americans do not differ enormously from those of members of collectivistic cultures.

**KEY TERM**

**Intelligence:** the ability to learn from experience and to adapt to the environment.

Most psychologists accept that the concept of intelligence is useful in accounting for some individual differences in behaviour. However, Howe (1990, p. 499) disputed this view:

*For the important task of helping to discover the underlying causes of differing levels of performance, there is no convincing evidence that the concept of intelligence can play a major role. So far as explanatory theories are concerned, the construct seems to be obsolete.*

It is certainly true that the concept of "intelligence" is sometimes used purely descriptively. For example, suppose we argue that Christine performs better than John on a range of complex cognitive tasks because she is more intelligent. This fails to provide an adequate explanation of Christine's superior performance. However, measures of intelligence often possess good predictive power. Intelligence tests administered at one point in time can predict future academic achievement and career success with moderate accuracy (see Mackintosh, 1998, for a review). Such findings suggest that the concept of "intelligence" possesses explanatory power.

Issues relating to the development of intelligence during childhood are covered in Chapters 14 and 15. Of most relevance, major theories of cognitive development (e.g., Piaget, Vygotsky) are discussed at length in Chapter 15. Other material of direct relevance to intelligence is dealt with in Chapter 8, especially the section concerned with skill acquisition and expertise.

## INTELLIGENCE TESTING

*How would you try to measure intelligence?*

The first proper intelligence test was devised by the Frenchman Alfred Binet. At the start of the twentieth century, he devised an intelligence test to allow mentally retarded children to be identified, so that they could be given special educational facilities. In 1905, Binet and his associate Simon produced a wide range of tests measuring comprehension, memory, and other cognitive processes. This led to numerous later tests. Among the best known of such tests are the Stanford–Binet test produced at Stanford University in 1916, the Wechsler Intelligence Scale for Children, the Revised Wechsler Adult Intelligence Scale (Wechsler, 1981), and the British Ability Scales in the 1970s.

These (and other) tests measure several aspects of intelligence. Many contain vocabulary tests in which individuals try to define the meanings of words. Tests often also include problems based on analogies (e.g., "Hat is to head as shoe is to——"), and tests of spatial ability (e.g., "If I start walking northwards, then turn left, and then turn left again, what direction will I be facing?").

All major intelligence tests share key similarities. They have manuals indicating how the test should be administered. This is important, because the wording of the instructions often influences the tested person's score. The major tests are also alike in that they are **standardised tests**. Standardisation of a test involves giving it to large, representative samples of the age groups for which the test is intended. The meaning of an individual's score can then be evaluated by comparing it against the scores of other people.

It is possible with most standardised tests to obtain several measures of an individual's performance. These measures are mostly of a fairly specific nature (e.g., arithmetical ability or spatial ability). However, the best-known measure is the very general **intelligence quotient** or IQ. This reflects performance on all of the sub-tests contained in an intelligence test, and is thus regarded as an overall measure of intellectual ability.

How is IQ calculated? An individual's test performance is compared against the scores obtained by other children of his/her age or by other adults in the standardisation sample. Most intelligence tests are devised so that the overall scores are normally distributed, but it should be noted that we do not know what the "real" distribution of intelligence looks like. The mean is an average worked out by dividing the total of all participants' scores by the number of participants, and the normal distribution is a bell-shaped curve in which there are as many scores above the mean as below it (see the figure on the right).

Most scores cluster fairly close to the mean, and there are fewer and fewer scores as you move away from it. The spread of scores in a normal distribution is usually indicated by a statistic known as the standard deviation, which is a measure of dispersal taking account of every score. In a normal distribution, 68% of the scores fall within one standard deviation of the mean or average, and 95% fall within two standard deviations.

Intelligence tests have a mean of 100 and a standard deviation of about 16. Thus, an IQ of 116 is one standard deviation above the mean, and indicates that the individual is more intelligent than 84% of the population. That is because 50% fall below the mean, and a further 34% between the mean and one standard deviation above it.

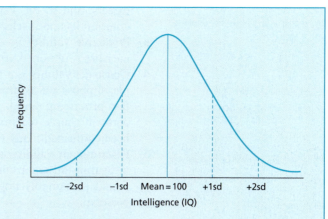

Those with high IQs do not usually perform well on all of the tests within an intelligence-test battery, nor do those with low IQs perform poorly on every test. As a result, tests are usually constructed to obtain measures of various abilities (e.g., numerical, spatial, reasoning, perceptual speed). We can obtain a more accurate assessment of an individual's intelligence by considering the profile of his/her performance across these abilities rather than by focusing only on IQ.

## Reliability

All good tests of intelligence have high reliability. **Reliability** refers to the extent to which a test provides consistent findings. Suppose someone obtained an IQ of 125 when taking an intelligence test on one occasion, but an IQ of 95 when re-taking the same test a short time later. If that happened, the test would clearly be unreliable, and could not be an adequate measure of something as relatively unchanging as intelligence.

*How would you know if your test was reliable?*

Reliability is generally assessed by the test–retest method. Numerous people take the same test on two separate occasions. The scores of all the participants on the two occasions are then correlated with each other. The higher the correlation (a measure of the relationship between the two scores), the greater is the reliability of the test. The highest possible correlation is +1.00, which would indicate perfect agreement or reliability between the two sets of scores. A correlation of 0.00 would indicate no reliability at all.

The test–retest method has the drawback that when participants are given the test for the second time, they may remember some answers they gave on the first administration. This can produce a high reliability coefficient for the wrong reason. In addition, there can be practice effects (improved performance as a result of practice) from taking an intelligence test with which the participants are already familiar. In fact, most standard intelligence tests have good reliability. Reliability correlation coefficients tend to be about +.85 to +.90. This is not far short of perfect reliability.

## Validity

All good intelligence tests possess good **validity**, which refers to the extent to which a test measures what it is supposed to be measuring. Please note that terminology in this area is rather variable, with two (or even three) terms being used to describe any given form of validity:

1. **Face validity** is the simplest form of validity. It is simply concerned with whether the content of the test seems to be relevant. For example, a test of mathematical ability that included a vocabulary test would have rather low face validity.
2. **Concurrent validity** involves relating IQ to some external criterion or standard about which we have information when the intelligence test is administered. For example, we would expect highly intelligent individuals to do well at school, to succeed in their

**KEY TERMS**
**Reliability:** the extent to which a test provides consistent findings.
**Validity:** the extent to which a test measures what it is designed to measure.
**Face validity:** an assessment of whether a test is measuring what it claims to be measuring by inspecting the content of its items.
**Concurrent validity:** an assessment of whether a test is measuring what it claims to be measuring by correlating scores with some currently available relevant criterion (e.g., school performance).

*How could you be sure that your test was really measuring intelligence?*

careers, and so on. Performance on an intelligence test is correlated with whatever criterion has been selected.

3. **Predictive validity** is very similar to concurrent validity, except that the criterion measure is obtained *after* the test has been given.

4. **Construct validity** is a form of validity based on the testing of hypotheses. For example, suppose we assume theoretically that an important aspect of high intelligence is fast processing speed. We might then predict that high scorers on our test would perform simple reaction-time tasks faster than low scorers, a prediction which has been confirmed many times (Jensen, 1998).

5. **Discriminant validity** is found when an intelligence test does *not* correlate with tests measuring different abilities or characteristics. For example, a good intelligence test would presumably not correlate with tests designed to measure various aspects of personality.

Much research on validity has focused on concurrent and predictive validity. The obvious limitation of approaches based on these two forms of validity is that nearly all the criteria that have been used are influenced by other factors as well as by intelligence. For example, academic success at school depends in part on intellectual ability. However, it also depends on motivation, amount of parental encouragement, and so on. In spite of these problems, moderate correlations between IQ and various criteria have been obtained (see Mackintosh, 1998, for a review). IQ scores typically correlate about +.50 with academic achievement. IQ correlates up to about +.5 to +.6 with occupational status, and it correlates about +.3 with income. In addition, IQ correlates between +.15 and +.30 with occupational performance.

Gottfredson (1997) reviewed in detail the literature on intelligence and ability to handle the complexities of everyday life. Comprehensive findings on the relationship between intelligence and occupational performance were reported by Hunter (1986). The predictive validity of intelligence (the correlation between intelligence and work performance) was only +.23 with low-complexity jobs (e.g., shrimp picker, corn-husking machine operator) but rose to +.58 for high-complexity jobs (e.g., biologist, city circulation manager). Thus, high intelligence is especially useful when dealing with complex information processing.

Intelligence is also important in other aspects of everyday life. As Gottfredson (1997, p. 79) concluded,

## The Rainbow Project

Robert J. Sternberg and colleagues at Yale University in the US have been working on an intelligence test that is broader than an IQ test (Sternberg, 2003). Their Rainbow Project has involved designing and then piloting this new test at 15 educational institutions. The test measures analytical skills, but also creative and practical skills. The data of the first 1000 students are very encouraging, indicating that the Rainbow Test "significantly and substantially improves the accuracy of prediction of later college success". And a further encouraging note is that the test seemed more inclusive than an IQ test, so increasing its diversity, as the students who did extremely well on the creative and practical tests were more ethnically diverse than those who excelled in the visual memory and analytical tests.

*Higher levels of cognitive ability systematically improve individuals' odds of dealing successfully with the ordinary demands of modern life (such as banking, using maps and transportation schedules, reading and understanding forms, interpreting news articles).*

We will now return to the moderately strong relationship between IQ and educational attainment. It has often been assumed (e.g., H.J. Eysenck, 1979) that IQ tests largely measure inborn ability, whereas educational attainment is merely a measure of acquired knowledge. As a result, intelligence tests are more valuable than measures of educational attainment, because they allow us to predict more accurately what individuals are likely to achieve in the future. H.J. Eysenck claimed in support that genetic factors are much more important in determining individual differences in IQ than in educational attainment. This is simply untrue, since individual differences in educational attainment depend almost as much as those in intelligence on genetic factors (Mackintosh, 1998).

The above findings are important for two reasons. First, the findings indicate that, "The distinction between tests of attainment, aptitude, and ability is at best a blurred one" (Mackintosh, 1998, p. 333). Second, the findings suggest that intelligence tests may not measure inborn ability or predict future achievements significantly better than does educational attainment.

# FACTOR THEORIES

During the first half of the twentieth century, theorists such as Spearman, Thurstone, and Burt tried to identify the main aspects of intelligence using a statistical technique known as factor analysis. The first step in factor analysis is to give a series of tests to numerous individuals, and to obtain scores for each individual on each test. The correlations between these tests are then calculated. If two tests correlate highly with each other, this means that those who perform well on one test tend to perform well on the other test. The key assumption is that two tests correlating highly with each other are assessing the same aspect or factor of intelligence. It is also assumed that two tests that correlate weakly or not at all with each other are *not* assessing the same factor of intelligence. Thus, the pattern of correlations is used to identify the same factors of intelligence.

We can see what happens in simplified fashion by considering the table on the right. How many factors should we extract from this correlation matrix? The answer is two. Tests 1 and 2 correlate highly with each other, and so are measures of the same factor. Tests 3 and 4 correlate highly with each other (but not with test 1 or test 2), and so they form a different, second factor.

|        | Test 1 | Test 2 | Test 3 | Test 4 |
|--------|--------|--------|--------|--------|
| Test 1 | –      | +.85   | +.12   | +.10   |
| Test 2 | +.85   | –      | +.08   | +.11   |
| Test 3 | +.12   | +.08   | –      | +.87   |
| Test 4 | +.10   | +.11   | +.87   | –      |

There are numerous forms of factor analysis. Of particular importance is the distinction between methods of factor analysis which identify independent or orthogonal factors essentially uncorrelated with each other, and methods that identify related factors which correlate moderately with each other.

## Spearman

Charles Spearman (1923) was a British psychologist who put forward the first factor theory of intelligence. In his two-factor theory, there is a general factor of intelligence, which he called "**g**". Spearman argued for this general factor, because practically all of the tests contained within an intelligence-test battery correlate positively with each other. Most of these positive correlations are fairly low, so we cannot account for all of the data simply in terms of a general factor. Accordingly, Spearman argued that there are specific factors associated with each test.

L. Thurstone (1938) was not convinced of the need to assume that there is a general factor of intelligence. He pointed out that the general factor extracted from one intelligence-test battery might differ from that extracted from another test battery. This issue was addressed by R. Thorndike (1987). He assessed the correlations or loadings of tests on the general factors extracted from six different independent test batteries. Thorndike found that the correlations between the g-loadings in two different test batteries varied between +.52 and +.94. Thus, the general factors obtained from different intelligence-test batteries are similar but by no means identical to each other.

*What factors do you consider contribute to intelligence?*

## Thurstone

L. Thurstone adopted a different approach to factor analysis based on simple structure. This led him to identify seven factors, which he termed primary mental abilities. These primary mental abilities were as follows: inductive reasoning, verbal meaning, numerical ability, spatial ability, perceptual speed, memory, and verbal fluency.

Thurstone (1938) ignored the general factor in his theory of intelligence. However, all seven primary abilities identified by Thurstone correlate positively with each other. As a result, factor analysis of Thurstone's seven factors produces the general factor (Sternberg, 1985).

## Cattell

Cattell (1963, 1971) used evidence from factor analyses to draw a distinction between two major types of intelligence: fluid ability and crystallised ability. **Fluid ability** is the type of intelligence used when dealing with novel situations and problems; it corresponds roughly to non-verbal reasoning. In contrast, **crystallised ability** is the type of intelligence used when previously acquired knowledge and ways of thinking are required; it corresponds to verbal intelligence. More generally, crystallised ability is claimed to depend on fluid ability, but the reverse is not the case.

*How useful is the distinction between crystallised ability and fluid ability?*

There is much support for the distinction between fluid and crystallised ability. For example, Beauducel and Kersting (2002) compared measures of fluid and crystallised ability with components assessed by the Berlin Model of Intelligence Structure (BIS). Fluid ability was associated with processing capacity and memory from the BIS, whereas crystallised ability was associated with the BIS components of knowledge and processing speed. In general terms, these differences between fluid and crystallised ability were meaningful and as predicted.

Cattell (1963, 1971) argued that genetic factors are more important in determining individual differences in fluid ability than in crystallised ability. Cattell (1971) claimed some support for his position from twin studies. However, Horn (1994) reviewed the relevant literature, and concluded that genetic factors are as important in crystallised ability as in fluid ability.

According to Cattell (1963), fluid ability declines at an earlier age than does crystallised ability. There is only limited support for Cattell. For example, Schaie (1996) reported the findings from a 28-year longitudinal study on people from the ages of 53 to 81. The decline in fluid ability was only slightly greater than the decline in crystallised ability.

In sum, the distinction between fluid and crystallised ability is important. However, there is little theoretical understanding of the nature of these two types of ability, with Cattell's views having attracted little empirical support.

## Hierarchical approach

Several theorists (e.g., Carroll, 1986; Vernon, 1971) have argued that a synthesis of the views of Spearman and Thurstone can provide an adequate account of the structure of human intelligence. This synthesis involves a three-level hierarchical approach. At the highest level of the hierarchy, there is the general factor of intelligence originally identified by Spearman. At the intermediate level of the hierarchy, there are six or seven group factors, which are more specific than the general factor. Thurstone's seven primary abilities are group factors. Carroll also identified seven group factors, but disagreed somewhat with Thurstone (1938) on the nature of these factors. According to Carroll, the seven group factors are as follows: general memory capacity, general auditory perception,

> **KEY TERM**
> **Crystallised ability:** the form of intelligence based on acquired knowledge and ways of thinking.

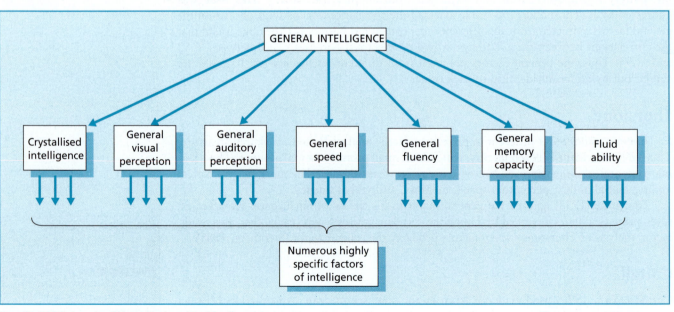

Carroll's (1986) three-level hierarchical model of intelligence.

general fluency, fluid ability, crystallised intelligence (knowledge), general visual perception, and general speed. At the lowest level of the hierarchy, there are numerous specific factors (e.g., spelling ability), as had been suggested by Spearman (1923).

Carroll (1993) discussed evidence relevant to his hierarchical theory based on factor analysis of over 460 data sets obtained over a 60-year period from more than 130,000 people. In essence, there appeared to be three levels or strata, and the abilities at the intermediate level or stratum corresponded closely to those put forward by Carroll (1986).

## Evaluation

⊕ The factorial approach has produced reasonable agreement on aspects of the structure of intelligence.
⊕ Evidence for a general factor of intelligence justifies the widespread use of IQ as a general measure of intelligence.
⊖ Factor analysis is descriptive rather than explanatory. As Mackintosh (1998, p. 230) argued, "Factor analysis can do no more than describe the relationships between different IQ tests. This is not the same as uncovering the structure of human abilities. That will only be achieved by the development and testing of psychological theory."
⊖ Factor analysis tells us little or nothing about the cognitive processes and mechanisms involved in intelligent behaviour.
⊖ Factor analysis is limited in that it is like a sausage machine: What you get out of it depends on what was put into it in the first place. If, for example, no tests of creativity are given to the participants, then no factor of creativity will emerge from the factor analysis.

## HEREDITY AND ENVIRONMENT

Why are some children and adults more intelligent than others? At the most general level, only two factors could be responsible: heredity and environment. Heredity consists of each person's genetic endowment, and environment consists of the situations and experiences encountered by people in the course of their lives. There is almost complete agreement that individual differences in intelligence depend on both heredity and environment.

*To what extent can our environment enhance our intelligence?*

It is sometimes assumed that heredity and environment have *independent* effects on an individual's level of intelligence. However, the reality is more complex. Plomin (1990) identified three types of covariation or *interdependence* of genetic endowment and environment:

1. *Active covariation.* This occurs when children of differing genetic ability look for situations reinforcing their genetic differences. For example, children of high genetic ability may read numerous books and become friends with other intelligent children, whereas those with less genetic ability may actively seek out less intellectually demanding situations.
2. *Passive covariation.* This occurs when parents of high genetic ability provide a more intellectually stimulating environment than parents of lower genetic ability.
3. *Reactive covariation.* This occurs when an individual's genetically influenced behaviour helps to determine how he/she is treated by other people.

Dickens and Flynn (2001) chose the example of basketball performance to show the implausibility of the assumption that heredity and environment have entirely independent effects. According to that assumption,

*Good coaching, practising, preoccupation with basketball, and all other environmental factors that influence performance must be unrelated to whether genes contribute to someone being tall, slim, and well co-ordinated. For this to be true, players must be selected at random for the varsity basketball team and get the benefits of professional coaching and intense practice, without regard to build, quickness, and degree of interest.*

We can see a person's phenotype, but their genotype lies hidden.

In fact, of course, individuals whose genes predispose them to be outstanding at basketball are more likely to put themselves into an environment supporting excellent basketball performance than are those whose genes do not.

A key problem faced by researchers in this area is that experimental control is lacking. We cannot ethically manipulate heredity by a breeding programme, nor can we achieve much control over the environment in which children develop. In addition, we cannot assess accurately an individual's genetic potential (known as the **genotype**). All we can measure directly are the observable characteristics (known as the **phenotype**).

The search is on for the so-called "intelligence genes". The completion of the human genome project means that all human genes have been identified, and some of these genes are relevant to intelligence. Chorney et al. (1998) found the gene IGF2R was present in 34% of children with very high IQs, but in only 17% of children with average IQs. This is a promising finding (even though it is only correlational), and IGF2R may be one of the genes forming intelligence. However, intelligence undoubtedly depends on numerous genes acting in combination, and so it is quite wrong to think in terms of any gene being *the* intelligence gene.

## Family studies

The most informative approach to assessing the respective roles played by heredity and environment in determining individual differences in intelligence is based on the study of twins. Identical or **monozygotic twins** derive from the same fertilised ovum, and so have essentially identical genotypes. In contrast, fraternal or **dizygotic twins** derive from two

The Collister twins: identical twin brothers, married to identical twin sisters.

different fertilised ova. As a result, their genotypes are no more similar than those of two ordinary siblings, i.e., they share on average 50% of their genes. If heredity influences intelligence, identical twins should be more alike in intelligence than fraternal twins. On the other hand, if environmental factors are all-important, then identical twins should be no more alike than fraternal twins.

The degree of similarity in intelligence shown by pairs of twins is usually reported in the form of correlations. A correlation of +1.00 would mean that both twins in a pair have very similar or the same IQs, whereas a correlation of 0.00 would mean that there was no relationship at all between the IQs of twins. Bouchard and McGue (1981) reviewed 111 studies, and reported that the mean correlation for identical twins was +.86, and it was +.60 for fraternal twins. Similar findings from a later meta-analysis were reported by McCartney, Harris, and Bernieri (1990). The mean correlation for identical twins was +.81, compared to +.59 for fraternal twins.

The fact that monozygotic or identical twins are much more similar than dizygotic or fraternal twins suggests that heredity is of major significance in determining individual differences in intelligence. However, that conclusion rests on the assumption that the degree of environmental similarity experienced by identical twins is the same as that experienced by fraternal twins. In fact, however, identical twins are treated in a more similar fashion than fraternal twins in the following ways: paternal treatment, playing together, dressing in a similar style, and being taught by the same teachers (Loehlin & Nichols, 1976).

It is important not to over-interpret the above findings. Even though identical twins are treated in a more similar way than fraternal twins, the differences are relatively small, and seem to have little impact on twins' differences in intelligence (Loehlin & Nichols, 1976). Furthermore, it is possible that parents treat identical twins more similarly than fraternal twins, because they are responding to the greater genetically influenced similarities in the behaviour of identical twins (i.e., reactive covariation).

**KEY TERMS**

**Genotype:** an individual's genetic potential.

**Phenotype:** an individual's observable characteristics, which depend on his/her genotype plus experiences.

**Monozygotic twins:** identical twins derived from a single fertilised ovum and sharing 100% of their genes.

**Dizygotic twins:** fraternal twins derived from two fertilised ova and sharing 50% of their genes.

There is another aspect of the environment we need to consider: the prenatal environment. All fraternal twins have separate placentas in the womb, whereas two-thirds of identical twins share a single placenta. This means that the prenatal environment of most identical twins is more similar than is the prenatal environment of fraternal twins. Does this matter? Phelps, Davis, and Schartz (1997) discussed evidence indicating that it probably does. They reviewed several studies in which it was found that identical twins sharing a single placenta were more similar in intelligence than were identical twins having separate placentas.

*What problems arise in drawing conclusions about intelligence from twin studies?*

In some studies, use has been made of identical twins brought up apart in different families. Such twin pairs would seem to be of particular value in deciding on the relative importance of genetic and environmental factors in determining intelligence. Those arguing that genetic factors are of most importance would expect such twins to resemble each other closely in intelligence. In contrast, those favouring an environmentalist position would argue that placing twins in different environments should ensure that they are not similar in intelligence.

The findings broadly favour the hereditarian position. According to Bouchard and McGue's (1981) review (leaving out the very dubious data of Burt, 1955), the mean correlation coefficient for identical twins is +.72. This figure is certainly higher than would be expected from an environmentalist position. However, the fact that the correlation is lower than it is for identical twins brought up together provides evidence that environmental factors are also important.

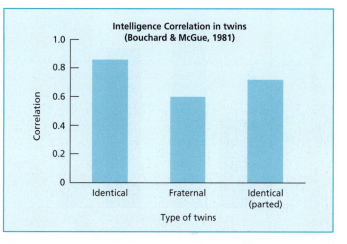

There are limitations with the evidence from monozygotic twins brought up apart. Over half of monozygotic twins brought up apart were, in fact, brought up in different branches of the same family. Other monozygotic twins were actually brought up together for several years before being separated. Thus, many pairs of identical twins actually experience rather similar environments.

Bouchard, Lykken, McGue, Segal, and Tellegen (1990) studied more than 40 adult monozygotic twin pairs who had been separated at a mean age of 5.1 months, and who had spent on average 9.2 months together during their lives. In spite of the fact that these twin pairs had been separated in infancy, their IQs correlated +.75. Bouchard et al. also found that the similarity in IQ of identical twins brought up apart depended very little on their age at separation or on the total amount of contact they had had thereafter.

The findings of Bouchard et al. (1990) suggest that the similarity of IQ of identical twins brought up apart depends mainly on genetic factors rather than on environmental similarity. However, the identical twins involved in the various studies are not representative of the general population: Very few of them were intellectually retarded or had extremely poor parents. Thus, it remains unclear whether the findings from identical twins brought up apart can be generalised to the population at large.

There have been several attempts to assess the similarity of IQ between different groups of relatives. Bouchard and McGue (1981) carried out various meta-analyses, and produced the following mean correlations:

| *Relationship* | *Mean correlation* |
| --- | --- |
| Siblings reared together | +.47 |
| Siblings reared apart | +.24 |
| Single parent–offspring reared together | +.42 |
| Single parent–offspring reared apart | +.22 |
| Half-siblings | +.31 |
| Cousins | +.15 |
| Adopted parent–offspring | +.19 |

These findings indicate that relatives sharing greater genetic similarity tend to be more similar in IQ. However, relatives having greater genetic similarity tend to live in more similar environments than those with less genetic similarity, which makes it difficult to interpret the findings. As Bouchard and McGue (1981) concluded, "Most of the results of studies of family resemblance … can be interpreted as either supporting the genetic or environmentalist theory."

## Adoption studies

Adoption studies provide another way of assessing the relative importance of heredity and environment in determining individual differences in intelligence. If heredity is more important than environment, then adopted children's IQs will be more similar to those of their biological parents than their adoptive parents. The opposite pattern will be found if environment is more important.

The IQs of adopted children are generally more similar to those of their biological parents than of their adoptive parents (see Mackintosh, 1998). These findings suggest that heredity may be more important than environment in determining individual differences in intelligence.

It is often hard to interpret the findings from most adoption studies. A key problem is that of **selective placement**: Adoption agencies often have a policy of trying to place infants in homes with similar educational and social backgrounds to those of their biological parents. As a result, some of the similarity in IQ between adopted children and their biological mothers may occur because they are living in an environment resembling the one their mother would have provided.

Capron and Duyne (1989) carried out an important study on adopted children. It has the great advantage over most other adoption studies that there was little or no evidence of selective placement. Capron and Duyne used four very different groups of adopted children, involving all four possible combinations of biological parents of high or low socioeconomic status and adoptive parents of high or low socioeconomic status. The predictions are fairly straightforward. The measured intelligence of the adopted children should depend mainly on the socioeconomic status of the biological parents if genetic factors are of more importance, but should depend mostly on the socioeconomic status of the adoptive parents if environmental factors are more important. In fact, the effects of the socioeconomic status of the biological and of the adoptive parents were comparable (see Figure above). Thus, genetic and environmental factors were of about equal importance in determining the intelligence of the adopted children.

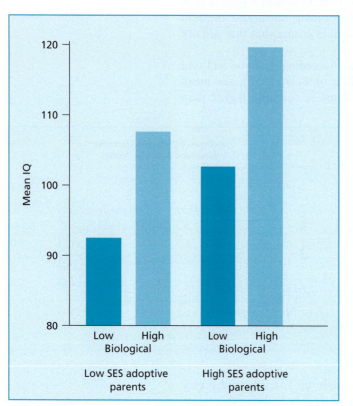

Mean IQs of adopted children as a function of socioeconomic status (SES) of their biological parents (low vs. high) and their adoptive parents (low vs. high). Data from Capron and Duyne (1989).

## Heritability

The evidence indicates that heredity and environment both play a major role in determining intelligence. Researchers trying to be more specific about the contributions of heredity and environment have made extensive use of the concept of heritability. **Heritability** is the ratio of genetically caused variation to total variation (a combination of genetic and environmental variation) within any given population. Thus, measures of heritability provide only limited information. More specifically, heritability tells us something about the role of genetic factors in producing individual differences in intelligence, but this is *not* the same as genetic determination.

We can make sense of the distinction between heritability and genetic determination if we consider an instructive example (Block, 1995a). The number of fingers that human beings have on each hand is determined almost entirely by genetic factors. However, heritability is concerned *only* with individual differences, and so to assess heritability in this case we need to consider the factors causing a few individuals to have more (or fewer) than five fingers on each hand. Such individual differences depend mainly on environmental factors such as being involved in industrial or car accidents, or experiencing complications in foetal development. Thus, the genetic determination of the number of fingers is extremely *high*, whereas heritability is very *low*.

There is another important limitation of heritability. It is a population measure, and varies greatly from one population to another. In general terms, the more similar the environmental factors experienced by those living in a given culture, the greater will be the effect of genetic factors in determining individual differences in intelligence. Evidence that heritability varies across cultures was discussed by Brace (1996). The heritability of intelligence was found to be much higher among people living in affluent white American suburbs than among people living in American urban ghettos.

Mackintosh (1998, p. 93) provided a suitably cautious conclusion after reviewing the evidence:

> *The broad heritability of IQ in modern industrialised societies is probably somewhere between 0.30 and 0.75, and neither the data nor the models justify much greater precision ... without some arbitrary, simplifying assumptions, it would be impossible to derive any estimate of heritability at all.*

Thus, between 30% and 75% of individual differences in intelligence are due to genetic factors.

There is one final point which needs to be made. Plomin (1988, p. 420) argued that the genetic influence on individual differences in IQ, "increases from infancy (20%) to childhood (40%) to adulthood (60%)". Much of the evidence supports this argument (e.g., Bishop, Cherny, Corley, Plomin, DeFries, & Hewitt, 2003). It is not known *why* the heritability of intelligence increases during development. However, one possible reason is that adolescents and adults can select and control their own environment to a greater extent than children, and this reduces the direct impact of the environment on intelligence. Thus, the increase in heritability of intelligence during the course of development may reflect what Plomin (1990) called active covariation (discussed earlier).

## Group differences

The mean difference in IQ between white people and black people in the United States is about 15 points, but about 20% of black people have a higher IQ than that of the average white person. Most psychologists have assumed that the difference between white and black people is due to the environmental deprivation suffered by black people. However, Jensen (1969) and H.J. Eysenck (1971) argued controversially that genetic differences might be involved.

*What problems might arise in trying to explore IQ differences between different cultures?*

### General criticisms of IQ tests, adoption studies, and twin studies

| IQ tests | Adoption studies | Twin studies |
|---|---|---|
| Debatable whether IQ is an adequate measurement of intelligence | Selective placement makes it hard to determine the effects of heredity and environment | Environmental similarity often occurs |
| Cultural differences not always considered | Heredity is less well controlled than in twin studies | Twins raised separately actually raised by different branches of the same family |
| | | Twins had spent some years together before being separated |

The first point to make about this controversial issue is that we cannot carry out definitive research. We cannot measure accurately the levels of deprivation experienced by black people, nor can we compare the genetic endowment of white and black people.

The second point is that evidence that genetic factors *within* a population play an important role in determining individual differences in intelligence does *not* support the notion that differences in intelligence *between* groups also depend on genetic factors. Suppose we compare the heights of everyone in the United Kingdom currently in their 20s. We would probably find that about 95% of individual differences in their height depend on heredity. However, if we had detailed records of the heights of British people who were in their 20s 100 years ago, we would find that they were on average several inches shorter. This is because of considerable improvements in nutrition and diet over the past century. In this case, variations *within* a population (e.g., those currently in their 20s) depend almost entirely on heredity, while variations *between* populations are heavily influenced by environmental factors.

## Evidence

A major reason why black people perform less well than white people on intelligence tests is because of environmental deprivation. Mackintosh (1986) compared white and West Indian children in England. Some of the children were matched for father's job, number of brothers and sisters, family income, and other measures relevant to deprivation, whereas the others were unmatched. In one study, there was a 9 point difference between unmatched groups, but only a 2.6 point difference in the matched groups. Thus, the two groups hardly differed in intelligence when they were equated for the level of deprivation.

Most intelligence tests are devised by white, middle-class psychologists from Western societies. Tests may, therefore, underestimate the intelligence of those from other cultures or social backgrounds.

Tizard, Cooperman, and Tizard (1972) reported a study of black, white, and mixed children living in similar environments in residential nurseries in the United Kingdom. White children had a mean IQ of 101, mixed children a mean IQ of 105, and black children a mean IQ of 104. In the United States, Scarr and Weinberg (1983) found that children adopted by white parents had very similar IQs regardless of the colour of their biological parents.

It has been claimed that most intelligence tests are biased in favour of white individuals. We can try to avoid bias by constructing "culture-fair" tests consisting mainly of abstract and non-verbal items that should not be more familiar to members of one group than another. However, such culture-fair tests typically produce larger differences in intelligence across cultural groups than do conventional tests (Sternberg, 1994). Rather different findings were obtained with the Black Intelligence Test of Cultural Homogeneity (BITCH), which was designed for black Americans. White American children did no better than black American children on this test, and sometimes performed worse (Williams, 1972).

## Evaluation

● The issue of race differences is essentially meaningless, being based on the incorrect assumption that whites and blacks form separate biological groups.
● The issue lacks scientific interest, in that it is unlikely to tell us anything about the processes involved in human intelligence. Whatever the findings, we should strive to provide good opportunities for everyone.
● It is profoundly regrettable that some psychologists have publicised unjustified and politically inflammatory views.

# ENVIRONMENTAL INFLUENCES

We have seen that environmental factors (as well as genetic factors) are important in determining individual differences in intelligence. Twin studies and studies on adopted children have been used to assess two types of environmental influence: shared environment and non-shared environment. **Shared environment** refers to all the common influences within a family that make children resemble each other; such influences include parental attitudes to education and parental income. **Non-shared environment** refers to all those influences that are unique to any given child (e.g., different experiences with peers). Plomin (1988, 1999) has considered the relevant evidence. Twin and adoption studies suggest that about 20% of individual differences in intelligence are due to non-shared environment. So far as shared environment is concerned, "Such shared environmental influences that contribute to the resemblance of family members for *g* are important in childhood, accounting for about a quarter of the variance, but they are not important after adolescence" (Plomin, 1999, p. C26). This probably happens because adolescents and adults seek out environments that are suitable for them to a greater extent than do children.

Surprising evidence that environmental factors can have a substantial effect on intelligence was reported by Flynn (1987, 1994). He has obtained evidence from 20 Western countries, each of which showed the **Flynn effect**: a rapid rise in average IQ in most Western countries in recent decades. More specifically, Flynn (1987) reported that there has been an increase of 2.9 points per decade on non-verbal IQ and of 3.7 points on verbal IQ. This rapid increase cannot be due to genetic factors. What aspects of the environment account for the Flynn effect? Here are some likely factors:

- Increases in the number of years of education.
- Greater access to information (e.g., television, internet).
- The increased cognitive complexity of the average person's job now compared to several decades ago.
- More generally, a large increase in the number of middle-class families.

Dickens and Flynn (2001) tried to reconcile the Flynn effect (showing large environmental influences on intelligence in Western societies) with other evidence indicating that the heritability of intelligence in the same countries is fairly high. In essence, they argued that there are strong effects of environment on intelligence, but measures of heritability *under-estimate* environmental impact on intelligence. How does this happen? According to Dickens and Flynn (p. 347), "Higher IQ leads one into better environments causing still higher IQ, and so on." In other words, individuals seek out environments *matching* their genotype or intellectual potential. Measures of heritability combine the *direct* influence of the genotype with the *indirect* effects of the genotype on the environments that individuals choose for themselves. The take-home message is that heritability measures depend in part on environmental influences as well as on genetically determined ones, and that is why such measures exaggerate the impact of genetic factors on individual differences in intelligence.

Gottfried (1984) carried out a meta-analysis to assess the relative importance of several environmental factors in influencing children's intelligence. Provision of appropriate play materials, parental involvement with the child, and opportunities for variety in daily stimulation were the best predictors of children's subsequent IQs. Unfortunately, Gottfried's findings are correlational in nature, and so cannot show causality. Yeates, MacPhee, Campbell, and Ramey (1983) considered the causality issue in a longitudinal study of young children. The mother's IQ

> **KEY TERMS**
> **Shared environment:** environmental influences that are common to the children within a given family.
> **Non-shared environment:** environmental influences that are unique to a given individual.
> **Flynn effect:** a rapid rise in average IQ in several Western countries in recent decades.

## KEY STUDY EVALUATION—Sameroff et al.

It is not clear whether all of the 10 factors identified by Sameroff et al. were causally related to the children's IQ. For example, consider their evidence that the mother not going to high school and the head of household having a semi-skilled job were associated with low IQ in the children. It is possible that genetic factors play a part in producing these environmental factors and in leading to low IQ in children.

# Sameroff et al.: The Rochester Longitudinal Study

Sameroff et al. (1987, 1993) conducted a longitudinal study in New York State to investigate the factors that might be linked to intellectual delay in young children. They selected pregnant women to be part of their study and followed 215 children, testing the children's IQs at ages 4 and 13 (at this point 152 families remained in the sample). The families represented a range of socioeconomic backgrounds, maternal age groups, and number of other siblings.

Sameroff et al. identified 10 family risk factors that were related to lower IQ:

- Mother has a history of mental illness.
- Mother did not go to high school.
- Mother has severe anxiety.
- Mother has rigid attitudes and values about her child's development.
- Few positive interactions between mother and child during infancy.
- Head of household has a semi-skilled job.
- Four or more children in the family.
- Father does not live with the family.
- Child belongs to a minority group.
- Family suffered 20 or more stressful events during the child's first 4 years of life.

There was a clear negative association between the number of risk factors associated with a child and the child's IQ, as illustrated in the graph on the left. At age 4 this correlation was −.58. At age 13 it was −.61. At the age of 4, high-risk children were 24 times more likely to have IQs below 85 than low-risk children. It was calculated that, on average, each risk factor reduced the child's IQ score by 4 points.

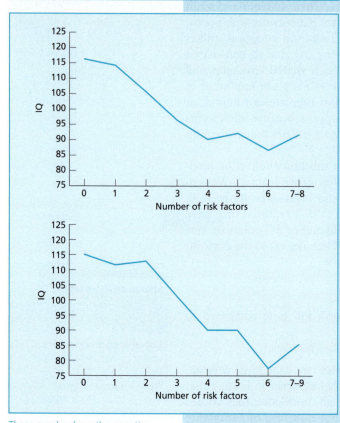

These graphs show the negative association between IQ and number of environmental risk factors. The top graph presents data for mean 4-year IQ scores, and the bottom graph presents data for mean 13-year IQ scores.

## Discussion points

1. Select one of the risk factors and suggest how it might affect intellectual development.
2. What are the political implications of this study?

predicted children's IQs at the age of 2 better than did various environmental factors. However, environmental factors (e.g., parental involvement with the child) predicted the IQs of the same children at the age of 4 better than did the mother's IQ. Thus, the beneficial effects of a stimulating home environment may become stronger as children develop.

Sameroff, Seifer, Baldwin, and Baldwin (1993) reported the findings of a study in which hundreds of children were followed from birth to adolescence (see Key Study above).

## Cultural differences

As we saw earlier, what is regarded as intelligent behaviour varies from one culture to another. That makes it difficult to compare intelligence across different cultures, as was emphasised by Triandis (1994, p. 58):

*When we measure something in another culture, we are most likely to get an answer to the question, Do they do our tricks as well as we do our tricks? rather than, Do they do their tricks well? ... Different ecologies [environments] reward different tricks.*

Cole, Gay, Glick, and Sharp (1971) reported an interesting difference between members of Western cultures and members of the Kpelle tribe in Africa. When we sort concepts, we typically sort them hierarchically (e.g., we sort different kinds of animals into groups such as fish, birds, and so on, with the concept "animal" put over them). In contrast, the Kpelle sorted in terms of function (e.g., "fish" and "eat" might be sorted together because we eat fish). However, the findings differed when Cole et al. asked the Kpelle to sort as a stupid person would. Members of the Kpelle tribe given those instructions sorted concepts hierarchically in the same way as Westerners!

Not surprisingly, members of any given culture tend to emphasise skills and knowledge of particular relevance within that culture. For example, Sternberg (reported in Sternberg & Ben-Zeev, 2001) studied Kenyan children who possessed considerable knowledge about natural herbal medicines that can be used to fight infection in that country. Those Kenyan children possessing most knowledge tended to perform *worse* than the other children on standard verbal tests of intelligence. The implication is that the skills that are important in the Kenyan culture differ considerably from those deemed important in Western cultures.

Street skills such as the commercial, bargaining, and economic abilities these children possess are not measured by conventional intelligence tests.

An important cultural difference may be that children in non-Western cultures have much less experience than those in Western cultures in considering hypothetical and rather abstract problems at school. For example, consider a study by Nunes (1994) on very poor Brazilian children. These children worked as street vendors, and many of them were very successful because they could carry out complex arithmetical calculations when they were selling goods. However, their mathematical performance was considerably worse when they tried to solve similar arithmetical problems at school.

*How might cultures differ in their perception of what makes someone intelligent?*

We have seen that there are various problems in assessing intelligence in other cultures. How can we obtain more accurate information about the intellectual capabilities of members of other cultures? Sternberg et al. (2002) argued for the usefulness of dynamic testing, in which individuals are tested on two different occasions and there is an emphasis on the processes involved in learning and change. This contrasts with conventional static testing, in which an individual's pre-existing skills are assessed at a single testing session.

Sternberg et al. (2002) gave various tests of fluid ability to children in Tanzania on two occasions. Some of the children received brief interventions (less than 1 hour each) between the two testing occasions in order to teach some of the skills assessed by the tests. There were substantial improvements in performance on all tests of fluid ability on the second testing occasion. Sternberg et al. (p. 154) concluded that children growing up in difficult circumstances, "have substantial levels of underlying capacities that are reflected in developing but not in developed abilities. Dynamic testing is one way of trying to get past conventional static measures of developed abilities, and to assess as well developing abilities generated by these underlying capacities."

## Evaluation

➕ Environmental factors have substantial effects on the development of IQ; this is clearly seen in the Flynn effect.

➕ Various specific aspects of the environment having beneficial or adverse effects on intelligence have been identified.

➕ There seem to be important cultural differences in the skills and knowledge regarded as important.

➕ Children in other cultures may have underlying capacities that are better assessed by dynamic testing than by static testing.

- It has proved difficult to establish causal links between environmental factors and intelligence.
- We have no clear theoretical understanding of *why* or *how* certain environmental factors influence IQ.

## Enriched environment

If we can identify environmental factors enhancing intelligence, then it should be possible to provide an enriched environment to benefit disadvantaged children. The best-known attempt to do this is probably Operation Headstart, introduced in the United States during the 1960s. However, there have been various other enrichment programmes (e.g., the Carolina Abecedarian project).

### Operation Headstart

Operation Headstart focused on the provision of extensive preschool education, but was sometimes extended to provide care and education for the children's parents. Medical and motivational advice was also included.

Headstart programmes typically produced fairly rapid increases in IQ of about 10 points (Lazar & Darlington, 1982). In addition, there were beneficial effects on educational achievement. However, these gains in IQ mostly disappeared when the children moved on to school. Within 2 years of entering the school system, there was generally no difference in academic achievement between those children who had undergone a Headstart programme and those who had not.

Headstart programmes varied considerably in the competence of the teachers involved and in resourcing. Schweinhart and Weikart (1985) concluded that the benefits of good Headstart programmes included, "improved intellectual performance during early childhood, better scholastic placement and improved scholastic achievement during the elementary school years; and, during adolescence, a lower rate of delinquency and higher rates of both graduation from high school and employment at age 19."

Lee, Brooks-Gunn, Schnur, and Liaw (1990) carried out a 20-year follow-up on children who had taken part in a Headstart programme, or had attended preschool, or had done neither. The benefits of the Headstart programme had reduced over the years, but those who had been involved in it still showed some advantages compared to those who had not and who had not attended preschool either. However, there was very little difference between those who had taken part in Headstart and those who had attended preschool.

### Carolina Abecedarian project

In the Carolina Abecedarian project, Ramey, Bryant, and Suarez (1985) studied disadvantaged children whose mothers had IQs between 70 and 85. Some of these children received a 5-day-a-week educational programme starting when they were only a few weeks old and continuing until they were 5. This was far more than was typically the case with Headstart programmes. There was also a control group of similarly disadvantaged children who did not receive the educational programme.

---

**Are music lessons enrichment?**

Wells Cathedral School in Somerset, England, educates children from age 4 to 18, and teachers report that musicians do achieve better exam results than non-musicians. This might tie in with Shaw's research in California (Shaw, 1997). Seventy-eight 3- and 4-year-olds were tested for jigsaw-puzzle ability. Then one-third were given piano lessons, one third were given computer lessons, and the remaining third were the control group with no extra enrichment. Nine months later the children were retested. Only the group learning the piano had improved, and this improvement measured an increase of 35%. This research suggests that extra musical experience may have an influence on those parts of the brain concerned with creative and intellectual ability.

Some research suggests that music lessons may enhance intellectual ability.

The mean IQ of children in the programme was much higher than that of the control children at the age of 3 (102 vs. 84, respectively). The gap was still fairly large at the age of 5 (102 vs. 93, respectively), and some difference remained at the age of 12.

Other groups were also studied in the Carolina Abecedarian project, including disadvantaged children receiving the intervention programme between the ages of 5 and 8 (Campbell & Ramey, 1994). The benefits of the programme were much smaller among those children, presumably because they had already started school.

Enrichment programmes, such as Operation Headstart, provide children with extensive preschool education.

## Evaluation

➕ Enrichment programmes for disadvantaged children typically produce fairly rapid increases in IQ and in educational achievement.

➖ Many beneficial effects of enrichment programmes disappear during the early years of full-time schooling.

➖ We do not know *how* and *why* enrichment influences children's development. However, detailed teaching of knowledge and enhanced motivation are two likely reasons.

➖ High IQ scores produced through intervention programmes are less predictive of school success than are high IQ scores occurring "naturally" (Miller & Bizzell, 1983). Thus, a high IQ produced via enrichment may be less useful than the same IQ occurring in the absence of enrichment.

## THEORIES OF INTELLIGENCE

Throughout much of this chapter, we have considered aspects of the traditional theory of intelligence. This theory had its origins in the work of Spearman (1927), but was subsequently endorsed by several other theorists including H.J. Eysenck (1979) and Herrnstein and Murray (1994). Key assumptions of the traditional theory are as follows:

* Individuals differ in a single psychological process that can be assessed by the general factor of intelligence or by IQ.
* Intelligence tests provide an adequate assessment of human intelligence.
* Intelligence depends mainly on genetic factors. For example, H.J. Eysenck (1979) argued that, "Intelligence as measured by IQ tests has a strong genetic basis; genetic factors account for an estimated 80% of the total variance."
* The fact that intelligence is largely inherited means it is difficult to change an individual's level of intelligence.

*How might the traditional theories of intelligence be criticised?*

All these assumptions are only approximately correct. The fact that nearly all individual tests in an intelligence-test battery correlate with each other is consistent with the assumption that a single underlying psychological or cognitive process is responsible. However, there are other possibilities. As Mackintosh (1998, p. 230) pointed out, "It is possible that all IQ tests tap a large number of different processes, but that there is some overlap in the set of processes tapped by different groups of tests."

Recent support for the notion of general intelligence has come from research by Duncan et al. (2000). They used PET scans to identify brain regions most active when participants performed a wide range of tasks correlating highly with the general factor of intelligence. The key finding was that a specific region of the frontal cortex was highly active during the performance of virtually all the tasks. Duncan et al. (p. 457) concluded that, "The results suggest that 'general intelligence' derives from a specific frontal system important in the control of diverse forms of behaviour."

Gardner's seven intelligences

Logical-mathematical

Spatial

Musical

Bodily-kinaesthetic

Linguistic

Intrapersonal

Interpersonal

The assumption that traditional intelligence tests assess all the main aspects of intelligence has come under increasing attack. As we will see shortly, many contemporary theorists refute that assumption. They point to important omissions from traditional intelligence tests, and argue that traditional intelligence tests provide an inadequate assessment of the kinds of practical intelligence needed for success in life.

The assumption that intelligence depends mainly on heredity is dubious. As we have seen, we cannot assess the genetic determination of intelligence in individuals. All that can be done is to assess heritability, which measures only the role of genetic factors in producing individual differences in intelligence within a population. Heritability estimates suggest that about 50% (not 80%) of individual differences in intelligence depend on genetic factors, and even that may be an over-estimate.

The assumption that an individual's level of intelligence is difficult to change follows from the notion that heredity is all-important in determining intelligence. Since that notion is incorrect, it is unsurprising that large changes in intelligence can occur. A notable example is the Flynn effect, in which IQ across several countries has increased substantially over recent decades.

If the traditional theory of intelligence is limited, then we must consider alternative theoretical approaches, some of which are discussed below.

## Gardner: Multiple intelligences

Gardner (1983) argues strongly that conventional theoretical approaches are based on a rather narrow view of intelligence. According to Gardner, there are seven separate intelligences rather than a single general factor. The seven intelligences he identified were as follows:

1. *Logical-mathematical intelligence.* This is of special value in handling abstract problems of a logical or mathematical nature.
2. *Spatial intelligence.* This is used when deciding how to go from one place to another, how to arrange suitcases in the boot of a car, and so on.
3. *Musical intelligence.* This is used both for active musical processes such as playing an instrument or singing, and for more passive processes such as appreciating music one hears.
4. *Bodily-kinaesthetic intelligence.* This is involved in the fine control of bodily movements in activities such as sport and dancing.
5. *Linguistic intelligence.* This is involved in language activities on both the input (reading and listening) and the output (writing and speaking) sides.
6. *Intrapersonal intelligence.* According to Gardner et al. (1996, p. 211), "*Intrapersonal intelligence* depends on core processes that enable people to distinguish among their own feelings."
7. *Interpersonal intelligence.* According to Gardner et al. (1996, p. 211), "*Interpersonal intelligence* makes use of core capabilities to recognise and make distinctions among *others*' feeling, beliefs, and intentions."

Gardner (1998) proposed adding *naturalist intelligence* to the seven intelligences he had previously identified. Naturalist intelligence is shown by individuals who can perceive patterns in nature. Charles Darwin is an example of a famous person having outstanding naturalist intelligence. More speculatively, Gardner suggested that there may be two additional intelligences: *spiritual intelligence* and *existential intelligence*. Spiritual intelligence is based on a concern for cosmic issues, and with the achievement of the spiritual as a state of being. Existential intelligence is based on concerns about ultimate issues of existence.

## What is an intelligence?

In order to decide whether there are really seven intelligences, we need to consider what we mean by an intelligence. According to Walters and Gardner (1986, p. 165), an intelligence can be defined as, "an ability or set of abilities that permits an individual to solve problems or fashion products that are of consequence in a particular cultural setting".

As we have seen, factor analysis used to be the main way in which different types of intelligence were identified. However, Gardner (1983) put forward a different approach based on a new set of criteria including the following. First, an intelligence should depend upon identifiable brain structures. Second, studies of brain-damaged patients should indicate that an intelligence can be impaired without the other intelligences being disrupted. Third, an intelligence should involve the use of certain specifiable cognitive operations. Fourth, there should be exceptional individuals showing a remarkable ability (or deficit) with respect to the intelligence. Fifth, there should be a relevant evolutionary history, with development of the intelligence leading to improved adaptation to the environment. Sixth, an intelligence should receive support from appropriate intelligence tests.

It is possible that the seven (or eight, or ten) intelligences proposed by Gardner satisfy his criteria, but it is hard to be sure. A major problem is that there are no good measures of some of the intelligences he has proposed. For example, it is very difficult to assess interpersonal intelligence. Ford and Tisak (1983) administered several tests of interpersonal or social intelligence, and found that on average they only correlated +.36 with each other. Thus, there was no evidence for a major factor of interpersonal or social intelligence. It is very likely that similar problems would arise in trying to measure very vague notions such as spiritual or existential intelligence.

*How would you try to measure interpersonal intelligence?*

There are other problems with the criteria for an intelligence proposed by Gardner (1983). They are very lenient, and so there appear to be several specific skills which meet them. Two examples are face recognition and the ability to learn foreign languages (Mackintosh, 1998).

## Evidence

In spite of the popularity of Gardner's (1983) theory of multiple intelligences, there is surprisingly little directly relevant evidence to support it. An exception is the work of Gardner (1993), who used the theory to study creativity. He selected seven individuals who displayed outstanding creativity during the early part of the twentieth century with respect to one of the seven intelligences. The representative of logical-mathematical intelligence was Albert Einstein, and the other outstanding figures were Pablo Picasso (spatial intelligence), Igor Stravinsky (musical intelligence), Martha Graham (bodily-kinaesthetic intelligence), T.S. Eliot (linguistic intelligence), Sigmund Freud (intrapersonal intelligence), and Mahatma Gandhi (interpersonal intelligence).

Gardner (1993) found there were great similarities in the upbringing of these creative geniuses. With the exception of Martha Graham, they were brought up in families which imposed high moral requirements on them, and which forced them to meet standards of excellence. Unsurprisingly, all seven were extremely ambitious. This led them to sacrifice other aspects of their lives and to cause suffering to their own families. Gardner (p. 32) was also impressed by their childlike qualities, with each of them showing signs of behaving like a "wonder-filled child". Finally, the lives of these creative geniuses suggested that environmental factors played a major role in allowing them to develop one intelligence to an outstanding extent. Picasso was the only one who displayed any obvious talent at an

Three of the individuals selected by Gardner (1993) to demonstrate his theory of multiple intelligence: Igor Stravinsky (for musical intelligence), Pablo Picasso (for spatial intelligence), and Mahatma Gandhi (for interpersonal intelligence).

early age. The other six showed no clear signs of their outstanding creativity and future career success even at the age of 20.

The obvious limitation with Gardner's (1993) approach is that his findings may apply only to the seven outstanding individuals he selected for study. For example, nearly all of Gardner's creative geniuses had relatively easy childhoods. However, many outstanding individuals not considered by Gardner had extremely difficult childhoods. Linus Pauling, who won two Nobel prizes, lost his father when he was seven and later on became an orphan. Michelangelo started an apprenticeship at the age of 13, because his father's inability to earn enough money meant that he had to leave school early. Leonardo da Vinci was illegitimate, and spent very little time with his mother during his childhood.

Another way of testing the theory of multiple intelligences is by basing educational interventions or programmes on it, and this has been done by several research groups. However, as Sternberg and Kaufman (1998, p. 493) pointed out, "Many of the programs are unevaluated, and evaluations of others of these programs seem still to be ongoing, so it is difficult to say at this point what the results will be." An exception is an intervention programme carried out and evaluated by Callahan, Tomlinson, and Plucker (1997). Their programme was based on Gardner's theory, but it failed to produce significant improvements in student achievement or in student self-concept.

## Evaluation

⊕ Gardner's approach to intelligence is broader in scope than most others.
⊕ There is some supporting evidence for each of the seven intelligences originally proposed by Gardner.
⊖ The seven intelligences correlate positively with each other, whereas Gardner (1983) assumed that they were independent. According to Gardner et al. (1996, p. 213), "Positive correlations are obtained because psychometric measures detect not only aptitude within a given intelligence, but also skill in taking short-answer, paper-and-pencil tests." There is no strong support for this contention.
⊖ Musical and bodily kinaesthetic intelligences are less important than the other intelligences in everyday life in Western cultures, with many very successful people being tone-deaf and poorly co-ordinated.

● The theory is descriptive rather than explanatory, and fails to explain how each intelligence works. As Howe (1997, p. 131) pointed out, "Gardner's largely descriptive contribution ... does not even attempt a fundamental question that traditional theory does at least try to answer, namely concerning why some people are more intelligent than others."

## Emotional intelligence

There has been controversy about emotional intelligence in recent years (see Matthews, Zeidner, & Roberts, 2002, for an extensive review). The term was popularised by Goleman (1995). However, it seems to have originated with Salovey and Mayer (1990, p. 189), who defined **emotional intelligence** as, "the ability to monitor one's own and others' emotions, to discriminate among them, and to use the information to guide one's thinking and actions". Thus, they seem to have regarded emotional intelligence as involving aspects of what Gardner (1983) termed intrapersonal intelligence and interpersonal intelligence. In contrast, Goleman adopted an even broader and vaguer definition, which is probably of little use in a scientific context.

Mayer, Caruso, and Salovey (1999) developed the Multi-Factor Emotional Intelligence Scale. This is based on the notion that four main abilities underlie emotional intelligence:

1. Identification of emotion in oneself and in others (e.g., identifying facial emotions).
2. Using emotion to facilitate thought and action (e.g., imagining a feeling until the appropriate emotion is experienced).
3. Understanding and reasoning about emotions (e.g., knowing how emotions develop and change over time).
4. Regulation of emotion in oneself and others (e.g., evaluating various courses of action in emotional circumstances).

> **Test your own EQ**
>
> It's really difficult to test any sort of intelligence, but emotional intelligence includes whether a person is basically optimistic or pessimistic in outlook. It is suggested that how we respond to hassles, setbacks, and obstacles is a clue to this aspect of EQ.
>
> Test yourself! Look at these five sample statements and choose either A or B as your response to each.
>
> 1. You put on weight on holiday and now can't lose it.
>    A. I'll never be thin
>    B. The latest fad diet isn't right for me
>
> 2. You've had a nasty fall playing sport
>    A. I'll never be any good at sport
>    B. The ground was very slippery
>
> 3. You've lost your temper with a friend.
>    A. We always end up arguing
>    B. Something must have upset her/him
>
> 4. You are feeling really run-down and exhausted
>    A. I never get the chance to relax
>    B. I've been unusually busy this month
>
> 5. You've forgotten your best friend's birthday
>    A. I'm just bad at remembering birthdays
>    B. I have had so much on my mind this week
>
> *More As:* You tend to take setbacks personally—you are naturally pessimistic.
> *More Bs:* You believe that life's obstacles can be overcome—you are naturally optimistic.

### Evidence

Davies, Stankov, and Roberts (1998) reported a systematic attempt to clarify what is being assessed by questionnaire and other measures of emotional intelligence. They administered several measures of emotional intelligence, together with tests designed to measure intelligence and major dimensions of personality. They found that emotional intelligence was unrelated to intelligence as traditionally assessed. Emotional intelligence as assessed by self-report questionnaires (e.g., measure of emotional empathy, measure of emotional control) was related to various personality dimensions. More specifically, high levels of emotional intelligence are associated with high levels of extraversion and low levels of neuroticism (see Chapter 13).

Davies et al. (1998) also used various objective tests to assess emotional intelligence. For example, different tests required the participants to decide on which emotions were present when exposed to faces, colours, pieces of music, and sound intervals. The reliabilities of these tests were generally low, suggesting they did not assess emotional intelligence adequately. Davies et al. (p. 1013) came to the following disappointing conclusion: "Questionnaire measures [of emotional intelligence] are too closely related to 'established'

**KEY TERM**

**Emotional intelligence:** the ability to understand one's own emotions as well as those of others.

To what extent is the concept of emotional intelligence useful?

personality traits, whereas objective measures of emotional intelligence suffer from poor reliability."

More promising findings have been obtained from the Multi-Factor Emotional Intelligence Scale, which involves assessing the four aspects of emotional intelligence identified by Mayer et al. (1999). In essence, the participants are asked to carry out a range of tasks relating to emotional intelligence (e.g., identifying the emotions present in faces, musical scores, graphic designs, and stories). How can we decide whether any given answer is "correct"? Mayer et al. assessed correctness in two different ways: (1) consensus scoring (the extent to which the participant's answer corresponded to that of other participants; and (2) expert scoring (the extent to which the participant's answer corresponded to that of two "experts", Mayer and Caruso). There was reasonable reliability of measurement with both types of scoring.

There were moderate relationships between overall scores on the Multi-Factor Emotional Intelligence Scale and general intelligence. Consensus-based scores correlated +.29 with general intelligence, and expert-based scores correlated +.40 with general intelligence. These correlations indicate that the Emotional Intelligence Scale can be regarded as a form of intelligence which is nevertheless reasonably separate from intelligence as traditionally assessed. Consensus-based overall scores correlated modestly with several personality measures (e.g., agreeableness, low neuroticism), but expert-based overall scores had very low correlations with nearly all aspects of personality. Accordingly, emotional intelligence as assessed by the Multi-Factor Emotional Intelligence Scale is *not* simply measuring personality.

There is one troubling problem with the Multi-Factor Emotional Intelligence Scale. Overall scores based on consensus only correlated +.48 with overall scores based on expert judgement. Thus, emotional intelligence as assessed by consensus scoring is substantially different from emotional intelligence as assessed by expert scoring. Unfortunately, we have no solid grounds for preferring one type of scoring over the other.

## Evaluation

● Emotional intelligence probably refers to an ability that is very important in coping successfully with everyday life.
● The Multi-Factor Emotional Intelligence Scale represents a clear advance over previous ways of assessing emotional intelligence. It possesses reasonable reliability, and its measure of emotional intelligence is distinct from personality and from traditional measures of intelligence.
● Most measures of emotional intelligence are seriously deficient. Self-report tests assess traditional personality traits, and objective tests often lack adequate reliability.
● "It remains uncertain whether there is anything about EI [emotional intelligence] that psychologists working within the fields of personality, intelligence, and applied psychological research do not already know" (Roberts, Zeidner, & Matthews, 2001, p. 200).

## Working memory

It seems reasonable to assume that cognitive psychology should have much to contribute to our understanding of intelligence. After all, many of the topics within cognitive psychology (e.g., reasoning, problem solving) are of obvious relevance to intelligence. Surprisingly, it is only within the past 25 years or so that cognitive psychologists have had a substantial impact on our thinking about intelligence. We will consider one such approach here, based on the notion of a working memory system that is involved in processing and storage of information (Baddeley, 1986). In essence, there is plentiful evidence (see Chapter 9) that working memory (especially the central executive) is involved in co-ordinating and supervising a wide range of cognitive processes. As such, several theorists (e.g., Conway, Cowan, Bunting, Therriault, & Minkoff, 2002; Engle, 2002; Lohman, 2001) have argued that individual differences in working memory capacity may underlie individual differences in intelligence. According to Engle (pp. 21–22), working memory is "closely associated with general fluid intelligence ... and may be isomorphic [similar in form] to general intelligence."

*To what extent is intelligence linked to memory?*

There are several ways of assessing working memory capacity. One of the most popular measures is **reading span** (Daneman & Carpenter, 1980). Participants read a series of sentences for comprehension and then recall the final word of each sentence. The reading span is the maximum number of sentences for which they can do this.

## Evidence

Conway et al. (2002) gave their participants tests of fluid intelligence and various measures of working memory capacity (e.g., reading span). They found that there was a strong relationship between working memory capacity and fluid intelligence. In order to explore this relationship further, they also used tests of short-term memory capacity (word span) and of processing speed (e.g., deciding rapidly whether two letters or patterns were the same or different). Short-term memory capacity and processing speed both failed to predict fluid intelligence, indicating that neither of these factors explained the relationship between working memory capacity and fluid intelligence.

What conclusions did Conway et al. (2002) draw from their study? First, they speculated that working memory capacity may form the basis of general intelligence. Second, they suggested that what working memory tasks and tests of fluid intelligence have in common is that they both require controlled attention and the use of appropriate strategies.

Ackerman, Beier, and Boyle (2002) carried out a similar study in which they assessed working memory capacity, general intelligence, and processing speed. They found that working memory capacity correlated approximately +.57 with general intelligence, suggesting that working memory may be important in determining individual differences in intelligence. However, they also found that processing speed was much more strongly associated with working memory capacity than with intelligence. Thus, there may be important differences in the abilities involved in working memory capacity and intelligence.

> **The influence of Western education**
>
> Sternberg (1997, 2003) identifies two key processes, memory and analysis, in intelligence. But he also points out that traditional Western education and skills learning are based on these processes and therefore we have a kind of self-fulfilling prophecy: Students naturally gifted in memory and analysis abilities do well and are considered intelligent as the educational system uses memory and analysis skills to measure learning and assess intelligence.

We have assumed so far that there is a single working memory capacity. However, this was disputed by Shah and Miyake (1996), who suggested instead that there are separate verbal and spatial working memory systems. They obtained the following measures: verbal IQ, spatial IQ, word span, and spatial span. This last task involved participants deciding whether each of a set of letters was in normal or mirror-image orientation. After that, they had to indicate the direction in which the top of the letter had been pointing. The spatial span was the maximum number of letters for which they could do this. Reading span correlated highly with verbal IQ but not spatial IQ, and spatial span correlated highly with spatial IQ but not verbal IQ. This pattern of findings is consistent with the notion of separate verbal and spatial systems.

## Evaluation

- ⊕ Much can be learned about individual differences in intelligence by focusing on key systems (e.g., working memory) identified by cognitive psychologists.
- ⊕ There is a moderately strong relationship between working memory capacity and intelligence.
- ⊖ There may be important differences in the abilities involved in working memory capacity and in intelligence (Ackerman et al., 2002).
- ⊖ The evidence relating working memory capacity and intelligence is correlational. Thus, it is hard to know whether working memory capacity influences intelligence or vice versa.
- ⊖ It is generally assumed that there is a single working memory. However, there may be somewhat separate verbal and spatial working memories (Shah & Miyake, 1996).

**KEY TERM**

**Reading span:** the largest number of sentences read for comprehension from which an individual can recall all the final words; a measure of working memory capacity.

# SUMMARY

**Intelligence testing**

All good intelligence tests possess three features. They are standardised tests, they have good reliability, and they have good validity. Reliability is generally assessed by the test–retest method, and validity is assessed by means of concurrent and predictive validity. IQ correlates moderately with educational attainment and with occupational status. The assumption that IQ measures inborn ability whereas educational attainment is merely a measure of acquired knowledge is not supported by the evidence.

**Factor theories**

Factor analysis can be used to identify the structure of human intelligence. Spearman claimed that there is a single general factor ("g") and numerous specific factors, whereas Thurstone argued that there are seven primary mental abilities. These two views can be combined into a three-level hierarchical model with the general factor at the top level, primary mental abilities or group factors at the intermediate level, and specific factors at the bottom level. Factor analysis is descriptive rather than explanatory, and it tells us little about the cognitive processes underlying intelligent behaviour.

**Heredity and environment**

Some effects of heredity and environment on intelligence are interdependent rather than independent. Findings from twin studies suggest that genetic factors play an important role in determining individual differences in intelligence, and the same conclusion follows from adoption studies. The heritability of intelligence in Western societies is probably approximately .5. However, heritability is a limited measure and does *not* assess genetic determination. Studies of group differences have indicated that environmental factors (e.g., deprivation) account for most (or all) differences between blacks and whites in intelligence.

**Environmental influences**

Shared environment and non-shared environment both influence differences in children's levels of intelligence, but shared environment becomes unimportant in adulthood. Compelling evidence that environmental factors can have a substantial effect on IQ is available in the Flynn effect, which is the rapid rise in IQ in most Western countries over the past 50 years or so. Several environmental factors (e.g., mother has a history of

mental illness, few positive interactions between mother and child) are associated with children's intelligence, but it is hard to show that there are causal effects. Attempts to provide an enriched environment for disadvantaged children (e.g., Operation Headstart) typically produced beneficial effects which reduced over time. It is hard to compare intelligence in different cultures. Use of dynamic testing may be preferable to static testing when assessing intelligence in some other cultures.

The traditional theory of intelligence assumed that intelligence is mostly determined by heredity, is relatively unchanging, and can be adequately assessed by intelligence tests. These assumptions are no more than partially correct. Gardner proposed a theory of multiple intelligences, in which he claimed to have identified seven or eight independent intelligences. However, these intelligences are not independent, and Gardner's approach is mainly descriptive. Emotional intelligence may be important. It has proved difficult to show that emotional intelligence differs from previously established measures of intelligence and/or personality, but there has been recent progress. There are strong links between working memory capacity and intelligence, but the extent to which working memory capacity forms the basis of intelligence is controversial.

*Theories of intelligence*

# FURTHER READING

- Mackintosh, N.J. (1998). *IQ and human intelligence*. Oxford, UK: Oxford University Press. This is a truly excellent book by a leading British psychologist. It is notable for its fair-minded approach and numerous insights.
- Matthews, G., Zeidner, M., & Roberts, R.D. (2002). *Emotional intelligence: Science and myth*. Cambridge, MA: MIT Press. This book provides a balanced assessment of our current knowledge of emotional intelligence.
- Sternberg, R.J., & Ben-Zeev, T. (2001). *Complex cognition: The psychology of human thought*. Oxford, UK: Oxford University Press. Several chapters (especially Chapter 11) contain good introductory discussions of topics relating to intelligence.

- **Freud's psychoanalytic approach**
  Theory based on the importance of early childhood in the development of personality.

  *General introduction to Freud's ideas: id, ego, superego*
  *His three levels of the mind: conscious, preconscious, unconscious*
  *Defence mechanisms, including repression*
  *Freud's five-stage theory of psychosexual development: oral, anal, phallic, latency, genital*

- **Humanistic approach**
  Rogers' application of the humanistic approach to personality.

  *Rogers' client-centred theory*
  *The emphasis on self-concept, ideal self, and self-actualisation*
  *The defence mechanisms of distortion and denial*

- **Personality assessment**
  Discussion of four ways to measure personality.

  *Explanation of reliability and five main types of validity*
  *Self-report questionnaires and the criterion-keying approach*
  *Ratings*
  *Objective tests*
  *Projective tests*

- **Trait theories of personality**
  Attempts to define personality using a variety of traits.

  *The application of factor analysis*
  *Cattell's trait theory and the 16PF*
  *Eysenck's trait theory: neuroticism, extraversion, psychoticism*
  *The five-factor theory: extraversion, agreeableness, conscientiousness, emotional stability, and culture*
  *Cross-cultural trait studies*

- **Social cognitive theory**
  Bandura's individual differences approach.

  *The idea of observational learning*
  *The vicarious reinforcement mechanisms*
  *The association between self-efficacy and personality*
  *Self-regulation of behaviour*

# Personality

# 13

One of the most fascinating things about our dealings with other people is the endless variety of human personality. Some people are nearly always cheerful and friendly, others are unfriendly and depressed, and still others are aggressive and hostile. This chapter is concerned with attempts to understand these individual differences in personality.

What is meant by the word "personality"? According to Child (1968, p. 83), personality consists of "the more or less stable, internal factors that make one person's behaviour consistent from one time to another, and different from the behaviour other people would manifest in comparable situations." There are four key words in that definition:

1. *Stable*. Personality remains relatively constant or unchanging over time.
2. *Internal*. Personality lies within us, but how we behave is determined in part by our personality.
3. *Consistent*. If personality remains constant over time, and if personality determines behaviour, then we would expect people to behave fairly consistently.
4. *Different*. When we talk of personality, we assume there are considerable individual differences, leading different people to behave differently in similar situations.

What are the main factors determining adult personality? If you ask six psychologists this question, you can expect to get six different answers. According to Freud, adult personality is influenced mainly by childhood experiences, although he accepted that biological factors were also important. According to humanistic psychologists such as Carl Rogers and Abraham Maslow, personality depends importantly on one's adult experiences. In contrast to Freud, they argued that personality can easily be changed, provided the individual alters his/her self-concept. Trait theorists such as Raymond Cattell, H.J. Eysenck, Paul Costa, and Robert McCrae emphasised the importance of genetic factors in determining personality. Finally, cognitive social psychologists such as Albert Bandura claim that individual differences in behaviour depend mainly on specific learning experiences (e.g., those involving reward or punishment).

Which of the above views is correct? There is some truth in all of them. Thus, adult personality depends in complex ways on heredity, on childhood experiences, on the development of the self-concept, and on specific learning experiences.

You may be surprised to learn that the notion that everyone has their own personality has only gained general acceptance fairly recently in the history of the human species. Before the Renaissance, people regarded themselves as members of a family, village, or other group rather than as individuals. Indeed, many people in Asian countries continue to do so to this day (see later in the chapter).

According to Winter and Barenbaum (1999), the modern study of human personality had its origins in three important developments occurring during the nineteenth and early twentieth centuries. First, there was the growth of individualism, with people becoming more aware that everyone has a separate identity. Second, there was increased interest in human irrationality and the unconscious, which owed much to Freud's enormous influence. Third, there was a growing emphasis on measurement. For example, Galton (1883, p. 79) argued that, "The character which shapes our conduct is a definite and durable 'something', and therefore … it is reasonable to attempt to measure it."

In this chapter, we focus on important theorists who have contributed to our understanding of personality. This is the most common way of dealing with the area of personality. However, it raises an interesting point:

*It is true that the lives and insights of Freud, Jung, Adler, Sullivan, Rogers, Maslow, etc. make extremely interesting reading, and their historical contributions highlight some of the issues of human relationships that must continue at the centre of personality research. But we may well ask why no one teaches cognition, social psychology, developmental psychology, or abnormal psychology by using the views of famous people as the centrepiece for the entire course (Singer & Kolligan, 1987, p. 535).*

Why do most books and courses on personality seem like a walk through the graveyard? One reason is that most major personality theories are strongly associated with a given individual. In addition, different theorists have had very different views about human personality. As a result, we can understand the key issues and controversies in personality research by focusing on the (sometimes extreme) views of the leading personality theorists.

## FREUD'S PSYCHOANALYTIC APPROACH

Sigmund Freud (1856–1939) is the most influential psychologist of all time. He is best known for developing psychoanalysis, which was the first systematic form of therapy for mental disorders (see Chapter 22). However, he made numerous other contributions to psychology. Of most relevance for this chapter is his theory of psychosexual development, which was in many ways a theory of personality. We will turn to this theory shortly, after a more general introduction to some of Freud's key theoretical ideas (see Chapter 16).

Sigmund Freud (1856–1939) made numerous contributions to psychology, including the development of psychoanalysis, and his theory of psychosexual development.

Freud assumed that the mind is divided into three parts. First, there is the **id**. This contains the sexual and aggressive instincts, and is located in the unconscious mind. The sexual instinct is known as libido. The id works in accord with the pleasure principle, with an emphasis on immediate gratification. Second, there is the **ego**. This is the conscious, rational mind, and develops during the first 2 years of life. It works on the reality principle, taking account of what is going on in the environment. Third, there is the **superego**. It develops at about the age of 5, when the child adopts many of the values of the same-sexed parent in a process known as **identification**. The superego is partly conscious and partly unconscious, and consists of the conscience and ego-ideal. The conscience is formed as a result of the child being punished, and it makes the child feel guilty about behaving badly. The ego-ideal is formed through the use of reward. It makes the child feel proud after behaving well.

Freud also assumed that there are three levels of the mind: the conscious, the preconscious, and the unconscious. The conscious consists of those thoughts which are currently the focus of attention. The preconscious consists of information and ideas which can be retrieved easily from memory and brought into consciousness. The unconscious consists of information which is either very hard (or almost impossible) to bring into conscious awareness.

The emergence of the ego and superego during the course of development has important implications, particularly when conflicts arise among the three parts of the mind. For example, there are frequent conflicts between the id and the superego. The reason for this is that the id desires immediate gratification, but the superego takes account of moral standards. Conflicts produce anxiety, which are perceived as being very threatening by the

**KEY TERMS**

**Id:** that part of the mind containing the sexual instinct.
**Ego:** the conscious, rational mind.
**Superego:** the part of the mind concerned with moral issues and cultural values.
**Identification:** children's imitation of the beliefs and behaviour of the same-sexed parent.

ego. The ego defends itself by using various **defence mechanisms**, which are various ways in which anxiety can be reduced (see Chapter 22). The most important defence mechanism is **repression**, which involves keeping anxiety-provoking material out of consciousness. Other defence mechanisms are displacement (shifting impulses away from a threatening object towards a less threatening object) and denial (refusing to accept the existence or reality of a threatening event). An example of displacement is kicking your cat or dog when someone in authority has criticised you publicly. An example of denial is refusing to accept that an important relationship is in great danger of breaking up.

An important implication of Freud's views is that information about threatening and/or traumatic childhood events can be stored in the unconscious for many years. As a result, such information can influence the individual concerned in adult life. Indeed, one of Freud's central assumptions was that treatment of adults suffering from a mental disorder should revolve around gaining access to this threatening material going back to the years of childhood (see Chapter 22).

In sum, Freud's theory of the mind represents a theory of motivation, a cognitive theory, and a social psychological theory. The id contains basic motivational forces, the ego corresponds to the cognitive system, and the superego or conscience internalises the values of family and of society generally. However, Freud did not really develop the social and cognitive aspects, and it would be misleading to regard him as a social or cognitive theorist.

## Theory of psychosexual development

According to Freud, the experiences children have during the first 5 years of life are very important. Their personalities are developing during that period, and adult personality depends very much on the experiences of early childhood. Most of Freud's approach to personality development was contained in his theory of psychosexual development. According to this theory, children pass through five stages:

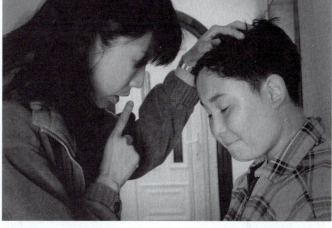

According to Freud, the conscience is formed as a result of being punished as a child.

1.  *Oral stage.* This lasts up to the age of 18 months; infants in this stage enjoy various activities involving their mouths, lips, and tongues. Children may experience problems at this stage (e.g., due to rapid weaning). These problems can produce adults with an oral receptive character (very dependent on other people) or an oral aggressive character (hostile and domineering).

2.  *Anal stage.* This lasts between 18 and 36 months, and involves the anal area as the main source of satisfaction. This is the stage at which toilet training occurs. Children experiencing problems at this stage may become adults with an anal retentive character (mean, stubborn, and orderly) or they may become very generous and giving.

3.  *Phallic stage.* This stage lasts between the ages of 3 and 6. During this stage, the penis or clitoris becomes the major source of satisfaction. At about the age of 5, boys acquire the **Oedipus complex**, in which they have sexual desires for their mother and consequent fear of their father. This complex is resolved by identification with their father. A similar process in girls is based on the Electra complex (not a term used by Freud), in which they desire their fathers. Those experiencing problems at this stage develop a phallic character. Men with a phallic character are vain and self-assured, whereas women with a phallic character fight hard for superiority over men.

4.  *Latency stage.* This lasts from the age of 6 until puberty. During this stage, boys and girls experience relatively few sexual feelings, and ignore each other.

5.  *Genital stage.* This lasts from puberty onwards. In this stage, the main source of sexual pleasure is the genitals. The key difference from the phallic stage is that the focus in the genital stage is on sexual pleasure with another person. Children who have avoided problems during the earlier stages develop a genital character in adulthood. People with this character are mature, and are able to love and to be loved.

**KEY TERMS**

**Defence mechanisms:** strategies used by the ego to defend itself against anxiety.

**Repression:** Freud's notion that very anxiety-provoking material is kept out of conscious awareness.

**Oedipus complex:** the Freudian notion that boys at about the age of 5 are frightened of their father and desire their mother.

The Greek writer Sophocles wrote the play *Oedipus Tyrannus*, which was first performed in Athens in about 425 BC. It was based on the myth of Oedipus, King of Thebes, who unwittingly kills his father and marries his mother.

**Freud's stages of psychosexual development**

| Stage | Approximate age | Summary |
| --- | --- | --- |
| Oral | 0–18 months | Satisfaction from eating, sucking, etc. |
| Anal | 18–36 months | Interest in and satisfaction from anal region |
| Phallic | 3–6 years | Genitals become source of satisfaction |
| Latency | 6 years old–puberty | Boys and girls spend little time together |
| Genital | From onset of puberty | Genitals main source of sexual pleasure |

According to Freud, there can be serious consequences if a child is frustrated by receiving insufficient gratification at any psychosexual stage. There can also be serious consequences if a child receives excessive gratification at a given stage. What consequences are likely to follow? Freud argued that frustration or excessive gratification leads to **fixation**, in which basic sexual energy remains attached to that stage during adulthood. When an adult has great problems, he/she will show **regression**, with their behaviour becoming more like their behaviour when they were children. Adults typically regress to the psychosexual stage at which they fixated as children. An important implication of this part of the theory is that adult mental disorders typically have their origins in childhood problems and difficulties.

## Evidence

We will make a start by considering the implications of Freud's views for the measurement of personality. Freud would undoubtedly be very surprised if he knew that psychologists in the twenty-first century typically assess personality by means of self-report questionnaires. His surprise would be due to the fact that individuals completing such questionnaires can only make use of information about themselves that is consciously accessible. Freud's emphasis on the power of the unconscious means that he would have regarded the questionnaire-based approach as inadequate.

There is much evidence to indicate that the information available to conscious awareness is often very limited. For example, Nisbett and Wilson (1977) carried out a study in which participants were presented with five essentially identical pairs of stockings, and were asked to decide which pair was the best. Most of them chose the right-most pair, and so their decisions were actually influenced by relative spatial position. However, the participants did not suggest spatial position as a reason for their choice. Indeed, they

**Useful mnemonic**

To help you remember Freud's stages of psychosexual development, the following mnemonic is made from the initial letter of each stage: Old Age Pensioners Love Greens!

**KEY TERMS**

**Fixation:** spending a long time at a given stage of psychosexual development.

**Regression:** returning to earlier stages of development when severely stressed.

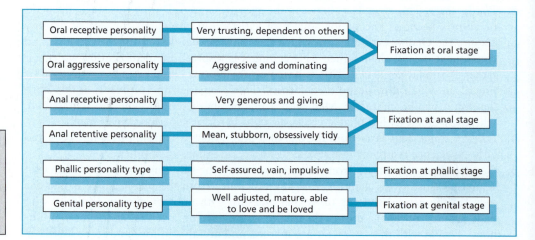

vehemently denied that it had played any part in their decision, referring instead to slight differences in colour, texture, and so on among the pairs of stockings as having been important.

There is reasonable support for the *general* approach taken by Freud, in that childhood experiences clearly influence the development of human personality (see Westen, 1998, for a review). However, this is *not* the same as arguing that there is support for Freud's specific theoretical assumptions. Mickelson, Kessler, and Shaver (1997) considered a random sample of more than 5000 adults. Parental loss or separation in childhood was associated with low attachment security and high ratings of insecure attachment in adulthood. Those adults who had experienced serious traumas in childhood (e.g., serious neglect, sexual assault) were more likely than other adults to have anxious attachments.

*In what ways might our early childhood experiences influence our personality?*

Franz et al. (1996) also reported evidence suggesting that childhood experiences have a long-term impact. Adult levels of depression at the age of 41 were predicted well by parental coldness when they were only 5 years old. In addition, an overall measure of difficult childhood experiences (e.g., divorce, frequent moves, loss) predicted depression in middle age.

There is a real problem with interpreting the findings of most studies finding a relationship between childhood experiences and adult problems. What we have is only correlational evidence, and we cannot use correlations to prove causes. For example, suppose an adult with serious emotional problems had parents who made his childhood miserable. It is possible that the unhappy childhood experiences helped to create the emotional problems in adulthood. However, it is also possible that genetic factors common to the parents and to their child are responsible. Kendler et al. (1992) carried out a twin study, and attempted to remove statistically the influence of genetic factors from their findings. They still found that parental loss through separation (e.g., divorce) was associated with depression in adult life, whereas parental loss through death was not. In a similar twin study, Kendler et al. (1996) found that childhood parental loss through separation was associated with a tendency to alcoholism, and this association was still present when the impact of genetic factors was removed.

There is support for some of the personality types identified by Freud. For example, Kline and Storey (1977) found the three main characteristics of the anal retentive character (stubbornness, meanness, orderliness) were often found together in the same person. There is also evidence that some people possess all of the characteristics of the oral receptive character, with others possessing all the features of the oral aggressive character (Kline, 1981).

Evidence for the existence of some of the personality types suggested by Freud does *not* show the theory is correct. Freud assumed these adult personality types depend on specific childhood experiences, but there is practically no convincing evidence that that is the case.

There has been fierce controversy concerning Freud's assumption that threatening and/or traumatic events in childhood are repressed and can subsequently be recovered. The relevant evidence is discussed more fully in Chapter 9, but will be briefly referred to here. Andrews et al. (1999) obtained detailed information about such recovered memories from over 200 adult patients, and their findings suggested that many recovered memories are likely to be genuine. For example, there was supporting evidence (e.g., other people reported being abused by the same person) for the claims of 41% of the patients.

In contrast, some patients have admitted that they have reported false memories of childhood abuse. For example, Lief and Fetkewicz (1995) studied 40 patients who had retracted their "memories" of childhood abuse. These patients generally claimed they had done so under pressure from their therapist. In about 80% of these cases, the therapist had made direct suggestions that the patient was the victim of sexual abuse. In contrast, there was little evidence of excessive pressure from the therapist among the patients studied by Andrews et al. (1999). Overall, the evidence for recovered memories is inconclusive.

> ## CASE STUDY: *Recovered memories?*
>
> The case of Lydia Carvey was reported in the *Sunday Times* (Driscoll, 1998). Ms Carvey suffered from depression in middle age and was hospitalised. Under drug treatment and psychotherapy she recalled years of childhood sexual abuse by her own father, memories that, later, she realised were false. Unhappily her father died before she came to this realisation.
>
> Case studies like these were scrutinised by a working party from the Royal College of Psychiatrists in the UK, chaired by Professor Sydney Brandon. The report concluded that these recovered memories should not be regarded as literal truth.

The evidence that Freud himself reported to support his own theoretical approach was very flimsy. It consisted mainly of about a dozen case studies, most of which are not at all convincing. For example, consider the famous case of Little Hans, which was claimed to illustrate the development of the Oedipus complex. When Hans was 3 years old, he began to exhibit a lot of interest in his penis, which caused his mother to threaten to cut it off. When he was about 5, he saw a horse-drawn van tip over on its side. This caused him to develop a fear of horses, and to refer to "black things around horses' mouths and the things in front of their eyes". As a result of his fear of horses, he was unwilling to leave the safety of his own home.

Freud's diagnosis was that Little Hans was suffering from an Oedipus complex. According to Freud, he was sexually attracted to his mother, but was very frightened his father would punish him for this. The fear that Hans had for his father turned into a fear of horses, with Freud arguing that horses' black muzzles and blinkers resembled the moustache and glasses of Hans' father. The fact that Hans' fear of horses caused him to remain at home had the significant advantage that he could spend more time with his mother, to whom allegedly he was sexually attracted.

Most people are unconvinced by Freud's account of Little Hans. There is very little evidence that Hans desired sexual contact with his mother or that he was very frightened of his father. Furthermore, the idea that Hans' great sexual excitement somehow turned into a state of high anxiety is fanciful.

*What problems arise from using case studies to generate or support personality theories?*

## Evaluation

- ⊕ "Freud ... drew the big picture, and proposed broad stages and structures that could account for an astonishing array of observable phenomena" (Westen & Gabbard, 1999, pp. 89–90).
- ⊕ Adult personality depends in part on the experiences of early childhood.
- ⊕ Freud put forward what is probably the first systematic theory of personality.
- ⊕ At least some of the personality types suggested by Freud do seem to exist.
- ⊕ The notion that individuals with certain types of personality are more vulnerable than others to the development of mental disorders is both powerful and convincing (see Chapter 22).
- ⊖ It is hard to establish accurately what childhood experiences any given adult has had.
- ⊖ It is very hard to prove that early childhood experiences have actually determined adult personality many years later, and so the theory is difficult to test.
- ⊖ What Freud said about the role of motivation in human personality is greatly oversimplified. As Westen and Gabbard (1999, p. 66) pointed out, "Not all motives can be reduced to sex and aggression; motives for intimacy are not uniformly reducible to sexual desire; not all motives (particularly aggressive motives) build up and require discharge."
- ⊖ Adult personality depends more on heredity and on the experiences of adolescence and adulthood than was assumed by Freud (discussed later in the chapter).
- ⊖ Freud's stage-based theory implies that personality development occurs in a more orderly way than is actually the case.
- ⊖ "Psychoanalysts seriously shot themselves in the foot by never evolving from case study methods [based on individual patients] as their primary mode of knowledge generation and hypothesis testing" (Westen & Gabbard, 1999).

## HUMANISTIC APPROACH

The humanistic approach to psychology was developed mainly by Carl Rogers and Abraham Maslow in the United States during the 1950s, but Rogers applied the approach more systematically to personality. According to Cartwright (1979, pp. 5–6), humanistic psychology, "is concerned with topics that are meaningful to human beings, focusing especially upon subjective experience and the unique, unpredictable events in individual human lives". Humanistic psychologists have focused on issues such as personal responsibility, free will, and the individual's striving towards personal growth and fulfilment. Of particular importance, the humanistic psychologists strongly favoured a reliance on **phenomenology**, which involves reporting pure experience with no attempt at interpretation by the person doing the reporting. According to Rogers (1951, p. 133), "This kind of personal, phenomenological type of study … is far more valuable than the traditional 'hard-headed' empirical approach. This kind of study, often scorned by psychologists as being 'merely self-reports', actually gives the deepest insight into what the experience has meant."

## Rogers' client-centred theory

Carl Rogers (1902–1987) devoted much of his working life to the search for improved methods of treating patients with mental disorders. This search led him to develop client-centred therapy, but which was later called person-centred therapy (see Chapter 22). Here we will focus mainly on the general theoretical ideas underlying person-centred therapy.

Rogers (e.g., 1951, 1959, 1967) argued that the concept of "self" is of fundamental importance to an understanding of human behaviour. For example, Rogers (1967, p. 108) had this to say when discussing what mattered to his clients:

> *Below the level of the problem situation about which the individual is complaining—behind the trouble with studies or wife or employer …—lies one central search. It seems to me that at the bottom each person is asking "Who am I, really? How can I get in touch with this real self, underlying all my surface behaviour? How can I become myself?"*

A key notion in Rogers' approach is that of the **self-concept**, which is an individual's thoughts and feelings about him/herself as an individual and in relation to others. The focus was mainly on those parts of the self accessible to consciousness, because Rogers argued that it is impossible to study systematically any parts of the self existing below the level of conscious awareness. Another key notion is that of the **ideal self**, which is the self-concept that the individual would most like to possess. Not surprisingly, Rogers assumed that happy people have a much smaller discrepancy between their self-concept and ideal self than those who are relatively unhappy.

Abraham Maslow (top) and Carl Rogers (bottom), two of the main developers of the humanistic approach to psychology.

### A humanistic perspective of personality development

In 1951 Carl Rogers published *Client-centred therapy*, a book outlining his approach to therapy and his theory of personality.

He began from the assumption that each individual is the centre of his world of experience. The sensations and thoughts of this private world can only ever truly be known by the individual and cannot be represented by external measurement. There is no need to have a concept of a "true" reality. Reality for each individual is what they perceive. The best vantage point for understanding behaviour is from the internal frame of reference of the individual him/her self.

Rogers' belief is that the individual reacts as an organised whole, rather than a set of stimulus–response (S–R) links. He also says that people have one basic tendency that causes them to strive to actualise, maintain, and enhance their lives. People have a self-righting tendency—an urge for independence, the desire to be self-determined and strive toward socialised maturity.

As a child grows up he or she learns to differentiate what is "me" (the conscious concept of self) from the rest of the world. This self-concept is formed as a result of interaction with the environment. The values attached to the self concept (i.e., self-esteem) are derived either from direct experience or from what other people tell you about yourself.

Through life the individual can assimilate experience in one of three ways: (a) organise them into the self concept, (b) ignore them entirely as being irrelevant, (c) distort the experience because it is inconsistent with self. Assimilation into the self-concept is most usual and most healthy. When a person does something that is apparently inconsistent with their self concept they will disown it, for example by saying "I was not myself". In many cases of psychological maladjustment individuals say "I don't know why I do it" or "I'm just not myself when I do those things". Rogers points out that the problem here is that their behaviour has not been incorporated into their self concept and therefore cannot be controlled. When they can accept themselves, then they are able to grow psychologically.

*How would you describe your ideal self?*

How can we assess the self-concept and the ideal self? One way is by using the **Q-sort method**. With this method, the person being assessed is presented with a pile of cards, each containing a statement of personal relevance (e.g., "I am a friendly person"; "I am tense most of the time"). The person's first task is to decide which statements best describe his/her own self, which statements are the next best in their descriptive power, and so on right down to the least descriptive statements. After that, precisely the same procedure is followed with respect to the individual's ideal self. Finally, the investigator calculates the discrepancy between the two categorisations.

Rogers emphasised the importance of **congruence**, by which he meant a lack of conflict between an individual's perceived self and their experience and behaviour. In general, we try to preserve congruence in our daily lives: "Most of the ways of behaving which are adopted by the organism are those which are consistent with the concept of the self" (Rogers, 1951, p. 507). Thus, we are motivated to achieve congruence. Rogers (p. 487) also argued that we are strongly motivated towards **self-actualisation** or full realisation of our potential as human beings: "The organism has one basic tendency and striving—to actualise, maintain, and enhance the experiencing organism."

What happens if we experience incongruence (e.g., behaving aggressively even though we regard ourselves as gentle)? According to Rogers, incongruence often creates anxiety, and can cause us to respond defensively. Two key defensive processes are denial and distortion. **Denial** involves refusing to accept at the conscious level that the experience happened. **Distortion**, which occurs more often than denial, involves misremembering the experience to make it consistent with the perceived self (e.g., "I didn't really behave aggressively at all").

According to Rogers, in healthy development parents give their children **unconditional positive regard**, meaning they are fully accepted by their parents regardless of how they behave. As a consequence, the children have no need to deny or distort their experiences to achieve congruence. In contrast, some parents impose **conditions of worth** on their children, meaning the children have to behave in certain ways to be accepted by their parents. This can easily produce incongruence. Suppose the parents require politeness at all times from their children for them to be regarded positively. That creates incongruence when the children are rude.

## Evidence

Rogers' entire approach was rather anti-scientific. As a result, there is little in the way of convincing evidence for or against his theoretical approach. However, we will consider a few relevant studies. Gough, Lazzari, and Fioravanti (1978) used the Q-sort method to identify air force officers having a large discrepancy between their self-concept and their ideal self, and those having only a small discrepancy. According to Rogers, those with a small discrepancy should have been better adjusted psychologically. When all the air force officers were rated by other people, those with a small discrepancy were perceived as being efficient, co-operative, and outgoing, whereas those with a large discrepancy were perceived as unfriendly, awkward, and confused.

Rogers' view that a small discrepancy between the real and ideal selves can be regarded as a sign of maturity is probably oversimplified. Katz and Zigler (1967) assessed the real and ideal selves of students between the ages of 11 and 17. According to Rogers' theory, the older students should have had smaller discrepancies between their real and ideal selves than the younger ones, but precisely the opposite was found. In addition, the discrepancy was larger in the most intelligent students. We could account for these findings by assuming that increasing maturity allows individuals to become more sensitive to differences between their own behaviour and their internal standards.

Rogers assumed that we are motivated to preserve congruence between our self-concept and our experience. There is indirect evidence in support of this assumption. Suinn, Osborne, and Winfree (1962) gave their participants the task of recalling adjectives that other people had used to describe them. The participants' recall was best for those adjectives consistent with their self-concept, and it was worst for adjectives inconsistent with their self-concept. Aronson and Mettee (1968) considered the relationship between self-concept and behaviour.

They argued that individuals high in self-esteem would be unlikely to cheat, because such behaviour would be inconsistent with their self-concept. In contrast, there would be much less incongruence between low self-esteem and cheating, and so cheating should be more common among those low in self-esteem. Their findings supported these predictions.

According to Rogers, the self-concepts of well-adjusted individuals are coherent and integrated. This assumption was investigated by Donahue, Robins, Roberts, and John (1993). Participants indicated the extent to which their feelings and behaviour were similar across their various social roles (e.g., daughter, student, friend). Individuals who seemed well-adjusted (i.e., high self-esteem, non-anxious, not depressed) typically had an integrated self-concept, in that they perceived themselves as being essentially the same person across their social roles. In contrast, poorly adjusted individuals with low self-esteem differed greatly across their social roles. Thus, the findings provided reasonably strong support for Rogers.

*How does our self-esteem influence our behaviour?*

## Evaluation

- ➕ Rogers was concerned with issues of major concern to people, such as making their self-concept resemble their ideal self more closely.
- ➕ Rogers' theoretical approach led him to develop client-centred (or person-centred) therapy, which has proved of moderate effectiveness (see Chapters 22 and 23).
- ➖ "It is difficult to evaluate Rogers' theory, since it is more of a philosophical view of the person than a formal, concrete psychological theory" (Cooper, 1998, p. 22).
- ➖ Rogers' great reliance on phenomenology means he did not explore systematically unconscious processes and structures.
- ➖ There is very little research directly addressing the assumption that our major motivating force is to achieve self-actualisation.
- ➖ Rogers' approach is limited. Adult personality is partly determined by childhood experiences and partly by genetic factors, but these influences on adult personality were largely ignored by Rogers.

## PERSONALITY ASSESSMENT

If we are to achieve a good understanding of personality, it is important to develop effective ways of measuring it. Four major kinds of personality tests have been developed:

1. Questionnaires.
2. Ratings.
3. Objective tests.
4. Projective tests.

We will consider all four kinds of personality tests shortly. As with intelligence tests (see Chapter 12), useful personality tests possess three characteristics: (1) high reliability, (2) high validity, and (3) standardisation. **Reliability** is the extent to which a test produces consistent results. One common way of assessing reliability is the test–retest method, in which a personality test is given to the same individuals on two occasions, and the scores are then correlated. As you might imagine, the correlation goes down when there is a long interval of time between test and retest, presumably because personality changes somewhat over time. Another way of assessing reliability is to calculate the internal consistency or cohesiveness of the items within it. The standard measure of internal consistency is Cronbach's alpha. The technical definition of this measure

*There are great differences in personality, sometimes within the same family.*

is that it is the estimated correlation of the test with any other test of the same length with similar items.

**Validity** refers to the extent to which a test measures what it claims to be measuring. Validity is important because, "the conclusions of researchers and assessors of personality are going to be formed in terms of what they *think* they are measuring. If what they're measuring isn't what they think they're measuring, the researcher will draw false conclusions" (Carver & Scheier, 2000, p. 43).

Some of the main forms of assessing the validity of a test are as follows:

1. **Concurrent validity**. This is the most important type of validity. The test is correlated with a relevant external measure or criterion of the underlying construct the test is supposed to be measuring. For example, suppose a test is designed to measure extraversion. We could use the opinions of other people as the criterion. If those scoring highly on the test are regarded as extraverted by other people, and those who obtain low test scores are regarded as introverted by others, then we would have high concurrent validity. Concurrent validity is typically expressed in the form of a correlation coefficient. The value of this correlation coefficient runs between 0.00 (indicating the test's ability to predict some other measure is non-existent) to +1.00 (indicating perfect predictions).
2. **Predictive validity**. This is the same as concurrent validity, except that the criterion is assessed *after* the assessment of personality. For example, we might use scores on a test of **trait anxiety** (the tendency to experience high levels of anxiety) to predict the likelihood of developing an anxiety disorder over the following 5 years.
3. **Construct validity**. This involves testing one or more hypotheses involving the personality dimension of interest. For example, suppose a theory states that anxiety makes people worry and thus impairs their ability to perform complex tasks. We could test this hypothesis by comparing individuals high and low in trait anxiety on their ability to perform a complex task.
4. **Discriminant validity**. It is important to show that a test doesn't measure characteristics it is not supposed to be measuring, and that is what is assessed by discriminant validity. For example, suppose that we obtain construct validity for a test of trait anxiety by showing that it correlates negatively with academic performance. This finding might be obtained because trait anxiety correlates negatively with intelligence, and low intelligence produces poor academic performance. Accordingly, it would be useful to show discriminant validity by demonstrating that the test of trait anxiety is uncorrelated with intelligence. We can see the importance of discriminant validity by considering tests devised to assess individual differences in anxiety and depression. Watson and Clark (1984) considered many of these tests. They discovered that tests allegedly measuring anxiety often correlate very highly (about +.7) with tests of depression, and vice versa. Thus, these tests are unsatisfactory because they lack discriminant validity.
5. **Face validity**. This is the simplest form of validity. It refers to the extent to which the kinds of items contained within a test seem to be of obvious relevance to the construct the test is designed to measure. However, high face validity can be a problem if the test is designed to measure characteristics (e.g., dishonesty, tendency to criminality) that people find threatening or undesirable. In those circumstances, high face validity can make it easier for respondents to distort their responses.

Before leaving the issue of validity, you should be warned that the terms used to refer to different forms of validity vary from textbook to textbook. Accordingly, do not be surprised if the definitions provided here don't all match up with those in other books!

Finally, there is standardisation. **Standardisation** involves giving a test to large, representative samples of people so that the significance of an individual's score on the test can be evaluated by comparing it against the scores of other people. Thus, for example, a score of 19 on a test of extraversion is meaningless on its own. However, it immediately becomes meaningful if we know that only 10% of the population have such a high score.

There is an important issue concerning standardisation. Suppose, for example, we develop a test of trait anxiety and then make sure it is properly standardised. Can we assume the standardisation norms will still be appropriate several years later? Twenge (2000) reported convincing evidence that the answer is, "No". She carried out **meta-analyses** (analyses combining the findings from several studies) on investigations assessing trait anxiety in children or college students. She found in both children and college students that the mean score for trait anxiety has increased substantially over the past 50 years. For example, consider scores on the Spielberger State-Trait Anxiety Inventory (Spielberger, Gorsuch, & Lushene, 1970). Over the period 1968–1993, the mean trait anxiety score of male college students increased from 36.37 to 40.73. Over the same time period, the mean score of female students went up from 37.94 to 41.92. More dramatically, "The average American child in the 1980s reported more anxiety than child psychiatric patients in the 1950s" (p. 1007). The implication is that tests need to be restandardised from time to time to maximise their usefulness.

*What factors could explain why the mean score for trait anxiety has increased over the last 50 years?*

## Questionnaires

The most common way of assessing personality is by self-report questionnaires. This method requires people to decide whether various statements about their thoughts, feelings, and behaviour are true. Sample questions are as follows: Do you tend to be moody? Do you have many friends? Do you like to be involved in numerous social activities? The questionnaire approach is easy to use. It also has the advantage that the individual presumably knows more about him/herself than do other people.

Three main approaches can be taken when constructing a personality questionnaire. First, there is the theoretical approach, which is the most popular one. In essence, the test designer uses theoretical considerations to decide what to measure, and then devises a questionnaire to measure it. This approach is exemplified in the work of H.J. Eysenck, which is discussed below. Second, there is the empirical approach. This approach is very different from the theoretical approach, in that the test designer has no clear initial idea of the number or nature of personality traits contained in the questionnaire. He/she produces questionnaire items to cover as much of human personality as possible, and then relies on appropriate statistical procedures to reveal precisely what the test is measuring. This empirical approach was followed by Cattell (see p. 160).

Third, there is what is sometimes called the **criterion-keying approach**. We start with some criterion group (e.g., hypochondriacs, who are excessively concerned about their health). We then devise numerous questionnaire items, which are administered to hypochondriacs and to various other groups. Those items that hypochondriacs answer differently to other groups form the hypochondria scale. For example, if hypochondriacs tend to answer, "Yes", to a question such as, "Do you prefer apricot jam to marmalade?", whereas other groups answer, "No", then that item would be included in the hypochondria scale. This is the case, even though there is no obvious reason why that item should discriminate between hypochondriacs and other people.

*The questionnaire approach is easy to use and has the advantage that large amounts of data can be collected at relatively little cost.*

### Limitations

There are various limitations associated with many personality questionnaires. One problem is **acquiescence response set**. This is the tendency to answer, "Yes", to all items regardless of their content. Acquiescence response set can be assessed by selecting items carefully. If, for example, we want to measure trait anxiety, then half the items can be written so that a "Yes" answer indicates high anxiety, with the rest being written so that

### The Minnesota Multiphasic Personality Inventory

Probably the best-known example of the criterion-keying approach is the Minnesota Multiphasic Personality Inventory (MMPI) (Hathaway & McKinley, 1940). The MMPI was originally published in 1940 and revised subsequently. The original MMPI contained 10 scales, most of which have a psychiatric feel about them. Items for these scales (listed below) were selected simply because they discriminated between patients with the relevant diagnosis and other patients:

- Hypochondria.
- Depression.
- Conversion hysteria.
- Psychopathic deviate.
- Masculinity–femininity.
- Paranoia.
- Neurosis.
- Schizophrenia.
- Hypomania.
- Social introversion.

The criterion-keying approach has the clear advantage that it focuses directly on the relationship between scales and relevant criteria. However, there are some problems with the MMPI. First, the test designers relied heavily on the assumption that the psychiatric diagnoses they used (e.g., schizophrenia) were valid. In view of the general unreliability and low validity of psychiatric diagnoses (see Chapter 22), this is a dubious assumption. Second, the sample used during test development was limited ethnically and geographically, with most of the participants coming from Minnesota. What was found with this limited sample may not apply to other ethnic groups in other areas.

Different jobs suit different people. In the highly stressful work atmosphere of the stock exchange an introverted, nervous person with low confidence in his or her judgement and decision making would be unlikely to succeed or to be happy.

### KEY TERMS

**Social desirability bias:** the tendency to produce socially desirable rather than honest answers to questionnaire items.

**Consensual validity:** the extent to which scores on a self-report measure correlate with scores obtained from ratings.

a "No" answer indicates high anxiety. Anyone who consistently answers "Yes" to both sets of items is showing acquiescence response set.

Probably the most serious problem with personality questionnaires is that individuals may fake their responses. Such faking typically takes the form of **social desirability bias**, the tendency to respond to questionnaire items in the socially desirable way. Thus, for example, the socially desirable answer to the question, "Do you tend to be moody?", is clearly "No" rather than "Yes".

One way of trying to deal with social desirability effects is to use a lie scale or a scale of social desirability. Such scales usually consist of items where the socially desirable answer is unlikely to be the true answer (e.g., "Do you ever gossip?", "Do you always keep your promises?"). If someone answers most of the questions in the socially desirable direction, it is assumed they are faking their responses. Of course, this is unfair on the genuinely saintly people in the population!

The issue of social desirability bias would seem to be especially important in personnel selection. As Cook (1993, p. 144) pointed out, "No one applying for a sales job is likely to say true to 'I don't much like talking to strangers', nor is someone trying to join the police force likely to agree that he/she has pretty undesirable acquaintances." However, it does not necessarily follow that "correcting" scores for social desirability will improve matters. This issue was addressed by Ones, Viswesvaran, and Reiss (1996), who found that the ability of personality measures to predict ratings of job performance was hardly affected when the effects of social desirability were removed statistically. This led Ones et al. (p. 671) to conclude that, "The reservation of industrial-organisational psychologists about using personality inventories for personnel selection because of the potential of social desirability is unfounded."

Most of the well-known personality questionnaires (e.g., Cattell's Sixteen Personality Factor Questionnaire or 16PF; the Eysenck Personality Questionnaire or EPQ; the Neuroticism Extraversion Openness Personality Inventory or NEO-PI ) are standardised tests. Nearly all of the major personality questionnaires have good or very good reliability. For example, the test–retest reliability for Cattell's 16PF and the Eysenck Personality Questionnaire is about +.80 or +.85, provided there is a short interval between test and retest.

It has proved much harder to devise questionnaires with high validity than with high reliability. Why is this? Remember that most ways of assessing validity involve correlating questionnaire scores with some external criterion (e.g., extraversion score with number of friends). The problem in a nutshell is that we have not yet found anything like a perfect external criterion. We can illustrate this problem by considering the concrete example of using number of friends as an external criterion for extraversion. Most people would agree that extraverts tend to have more friends than introverts, but no-one believes that an individual's level of extraversion is the *only* factor determining how many friends he/she has. As a result, the validity of most personality questionnaires generally appears to be moderate at best.

Is there a superior way of measuring validity? A very promising approach involves assessing what is often known as consensual validity. **Consensual validity** is a form of concurrent or predictive validity that involves comparing two kinds of information: (1) self-report questionnaire scores obtained from participants, and (2) ratings of those participants by observers (e.g., friends) for the same aspect of personality. This approach is based on the assumption that the limitations of self-report questionnaires and of ratings are different. Self-report questionnaires have the disadvantage that people may provide too favourable an impression of themselves, whereas ratings have the disadvantage that the rater may have limited information about the person being rated. Thus, it would be an impressive achievement if there were reasonable similarity between self-report and rating data.

*How would you try to assess someone's personality?*

Promising findings were reported by McCrae and Costa (1990). They used the NEO-PI, which provides measures of five major personality factors. Self-report questionnaire data were obtained from a large number of participants, and ratings on the same five personality factors were obtained from spouses and peers. The mean correlation between self-report scores and spouse scores was +.56, and it was +.50 between self-report scores and peer scores. Thus, there was reasonable agreement between self-report and rating data, and so fairly good consensual validity.

## Ratings

The second form of personality assessment is by ratings, in which observers provide information about other people's behaviour. Typically, the raters are given a list of different kinds of behaviour (e.g., "initiates conversations"), and they then rate their ratees (i.e., those being rated) on those aspects of behaviour. The more different situations in which the raters observe the ratees, the more accurate their ratings are likely to be.

Ratings have some advantages over self-report questionnaires. In particular, the problem that people filling in a questionnaire may distort their responses to present a favourable impression (social desirability bias) does not apply to observers' ratings. However, ratings pose problems of their own. First, the items of behaviour to be rated may be interpreted somewhat differently by different raters. For example, an item such as, "behaves in a friendly way towards others", might be thought to imply much more interaction with other people by a very sociable rater than by an unsociable one. Second, most raters are likely to observe other people in only some of the situations in which they find themselves in everyday life. Someone who appears distant and aloof at work may relax and be very friendly outside the work environment. The partial view which a rater has of his or her ratees may obviously lead to inaccurate assessment of the ratees' personalities.

*What particular difficulties emerge from using rating scales to measure personality?*

In spite of the limitations of using ratings to assess personality, they typically possess good reliability. What about validity? The most convincing evidence of the validity of rating data is based on assessment of consensual validity, in which rating data are correlated with self-report data. As we saw earlier, consensual validity is moderately high (McCrae & Costa, 1990).

## Objective tests

The third form of personality assessment involves the use of **objective tests**. There are several hundred objective tests, which measure behaviour under laboratory conditions with the participants not knowing what the experimenter is looking for. For example, asking participants to blow up a balloon until it bursts is a measure of timidity, and the extent to which people sway when standing on tiptoe is a measure of anxiety.

Objective tests are relatively free from the problems of deliberate distortion that can influence the responses on self-report questionnaires. The reason is that the participants are not aware that their personality is being assessed, and so have no particular motivation to respond in one way rather than another. However, there are various substantial problems with objective tests. It is often hard to know what any given objective test is actually measuring, and the results are often much influenced by apparently minor changes in procedure. Most objective tests have low reliability and validity, and so are not of much value in terms of assessing personality (Cooper, 2002).

An example of a Rorschach inkblot.

# Projective tests

The fourth form of personality assessment is by **projective tests**. Participants are given an unstructured task to perform (e.g., devising a story to fit a picture, describing what can be seen in an inkblot). The underlying rationale of projective tests is that people confronted by such unstructured tasks will reveal their innermost selves. Many users of projective tests favour the psychodynamic approach.

The best-known projective tests are the Rorschach Inkblot Test, introduced by the Swiss psychologist Hermann Rorschach in 1921, and the Thematic Apperception Test developed by Henry Murray (Morgan & Murray, 1935). The standard form of the Rorschach test involves presenting 10 inkblots. The participants suggest what each inkblot might represent, and indicate which part of the inkblot formed the basis of their response. The main emphasis with the Thematic Apperception Test is on content. The participants are presented with various pictures, and asked to say what is happening, what led up to the situation depicted, and what will happen next. These stories are interpreted flexibly, taking the individual's case history into account. The goal is to identify the individual's underlying motivational conflicts.

How successful are projective tests? In spite of their popularity, such tests are generally low in both reliability and validity (Eysenck, 1994a). There are two main reasons for this state of affairs. First, the unstructured nature of the tests means that the participants' responses are often determined by their current moods or concerns rather than by deep-rooted characteristics. Second, the very subjective nature of the interpretation of responses on projective tests means that much depends on the expertise of the person carrying out the interpretation. Non-expert interpretation will reduce the validity of the tests, and the subjectivity of interpretation reduces their reliability.

Zubin, Eron, and Shumer (1965) discussed validity in connection with the claim that creativity is indicated by numerous human movement responses. In fact, eminent artists did not produce more of such responses than ordinary individuals. More generally, three aspects of a participant's responses are used to interpret their meaning: content, location, and determinants. Content refers to the nature of what is seen by the participant, location refers to the part of the inkblot used to produce the response, and determinants are the characteristics of the inkblot (e.g., colour, form) influencing the choice of response. Most Rorschach experts argue that location and determinants are more informative than content. However, the evidence suggests that content possesses more validity than the other two measures (see Eysenck, 1994a).

# TRAIT THEORIES OF PERSONALITY

One of the most influential approaches to personality is based on the notion that human personality consists of a variety of traits. **Traits** can be defined as "broad, enduring, relatively stable characteristics used to assess and explain behaviour" (Hirschberg, 1978, p. 45). For example, smiling, talkativeness, participation in social events, and having many friends could together underlie a personality trait such as sociability. Most traits are normally distributed, with large numbers of people being close to the mean on sociability, trait anxiety, and so on.

## Factor analysis

Factor analysis (which has been used by most trait theorists) uses information about the inter-correlations of items from questionnaires, ratings, or other measures of personality. If two items correlate highly with each other, it is assumed they measure the same factor or personality trait. If two items do *not* correlate, they are measuring different factors. For example, items such as being outgoing, at ease in social situations, and wanting to take part in group activities would be correlated highly under the factor of extraversion.

Factor analysis as applied to personality has various limitations. First, it can only reveal the factors contained within the items included in the factor analysis. If, for example, no items dealing with sociability are included in a factor analysis, then a factor of sociability cannot emerge from the factor analysis. Thus, factor analysis is like a sausage machine, in that what comes out of it depends on what you put into it in the first place.

Second, factor analysis is a statistical technique, and so can only suggest guidelines for theory and research. In order to be confident that any personality trait is important, it is necessary to collect additional evidence that that trait is of significance in everyday life. For example, consider trait anxiety. Its relevance to the real world has been established in part by finding that patients suffering from anxiety disorders typically have very high scores on tests of trait anxiety (Eysenck, 1997).

Third, factor analysis involves making various arbitrary decisions. The number (and nature) of factors or traits extracted from any given set of data depend on decisions concerning the precise form of factor analysis to be performed on the data. For example, factor theorists have to decide whether to allow factors or traits to be correlated with each other. With **orthogonal factors**, all the factors must be uncorrelated with each other. Orthogonal factors are found in the approaches of Eysenck and the Big Five model. However, Cattell preferred to make use of **oblique factors**, which are factors or traits correlating with each other to some extent. The potential advantage of this approach is that a large number of personality traits can be identified, and it appears to provide a richer and more informative description of the structure of human personality.

Both of the above approaches have limitations. Reliance on orthogonal or independent factors is arbitrary, as there is no obvious reason *why* important personality traits should be uncorrelated with each other. Reliance on oblique factors often produces traits which are very similar to each other, and these traits can be hard to obtain consistently across studies. Which approach is superior? The only way to decide which approach is preferable is to study the empirical evidence (discussed below).

Smiling, talkativeness, participation in social events, and having many friends could together underlie a personality trait such as sociability.

## Cattell's trait theory

One of the greatest problems faced by trait theorists is how to ensure that all the important personality traits are included in their questionnaires. Raymond Cattell adopted an ingenious empirical approach to that problem. He used the **fundamental lexical hypothesis**, according to which any major language will contain words describing all the main personality traits.

Cattell's use of this hypothesis led him to the work of Allport and Odbert (1936). They found a total of 18,000 words in the dictionary of relevance to personality, with 4500 of them representing personality descriptions. These 4500 words were reduced to 160 trait words, in part by eliminating synonyms and removing unfamiliar words. Cattell (1946) then added 11 traits from the personality literature, producing a total of 171 trait names. He claimed that these trait names covered almost everything of importance in the personality sphere.

Cattell was still left with an unwieldy number of potential traits. As a result, he used findings from several previous rating studies to identify highly correlated traits. He argued that such traits were basically similar to each other, and reflected a single underlying trait. By this means, Cattell was left with 35 traits. He called them *surface traits*, because they were readily observable. These surface traits were investigated in rating studies. The findings from these rating studies suggested to Cattell that there are about 16 *source traits*, which are basic traits underlying the surface traits.

Having found 16 traits in rating data, life (L) data in his terms, the unflagging Cattell then studied personality traits with questionnaire (Q) and objective test (T) data. Q data were obtained by asking multiple choice questions, such as: "Do your moods sometimes

**KEY TERMS**

**Orthogonal factors:** personality factors or traits that are independent or uncorrelated with each other.

**Oblique factors:** personality factors or traits that correlate with each other to some extent.

**Fundamental lexical hypothesis:** the notion that the dictionary contains words describing all of the main traits.

make you seem unreasonable, even to yourself? Yes/No". T data were obtained by using various objective tests (see earlier). Cattell assumed initially that L, Q, and T data would all give rise to the same personality traits. In fact, he found reasonable similarity between the traits emerging from L and Q data, but T data produced rather different traits.

## Evidence

The best-known measuring instrument devised by Cattell is the Sixteen Personality Factor Questionnaire, generally known as the 16PF. It was intended to assess 16 personality factors, some relating to intelligence and social attitudes rather than to personality in the narrow sense. The construction of the 16PF was based on Cattell's assumption that personality traits are often correlated with each other, so the factors contained in the 16PF are oblique rather than orthogonal.

In spite of the massive popularity of the 16PF, it is inadequate. All systematic factor analyses of this test have shown that it does *not* actually measure anything like 16 different personality traits. For example, Barrett and Kline (1982) gave the 16PF to almost 500 participants. They then carried out five different factor analyses on their data, some precisely in line with Cattell's recommendations. Barrett and Kline obtained between seven and nine factors in each factor analysis, and these factors generally did not relate closely to those proposed by Cattell.

What is going on here? A key problem is that several of Cattell's factors are very similar. For example, the following factors assessing anxiety all correlate very highly with each other: placid–apprehensive; relaxed–tense; affected by feelings–emotionally stable. Any thorough factor analysis will reveal that these three factors are simply too similar to distinguish from each other.

> **The factors of Cattell's 16PF**
>
> Remember that each pair represents a continuum.
>
> Reserved .......................................................Outgoing
> Less intelligent ...............................................More intelligent
> Affected by feelings ........................................More emotionally stable
> Humble...........................................................Assertive
> Sober .............................................................Happy-go-lucky
> Expedient .......................................................Conscientious
> Shy .................................................................Venturesome
> Tough-minded.................................................Tender-minded
> Trusting..........................................................Suspicious
> Practical .........................................................Imaginative
> Forthright .......................................................Shrewd
> Placid .............................................................Apprehensive
> Conservative ..................................................Experimenting
> Group-dependent ...........................................Self-sufficient
> Casual.............................................................Controlled
> Relaxed...........................................................Tense

## Evaluation

- ➕ Cattell's use of the fundamental lexical hypothesis was potentially a suitable way of identifying the main personality traits.
- ➕ Cattell's attempt to combine information from several methods (questionnaires, ratings, objective tests) was thorough and systematic.
- ➖ As a result of several decades of research, it is reasonably clear that Cattell's approach based on oblique factors is less useful than an approach based on orthogonal or uncorrelated factors (see below).
- ➖ Cattell's approach was not very theoretical or explanatory. As Cattell (1957, p. 50) admitted, "I have always felt justifiably suspicious of theory built much ahead of data."
- ➖ There are only about eight different personality traits in the 16PF, and so Cattell's main questionnaire is badly flawed.

## Eysenck's trait theory

H.J. Eysenck (e.g., 1947) agreed with Cattell that factor analysis can assist in discovering the structure of human personality. However, the two theorists disagreed over the use of orthogonal or uncorrelated factors versus oblique factors. Cattell always emphasised oblique or correlated factors, because he argued that it is at this level that the most informative description of personality is possible. In contrast, Eysenck argued that orthogonal or independent factors are preferable, because oblique factors are often so weak that they cannot be found consistently.

Eysenck's (1944) initial attempt to use factor analysis to identify the main orthogonal factors involved 700 patients suffering from neurotic disorders. Psychiatrists' ratings on 39 scales were accounted for fairly well by the two factors or traits of neuroticism and extraversion. **Neuroticism** is a trait consisting of anxiety, tension, depression, and other negative emotional states. It closely resembles trait anxiety, with measures of neuroticism and trait anxiety correlating about +.7 with each other. **Extraversion** is a personality trait consisting mainly of sociability, but with an element of impulsiveness.

Most subsequent research on normal and abnormal groups has confirmed the importance of the factors of neuroticism and extraversion. The Eysenck Personality Inventory was devised to measure these two factors. Of importance, these two factors are contained in Cattell's 16PF. The oblique or correlated factors identified by Cattell are known as first-order factors. When a factor analysis is performed on these first-order factors, it is possible to obtain orthogonal, second-order factors from the 16PF. Saville and Blinkhorn (1981) did precisely that, finding that second-order factors resembling extraversion and neuroticism emerged from the 16PF.

Eysenck (1978) added a third personality factor, which he called **psychoticism**. High scorers on psychoticism are "egocentric, aggressive, impulsive, impersonal, cold, lacking in empathy and concern for others, and generally unconcerned about the rights and welfare of other people" (Eysenck, 1982, p. 11). Neuroticism, extraversion, and psychoticism are measured by the Eysenck Personality Questionnaire (EPQ). As assessed by the EPQ, these three factors are all almost uncorrelated, i.e., they are independent or orthogonal factors.

Where do the personality dimensions of extraversion, neuroticism, and psychoticism come from? According to Eysenck (1982, p. 28), "genetic factors contribute something like two-thirds of the variance in major personality dimensions". How do genetic factors produce individual differences in personality? According to Eysenck (e.g., 1967), heredity influences the responsiveness of parts of the physiological system. Introverts were assumed to have a higher level of cortical arousal (activity in the brain) than extraverts based on greater activity in the reticular formation (see Chapter 4). Suppose we assume that most people prefer an intermediate level of arousal, with low levels perceived as boring and high levels as stressful. Under-aroused extraverts seek stimulation to achieve the desired intermediate level of arousal, whereas over-aroused introverts avoid stimulation. This makes some sense in terms of the observed behaviour of extraverts and introverts. Extraverts spend much more of their time than introverts socialising with others and behaving impulsively, whereas introverts adopt a more cautious and reserved approach to life.

According to H.J. Eysenck (1967), those high in neuroticism have greater activity than those low in neuroticism in the **visceral brain**, which consists of several parts of the brain (hippocampus, amygdala, cingulum, septum, and hypothalamus). The physiological differences between those high and low in neuroticism are claimed to be greater when the situation is stressful. Finally, the physiological system underlying psychoticism remains obscure.

In sum, H.J. Eysenck's theoretical approach to personality was based on four major assumptions. First, he argued that we can arrive at a better understanding of personality by focusing on a small number of independent or uncorrelated personality factors than on a much larger number of correlated traits. Second, he argued that individual differences

---

**Personality dimensions**

Personality dimensions such as extraversion are at one end of a continuum, with their opposite at the other end. Personality testing does not simply determine that a person is either extraverted or introverted, but places them at the relevant point on the continuum, showing their degree of extraversion/introversion, as in the diagram below. This person is more extraverted than introverted.

**1  2  3  4  5  6  7  8  9  10**

EXTRAVERSION.....................●.....................................INTROVERSION
(Social, outgoing, active)                              (Unsocial, quiet, passive)

Jack Nicholson in *The Shining*—perhaps this character would score highly on Eysenck's psychoticism personality factor—he is aggressive, impulsive, impersonal, cold, and lacking in empathy and concern for others.

**KEY TERMS**

**Neuroticism:** a personality dimension identified by H.J. Eysenck, with high scorers being characterised by anxiety, depression, and tension.

**Extraversion:** a personality dimension identified by H.J. Eysenck, with high scorers being much more sociable and impulsive than low scorers.

**Psychoticism:** a personality identified by H.J. Eysenck, with high scorers being aggressive, hostile, and uncaring.

**Visceral brain:** the hippocampus, amygdala, hypothalamus, and other parts of the autonomic nervous system underlying individual differences in neuroticism in H.J. Eysenck's theory.

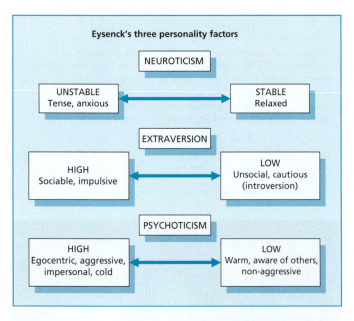

Eysenck's three personality factors

NEUROTICISM

| UNSTABLE | STABLE |
| Tense, anxious | Relaxed |

EXTRAVERSION

| HIGH | LOW |
| Sociable, impulsive | Unsocial, cautious |
| | (introversion) |

PSYCHOTICISM

| HIGH | LOW |
| Egocentric, aggressive, | Warm, aware of others, |
| impersonal, cold | non-aggressive |

in personality depend mostly on genetic factors. Numerous other theorists had suggested that possibility, but remarkably little research had been carried out to test it. Third, H.J. Eysenck argued that the personality factors revealed by factor analysis are not necessarily important ones. In order to demonstrate that they are important, it is essential to show that those scoring high and low on each factor differ predictably in their behaviour. Fourth, he argued that we should develop explanatory theories to account for individual differences in each personality factor or trait, which can be done by investigating individual differences in physiological functioning.

## Evidence

We will start our discussion of the evidence by considering the extent to which individual differences in Eysenck's three personality factors depend on genetic factors. The best approach to this issue involves monozygotic or identical twin pairs and dizygotic or fraternal twin pairs. In essence, identical twins share 100% of their genes, whereas fraternal twins share only 50% of their genes. Thus, if heredity is important in determining individual differences in personality, identical twins should be much more similar in personality than fraternal twins. More precise conclusions can be drawn if the study includes twin pairs brought up apart as well as twin pairs brought up together. As you can imagine, it is very difficult to find many pairs of identical twins brought up apart!

The most thorough twin study was reported by Pedersen, Plomin, McClearn, and Friberg (1988). They assessed extraversion and neuroticism in 95 identical twin pairs brought up apart, 150 identical twin pairs brought up together, 220 pairs of fraternal twins brought up apart, and 204 pairs of fraternal twins brought up together. Almost half of the twin pairs had been separated when they were under 1 year old, and most of the rest were separated before the age of 5. However, in many cases, separated twins were brought up in different branches of the same family, which would often mean that they were not exposed to very different environments. It should also be borne in mind that identical twins brought up together tend to be treated in a more similar way than fraternal twins brought up together (Loehlin & Nichols, 1976).

What did Pedersen et al. (1988) find? So far as extraversion was concerned, identical twins brought up together had a correlation of +.54, compared to +.06 for fraternal twins brought up together. The correlation was +.30 for identical twins brought up apart, and +.04 for fraternal twins brought up apart. According to Pedersen et al., these findings indicate that about 41% of individual differences in extraversion are attributable to genetic factors. For neuroticism, identical twins brought up together had a correlation of +.41, against +.24 for fraternals brought up together. For twins brought up apart, the correlations were +.25 for identicals and +.28 for fraternals. These figures suggest that about 31% of individual differences in neuroticism depend on heredity.

What about psychoticism? Zuckerman (1989) discussed the findings from four twin studies. The median correlation was +.52 for identical twins and +.21 for fraternal twins. It appears that somewhere between 40% and 50% of individual differences in psychoticism stem from genetic factors.

The findings discussed so far are typical of those reported in the literature. Plomin, DeFries, and McClearn (1997) reviewed numerous twin studies and concluded

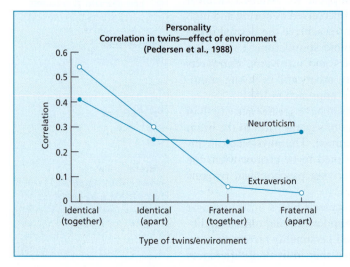

Personality
Correlation in twins—effect of environment
(Pedersen et al., 1988)

that genetic factors account for 40% of individual differences in personality. However, the methodological limitations of all twin studies (e.g., twins brought up apart not being put in very different environments) mean that we need to be cautious in our conclusions. However, the estimated figure of 40% of individual differences in each of the three personality dimensions being due to genetic factors is, of course, considerably less than claimed by H.J. Eysenck (1982).

We turn now to evidence concerning the physiological basis of Eysenck's personality factors. The only factor for which there is much support is extraversion, for which it will be remembered that H.J. Eysenck (1967) claimed that introverts are generally more cortically aroused than extraverts. One way of testing this hypothesis is by making use of electroencephalography (EEG), which provides a measure of brain-wave activity. Gale (1983) considered 33 EEG studies reporting a total of 38 experimental comparisons. Extraverts were significantly less cortically aroused than introverts in 22 comparisons, whereas introverts were significantly less aroused than extraverts in 5 comparisons. Introverts and extraverts did not differ in the remaining 11 cases. Thus, introverts are generally more cortically aroused than extraverts, but there are obviously some situations in which that is not the case.

H.J. Eysenck (1967) argued that individual differences in neuroticism depend on the level of activity within the "visceral brain". This hypothesis has been tested by taking a variety of indirect measures (e.g., heart rate, skin conductance) from individuals high and low in neuroticism (or the closely related personality factor of trait anxiety) in stressful and non-stressful conditions. The evidence was reviewed by Fahrenberg (1992, pp. 212–213), who concluded as follows: "Over many decades research has failed to substantiate the physiological correlates that are assumed for emotionality [neuroticism] and trait anxiety. There is virtually no distinct finding that has been reliably replicated across studies and laboratories."

H.J. Eysenck (1967) failed to distinguish between two types of individuals scoring low on neuroticism or trait anxiety. Weinberger, Schwartz, and Davidson (1979) distinguished between the truly low anxious (who are easy-going and non-defensive) and repressors (who are very controlled and defensive). Even though both groups are low in trait anxiety and neuroticism, they differ considerably in their physiological responses. For example, consider a study by Derakshan and Eysenck (1997), in which heart rate was recorded while students gave a public talk. As can be seen in the figure on the next page, the truly low-anxious were less physiologically active than the high-anxious, which is in line with Eysenck's theory. However, the repressors provide strong evidence against the theory: They are low in trait anxiety or neuroticism, but their level of physiological activity is as great as that of individuals high in trait anxiety or neuroticism.

What do the above findings means? In essence, H.J. Eysenck was wrong to assume that all low scorers on neuroticism or trait anxiety are similar to each other. In fact, there are numerous differences between the truly low-anxious and repressors (M. Eysenck, 1997).

Some of the theoretical assumptions of H.J. Eysenck have been tested by means of studies of behaviour or performance. For example, consider the assumption that introverts have a higher level of cortical arousal than extraverts. This can be tested by making use of a **vigilance task**, which is long and monotonous. An example of a vigilance task is watching a pointer moving around a clock face in order to detect occasional double jumps. As you might imagine, performance on most vigilance tasks deteriorates over time. The level of physiological arousal also tends to decrease over time on vigilance tasks (Davies & Parasuraman, 1982), suggesting that a low level of arousal may help to cause poor vigilance performance. If that is the case, then introverts (being generally more aroused) should perform better than extraverts on vigilance tasks.

M. Eysenck (1988) reviewed 12 studies concerned with extraversion and vigilance performance. Introverts performed significantly better than extraverts in five of those studies, but there were no differences between introverts and extraverts in the remaining seven

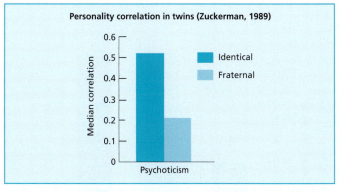

Personality correlation in twins (Zuckerman, 1989)

Median correlation — Identical / Fraternal — Psychoticism

A young woman (background) undergoing an EEG examination. The EEG test records the electrical activity of the brain via small electrodes attached to the scalp. Gale (1983) reviewed studies using this technique to test the hypothesis that introverts are more cortically aroused than extraverts.

**KEY TERM**

**Vigilance task:** typically a long and monotonous task in which occasional target stimuli need to be detected.

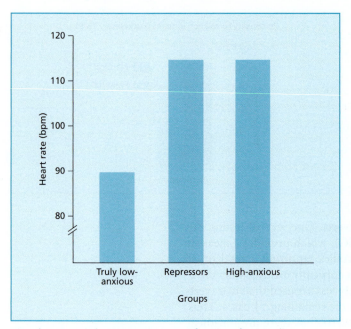

Mean heart rate in beats per minute as a function of personality group (truly low-anxious, repressors, and high-anxious). Data from Derakshan and Eysenck (1997).

*What might psychologists do if a link between mortality and personality were established?*

studies. Thus, there was limited support for the theoretical prediction.

The findings we have discussed suggest that individual differences in personality have only modest predictive value. However, H.J. Eysenck and Grossarth-Maticek reported in several studies funded by large tobacco companies that how long people live depends dramatically more on their personality than on other factors (e.g., whether or not they smoke). Grossarth-Maticek, Eysenck, and Vetter (1988) considered four personality types: type 1 (hopelessness and depression), type 2 (arousal and aggression), type 3 (ambivalence: fluctuation between the reactions of type 1s and type 2s), type 4 (personal autonomy or control). Subsequent research by Amelang and Schmidt-Rathjens (1992) showed that type 1s and type 2s are basically high in neuroticism, whereas type 4s are low in neuroticism. Grossarth-Maticek et al. predicted that type 1s would be susceptible to cancer and type 2s to coronary heart disease, whereas type 4s would be the healthiest. They tested these predictions by studying a large group of people over a 15-year period.

What did Grossarth-Maticek et al. (1988) find? We can express their findings in terms of relative risk. If, for example, 20% of type 1s die of cancer and 10% of type 4s die of cancer, then the relative risk for type 1s is 20%/10% = 2.00. The relative risk of dying over a 40-year period has been found to be 3.15 for smokers compared to non-smokers (Doll, Peto Wheatley, Gray, & Sutherland, 1994). Since smoking is generally regarded as the major cause of preventable death, a relative risk of 3 is very large. The relative risk of type 1s dying of cancer compared to type 4s in one of Grossarth-Maticek et al.'s studies was 55.6, and the relative risk of type 2s dying of coronary heart disease was 58.8 (Lee, 1991). Thus, the risks to health of having a type 1 or type 2 personality are almost 20 times greater than the risks associated with smoking! Lee concluded that, "Eysenck's results are so outside my experience as an epidemiologist that I find it very difficult indeed to accept them as real."

Amelang, Schmidt-Rathjens, and Matthews (1996) completely failed to replicate the findings of Grossarth-Maticek et al. (1988). In addition, the prediction that individuals low in neuroticism should live much longer on average than those high in neuroticism has received practically no support (see Watson & Pennebaker, 1989, for a review).

Grossarth-Maticek et al. (1988) claimed that type 1s have very different personalities to type 2s, and that is why they are susceptible to different diseases. However, Amelang and Schmidt-Rathjens (1992) found that questionnaire measures of type 1 and type 2 correlated very highly with each other (+.81). Thus, they are actually measuring the same underlying personality factor (i.e., neuroticism).

Very dramatic findings were reported by Grossarth-Maticek and Eysenck (1995). They devised the Self-Regulation Inventory, with high scorers having low neuroticism. Grossarth-Maticek and Eysenck assessed mortality over a 15-year period. The correlation between self-regulation and mortality was −.79 (John Valentine, personal communication), with self-regulation accounting for 62% of the variance or variation in mortality. This is *six* times greater than any association between personality and mortality previously reported by other researchers!

How can we explain the above findings? The obvious answer is that the questionnaires devised by H.J. Eysenck and Grossarth-Maticek are greatly superior to those devised by anyone else. Bearing in mind that good test items are short and unambiguous, consider this typical item taken from one of their questionnaires:

*Do you change your behaviour according to consequences of previous behaviour, i.e., do you repeat ways of acting which have in the past led to positive results, such as contentment, well being, self-reliance, etc., and to stop acting in ways which lead to negative consequences, i.e., to feelings of anxiety, hopelessness, depression, excitement, annoyance, etc.? In other words, have you learned to give up ways of acting which have negative consequences, and to rely more and more on ways of acting which have positive consequences?*

Since the items used by H.J. Eysenck and Grossarth-Maticek are extraordinarily long and ambiguous, it is clear that the obvious answer to the question posed in the previous paragraph is not correct.

*What criticisms can be made of H.J. Eysenck's trait theory of personality?*

## Evaluation

● It has proved more useful to identify a small number of unrelated personality factors than a larger number of correlated factors.
● Extraversion and neuroticism are major personality traits.
● H.J. Eysenck made a thorough attempt to explain the processes underlying individual differences in his three personality traits.
● Psychoticism is not a major personality trait. It is poorly named, being more closely related to psychopathy than psychosis.
● The role of heredity in determining individual differences in the three personality dimensions is much less than claimed by H.J. Eysenck.
● There is little support for the physiological bases of personality proposed by H.J. Eysenck.
● The theory emphasises individual differences in physiological activity but virtually ignores the possibility that individual differences in cognitive processes may also be important. For example, there is convincing evidence that individuals high in neuroticism or trait anxiety interpret ambiguous stimuli in a more threatening way than do those low in neuroticism or trait anxiety (see M. Eysenck, 1997). This could help to explain the greater levels of anxiety experienced by individuals high in neuroticism.
● The notion that longevity depends almost entirely on self-regulation or neuroticism is not generally accepted.
● There is an unacceptable lack of scientific objectivity running through H.J. Eysenck's writings. Pervin (1993, p. 290) referred to "Eysenck's tendency to dismiss the contributions of others and exaggerate the empirical support for his own point of view ... frequently he ignores contradictory findings".

## Five-factor theory

In recent years, several theorists have argued that there are five major personality traits. This approach became known as the Big Five model or the five-factor model of personality, but is now increasingly referred to as a theory. Note that there are minor differences of opinion concerning the exact nature of some of these factors or traits.

Important early research was reported by Norman (1963). Small groups of students all rated each other on several of Cattell's rating scales. The rating scales were then submitted to a factor analysis, and the following five orthogonal or unrelated factors emerged:

1. Extraversion (e.g., talkative, sociable).
2. Agreeableness (e.g., good-natured, co-operative).
3. Conscientiousness (e.g., responsible, hard-working).
4. Emotional stability (e.g., calm, composed; essentially the opposite of neuroticism).
5. Culture (e.g., artistically sensitive, imaginative).

McCrae and Costa (1985) put forward the most influential version of the five-factor theory, based on the five factors of neuroticism, extraversion, agreeableness, conscientiousness, and openness to experience. This last factor replaced culture, and is defined by curiosity, broad interests, creativity, and imagination. Costa and McCrae (1992) produced

*In what ways might gender contribute to personality differences?*

the NEO-PI Five-Factor Inventory to measure these five factors, with each factor being subdivided into six facets. For example, the facets for extraversion were warmth, gregariousness, assertiveness, activity, excitement seeking, and positive emotions. (If you want to remember the names of Costa and McCrae's five factors, note that the initial letters can be rearranged to form the word OCEAN.)

What causes individual differences in the five factors? Advocates of the five-factor theory generally assume that individual differences in each factor depend partly on genetic factors. It is also assumed that environmental factors are important, but there has been no systematic attempt to identify them in detail.

Costa and Widiger (1994, p. 2) argued that, "It seems reasonable to hypothesise that different forms of psychopathology [mental disorder] might be related to normal variations in basic personality dispositions." This hypothesis is most clearly relevant to the various personality disorders (e.g., anti-social personality disorder, avoidant personality disorder) (see Chapter 22). Costa and Widiger argued that the personality disorders can be regarded as extreme variants of personality traits. What predictions follow from that assumption? First, individuals having a personality disorder should tend to have extreme scores on some of the Big Five factors.

Second, if all the personality disorders involve extreme scores on a small number of personality factors, it would be expected that many individuals would suffer from more than one personality disorder. The joint occurrence of two or more disorders is known as **comorbidity**. According to the theory, comorbidity would be more likely to occur between personality disorders associated with similar patterns of scores on the Big Five factors.

## Evidence

Five traits or factors closely resembling those put forward by McCrae and Costa (1985, 1990) have been found numerous times. For example, Goldberg (1990) collected more than 1000 words describing personality. Students produced self-descriptions based on these terms, and the data were factor analysed in 10 different ways. The consistent finding was that five factors were extracted: emotional stability (opposite of neuroticism), agreeableness, conscientiousness, surgency (very similar to extraversion), and intellect (resembling openness).

Goldberg (1990) carried out a second study based on 479 common trait terms. In this study, he obtained self-report and rating data. He found strong evidence for the same five factors in both kinds of data, and (p. 1223) came to the following conclusion: "Analyses of any reasonably large sample of English trait adjectives in either self- or peer-descriptions [ratings] will elicit a variant of the Big-Five factor structure."

There is reasonable evidence that questionnaires of the Big Five factors are valid. For example, McCrae and Costa (1990) compared self-report measures on each of the five personality factors with ratings by spouses. All the correlations between self-report and rating data were moderately high: +.53 for neuroticism, +.53 for extraversion, +.59 for agreeableness, +.57 for conscientiousness, and +.59 for openness. McCrae, Costa, del Pilar, Rolland, and Parker (1998) obtained similar findings. Why aren't the correlations even higher? McCrae et al. asked couples to identify the reasons for any substantial disagreements on particular items. Idiosyncratic understanding of items and relating items to different time periods were two main reasons. Perhaps surprisingly, distortions of self-report data by social desirability bias seemed rare.

Additional evidence on validity comes from a study on concurrent validity by Paunonen (2003). He found that all five factors correlated significantly with various external criteria (see the figure on the next page, based on averaging across four samples of students). In general terms, these correlations are in line with theoretical predictions.

There have been various attempts to work out the role of heredity in determining individual differences on the five factors. For example, Loehlin, McCrae, Costa, and John (1998) carried out a twin study on the Big Five factors. Individual differences in all five factors were determined to a moderate extent by genetic factors. As was mentioned earlier, the available evidence suggests that about 40% of individual differences in personality are due to genetic factors (Plomin et al., 1997). Plomin et al. drew a distinction

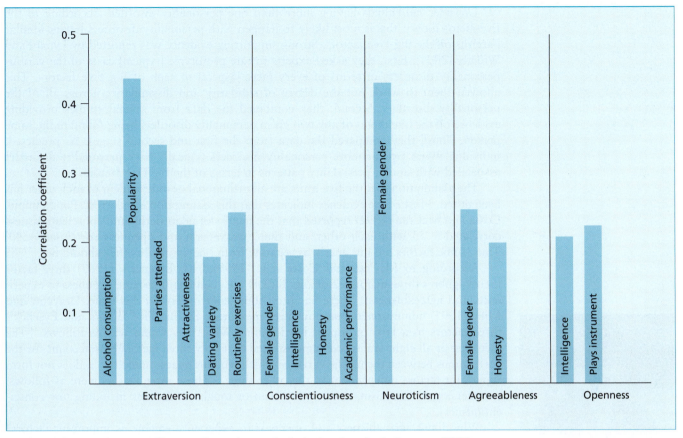

Correlations between the Big Five factors and several external criteria. Based on data in Paunonen (2003).

between shared environment (environmental factors having a similar effect on twins or siblings) and non-shared environment (environmental factors unique to a given individual). They concluded from a review of the evidence that non-shared environment accounts for 60% of variation in personality, whereas shared environment contributes practically nothing. Thus, the notion that a stressful family environment creates anxious children seems incorrect.

Borkenau, Riemann, Angleitner, and Spinath (2001) pointed out that nearly all estimates of the contributions of genetic and environmental factors to individual differences in personality depend on self-report data (i.e., participants completing questionnaires). They had identical and fraternal twins rated by judges on various adjective scales related to the Big Five factors. These rating data suggested that 40% of individual differences in the Big Five factors are due to heredity, 35% to non-shared environment, and 25% to shared environment. These findings suggest that the contribution of genetic factors to individual differences in personality remains fairly constant across self-report and rating data. However, it is puzzling that shared environment seems so much more important in rating data than in self-report data, and we cannot as yet explain this finding.

The general notion that personality disorders can be understood in terms of the five-factor theory has been investigated in several studies (see Chapter 22 for further coverage). The specific prediction that individuals with personality disorders should have extreme scores on the Big Five factors has received much support (see Widiger, Verheul, & van den Brink, 1999, for a review). For example, Widiger and Costa (1994) found that patients with schizoid personality disorder and with avoidant personality disorder obtained very low scores on the extraversion factor. In addition, both groups obtained high scores on neuroticism. Patients with borderline personality disorder, paranoid personality disorder, and anti-social personality disorder all obtained very low scores on the agreeableness factor.

In order to determine whether individual differences in personality are due to genetic factors or environment a number of studies using twins have been carried out. Resulting evidence suggests that 40% of individual differences in personality are due to genetic factors.

Consider individuals having more than one personality disorder. According to the five-factor theory, this is most likely to happen with personality disorders having similar patterns on the Big Five factors. Strong supporting evidence was reported by Lynam and Widiger (2001). First, they asked experts to rate prototypic [typical] cases of the various personality disorders in terms of every facet [aspect] of each of Big Five factors. This allowed them to work out the degree of similarity and dissimilarity across all of the personality disorders. Second, they combined the data from several studies providing evidence on the likelihood of any two given personality disorders being found in the same person. Third, they compared the data from the first and second stages. As predicted, individuals with two or more personality disorders typically have personality disorders associated with similar personality patterns in terms of the Big Five factors.

The assumption that the five traits are all orthogonal or independent of each other has been tested. Most of the evidence indicates that this assumption is incorrect. For example, Costa and McCrae (1992) reported that the factors of neuroticism and conscientiousness correlated $-.53$ with each other, and that extraversion and openness correlated $+.40$. Thus, some factors are not nearly as separate from one another as they should be.

According to McCrae and Costa (e.g., 1999), H.J. Eysenck's (1967) three-factor theory ignores three major personality factors (i.e., conscientiousness, openness to experience, and agreeableness). There has been some controversy on this issue. Draycott and Kline (1995) administered questionnaires measuring the Big Five factors and Eysenck's three factors to a large group of participants. What they found was as follows: "The factoring of all eight scales has demonstrated that only three factors best account for the correlations between them. The variance which remains unaccounted for … does not form significant factors independent of the other three." Those three factors were as follows: extraversion, neuroticism, and psychoticism or tough-mindedness including low conscientiousness.

Why didn't agreeableness and openness to experience emerge as important factors? Agreeableness correlated $-.47$ with the psychoticism factor and $-.41$ with the neuroticism factor, and so represented a combination of those two Eysenckian factors. Openness to experience correlated $+.61$ with the extraversion factor, probably because high scorers on both factors enjoy novelty.

Some individual differences in personality factors have been observed in other species. For example, Gosling and John (1999) observed individual differences in extraversion and neuroticism in chimpanzees as well as differences in conscientiousness.

It has sometimes been argued that fundamental personality factors should be observable in other species. Gosling and John (1999) considered cross-species evidence with respect to the Big Five. They reported evidence of individual differences in extraversion and neuroticism in numerous species, including chimpanzees, other primates, and even guppies and octopuses. Many species (but not guppies and octopuses) show variations in agreeableness, perhaps because all octopuses are disagreeable. Individual differences in various aspects of openness to experience (e.g., curiosity) are found in some other species, but only chimpanzees showed individual differences in conscientiousness.

## Evaluation

➕ The Big Five personality traits have been obtained repeatedly in self-report and rating data, and individual differences in each trait are moderately influenced by genetic factors.

➕ The Big Five approach builds on and extends the earlier theory of H.J. Eysenck.

➕ Consensual and concurrent validity have been established for all five factors.

➕ The Big Five personality traits are related meaningfully to the various personality disorders, and the theory allows us to predict which personality disorders are most likely (and least likely) to be found together.

➖ Some of the Big Five factors correlate with each other, and thus are not truly independent.

➖ Some of the factors (e.g., openness, conscientiousness) may be less important than others.

➖ The Big Five approach is essentially descriptive, and fails to provide an adequate explanation of the processes underlying the various factors.

- As McCrae and Costa (1999, p. 147) admitted, we don't have answers to certain key questions: "Shouldn't a five-factor theory explain why there are five factors and not six? And why these factors and not others?"
- The Big Five traits may reflect rather superficial aspects of personality. According to McAdams (1992, p. 333), "The five-factor model is essentially a psychology of the stranger—a quick and simple portrait of someone."

## Cross-cultural perspectives

Most attempts to identify the structure of human personality have focused on various Western cultures. Accordingly, it is important to discover whether the main personality dimensions (e.g., the Big Five) are universal or culture specific. Unfortunately, the approach generally adopted to address this issue is a limited one, in which personality questionnaires developed in Western cultures are administered to individuals in several other cultures. Why is this approach limited? Suppose we find that the Big Five personality factors can be found in several non-Western cultures. That indicates that the Big Five are not entirely culture specific. However, this approach cannot tell us whether there are additional personality dimensions unique to any of the cultures being tested. In order to obtain a more complete picture, we also need to make use of indigenous personality measures, which are assessments of personality developed in each particular culture. What is of interest is to see whether these indigenous measures assess aspects of personality missing from Western personality questionnaires.

*Why is it problematic to use personality tests devised for Western cultures on other cultural groups?*

### Evidence

Triandis and Suh (2002) have reviewed cross-cultural studies of personality. The major personality dimensions identified from Western studies are generally also found in non-Western cultures. For example, Barrett, Petrides, Eysenck, and Eysenck (1998) analysed data from the Eysenck Personality Questionnaire obtained in 34 different countries. This test measures extraversion, neuroticism, and psychoticism, and the key finding was that these factors were clearly present in all 34 countries. In similar fashion, McCrae et al. (1998) found that the factor structure of measures designed to assess the Big Five factors was very similar across several different cultures. John and Srivastava (1999, p. 109) concluded their review as follows: "Cross-language research suggests that the Big Five can be replicated in Germanic languages. The evidence for non-Western languages and cultures is more complex, and Factor V [Openness] generally shows the weakest replicability."

Steel and Ones (2002) discussed findings from the Eysenck Personality Questionnaire reported from 40 different countries. They kindly supplied the author with a detailed breakdown of these findings (including mean scores on the lie scale designed to detect deliberately distorted responding), which are shown in the table on the next page. National subjective well-being tended to be higher in those countries with high extraversion, low neuroticism, and low scores on the lie scale. This allows you to obtain some idea of your country's relative level of subjective well-being!

Studies using indigenous measures have often indicated that some aspects of personality are culture specific. For example, Cheung and Leung (1998) administered the Chinese Personality Assessment Inventory and the Big Five items in China and in Hong Kong. They found evidence for four of the Big Five factors but not for openness. In addition, they obtained a Chinese tradition factor having no relationship with the Big Five.

Katigbak, Church, Guanzon-Lapensa, Carlota, and del Pilar (2002) administered a Filipino version of a test of the Big Five personality factors together with three indigenous questionnaires to students in the Philippines. There was moderately strong evidence

### Mean scores for psychoticism, extraversion, neuroticism, and lie scales for 40 countries or regions

| Country or region | Psychoticism | Extraversion | Neuroticism | Lie | Sample size |
|---|---|---|---|---|---|
| Australia | 6.96 | 19.31 | 15.48 | 7.58 | 654 |
| Bangladesh | 4.24 | 19.05 | 12.29 | 19.15 | 1075 |
| Brazil | 3.99 | 17.63 | 14.20 | 17.93 | 1396 |
| Bulgaria | 4.17 | 18.60 | 14.96 | 15.12 | 1038 |
| Canada | 4.28 | 18.05 | 12.77 | 13.92 | 1257 |
| China | 6.79 | 13.75 | 14.50 | 20.41 | 1000 |
| Czechoslovakia | 9.14 | 19.52 | 14.09 | 11.47 | 1912 |
| Egypt | 4.40 | 18.57 | 17.36 | 21.37 | 1330 |
| Finland | 4.90 | 16.26 | 14.60 | 11.57 | 949 |
| France | 5.49 | 17.75 | 15.09 | 14.59 | 811 |
| Germany FR | 6.23 | 18.40 | 13.68 | 10.96 | 1336 |
| Greece | 5.49 | 20.40 | 18.32 | 16.61 | 1301 |
| Hong Kong | 7.05 | 16.73 | 14.61 | 14.37 | 732 |
| Hungary | 3.86 | 16.57 | 14.58 | 15.63 | 962 |
| Iceland | 3.52 | 19.19 | 13.90 | 10.53 | 1144 |
| India | 8.17 | 22.80 | 16.26 | 18.38 | 981 |
| Iran | 4.52 | 17.69 | 16.05 | 17.13 | 624 |
| Israel | 3.60 | 22.62 | 8.51 | 17.39 | 1050 |
| Italy | 4.43 | 18.37 | 16.66 | 16.89 | 802 |
| Japan | 4.80 | 16.50 | 16.78 | 9.62 | 1318 |
| Korea | 4.97 | 16.49 | 18.71 | 15.74 | 1200 |
| Lebanon | 2.30 | 19.26 | 14.17 | 20.30 | 1239 |
| Lithuania | 5.01 | 16.45 | 15.10 | 17.50 | 1404 |
| Mexico | 4.49 | 20.63 | 14.15 | 15.41 | 988 |
| Netherlands | 2.88 | 17.36 | 11.52 | 16.09 | 876 |
| Nigeria | 3.58 | 24.50 | 9.43 | 17.76 | 430 |
| Norway | 2.22 | 18.65 | 10.33 | 11.68 | 802 |
| Portugal | 2.49 | 18.94 | 15.27 | 14.12 | 1163 |
| Puerto Rico | 4.43 | 21.01 | 14.15 | 17.01 | 1094 |
| Romania | 3.51 | 18.45 | 13.31 | 17.14 | 1014 |
| Russia | 3.41 | 16.55 | 18.04 | 14.18 | 1067 |
| Sicily | 5.89 | 17.36 | 17.16 | 16.42 | 785 |
| Singapore | 4.36 | 17.42 | 13.02 | 16.32 | 994 |
| Spain | 2.97 | 17.11 | 16.24 | 15.81 | 1030 |
| Sri Lanka | 4.27 | 18.67 | 12.09 | 20.86 | 1027 |
| Uganda | 6.06 | 19.44 | 15.78 | 13.56 | 1476 |
| United Kingdom | 3.84 | 18.03 | 14.97 | 12.11 | 1198 |
| United States | 3.32 | 21.53 | 15.20 | 9.46 | 879 |
| Yugoslavia | 7.46 | 17.32 | 14.37 | 17.94 | 971 |
| Zimbabwe | 6.50 | 19.75 | 14.65 | 15.20 | 838 |

Data supplied by Steel and Ones (2002).

*How would you explain some of the wide variations in mean personality scores for the cultures listed here?*

for the existence of the Big Five factors. Analysis of the indigenous questionnaires suggested in addition personality dimensions of social curiosity (e.g., gossiping) and risk taking.

There may be more profound differences among cultures than has been suggested so far. It has often been argued that there is a major distinction between individualist and collectivistic cultures (see Chapter 1), with the former emphasising personal responsibility and the latter focusing on group obligations. The entire notion of semi-permanent personality traits determining behaviour may be less applicable in collectivistic cultures, in which it is assumed that individuals will be changeable and do whatever is needed to fit in with group expectations. For example, Norenzayan, Choi, and Nisbett (1999) found that people from Western cultures regard personality traits as stable, whereas East Asians regard traits as much more flexible and changeable. In line with this analysis, there is evidence that personality traits do not predict behaviour as well in collectivistic cultures as they do in individualistic ones (Church & Katigbak, 2000).

## Evaluation

● There has been an impressive increase in the number of studies concerned with cultural similarities and differences in personality.

● Evidence for H.J. Eysenck's three personality factors and the Big Five factors has been found in numerous cultures.

● When indigenous measures of personality have been used, there is often evidence for the existence of personality dimensions over and above those emphasised in Western cultures.

● Most cross-cultural studies have relied heavily on data collected from student samples. Students in non-Western cultures are more likely than non-students to be influenced by Western values and ideas (Triandis & Suh, 2002). As a result, such studies may minimise the differences in personality among cultures.

● The notion that individual differences in behaviour are determined by semi-permanent personality traits or factors is probably more relevant in individualistic than collectivistic cultures.

*What are the drawbacks in using student samples for research into personality?*

## Overall evaluation of the trait approach

The trait approach to personality has several strengths. First, it is reasonably scientific, and has shown real progress over time. Second, the trait approach has produced an approximate description of the structure of human personality. Several lines of research converge on the conclusion that conscientiousness, extraversion, agreeableness, and neuroticism are all major personality traits, with openness to experience probably forming a fifth trait. Third, twin studies have shown that genetic factors are important in determining individual differences in personality.

What about weaknesses with the trait approach? First, "Trait theories have had extraordinarily little to say about how personality works … or how it influences behaviour, how the person gets from trait to action" (Carver & Scheier, 2000, p. 86). Second, trait theorists typically assume that personality is stable over time. It is fairly stable, but less so than intelligence (Conley, 1984). As Pervin and John (1997, p. 295) pointed out, "It is one thing to document the stability of personality and to suggest reasons for such stability—genetic (temperament) factors, selection and shaping of situations … It is another thing to entirely omit an account of how change comes about." Third, critics of the trait approach have attacked the assumption that individuals behave consistently in different situations. According to Mischel (1968), there is actually very little **cross-situational consistency**, which would involve any given individual behaving in similar ways across different situations. Trait theorists assume that behaviour can be predicted on the basis of personality traits, and so they predict that there will be fairly high levels of cross-situational consistency. Mischel's literature review revealed that personality measures rarely correlate more than about +.30 with behaviour in any given situation.

*To what extent do you think it is possible for people to change their personality?*

Novel, formal, and public situations            Familiar, informal, and private situations

**KEY TERM**
**Cross-situational consistency:** the extent to which an individual responds in the same way in different situations.

*Can you think of any circumstances where situational variables might determine our behaviour more than our personality traits?*

This means that personality accounts for no more than 9% of the individual differences in behaviour. Mischel concluded that personality predicts behaviour poorly, and that behaviour is overwhelmingly determined by the situation in which the individual finds him/herself.

There is some mileage in Mischel's criticisms of the trait approach. However, he failed to compare the effects of personality and of the situation directly, so he really did not know that situational factors predict behaviour much better than personality. Sarason, Smith, and Diener (1975) calculated the percentage of the variance (differences in behaviour among individuals) accounted for by personality and by the situation across 138 experiments. On average, the situation accounted for 10.3% of the variance, whereas personality accounted for 8.7% of the variance. Thus, it is not the case that behaviour is determined substantially more by the situation than by personality.

Further evidence that situational factors are not overwhelmingly important was reported by Funder and Ozer (1983). They focused on the impact of situational factors in classic studies such as Milgram's (1974) research on obedience to authority (see Chapter 20) and Darley and Latané's (1968) work on bystander intervention (see Chapter 19). The average correlation between the theoretically important situational factors manipulated in these studies and behaviour was about +.38 or 14% of the variance, which is only slightly greater than associations between personality and behaviour.

Epstein (1977) made the point that cross-situational consistency will be low if we correlate small and unreliable pieces of behaviour. He correlated ratings of sociability based on two samples of behaviour. When each sample was only one day in duration, the correlation was only +.37. However, this rose to +.81 when each sample was 14 days in duration. He concluded that there is considerable cross-situational consistency when extended samples of behaviour are considered.

We ignore some of the complexities of what is happening if we just focus on the issue of whether behaviour depends more on personality or on the situation. Behaviour often involves an interaction between personality and situation. Atkinson, Atkinson, Smith, and Bem (1993) distinguished three different kinds of interaction:

1. *Reactive interaction.* There are individual differences in behaviour in a given situation, because individuals differ in how they interpret that situation.
2. *Evocative interaction.* Other people's behaviour towards us depends to some extent on our behaviour towards them.
3. *Proactive interaction.* We often decide which situation to put ourselves in. For example, Furnham (1981) found that extraverts select social situations more often than introverts.

## SOCIAL COGNITIVE THEORY

Albert Bandura, an American psychologist born in 1925, has spent many years developing his approach to individual differences in behaviour. Initially, he worked very much within the behaviourist tradition (see Chapter 8). Thus, he argued that we need to study the environment very carefully to understand why people behave as they do. He also argued that learning occurs through performing responses that are rewarded and not performing responses that are punished. However, he gradually developed a more complex approach (Bandura, 1986, 1999). He identified some of the key differences between his social cognitive theory and behaviourism as follows: "People are self-organising, proactive, self-reflecting, and self-regulating, not just reactive organisms shaped and shepherded by external events [as in the behaviourist approach]" (Bandura, 1999, p. 154). More specifically, various cognitive processes and strategies are important in determining how someone will behave. Individual differences in behaviour in a given situation occur in part because individuals differ in their cognitive processes.

*How might cognitive processes account for individual differences?*

We can see more clearly how Bandura's social cognitive approach differs from some other approaches if we consider the figure on the next page. The behaviourists and some trait theorists argued in favour of what Bandura (1999) called unilateral causation. In the case of behaviourists, the emphasis was on the notion that the external environment determines behaviour. In the case of trait theorists, it was assumed that personal factors (e.g., personality traits) determine behaviour. Bandura argued that both approaches were far too simple-minded, and that it is more realistic to think in terms of triadic reciprocal causation (see the figure on the right). What is **triadic reciprocal causation**? The basic idea is that personal factors (e.g., cognitive and affective events), the environment, and behaviour all influence each other. For example, our behaviour and our motives often influence the precise environment in which we find ourselves. Thus, the environment influences us, but we also help to determine our own environment.

Bandura (1999) argued strongly that we can only predict people's behaviour when we take full account of the particular situation or context in which they find themselves. He contrasted this point of view with that of most trait theorists, who typically make use of questionnaires containing very general kinds of questions:

> *In this "one size fits all" approach, the items are decontextualised by deleting information about the situations with which people are dealing ... it is unrealistic to expect personality measures cast in non-conditional generalities to shed much light on the contribution of personal factors to psychosocial functioning in different task domains under diverse circumstances across all situations (p. 160).*

Bandura (1999) was highly critical of the traditional trait-based approach to personality. What, then, is his preferred view of personality? According to Bandura (p. 187):

> *The self embodies all of the endowments, belief systems, and distributed structures and functions through which personal agency is exercised rather than residing as a discrete [separate] entity in a particular place ... "Personality" is the integrated self system within which the previously identified constituents operate in complex mutual interaction.*

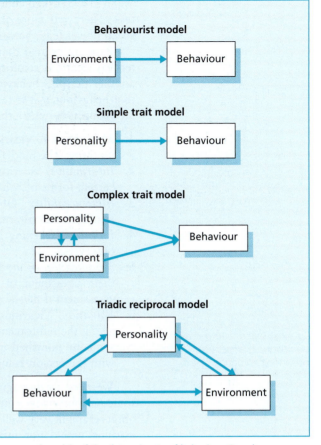

Various causal models of the determinants of behaviour. Based on Bandura (1999).

Some of the most important components of this integrated self system are discussed below.

## Observational learning

According to Bandura (1977b, p. 12):

> *Virtually all learning phenomena resulting from direct experience occur on a vicarious [second-hand] basis by observing other people's behaviour and its consequences for them. The capacity to learn by observation enables people to acquire large, integrated patterns of behaviour without having to form them gradually by tedious trial and error.*

The term **observational learning** or modelling is used to refer to learning by observing someone else's behaviour (see Chapter 8).

This emphasis on observational learning is very different from the behaviourist emphasis on learning to produce rewarded responses and to avoid producing punished responses. Observational learning may well have become increasingly important in the modern era, because much of what we learn is based on observing people on television and films.

According to Bandura (1986), the amount of observational learning obtained in any given situation depends on the model's characteristics. There is more observational learning with models who are attractive, trustworthy, similar to the observer, and who appear competent than there is with models lacking these characteristics. Brewer and

Wann (1998) asked college students to watch a videotape of a model performing a puzzle task. There was more observational learning when the model was described as possessing social power (e.g., he was an expert) than when he was not.

Bandura argued that a key factor associated with observational learning is what he termed vicarious reinforcement. **Vicarious reinforcement** occurs when someone observes another person's behaviour being rewarded or punished; they are more likely to imitate that behaviour if it is rewarded rather than punished. Bandura (1977b) specified several mechanisms by which the behaviour of observers is influenced by vicarious reinforcement:

1. *Motivational*. Vicarious reinforcement can motivate observers to imitate (or avoid imitating) the model's behaviour.
2. *Informative*. Vicarious reinforcement supplies information about the consequences of certain forms of behaviour.
3. *Influenceability*. Observers may become more affected by a particular form of reinforcement after they see how the model responds to similar reinforcements.
4. *Emotional learning*. Vicarious reinforcement can generate emotional arousal or fear in observers.
5. *Modification of model status*. Vicarious reinforcement can lead observers to increase their assessment of the model's status if he/she is rewarded, or to decrease their assessment if he/she is punished.
6. *Valuation*. Vicarious reinforcement can change how observers perceive the person giving the reinforcement as well as how they perceive the model. For example, seeing someone punished unjustly may lead observers to dislike the punisher and identify with the person being punished.

*To what extent can our own behaviour change after observing someone else?*

We need to distinguish between learning and performance. Consider, for example, someone observing a model behaving in a certain way and then being punished. The observer might very well *learn* something about the behaviour of the model. However, this learning would not influence *performance*, because the observer would not want to experience the negative consequences of behaving in the same way as the model.

## Evidence

Observational learning has been observed many times (see Chapter 16). For example, Bandura and Rosenthal (1966) carried out a study in which the participants watched a model. The model, who was a confederate of the experimenter, was attached to various pieces of electrical apparatus. When a buzzer sounded, the model withdrew his hand rapidly from the arm of the chair in which he was sitting, and pretended to be in pain. What happened after a while was that the participants started to react in a fearful way to the buzzer.

The importance of the distinction between learning and performance was shown by Bandura, Ross, and Ross (1963). Children were much more likely to imitate the behaviour of a model when the model's behaviour was rewarded than when it was punished. Thus, the consequences of the model's behaviour influenced the observer's performance. However, when the children were offered attractive incentives for copying the model's behaviour, there was no difference between the children who had seen that behaviour rewarded and those who had seen it punished. Thus, both groups of children had learned about the model's behaviour to the same extent.

Cook and Mineka (1989) obtained evidence of observational learning in rhesus monkeys. These monkeys all saw a videotape in which a monkey seemed to be responding with intense fear to a toy snake, a toy crocodile, a toy rabbit, or flowers. Those monkeys who saw the videotape involving the toy snake or crocodile developed a fear reaction to that object. However, this did not happen with the rabbit or flowers, presumably because they pose no danger in the real world. These findings present some problems for Bandura's approach: They suggest that observational learning can depend on our evolutionary history, in which it was desirable to develop fears of snakes and crocodiles. Bandura has not explicitly considered the relevance of our evolutionary history in influencing whether or not observational learning occurs.

**KEY TERM**

**Vicarious reinforcement:** a situation in which the reinforcement or reward obtained by someone else has a reinforcing effect on one's own behaviour.

## Evaluation

● Observational learning and vicarious reinforcement are both important phenomena that have been demonstrated in numerous studies.

● Observational learning helps us to understand why there are individual differences in behaviour in any given situation.

● Our evolutionary history influences whether or not we acquire fear responses through observing a fearful model.

● According to Bandura (1999, p. 173), "Modelling is not simply a process of response mimicry as commonly believed. Modelled judgements and actions may differ in specific content but embody the same rule." This is rather vague, and it may often be hard to decide whether the observer's behaviour does (or does not) "embody the same rule" as the model's behaviour.

## Self-efficacy

The notion of self-efficacy is of central importance within Bandura's social cognitive theory. **Self-efficacy** refers to the beliefs that individuals have concerning their ability to cope with a particular task or situation and achieve the desired outcome. In the words of Bandura (1977a, p. 391), self-efficacy judgements are concerned, "not with the skills one has but with judgements of what one can do with the skills one possesses". Self-efficacy is claimed to predict several aspects of behaviour. According to Bandura (p. 194):

*Given appropriate skills and adequate incentives, ... efficacy expectations are a major determinant of people's choice of activities, how much effort they will expend, and how long they will sustain effort in dealing with stressful situations.*

An individual's sense of self-efficacy in any given situation is determined by four main factors:

1. The individual's *previous experiences* of success and/or failure in that situation.
2. *Relevant vicarious experiences* (e.g., if you see someone else cope successfully with a situation, this may increase your self-efficacy beliefs).
3. *Verbal (or social) persuasion.* Your feelings of self-efficacy may increase if someone argues persuasively that you have the skills needed to succeed in that situation.
4. *Emotional arousal.* High levels of arousal are often associated with anxiety and failure, and can serve to reduce feelings of self-efficacy.

*What might result in some people under-estimating their abilities?*

Previous success in a situation may make an individual more likely to believe they will succeed again, whereas previous failure may lead to reluctance to put much effort in or show much interest.

## Evidence

Self-efficacy beliefs have often been found to predict behaviour. For example, Dzewaltowski (1989) recorded the amount of exercise taken by 328 students over a 7-week period. Before this period, Dzewaltowski obtained measures of various factors (e.g., the students' behavioural intentions) that might predict how much exercise they would take. Self-efficacy beliefs concerning their ability to participate in an exercise programme when faced with competing demands emerged as the best single predictor. Perceived self-efficacy correlated +.34 with exercise behaviour.

*How can we increase a person's sense of self-efficacy?*

Dennis and Goldberg (1996) carried out a study on 54 obese women involved in a 9-month nutrition and weight-loss programme. Those women high in self-efficacy were categorised as assured, whereas those who were low in self-efficacy were categorised as disbelievers. The assured lost significantly more weight than the disbelievers over the 9-month period, suggesting that self-efficacy plays a role in successful weight loss.

Stajkovic and Luthans (1998) carried out a meta-analysis of 114 studies concerned with the relationship between self-efficacy and work-related performance. The mean correlation between self-efficacy and performance was +.38, meaning that self-efficacy accounted for 14% of the variance or variation in performance across individuals. Stajkovic and Luthans (p. 252) then worked out that this correlation was equivalent to a 28% increase in performance, which compared favourably against the increase associated with other variables: "This 28% increase in performance due to self-efficacy represents a greater gain than, for example, those obtained in meta-analysis examining the effect on performance of goal setting (10.39% …), feedback interventions (13.6% …), or organisational behaviour modification (17% …)."

Stajkovic and Luthans (1998) also found that the strength of the relationship between self-efficacy and performance was influenced by two factors: task complexity and study setting (laboratory vs. field). Self-efficacy was more strongly associated with high task performance on easy tasks than on complex ones. In addition, the strength of the association was consistently higher in laboratory settings than in more naturalistic field settings. Thus, the mean correlation between self-efficacy and performance on easy tasks in the laboratory was +.54, whereas it was only +.20 on hard tasks in field settings. Why did these differences occur? Presumably the relationship between self-efficacy and performance will be greatest when the participants possess detailed information about task demands, the best strategy to adopt to perform the task successfully, and so on. Participants performing hard tasks in field settings will often have insufficient information to make an accurate judgement of self-efficacy.

*In what ways can self-efficacy improve performance?*

Caprara, Barbaranelli, and Pastorelli (1998) compared the power of self-efficacy and of the Big Five personality factors to predict academic achievement and peer preference. The Big Five factors nearly all failed to have any predictive power, except that openness predicted academic achievement. In contrast, academic and self-regulatory self-efficacy both predicted academic achievement and peer preference.

Judge and Bono (2001) carried out a meta-analysis to consider the effects of generalised self-efficacy and of emotional stability (low neuroticism) on job performance. Both factors were significantly related to job performance. The mean correlation between generalised self-efficacy and job performance was +.23, and it was +.19 between emotional stability and job performance.

## Evaluation

⊕ Strong associations have often been found between self-efficacy and performance (Stajkovic & Luthans, 1998), and these associations are often larger than those of other variables with performance.

⊕ Cognitive processes (e.g., self-efficacy judgements) play an important role in determining individual differences in motivation (see also research on goal setting discussed in Chapter 3).

● Self-efficacy predicts performance less well when the task is difficult and/or the task is performed under naturalistic conditions rather than in the laboratory.
● Self-efficacy judgements are based only on internal processes of which the individual has conscious awareness.
● There are tricky issues about causality. It is assumed that self-efficacy plays a role in determining performance. However, past performance undoubtedly helps to determine self-efficacy judgements, so the association between self-efficacy and performance is hard to interpret.

## Self-regulation

According to Bandura (1986), our behaviour is often determined by self-regulation. **Self-regulation** involves using one's cognitive processes to regulate and control one's own behaviour, often involving a process of self-reward if a given standard of performance is achieved. Thus, our behaviour is often controlled by internal factors rather than the external ones (e.g., reward or reinforcement) emphasised by the behaviourists. Bandura (1977a, pp. 128–129) provided vivid examples to support this point of view: "Anyone who attempted to change a pacifist into an aggressor or a devout religionist into an atheist would quickly come to appreciate the existence of personal sources of behavioural control."

*Under what circumstances might you make a conscious effort to control your own behaviour?*

Bandura (1986) spelled out the processes involved in self-regulation in some detail:

1. *Self-observation.* Individuals observe their own behaviour (e.g., the quality of their work, their productivity).
2. *Judgemental processes.* Individuals take account of their personal standards, of standard norms (i.e., the performance of other people), and of the role of personal and external factors in influencing their performance.
3. *Self-reaction.* Individuals experience positive self-reactions of pride or self-satisfaction when their behaviour reaches or exceeds their personal standards. In contrast, they experience self-criticism or dissatisfaction when their behaviour falls short of their personal standards.

According to the behaviourists, we are strongly influenced by the external rewards (e.g., money) provided for behaving in certain ways. Central to the notion of self-regulation is

> **KEY TERM**
> **Self-regulation:** this involves using one's own cognitive processes to control and regulate one's own behaviour and goals.

According to the behaviourists, the way we behave is strongly influenced by external rewards.

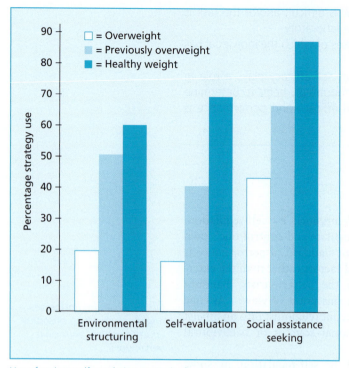

Use of various self-regulation strategies by overweight, previously overweight, and healthy weight participants. Data from Kitsantas (2000).

that what is also important is self-reinforcement, which is based on our internal reactions to our own behaviour. In the words of Bandura (1999, p. 176):

*People pursue courses of action that give them self-satisfaction and a sense of self-worth, but they refrain from behaving in ways that result in self-censure … The self-regulation of behaviour by self-evaluative reactions is a uniquely human capability … Self-evaluation gives direction to behaviour and creates motivators for it.*

Self-regulation should not be regarded as being totally separate from observational learning and self-efficacy. For example, observing others can help to determine what we regard as a reasonable standard of performance, and can influence which aspects of our behaviour or performance are the main focus of our self-observations. Part of the relationship between self-regulation and self-efficacy was spelled out by Bandura (1999, p. 176):

*After people attain the standard they have been pursuing, those who have a strong sense of efficacy generally set a higher standard for themselves.*

## Evidence

People using self-regulation strategies generally perform better than those who make less use of such strategies. For example, Kitsantas (2000) considered self-regulation and self-efficacy in college students belonging to three groups: overweight students who had failed to lose weight, previously overweight students who had successfully lost weight, and students with no weight problems. All participants completed a questionnaire indicating the types of self-regulation strategies they used, and their self-efficacy beliefs concerning their ability to use these strategies successfully. The self-regulation strategies considered included the following: goal setting and/or planning (e.g., desired weight), self-monitoring to keep track of progress in losing weight, self-evaluation of progress in weight control, and attempts to seek help in efforts to lose weight.

What did Kitsantas (2000) find? First, the overweight students who didn't lose weight used fewer self-regulation strategies than did the other two groups (see the top figure). This was especially the case for self-evaluation of progress, which was a strategy used by far fewer overweight students than students in the other groups. Second, the overweight students who didn't lose weight

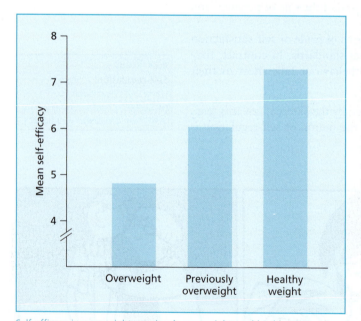

Self-efficacy in overweight, previously overweight, and healthy weight groups. Data from Kitsantas (2000).

also had lower levels of self-efficacy than students in the other two groups (see the bottom figure). Third, the use of several self-regulation strategies was only effective when combined with high self-efficacy. Overall, individuals who want to lose weight (or to maintain a healthy weight) should use many self-regulation strategies and should have strong self-efficacy beliefs that they can carry out these strategies successfully.

## Evaluation

● Much human behaviour is motivated by self-reinforcement rather than directly by external rewards.

● The role of internal factors (e.g., self-observation, self-reaction) in determining motivation and behaviour was de-emphasised in most previous theories.

● Numerous factors influence self-regulation, and so an apparent failure to support the theory can be explained away with reference to factors not explicitly included in the study.

● "Sometimes a behaviour is maintained with no obvious external reinforcer. In such a case, the [social cognitive] theorists assert that the behaviour is being supported by self-reinforcement … If self-reinforcement accounts for behaviour sometimes, why isn't it adequate all the time? Why is external reinforcement ever necessary? How do you decide when it's needed and when it isn't?" (Carver & Scheier, 2000, p. 372).

## Overall evaluation

● Observational learning, self-efficacy, and self-regulation are all important in determining how any given individual will behave in a particular situation.

● "Social cognitive theory investigates and attempts to account for the very phenomena that are of interest to most people—aggression, the effects of parents and mass media on children, … and the increase of control over one's life" (Pervin & John, 1997, p. 445).

● Bandura's approach has deservedly been very influential within health psychology. The extent to which people adopt healthy forms of behaviour (e.g., giving up smoking, losing weight, taking exercise) depends to an important extent on factors such as self-efficacy.

● The theory has been open to change, and there has been an appropriate increasing emphasis on cognitive processes and on self-regulation.

● "Social cognitive theory has been criticised for being neither systematic nor unified. Several important topics have been studied extensively … but how these topics are related to each other is not clear" (Hergenhahn & Olson, 1999, p. 372). For example, the relationships among observational learning, self-efficacy, and self-regulation are not entirely clear.

● The emphasis in social cognitive theory is too much on cognitive factors and not enough on emotional ones. Much human motivation and behaviour is influenced by our emotions rather than by cool calculation.

● "Little is said in social cognitive theory about the biological, hormonal, or maturational influences on personality development" (Hergenhahn & Olson, 1999, p. 372).

● Bandura has focused mainly on predicting and understanding people's behaviour in specific situations rather than in broad areas of life. As a result, it is not clear that his social cognitive theory provides much understanding of individual differences in personality.

# SUMMARY

### Freud's psychoanalytic approach

According to Freud, the development of adult personality depends on the experiences of early childhood. He identified five stages of psychosexual development: oral, anal, phallic, latency, and genital. Adults encountering problems tend to regress to the stage of psychosexual development at which they fixated (experienced problems as children). Certain personality types are associated with fixation at each stage. Freud was correct in assuming that childhood experiences influence the development of adult personality. There is evidence for some of the personality types identified by Freud, but it is not clear that these personality types develop for the reasons he proposed. Freud exaggerated the importance of sexual impulses in the development of personality, and de-emphasised the role of genetic factors and adult experiences.

### Humanistic approach

Humanistic psychologists strongly favour a reliance on phenomenology. According to Rogers, individuals will be unhappy if there is a large discrepancy between their self-concept and their ideal self. There is evidence to support that assumption. According to Rogers, people are motivated to eliminate incongruence between their self-concept and experience, an assumption for which there is some support. The theory is limited in various ways: Unconscious processes are not studied; the approach is not properly scientific; and the influences of genetic factors and childhood experiences on adult personality are largely ignored.

### Personality assessment

Useful personality tests possess high reliability and moderate validity, and they have been standardised. Standardisation allows the meaning of an individual's test score to be evaluated by comparing it against the scores of other people. The development of personality measures can be based on some theoretical approach or on a more purely empirical approach. There are four main types of personality assessment: self-report questionnaires, ratings, objective tests, and projective tests. Many questionnaires have high reliability and moderate validity, but their value can be limited because of social desirability bias. Ratings often have high reliability and moderate validity. Raters may have only partial knowledge of the person being rated, because they have only observed them in certain situations. Objective tests are typically free from problems of deliberate distortion. However, most objective tests suffer from low reliability and validity, and the same is true of nearly all projective tests.

### Trait theories of personality

Cattell used the fundamental lexical hypothesis in the construction of his 16PF test. He found reasonable agreement between the traits emerging from questionnaire and rating data, but rather different traits were found in objective-test data. The 16PF contains far fewer traits than Cattell claimed, and his approach was not very theoretical. Eysenck identified three uncorrelated personality factors (extraversion, neuroticism, and psychoticism). As predicted, individual differences in Eysenck's three factors depend to a moderate extent on genetic factors. Little progress has been made in identifying the physiological bases of these personality factors. Eysenck virtually ignored the cognitive system, and often failed to adhere to generally accepted rules for the conduct and reporting of scientific research. According to the five-factor theory, there are five major personality factors. Individual differences in these depend in part on genetic factors, but the factors correlate more with each other than they should. Some of the five factors (e.g., openness) may be less useful than others, and the five-factor theory is descriptive rather than explanatory. Individuals show less cross-situational consistency than suggested by trait theorists. However, behaviour is influenced by personality almost as much as by the situation.

According to Bandura's social cognitive theory, personal factors (e.g., cognitive events), the environment, and behaviour all influence each other, and we can only predict people's behaviour accurately when account is taken of the current situation. Bandura claims that behaviour is determined by observational learning, self-efficacy beliefs, and self-regulation. Self-efficacy judgements are fairly strongly associated with performance, especially on simple tasks performed under laboratory conditions. Self-regulation involves processes of self-observation, judgemental processes, and self-reaction, with a reliance on self-reinforcement rather than on external rewards. Social cognitive theory focuses too much on cognitive factors and not enough on emotional ones, and the role of genetic factors in determining individual differences is ignored. In addition, the theory sheds little light on individual differences in personality observed over a broad range of situations.

*Social cognitive theory*

## FURTHER READING

- Carver, C.S., & Scheier, M.F. (2000). *Perspectives on personality* (4th ed.). Boston: Allyn & Bacon. The authors of this textbook provide an accessible and clear account of the main theoretical approaches to personality.
- Cooper, C. (2002). *Individual differences* (2nd ed.). London: Arnold. This book provides an interesting introduction to both personality and intelligence research. It has the advantage over most other textbooks of discussing methods of assessment as well as theory and research.
- Pervin, L.A., & John, O.P. (Eds.) (1999). *Handbook of personality* (2nd ed.). New York: Guilford Press. This edited book has contributions by leading theorists in personality research (e.g., McCrae & Costa, Bandura).
- Triandis, H.C., & Suh, E.M. (2002). Cultural influences on personality. *Annual Review of Psychology, 53,* 133–160. This review chapter provides a detailed account of cross-cultural similarities and differences in personality.

# Developmental Psychology

# IV

This section of the book (Chapters 14–17) is concerned with developmental psychology. Developmental psychology is mainly concerned with the psychological changes occurring during the time between birth and adulthood. However, some developmental psychologists are interested in changes throughout the life span. Our primary focus will be on infancy and childhood, because that is the period of life in which the most dramatic changes in development occur.

Developmental psychology is of crucial importance to the understanding of adult behaviour. What we are now as adults depends to a large extent on the experiences we had during the years of childhood. In other words, as the poet William Wordsworth pointed out in *The Rainbow*, "The Child is father of the Man". The fact that the childhood years are vitally important means society has a responsibility to ensure that all children are provided with the opportunities and support they need to develop into well-adjusted and successful adults.

It should also be pointed out that the study of children is intrinsically fascinating, especially to parents. As a parent myself, I still remember very clearly being put in my place by my daughter Fleur, who was 2¼ at the time. We were on a cross-channel ferry, and I said to her, "Look, Fleur, there's a boat." I instantly felt deflated when she replied, "It's not a boat, Daddy, it's a yacht!" At the age of 4, Juliet (my other daughter) also managed to deflate me when she said earnestly, "A professor should know at least everything."

## ECOLOGY OF DEVELOPMENT

Bronfenbrenner (1979) proposed an influential approach within developmental psychology. According to his ecological model, we should study children in terms of the ecology or social and cultural environment in which they grow up. More specifically, Bronfenbrenner argued that development occurs within various environmental structures arranged "like a set of Russian dolls" (p. 3). There are four basic structures or systems:

- *Microsystem*. A microsystem consists of a child's direct experiences in a particular setting. Children typically encounter various microsystems in their everyday lives (e.g., school microsystem, home microsystem). Most developmental research focuses on children's behaviour within a single microsystem.
- *Mesosystem*. This consists of the inter-relationships among the child's various microsystems. For example, the child's ability to form friendships at school may depend in part on how securely attached he/she is to his/her parents at home.

- *Exosystem*. This consists of factors (e.g., parents' workplaces, mass media) that are not experienced directly by the child, but which nevertheless have an indirect impact on him/her.
- *Macrosystem*. This consists of the general beliefs and ideology of the culture, which can have various indirect effects on children. For example, if a child's parents have occupations that are highly valued by society, this may influence their behaviour at home.

Bronfenbrenner's (1979) ecological approach is attractive for two reasons. First, it helps to integrate the closely related areas of developmental and social psychology. Second, it is much broader in scope than most developmental theories, in which the emphasis is often primarily at the level of specific microsystems. However, a limitation of Bronfenbrenner's approach is that it does not lead to many precise and testable predictions.

It follows from Bronfenbrenner's approach that developmental psychologists should carry out cross-cultural studies. Such studies would help to clarify the role played by the macrosystem in influencing children's development. Most developmental research is still carried out in the United States and Europe, but there has been a welcome increase in cross-cultural research in recent years (see below).

## Evidence

Cross-cultural research is considered at various points over the next four chapters. For example, cross-cultural differences in expectations of males and females are discussed in Chapter 16, and cross-cultural differences in child rearing are dealt with in Chapter 17. Here we will consider two cultural differences of general importance. First, many cultures can be categorised as individualistic (with an emphasis on individual responsibility and achievement) or collectivistic (with an emphasis on the group) (see Chapter 1). We would expect to find more co-operative and conforming behaviour by children in collectivistic than in individualistic cultures (see below).

Tobin, Wu, and Davidson (1989) observed what happened in preschools in the United States (an individualistic culture) and in China (a collectivistic culture). The American children differed considerably from each other in their behaviour, and sometimes fought over attractive toys. The adults in charge made little effort to try to persuade them to behave in the same way, and allowed a certain amount of fighting to occur. In contrast, the Chinese children were highly regulated. They all went to the toilet at the same time, and the adults in charge expected them to play in a co-operative and helpful way with each other. Fighting over toys was simply not tolerated.

Co-operative behaviour in the form of altruistic or unselfish helping of others was considered by Eisenberg and Mussen (1989; see Chapter 16). They reported that altruistic behaviour by children was much more common in non-industrialised or collectivistic cultures than it was in industrialised or individualistic cultures.

Individualistic and collectivistic cultures even differ in what they regard as constituting intelligent behaviour in children and adults (see Chapter 12). Sternberg and Kaufman (1998) reviewed the evidence, concluding that the definition of intelligence includes many more social factors (e.g., consideration for others, social responsibility) in collectivistic cultures than in individualistic ones. For example, people living in a village in Kenya argued that intelligence involves obedience, sharing with others, and caring behaviour. These cultural differences influence the ways in which children are brought up and thus how they behave (Smith, Cowie, & Blades, 2003).

Second, cultures differ considerably in wealth and longevity, but note that wealthy countries are much more likely than poor ones to be individualistic (Hofstede, 1980). Childhood and adolescence typically last many more years in affluent cultures where life expectancy is high than in poor cultures with low life expectancy. Indeed, it is sometimes argued that adolescence exists only in Western cultures! For example, consider the !Kung San people who live in the Kalahari desert. When children in this culture reach puberty, they have already acquired good hunting and gathering skills that allow them to be self-sufficient and economically independent (Cole & Cole, 2001).

# METHODS IN DEVELOPMENTAL PSYCHOLOGY

Much research in developmental psychology still involves laboratory studies. There is a danger with laboratory studies that the findings may be of limited relevance to everyday life. However, researchers are well aware of this danger, and increasing numbers of studies are being carried out in naturalistic surroundings (e.g., school playgrounds; see Chapters 16 and 17).

The main advantage of naturalistic studies is that they are more likely to provide findings of relevance to children's everyday lives and behaviour. However, such studies tend to suffer from the disadvantage that they are less well controlled than laboratory studies. For example, it would be very difficult to control the activities of children in a playground. The appropriate way of dealing with these issues is to carry out both laboratory and naturalistic studies. If broadly similar findings can be obtained from both kinds of studies, then we can have some confidence that the findings are genuine and applicable to everyday life.

Most research on children used to involve obtaining relatively simple response measures (e.g., reaction times). However, there has been a substantial increase in studies in which much more complex types of behaviour have been assessed. There are perhaps two key reasons for this change. First, the ready availability of video-recording equipment means that children's behaviour can be replayed over and over again so that its full richness can be analysed. Second, computer-based software packages for analysing complex sets of data are now in wide use, and greatly simplify data analyses.

# ORGANISATION OF CHAPTERS 14–17

Developmental psychology is extremely broad in scope, but it can be argued that it deals largely with cognitive and social development. The four chapters on developmental psychology reflect that basic distinction. Chapter 14 and Chapter 15 are concerned with cognitive development, whereas Chapters 16 and 17 deal with social development. Chapter 14 focuses on the development of various important abilities, including perception, memory, language, and theory of mind. In Chapter 15, the emphasis shifts to general theories of cognitive development, including the very influential approaches proposed by Jean Piaget and by Lev Vygoysky. Chapter 16 deals with the development of several aspects of social development, such as moral development, development of pro-social and anti-social behaviour, and gender development. Finally, in Chapter 17, we consider the most general and important aspects of social development. These include the child's attachment to its parents or significant caregivers, the consequences of parental deprivation and divorce, friendships, and relationships with peers (children of the same age).

Please do not infer from the organisation of these chapters that cognitive and social development are completely separate from each other. In fact, cognitive development is influenced by social development, and social development depends in part on cognitive development. Accordingly, the links between these two major forms of development are emphasised at several points across the four chapters.

- **Perceptual development**
  Assessing the perceptual capabilities of infants.

  *Different research methods*
  *Visual and auditory abilities of newborns*
  *Studies into, and theories of, face perception*
  *Depth perception*
  *Size and shape constancy*
  *Theoretical views of perception*

- **Memory development**
  Explanations of the process of memory improvement.

  *Basic processes and capacity: working memory*
  *Memory strategies: rehearsal, organisational strategies*
  *Metamemory*
  *Content knowledge; scripts*
  *Explicit and implicit memory*
  *Infantile amnesia*
  *Eyewitness testimony; interviewer bias*

- **Language acquisition**
  The development of language.

  *Stages of language development: cooing, single words, telegrams, further development*
  *Inside-out theories: Chomsky's language acquisition device and linguistic universals; critical period hypothesis*
  *Outsite-in theories: child-directed speech; Piaget's cognitive approach and Tomasello's constructivist approach*

- **Animal language acquisition**
  Attempts to teach animals language.

  *Definitions of language*
  *Discussion of various studies using chimpanzees: Washoe, Kanzi, Panabanisha, Nyota*

- **Theory of mind**
  The development of attribution.

  *Assessment using false-belief tasks*
  *Exploration of the theory-of-mind deficit in autistic children*

# Cognitive development: Specific abilities

## PERCEPTUAL DEVELOPMENT

How much can the newborn baby (or neonate) see and hear? It used to be assumed the answer was "very little". William James, towards the end of the nineteenth century, described the world of the newborn baby as a "buzzing, blooming confusion, where the infant is seized by eyes, ears, nose and entrails all at once". This suggests that the infant is bombarded by information in all sense modalities, and cannot attach meaning to this information. That view under-estimates the capabilities of infants. Many basic perceptual mechanisms are working at a very early age, and infants are not merely helpless observers of their world.

A fascinating research development has involved the recognition that even foetuses are capable of some perceptual learning. For example, Kisilevsky et al. (2003) exposed 38-week-old foetuses to a tape recording of their mother or a female stranger reading a poem. They found that foetal heart rate increased when the poem was read by the mother but decreased when it was read by the stranger. These findings indicate that foetuses can discriminate between different voices prior to birth.

### Research methods

It is hard to assess perception in infants, because they cannot tell us what they can see. However, several techniques have been developed to assess their visual abilities. These techniques or methods are more likely to *under-estimate* than *over-estimate* the perceptual abilities of infants:

- *Behavioural method.* Various behavioural measures can be taken to discover what infants can perceive. For example, Butterworth and Cicchetti (1978) tested infants in a room in which the walls and the ceiling moved towards and away from them. The infants lost balance, and this loss of balance was always in the expected direction.
- *Preference method.* Two or more stimuli are presented together, and the experimenter simply observes which stimulus attracts the most attention. If infants systematically prefer one stimulus to another, they can discriminate between them. The use of video recordings means that the infant's direction of gaze can be established very accurately.
- *Habituation method.* A stimulus is presented repeatedly until the infant no longer attends to it; this is known as **habituation**. When the infant shows habituation to one stimulus, he/she is shown a different stimulus. If the infant responds to the new stimulus, he/she must have discriminated between the two stimuli. Habituation is useful for infants, because it leads them to explore their environment.
- *Eye-movement method.* The eye movements of infants can provide information about their visual perception. For example, if infants are presented with a moving stimulus, the tracking response can be recorded. This indicates whether or not they can distinguish between the moving stimulus and the background.

A drawing of the Butterworth and Cicchetti moving room. The walls and ceiling of the room can be moved, although the floor is fixed. The children experience loss of balance, swaying forwards or backwards depending on which way the room appears to move.

*Can you think of any unwanted factors that might influence infants' behaviour when using the methods outlined above?*

- *Physiological method.* Various physiological measures can be used. One way of telling whether infants can discriminate between two stimuli is to measure their event-related potentials (brain-wave activity) to each stimulus. Alternatively, if infants show different patterns of heart rate and/or breathing rate to two stimuli, this suggests that the infants perceive the two stimuli differently.
- *Visual reinforcement method.* The infant is given control over the stimulus or stimuli presented to it. For example, Siqueland and DeLucia (1969) gave infants a dummy wired up so their sucking rate could be assessed. A stimulus was presented only while it produced a high sucking rate, being replaced when it did not. Stimuli of interest to infants are associated with a high sucking rate.

## Basic aspects of vision

Newborns are at a great disadvantage to adults with respect to several basic aspects of vision. For example, they have very poor visual acuity. We can assess visual acuity by presenting a display of alternating black and white lines, and then making the lines progressively narrower until they can no longer be separated in vision. In order for newborns to detect the separation of the lines, they need to be about 30 times wider than is the case for adults (Braddick & Atkinson, 1983).

Another visual limitation in newborns results from the fact that their eyes have a fixed focal length for the first 3 months of life. Older children and adults show accommodation, in which the curvature of the eye's lens alters to bring objects at different distances into focus (see Chapter 7). Newborns do not show accommodation, and so only objects 8 inches in front of them can be seen clearly. As Harris and Butterworth (2002) pointed out, it may not be a coincidence that this is approximately the distance between the infant and its mother's face when she is holding it in her arms.

The evidence suggests that the eye movements of newborns are fairly systematic rather than random, although their scanning abilities improve during the first 3 months of life (Haith, 1980). Of particular importance, the eye movements of newborns suggest they are searching for the edges of objects. When an edge is detected, a newborn's next few eye movements tend to be small so as to keep the visual focus close to it (Haith, 1980). Such findings suggest that visual perception in newborns emphasises specific or local features of stimuli. In contrast, adults' perception tends to be dominated by the global or general pattern of stimuli rather than local visual information (Kimchi, 1992; see Chapter 7). However, Cassia, Simion, Milani, and Umiltà (2002) found that newborns aged between 1 and 3 days resembled adults in that global visual information dominated over local visual information.

Colour vision is either non-existent or nearly so during the first weeks of life. Teller (1997) considered the evidence, and argued that newborns probably have no colour vision. However, "By two months, rudimentary colour vision has arrived. Most infants can probably discriminate red, blue, and green from each other, but not yet yellows and yellow-greens" (p. 2197).

Another basic aspect of visual perception is binocular disparity (see Chapter 7). There is a disparity or difference in the images projected on to the retinas of the two eyes that assists depth perception. Teller (1997) reviewed evidence suggesting that binocular disparity is first found in infants between the ages of 3 and 6 months.

So far we have considered only visual abilities. How good are newborns at relating visual and auditory information so as to establish the source of a sound? The evidence suggests they are surprisingly good at doing this. For example, newborn infants in one study (Muir & Field, 1979) were presented with two rattles in motion, one to their left and one to their right. Only one of these rattles made a sound, and most of the newborns showed a preference for looking at that rattle rather than the soundless one.

Further evidence that newborns can relate visual and auditory information was reported by Slater, Brown, and Badenoch (1997). Initially the newborns were presented several times with visual-auditory pairings (e.g., hearing the word "um" while seeing a red line). After that, they were presented with a familiar pairing and a novel pairing. The newborns preferred the novel pairing, indicating that they had learned the original pairing and had habituated to it.

Newborns are able to relate visual and auditory information, for example, the sight and sound of a rattle.

## Developmental processes

As we have seen, even newborns possess some basic perceptual abilities, including non-random eye movements, some ability to relate visual and auditory information, and a dominance of global over local visual information in perception. In addition, other visual abilities develop surprisingly rapidly during the early months of life. What processes underlie these developmental changes? So far as visual acuity and accommodation are concerned, maturational changes are of primary importance. For example, the eye is shorter in the newborn than in older infants, and the pupil is smaller. As a consequence, the image of a visual stimulus falls on a smaller area of the retina of newborns than of older infants. The development of colour vision also probably depends on maturational changes (Teller, 1997).

The position with respect to binocular disparity is more complicated. Banks, Aslin, and Letson (1975) studied adults who had had problems with binocular vision because of having a squint in childhood that was subsequently corrected. Their degree of binocular disparity was assessed as follows: The participants first stared at tilted gratings with one eye, and then stared at vertical gratings with the other eye. Individuals with normal binocular disparity show a tilt after-effect, in which the vertical gratings appear tilted in the opposite direction to the original gratings.

The findings obtained by Banks et al. (1975) depended on the age at which the squint was detected, and the age at which corrective surgery was carried out:

1. *Squint at birth or shortly thereafter, and surgery by 30 months of age.* There was a nearly normal tilt after-effect, indicating reasonable binocular disparity.
2. *Squint diagnosed between 2 and 7 years of age, and surgery 2 or 3 years after diagnosis.* Reasonable levels of tilt after-effect, and thus binocular disparity.
3. *Squint at birth or shortly thereafter, and surgery between the ages of 4 and 20.* Little evidence of tilt after-effect, and thus little or no binocular disparity.

The above findings suggest there is a critical or sensitive period for the development of binocularity during the early years of life. If children are unable to develop binocularity during the first few years of life because of an uncorrected squint, then it may be virtually impossible to develop it thereafter.

## Face perception

Fantz (1961) used the preference method to study face perception. He showed infants (aged between 4 days and 5 months) pairs of face-shaped discs and measured the amount of time spent fixating each one. There were realistic faces, scrambled faces, and blank faces. Infants of all ages looked most at the realistic face and least at the blank face, suggesting the ability to recognise faces is either innate or learned shortly after birth. Clearer evidence as to whether face recognition is innate requires

Faces used in Fantz's study

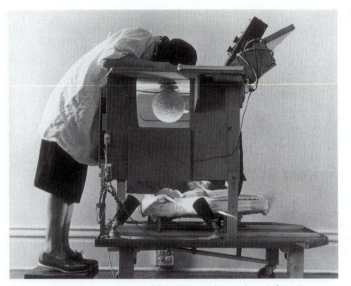

The experimental apparatus used by Fantz to observe how infants respond to visual stimuli.

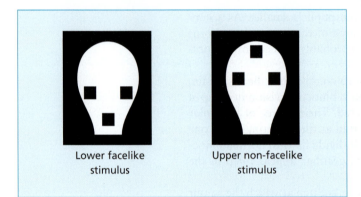

Lower facelike stimulus

Upper non-facelike stimulus

Newborns preferred an upper non-facelike stimulus (shown on the right) to the lower facelike stimulus (shown on the left). From Turati et al. (2002).

the use of newborn infants. Johnson et al. (1991) studied newborns in the first hour after birth. The newborns showed more visual tracking of realistic faces than of scrambled but symmetrical faces, suggesting that some aspects of face perception do not depend on learning.

Walton, Bower, and Bower (1992) presented infants between 1 and 4 days of age with videotapes of their mother's face and the face of a similar looking woman. Eleven out of twelve infants preferred their mother's face, indicating that infants can discriminate among faces at a very early age. Pascalis et al. (1995) replicated those findings in infants 4 days old. However, the infants could not distinguish between their mother and an unfamiliar woman when both wore scarves to hide their external facial features (e.g., hair).

Simion, Valenza, Macchi Cassia, Turati, and Umiltà (2002) argued that newborns' apparent preference for facelike stimuli may reflect a more general tendency for them to prefer *any* visual stimuli having more elements in their upper part. They found newborns preferred visual stimuli having more elements in the top half than the bottom half even with stimuli not looking anything like faces. Additional evidence was reported by Turati, Simion, Milani, and Umiltà (2002). Newborns aged between 1 and 3 days did *not* prefer facelike stimuli to non-facelike stimuli when the number of elements in the upper part was held constant. Of key importance, newborns preferred a stimulus consisting only of a non-facelike arrangement in the upper part to a stimulus consisting only of a facelike arrangement in the lower part (see the figure opposite). These findings suggest that, "Newborns direct their gaze toward faces because they belong to a broader stimulus category that is characterised by a greater number of high-contrast areas in the upper portion of the pattern" (p. 881).

## Theoretical views

*Why might it be useful for newborns to have a preference for facelike stimuli?*

Most of the evidence indicates that newborns prefer to look at facelike stimuli with the features arranged naturally than at facelike stimuli with the features arranged unnaturally or at non-facelike stimuli. It is also clear that infants a few days old prefer to look at their mother than at another woman. However, there has been considerable theoretical controversy concerning how to interpret the findings. Here we will consider three main theories.

First, there is the theory of Morton and Johnson (1991). They argued that human infants are born with a mechanism containing information about the structure of human faces. This mechanism is known as CONSPEC, because the information about faces it contains relates to conspecifics (members of the same species). More specifically, CONSPEC responds to the presence of three blobs in a triangular formation corresponding to the two eyes and the mouth within a face-sized stimulus.

Second, there is the theory proposed by Bushnell (1998). He argued that newborns do not possess an innate mechanism specialised for faces. Instead, he argued that a preference for faces in newborns occurs as a result of rapid learning. Newborns spend more time looking at their mother's face than at any other stimulus, and this allows them to develop a preference for looking at her face within about 4 days of being born. According to this theoretical perspective, the development of face perception is very similar to that for other objects. The main distinctive feature of the development of face perception is that it happens more rapidly, but this occurs only because newborns devote more of their time to looking at faces than at other objects.

Third, there is the sensory hypothesis proposed by Simion et al. (2002) and by Turati et al. (2002). According to this hypothesis, there is nothing special about faces. The only reason they are preferred to other visual stimuli is because they contain more elements in the upper part than in the lower part.

And the winner is … ? Unfortunately, it is still not clear which theory accounts best for the development of face recognition and perception. However, the findings of Simion et al. (2002) and of Turati et al. (2002) are hard to reconcile with Morton and Johnson's (1991) CONSPEC mechanism. CONSPEC should always prefer facelike stimuli to non-facelike ones, but Turati et al. reported several findings inconsistent with this prediction.

What about the other two theories? The findings of Simion et al. (2002) and of Turati et al. (2002) are consistent with the sensory hypothesis, according to which a preference for stimuli with more elements in the upper part leads to a preference for faces. However, these findings are also consistent with an alternative view based on Bushnell's (1998) position, according to which the early experiences newborns have with human faces leads to a preference for stimuli sharing similar qualities. The jury is still out.

## Depth perception

Gibson and Walk (1960) studied depth perception by designing a "visual cliff" involving a glass-top table (see the figure below). A check pattern was positioned close to the glass under one half of the table (the "shallow" side) and far below the glass under the other half (the "deep" side). Infants between the ages of 6½ and 12 months were placed on the shallow side of the table, and encouraged to crawl over the edge of the visual cliff on to the deep side. Most failed to respond to these incentives, suggesting they possessed some elements of depth perception. This is consistent with the evidence that binocular vision (which is helpful in depth perception) has typically developed by the age of 6 months (Teller, 1997).

Adolph (2000) argued that the development of depth perception is more complex than was assumed by Gibson and Walk (1960). She started by arguing that motor development in infancy involves a series of achievements, starting with sitting, followed by crawling, moving sideways, and then walking. Previous theorists had emphasised the notion that infants acquire *general* knowledge (e.g., an association between depth information and falling) that stops them from crossing the visual cliff. In contrast, Adolph's sway model is based on the assumption that infants' knowledge is highly *specific*. According to this model, infants learn how to avoid risky gaps when sitting, but subsequently have to learn how to avoid such gaps when they are crawling.

Adolph (2000) obtained support for her sway model by studying 9-month-old infants more familiar with sitting than with crawling. The key findings were that, "The babies avoided reaching over risky gaps in the sitting posture but fell into risky gaps while attempting to reach in the crawling posture" (p. 290). Adolph (p. 294) concluded as follows: "Infants must learn, posture by posture … how to discover … their region of permissible sway and to use this information for prospective control of action."

Arterberry, Yonas, and Bensen (1989) studied depth perception in a different way. Infants aged between 5 and 7 months were presented with two visual objects that were the same distance away from them. However, the objects were placed on a grid using linear perspective (a cue to depth based on the convergence of parallel lines) and texture

A drawing of Gibson and Walk's "visual cliff". Babies between 6½ and 12 months of age were reluctant to crawl over the "cliff" edge, even when called by their mothers, suggesting that they perceived the drop created by the check pattern.

gradient (increased rate of change of texture density from front to back) to suggest that one object was closer than the other. Most 7-month-old infants showed evidence of depth perception by reaching for the "closer" object, but 5-month-old infants did not.

In sum, most aspects of depth perception are present by about 6 months of age. However, infants' ability to use depth information effectively depends on the task and on their stage of motor development.

## Size and shape constancy

Nearly all adults display **size constancy** and **shape constancy**. Size constancy means that a given object is perceived as having the same size regardless of its distance from us, and shape constancy means that an object is seen to have the same shape regardless of its orientation. Thus, we see things "as they really are", and are not taken in by variations in the information presented to the retina. It is of interest to discover whether infants show size and shape constancy. As we will see, there is evidence that infants have at least partial size and shape constancy. Other evidence not discussed here suggests that infants possess various other constancies as well.

Studies using the habituation method suggest size constancy is an innate visual capacity. For example, Slater, Mattock, and Brown (1990) familiarised newborns with either a small or a large cube over a number of trials. After that, the two cubes were presented successively. The larger cube was presented at a greater distance from the newborns than the smaller cube, with the size of the retinal image being the same in both cases. All the newborns looked longer at the new cube, because they had habituated to the old one. The fact that they could distinguish between two cubes having the same-sized retinal image suggests the newborns possessed at least some of the elements of size constancy.

Slater and Morison (1985) used the habituation method to study shape constancy in newborns (average age 1 day, 23 hours). The newborns were shown a given shape (a square or a trapezium) at various angles of slant until they had habituated to it. Then they were shown the same shape at a novel angle together with a new shape. The newborns paid much more attention to the new shape than to the same shape presented at a novel angle. Thus, there was habituation to the same shape at a novel angle, and this indicates that newborns possess at least partial shape constancy.

Do findings such as those of Slater et al. (1990) and Slater and Morison (1985) indicate that newborns possess adult levels of size and shape constancy? By no means. All that can safely be concluded is that newborns have some ability to discriminate between a familiar object having a given size or shape and a novel object of a different size or shape, which is a very different kettle of fish.

## Theoretical approaches

Perceptual development is a complex matter, with different perceptual abilities developing at different ages and in various ways. Some aspects of visual perception (e.g., relating visual and auditory information, aspects of face perception, aspects of size and shape constancy, dominance of global over local features) seem to be present at birth or very shortly thereafter. These aspects reflect either innate visual capacities or very rapid learning. Other aspects of visual perception (e.g., visual acuity, colour vision) develop several weeks after birth, and may well depend on maturational factors. There are still other

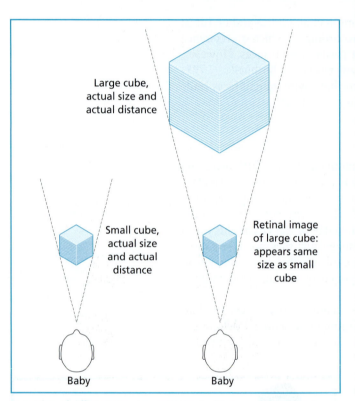

Large cube, actual size and actual distance

Small cube, actual size and actual distance

Retinal image of large cube: appears same size as small cube

Baby            Baby

Two cubes of different sizes may project retinal images of the same size, depending on their distance from the viewer.

*What could we learn from the study of size constancy in infants from other cultures?*

**KEY TERMS**

**Size constancy:** objects are perceived to have a given size regardless of the size of the retinal image.

**Shape constancy:** objects are perceived to have a given shape regardless of the angle from which they are viewed.

aspects of perception for which there may be a critical or sensitive period for their development (e.g., binocular disparity). Finally, there are other aspects of perception (e.g., those relating to depth perception) that develop only after several months of life, and probably require certain kinds of learning.

The notion that specific forms of learning are important has been confirmed in animal research. For example, Blakemore and Cooper (1970) reared kittens in an environment consisting only of horizontal or vertical black-and-white stripes. Thereafter, the kittens responded to visual stimuli in the familiar orientation, but failed to respond to stimuli in the unfamiliar orientation (e.g., horizontal stripes were ignored by cats reared in the presence of vertical stripes). Recordings taken from neurons in the visual cortex revealed that neural activity was present only when stripes in the familiar orientation were presented.

How can we explain the order in which the various visual capacities appear developmentally? Kellman (1996, pp. 40–41) argued as follows:

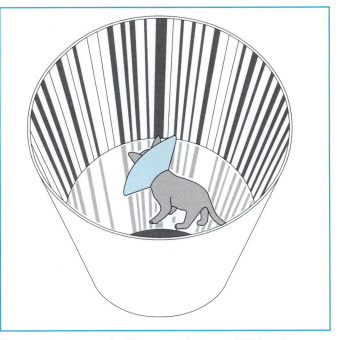

The experimental set-up for Blakemore and Cooper's (1970) studies on visual development in kittens.

> *The order of appearance of perceptual capacities closely parallels their ecological validity; that is, information that most closely specifies the environment is usable first ... For infants, perceiving comprehensively is not nearly so crucial as perceiving accurately. If the infant is built as risk aversive in this sense, we would expect perceptual abilities to appear in order of ecological validity.*

Evidence consistent with the predictions of this approach was reported by Spelke et al. (1993). They presented infants aged 3, 5, and 9 months and adults with simple but unfamiliar displays (see the figure on the right). Each display could be perceived as a single object or as two joined objects. What determined whether each display was seen as consisting of one or two objects? The Gestalt psychologists argued that we use various principles to decide which parts of the visual scene belong together. For example, there is the law of similarity: If parts of a

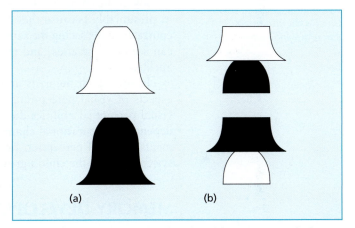

Schematic depiction of two types of displays: (a) homogeneous displays and (b) heterogeneous displays. From Spelke et al. (1993).

scene are similar (e.g., in colour and texture), we tend to assume those parts belong to the same object. Adults used the various principles as expected by Gestalt theory. In contrast, the infants saw most displays as single objects. They used the law of proximity (visual elements close to each other belong together), and largely ignored the other Gestalt principles (e.g., law of similarity). This makes sense if we assume that proximity is the most accurate predictor of which visual elements belong to the same object.

Other theoretical views of infant perception have been expressed by Teller (1997) and by Slater (1990, 1998). Teller (p. 2196) focused on the situation in which newborn infants find themselves:

> *Their acuity and contrast sensitivity are very poor but are measurable. Their ... eye movements reveal the capacity to analyse the direction of motion of large, high-contrast objects ... However, they should reveal no appreciation of stereo depth, no capacity to respond to low contrasts or to fine spatial details, and probably no colour vision. Their visual worlds are probably marked less by blooming and buzzing than by the haziness of low-contrast-sensitivity, the blurriness of spatial filtering, and the blandness of monochrome [black-and-white].*

Slater (1990, p. 262) summarised infants' perceptual skills:

*No modality [none of the senses] operates at adult-like levels at birth, but such levels are achieved surprisingly early in infancy, leading to recent conceptualisations of the "competent infant" ... early perceptual competence is matched by cognitive incompetence, and much of the reorganisation of perceptual representation is dependent upon the development and construction of cognitive structures that give access to a world of objects, people, language, and events.*

Slater (1998) provided more detailed support for the notion of the "competent infant".

It is undoubtedly the case that infants' visual perception differs substantially from that of an adult in many ways, especially with respect to the meaning or significance attached to visual stimuli. For example, suppose that you are looking at an object, but then someone covers it up with a cloth. I am sure you would expect the object to be there when the cloth is subsequently removed, but young children do not seem to have this expectation (see Chapter 15). According to Piaget, such findings mean that infants lack object permanence, meaning that they do not realise that objects continue to exist even when not in sight.

Evidence that infants sometimes do not perceive objects as we do was provided by Slater et al. (1990). They presented newborns with a visual display in which a rod was seen moving from side to side behind a box. The newborns never saw the entire rod; instead, they could see the top and bottom of the rod above and below the box. When a complete rod and a broken rod were subsequently presented to the newborns, they chose to look at the complete rod. They ignored the broken rod because they had habituated to it, presumably because they had perceived the rod behind the box as a broken one. In contrast, adults seeing the same display would assume there was a single rod of which they can see only the ends, and the same is true of infants aged 3 or 4 months (Kellman & Spelke, 1983).

In sum, both theorists accept that newborns immediately possess some of the main aspects of visual perception, and that there are rapid and substantial improvements in visual perceptual abilities during the early months of life. Many of these improvements depend on maturational changes in basic aspects of vision (Teller, 1997). Other developments in visual perception probably depend more on the development of the cognitive system, and on the child's growing store of knowledge (Slater, 1990, 1998).

*Can you think of an alternative explanation for these findings? (Clue: what else might preference indicate?)*

## MEMORY DEVELOPMENT

Children's ability to remember information becomes progressively better during the process of development. A key issue is to try to understand the main reasons for this progressive improvement. Siegler (1998) argued there are four possible explanations:

1. *Basic processes and capacity.* For example, the capacity of short-term or working memory may increase.
2. *Strategies.* Children possess more memory strategies as they develop, and may use these strategies more efficiently.
3. *Metamemory.* **Metamemory** "is knowledge *about* memory. The development of metamemory is the development of the ability to monitor and regulate one's own memory behaviour" (Goswami, 1998, p. 206).
4. *Content knowledge.* Older children possess more knowledge than younger ones, and this can make it easier to learn and remember new information.

All four explanations are discussed below. The evidence indicates that all four explanations possess some validity. However, there are some important limitations of most of the research in this area. As Ornstein and Haden (2001, p. 204) pointed out, "Because the bulk of the literature is based on cross-sectional experiments, little can be said about the developmental course of memory within individual children." In other words, we know older children possess memory skills and strategies not possessed by younger children.

**KEY TERM**

**Metamemory:** knowledge about one's memory and about how it works.

However, we lack a clear sense of the processes involved in the development of these skills and strategies. This can only be provided by longitudinal studies, but relatively few such studies have been carried out.

## Basic processes and capacity

One of the most important parts of the human information-processing system is working memory (see Chapter 9). **Working memory** allows us to process one kind of information while temporarily storing some other information. An example of a task requiring the use of working memory is as follows (Swanson, 1999). The participants are given a sentence such as, "Now suppose somebody wanted to have you take them to the supermarket at 8651 Elm Street." The task was to recall the name of the street, and then to recall the number.

The task just described provides an assessment of verbal working memory. Swanson (1999) used this and other tasks to measure verbal working memory and visuo-spatial working memory in people of various ages between 6 and 57. Both forms of working memory improved continuously throughout childhood and adulthood up to the age of 45. There are two main ways working memory might develop during childhood: (1) its capacity might increase; and (2) the capacity of working memory might remain constant, but it might be used with increasing efficiency. Swanson tried to distinguish between these explanations in the following way. If the participants could not produce the correct answer on a working-memory task, they were provided with cues consisting of part of the answer (e.g., "the last digit was 1"). If young children perform poorly on working-memory tasks because of limited capacity, then such cues would be relatively ineffective in improving performance. However, if the information is stored inefficiently, then cues might enable the children's performance to improve substantially.

Swanson (1999) found that the presentation of cues benefited the younger children no more than the older children and adults. Thus, Swanson (p. 986) concluded that the capacity of working memory increases during childhood. Swanson also found that age differences in working memory predicted reasonably well children's performance in reading and arithmetic. This suggests that working memory capacity is an important factor in cognitive development.

## Memory strategies

Adults use several memory strategies (e.g., verbal rehearsal) to assist them in learning and remembering. Older children make more use of rehearsal than do younger children. For example, Flavell, Beach, and Chinsky (1966) found on a picture-learning task that only 10% of 5-year-olds rehearsed, whereas the figure was 60% for 7-year-olds, and 85% for 10-year-olds. Age also influences the nature of rehearsal activity. When children 7 years old and above were told to rehearse out loud during the learning of several lists, the overall amount of rehearsal was similar in all groups (Cuvo, 1975). However, the younger children's rehearsal was often limited to repetition of a single word, whereas older children and adults typically rehearsed several words together.

Suppose adults try to remember a list consisting of, say, four words belonging to each of six categories presented in a random order. They typically use an organisational strategy, in which the words are rehearsed and recalled category by category. This organisational strategy leads to improved recall of the list. Do children use this strategy? Schneider (1986) presented 7- and 10-year-olds with pictures belonging to categories. The pictures

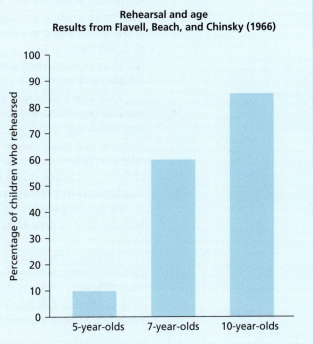

**Rehearsal and age**
**Results from Flavell, Beach, and Chinsky (1966)**

What does this suggest about the way in which memory is organised in older and younger children?

within each category were either highly associated (e.g., desk, lamp, sofa) or weakly associated (e.g., stove, bookcase, rocking chair). The children were told to sort the pictures, and then their picture recall was tested. About 60% of the 10-year-olds organised the pictures in categories, compared to only 10% of the 7-year-olds. The older children grouped pictures in a deliberate way on the basis of category labels, and were as likely to group weakly associated pictures as strongly associated ones. In contrast, the younger children were much more likely to group together highly associated pictures than weakly associated ones, and made very little use of categories.

Even very young children sometimes make spontaneous use of memory strategies. According to Ornstein and Haden (2001, p. 203), "18-month-olds begin to evidence rudimentary strategies such as verbalising, looking, and pointing when they are faced with the task of remembering the location of an attractive object that they had watched a researcher hide."

## Metamemory

As children grow older, they show increasing evidence of metamemory, which is knowledge about one's own memory, and how it works. For example, Yussen and Levy (1975) asked various groups (preschoolers, 9-year-olds, college students) to predict their own memory span, and then compared the predictions against the actual span. The preschoolers showed a much larger discrepancy between predicted and actual performance than either of the other two groups. The preschoolers on average thought they would be able to recall eight items, but actually averaged only just over three items. In contrast, the 9-year-olds showed a modest over-estimate of about one item, and the college students' predictions were accurate.

A key issue is whether children's metamemory knowledge predicts their memory performance. Schneider and Pressley (1989) carried out a meta-analysis based on 60 studies. The mean correlation coefficient between metamemory and memory performance was +.41, indicating a moderate relationship. Why isn't the relationship stronger? According to Schneider and Pressley, children may not be motivated to use effective memory strategies they possess, they may feel a good memory strategy is not needed when a word list is relatively short, and so on.

Fabricius and Hagen (1984) devised a situation in which 6- and 7-year-olds sometimes used an organisational strategy and sometimes did not. Recall was much higher when the organisational strategy was used. The children were then asked to explain their success on some of the trials. Some attributed their success to use of the organisational strategy, whereas others came up with other explanations (e.g., using their brain more). The children were then tested one week later in a somewhat different situation. Of those who attributed their previous success to the organisational strategy, 99% used it on the second occasion, compared to only 32% of those who attributed their previous success to other factors. Thus, a little metamemory knowledge may be a dangerous (or at least ineffective) thing.

There is a final note of caution. Self-reports or interviews are generally used to assess children's metamemory knowledge. However, as Schneider and Pressley (1997) pointed out, "There is a long history of scepticism about the validity of self-reports and interview data ... Young children's verbal skills are often inadequate for them to articulate their knowledge about memory."

## Content knowledge

If the amount of relevant knowledge is of major significance in determining memory performance, then a well-informed child might remember some things better than an ill-informed adult. This prediction was tested by Chi (1978), who looked at digit recall and reproduction of chess positions in 10-year-olds who were skilled chess players and in adults knowing little about chess. The adults performed better than the children on digit recall. However, the children's recall of chess positions was more than 50% better than that of the adults (see the figure on the next page).

Schneider, Gruber, Gold, and Opwis (1993) compared children who were experts at chess with adults with a comparable level of expertise. The expert children remembered chess positions as well as the expert adults, and both groups performed much better than non-expert children and adults. Thus, memory for chess positions depends largely on expertise and hardly at all on age.

Children learn at an early age that many events in their lives recur in similar forms. For example, a meal in a restaurant involves being shown to a table, ordering the food you want, eating the food, paying for it, and then leaving the restaurant. Young children store away much of this kind of information in the form of **scripts**, which are knowledge structures indicating the typical sequence for common events. These scripts make it easier for children (and adults) to make immediate sense of everyday events.

Very young children have already acquired various scripts. Bauer and Thal (1990) studied script knowledge in children aged 21 or 22 months. They presented children with a sequence of actions (e.g., giving teddy a bath involved putting the bear in the tub, washing it with the sponge, and then drying it with the towel). In one condition, sequences of actions were presented in the wrong or unnatural order. The children tended to recall the sequences in the correct order even when they had been presented in the wrong order. Presumably this occurred because the children already possessed the relevant scripts.

Schemas are similar to scripts in that both involve organised sets of information. However, schemas contain information about objects or scenes rather than about typical sequences of actions (see Chapter 9). Young children possess schemas as well as scripts. For example, Blades and Banham (1990) presented young children with a model of a kitchen that was realistic except that it lacked a cooker. When the children subsequently tried to reconstruct the kitchen, their performance was generally accurate. However, about 60% of them included a cooker in the reconstruction, suggesting that their schematic knowledge of kitchens distorted their memory for what they had seen previously. Schematic knowledge impaired memory in this particular study, but it generally leads to improved memory performance (see Chapter 9).

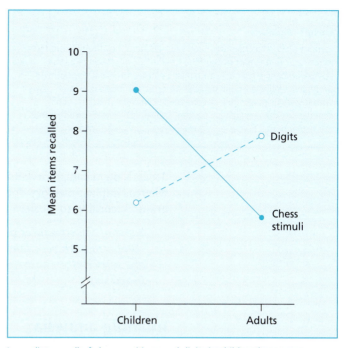

Immediate recall of chess positions and digits in children (mean age = 10 years 6 months) with expert knowledge of chess and in adults with limited knowledge of chess. Adapted from Chi (1978).

Schneider et al. (1993) found that age does not affect memory for chess positions.

# Implicit memory

The research discussed so far has been concerned with **explicit memory**, because the memory tests required conscious recollection of information. Explicit memory can be contrasted with **implicit memory**, a form of memory *not* dependent on conscious recollection (see Chapter 9). Implicit memory is surprisingly good even at a very early age. Indeed, implicit memory is often as good in young children as in adults. For example, Naito (1990) studied 5-, 8-, and 11-year-olds, and adults. They carried out a word-fragment completion task, in which they were given some of the letters of a word, and thought of the first word that came to mind (the target word). Before doing this task, the participants carried out other tasks involving some of the target words. The participants showed implicit memory by completing more word fragments successfully when the target words had been encountered before than when they had not. Implicit memory performance was the same at all age levels from 5 to adult. In contrast, Naito found that explicit memory

**KEY TERMS**

**Scripts:** knowledge structures relating to general events.

**Explicit memory:** memory that depends on conscious recollection; see implicit memory.

**Implicit memory:** memory not involving conscious recollection; see explicit memory.

**Earliest memories**

Lamont (2001) has demonstrated musical memories from before birth in research that is part of the BBC Child of Our Time project. She compared babies from eleven families where in the last 3 months of pregnancy daily half-hour sessions of particular music had been played with babies from another eleven families who had had no such experience. The research is ongoing, but results indicate strongly that the experimental babies do have a musical long-term memory.

(recalling the target words) was much better in older children and adults than in younger children.

Russo, Nichelli, Gibertoni, and Cornia (1995) obtained similar findings. They tested explicit and implicit memory for pictures in 4-year-olds, 6-year-olds, and young adults, all of whom showed comparable levels of implicit memory. However, explicit memory was highest in the adult group and lowest in the 4-year-olds.

Why does implicit memory develop fully much earlier than explicit memory? One reason is that explicit memory depends on metamemory and various complex memory strategies which develop with age, whereas implicit memory does not. Another reason has to do with the development of the brain. According to Siegler (1998, p. 181):

*Some of the structures associated with explicit memory, especially the prefrontal cortex, mature very late ... other structures—in particular, the hypothalamus— are sufficiently mature in the first few months after birth to support implicit processing.*

## Infantile amnesia

Infants start to show visual self-recognition, and therefore a sense of self, at about 20 months of age.

What happens when adults try to remember events and experiences from their own childhood? The most striking finding is that most people find it difficult (or impossible) to remember any events dating back to the first 3 or 4 years of life. The term **infantile amnesia** is used to describe this inability of adults to recall early experiences (see Chapter 9).

The most obvious explanation of infantile amnesia is that very young children are simply unable to form long-term memories. However, that is *not* the case. It is hard to assess memory in infants who possess very little language. However, much recent research (see Bauer, 2002, for a review) has used an effective method known as elicited imitation. What happens in **elicited imitation** is that objects are used to produce an action sequence (e.g., using a mallet to hit a metal plate), which the infant then tries to imitate. Most infants as young as 9 months remember the individual actions over a period of 1 month, and about 40% of them produce the actions in the correct sequence (Bauer, 2002). These abilities develop rapidly, with 60% of 16-month-olds exposed to an action sequence producing the actions in the right order after a 12-month delay (Bauer, Wenner, Dropik, & Wewerka, 2000).

According to Freud (1915), infantile amnesia is due to repression or banishing from consciousness of early traumatic and other threatening experiences. This explanation is clearly inadequate, because it cannot account for our inability to recall early positive and neutral experiences.

Howe and Courage (1997) related infantile amnesia to the emergence of the self towards the end of the second year of life. Infants at about 20 months show signs of developing a sense of self in the phenomenon of visual self-recognition, which involves responding to their own image in a mirror with self-touching, shy smiling, and gaze aversion (see Chapter 16). A few months after that, infants start to use words such as I, me, and you. The crucial theoretical assumption of Howe and Courage (p. 499) is as follows:

*The development of the cognitive self late in the second year of life (as indexed by visual self-recognition) provides a new framework around which memories can be organised. With this cognitive advance ..., we witness the emergence of autobiographical memory and the end of infantile amnesia.*

Howe and Courage also assumed that the processes (e.g., rehearsal) used in learning and memory develop during the years of childhood, and so relatively few autobiographical memories should come from the years 2 to 5.

As predicted from the above theoretical perspective, very few earliest memories come from the first 2 years of life, and relatively few come from the years between 2 and 5.

**KEY TERMS**

**Infantile amnesia:** an inability on the part of adolescents and adults to remember the events of early childhood.

**Elicited imitation:** a method of assessing memory in which an action sequence is shown to infants, who then try to imitate it.

However, we cannot conclude that there is clear evidence that the emergence of a sense of self is causally related to age of first memory. The fact that the age at which a sense of self develops is approximately the same as the age of earliest autobiographical memories could simply be a coincidence.

Social interactionist accounts (e.g., Fivush, Haden, & Reese, 1996) can also explain infantile amnesia. According to the social interactionist perspective, "The primary functions of autobiographical memory are to develop a life history and to tell others what one is like through relating one's past experiences" (Harley & Reese, 1999, p. 1338). Harley and Reese argued that the way in which parents talk to their children about the past should influence the children's autobiographical memories. More specifically, they distinguished between two maternal reminiscing styles: high elaborative (in which past events are discussed in detail) and low elaborative. They assumed that children whose mothers adopted the high-elaborative style would be able to report fuller and earlier childhood memories than children whose mothers used the low-elaborative style.

Harley and Reese (1999) assessed mothers' maternal styles of talking to their children about the past, and children's self-recognition at the age of 19 months. They also assessed children's language production at the same age. They then considered children's autobiographical memories when the children were aged between 19 and 32 months. Their findings supported the social interactionist and cognitive self positions: "Both maternal reminiscing style and children's self-recognition were strong ... predictors of children's very early ability to talk about the past, regardless of children's linguistic or non-verbal memory skill."

There are important cultural differences in parents' interactions with their children and in the importance attached to the past. According to the social interactionist perspective, there should therefore be cultural differences in infantile amnesia. This prediction was confirmed by MacDonald, Uesiliana, and Hayne (2000). The mean age of earliest memory was 58 months for Asian (mainly Chinese) adults, 43 months for New Zealand Europeans, and 33 months for New Zealand Maoris. MacDonald et al. argued that the Maoris had the earliest memories because of their strong cultural emphasis on the importance of the past. There was a large gender difference for age of earliest memory among the Asian participants, with females reporting much later memories than males. This may reflect a tendency for Chinese families to attach more importance to the experiences and achievements of sons than of daughters.

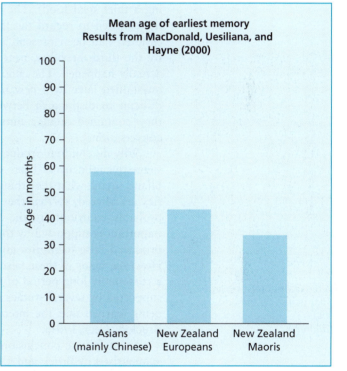

Mean age of earliest memory
Results from MacDonald, Uesiliana, and Hayne (2000)

Age in months (y-axis: 0, 10, 20, 30, 40, 50, 60, 70, 80, 90, 100)

Asians (mainly Chinese) | New Zealand Europeans | New Zealand Maoris

*Think about your own earliest memories, and estimate how old you might have been when the events occurred. Do your experiences fit in with Howe and Courage's theoretical perspective?*

## Eyewitness testimony

There has recently been a dramatic increase in the number of children testifying in sexual abuse cases in several countries. This has raised important questions about the accuracy of the information provided by children, and has led to much research (see Bruck & Ceci, 1999, for a review). As we will see, the evidence generally indicates that children are suggestible, which can result in systematic errors in their recall of events (suggestibility in adult eyewitnesses is discussed in Chapter 9). In general, suggestibility tends to decrease during the years of childhood (see Bruck & Ceci, 1999).

Thompson, Clarke-Stewart, and Lepore (1997) studied the effects of interviewer bias on children's memories. Five- and six-year-olds witnessed one of two events. In the innocent event, a janitor called Chester cleaned some dolls and other toys in a playroom. In the abusive event, Chester handled the dolls roughly and in a mildly abusive way. Some children were then questioned by an accusatory interviewer (who suggested that the janitor had been abusive), others were questioned by an exculpatory [free from blame] interviewer (who suggested that the janitor's behaviour was innocent), and the remainder were questioned by a neutral interviewer (who avoided making suggestions). The children were asked by their parents to describe what the janitor had done immediately after the interview and 2 weeks later.

Thompson et al. (1997) found that children's eyewitness memories were generally accurate when questioned by the neutral interviewer. This is important, because it shows that children can remember events accurately when not exposed to suggestive influences. However, when questioned by the accusatory or exculpatory interviewer, the children's accounts typically conformed to the interviewer's suggestions. Thus, the janitor was reported by the children as having behaved abusively when the interviewer was accusatory, but as having behaved innocently when the interviewer was exculpatory. When the children were then asked neutral questions by their parents, their descriptions of the event were consistent with what they had said to the interviewer.

It is perhaps not surprising that young children are influenced by blatant interviewer bias as in the study by Thompson et al. (1997). However, there is convincing evidence of children's suggestibility in numerous situations (see Bruck & Ceci, 1999). For example, Bruck, Ceci, and Hembrooke (1997) asked preschool children on five separate occasions to describe two true events (e.g., a recent punishment) and two false events (e.g., witnessing a thief steal food). The interviewer used various suggestive techniques to persuade the children to regard the false events as true. For example, they were told that other children had been present, and that they should try to imagine the event in question. By the third interview, nearly all the children accepted that both the false events had actually happened. The children continued to argue that the false events were true when questioned later by a new interviewer who adopted a non-suggestive approach. It was difficult to distinguish between the descriptions of the true and false events, because they contained similar numbers of spontaneous statements and details (e.g., about conversations).

Why do children produce systematically distorted reports of events when exposed to suggestive influences? There are two major possible reasons: (1) children are socially compliant, saying what they think the interviewer wants them to say; or (2) children's memories are altered, so that they come to believe their own distorted reports. Both reasons probably contribute to the effects of suggestion. The notion that social compliance is important is supported by the findings of a study by Poole and Lindsay (1996). Children produced false memories after being repeatedly questioned by a suggestive interviewer. However, many of these false memories faded when the children were not interviewed for a reasonably long period of time. The notion that children's memories may be altered is supported by several studies in which children continued to produce false memories after being warned that the interviewer may have been mistaken in his/her suggestions (see Bruck & Ceci, 1999).

*In the light of this research, what would be the best way to obtain reliable evidence from children?*

No definitive conclusions are possible as yet. The present state of knowledge was summarised by Bruck and Ceci (1999, p. 434):

> *Children may start out knowingly complying to suggestions, but with repeated suggestive interviews, they may come to believe and incorporate the suggestions into their memories. However, depending upon the strength of the false belief, children may eventually come to forget their misreports and thus recant their previous allegations, especially if suggestive interviewing has ceased for a long period.*

## LANGUAGE ACQUISITION

Young children seem to acquire language with breathtaking speed. By the age of 2, most children use language to communicate hundreds of messages. By the age of 5, children have mastered most of the grammatical rules of their native language. However, very few parents are consciously aware of the rules of grammar. Thus, young children simply "pick up" the complex rules of grammar without much formal teaching.

# Stages of language development

Language development can be divided into *receptive language* (language comprehension) and *productive language* (language expression or speaking). One-year-old children (and adults) have better receptive than productive language. Sometimes the difference is extreme. Bates, Bretherton, and Synder (1988) found some young children who produced only a few words nevertheless had a comprehension vocabulary in excess of 150 words.

Children need to learn four kinds of knowledge about language:

1. *Phonology*. The sound system of a language.
2. *Semantics*. The meaning conveyed by words and sentences.
3. *Syntax*. The set of grammatical rules indicating how words may be combined to make sentences.
4. *Pragmatics*. The principles determining modifications of language to fit the context (e.g., we speak more simply to a child than an adult).

Children typically acquire these kinds of knowledge in the order listed. They initially learn to make sounds, followed by developing an understanding of what those sounds mean. After that, they learn grammatical rules, and how to change what they say to fit the situation.

Evidence that some aspects of phonological development occur very early in life was reported by Mehler, Jusczyk, Dehaene-Lambertz, Dupoux, and Nazzi (1994). They found that 4-day-old French infants could discriminate between the French and Russian languages, showing a clear preference for French. Evidence of more complex phonological learning was provided by Saffran, Aslin, and Newport (1996), who created very small artificial languages of "words" consisting of three nonsense syllables each. Eight-month-old infants were presented with a continuous speech stream that included these "words". The key finding was that these infants were able to discriminate those syllable sequences forming words from those syllable sequences that did not.

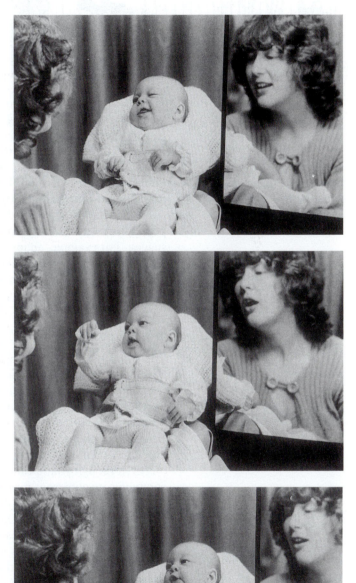

## *Early vocalisations*

Infants between the ages of about 3 and 5 weeks start to coo, producing vowel-like sounds (e.g., "ooooh") over and over again. Between 4 and 6 months of age, infants start to babble. Babbling consists of combinations of vowels and consonants that seem to lack meaning for the infants.

The babbling of infants up to about 6 months of age is similar in all parts of the world and in deaf infants as well as hearing ones. However, by about 8 months of age, infants show signs of the language they have heard. Indeed, adults can sometimes guess accurately from their babbling whether infants have been exposed to French, Chinese, Arabic, or English (De Boysson-Bardies, Sagart, & Durand, 1984).

## *One-word stage*

Up until the age of about 18 months, young children are limited to single-word utterances. Nelson (1973)

A six-week-old girl smiles at her mother's face, then responds to gentle baby-talk with cooing vocalisation and conspicuous hand movement. In the third picture the mother is imitating the preceding vocalisation of her baby. From Trevarthen (1980).

*What do these mistakes reveal about the way children are thinking about the objects they come across?*

categorised the first 50 words used by infants. The largest category was classes of objects (e.g., cat, car), followed by specific objects (e.g., Mummy, Daddy). The other four categories used by young children were (in descending order of frequency): action words such as "go" and "come"; modifiers (e.g., "mine", "small"); social words (e.g., "please", "no"); and function words (e.g., "for", "where").

Almost two-thirds of the words used by young children in the United States and Europe refer to objects or to people. Why is this? Children naturally refer to things of interest to them, which consist mainly of the people and objects surrounding them. Gentner (1982) carried out a study to see whether the tendency for children to learn more nouns than other classes of words initially is found in a range of countries. Five languages were studied (German, Japanese, English, Turkish, and Kaluli), and nouns formed the earliest and largest group of words learned in all five languages.

Young children often make mistakes with word meanings. Some words are initially used to cover more objects than they should (over-extension). It can be embarrassing, as when my younger daughter referred to every man as "Daddy". The opposite mistake is known as under-extension. For example, a child may think the word "cereal" refers only to the brand of cereal he/she eats for breakfast.

McNeill (1970) referred to the one-word stage as the **holophrastic period**. In this period, young children try to convey much more meaning than their utterances would suggest. For example, an infant who says "ball" while pointing to a ball may mean he/she would like to play with the ball. Infants produce one-word utterances because of a limited attention span and a small vocabulary (McNeill, 1970). However, their limited cognitive development is another relevant factor.

## Telegraphic period

The second stage of language development is the **telegraphic period**, starting at about 18 months of age. Its name arises because the speech of children in this stage is like a telegram. Telegrams cost so much per word, and so senders of telegrams make them short. Content words such as nouns and verbs are included, but function words such as "a", "the", "and", pronouns, and prepositions are omitted. The same is true of the speech of young children. However, they leave out even more than is left out of a telegram (e.g., plurals and tenses).

Even though young children are largely limited to two-word utterances, they can still communicate numerous meanings. A given two-word utterance can mean different things in different situations. "Daddy chair" may mean "I want to sit in Daddy's chair", "Daddy is sitting in his chair", or "Daddy, sit in your chair!" However, we need to be aware that deciding on the precise meaning intended by the child is subjective, and may involve wishful thinking on the part of the researcher or parent!

Brown (1973) argued that young children possess a basic order rule: a sentence consists of agent + action + object + location (e.g., "Daddy eats lunch at home"). Their two-word utterances follow the basic order rule. For example, an utterance containing an agent and an action will be in the order agent–action (e.g., "Daddy walk") rather than the reverse ("walk Daddy"). Similarly, action and object will be spoken in the order action–object (e.g., "drink Coke"). Children everywhere construct two-word utterances obeying the basic order rule.

## Subsequent developments

Children's language develops considerably between 2 years and 5 years of age. For example, the maximum sentence measured in terms of the number of morphemes (meaningful units) produced increases from four morphemes at 24 months to eight morphemes

**KEY TERMS**

**Holophrastic period:** a stage of speech development in which infants produce meaningful one-word utterances.

**Telegraphic period:** a stage of language development in which children's speech is abbreviated like a telegram.

at 30 months (Fenson et al., 1994). One important change is based on the learning of **grammatical morphemes**. These include prepositions, prefixes, and suffixes (e.g., "in", "on", plural -s, "a", "the"), and they serve to alter the meaning of words or phrases. All children learn the various grammatical morphemes in the same order, starting with simple ones (e.g., including "in" and "on" in sentences) and moving on to more complex ones (e.g., reducing "they are" to "they're").

Do children simply imitate the speech of adults rather than learning rules? Evidence they do not comes from children's grammatical errors. For example, a child will say, "The dog runned away", which adults are unlikely to produce. Presumably the child makes that mistake because he/she is applying the rule that the past tense of a verb is usually formed by adding -ed to the present tense. Using a grammatical rule in situations in which it does not apply is known as **over-regularisation**.

It could be argued that over-regularisation occurs because children imitate what other children say. However, this cannot explain the findings of Berko (1958). Children were shown two pictures of an imaginary animal or bird. They were told, "This is a wug. This is another wug. Now there are two …" Even young children produced the regular plural form "wugs", despite the fact they had never heard the word before.

Finally, children at this stage develop a good grasp of pragmatics, in which what they say fits the situation. Shatz and Gelman (1973) analysed the speech of 4-year-old children when talking about a new toy to a 2-year-old or to an adult. They used longer and more complex sentences when talking to the adult.

This is a wug

Now there is another one.
There are two of them.
There are two_____.

## Vocabulary and syntax

As we have seen, young children show rapid development in vocabulary and in syntax. For example, vocabulary size increases from 20 words at 18 months to about 200 words at 21 months (Harris & Butterworth, 2002). Shortly after this, from about 22 months of age, children show a rapid increase in the complexity of the sentences they produce, due in large measure to their development of syntax (Fenson et al., 1994).

Bates and Goodman (1999) argued that we should not think of vocabulary development and syntax development as occurring in isolation from each other. Instead, the two forms of development are actually closely related. As evidence for that, they found that children's vocabulary size at the age of 20 months was the best predictor of syntactic development at the age of 28 months. Bates and Goodman also discussed findings from children whose language development is severely impaired (e.g., through brain damage). Such children typically have comparable impairments for vocabulary and syntactic development.

## Theories of language acquisition

Numerous theories have been put forward to account for children's language acquisition, most of which can be categorised as inside-out theories or outside-in theories (Hirsch-Pasek & Golinkoff, 1996). According to inside-out theorists (e.g., Chomsky, Pinker), language acquisition depends heavily on innate factors and only modestly on the child's own experiences. In contrast, outside-in theorists (e.g., Bruner, Tomasello) argue that the role of experience is of central importance in children's language acquisition.

**Early language acquisition**

| Age | 0–6 months | 6 months–1 year | 1–2½ years | 2–5 years |
|---|---|---|---|---|
| Babbling | ✓ | | | |
| Some phonemes learned | ✓ | ✓ | | |
| First spoken word | | ✓ | | |
| Beginning of grammatical rules | | | ✓ | |
| Basic rules of grammar acquired | | | | ✓ |

**Key Terms**

**Grammatical morphemes:** modifiers (e.g., prefixes, suffixes) that modify meaning.

**Over-regularisation:** using a grammatical rule in situations in which it does not apply.

There are other differences between inside-out and outside-in theorists (Harris & Butterworth, 2002). For example, most inside-out theorists claim that language development occurs in relative isolation from other forms of cognitive and social development. In contrast, outside-in theorists argue that general cognitive and social mechanisms (e.g., those involved in perception or thinking) are involved in language development. Evidence for and against these two theoretical approaches is discussed below. Bear in mind that innate factors *and* experience may both be of vital importance in language acquisition. If so, a theoretical compromise between current inside-out and outside-in theories may be called for.

## Inside-out theories

*How might this theory be put to the test?*

Inside-out or nativist theorists argue that infants are born with knowledge of the structure of human languages. For example, Chomsky (1965) argued that humans possess a **language acquisition device** consisting of innate knowledge of grammatical structure. Children need to have some exposure to (and experience with) the language environment provided by their parents and people to develop language. At the simplest level, such experience determines which specific language any given child will learn.

Chomsky (1986) later replaced the notion of a language acquisition device with the idea of a universal grammar, which forms part of our innate knowledge of language. According to Chomsky's Principles and Parameters Theory, there are **linguistic universals**, which are features found in nearly every language. There are substantive universals and formal universals. Substantive universals concern categories common to all languages (e.g., noun and verb categories). Formal universals are concerned with the general form of syntactic or grammatical rules.

Chomsky (1986) argued that there are various language parameters which differ across languages. For example, there are some languages (e.g., English) in which all sentences must have a grammatical subject, whereas this is not the case for other languages (e.g., Italian). This difference between languages is dealt with by a parameter called "pro-drop" (short for pronoun drop). This parameter has two possible settings, one for languages like English and one for languages such as Italian. How is the parameter set? According to Chomsky, any parameter setting is "triggered" by exposure to sentences in any given language.

Pinker (1984, 1989) is broadly sympathetic to Chomsky's approach. However, he argued that exposure to language plays a more important role than simply "triggering" parameter settings. According to Pinker (1989), children use a process that he calls "semantic bootstrapping" to allocate words to their appropriate word class. This is done by what Pinker calls "linking rules". For example, suppose a young child hears the sentence, "William is throwing a stone", while watching a boy carrying out that action. The child will realise from his/her observations that "William" refers to the actor, "stone" refers to an object, and "is throwing" refers to an action. The child has innate knowledge of word categories, and can use linking rules to decide that "William" is the subject of the sentence, "stone" is the "object", and "throwing" is the verb.

## Evidence

Chomsky (1986) assumed there are numerous linguistic universals (e.g., word order). Consider the preferred word order for expressing the subject, verb, and object within sentences. There are six possible orderings, two of which (object–verb–subject, object–subject–verb) are not found among the world's languages (Greenberg, 1963). The most popular word order is subject–object–verb (44% of languages), followed by the subject–verb–object word order found in English (35% of languages). The subject precedes the object in 98% of languages, presumably because it makes sense to consider the subject of a sentence before the object.

Chomsky (1986) assumed that linguistic universals are innate, but there are other possibilities. Consider the linguistic universals of nouns and verbs, with nouns referring to objects and verbs to actions. Perhaps objects and actions are distinguished in all languages simply because the distinction is such an obvious feature of the environment.

Another line of research supporting the notion of an innate grammar was developed by Bickerton (1984). He proposed the language bioprogramme hypothesis, according to which children will create a grammar even if not exposed to a proper language during their early years. Evidence for this hypothesis was obtained by considering labourers from China, Japan, Korea, Puerto Rico, Portugal, and the Philippines who were taken to the sugar plantations of Hawaii about 100 years ago. In order to communicate with each other, these labourers developed a pidgin language, which was very simple and lacked most grammatical structures. Here is an example of this pidgin language: "Me cape buy, me check make", which was intended to mean, "He bought my coffee; he made me out a cheque" (Pinker, 1984).

Bickerton's (1984) key finding was that the offspring of these labourers developed a language known as Hawaiian Creole. This is a proper language and is fully grammatical. Here is an example of this language: "Da firs japani came ran away from japan come." This means, "The first Japanese who arrived ran away from Japan to here."

Research in genetic linguistics has been claimed to support the view that language is partly innate. Gopnik (1990, 1994a) considered three generations of a family known as the Ks. About half the members of this family displayed specific language impairment (very poor acquisition of language but near-normal non-verbal IQ). The pattern of affected and unaffected individuals within this family suggested that a single dominant gene was involved. Gopnik (1990) proposed the feature-blindness hypothesis, according to which the genetic make-up of the affected individuals made it very hard to mark grammatical features such as number, gender, and tense. Another possibility is that the gene involved is involved in articulation.

## Evaluation

⊕ Chomsky's theory potentially explains why nearly all children master their native language very rapidly.

⊕ Chomsky's theory is supported by the way in which pidgin languages develop into creole languages. It is also supported (but more controversially) by studies of genetic linguistics, in which specific language impairment runs in families.

⊕ The theory makes sense of the fact that language is rule based even though few speakers of a language can express these rules explicitly.

⊖ Chomsky (1980, p. 80) argued that, "An innatist hypothesis is a refutable hypothesis", but there are formidable obstacles to doing so. For example, Chomsky assumed that very young children have access to a considerable amount of grammatical knowledge. However, when their language performance fails to match up to this alleged knowledge or competence, there are several ways of salvaging the theory. As Bishop (1997, p. 130) pointed out, "The problem is … that limitations of memory and attention, biases to prefer particular options, or motivational factors interfere with their ability to demonstrate this knowledge."

⊖ Chomsky argued that the language children hear contains insufficient information to allow them to work out grammatical rules from scratch. This argument is not very persuasive. As is discussed later, mothers and other adults typically talk to young children in simple, short sentences, which facilitates children's language acquisition.

⊖ The whole idea of an innate grammar seems implausible. According to Bishop (1997, p. 123), "What makes an innate grammar a particularly peculiar idea is the fact that innate knowledge must be general enough to account for acquisition of Italian, Japanese, Turkish, Malay, as well as sign language acquisition by congenitally deaf children."

## Critical period hypothesis

Did you find it easier to learn your native language as a young child than other languages that you learned later? It probably seemed much easier to learn your own language.

## CASE STUDY: *Genie*

Genie spent most of her time up to the age of 13 in an isolated room (Curtiss, 1977). She had practically no contact with other people, and was punished if she made any sounds. After Genie was rescued in 1970, she learned some aspects of language, especially vocabulary. However, she showed very poor learning of grammatical rules. There are problems in interpreting the evidence from Genie. She was exposed to great social as well as linguistic deprivation, and her father's "justification" for keeping her in isolation was that he thought she was very retarded. Thus, there are various possible reasons for Genie's limited ability to learn language.

Ethical issues: Deprivation studies are useful examples from which we can draw some inferences, but they rarely provide data that can be regarded as scientific. What are some of the ethical issues that arise from looking at the effects of deprivation? Should the psychologist be concerned with compensation for deprivation experienced, e.g., linguistic support for individuals like Genie?

Do the ethical problems concerning work like this outweigh any practical advancement of our understanding as psychologists?

*Does this support the critical period hypothesis? What other possible explanations can you think of?*

Lenneberg (1967) and other nativists argued that this common experience supports the **critical period hypothesis**. According to this hypothesis, language learning depends on biological maturation, and is easier before puberty. Supporting evidence was reported by Johnson and Newport (1989), who studied Chinese and Korean immigrants to the United States. Those who had arrived in the United States at an early age performed much better than those who had arrived later when asked to decide whether sentences were grammatically correct. This suggests that there may be a critical period for the learning of syntax.

Lenneberg (1967) claimed the two hemispheres of the brain have the same potential at birth. However, their functions become more specialised and rigid over the years (this is known as lateralisation), with language functions typically being located mainly in the left hemisphere. It follows that damage to the left hemisphere at an early age can be overcome by language functions moving to the right hemisphere. This would be harder if the brain damage occurred during adolescence, by which time language is well-established in the left hemisphere. There is support for these predictions. Some epileptic patients undergo hemi-decortication, in which an entire hemisphere of the brain is removed. Removal of the left hemisphere in children under the age of 4 or 5 typically does not prevent fairly normal language development, whereas the effects on language are devastating in adults (Harley, 2001).

In principle, the best way to test the critical period hypothesis is to consider children having little chance to learn language during their early years. There have been various reports on wild or feral children abandoned at birth. For example, the "Wild Boy of Aveyron" was found in an isolated place in the south of France. A French educationalist, Dr Itard, tried to teach him language, but he only managed to learn two words.

## Evaluation

● There is probably a critical period (or at least a sensitive period) for the learning of syntax, as well as for phonology.

● There is support for a weakened version of the critical period hypothesis, according to which some aspects of language are harder to acquire outside the critical period (Harley, 2001).

● There is little evidence of a critical period for the learning of vocabulary, and many language skills can be acquired after the critical period.

● Some lateralisation is present at birth or shortly thereafter, which is much earlier than was assumed by Lenneberg. For example, the left hemisphere responds more to speech than to non-speech sounds in infants as young as 1 week (Molfese, 1977).

## Outside-in theories

There are several outside-in theories emphasising the central role of experience in allowing young children to acquire language. We will discuss one of the most important of such theories, the constructivist theory proposed by Tomasello (e.g., Tomasello & Brooks, 1999). Before that, we consider one of the main points of disagreement between outside-in theorists and inside-out theorists. In essence, outside-in theorists argue that the language input to which young children are exposed is adequate for language acquisition, whereas inside-out theorists are sceptical. We start with a discussion of research on child-directed speech, which is very relevant to this disagreement.

**KEY TERM**

**Critical period hypothesis:** the assumption that language learning depends on biological maturation, and is easier to accomplish prior to puberty.

## Child-directed speech

A key environmental factor in children's language learning in most cultures is the guidance provided by the mother and/or caregiver. When mothers (and fathers) talk to their young children, they use very short, simple sentences; this is known as **child-directed speech**. The length and complexity of what the mother says to her child gradually increase as the child's own use of language develops. Perhaps even more importantly, the mother uses sentences that are slightly longer and more complicated than those produced by her child (Bohannon & Warren-Leubecker, 1989). In addition, child-directed speech typically involves a slow rate of speaking, use of a restricted vocabulary, and extra stress put on key words (Dockrell & Messer, 1999).

Mothers, fathers, and other adults also try to help children's language development by expansions. **Expansions** consist of fuller and more grammatical versions of what the child has just said. For example, a child might say, "Dog out", with its mother responding, "The dog wants to go out." Saxton (1997) argued that many expansions provide children with an immediate contrast between their own incorrect speech and the correct version. For example, a child may say, "He shooted the fish", to which the adult might reply, "He shot the fish!". Children typically process expansions reasonably thoroughly, because they are more likely to repeat adult expansions than other adult utterances (Farrar, 1992).

What factors determine the precise form of child-directed speech used by mothers and other adults? Clarke-Stewart, Vanderstoep, and Killian (1979) found that child-directed speech was influenced mainly by the child's level of comprehension rather than by his/her level of speech production. This makes sense, because adults use child-directed speech in order to communicate effectively with children.

Evidence that the way in which the mother talks to her child affects its language development was reported by Harris et al. (1986; see the figure on the right). They found that 78% of what mothers said to their 16-month-old children related to the objects to which the children were attending. However, the situation was different in children whose language development at the age of 2 years was poor. Among these children, only 49% of what mothers said to their children at the age of 16 months related to the object of the child's attention.

Child-directed speech helps children to learn vocabulary. For example, Weizman and Snow (2001) considered factors influencing children's vocabulary at the age of seven. Children with the largest vocabularies had mothers who included many sophisticated words when speaking to them. In addition, their mothers tended to introduce these sophisticated words in helpful ways (e.g., providing explicit information about the meaning of each word).

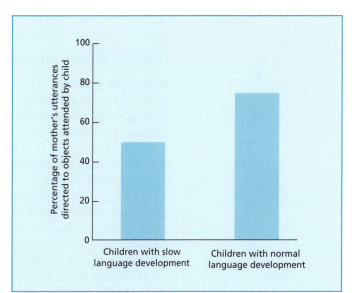

The percentages of mother's utterances related to an object currently attended by her child in children with slow or normal language development. Data from Harris et al. (1986).

From what has been discussed so far, you may have formed the opinion that language acquisition relies heavily on child-directed speech. However, most of the evidence is only correlational. Finding that children having the greatest exposure to child-directed speech acquire language the fastest does not prove that the child-directed speech was responsible for the speed of language acquisition. Another possibility is that adults use more child-directed speech with children who find it easiest to acquire language.

Cross-cultural research suggests that child-directed speech may *not* be essential for language acquisition. Schieffelin (1990) studied the Kaluli of New Guinea. Adults talk to children as if they were adults, but Kaluli children develop language at about the normal rate. However, cultures in which child-directed speech is little used may provide alternative assistance to children learning language. For example, Ochs and Schieffelin (1995) argued that children in such cultures become involved in its social and communal activities, which can facilitate shared understanding and language development.

*Why might involvement in communal activities be more motivating in other cultures? See if you can think of any examples of cultures where this might apply.*

What may be important for rapid language acquisition in any culture is that attempts are made to *motivate* young children to learn language. For example, children having the fastest language acquisition in a Western culture had mothers who asked the most questions and replied most fully to their questions (Howe, 1980). In other cultures, motivation to learn language may depend more on involving young children in communal activities.

## Evaluation

- ● The language that young children hear is generally tailored to their current comprehension level.
- ● Child-directed speech may be especially helpful in learning vocabulary.
- ● Cross-cultural research sheds doubt on the notion that child-centred speech is essential for normal language acquisition.
- ● "Some studies report positive correlations between CDS [child-directed speech] and later speech, but more fail to find such a relationship. Also, because these studies are not experiments …, it is difficult to be sure whether there is a causal relation between CDS and children's language acquisition" (Messer, 2000, p. 138).

## Cognitive and constructivist approaches

Piaget (see Chapter 15) argued that children acquire language only after they have developed the appropriate cognitive abilities. More specifically, he claimed that children form schemas consisting of organised knowledge about the world and events they have experienced. Children need to have developed various cognitive processes and structures (e.g., schemas) *before* they can develop language; this is known as the cognition hypothesis. The essence of this hypothesis is that language development is dependent on prior cognitive development.

There is some support for this theoretical approach. At the cognitive level, young children are able to think about objects which are present at an earlier age than objects which are not. This is reflected in their language learning. Children learn words (e.g., "move", "up") relating to changes affecting visible objects earlier than words (e.g., "gone") referring to absent objects (Tomasello & Farrar, 1986).

It follows from Piaget's cognition hypothesis that children having slow cognitive development should also have slow linguistic development. This is often (but by no means always) the case. For example, consider children with **Williams syndrome**, which is a rare genetic disorder involving unusual facial characteristics ("elfin face") and typically an IQ of about 50. They have slow cognitive development, and their visuo-spatial abilities are especially poor. However, their language abilities are relatively good, and they typically have surprisingly large vocabularies (Tager-Flusberg, 1999). Such findings seem inconsistent with the cognition hypothesis. However, it should be noted that the onset of language in children with Williams syndrome is later than in healthy children.

Tomasello has developed a theory of language acquisition based in part on Piaget's views. The essence of his constructivist theory is as follows:

> *Children acquire linguistic competence in the particular language they are learning only gradually, beginning with more concrete linguistic structures based on particular words and morphemes, and then building up to more abstract and productive structures based on various types of linguistic categories, schemas, and constructions"* (Tomasello & Brooks, 1999, p. 161).

According to Tomasello's theory, children's language development is based on their cognitive understanding of the scenes or events they experience in their everyday lives. They generally find it easiest to learn nouns, in part because nouns refer to concrete objects or people within scenes. In contrast, it is harder to learn verbs, because their

**KEY TERM**

**Williams syndrome:** a rare genetic disorder involving low IQ but reasonable language development.

meaning is typically more abstract. Tomasello (1992) put forward the Verb Island hypothesis, according to which children initially treat each verb independently as if it had its own island of organisation.

The notion that most aspects of language are acquired relatively slowly by children contrasts with inside-out or nativist theories. According to such theories, children rapidly link the specific features of the language they are learning to an abstract universal grammar, and can then produce an essentially infinite number of grammatical utterances. We can relate the contrasting assumptions of constructivist and nativist theories to the issue of language productivity or creativity. According to Tomasello's constructivist theory, young children should initially show very limited productivity. According to nativist theories, young children should rapidly show high levels of productivity or creativity in their language utterances.

## Evidence

A central assumption of the constructivist approach is that initial language learning (especially of verbs) should be slow. Supporting evidence was reported by Tomasello (1992), based on observations of his daughter in the second year of her life. She used some verbs in only one kind of sentence frame (e.g., "Cut ___"), which indicates limited learning. Other verbs were used in several kinds of sentence frame (e.g., "Draw ___"; "Draw ___ on ___", "Draw ___ for ___"). Such differences among verbs are consistent with the Verb Island hypothesis (discussed above).

Tomasello, Akhtar, Dodson, and Rekau (1997) taught children aged between 18 and 23 months two new nouns and two new verbs. The children showed much more productivity with the nouns than with the verbs: They produced 10 times as many combinations of words using the novel nouns than using the novel verbs. This relative lack of productivity with novel verbs is more consistent with the constructivist approach than the nativist one.

One of the main assumptions of the constructivist approach is that learning language resembles other kinds of learning in many ways. This issue was addressed by Childers and Tomasello (2002) in a study in which 2-year-old children were taught novel nouns or verbs. The learning was either after massed (all on the same day) or distributed (spread out over 2 weeks). The children's ability to produce the novel nouns and verbs subsequently was greater after distributed than after massed learning. Distributed learning has been found to be more effective than massed learning with numerous tasks (see Dempster, 1996), and so the findings of Childers and Tomasello (2002) point to an important similarity between language learning and other forms of learning.

Several studies have found that young children learning English typically have more nouns than verbs in their vocabularies. According to Tomasello's theory, the reason is that verbs are more abstract and complex, and thus are harder to learn. However, the most obvious explanation is simply that most young children hear far more nouns than verbs. Childers and Tomasello (2002), in the study discussed above, addressed this issue by equating the frequency with which novel nouns and verbs were presented. The children produced three times as many novel nouns as novel verbs when asked to recall them, thus providing empirical support for Tomasello's theory.

## Evaluation

⊕ The notion that language acquisition depends on various perceptual and cognitive processes is plausible.
⊕ Children show relatively little productivity early in language acquisition (especially with verbs), which is as predicted from the constructivist approach.
⊕ There is some evidence that language learning is similar to other kinds of learning (e.g., Childers & Tomasello, 2002).
⊕ Noun learning is slower than verb learning by children learning English, which is as predicted by Tomasello's theory.

● More thorough longitudinal research is needed to show how cognitive processes influence language acquisition.
● At the theoretical level, we need more detail on the processes children use in proceeding from initial concrete linguistic structures to more general abstract schemas.

# ANIMAL LANGUAGE ACQUISITION

The issue of whether animals can acquire language is intrinsically fascinating. It can also tell us something about the nature of language, because it forces us to consider carefully what we mean by language. Finally, the issue has theoretical significance. According to some theorists (e.g., Chomsky), language is unique to the human species, because only members of the human species possess a language acquisition device. Thus, proof that members of some other species could acquire language would disprove Chomsky's theory.

Before proceeding, we need to have some criteria or standards for defining language. Hockett (1960) put forward several criteria for language, including the following:

● *Semanticity*. The words or other symbols must have meaning.
● *Arbitrariness*. There must be an arbitrary connection between the form or sound of the word and its meaning.
● *Displacement*. Language can be produced in the absence of the object or objects being described.
● *Prevarication*. There is an ability to tell lies and make jokes.
● *Productivity*. There is an essentially infinite number of different ideas that can be communicated.

## Evidence

Most research on language acquisition in other species has involved studying chimpanzees, mainly because they are intelligent and social creatures. Research on teaching language to chimpanzees started in earnest with the work of Allen and Beatrice Gardner (1969). They taught American Sign Language to a 1-year-old female chimpanzee called Washoe. After 4 years of training, Washoe knew 132 signs, and could arrange them in novel ways (showing very limited evidence of productivity). For example, when she saw a swan, she signed "water bird". She had also apparently grasped some aspects of grammar. For example, she signed "tickle me" much more often than "me tickle", and "baby mine" more often than "mine baby". In view of her achievements, the Gardners concluded she had learned language.

*Which of Hockett's criteria have been demonstrated by Washoe?*

We should probably not accept the Gardners' conclusion. Terrace, Petitto, Sanders, and Bever (1979) analysed Washoe's behaviour as revealed in a film made about her. Most of Washoe's grammatical sequences of signs occurred when she simply imitated the signs produced by her teacher. The ability to imitate is very different from the ability to grasp grammatical rules. In addition, many of the signs Washoe learned are the same as gestures occurring naturally in chimpanzees. These include "tickle" (signed by tickling) and "scratch" (signed by scratching). Such signs do not fulfil Hockett's criterion of arbitrariness. Finally, the Gardners engaged in some wishful thinking: Deaf signers observed far fewer signs in Washoe's behaviour than did her trainers (Pinker, 1994).

Washoe was a common chimpanzee, and bonobo chimpanzees seem to be more intelligent and to communicate more with other chimpanzees. As a result, Savage-Rumbaugh, McDonald, Sevcik, Hopkins, and Rupert (1986) studied a male bonobo chimpanzee called Kanzi (see Key Study on the next page).

### The benefits of being able to communicate with Washoe

When Washoe was 5 years old she left the Gardners' care. Twelve years later they were reunited and Washoe immediately recognised them, and began to play a game she had not been seen playing since she left them. This clearly raises ethical questions concerning the nature of the experience from Washoe's point of view and whether the findings justified the research process.

Another story relates to a time when Washoe had a baby who was born unwell. The trainer removed the infant for treatment and later returned to tell Washoe the infant had died. Washoe thought he was returning with her child and signed "baby" enthusiastically. The trainer signed back, "He is dead, finished". And Washoe dropped her head, moved to a corner and stopped signing. Being able to communicate with humans may have been a good thing for Washoe—or a bad thing, depending on how you view it.

## Savage-Rumbaugh et al.: Kanzi

Savage-Rumbaugh et al. (1986) taught Kanzi using a keyboard containing geometric patterns known as lexigrams. Initially, he learned by observing the training of his mother (Matata). In 17 months, he learned to understand nearly 60 lexigrams and he could produce nearly 50. His comprehension skills were especially good. Kanzi responded correctly to 109 words on a speech comprehension test, and behaved appropriately in response to 105 utterances (e.g., "Kanzi, go get me a knife").

Sometimes Kanzi received spoken instructions through headphones.

Kanzi's language learning was greater than that of Washoe and other chimpanzees who had received language training. For example, more than 80% of his utterances were spontaneous, whereas most of Washoe's were not. Kanzi understood the difference between "Chase Kanzi" and "Kanzi chase". He could even make fairly subtle distinctions, such as that between, "Put the pine needles in your ball", and "Can you put the ball on the pine needles?" In addition, Kanzi by the age of 46 months had learned nearly 50 symbols and had produced 800 combinations of them (e.g., "Grape eat", "More drink").

Savage-Rumbaugh, Murphy, Sevcik, Brakke, Williams, and Rumbaugh (1993) compared Kanzi's language abilities against those of a 2-year-old girl called Alia, both of whom were given extensive training in understanding lexigrams and spoken English. Kanzi and Alia both used word order to distinguish the meanings of sentences, and showed similar levels of performance overall. However, Kanzi performed much better than Alia when given sentences of the type (Go to location Y and get object X): He was correct 82% of the time, whereas she was correct on only 45% of occasions. This difference may have occurred because Kanzi spent much of his time retrieving objects from specific locations.

Do the above findings show that Kanzi has mastered language? Most experts remain sceptical for various reasons. First, Kanzi showed a limited grasp of syntax, especially with his effective use of word order to understand sentences. However, syntax also depends on morphology (modifying language to indicate plurals) and the use of function words (e.g., the, a, to, in). Kanzi did not use morphology or function words (Kako, 1999). Second, Kanzi's use of language was much less complex than that of young children. For example, the mean length of utterance produced by Kanzi peaked at 1.15 morphemes (smallest units of meaning), whereas Alia's mean length of utterance was nearly two morphemes at 18 months and went up to more than three morphemes by the age of two. Third, there are real doubts as to whether Kanzi's use of language satisfied several of Hockett's (1960) criteria for language. For example, his language showed very limited productivity or displacement (e.g., he rarely referred to past or future events). More controversially, there are concerns about semanticity (the meanings he attached to words and lexigrams). For example, as Seidenberg and Petitto (1987) pointed out, Kanzi used the word 'strawberry' to indicate that he wanted strawberries or that he wanted to go to where strawberries were growing as well as to refer to the object itself. Thus, the meanings he attached to words often differed from the meanings we attach to words.

### KEY STUDY EVALUATION—Savage-Rumbaugh et al.

Savage-Rumbaugh's research has been the most promising to date and has indicated considerable abilities in non-human animals. However, Terrace (1979) says Kanzi is simply "going through a bag of tricks in order to get things". Other critics say there is nothing surprising about chimpanzees associating vocal sounds with objects. On one occasion Kanzi was recorded on videotape being told, "Give the dog a shot." The chimpanzee picked up a hypodermic syringe lying on the ground in front of him, pulled off the cap, and injected a toy dog. But was Kanzi just trained to associate the sound "dog" with the furry thing in front of him and programmed to carry out a stylised routine when he heard "shot"? Does the chimp really understand what he is doing?

## Discussion points

1. How impressed are you by Kanzi's command of language?
2. What are the limitations in the achievements of Kanzi and other apes?

Sue Savage-Rumbaugh holds a board displaying lexigrams that Kanzi uses to communicate with her.

Savage-Rumbaugh subsequently obtained even more impressive findings (see Leake, 1999). Another bonobo chimpanzee, Panbanisha, has spent her entire life in captivity receiving training in the use of language. Savage-Rumbaugh aimed to teach Panbanisha language in the same way that children are taught: they are exposed to it in the course of everyday life, use it to talk about future plans, and they are encultured by it. She uses a specially designed keypad with about 400 lexigrams on it. When she presses a sequence of keys, a computer translates the sequence into a synthetic voice. Savage-Rumbaugh continued to converse using lexigrams while roaming around the large forest surrounding her home, to ensure that language was being learned in a natural and social setting. Panbanisha learned a vocabulary of 3000 words by the age of 14 years, and became very good at combining a series of symbols in the grammatically correct order. For example, she can construct sentences such as, "Please can I have an iced coffee?", and "I'm thinking about eating something."

Panbanisha also demonstrated prevarication. An experiment replaced a sweet that was in a box with an insect. When another person was about to open the box, Panbanisha was asked by the first experimenter what the second person was looking for. Panbanisha answered "a sweet". This suggests both prevarication and the ability to have insight into the mental state of another.

---

## CASE STUDY: *An interview with Sue Savage-Rumbaugh*

**Q.** Do your apes speak?

**A.** They don't speak. They point to printed symbols on a keyboard. Their vocal tract isn't like ours, and they don't make human noises. However, they do make all kinds of ape noises. And I believe they use them to communicate with one another. Now, the apes may not always elect to talk about the same things we do. They might not have a translation for every word in our vocabulary to theirs. But from what I've seen, I believe they are communicating very complex things. Let me give you an example. A few weeks ago, one of our researchers, Mary Chiepelo was out in the yard with Panbanisha. Mary thought she heard a squirrel and so she took the keyboard and said, "There's a squirrel." And Panbanisha said "DOG." Not very much later, three dogs appeared and headed in the direction of the building where Kanzi was. Mary asked Panbanisha, "Does Kanzi see the dogs?" And Panbanisha looked at Mary and said, "A-frame." A-frame is a specific sector of the forest here that has an A-frame hut on it. Mary later went up to "A-frame" and found the fresh footprints of dogs everywhere at the site. Panbanisha knew where they were without seeing them. And that seems to be the kind of information that apes transmit to each other: "There's a dangerous animal around. It's a dog and it's coming towards you."

**Q.** How do you know when the chimps point to symbols on the keyboard that they are not just pointing to any old thing?

**A.** We test Kanzi and Panbanisha by either saying English words or showing them pictures. We know that they can find the symbol that corresponds to the word or the picture. If we give similar tests to their siblings who haven't learned language—they fail. Many times, we can verify through actions. For instance, if Kanzi says "Apple chase," which means he wants to play a game of keep away with an apple, we say, "Yes, let's do." And then, he picks up an apple and runs away and smiles at us.

**Q.** Some of your critics say that all your apes do is mimic you?

**A.** If they were mimicking me, they would repeat just what I'm saying, and they don't. They answer my questions. We also have data that shows that only about two percent of their utterances are immediate imitations of ours.

**Q.** Nonetheless, many in the scientific community accuse you of over-interpreting what your apes do.

**A.** There are SOME who say that. But none of them have been willing to come spend some time here. Their belief is that there is a thing called human language and that unless Kanzi does everything a human can, he doesn't have it. They refuse to consider what Kanzi does—which is comprehend—as language. And it's not even a matter of disagreeing over what Kanzi does. It's matter of disagreeing over what to call these facts. They are asking Kanzi to do everything that humans do, which is specious. He'll never do that. It still doesn't negate what he can do.

From Claudia Dreifus (1998) "She talks to apes and, according to her, they talk back". *New York Times*, 14 April.

Panbanisha has a son called Nyota, who at the age of 1 had a vocabulary similar in size to that of a child of about 18 months. He could point to symbols representing his favourite foods, which are M&Ms, strawberries, and grapes. According to Savage-Rumbaugh (reported in Leake, 1999), "He [Nyota] is more advanced than either Kanzi ... or Panbanisha were at that age."

## Evaluation

+ Chimpanzees have learned dozens or hundreds of words in the form of signs or lexigrams. Their signing shows evidence of satisfying several of Hockett's (1960) criteria for language, including arbitrariness, prevarication, and perhaps semanticity.
+ Chimpanzees have some understanding of the signs and lexigrams they use, although that understanding may differ from ours.
+ Bonobo chimpanzees such as Kanzi and Panbanisha have shown some ability.
- Chimpanzees show relatively little evidence of productivity, and rarely refer to objects they have not seen for some time (displacement). Thus, some of the criteria for language are missing or almost so.
- Chimpanzees have not been shown to acquire syntax fully, since they do not use morphology or function words.
- The utterances of chimpanzees tend to be much shorter and less informative than those of young children.
- As Chomsky (quoted in Atkinson, Atkinson, Smith, & Bem, 1993) pointed out, "If animals had a capacity as biologically advantageous as language but somehow hadn't used it until now, it would be an evolutionary miracle, like finding an island of humans who could be taught to fly."

"He says the downturn in world trade is adversely affecting banana supply, and warrants a reduction in interest rates".

*Do you consider teaching language to captive primates to be ethically sound?*

# THEORY OF MIND

There has been a massive increase in research on theory of mind. For example, Wellman, Cross, and Watson (2001) reported a meta-analysis based on 178 studies. What exactly is theory of mind? According to Astington and Jenkins (1999, p. 1311), **theory of mind** "conveys the idea of understanding social interaction by attributing beliefs, desires, intentions, and emotions to people". In order for someone to have a theory of mind, it is crucially important they understand that other people's beliefs about the world may differ from their own. The development of a theory of mind seems to represent a milestone in children's social development, because social communication is necessarily limited if a child assumes everyone else has the same beliefs as him/her about the world.

Theory of mind has been assessed by using various false-belief tasks. For example, Wimmer and Perner (1983) used models to present children with the following story. A boy called Maxi puts some chocolate in a blue cupboard. While he is out of the room, his mother moves the chocolate to a green cupboard. The children indicated where Maxi would look for the chocolate when he returned to the room. Most 4-year-olds argued mistakenly that Maxi would look in the green cupboard, thus failing to show evidence for a theory of mind. In contrast, most 5-year-olds produced the right answer.

> **KEY TERM**
>
> **Theory of mind:** the understanding that other people may have different beliefs, emotions, and intentions than one's own.

Several explanations for children's development of theory of mind have been proposed. Many theorists argue that children's developing information processing, memory, and language skills play a key role in the acquisition of theory of mind (e.g., Flavell, 1999). Astington and Jenkins (1999) proposed a more specific account, in which language development was seen as central to success on false-belief tasks.

Riggs et al. (1998) argued that children need to develop their reasoning ability to succeed on false-belief tasks. For example, children given the Maxi problem have to imagine a state of affairs (chocolate in the blue cupboard) that would exist if his mother hadn't moved the chocolate to the green cupboard. This is known as counterfactual reasoning, and is claimed by Riggs et al. to be crucially important on false-belief tasks.

Harris (1992) argued that children do not have a *theory* about the beliefs of others. Children are aware of their own mental states and beliefs, and use a process of *simulation* or role-taking to work out the mental states and beliefs of others. It is certainly true that adults often engage in simulation to predict the reactions of other people to various situations. For example, if we hear that a friend's relationship has just ended, we can work out her likely reaction by imagining ourselves in the same situation. This explanation can be related to the one proposed by Riggs et al. (1998). We can only predict someone else's beliefs accurately in false-belief tasks when we have imagined the hypothetical situation in which they perceive themselves to be.

## Evidence

Wellman et al. (2001) in their meta-analysis showed convincingly that there are large developmental changes between the ages of 3 and 5 on nearly all false-belief tasks. In general, most 3-year-olds perform poorly on false-belief tasks, whereas a substantial majority of 5-year-olds are correct. Thus, it is at about the age of 4 that a theory of mind seems to develop.

Does theory of mind develop in similar ways in different cultures? Wellman et al. (2001) reported relevant findings from seven countries (United States, United Kingdom, Korea, Australia, Canada, Austria, and Japan). There were substantial improvements in performance on false-belief tasks in all seven countries between the ages of 3 and 5, suggesting that an understanding of false beliefs develops similarly in different cultures. However, children in Australia and Canada developed a theory of mind the fastest, and those in Austria and Japan the slowest.

*How might these similarities and differences be explained?*

The finding that a given child succeeds on a standard false-belief task does *not* necessarily mean that he/she has developed a complete theory of mind. Perner and Wimmer (1985) considered "second order" beliefs, which are more complex than the first order beliefs typically studied. Second order beliefs involve understanding that another person can have beliefs about a third person (e.g., "I think that John thinks that Mary went to the shop to buy ice cream"). Perner and Wimmer found it was only at about the age of 6 that children started showing evidence of these second order beliefs.

There is much controversy as to whether some elements of a theory of mind may be present before the age of 4. For example, consider a study by O'Neill (1996). Children 2 years of age (and so allegedly too young to have a theory of mind) watched an attractive toy being placed on a high shelf in the presence or absence of their parent. The children subsequently asked their parent to let them have the toy. Those children whose parent had been absent previously were much more likely to name the toy and to gesture towards it than were those whose parent had been present. Thus, even 2-year-olds may have some awareness of the knowledge possessed by other people.

According to Riggs et al. (1998), the ability to engage in counterfactual reasoning underlies successful performance on false-belief tasks. It follows that young children who fail on false-belief tasks should also fail on other tasks requiring counterfactual reasoning. Zaitchik (1990) used a photograph task of similar complexity to false-belief tasks, but which did not require a theory of mind. Young children saw a Polaroid camera taking a picture of a doll sitting on a mat. While they waited for the camera to develop the photograph, the experimenter moved the doll to the top of a box. When the children were asked where the doll would appear in the photograph, most 3-year-olds said on top of the box, whereas a majority of 4-year-olds said on the mat. These findings are very similar to those obtained on false-belief tasks, and are consistent with the notion that counterfactual reasoning rather than a theory of mind is needed to succeed on false-belief tasks.

Riggs et al. (1998) tested their theory by presenting a story to 3- and 4-year-old children. In this story, Maxi and his mother put chocolate in a cupboard. While Maxi is out at school, his mother uses some of the chocolate to make a cake, putting the rest of it in the fridge. After that, Maxi comes home. The children were asked a standard false-belief question ("Where does Maxi think the chocolate is?"). They were also asked a second question ("If mum had not made a cake, where would the chocolate be?"). Answering this question correctly required counterfactual reasoning but not an understanding of false beliefs.

What did Riggs et al. (1998) discover? They found that children who were correct on the false-belief question were nearly always also correct on the reasoning problem, and those who were incorrect on the false-belief question nearly always failed the reasoning question. Thus, they concluded that deficient counterfactual reasoning is the prime reason for failure on false-belief tasks. However, this may not be the whole story. Harris, German, and Mills (1996) found that many 3-year-old children could engage in counterfactual reasoning even though they were too young to succeed on most false-belief tasks. They were told a story about a girl who got cold because she went out wearing a cardigan rather than a coat. Many of them realised (using counterfactual reasoning) that the girl could have avoided getting cold if she had worn a coat.

Astington and Jenkins (1999) carried out a longitudinal study on 3-year-olds to test their theory that language development underlies improvement on false-belief tasks with age. The children were given various theory-of-mind tasks (e.g., false-belief tasks) and measures of language competence. The results strongly supported the theory: "Earlier language abilities predicted later theory-of-mind test performance …, but earlier theory of mind did not predict later language test performance … language is fundamental to theory of mind development" (p. 1311).

## Autism

It has been argued by several theorists (e.g., Baron-Cohen, Leslie, & Frith, 1985; Leslie, 1987) that children with autism lack a theory of mind. **Autism** is a very serious condition involving three categories of symptoms according to the *Diagnostic and Statistical Manual of Mental Disorders* (American Psychiatric Association, 1994; see Chapter 22):

1. *Qualitative impairment in social interaction* (e.g., great impairment in the use of several non-verbal behaviours).
2. *Qualitative impairments in communication* (e.g., reluctance to use speech to initiate or maintain a conversation).
3. *Restricted repetitive and stereotyped patterns of behaviour* (e.g., compulsive adherence to specific routines or rituals).

The film *Rainman* has been praised for Dustin Hoffman's accurate portrayal of an autistic adult.

Leslie (1987) argued that the central problem of autistic children is that they lack an understanding that other people have different ideas and knowledge to their own; this is known as "mind-blindness". They also fail to understand how behaviour is influenced by beliefs and thoughts. Thus, they do not have a theory of mind. As a result, autistic children cannot make sense of the social world, and cannot communicate effectively with other people.

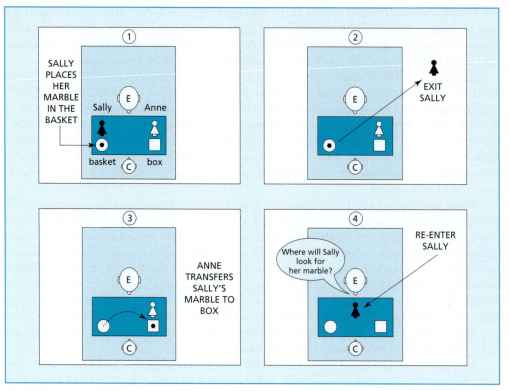

The Sally–Anne test. C denotes the child observer, and E is the experimenter.

Relevant evidence was reported by Baron-Cohen et al. (1985). Autistic and Down's syndrome children with a mental age of 4 years or more, plus normal 4-year-old children, were presented with the following story: "Sally puts her marble in the basket. Then she goes out. Anne takes Sally's marble, and puts it into her box. Then Sally comes back from her walk. Where will she look for her marble?" Over 80% of the normal children and of the Down's syndrome children correctly pointed to the basket, compared to only 20% of the autistic children. Thus, the autistic children failed to take account of the fact that they possessed knowledge that Sally did not, and did not seem to understand that other children may have a different perspective from their own.

Autistic children have great difficulty on most false-belief tasks, and thus seem to lack a theory of mind. However, it is possible that their performance on such tasks reflects general cognitive limitations rather than being specific to theory of mind. This issue was addressed by Leslie and Thaiss (1992) using two groups of children: autistic children with a mean age of 12 years and a mental age of 6 years, and normal children with a mean age of 4 years and a mental age of 4 years. They were given a false-belief task and a photograph task based on the one used by Zaitchik (1990).

The pattern of performance was very different for the two groups of children (see the figure on the left). The normal children found the two tasks comparably easy, whereas the autistic children performed markedly worse on the false-belief task than on the photograph task. Since only the false-belief task required a theory of mind, these findings suggest that autistic children have a relatively specific deficit relating to a theory of mind.

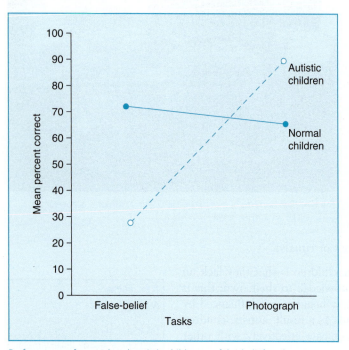

Performance of normal and autistic children on false-belief and photograph tasks. Based on data in Leslie and Thaiss (1992).

## CASE STUDY: *Autistic talents*

Not all aspects of autism are as negative as might be imagined. Some autistic children have startling artistic abilities and can produce drawings in full detail and perspective much earlier than other children.

An autistic girl named Nadia was studied by Selfe (1983). When she was only 5 years old, Nadia could draw realistic pictures of horses, cockerels, and cavalrymen from memory, although she did not speak and had various severe motor problems.

Other talents shown by autistic children and adults include feats of mental arithmetic, for example being able to calculate the day of the week for any given date in the previous 500 years. There have also been gifted autistic musicians who learn to play musical instruments by ear, with no formal training.

These talents may all be linked in some way to the autistic child's narrow focus on the world, through which they can become preoccupied with certain objects or processes in great detail.

Kanner (1943) called gifts like these "islets of ability", which suggests that other aspects of autistic children's intelligence are hidden beneath the surface of a sea of difficulties.

Drawings by 5-year-old Nadia, who is autistic (left) and an average 6½-year-old child (right).

## Evaluation

- ⊕ The acquisition of a theory of mind is probably of major importance in cognitive and social development.
- ⊕ Some of the aspects of cognitive development (e.g., counterfactual reasoning) associated with the development of a theory of mind have been identified.
- ⊕ Autistic children's difficulties with the false-belief task seem to stem from a specific theory-of-mind deficit rather than a more general cognitive impairment (e.g., Leslie & Thaiss, 1992).
- ⊖ Successful performance on false-belief tasks by normal children may reflect the development of various general cognitive abilities (e.g., counterfactual reasoning, language) rather than abilities *specific* to theory of mind.
- ⊖ There is no *single* theory of mind; rather, children acquire a progressively deeper understanding of others' beliefs over a period of years.
- ⊖ The theory-of-mind approach provides an incomplete account of the problems faced by autistic children. As Smith, Cowie, and Blades (2003, p. 481) noted, "It is not obvious how specific language problems …, obsessive behaviours, or 'islets of ability' [in autistic children] could be linked to a lack of understanding minds."

## SUMMARY

Infants cannot tell us what they see. However, various methods of assessing their visual abilities have been developed, including those based on behaviour, preference, habituation, eye movements, physiology, and visual reinforcement. Newborns are deficient in some of the basic aspects of vision, having poor visual acuity, an inability to see colour, and a lack of binocular disparity. Infants show a preference for faces over non-faces almost from birth, but whether this reflects rapid learning or a preference for objects with more elements in the top half is unclear. The visual constancies are present to some extent

*Perceptual development*

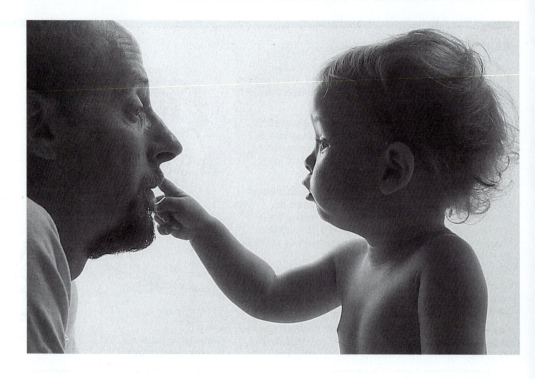

at an early age. Some developments in visual perception (e.g., visual acuity) depend on maturational changes, whereas others (e.g., aspects of depth perception, attachment of meaning to stimuli) depend on learning.

**Memory development**

Children show a general improvement in memory functioning during the years of childhood. One reason for this is an increase in the capacity of working memory. A second reason is that older children are more likely than younger ones to use rehearsal or organisational strategies during learning. A third reason is that children develop improved metamemory. However, the relationship between metamemory and memory performance is only moderate, suggesting that children often fail to use their knowledge about memory in an effective way. A fourth reason is that older children possess far more knowledge than younger ones, and relevant knowledge generally leads to enhanced memory performance. Much of this knowledge is stored in the form of scripts. Implicit memory tends to develop fully a few years earlier than explicit memory. The age of earliest memories probably depends on the development of a coherent sense of self and on interactions between parents and children. Children's eyewitness reports are often inaccurate; this is probably due to a combination of social compliance and genuine alterations in memory following questioning.

**Language acquisition**

Up until the age of about 18 months, infants are limited to single-word utterances. This is followed by the telegraphic period, during which inessential words are omitted. After that, children learn grammatical morphemes. There are close links between vocabulary development and grammatical development. The notion that we possess a language acquisition device is supported by evidence that children can create a grammar even if they are not exposed to a proper language early in life. However, the idea of an innate grammar has little convincing evidence in its favour. Child-directed speech assists language acquisition, but is probably not essential. According to the constructivist approach, language learning resembles other kinds of learning, proceeding from the concrete/specific to the abstract/general.

**Animal language acquisition**

Attempts to teach chimpanzees language are of relevance to the theoretical controversy as to whether the ability to learn language is unique to humans. Some bonobo chimpanzees have acquired a vocabulary of several hundred signs or lexigrams, and have shown some ability to understand them and to combine them to convey more complex meanings. However, chimpanzees show relatively little evidence of productivity or displacement, and have not fully mastered syntax.

Children by the age of 4 develop the ability to attribute beliefs, intentions, and emotions to others. The development of a theory of mind in normal children seems to depend on general cognitive abilities and skills (e.g., language development, counterfactual reasoning). Acquisition of a theory of mind is typically assessed by false-belief tasks, but these tasks may not assess accurately what children know about theory of mind. Autistic children find false-belief tasks especially difficult, and seem to have a specific theory-of-mind deficit. However, autistic children have many symptoms (e.g., specific language problems) that cannot readily be explained by a lack of theory of mind.

*Theory of mind*

# FURTHER READING

- Harley, T. (2001). *The psychology of learning: From data to theory* (2nd ed.). Hove, UK: Psychology Press. The processes involved in language acquisition are discussed in an approachable way in Chapters 3 and 4 of this textbook.
- Harris, M., & Butterworth, G. (2002). *Developmental psychology: A student's handbook*. Hove, UK: Psychology Press. The development of language in the early years of life is covered in a readable way in Chapters 7 and 8 of this textbook.
- Smith, P.K., Cowie, H., & Blades, M. (2003). *Understanding children's development* (4th ed.). Oxford, UK: Blackwell. Several chapters in this textbook (e.g., Chapters 10 and 11) provide detailed coverage of important aspects of cognitive development.

- **Piaget's theory**
  Outline of Piaget's self-discovery approach.

  *Piagetian concepts: accommodation, assimilation, schema, equilibration*
  *Sensori-motor stage*
  *Pre-operational stage*
  *Concrete operations stage*
  *Formal operations stage*
  *Evaluation of his theory*
  *Lourenço and Machado's defence*
  *Implications for education*

- **Vygotsky's theory**
  Outline of Vygotsky's social interaction approach.

  *Vygotsky's four stages*
  *Zone of proximal development and scaffolding*
  *The development of language*
  *Evaluation of his theory*
  *Implications for education; peer tutoring*
  *Comparison of Vygotsky and Piaget*

- **Information-processing approach**
  The information-processing theories.

  *Neo-Piagetians: Pascual-Leone and Case*
  *Siegler's overlapping waves model*
  *Implications for education*

# Cognitive development: General theories

**15**

In the last chapter, we considered the dramatic changes in various cognitive abilities (e.g., perception, memory, language) occurring during the years of childhood. In this chapter, the emphasis shifts to more general or all-inclusive approaches to cognitive development. The first general, systematic theory of cognitive development was proposed by Jean Piaget. However, several other major theoretical approaches to cognitive development have been proposed, including those of Vygotsky and information-processing theorists.

One reason why it is important to study cognitive development is because of its relevance to education. If we can understand the processes involved in learning and cognitive development, then it should be possible to improve the educational system for the benefit of students. The implications of the various theories for education are discussed.

## PIAGET'S THEORY

Jean Piaget (1896–1980) was an expert in many fields. He studied biology and philosophy at university, after which he did a PhD on the adaptations of molluscs in the lakes of his native Switzerland. After that, he went to Zurich to study experimental psychology. However, it is as the most influential developmental psychologist of all time that he is best known. Piaget put forward the most thorough account ever offered of cognitive development, and only a sketchy account can be provided here.

Piaget was interested in how children learn and adapt to the world. In order for adaptation or adjustment to occur, there must be constant interactions between the child and the outside world. According to Piaget, two processes are of key importance:

- **Accommodation**. The individual's cognitive organisation is altered by the need to deal with the environment; in other words, the individual adjusts to the outside world.
- **Assimilation**. The individual deals with new environmental situations on the basis of his/her existing cognitive organisation; in other words, the interpretation of the outside world is adjusted to fit the individual.

The clearest example of the dominance of assimilation over accommodation is play, in which reality is interpreted according to the individual's whim (e.g., a stick becomes a gun). In contrast, dominance of accommodation over assimilation is seen in imitation, in which the actions of someone else are simply copied.

There are two other key Piagetian concepts: schema and equilibration. **Schema** refers to organised knowledge used to guide action. The first schema infants develop is the body schema, when they realise there is an important distinction between "me" and "not me". This body schema helps the infant in its attempts to explore and make sense of the world.

**Equilibration** is based on the notion that the individual needs to keep a stable internal state (equilibrium) in a changing environment. When a child tries unsuccessfully to understand its experiences in terms of existing schemas, there is an unpleasant state of *disequilibrium* or lack of balance. The child then uses assimilation and accommodation to restore a state of equilibrium or balance. Thus, disequilibrium motivates the child to learn new skills and knowledge to return to the desired state of equilibrium.

The Swiss psychologist Jean Piaget, 1896–1980.

We can distinguish hypothetically between two kinds of theorists. One group argues that cognitive development only involves changes in the *amount* of knowledge available to the child, and the efficiency with which that knowledge is used in thinking. According to such theorists, there are no fundamental differences in cognition during development. The second group of theorists (e.g., Piaget) claims that the ways of thinking found in adolescence differ profoundly from those of early childhood.

Piaget argued that all children pass through various stages. His stage theory is discussed in detail below. However, some of its main assumptions will be considered here. First, there must be sufficient changes in cognitive development to permit the identification of separate cognitive stages. Second, while the ages at which different children attain any given stage can vary, the *sequence* of stages should remain the same for all. Third, the cognitive operations and structures defining a stage should form an integrated whole.

Stage theories can potentially explain the complexities of developmental change. However, they often *over-estimate* the differences between stages and *under-estimate* the variations within a given stage. In other words, they can make cognitive development look neater and tidier than is actually the case. Piaget accepted that children in a given stage do not always adopt the mode of thought typical of that stage, and he coined the term **horizontal decalage** to refer to this state of affairs.

An example of the dominance in play of assimilation over accommodation—pretending that cardboard boxes are vehicles.

Piaget argued there are four major stages of cognitive development. The first is the sensori-motor stage, lasting from birth to about 2 years of age. The second is the pre-operational stage, spanning the years between 2 and 7. The third is the concrete operations stage, which usually occurs between the ages of 7 and 11 or 12. The fourth stage is the formal operations stage, which follows on from the stage of concrete operations.

According to Piaget, very young children deal with the environment by manipulating objects. Thus, sensori-motor development is basically *intelligence in action*. After that, thinking becomes dominated by *perception* during the stage of pre-operational thought. From 7 years onwards, thinking is more and more influenced by logico-mathematical considerations. During the stage of concrete operations, logical reasoning can only be applied to objects that are real or can be seen. During the stage of formal operations, the older child or adult can think logically about potential events or abstract ideas.

*What type of play might demonstrate the dominance of accommodation over assimilation?*

**KEY TERM**

**Horizontal decalage:** apparent inconsistency in a child's performance, in which a certain cognitive ability is shown in some circumstances but not in others.

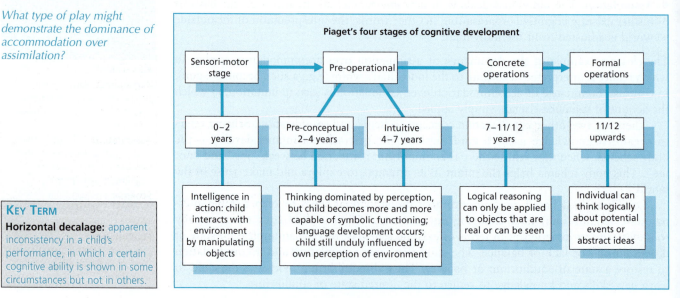

**Piaget's four stages of cognitive development**

| Sensori-motor stage | Pre-operational | | Concrete operations | Formal operations |
|---|---|---|---|---|
| 0–2 years | Pre-conceptual 2–4 years | Intuitive 4–7 years | 7–11/12 years | 11/12 upwards |
| Intelligence in action: child interacts with environment by manipulating objects | Thinking dominated by perception, but child becomes more and more capable of symbolic functioning; language development occurs; child still unduly influenced by own perception of environment | | Logical reasoning can only be applied to objects that are real or can be seen | Individual can think logically about potential events or abstract ideas |

How did Piaget set about obtaining evidence to support his theoretical views? He was sceptical about the value of the typical experimental approach, preferring instead to use a less structured and formal approach. More specifically, Piaget made extensive use of the **clinical method**, in which the experimenter questions children in an informal way to ascertain the nature of their understanding of various problems.

## Sensori-motor stage (0–2 years)

This stage of cognitive development lasts from birth to about 2 years of age, with the infant learning a great deal by moving around and exploring its environment. Initially, the baby's schemas consist largely of inborn reflexes such as sucking. However, these reflexes change somewhat with experience. For example, babies learn at a very early age to alter the shape of their lips so that they can suck more efficiently.

The key achievement of this stage is **object permanence**. This involves being aware that objects continue to exist when they are no longer in view. In the early part of the sensori-motor stage, the infant has no awareness at all of object permanence: It is literally a case of "out of sight, out of mind". Object permanence develops as the child actively explores his/her environment. Towards the end of its first year, the infant starts to display what is known as **perseverative search**. This involves the infant searching for a concealed object in the place in which it was found some time earlier rather than in the place in which it was last seen. More specifically, the experimenter hides an object at location A, which the infant finds successfully. After that, the object is hidden at location B, but the infant mistakenly searches at location A. It is for this reason that perseverative search is often known as the A-not-B error.

According to Piaget, the A-not-B error happens because the infant does not regard the object as existing independently of its own behaviour. Perseverative search shows some features of object permanence. However, full object permanence is only achieved towards the end of the sensori-motor stage according to Piaget.

The development of imitation is a major achievement of the sensori-motor stage. Imitation allows the infant to add considerably to the range of actions of which it is capable. It develops slowly, becoming more precise over time. Towards the end of the sensori-motor stage, the infant shows evidence of **deferred imitation**, which is the ability to imitate behaviour seen before.

Just as children must learn the alphabet before they can read, Piaget defined a set of stages that all children must pass through as they develop.

## *Evidence*

Object permanence seems to develop more rapidly than indicated by Piaget. For example, Bower (1982) hid a toy behind a screen. When the screen was lifted a few seconds later, the toy was no longer there. Infants who were 3 or 4 months old showed surprise. This suggests that at least some aspects of object permanence are present much earlier than was claimed by Piaget.

In the left-hand picture, the baby is reaching for a toy he can see. In the right-hand one, he searches in the same place for it, although in fact it is hidden under the cloth on his right.

Baillargeon (1987) showed evidence of object permanence in infants who were only 3½ to 5½ months of age. All the infants saw a solid screen, which was initially flat on the table, lift up and move through 180 degrees until it was flat again. A box was then placed in the way, so that the screen could only move 112 degrees before hitting it. However, the box was hidden from view by the screen as it was raised, and so the infants could not actually see the screen hit the box. There were two conditions. In the control condition, the infants saw the screen move through 112 degrees and stop. In the experimental condition, they saw the screen move through 180 degrees, which should have been impossible because of the obstruction provided by the box. Unknown to the infants, the box was removed via a trap door when the screen was upright at 90 degrees. The key finding was that the infants looked longer at the screen in the "impossible" condition. According to Baillargeon, this happened because the infants remembered that the box had been present, and were surprised that it did not stop the movement of the screen. In other words, they showed object permanence for the box several months earlier than Piaget thought was possible.

Rivera, Wakeley, and Langer (1999, p. 433) disagreed with Baillargeon (1987), arguing that, "Accounting for the findings does not require the rich interpretation that infants' behaviour in this paradigm is based on representational reasoning about what is physically possible with solid objects." Rivera et al. found that 5-month-old infants looked for the same amount of time at a screen moving through 180 degrees regardless of whether its movement was possible or "impossible". What conclusion follows from these new findings? According to Rivera et al. (p. 433), "These findings support the hypothesis that infants' longer looking at the apparently impossible 180 degree rotations [than at the 112 degree rotations] is due only to simple perceptual preference for events that display more motion." However, most of the evidence suggests that object permanence does develop earlier than predicted by Piaget.

According to Piaget, deferred imitation only develops towards the end of the second year of life. However, Meltzoff (1985, 1988) found it could occur several months earlier than Piaget believed. Meltzoff (1985) made use of a dumb-bell consisting of two wooden blocks connected by a plastic tubing. Three groups of 14-month-old infants were exposed to one of the following conditions: (1) observing the experimenter pull the toy apart (imitation condition); (2) observing the experimenter moving the toy in a circle (control condition); and (3) giving the toy to the infant (baseline condition). Twenty-four hours later all the infants were given the toy. Of those in the imitation condition, 45% immediately pulled it apart, compared to an average of only 7.5% in the other two conditions. Thus, the infants in the first condition showed clear evidence of deferred imitation.

Meltzoff (1988) extended the findings of his previous study. He again made use of imitation, control, and baseline conditions with 14-month-old infants. However, this time there were six actions that the infants could imitate, and the interval of time between observing the initial session and the test of imitation was 1 week. There was clear evidence of deferred imitation in the imitation group, in spite of the fact that the infants had to remember six actions over a relatively long period of time.

Some of Piaget's explanations have not been supported. Piaget assumed that infants showing perseverative search or the A-not-B error did not remember where the toy had been hidden. However, Baillargeon and Graber (1988) carried out a study in which 8-month-old infants saw a toy being hidden behind one of two screens. Fifteen seconds later they saw a hand lift the toy out either from the place in which it had been hidden or from behind the other screen. The infants were only surprised when the toy was lifted from behind the "wrong" screen, indicating they *did* remember where it had been put. Thus, perseverative search does *not* occur simply because of faulty memory.

More evidence that failures of memory may not account for the A-not-B error was reported by Butterworth (1977).

*Can you explain why it was necessary to have the control and baseline conditions in this study?*

Baillargeon and Graber found that 8-month-old infants were surprised when a cup they had seen being put behind the left-hand screen was then retrieved from behind the right-hand screen.

He discovered that infants still make this error and search at location A even when the object is in full view at location B!

There is another problem with Piaget's explanation of perseverative search. He argued that perseverative search occurs because young children believe an object's existence depends on their own actions. It follows that children who only passively observed the object in its first location should *not* show perseverative search. In fact, infants show as much perseverative search under those conditions as when they have been allowed to find the object in its first location (see Eysenck, 2000).

## Evaluation

- ⊕ Piaget proposed a detailed and coherent account of children's cognitive development over the first 2 years of life.
- ⊕ Piaget identified many of the main kinds of learning shown by infants during the first 2 years (e.g., development of object permanence).
- ⊖ Deferred imitation and object permanence both develop earlier in life than was suggested by Piaget.
- ⊖ Piaget's view that perseverative search or the A-not-B error occurs because of faulty memory is an over-simplification.
- ⊖ The notion that young children believe that an object's existence depends on their own actions has not been supported by the evidence.

## Pre-operational stage (2–7 years)

The child who completes the sensori-motor stage of cognitive development is still not capable of "true" thought. He/she operates largely at the level of direct action, whereas the pre-operational child becomes more and more capable of symbolic functioning. The development of language is associated with the cognitive advances of pre-operational children. However, Piaget regarded language development as largely a consequence of more fundamental cognitive changes rather than as itself a cause of cognitive advance.

Children show considerable cognitive development during the 5 years covered by the pre-operational stage. Accordingly, Piaget divided the pre-operational stage into two sub-stages: the pre-conceptual (2–4 years) and the intuitive (4–7 years). Two of the cognitive differences between children at the pre-conceptual and intuitive stages involve seriation and syncretic thought. Seriation tasks require children to arrange objects in order on the basis of a single feature (e.g., height). Piaget and Szeminska (1952) found that pre-conceptual children found this very hard to do, and even intuitive children often used a trial-and-error approach.

Syncretic thought is a limited form of thinking in which only some of the relevant information is considered. It is revealed on tasks where children are asked to select various objects that are all alike. Intuitive children tend to perform this task accurately, for example selecting several yellow objects or square objects. Pre-conceptual children show syncretic thought. The second object they select is the same as the first on one dimension (e.g., size), but then the third object is the same as the second on another dimension (e.g., colour). Thus, syncretic thought occurs because young children focus on two objects at a time, and find it hard to consider the characteristics of several objects at the same time.

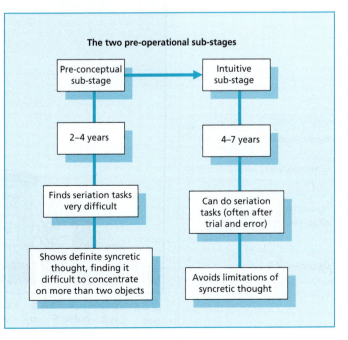

**The two pre-operational sub-stages**

Pre-conceptual sub-stage → Intuitive sub-stage

2–4 years | 4–7 years

Finds seriation tasks very difficult | Can do seriation tasks (often after trial and error)

Shows definite syncretic thought, finding it difficult to concentrate on more than two objects | Avoids limitations of syncretic thought

# Piaget: Conservation

Pre-operational children are unduly influenced by their own perception of the environment. They tend to pay attention to only one aspect of the total situation (this is called **centration** by Piaget). The way in which centration produces errors is shown in studies of conservation. **Conservation** refers to the understanding that certain aspects of a visual display do not vary in spite of changes in perceptual aspects. According to Piaget, conservation underlies children's understanding of invariance, which involves knowing that quantities do not change unless something has been added or taken away from them.

In his classic studies on conservation of quantity, Piaget presented children with two glasses of the same size and shape containing the same quantity of liquid. When the child agrees there is the same quantity of liquid in both glasses, the liquid from one of the glasses is poured into a different glass that is taller and thinner. The child is then asked if the two glasses (the original one and the new one) contain the same amount to drink, or if one contains more. Pre-operational children fail to show conservation. They argue either that there is more liquid in the new container ("because it's higher") or that there is more liquid in the original glass ("because it's wider"). In either case, the child centres or focuses on only one dimension (height or width).

## KEY STUDY EVALUATION—Piaget

Piaget used the conservation of liquid task to show that pre-operational children lack the internalised cognitive operations of reversibility and decentration. However, it might be interesting to try the same experiment with children from a non-Western environment, such as the bush people of the African Kalahari desert, who are not likely to be familiar with glass beakers filled with water. Would they show conservation or not? Would a lack of conservation necessarily mean that these children could not decentre?

The pre-operational child fails on conservation tasks partly because of centration. However, the child also lacks crucial internalised cognitive operations according to Piaget. Two cognitive operations are of special relevance on conservation tasks: reversibility and decentration. **Reversibility** involves the ability to undo, or reverse mentally, some operation that has been carried out. Reversibility allows the realisation that the effect of pouring liquid from one container into another could be negated by simply pouring the liquid back into its original container. **Decentration** involves the ability to take account of two or more aspects of a situation at the same time. In the case of conservation of quantity, it involves considering height and width together.

*Children are asked the same question twice in this classic study. What effect might this have on their responses?*

## KEY TERMS

**Centration:** attending to only one aspect of a situation.

**Conservation:** the principle that quantities remain constant under various changes to their appearance.

**Reversibility:** the ability to undo, or reverse mentally, an action or operation.

**Decentration:** a cognitive operation involving the ability to take account of two or more aspects of a situation at the same time.

*Seriation tasks require children to arrange objects in order on the basis of a single feature, such as height.*

## Egocentrism

Piaget argued that the thinking of pre-operational children is characterised by egocentrism. **Egocentrism** is the tendency to assume that one's way of thinking about things is the only possible way. Piaget studied egocentric thinking in pre-operational children by using the three mountains task. Children looked at a model of mountains, and then decided which picture showed the view that would be seen by someone looking at the display from a different angle. Children younger than 8 nearly always selected the photograph of the scene as they themselves saw it. According to Piaget, this error occurred because of their inability to escape from an egocentric perspective.

Egocentrism also involves a lack of differentiation between the self and the world, which makes the child unable to distinguish clearly between psychological and physical events. This produces:

A drawing of the model used in Piaget's three mountains task. Children were shown the model from one angle, then shown photographs of the model from other viewpoints, and asked to choose which view someone standing at one of the other labelled points would see. Pre-operational children usually selected the view from the point at which they themselves had seen the model.

- *Realism*. The tendency to regard psychological events as having a physical existence.
- *Animism*. The tendency to endow physical objects and events with psychological qualities.
- *Artificialism*. The tendency to consider that physical objects and events were created by people.

Piaget (1967) provided the following example of realism: "Engl (8½): Where is the dream whilst you are dreaming? Beside me.—Are your eyes shut when you dream?—Where is the dream?—Over there" (p. 95).

Children show animism when they claim that the wind feels it when it blows against a mountain. Young children often attribute consciousness to all things. An example of artificialism concerns my daughter Fleur at the age of 3. We were on Wimbledon Common, and I told her that the sun would come out when I had counted to ten. When it did so, she was very confident that Daddy could control the sun, and often begged me to make the sun appear on gloomy days!

## Evidence

Many people argue that Piaget under-estimated the extent to which young children can exhibit conservation. More specifically, they claim the tasks he used made it difficult for children to reveal the full extent of their relevant knowledge. For example, Wheldall and Poborca (1980) argued that children often fail on conservation tasks such as those used by Piaget because they do not understand the question. Accordingly, they devised a non-verbal version of the liquid conservation task. This version was based on operant discrimination learning, and did not involve the use of language. Only 28% of their 6- and 7-year-old participants showed conservation with the standard verbal version, but 50% did so when tested on the non-verbal version. These findings suggest that misunderstanding of language is one factor involved in non-conservation. However, the fact that one-half of the participants were non-conservers with the non-verbal version indicates that other factors must also be involved.

The notion that children may fail to show number conservation because they think the experimenter intended to change the number (see Key Study on the next page) was supported by Light, Buckingham, and Robbins (1979). They tested 5- and 6-year-olds in pairs, with both members of each pair being given glass beakers of the same size and containing the same number of pasta shells. They were told the shells would be used to play a

**KEY TERM**

**Egocentrism:** the assumption that one's way of thinking is the only possibility.

## McGarrigle and Donaldson: The "naughty teddy"

McGarrigle and Donaldson (1974) also showed that changing the way in which a conservation task is presented can make a large difference. They presented 6-year-old children with two rows of counters. All the children agreed there were equal numbers of counters in each row. In one condition, the experimenter deliberately messed up one of the rows. Number conservation was shown on 40% of the trials. This finding suggests that most of the children lacked the underlying competence necessary to show number conservation. However, the findings were rather different in a second condition, in which a "naughty teddy bear" messed up one of the rows in what looked like an accidental way. In this condition, number conservation was obtained on 70% of the trials.

Why did McGarrigle and Donaldson (1974) find such a large difference between the two conditions? The high level of performance in the "naughty teddy" conditions presumably occurred because most of the children had some understanding of number conservation. In the other condition, the fact that the experimenter deliberately altered the situation may have led the children to assume that the experimenter *intended* to change the number of counters in one of the rows. Whether or not that is correct, the fact remains that performance in that condition failed to reflect the underlying level of competence. However, it should be noted that Eames, Shorrocks, and Tomlinson (1990) failed to replicate McGarrigle and Donaldson's findings.

### KEY STUDY EVALUATION—McGarrigle and Donaldson

Recent research suggests that McGarrigle and Donaldson may also have been mistaken. It is possible that the children were so absorbed in the "naughty teddy" routine that they didn't actually notice the transformation and that is why, with naughty teddy, they said the display hadn't changed. To test this possibility, Moore and Frye (1986) arranged for naughty teddy to actually add a counter (or take one away). Children said no change had taken place, which suggests that they were simply not attending to the display at all.

However, other evidence provides support to McGarrigle and Donaldson's (1974) findings. As we have seen, Light et al. (1979) found that the existence of number conservation in children depended very much on whether or not the changes introduced by the experimenter seemed deliberate. It is likely that the percentage of children showing conservation is influenced by a number of factors (e.g., whether the experimenter changes the situation deliberately; whether the children attend to the changes).

## Discussion points

1. Why do you think that McGarrigle and Donaldson found such a large difference between their two conditions?
2. What problems for Piaget's theory arose from his failure to distinguish carefully between performance and competence?

competitive game, and so it was essential they had the same number. Then the experimenter pretended to notice that one of the beakers had a badly chipped rim and so might be dangerous to handle. The shells were then transferred to another beaker of a different shape, and the children were asked whether the number of shells in each beaker was the same. Conservation was shown by 70% of the children in this incidental transformation condition, against only 5% in a standard intentional transformation condition. Presumably the change seemed less important when it was seen as merely incidental.

Piaget claimed that conservation involves an understanding of invariance, and argued that his conservation task was an appropriate way of assessing children's understanding of invariance. However, Elkind and Schoenfeld (1972) disagreed. According to them, the simplest way to decide whether children have an understanding of invariance would be to present them with a *single* quantity (e.g., glass of liquid), and then to transform that quantity (e.g., pour it into a container of a different shape). Children who argue that the quantity remains the same show conservation and an understanding of invariance.

In contrast, children have to go through three steps on Piaget's conservation task: (1) decide that the two quantities are equal initially; (2) decide that the quantity that has changed is still equivalent to what it was initially; and (3) decide that the changed quantity is equal to the other unchanged quantity. According to Elkind and Schoenfeld (1972), this task assesses the conservation of equivalence rather than of identity.

Elkind and Schoefeld (1972) assessed conservation of identity (i.e., only one quantity is presented initially) and conservation of equivalence (i.e., two quantities were presented initially as in Piaget's studies). Four-year-olds performed much better on conservation of identity than on conservation of equivalence. What do these findings mean? According to Goswami (1998, p. 244), "Although both [kinds of task] were measures of the understanding of invariance, the conservation of identity provided a relatively pure measure of this understanding whereas the conservation of equivalence required in addition an understanding of transitivity [arranging objects in order]."

Hughes (1975) argued that poor performance on the three mountains task (used to test egocentric thinking) occurred because it did not relate to children's experience. He tested this argument by using a piece of apparatus in which two walls intersected at right angles to form what looked like a plus sign. A boy doll and a policeman doll were put into the apparatus, and the child was asked whether the policeman doll could see the boy doll. After that, the child was told to hide the boy so that the policeman could not see him. Nearly all the children could do this, and any errors were corrected. Finally, a second policeman was used, and the children were told to hide the boy doll so that neither of the policemen could see him. According to Piaget, the children should have hidden the boy so that they could not see it, and so should have failed the task. In fact, 90% of children between the ages of 3½ and 5 performed the task successfully. Hughes concluded that the main reason why performance was much higher on his task than on the three mountains task used by Piaget was because his task was much more meaningful and interesting for young children. However, it could also be argued that the task was much simpler than the one used by Piaget.

Convincing evidence that young children are not entirely egocentric comes from listening to them talking to even younger children (Eysenck, 2001). For example, I used to listen to my son William talking to his sister Juliet, who is 2 years younger than him. By the time he was 4, he spoke in a simpler way to her than to his parents.

## Evaluation

- ➕ Piaget identified several limitations in the thinking of pre-operational children.
- ➕ Piaget provided a coherent theoretical account, arguing that children at this stage lack important cognitive operations (e.g., reversibility).
- ➖ Piaget often used tasks which children found difficult to understand, and different findings have often been obtained using more child-friendly versions of these tasks.
- ➖ Piaget's conservation task may assess conservation of equivalence even though it was intended to assess conservation of identity.
- ➖ Piaget under-estimated the cognitive abilities of pre-operational children and exaggerated the extent to which they show egocentric thinking. However, some of Piaget's critics may have over-estimated the cognitive skills of pre-operational children (see below).

## Concrete operations stage (7–11 years)

Children during the stage of concrete operations cease to show many of the cognitive limitations they exhibited during the stage of pre-concrete operations. For example, they show an understanding of conservation, reversibility, decentration, and so on. More generally, Piaget argued that the shift from pre-operational to concrete operational thinking involves an increasing independence of thought from perception. Underlying this shift is the development of various cognitive operations of a logical or mathematical nature, including the actions implied by mathematical symbols (e.g., $+$, $-$, $\div$, $\times$, $>$, $<$, $=$). The most important cognitive operation is reversibility, which involves the ability to cancel out the effects of a perceptual change by imagining the opposite change. During the concrete operations stage, children can use the various cognitive operations only with respect to specific concrete situations. In the subsequent stage of formal operations, thinking is freed from the immediate situation.

Piaget argued that cognitive operations are usually combined or organised into a system or structure. For example, the operation "greater than" cannot really be considered independently of the operation "less than". Someone has failed to grasp the full meaning of "A is greater than B" unless he/she realises this statement means that "B is less than A". Piaget coined the term **grouping** to refer to such sets of logically related operations.

> **KEY TERM**
> **Grouping:** in Piaget's theory, a set of logically related operations.

One of the tasks used to test conservation of number. Children are asked if there are the same number of beads in the two rows before and after they are rearranged.

What kinds of tasks can children perform in the concrete operations stage they could not perform previously? One example is based on the notion of **transitivity**, which allows three elements to be placed in the correct order. For example, if Mark is taller than Peter, and Peter is taller than Robert, then it follows from the notion of transitivity that Mark is taller than Robert. Concrete operational children can solve problems such as the one just discussed, but cannot apply the notion of transitivity to abstract problems.

Piaget argued that it was during the stage of concrete operations that children were able to demonstrate transitivity. However, there is contrary evidence. For example, Pears and Bryant (1990) found a relatively simple way of testing children's understanding of transitivity. Four-year-old children were initially presented with a number of small towers, each consisting of two coloured bricks (e.g., a red brick on a yellow brick, a yellow brick on a green brick, and a green brick on a blue brick). These small towers provided information as to the way in which the children should construct a large tower, since the order of the bricks in this large tower was to correspond with that in the small towers. Thus, the large tower would have red at the top, followed in sequence by yellow, green, and blue. Before the children built the large tower, they were asked various questions to test their knowledge of transitivity (e.g., "Which will be the higher in the tower that you are going to build, the yellow brick or the blue one?"). The children performed reasonably well on this task, indicating they could make transitive inferences several years earlier than was assumed by Piaget.

Piaget argued that children should find it easier to achieve conservation on some tasks than on others. Conservation of number (e.g., realising that two rows of objects contain the same number of objects even when the objects are closer together in one row) involves fairly simple operations. All the child has to do is to pair each object in one row with an object in the other row. In contrast, consider conservation of volume. This can be tested by placing two identical balls of clay into two identical transparent containers

This apparatus tests conservation of volume. Children are asked if the liquids will be at the same level again when the new shape of clay is put back into the glass. Conservation of volume is not usually attained until about the age of 11 or 12.

filled to the same level. One ball of clay is then moulded into a new shape, and conservation is shown if the child realises that this will not change the amount of water it displaces. Conservation of volume is said to be harder to achieve than conservation of number because it involves taking account of the operations involved in the conservation of liquids and of mass. As predicted, conservation of volume is generally attained some years after conservation of number (e.g., Tomlinson-Keasey, Eisert, Kahle, Hardy-Brown, & Keasey, 1979).

Most children acquire the various forms of conservation in the same order. First comes conservation of number and liquid at the age of about 6 or 7. Then comes conservation of substance or quantity and of length at about 7 or 8, followed by conservation of weight between the ages of 8 and 10. Finally, there is conservation of volume at about the age of 11 or 12. However, cultural differences (which Piaget tended to ignore) are of importance. For example, Price-Williams, Gordon, and Ramirez (1969) found that the children of Mexican potters had slow development of conservation of volume using beakers, but fast development when a ball of clay was stretched into an oblong shape. Ghuman (1982) studied the children of farmers living in the Punjab region of India. These children helped their parents to weigh farm products such as rice and corn, and their understanding of conservation of weight was advanced for their age. Thus, the specific experiences of children in any given culture influence the speed with which conservation is achieved.

*What are the implications of these findings for the education of children?*

## Evaluation

● The cognitive development of children between the ages of 7 and 11 is approximately as described by Piaget.

● Children in the stage of concrete operations typically learn a range of cognitive operations (e.g., reversibility, decentration) related to mathematics and to logic.

● Much of the new knowledge acquired by children during the concrete operations stage owes little to either mathematics or logic.
● There are greater cross-cultural differences in achievement of conservation than would be expected on Piaget's theory.
● Piaget under-estimated the importance of specific experiences in determining performance on conservation tasks. For example, children often show conservation of volume for substances with which they are familiar some time before they show conservation of volume for less familiar ones (Durkin, 1995). This is somewhat inconsistent with Piaget's stage-based account of cognitive development.

## Formal operations stage (11 upwards)

Formal operational thought involves the ability to think in terms of many possible states of the world. This permits an escape from the limitations of immediate reality. Thus, adolescents and adults in the formal operations stage can think in an abstract way as well as the concrete way found in the previous stage of cognitive development. Initially, Piaget argued that this stage starts at the age of 11 or 12. However, he and other researchers found that most children of this age showed very little evidence of formal operations. Accordingly, he changed the proposed age of onset to 15 to 20 years of age (Piaget, 1972).

Inhelder and Piaget (1958) put forward the following suggestions for deciding whether someone is using formal operations:

*Analyse the proofs employed by the subject. If they do not go beyond observation of empirical correspondences [observable similarities], they can be fully explained in terms of concrete operations, and nothing would warrant our assuming that more complex thought mechanisms are operating. If, on the other hand, the subject [participant] interprets a given correspondence as the result of any one of several possible combinations, and this leads him to verify his [sic] hypotheses by observing their consequences, then we know that propositional operations are involved (p. 279).*

Thus, formal operational thinking involves considering most or all of the possible combinations of factors, whereas concrete operational thinking involves considering only a small number of combinations.

What kinds of problems have been used to study formal operational thought? One task used by Piaget involved presenting the participants with a set of weights and a string that could be lengthened or shortened. The goal was to work out what determines the frequency of the swings of a pendulum formed by suspending a weight on a string from a pole. The factors often considered include the length of the string, the weight of the suspended object, the force of the participant's push, and the position from which the pendulum is pushed. In fact, only the length of the string is relevant.

When pre-operational children are presented with this problem, they typically argue mistakenly that the strength of the push they give to the pendulum is the main factor. Concrete-operational children often argue that the frequency of swinging of the pendulum is affected by the length of the string, but they cannot isolate that factor from all the others. In contrast, many formal-operational children manage to solve the problem. According to Piaget, the ability to solve the pendulum problem requires an understanding of a complicated combinatorial system.

Bradmetz (1999) assessed formal operational thinking in 62 15-year-olds using various Piagetian tasks. He also assessed general intelligence. Two key findings emerged from this research. First, only 1 out of the 62 participants showed substantial evidence of formal operational thought. This

Children were asked to work out what would affect the frequency of the swings of the pendulum. They were asked to consider changing the weights on the pendulum, the length of the string, how hard they pushed it, and which direction it was pushed in.

finding runs counter to Piaget's theorising, since he assumed that many (or most) 15-year-olds would have attained the stage of formal operations. It should be noted that Bradmetz's finding is in line with those of other researchers. Second, overall performance on the tests of formal thought correlated +.61 with general intelligence. This indicates that the cognitive abilities associated with formal thought are fairly similar to those assessed by traditional IQ tests.

## Evaluation

⊕ The tasks used by Piaget to assess formal operations are fairly closely related to general intelligence.

⊖ Relatively few adolescents and adults show clear evidence of having reached the stage of formal operations (e.g., Bradmetz, 1999).

⊖ Even adults who appear to have reached the stage of formal operations on some tasks generally do not do so on all tasks. For example, the author of this book responds to almost all computer problems with angry mutterings under his breath rather than the application of formal operational thought!

⊖ Adults in their everyday lives typically deal with problems having no single perfect solution, and that cannot be solved simply by using logico-mathematical structures. Thus, a detailed understanding of mathematics and of logic is of limited value in most adult thinking.

*Do you think that there is any cognitive development beyond formal operations? What form might it take if there is?*

## In defence of Piaget

Most experts argue that Piaget's theoretical approach is inadequate, and many of their criticisms have been discussed already. However, Lourenço and Machado (1996) made a spirited attempt to defend Piaget from his critics, and we will consider their views. The central argument put forward by Lourenço and Machado (p. 146) was that many researchers have *over-estimated* the abilities of children: "Having concluded that Piaget under-estimated the competence of young children, his critics failed to realise how often they were victims of the converse, false-positive error (i.e., of ascribing to children operational competencies that … turn out to be only preoperational)."

The general issue of whether the abilities of young children have been over-estimated or exaggerated will be considered with reference to the studies of Baillargeon (1987) and of McGarrigle and Donaldson (1974), both of which were discussed earlier. Baillargeon found that infants seemed surprised when the movement of a screen was not impeded by a box, and she concluded that this indicated that the infants had achieved object permanence. According to Lourenço and Machado (1996, p. 144), such findings "indicate that something in a perceptual array has changed but provide no conclusive evidence that a conceptual competence (i.e., object permanence) is responsible for the infant's reaction of surprise".

There is some substance to the arguments put forward by Lourenço and Machado (1996). As we saw earlier, the infants who showed surprise in Baillargeon's (1987) study probably lacked complete object permanence. However, we then have to ask what evidence would prove that an infant has object permanence. There is a danger that discounting apparently convincing evidence for object permanence such as that provided by Baillargeon may make Piaget's theoretical ideas essentially untestable.

McGarrigle and Donaldson (1974) found that number conservation was shown by 40% of 6-year-olds when a row of counters was deliberately disrupted by the experimenter but by 70% when the row of counters was "accidentally" disrupted by "naughty teddy". Can we assume that 70% of 6-year-olds have achieved number conservation? Not really. When the accidental condition followed the deliberate condition, only 55% of children showed number conservation (compared to 85% when the accidental condition preceded the deliberate condition). The finding that merely changing the order of conditions had a large effect on their performance indicates that many 6-year-olds have a very shaky grasp of number conservation!

What is the take-home message from this section? Experimenters have found ingenious ways of simplifying Piagetian problems so that most children can solve them at earlier ages than Piaget predicted. However, children can provide accurate answers on, for example, conservation tasks without any deep understanding of conservation. The crucial point is that Piaget's critics have focused on whether children can produce correct answers, whereas Piaget was much more interested in whether children had a deep understanding.

## Overall evaluation

- ⊕ Piaget's theory was an extremely ambitious attempt to explain how children move from being irrational and illogical to being rational and logical.
- ⊕ Piaget provided the first detailed account of the ways in which children's thinking changes during childhood, and he remains the most important theorist on cognitive development.
- ⊕ The notions that children learn certain basic operations (e.g., reversibility), and that these operations then allow them to solve numerous problems, are valuable ones.
- ⊖ Stage theories such as Piaget's *over-estimate* the differences between stages and *under-estimate* the differences within stages. For example, children in the concrete operations stage show conservation of quantity for familiar materials some time before they show it for unfamiliar materials (see Durkin, 1995). Thus, successful performance depends on *specific* learning experiences as well as on the *general* cognitive operations emphasised by Piaget. In essence, cognitive development proceeds less systematically than Piaget assumed.
- ⊖ Piaget under-estimated the cognitive skills of young children, but probably less than his critics have claimed. He used tasks that were rather abstract and lacking in meaning for children, and which made great demands on their language abilities. Children performed much worse on such tasks than on similar ones which were more meaningful to them, and which were explained to them in simple language.
- ⊖ Piaget gave a detailed *description* of the major cognitive changes in development, but did not provide an adequate *explanation* of the factors producing these changes. Thus, Piaget told us *what* cognitive development involves, but not *why* or *how* this development occurs.
- ⊖ Piaget de-emphasised the role of social factors in cognitive development. For example, children learn much from social interactions with adults and other children, but such learning was not considered in detail by Piaget (see below).

## Educational implications

Piaget himself did not focus very much on the usefulness of his theory for educational practice. However, many people working in education have done precisely that. The Plowden Report in the late 1960s suggested Piaget's ideas should be used in schools (see Peaker, 1971, for a follow-up to the Report). Years later, the Nuffield Science approach to education was based on the Piagetian notions that children should be actively involved in learning, and that concrete practical work should precede the more abstract aspects of science. Below we consider three ways in which Piagetian theory has been applied in education (see Gross, 1996).

## 1. What can children learn?

According to Piaget, what children can learn is determined by their current stage of cognitive development. Thus, it is very much limited to what they are "ready" to learn. Children can only deal successfully with tasks that make use of the various cognitive structures and operations they have already mastered.

The above prediction has received only partial support. Several attempts have been made to teach concrete operations to preschool children. The ability to perform concrete operational tasks is normally learned at about the age of 7. Thus, it should not be possible on Piagetian theory for much younger children to perform them successfully. However, provision of suitable training to 4-year-olds usually leads to reasonably good performance on such tasks (Brainerd, 1983). Piaget seems to have under-estimated the ability of children to cope with new kinds of intellectual challenge.

## 2. How should children be taught?

According to Piaget, children learn best when engaging in active **self-discovery**. Children apply the processes of assimilation and accommodation to their active involvement with the world around them. Teachers can encourage this by creating a state of *disequilibrium*, in which the child's existing schemas or cognitive structures are shown to be inadequate. Disequilibrium can be created by asking children difficult questions, and by encouraging them to ask questions.

Some of the above ideas can be applied to playgroup practices and to children playing with toys. According to Piaget, children will obtain the most benefit from playgroups and from toys when actively involved in a process of self-discovery. In what Piaget called mastery play, the child uses new motor schemas in several different situations. This helps to strengthen the child's learning.

Piaget's preferred educational approach can be contrasted with the more traditional approach, in which the teacher provides relatively passive children with knowledge. Piaget argued that this approach (called **tutorial training**) is much less effective than self-discovery. In his own words, "Every time we teach a child something, we prevent him from discovering it on his own."

Cross-cultural research provides little support for Piaget's views. For example, most teachers in Asian countries use tutorial training rather than the active self-discovery favoured by Piaget. However, Asian children have superior academic achievement to those in most other cultures (see Dworetzky, 1996). In fairness to Piaget, it should be noted that social and cultural factors not directly related to teaching style seem to be important. For example, Stigler, Lee, and Stevenson (1987) found that Japanese and Taiwanese students spent only 5% of their time in mathematics classes doing non-work activities (e.g., talking to classmates, wandering around the room), whereas American students spent 20% of their time engaged in such activities. Probably the most important single factor in explaining the Asian students' superior mathematics performance was that Asian teachers devoted two or three times as many hours per week to teaching the subject than did American teachers.

> **The French connection**
>
> Larivee et al.'s (2000) overview of French-speaking researchers' work in Switzerland and France shows how Piaget's ideas have developed. The normal variations between children—what psychologists call individual differences—are seen as important areas for further research. Differing sensitivities to situations and differing preferences for strategies or ways of problem solving could lead to different developmental pathways. Nowadays one pathway of developmental stages is not thought to be applicable to the child population of even one or two cultures.

Brainerd (1983) reviewed studies on different teaching styles. He concluded that, "although self-discovery training can produce learning, it is generally less effective than tutorial learning". Meadows (1994) arrived at a similar, but broader conclusion: "Piagetian theory emphasises the individual child as the virtually independent constructor of his own development, an emphasis that under-values the contribution of other people to cognitive development and excludes teaching and cultural influences."

## Socio-cognitive conflict

The notion of disequilibrium was developed by neo-Piagetians such as Doise and Mugny (1984). They argued that cognitive development involves the resolution of **socio-cognitive conflict** produced by exposure to the differing views of others. Thus, they emphasised social factors in learning more than did Piaget.

Evidence indicating the importance of socio-cognitive conflict was reported by Ames and Murray (1982), in a study on children of 6 and 7 who had failed on conservation

> **KEY TERMS**
>
> **Self-discovery:** an active approach to learning in which the child is encouraged to use his or her initiative in learning.
>
> **Tutorial training:** a traditional approach in which the teacher imparts knowledge to fairly passive students.
>
> **Socio-cognitive conflict:** intellectual conflict created as a result of being exposed to the differing views of other people.

tasks. Some children were given corrective feedback, and others were exposed to children who already knew about conservation. Still others were paired with children who had also failed to conserve, but who had provided a different wrong answer to the one they had produced. Children in the last condition showed the greatest improvement in ability to conserve. Presumably this happened because socio-cognitive conflict and the need to consider the task in detail were greatest in this condition.

The neo-Piagetians also emphasised the importance of **social marking**, which involves conflict between an individual's cognitive understanding and some social rule. Doise, Rijsman, van Meel, Bressers, and Pinxten (1981) studied conservation of liquid in children between the ages of 4 and 6 not initially showing conservation. Social marking was induced in some pairs of children by reminding them of the social rule that both children deserved the same reward. Other pairs of children were not reminded of this rule. The children in the social marking condition saw a conflict between the social rule and the apparently different amounts of liquid in the two containers, and this helped them to show conservation.

## 3. What should children be taught?

Piaget claimed that cognitive development involves children acquiring numerous schemas or cognitive structures (e.g., operations). Many of these schemas are based on mathematical or logical principles. Thus, it should be useful for children to study mathematics and logic, as well as science subjects providing illustrations of these principles at work. Of crucial importance is the notion that the learning material must not be too complex and far removed from the child's existing schemas. According to Piaget, children can only learn effectively when they possess the relevant underlying schemas. Unfortunately, the cognitive structures Piaget emphasised are of rather limited value for many kinds of learning (e.g., foreign languages, history). Thus, his approach applies only to some school subjects.

Piaget recommended that a child's learning material should not be too complex or advanced for the child as children only learn effectively when they possess the relevant underlying schemas.

## VYGOTSKY'S THEORY

Lev Vygotsky (1896–1934) was a Russian psychologist who emphasised the notion that cognitive development depends very largely on social factors. He graduated from Moscow University in 1917, which was the year of the Soviet Revolution. Vygotsky was one of untold millions who suffered under Stalin, with his various writings being suppressed in Russia. As a result, few people knew of his work during his life, which came to an early end because of tuberculosis. In fact, his work only began to be translated into other languages in the 1960s and 1970s.

According to Vygotsky (1930/1981, p. 163), "Social relations or relations among people genetically [developmentally] underlie all higher functions and their relationships." More specifically, Vygotsky (p. 163) argued as follows: "Any function in the child's cultural development appears twice, or on two planes. First, it appears on the social plane, and then on the psychological plane." As Durkin (1995) pointed out, the child is an apprentice who learns directly from social interaction and communication with older children and adults having the knowledge and skills the child lacks. It may seem obvious that Vygotsky is correct. However, you only have to look at any textbook on cognitive psychology (including Eysenck & Keane, 2000!) to see that few cognitive psychologists consider social factors at all.

Vygotsky's approach contrasts with that of Piaget, who emphasised that the individual acquires knowledge through a process of self-discovery. However, there are also some similarities. For example, Vygotsky and Piaget both agreed that activity forms the basis for learning and for the development of thinking. In addition, they both argued that learning is most effective when the information presented to children is closely related to their current knowledge and abilities.

The Russian psychologist Lev Semeonovich Vygotsky, 1896–1934.

> **KEY TERM**
> **Social marking:** conflict between an individual's cognitive understanding and a social rule.

Vygotsky argued that there are four stages in the formation of concepts. He identified these four stages on the basis of a study in which children were presented with wooden blocks provided with labels consisting of nonsense symbols. Each nonsense syllable was used consistently to refer to blocks having certain characteristics (e.g., circular and thin). The children were given the concept-formation task of working out the meaning of each nonsense syllable. Vygotsky's four stages were as follows:

1. *Vague syncretic stage.* The children failed to use systematic strategies and showed little understanding of the concepts.
2. *Complex stage.* Non-random strategies were used, but these strategies were not successful in finding the main features of each concept.
3. *Potential concept stage.* Systematic strategies were used, but they were limited to focusing on one feature at a time (e.g., shape).
4. *Mature concept stage.* Systematic strategies relating to more than one feature at a time were used, and led to successful concept formation.

The above study is one of the very few carried out by Vygotsky, and it is of interest because of that. It is also of interest because Vygotsky's findings resemble those of Piaget with very different tasks. Vygotsky found that children had problems with concept formation because they focused on only one salient or obvious feature of stimuli. This is very similar to Piaget's discovery that pre-operational children fail on conservation tasks because they attend to only one aspect of the situation.

## Zone of proximal development and scaffolding

One of the key notions in Vygotsky's approach to cognitive development is the **zone of proximal development**. This was defined by Vygotsky (1978, p. 86) as "the distance between the actual developmental level as determined by independent problem solving and the level of potential development as determined through problem solving under adult guidance or in collaboration with more capable peers".

Two aspects of the zone of proximal development are of particular importance. First, children apparently lacking certain skills when tested on their own may perform more effectively in the social context provided by someone with the necessary knowledge. Second, when a given child's level of understanding is moderately challenged, he/she is most likely to acquire new knowledge rapidly and without a sense of failure. Vygotsky assumed that children differ in the size of the zone of proximal development: Those deriving the greatest benefit from instruction have larger zones of proximal development than those deriving less benefit.

Wood, Bruner, and Ross (1976) developed Vygotsky's notion of a zone of proximal development. They introduced the concept of **scaffolding**, which refers to the context provided by knowledgeable people such as adults to help children to develop their cognitive skills. Effective scaffolding means that the child does not need to climb too far at any point.

*How can these Vygotskian ideas be applied to education?*

**KEY TERMS**
**Zone of proximal development:** in Vygotsky's theory, capacities that are being developed but are not as yet functioning fully.
**Scaffolding:** the context provided by an adult or other knowledgeable person, which helps the child to develop its cognitive skills.

Left to his own devices, could this boy make his sister a birthday cake? His mother uses scaffolding to create a situation within which he can begin to move into a zone of proximal development.

Another important aspect of scaffolding is that there is a gradual withdrawal of support as the child's knowledge and confidence increase.

Wood et al. (1976) identified five major components of scaffolding. First, there is recruitment, which involves making sure the child is interested in the task. Second, there is reduction of degrees of freedom, with the tutor simplifying the task for the benefit of the learner. Third, there is direction management, which involves the tutor providing encouragement to persuade the child to persevere with the task. Fourth, there is marking of critical features, with the tutor focusing on important aspects of the task. Fifth, there is demonstration, in which the tutor turns the child's partial solution into a complete solution in the hope that the child will then be able to copy (or improve on) this solution.

# Language

Vygotsky attached great importance to the development of language. He argued that language and thought are essentially unrelated during the first stage of development. As a result, young children have "pre-intellectual speech" and "pre-verbal thought". During the second stage, language and thought develop in parallel, and continue to have very little impact on each other. During the third stage, children begin to make use of the speech of others and talking to themselves (private speech) to assist in their thinking and problem solving. An important notion here is that of **intersubjectivity**. This refers to the process by which two individuals whose initial views about a task are different move towards an agreed understanding of what is involved.

Finally, private speech is used routinely in problem solving, and language plays a part in the development of thinking. Thus, language becomes increasingly central to cognitive development over the years. Private speech is initially spoken out loud, but then becomes more and more internal. Language generally plays a crucial role when children learn from social interactions with others. Some of the processes involved were described by Berk (1994, p. 62): "When a child discusses a challenging task with a mentor [someone providing guidance], that individual offers spoken directions and strategies. The child incorporates the language of those dialogues into his or her private speech and then uses it to guide independent efforts."

Vygotsky's views on the functions of language were complex. However, his central point was that language serves two very different functions: "In the beginning, speech serves a regulative, communicative function. Later, it also serves other functions and transforms the way in which children learn, think, and understand. It becomes an instrument or *tool* of thought, not only providing a 'code' or system for representing the world but also the means by which *self-regulation* comes about" (Wood, 1998, p. 29). Vygotsky (1962, p. 17) gave the following example of this self-regulatory function in a child who discovered that he did not have a blue pencil to colour a drawing: "Where's the pencil? I need a blue pencil. Never mind, I'll draw with the red one and wet it with water; it will become dark and look blue."

Vygotsky's views on the role of language in cognitive development are very different from those of Piaget. At the risk of over-simplification (a crime of which the author is often accused!), Vygotsky argued that cognitive development depends crucially on language development and use. In contrast, Piaget argued that cognitive development typically precedes (and is little affected by) language development.

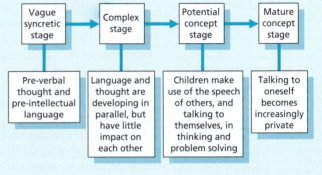

**Language development in Vygotsky's four stages**

| Vague syncretic stage | Complex stage | Potential concept stage | Mature concept stage |
|---|---|---|---|
| Pre-verbal thought and pre-intellectual language | Language and thought are developing in parallel, but have little impact on each other | Children make use of the speech of others, and talking to themselves, in thinking and problem solving | Talking to oneself becomes increasingly private |

Parents can provide their children with an excellent start in acquiring skills if they support and encourage attempts to learn through play.

**KEY TERM**
**Intersubjectivity:** a process by which two individuals with different views about a task adjust those views so they become more similar.

Finally, Vygotsky argued that children can learn much through play. According to Vygotsky (1976), "In play, the child functions above his average age, above his usual everyday behaviour, in play he is head high above himself" (p. 552). Why is this? Children at play generally make use of some aspects of their own culture. For example, they may pretend to be a fireman or a doctor, or they may play with toys specific to their culture. This relationship to their own culture enhances learning.

## Evidence

Approaches to teaching based on the zone of proximal development and on scaffolding can be very effective. The first systematic study of scaffolding was carried out by Wood et al. (1976). An adult tutor (Gail Ross) was given the task of teaching 3-, 4-, and 5-year-old children to build a three-dimensional structure. What the tutor said and did were largely determined by the child's efforts to perform the task. Her interventions were categorised as showing (e.g., joining blocks together) or telling (e.g., asking the child whether incorrectly assembled blocks were correct). The tutor engaged in more showing than telling with the 3-year-olds, but there was much more telling than showing with the 4- and 5-year-olds. In addition, the 5-year-olds received much less help from the tutor than did the 4-year-olds, because they needed less assistance or scaffolding.

Conner, Knight, and Cross (1997) studied the effects of scaffolding on 2-year-olds performing various problem-solving and literary tasks. Most previous studies had focused only on mothers' scaffolding, but they also considered fathers' scaffolding. Mothers and fathers were equally good at scaffolding, and the quality of scaffolding predicted the children's performance on the various tasks during the teaching session.

If scaffolding is to be of real value in education, its beneficial effects need to last well beyond the original teaching session. Accordingly, Conner et al. (1997) conducted a follow-up session. The children who had originally received better scaffolding continued to perform better than those who had received poor scaffolding.

Moss (1992) reviewed studies on the scaffolding provided by mothers during the preschool period. There were three main aspects to the mothers' scaffolding strategies. First, the mother instructed her child in new skills the child could not use on its own. Second, the mother encouraged her child to maintain useful problem-solving tactics it had shown spontaneously. Third, the mother tried to persuade the child to discard immature and inappropriate forms of behaviour. In general, scaffolding seemed to be an effective technique for promoting learning in preschool children.

Wertsch, McNamee, McLane, and Budwig (1980) obtained evidence supporting Vygotsky's view that learning initially emerges in a social context. Mothers and children between the ages of 2 and 4 built a truck to look like a model they could see. When the mothers of the younger children looked at the model, their children looked at the model on about 90% of occasions. However, the older children's looking behaviour was much less influenced by what their mothers were doing. Thus, social factors in the form of the mothers' looking behaviour had much more impact on younger than on older children, as expected on Vygotsky's theory.

Vygotsky's notion that inner speech can be of value in thinking has received support. Behrend, Harris, and Cartwright (1992) used whispering and observable lip movements as measures of inner speech. Children using the most inner speech performed hard tasks better than children making little use of inner speech. Berk (1994) found that 6-year-olds spent an average of 60% of the time talking to themselves while solving problems in mathematics. Those whose speech contained numerous comments about what needed to be done on the current problem did better at mathematics over the following year. This confirmed Vygotsky's view that self-guiding speech makes it easier for children to direct their actions. This self-guiding speech probably made it easier for the children to focus their attention on the task in hand.

Vygotsky argued that private speech becomes more internal as children's level of performance improves. Berk (1994) discussed a study in which 4- and 5-year-old children made Lego models in each of three sessions. As predicted by Vygotsky, the children's speech become increasingly internalised from session to session as their model-making performance became better. Thus, as Vygotsky assumed, private speech is of most value to children when confronted by novel tasks they do not fully understand.

Children who make use of inner speech tend to perform better on difficult or novel tasks than children who do not use much inner speech

## Evaluation

● Children's cognitive development depends on the social context and on guidance provided by adults and other children. Piaget under-estimated the importance of the social environment, and Vygotsky deserves credit for acknowledging its key role in cognitive development.

● It follows from Vygotsky's approach that there should be major differences in cognitive development from culture to culture, whereas Piaget argued that children everywhere go through the same sequence of cognitive stages in the same order. The fact that there are large cultural differences in what is regarded as intelligent behaviour (Chapter 12) suggests that Vygotsky was correct.

● The evidence suggests that inner speech helps the problem-solving activities of young children.

● "Much of what he [Vygotsky] wrote was speculative and, in places, self-contradictory … Vygotsky's perspective on human development can hardly be called a fully fledged theory" (Wood, 1998, pp. 37–39).

● Vygotsky exaggerated the importance of the social environment. Children's rate of cognitive development is determined more by internal factors (e.g., level of motivation, interest in learning) than was believed by Vygotsky.

● Vygotsky did not specify clearly what kinds of social interaction were most beneficial for learning (e.g., general encouragement versus specific instructions). Vygotsky and his followers have focused relatively little on the precise ways in which language is used in social interactions.

● Social interactions between, for example, parent and child do not always have beneficial effects, as all parents know to their cost. They can lead to confrontations, stubbornness, and a failure to listen to each other rather than to enlightenment. Indeed, social interactions can make matters worse rather than better.

● Vygotsky assumed that social interactions enhance cognitive development because of the instruction provided. However, Light, Littleton, Messer, and Joiner (1994) found on a computer-based task that children learned better in pairs than on their own, even when the other child was merely present and said nothing. This is known as *social facilitation*, and occurs because the presence of others can have a motivational effect (see Chapter 20).

● Most early research on scaffolding involved adults deciding what children should learn, and then arranging the situation to maximise learning. However, children in everyday life are more likely than adults to initiate interactions and decide what is going to be discussed (Smith, Cowie, & Blades, 2003).

*Think about the occasions when you use inner speech or talk to yourself when doing things (or when you have observed children using it). Do they fit in with Vygotsky's view of self-guiding speech?*

## Educational implications

Much of the evidence we have considered already is of relevance to education. Vygotsky's key contribution to educational practice was the notion that children typically learn best in a social context in which someone more knowledgeable guides and encourages their learning efforts. Thus, children are typically taught the necessary skills by those who already possess them via scaffolding and the zone of proximal development. Effective teachers or tutors will generally reduce their control over the learning process when children are performing successfully, but will increase their control when children start making errors.

There are several ways in which those involved in educating children might focus on the child's zone of proximal development, and Vygotsky was not very explicit on the matter. However, Vygotsky (1934/1987, p. 209) did mention assisting children "through demonstration, leading questions, and by introducing the initial elements of a task's solution". Goodman and Goodman (1990)

To be an effective tutor, this father needs to avoid interfering while his son is managing alone, but be prepared to help when the boy gets stuck.

## CASE STUDY: *Weaving*

Evidence that the zone of proximal development and scaffolding are used effectively in cultures other than typical Western ones was reported by Greenfield and Lave (1982) in a study on the Zinacanteco Mexicans. Young girls who wanted to learn weaving skills started by spending almost half their time simply watching expert women weavers. After that, the girls were closely supervised by the skilled weavers as they acquired the necessary skills. The skilled weavers were generally successful at structuring the assistance they provided so that the girls remained within the zone of proximal development. Finally, the girls developed sufficient skills so that they could take responsibility for their own weaving.

discussed the ways in which teachers try to make use of the zone of proximal development in their teaching, and identified five guidelines: (1) interfere as little as possible; (2) ask questions; (3) offer useful hints; (4) direct attention at anomalies or inconsistencies; and (5) direct attention at overlooked pieces of information.

Hedegaard (1996) carried out a longitudinal study on Danish children aged between about 9 and 11 in which the focus was on the zone of proximal development. The ambitious goal was for the children to integrate information about the evolution of species, the origins of the human species, and the ways in which societies have changed historically. The essence of the approach involved the children working together in groups within the zone of proximal development. For example, the children sometimes engaged in co-operative work in groups, and at other times joined in discussions involving the entire class. Most of the children showed high levels of motivation, with their interests moving from the concrete and specific (e.g., adaptation of polar bears to the Arctic) to the more abstract and general (e.g., principles underlying evolutionary change).

## Peer tutors

Peer tutoring: a girl teaches her younger sister to count.

It could be argued that the ideal tutors are children slightly older and more advanced than the children being taught. Such tutors have useful knowledge to communicate to the children being taught. They should also remember the limitations in their own knowledge and understanding when they were 1 or 2 years younger, which might make it easier for them to work within the younger child's zone of proximal development. The approach we have just described is known as **peer tutoring**, and it has become increasingly popular in schools.

Peer tutoring is generally effective. Barnier (1989) looked at the performance of 6- and 7-year-olds on various spatial and perspective-taking tasks. Those exposed to brief sessions of peer tutoring with 7- and 8-year-old tutors performed better than those who were not. The benefits of peer tutoring have been found in various cultures. Ellis and Gauvain (1992) compared 7-year-old Navaho children and Euro-American children performing a maze game. They were tutored by one or two 9-year-old tutors working together. The children from both cultures benefited more from the paired tutors than from the individual ones, and the benefit was the same in both cultures. However, there were some cultural differences in the teaching style of the tutors. For example, the Euro-American tutors gave many more verbal instructions, and were generally less patient. This impatience may explain why the Navaho children made fewer errors than the Euro-American children.

## Vygotsky vs. Piaget

*To what extent do you think cultural differences may affect whether conflict or collaboration is more useful in teaching situations?*

Forman and Cazden (1985) found that collaboration as recommended by Vygotsky and conflict as recommended by the neo-Piagetians are both important. They studied 9-year-olds carrying out an experiment on chemical reactions. Collaboration among the children was very useful early on when the apparatus had to be set up. Later on, however, when they had to decide how to carry out the experiment (e.g., which combinations of elements would produce which effects), conflict seemed more useful than collaboration. The message is that any given teaching method is likely to work better in some situations than in others.

At a superficial level, it may appear that the approach to education following from Vygotsky's ideas is radically different from that of Piaget. As DeVries (2000) pointed out, Vygotsky seemed to emphasise factors external to the child (e.g., tutors, teachers) in promoting learning, whereas Piaget emphasised internal factors (e.g., adaptation), with the child in charge of the learning process. In fact, however, Vygotsky and Piaget were

**KEY TERM**

**Peer tutoring:** teaching of one child by another, with the child doing the teaching generally being slightly older than the child being taught.

both fully aware of the importance of external and internal factors, and it is possible to develop educational practices which reconcile their views (see DeVries, 2000).

## Evaluation

⊕ Much effective learning arises out of social situations.
⊕ The scaffolding provided by peers or by teachers can be very effective in promoting effective learning at school.
⊖ As Durkin (1995, p. 375) pointed out, the whole approach is based on the dubious assumption that, "helpful tutors team up with eager tutees to yield maximum learning outcomes". In fact, as Salomon and Globerson (1989) pointed out, this assumption is often incorrect. For example, if there is too much status difference between the tutor and the learner, the learner may become uninvolved in the learning process. Another possibility is what Salomon and Globerson called "ganging up on the task", in which the tutor and learner agree the task is not worth doing properly.
⊖ The Vygotskyan approach is better suited to some kinds of tasks than to others, with many of the successful uses of scaffolding involving various construction tasks. In contrast, Howe, Tolmie, and Rodgers (1992) studied peer tutoring on a task concerned with understanding motion down an incline. Peer tutoring was of very little benefit, whereas thinking about the underlying ideas proved useful.
⊖ Vygotsky (1930/1981, p. 169) de-emphasised the importance of children's natural curiosity and motivation in the learning process: "We never find a child who would naturally develop arithmetic functions in nature … These are external changes coming from the environment and are not in any way a process of internal development."

## INFORMATION-PROCESSING APPROACH

Several information-processing theories of cognitive development have been put forward over the past 30 years. These theories share key assumptions (Siegler, 1998). First, thinking involves information processing, and so the emphasis is on the processes and structures associated with information processing. Second, it is important to provide a detailed account of the processes underlying cognitive changes rather than simply describing children's performance at different ages. Third, cognitive change occurs as a result of a process of self-modification (Siegler, 1998): Children notice the outcomes of their own activities, which leads to changes in their subsequent thinking and behaviour.

Some theorists have tried to incorporate Piaget's key insights into information-processing theories. However, information-processing theories are much less comprehensive than Piaget's theory. In addition, information-processing theories often provide more detailed accounts of specific aspects of cognitive development than were offered by Piaget.

We will consider two of the main information-processing approaches to cognitive development. First, there are the neo-Piagetian theories of Pascual-Leone and of Case. Second, there is Siegler's overlapping waves model, which has become influential in recent years. In addition, the information-processing approach is discussed with reference to perception, memory, and language in Chapter 14.

> **Nature or nurture?**
> Many child development theories assume cognitive development to be more nurture—influenced by environmental factors—than nature—determined by genes. However, Price et al.'s (2000) study of nearly 2000 pairs of same-sex, 2-year-old Welsh and English twins compared verbal and non-verbal cognitive development and could challenge this assumption. The findings suggest that there is a high heritability for delayed development of verbal skills compared to what they call "a modest heritability" for the normal range of individual differences. This means that genetic influences could be a main factor in information processing and cognitive development, perhaps as important as the child's environment.

## Neo-Piagetian theories

Pascual-Leone (1984) and Case (1974) were both strongly influenced by Piaget's theoretical approach. They agreed with Piaget that children actively structure their understanding, and that children move from pre-concrete to concrete thinking, and then on to abstract thinking.

However, their views differed from those of Piaget in some important ways. First, they emphasised the need to consider cognitive development within an information-processing approach. Second, they claimed it is preferable to focus on specific components of cognitive processing rather than the more general schemas emphasised by Piaget. Third, they argued cognitive development depends on an increase in mental capacity or mental power.

According to Pascual-Leone (1984), a key aspect of mental capacity is M. This refers to the number of schemes or units of cognition that a child can attend to or work with at any given time. M increases as children grow up, and this is important for cognitive development. Pascual-Leone assumed that increased M or processing capacity resulted from neurological development.

The information-processing approach of Pascual-Leone and Case revolves around the notion of a scheme or basic unit of cognition, which resembles Piaget's schema. Case (1974) identified three kinds of scheme:

1. *Figurative schemes.* "[I]nternal representations of items of information with which a subject is familiar, or of perceptual configurations which he can recognise." Recognising one's own school from a photograph involves using a figurative scheme.
2. *Operative schemes.* "[I]nternal representations of functions (rules), which can be applied to one set of figurative schemes, in order to generate a new set." For example, deciding that two photographs of a school depict the same school involves an operative scheme.
3. *Executive schemes.* "[I]nternal representations of procedures which can be applied in the face of particular problem situations, in an attempt to reach particular objectives." These schemes determine which figurative and operative schemes are being used in a given situation.

According to this theory, a child's ability to solve a problem depends on four basic factors. First, there is the range of schemes the child has available. Second, there is the child's M-power or mental capacity, which increases with age. Third, there is the extent to which the child uses all of its available M-power. Fourth, there is the relative importance which the child gives to perceptual cues versus all other cues.

Case (1974) suggested that new schemes can be formed by modifying existing schemes. Alternatively, new schemes can be acquired by the combination or consolidation of several existing schemes.

## Evidence

This theory can be applied to many of Piaget's findings. For example, Piaget found children below the age of 7 generally did not realise that the amount of water remains the same when poured from one container into another that is taller and thinner. According to Piaget, this is because these children do not understand the logic of conservation. According to Pascual-Leone (1984), this is often because the children do not have enough mental capacity to hold all the relevant schemes in mind. Suppose the conservation task were made easier by filling the containers with beads and allowing children to count the number of beads? Piaget would still expect the children to fail, because they have not learned the underlying logic, whereas Case and Pascual-Leone would predict more success because the demands on mental capacity have been reduced. When this study was carried out, the findings supported the neo-Piagetians rather than Piaget (Bower, 1979).

The value of the neo-Piagetian approach can also be seen in a study discussed by Case (1992). Children and adolescents aged between 10 and 18 drew a picture of a mother who was looking out of the window of her home and could see her son playing peekaboo with her in the park on the other side of the road. The younger participants found it very hard to do this. They could draw the mother in the house and the boy in the park, but they did not have enough mental capacity to integrate the two parts of the drawing. In contrast, the older participants produced an integrated drawing, because they had greater M-power.

**Learning a second language**

Pascual-Leone (2000) points out that higher cognitive functions may evolve developmentally from lower cognitive functions, and this is a process that is not easy to research experimentally. This is why theory-guided research, such as the information-processing approach uses, is so important. For example, research into the acquisition of a second language before adolescence shows that the later it is acquired the less adequate the use of the second language is. The conclusion is that in the very young the limited but increasing information-processing capacity matches the simple components of basic language. And as the language structure being learned increases in complexity the information-processing capacity will have developed in a complementary fashion, so the two go hand in hand.

There are close similarities between the notion of M-power or mental capacity on the one hand and working memory capacity on the other (see Chapter 9). Working memory is concerned with the ability to store some information at the same time as processing other information. Swanson (1999) found there was a progressive increase in the capacity of working memory during childhood (see Chapter 14). She also found that age differences in working memory capacity predicted children's performance in reading and in arithmetic. Both of these findings are consistent with the neo-Piagetian approach.

*How might a student's level of M-power affect the quality of essays written?*

## Evaluation

➕ Many of Piaget's tasks lend themselves to an information-processing account.

➕ Many problem-solving failures in children depend on memory limitations or insufficient M-power rather than on the absence of the necessary logical or other structures as Piaget claimed.

➕ The concepts (e.g., different types of schemes) used by theorists such as Case and Pascual-Leone are easier to assess than the schemas included in Piaget's theory.

➖ It is often hard to work out how many schemes are required to solve a task, or to decide how many schemes are actually being used by a given child.

➖ It is hard to calculate someone's mental capacity. There is. a danger of simply assuming that success results from sufficient mental capacity and failure results from insufficient mental capacity.

➖ It is very hard to distinguish between changes in strategies and changes in M-space or mental capacity. As Meadows (1986) pointed out, "Attempts to measure the size of M-space have to hold strategy and strategy demands constant if they are to distinguish between changes in the size of M-space and changes in the way a stably-sized space is used" (p. 41). In fact, Case (1985) admitted that children's cognitive development may depend more on changing strategies than on basic mental capacity.

## Overlapping waves model

According to Siegler (1998), even fairly young children confronted by a complex task often use rules or systematic goal-directed approaches to solving a problem. Children are especially likely to use rules when the task is unfamiliar, when it involves comparing quantities (e.g., weight, distance), and when one of the dimensions involved in the problem is much more salient or obvious than the other(s). However, most problems (e.g., arithmetic, spelling, language use) do not possess these characteristics. According to Siegler, children are likely to approach such problems by using strategies, which are goal-directed approaches varying from trial to trial. Siegler and Chen (2002) provide a good account of the similarities and differences between rules and strategies.

Siegler (1998) proposed the overlapping waves model to account for children's use of strategies and of rules. The key assumption is that children at any given time typically have various strategies or ways of thinking about a problem. These strategies compete with each other, with the more effective ones gradually displacing the less effective ones (see the figure on the right).

What processes lead to improved strategy selection by children? According to the model, children acquire increasingly detailed knowledge by taking account of the speed and accuracy of problem solution with each strategy. This allows them to select the best strategy more often, and to learn that a strategy which is generally the most effective one may not be so for all types of problems.

A key feature of Siegler's approach is his use of the **microgenetic method**. This involves carrying out short-term longitudinal studies in which changes in cognitive strategies

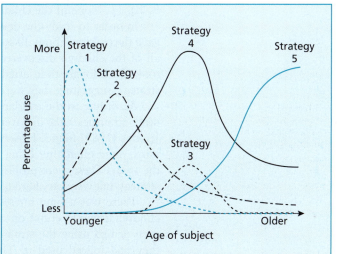

Siegler's overlapping waves model.

*What difficulties might be associated with longitudinal studies (whether short- or long-term)?*

are observed as they happen. This is a more useful approach than you might think. For example, Piaget and his followers were very interested in developmental changes in cognition. However, the cross-sectional experiments they carried out (i.e., children of different ages tested at the same time) did not permit them to observe these changes as they happened!

## Evidence

Siegler (1976) carried out a well-known study on rule use based on the balance-scale problem. Children were presented with a balance scale having four pegs on each side of the fulcrum or pivot. Weights were then attached to some of the pegs while the balance was held

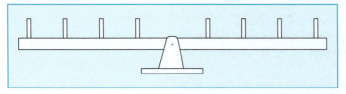

A balance-scale of the type used by Siegler (1976).

immobile by means of a wedge. The children predicted what would happen when the wedge was removed. Children aged 5 years and upwards generally gave rule-based answers, but the nature of the rule changed as a function of age. Five-year-olds generally adopted the simple rule of predicting that the side with more weights would go down (Rule 1), taking no account of the distance of the weights from the fulcrum. Nine-year-olds typically used one of two rules (Rule 2 or Rule 3), taking account of both the number of weights and their distance from the fulcrum. According to Rule 2, the side with more weights is predicted to go down. If the number of weights is equal, then the side with weights further from the fulcrum is predicted to go down. Rule 3 is similar to Rule 2, except that guessing occurs when one side has more weights but the weights are further from the fulcrum on the other side.

Siegler and Chen (1998) carried out a study in which 4- and 5-year-olds were presented with balance problems. The weights on both sides of the scale were the same, but those on one side were further from the fulcrum. The children received feedback concerning the right answer on each trial, and were then asked to explain it. What was of interest was to identify the factors allowing children to acquire Rule 2 on this task. The single most important factor was noticing the potential value of distance in explaining the movement of the balance scale. For example, children who said, "These weights are here, and these are here", generally acquired Rule 2.

Siegler (1998) discussed the findings from various kinds of tasks (e.g., addition, multiplication, spelling, and memory) involving the use of strategies rather than rules. A consistent finding was that most children used at least three different strategies when dealing with each type of task. Thus, the central prediction of the overlapping waves model has been confirmed using several kinds of tasks.

How do children start to use new strategies? Relevant evidence was reported by Siegler and Jenkins (1989). They studied 4- and 5-year-olds given the task of solving addition problems (e.g., 3 + 8). One of the most effective strategies used by young children is the count-on or min strategy, which involves starting with the larger number and counting on from that point. Thus, in our example, children would start with 8, and count 9, 10, 11. None of the children in this study used the count-on strategy initially.

In order to study the development of the count-on strategy, Siegler and Jenkins (1989) gave the children about 30 sessions devoted to solving addition problems. As a result, nearly all of the children discovered the count-on strategy at some point. The children typically took much longer than usual on the problem immediately before their first use of the new strategy, suggesting they were thinking carefully about the best strategy to use.

According to the overlapping waves model, the children should have continued to use other strategies after discovering the count-on strategy. That was exactly what Siegler and Jenkins (1989) found. However, children who had discovered the count-on strategy used it much more often after being presented with some *challenge* problems in the eighth week of the study. These were problems such as 26 + 2 that were easy to solve using the count-on strategy, but were very hard to solve with other strategies (e.g., counting all the way from one).

There was a final interesting finding from Siegler and Jenkins' (1989) study. Several children using the count-on strategy showed little explicit understanding of it. Indeed, some even denied using the strategy at all, in spite of videotape evidence showing very clearly they had indeed used it! This finding suggests implicit knowledge can guide children's choice of strategy.

Siegler and Stern (1998) also obtained evidence that children can adopt an effective strategy based only on implicit knowledge. Seven-year-olds were given inversion problems of the form $A + B - B$ (e.g., $18 + 24 - 24$). We can see that the best strategy for such problems is simply to say the first number. However, most of the 7-year-olds started by adding the first two numbers and then subtracting the third. After considerable practice, the children started to perform inversion problems much faster than initially, indicating they were using the best strategy. Siegler and Stern assessed whether the best strategy was being used consciously by asking the children to explain what they had done on each trial. The key finding was that almost 90% of the children used the best strategy on one or more trials before they were able to report using it. Thus, adopting an effective strategy does not depend on conscious awareness of that strategy.

Strategy changes do not always happen gradually. For example, Alibali (1999) studied children aged between 9 and 11 years of age who learned to solve mathematical equivalence problems (e.g., $3 + 4 + 5 = ? + 5$). Some children received direct instruction in how to solve such problems as well as feedback about whether their answer was correct, others received feedback only, and still others received neither direct instruction nor feedback. Although most of the children showed gradual strategy changes, several children receiving detailed direct instruction showed abrupt strategy change.

What factors lead to strategy change? Alibali (1999) found that feedback on its own led to strategy change, but was ineffective in leading children to adopt the correct strategy. Direct instruction plus feedback led children to adopt the correct strategy, especially when the direct instruction included detailed information about the correct procedure.

The microgenetic method has revealed interesting ways in which children's use of strategies can change over a relatively short period of time when special training is provided. However, doubts have been expressed as to whether such strategic changes are the same as those shown by children in the natural environment over a longer period of time. In other words, findings based on use of the microgenetic method may not be applicable to the real world.

The above issue was addressed by Siegler and Svetina (2002) in a study in which children were given matrix problems in which they had to select an object to complete a matrix or visual display. Six-year-old children exposed to the microgenetic method were given seven sessions on this task over an 11-week period. Those children receiving feedback as to the correct answer showed a substantial improvement in performance across the seven sessions from about 25% to 50% correct. There was also a cross-sectional part to the study, in which 6-, 7-, and 8-year-olds were tested on matrix problems in a single session. Eight-year-olds had the most correct answers (78%), compared to 48% for 7-year-olds and 20% for 6-year-olds. The majority of errors in both the microgenetic and cross-sectional parts of the study were duplicates (incorrectly completing the matrix with an object that was already present). The overall conclusion was as follows: "Microgenetic and age-related change proved to be quite similar. On all but one of the measures that could be assessed in both microgenetic and cross-sectional contexts, significant changes were present either in both contexts or in neither" (p. 806).

## Evaluation

⊕ It is valuable to study changes in children's strategies in short-term longitudinal studies, so changes can be observed as they happen. Thus, the microgenetic method represents a significant advance on previous approaches to cognitive development.

⊕ Children systematically use rules on certain tasks, and factors leading children to change rules have been identified.

⊕ The microgenetic method produces changes in cognitive strategies more rapidly than would happen in more naturalistic conditions, but the changes produced in both cases are similar (Siegler & Svetina, 2002).

⊕ Children often have several strategies available for solving a given type of problem, and cognitive development depends in part on competition among these strategies.

- ⊕ Effective strategies are often initially used unconsciously (Siegler & Stern, 1998).
- ⊖ "Whereas the computer simulations of strategy choice indicate in detail … how choices among the strategies change over time, no similarly detailed model exists for how new strategies are discovered" (Siegler, 1998, p. 97).
- ⊖ "The theory seems most applicable to domains in which children use clearly-defined strategies; its applicability to areas in which strategies are less well defined remains to be demonstrated" (Siegler, 1998, p. 97).

## Educational implications

There are several implications of the information-processing approach for education. For example, teachers should engage in a careful task analysis of the information they want to communicate to their students. This is valuable in ensuring that the material is presented effectively. It is also of value in identifying the reasons why some children perform a task inaccurately. If teachers have a clear idea of the information and processes needed to perform the task, they can analyse children's errors to see which rules or processes are being used wrongly.

Siegler's research provides clear evidence that children frequently adopt rules or strategies which are inadequate because they are based on only some of the relevant information (e.g., Siegler, 1976). It is essential for children to start taking account of all the relevant information if they are to develop adequate rules or strategies. This can happen spontaneously (e.g., Siegler & Chen, 1998), or children's attention can be drawn to such information by using detailed direct instruction (e.g., Alibali, 1999).

Other implications of the information-processing approach are as follows:

1. Parts of the information-processing system (e.g., attention, short-term memory) have very limited capacity. Thus, teachers should present tasks so that these limited capacities are not overloaded.
2. Children benefit from gaining **metacognitive knowledge** about cognitive processes. Such knowledge involves understanding the value of various cognitive processes (e.g., knowing that processing of meaning will enhance long-term memory).

With respect to the first implication, Beck and Carpenter (1986) argued that children often find it hard to understand what they read because their processing capacity is focused on identifying individual words and parts of words. Accordingly, they gave children huge amounts of practice in identifying and using sub-word units such as syllables. This led to substantial increases in the speed and accuracy of word recognition, and also produced enhanced comprehension of reading material.

With respect to the second implication, children and even adults often lack important metacognitive knowledge. For example, in order to understand a text fully, readers need to focus on the structure of the text, including identifying its main theme. However, children typically lack this metacognitive knowledge, and focus on individual words and sentences rather than the overall structure. Palincsar and Brown (1984) gave children specific training in thinking about the structure of the texts they were reading. This led to a significant increase in their comprehension ability.

*To what extent could these points be applied to your own educational experiences (past and present)?*

## *Evaluation*

- ⊕ The information-processing approach has proved of use in education. It provides techniques for identifying the processes and strategies required to complete tasks successfully.
- ⊖ There are many tasks where it is hard to identify the underlying processes.
- ⊖ It is often hard to assess accurately a child's capacity limitations and so the point at which overload will occur is not easy to predict.
- ⊖ The information-processing approach often indicates *what* processes are involved in task performance without specifying *how* children acquire those processes.

**KEY TERM**

**Metacognitive knowledge:** knowledge about the usefulness of various cognitive processes relevant to learning.

# SUMMARY

According to Piaget, a state of equilibrium or balance is achieved through processes of accommodation and assimilation. He proposed four stages of cognitive development: sensori-motor, during which development is intelligence in action; pre-operational, during which thinking is dominated by perception; concrete operations, during which logical thinking is applied to objects that are real or can be seen; and formal operations, during which logical thinking can be applied to potential events or abstract ideas. There is general support for his theory of cognitive development. However, Piaget under-estimated somewhat the cognitive abilities of children, he under-estimated the piecemeal and unsystematic nature of cognitive development, and he described rather than explained cognitive development. According to Piaget, what children can learn is determined by their current stage of cognitive development. He claimed that children learn best when engaged in a process of active self-discovery. He also argued that the study of subjects such as mathematics, logic, and science is valuable for the development of cognitive schemas. In fact, active self-discovery is generally less effective than the more traditional approach of tutorial training. The neo-Piagetians attach much importance to conflict, and especially socio-cognitive conflict, as a way to promote effective learning at school.

Vygotsky emphasised the notion that cognitive development depends largely on social factors and on language acquisition. What children can achieve with the assistance of others is more than they can achieve on their own; the difference between the two is the zone of proximal development. Scaffolding plays an important role in cognitive development. Social learning is not always effective, and Vygotsky under-estimated the contribution of the individual child to his/her own cognitive development. According to Vygotsky's followers, scaffolding provided by teachers or by peer tutors is an effective form of learning. The evidence indicates that teaching based on scaffolding and the zone of proximal development is effective in several cultures.

According to the information-processing approach, cognitive development is associated with increases in knowledge and mental capacity or M-power. Within Case's theory, children over time increase their range of schemes (basic units of cognition), their M-power, and their ability to use their M-power. It is hard to assess which schemes are being used and to measure M-power. According to Siegler's overlapping waves model, any given child will typically use various strategies to deal with a problem. These strategies compete with each other, with the more effective ones gradually displacing the less effective ones. Siegler has made extensive use of the microgenetic method, which involves using short-term longitudinal studies to observe changes in strategies as they occur. Changes of strategy are influenced by feedback, by direct instruction, and by implicit knowledge. According to the information-processing approach, teaching should be based on a sound understanding of the knowledge and processes required to perform different tasks. Teaching should also focus on preventing overload of short-term memory, on analysing the errors made by children, and on developing children's metacognitive knowledge.

*Piaget's theory*

*Vygotsky's theory*

*Information-processing approach*

# FURTHER READING

- Goswami, U. (1998). *Cognition in children*. Hove, UK: Psychology Press. An excellent introduction to the main theories and research on cognitive development.
- Harris, M., & Butterworth, G. (2002). *Developmental psychology: A student's handbook*. Hove, UK: Psychology Press. This book provides good coverage of Piaget's and Vygotsky's theoretical approaches to cognitive development.
- Smith, P.K., Cowie, H., & Blades, M. (2003). *Understanding children's development* (4th ed.) Oxford, UK: Blackwell. Chapters 12, 13, and 15 provide detailed introductory coverage of the main theories of cognitive development.

# Social development in everyday life

As children grow up, they have a rapidly developing sense of who they are, a large increase in their social involvement with other people, and a clearer sense of their place in society. Several kinds of learning underlie children's development of social behaviour, and these different kinds of learning interact with each other in complex ways. However, at the risk of over-simplification, it is possible to draw a distinction between (1) the knowledge children acquire about themselves and about the kind of person they are; and (2) the kinds of learning that permit children to assume increasing responsibility for their own behaviour.

The first part of this chapter is concerned with the knowledge about themselves that children acquire. Of central importance here is the development of the self-concept, which provides the child with answers to the question, "Who am I?" There are many aspects to the self-concept. However, an especially important aspect is provided by the child's sex, with children's self-concept being influenced strongly by whether they are male or female.

The second part of this chapter is concerned with the ways in which children learn to control their own behaviour so they can function effectively in numerous social situations. One important aspect here is the child's gradual increase in pro-social or helping behaviour, and his/her realisation that anti-social or aggressive behaviour is generally counterproductive. Another important aspect is moral development. If children are to be integrated into society, then they must learn to distinguish between right and wrong, and thus acquire the rules governing most people's behaviour.

In sum, this chapter deals with aspects of social development relating to children's increasing self-knowledge and self-control, which allow them to relate to others in everyday life. Broader issues of social development relating to children's main social attachments and friendships are considered in the next chapter.

## DEVELOPMENT OF THE SELF

It is hard to exaggerate the importance of the development of the self within social development. According to Schaffer (1996, pp. 154–155), "Of all social concepts that of the self is the most basic … It has a key role because it determines how each of us construes reality and what experiences we seek out in order to fit in with the self-image." The self-concept in adults is discussed in detail in Chapter 18.

There are two major problems in trying to understand the development of the self. First, the self is something inside an individual, and so it is difficult to study experimentally. Second, the self is complex and consists of several aspects. For example, William James (1890) drew an important distinction between two aspects of the self:

1. *The "I" or self as the subject of experience*. This self is the self-as-knower, and is used to interpret our daily experiences.
2. *The "me" or self as the object of experience*. This self is the self-as-known, and is used when we try to understand ourselves in terms of our age, ability, gender, personality, and so on.

The above distinction is very similar to the one drawn by Lewis (1990) between an existential self (resembling "I") and a categorical self (resembling "me"). The categorical self involves an awareness of the self as an object that can be perceived by others. According to Lewis, we are the only species having a categorical self or self-awareness.

There are other ways of referring to aspects of the self. Of particular importance are the following two terms:

- **Self-concept.** This is the cognitive component of the self. It consists of the knowledge and information that we possess about the kind of person we are.
- **Self-esteem.** This is the evaluative component of the self. It concerns how worthwhile and confident an individual feels him/herself to be.

*Do you think that an individual who grew up in total isolation would have any sense of self?*

There is much overlap between the self-concept and self-esteem. For example, the wealth of information about ourselves that forms the self-concept plays a major role in determining our self-esteem. The self-concept is influenced by numerous factors. However, our relationships with other people are of great importance. Charles Cooley (1902) used the term "looking-glass self" to convey the idea that our self-concept reflects the evaluations of other people. Thus, we tend to see ourselves as others see us. Those of greatest importance in our lives (e.g., partners, parents, close friends) have most influence on our self-concept.

The notion that the self-concept emerges from our interactions with other people was developed by George Herbert Mead. According to Mead (1934), "The self is something which … is not initially there at birth but arises in the process of social development. That is, it develops as a result of his [sic] relations to that process as a whole and to other individuals within the process."

## Early childhood: Self-awareness

It is hard to study the development of self-awareness in early childhood, in part because young children possess insufficient language to express any thoughts they might have about themselves. However, an impressive series of studies by Lewis and Brooks-Gunn (1979) and others has shed light on one aspect of self-awareness, that involved in visual self-recognition. In essence, infants who have had a red spot applied to their nose are held up to a mirror. Those recognising their own reflection and so reaching for their own nose rather than the one in the mirror show at least some self-awareness. By the way, it has been found with this task that chimpanzees learn to recognise themselves in a mirror, but macaques, baboons, and gibbons do not (Gallup, 1979).

The findings on human infants reported by Lewis and Brooks-Gunn (1979) were clear-cut. Practically no infants in the first year of life showed clear evidence of self-awareness, whereas about 70% of infants aged between 21 and 24 months did so. Infants aged between 15 and 18 months were intermediate, with about 25% of them touching their own noses. What information do the infants use to show visual self-recognition? There are two main possibilities:

- *Contingency clues*, based upon the fact that the movements of the mirror image correspond precisely to the infant's own movements.
- *Feature clues*, based upon the details of the infant's face and body.

Chimpanzees can learn to recognise themselves in a mirror and use the mirror to investigate parts of themselves they cannot easily see.

These possibilities can be distinguished by presenting children with previously filmed videotapes of themselves or with photographs. Self-awareness with these stimuli must be due to the use of feature clues rather than contingency clues.

Lewis and Brooks-Gunn (1979) carried out various studies, and concluded that the development of self-awareness involves four stages:

1. Up to about 3 months of age, there is little or no reaction to the child's own image or that of anyone else.
2. Between about 3 and 8 months of age, there are the first signs of visual self-recognition, with the child relying exclusively on contingency clues.
3. Between 8 and 12 months of age, infants improve their self-awareness based on contingency clues, and begin to use feature clues.
4. Between 12 and 24 months of age, children develop the ability to recognise themselves from feature clues only.

Can we conclude that the ability to show visual self-recognition is fully present in nearly all children aged 2 and above? Povinelli, Landau, and Perilloux (1996) showed the answer is, "No." They had the ingenious idea of showing young children Polaroid photographs or videos of themselves taken a few minutes earlier. When the photograph or video showed that the child had a large sticker on its head, most children who were 4 years old reached for it. In contrast, children who were 2 years old or had only been 3 for a few months tended not to reach for the sticker. Thus, younger children find it harder than older ones to appreciate that the way they looked a few minutes earlier can predict the way they look now, suggesting they only have an immediate sense of self.

Visual self-recognition is only one aspect of self-awareness, and its development may not correspond to the development of other aspects of self-awareness. Lewis, Sullivan, Stanger, and Weiss (1989) addressed this issue. They argued that many emotions (which they called "self-referential emotions") involve self-awareness and thinking about oneself in relation to others. For example, we are embarrassed when we feel we have behaved in a way someone else finds inappropriate. Lewis et al. tested for the presence of self-awareness in the form of self-referential emotions by observing the reactions of young children when dancing in front of an adult. They also tested for the presence of self-awareness in the form of visual self-recognition by using the mirror test to see whether the young children would rub the red spot off their nose. It was mostly the children who recognised themselves in the mirror who became embarrassed when asked to dance, suggesting that both activities reflect the same underlying self-awareness.

## Evaluation

⊕ Self-awareness develops mainly during the second year of life.
⊕ The development of visual self-recognition depends initially on contingency clues and later on both contingency and feature clues.
⊖ Little is known of the factors leading to development of the self. However, Case (1991) argued that the origins of the "I" self occur when infants learn their behaviour has effects on people and objects. In contrast, the origins of the "me" self occur when infants observe their own movements (e.g., watching their own hand take hold of a toy).
⊖ The development of self-awareness is complex, with different aspects occurring at different times. Bullock and Lutkenhaus (1990) found that visible aspects of the self (e.g., visual self-recognition) emerged earlier than non-visible aspects (e.g., the child's own name).

## Self-concept

How does the self-concept change during the course of development? It clearly becomes more complex as children acquire increasing information about themselves as they interact with more people in a greater variety of situations. In addition, the self-concept becomes more consistent in the later years of childhood (see Schaffer, 1996). Young children's self-concept is often rather variable, and changes in response to particular experiences.

## Damon and Hart

Damon and Hart (1988) argued that children's self-descriptions fall into four major categories:

1. *Physical features*. These are external characteristics (e.g., being tall, being overweight).
2. *Activities*. These are the things the child spends time doing (e.g., "I like playing football").
3. *Social characteristics*. These are self-descriptions that relate the self to other people (e.g., "I have a brother and a sister").
4. *Psychological characteristics*. These are internal characteristics (e.g., "I am very friendly").

According to Damon and Hart (1988), there are common themes in the self-concept throughout childhood, with all four categories being included in most self-descriptions. However, physical characteristics become less important during childhood, whereas psychological characteristics become more important.

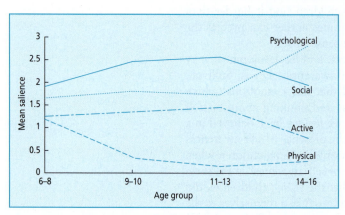

Mean salience of four self-descriptive characteristics (psychological, social, active, and physical) as a function of age. From Hart et al. (1993).

Detailed evidence on the salience or centrality of the four categories of self-descriptions among 6- to 16-year-olds was reported by Hart, Fegley, Chan, Mulvey, and Fischer (1993). The relative importance of most of the categories does not change much between the ages of 6 and 16. However, children of 9 or 10 define themselves less in terms of their activities than do children of 6 to 8, and adolescents attach much more significance than 11- to 13-year-olds to psychological characteristics.

Wellman and Gelman (1987) pointed out that there are two kinds of psychological or internal characteristics contained in self-descriptions: (1) dispositions (e.g., personality traits), which are relatively permanent; and (2) internal states (e.g., feeling sad), which are short-lived. Children typically do not include dispositions in their self-descriptions before the age of 7, but psychological characteristics in the form of internal states are applied to themselves by 3-year-olds (Eder, 1990). Schaffer (1996) offered an interesting explanation of this difference. Internal states are often directly related to the current, visible situation, and so are fairly easy to identify. In contrast, dispositions are more abstract, and involve complex inferences based on numerous situations.

Damon and Hart (1988) argued that children increasingly think of themselves in relationship to other people as they grow up, and so the self-concept becomes increasingly defined in social terms. They proposed a theory based on three different levels of the self-concept:

1. *Categorical identification* (4–7 years). At this level, children describe themselves in terms of various personal or individual characteristics (e.g., "I am 7 years old", "I'm happy").
2. *Comparative assessments* (8–11 years). At this level, self-descriptions are often based on comparisons with other children (e.g., "I'm better at running than most children", "I'm cleverer than other children").
3. *Interpersonal implications* (12–15 years). At this level, the impact of children's characteristics on their relationship with other people is included in their self-descriptions (e.g., "I'm very sociable, so I have a lot of friends", "I understand people, so they come to me with their problems").

Evidence that children only start to compare themselves systematically with other children at about the age of 7 or 8 was reported by Ruble, Boggiano, Feldman, and Loebl (1980). Children aged between 5 and 9 threw balls into a concealed basketball hoop, and

*What could potentially limit the self-descriptions produced by younger children?*

were told how their performance compared to that of other children. Children of 9 judged their performance by taking account of the performance of the other children, but children under the age of 7 rarely did. However, Ruble (1987) pointed out that children under the age of 7 *do* compare themselves to other children with respect to very visible characteristics (e.g., "I am taller than Tom").

There is a final development of the self-concept that we have not considered so far. Selman (1980) distinguished between the self-as-public and the self-as-private. Children under the age of 6 find it difficult to distinguish between their public behaviour and their private thoughts and feelings. Thus, they do not possess separate public and private selves. Children from about the age of 8 do make the distinction between two selves, and argue the private self is more important and genuine.

## Self-esteem

People's self-esteem is based on their evaluation of themselves. The discrepancy between our real or actual self and our ideal self (the kind of person we would most like to be) is important. The greater the discrepancy between the real and ideal selves, the lower will be the level of self-esteem. There are significant problems in assessing self-esteem, especially among younger children. Davis-Kean and Sandler (2001) carried out a meta-analysis of studies assessing self-esteem in children, and found that the reliability (or consistency) of measurement was lower in 4- and 5-year-olds than in children aged 6. There are two likely reasons why it is hard to measure self-esteem in younger children. First, they have a less developed sense of self. Second, their limited mastery of language makes it difficult for them to understand some of the items.

### Harter's theory

Harter (1987) argued that children in early childhood have a rather incoherent sense of self, but generally have a very positive view of themselves. During the years of middle childhood, children's level of self-esteem tends to decrease. Why does this happen? According to Harter, children's self-esteem is increasingly influenced by the opinions of others (e.g., friends, teachers), and their views are generally more realistic and less optimistic than those of the individual child.

Harter (1987) also emphasised the importance to their self-esteem of children's assessments of their own competence. Children become concerned about their level of competence in an increasing number of areas. This reflects their growing involvement with other people as they start going to school, developing friendships, and so on. Harter argued that children's level of self-esteem depends in large measure on their perceived competence. Children regarding themselves as competent in most ways have higher self-esteem than those regarding themselves as incompetent.

The development of self-esteem was studied by Harter and Pike (1984) and by Harter (1982). In the study by Harter and Pike, children between the ages of 4 and 7 were presented with pairs of pictures, and indicated the member of each pair corresponding more closely to themselves. The pictures related to the four areas of cognitive competence, physical competence, peer acceptance, and maternal acceptance. The children's responses indicated they assessed their self-esteem in terms of two categories: (1) competence (cognitive and physical); and (2) acceptance (peer and maternal).

Harter (1982) assessed self-esteem in children between the ages of 8 and 12 by giving them the Harter Self-esteem Scale. These children distinguished among cognitive, social, and physical competence, in addition to general self-worth (e.g., "I am a good person"). Thus, they seemed to view self-esteem in a more complex way than the younger children studied by Harter and Pike (1984).

Harter (1987) extended this line of work. Children rated themselves in five areas: scholastic competence, athletic competence, social acceptance, physical appearance, and behavioural conduct. They rated their competence in each area, and how important it was to do well in each area to feel good about themselves. Finally, the children completed a global self-worth scale.

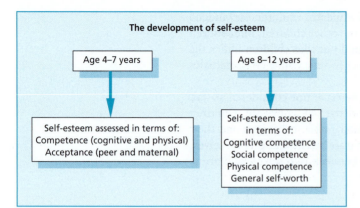

**The development of self-esteem**

Age 4–7 years

Self-esteem assessed in terms of:
Competence (cognitive and physical)
Acceptance (peer and maternal)

Age 8–12 years

Self-esteem assessed
in terms of:
Cognitive competence
Social competence
Physical competence
General self-worth

What did Harter (1987) find? First, incompetence in any area was associated with low self-esteem. Second, incompetence in an area the children regarded as important was especially associated with low self-esteem. Thus, for example, poor athletic competence had little effect on the self-esteem of children who did not regard sport as important. Third, self-esteem in individual children often varied a lot between areas. Children from the age of about 7 or 8 combined information from all five areas to achieve a global or general level of self-esteem. In contrast, younger children's feelings of self-esteem were much more tied to specific areas of competence and incompetence.

Why are there large individual differences in self-esteem among children of any given age? Harter (1987) considered the strength of social support available to children from four sources: parents, classmates, friends, and teachers. Among children aged 8 to 11, all four sources of support predicted global self-esteem, with classmates and parents being the most important sources. The same basic pattern was also present in 11- to 13-year-olds.

Coopersmith (1967) considered the role of the parents in boys aged 10 to 12. The parents of boys with high self-esteem tended to have the following characteristics:

- They had general acceptance of their children.
- They set clearly defined limits on their children's behaviour.
- They allowed their children to control their own lives and to behave with reasonable freedom within those limits.

*Which factors mentioned here might be the cause of low self-esteem in immigrants entering another country with a different culture?*

The boys with high self-esteem mostly had parents who also had high self-esteem. In contrast, the boys with low self-esteem tended to have parents who were either domineering or too permissive.

## Evaluation

- ⊕ There are fairly close links between children's ratings of competence in various areas and their level of self-esteem.
- ⊕ The number of areas in which children try to be competent increases as they enter more fully into society.
- ⊕ Individual differences in self-esteem depend in part on the support provided by parents, classmates, friends, and teachers.
- ⊖ Harter relied heavily on children's self-reports. This approach is limited, because children lack detailed conscious awareness of themselves, and may provide distorted responses.
- ⊖ Most of Harter's findings are correlational, which makes it hard to assess causality. For example, he assumed that feelings of incompetence produce low self-esteem. However, low self-esteem may cause children to underestimate their level of competence.
- ⊖ Harter (1987) focused on environmental factors influencing self-esteem. However, McGuire, Neiderhiser, Reiss, Hetherington, and Plomin (1994) carried out a study on twins, siblings, and step-siblings, finding that genetic factors influence individual differences in self-esteem. Shared environmental factors (e.g., social class, family size) common to all the children within a family were almost irrelevant in determining self-esteem, but non-shared environmental factors specific to each child had a major effect.

## GENDER DEVELOPMENT

When a baby is born, a key question everyone asks is, "Is it a boy or a girl?" As the baby develops, how it is treated by its parents and other people is influenced by its sex. The growing child's thoughts about itself and its place in the world increasingly depend on whether it is male or female. For example, most children by the age of 2 label themselves and others accurately as male or female. Indeed, photographs of male and female strangers are responded to differently by infants as early as 9–12 months of age (Brooks-Gunn & Lewis, 1981). By about the age of 3, almost two-thirds of children prefer to play with children of the same sex (LaFreniere, Strayer, & Gauthier, 1984). From the age of 3 or 4, children have fairly fixed stereotypes about the activities (e.g., housekeeping) and occupations (e.g., doctor, nurse) appropriate for males and females. These are known as **sex-role stereotypes**. All in all, an individual's gender is typically of major importance in influencing his/her self-concept.

The literature on sex-role development contains a bewildering variety of terms describing the phenomena of interest. The term "sex" has often been used to refer to biological differences, whereas "gender" refers to aspects that are socially determined. However, this sharp distinction is often blurred in practice. Other terms in common use are gender identity and sex-role behaviour. **Gender identity** refers in essence to a child's or adult's awareness of being male or female. **Sex-typed behaviour** is behaviour that is consistent with the prevailing sex-role stereotypes.

Egan and Perry (2001) pointed out that there is more to gender identity than simply being aware that one is male or female. More specifically, gender identity involves feeling one is a typical member of one's sex; feeling content with one's own biologically determined sex; and experiencing pressure from parents and peers to conform to sex-role stereotypes. Egan and Perry assessed these various aspects of gender identity in boys and girls between the ages of 10 and 14. Boys on average had much higher scores than girls on feeling oneself to be a typical boy or girl, on feeling content with one's biological sex, and on experiencing pressure from others to behave in conformity with sex-role stereotypes. These findings suggest that it is regarded as more important by individual children and by society at large for boys to conform to stereotypical views of male behaviour than is the case for girls.

## Observed sex differences

Some ideas about sex-typed behaviour are in decline. Few people accept any more that men should go out to work and have little to do with looking after the home and the children, whereas women should stay at home and concern themselves only with home and children. However, many stereotypes still exist, and it is important to consider the actual behaviour of boys and girls.

Most observed sex differences in behaviour are fairly modest. However, Golombok and Hines (2002) in a review identified a small number of sex differences present in the first 2 years of life. Girl infants tend to stay closer to adults than do boy infants, but boys are more upset by situations outside their control than are girls. In addition, girls on average learn to talk at an earlier age than boys.

In Britain, girls are outperforming boys in nearly all school subjects. In 1997, the percentages of 14-year-old boys and girls reaching the expected standards in different subjects were as follows (boys' percentages in brackets): modern foreign languages: 67% (51%); history: 62% (50%); geography: 63% (54%); design and technology: 64% (49%); and information technology: 52% (47%). If anything, most of the differences in the academic performance of boys and girls have increased in the years since then.

In general, there are fewer and smaller differences between the sexes than is generally assumed. Why is there this gap between appearance and reality? One reason is that we tend to misinterpret the evidence of our senses to fit our stereotypes. Condry and Condry (1976) asked college students to watch a videotape of an infant. The ways in which the infant's behaviour was interpreted depended on whether it was referred to as David or Dana. The infant

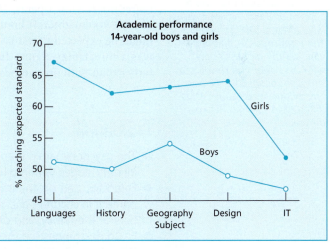

Academic performance 14-year-old boys and girls

### Studying and gender behaviour

Girls regularly outperform boys in GCSE exams in the UK, and also, since 2000, in A-levels and the National Curriculum tests. However, at some universities, e.g., Oxford University, men outperform women in getting first class honours degrees. This apparent anomaly could be caused by studying being perceived as "uncool" by boys, and so they don't study as long or as hard as girls. But at university a study by Mellanby et al. (2000) found that men took greater risks in the ways they revised but were more ambitious than women.

was said to be "angry" in its reaction to a jack-in-the-box if it had been called David, but "anxious" if it had been called Dana.

## Psychodynamic theory

Freud argued that "anatomy is destiny." He claimed that boys develop an Oedipus complex, in which they have sexual desires for their mother combined with intense fear of their father. Part of this fear arises because boys think their father may castrate them. The Oedipus complex is resolved via identification with the father. According to Freud, identification plays a major role in the development of sex-typed behaviour.

Freud (1933) argued that girls are "mortified by the comparison with boys' far superior equipment", for which they blame their mother. Girls develop an Electra complex, in which they have sexual desires for their father and regard their mother as a rival. Girls develop sex-typed behaviour because they are rewarded by their father, who is the central focus of their affection.

Chodorow (1978) developed an alternative psychodynamic theory, according to which most young children develop a close relationship with their mother. This relationship then sets the pattern for future relationships. Girls develop a sense of gender identity based on their close relationship with another female (their mother) and associate femininity with feelings of closeness. In contrast, boys have to move away from their close relationship with their mother to develop gender identity, and this can make them regard masculinity and closeness as separate.

### Evidence

The father often plays a major role in the development of sex-typed behaviour in boys. Boys whose fathers were missing when the Oedipus complex allegedly develops (around the age of 5) showed less sex-typed behaviour than boys whose fathers were present throughout (Stevenson & Black, 1988).

Freud's psychodynamic theory of the development of gender identity is incorrect in nearly all other respects. There is no real evidence that boys fear castration or that girls regret not having a penis. (As a father, I certainly never detected any such regret in either of my two daughters!) Freud argued that the identification process depends on fear, so it might be expected that a boy's identification with his father would be greatest if his father was a threatening figure. In fact, boys identify much more with a warm and supportive father than with an overbearing and threatening one (Mussen & Rutherford, 1963).

*According to this theory, boys suffer more fear than girls because castration has yet to happen to them, whereas girls have already lost the penis. The implication is that boys will identify more strongly with the father and develop a stronger gender role. Is there any evidence of gender roles differing in strength between the sexes?*

### Evaluation

⊕ The psychodynamic theory of gender development was the first systematic attempt to identify stages within which gender development can be understood.

⊖ Freud focused on the influence of the same-sexed parent in influencing gender development in children, and minimised the impact of the opposite-sexed parent, other members of the family, and other children.

⊖ Freud de-emphasised the importance of cognitive factors in the development of sex-role behaviour (see Kohlberg's theory below).

## Social learning theory

According to social learning theory (e.g., Bandura, 1977a), the development of gender occurs as a result of the child's experiences. In general terms, children learn to behave in ways which are rewarded and to avoid behaving in ways which are punished. Since society has expectations about the ways in which boys and girls should behave, the operation of socially delivered rewards and punishments will produce sex-typed behaviour.

Bandura (1977a) also argued that children can learn sex-typed behaviour by observing the actions of various models of the same sex, including other children, parents, and teachers. This is known as **observational learning**. It has often been argued that much observational learning of sex-typed behaviour in children depends on the media, and especially television.

## Evidence

Sex-typed behaviour is learned in part through direct tuition. Fagot and Leinbach (1989) carried out a long-term study on children. Parents encouraged sex-typed behaviour and discouraged sex-inappropriate behaviour in their children even before the age of 2. For example, girls were rewarded for playing with dolls, and discouraged from climbing trees. Those parents making most use of direct tuition tended to have children who behaved in the most sex-typed way. However, these findings are not altogether typical. Lytton and Romney (1991) and Golombok and Hines (2002) have reviewed numerous studies on the parental treatment of boys and girls. There is a modest tendency for parents to encourage sex-appropriate activities and to discourage sex-inappropriate ones. However, it is hard to interpret this difference. It may occur because parents want to promote sex-role stereotypes. Alternatively, it may occur because their sons have pre-existing tendencies to behave differently from their daughters, and the parents simply respond to this state of affairs. (That rings true to me, because initially I had every intention of treating my two daughters and my son in exactly the same way.) The reviews also indicate that boys and girls receive equal parental warmth, encouragement of achievement, discipline, and amount of interaction.

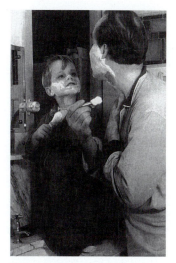

Fathers may play a major role in the development of sex-typed behaviour in their sons.

Reward or reinforcement is often less effective than might be expected by social learning theorists. For example, Fagot (1985) studied the behaviour of children aged between 21 and 25 months. Boys' behaviour was influenced when it was rewarded or reinforced by other boys, but was affected very little when it was rewarded by the teacher or by girls. Of particular note, Fagot found the teacher typically reinforced or rewarded quiet activities carried on close to him/her, but this had no effect on boys' tendency to engage in rough-and-tumble play or to play with toy trucks and cars. Girls' behaviour was influenced by the teacher and by other girls, but was only modestly affected by boys.

Observational learning was studied by Perry and Bussey (1979). Children aged 8 or 9 watched male and female adult models choose between sex-neutral activities (e.g., selecting an apple or a pear). Afterwards, they typically made the same choices as the same-sex models. These findings suggest that observational learning plays an important role in gender development. However, Barkley, Ullman, Otto, and Brecht (1977) reviewed the literature, and found children showed a bias in favour of the same-sex model in only 18 out of 81 studies.

Children between the ages of 4 and 11 watch about 3 hours of television a day, which adds up to 1000 hours a year. It would be surprising if this exposure had no impact on children's views on themselves and on sex-typed behaviour via observational learning. Most research indicates a modest link between television watching and sex-typed behaviour. Frueh and McGhee (1975) studied the television-viewing habits of children aged between 4 and 12. Those children who watched the most television tended to show more sex-typed behaviour in terms of preferring sex-typed toys. However, this is only correlational evidence, and so we do not know that watching television caused sex-typed behaviour.

Williams (1986) examined sex-role stereotypes in three towns in Canada: "Notel" (no television channels), "Unitel" (one channel), and "Multitel" (four channels). Sex-role stereotyping was much greater in the towns with television than in the one without. During the course of the study, Notel gained access to one television channel, which was followed by increased sex-role stereotyping among children.

Evidence that television can influence gender development was reported by Johnston and Ettema (1982). In the *Freestyle* project, there was a series of television programmes in which non-traditional opportunities and activities were modelled. These programmes

KEY TERM
**Observational learning:** learning to imitate others by observing their behaviour.

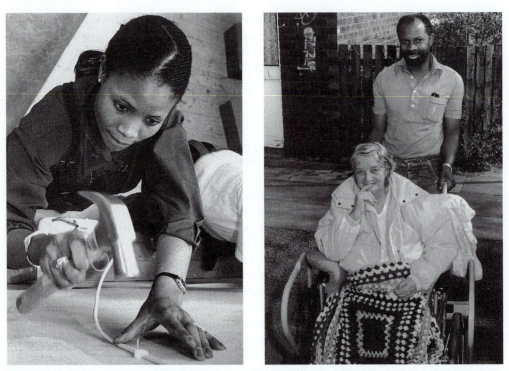

Television programmes that showed men and women taking part in non-traditional sex-typed activities have been found to produce some attitude changes among viewers, but the effects on behaviour were small.

produced significant attitude changes away from sex-role stereotypes, and these changes were still present 9 months later. However, the effects on behaviour were rather small.

## Evaluation

● The social learning approach emphasises the social context in which the development of gender occurs.

● As social learning theorists have claimed, some sex-typed behaviour occurs because it has been rewarded, and sex-inappropriate behaviour is avoided because it has been discouraged or punished.

● Observational learning probably plays a part in the development of sex-role behaviour.

● The effects of direct tuition and observational learning on sex-role behaviour are rather modest.

*Cultural differences in gender roles have been observed many times. To what extent does this support social learning theory?*

● Social learning theorists regarded young children as *passive* individuals who are taught how to behave by being rewarded and punished. In reality, children make an active contribution to their own development. This criticism applies less well to Bussey and Bandura's (1999) social cognitive theory, which is discussed shortly.

● Social learning theorists mistakenly assumed that learning processes are very similar at any age. For example, consider young children and adolescents watching a film in which a man and a woman are eating a meal together. The observational learning of the young children might focus on the eating behaviour of the same-sexed person, whereas the adolescents might focus on his/her social behaviour.

● Social learning theory focused on the learning of *specific* ways of behaving. However, children also engage in much *general* learning. For example, children seem to acquire gender schemas (organised beliefs about the sexes; Martin & Halverson, 1987), and it is hard to explain this within social learning theory.

# Cognitive-developmental theory: Kohlberg

Lawrence Kohlberg (1966) proposed a cognitive-developmental theory to account for sex-typed behaviour. The essence of his approach can be seen by contrasting it with social learning theory. According to Kohlberg (p. 85), "The child's sex-role concepts are the result of the child's active structuring of his own experience; they are not passive products of social training." More generally Kohlberg assumed that gender development is closely related to children's basic cognitive development.

There are other important differences between social learning theory and Kohlberg's theory. According to social learning theory, children develop a gender identity as a result of attending to same-sex models. According to Kohlberg, the causality goes in the other direction: Children attend to same-sex models because they have already developed a consistent gender identity. More generally, children find it rewarding to behave in line with their consistent gender identity: "I am a boy; therefore I want to do boy things; therefore the opportunity to do boy things … is rewarding" (Kohlberg, 1966, p. 89). In contrast, social learning theorists argue that rewarding behaviour is behaviour *others* regard as appropriate.

The notion of gender identity is of great importance within Kohlberg's cognitive-developmental theory. Gender development involves three stages:

1. *Gender identity* (age 2 to 3½ years). Boys know they are boys, and girls know they are girls. However, they believe it would be possible to change sex.
2. *Gender stability* (3½ to 4½ years). There is an awareness that sex is stable over time (e.g., boys will become men), but less awareness that sex remains stable across different situations (e.g., wearing clothes normally worn by members of the opposite sex). When a doll was dressed in transparent clothes so there was a discrepancy between its clothing and its genitals, children in this stage decided on its sex on the basis of clothing (McConaghy, 1979).
3. *Gender consistency* (4½ to 7 years upwards). Children at this stage realise that sex remains the same over time and over situations. There are clear similarities between the achievement of gender consistency and Piaget's notion that children of this age achieve conservation of physical properties (see Chapter 15).

## *Evidence*

Children do seem to progress through the three stages proposed by Kohlberg. In a cross-cultural study, Munroe, Shimmin, and Munroe (1984) found that children in four cultures had the same sequences of stages on the way to full gender identity.

One of the predictions of Kohlberg's theory is that children who have reached the stage of gender consistency will pay more attention to the behaviour of same-sex models than children at earlier stages of gender development. Slaby and Frey (1975) tested this prediction. Children between the ages of 2 and 5 were assessed for gender constancy, and assigned to a high or a low gender constancy group. They were then shown a film of a male and a female performing a variety of activities. Those high in gender constancy showed a greater tendency to attend to the same-sexed model than did those low in gender constancy.

There is much evidence in young children for a moderately strong association between consistency of gender identity and sex-typed behaviour. This is consistent with the theory, in that it is assumed that children having more consistent gender identity will exhibit more sex-typed behaviour. However, correlational studies do not provide evidence about causality. It is necessary to carry out longitudinal studies to provide clearer evidence.

| KOHLBERG'S STAGES IN THE DEVELOPMENT OF GENDER IDENTITY | | |
|---|---|---|
| **Basic gender identity** | **Gender stability** | **Gender consistency** |
| 2–3½ years | 3½–4½ years | 4½–7 upwards |
| Aware of sex, but believes it can change. | Aware that sex is stable over time, but not over situations. | Realises sex remains the same, regardless of time or situation. |

Fagot and Leinbach (1989) studied children from the age of 16 months to 4 years. They divided their participants into early labellers (showing gender labelling or gender identity by 27 months) and late labellers (showing gender labelling later on). Early labellers showed increased amounts of sex-typed play between 16 months and 27–28 months, whereas late labellers did not.

Critics of Kohlberg's theory (e.g., Huston, 1985) have claimed that sex differences in behaviour are found several months before children show gender identity or gender stability. More specifically, Huston discussed studies in which sex-typed behaviour was present in infants aged between 14 months and 2 years. If such findings can be taken at face value, they seem to provide striking evidence against Kohlberg's cognitive-developmental theory. However, there are arguments against taking these findings at face value. First, as Martin, Ruble, and Szkrybalo (2002, pp. 917–918) pointed out:

> *These early sex differences (before 24 months old) have been documented in only a limited number of studies, often with parents present (who may influence children's toy choices), and gender differences have been apparent on only a few toys and behaviours ... much of the available research in which children are observed in natural or laboratory settings suggests that gender-differentiated behaviour is more clearly evident around the age of 2 years or soon after.*

*Which theories could be supported by this finding?*

Second, infants below the age of 24 months may possess more gender knowledge than appears from most studies. For example, many children in the first year of life can discriminate male and female faces, can discriminate voices of males and females, and can detect correlations between faces of men and women and gender-related objects (see Martin et al., 2002).

## Evaluation

➕ Gender identity seems to develop through the three stages proposed by Kohlberg.

➕ As predicted by the theory, the achievement of full gender identity increases sex-typed behaviour.

➕ The notion that gender development involves children actively interacting with the world around them is valuable, as is the notion that how they interact with the world depends on the extent to which they have reached gender identity.

➖ It has been argued that some sex-typed behaviour occurs in young children before they achieve gender identity, but the evidence is not conclusive.

➖ Kohlberg (1966, p. 98) argued that, "the process of forming a constant sexual identity is ... a part of the general process of conceptual growth." This approach tends to ignore the external factors (e.g., reward and punishment from parents) determining some early sex-typed behaviour. More generally, Kohlberg's focus was too much on the individual child, and not enough on the social context influencing gender development.

➖ Kohlberg probably exaggerated the importance of cognitive factors in producing sex-typed behaviour.

## Gender-schema theory

Martin and Halverson (1987) put forward a rather different cognitive-developmental theory known as gender-schema theory. They argued that children as young as 2 or 3 who have acquired gender identity start to form **gender schemas** consisting of organised sets of beliefs about the sexes. The first schema formed is an ingroup/outgroup schema, consisting of organised information about which toys and activities are suitable for boys and which for girls. Another early schema is an own-sex schema containing information about how to behave in sex-typed ways (e.g., how to dress dolls for a girl). Some of the processes involved in the initial development of gender schemas may include those emphasised by social learning theorists.

A key aspect of gender-schema theory is the notion that children do not simply respond passively to the world. Instead, the gender schemas possessed by children help to determine what they attend to, how they interpret the world, and what they remember of their experiences. Thus, "Gender schemas 'structure' experience by providing an organisation for processing social information" (Shaffer, 1993, p. 513).

## Evidence

According to the theory, gender schemas are used by children to organise and make sense of their experiences. If they are exposed to information inconsistent with one of their schemas (e.g., a boy combing the hair of his doll), then the information may be distorted to make it fit the schema. Martin and Halverson (1983) tested this prediction. They showed 5- and 6-year-old children pictures of schema-consistent activities (e.g., a girl playing with a doll) and schema-inconsistent activities (e.g., a girl playing with a toy gun). Schema-inconsistent activities were often mis-remembered 1 week later as schema-consistent (e.g., it had been a boy playing with a toy gun).

Another study supporting gender-schema theory was reported by Bradbard, Martin, Endsley, and Halverson (1986). Boys and girls between the ages of 4 and 9 were presented with gender-neutral objects (e.g., burglar alarms, pizza cutters). They were told some of the objects were "boy" objects, whereas others were "girl" objects. There were two key findings. First, children spent much more time playing with objects allegedly appropriate to their sex. Second, even a week later, the children remembered whether any given object was a "boy" or a "girl" object.

A study by Masters, Ford, Arend, Grotevant, and Clark (1979) also supports gender-schema theory. Young children of 4 and 5 were influenced in their choice of toy more by the gender label attached to the toy (e.g., "It's a girl's toy") than by the sex of the model seen playing with the toy. Thus, children's behaviour is determined more by gender schemas than by a wish to imitate a same-sexed model.

Serbin, Powlishta, and Gulko (1993) found that boys and girls in middle childhood possessed comparable amount of gender stereotypic knowledge in their gender schemas. The natural prediction from gender-schema theory is that there would be no difference between boys and girls in sex-typed behaviour. In fact, however, boys exhibited more sex-typed behaviour than girls, and this sex difference is hard to explain on the theory.

Schema-consistent activities

Schema-inconsistent activities

**Stereotyped toys**

Holloway (1999) cites a study at Loughborough University in the UK that found the much lower popularity of computers with girls compared to boys was linked to these machines being stereotyped as "boys' toys". This was because, apart from email, computers were regarded as vehicles for combat or sports-based games, which girls did not find attractive.

## Evaluation

- ⊕ Gender-schema theory helps to explain why children's sex-role beliefs and attitudes often change rather little after middle childhood. Gender schemas tend to be maintained because schema-consistent information is attended to and remembered.
- ⊕ The theory regards the child as being actively involved in making sense of the world in the light of its present knowledge.
- ⊖ The theory exaggerates the role of the individual child in gender development, and de-emphasises the importance of social factors.

- The linkage between possession of gender schemas and behaviour is unlikely to be strong. As Bussey and Bandura (1999, p. 679) pointed out, "Children do not categorise themselves as 'I am a girl' or 'I am a boy' and act in accordance with that schema across situations and activity domains."
- The theory does not really explain *why* gender schemas develop and take the form they do.
- The theory fails to account for the finding that boys exhibit more sex-typed behaviour than girls (Serbin et al., 1993).

# Biological theories

There are various obvious biological differences between boys and girls. These biological differences produce hormonal differences between the sexes at a very early stage of development (see Chapter 3). For example, the male sex hormone testosterone is present in greater amounts in male than female foetuses from about the age of 6 weeks, whereas the opposite is the case for the female sex hormone oestrogen. It has been argued that basic biological and hormonal factors are important in gender development. However, as Willerman (1979) pointed out, "One should not expect too much of the genetic differences between males and females. The two sexes have forty-five/forty-six of their chromosomes in common, and the one that differs (the Y) contains the smallest proportion of genetic material."

The ideal way of testing biological theories of gender development would be to study individuals in whom there is a clear distinction between **sexual identity** (based on biological factors) and the way in which they are treated socially. Thus, for example, if an individual was born a boy but treated as a girl, would biological or social factors be more important in their gender development? The ideal study has not been carried out, but approximations to it are discussed below.

*What would be the ideal study and why has it not been carried out?*

## Evidence

Suggestive evidence in support of the biological approach to gender development has been obtained in animal studies. For example, Young, Goy, and Phoenix (1964) gave doses of testosterone to pregnant monkeys. This male sex hormone produced greater aggressiveness and higher frequency of rough-and-tumble play in the mothers' female offspring. Hormonal abnormalities are found in some human babies. For example, in congenital adrenal hyperplasia, the adrenal glands produce large quantities of male sex hormones early in life.

Money and Ehrhardt (1972) discussed cases of females exposed to male sex hormones prior to birth, including some with congenital adrenal hyperplasia. Even though their parents treated them as girls, they tended to be tomboys. They played and fought with boys, and avoided more traditional female activities. In addition, they preferred to play with blocks and cars rather than with dolls. However, many of these girls were given the hormone cortisone to prevent them from becoming too masculine anatomically. Cortisone increases activity level, and this may have made their behaviour more like that expected of boys. In addition, the parents knew about their child's hormonal abnormalities, which may have influenced their behaviour.

Evidence that social factors can override biology was also reported by Money and Ehrhardt (1972). They studied male identical twins, one of whom had his penis very severely damaged during circumcision. He had an operation at the age of 21 months to make him anatomically a girl. His parents treated him like a girl, and this affected his behaviour. He asked for toys such as a doll and a doll's house, whereas his brother asked for a garage. He was neater and more delicate in his behaviour than his identical twin. Diamond (1982) carried out a follow-up study on the identical twin who grew up as a girl. This study suggested biological factors are important. The girl had few friends, did not feel securely female or male, and believed life was better for boys than girls.

There are rare cases in which the development of biological gender is complex. For example, about 500 people in Britain have testicular feminising syndrome. They are male in that they have male chromosomes and testicles. However, their bodies do not respond to the male sex hormone testosterone. As a result, they develop a female body shape and their breasts develop. Mrs Daphne Went has testicular feminising syndrome. In spite of her male chromosomes, she looks like a woman, is married with two adopted children, and has succeeded in her role as a woman (Goldwyn, 1979).

Imperato-McGinley, Guerro, Gautier, and Peterson (1974) studied the Batista family in the Dominican Republic. Four sons in the family appeared biologically to be female when born, and they were reared as girls. However, at the age of about 12, they developed male genitals and started to look like ordinary adolescent males. In spite of the fact that all four of them had been reared as girls (and had thought of themselves as females), they adjusted well to the male role. According to Gross's (1996) account, "They have all taken on male roles, do men's jobs, have married women and are accepted as men" (p. 584). Thus, biological factors can be more important than social ones.

Collaer and Hines (1995) reviewed the sometimes confusing and inconsistent findings from numerous studies. They argued there is good evidence for at least three effects. First, male sex hormones increase the likelihood that the child will enjoy rough-and-tumble play and physical activity generally. Second, exposure to high levels of male sex hormones at an early age affects sexual orientation in adolescence. Third, male sex hormones lead to an increase in aggressive behaviour.

## Evaluation

⊕ Biological factors play some role in gender development.
⊕ Excessive male sex hormones can make children more physically active and aggressive.
⊖ Biological theories do not explain the impact of social factors on gender development.
⊖ Biological theories cannot account for the substantial changes in gender roles that have occurred in Western societies in recent decades.
⊖ Biological theories predict that the roles and status of men and women should be fairly constant across cultures, but there are actually substantial cross-cultural differences (Wood & Eagly, 2002, see below).

## Recent theoretical developments

You have probably got the impression by now that most theories of gender development are radically different from each other. That is much less the case now than it used to be. As Martin et al. (2002, p. 904) pointed out, "It is now widely acknowledged that regardless of one's preferred theoretical orientation, cognitive, environmental, and biological factors are all important." For example, the social learning approach to gender development has been broadened into a social cognitive theory (Bussey & Bandura, 1999).

Social cognitive theory resembles social learning theory in that three modes of influence promoting gender development are identified. First, there is observational learning or modelling. Second, there is enactive experience, in which children learn about sex-typed behaviour by discovering the outcomes (positive or negative) resulting from their actions. Third, there is direct tuition, in which other people teach children about gender identity and sex-typed behaviour. These modes of influence depend mostly on the external environment (e.g., presence of a model).

In addition to the above modes of influence, Bussey and Bandura (1999) identified various other mechanisms influencing gender development. For example, children use self-regulatory mechanisms to compare their own behaviour against their own standards of how they should behave. In addition, when children decide which aspects of others' behaviour to imitate, they typically choose forms of behaviour they think will increase their feelings of self-efficacy or mastery. In sum, social cognitive theory as proposed by Bussey and Bandura differs from traditional social learning theory in that gender development depends on a range of internal cognitive mechanisms as well as on external factors (e.g., rewards and punishments). As such, it is much closer to cognitive theories such as Kohlberg's

Parents may try to discourage what they see as sex-inappropriate behaviour in a variety of ways. Climbing trees while wearing a skirt is more difficult than in trousers or shorts.

cognitive-developmental theory and gender-schema theory. However, an important difference is that Bussey and Bandura assume that young children engage in sex-typed behaviour *before* they have a conception of gender, but fail to indicate clearly how that is possible.

Maccoby (1998, 2002) pointed out that children have a preference for same-sex peers in nearly all cultures, with this preference typically increasing during childhood and adolescence. In most cultures, peer groups of boys tend to be relatively large and competitive, whereas peer groups of girls are smaller and co-operative. According to Maccoby, children's experiences in these same-sex groups may have substantial effects on gender development.

There seems to be a natural tendency for boys to prefer larger groups than girls. Benenson, Apostolaris, and Parnass (1997) allowed same-sex groups of six children to organise themselves as they wanted for play activities. The girls tended to divide up into groups of two or three, whereas the boys tended to form much larger groups. The size of the group influences the kinds of interaction that occur. Benenson, Nicholson, Waite, Roy, and Simpson (2001) found that there was more conflict and competition in larger groups than in smaller ones (whether the groups consisted only of boys or only of girls). In contrast, the needs and views of others were taken more into account in smaller groups than in larger ones. It is an interesting notion that sex differences in preferred group size may influence the development of sex-typed behaviour.

Evidence supporting Maccoby's (2002) position was reported by Martin and Fabes (2001). Boys who spent the most time in same-sex groups showed the greatest increases in sex-typed behaviour (e.g., more rough-and-tumble play, greater preference for sex-typed toys, less time near adults). In similar fashion, girls spending the most time in same-sex groups had the largest increases in sex-typed behaviour (e.g., greater preference for sex-typed toys, decreased aggression, more time near adults). However, it remains to be seen whether there is a direct causal effect of time spent in same-sex groups on sex-typed behaviour.

What leads children to belong to same-sex groups in the first place? Part of the answer was provided by Fagot (1985), who found that young children showing gender identity spent more of their time in same-sex groups than did children who could not identify or label the sexes.

## Cultural differences

In Western societies, boys are encouraged to develop an *instrumental role*, in which they are assertive, competitive, and independent in their behaviour. In contrast, girls are encouraged to develop an *expressive role*, in which they are co-operative, supportive, and sensitive in their dealings with other people. These are stereotypes, of course, and we have already seen there are rather small differences in actual behaviour.

In most Western societies, there are now more female than male university students.

There have been great changes in most Western societies in recent years. Thirty years ago, many fewer women than men went to university. Nowadays the number of female university students exceeds that of male students in several countries (e.g., Spain). There is a similar pattern in employment. In spite of these changes, many stereotypes have changed very little. Bergen and Williams (1991) found in the United States that stereotypical views of the sexes in 1988 were remarkably similar to those expressed in 1972.

Socialisation pressures in 110 non-industrialised countries were explored by Barry, Bacon, and Child (1957). They considered five characteristics:

- Nurturance (being supportive).
- Responsibility.
- Obedience.
- Achievement.
- Self-reliance.

There was more pressure on girls than on boys to be nurturant in 75% of the non-industrialised societies, with none showing the opposite pattern. Responsibility was regarded as more important in girls than in boys in 55% of the societies, with 10% showing the opposite pattern. Obedience was stressed for girls more than for boys in 32% of societies, with 3% showing the opposite. There was more pressure on boys than on girls to acquire the other two characteristics. Achievement was emphasised more for boys in 79% of societies (3% showed the opposite), and self-reliance was regarded as more important in boys in 77% of societies, with no societies regarding it as more important in girls.

These findings indicate that the sex-role stereotypes of females being expressive and males being instrumental are very widespread. Related findings were obtained by Williams and Best (1990). Similar gender stereotypes to those found in the United States were present in 24 other countries in Asia, Europe, Oceania, Africa, and the Americas.

In spite of the evidence for various cross-cultural similarities in sex-role stereotypes, there are also important differences across cultures. Wood and Eagly (2002; see Chapter 1) considered sex roles in 181 non-industrialised societies. Men were dominant in 67% of those societies, especially those in which there was much warfare and men's economic contribution was much greater than that of women. However, neither sex was dominant in 30% of societies, and women were dominant in 3%. There were also large cultural differences in terms of responsibility for obtaining food. Men had the primary role in obtaining food in societies which depend on hunting or fishing, but women had the main role when food gathering was involved.

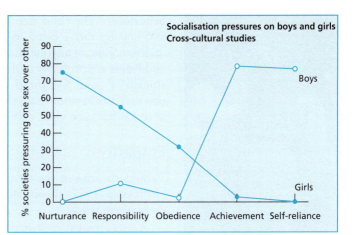

*Which theory would not be supported by the demonstration of cultural differences in gender roles?*

## Evaluation

⊕ Some cultural expectations and stereotypes for boys and girls are similar in otherwise very different cultures.

⊕ The notion that men should adopt an instrumental role and women an expressive role is common across numerous cultures.

⊖ There is increasing evidence (e.g., Wood & Eagly, 2002) that there are greater cultural variations in the expectations for men and women and in their behaviour than used to be assumed to be the case.

⊖ There may be large differences between *expectations* and actual *behaviour*. What is needed is more research in which the behaviour of boys and girls of different ages is observed systematically to see whether differences in cultural expectations are matched by differences in behaviour.

## PRO-SOCIAL BEHAVIOUR

You must have met some people who were very helpful and co-operative, and others who were aggressive and unpleasant. Psychologists use the terms "anti-social behaviour" and "pro-social behaviour" to describe these very different ways of treating other people. Anti-social behaviour is behaviour that harms or injures someone else. In contrast, **pro-social behaviour** is "any voluntary, intentional action that produces a positive or beneficial outcome for the recipient regardless of whether that action is costly to the donor, neutral in its impact, or beneficial" (Grusec, Davidov, & Lundell, 2002, p. 2). Pro-social behaviour is more general than **altruism**, which is voluntary helping behaviour that benefits someone else but provides no obvious self-gain to the person who behaves altruistically. It has often been assumed that altruism typically depends on empathy. **Empathy** is the ability to share the emotions of another person in order to understand his or her needs.

Is pro-social behaviour or anti-social behaviour more common in young children? As Schaffer (1996, p. 269) pointed out, Freud and Piaget provided rather negative accounts of children, emphasising their tendency to engage in anti-social rather than pro-social

Even quite small children can show concern when they see others are unhappy.

behaviour: "The child emerged from these accounts as a selfish, self-centred, aggressive, and uncooperative being, with little interest in other people in their own right and little understanding of anyone else's needs and requirements." As we will see, the views of Freud and Piaget are probably unduly pessimistic. For example, Eisenberg-Berg and Hand (1979) studied 4- and 5-year-old children in preschool classes. They recorded evidence of pro-social behaviour (e.g., sharing, comforting) whenever it was observed, and found on average that each child exhibited such behaviour five or six times every hour.

## Empathy

Various theories of the development of empathy have been proposed. We will focus on Hoffman's (1987) theory, according to which there are four main stages in the development of empathy:

- *Stage 1: Global empathy.* This stage starts during the first year of life, before the infant can distinguish clearly between self and other. The infant will sometimes start crying when another infant cries, but this is an involuntary reaction rather than genuine empathy.
- *Stage 2: "Egocentric" empathy.* This stage starts in the second year of life. The developing sense of self allows the child to realise it is someone else rather than the child itself who is in distress. However, the child still cannot distinguish clearly between someone else's emotional state and its own.
- *Stage 3: Empathy for another's feelings.* This stage starts at about 2 or 3. It involves genuine empathy based on a clear awareness of (and empathy for) the various emotions others experience.
- *Stage 4: Empathy for another's life condition.* This stage starts in late childhood. Children in this stage are aware that other people have separate identities and life experiences, and this permits them to understand how others are likely to be feeling even when it is not clear from their behaviour.

### *Evidence*

*Why might it be difficult to study empathy in children using studies such as these?*

A key prediction from Hoffman's (1987) theory is that children even as young as 2 years of age should show evidence of genuine empathy. This prediction was supported in a study by Zahn-Waxler, Robinson, and Emde (1992). In this study, the mothers of children in their second year of life recorded the reactions of their children to situations in which someone else experienced distress, divided into whether or not this distress had been caused by the child. As might be expected, the children were generally less likely to show signs of empathy and of altruism when they had caused the distress.

Zahn-Waxler et al. (1992) obtained evidence of empathic concern in children of between 13 and 20 months on about 10% of occasions on which someone else's distress was not caused by the child. This empathic concern took several forms, including sad or upset facial expressions and expressing concern (e.g., "I'm sorry"). There was much more empathic concern among children aged between 23 and 25 months: They showed empathy on 25% of occasions when they encountered distress for which they were not responsible.

Zahn-Waxler et al. (1992) also obtained evidence about altruistic behaviour in response to another person's distress. The kinds of altruistic behaviour exhibited by the children included sharing food, hugging, and giving a bottle to a crying baby. There was a marked increase with age in altruistic behaviour in response to distress not caused by the child. More specifically, there was an altruistic response by children aged 13–15 months on 9% of occasions, compared to

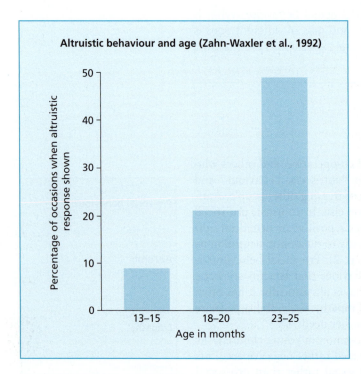

**Altruistic behaviour and age (Zahn-Waxler et al., 1992)**

Percentage of occasions when altruistic response shown

Age in months

21% of occasions by children aged 18–20 months, and to 49% of occasions by children between 23 and 25 months.

After the age of 2, children develop more awareness of their own emotions and those of others, of the kinds of situations that produce different emotions, and of the most effective kinds of help in those situations (see Schaffer, 1996). However, that does not necessarily mean that children show a progressive increase in pro-social behaviour throughout childhood. The evidence is rather inconsistent on this point. Hay (1994) reported a decrease in pro-social behaviour between the ages of 3 and 6, but others (e.g., Eisenberg, 1989) have not found a decrease. What is clear is that the frequency and types of pro-social behaviour shown by children come to depend increasingly on the specific aspects of the situation and of the distressed person (Eisenberg, 1989).

Why are there substantial differences in pro-social behaviour among children of a given age? Part of the answer seems to involve genetic factors. Zahn-Waxler et al. (1992) carried out a study on identical and fraternal twins aged between 14 and 20 months. Their mothers *reported* on various types of pro-social behaviour (e.g., expressions of concern, attempts to help). There was more similarity in the amount of pro-social behaviour shown by identical twins than by fraternal twins, suggesting that genetic factors play an important role. However, Zahn-Waxler et al. obtained rather different findings when *observing* the reactions of the twins to simulated distress. There was no clear evidence that the pro-social behaviour of the identical twins was more similar than that of the fraternal twins.

## Evaluation

⊕ As predicted by the theory, there is evidence of genuine empathy at a surprisingly early age.
⊕ There is general support for the four stages of empathy development proposed by Hoffman (1987).
⊖ The role of genetic factors in influencing individual differences in empathy is de-emphasised in the theory.
⊖ The theory says relatively little about the precise ways in which parental behaviour influences the development of empathy (see below).

## Parental influence

Parental behaviour is of major importance in determining how much pro-social behaviour their children will display. According to Grusec et al. (2002), there are three ways in which parents can help their children to internalise pro-social values. First, the parents need to be perceived as sensitive and empathic by the child. Second, the parents need to provide their child with unconditional approval. Third, the parents need to respond positively whenever the child's demands are reasonable. As we will see, there is reasonable support for this position.

Studies by Zahn-Waxler, Radke-Yarrow, and King (1979) and by Robinson et al. (1994) have revealed that children having a warm and loving relationship with their parents are most likely to show high levels of pro-social behaviour. In addition, specific forms of parental behaviour are consistently associated with pro-social behaviour in their children. It is probably important that children learn to attribute their pro-social behaviour to internal factors (e.g., "I am a helpful person") rather than to external factors (e.g., "I am being helpful in order to be praised"). For example, Fabes, Fultz, Eisenberg, May-Plumlee, and Christopher (1989) found that external rewards are not an effective way of producing pro-social behaviour. They promised toys to some children if they sorted coloured paper squares for children who were sick in hospital. Other children were not offered any reward for carrying out the same task. After a while, all the children were told they could continue to sort the coloured squares, but they would not receive any reward for doing so. The children who had been rewarded were less likely to continue to be helpful than those who had not been rewarded. This effect was strongest among those children whose mothers believed in using rewards to make their children behave well.

Why are rewards so ineffective in producing pro-social or altruistic behaviour? Those who are rewarded for behaving helpfully are motivated by the thought of the reward rather than by the desire to help others. As a result, removal of the rewards often causes the helpful behaviour to stop.

Grusec (1988) asked the mothers of children aged between 4 and 7 to record their child's deliberate acts of helping. The mothers nearly always responded positively to such pro-social behaviour (e.g., thanking, smiling, praising). In contrast, mothers tended to respond with moral exhortations, frowning, or requests to their child to be altruistic when he/she failed to be helpful.

Schaffer (1996) argued that five types of parental behaviour are of particular value in teaching children to be altruistic:

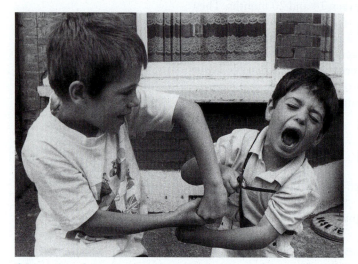

If the mother of an aggressive child emphasises how much the other child is being hurt, the aggressive child is more likely to feel empathy and stop the undesirable behaviour.

*What kind of model would be most effective in producing imitation here?*

1. *Provision of clear and explicit guidelines* (e.g., "You mustn't hit other people, because you will hurt and upset them"). For example, Krevans and Gibbs (1996) found that children were more likely to show empathy for other people and to exhibit pro-social behaviour when their mothers repeatedly asked them to consider the likely effects of their behaviour on others.
2. *Emotional conviction.* Guidelines to children should be given in a fairly emotional way.
3. *Attributing altruistic or pro-social characteristics to the child* (e.g., "You are a really helpful boy").
4. *Parental modelling.* The parent should behave altruistically.
5. *Empathic and warm parenting.* Children who form secure attachments in infancy show more empathy later in childhood (e.g., Waters, Wippman, & Sroufe, 1979).

Grusec, Saas-Kortsaak, and Simutis (1978) addressed the issue of whether pro-social behaviour is facilitated more by the behaviour of a model or by what the model says. Children aged between 8 and 10 played a game to win marbles, some or all of which could be donated to help poor children. The participants observed an adult playing the game before them. This adult either gave away half or none of her marbles, and she either exhorted or did not exhort the children to give away half of their marbles. Most children who saw the adult give marbles did so themselves, whereas exhortations to give marbles had only a small effect. Thus, children were more influenced by the model's behaviour than by her exhortations. Disappointingly, only a few children donated any marbles when they played the marble game again 3 weeks later.

Many studies on altruism or pro-social behaviour are rather artificial. Zarbatany, Hartmann, and Gelfand (1985) argued it is important to distinguish between "true" altruism and conformity to adult expectations. They found that older children seemed more generous than younger ones, but this was mainly because older children were more responsive to adult expectations. The finding by Grusec et al. (1978) that there were no long-term effects of observational learning on pro-social behaviour is what might be expected if the children were simply conforming to what they perceived to be the model's expectations.

## Evaluation

➕ Parents have a substantial impact on the pro-social and altruistic behaviour of children.
➕ Various parental characteristics associated with high levels of pro-social behaviour in their children have been identified (e.g., warm and loving relationship, attributing pro-social behaviour to internal factors, showing by example).

● Individual differences in the development of pro-social behaviour probably depend in part on genetic factors as well as on parental influence (e.g., Zahn-Waxler et al., 1992).
● Some laboratory studies allegedly studying altruistic behaviour may mainly be assessing conformity to adult expectations.

## Media influences

Can pro-social or helping behaviour be increased by watching television programmes? Evidence that it can has been reported in several studies. Friedrich and Stein (1973) studied American preschool children, who watched episodes of a pro-social television programme called *Mister Rogers' Neighbourhood*. These children remembered much of the pro-social information contained in the programmes, and behaved in a more helpful and co-operative way, than did children watching television programmes with neutral or aggressive content. They became even more helpful if they role-played pro-social events from the programmes.

Hearold (1986) reviewed more than 100 studies on the effects of pro-social television programmes on children's behaviour. She concluded that such programmes do generally make children behave in more helpful ways. Indeed, the beneficial effects of pro-social programmes on pro-social behaviour were almost twice as great as the adverse effects of television violence on aggressive behaviour. However, helping behaviour was usually assessed shortly after watching a pro-social television programme, and it is not clear whether pro-social television programmes have long-term beneficial effects.

Why is children's helping behaviour increased by watching pro-social television programmes? One possibility is that observational learning is involved, with the children simply imitating the pro-social behaviour they have observed. In a study by Sagotsky, Wood-Schneider, and Konop (1981), children of 6 and 8 saw co-operative behaviour being modelled. Children of both ages showed an immediate increase in co-operative behaviour. However, only the 8-year-olds continued to show increased co-operation 7 weeks later.

### *Lassie* and helping behaviour

Sprafkin, Liebert, and Poulos (1975) studied 6-year-olds. Some watched an episode of *Lassie*, in which a boy was seen to risk his life to rescue a puppy from a mine shaft. Other groups of children saw a different episode of *Lassie*, in which no helping was involved, or they saw an episode of a situation comedy called *The Brady Bunch*. After watching the programme, all the children had the chance to help some distressed puppies. However, to do so they had to stop playing a game in which they might have a won a big prize. The children who had watched the rescue from the mine shaft spent an average of over 90 seconds helping the puppies, compared to under 50 seconds by the children watching the other programmes.

### Evaluation

● Pro-social television programmes can promote pro-social behaviour in children.
● The long-term beneficial effects of pro-social television programmes on children's behaviour may be rather weak or even non-existent.
● We do not have clear explanations of precisely *why* pro-social television programmes have beneficial effects, although observational learning probably plays a part.

## Gender differences

It is assumed in most Western cultures that girls are more empathic and show more pro-social behaviour than boys. There is some support for that assumption. For example, Olweus and Endresen (1998) studied the ability of adolescent boys and girls to show empathy when reading a description of a distressed fellow student. Older adolescent girls showed greater empathic concern than younger adolescent girls regardless of whether the distressed student was male or female. Boys showed the same developmental pattern as girls when the description referred to a girl. However, older adolescent boys showed *less* empathic concern for a distressed boy than did younger adolescent boys, presumably because being concerned about another boy was perceived as being in conflict with their masculine identity.

Girls generally seem to be more skilful than boys at using pro-social behaviour to resolve difficult situations. For example, Osterman, Bjorkqvist, Lagerspetz, Landau, Fraczek, and Pastorelli (1997) studied children aged 8, 11, and 15 in Finland, Israel, Italy, and Poland. Girls in all four cultures were more likely than boys to resolve conflicts in constructive ways or by making use of a third party. Why is there this gender difference? One possibility is that females are better than males at interpreting the behaviour of others, and another possibility is that their lesser physical strength means they have to find non-physical ways of resolving conflicts.

Grusec et al. (2002) have reviewed the evidence on gender differences in pro-social behaviour. They pointed out that gender differences in pro-social behaviour are usually smaller when such behaviour is assessed by direct observation rather than by self-report measures. In addition, gender differences in pro-social behaviour are smaller when the behaviour involves sharing or helping than when it involves showing consideration or kindness.

## Cross-cultural differences

We have already referred to a study by Osterman et al. (1997) on children from four cultures (Finland, Italy, Israel, and Poland). They found that developmental *changes* between the ages of 8 and 15 in the strategies used to resolve conflicts were very similar in all four cultures. In spite of these similarities, there were some differences. The approaches towards conflict resolution were generally more constructive in Israeli and Finnish children than in those from Italy or Poland.

Most of the research we have discussed so far has been carried out in Western cultures which are individualistic, meaning that the emphasis is on individuals' own welfare rather than that of other people (see Chapter 1). It is reasonable to assume there would be more evidence of altruistic and pro-social behaviour in collectivistic cultures, in which the emphasis is on the well-being of the group. Evidence that there are important cross-cultural differences in altruism was reported by Whiting and Whiting (1975). They considered the behaviour of young children between the ages of 3 and 10 in six cultures (United States, India, Okinawa—an island in South West Japan, Philippines, Mexico, and Kenya). At one extreme, Whiting and Whiting found that 100% of young children in Kenya were high in altruism. At the other extreme, only 8% of young children in the United States were altruistic. Those cultures in which children showed the most pro-social behaviour were those in which women contributed the most to the family economy, and frequently assigned tasks to their children.

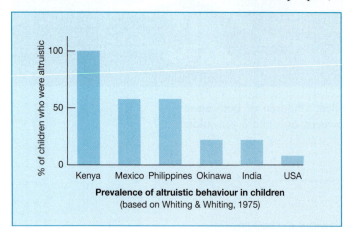

**Prevalence of altruistic behaviour in children**
(based on Whiting & Whiting, 1975)

Robarchek and Robarchek (1992) compared two cultures:

1. The Semai live in the Malaysian rainforest, and have a culture emphasising co-operation and mutual support within the family and within the society as a whole.
2. The Waorani people from the Amazon region have a very individualistic society, and consistently behave in a warlike fashion. If they are attacked, the members of the Waorani focus on saving themselves rather than on helping other members of their family or their society.

As might be imagined, there is considerably more evidence of pro-social and altruistic behaviour among the children of the Semai than among those of the Waorani.

Eisenberg and Mussen (1989) reviewed several studies on cross-cultural differences in altruism, and came to the following conclusion: "Most children reared in Mexican villages, Hopi children on reservations in the Southwest [of America], and youngsters on Israeli kibbutzim are more considerate, kind, and co-operative than their 'typical' middle-class American counterparts."

What do the above findings mean? Two main factors are involved. First, industrialised and individualistic cultures such as those in most parts of the United States and Okinawa place much emphasis on competition and personal success. This emphasis is likely to reduce co-operation and altruism. Second, the family structure in non-industrialised and collectivistic cultures such as those of Kenya, Mexico, and the Hopi is quite different from that in industrialised cultures. Children in non-industrialised societies are often given major family responsibilities (e.g., caring for young children), and these responsibilities help to develop altruistic behaviour.

Most experts have assumed that members of non-industrialised and collectivistic cultures are more altruistic than those of industrialised and individualistic cultures. However, this may well not be altogether correct. Fijneman, Willemsen, and Poortinga (1996) found that people living in collectivistic societies expect more help from others than do those living in individualistic societies. Thus, their motives in helping others may be based on what they expect to receive in return rather than being altruistic. Collectivistic and individualistic societies are similar, in that individuals expect to give only a little more help than they receive in return. Thus, there is a norm of reciprocity or mutual exchange in both individualistic and collectivistic cultures, and the two kinds of cultures may differ little in their levels of altruism.

*If this is the case, can we label the same behaviours as altruistic in all cultures?*

## Evaluation

⊕ There are clear cross-cultural differences in the amount of pro-social behaviour shown by children.

⊕ Children generally show more pro-social behaviour in collectivistic cultures than in individualistic ones.

⊖ Evidence is needed from a wider range of cultures to clarify which cultural factors are the most important determinants of children's pro-social behaviour.

⊖ There is some controversy as to whether children in collectivistic cultures exhibit more pro-social behaviour because they are genuinely more altruistic or because they expect to receive more help in return.

## ANTI-SOCIAL BEHAVIOUR

There are various forms of anti-social behaviour. Delinquency is the legal definition of anti-social behaviour, and it includes shoplifting and vandalism as well as behaviour that is aggressive and violent. However, aggression is of particular importance, and will be our central focus in this section. **Aggression** involves hurting others on purpose (see Chapter 19), and can be defined as, "any form of behaviour directed towards the goal of harming or injuring another living being who is motivated to avoid such treatment" (Baron & Richardson, 1993). The hurting has to be deliberate. For example, someone who slips on the ice and crashes into someone by accident is not behaving aggressively. Children who are aggressive often lack friends and are rejected by other children (see Chapter 17).

A distinction has often been drawn between hostile aggression and instrumental aggression (see Chapter 19). Hostile aggression involves angry, impulsive behaviour designed to harm another person, whereas instrumental aggression is calculated, and is designed to achieve some goal (e.g., stealing money). However, this distinction oversimplifies a complex reality. Most aggressive behaviour is determined by several factors, and it often involves instrumental motives as well as anger (Bushman & Anderson, 2001).

There are problems in deciding whether a certain piece of behaviour is aggressive. The key measurement problem is that aggression involves the *intent* to harm someone, and it is sometimes hard to know whether a child intended to cause harm. However, Jones

**KEY TERM**

**Aggression:** behaviour that is designed or intended to harm or to injure another living being.

We can distinguish between aggression and rough-and-tumble play by the facial expressions and bodily movements used.

*Why do you think that girls did not show an increase in aggressive actions between 9 and 14 years?*

(1972) argued that we can distinguish reasonably clearly between aggressive behaviour and a form of play known as rough-and-tumble. Analyses of facial expressions and bodily movements in both situations indicated that children acting aggressively frown, push, take–tug–grab, and hit the other child. In contrast, children engaged in rough-and-tumble often laugh, and they jump, run, wrestle, and hit at the other child. Another major difference is that aggression often occurs when two children both want the same toy, whereas rough-and-tumble does not.

## Developmental trends

There are fairly pronounced changes during the course of development in both the amount of aggression and the types of aggression displayed. The amount of aggression typically decreases during the first few years of life, but may then increase again. Holmberg (1980) studied children between the ages of 12 and 42 months. At 12 months, about 50% of all behaviour directed at another child seemed to have an aggressive intent, but this dropped dramatically to 17% at 42 months. A subsequent increase in aggressive behaviour was reported by Cairns (1986) in a study on self-reported and observed aggressive actions in boys and girls. Boys (but not girls) showed an increase in such aggressive actions between 9 and 14 years of age.

There are several changes during development in the expression of aggression. As Schaffer (1996, p. 279) pointed out:

*As children get older there is a tendency for aggression to become increasingly expressed in verbal rather than physical form. The 2-year-old has little choice but to express anger through direct bodily action; by the age of 10 shaming, humiliation, sarcasm, and teasing have all been added to the repertoire of responses for hurting others.*

Eron (1987) found that children who were aggressive at a young age were more likely than other children to be involved in criminal activities when they were adults.

Hartup (1974) studied children between the ages of 4 and 7. There was a steady decrease in the total number of aggressive actions. However, more detailed analysis revealed that there was only a decrease in calculated aggression (sometimes known as instrumental aggression), with the amount of anger-based aggression remaining more or less constant.

A striking finding from longitudinal studies of aggression is that most children show reasonable stability in their level of aggression throughout childhood. For example, Eron (1987) found that children who were aggressive at the age of 8 tended to be aggressive at the age of 18. Indeed, those who were aggressive at 8 were *three* times more likely than other children to have a police record at the age of 18. These same children were more likely than other children to have been involved in criminal activities and to have behaved violently towards their spouse by the age of 30.

Patterson, DeBaryshe, and Ramsey (1989) argued that the factors causing anti-social behaviour change in the course of development. So far as early childhood is concerned, a lack of parental monitoring and discipline can lead to behaviour problems. In middle childhood, such behaviour problems can produce academic failure and lead to rejection by most other children. As a result, there is commitment to a group of other deviant children in late childhood, which can lead to delinquency.

Support for Patterson et al.'s (1989) theory was reported by Berndt and Keefe (1995) and by Pettit et al. (1999). Berndt and Keefe found in children aged 13 and 14 that those who had disruptive friends often showed an increase in disruptive behaviour over the following 6 months. Pettit et al. found in 12- and 13-year-olds that those who were rated by teachers as having behaviour problems tended to come from unsafe neighbourhoods and to have parents who failed to monitor them or to supervise their activities with other children.

Patterson, Reid, and Dishion (1992) studied adolescent delinquents. They distinguished between "early starters" and "late starters". Early starters are typically rejected by other children in middle childhood, and then become key members of anti-social peer groups. They generally start to commit crimes when they are about 10 or 11, and often reoffend. In contrast, late starters show relatively normal social behaviour during early and middle childhood, but become involved in anti-social behaviour in adolescence when they join an anti-social peer group. Their initial offences start at about 15, and they are more likely to stop offending altogether.

Farrington (1995) carried out a longitudinal study on working-class boys in London. Early starters were convicted of about twice as many offences on average as later starters. Farrington identified seven risk factors for delinquency: hyperactivity, poor concentration, low intelligence and school performance, family poverty, poor parenting, family criminality, and causing trouble at school. As someone who has always lived in London and regards it as one of the great cities of the world, it is sad to report that those boys who moved away from London were less likely to become delinquents.

## Media influences

The average 16-year-old in Western society has seen about 13,000 violent murders on television, and this presumably has some effects on his/her behaviour. There is, indeed, a positive relationship between the amount of television violence children have seen and the aggressiveness of their behaviour. It may be that watching violent programmes causes aggressive behaviour. On the other hand, it may be that naturally aggressive children choose to watch more violent programmes than non-aggressive children.

Why might aggression be increased by watching violent television programmes? According to Bandura's (1973) social learning theory, one of the factors involved is observational learning or modelling (see Chapter 8). The basic idea is that we learn ways of behaving aggressively from observing people on television behaving violently, and this behaviour may be imitated subsequently. Another possibility is that we gradually become less responsive to (and emotionally concerned by) acts of violence, because we have seen so many on television and in films. This reduced responsiveness may produce an increased acceptance of violent behaviour.

The question of whether or not violence depicted in films and on TV leads to violent behaviour is often discussed and was hotly debated in relation to the Oliver Stone film *Natural Born Killers*. The film itself looks at media focus on violence and how it can be glamorised.

Another reason why television violence may lead to aggressive behaviour is because of cognitive priming (Josephson, 1987). According to this viewpoint, the aggressive cues presented in violent television programmes and films lead to aggressive thoughts and feelings. For example, when college students were asked to write down their thoughts while watching violent films (e.g., *The French Connection*), they reported numerous aggressive thoughts, increased anger, and a high level of physiological arousal.

### Evidence

Eron (1987) conducted a major longitudinal study on aggression, in which over 600 8-year-olds were studied for 22 years. The amount of television violence watched at the age of 8 predicted well the level of aggression and of criminality in the same children at the age of 18. However, the 8-year-olds who watched the most television violence were already significantly more aggressive than other 8-year-olds. Thus, the evidence of this

## CASE STUDY: *Movie violence*

Since its release in 1994, the film *Natural Born Killers* has been surrounded by controversy and has sparked a long-standing debate about the effect of viewing intense violence on the human mind. The film follows the story of Mickey and Mallory Knox, a young couple who go on a killing spree across America, claiming 52 lives at random. Their flippant attitude towards the crimes they commit is portrayed as exciting and thrilling by the media and as a result their murderous behaviour catches the imagination of a generation of young impressionable people who idolise them. The notion of admiring cold-blooded killers may seem to be far-fetched, but alarming similarities have emerged between the reaction to the fictional Mickey and Mallory and other real-life killers. *Natural Born Killers* has been linked to at least a dozen murders, including two cases in France where the defence has blamed the film as providing inspiration for the crime.

In October 1998 the French courts sentenced Florence Rey to 20 years in prison for her part in a shoot-out that left five people dead. She committed the crime with her boyfriend, Audry Maupin, who was killed in the shoot-out. Publicity material from the film was found in the flat that Rey shared with her boyfriend at the time of the shootings. The press latched on to this and called the pair "France's Natural Born Killers", and as in the film the vulgarity of the multiple murder was lost and replaced by a glamorous image of

rebellion that was both enticing and thrilling. Before long, young Parisians were wearing a picture of the convicted woman on their T-shirts. This was the first time a real-life murderer had been idolised in public.

Stronger links between the film and a murder were discovered in the case of Véronique Herbert and her boyfriend Sébastian Paindavoine who lured their victim into a trap and then stabbed him to death. There was no motive for the attack and Herbert placed the blame on *Natural Born Killers*. She said, "The film coincided with my state of mind. Maybe I muddled up dream and reality. I wanted to eliminate someone, as if by magic … The idea of killing invaded me." In the light of such a testimony, can anyone deny the link between the sort of violence depicted in *Natural Born Killers* and Herbert and Paindavoine's gruesome act?

The pro-censorship lobby says the film and subsequent murders provide conclusive evidence that screen violence is rapidly translated into street violence. The image of killing, especially in a fictional world where the characters do not have to live with the consequences of their actions, can become a reality. Such allegations against a film cannot be dismissed and the controversy surrounding the subject matter has been fuelled by the similarities between Mickey and Mallory and the real-life murderers. However, there is an argument against censorship which states that *Natural Born Killers* was intended as a satire on the bloodlust of the media and American society and that it is society that should be held responsible for any acts of violence rather than the film itself.

---

study suggests that watching violent programmes causes aggressive behaviour *and* that being aggressive leads to increased watching of violent programmes.

Anderson et al. (2001) reported a longitudinal study in which children's television viewing at the age of 5 and in adolescence (16–18 years) was related to aggression and academic performance in adolescence. There was modest evidence that watching violent television programmes at the age of 5 was related to adolescent aggression and to poor academic achievement in girls only. Watching violent television programmes in adolescence was not related to aggression or academic performance in boys or girls.

One of the most thorough experimental studies was reported by Leyens, Camino, Parke, and Berkowitz (1975), using juvenile delinquents at a school in Belgium as the participants. They lived in four dormitories, two of which had high levels of aggressive behaviour and two of which had low levels. During a special Movie Week, the boys in two of the dormitories (one high in aggression and the other low) watched only violent films, whereas the boys in the other two dormitories watched only non-violent films.

*Are any ethical issues raised by carrying out this type of study?*

There was an increased level of physical aggression among the boys watching the violent films, but not among those watching the non-violent films. The findings were more complex for verbal aggression. This increased among boys in the aggressive dormitory who saw violent films, but it actually decreased among boys from the non-aggressive dormitory who saw violent films. Finally, the effects of the violent films were much stronger shortly after watching them than later on. A general limitation of this study is that the experimenters did not distinguish clearly between real and pretend aggression.

The studies considered so far suggest that violent television and films lead to increased aggression. However, no effects of television on aggression have been found in other studies. One such study was carried out by Hennigan, Del Rosario, Cook, and Calder (1982). They made use of the fact that the Federal Communications Commission in the United States refused to issue any new

## CASE STUDY: *St Helena*

A study was carried out on the island of St Helena in the south Atlantic, which is best known for the fact that Napoleon spent the last few years of his life there. Its inhabitants received television for the first time in 1995, but there is no evidence of any adverse effects on the children. According to Charlton (1998):

*The argument that watching violent television turns youngsters to violence is not borne out, and this study on St. Helena is the clearest proof yet. The children have watched the same amounts of violence, and in many cases the same programmes as British children. But they have not gone out and copied what they have seen on TV.*

What are the factors preventing television violence from influencing the children of St Helena? According to Charlton (1998), "The main ones are that children are in stable home, school and community situations. This is why the children on St. Helena appear to be immune to what they are watching."

television licences between the end of 1949 and the middle of 1952. As a result, television arrived in some parts of the United States 2 or 3 years before others. According to FBI crime statistics, the level of crime did not differ between those areas having and not having television. When television was introduced into new areas, it did not lead to an increase in violent crime.

Wood, Wong, and Chachere (1991) reviewed 28 laboratory and field studies concerned with the effects of media violence on aggression in children and in adolescents. With both types of studies, exposure to media violence led to more aggressive behaviour towards strangers, classmates, and friends, but the overall effects were weak and not statistically significant. The studies reviewed by Wood et al. showed that media violence has relatively immediate or short-term effects on children's aggressiveness.

Comstock and Paik (1991) reviewed more than 1000 findings on the effects of media violence. They argued that there were strong short-term effects, especially with respect to minor acts of aggression, but the long-term effects were weaker. They identified five factors tending to increase the effects of media violence on aggression:

Children are exposed to violent images at an early age and often incorporate them into their play. How well do they distinguish between a play scenario and how they behave in real life?

1. Violent behaviour is presented as being an efficient way to get what you want.
2. The person behaving violently is portrayed as similar to the viewer.
3. Violent behaviour is presented realistically rather than, for example, in cartoon form.
4. The suffering of the victims of violence is not shown.
5. The viewer is emotionally excited while watching the violent behaviour.

The second factor identified by Comstock and Paik (1991) suggests that observational learning or modelling helps to explain why media violence can produce aggression in children. There is also evidence that **cognitive priming** may be involved. Josephson (1987) showed Canadian boys a television programme involving violence in the form of a gun battle, in which the snipers communicated with each other using walkie-talkies. The other boys watched a non-violent programme about a motocross team. After they had watched the television programme, all the boys played floor hockey. Before the game started, the referee gave the boys instructions either by walkie-talkie or in a tape recording. The boys who had watched the violent programme and had received instructions by walkie-talkie were more aggressive during the hockey game than the boys who had watched the same programme but had received instructions by tape recording. Thus, the walkie-talkie acted as a cognitive primer or cue to aggression.

> **KEY TERM**
> **Cognitive priming:** a phenomenon in which the presentation of cues previously associated with aggression can cause someone to behave aggressively.

There has been a dramatic increase in the amount of time children spend playing video games in recent years. This is also true of some adults, with the author of this book having spent dozens of hours fruitlessly trying to match his children's performance on the video game Tetris. What has been of particular concern is that so many video games involve violence. Very young children often behave more aggressively after playing a violent video game, but the effects are generally much smaller in older children (Griffiths, 2000). However, Wiegman and van Schie (1998) found in Dutch children aged about 11 that those who preferred aggressive video games were more aggressive than those who did not. This was especially the case among boys, perhaps in part because four times as many boys as girls spent more than 30 minutes a day playing video games. The findings are hard to interpret, because it is possible that naturally aggressive boys are more attracted to violent video games.

Is it that aggressive children choose to play aggressive video games, or do the games make children aggressive?

## Evaluation

⊕ Media violence and playing violent video games can lead to short-term increases in children's aggression, but the effects are generally weak.

⊕ Observational learning and cognitive priming are two ways in which media violence leads to increased aggression.

⊖ Most studies have focused only on the short-term effects on behaviour of exposure to a single violent programme, and so are uninformative about the long-term effects of prolonged exposure to numerous violent programmes.

⊖ There is only a limited theoretical understanding of the reasons *why* media violence produces increased aggression.

---

### Observational learning

Of the hundreds of studies Bandura was responsible for, one group stands out above the others—the Bobo doll studies. He made a film of one of his students, a young woman, essentially beating up a Bobo doll. In case you don't know, a Bobo doll is an inflatable, egg-shape balloon creature with a weight in the bottom that makes it bob back up when you knock it down. Nowadays, it might have Darth Vader painted on it, but back then it was simply "Bobo" the clown.

The woman punched the clown, shouting "sockeroo!" She kicked it, sat on it, hit it with a little hammer, and so on, shouting various aggressive phrases. Bandura showed his film to groups of kindergartners who, as you might predict, liked it a lot. They then were let out to play. In the playroom, of course, were several observers with pens and clipboards in hand, a brand new Bobo doll, and a few little hammers.

And you might predict as well what the observers recorded: a lot of little kids beating the daylights out of the Bobo doll. They punched it and shouted "sockeroo", kicked it, sat on it, hit it with the little hammers, and so on. In other words, they imitated the young lady in the film, and quite precisely at that.

This might seem like a real nothing of an experiment at first, but consider: these children changed their behaviour without first being rewarded for approximations to that behaviour! And while that may not seem extraordinary to the average parent, teacher, or casual observer of children, it didn't fit so well with standard behaviouristic learning theory. Bandura called the phenomenon observational learning or modelling, and his theory is usually called social learning theory.

From http://www.ship.edu/~cgboeree/bandura.html

---

## Social learning theory

According to Bandura's social learning theory, aggressive behaviour is learned as a result of the child's particular experiences. According to Bandura (1973), "The specific forms that aggressive behaviour takes, the frequency with which it is displayed, and the specific targets selected for attack are largely determined by social learning factors."

According to Bandura's theory, observational learning or modelling is of great importance in producing aggressive behaviour. Observational learning involves imitating or copying the behaviour of others. Aggressive behaviour can also be acquired when the child's aggressive behaviour is reinforced or rewarded by getting its own way or by gaining attention.

### Evidence

Bandura, Ross, and Ross (1963) showed young children one of two films. One film showed a female adult model behaving aggressively towards a large Bobo doll. The other film showed the adult model behaving non-aggressively towards the doll. Those children who had seen the model behave aggressively were much more likely to attack the Bobo doll.

Bandura (1965) carried out another study on aggressive behaviour towards the Bobo doll (see Chapter 8). One group of children simply saw a film of an adult model kicking and punching the Bobo doll. A second group saw the same aggressive behaviour performed by the adult model, but this time the model was rewarded by another adult for his aggressive behaviour. A third group saw the same aggressive behaviour, but the model was punished by another adult.

Those children who had seen the model rewarded, and those who had seen the model neither rewarded nor punished, behaved much more aggressively towards the Bobo doll than did those who had seen the model punished. It could be argued that the children who had seen the model being punished remembered less about the model's behaviour than did the other groups of children. However, all three groups showed the same ability to reproduce the model's aggressive behaviour when rewarded for imitating it.

Evidence consistent with Bandura's approach was reported by Huesmann, Lagerspitz, and Eron (1984) and by Eron, Huesmann, and Zelli (1991). Huesmann et al. found that there was great similarity in aggressive behaviour across two generations when assessed at the same age for parents and their children. Eron et al. extended this finding, observing similarity of aggressive behaviour across three generations. Similarity of aggression across

A child attacks a Bobo doll.

generations may depend in part on genetic factors, but probably also involves observational learning.

## Evaluation

⊕ Much aggressive behaviour is learned, and observational learning or modelling is often involved.

⊕ Social learning theory helps to explain the precise forms of aggressive behaviour exhibited by individuals.

⊖ Bandura consistently failed to distinguish between real aggression and playfighting, and much of the aggressive behaviour observed by Bandura was only playfighting (Durkin, 1995).

⊖ Bandura over-estimated the extent to which children imitate the behaviour of models. Children readily imitate aggressive behaviour towards a doll, but are much less likely to imitate aggressive behaviour towards another child.

⊖ The Bobo doll has a weighted base and so bounces back up when knocked down. This gives it a novelty value. Cumberbatch (1990) reported that children who were unfamiliar with the doll were five times more likely to imitate aggressive behaviour against it than children who had played with it before.

⊖ Bandura focused on *external* or environmental factors producing aggressive behaviour, but de-emphasised the *internal factors* (e.g., heredity, hormonal factors) that are also involved.

# Biological approach

According to the biological approach, some individuals are genetically more predisposed than others to high levels of aggressiveness. It has also been argued that the tendency for males to be more aggressive than females can be attributed to biological factors. For example, males have higher levels of the sex hormone testosterone, and this may help to explain their greater aggressiveness.

> **KEY TERM**
> **Anti-social behaviour:**
> behaviour that harms or injures another person.

## Evidence

The findings from twin and adoption studies indicate that genetic factors play a role in producing individual differences in aggression and in **anti-social behaviour**. For example, Rhee and Waldman (2002) carried out a meta-analysis of 51 twin and adoption studies investigating anti-social behaviour (e.g., anti-social personality disorder, aggressive behaviour, delinquency). They found that 41% of the variability in anti-social behaviour was due to genetic factors, 43% was due to non-shared environmental influences (influences differing among the children within a family), and 16% was due to shared environmental influences. The figures were very similar for males and females, and indicate that anti-social behaviour is fairly strongly influenced by genetic factors in both sexes. The impact of genetic factors was similar in children, adolescents, and adults. However, shared environmental influences decreased with age, whereas non-shared environmental influences increased.

Eley, Lichtenstein, and Stevenson (1999) found in a study of Swedish and British identical and fraternal twins that it may be important to distinguish between aggressive behaviour (e.g., fighting, bullying) and non-aggressive anti-social behaviour (e.g., theft, truancy). Their key finding was

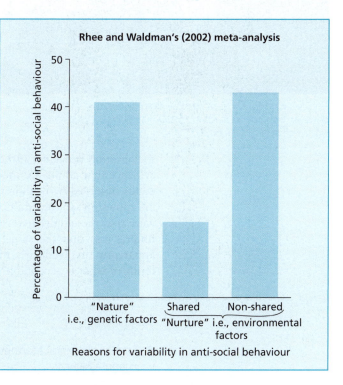

**Rhee and Waldman's (2002) meta-analysis**

Percentage of variability in anti-social behaviour

"Nature" i.e., genetic factors — "Nurture" i.e., environmental factors — Shared — Non-shared

Reasons for variability in anti-social behaviour

that aggressive anti-social behaviour is influenced far more by genetic factors than is non-aggressive anti-social behaviour.

Miles and Carey (1997) carried out a meta-analysis of studies concerned with the impact of genetic factors on individual differences in aggression. They came to the following conclusion: "There was a strong overall genetic effect that may account for up to 50% of the variance in aggression" (p. 207). However, this conclusion applied only to studies based on self-report data and on parental ratings. When aggression in children was assessed by observational ratings of laboratory behaviour, there was no evidence that genetic factors influenced individual differences in aggression. As Miles and Carey (p. 207) concluded, "Given that almost all substantive conclusions about the genetics of personality have been drawn from self or parental reports, this last finding has obvious and important implications for … aggression research."

*What kinds of biases could result from a) self-report, b) parental ratings, and c) observational ratings of aggression?*

The assumption that males are more aggressive than females has received only limited support. Eagly and Steffen (1986) carried out a meta-analysis based on numerous relevant studies on gender differences. There was only a small overall tendency for males to be more aggressive than females. Sex differences were greater with respect to physical aggression than verbal and other psychological forms of aggression. Why are males more aggressive than females? According to Eagly and Steffen, women feel more guilty and anxious about behaving aggressively, and they are also more concerned about possible dangers to themselves if they behave aggressively.

Most studies reviewed by Eagly and Steffen (1986) were based on adolescent or adult participants. Tieger (1980) reviewed studies that considered developmental trends in aggression, and found that there was very little evidence of sex differences in aggression below the age of 5.

Studies have shown boys to be more physically aggressive than girls. However, Bjorkqvist et al. (1992) found that girls show more indirect aggression than boys.

We have seen that there is some evidence that men are more aggressive than women. However, there is an important exception so far as indirect aggression is concerned. Bjorkqvist, Lagerspetz, and Kaukiainen (1992) studied physical aggression, verbal aggression, and indirect aggression (e.g., gossiping, writing unkind notes, spreading false stories) in adolescent boys and girls. The boys displayed much more physical aggression than the girls, but the girls showed significantly more indirect aggression than the boys.

As has already been mentioned, males have higher levels of the sex hormone testosterone, and this hormone may be related to aggressiveness. For example, adolescent boys who are aggressive and anti-social in their behaviour have especially high levels of testosterone (Olweus, 1985). However, such evidence is correlational in nature, which makes the findings hard to interpret. High testosterone levels may lead to aggression, but it is also possible that aggression produces high testosterone levels.

Any sex differences in aggression may depend on socialisation processes rather than biological factors. Condry and Ross (1985) obtained evidence that adults are more tolerant of aggressive behaviour in boys than in girls. The adults observed two children playing in a rough way in the snow. The children were wearing snowsuits, so the adults could not tell whether they were boys or girls. Half the adults were told the children were boys, and the other half were told they were girls. The key finding was that the same behaviour was perceived as being more aggressive when it apparently involved girls than when it involved boys. Thus, adults are more lenient in terms of what is acceptable behaviour with boys than with girls.

## Evaluation

➕ Twin studies indicate that genetic factors play a role in producing individual differences in aggressiveness.

➕ Testosterone levels are associated with level of aggression, but it is not clear that the former causes the latter.
➖ Sex differences in aggression are generally smaller than expected by advocates of the biological approach.
➖ The complex ways in which biological factors interact with social and other environmental factors are de-emphasised.

## Coercive family processes

There have been numerous studies in which aspects of parental behaviour have been correlated with the aggressiveness of their children. For example, very aggressive children have parents who administer physical punishment frequently and for unpredictable reasons (Eron & Huesmann, 1984), and aggressive adolescent boys often have mothers who are very tolerant of aggressive behaviour in their sons (Olweus, 1980). The problem with such correlational studies is that we cannot be confident it is the parental behaviour *causing* the aggressive behaviour in their children. For example, children who are naturally aggressive may lead their parents to administer physical punishment, rather than parental punitiveness causing aggression in the children. Evidence that that is part of the story was reported by O'Connor, Deater-Deckard, Fulker, Rutter, and Plomin (1998; see Chapter 17). They carried out a study on adopted children. Some of these children had biological mothers with a history of anti-social behaviour, and so the children were regarded as being at genetic risk. These children received more negative control (e.g., hostility) from their adoptive parents, presumably because their genetic inheritance led them to behave more aggressively than children not at genetic risk.

Patterson (1982) argued that we need to study in detail the dynamics of family interactions to understand more fully why some children are much more aggressive than others. At a theoretical level, Patterson claimed that what is important is the functioning of the family as a whole rather than merely the behaviour of the child or parents. More specifically, Patterson argued there is mutual provocation in families with a highly aggressive child. The behaviour of the parents and of the child has what Patterson called a coercive quality about it, because it leads directly to increased aggression by other members of the family.

### Evidence

Patterson (1982) and Patterson et al. (1989) carried out research in which highly aggressive children were observed in their homes in interaction with other family members. The interaction patterns in such families were compared with those in the families of non-aggressive children. Patterson and Patterson et al. found there was a typical pattern of escalating aggression in the families of aggressive children. First of all, the child behaves aggressively (e.g., he refuses to do what his mother asks him to do). Second, the mother responds aggressively (e.g., she shouts angrily at her son). Third, the child reacts in a more aggressive and hostile way (e.g., he shouts back loudly at his mother). Fourth, the mother responds more aggressively than before (e.g., she hits her son). The pattern of behaviour we have just described was termed by Patterson (1982) a **coercive cycle**: A small increase in aggression by the parent or the child is matched or exceeded by the aggression of the other person.

According to Patterson et al. (1989), most aggressive behaviour displayed by parents and their children in aggressive families can be regarded as attempts to stop the other person from being aggressive to them. In such families, however, these attempts often serve to provoke further aggression. Children who have developed this type of aggressive approach to difficult situations are often rejected by their peers, and thus suffer severe problems in social adjustment.

Patterson et al. (1989) also reported that the parents in aggressive families rarely provided their children with affection or even with encouragement. This lack of affection may lead aggressive boys to behave aggressively to attract attention from their parents.

**KEY TERM**

**Coercive cycle:** a pattern of behaviour in which aggressive behaviour by one person within a family (e.g., a child) produces an aggressive response, and so on.

## *Evaluation*

⊕ Coercive cycles frequently occur in aggressive families.
⊕ It is valuable to focus on the role of family dynamics in producing aggressive children.
⊖ The factors responsible for the development of coercive cycles in the first place remain unclear.
⊖ Genetic factors are probably of importance in explaining why some families have aggressive parents and aggressive children (e.g., McGue, Brown, & Lykken, 1992).

## Cultural differences

Most research on the development of anti-social behaviour has been carried out in Western cultures. However, Chen, Greenberger, Lester, Dong, and Guo (1998) investigated misconduct (e.g., cheating in a test, fighting, destroying property on purpose) among 13- and 14-year-old European Americans, Chinese Americans, and Chinese individuals in Taipei, and Beijing. The levels of self-reported misconduct were comparable in all four groups, with males having higher levels of misconduct than females in every group. The amount of misconduct shown by European and Chinese Americans was much more influenced by peer approval or disapproval than was the case for the Chinese adolescents, perhaps because American adolescents spend much more time with peers than do Chinese ones.

Feldman et al. (1991) studied older adolescents in Hong Kong, Australia, and America. They found that the levels of misconduct were lower in Chinese adolescents than in Australian and American adolescents. How can we explain the differences in findings between this study and that of Chen et al. (1998)? Peer approval of misconduct is responsible for much of the misconduct shown by adolescents in Western cultures. However, younger Western adolescents are more influenced than older adolescents by their families, and it may well be waning family influences which help to produce high levels of misconduct in older Western adolescents.

Genta et al. (1996) studied bullying among Italian children aged between 8 and 14, and related their findings to those obtained in Norway, Spain, Japan, and England. In all of these cultures, boys were responsible for most of the bullying, and older children were less likely to be bullied than younger ones. There was one significant cultural difference: There was more bullying in Italy than in the other four cultures.

*From what you know about these cultures, can you suggest why bullying might be more common in Italy?*

## MORAL DEVELOPMENT

What is meant by the term "morality"? According to Shaffer (1993), **morality** implies "a set of principles or ideals that help the individual to distinguish right from wrong and to act on this distinction". Morality is important because society cannot function effectively unless there some agreement on what is right and wrong. Of course, there are moral and ethical issues (e.g., animal experiments) on which members of a given society have very different views. However, if there were controversy on all major moral issues, society would become chaotic. We will be concerned with the changes in moral development during the course of childhood.

Human morality has three components:

1. *The cognitive component.* This is concerned with how we think about moral issues, and make decisions about what is right and wrong.
2. *The emotional component.* This is concerned with the feelings (e.g., guilt) associated with moral thoughts and behaviour.
3. *The behavioural component.* This is concerned with how we behave. It includes the extent to which we lie, steal, cheat, or behave honourably.

Why should we distinguish among these components? First, there are often significant differences between components. For example, we may know at the cognitive level it is wrong to cheat, but we may still cheat at the behavioural level. Some people lead blameless lives (behavioural component), but still feel guilty (emotional component). Second, the distinction among different moral components is useful in comparing theories of moral development. Freud emphasised the emotional component, Piaget and Kohlberg focused on the cognitive component, and social learning theorists concentrated on the behavioural component.

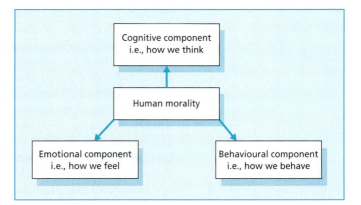

## Freudian theory and beyond

Sigmund Freud (1856–1939) argued that the human mind consists of three parts: the id, ego, and superego (see Chapter 22). The id deals with motivational forces (e.g., the sexual instinct); the ego is concerned with conscious thinking; and the superego is concerned with moral issues. The superego is divided into the conscience and the ego-ideal. Our conscience makes us feel guilty or ashamed when we have behaved badly, whereas our ego-ideal makes us feel proud when we have behaved well in the face of temptation.

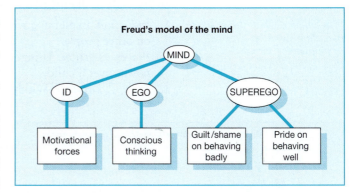

Freud suggested that the superego develops at the age of 5 or 6. Boys develop sexual desires for their mother, leading to an intense rivalry with their father. This is known as the **Oedipus complex**. It makes boys feel very fearful, because they are much weaker than their father. This situation is resolved through the process of **identification**, in which boys imitate or copy their father's beliefs and behaviour. During the identification process, boys adopt their father's moral standards, and this leads to the formation of the superego. According to Freud, the superego is "the heir of the Oedipus complex".

Freud argued that a similar process occurs in girls at about the same age. They develop an **Electra complex** based on their desires for their father. This complex is resolved by girls through identification with their mother and through adopting her moral standards. Freud claimed girls do not identify with their mother as strongly as boys identify with their father, and so girls develop weaker superegos than boys. This is an example of gender bias, an issue discussed later. However, Freud admitted that, "the majority of men are far behind the masculine ideal [in terms of superego strength]".

### Evidence

The main evidence available to Freud consisted of his patients' accounts of their childhood. Such evidence is weak because of its reliance on patients' fallible memories. Another problem was identified by Meadows (1986, p. 162): "There could be no refuting evidence since a demonstration that a person did not experience an Oedipus complex, feel penis-envy, etc., might be taken as evidence for the perfect repression [motivated forgetting] of the person's Oedipus complex, penis-envy, etc."

Freud argued that fear of the same-sexed parent influenced the development of the superego. Thus, parents who are aggressive and administer a lot of punishment might be expected to have children with strong superegos. In fact, the opposite is the case. Parents who make the most use of spanking and other forms of punishment tend to have children who behave badly and who experience little guilt or shame (Hoffman, 1988).

Freud's hypothesis that girls have weaker superegos than boys has been disproved. Hoffman (1975) discussed studies in which the behaviour of children on their own was assessed to see whether they did what they had been told not to do. There was no difference between boys and girls in most of the studies. When there was a sex difference, it was the girls (rather than the boys) who were better at resisting temptation. However, ability to resist temptation may not be a good measure of superego strength. Cross-cultural studies have confirmed the findings of Hoffman. Snarey (1985) reviewed 17 studies from 15 cultures around the world. Sex differences in moral development were found in only three of those studies.

What about Freud's assumptions that the conscience or superego develops at about the age of 5 or 6 and that it has a strong influence on children's behaviour? Kochanska, De Vet, Goldman, Murray, and Putnam (1994) studied children aged between 26 and 41 months. Some of these children showed evidence of a conscience (e.g., appeared guilty after transgressing, confessed to wrongdoing), in spite of being much younger than 5 years old. Those children with a conscience transgressed less than those without in an experimental situation, thus supporting Freud's view that the possession of a conscience is associated with more moral behaviour.

In spite of the problems with Freud's theory, his assumption that children's moral development depends very much on their parents has received support. Hoffman (1970) identified three major styles used by parents:

*Why might each of these parenting styles be effective in influencing moral development? Which do you expect to be the most effective?*

1. *Induction*. Explaining why a given action is wrong, with special emphasis on its effects on other people.
2. *Power assertion*. Using spankings, removal of privileges, and harsh words to exert power over a child.
3. *Love withdrawal*. Withholding attention or love when a child behaves badly.

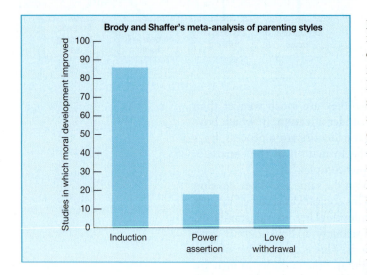

**Brody and Shaffer's meta-analysis of parenting styles**

Brody and Shaffer (1982) reviewed studies in which parental style influenced moral development. Induction improved moral development in 86% of those studies. In contrast, power assertion improved moral development in only 18%, and love withdrawal in 42%. Power assertion had a negative effect on moral development in 82% of the studies, and so is a very ineffective parenting style. Power assertion often produces children who are aggressive and do not care about others (Zahn-Waxler et al., 1979). Physical punishment forms an important part of the power assertion approach. Many people disapprove of physical punishment on principle, but its effects are not always negative. Larzelere (2000) reviewed the literature on physical punishment applied to children, and concluded that it was sometimes reasonably effective. However, for physical punishment to be effective, it has to be not severe, not used when the parent is angry, accompanied by reasoning, and limited to children between the ages of 2 and 6.

Induction is an effective parenting style because it provides the child with useful information that helps the development of moral reasoning. It also encourages children to think about other people. Considering the needs and emotions of others is of importance if moral development is to occur.

The findings tell us there is an association between parental use of induction and good moral development. The main reason for this association is probably that inductive parenting benefits children's moral development, but that may not be the whole story. Children who are well-behaved are more likely to be treated in a reasonable, inductive way by their parents. In contrast, children who are badly behaved and aggressive may cause their parents to use power assertion. Thus, parenting style affects children's behaviour, but children's behaviour also affects parenting style.

## Evaluation

➕ Freud put forward the first detailed theory of moral development.
➕ Freud's basic assumptions that parents have a major influence on the moral development of their children, and that many moral values are acquired in the early years of life, are correct.

⊕ The growth of conscience in young children plays an important role in moral development.

⊖ Freud exaggerated the role of the same-sexed parent in the development of children's morality. The other-sexed parent and other children also generally play an important role (Shaffer, 1993).

⊖ The conscience seems to develop earlier than was assumed by Freud (Kochanska et al., 1994).

⊖ Freud attached too much weight to emotional factors in morality and not enough to cognitive processes.

⊖ Freud claimed that children make more dramatic progress in moral development at about the age of 5 or 6 than later in childhood or adolescence. In fact, large changes in moral reasoning occur between the ages of 10 and 16 (e.g., Colby, Kohlberg, Gibbs, & Lieberman, 1983).

## Freud's methods

The main source of evidence used by Freud was adults' memories of their childhood. However, not only is this evidence prone to distortion by the person who is remembering, it also cannot be proved or disproved. Freud did not see child patients, but dealt with parents, sometimes only through letters, which has led to speculation about his interpretations of particular behaviours. Freud claimed that the Oedipus and Electra complexes were unconscious phases that a child passed through on his or her way to identifying with the same-sex parent. However, if these phases are unconscious we have no way of proving that they did in fact happen, except indirectly through interpretations of children's behaviour.

A more general criticism of the psychodynamic approach stems from the way in which the theories are formulated. Freud's theory tends to "work backwards", for example, the result leads to the formation of a hypothesis. Freud did not so much predict behaviour as analyse it once it had happened. Finally, the period in which Freud was working must be considered. His patients mostly came from middle-class families, which at the time were ruled by strict disciplinarian regimes. At that point in history, the family would have had the most influence on the developing child. However, today outside pressures such as peer groups, school, and even television may prove as influential as the family in a child's development.

## Piaget's cognitive-developmental theory

According to Jean Piaget (1896–1980), children's thinking goes through a series of stages (see Chapter 15). The early stages focus on what the child can see and hear, whereas the later stages involve the ability to think in an abstract way about possible events that may never happen. Piaget argued that children's moral reasoning also proceeds through a number of different stages.

Piaget developed his ideas about moral reasoning by playing marbles with children of different ages. He was interested in seeing how well they understood the rules of the game, how important they thought it was to obey those rules, and so on. His observations led him to propose the following stages of moral development:

1. *Pre-moral period* (0–5 years). Children in this stage have very little understanding of rules or other aspects of morality.

2. *Stage of moral realism or heteronomous morality* (heteronomous means "subject to externally imposed rules") (5–10 years). Children at this stage are rather rigid in their thinking—they believe rules must be obeyed no matter what the circumstances (e.g., it's wrong to tell a lie even if it will spare someone's feelings). Children at this stage think rules are made by important other people (e.g., parents), and that how bad an action is stems from its consequences rather than the actor's intentions. There are two other key features of children's moral reasoning at this stage. First, they believe in **expiatory punishment**: The naughtier the behaviour, the greater should be the punishment. However, there is no idea that the punishment should fit the crime. For example, a child who drops a freshly baked cake on the floor should be spanked rather than having to help to bake another cake. Second, children between the ages of 5 and 10 strongly favour the notion of fairness. This leads them to believe in *immanent justice*, which is the idea that naughty behaviour will always be punished in some way.

3. *Stage of moral relativism or autonomous morality* (10 years upwards). Children at this stage think more flexibly about moral issues. They understand that moral rules evolve from human relationships, and that people differ in their standards of morality. They also understand that most rules of morality can be broken sometimes. If a violent man with a gun demands to be told where your mother is, it is perfectly acceptable to tell a lie, and say you do not know. There are other major differences from the previous stage. First, the child now thinks that the wrongness of an action depends far more on the individual's intentions than on the consequences of his/her behaviour. Second, children in this stage believe in **reciprocal punishment** rather than expiatory punishment. Thus, the punishment should fit the crime. Third, children in this stage have learned that people often behave wrongly but manage to avoid punishment. Thus, they no longer believe in immanent justice.

### KEY TERMS

**Expiatory punishment:** the view that the amount of punishment should match the badness of behaviour, but without the idea that the form of punishment should fit the crime.

**Reciprocal punishment:** the view that the form of punishment should fit the crime.

| PIAGET'S STAGES OF MORAL DEVELOPMENT | | |
|---|---|---|
| **Pre-moral** | **Moral realism (Heteronomous morality)** | **Moral relativism (Autonomous morality)** |
| 0–5 years old | 5–10 years old | 10 years upwards |
| Little understanding of rules and other aspects | Rigid thinking: rules must be obeyed<br>Actions are judged by their consequences | Development of flexibility in moral issues<br>Understanding that people differ in moral standards. Rules can be broken and wrong behaviour is not always punished |
| | Belief in:<br>● Expiatory punishment<br>● Immanent justice | Belief in:<br>● Reciprocal punishment |

Why does moral reasoning change during childhood? According to Piaget, two main factors are involved. First, young children are egocentric in their thinking, seeing the world only from their own point of view. At about the age of 7, they become less egocentric. Their growing awareness that other people have different points of view leads to more mature moral reasoning. Second, older children develop flexible ideas of morality because they are exposed to the different views of other children of the same age. This leads them to question their own values. In contrast, most younger children have rather rigid ideas of morality. What counts as good or bad behaviour is determined very much by the reactions of their parents.

At a more general level, Piaget argued that disequilibrium provides the motivational force triggering developments in moral reasoning. Children become aware that there are inconsistencies in their reasoning, and this leads them to change their reasoning to restore equilibrium.

## Evidence

Children in most Western societies go through Piaget's stages of moral development in the order specified by Piaget. There is also evidence to support many of the details of the theory. For example, Piaget argued that children in the stage of moral realism judge actions by their consequences rather than by the actor's intentions. Piaget (1932) obtained evidence for this. Children in this stage were told about a boy called John who opened a door, and by so doing broke 15 cups on the other side of the door. They were also told about Henry, who broke one cup while trying to reach some jam. Even though John had no idea there were any cups there, he was still regarded as being naughtier than Henry because he broke more cups.

Serious criticisms have been made of Piaget's empirical studies on moral development. For example, the moral problems given to the children often made substantial demands on their memory, and the problems themselves were rather abstract and removed from the social realities of everyday life. The validity of some of these criticisms can be seen if we consider Dunn's (1987) attempts to test Piaget's claim that children up to the age of about 5 have essentially no understanding of rules or moral reasoning. She found through naturalistic observation of children that they acquire aspects of moral reasoning considerably earlier than appeared to be the case in Piaget's studies. For example, 2-year-old children played games with older siblings while taking account of the rules and roles involved. Two-year-olds only showed an ability to play games properly with older siblings rather than with other children or their parents. Why was this? Young children are often motivated to

*What are the limitations of naturalistic observation when studying moral reasoning?*

match up to the achievements of an older sibling, and the older sibling may be especially good at communicating with a younger sibling.

Dunn (1987) also found that 2-year-olds showed a generally good awareness that they were transgressing rules. For example, several children laughed while doing a forbidden action in a joking way in the presence of their mothers, and one child went behind a sofa to pick her nose after she had been forbidden to do it. In sum, it appears that young children within the emotionally significant family environment can reveal a much greater ability to engage in moral reasoning than is apparent when they confront artificial moral problems.

Piaget also underestimated the ability of children in the stage of moral realism to take account of the actor's intentions. Costanzo, Coie, Grumet, and Famill (1973) used stories in which the characters had good or bad intentions, and in which the outcomes were positive or negative. As Piaget had found, young children almost always ignored the actor's intentions when the consequences were negative. However, they were as likely as older children to take account of the actor's intentions when the consequences were positive.

Piaget argued that children at the stage of moral realism follow uncritically the rules of parents and other authority figures. However, this only applies to certain parental rules, such as those about honesty and stealing. They are much less willing to allow their parents to make and enforce rules about who they may have as their friends or what they should do in their free time (Shaffer, 1993).

We have seen that Piaget greatly *underestimated* the development of moral reasoning in young children. However, he *overestimated* moral reasoning in older children, because he assumed that 10- and 11-year-old children have reached an adult level of moral reasoning. For example, Colby et al. (1983), in a study discussed in more detail shortly, found large changes in moral thinking between the ages of 10 and 16.

## Evaluation

➕ Piaget was right that there are reasonably close links between cognitive development in general and moral development in particular.

➕ Most children in Western societies show the shift from moral realism to moral relativism predicted by Piaget.

➕ Piaget developed research in the area of moral development by devising short stories to illustrate moral points.

➖ Naturalistic observation has failed to support several of Piaget's findings based on moral problems (Dunn, 1987).

➖ Young children have more complex ideas about morality than assumed by Piaget, and their moral thinking is more advanced than claimed by Piaget.

➖ Piaget exaggerated the level of moral reasoning attained by children of 10 and 11 (Colby et al., 1983).

➖ Piaget failed to obtain clear evidence that developments in moral reasoning occur as a result of disequilibrium or inconsistencies in children's thinking about moral issues.

➖ Piaget focused on children's views concerning moral issues, and de-emphasised the behavioural and emotional components of morality.

---

**Piaget's moral stories**

Piaget used moral stories to investigate what moral decisions children reached. An example is given below with a sample interview with a child.

**STORY 1**: A little boy who is called John is in his room. He is called to dinner. He goes into the dining room. But behind the door there was a chair, and on the chair there was a tray with 15 cups on it. John couldn't have known that there was all this behind the door. He goes in, the door knocks against the tray, "bang" to the 15 cups and they all get broken!

**STORY 2**: Once there was a little boy whose name was Henry. One day when his mother was out he tried to get some jam out of the cupboard. He climbed up on a chair and stretched out his arm. But the jam was too high up and he couldn't reach it and have any. But while he was trying to get it, he knocked over a cup. The cup fell down and broke.

Below is a characteristic response for a child in the stage of moral realism:

*Questioner:* "What did the first boy do?"
*Child:* "He broke 15 cups."
*Questioner:* "And the second one?"
*Child:* "He broke a cup by moving roughly."
*Questioner:* "Is one of the boys naughtier than the other?"
*Child:* "The first one is because he knocked over 15 cups."
*Questioner:* "If you were the daddy, which one would you punish most?"
*Child:* "The one who broke 15 cups."
*Questioner:* "Why did he break them?"
*Child:* "The door shut too hard and knocked them over. He didn't do it on purpose."
*Questioner:* "And why did the other boy break a cup?"
*Child:* "Because he was clumsy. When he was getting the jam the cup fell down."
*Questioner:* "Why did he want to get the jam?"
*Child:* "Because he was alone. Because the mother wasn't there."

Piaget (1932), pp. 122 and 129

# Kohlberg's cognitive-developmental theory

Lawrence Kohlberg (1927–1987) agreed with Piaget that we need to focus on children's cognitive structures to understand how they think about moral issues. However, Kohlberg's

## Kohlberg: Moral dilemmas

The main experimental approach used by Kohlberg involved presenting his participants with a series of moral dilemmas. Each dilemma required them to decide whether it is preferable to uphold some law or other moral principle or to reject the moral principle in favour of some basic human need. To clarify what Kohlberg (e.g., 1963) did, we will consider one of his moral dilemmas:

### KEY STUDY EVALUATION—Kohlberg

Kohlberg's theory addresses some of the problems of Piaget's approach, in that it is more flexible and less tied to specific age-based stages of development. Meta-analyses have shown that the six stages of Kohlberg's theoretical framework apply across most cultures, and it is almost universally the case that individuals work through the various stages in the same order. However, individual differences in experience or cultural differences may affect the speed with which a person moves through the stages. For example, in some cultures children can work, be married, or be regarded as full members of adult society at much younger ages than Western children. It is possible that these individuals move through Kohlberg's stages much earlier than Western children do. In addition, some Western children's lives do not conform to the stereotypical well-balanced family background with a strong moral sense of right and wrong that seems to lie behind some of Kohlberg's stages. This may also have a profound effect on a child's moral development.

*In Europe, a woman was dying from cancer. One drug might save her, a form of radium that a druggist in the same town had recently discovered. The druggist was charging 2,000 dollars, ten times what the drug cost him to make. The sick woman's husband, Heinz, went to everyone he knew to borrow the money, but he could only get together about half of what it cost. He told the druggist that his wife was dying and asked him to sell it cheaper or let him pay later. But the druggist said "No". The husband got desperate and broke into the man's store to steal the drug for his wife.*

The moral principle in this dilemma is that stealing is wrong. However, it was the good motive of wanting to help his sick wife that led Heinz to steal the drug. It is precisely because there are powerful arguments for and against stealing the drug that there is a moral dilemma.

Kohlberg used evidence from such moral dilemmas to develop his theory. He agreed with Piaget that all children follow the same sequence of stages during moral development. However, Kohlberg's three levels of moral development (with two stages at each level) differ from Piaget's:

*Level 1: Pre-conventional morality.* At this level, what is regarded as right and wrong is determined by the rewards or punishments that are likely to follow, rather than by thinking about moral issues. Stage 1 of this level is based on a *punishment-and-obedience orientation*. Stealing is wrong because it involves disobeying authority, and leads to punishment. Stage 2 of this level is based on the notion that the right way to behave is the way that is rewarded. There is more attention to the needs of other people than in Stage 1, but mainly on the basis that if you help other people, then they will help you.

*Level 2: Conventional morality.* The greatest difference between Level 1 and Level 2 is that the views and needs of other people are much more important at Level 2 than at Level 1. At this level, people are very concerned to have the approval of others for their actions, and to avoid being blamed by them for behaving wrongly. At Stage 3, the emphasis is on having good intentions, and on behaving in ways that conform to most people's views of good behaviour. At Stage 4, children believe it is important to do one's duty, and to obey the laws or rules of those in authority.

*Level 3: Post-conventional or principled morality.* Those at the highest level of post-conventional or principled morality recognise that the laws or rules of authority figures should sometimes be broken. Abstract notions about justice and the need to treat other people with respect can override the need to obey laws and rules. At Stage 5, there is a growing recognition that what is morally right may differ from what is legally right. Finally, at Stage 6, the individual has developed his/her own principles of conscience. The individual takes into account the likely views of everyone who will be affected by a moral decision. Kohlberg (1981) described this as a kind of "moral musical chairs". In practice, it is very rare for anyone to operate most of the time at Stage 6.

### Discussion points

1. How adequate do you find Kohlberg's use of moral dilemmas to study moral development?
2. What do you think of Kohlberg's stage-based approach to moral development?

*Do you think that people from individualistic and collectivistic cultures are likely to feel differently about conventional and post-conventional morality?*

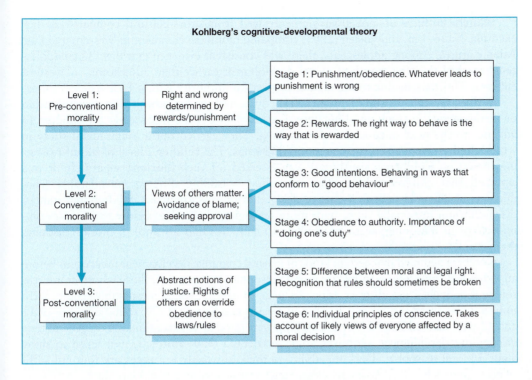

theory differs in several ways from that of Piaget. For example, Kohlberg (e.g., 1976) believed that moral reasoning often continues to develop through adolescence and early adulthood.

Why are there changes in children's moral reasoning in the course of development? Kohlberg (e.g., 1976) agreed with Piaget that disequilibrium (inconsistency among an individual's views) provides the motivational force which leads to developments in moral reasoning.

## Evidence

Kohlberg assumed that all children follow the same sequence of moral stages. The best way of testing this assumption is to carry out a longitudinal (long-term) study to see how children's moral reasoning changes over time. Colby et al. (1983) conducted a 20-year study of 58 American males. There was a substantial drop in Stage 1 and Stage 2 moral reasoning between the ages of 10 and 16, with a compensatory increase in Stage 3 and Stage 4 moral reasoning occurring during the same time period (see the figure below). Most impressively for Kohlberg's theory, all the participants progressed through the moral stages in exactly the predicted sequence. More worryingly for the theory, only about 10% of individuals in their 30s showed Stage 5 moral reasoning, and there was practically no evidence of Stage 6 reasoning at all.

Snarey (1985) reviewed 44 studies from 27 cultures. People in nearly all cultures went through the first four stages of moral development identified by Kohlberg in the same order and at about the same time. There was little evidence of people omitting any stage of moral development or returning to an earlier stage. However, there was more evidence of Stage 5 reasoning in Western cultures than in most rural or village cultures. According to Snarey, this does *not* mean that the moral reasoning of those living in Western cultures is superior to that of those living in other cultures. Instead, it reflects the individualistic emphasis of most Western cultures; for example, the greater value attached to human life.

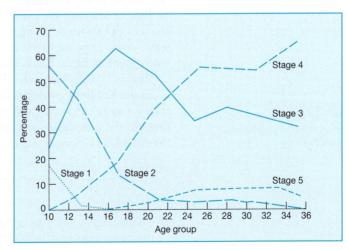

Western cultures do not always emerge well from cross-cultural comparisons. For example, Naito, Lin, and Gielen (2001) compared moral development in Western and East Asian cultures. Among adolescents, there was consistent evidence that East Asian adolescents reached the later stages of moral development earlier than adolescents in Western cultures. This may be due to the greater respect for authority within East Asian cultures.

Walker, Gustafson, and Hennig (2001) considered the hypothesis that disequilibrium or inconsistency in thinking about moral issues provides the motivation for children to advance to the next stage of moral reasoning. They carried out a longitudinal study in which children were given various moral dilemmas. The children's level of moral reasoning (based on Kohlberg's six stages) was assessed for each dilemma separately. It was assumed that children whose stage of moral reasoning differed considerably from dilemma to dilemma were in a state of disequilibrium. As predicted, children in a state of disequilibrium (especially those with more reasoning above than below their most common stage of reasoning) were most likely to show a rapid advance in moral reasoning thereafter.

Kohlberg assumed that certain kinds of general cognitive development must occur before an individual can progress in his/her moral reasoning. For example, those whose moral reasoning is at Stage 5 use abstract principles (e.g., of justice), which presumably require them to be good at abstract thinking. Tomlinson-Keasey and Keasey (1974) found that girls of 11 and 12 who showed Stage 5 moral reasoning were good at abstract thinking on general tests of cognitive development. However, some girls could think abstractly, but failed to show Stage 5 moral reasoning. Thus, the ability to think abstractly is a necessary (but not sufficient) requirement for someone to attain Stage 5 of post-conventional morality.

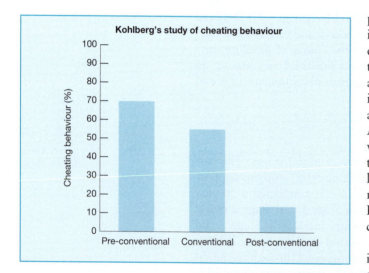

**Kohlberg's study of cheating behaviour**

Cheating behaviour (%)

Pre-conventional    Conventional    Post-conventional

Individuals' judgements on moral dilemmas may not predict their behaviour in real-life situations. The evidence is somewhat inconsistent. Santrock (1975) found that children's level of moral reasoning did not predict whether they would cheat. However, there is more evidence among adults that the stage of moral reasoning can predict behaviour. Kohlberg (1975) compared cheating behaviour among students at different levels of moral reasoning. About 70% of the students at the pre-conventional level were found to cheat, compared to only 15% of those at the post-conventional level. Students at the conventional level were intermediate (55%). Kutnick and Brees (1982) reviewed the evidence on the relationship between Kohlberg's stages of moral reasoning and behaviour, and concluded the relationship is generally not close.

Cross-cultural studies indicate there is more diversity in moral reasoning than was suggested by Kohlberg. For example, Shweder (1990) compared Hindus in India with Americans living in Chicago. After the death of a relative, Hindus regard eating chicken or fish, or cutting one's hair, as serious transgressions, because they would reduce the chances of salvation. None of these acts was regarded as immoral by Americans. In contrast, many children living in Chicago regarded sexual inequality as an important moral issue, much more so than children living in India.

Isawa (1992) compared the reasoning used by Japanese and American people when given the Kohlberg problem about a man stealing a drug for his wife who has cancer. The stage of moral reasoning was the same in both groups. However, the Japanese participants thought the man should not steal the drug so as to make his life cleaner and purer, whereas the Americans thought the man should steal the drug to prolong his wife's life.

*Why is it likely that moral reasoning and behaviour may differ?*

## Evaluation

➕ Children in virtually all cultures work through the various stages of moral reasoning in the order specified by Kohlberg.

⊕ Kohlberg's theory has the advantage over Piaget's that it provides a more detailed and accurate account of moral development.

⊕ Disequilibrium seems to motivate children's developments in moral reasoning (e.g., Walker et al., 2001).

⊖ Most people do not seem to develop beyond Stage 4 (Colby et al., 1983; Snarey, 1985).

⊖ It is hard to distinguish clearly between Stage 5 and Stage 6 moral reasoning (Colby et al., 1983).

⊖ Kohlberg focused on moral judgements made in response to artificial dilemmas rather than on actual moral behaviour, but such judgements typically fail to predict behaviour accurately (Kutnick & Brees, 1986).

⊖ Kohlberg did not consider the emotional component of morality in any detail. For example, the development of emotions such as shame and guilt is important within moral development (see Eisenberg, 2000, for a review).

⊖ Kohlberg paid insufficient attention to differences in moral reasoning from one culture to another.

## Gilligan's theory

Carol Gilligan (1977, 1982) disliked what she regarded as the sexist bias of Kohlberg. Kohlberg initially based his theory on interviews with male participants, so bias may have been introduced. In addition, Kohlberg reported that most women were at Stage 3 of moral development, whereas men were at Stage 4.

Gilligan (1982) argued that boys develop the **morality of justice**, in which they focus on the use of laws and moral principles. In contrast, girls develop the **morality of care**, in which their main focus is on human well-being and compassion for others. According to Gilligan, Kohlberg showed sexist bias by regarding the morality of justice as superior to the morality of care. More generally, Gilligan argued that theories of moral reasoning should accord equal importance to the care orientation and the justice orientation.

According to Gilligan and Wiggins (1987), the above gender differences have their origins in early childhood. Women are the main caretakers in most societies, and girls learn the morality of care through their strong attachment to their mother. In contrast, boys are less attached to their mother. They tend to identify with their father, who is often perceived as an authority figure. This identification process leads boys to develop the morality of justice.

### Evidence

As Jaffee and Hyde (2000) pointed out, it is hard to test Gilligan's views on the origins of moral orientation. However, Benenson, Morash, and Petrakos (1998) studied mothers playing with their children who were 4 or 5 years old. The girls seemed more attached to their mothers than the boys. For example, girls remained closer to their mothers, had more mutual eye contact with their mothers, and seemed to derive more enjoyment from the play session. However, it would be going beyond the evidence to claim that these findings showed that girls identify more strongly than boys with their mothers.

The most thorough review of studies focusing on possible gender differences in moral orientation was reported by Jaffee and Hyde (2000). They carried out a meta-analysis of 113 studies of moral reasoning. Overall, there was a very small tendency for males to show more justice reasoning than females, and a slightly larger (but still small) tendency for females to show more care reasoning than males. According to Jaffee and Hyde (p. 719):

> *The small magnitude of these effects [the ones just described], combined with the finding that 73% of the studies that measured justice reasoning and 72% of the studies that measured care reasoning failed to find significant gender differences, leads us to conclude that, although distinct moral orientations may exist, these orientations are not strongly associated with gender.*

**KEY TERMS**

**Morality of justice:** morality based on moral principles and on the application of laws.

**Morality of care:** morality based on compassion and on human well-being.

## Evaluation

⊕ There are gender differences in moral reasoning, and these differences are as predicted by Gilligan.

⊖ The magnitude of gender differences in moral reasoning is small, and males and females both use a mixture of justice and care moral reasoning.

⊖ It has proved difficult to study the proposed origins of gender differences in moral reasoning. Part of the problem is that some of the concepts used by Gilligan (e.g., parental identification, equality vs. inequality) cannot readily be measured.

# SUMMARY

*Development of the self*

There is an "I" (the self as the subject of experience) and a "me" (the self as the object of experience). Children's reactions to their mirror images suggest their sense of self starts to develop towards the end of their second year. The self-concept becomes increasingly complex in the course of development, and contains more interpersonal implications. Harter argued that children's self-esteem depends on their perceived competence in five domains. Children whose parents accept them, who set clearly defined limits on their behaviour, and who permit them to develop a sense of control, tend to be high in self-esteem.

*Gender development*

Most societies have expectations about the attitudes and behaviour of males and females. However, there are smaller differences between the sexes than is generally assumed. According to psychodynamic theory, anatomy is destiny, meaning that gender development is largely determined by biological factors. Freud argued that identification with the same-sexed parent plays a major role in the development of sex-typed behaviour. The evidence does not support this. According to social learning theory, gender development occurs through direct learning and observational learning. As predicted, sex-typed behaviour sometimes occurs because it is rewarded, whereas sex-inappropriate behaviour is avoided because it is discouraged. Social learning theorists focus on learning specific forms of behaviour rather than on general types of learning, and they tend to regard children as passive rather than active. According to Kohlberg's theory, children develop gender identity in three stages: basic gender identity, gender stability, and gender consistency. There is evidence for these three stages, and the achievement of gender consistency leads to the predicted increase in sex-typed behaviour. However, Kohlberg focused too much on the internal processes involved in the development of gender identity and not enough on external factors (e.g., rewards). According to gender-schema theory, young children who have acquired basic gender identity start to form gender schemas. Information that is inconsistent with a gender schema tends to be misremembered. There is limited support for biological theories of gender development. Stereotypes of females being nurturant and males being instrumental are very widespread across cultures.

*Pro-social behaviour*

Empathy plays an important role in pro-social behaviour. According to Hoffman, there are four stages in the development of empathy: global empathy, egocentric empathy, empathy for another's feelings, and empathy for another's life conditions. Individual differences in the amount of pro-social behaviour shown by children of any given age depend in part on genetic factors and in part on parental behaviour. Watching pro-social or helping behaviour on television can lead children to behave in a more pro-social way.

*Anti-social behaviour*

As children develop, they increasingly express their aggression in verbal rather than physical form. Media violence sometimes leads to short-term increases in children's aggression, and there may also be long-term effects. However, observational learning can lead to playfighting rather than to genuine aggression. Genetic factors influence individual differences in aggression. There are only small sex differences in aggression, but males tend to show more physical aggression. Childhood aggression can increase as a result of the dynamics of family interactions (e.g., coercive cycles).

There are emotional, cognitive, and behavioural components associated with morality. Freud emphasised the notion that moral development depends on children's identification with the same-sexed parent at about the age of 5 or 6. This is a very limited theory. According to Piaget, children's moral reasoning goes through three major stages. Moral development occurs as children become less egocentric and more influenced by their peers. Young children have more complex and mature ideas about morality than Piaget assumed. Piaget focused on moral reasoning rather than moral behaviour. Kohlberg expanded Piaget's theory in his six-stage theory. This theory tells us more about moral reasoning than moral behaviour, and de-emphasises emotional factors and cross-cultural differences in moral reasoning. Gilligan's notion that males favour a morality of justice whereas females favour a morality of care has received only modest support.

*Moral development*

# FURTHER READING

- Cole, M., & Cole, S.R. (2001). *The development of children* (4th ed.). New York: Worth. This book provides an introduction to key topics in social development.
- Shaffer, D.R. (2000). *Social and personality development* (4th ed.). Belmont, CA: Wadsworth. There is detailed and up-to-date material on topics such as moral development and sex-role identity in this book.
- Smith, P.K., Cowie, H., & Blades, M. (2003). *Understanding children's development* (4th ed.). Oxford, UK: Blackwell. Several chapters in this excellent textbook (especially 6 and 8) contain good introductory accounts of topics discussed in this chapter.

# Social development: Attachments and friendships

**17**

Human beings are social creatures, and so it is unsurprising that much of the early learning of infants is in the area of social development. In the last chapter, we considered some aspects of social development, including the development of the self, gender development, moral development, and changes in pro-social and anti-social behaviour. However, what is of central importance to social development are the warm, positive, and deep relationships which infants and children form with other people. This chapter focuses on relationships of all kinds, ranging from relatively weak and short-lived ones to very strong and long-lasting ones. It is probably true that nothing in human development is more important than the formation of such relationships.

Of special importance to infants is the **attachment** (a strong and long-lasting emotional tie) they typically form to their mother or other significant caregiver. As we will see, much evidence indicates that the nature and strength of the attachments formed by infants have long-term consequences for their future psychological well-being. Some children either never form strong attachments with other adults, or these attachments are disrupted. There has been much concern that deprivation (and especially maternal deprivation) may have severe long-term effects on children socially and intellectually.

Children's social and emotional development depends in part on their parents' child-rearing practices. Styles of child rearing vary considerably across cultures, and this makes it important to carry out cross-cultural studies. As might be expected, child-rearing practices reflect the dominant values of the culture, and this is one way in which parents pass on those values to the next generation.

The success or otherwise of young children's attachment to their parents or other significant adults only forms part of their social development. It is also very important for children to develop social skills and competence so they can interact successfully with other children. Related to this, children typically form friendships with their peers (other children of the same age). As we will see, children who have friends are happier and more successful than those who do not.

## ATTACHMENT

According to Shaffer (1993), an attachment is "a close emotional relationship between two persons, characterised by mutual affection and a desire to maintain proximity [closeness]". Developmental psychologists disagree about many things, but virtually all agree it is crucially important for infants and children to form strong attachments.

The main attachment of the infant is typically to its mother. However, strong attachments can be formed to other people with whom the infant has regular contact (Schaffer & Emerson, 1964). This is generally the father, but is sometimes other relatives. The first attachment that infants form in early childhood is very important because it is the starting point for their lifelong social and emotional involvements with other people. It gives them

an idea of what they might expect from adults as they grow up, and also forms the basis for the development of their own personality.

Evidence that infants often form attachments to their father as well as their mother was obtained by Weston and Main (1981). They used the Strange Situation procedure (described later) with 44 infants. Twelve infants were securely attached to both parents, eleven were securely attached only to their mother, ten were securely attached only to their father, and eleven were insecurely attached to both parents.

Bowlby (1969, 1988) provided a very influential account of the five major phases involved in the development of attachment:

1. The infant responds to other people, but does so in a similar way to everyone.
2. At around 5 months of age or perhaps earlier, the infant begins to discriminate consistently among other people (see Chapter 14). For example, the infant smiles much more at its mother or other significant caregiver than at other people. In addition, when the infant is distressed, the mother or caregiver is more effective than others at comforting him/her. This phase witnesses the start of attachment.
3. At around 7 months of age, the infant tries to remain close to its mother or important caregiver. During this phase, the infant shows "separation protest" by becoming obviously upset (e.g., crying) when its mother leaves. Another feature of this phase is that the infant begins to exhibit a fear of strangers.
4. From about the age of 3, the attachment between child and caregiver develops into what Bowlby referred to as a goal-corrected partnership. This means the child takes some account of the caregiver's needs, and does not focus exclusively on what the caregiver can provide for him/her.
5. From about the age of 5 upwards, the child's attachment to the mother or other caregiver depends much less on proximity. The child has developed an internal working model of the relationship, so the attachment can remain strong when the child does not see the caregiver for some time.

## Early approaches

Sigmund Freud (1924) proposed a simple account of the infant's attachment to its mother: "The reason why the infant in arms wants to perceive the presence of its mother is only because it already knows by experience that she satisfies all its needs without delay." Thus, babies are initially attached to their mothers because they are a source of food as well as comfort and warmth.

Freud's views on early attachment stemmed from his theory of psychosexual development (see Chapter 13). According to that theory, the first stage of psychosexual development is the oral stage. This lasts for about 18 months, and during it the infant obtains much satisfaction through oral experiences such as sucking the mother's breast. As a result, Freud (1924, p. 188) argued that the mother's status was "unique, without parallel, established unalterably for a whole lifetime as the first and strongest love-object and as the prototype of all later love-relations".

Freud's approach is far too simple. Attachment behaviour even in monkey babies does *not* depend only on the provision of food. Harry Harlow (1959) carried out several studies on very young monkeys. These monkeys had to choose between two surrogate (or substitute) mothers, one made of wire and the other covered in cloth. Milk was provided by the wire mother for some of the monkeys, whereas it was provided by the cloth monkey for the others. The findings were clear-cut. The monkeys spent most of their time on the cloth mother even when she did not supply milk.

More evidence against Freud's theory was provided by Schaffer and Emerson (1964). In about 40% of human infants, the adult who fed and changed him/her was not the person to whom the infant was most attached. Thus, there is not the simple link between food and attachment behaviour assumed by Freud. Infants were most likely to become attached to adults who were responsive to them, and who provided them with much stimulation in the form of touching and playing.

The ethologists studied animals in their natural environment. One of the ethologists (Konrad Lorenz) found among the young of some species of birds that they tended to follow the first moving object they saw, and continued to follow it thereafter. This is known as **imprinting**. It only occurs during a short critical period in the bird's life. When imprinting has occurred, it tends to be irreversible, in the sense that the bird will continue to follow the object on which it is imprinted.

Although the wire mother on the left is where the baby monkey receives his food, he runs to the cloth mother for comfort when he is frightened by the teddy bear drummer (Harlow, 1959).

According to Bowlby (1969), something like imprinting occurs in infants. He discussed the notion of **monotropy**, according to which human infants have an innate tendency to form strong bonds with one particular individual. This will usually (but not always) be the

Lorenz hatched some goslings and arranged it so that he would be the first thing that they saw. From then on they followed him everywhere and showed no recognition of their actual mother. The goslings formed a picture (imprint) of the object they were to follow.

> ### KEY TERMS
> **Imprinting:** a strong tendency for the young of some species (e.g., geese) to follow and to bond with the first moving object they encounter.
> **Monotropy:** the notion that infants have an innate tendency to form strong bonds with their mother; proposed by Bowlby.

### CASE STUDY: *Amorous turkeys*

Some psychologists were conducting research on the effects of hormones on turkeys. In one room there were 35 full-grown male turkeys. If you walked into the room, the turkeys fled to the furthest corner and if you walked towards them, the turkeys slid along the wall to maintain a maximum distance between you and them. This is fairly normal behaviour for wild turkeys. However, in another room, there was a group of turkeys who behaved in a very different manner. These turkeys greeted you by stopping dead in their tracks, fixing their eyes on you, spreading their tail into a full courtship fan, putting their heads down and ponderously walking towards you, all at the same time. Their intention was clearly one of mating. (Fortunately turkeys in mid-courtship are famously slow so it is easy to avoid their advances.)

What was the difference between these two groups? The first set were raised away from humans, whereas the second group had received an injection of the male hormone, testosterone, when they were younger. The hormone created an artificial sensitive period during which the turkeys imprinted on their companion at the time—a male experimenter. Subsequently, these turkeys showed little interest in female turkeys, however they were aroused whenever they saw a male human—displaying their tail feathers and strutting their stuff.

It has been suggested that the reason this learning was so strong and apparently irreversible was because it took place at a time of high arousal—when hormones were administered. In real life, hormones may be involved as well. Perhaps, for these birds, a moving object creates a sense of pleasure and this pleasure triggers the production of endorphins, opiate-like biochemicals produced by the body, which in turn create a state of arousal that is optimal for learning.

From Howard S. Hoffman, 1996.

*What implications might this have for adult relationships and parenting?*

infant's mother. He also argued there is a critical period during which the infant's attachment to the mother or other caretaker must occur. This critical period ends at some point between 1 and 3 years of age. After that, it is no longer possible to establish a powerful attachment to the mother or other person.

## Strange Situation test

In order to develop a full understanding of infants' attachment behaviour, we need to have good ways of measuring it. Ainsworth and Bell (1970) developed the Strange Situation procedure. The infant (normally about 12 months old) is observed during a sequence of eight short episodes. For some of the time, the infant is with its mother. At other times, it is with its mother and a stranger, just with a stranger, or on its own. The child's reactions to the stranger, to separation from the mother, and to being reunited with its mother are all recorded. Cross-cultural studies using the Strange Situation are discussed in detail later in the chapter.

The infant's reactions to these episodes allow its attachment to its mother to be placed in one of three categories:

1. **Secure attachment.** The infant is distressed by the mother's absence. However, it rapidly returns to a state of contentment after the mother's return, immediately seeking contact with her. There are clear differences in the infant's reaction to the mother and to the stranger. About 70% of American infants show secure attachment.
2. **Resistant** (or ambivalent) **attachment.** The infant is insecure in the presence of the mother, and becomes very distressed when the mother leaves. It resists contact with the mother upon her return, and is wary of the stranger. About 10% of American infants are resistant.
3. **Avoidant attachment.** The infant does not seek contact with the mother, and shows little distress when separated from her. The infant avoids contact with the mother upon her return. The infant treats the stranger in a similar way to the mother, often avoiding him/her. About 20% of American infants are avoidant.

**KEY TERMS**

**Secure attachment:** a strong and contented attachment of an infant to its mother, combined with resumption of contact with her when she returns after an absence.

**Resistant attachment:** an insecure attachment of an infant to its mother.

**Avoidant attachment:** an insecure attachment of an infant to its mother, combined with avoidance of contact with her when she returns after an absence.

| The eight stages of the Strange Situation experiment | | |
|---|---|---|
| **Stage** | **People in the room** | **Procedure** |
| 1 (30 seconds) | Mother or caregiver and infant plus researcher | Researcher brings the others into the room and quickly leaves |
| 2 (3 minutes) | Mother or caregiver and infant | Mother or caregiver sits; infant is free to explore |
| 3 (3 minutes) | Stranger plus mother or caregiver and infant | Stranger comes in and after a while talks to mother or caregiver and then to the infant. Mother or caregiver leaves the room |
| 4 (3 minutes) | Stranger and infant | Stranger keeps trying to talk and play with the infant |
| 5 (3 minutes) | Mother or caregiver and infant | Stranger leaves as mother or caregiver returns to the infant. At the end of this stage the mother or caregiver leaves |
| 6 (3 minutes) | Infant | Infant is alone in the room |
| 7 (3 minutes) | Stranger and infant | Stranger returns and tries to interact with the infant |
| 8 (3 minutes) | Mother or caregiver and infant | Mother or caregiver returns and interacts with the infant, and the stranger leaves |

The original version of the Strange Situation test (described above) was designed for infants. Thus, there is a focus on the infant's movements towards or away from its mother and on whether or not it cries. Attachment in 3- and 4-year-olds can still be assessed by the Strange Situation test. However, it is important to take account of the much greater variety of behaviour shown by such children (e.g., content and manner of speech to parents; verbal expressions of emotion; see Bar-Heim et al., 2000). When this is done, the same three categories (secure, resistant, avoidant) are present in 4-year-olds as in infants (Bar-Heim et al., 2000).

There is evidence for a fourth type of attachment behaviour in the Strange Situation. Main, Kaplan, and Cassidy (1985) argued that some infants display what they called disorganised and disoriented attachment. These infants seemed to lack any coherent strategy for coping with the Strange Situation, and their behaviour was often a confusing mixture of approach and avoidance.

Fraley and Spieker (2003) argued that it is an oversimplification to allocate all children's attachment patterns to three (or four) categories. For example, two children might both be classified as showing avoidant attachment, but one might show much more avoidant behaviour than the other. Accordingly, Fraley and Spieker (2003) suggested it would make more sense to assess children's attachment behaviour in terms of two dimensions. First, there is a dimension of proximity seeking versus avoidant strategies, which is concerned with the extent to which the child tries to maintain physical closeness to his/her mother. Second, there is a dimension of angry and resistant strategies versus emotional confidence, which is concerned with the child's emotional reactions to the attachment figure's behaviour. As can be seen in the figure on the right, secure

*This study was carried out on American infants. Do you think that children from other cultures are all likely to behave in the same way?*

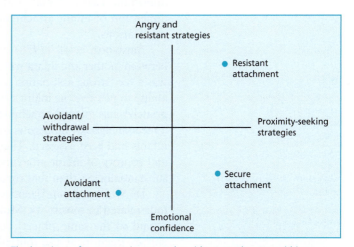

The locations of secure, resistant, and avoidant attachments within a two-dimensional framework (proximity seeking vs. avoidance/withdrawal, angry and resistant vs. emotional confidence.). Based on Fraley and Spieker (2003).

attachment is associated with high proximity seeking and high emotional confidence, resistant attachment is associated with high proximity seeking and high anger and resistance, and avoidant attachment is associated with low proximity seeking and high emotional confidence.

Is this dimensional approach preferable to Ainsworth's categorical approach? There are two advantages of focusing on dimensions. First, the dimensional approach is more flexible than the categorical approach, since it does not require every child's attachment behaviour to be assigned to one out of a very small number of categories. Second, it is more sensitive. For example, small differences in attachment behaviour between children are taken into account in a dimensional approach but are typically ignored in a categorical approach.

Does infant attachment predict attachment later in childhood? There is some evidence for stability over a period of several years. For example, Wartner et al. (1994) found much similarity between attachment classifications at 12 months in the Strange Situation and attachment at 6 years. However, a more complicated picture emerged in a study by Bar-Heim et al. (2000). Attachment classifications were reasonably constant between 14 and 24 months of age, with 64% of children remaining in the same attachment category. However, there was much less stability between 14 and 58 months of age, with only 38% of children staying in the same attachment category. Bar-Heim et al. found that children whose attachment category altered between 14 and 58 months were significantly more likely than children whose attachment category remained the same to have mothers who reported a large number of negative life events.

Does infant attachment predict social and cognitive development several years later? The evidence is somewhat inconsistent, but positive findings were reported by Stams, Juffer, and van IJzendoorn (2002) on adopted children. They assessed child–mother attachment security at the age of 12 months, and then assessed social and cognitive development 6 years later. Children who were securely attached at the age of 12 months had superior social and cognitive development at the age of 7. Difficult early temperament and maternal sensitive responsiveness (discussed below) also predicted social and cognitive development, but did so to a lesser extent than attachment security.

## Theories of attachment

Why do some infants have a secure attachment with their mother, whereas others do not? According to Bowlby (1969), the attachment figure's sensitivity in responding to the infant's signals is of major importance. This view was also expressed by Ainsworth et al. (1978, p. 152), who put forward the maternity sensitivity hypothesis: "The most important aspect of maternal behaviour commonly associated with the security–anxiety dimension of infant attachment is ... sensitive responsiveness to infant signals and communications."

Ainsworth et al. (1978) carried out a study on 26 families in which the interactions between mother and infant were observed in great detail throughout the first year of life. There was a very strong association (correlation of +.78) between maternal sensitivity (involving the ability to perceive the infant's signals accurately and to respond to them promptly and appropriately) and infants' attachment security. De Wolff and van IJzendoorn (1997) carried out a meta-analysis of numerous studies in which maternal sensitivity and attachment security in infants had been assessed. They reported a correlation of +.24 between maternal sensitivity and security of infant attachment. This indicates a moderate strength of association, but is substantially less than that reported by Ainsworth et al.

De Wolff and van IJzendoorn (1997) also considered other aspects of maternal behaviour related to sensitivity. Mutuality (e.g., positive exchanges in which mother and infant attend to the same object) correlated +.32 with infants' attachment security, and synchrony (reciprocal and mutually rewarding interactions of mother and infant) correlated +.26 with infants' attachment security. Finally, de Wolff and van IJzendoorn found that aspects of mothers' behaviour having little resemblance to sensitivity were also important. Stimulation (any action of the mother directed at her baby) correlated +.18 with infants' attachment security, as did attitude (e.g., mother's expression of positive emotion to her baby). Thus, maternal sensitivity is important, but several other aspects of maternal behaviour are of comparable importance in determining infants' attachment type.

Most of the research on the maternal sensitivity hypothesis is limited because it is correlational, and is based on finding an association between maternal sensitivity and attachment type. Such research cannot show that differences in maternal sensitivity *cause* differences in attachment type. It may be, for example, that children predisposed to be securely attached elicit more sensitive behaviour from their mothers. One useful way of addressing the causality issue is to use interventions designed to increase parental sensitivity. According to the maternal sensitivity hypothesis, such interventions based on an experimental approach should lead to a significant increase in the number of infants being securely attached.

Bakermans-Kranenburg, van IJzendoorn, and Juffer (2003) carried out a meta-analysis of 51 studies in which interventions were used to increase positive maternal behaviour (e.g., sensitivity, responsiveness, involvement). The interventions were generally successful in enhancing the sensitivity of mothers' parenting, and the interventions tended to make infants more securely attached. More specifically, 58% of infants whose mother received training in sensitive parenting were more securely attached than the average infant whose mother didn't receive training.

The maternal sensitivity hypothesis has been criticised because it exaggerates the role of the mother in the development of infant attachment. For example, you may be wondering what role (if any) is played by the father in influencing infants' attachment pattern. Van IJzendoorn and de Wolff (1997) carried out a meta-analysis on eight studies in which paternal sensitivity had been assessed. The key finding was that there was a correlation of +.13 between the father's sensitivity and infant–father attachment. Thus, paternal sensitivity is modestly associated with the infant's security of attachment to the father. However, the association is significantly smaller than that between maternal sensitivity and security of infant–mother attachment.

Another possible limitation with the maternal sensitivity hypothesis is that it ignores the role played by the infant him/herself. We know, for example, that genetic factors play a role in determining individual differences in personality (see Chapter 13), and genetic factors may influence infants' attachment pattern. This hypothesis can be tested by comparing monozygotic (identical) twins who share 100% of their genes with dizygotic (fraternal) twins who share only 50% of their genes. If the hypothesis is correct, then identical twins should show more agreement (concordance) than dizygotic or fraternal twins with respect to attachment pattern.

Finkel, Wille, and Matheny (1999) reported support for the genetic hypothesis. The concordance rate for attachment category was 66% for identical twins, which was much higher than the figure of 48% for fraternal twins. However, the concordance rate for fraternal twins is remarkably low, being even lower than chance expectation. O'Connor and Croft (2001) carried out a study on identical and fraternal twins of preschool age. The concordance rate was 70% for identical twins compared to 64% for fraternal twins. This small difference suggested that 14% of individual differences in attachment type were due to genetic factors. In sum, genetic factors probably influence young children's attachment type to a small extent.

Suppose infants' attachment patterns were determined in a large part by genetic factors possessed by the infant. Infants securely attached to their mother would typically also be securely attached to their father, and those insecurely attached to their mother would be insecurely attached to their father. In fact, however, there is only a modest correlation of +.17 between infant–mother attachment and infant–father attachment. This suggests that an infant's attachment to his/her mother and father depend primarily on characteristics of his/her parents.

## Evaluation

*Do you think that loss of an attachment figure would have the same effects as never forming an attachment in the first place?*

➕ Much research has confirmed the usefulness of the Strange Situation test, and of the three types of attachment identified by Ainsworth and Bell (1970).

➕ Various factors determining attachment type (e.g., maternal sensitivity; paternal sensitivity) have been identified.

➕ Attachment type in infancy predicts future social and cognitive development to some extent (Stams et al., 2002).

➕ Some of the most thorough cross-cultural research in developmental psychology has involved use of the Strange Situation test (see below).

➖ The Strange Situation procedure is laboratory-based, and represents a rather artificial approach to the study of attachment. Bronfenbrenner (1979) pointed out that infants' attachment behaviours are typically much stronger in the laboratory than they are at home.

➖ It is unclear whether strong early attachment *directly* influences later social and emotional development because of the reliance on correlational data.

➖ It may be preferable to replace Ainsworth's attachment types with a dimensional approach.

The child psychoanalyst John Bowlby (1907–1990). "Mother love in infancy and childhood is as important for mental health as are vitamins and proteins for physical health." (Bowlby, 1953).

# EFFECTS OF DEPRIVATION

We have already considered some factors determining the nature of the attachment that a young child forms with its mother or other caregiver. In the real world, of course, there are circumstances (e.g., divorce or death of a parent) that can disrupt the child's attachments or even prevent them from being formed at all. In this section of the chapter, we will discuss the effects on the young child of being separated from one or more of the most important adults in its life. However, note that deprivation can have severe effects on much older children as well. For example, girls whose mothers died before they reached the age of 12 are much more likely than other girls to become severely depressed in adult life (Brown & Harris, 1978).

## Maternal deprivation hypothesis

John Bowlby (1907–1990) was a child psychoanalyst who focused on the relationship between mother and child. According to Bowlby (1951), "an infant and young child should experience a warm, intimate and continuous relationship with his [sic] mother (or permanent mother-figure) in which both find satisfaction and enjoyment". No-one would disagree with that. However, Bowlby went on to propose the more controversial maternal deprivation hypothesis. According to this hypothesis, breaking the maternal bond with the child during the early years of its life is likely to have serious effects on its intellectual, social, and emotional development. Bowlby also claimed that many of these negative effects of maternal deprivation are permanent and irreversible.

Most studies have focused on long-term effects of deprivation. However, we will first consider some short-term effects. Even fairly brief separation from the mother has severe emotional effects on the child. Robertson and Bowlby (1952) studied young children separated from their mother for some time, often because she had gone into hospital. There were three stages in the child's response to separation:

Separation from the mother can have severe emotional effects on a child. The first stage of the child's response to the separation is known as protest: an intense period during which the child cries for much of the time.

1. *Protest*, which was often very intense; the child cried much of the time, and sometimes seemed panic stricken.

2. *Despair*, involving a total loss of hope; the child was often apathetic and showed little interest in its surroundings.

3. *Detachment*, during which the child seemed to behave in a less distressed way. If the mother reappeared during this stage, she was not responded to with any great interest.

It used to be thought that children in the third stage of detachment had adjusted fairly well to separation from their mother. In fact, the calm behaviour shown by the child often hides underlying distress. The indifference shown by the child when its mother reappears is generally apparent rather than real, as shown by the fact that the child will re-establish an attachment to the mother over time.

Is it inevitable that short-term separation will produce these negative effects? Evidence reported by Robertson and Robertson (1971) suggests it is not. They used their own home to look after young children who had been separated from their mother, and took various steps to minimise any distress the children might experience. First, they ensured that the children visited their home before the actual separation, so the children could become familiar with their new surroundings. Second, they did their best to provide the children with the kind of daily routine with which they were familiar. Third, they discussed the children's mothers with them. This approach proved successful, with the children showing much less distress than do most separated children.

## Evidence

Bowlby's maternal deprivation hypothesis was based in part on the work of Goldfarb (1947) and Spitz (1945). Spitz (1945) visited several very poor orphanages and other institutions in South America. Most children in these orphanages received very little warmth or attention from the staff, as a result of which they became apathetic. Many of the children suffered from **anaclitic depression**, a state involving resigned helplessness and loss of appetite.

Goldfarb (1947) compared two groups of infants from a poor and inadequately staffed orphanage. One group had spent only the first few months of their lives there before being fostered. The other group consisted of infants who had spent 3 years at the orphanage before fostering. Both groups were tested at various times up to the age of 12. Those children who had spent 3 years at the orphanage did less well than the others on intelligence tests. They were less socially mature, and were more likely to be aggressive.

The findings of Goldfarb (1947) and Spitz (1945) provide less support for the maternal deprivation hypothesis than Bowlby assumed. The institutions they studied were deficient in several ways, with the children suffering from a general lack of stimulation and attention as well as maternal deprivation. Thus, we cannot interpret the findings: They may be due to absence of the mother, or they may be due to presence of poor institutional conditions, or to a combination of both factors.

Bowlby (1946) presented evidence that maternal deprivation can have severe long-term effects. He compared juvenile delinquents who had committed crimes with other emotionally disturbed adolescents who had not committed any crimes. Thirty-two per cent of the juvenile delinquents, but none of the emotionally disturbed adolescents, showed **affectionless psychopathy**, a disorder involving a lack of guilt and remorse. Bowlby (1946) found 64% of the juvenile delinquents with affectionless psychopathy had experienced deprivation in early childhood. In contrast, only 10% of the juvenile delinquents *without* affectionless psychopathy had been maternally deprived. These findings suggested that maternal deprivation can lead to affectionless psychopathy, but were not repeated in later studies.

## Deprivation and privation

Rutter (1981) argued that Bowlby's (1946) findings on affectionless psychopathy should be re-interpreted. He pointed out there is an important difference between deprivation and privation. **Deprivation** occurs when a child has formed an important attachment, but is then separated from the major attachment figure. In contrast, **privation** occurs when a child has never formed a close relationship with anyone. Many of Bowlby's juvenile delinquents had experienced several changes of home and of principal caretaker during their early childhood. This indicated to Rutter that their later problems were due to privation rather than deprivation as Bowlby had claimed. Rutter argued that the effects of privation are much more severe and long-lasting than those of deprivation, concluding that privation often leads to "an initial phase of clinging, dependent behaviour, followed by attention-seeking, uninhibited, indiscriminate friendliness and finally a personality characterised by lack of guilt, an inability to keep rules and an inability to form lasting friendships".

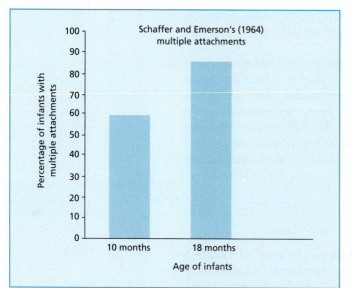

Schaffer and Emerson's (1964) multiple attachments

Percentage of infants with multiple attachments

Age of infants

## Monotropy hypothesis

According to Bowlby's monotropy hypothesis, infants form only one strong attachment, and this is typically to the mother. In fact, this is often not the case. Schaffer and Emerson (1964), in a study mentioned before, visited the homes of babies several times during their first year of life. By the age of 10 months, 59% of infants had formed more than one attachment, and the figure rose to 87% by the age of 18 months. At the older age, only about half the infants were mainly attached to their mother, with 30% being mainly attached to their father. Thus, relatively few children only have a strong attachment to their mother as assumed by Bowlby.

In spite of the above findings, it may still be the case that social development is adversely affected if young children are exposed to several caregivers. Roy, Rutter, and Pickles (2000) considered 6-year-old children removed from their troubled families. Some of the children were receiving foster care, and so the main caregiving was provided by the family fostering them. In contrast, other children were receiving institutional care, and so had several caregivers. The school achievement of both groups of children was below that of children from intact families. However, the institutional children exhibited more emotional disturbance, inattention, and hyperactivity than those in foster care, which may well be due to having many more caregivers.

## Reasons for deprivation

Bowlby (1951) argued that deprivation in and of itself causes long-term difficulties. In contrast, Rutter (1981) suggested the effects of deprivation depend on the precise reasons for the separation. He studied boys aged between 9 and 12 years of age who had been deprived of their mothers for a period of time when they were younger. In general, the well-adjusted boys had been separated because of factors such as housing problems or physical illness. In contrast, the maladjusted boys had mostly been separated because of problems with social relationships within the family (e.g., psychiatric illness). Thus, family discord rather than separation as such causes difficulties for children.

Bowlby (1951) argued the negative effects of maternal deprivation could not be reversed or undone. However, most of the evidence does not support his argument, and indicates that even privation does not always have permanent effects. Thorough evidence on this issue was reported by Tizard (1977, 1986) and Tizard and Hodges (1978) (see Key Study opposite).

*What kinds of factors might influence whether or not the effects are severe and long-lasting?*

## Irreversibility of damage: Extreme privation

A few researchers have looked at the effects of very extreme privation and isolation on children. It is surprising how resilient these children often seem to be. Koluchová (1976) studied identical twins who had spent most of the first 7 years of their lives locked in a cellar. They had been treated very badly, and were often beaten. They were barely able to talk, and relied mainly on gestures other than speech. The twins were fostered at about the age of 9. By the time they were 14, their behaviour was essentially normal. By the age of 20, they were of above-average intelligence, and had excellent relationships with the members of their foster family.

Curtiss (1989) discussed the case of Genie, who spent most of her childhood in a cupboard at her home in Los Angeles (see Chapter 14). She had had very little contact with other members of her family, and was discouraged from making any sounds. She was found when she was 13½ years old. She had not been fed adequately, could not stand erect, and had no social skills. At that time, she did not understand language and could not speak. Genie was given a considerable amount of education and assistance in the years after she was found. Her ability to perform tasks not dependent on language improved

## Hodges and Tizard: Long-term effects of privation

Tizard (1977, 1986) and Tizard and Hodges (1978) studied children who spent up to the first 7 years of their lives in an institution. Each child had been looked after on average by 24 different caregivers by the age of 2. The lack of opportunity to form a strong, continuous relationship with any one adult meant that they suffered from maternal deprivation. In spite of this, the children had a mean IQ of 105 at the age of 4½. Thus, the institutions probably did not hold back the children's cognitive development.

The progress of these children was also studied at the ages of 8 and 16. Some of them had returned to their own families, whereas others had been adopted. Most of the adopted children had formed close relationships with their adoptive parents. This was less true of the children who returned to their own families, because their parents were often not sure they wanted to have their children back. Both groups of children experienced difficulties at school. According to Tizard and Hodges (1978), they had "an almost insatiable desire for adult attention, and a difficulty in forming good relationships with their peer group" (p. 114).

Hodges and Tizard (1989) found that the family relationships of the adopted children at the age of 16 were as good as those of families in which none of the children had been removed from the family home. However, the 16-year-olds who had returned to their families showed little affection for their parents, and their parents were not very affectionate towards them. Both groups were similar in their relationships with other adolescents of the same age. They were less likely than other children to have a special friend or to regard other adolescents as sources of emotional support.

### KEY STUDY EVALUATION—Hodges and Tizard

One of the criticisms of this study is that some of the children "dropped out" before the end of the study. This left a biased sample because children who could not be traced or were not willing to take part may well have been different from those left in the study. In fact Hodges and Tizard reported that those adopted children who remained in the study had earlier shown somewhat more adjustment problems than the restored children who dropped out. This left a "better" sample of adopted children and might explain why they did better.

It is also important to note that there were considerable individual differences within each group: some of the restored children actually had good family relations and some of the adopted children didn't.

As this was a natural experiment, cause and effect cannot be assumed, so it cannot be said that privation causes long-term negative social effects; it can only be inferred.

### Discussion points

1. How has the research of Hodges and Tizard added to our knowledge of the effects of deprivation?
2. How might we account for the different patterns of behaviour shown by adopted children and children who returned to their families?

rapidly, and reached normal levels on several perceptual tasks (Curtiss, 1989). However, Genie's social skills remained limited, in part because "her use of intonation was poor, and only people who knew her well could understand much of what she was trying to say" (Curtiss, 1989, p. 216).

Freud and Dann (1951) provided interesting evidence that young children who form strong attachments with other young children can avoid severe damage resulting from the loss of both parents and living in terrible circumstances. They studied six war orphans whose parents had been murdered in a concentration camp when they were only a few months old. The infants lived together in a deportation camp for about 2 years until the age of 3, and had distressing experiences such as watching people being hanged. In this camp, they were put in the Ward for Motherless Children, and had very limited contact with anyone other than each other. After the camp was liberated at the end of the Second World War, they were flown to England. When they were freed from the camp, the children had not yet developed speech properly, they were underweight, and they expressed hostility towards adults. However, they were greatly attached to each other.

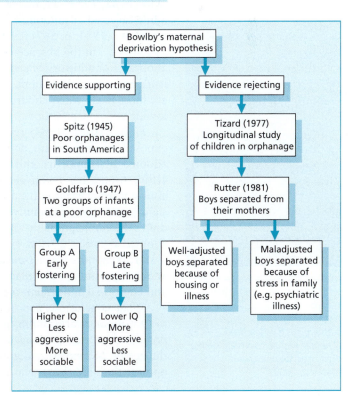

Orphaned children held in concentration camps who underwent terrible experiences in their early lives showed rapid social and language development once they had been removed from the camps. These children were photographed awaiting their release from Auschwitz in January 1945.

*What is the difficulty with conclusions based on case studies?*

According to Freud and Dann (1951), "The children's positive feelings were centred exclusively in their own group … They had no other wish than to be together and became upset when they were separated from each other, even for short moments" (p. 131).

As time went by, the six children became attached to their adult caretakers. In addition, they developed rapidly at a social level and in their use of language. It is hard to say whether their early experiences had any lasting adverse effects. One of them (Leah) received psychiatric assistance, and another (Jack) sometimes felt very alone and isolated (Moscovitz, 1983). However, it would not be exceptional to find similar problems in six adults selected at random.

Skuse (1984, p. 567) reviewed studies on cases of extreme deprivation, and concluded as follows: "In the absence of genetic or congenital [non-hereditary and present at birth] anomalies or a history of gross malnourishment, victims of such deprivation have an excellent prognosis. Some subtle deficits in social adjustment may persist." Positive outcomes are most likely when children are looked after by a caring and sympathetic caregiver following severe deprivation.

Since Skuse's (1984) review, findings have been reported from Romanian children exposed to very severe deprivation and neglect in their native country before being adopted by supportive and caring British families in the United Kingdom. Rutter et al. (1998) found that 4-year-old Romanian children adopted before the age of 6 months had almost normal levels of cognitive development, whereas those adopted after 6 months had significantly poorer cognitive development. O'Connor et al. (2000b) reported on the children's development at the age of 6, including a comparison between Romanian children adopted between 24 and 42 months (late-placed adoptees) and those adopted between 6 and 24 months (earlier-placed adoptees). The cognitive development of the late-placed adoptees was inferior to that of the earlier-placed adoptees, and their general development and emotional adjustment were poor.

What conclusions can be drawn from this study on Romanian children? According to O'Connor et al. (2000b, p. 387), "Significant catch-up, but not complete recovery, is possible even after prolonged exposure to deprivation." Children who were adopted after the age of 24 months had greater difficulty in achieving good cognitive and social development than did those who were adopted at a younger age.

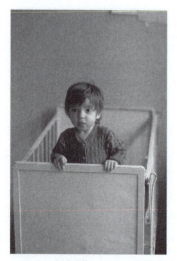

Many of the charity workers who went in to Romania after the collapse of Ceauşescu's regime found widespread privation—one such worker has described "children kept like animals, tied to their beds, kept in cages" (Dennett, 2003).

## Evaluation

- ⊕ Maternal deprivation often has adverse short- and long-term effects on children.
- ⊖ The negative effects of privation are typically greater than those of deprivation. Contrary to popular belief, Bowlby argued that about 25% (rather than 100%) of children suffer long-term damage from maternal deprivation (Diana Dwyer, personal communication). Thus, his theory is more accurate than is generally assumed.
- ⊖ The assumption of the monotropy hypothesis that infants form only one strong attachment is incorrect, but there may be disadvantages in having several caregivers.
- ⊖ Maternal deprivation has more damaging effects on children when it is due to factors related to social relationships within the family than when it is due to other factors (e.g., physical illness). Thus, family discord is more important than deprivation itself in producing negative effects on children.
- ⊖ Many (or even most) of the adverse effects of maternal deprivation (and even privation) are reversible, especially when the privation or deprivation is relatively short-lived.

> ### CASE STUDY: *The Riley family*
>
> Jean Riley (54) and her husband Peter (58) adopted two children from Romania who are now aged 17 and 9. Cezarina, when they first saw her, was cross-eyed, filthy, and about 4 years behind in her physical development. First Cezarina's physical problems had to be sorted out, but from then on she made good progress. However, Cezarina is "laid back" about things that seem important to Jean and Peter. Jean understands this attitude, though, because clearly examinations seem less important when a child has had to struggle to survive.
>
> According to Jean, Cezarina is bright, but needs to have information reinforced over and over again. She has also struggled to understand jokes and sarcasm, although this may be due to difficulties with learning the language. Jean sees Cezarina as naive and emotionally immature. Cezarina says herself that initially she was frustrated because she couldn't communicate. She does see herself as being different from other girls, although she likes the same things, such as fashion and pop music. Jean runs The Parent Network for the Institutionalised Child, a group for people who have adopted such children. Cezarina has partly recovered from her poor early experiences. (Account based on an article in *Woman*, 21 September 1998.)
>
> An important study has been carried out by Rutter et al. (1998) on 111 Romanian children adopted in the UK before the age of 2. The children arrived with severe developmental impairment, but in 2 years their progress has been described as dramatic.
>
> These findings provide further support for the notion that most children are able to recover even from very difficult and distressing childhoods.

# EFFECTS OF DIVORCE AND DAY CARE

Some of the major sources of disruption to children's attachments in Western society (and in many other cultures around the world) have become markedly more common in recent decades. For example 50 years ago, fewer than 5% of marriages in the United Kingdom ended in divorce. Nowadays, the figure is 40%, and it is even higher in the United States. Not surprisingly, the possible negative effects of divorce on children are receiving increasing attention from researchers.

Another major change in most Western societies has been the substantial increase in the number of mothers going out to work. In several countries, approximately 50% of young children are put into day care for several days a week while their mothers go out to work. In contrast, it was relatively rare for mothers with young children to go out to work until recent decades.

In this section, we will be considering the effects on children of these large increases in divorce and in day care. More specifically, we will address the issue of whether children are likely to suffer as a result. Of course, common sense would suggest that the adverse effects of divorce are likely to be much greater than those of day care. Divorce produces a major and permanent change in the situation of the children affected by it, whereas children in day care typically experience many hours a week of loving attention from both their parents. However, according to Bowlby's (e.g., 1969) attachment theory, any disruption of the bond between mother and child during the first few years of life can impair the child's social and emotional development.

## Divorce

A key point to bear in mind is that, "Divorce is not a single event but a complex series of transitions requiring considerable adjustment" (Dworetzky, 1996, p. 381). First, there are marital conflicts which are distressing to children. Second, there is the actual separation, followed by divorce. Third, there are the various adjustments which need to be made by the parents and children. These often include moving house, having less money available, and reacting to new relationships as the parents find new partners and perhaps remarry.

More than half of children whose parents divorce lose contact with the parent who is not looking after them (nearly always the father) within 2 years. The effects are generally more serious than losing a father through death. As Hetherington (1979, 1989) pointed out, children of divorced parents usually feel the parents chose to divorce even though the children themselves were opposed to it. This creates feelings of anger rarely found when the father dies. In addition, children often experience guilt, feeling they may be partially responsible for the divorce.

## Evidence

Hetherington, Cox, and Cox (1982) studied the effects of divorce on 4-year-old middle-class children over a 2-year period. They called the first year after divorce the *crisis phase*. During that time, the mothers (who were looking after the children) became stricter than before, and were less affectionate. In return, the children behaved in more aggressive and unchanging ways, and this was especially the case with boys. During this year, the non-custodial fathers tended to become less strict and often gave treats to their children.

The *adjustment phase* was usually reached about 2 years after divorce. There was more routine and order about the children's everyday lives. In addition, the mothers had gone back to treating their children in a more patient and understanding fashion. Overall, there was less emotional distress in this phase than the previous phase. However, there was a tendency for boys to have worse relations with their mothers than did boys whose parents had not divorced. In addition, the boys of divorced parents showed more anti-social and disobedient behaviour.

*Do you think that the effects of divorce would be the same in all cultures?*

Hetherington (1988) carried out a follow-up 6 years after divorce. At that stage, 70% of the divorced mothers had remarried. The children of divorced parents were more independent and had more impact on decision making than children in intact families. Sons still tended to be disobedient in their interactions with their mothers, with mothers finding it hard to exercise control.

Girls often find it harder than boys to adjust to their mother's remarriage. Why is this? According to Hetherington (1989, p. 7), "Daughters in one-parent families have played more responsible, powerful roles than girls in non-divorced families and have had more positive relationships with their divorced mothers than have sons. They may see both their independence and their relationship with the mother as threatened by a new stepfather." In contrast, sons often regarded their stepfather as a role model and as someone who would provide support (Vuchinich et al., 1991).

How long-lasting are the negative effects of divorce? Wallerstein (1987) carried out a study on children whose parents had divorced when they were between 2½ and 18 years of age. Nearly all the children were extremely distressed when their parents separated and divorced, and the situation was similar 18 months later. Five years after their parents' divorce, it was still the case that about 30% of the children showed clear signs of depression.

Wallerstein (1987) found that, even 10 years after a divorce, the children involved regarded the divorce as the most stressful event in their lives. They typically felt that they had been seriously deprived by not growing up in a family with both parents. In contrast to the short-term effects, girls suffered more in the long term. Many feared rejection and betrayal by men.

The adverse effects of divorce reported by Wallerstein (1987) are greater than those obtained in most other studies. A possible reason for this is that Wallerstein obtained participants by offering them counselling if they wanted it. This may well have encouraged especially distressed families to participate in the study.

The effects of divorce as described in this section apply to children of most ages. However, there are two reasons why some effects can be less serious in adolescents than in younger children. First, adolescents are often better able to understand that their parents have divorced because of the poor relationship between them rather than because of anything their children have done. Second, most adolescents have begun to develop close attachments to other adolescents, and so their family is of less central importance in their lives.

We have focused on the negative effects of divorce on children. However, Hetherington and Stanley-Hagan (1999) emphasised that the effects of parental divorce are extremely variable. Some children of divorced parents suffer long-term adverse effects persisting into adulthood. For example, O'Connor, Thorpe, Dunn, and Golding (1999) found among women, mostly in their twenties, that those who had experienced divorce in childhood were more likely to be severely depressed than those whose parents had not divorced (17% vs. 12%, respectively). In contrast, some children of divorced parents become very competent and caring adults as a result of having had to cope with the consequences of experiencing divorce (Hetherington & Stanley-Hagan, 1999).

There is a major limitation with most research on the effects of divorce. As O'Connor, Caspi, DeFries, and Plomin (2000a, p. 435) pointed out, "Research into the frequently observed association between divorce and children's outcomes has assumed an exclusively environmentally mediated process. Rarely is there a consideration that the connection between divorce and children's adjustment may reflect shared genetic effects on parents' and children's behaviour." This is unfortunate, because genetic factors play a part in determining which couples will divorce. For example, Jockin, McGue, and Lykken (1996) found there were significant associations between personality and likelihood of divorcing, and it is known that individual differences in personality depend in part on genetic factors (see Chapter 13).

How can we study the influence of genetic factors on children's reactions to divorce? The answer is not straightforward, because parents contribute genes *and* environment to their biological children. O'Connor et al. (2000a) argued the best approach is to consider four types of families:

1. Biological families; no divorce.
2. Biological families; divorce.
3. Adoptive families; no divorce.
4. Adoptive families; divorce.

The children in adoptive families do not share genes with their adoptive parents, and so any adverse effects of divorce in such families must presumably be due to environmental factors. In contrast, adverse effects of divorce in biological families could be due to genetic factors, environmental factors, or both. If the adverse effects of divorce are comparable in biological and adoptive families, these effects can be attributed to environmental factors. If the adverse effects of divorce are greater in biological than adoptive families, then this would suggest that genetic factors play a role.

O'Connor et al. (2000a, p. 435) used the four types of families discussed above within the context of the Colorado Adoption Project. Their findings were as follows: "Whereas the associations between parental divorce history and indicators of self-esteem, social competence, and academic competence may be partly genetically influenced, the connections between divorce and children's psychopathology [mental disorder] may be attributed to environmentally mediated processes." Thus, genetic factors seem to play some part in producing the ill-effects of divorce on children, but environmental factors are also important.

There is a final point that needs to be made. Divorce is nearly always preceded by bitter conflicts and unpleasantness, and some of the adverse effects of divorce on children are probably due to such conflicts rather than to the divorce itself. Cherlin et al. (1991) addressed this issue. They considered longitudinal studies in Britain and in the United States in which children's behaviour problems and academic achievement were assessed before and after divorce. The key finding was that the children showed behaviour problems and poor achievement *before* their parents were divorced as well as afterwards. The implication is that children suffer from parental conflict in the pre-divorce period as well from divorce itself.

> **Have the effects of divorce been over-estimated?**
> Hetherington's (2002) study of 2500 people, 1400 families in total, over 25 years suggests that the adverse effects of divorce on children could have been over-estimated. Her conclusion is that 2 years after the divorce the vast majority of children are functioning quite well. Overall, about 80% of children cope and function well. But this does mean that 20% of children do not cope or function well—twice the proportion from families that are still together. These children have social and/or emotional problems and should receive help.

## Day care

Do infants who are placed in day care several days a week suffer as a result? As we will see, the answer may depend on the nature of the family and on the kinds of caregiving provided while the mother is working.

Several studies have been carried out in the Strange Situation test, which was discussed earlier. Overall, 36% of infants whose mothers work full time are insecurely attached (avoidant or resistant attachment), compared to 29% of infants whose mothers do not go out to work or who work part time (see Clarke-Stewart, 1989, for a review). It is hard to interpret these findings. For example, it may be that mothers who decide to work full time tend to be less emotionally attached to their babies than are mothers who stay at home. Another possible reason why the infants of working mothers are insecurely attached, "is not that 40 hours of day care is hard on infants but that 40 hours of work is hard on mothers" (p. 270).

*How would you explain these differences between types of day care?*

Belsky (1988) studied infants in the first year of life who were regularly placed in day-care settings. These infants were more likely than other infants to show an avoidant attachment to their mothers. According to Belsky (p. 401), there is "a rather robust association between extensive non-maternal care experience initiated in the first year of life and insecure infant–mother attachment assessed in the Strange Situation". Some support for Belsky's contention that any negative effects of day care are most likely to occur in children under the age of 1 was reported by Baydar and Brooks-Gunn (1991). When mothers started work when their child was under 1 year old, there were negative effects on its cognitive development. However, there were no negative effects when the mother waited until the child was over 1 year old before returning to work.

Most studies of day care have found few, if any, differences in emotional and intellectual development between children whose mothers do and do not go out to work (Clarke-Stewart, 1989). For example, Kagan et al. (1980) considered the impact of day care on young children over a 5-year period. Their rate of language development and their relationships with other children and with their mothers were as good as those of children raised at home. There is evidence that disadvantaged children actually benefit from high-quality day care (McCartney et al., 1985).

Children whose mothers go out to work can be looked after in various ways, and it is of interest to compare these ways. Melhuish et al. (1990) studied infants receiving nursery care, childminding, or being cared for by relatives. At 18 months of age, there were no differences among the three groups in terms of attachment to their mothers. At 3 years of age, all groups of children showed the same level of cognitive development. However, the children in nursery care had the lowest naming vocabulary. On the social side, children receiving nursery care showed rather more pro-social behaviour (e.g., co-operation, sharing) than did children in the other two groups.

Kagan et al. (1980) found that language development and relationships with other children were as good in day-care children as in children raised at home.

Scarr (1997) reviewed the evidence on the effects of child care. She discussed a study on more than 1000 infants, in which it was found that attachment to the mother as assessed by the Strange Situation was not affected at all by the amount of stimulation which infants received. Scarr pointed out that the care received within the home is far more important than day care in determining children's social development. However, children from low-income families often benefit substantially from high-quality day care. Scarr (p. 147) concluded her review in the following positive way: "Within a broad range of safe environments, quality variations in child care have only small and temporary effects on most children's development. With a few exceptions …, studies both in the United States and elsewhere fail to find any long-term effects."

Similar findings were reported by Erel, Oberman, and Yirmiya (2000), who carried out probably the most thorough series of meta-analyses on studies of the effects of day care. In all, they related day care to seven measures of child development, which they described as outcome variables:

1. *Secure vs. insecure attachment to the mother.*
2. *Attachment behaviours*: avoidance and resistance (reflecting insecure attachment), and exploration (reflecting secure attachment).
3. *Mother–child interaction*: responsiveness to mother, smiling at mother, obeying mother, and so on.
4. *Adjustment*: self-esteem, lack of behaviour problems, and so on.
5. *Social interaction with peers.*
6. *Social interaction with non-parental adults.*
7. *Cognitive development*: school performance, IQ, and so on.

Erel et al. (2000) also considered various other factors which might influence the effects of day care on the above measures of child development. Among the factors included were the number of hours of day care per week, the age at which the child started in day care, the number of months in day care, and the child's gender.

The key findings of Erel et al. (2000, p. 737) were very straightforward: "The fact that the composite mean weighted effect sizes of all seven outcome variables were non-significant and of very small magnitude indicates that research to date offers no support for the notion that child development is either positively or negatively associated with type of care per se." This conclusion was strengthened by the additional finding that the lack of impact of day care on all seven measures was obtained regardless of the amount of day care per week, the number of months the child had had in day care, the child's gender, and so on.

Suppose we focus on children receiving day care. What are the effects of day-care quality (e.g., language stimulation provided by caregiver, provision of stimulating toys) on young children's development? The National Institute of Child Health and Development (NICHD) has carried out an extensive study on over 1000 children. They found that the effects of the mother and family on young children were greater than the effects of day-care quality. However, there was an interaction between these factors: Children were more likely to show insecure attachment if there was a lack of maternal sensitivity and day care was of poor quality (NICHD, 1997b).

Finding an association between day-care quality and children's development is *not* sufficient to show that day-care quality has had a causal effect on children's development. Why is that? Those children who experience high-quality care tend to have parents who are better educated and more responsive than those children experiencing low quality care (NICHD, 1997b). As a result, it is hard to determine whether it is the parenting or the day care which is responsible for the association between day-care quality and children's development.

The above issue was addressed in the large NICHD study referred to above, in which over 1000 children were studied from birth to 4½ years. Detailed information about family environments was obtained, so that effects of day-care quality could be distinguished from those of family environment. When the effects of family environment were controlled, the influence of day-care quality was surprisingly modest: "Although there may be a causal link between child-care quality and child outcomes, the evidence for it is mixed and the 'effect', if any, is not large … and is restricted to cognitive outcomes" (NICHD, p. 467). More specifically, day-care quality influenced memory and

Melhuish et al. (1990) found that children receiving nursery care show more co-operative and sharing behaviour than those that were cared for by a relative or childminder.

---

### The importance of the quality of childcare

The USA's Early Child Care Research Network, funded by the National Institute of Child Health and Human Development (NICHD), has 26 principal researchers at 10 different sites. Their findings, reported at the APA (1999) Annual Convention, emphasised the vital importance of the quality of childcare, and not its duration, as an influence on development. High quality leads to improved cognitive development—but high quality requires child–staff ratios of 3 : 1 in the under 2s, group sizes of six in that age group, and formally trained child carers. Low-quality care, out of or in the home, is linked to poor readiness for starting school and poor language skills (Early Child Care Research Network, 1999).

language quality, but didn't affect social development (e.g., social competence, behaviour problems).

In sum, day care generally has no negative effects on young children. The one exception may be extensive day care for infants in the first year of life (Baydar & Brooks-Gunn, 1991; Belsky, 1988), but even there the effects are rather small. In addition, day care of poor quality may have minor adverse effects on cognitive development (NICHD, 2003). In assessing the effects of day care on young children, we need to consider the position of the mother. For example, Harrison and Ungerer (2002) studied families in which the mother had returned to paid employment during the first year of her infant's life. Infants were most likely to be securely attached to their mothers at 12 months when their mother was strongly committed to work and had little anxiety about using non-family child care than when the mother was not committed to work and had anxieties about making use of child care.

## CROSS-CULTURAL DIFFERENCES IN CHILD REARING

So far in this chapter the focus has been largely on processes of early attachment and socialisation among young children in the United States and United Kingdom. However, there are substantial differences in child-rearing practices from one culture to another, and these differences inevitably influence children's social behaviour.

Two cautions are needed before we proceed. First, when we discover interesting cross-cultural differences in child-rearing practices and in children's behaviour and development, it is tempting to conclude the former have caused the latter. However, cross-cultural studies are essentially correlational, and so cannot prove there are causal relationships between child-rearing practices and children's development.

Second, it is dangerous to assume that some cultures have better child-rearing practices than others. Full account needs to be taken of the *appropriateness* of a culture's child-rearing practices within that particular culture. For example, parents may spend very little time looking after their children if the culture to which they belong is very poor and under threat. An example of this is found among deprived families in the north east of Brazil (Scheper-Hughes, 1992). Children in this area who fail to develop at the normal rate

Child-rearing practices vary from culture to culture. Although in many countries it would be unacceptable to expect children as young as these to earn their own livings, these Bangladeshi rubbish collectors make an important financial contribution to their family's well-being.

typically receive very little care if they become ill. This sounds very harsh. However, it becomes more understandable when one realises that these families are living in such difficult conditions that about 50% of the children die before the age of 5. In those circumstances, it makes sense to give proper care only to those children having the best chance of survival.

The dangers of trying to impose cultural values were shown by Raven (1980) in a Home Visiting project in Edinburgh. In this project, working-class mothers were encouraged to adopt what was regarded as the middle-class approach of communicating very frequently with their children. As a result, the mothers became less confident of their own mothering skills. As Meadows (1986) commented, "Some part of what is 'good parenting' depends on what society outside the family allows to, and demands of, the child and family" (p. 183). Thus, child-rearing practices develop because they "work" within that culture.

## Child-rearing practices

We saw earlier in the chapter that infants in Western cultures often have more than one caregiver, and so form strong attachments to more than one person (e.g., Weston & Main, 1981). Cross-cultural research has indicated that it is common practice in numerous cultures for more than one person to be responsible for caregiving. For example, Weisner and Gallimore (1977) considered caregiving in nearly 200 non-industrialised cultures. The mother was virtually the only caregiver in only 3% of these cultures. One or more individuals other than the mother was much involved in caregiving during infancy in 40% of the cultures, and this figure increased to 80% in early childhood.

Some studies have found important similarities in child-rearing practices across cultures, whereas others have not. Among those studies reporting similarities was one by Keller et al. (1988). They observed mothers and their infants in four cultures: German, Greek, Yanomani Indian, and Trobriand Island, and found evidence that mother–infant communication patterns were similar in all four cultures. For example, conversations between mothers and infants and patterns of eye contact showed clear similarities in each culture.

In contrast, Rabain-Jamin (1989) found French mothers and West African mothers living in Paris treated their 10- to 15-month infants rather differently. Native French mothers spoke more to their children. They were also more likely to integrate verbal and non-verbal information, for example, by naming and talking about an object while pointing to it. The essence of the difference in child-rearing practices was expressed as follows by a West African mother: "We give toys to play with. You give them toys to teach, for the future. We feel that children learn better when they are older" (p. 303).

When would we expect to find cultural differences in child-rearing practices? Such differences typically reflect differences in the cultural expectations of older children and adults. For example, consider the differences between French and West African mothers reported by Rabain-Jamin (1989). The expectation within French culture is that children will devote several years to formal education, with high-level language skills forming an important part of that education. In contrast, the expectation within West African culture is that children will become equipped at a fairly young age to handle the practical demands of everyday living. The differences in child-rearing practices seem well-designed to achieve these cultural goals.

### Cultural values

Child-rearing practices in different cultures are of importance in passing on cultural values from one generation to the next. For example, cultures differ in their emphasis on individualism versus collectivism (e.g., Hofstede, 1980; see Chapter 1). Individualistic cultures (e.g., the American) focus on personal achievement, whereas collectivistic cultures (e.g., the Japanese and Chinese) focus on group effort and co-operation. Bornstein et al. (1990) found that Japanese mothers encouraged their babies to attend to them, after which the mothers directed their child's attention to some aspect of the environment. In contrast, American mothers provided support and encouragement to their babies, regardless of whether they attended to the environment or to their mother. These findings suggest that Japanese mothers focus mainly on the interpersonal development of their infants, whereas American mothers focus on developing initiative in their infants.

Similar findings were reported by Harwood and Miller (1991). Anglo-American mothers reacted favourably to signs of independence in their infants, which fits with the individualistic British and American cultures. In contrast, Puerto Rican culture is more collectivistic, and mothers in that culture reacted favourably to obedient and social behaviour by their infants.

Reasonable evidence that child-rearing practices can influence social development by fostering collectivism was reported by Bronfenbrenner (1970). He interviewed 12-year-olds in the old Soviet Union, Great Britain, the United States, and what was then West Germany. Some of the children were told their interview answers would be entirely confidential, whereas others were told that only their peers would know what they had said, and still others were informed that the results would be shown at a parent–teacher meeting.

The answers of the Soviet children revealed much less anti-social behaviour in every condition than did those of any of the other three groups of children. The German, British, and American children were more willing to admit to anti-social behaviour when they thought only their peers would know what they had said, whereas the Soviet children refused to admit to anti-social behaviour even in that condition. In those days, the Soviet educational system was designed to make children develop a sense of collective belonging, and this provides the most obvious explanation of the very low level of anti-social behaviour among Soviet children.

## Parenting style

Several styles of parenting have been identified. One of the most influential approaches is that of Maccoby and Martin (1983). They identified two dimensions of parenting style: (1) demanding vs. undemanding; and (2) responsive vs. unresponsive. According to this approach, there are four major parenting styles:

- Authoritative: demanding + responsive;
- Authoritarian: demanding + unresponsive;
- Permissive: undemanding + responsive;
- Uninvolved: undemanding + unresponsive.

Dekovic and Janssens (1992) studied children aged between 6 and 11 years. Children whose parents were authoritative tended to be friendly and popular, whereas those whose parents were authoritarian tended to be rejected by other children. The distinction between authoritative and authoritarian parents seems to be important in non-Western cultures as well. Chen, Dong, and Zhou (1997) found among 8-year-old children in Beijing that those having authoritative parents were better liked and were less likely to be rejected than those having authoritarian parents.

Collectivistic and individualistic societies differ in parenting style along the demanding–undemanding dimension (Triandis, 1994). Parents in collectivistic societies are relatively demanding, because they want their children to become co-operative and obedient members of society. In contrast, parents in individualistic societies tend to be undemanding to encourage their children to become independent. Children seem to be influenced by these cultural expectations regarding child-rearing practices. For example, children in South Korea (a moderately collectivistic culture) regard parents who are accepting and demanding as much more loving than parents who are accepting and undemanding (Rohner & Pettengill, 1985).

What about the responsive–unresponsive dimension? Cross-cultural studies indicate that children in virtually all societies do better in terms of social development if their

Rohner and Pettengill (1985) found that children in collectivistic cultures, such as South Korea, view parents who are accepting and demanding as more loving than parents who are accepting and permissive.

*To what extent could these variations lead to different behaviours being seen as problematic in children in these cultures?*

parents are responsive (accepting) rather than unresponsive (rejecting). Unresponsive parenting is associated with aggression, delinquency, difficulty in maintaining intimate relationships, and moodiness (Rohner, 1986). Rohner (1975) carried out a large cross-cultural study in which cultures were assessed for parental acceptance versus rejection. Across cultures there was a correlation of +.72 between parental acceptance and self-esteem in children, indicating an almost universal tendency for high self-esteem in children to be associated with parental acceptance. Cultures with accepting or loving parents also had children who were low in hostility (a correlation of −.48) and low in dependence (a correlation of −.30).

It is useful to consider parenting styles when trying to understand children's social development. However, most attempts to categorise parenting styles are limited. For example, the two-dimensional approach put forward by Maccoby and Martin (1983) does not explicitly refer to parental warmth, which is likely to have an important impact on children's social development. There is some evidence that most of the ways of categorising parenting styles developed by Western psychologists are less relevant when applied to non-Western cultures. For example, Darling and Steinberg (1993) discussed a study in which parenting styles predicted American children's social behaviour better when their family had emigrated from Europe rather than Africa.

## Attachment styles

Infant attachment styles in various cultures have been studied using the Strange Situation test devised by Ainsworth and Bell (1970), and discussed earlier in the chapter. Findings for infants in the United States, Israel, Japan, and Germany were reported by Sagi et al. (1991). Their findings for the American infants were similar to those reported by Ainsworth and Bell (1970): 71% showed secure attachment, 12% showed resistant attachment, and 17% were avoidant. The Israeli infants behaved rather differently from the American ones. Secure attachment was shown by 62% of them, 33% were resistant, and only 5% were avoidant. These infants lived in a kibbutz or collective farm, and were looked after by adults who were not part of their family much of the time. However, they had a close relationship with their mothers, and so tended not to be anxious and avoidant.

Japanese infants are treated very differently from Israeli infants. Japanese mothers practically never leave their infants alone with a stranger. In spite of the differences in child-rearing practices in Japan and Israel, the Japanese infants showed similar attachment styles to the Israeli ones. Two-thirds of them (68%) had a secure attachment, 32% were resistant, and none was avoidant. The complete absence of avoidant attachment may have

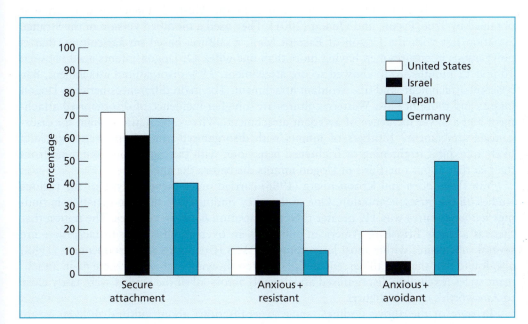

Children from different countries vary in their attachment types. The graph summarises research from Sagi et al. (1991) and Ainsworth and Bell (1970).

*To what extent do you think that these variations between cultures are likely to be greater than variations within cultures?*

occurred because the infants were faced with the totally new situation of being on their own with a stranger.

Israeli and Japanese children showed resistant attachment for rather different reasons. Israeli children are accustomed to being separated from their mother, but rarely encounter complete strangers. Thus, their resistant behaviour was due to the presence of the stranger. In contrast, Japanese children are practically never separated from their mother during the first year of life, and this was the main cause of their resistant attachment behaviour. Takahashi (1990) confirmed that many 12-month-old Japanese infants show resistant attachment, but also found that far fewer infants showed resistant attachment at 24 months. The reason for this is probably that Japanese infants spend increasing amounts of time away from their mothers after the first year of life.

The notion that Japanese infants behave as they do because they have not had the experience of being separated from their mother receives support from a study by Durrett et al. (1984). They focused on Japanese families in which the mothers were pursuing careers, and so had to leave their children in the care of others. The children of these mothers showed a similar pattern of attachment styles to that found in the United States.

Finally, the German infants showed a different pattern of attachment to the other three groups of infants. Only 40% of them were securely attached, which was less than the number of infants (49%) who were avoidant. The remaining 11% were resistant. Grossman, Grossman, Spangler, Syess, and Unzner (1985) obtained very similar findings. They suggested that German culture requires keeping some interpersonal distance between parents and children: "The ideal is an independent, non-clinging infant who does not make demands on the parents but rather unquestioningly obeys their commands" (p. 253).

Further evidence on why it is that German children are less likely to be securely attached than infants from other cultures was reported by Sagi and Lewkowicz (1987). German parents regarded some aspects of securely attached behaviour in a negative way, as indicating that the infants were spoiled.

The very different child-rearing practices in the United States, Israel, Japan, and Germany have a significant impact on infants' attachment styles. However, about two-thirds of infants in the United States, Israel, and Japan show secure attachment to their mothers. This suggests that the goal of producing securely attached children can be reached in various ways.

Can the Strange Situation test be used successfully to study children's attachment in cultures radically different from those found in the West? Evidence that it can was obtained by True, Pisani, and Oumar (2001). They used a modified version of the Strange Situation test with the Dogon of Eastern Mali, a culture, based on agriculture, that is polygamous in nature (men having more than one wife). Of Dogon infants aged between 10 and 12 months, 67% showed secure attachment, 25% disorganised attachment, 8% resistant attachment, and 0% avoidant attachment. The main differences between Dogon infants and those in most Western cultures are a higher incidence of disorganised attachment and a lower incidence of avoidant attachment. Why is the figure so high for disorganised attachment? Mothers of infants with disorganised attachment were especially likely to exhibit frightening or frightened behaviour, with this behaviour stemming from the fact that about one-third of Dogon infants die before the age of 5.

Van IJzendoorn and Kroonenberg (1988) carried out a meta-analysis of the various studies on the Strange Situation. One of their key findings was that the variation in findings *within* cultures was 1½ greater than the variation *between* cultures. The notion that there is a *single* British or American culture is an oversimplification: In fact, there are several subcultures within most large countries. Van IJzendoorn and Kroonenberg (1988) also found that the overall percentages of children showing each of the three main attachment styles (excluding disorganised attachment) across all of the studies were fairly close to Ainsworth's original figures.

In spite of the above findings, some generalisations about cultural differences are possible. According to Durkin (1995), "While Type Bs [securely attached] are the most common type, Type As [avoidant] are relatively more common in Western European countries, while Type Cs [resistant] are relatively more frequent in Israel and Japan" (p. 106).

## Evaluation

- ⊕ Cross-cultural studies reveal important cultural differences in child-rearing practices and in the relationship between infants and their mothers.
- ⊕ Cultural differences in parenting style seem to influence children's attachment pattern and social development.
- ⊖ As Cole and Cole (1993, pp. 235–236) pointed out, "cultural differences in the meaning attached to the Strange Situation make it difficult to infer the true nature of the emotional bonds between the mothers and their children, leading to false conclusions when patterns discovered in one culture are used to reason about another."
- ⊖ The great reliance on the Strange Situation in cross-cultural research means that conclusions about cultural differences in attachment behaviour are based on a rather narrow set of empirical findings.

## PEER RELATIONSHIPS

Children of nearly all ages spend significant amounts of time with their peers (individuals of about the same age). Even at a very early age, infants show clear signs of being interested in their peers and in social interaction. For example, Tremblay-Leveau and Nadel (1996) carried out a study involving pairs of infants of 11 or 24 months of age who already knew each other. Each pair of infants interacted with a familiar experimenter. Of interest was the reaction of an infant when excluded from an interaction between the experimenter and the other child. Children at 11 months were five times more likely to interact with the other child (e.g., smiling, putting their body between the experimenter and the other child) when excluded than when not excluded. There was an eightfold increase in interactions with the other child among 24-month-old children who were excluded. Thus, even infants seek attention from their peers.

Infants start to play with each other at about 6 months old and gradually improve their communication as they develop physical, cognitive, and language skills.

One of the most striking developmental changes in peer relationships is a marked increase in the preference for associating with same-sex peers. Maccoby (1998) has reviewed evidence showing that this occurs in numerous cultures around the world. From about the age of 3, children prefer to play with same-sex rather than opposite-sex peers. When they start going to school, the percentage of children associating with same-sex children in the playground increases steadily between the ages of 4 and 12. This same-sex preference is also found with respect to friendship. Children's best friend between middle childhood and adolescence is typically someone of the same sex.

Children interact with their peers in various ways. However, research on children's peer interactions can conveniently be divided into two major areas. First, we can focus on children's ability to interact constructively and happily with their peers. Such research allows us to identify individual differences among children in social competence and social status. Second, we can study friendship patterns among children. In such research, the emphasis is on relatively close relationships with specific peers. The two areas are linked, in the sense that we would expect socially competent children to have more friends than socially incompetent children. However, it is perfectly possible for a child lacking in social competence to have a close friend, or for a socially competent and popular child to have no close friend. We will consider these two lines of research in turn.

## Social competence

There are various methods for assessing how well children relate to their peers. For example, observational techniques can be used to measure different kinds of social behaviour (e.g., smiling, aggressive actions). Another method is to use peer ratings, in which all the

*Can you think of any possible cultural variation in behaviours involved in social competence?*

children in a group rate each other in terms of likeability or some similar dimension. The information from such ratings can be used to work out the most and least popular children within the group. The two methods often produce comparable findings (Bukowski & Hoza, 1989).

Methods such as those described above allow us to categorise children on the basis of how accepted they are by other children. Theorists differ in the number and nature of the social categories which they propose. However, the scheme put forward by Coie, Dodge, and Coppotelli (1982) is fairly representative. They studied large numbers of children aged 8, 11, and 14, asking all of them to identify three classmates whom they liked most, and three whom they liked least. On the basis of that information (and several behaviour descriptions), Coie et al. proposed five categories:

1. *Popular* (often liked most; seldom liked least).
2. *Controversial* (often liked most; often liked least).
3. *Average* (sometimes liked most; sometimes liked least).
4. *Neglected* (seldom liked most; seldom liked least).
5. *Rejected* (seldom liked most; often liked least).

What factors were associated with being liked most and being liked least? The main factors associated with being liked most were being supportive, co-operating with peers, leading peers, and being physically attractive. The main factors associated with being liked least were disrupting the group, getting into trouble with the teacher, starting fights, and being snobbish.

It would be tempting (but wrong!) to assume that all children assigned to the same category have similar behaviour. For example, Cillessen et al. (1992) studied almost 100 rejected children in detail by considering several kinds of evidence (e.g., peer ratings, behavioural observations, teacher ratings). Almost half of the rejected children were aggressive, and also tended to be unco-operative and dishonest. About one-eighth of the rejected children were submissive and shy, and the remaining rejected children exhibited few extreme forms of behaviour. As might be expected, the children rejected because they were aggressive were much more likely than the other rejected children to continue to be in the rejected group 1 year later (58% vs. 34%, respectively).

It might be imagined that rejected children lack insight into the opinions held about them by their peers. This issue was investigated by MacDonald and Cohen (1995) in a study on children between the ages of 7 and 12. Rejected children were less accurate than other children at predicting which other children liked them. However, they were very good at predicting who disliked them, and showed more ability here than did the popular children. Perhaps rejected children focus too much on the negative reactions of other children and not enough on the positive reactions they evoke.

## What underlies social competence?

As we have seen, some children are socially competent (and so tend to be popular), whereas others lack social competence (and so tend to be rejected or ignored). Not surprisingly, one of the factors associated with children's level of social competence is the security of their attachment to their mother or other significant adult. For example, Stams et al. (2002) in a study discussed earlier assessed the attachment of adopted children to their adoptive mother at 12 months of age. Children who were securely attached at 12 months had better social competence and general social development at the age of 7 years than did children who were not securely attached at 12 months.

What are the key differences between children high and low in social competence? As Lemerise and Arsenio (2000) pointed out, two main answers have been proposed in the literature. First, there may be cognitive differences, with socially competent children being more skilled at social information processing (e.g., Crick & Dodge, 1994). Second, there may be emotional differences, with socially incompetent children experiencing many negative emotions and having poor emotional regulation or control (e.g., Eisenberg & Fabes, 1992). These two approaches to understanding social competence are discussed below.

## Social information processing

Crick and Dodge (1994) put forward a model emphasising the importance of social information processing. They proposed that six steps are involved in social behaviour, with every step needing to be completed successfully for social competence to be demonstrated:

1. Attend to and encode the social cues (e.g., the non-verbal behaviour of another child) in a situation.
2. Interpret or make sense of those social cues (e.g., deciding why someone else has behaved in a certain way).
3. Select a goal or desired outcome for the situation (e.g., making a new friend).
4. Consider possible responses to the situation (e.g., offer help to the other person).
5. Evaluate possible responses and select the one offering the greatest possibility of achieving the desired goal or outcome.
6. Produce the chosen response.

From what has been said so far it might be assumed that these six steps occur one after the other in a rigid sequence. However, the cyclical structure and feedback loops contained in the figure below indicate that assumption is incorrect. According to Crick and Dodge (p. 77), "Individuals are engaged in multiple social information-processing activities at the same time … individuals are perpetually engaging in each of the steps of processing proposed."

How does the model explain why older children have higher levels of social competence and adjustment than younger ones? First, children's database of social knowledge increases over time. As a result, they have more possible responses from which to choose, and they gradually learn more about the likely consequences of producing any given response. Second, children show developmental increases in capacity and/or speed of processing, and these increases allow them to process social information more efficiently.

## Evidence

Strassberg and Dodge (1987) found that individual differences in interpreting social cues (step 2) help to explain why some children are better adjusted socially. Rejected and

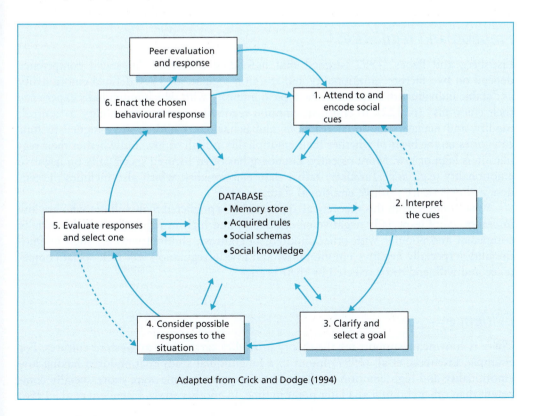

Adapted from Crick and Dodge (1994)

non-rejected children watched videotapes of other children at play, and were asked to interpret what they saw. Rejected children were more likely than non-rejected children to provide aggressive interpretations of the social interactions in the videotapes.

Crick and Ladd (1990) assessed the role of response evaluation (step 5) in social competence. Children were presented with a situation, and evaluated what would happen if they responded in a given way. Children who predicted verbal aggression would produce positive outcomes tended to be children rejected by their peers. In addition, neglected children predicted that behaving assertively would lead to more negative outcomes than did non-neglected children.

Dodge et al. (1986) applied the model to children who were at kindergarten or had just started school. The children were first shown videotapes of children playing, and were asked questions to assess their awareness of what should happen at each of the various steps of social information processing. After that, they joined two other children already involved in playing a building game. As predicted, children performing best on the videotape task showed the greatest social competence on the group entry task.

## Evaluation

⊕ The model provides a detailed account of children's cognitive processing of social information.

⊕ There is reasonable evidence relating skill at social information processing to measures of social competence.

⊖ The relationship between social information processing and social competence is not very strong, indicating that social competence depends on factors omitted from the model.

⊖ Thinking about one's own behaviour and that of others in social situations is very different from thinking about things. A key difference is that powerful emotions are much more likely to be involved in social information processing, but Crick and Dodge's (1994) model has relatively little to say about emotional processes.

## Emotion and regulation

Eisenberg and Fabes (1992) argued that individual differences in social competence depend on two factors: emotionality and emotion regulation. They defined emotionality as "stable individual differences in the typical intensity with which individuals experience their emotions" (p. 122). In contrast, emotion regulation involves the ability to control, modify, and manage emotional reactions and behaviour. Children are assigned to four categories on the basis of whether their emotionality is high or low and whether their regulation is high or low. More recently, Eisenberg has often focused specifically on negative emotionality (e.g., anger, anxiety) rather than emotionality, which also includes the tendency to experience positive emotional states.

What follows from this theoretical approach? It is predicted that children who are low in emotionality (especially negative emotionality) and high in regulation will be socially competent and popular with other children. In contrast, children who are high in emotionality (especially negative emotionality) and low in regulation will lack social competence and will tend to be rejected by their peers.

## Evidence

There is convincing support for the theory in studies carried out in Western cultures. For example, Eisenberg et al. (1997) found in a longitudinal study that children having low emotionality and high emotion regulation at one point in time were more socially competent than other children at a later point in time. In another study, Eisenberg et al. (1996)

found that children having high emotionality and low regulation subsequently had poorer social functioning and exhibited more problem behaviour than other children.

Eisenberg, Pidada, and Liew (2001) wanted to see whether negative emotionality and regulation are important in a culture very different from most Western ones. They selected Java in Indonesia, which is a very collectivistic or group-centred culture, and one in which emotion regulation is valued very highly. The findings were very similar to those previously obtained in the United States. Children who were rejected by their peers had lower scores on emotion regulation than children who were not rejected. In addition, rejected children had higher scores on negative emotionality than did children who were popular, neglected, or average.

Eisenberg et al. (2001) also found gender differences which were similar to those obtained in Western cultures. Males were rated higher than females on negative emotionality and lower on regulation. Perhaps as a result, more males than females were disliked, and males were rated lower in social skills.

## Evaluation

- ⊕ When trying to understand individual differences in social competence, it makes sense to emphasise emotional factors.
- ⊕ Emotionality (particularly negative emotionality) in combination with poor emotion regulation is associated with lack of social competence, rejection, and behaviour problems.
- ⊖ There is a moderately negative association between negative emotionality and emotion regulation (e.g., Eisenberg et al., 2001), and so the two dimensions are not entirely separate.
- ⊖ The theory is relatively uninformative about the cognitive processes involved in peer interactions. Lemerise and Arsenio (2000) suggested that progress could be made by relating this theory to Crick and Dodge's (1994) model. The central assumption is that children high in negative emotionality and low in emotion regulation have deficits at every step of social information processing.
- ⊖ The theory doesn't provide a detailed account of the processes underlying the development of emotion regulation.
- ⊖ The direction of causality is often unclear: High negative emotionality and poor regulation may cause children to be rejected, but rejection may itself increase negative emotionality and impair regulation.

## Consequences of social incompetence

There is much evidence indicating that children who are rejected or neglected by their peers may experience various emotional and behavioural problems subsequently (see Deater-Deckard, 2001, for a review). For example, Keiley, Bates, Dodge, and Pettit (2000) found that children were rejected by their peers in kindergarten were much more likely than other children to have behaviour problems in middle childhood and adolescence. Miller-Johnson, Cole, Maumary-Gremaud, Lochman, and Terry (1999) reported that children at school who were rejected by their peers were more likely to exhibit extreme forms of delinquency in adolescence. Children who are withdrawn and avoid social interactions with their peers are sometimes neglected and sometimes rejected. Such children have been found to be susceptible to disorders such as anxiety and depression (Rubin, Bukowski, & Parker, 1998).

It is not easy to interpret findings such as those described in the previous paragraph. Children who are rejected or neglected by their peers are more likely than socially competent children to live in poverty and to experience harsh parenting (Deater-Deckard, 2001). As a result, it is hard to show that children's difficulties with their peers are directly responsible for later problems such as delinquency or depression. Some light has been shone on this issue by considering what happens when children move school and have to adjust to a new peer group. Berndt, Hawkins, and Jiao (1999) found that children aged 11 or 12 who had a stable friendship during the period of transition from one school to another were less likely than other children to show an increase in withdrawn behaviour. In similar fashion, Fenzel (2000) found that children who experienced stress in forming a new peer group after moving school showed a substantial reduction in self-worth. Thus, there is suggestive evidence that difficulties with peers can cause various problems.

## Friendships

Much of the research on children's friendships has involved comparisons between children who have friends and those who do not. However, this is a gross over-simplification, because friendships differ enormously from each other (Hartup, 1996). For example, friendships obviously differ in terms of quality, whether the friend has high or low status in the peer group, and so on. There is evidence that friendship quality is more important than quantity. Berndt (1989) studied children of 11 or 12 who moved school. Friendship quality was positively related to the friendship support the children received during this period of transition. However, the number of friends was actually *negatively* related to friendship support.

Friendship is an important part of relationships with peers.

What characteristics are associated with friendship? Bukowski, Hoza, and Boivin (1994) provided relevant evidence by devising a Friendship Qualities Scale. This questionnaire contains five sub-scales designed to assess companionship, closeness, help, security, and conflict. Bukowski et al. asked children aged between 10 and 12 to rate friends and other peers on all sub-scales. Friends consistently received higher scores than non-friends on four of the sub-scales (companionship, help, security, and closeness). In addition, friends who remained friends 6 months later received higher scores on those sub-scales than did friends who did not remain as friends. In contrast, friends tended to receive lower scores than non-friends on the conflict sub-scale, although there was no difference between friends who remained or did not remain as friends over the following 6 months.

Newcomb and Bagwell (1995) obtained similar findings in a meta-analysis to identify factors characterising friendship relationships more than non-friendship ones. Not surprisingly, friendships showed more evidence of positive engagement (social contact, talking, co-operation, and positive affect). Friendships were also associated with various relationship properties such as closeness, loyalty, mutual liking, equality, and similarity. Two further factors associated with friendship were conflict management and task activity. Conflict management involved more effective negotiation when conflicts arose, and task activity involved effective focusing on the task in hand.

Fonzi et al. (1997) provided evidence of conflict management between 8-year-old friends who had to share equipment or task turns when playing a game. Friends were more likely than non-friends to make suggestions, to negotiate ways of proceeding, and were more likely to compromise and be agreeable.

As might be imagined, children's friends tend to be similar to them. However, friends are more similar with respect to some attributes than others. Of key importance is what is known as reputational salience, which is the importance of any given attribute in determining a child's status. Friends are typically more similar with respect to attributes having high reputational salience than attributes having low reputational salience. Challman (1932) found that friends were generally similar in terms of social co-operation, an attribute having high reputational salience. However, friends were not very similar with respect to intelligence, an attribute having low reputational salience. In similar fashion, Haselager et al. (1995) found with 11-year-olds that friends were more similar for antisocial behaviour (an attribute of high reputational salience) than for pro-social behaviour or social withdrawal.

## Does the nature of friendship change with age?

Newcomb and Bagwell (1995) considered whether there are systematic changes in the nature of friendship between the preschool years and early adolescence. There was a large increase in positive engagement with friends between preschool (up to about 5 years) and childhood years (between about 6 and 9 years of age), and a further small increase between the childhood years and early adolescence (about 10–13 years). However, there was also an increase in positive engagement with non-friends, producing the following somewhat surprising conclusion: "Although there were significant differences in the over-all behavioural manifestations of friendship compared with non-friendship relations at each of the three age levels, the relative magnitude of these overall differences did not vary between the three levels" (p. 340).

There were more convincing changes with age in the relationship properties associated with friendship (e.g., closeness, loyalty). These relationship properties increased systematically throughout the period from preschool up to early adolescence. According to Newcomb and Bagwell (1995, p. 340), "It has been hypothesised that adolescent friendships are characterised by greater intimacy than are the friendships of younger children … The current meta-analytic findings provide strong empirical support for this age-related difference."

Hartup and Stevens (1997, p. 356) argued that friendships possess a deep structure and a surface structure: "We use *deep structure* to refer to the social meaning (essence) of relationships and *surface structure* to refer to the social exchanges that characterise them at any given moment or in any given situation." Hartup and Stevens then proceeded to make two main predictions: (1) The deep structure of friendships doesn't change during development; (2) the surface structure of friendships changes in various ways during development.

According to Hartup and Stevens (1997), reciprocity or mutuality is of central importance in friendship deep structure. Thus, friendship at all ages is based on a fair balance between giving and taking. However, *what* is given and taken (the surface structure) varies as a function of age. Goodnow and Burns (1995) found that young children's expectations of friendship tended to revolve around rather concrete reciprocities and common interests (e.g., "And I given them food, so they give me food back", p. 120). Among school children, reciprocity takes the form of shared interests (e.g., "A good friend is someone who likes you and spends time with you and forgives you and doesn't actually bash you up", p. 120).

In adolescence, the types of reciprocity between friends are rather different. When adolescents described their ideal friend, they indicated that he/she was someone who was supportive in the sense of being understanding and trustworthy. Thus, there is a shift in the nature of reciprocity or mutuality from common activities in young children to shared interests during the main school years, to emotional reciprocity among adolescents.

## Evaluation

● Numerous studies indicate that children's friendships possess some similarities (e.g., reciprocity, positive engagement) throughout childhood and adolescence.

● Much research indicates that children's friendships are characterised by some differences (closeness, complexity) over the years from childhood to adolescence.

● Most studies on children's friendships provide empirical data about friendship patterns at various ages, but do not test any clear theoretical predictions.

● Most research has been cross-sectional, with the friendships of children of different ages being studied at a given point in time. As a result, relatively little is known about the dynamic changes occurring over time within many friendships. For example, we lack a detailed understanding of the processes causing friendships to become stronger and weaker.

## Consequences of having (or not having) friends

Not surprisingly, children who have friends typically have superior social development than those who do not. According to Hartup (1996, p. 4), "Not one data set suggests that children with friends are worse off than children who do not have them." However, it is hard to show that having friends is the decisive factor. After all, children with friends differ from those without friends in many ways, including having greater social competence, more responsive parents, and so on (Hartup, 1996). This issue has been addressed to some extent in a number of longitudinal studies in which children were followed up for a period of several months. For example, Berndt et al. (1999), in a study discussed earlier, found that children who changed school in the company of one or more good friends suffered from fewer psychological disturbances than those unaccompanied by good friends. Ladd (1990) found that young children who made new friends at kindergarten showed greater improvements in school performance than those who did not make new friends.

A study by Bagwell, Newcomb, and Bukowski (1998) was the first one which tested the assumption that childhood friendships play an important role in social and emotional development in a long-term longitudinal study. Bagwell et al. identified 11- and 12-year-olds who had or did not have a close friend. They also obtained a measure of social competence by assessing peer rejection. All the children were then followed up until they reached the age of 23. Children having friends had greater feelings of self-worth in adulthood. In addition, those having a friend at the age of 11 were less likely than friendless children to have symptoms of depression in adulthood. Children who were both friendless and suffered peer rejection were more likely than other children to become delinquents in adolescence and adulthood.

Peer rejection on its own was associated with some negative effects later on. For example, rejection by peers at the age of 11 or 12 was associated with inferior school performance, lower aspiration level, and reduced participation in social activities.

## PARENTS, PEERS, OR GENES?

The evidence considered in this chapter (and in the previous one) suggests that children's development is strongly influenced by the way they are treated by their parents. However, matters may not be so simple. Consider, for example, the association between high levels of parental negativity and/or hostility and anti-social behaviour in their adolescent children. It may seem natural to assume it is the parents' behaviour causing poor adjustment in their children. However, there are other possibilities. For example, anti-social behaviour by children may cause their parents to react in a hostile way. In this section of the chapter we will focus on attempts to clarify the meaning of such findings.

## Behavioural genetics

An approach for understanding some causal factors responsible for children's social development is known as behavioural genetics. **Behavioural genetics** can be defined as, "the scientific study of how genotype interacts with environment to determine behavioural attributes such as intelligence, personality, and mental health" (Shaffer, 2000). Some of the main findings emerging from this approach are discussed below.

We will make a start by returning to the issue of how to explain the fact that negative parental behaviour is associated with anti-social behaviour in their children. O'Connor, Deater-Deckard, Fulker, Rutter, and Plomin (1998) considered this issue from the perspective of behavioural genetics (see Chapter 16). They studied adopted children, some of whose biological mothers had a history of anti-social behaviour prior to the birth of their child. It was assumed that adopted children whose mother had such a history would be genetically at risk for anti-social behaviour. The tendency of the adoptive parents to use negative control in the form of hostility, guilt induction, and withdrawal from the relationship was assessed.

The key finding obtained by O'Connor et al. (1998) was as follows: "Children at genetic risk received more negative control from their adoptive parents than children not at genetic risk from middle childhood to early adolescence." Thus, children at genetic risk for anti-social behaviour evoke or produce negative behaviour from their adoptive parents. Thus, genetic factors in the children influence the association between negative parental behaviour and anti-social behaviour in children.

*Why did these researchers choose to study adopted children?*

O'Connor et al. (1998) did *not* find that negative parental behaviour is due entirely to genetic factors in their adopted children. Parental behaviour depends on numerous factors, including financial problems, the quality of the marital relationship, and the parent's own experiences as a child (Hetherington, 1993).

Behavioural geneticists identify three types of influences determining the extent to which children within the same family will be similar or dissimilar. First, there are genetic influences. Second, there are shared environmental influences, consisting of those environmental influences (e.g., parental behaviour) which children of the same family have in common. If Freud and many other theorists are correct, then shared environmental influences provided within the family should have a major impact on children's personality development. Third, there are non-shared environmental influences, which are the experiences unique to one child. Note that the term "non-shared environment" is somewhat misleading. As Westen (1998, p. 349) pointed out, "It [non-shared environment] includes shared events to which different children respond differently ... Thus, early separation from a parent may have a substantially greater effect on a child who is temperamentally higher in negative affect than one with an easier temperament, even though the environmental event is identical and hence shared."

Loehlin (1985) obtained fairly typical findings, and we will focus on his study. He measured several personality traits in monozygotic or identical twins, dizygotic or fraternal twins, and in unrelated children brought up in the same household (see Chapter 13). Correlations were used to assess the degree of similarity in personality between children belonging to these various categories. Identical twins were fairly similar in personality, as was indicated by a mean correlation of +.50 across the various traits. Fraternal twins were less similar, with a mean correlation of +.30. Of most relevance to the present discussion, unrelated children brought up in the same household had a mean correlation of +.07, meaning they scarcely resembled each other at all. Thus, shared environment had minimal impact on their personality development.

One problem with researching twins is that identical twins are very rare. Identical twins who are identifiable *and* have been brought up apart are extremely rare. This means that the twin sample is never going to be representative of the general population and is also going to be very small in size. So this type of research cannot really be conclusive, though it can give us useful ideas to consider.

There is another way of investigating the influence of shared environment on personality. We can compare the similarity in personality between identical twins brought up together and apart and between fraternal twins brought up together and apart (see Chapter 13). If shared environment is important, identical twins brought up together in the same family should be more similar in personality than identical twins brought up apart, and the same should be true when fraternal twins brought up together are compared against those brought up apart. In fact, twins brought up together resemble each other only slightly more than twins brought up apart (Bouchard, Lykken, McGue, Segal, & Tellegen 1990; Pedersen, Plomin, McClearn, & Friberg 1988; Shields, 1962).

Genetic factors account for about 40% of individual differences in personality (see Chapter 13), and shared environment has little impact. It follows that non-shared environment is important. According to Harris (1995, p. 459), "On the average, from 40% to 50% of the variance in adult personality characteristics falls into the unexplained or non-shared sector." Harris' attempt to identify the main non-shared environmental factors which influence personality will be discussed shortly.

## Evaluation

● Behavioural geneticists have shown that genetic factors influence important aspects of the child's environment (e.g., the ways in which parents treat him/her).
● Individual differences in personality development have been shown to depend much more on non-shared environmental factors than on shared ones.

● "Behavioural geneticists [make] few if any attempts to measure environmental influences directly or to specify *how* environments act on individuals to influence their behaviour … one has not *explained* development by merely postulating that *unspecified* environmental forces influenced in *unknown* ways by our genes *somehow* shape our abilities, conduct, and character" (Shaffer, 2000, p. 85).

## Group socialisation theory

Harris (1995, 2000) used the findings of behavioural geneticists and other researchers in putting forward her group socialisation theory of development. She argued there are two main ways of explaining *why* shared environment has little influence on the development of personality. First, it is possible that, "parental behaviours have no effect on the psychological characteristics their children will have as adults" (p. 458). Second, children growing up in the same family may have different experiences within the home, for example, because they are treated very differently by their parents. When I became a parent, I was determined to treat all my children (two girls and a boy) in the same way. However, it rapidly became clear that wasn't a good strategy, because they all had such different personalities and interests.

*Why might individual children in a family be treated differently by their parents?*

According to Harris's (1995, 2000) group socialisation theory, parents have no long-term effects on their children's personality development. In other words, "Children would develop into the same sort of adults if we left them in their homes, their schools, their neighbourhoods, and their cultural or sub-cultural groups, but switched all the parents around" (Harris, 1995, p. 461). This is clearly a provocative hypothesis, and one which seems inconsistent with much of the evidence discussed in this chapter and the previous one.

Harris (1995) accepted that children learn much about social behaviour within the family environment. However, a key theoretical assumption is that such learning does not generalise to other situations. Thus, learning within the family environment is very context dependent. According to Harris (p. 462), "Children learn separately how to behave at home (or in the presence of their parents) and how to behave when they are not at home … In the home, they may be reprimanded for mistakes and praised when they behave appropriately; out of the home they may be ridiculed for mistakes and ignored when they behave appropriately."

According to the theory, environmental factors within the family are regarded as being unimportant in social development. Which factors are thought to be important? According to Harris (1995, p. 481), "Experiences in childhood and adolescent peer groups … account for environmental influences on personality development." We can relate this assumption to our earlier discussion, in which we saw that non-shared environmental factors are much more important than shared environmental factors in determining personality development. According to group socialisation theory, experiences in peer groups are the central non-shared environmental factors.

### Evidence

According to group socialisation theory, the development of socialisation and personality depends very much on the experiences which children have within peer groups. Support for this viewpoint was discussed earlier in the chapter. For example, Bagwell et al. (1998) found that those 11-year-old children who were rejected by their peers had less social life and poorer job performance than other children 12 years later. Deater-Deckard (2001) reviewed evidence showing that peer rejection and avoidance of peer interaction in childhood are both associated with various emotional and behavioural problems later on (e.g., anti-social behaviour, depression). In Chapter 16, we discussed research indicating the importance of experiences in peer groups in gender development (Maccoby, 1998). At a more trivial level, my children's accents degenerated into cockney almost as soon as they started full-time schooling and were exposed to a wide range of peers.

A key theoretical prediction is that parental and family influences on children's social development are very small. Some of the evidence discussed earlier is relevant to that prediction. For example, O'Connor et al. (1998) found that some of the apparent effects of parental behaviour on children's behaviour were caused by genetic factors in the children. Such evidence suggests that many theorists have exaggerated the importance of parental factors in determining children's development.

Harris (1995, 2000) accepted that parental behaviour has various effects on their children. However, she predicted such effects would be limited to the home environment and would not generalise to other situations. Evidence consistent with that prediction was reported by Forgatch and DeGarmo (1999). They observed the effects of an intervention programme designed to improve parental child-rearing style. The intervention produced significant improvement in the children's behaviour at home, but had no effect on teachers' ratings of the children at school.

Other evidence seems to contradict the assumption that what happens within the family has very little effect on children's socialisation. For example, as we saw earlier in the chapter, parents often influence strongly children's attachment behaviour. In addition, as we also saw earlier in the chapter, there can be serious consequences if children lack emotional support from their parents through deprivation or privation. Family influences were also shown to be important by East and Rook (1992). They studied children who were relatively isolated from their peers at school. Those children having a strong relationship with a sibling showed fewer adjustment problems at school than did those without such a relationship.

> **Do parents matter?**
> David Bell, the Chief Inspector of Schools in England, certainly seems to think so. His statement (2003) that today's rising 5-year-olds are "less prepared to start school than ever" is based on his opinion that social, behavioural, and verbal skills in this group are at an all-time low. He describes these children as unable to listen, settle down, and be quiet. He also says that some are unable to speak properly or use a knife and fork. Bell cites lack of parental discipline and poor stimulation as causes. Others have identified use of television and videos as "child minders" rather than real humans to interact with these children.

It might seem as if birth order is a factor within the family likely to have a significant impact on children's socialisation. First-born children are generally larger and stronger than their siblings, and they have the advantage of not having to compete for their parents' attention for at least the first year of their lives. In addition, 80% of American mothers and 86% of British mothers admitting they loved one child more than another said it was the younger child (Dunn & Plomin, 1990). In spite of all this, birth order has often been found to have no effect on adult personality (Dunn & Plomin, 1990), which is consistent with the theory.

Evidence that birth order may be important was reported by Paulhus, Trapnell, and Chen (1999). They pointed out that most previous studies had used between-family designs, meaning that individuals differing in birth order came from different families. The problem with this approach is that it is hard to ensure that the various families are comparable in terms of social class, parental personality, and so on. A preferable (and more sensitive) approach is to use a within-family design, in which individuals differing in birth order come from the same family. This was the approach adopted by Paulhus et al. (1999). They found that first-borns tended to be most achieving and conscientious, whereas later-borns were most likely to be liberal, rebellious, and agreeable. These findings are opposed to the predictions of group socialisation theory, because they indicate that influences within the family can have strong effects on personality and achievement.

The finding that non-shared environmental factors are often much more important than shared environmental factors in accounting for individual differences in socialisation is consistent with the notion that parents have little influence on their children. However, there are other possibilities. For example, suppose that parents treat their children differently, and this differential treatment influences their development. Such parental influences would be classified as non-shared environmental influences. Alternatively, suppose that children respond differently to their parents' behaviour. Any effects of such parental behaviour on children's development would also be classified as non-shared environmental influences.

There is support for the possibilities mentioned in the previous paragraph. For example, Bergeman, Plomin, McClearn, Pedersen, and Friberg (1988) found in identical twins brought up apart that high family conflict was associated with increased impulsivity only in children predisposed to impulsivity. Frequent family activities were associated with reduced neuroticism (tendency to experience negative emotions; see Chapter 13) among children predisposed to neuroticism. However, frequent family activities were associated with *increased* neuroticism among children not predisposed to neuroticism. Thus, some non-shared environmental influences reflect the different effects of parental behaviour on the children within a family.

## Evaluation

⊕ Group socialisation theory represents a systematic attempt to account for the finding that non-shared environmental factors have much more impact than shared environmental factors on the development of socialisation in children.

⊕ Many previous theorists exaggerated the importance of shared experiences within the family in influencing children's social development.

⊕ There is increasing evidence that childhood experiences in peer groups have lasting effects on social development.

⊖ The finding that individual differences in socialisation depend much more on non-shared environmental factors than shared ones can be explained in several ways, and does not necessarily imply that parental influences are weak or non-existent.

⊖ "In adopting the view that experiences in one context have absolutely no influence outside of that context, Harris has proposed a highly compartmentalised self that is at odds with recent research and theory" (Vandell, 2000, p. 703).

⊖ Harris's (1995, 2000) claim that parents, siblings, and teachers all have very small effects on the socialisation of children is too extreme and is not supported by the evidence.

## SUMMARY

**Attachment**

The main attachment of an infant is usually to its mother, but there are often strong attachments to other people. According to Bowlby, the development of attachment in children goes through several stages, with the child gradually developing a goal-corrected partnership and an internal working model of the relationship. According to the psycho-dynamic approach, babies are initially attached to their mother because she is a source of food. This is very oversimplified. Bowlby claimed that infants have an innate tendency to form strong bonds with one particular individual, and there is a critical period (ending by the age of 3) during which this bonding must occur. In fact, the relationship between mother and baby develops over time rather than being fixed shortly after birth. Evidence from the Strange Situation test indicates that there are four main types of attachment of infants to their mother: secure attachment, resistant attachment, avoidant attachment, and disorganised and disoriented attachment. According to Ainsworth's caregiving hypothesis, the sensitivity of the mother (or other caregiver) is of crucial importance in determining the type of attachment. This hypothesis ignores the part played by the infant and by the father, and is clearly only part of the story.

**Effects of deprivation**

According to Bowlby's maternal deprivation hypothesis, breaking the child's bond with its mother in early life has severe long-term effects on its social, emotional, and intellectual development. There are also short-term effects in the form of protest, despair, and detachment. However, the effects of privation are generally more severe than those of deprivation, and few children only have a strong attachment to their mother. Deprivation is much more likely to lead to long-term difficulties when it occurs because of problems with social relationships within the family than when it is due to physical illness or housing problems. Bowlby argued the adverse effects of maternal deprivation are generally irreversible. Most studies on children who have experienced extreme privation and isolation have failed to support the notion of irreversibility.

After their parents' divorce, children typically go through a crisis phase followed by an adjustment phase. Girls tend to cope better with the divorce of their parents than boys, but sometimes find it harder to adjust to their mother's remarriage. Some children and adolescents are still depressed 10 years after their parents' divorce. Some of the apparent effects of divorce on children's self-esteem and social competence depend on genetic influences from the parents. There are adverse effects on children from parental conflict before divorce, as well as from the divorce itself. Most studies on day care indicate that it has few (or no) effects on attachment to the mother, on social development, or on academic development. However, this may not be the case among infants under 1 year of age who experience day care for many hours every week.

*Effects of divorce and day care*

Cultural differences in child-rearing practices typically reflect differences in adults' cultural expectations and values. Parents in collectivistic societies are demanding, and want their children to be obedient and co-operative. In contrast, parents in individualistic societies are undemanding, and want their children to become independent. Cultures vary in terms of parental responsiveness, but parental unresponsiveness or rejection is almost universally associated with undesirable outcomes in the children (e.g., low self-esteem, delinquency, aggression). Most infants in most cultures have a secure attachment style. However, an avoidant attachment style is more common in Western Europe than elsewhere, whereas a resistant style is relatively more common in Israel and Japan. Most cross-cultural studies cannot demonstrate causal relationships.

*Cross-cultural differences in child rearing*

Peer ratings of those children they like most and least produce five social categories: popular, controversial, average, neglected, and rejected. Social competence involves attending to social cues, interpreting those social cues, selecting a goal, accessing possible responses, selecting a response, and producing the response. However, social competence undoubtedly depends on emotional factors such as low negative emotionality and emotion regulation. Friendships involve positive engagement and various relationship properties (e.g., closeness). Older children's friendships exhibit more positive engagement and relationship properties such as closeness than do those of younger children. The deep structure (reciprocity) of friendships does not change during development, whereas the surface structure (i.e., social exchanges) does change. Children who have friends seem to be better off than those without in various ways (e.g., greater self-worth, fewer depressive symptoms).

*Peer relationships*

Behavioural geneticists study interactions between genetic and environmental factors in determining behaviour. The association between parental negative control and children's anti-social behaviour is due in part to genetic factors in the children influencing parental behaviour. Individual differences in personality depend mainly on genetic factors and on non-shared environment. According to group socialisation theory, peer influences are the most important environmental factor influencing socialisation, and parental and family influences have little long-term effect outside the home. Group socialisation theory is too extreme in its assumption that parents, siblings, and teachers do not affect children's socialisation, and it is incorrect that experiences in one social context have no influence in other contexts.

*Parents, peers, or genes?*

## FURTHER READING

- Harris, M., & Butterworth, G. (2002). *Developmental psychology: A student's handbook*. Hove, UK: Psychology Press. The course of social development from infancy, through the preschool years and the school years is discussed in an authoritative way in this excellent textbook.
- Shaffer, D.R. (2000). *Social and personality development* (4th. Ed.). Belmont, CA: Wadsworth. Most of the main topics in social development are discussed in detail.
- Smith, P.K., Cowie, H., & Blades, M. (2003). *Understanding children's development* (4th Ed.). Oxford, UK Blackwell. This textbook contains a detailed but accessible introductory account of the processes involved in social development.

# Social Psychology

The next four chapters are all concerned with social psychology. Allport (1935) defined **social psychology** as "the scientific investigation of how the thoughts, feelings and behaviours of individuals are influenced by the actual, imagined, or implied presence of others". Of course, other areas of psychology (e.g., cognitive psychology, psychology of emotion) are concerned with individuals' thoughts and feelings. However, social psychology focuses on the impact of other people on individuals, even when those other people are not actually present. For example, most people would not drop litter in the street even if no-one was observing them (Hogg & Vaughan, 2002). A key reason is the social convention that dropping litter is unacceptable. Thus, we do not drop litter because most people within our society disapprove of such behaviour.

Some psychologists claim there is a social dimension to virtually all of our behaviour. For example, Heather (1976, pp. 31–33) discussed the social nature of laboratory experiments:

> *Experiments in psychology ... are social situations involving strangers ... the main kind of knowledge gleaned from years of experimentation with human subjects is information about how strangers interact in the highly artificial and unusual social setting of the psychological experiment.*

In my opinion, social psychology is both the most fascinating *and* the most frustrating area of research in psychology. It is fascinating because most of us enjoy trying to understand our own social behaviour and that of our friends and acquaintances. It is frustrating, because it has proved very hard to come to grips with the complexities of social behaviour. Almost any aspect of social behaviour is influenced by so many factors that it is fairly difficult to find a factor having no influence whatsoever!

## RESEARCH METHODS IN SOCIAL PSYCHOLOGY

As Manstead and Semin (2001, p. 84) pointed out, "Experimentation has been the dominant research method in social psychology ... Standard guides to research in social psychology ... tend to treat experimentation as the preferred research method." The experimental method is often used in laboratory studies of social phenomena. In addition, social psychologists carry out field experiments, in which experimentation occurs under naturalistic conditions in the real world. We have certainly learned a huge amount about human social behaviour through experimentation, as we will see in the following four chapters. However, experimentation has various limitations (discussed on the next page).

### KEY TERM

**Social psychology:** the study of the thoughts, feelings, and behaviour of individuals and groups as influenced by other people.

First, most experiments involve manipulation of some aspect of the situation (the independent variable) to observe its effects on behaviour (the dependent variable). Suppose we want to study the effects of social disapproval (e.g., "Please stop doing that!") on someone's behaviour. Such effects depend heavily on the current social context. For example, your behaviour is more likely to be influenced if the disapproving person is an authority figure (e.g., your boss) and the situation is a formal one than if the disapproving person is a stranger and the situation is an informal one (e.g., a pub). The influence of the prevailing social context means that, "few stimulus events considered independently have the capacity to elicit predictable social behaviour" (Gergen, 1978, p. 509).

Second, it can be hard to interpret the findings even when we discover that the manipulation of some independent variable has consistent effects on behaviour. The problem was described clearly by Manstead and Semin (2001, p. 106): "What one experimenter believes to be a demonstration of the effect of X on O via the mediating process Z, another will prefer to explain in terms of an alternative mediating process ... The heart of the problem ... is that phenomena of interest to social psychologists often entail chains of events." Thus, social behaviour is often influenced by various internal processes (e.g., interpretation of the situation; thoughts about reactions to one's behaviour by other people), and experimentation does not necessarily allow us to identify these internal processes.

Third, Giddens (1982, p. 16) argued that, "Human beings are ... agents able to—and prone to—incorporate theory and research within their own action." Thus, learning about findings in social psychology can cause individuals to modify their behaviour, and so make the theory obsolete. For example, suppose you read in a social psychology textbook that people who are lying tend to look fixedly at the person to whom they are speaking. Thereafter, you will probably make sure that you don't stare at the other person when distorting the truth!

There are several non-experimental methods available to social psychologists, and some of them will be mentioned briefly here. First, there are surveys, in which questionnaires and/or interviews are used to obtain detailed information. One of the advantages of survey research is that a considerable amount of information can be obtained from a large number of individuals in a relatively short space of time.

Second, there are field studies, in which the researcher simply observes the social behaviour of groups (e.g., children in a playground, adolescent gangs). Field studies are rich sources of information, but such information is often hard to interpret.

Third, there is archival research, in which interesting data previously collected by non-psychologists (e.g., government agencies) are used to shed light on social issues. For example, Hovland and Sears (1940) wanted to test the frustration–aggression hypothesis, according to which frustration produces aggression. Drops in cotton prices in the United States were assumed to cause frustration and the number of lynchings was taken as a measure of aggression. As predicted, those years in which the cotton prices were lowest tended to be the ones with the most lynchings.

Fourth, there are case studies, in which an individual or a group is studied in great detail. Case studies are especially valuable in the investigation of rare phenomena (e.g., coping with natural disasters, weird cults). A limitation of most case studies is that the researcher's theoretical convictions may influence his/her interpretation of the evidence.

In sum, social psychologists use various methods in their research, and have discovered an enormous amount about people as social animals. However, you need to bear in mind that social behaviour is complex, and that the methods available for studying it have their limitations.

## LEVELS OF EXPLANATION

Social psychology is a complicated area of research, in part because it has connections to several other disciplines and areas of psychology. For example, disciplines such as social anthropology, sociology, and socio-linguistics are all relevant to social psychology, as are areas of psychology such as cognitive psychology and the study of individual differences.

It follows that social psychologists make use of several levels of explanation. Doise (1986) argued that there are four levels of explanation in social psychology:

1. *Intrapersonal level.* This is concerned with each individual's psychological processes (e.g., interpretation of social situations).
2. *Interpersonal and situational level.* This focuses only on the interactions among individuals within a given situation at a given time.
3. *Positional level.* This resembles the previous level, but some account is taken of role or social position (e.g., status, identity) outside of the immediate situation.
4. *Ideological level.* This level is concerned with the impact of general social beliefs and social identity on social behaviour.

Social psychology in Europe differs substantially from that in the United States. Most European social psychologists would accept that social psychology should encompass all four levels identified by Doise (1986). In contrast, many American social psychologists are mainly interested in the intrapersonal level, especially the ways in which individuals make sense of their social environment.

## ORGANISATION OF CHAPTERS 18–21

What topics within social psychology are covered in Chapter 18 and the three following ones? Chapter 18 is concerned with cognitive approaches to social psychology, which have become of increasing interest and importance in recent decades. Such approaches involve an emphasis on **social cognition**, "the cognitive processes and structures that influence and are influenced by social behaviour" (Hogg & Vaughan, 2002, p. 651). Most research in this area is at the intrapersonal level, because the focus is on the ways in which individuals think about and make sense of their social behaviour and that of others.

We will begin our discussion of cognitive approaches to social psychology with attitudes, which involve beliefs and feelings about other people, groups, or objects. In everyday life, we often try to understand *why* we or other people are behaving in certain ways. Various attribution theories have addressed that issue directly, and are also considered in Chapter 18. Of all the socially-relevant information we have stored in long-term memory, information about ourselves and our self-concept is regarded as being of particular importance. Chapter 18 concludes by considering various perspectives on the self. Note that cognitive processes and structures are important in virtually every area of social psychology, and so are discussed at several points in Chapters 19–21. For example, much of Chapter 21 is devoted to the ways in which we think about other groups within society.

Chapter 19 focuses on our dealings with other people as individuals, with an emphasis on the emotional level. For example, if we feel positively about someone else, we are likely to behave in a helpful way towards them. In contrast, we may behave aggressively if we feel negatively about another person. At a more intimate level, close emotional relationships may lead to marriage. Such interpersonal relationships are discussed at length in Chapter 19.

Chapter 20 deals with a wide range of group processes. There are various important phenomena associated with groups, including pressures to conform, the emergence of a leader, and the development of group cohesiveness. Explanations for such phenomena are discussed, and there is some analysis of the behaviour of very large groups or crowds.

Chapter 21 deals with various intergroup processes, especially those in which groups are in conflict. The key topics in this chapter are prejudice and discrimination, and what can be done to reduce them. In order to understand prejudice fully, it is important to consider why and how we form stereotypes of other groups in our society.

In sum, there is a natural progression as we move through the chapters. Chapter 18 focuses on individual thoughts and cognitive structures, Chapter 19 deals mainly with our treatment of other individuals, Chapter 20 analyses group phenomena, and Chapter 21 provides explanations of intergroup conflict. As you can see, the scope of social psychology is very broad!

**KEY TERM**

**Social cognition:** processing and understanding social situations and behaviour.

- **Attitudes**
  How attitudes can influence our behaviour.

  *Measurement: self-report questionnaires*
  *Measurement problems: social desirability bias, the bogus pipeline, implicit attitudes*
  *The function of attitudes*
  *Relationship between attitudes and behaviour*
  *Theories for predicting behaviour from attitudes: reasoned action, planned behaviour*

- **Attitude change and persuasion**
  Research into ways to alter attitudes.

  *The importance of persuasive messages*
  *McGuire's five factors of persuasion*
  *Petty & Wegener's elaboration likelihood model*
  *The heuristic-systematic model*
  *Festinger's cognitive dissonance theory*

- **Attribution theories**
  Why people behave in certain ways.

  *Dispositional and situational attributions*
  *Correspondent inference theory*
  *Kelley's attribution theory—the covariation principle*
  *The fundamental attribution error*
  *Actor–observer effect*
  *Cross-cultural differences*
  *Gilbert & Malone's correction model*
  *Trope & Gaunt's integration model*

- **The self**
  The effect of social factors on the self-concept.

  *Definition of the self*
  *Social identity theory*
  *Cultural differences between the independent and the interdependent self*
  *Changing the self-concept*
  *Self-presentation motives*
  *Self-esteem: Tesser's self-evaluation maintenance model; self-serving bias; false uniqueness bias*
  *The importance of self-esteem, and cultural differences*

# Cognitive approaches to social psychology

**18**

## ATTITUDES

What factors influence our behaviour in social situations? Numerous factors are at work, including our personalities, our previous experiences in similar situations, the expectations of others, and our relationships with them. Social psychologists increasingly argue that one important way of understanding social behaviour is by studying the ways in which individuals think about themselves, about the groups to which they belong, and about other groups in society.

Much of the early research in social cognition was concerned with **attitudes**. According to Augoustinos and Walker (1995, p. 13), "Attitudes are evaluations. They denote a person's orientation to some object, or attitude reference. All attitudes have a referent, an 'object of thought', a 'stimulus object' … they convey information from one person to another; attitudes are social." More specifically, attitudes have an affective component (i.e., they indicate our feelings towards some object) and they also have a cognitive component (i.e., they indicate our thoughts and beliefs about that object). As we will see, there have been numerous attempts to find out the extent to which attitudes predict behaviour.

Most of the discussion of attitudes is in this chapter. In addition, however, there is additional relevant material in Chapter 21, especially the section concerned with stereotypes.

## Measurement issues

Attitudes cannot be observed directly, which poses issues for attitude measurement. The commonest way of measuring attitudes is by self-report questionnaires. What typically happens is that participants are presented with various statements (e.g., "American films are generally better than British films", "Most American films are too superficial"). For each statement, they indicate their level of agreement or disagreement on a 5-point (sometimes 7-point) scale (e.g., strongly agree, agree, neither agree nor disagree, disagree, strongly disagree). What I have just described is known as a **Likert scale**.

The single greatest problem with the measurement of attitudes is that people may be unwilling to be honest. More specifically, they may show **social desirability bias**, deliberately distorting their responses to make them more socially desirable than is actually the case. This type of bias is especially likely to occur when their actual attitudes are disapproved of within society (e.g., negative views of minority groups). More generally, "The use of such measures [self-report questionnaires] necessarily assumes that individuals have both the ability and the motivation to report attitudes and beliefs accurately, assumptions that do not stand up to scrutiny" (Cunningham, Preacher, & Banaji, 2001).

There have been various attempts to minimise these problems, and we will discuss three of them here. First, we can use physiological measures. For example, Cacioppo and Petty (1979) recorded the movements of facial muscles before and during a talk in which the speaker argued for stricter or more lenient university rules concerning alcohol or visiting hours. Before the talk, there was one pattern of facial muscles in those students

**KEY TERMS**

**Attitudes:** beliefs about some person, group, or object, with these beliefs having an evaluative component (good vs. bad).

**Likert scale:** an approach to attitude measurement in which respondents indicate the strength of their agreement or disagreement with various statements.

**Social desirability bias:** the tendency when answering questionnaires to produce answers that are more socially desirable than honest answers would be.

Facial expressions give clues to our attitudes.

who agreed with what was going to be said and another pattern in students who disagreed. Cacioppo and Petty also found that the differences between these two patterns were greater during the talk. These findings suggest that facial muscles can provide useful information as to whether someone's attitudes towards a given topic are favourable or unfavourable.

Second, there is what is known as the **bogus pipeline**: Participants are connected to an impressive-looking machine, and are told that the machine will detect any lies they tell. The key finding is that participants are much more likely to reveal socially undesirable attitudes (e.g., racial and other kinds of prejudice) when attached to the bogus pipeline than when completing attitude scales under standard conditions (see Jones & Sigall, 1971). For example, Tourangeau, Smith, and Rasinski (1997) found that use of the bogus pipeline led people to admit to cocaine use, frequent oral sex, and excessive drinking. In spite of its effectiveness in reducing social desirability bias, the bogus pipeline is little used nowadays. It raises important ethical issues, including the use of deception and the invasion of privacy.

Third, there has been a rapid increase in the use of various techniques to assess **implicit attitudes**, which are outside conscious awareness and control (see fuller discussion in Chapter 21). For example, Cunningham et al. (2001) studied evaluative priming. The participants had to decide rapidly whether words had a positive or a negative meaning by pressing one key for good words and another key for bad words. Immediately before each word was presented, a white or a black face was presented briefly. Participants' performance was scored by dividing the trials into two sets: (1) the white face followed by a positive word and the black face followed by a negative word; and (2) the white face followed by a negative word and the black face followed by a positive word. Significantly fewer errors were made on trials belonging to the first set than on those belonging to the second set. The implication is that the participants had negative implicit attitudes towards blacks. Of interest, a standard self-report questionnaire of explicit attitudes (the Modern Racism Scale) did *not* reveal prejudiced attitudes.

## Why do we have attitudes?

Nearly everyone possesses thousands of attitudes about a huge range of groups, objects, and topics, which suggests that attitudes must possess some value for us. Shavitt (1989) argued that attitudes can fulfil four major functions:

1. *Knowledge function.* Attitudes contain a limited amount of information about objects, and provide an efficient and relatively effort-free way of responding towards those objects.
2. *Utilitarian function.* Attitudes assist us in behaving in ways likely to produce rewards and avoid punishments. This happens because our attitudes towards any given object are favourable or unfavourable on the basis of our past experience with that object.
3. *Self-esteem maintenance.* Attitudes can lead us to align ourselves with liked objects (e.g., a successful football team), and this can maintain or enhance our self-esteem.
4. *Social identity function.* Attitudes provide a way of expressing our personal values and identifying with social groups perceived as endorsing the same attitudes.

## Attitudes and behaviour

What is the relationship between attitudes and behaviour? It seems reasonable to assume that we start with various attitudes, and that these attitudes then help to determine our behaviour towards the objects of those attitudes. These assumptions seem commonsensical, but have received only modest empirical support. For example, LaPiere (1934) reported a classic study showing how great a difference there can be between attitudes and behaviour. He was a white man who travelled around the United States with a young Chinese couple. In spite of the high level of prejudice against Asians at that time, LaPiere found only 1 out of 66 hotels turned them away, and they were served at all 184 restaurants at which they stopped. Afterwards, LaPiere sent a letter to all the establishments

**KEY TERMS**

**Bogus pipeline:** a set-up in which participants are attached to a machine that they are told can detect any lies they tell.

**Implicit attitudes:** attitudes that are outside conscious awareness and control.

asking whether they would accept Chinese guests. In all, 128 of the establishment owners replied, and more than 90% of them said they would not.

For the broader picture we can turn to Wicker (1969). He summarised the findings from 32 studies in which the relationship between attitudes and behaviour was examined. The correlation between attitude and behaviour only rarely exceeded +.3, and the mean correlation was +.15. As Wicker (p. 65) concluded, "Taken as a whole, these studies suggest that it is considerably more likely that attitudes will be unrelated or only slightly related to overt behaviours than that attitudes will be strongly related to actions."

*To what extent do our attitudes determine our behaviour?*

There is not always a large discrepancy between attitudes and behaviour. For example, there is a fairly strong relationship between people's attitudes towards major political parties and their actual voting behaviour (see Franzoi, 1996). What factors determine whether the association between attitudes and behaviour is strong or weak? First, it matters whether attitudes and behaviour are measured at the same *level of specificity*. General measures of attitudes usually fail to predict very specific types of behaviour. This was the case in the LaPiere (1934) study. The behaviour of the owners of the establishments was in response to a specific, well-dressed, well-spoken Chinese couple in the company of a white person. In contrast, the attitude questionnaire the owners filled in referred to Chinese guests in general.

Second, there is the *time interval*. As we would expect, the relationship between attitudes and behaviour is weaker when there is a long interval of time between the assessments of attitudes and behaviour (it was 6 months in the LaPiere, 1934, study). For example, we can predict voting behaviour more accurately from opinion polls 1 week beforehand than from polls carried out 1 month before election day (Fishbein & Coombs, 1974).

Third, there is *direct experience*. Attitudes formed through direct experience predict behaviour much better than do attitudes formed without such experience (Fazio & Zanna, 1981). This may be because attitudes based on direct experience tend to be stronger and clearer.

## Theories of reasoned action and planned behaviour

We have seen it is often possible to predict behaviour from attitudes reasonably well, provided that the research is carried out carefully. However, there is a huge amount of evidence (e.g., Asch, 1951; Milgram, 1963; see Chapter 20) that people's behaviour in social situations is often strongly influenced by social factors (e.g., the opinions and expectations of others). Thus, we need theories based on the assumption that behaviour depends on both attitudes and social factors. Precisely this was done by Fishbein and Ajzen (1975) in their theory of reasoned action. This theory was subsequently developed and extended by Ajzen (e.g., 1985, 1991) in the theory of planned behaviour.

*How might social factors influence the attitudes we hold?*

The key assumptions of the theory of reasoned action are as follows:

- Measures of attitudes should be compatible with measures of behaviour in terms of action, object, context, and time (the principle of compatibility).
- Behaviour depends in part on a subjective norm reflecting the perceived social pressure on the individual to carry out (or avoid) the behaviour in question.
- An individual's behaviour is determined by his/her behavioural intention, i.e., how he/she intends to behave. This behavioural intention is determined in turn by attitude towards the behaviour and by the subjective norm.
- Attitude towards the behaviour depends on behavioural beliefs (beliefs about the likely consequences of performing the behaviour) and on outcome evaluations (the person's evaluation of each consequence).
- Subjective norms depend on normative beliefs (the extent to which the individual believes that other people expect him/her to behave in a given way) and on motivation to comply (the extent to which the individual wants to conform to those expectations).

Ajzen (1985, 1991) argued that the theory of reasoned action was limited, because it focused only on forms of behaviour under the individual's control. Accordingly, Ajzen extended the theory by adding perceived behavioural control as another factor influencing behavioural intentions and behaviour itself, thereby producing the theory of planned

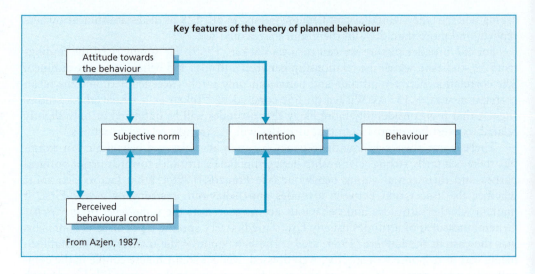

**Key features of the theory of planned behaviour**

From Azjen, 1987.

behaviour (see the figure above). It was assumed that people will be more likely to form the intention to perform a particular action if they perceive themselves to have a high level of behavioural control with respect to that action.

The theory of planned behaviour is better equipped than the theory of reasoned action to handle situations in which there is a low level of perceived behavioural control. Consider, for example, a smoker with very positive attitudes about quitting smoking, and the subjective norm also favours the intention to stop smoking. It follows from the theory of reasoned action that the smoker would stop smoking. In practice, however, many smokers feel that smoking is an addiction and thus is very hard to stop. Such smokers will have low perceived behavioural control, and this leads to the (accurate) prediction that they will typically be unsuccessful in their attempts to stop smoking.

## Evidence

Much evidence supports the theory of reasoned action. For example, Smetana and Adler (1980) obtained questionnaire data from 136 women waiting to learn the results of a pregnancy test. The questionnaire covered all the components of the theory (e.g., beliefs about the consequences of having or not having an abortion, attitudes towards abortion). The key finding was that the correlation between intention to have (or not have) an abortion correlated +.96 with their behaviour among those women who were pregnant.

Van den Putte (1993) carried out a meta-analysis on the findings from 150 tests of the theory of reasoned action. There were two main findings. First, the overall correlation between attitude plus subjective norm and behavioural intention was +.68. Second, the overall correlation between behavioural intention and behaviour was +.62. Thus, the theory provides reasonably accurate predictions of behaviour.

There is a major limitation in most of the studies considered by van den Putte (1993). The studies were *correlational*, and measures of attitudes, intentions, and behaviour were often obtained at the same time. It is unclear from such evidence whether behaviour is causally determined by attitudes and intentions. Kraus (1995) carried out a meta-analysis on 88 studies in which attitudes were assessed some time prior to behaviour. There was an overall correlation of +.38 between attitudes and behaviour, suggesting (but not proving) that attitudes can cause or determine behaviour.

In spite of the successes of the theory of reasoned action, the theory of planned behaviour is preferable. Armitage and Conner (2001) carried out a meta-analysis on 185 studies. Perceived behavioural control (included only in the theory of planned behaviour) contributed significantly to the prediction of behaviour. Overall, the theory of planned behaviour accounted for 39% of the variance in intention, and it accounted for 27% of the variance in behaviour. The theory was more effective at predicting behaviour when behaviour measures were self-report rather than objective or observed, accounting for

The theory of planned behaviour perhaps accounts better for a dieter's failure to lose weight than the theory of reasoned action. Low perceived behavioural control prevents success.

31% of the variance in behaviour in the former case and 21% in the latter. Overall, the findings from this meta-analysis indicate that the theory of planned behaviour is moderately effective in predicting intentions and behaviour.

Behaviour is often predicted better by past behaviour than by the cognitions or beliefs included in the theories of reasoned action and planned behaviour. Relevant findings were discussed by Conner and Armitage (1998), who identified seven experiments in which information about past behaviour and the factors emphasised by the theory of planned behaviour was available. Conner and Armitage (p. 1438) found that, "Past behaviour explained a mean 13.0% of variance in behaviour after taking account of intentions and PBC [perceived behavioural control]." For example, Norman and Smith (1995) found that the amount of physical exercise that participants took over a period of several weeks was predicted to a greater extent by the amount of exercise they had taken in the past than by their cognitions (e.g., intentions).

Ouellette and Wood (1998) carried out a meta-analysis of studies on past behaviour, attitudes, and present behaviour. They argued there are two main ways in which current behaviour is influenced by past behaviour. First, well-practised types of behaviour typically occurring in a particular situation (e.g., using a seatbelt in your car) become habitual and are produced as a result of automatic processes. Second, types of behaviour that are not well learned and that have been used in several situations are under the control of conscious processes. With these types of behaviour, past behaviour influences current behaviour indirectly by altering intentions. Evidence for this was reported by Conner and Armitage (1998), who found across 11 studies that past behaviour accounted for 7.2% of the variance in intentions. Thus, some of the influence of past behaviour on current behaviour (i.e., via altered intentions) can be accounted for by the theory of planned behaviour, but some (based on automatic processes) cannot.

New Year resolutions, such as attending a gym, do not always last. Despite the intentions (planned behaviour) it is past behaviour that often determines our actions.

## Evaluation

● The theories of reasoned action and planned behaviour provide a general framework within which the relationship between attitudes and behaviour can be understood.

● The factors emphasised by the theories typically influence behavioural intentions and actual behaviour.

● The theory of planned behaviour represents an advance on the theory of reasoned action.

● It is assumed within theory of planned behaviour that we make rational decisions about how to behave. However, our behaviour is often influenced by emotional considerations.

● The theories are basically designed to explain behaviour resulting from a conscious consideration of various possibilities. However, people frequently behave in habitual ways based on automatic or implicit processes. This may explain why very few New Year resolutions produce lasting changes in behaviour.

● The whole approach represented by the theories of reasoned action and planned behaviour is based on a very specific and limited view of attitudes. According to Böhner (2001, p. 280), these theories "have used a narrow definition of *attitude towards behaviour* (beliefs about the likelihood and value of behavioural consequences) and have relegated the attitude concept to the background as one among many predictors of behaviour."

*To what extent is our behaviour the result of rational decision making?*

## ATTITUDE CHANGE AND PERSUASION

Why is it important to understand the factors involved in persuasion and attitude change? One important reason relates to the growing field of preventive medicine, in which the emphasis is on preventing diseases from happening rather than on providing cures.

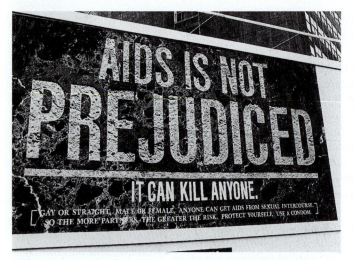

Despite prominent public health campaigns to encourage safer sexual practices, a study in the US found that only 17% of heterosexuals use condoms regularly.

People need to adopt healthier life styles for preventive medicine to work, and techniques of persuasion are very important in making this happen. This is often easier said than done, as we will see in the example below.

About 1.5 million Americans are infected with the human immunodeficiency virus (HIV) that causes AIDS, and HIV is also common throughout Western Europe and many other parts of the world. It is often wrongly believed that the disease is found mainly among homosexuals. In fact, about 75% of HIV-positive people in the world are heterosexual. Thus, it is very important for everyone to behave in ways which minimise the risks of contracting HIV and AIDS. The most effective approach is to use condoms (apart from avoiding all sexual contact!). Persuasive messages have emphasised the importance of using condoms (so-called safer sex), and have stressed the life-threatening consequences of not doing so. In spite of the importance of these messages, they are generally disregarded. For example, a study in the United States reported that only 17% of heterosexuals use condoms on a regular basis (Miller, Turner, & Moses, 1990).

Kimble, Robinson, and Moon (1992) shed light on the mystery of why persuasive messages about safer sex and AIDS have had little impact. They studied college students, most of whom regarded relative strangers and those over-anxious for sex as potentially risky sexual partners. College students believed the risk was very small when they were in a caring relationship. In the words of one student (p. 926), "When you get to know the person ... as soon as you begin trusting the person ... you don't really have to use a condom." Unfortunately, there is no evidence to support these views on which sexual partners are risky and which are safe.

## Five factors

What is the most effective way of persuading someone to change his or her attitudes? According to McGuire (1969), five kinds of factors are involved in persuasion:

1. *Source.* Sources differ greatly in attractiveness, power, credibility, and so on.
2. *Message.* The information presented may appeal to reason or to emotion, it may or may not contain many facts, and so on.
3. *Channel.* The message may be presented visually or aurally, and may be most effective when both sensory channels are used (e.g., television advertisements).
4. *Recipient.* The effectiveness of a persuasive message depends in part on the amount of attention paid to it by the recipient, and by his/her personality, pre-existing attitudes, and level of intelligence.
5. *Target behaviour.* It is easier to persuade people to perform small actions (e.g., voting for a given political party) than large ones (e.g., spending weeks canvassing for that party). Note that behaviour can be changed without changing attitudes, and vice versa.

*What strategies have you used to try to persuade someone to change their attitude?*

## Source

What characteristics should the source of a communication have to be persuasive? Communicators who are trustworthy, attractive, who have expertise and credibility, and who are similar to the receiver of the message usually produce more attitude change than communicators lacking these characteristics (Petty & Cacioppo, 1981). The importance of the source's characteristics was shown by Hovland and Weiss (1951). Their participants were given information about drug taking, and were led to believe that the source was either a prestigious medical journal or a newspaper. The amount of attitude change

It is easier to persuade people to perform small actions than large ones.

produced by the communication was more than twice as great when the source was thought to be the medical journal.

Two biases may lead us to disregard the source's message (Deaux & Wrightsman, 1988). First, there is **reporting bias**, which occurs when we think the source is unwilling to tell the truth. For example, a politician seeking re-election may argue that the economy is performing better than it is. Second, there is **knowledge bias**, which occurs when we think the source's knowledge is likely to be inaccurate. For example, someone who is very wealthy may know little about the problems experienced by homeless people.

## Message

When trying to persuade other people of a given point of view, we may decide to present only one side of the argument. An alternative approach is to present both sides of the argument, but to try to identify weaknesses in the opposing side. Which approach is more effective? Hovland, Lumsdaine, and Sheffield (1949) reported a study in which American soldiers listened to a radio broadcast claiming the war against Japan would last for more than 2 years. The broadcast presenting both sides of the argument produced more attitude change than the one-sided broadcast among soldiers who initially believed the war would last less than 2 years. They were already familiar with some of the arguments in favour of a rapid end to the war, and so found the one-sided broadcast biased. In contrast, those soldiers who initially believed the war would last for a long time were more influenced by the one-sided message.

Lumsdaine and Janis (1953) carried out a study on people given either a one-sided or a two-sided message. Those receiving the two-sided message were less influenced by a later message arguing against the position favoured in the original one. This happened because they were already aware of the counter-arguments presented in the second message, and also knew about weaknesses in those counter-arguments.

Rothman and Salovey (1997) reviewed studies on the effectiveness of messages designed to promote healthy behaviour. They found that the way the message was framed was important. If the behaviour being promoted produces a positive outcome

> **Pre-existing beliefs**
>
> The findings of Hovland et al. (1949) demonstrate that pre-existing beliefs will greatly influence the ways in which a particular message is received. In lay terms, we "like to have our prejudices confirmed". Other factors that may strongly influence our susceptibility to attitude changes are group conformity and self-image or self-concept. How we see ourselves and those with whom we identify may have a much greater influence on our views than advertising or propaganda. There are many examples of behaviours that receive little or even negative attention in the media, but have great popularity, for example tattooing and body piercing.

**KEY TERMS**

**Reporting bias:** the tendency to disregard a message if we perceive the source to be untrustworthy.

**Knowledge bias:** the tendency to disregard a message if we believe that the source lacks accurate and detailed knowledge.

(e.g., jogging every day), then the message was more effective when it was framed in terms of gain rather than preventing loss. However, the opposite was the case when the behaviour being promoted involved disease detection (e.g., breast self-examination).

## Fear

Are emotional messages more effective than non-emotional ones? The evidence is mixed, and we must distinguish between attitude change and behavioural change. Leventhal, Singer, and Jones (1965) showed films about tetanus. The participants shown the high-fear film had a greater change in their attitudes towards tetanus and the value of having tetanus inoculations than did those shown the low-fear film. However, the two groups did *not* differ in terms of actually going to have a tetanus inoculation. Thus, communications can have rather different effects on attitudes than on behaviour.

How can we ensure that high-fear communications influence behaviour as well as attitudes? Leventhal (1970) found this happened when a high-fear communication was accompanied by specific instructions on what to do to avoid the feared outcome. Smokers were exposed to a film showing a young man whose X-rays revealed that he was suffering from lung cancer, followed by a film showing an operation for lung cancer. The film was much more effective in reducing smoking behaviour when the smokers were also instructed to buy magazines instead of cigarettes, and to drink water when they felt the urge to smoke.

Rogers (1983) put forward protection motivation theory to account for the effects of threatening messages. According to this theory, threatening messages initiate two processes in the recipient:

1. *Threat appraisal.* This involves assessing the severity of the danger, and of the individual's vulnerability to the possible consequences.
2. *Coping appraisal.* This involves the recipient assessing his or her ability to perform the requiring coping behaviour to avoid the negative consequences.

The key prediction of protection motivation theory is that threat and coping appraisal interact. More specifically, increasing threat leads to *stronger* intentions to adopt the recommended behaviour when coping appraisal is high, but to *weaker* intentions when coping appraisal is low. If you are warned of a serious threat but doubt whether you can avoid it, you may focus more on reducing your fear level than on adopting the appropriate coping strategy. Indeed, there may even be a "boomerang" effect, in which the intention to adopt the coping behaviour becomes lower than it was initially.

Sturges and Rogers (1996) tested the theory in a study concerned with the dangers of tobacco use. Young adults listened to audiotaped persuasive messages arguing that the dangers of tobacco were modest or great, and that it was easy or difficult to keep away from tobacco. The predicted interaction between threat and coping was obtained, and there was some suggestion of a "boomerang" effect for the group exposed to high threat and low coping (see the graph above).

**Fear and smoking**

Fear messages on their own do not seem very effective in changing attitudes to cigarette smoking. After decades of such messages, deaths from lung cancer in England in the early 1990s were over 25,000 a year, with over 75,000 deaths a year from related diseases such as coronary heart disease (Department of Health, 1992). In Europe, about 30% of adults smoke cigarettes regularly, but there are variations, such as 45% of young Portuguese men still continuing to smoke (Steptoe & Wardle, 1992).

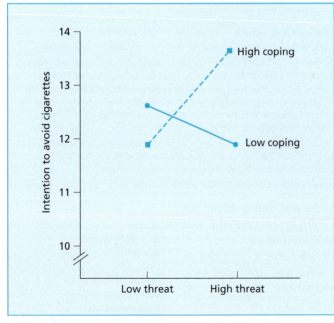

Strength of intention to avoid cigarettes as a function of degree of threat (low vs. high) and ease of coping (low vs. high). Based on data in Sturges and Rogers (1996).

## Channel

Chaiken and Eagly (1983) compared the amount of attitude change as a function of whether a message was presented in audio, video, or written form. With simple messages, videotape was the most effective and the written form was the least effective. However, with complex messages the written form was the most effective and audiotape was the least effective. Presumably the advantage of the written form with complex messages occurred because a written message can be processed slowly and the participants can go back over it if necessary.

## Recipient

Are women more easily persuaded by messages than men? Some early studies suggested that the answer to that question was "Yes". However, that conclusion has not been supported by subsequent research. Eagly and Carli (1981) carried out a meta-analysis on this issue, and found that what matters is the relative familiarity of the subject of the message for men and women. Women are influenced more than men by messages on topics with which men are more familiar, but the opposite is the case with messages on topics with which women are more familiar. In other words, familiarity and knowledge make us less susceptible to attitude change.

*Why are some people more easy to persuade than others?*

Duck, Hogg, and Terry (1999) studied the **third-person effect**, which is the belief held by most individuals that they are personally less influenced than other people by persuasive messages. Students were asked to indicate their perceptions of the impact of advertisements discussing AIDS on them personally, on other students, on non-students, and on people in general. There was a clear overall third-person effect, with students believing themselves to be less influenced by the AIDS advertisements than other groups. However, students who identified themselves strongly as students did not show any third-person effect when comparing themselves against other students.

## Target behaviour

Not surprisingly, people are more easily persuaded when they are asked to do something relatively small and undemanding than when asked to do something which is more difficult. This was shown by Cialdini et al. (1978). When they asked some people to volunteer to take part in an experiment, 56% agreed. Other people were asked to agree to a more unpleasant experience by volunteering to take part in an experiment starting at 7am. Only 31% of those approached agreed to do this. The sneaky experimenters told the former group that the experiment would start at 7am after obtaining their agreement to take part, and found that most of them honoured the appointment. Thus, you can often persuade people to change their attitude and their behaviour by initially not telling them everything that is involved!

# Dual-process models

We have considered several factors which influence attitude change. What is lacking in most of the research discussed so far is a theoretical account of what is going on. This situation has been remedied by two major dual-process models: the elaboration likelihood model (e.g., Petty & Wegener, 1998) and the heuristic-systematic model (e.g., Chaiken, Giner-Sorolla, & Chen, 1996). According to both models, people are generally motivated to hold correct attitudes. However, they may be unable or unwilling to process persuasive messages thoroughly for various reasons (e.g., lack of relevant knowledge, low personal relevance of the message).

It is assumed within the elaboration likelihood model that recipients of messages can be persuaded in two rather different ways, involving two distinct routes:

1. *Central route.* This involves detailed consideration and elaboration of the persuasive message.

> **KEY TERM**
>
> **Third-person effect:** the belief that one is personally less influenced than most other people by persuasive messages (e.g., advertisements).

2. *Peripheral route.* This involves being influenced more by non-content aspects of the message (e.g., the number of arguments produced) and by the context (e.g., the attractiveness of the communicator) than by the message content. Individuals using this route pay relatively little attention to the persuasive message.

What determines which processing route will be used? People often use the peripheral route, because they have limited time and resources to devote to most messages. They will use the central route if their motivation and ability are high. Thus, individuals interested in the topic discussed in the message and who possess relevant background knowledge are especially likely to engage in central processing.

A final assumption of the elaboration likelihood model is that there are consistent individual differences in the need for cognition. Individuals high in need for cognition are motivated to engage in effortful thinking on many topics. Such individuals should be more likely than those low in need for cognition to engage in central-route processing when receiving a message, a prediction that has generally been supported (see Cacioppo et al., 1996, for a review).

According to the elaboration likelihood model, central processing typically produces stronger and longer-lasting attitudes than peripheral processing. The main reason for this prediction was explained by Petty (1995, p. 230):

> *When we do a lot of thinking before changing our attitudes, we are likely to be accessing the attitude and the corresponding knowledge structure quite frequently. This cognitive activity should tend to increase the number of linkages and strengthen the associations among the cognitive elements in the underlying attitude structure. This would tend to make the attitude structure more internally consistent, accessible, and enduring.*

*Under what circumstances have you changed your attitudes about people or ideas?*

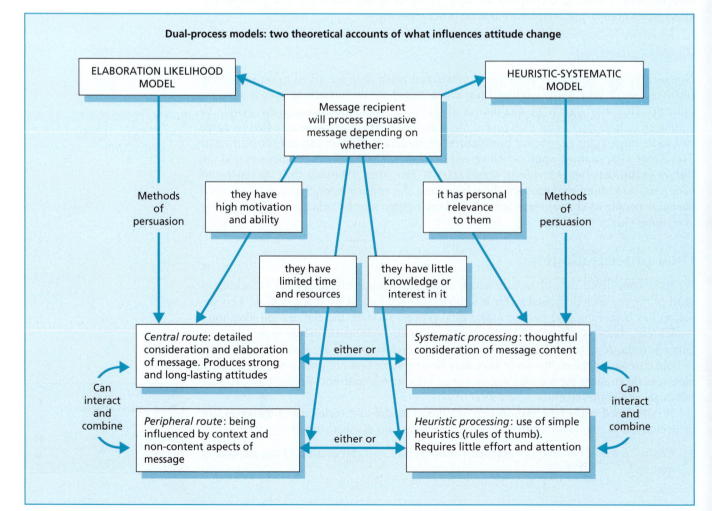

**Dual-process models: two theoretical accounts of what influences attitude change**

The heuristic-systematic model is similar to the elaboration likelihood model, being based on the assumption that two kinds of processes can be applied to persuasive messages. Systematic processing closely resembles the central route since it involves thoughtful consideration of message content. This form of processing is most likely to be used when messages have personal relevance, when the recipient already possesses strong attitudes on the message topic, and when the recipient is high in need for cognition.

Heuristic processing resembles the peripheral route, in that it requires relatively little effort and attention. Individuals who are not very interested in (or knowledgeable about) a persuasive message use simple heuristics or rules of thumb (e.g., "Statistics don't lie", "Agree with the expert", "People like me are usually right").

*Why do you think that some attitudes are more resistant to change than others?*

What is the relationship between heuristic and systematic processing within the heuristic-systematic model? When a message is ambiguous, recipients may initially engage in heuristic processing. This heuristic processing may then bias subsequent systematic processing, producing attitudes consistent with the implications of the initial heuristic processing.

What are the key differences between these two influential dual-process models? As Bohner (2001, p. 263) pointed out, "The ELM [elaboration likelihood model] provides the more comprehensive framework, incorporating effortful processing as well as a variety of low-effort processes." However, the heuristic-systematic model has the advantage of more specific assumptions about the ways in which its two processes interact with each other.

## Evidence

Petty, Cacioppo, and Goldman (1981) tested the elaboration likelihood model and obtained good evidence that there are two separate routes to persuasion (see Key Study below).

The prediction from the elaboration likelihood model that attitude change produced by central route processing will last longer has been tested several times. The relevant evidence was considered by Petty (1995, p. 232): "Research on attitude change persistence has shown that the more people process the arguments in a persuasive message carefully, the more any change induced by that message is likely to persist … over time."

## Petty et al.: Two routes to persuasion

Petty et al. (1981) tested the elaboration likelihood model. Students read a message strongly supporting the notion that a new large-scale examination should be introduced. All students would need to pass this examination to graduate. Some participants were told this examination might be introduced the following year in order to provide them with strong motivation to use the central route. The other participants were told there would be no change for 10 years, and thus any changes would not affect them personally. This was designed to produce low motivation to process the message thoroughly, so they would use the peripheral route.

Petty et al. (1981) prepared several versions of the message. The message was either attributed to a source high in expertise (the Carnegie Commission on Higher Education) or to a source low in expertise (a local high school class). The quality of the arguments in the message was also varied. There were either strong arguments based on statistics and other data, or weak arguments based on personal opinion and anecdotes.

What did Petty et al. (1981) find? For students expected to use the central route, the quality of the arguments was the main factor determining how persuaded they were. In contrast, for those students expected to use the peripheral route, the source of the message was the main factor influencing its persuasiveness. Thus, there seem to be two separate routes to persuasion.

### KEY STUDY EVALUATION—Petty et al.

A possible problem with Petty et al.'s study could be that the groups of participants were not balanced; factors relating to all levels of cognitive processing could be so different between the two groups that their responses could not reasonably be compared. The manipulation of the key variables, i.e., quality and source of message, does demonstrate the significance of these factors in determining the response to the message received, but the possibility of intervening variables such as low attention levels and/or low recall levels in the case of the second, peripheral-route group would suggest that direct comparison between the groups would be questionable. The feelings of the participants towards assessments would need to be measured before the study so that later comparison could be made. Students who perform badly in exams in general may respond negatively towards the message, irrespective of its content or context or whether it will affect them directly.

### Discussion points

1. Do persuasive messages influence you via the central or the peripheral route?
2. What kinds of motivational factors might lead someone to pay close attention to a persuasive message?

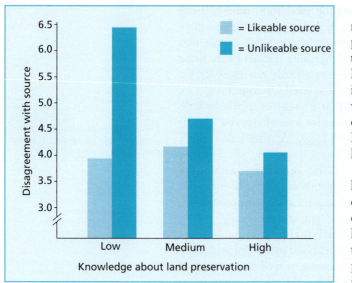

Disagreement with source as a function of knowledge about land preservation (low, medium, or high) and source likeability (likeable vs. unlikeable). Data from Wood and Kallgren (1988).

*How would you try to persuade a smoker to give up the habit?*

According to the two models we are considering, message recipients can use both central or systematic and peripheral or heuristic processing in parallel (at the same time). Supporting evidence was reported by Wood and Kallgren (1988). The participants read an account of an interview in which a student argued against land preservation. They were told the student was either an expert or a non-expert, and that he was likeable or unlikeable. Finally, students were assessed for their knowledge about land preservation.

What was found in the above study? First, those knowing the least about land preservation were the only ones influenced by the student's likeability (see the figure opposite). This suggests that people lacking relevant knowledge are most likely to use the heuristic, "disagree if the communicator is unlikeable". Second, all groups of participants were equally affected by the student's expertise, suggesting that they all used the heuristic, "agree with the expert". Third, the participants with most knowledge about land preservation made most use of central or systematic processing, and so recalled more of the message than did participants in the other two groups. Thus, those with high relevant knowledge used central/systematic *and* peripheral/heuristic processing.

More direct evidence that heuristics influence attitude change was reported by Chaiken (1987). In one study, some participants memorised eight phrases relevant to the heuristic that length implies strength (e.g., "the more the merrier"). After that, the participants received a message in which the speaker claimed to have either two or ten reasons supporting compulsory examinations. These participants showed more attitude change when the speaker claimed to have ten reasons rather than two, presumably because they used the heuristics contained in the phrases.

There is support for the notion that heuristic processing can bias subsequent systematic processing when messages are ambiguous. Chaiken and Maheswaran (1994) exposed their participants to a message about a new answerphone, the XT 100, with the message allegedly coming from a low-credibility source (Kmart, a chain of discount shops) or a high-credibility source (*Consumer Reports*, a well-regarded product-testing magazine). As predicted, source credibility *only* influenced systematic processing and attitudes towards the new answerphone when the message was ambiguous, presumably because source credibility affected heuristic processing in that condition.

## Evaluation

➕ The two models discussed in this section provide more adequate accounts of attitude change than previous theories.

➕ Attitude change typically depends on contextual information (e.g., likeability of the communicator, expertise of communicator) as well as on message content.

➕ Several factors determining whether processing is mainly central/systematic or peripheral/heuristic have been identified.

➖ The notion that there are two forms of processing of persuasive messages is oversimplified. As Petty (1995, pp. 208–209) admitted, "It is best to view the central and the peripheral routes to persuasion as falling along a continuum [continuous line] of attitude change strategies that differ in the amount of effortful message evaluation they require."

➖ It is assumed within the elaboration likelihood model that central and peripheral processes can occur at the same time. However, it is not made clear how these processes interact and combine with each other.

● According to the heuristic-systematic model, information not processed systematically (e.g., source likeability) influences attitudes via the retrieval of heuristics from long-term memory. However, there have been very few attempts to test this assumption directly.

## Cognitive dissonance theory

One of the most influential approaches to an understanding of attitudes (and the relationship between attitudes and behaviour) is Festinger's (1957) cognitive dissonance theory. According to this theory, someone holding two cognitions or thoughts which are psychologically discrepant experiences **cognitive dissonance** (an uncomfortable state produced by a discrepancy between two cognitions). This state motivates the person to reduce the dissonance. Dissonance can be reduced by changing one or both of the cognitions, or by introducing a new cognition.

A commonplace example of cognitive dissonance is found in smokers. They have the cognition or thought that smoking can cause several diseases and they also have the cognition that they frequently engage in smoking behaviour. How can they reduce cognitive dissonance? One way is to stop smoking, and another way is to persuade themselves that smoking is less dangerous than is generally assumed. Relevant evidence was reported by Gibbons, Eggleston, and Benthin (1997). Smokers about to quit smoking regarded smoking as very dangerous, and this was a factor in them deciding to quit. However, when these same individuals started to smoke again, they perceived smoking to be much less dangerous than they had before! This change of attitude helped them to justify their decision to start smoking again.

Festinger (1957) argued that people will often resolve a discrepancy between their attitudes and behaviour by altering their attitudes. Thus, rather than attitudes determining behaviour, it is sometimes the case that behaviour determines attitudes. How can we create a discrepancy between someone's attitudes and their behaviour? One approach is known as **induced compliance**, in which people are persuaded to behave in ways inconsistent with their attitudes. Another approach is known as **effort justification**, in which people exert much effort to achieve some fairly trivial goal.

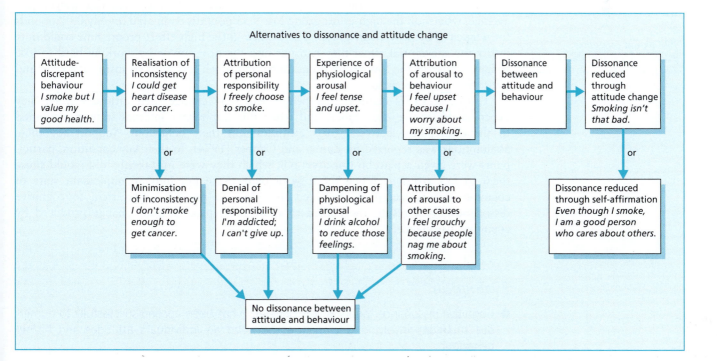

## Evidence

One of the best-known studies on induced compliance is that of Festinger and Carlsmith (1959). Their participants spent 1 hour performing very boring tasks (e.g., emptying and refilling a tray with spools). After that, the experimenter asked each participant to tell the next participant that the experiment had been very enjoyable. The participants were offered either $1 or $20 to lie in this way. Finally, all the participants were asked to provide their honest opinion of how much they liked the tasks they had performed.

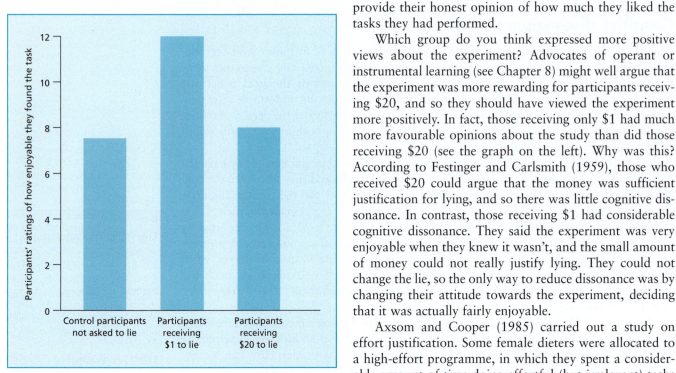

Which group do you think expressed more positive views about the experiment? Advocates of operant or instrumental learning (see Chapter 8) might well argue that the experiment was more rewarding for participants receiving $20, and so they should have viewed the experiment more positively. In fact, those receiving only $1 had much more favourable opinions about the study than did those receiving $20 (see the graph on the left). Why was this? According to Festinger and Carlsmith (1959), those who received $20 could argue that the money was sufficient justification for lying, and so there was little cognitive dissonance. In contrast, those receiving $1 had considerable cognitive dissonance. They said the experiment was very enjoyable when they knew it wasn't, and the small amount of money could not really justify lying. They could not change the lie, so the only way to reduce dissonance was by changing their attitude towards the experiment, deciding that it was actually fairly enjoyable.

Axsom and Cooper (1985) carried out a study on effort justification. Some female dieters were allocated to a high-effort programme, in which they spent a considerable amount of time doing effortful (but irrelevant) tasks such as reading out tongue twisters. Other women were allocated to a low-effort programme, in which the tasks were less time consuming and effortful, but were still irrelevant to weight loss. The women in the high-effort programme were much more likely than those in the low-effort condition to lose weight. For example, after 6 months, 94% of the former group but only 39% of those in the latter group had lost weight. On average, women in the high-effort group lost 8.55 pounds, compared to only 0.07 pounds for women in the low-effort group. The women in the high-effort programme could only justify the substantial effort they had put into the programme by working hard to lose weight. Those in the low-effort programme had much less need to justify the time and effort they had expended.

*How would cognitive dissonance explain the use of initiation ceremonies for new gang members?*

Festinger (1957) claimed that people will only change their attitudes when they experience cognitive dissonance, and when this unpleasant internal state is attributed to the discrepancy between their attitudes and their behaviour. Support for these assumptions was reported by Zanna and Cooper (1974). In their key condition, participants were given a placebo (inactive) pill, which they were mistakenly told would cause them to feel aroused. When these participants were put into an unpleasant state of cognitive dissonance, they attributed this state to the pill rather than to cognitive dissonance. As a result, they failed to show the typical attitude change produced by cognitive dissonance.

## Evaluation

➕ Cognitive dissonance theory is very general. It has been applied successfully to numerous situations involving discrepancies between an individual's attitudes and his/her behaviour.

⊕ There is much evidence in favour of the apparently paradoxical prediction from cognitive dissonance theory that the weaker the reasons for behaving inconsistently with one's attitudes, the stronger the pressure to change those attitudes (e.g., Festinger & Carlsmith, 1959).

⊖ Many findings can also be explained by Bem's (1972) self-perception theory, according to which we often infer our own attitudes by focusing on our behaviour and the circumstances in which it occurs. Self-perception theory often works better than dissonance theory when people argue for a position fairly close to their initial attitudes (Fazio, Zanna, & Cooper, 1977). However, dissonance theory works better than self-perception theory when people argue for positions very discrepant from their initial attitudes (Fazio et al., 1977).

⊖ The induced-compliance effect found by Festinger and Carlsmith (1959) was not replicated by Hiniker (1969) with Chinese participants or by Choi, Choi, and Cha (1992) with Korean ones. These failures to replicate may have occurred because the need for cognitive consistency is less strong in collectivistic societies than in individualistic ones (see Chapter 1). Kashima et al. (1992) found that Australians believed that consistency between attitudes and behaviour is more important than did the Japanese. People in collectivistic societies focus on behaving in a socially acceptable way even when it conflicts with their beliefs.

⊖ The theory ignores important individual differences. For example, consider the personality trait of **self-monitoring** (using cues from other people to control one's own behaviour). Those high in self-monitoring experience much less cognitive dissonance than those low in self-monitoring when there is a discrepancy between their attitudes and their behaviour (see Franzoi, 1996).

*Why might some cultures give less importance to the consistency between attitudes and behaviour than others?*

## ATTRIBUTION THEORIES

In our everyday lives, it is often important to work out *why* other people are behaving in certain ways. For example, suppose someone you have only just met is very friendly. They may really like you, or they may want something from you, or perhaps they are merely being polite. In order to know how to treat them, it is very useful to understand the reasons for their apparent friendliness.

According to Heider (1958), people are naïve scientists who relate observable behaviour to unobservable causes. We produce **attributions**, which are beliefs about the reasons why other people behave as they do. Heider distinguished between internal attributions (based on something within the individual being observed) and external attributions (based on something outside the individual). Internal attributions are called **dispositional attributions**, whereas external attributions are called **situational attributions**. A dispositional attribution is made when we decide that someone's behaviour is due to their personality or other characteristics. In contrast, a situational attribution is made when someone's behaviour is attributed to the current situation.

The above distinction can be exemplified by considering a male office worker who works very slowly and inefficiently. A dispositional attribution would be that he is lazy or incompetent. A situational attribution would be that he has been asked to do work inappropriate to his skills or that the company for which he works has failed to monitor sufficiently what he does.

Since Heider's (1958) contribution, various theorists have put forward attribution theories based on his ideas. Two of the most important of such theories are discussed next. First, we consider briefly the correspondent inference theory put forward by Jones and Davis (1965). Second,

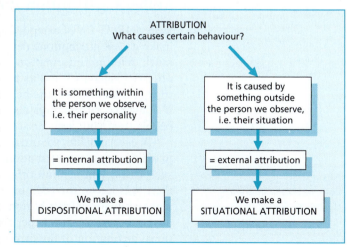

| NON-COMMON EFFECTS PRINCIPLE: WHICH CAR WILL YOU BUY? | | |
| --- | --- | --- |
| **Car A** | **Car B** | **Car C** |
| Lead-free petrol | Lead-replacement petrol | Diesel |
| Power steering | Power steering | Power steering |
| Air bag | Air bag | Air bag |
| Expensive to service | Cheap to service | Cheap to service |

If you buy Car A, we can infer that lead-free petrol is important to you. You will not have made your decision because of the power steering or air bags, as they are common to the other two cars. We might then infer that you also care about the environment.

we deal with Kelley's (1967, 1973) attribution theory. Later on, more recent attribution theories are considered.

## Correspondent inference theory

According to correspondent inference theory (Jones & Davis, 1965), we use information about another person's behaviour and its effects to draw a **correspondent inference**, in which the behaviour is attributed to a disposition or personality characteristic. How is this done? First, there is the issue of whether the effects of someone's behaviour were intended. We are more likely to draw a correspondent inference if the behaviour appears intentional than when it is unintentional.

Second, we are more likely to decide there is a correspondence when the effects of the behaviour are socially undesirable. For example, if someone is very rude in a social situation, we conclude that he/she is an unpleasant person. On the other hand, if someone is conventionally polite, we feel we have learned little about that person.

In deciding whether someone's behaviour corresponds to an underlying disposition, we also make use of the *non-common effects principle*. If the other person's actions have rare or non-common effects not shared by other actions, then we infer an underlying disposition.

Correspondent inference theory has various limitations. First, it is assumed that observers decide on the commonality of effects by comparing the actor's actual behaviour with several non-chosen actions. In fact, observers rarely consider non-chosen actions (Nisbett & Ross, 1980). Second, correspondent inferences are often drawn even when we judge someone's actions to be unintentional. As Hogg and Vaughan (2002) pointed out, careless behaviour is unintentional, but often leads us to conclude that the individual concerned is a careless person. Third, as we will see shortly, the processes involved in drawing inferences about others' behaviour are more complex than is suggested within correspondent inference theory.

## Kelley's attribution theory

Kelley (1967, 1973) extended attribution theory. He argued that the ways in which people make causal attributions depend on the information available to them. When you have much relevant information from several sources, you can detect the *covariation* of observed behaviour and its possible causes. For example, if a man is generally unpleasant to you, it may be because he is an unpleasant person or because you are not very likeable. If you have information about how he treats other people, and you know how other people treat you, you can work out what is happening.

In everyday life, we often only have information from a *single* observation to guide us in making a causal attribution. For example, you see a car knock down and kill a dog. In such cases, you use information about the configuration or arrangement of factors. If there was ice on the road or it was a foggy day, this increases the chances that you will make a situational attribution of the driver's behaviour. In contrast, if it was a clear, sunny day and there was no other traffic on the road, then you will probably make a dispositional attribution of the driver's behaviour (e.g., he is a poor or inconsiderate driver).

We think of Tom Hanks as an all-round nice guy because that is what he is often like in his films. We are making inferences about his true disposition on the basis of observable behaviours. This is an example of "correspondent inference".

**KEY TERM**

**Correspondent inference:** attribution of an actor's behaviour to some disposition or personality characteristic.

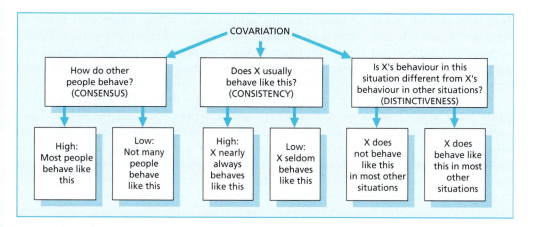

## Covariation

According to Kelley (1967), people making causal attributions use the **covariation principle**. This principle states that, "an effect is attributed to a condition that is present when the effect is present, and absent when the effect is absent" (Fincham & Hewstone, 2001, p. 200). According to Kelley, this principle is used when the individual has information from multiple observations. We use three types of information when interpreting someone's behaviour:

1. *Consensus*. The extent to which others in the same situation behave in the same way.
2. *Consistency*. The extent to which the person usually behaves in the way he/she is currently behaving.
3. *Distinctiveness*. The extent to which the person's behaviour in the present situation differs from his/her behaviour in the presence of other people.

*What helps you decide whether someone's negative behaviour is the result of their disposition, rather than the situation?*

Information about consensus, consistency, and distinctiveness is used when deciding whether to make a dispositional or a situational attribution. If someone's behaviour has high consensus, high consistency, and high distinctiveness, we typically make a situational attribution. Here is an example: Everyone is rude to Bella; Mary has always been rude to Bella in the past; Mary has not been rude to anyone else. Mary's behaviour is attributed to Bella's unpleasantness rather than her own unpleasantness.

In contrast, we make a dispositional attribution if someone's behaviour has low consensus, high consistency, and low distinctiveness. Here is an example: Only Mary is rude to Susan; Mary has always been rude to Susan in the past; Mary is rude to everyone else.

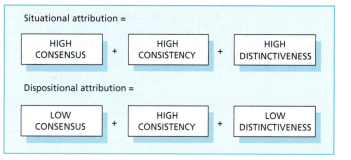

## Evidence

McArthur (1972) tested Kelley's attribution theory. He presented American participants with the eight possible patterns of information based on the three factors identified by Kelley: high vs. low on each of the three factors of consensus, consistency, and distinctiveness. The participants attributed causality for the events described. For example, consider the sentence, "Neil falls asleep during Professor Brown's lecture". The fact that Neil fell asleep might be attributed to something in the person (i.e., Neil), to something in the circumstances (e.g., hot lecture theatre), or to the entity (i.e., Professor Brown).

What findings would be expected? Suppose Neil has fallen asleep during Professor Brown's lectures in the past, that other students do not do so, and that Neil also falls asleep in other people's lectures. The fact that Neil fell asleep during one of Professor Brown's lectures should be attributed to Neil (the person). Suppose Neil has fallen asleep during Professor Brown's lectures in the past, that the other students do the same, and that

**KEY TERM**
**Covariation principle:**
attributing an effect to a factor that is present when the effect is present, but that is absent when the effect is absent.

Neil does not fall asleep in other people's lectures. Neil falling asleep during one of Professor Brown's lectures should be attributed to Professor Brown (the entity). Finally, suppose that Neil has not slept in Professor Brown's lectures in the past. This should lead participants to attribute the fact that Neil fell asleep during one of Professor Brown's lectures to the circumstances (e.g., Neil had too much to drink last night).

McArthur (1972) reported some support for Kelley's theory. However, the participants made much less use of consensus information than predicted by Kelley. Thus, people's causal attributions of an individual's behaviour were influenced very little by the information that "almost everyone" or "hardly anyone" behaves in the same way. High consensus suggests that situational factors are strong and low consensus suggests that such factors are weak. Thus, the findings suggest that Americans de-emphasise the importance of situational factors when making attributions of behaviour. In contrast, Cha and Nam (1985) found that Korean participants made effective use of consensus information, and thus took account of situational factors. Reasons for cultural differences in attributions are discussed at length below.

Subsequent research has provided support for the predictions that low consensus, high consistency, and low distinctiveness should be associated with person attributions, and that high consensus, high consistency, and high distinctiveness should be associated with entity attributions (e.g., Forsterling, 1989). However, as Fincham and Hewstone (2001, p. 201) pointed out, "There does not seem to be one specific pattern of information ... that clearly leads to circumstance attributions."

*To what extent do you think that people make use of the covariation principle before making causal attributions?*

## Evaluation

- ⊕ The notion that our causal attributions of others' behaviour depend in complex ways on the pattern of information we have available has proved very influential.
- ⊕ There is at least partial support for the covariation principle, and for the importance of the three factors of consistency, distinctiveness, and consensus.
- ⊖ "Although participants' attributions may appear *as if* they used the covariation principle, their actual information processing may be completely different from that set out by Kelley" (Fincham & Hewstone, 2001, p. 202).
- ⊖ Experiments to test the theory are mostly very artificial because they provide participants with all the covariation information needed to make causal attributions. In real life, people typically make causal attributions on the basis of much more limited information.
- ⊖ Even when information about consistency, consensus, and distinctiveness is available in everyday life, it is unlikely that such information typically influences our thinking (Pennington, personal communication).

## Fundamental attribution error

One of the best-known errors or biases in social cognition is the **fundamental attribution error** (also known as correspondence bias), which involves exaggerating the influence of dispositions (personality) as causes of behaviour while minimising the role of situational factors. For example, suppose you meet someone for the first time and find them rather irritable and rude. You may well conclude they have an unpleasant personality, ignoring the possibility they have a headache or are troubled by problems.

Why do people possess the fundamental attribution error? We like to think that life is fair, and an emphasis on dispositional factors is consistent with the notion that, "We get what we work for, get what we ask for, and get what we deserve" (Gilbert, 1995, p. 108). In addition, the fundamental attribution error helps to make our lives seem predictable. If the behaviour of other people is determined mainly by their personalities, this makes their future behaviour much more predictable than if their behaviour varies considerably from situation to situation.

## Evidence

The fundamental attribution error was obtained by Jones and Harris (1967). Their American participants were presented with short essays either for or against the Castro government in Cuba. They were told either that the essay writers had chosen which side of the argument to support (choice condition), or that the writers had been told to write a pro- or anti-Castro essay as part of an examination (no-choice condition). The participants' task was to estimate the essay writer's real attitudes towards Castro.

The participants paid some attention to the situation (whether or not the essay writer had a choice), but less than they should have done. Strictly speaking, nothing can be concluded about the writer's true attitudes in the no-choice condition. However, the participants were significantly influenced by the views expressed by the writer in that condition.

Fein, Hilton, and Miller (1990) argued that people will be less likely to underestimate the importance of situational factors in determining behaviour when the other person has strong reasons for suppressing his/her true attitudes. Their participants read an essay written by a student called "Rob Taylor" on a controversial topic. Some participants were told Rob had been assigned to write either in favour of (or against) a particular point of view. Other participants were told that Rob had been allowed to choose what point of view to express; however, the professor who would be evaluating Rob had very strong views on the topic. After that, they were told that Rob's essay expressed the same views as those held by his professor.

Those participants who thought Rob had been assigned a point of view made the fundamental attribution error, deciding Rob's true attitudes were those expressed in the essay. In contrast, those participants believing Rob had a good reason for hiding his true attitudes (i.e., pleasing his professor) concluded that the essay did *not* reflect his true attitudes. Thus, we do *not* make the fundamental attribution error when it is clear that people have a hidden motive for their behaviour. For example, we expect politicians to express agreement with the views of their party purely for situational reasons (e.g., to gain advancement).

What factors are responsible for the fundamental attribution error? Perhaps the most important factor is perceptual salience: Someone else's behaviour is usually more salient or prominent to an observer than is the situation. McArthur and Post (1977) reported evidence for the importance of salience. Observers watched and listened to a conversation between two people. One of those involved in the conversation was made salient by being illuminated by a bright light, whereas the other was made non-salient by being in a dim light. The behaviour of the person who was made salient was rated by observers of the conversation as being caused more by disposition or personality and less by the situation than was the behaviour of the non-salient person.

*Why is it easier for us to assume that people's behaviour is the result of their disposition rather than the situation?*

## Evaluation

⊕ People often exaggerate the importance of disposition and minimise that of the situation as causes of behaviour.

⊖ The fundamental attribution error may be less important in everyday life than in the laboratory. In everyday life, we realise that many people (e.g., politicians, secondhand car salespeople) have hidden motives which may influence their behaviour.

## Actor–observer effect

Suppose a mother is discussing with her son why he has done poorly in an examination. The son may argue that the questions were unusually hard, that the marking was unfair, and so on. However, his mother may focus on the child's laziness and general lack of motivation. Thus, the son sees his own behaviour as being determined by various external

or situational factors, whereas his mother focuses on internal or dispositional factors within her son.

Jones and Nisbett (1972) argued that the processes involved in the above example operate in numerous circumstances. According to them (p. 80), "there is a pervasive tendency for actors to attribute their actions to situational requirements, whereas observers tend to attribute the same actions to stable personal dispositions". This phenomenon is often referred to as the **actor–observer effect**.

## Evidence

Nisbett, Caputo, Legant, and Maracek (1973) asked their participants to rate themselves, their best friend, their father, an admired acquaintance, and Walter Cronkite (a well-known American television presenter) on a series of trait adjective pairs (e.g., tense–calm). They could either pick one of the adjectives or argue that it depended on the situation. The participants were much more inclined to argue that it depended on the situation when describing themselves than when describing any of the other people. According to Nisbett et al., people are much more aware of the importance of situational factors in determining their own behaviour than in determining that of others.

Why do actor–observer differences in attribution occur? One possible reason stems from the fact that we can see other people but cannot see ourselves. However, we can see the situation, and this may lead us to exaggerate its importance in determining our behaviour. The notion that focus of attention or salience accounts for the actor–observer effect was tested by Storms (1973). Two participants took part in a "get acquainted" conversation, and two additional participants observed them. Two videos were made of the conversations, one from the actor's point of view and the other from the observer's. The usual actor–observer effect was obtained when actors and observers viewed the video made from their own point of view. However, the actor–observer effect disappeared when actors and observers viewed the video taken from the opposite point of view. When people observed their own behaviour, they generally attributed it to dispositional rather than to situational factors.

Support for the findings of Storms (1973) was obtained by Frank and Gilovich (1989). They also used a "get acquainted" conversation. Some time thereafter, the participants were asked to remember their behaviour during the conversation from their own or an actor perspective or from an outside or observer perspective. Those who adopted the actor perspective mostly used situational attributions of their own behaviour. However, those who adopted the observer perspective made more dispositional attributions of their own behaviour.

Robins, Spranca, and Mendelsohn (1996) argued that the actor–observer effect is expressed too vaguely. Various internal and external factors might influence attributions, and we need to identify the *specific* factors involved. Pairs of students interacted, and then rated the importance of various factors in influencing their behaviour and that of their partner. There were two internal factors (personality, mood) and two external factors (partner, situation). The situational factor included being in an experiment and meeting someone for the first time.

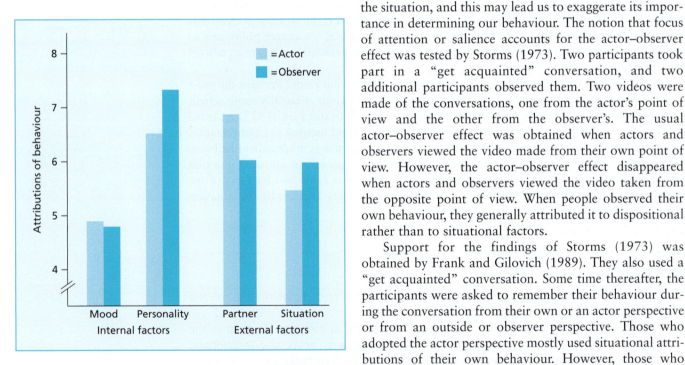

The key findings are shown in the graph on the previous page. There was support for the actor–observer effect for one internal factor (personality) and for one external factor (partner). However, there was *no* support for this effect for the other internal factor (mood), and the findings were opposite to those predicted for the other external factor (situation). Thus, the notion of a general actor–observer effect is greatly oversimplified. Why were actors' attributions strongly influenced by one external factor (partner) but not by another (situation)? Presumably the actors' focus of attention was more on their partner than on more general aspects of the situation.

## Evaluation

⊕ There is reasonably consistent evidence for the actor–observer effect in some circumstances.
⊕ The actor–observer effect explains some of the misunderstandings occurring between people. For example, students may attribute their poor exam marks to bad luck, whereas their parents may attribute those marks to a lack of motivation.
⊖ The actor–observer effect is less general than was originally thought to be the case.
⊖ "The assertion that observers attribute their behaviour to internal factors whereas actors attribute their behaviour to external factors is not meaningful without specifying which internal factors and which external factors" (Robins et al., 1996, p. 385).

## Cross-cultural differences

We have seen that people in Western cultures often exaggerate the importance of dispositional factors in determining the behaviour of others. However, the findings might be different in other cultures. Most Western cultures are individualistic, with an emphasis on individual responsibility and independence (see Chapter 1). It seems reasonable that such cultures would focus on internal or dispositional explanations of people's behaviour. In contrast, many cultures in other parts of the world (e.g., East Asia) are collectivistic, with an emphasis on group cohesiveness rather than individual needs (see Chapter 1). It seems reasonable that such cultures would focus on situational explanations of people's behaviour, because the members of such cultures have to be responsive to the wishes of other people.

*Why might collectivistic cultures be less likely than individualistic cultures to focus on dispositional factors when explaining other people's behaviour?*

What follows from the above analysis? The main prediction is that the fundamental attribution error and actor–observer effect should not exist (or should exist only in a weakened form) in collectivistic cultures compared to individualistic ones.

## Evidence

Choi and Nisbett (1998) asked American and Korean participants to read an essay supporting or opposing capital punishment. They were told that the essay writer had been told which side of the issue to support, and efforts were made to make explicit to the participants the situational pressure under which the essay had been written. The American participants showed a much stronger fundamental attribution error (i.e., arguing that the essay writer was expressing his/her true attitudes) than did the Korean participants.

Choi and Nisbett (1998) also examined cultural differences in the actor–observer effect. Participants carried out two tasks: (1) they rated the extent to which the essay writer was expressing his/her genuine attitudes; (2) they wrote an essay under the same conditions as the essay writer, and then rated the extent to which they themselves had expressed their genuine attitudes. American participants showed the actor–observer effect, arguing that the essay writer expressed his/her true attitudes to a greater extent than they had themselves. In contrast, the Korean participants argued that the essay writer was no more likely than they themselves to be expressing his/her true attitudes.

Choi, Nisbett, and Norenzayan (1999) discussed a study of theirs in which American and Korean students were presented with various points of view about the causes of behaviour. One point of view was dispositional (e.g., "How people behave is mostly determined by their personality"), and another point of view was situational (e.g., "How people behave is mostly determined by the situation in which they find themselves"). The two groups of students showed comparable levels of agreement with the dispositional point of view. However, the Korean students agreed much more than the American students with the situational point of view.

Choi et al. (1999) raised the interesting question of whether the individualistic or collectivistic approach to causal attribution is more accurate. There are complex issues here, and no definitive answer can be given as yet. However, the study by Choi and Nisbett (1998, discussed above) provides relevant evidence. They found that Korean participants realised that the behaviour of other people would be as strongly influenced by situational factors as was their own behaviour, whereas American participants did not. Such findings support the notion that the members of collectivistic cultures tend to be more accurate than those of individualistic cultures in explaining the behaviour of others.

## Evaluation

➕ There is increasing evidence that there are important cultural differences in attributions about the behaviour of other people.

➕ The fundamental attribution error and the actor–observer effect are more common in individualistic cultures than in collectivistic ones.

➕ There seems to be a strong relationship between individualistic cultures and an emphasis on dispositional factors, and between collectivistic cultures and an emphasis on situational factors.

➖ The notion that all cultures can be categorised as individualistic or collectivistic is an over-simplification.

➖ The notion that the members of any given culture always favour either situational or dispositional attributions of the behaviour of others is an over-simplification.

*To what extent is the distinction between individualistic cultures and collectivistic cultures an over-simplification?*

## Correction vs. integration models

In recent years, attempts have been made to develop theoretical models specifying in some detail the mechanisms underlying attributions of other people's behaviour. In this section, we will focus on two such models: the correction model and the integration model.

Gilbert and Malone (1995) proposed the correction model to explain our tendency to attribute other people's behaviour to dispositional factors. According to this model, three successive stages are involved:

1. *Categorisation.* The observer assigns the actor's behaviour to a general category (e.g., "Fred behaved anxiously").
2. *Characterisation.* The observer infers that the actor possesses the corresponding disposition or personality characteristic (e.g., "Fred is an anxious person").
3. *Correction.* Observers correct the inference in (2) by taking account of situational factors (e.g., "The situation is stressful, and so Fred is not really an anxious person").

Of key importance, it is assumed theoretically that the first two stages are carried out automatically and with minimal use of processing resources, whereas the third stage requires effort and much use of processing resources. This stage is omitted when observers are under cognitive load (i.e., busy doing something else) and so have insufficient spare processing capacity to engage in correction. The key predictions are that the tendency to attribute other people's behaviour to dispositional factors will be high when they are under cognitive load but will be less when they are not under cognitive load and so can correct their initial dispositional inference.

*What do you understand by the term "cognitive load"?*

Trope and Gaunt (e.g., 2000) proposed the integration model, which involves two successive stages:

1. *Behaviour identification.* The observer uses a mixture of dispositional and situational information to provide a description of the actor's behaviour (e.g., "Fred behaved anxiously"). This description is influenced most by information which is salient or conspicuous.
2. *Diagnostic evaluation.* The observer uses the identified behaviour from stage 1 to compare the dispositional hypothesis (e.g., "Fred is an anxious person") against situational hypotheses (e.g., "Fred was placed in a very stressful situation"). In other words, the observer integrates the available information to decide the causes of the actor's behaviour.

According to this model, the first stage is carried out relatively automatically, whereas the second stage is more effortful and demanding. Observers under cognitive load will make little or no use of the second stage, and so whatever explanation of the actor's behaviour (dispositional or situational) is salient or dominant at stage 1 will be favoured.

*How conscious are your thought processes when you make causal attributions?*

## Evidence

Gilbert, Pelham, and Krull (1988) asked participants to watch a videotape of a woman behaving anxiously. They could not hear what the woman was saying, but the topics she was supposed to be discussing were included as subtitles in the videotape. In one condition, the topics were anxiety-provoking (e.g., hidden secrets). In the other condition, the topics were fairly neutral (e.g., world travel). In fact, the participants in both conditions saw exactly the same videotape except for the subtitles.

Half the participants were told to memorise the list of topics (cognitive load), whereas the other half simply watched the videotape. Afterwards the participants indicated the extent to which the woman's anxiety was due to her disposition. As expected, participants who simply watched the videotape gave a stronger dispositional attribution when the woman was talking about neutral topics (see the figure below). The reason for this was that her anxious behaviour could not be attributed to the topic when she was discussing a neutral topic. However, the participants under cognitive load provided the same dispositional attribution regardless of the topics discussed. According to Gilbert et al. (1988), this occurred because these participants were too busy learning the list to engage in the effortful processing needed to produce a situational attribution.

The findings of Gilbert et al. (1988) can be explained by both theories. We can compare the two theories directly if two factors are present: (1) the participants experience cognitive load, and (2) situational information is salient or conspicuous. According to the correction model, dispositional attributions should be given in those circumstances. According to the integration model, situational attributions should be given. Suppose participants under cognitive load (holding digits in memory) read an essay allegedly written by someone instructed to favour the legalisation of marijuana in their essay. Situational information is made salient by presenting the instructions given for the essay in an audio recording. Trope and Gaunt (2000) found in those circumstances that reasonable account was taken of situational factors when deciding whether the essay writer was expressing his/her true attitudes towards marijuana. Thus, the findings supported the prediction of the integration model but not that of the correction model.

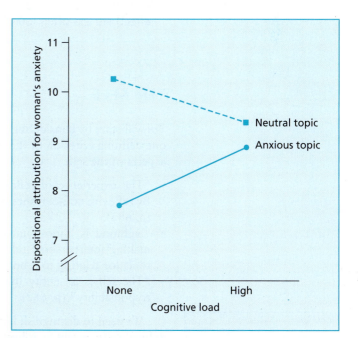

Strength of attribution of a woman's anxious behaviour to personality or disposition as a function of the topic she discussed (neutral vs. anxious) and the participant's cognitive load (none vs. high). Data from Gilbert et al. (1988).

## Evaluation

⊕ Our attributions of others' behaviour are influenced by relatively automatic and by more effortful processes.

⊕ Attributions of others' behaviour are often different when we engage in effortful cognitive processing than when we do not.

⊕ There is support for the correction and integration models, but the integration model has proved more successful.

⊖ The distinction between automatic and effortful processes is over-simplified (see Chapter 6).

⊖ More research is needed to identify more precisely the processes underlying our explanations of others' behaviour.

## General evaluation

⊖ Several factors determining our attributions of other people's behaviour have been identified.

⊖ It is important to study causal attributions, because our behaviour towards others is determined in part by our attributions of their behaviour. For example, attributions within marriage influence subsequent marital satisfaction or dissatisfaction (see Chapter 19).

⊖ The distinction between internal or dispositional causes and external or situational causes is often relatively unclear. For example, there is often little difference between internal attributions (e.g., "I bought the car because I like red cars") and external attributions (e.g., "I bought the car because it is red") (Robins et al., 1996).

⊖ "Psychology experiments ... are among the poorest vehicles for obtaining actuarial [statistically accurate] information about attributions. Because no effort is made to select representative situations or subjects, such experiments cannot reveal the kinds of attributions people usually, normally, routinely, generally, or typically make" (Gilbert & Malone, 1995, p. 28).

⊖ Attributional errors and biases (e.g., the fundamental attribution error, the actor–observer effect) are less often found in collectivistic cultures.

*What are the drawbacks of using experimental methods to help us understand how we explain others' behaviour?*

## THE SELF

We will start by considering the definition of the "self". According to Baumeister (1998), one defining criterion of the self is unity or oneness. He argued there are three other key aspects of the self:

- "The experience of reflexive consciousness ... is central to the nature of selfhood. By reflexive consciousness is meant the experience in which the person is aware of self" (p. 682).
- "Selfhood is almost unthinkable outside a social context, and selves are vital for making interpersonal relationships and interactions possible. Selves are handles and tools for relating to other people" (p. 680).
- "The self is an entity that makes choices and decisions, initiates actions, and takes responsibility" (p. 682).

We need to distinguish between the self and the self-concept. Baumeister (1995, p. 58) defined **self-concept** as follows: "The total organised body of information that any given person has about himself or herself ... the self-concept consists of a large number of self-schemas, organised or integrated in some coherent, usable fashion." Thus, the self-concept is composed of organised information about the self stored in long-term memory.

**KEY TERM**

**Self-concept:** the organised body of information that an individual possesses about him- or herself.

The self-concept is influenced by numerous factors. However, our relationships with other people are crucial. Charles Cooley (1902) used the term, "looking-glass self", to convey the notion that the self-concept reflects the evaluations of other people. Thus, we tend to see ourselves as others see us. Those of most importance in our lives (e.g., partners, parents, close friends) typically have the greatest effect on our self-concept.

*How would you describe yourself to someone else?*

William James (1890) distinguished two aspects of the self-concept: the "I" or self as the subject of experience, and the "me" or self as the object of experience. Young children initially begin to develop a sense of being separate from other people. This is the "I". After that, the "me" develops, which involves an awareness of the self as an object perceived by others. The development of the self is discussed at length in Chapter 16.

Stryker (1997) argued that the concept of the self is of fundamental importance to social psychology:

*Social psychology must incorporate a concept of self ... to get very far; for it is the set of self-conceptions, or self-definitions that make up self, that mediate the relation of society to behaviour and of behaviour to society. (p. 321)*

In view of the central importance of research on the self to social psychology, you might reasonably expect that we would by now have a clear picture of the self and its impact on social processes. However, this is not the case. As Baumeister (1995, p. 52) pointed out, "The diversity of approaches, methods, and ideas [in research on the self] is linked to a multiplicity of topics and issues, and so there is no coherent psychology of self."

## Social identity theory

One of the most important approaches to an understanding of the self-concept is social identity theory. This theory was originally proposed by Tajfel (e.g., 1969), but has since undergone considerable development (e.g., Turner et al., 1987). This theory is covered in detail in Chapter 21, and so we will focus here on those aspects most relevant to the self-concept. Of crucial importance is the distinction between personal identity and social identity, both of which help to define our sense of self. **Personal identity** is based on our personal relationships and characteristics, and includes those ways in which we differ from other people (e.g., in personality). In contrast, **social identity** is based on our membership of various groups (e.g., student, woman, European). Most other theoretical approaches to the self have focused almost exclusively on personal identity, and have ignored the notion that the self is strongly influenced by various social identities. However, social identities are of great importance. As Turner and Oakes (1997, p. 356) argued, "Minds belong to individuals ... but their content, structure, and functioning are nevertheless socially shaped and interdependent with society."

*What do you consider to be the difference between your personal identity and your social identity?*

We possess numerous personal and social identities: "We have as many social identities as there are groups that we feel we belong to, and as many personal identities as there are interpersonal relationships we are involved in and clusters of idiosyncratic attributes that we believe we possess" (Hogg & Vaughan, 2002, p. 126).

What determines which identity is dominant or salient in any given situation? According to social identity theory, several factors are involved (Turner, 1999). One important factor is the fit or match between the current situation and our various personal and social identities. For example, if I attend a function at my daughter's school, my identity as a parent will be dominant. However, if I attend a psychology conference, then my identity as a psychologist is likely to be dominant.

The personal or social identity that is dominant is also determined by our current motives and goals. For example, most people (at least in Western cultures) like to perceive themselves in ways that will increase their self-esteem. As a result, we are more likely to adopt a social identity based on the group in which we currently find ourselves if that group is prestigious and successful.

Turner (1999) discussed two other factors influencing the identity we adopt. First, there are our past experiences. For example, if it has made me happy to identify myself as a psychologist in the past, then that increases the likelihood I will do so across a range of situations. Second, there are present expectations. For example, if I expect that the

**KEY TERMS**

**Personal identity:** those aspects of the self-concept that depend on our personal relationships and characteristics or traits.

**Social identity:** those aspects of the self-concept that depend on the various groups to which we belong.

people I am interacting with will be more positively disposed towards a writer than a psychologist, then I may be tempted to adopt the identity of a writer rather than a psychologist!

What about the relationship between personal identity and social identity? According to Turner (1999, p. 12), "As shared social identity becomes salient, … individuals tend to define and see themselves less as differing individual persons and more as the interchangeable representatives of some shared social category membership [social identity]." Thus, for example, a woman who adopts the social identity of a woman will focus on the ways in which she is similar to other women and de-emphasise the ways in which she differs from most other women. In other words, it is typically the case that increased social identity is accompanied by a decrease in personal identity.

## Evidence

In view of the fact that most of the research discussed later in the chapter deals with personal identity, our central concern here will be with social identity. What are the circumstances in which our social identities are more important than our personal identities? According to Ellemers, Spears, and Doosje (2002), social identities are especially important when some group to which we are highly committed comes under threat. In such circumstances, social identity can lead to extreme individual self-sacrifice, as can be seen with kamikaze pilots or suicide bombers.

In many cases, individuals' commitment to a group is sufficiently strong that they are willing to accept very negative consequences from continued group involvement. For example, Baltesen (2000) discussed the employees of Baan, an IT company in the Netherlands. They all belonged to a very religious community, and so there was a strong sense of social identity among them. As a result, they remained in the company even when it encountered severe financial problems. Their reaction to these problems was to introduce daily prayers in the hope that the company might survive.

One of the main assumptions of social identity theory is that group members like their group to be distinct from other groups in positive ways (e.g., more successful, more dynamic). However, there are situations in which it is difficult for a group to be both distinctive *and* perceived positively. In such cases, one might predict that the need for a distinctive social identity based on group membership would be even more important than the group being perceived positively. For example, Poland has been invaded several times in its history, and so Polish people should have a strong sense of national identity. As predicted, Polish students were willing to accept that they possessed various negative characteristics (e.g., excessive drinking, quarrelsome, vulgar) associated with being Polish in order to maintain their national social identity (Mlicki & Ellemers, 1996).

What causes a change in social identity? According to Drury and Reicher (2000), a key factor is the existence of a discrepancy between ingroup and outgroup views of one's group. For example, many of those involved in a long-running campaign against the building of the M11 link road in north-east London regarded themselves initially as citizens having a neutral relationship with the police. However, the discovery that they were regarded as irresponsible by the police led many of them to change their social identity and become more radical in their thinking. In the words of one female campaigner, "I've got very determined just lately, determined to get on with things, and I don't ever think that I'm going to lead an ordinary life again" (p. 594).

What happens when a group to which we are *not* highly committed comes under threat? There are various possibilities, one of which is to cease identifying with the group in question. This was shown in a study by Cialdini, Borden, Thorne, Walker, Freeman, and Sloan (1976), in which students were asked to describe the outcome a few weeks after their college American football team had played a match. Students generally used the pronoun, "We", when the team had won, but the pronoun, "They", was preferred when the team had lost. Thus, a weak sense of social identity can be lost when the group in question is under threat.

*Under what circumstances might your social identity dominate over your personal identity?*

*What leads to changes in social identity?*

## Evaluation

⊕ Our sense of self is flexible, and the identity dominant at any given time is determined in part by the immediate situation (see Turner, 1999).

⊕ The distinction between personal identity and social identity has proved useful.

⊕ Previous theoretical approaches tended to ignore social identity, which appears to be of great importance to the sense of self.

⊖ It is not easy to determine precisely which personal and social identities are possessed by any given individual.

⊖ We often cannot predict which identity will be dominant in a given situation because so many factors are involved.

⊖ "It is [not] clear how we should conceive of the social self, which can be as varied as the groups to which we belong" (Ellemers et al., 2002, p. 164).

# Independent self vs. interdependent self

Markus and Kitayama (1991) argued that there are major cultural differences in the conception of the self. Those living in individualistic cultures such as the United States (see Chapter 1) have an **independent self**: The individual is seen as "an independent, self-contained autonomous entity who (a) comprises a unique configuration of internal attributes (e.g., traits, abilities, morals, and values), and (b) behaves primarily as a consequence of these internal attributes" (p. 224). In contrast, people living in collectivistic cultures (e.g., East Asia) have an **interdependent self**: They define themselves mainly with respect to their relationships and group memberships.

## Evidence

We can study cultural differences in the self-concept by using a simple technique known as the Twenty Statements Test. This test requires participants to provide 20 answers to the question, "Who am I?" The evidence from most studies using this test reveals the predicted cultural differences in the self-concept (see Smith & Bond, 1998). For example, Triandis, McCusker, and Hui (1990) compared the test responses of students from mainland United States, Hawaii, Hong Kong, Greece, and China. There were far more references to oneself as a member of a social category or group in the responses of Chinese students than in those of any other group.

When Masake Owado married Japan's Crown Prince Naruhito in 1993 she gave up a diplomatic career and her legal existence as a person. Although this may seem strange to many Western women, from the point of view of Japanese culture, with its valuing of connectedness to others and the greater good of the group, the decision may not have been so hard to understand.

Interesting evidence that these cultural differences in the conception of the self influence social processes was obtained by Gudykunst, Gao, and Franklyn-Stokes (1996a) in a study of American, British, Japanese, and Chinese participants. The American and British participants reported greater monitoring of their own behaviour in social situations than did the Japanese and Chinese participants. In contrast, the Japanese and Chinese participants reported greater monitoring of others' behaviour in social situations to ensure that their behaviour was socially appropriate.

Cross and Madson (1997) argued that the distinction between an independent self and an interdependent self can be applied to gender differences. They proposed that, "Men in the United States are thought to construct and maintain an independent self-construal, whereas women are thought to construct and maintain an interdependent self-construal" (p. 5).

Cross and Madson (1997) reviewed numerous studies supporting their position. For example, Clancy and Dollinger (1993) carried out a study in which men and women put

**KEY TERMS**

**Independent self:** a view of oneself as an independent person whose behaviour is determined mainly by one's own internal characteristics.

**Interdependent self:** a view of oneself as being defined primarily by one's relationships and group memberships.

*How might gender or culture influence our perception of ourselves as "independent" or "interdependent"?*

together sets of pictures which described themselves. Most of the pictures chosen by women showed them with others (e.g., family members). In contrast, most of the pictures chosen by men showed them on their own.

There have been various studies in which men and women have been asked to evaluate themselves with respect to various dimensions. Men typically evaluate themselves more positively with respect to independence (e.g., power, self-sufficiency) than with respect to interdependence (e.g., sociability, likeability). However, the opposite pattern is found with women (see Cross & Madson, 1997, for a review).

Another study showing gender differences in self-concept was reported by Stein, Newcomb, and Bentler (1992). A measure of interdependence predicted self-esteem 2 years later for women but not for men, suggesting the greater importance of interdependence for women. In addition, a measure of independence predicted self-esteem 2 years later for men but not for women, providing evidence that men's self-concept depends more than women's on independence.

## Evaluation

- ⊕ There are important cultural differences in the ways in which the self is regarded, and the distinction between independent and interdependent selves captures some of these differences.
- ⊕ The distinction between independent and interdependent selves sheds some light on gender differences in views of the self.
- ⊖ It is an over-simplification to use only two categories (i.e., independent, interdependent) to describe the self.
- ⊖ The theoretical approach is based on the assumption that the self is relatively unchanging over time. However, the evidence obtained by social identity theorists indicates that views of the self alter considerably with changing social contexts.
- ⊖ Cross and Madson (1997) may have misinterpreted the evidence when they argued that men are basically less concerned about other people than are women. The evidence is at least as consistent with the view that, "men and women are equally social and care equally how they relate to others—but within different spheres. Women … mainly orient toward and invest in a small number of close relationships, whereas men orient toward and invest in a larger sphere of social relationships" (Baumeister & Sommer, 1997, pp. 38–44).

## Changing the self

*To what extent can we change our self-concept?*

Our self-concept is strongly influenced by social factors, and so change in the self-concept should also depend on social factors. Jones et al. (1981) put forward an alternative view, according to which the self-concept can be changed merely by what they termed biased scanning. If people focus selectively on some of the stored information about the self, this can distort their self-concept. For example, if someone searches long-term memory for occasions in which they behaved in an introverted manner, this may lead them to think of themselves as introverted.

Tice (1992) carried out a study in which the participants answered loaded questions. For example, they might be asked questions pushing them into focusing on introverted aspects of their self-concept (e.g., "What annoys you most about loud, crowded parties?"). These loaded questions were asked either in a public, interpersonal setting or in a private, anonymous setting with no-one else present (speaking into a tape recorder). After that, there was an assessment of self-concept change.

What findings would be predicted? According to the biased scanning hypothesis, the loaded questions should have produced changes in self-concept in both conditions (i.e., public and private). In contrast, the self-concept should have changed only in the public condition if social and interpersonal factors are required to produce change, which is what was found. Thus, self-concept change depends on social factors (e.g., public commitment) rather than simply on biased scanning.

## Self-presentation

An important aspect of social life is **self-presentation**, which can be defined as "people's attempts to convey information about or images of themselves to others" (Baumeister, 1998, p. 703). According to Baumeister, two major kinds of motives influence our self-presentations. First, there are instrumental motives: We present ourselves to obtain rewards from other people. Second, there are expressive motives: We present ourselves in ways consistent with our values to establish our own identity.

### Evidence

People's self-presentations are often influenced by the potential rewards of presenting themselves in certain ways. Kowalski and Leary (1990) asked their participants to describe themselves to a supervisor, having been told this supervisor did or did not have the power to decide which tasks they did later. The participants only changed their self-presentations to impress the supervisor when he had power over them, presumably because it was only in those circumstances that there was any real advantage in so doing.

*What three factors would you use to describe yourself to someone new? Would you choose different factors for different people?*

We generally try to present ourselves in a favourable way. However, Tice et al. (1995) pointed out that most of this research had involved strangers, and might not be applicable to interactions between friends. They found that self-presentations tend to be modest and neutral when talking with friends, in contrast to the rather favourable self-presentations found when talking with strangers. Presumably this difference occurs because friends are much better than strangers at detecting any tendencies we may have to exaggerate our strengths.

What happens when our needs to present ourselves to obtain rewards from others *conflict* with our needs to present ourselves in accord with our own values? This issue was addressed by Wicklund and Gollwitzer (1982). The male participants completed a bogus personality test, and were given either encouraging or discouraging feedback. After that, they interacted with a girl called Debbie, who made it clear beforehand that she preferred either confident and self-enhancing people or modest and self-deprecating people. The participants who had received discouraging feedback presented themselves to Debbie in a confident and boastful way, even when they believed she disliked that type of person. In contrast, the participants who received encouraging feedback presented themselves modestly when led to believe that Debbie preferred modest people.

What can we conclude from the above study? First, self-presentation is sometimes determined mainly by the need to obtain rewards from others, and is sometimes determined by our need to establish our own identity. Second, individuals relatively secure in their own identity often manipulate their self-presentation to obtain rewards from others. Third, individuals insecure in their own identity are influenced in their self-presentations by the need to establish their own identity more clearly.

**KEY TERMS**
**Self-presentation:** the ways in which individuals try to convey information about themselves to other people.
**Self-esteem:** the evaluative part of the self-concept, concerned with feelings of worth and confidence.

## Self-esteem

An important part of the self-concept is **self-esteem**. This is the evaluative aspect of the self-concept, and concerns how worthwhile and confident an individual feels about him/herself. A brief definition of self-esteem was offered by Franzoi (1996, p. 51): "A person's evaluation of his or her self-concept."

Several theorists (e.g., Baumeister, 1995; Tesser, 1988) have argued that most people are highly motivated to maintain or enhance their self-esteem. As a result, much social behaviour can be regarded as serving the goal of maximising

A person's show of confidence can reflect how high their self-esteem is.

self-esteem. However, other theorists (e.g., Swann, 1987) have argued that people are motivated more to maintain *consistent beliefs* about themselves. According to this self-consistency theory, people like to feel they understand themselves. If they allow positive information about themselves to boost their level of self-esteem, they would have to change their self-concept, which could be disturbing and unsettling. Accordingly, people focus on maintaining consistent beliefs about themselves, even when many of those beliefs are negative.

Tesser (1988) proposed a self-evaluation maintenance model, which was concerned with the ways in which individuals maintain or enhance their self-esteem. He argued that an individual's self-esteem depends on his/her relationships with other people. Two main processes can raise self-esteem:

1. A *self-reflection process*. The individual basks in someone else's success; the closer the relationship, the greater the beneficial effect on self-esteem.
2. A *comparison process*. The individual enhances his/her self-esteem by performing better than someone else; again, the closer the relationship, the greater the effect.

These two processes are almost the opposite of each other, and so we need to know *when* each process will apply. According to Tesser, the comparison process is used when the success is in an area central to the individual's self-concept, whereas the self-reflection process is used when the successful performance is in an area of little relevance to the self-concept. These processes can also lead to reduced self-esteem if failure rather than success occurs. According to the theory, people will try to use the reflection and self-comparison processes to boost their self-esteem.

## Evidence

If people are motivated to enhance their self-esteem, then we might expect them to take credit for success by attributing it to internal or dispositional factors (e.g., "I worked very hard", "I have a lot of ability"). In contrast, they should deny responsibility for failure by attributing it to external or situational factors (e.g., "The task was very hard", "I didn't have enough time to prepare myself"). These tendencies to take the credit for success but accept no blame for failure define the **self-serving bias**.

There are several studies reporting evidence of the self-serving bias. For example, Bernstein, Stephan, and Davis (1979) considered students who had obtained a good or a poor grade on an examination. Those receiving a good grade typically attributed it to their intelligence, their hard work, or both. In contrast, those receiving a poor grade attributed it to bad luck or an unreasonable lecturer. Campbell and Sedikides (1999) carried out a meta-analysis of studies on self-serving bias. In line with the self-serving bias, success was consistently attributed to internal factors. However, failure was sometimes attributed to internal factors and sometimes to external factors.

Why are the attributions for failure so inconsistent? Duval and Silvia (2002) led self-focused participants to believe that failure could or could not be followed by improvement. Failure was attributed internally when subsequent improvement was likely, but it was attributed externally when subsequent improvement was improbable.

The self-serving bias is stronger in individualistic cultures than in collectivistic ones (see Smith & Bond, 1998, for a review). For example, Kashima and Triandis (1986) asked American and Japanese students to remember detailed information about landscapes shown on slides. Both groups tended to explain their success in terms of situational factors (e.g., luck) and their failures in terms of task difficulty. However, the Americans were more inclined to explain their successes in terms of high ability than their failures in terms of low ability, whereas the Japanese showed the opposite pattern.

Are attempts to maintain or enhance self-esteem at the heart of the self-serving bias? Individuals having generally high self-esteem show more evidence of self-serving bias than

**KEY TERM**

**Self-serving bias:** the tendency to take the credit for success but not to accept blame for failure.

those generally low in self-esteem (e.g., Shrauger, 1975). However, such findings do not prove that self-serving bias raises self-esteem. There are two reasons for doubting whether attempts to enhance self-esteem are always important. First, failure is often attributed to internal factors, and this leads to *reduced* self-esteem (e.g., Duval & Silvia, 2002). Second, as we have seen, members of collectivistic cultures are less likely than those of individualistic cultures to show the self-serving bias.

The emphasis on enhancing self-esteem can also be seen in the **false uniqueness bias**, the tendency to regard oneself as better than most other people. This bias has been found consistently in North Americans (e.g., Campbell, 1986). However, Japanese people do not show the false uniqueness bias, even when rating themselves on attributes seen as central to success within Japanese culture (see Heine, Lehman, Markus, & Kitayama, 1999).

There have been various attempts to test Tesser's (1988) self-evaluation maintenance model. For example, Tesser, Campbell, and Smith (1984) assessed American students'

It has been found that whereas American students over-estimate their own academic performance but not that of their close friend, Japanese students over-estimate their own performance but they over-estimate the performance of their friends even more, suggesting that collectivistic students are motivated to enhance others more than themselves.

estimates of their own and a close friend's performance in class. When the performance involved an activity regarded as relevant to the self-concept, they over-estimated their own performance (but not that of their close friend), presumably because the comparison process was involved. In contrast, they over-estimated their friend's performance (but not their own) on an irrelevant activity, presumably because the reflection process was involved.

Isozaki (1994) tried to replicate Tesser et al.'s (1984) study with Japanese students. He obtained partial support for Tesser's (1988) model, with students tending to over-estimate their own performance on relevant school subjects. However, they over-estimated the performance of their friends even more, suggesting the students were motivated to enhance others more than themselves. This is what one might expect in a collectivistic culture, in which the emphasis is on group solidarity rather than on individual achievement.

## Is high self-esteem important?

It may seem obvious that it is important for individuals to have high self-esteem, and that is certainly what most people in Western cultures believe. However, as Baumeister (1998, p. 695) pointed out, "There is a serious lack of evidence for beneficial or adaptive consequences of self-esteem." Nevertheless, there is reasonable evidence that high self-esteem is associated with pleasant emotional states. For example, Campbell, Chew, and Scratchley (1991) asked people to keep a diary in which they recorded their emotional reactions to their daily experiences. Individuals with low self-esteem experienced fewer pleasant and positive mood states than those with high self-esteem. The direction of causality is not clear: It is possible that high self-esteem helps to produce good moods, but it is also possible that experiencing many positive mood states enhances self-esteem.

Evidence that high self-esteem can have negative consequences was reported by Colvin, Block, and Funder (1995). They identified individuals whose opinions about themselves were significantly more favourable than those of their friends. When studied in the laboratory, such individuals interrupted other people, they expressed hostility, they were socially awkward, and they made others feel irritable. In general terms, these individuals with inflated self-esteem appeared to be arrogant and self-centred.

Baumeister, Smart, and Boden (1996) identified another downside associated with high self-esteem. They found interpersonal violence occurred more frequently among

Bullying is a real-life problem behaviour that may in some cases relate to having unrealistically high self-esteem. This condition is also termed the "narcissistic personality" and has a link to inappropriate behaviour such as over-reacting and aggressiveness (Ronningstam & Gunderson, 1990).

**KEY TERM**

**False uniqueness bias:** the mistaken tendency to think of oneself as being better than most other people.

those high in self-esteem than those low in self-esteem. Aggressive behaviour was especially likely when the very favourable view of themselves held by those high in self-esteem was disputed by someone else.

## Cultural differences

There are important cultural differences with respect to various biases related to self-esteem. Heine et al. (1999) argued that the notion that most people strive to maintain or enhance their self-esteem is not true of all cultures, especially collectivistic cultures. They supported this argument by considering a wide range of evidence from the North American and Japanese cultures. According to their theory, a key difference between the two cultures is in terms of the value of self-confidence, a concept closely related to self-esteem. North Americans attach great importance to self-confidence. In Japanese culture, in contrast:

> *To say that an individual is self-confident has negative connotations because it reflects how self-confidence gets in the way of interdependence, or it reveals one's failure to recognise higher standards of excellence and thus to continue to self-improve, or both. The motivation for individual self-esteem … is incongruent with motives to achieve connection and interpersonal harmony. (p. 785)*

*Why might self-esteem and self-confidence be thought to be more important for the North Americans than for the Japanese?*

In support of their theory, Heine et al. (1999) discussed unpublished research in which European Canadian and Japanese students ranked 20 traits in terms of how much they ideally would like to possess them. European Canadians rated self-confidence as the trait they would *most* like to possess, whereas the Japanese rated it as the trait they would *least* like to possess.

Kitayama, Markus, Matsumoto, and Norasakkunkit (1997) asked American and Japanese students to indicate how they would respond to various success and failure situations. Japanese students perceived failure situations as more relevant than success situations to their self-esteem, whereas American students showed the opposite pattern. The estimated decrease in self-esteem in failure situations was greater than the estimated increase in self-esteem in success situations for Japanese students, but it was the opposite for American students. Thus, Japanese people are more self-critical and less focused on enhancing their self-esteem.

The evidence suggests that Japanese people are much less motivated than Americans to enhance their self-esteem. Is it possible that Japanese people try to enhance their self-esteem by being very positive about the groups to which they belong? This possibility lacks empirical support. For example, Heine and Lehman (1997) found that North Americans had more positive appraisals of the groups to which they belonged than did Japanese people, and also felt that other people viewed their groups more positively than did the Japanese.

In sum, there are major cultural differences in the importance attached to high self-esteem. As Heine et al. (1999, p. 785) concluded:

> *Conventional theories of self-esteem are based on a North American individualised view of self that is motivated to achieve high self-esteem. In contrast, the most characteristic view of self in Japan (and elsewhere) is different from its North American counterpart … It is maintaining a self-critical outlook that is crucial to developing a worthy and culturally appropriate self in Japan.*

## SUMMARY

*Attitudes*

Self-report measures of attitudes are open to distortion, and have led to the development of physiological measures, assessment of implicit attitudes, and the bogus pipeline. Attitudes serve knowledge, utilitarian, self-esteem maintenance, and social identity functions. There is often a weak relationship between attitudes and behaviour. However, it is stronger when attitudes are measured at the same level of specificity and at similar points in time, and when attitudes have been formed through direct experience.

According to the theory of planned behaviour, our behaviour is influenced by our behavioural intentions, perceived behavioural control, and subjective norms as well as by our attitudes. The theory de-emphasises the extent to which our behaviour is determined by emotional factors and by automatic or implicit processes.

*Attitude change and persuasion*

Attitude change is maximal when the communicator is trustworthy, attractive, and similar to the recipient, and has relevant expertise. Presenting both sides of the argument is generally more effective than presenting only one side. Attitude or behaviour change is greatest when the perceived threat in the message is high and the perceived ability to cope is high. According to dual-process theories, people can be persuaded by messages via a central route (systematic processing) or via a peripheral route (heuristic processing). Attitude change generally lasts longer when produced by central route processing. Dual-route theories are over-simplified, and there are probably several processing strategies differing in the extent to which they involve effortful message evaluation. According to cognitive dissonance theory, a discrepancy between cognitions causes an uncomfortable state and the need for cognitive consistency. However, this need is less obvious in high self-monitors and in collectivistic societies.

*Attribution theories*

According to correspondent inference theory, we use information about people's behaviour and its effects to work out their intentions and their personal dispositions. According to Kelley's attribution theory, we use information about consensus, consistency, and distinctiveness to make attributions about others' behaviour based on the covariation principle. People often exaggerate the importance of disposition and minimise that of situational factors as the causes of other people's behaviour (fundamental attribution error, actor–observer effect). These effects are less common in collectivistic cultures than in individualistic ones. The attributions we make about others' behaviour often differ depending on whether we process the available information reasonably thoroughly or only superficially. Salient information (dispositional or situational) has more influence on our attributions when we are unable to engage in effortful processing.

*The self*

Our self-concept is strongly influenced by social factors, as are changes in self-concept. According to social identity theory, we have several personal and social identities, with the dominant identity at any point in time being determined by the situation in which we find ourselves. Those living in individualistic cultures have an independent self, whereas those in collectivistic cultures have an interdependent self, but the distinction between individualistic and independent selves is over-simplified. Many people are motivated to enhance their self-esteem, and this is reflected in the self-serving and false uniqueness biases. However, Japanese people are less motivated than Americans to enhance their self-esteem.

# FURTHER READING

- Baumeister, R.F. (1998). The self. In D.T. Gilbert, S.T. Fiske, & G. Lindzey (Eds.)., *The handbook of social psychology* (4th ed.). New York: McGraw-Hill. Baumeister provides a masterly account of theory and research on a notoriously complex topic.
- Hewstone, M., & Stroebe, W. (2001). *Introduction to social psychology* (3rd ed.). Chapters 5, 7, and 8 provide up-to-date accounts of several of the main topics in social cognition.
- Hogg, M.A., & Vaughan, G.M. (2002). *Social psychology* (3rd ed.). There is detailed coverage of nearly all the topics discussed in this chapter in Chapters 2–6 of this excellent textbook.
- Smith, E.R., & Mackie, D.M. (2000). *Social psychology* (2nd ed.). Philadelphia: Psychology Press. Several chapters in this textbook (e.g., 4, 7, and 8) deal with relevant key topics in an introductory way.

# Social behaviour and relationships

**19**

This chapter is concerned with the main ways we respond to (and interact with) other people. One important example is pro-social behaviour. This involves behaving positively towards others, doing our best to help them even at some cost to ourselves. Aggressive or anti-social behaviour is much more negative, since it involves deliberately trying to hurt someone else. In this chapter, we will be discussing key factors determining pro-social and anti-social or aggressive behaviour in adults.

You might imagine that pro-social and anti-social behaviour are simply opposite extremes of a single dimension, but this is *not* the case. Pro-social behaviour and aggressive or anti-social behaviour are largely *independent* of each other (Krueger, Hicks, & Mcgue, 2001). Thus, there is no general tendency for individuals who are high in pro-social behaviour to be low in aggressive behaviour or vice versa.

This chapter is also concerned with interpersonal relationships. It deals with the factors determining whether we are initially attracted to another person, the factors maintaining a friendship or other relationship, and the factors leading to its break-up. Several theories of the processes involved in interpersonal relationships will be considered in detail. As we will see, there are considerable differences in some aspects of interpersonal relationships (especially marriage) from one culture to another.

Some issues relating to the early stages of relationships can be studied in the laboratory. For example, suppose we want to know whether physical attractiveness is important in determining initial attraction. We could show our participants photographs of various people, with some biographical information attached to each photograph. We could then see whether willingness to go on a date with each person depended more on their physical attractiveness or on the biographical information. However, it is much harder to study the later stages of relationship development in the laboratory.

## PRO-SOCIAL BEHAVIOUR

This section of the chapter is concerned with pro-social behaviour, which is also discussed from the developmental perspective in Chapter 16. There is much overlap between helping behaviour and **pro-social behaviour**, but the distinction between them was clarified by Bierhoff (2001, p. 286): "The definition of 'pro-social behaviour' is narrower [than that of helping behaviour] in that the action is intended to improve the situation of the help-recipient, the actor is not motivated by the fulfilment of professional obligations, and the recipient is a person and not an organisation."

Some of the clearest examples of pro-social behaviour involve what is generally called altruism. **Altruism** is voluntary helping behaviour that is costly to the person who is altruistic, and typically involves empathy. **Empathy** is the ability to share the emotions of another person, and to understand that person's point of view. According to Batson (1995, p. 355), empathy involves:

> *other-oriented feelings congruent with the perceived welfare of another person. If the other is perceived to be in need, empathy includes feelings of sympathy, compassion, tenderness, and the like. Empathy is usually considered to be a*

**KEY TERMS**

**Pro-social behaviour:** co-operative, affectionate, or helpful behaviour intended to benefit another person.

**Altruism:** a form of pro-social behaviour that is costly to the individual, and which is motivated by the wish to help another person.

**Empathy:** the ability to understand someone else's point of view, and to share their emotions.

*product ... of adopting the perspective of the other, which means imagining how the other is affected by his or her situation.*

We will first of all consider two key general issues related to pro-social behaviour and altruism. After that, we will move on to some of the main theories.

## Why does altruism exist?

The issue of why altruism exists has been considered most systematically by theorists influenced by Darwin's (1859) theory of natural selection. According to that theory, there is natural selection or survival of the fittest (in the sense of reproductive success rather than physical fitness). Humans (or the members of other species) who behave in an altruistic or self-sacrificing way are probably less likely than non-altruistic individuals to produce many offspring. It seems to follow that the processes of natural selection should have led to the gradual disappearance of altruism. Why hasn't this happened?

*Why would anyone sacrifice their own life to save others?*

Advocates of **evolutionary psychology** (an approach based on the assumption that human behaviour can often be understood in evolutionary terms) claim that individuals are more concerned to make sure that their *genes* survive rather than that they *themselves* survive. Note that most people are unaware of this concern at the conscious level. This provides a potential explanation for altruistic behaviour: "If a mother dies in the course of saving her three offspring from a predator, she will have saved 1½ times her own genes (since each offspring inherits one half of its mother's genes). So, in terms of genes, an act of apparent altruism can turn out to be extremely selfish" (Gross, 1996, p. 413). The underlying notion behind this explanation is **kin selection**. This involves individuals ensuring the survival of their genes by helping the survival of their relatives.

Parents invest a lot of time and resources in their children, which may be explained by biological theories of relationships—the parents' chances of passing on their genes are improved if they can help their children to survive and succeed.

An important implication of the evolutionary approach is that altruistic behaviour is more likely to be shown towards close relatives than to other individuals, because we share more genes with close relatives. This idea was summed up by the geneticist J.B.S. Haldane. He argued that he would be willing to sacrifice his own life for the sake of two of his brothers or eight of his cousins.

The notion of kin selection helps to explain why people often behave altruistically towards members of their own families. However, other explanatory principles are needed to explain altruistic behaviour towards non-relatives. Evolutionary psychologists (e.g., Trivers, 1971) have done precisely this by emphasising the notion of **reciprocal altruism**, which is approximately summed up in the expression, "I'll scratch your back if you scratch mine." Thus, altruistic behaviour may occur because the individual behaving altruistically towards someone else expects that person to return the favour. According to Trivers, the strategy of offering help in the expectation that you will be helped in return is most likely to be adopted under certain conditions:

- The costs of helping are fairly low and the benefits are high.
- We can identify those who cheat by receiving help without helping in return.

### KEY TERMS

**Evolutionary psychology:** an approach based on the notion that much human behaviour can be understood in evolutionary terms.

**Kin selection:** the notion that the likelihood of survival of an individual's genes is increased by helping close relatives to survive.

**Reciprocal altruism:** the notion that individuals will behave altruistically towards another person if they anticipate that he/she will respond altruistically.

## Evidence

Relatively little research on pro-social behaviour and altruism is of direct relevance to kinship selection. One exception was a study by Burnstein, Crandall, and Kitayama (1994), in which they asked their participants to choose between helping various individuals differing in kinship (genetic relatedness), sex, age, health, and wealth. Their key findings were that choices were strongly influenced by kinship, and this tendency was especially great for life-and-death situations rather than for less important ones. In similar fashion, Fellner and Marshall (1981) found that 86% of people were willing to be a kidney donor for their children, 67% would do the same for their parents, and 50% would be a kidney donor for their siblings.

Korchmaros and Kenny (2001) argued that it is important to distinguish between genetic relatedness or kinship and emotional closeness. They asked college students to choose which family member they would be most likely to provide with life-saving assistance. Altruistic behaviour was determined in part by kinship or genetic relatedness and in part by emotional closeness,

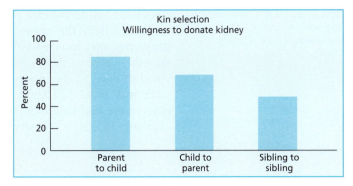

suggesting that evolutionary psychology cannot explain all altruistic behaviour. Not surprisingly, there was a fairly close association between genetic relatedness and emotional closeness.

Evidence supporting the notion of reciprocal altruism has been obtained from cross-cultural studies. Fijneman, Willemsen, and Poortinga (1996) found that individuals in collectivistic cultures gave more help to other people than was the case with individuals in individualistic cultures (see Chapter 1 for a discussion of collectivism and individualism). However, those living in collectivistic cultures expected more help from others than did those living in individualistic societies. As a result, there was reciprocal altruism in most cultures, with individuals typically giving approximately as much help as they expected to receive in return.

*What is it about collectivistic cultures that could lead to them being more likely to be altruistic than individualistic cultures?*

Reciprocal altruism is only an effective strategy when we can identify those who cheat by receiving help without offering any help themselves. It is easier to do this in small communities rather than large ones, and so there should be more evidence of altruism in small communities. Steblay (1987) carried out a meta-analysis, and concluded that individuals living in large cities are less willing to pass on a telephone message, less helpful to a lost child, less willing to do small favours, and less likely to post letters that have gone astray.

Reciprocal altruism or co-operation has been studied in the context of the prisoner's dilemma. In its typical format, the two players are given the hypothetical situation of being arrested for working together to commit a crime. The two "prisoners" are kept apart, and each is questioned by the "police". The same suggestion is made to each one: If he or she (A) agrees to confess and give evidence against the other prisoner (B), then A will be released and B will be severely punished. Each player has two choices: to keep silent in co-operation with their partner, or to confess all.

Both players gain when they co-operate with each other, as each will receive the same small punishment (there being little or no evidence against either). If both players confess, they both lose, because there is now evidence against both of them, and the penalties will be more severe. However, if one remains silent and the other confesses, the confessor gets away without a penalty while the other player receives the severe punishment. The dilemma is that each prisoner cannot be sure of the other prisoner's decision.

Axelrod (1984) asked 62 scientists to suggest winning strategies for the prisoner's dilemma when played repeatedly. The most effective strategy was tit-for-tat, which corresponds to reciprocal altruism. It involves the individual co-operating on the first occasion. On the second occasion, the individual behaves as the other individual had on the first occasion. After that, the individual simply copies the behaviour of the other individual on the previous occasion. This tit-for-tat strategy works, because it encourages the other person to be co-operative, while discouraging him/her from being selfish.

Kuhlman and Marshello (1975) compared the effects of the tit-for-tat strategy against two other strategies: 100% co-operation and 100% non-co-operation. The tit-for-tat strategy was the most effective strategy in producing high levels of co-operation in the other person. This was the case even among individuals mainly interested in pursuing their own self-interest.

The tit-for-tat strategy is unlikely to be used when the prisoner's dilemma is played only once, and so future co-operation is not needed. For example, consider a series called "Shafted" that was briefly seen on British television. At the end of the show, each

*How useful is the evolutionary approach to aiding our understanding of altruism*

contestant had to indicate privately (and without the other's knowledge) whether he/she wanted to share the money or have all of it for themselves. If they both voted to share the money, they received 50% each. If one person decided they wanted all the money and the other voted to share it, the former person received all the money. Finally, if they both voted to have all the money, no-one received anything. In the final show, the money at stake was about £220,000. Both players voted to have all the money. It was cruel to observe the looks on their faces when they realised that neither of them would receive anything. Indeed, it was so cruel that the series ended prematurely after that show.

## Evaluation

⊕ Evolutionary psychologists have put forward persuasive reasons (kin selection, reciprocal altruism) for the existence of helpful and altruistic behaviour.
⊕ The evolutionary approach explains why altruistic behaviour is much more likely to be shown to close relatives than to non-relatives.
⊕ Evolutionary psychologists (unlike other psychologists) address the important issue of *why* altruism is so important to the human species (McAndrew, 2002).
⊖ As we will see shortly, there is good evidence that people sometimes behave altruistically towards strangers, and such behaviour cannot be fully explained in terms of kin selection or reciprocal altruism.
⊖ The evolutionary approach ignores several factors (e.g., emotional closeness, social learning, personality) which help to determine the precise circumstances in which altruistic behaviour is and is not found.

## Who is helpful?

*Why are some people more helpful than others?*

Some people are generally more helpful than others, and there has been some research to identify the personal characteristics associated with helpful behaviour. For example, Schwartz (1977) argued that people possess a range of personal norms, or standards of behaviour based on the values they hold. Some of these norms relate to helping and to accepting responsibility for the welfare of others. According to Schwartz, individuals behaving in accord with their personal norms experience self-satisfaction, whereas those who do not experience shame and reduced self-esteem. As predicted, Schwartz found that those who were most helpful had personal norms relating to helping and to accepting responsibility for others.

Bierhoff, Klein, and Kramp (1991) studied first-aiders who helped those injured in traffic accidents. These first-aiders scored high on social responsibility. They also tended to have an internal locus of control, i.e., they believed they were in control of their own destiny.

Krueger et al. (2001) studied altruism in male identical and fraternal twins, finding that individual differences in altruism depended more on environmental factors than on heredity. Individuals high in the personality dimension of positive emotionality (i.e., high in sociability and extraversion) were more altruistic than those low in positive emotionality, with the two factors correlating $+.44$. In contrast, altruism scarcely correlated ($-.10$) with the personality dimension of negative emotionality (anxiety and depression).

## Empathy–altruism hypothesis

Batson (e.g., 1987) claimed that two main emotional reactions occur when we observe someone in distress (adjectives describing each reaction are in brackets):

● *Empathic concern.* A sympathetic focus on the other person's distress, plus the motivation to reduce it (compassionate, soft-hearted, tender).
● *Personal distress.* Concern with one's own discomfort, plus the motivation to reduce it (worried, disturbed, alarmed).

According to Batson's empathy–altruism hypothesis, altruistic or unselfish behaviour is motivated mainly by empathy rather than by personal distress.

## Evidence

Batson, Duncan, Ackerman, Buckley, and Birch (1981) and Batson et al. (1988) tested the empathy–altruism hypothesis and concluded that altruistic behaviour is motivated by empathy—see Key Study below.

Cialdini, Brown, Lewis, Luce, and Neuberg (1997) challenged the notion that pro-social behaviour is determined by empathic concern. They argued that the most important factor is oneness, defined as "a sense of shared, merged, or interconnected personal identities" (Cialdini et al., 1997, p. 483). They used scenarios in which someone needed help (e.g., there are two children whose parents have died in an accident). The person needing help was a near stranger, an acquaintance, a good friend, or a close family member of the participants. Pro-social behaviour was predicted better by feelings of oneness than by feelings of empathy. More importantly, after controlling for the effects of oneness, the influence of empathic concern on pro-social behaviour was very small.

## Batson et al.: Testing the empathy–altruism hypothesis

Batson et al. (1981) devised a situation to test the empathy–altruism hypothesis. Female students observed a student called Elaine receiving several mild electric shocks, and were asked whether they would take the remaining shocks instead of Elaine. Some students were told they were free to leave the experiment if they wanted, whereas other students were told they would have to stay and watch Elaine being shocked if they refused to take the shocks themselves. All of the students received a placebo drug (i.e., one having no effects). However, the students were given misleading information about the drug, so that they would interpret their reactions to Elaine as either empathic concern or personal distress. (It must be open to doubt whether all the participants believed this somewhat unlikely story!)

Most of the students feeling empathic concern offered to take the remaining shocks regardless of whether they could easily escape from the situation. In contrast, most of those who felt personal distress offered to take the shocks when escape was difficult, but far fewer did so when escape was easy. Thus, those feeling personal distress were motivated to help by fear of disapproval if they did not help, rather than by any real desire to help Elaine.

Batson et al. (1981) argued that the students feeling empathic concern helped Elaine for unselfish reasons. However, there are other possibilities. For example, they might have wanted to avoid self-criticism or social disapproval. In order to test these possibilities, Batson et al. (1988) carried out a modified version of the 1981 study. Some female participants were told that they would only be allowed to help Elaine by taking some of her electric shocks if they did well in a difficult mathematical task. Someone motivated to help Elaine only to avoid social disapproval and self-criticism might well offer to help, but then deliberately perform poorly on the mathematical task. This could be regarded as taking the easy way out. Many of those feeling personal distress did just that, and performed at a low level on the mathematical task. However, most students feeling empathic concern volunteered to help Elaine and did very well on the mathematical task. Their refusal to take the easy way out suggests that their desire to help was genuine.

### KEY STUDY EVALUATION—Batson et al.

Batson et al.'s study was intended to test the empathy–altruism hypothesis, however, mechanisms other than empathy may have played a part, including fear of social disapproval, or even the demand characteristics of the experimental situation. The students might easily have guessed that the experimenter was interested in their level of care for another person and behaved in what they thought was the expected or socially acceptable way.

It might also be interesting to speculate on the reasons why psychologists so often use the inflicting of electric shocks in their experiments, even if the shocks are only simulated. Mild shocks are often used in animal experiments, but their use in human experiments often seems contrived and artificial. How often do people find themselves in such a situation in real life?

## Discussion points

1. Does this study seem to provide a good test of the empathy–altruism hypothesis?
2. Do you think that someone needs to experience empathy in order to behave altruistically?

### Empathy and conduct disorders

Strayer and Cohen (1988) researched empathy and altruism in children. They showed them video clips portraying various emotional behaviour such as sadness, happiness, anger, and so on. They then scored the children on two scales. One was a cognitive measure relating to the understanding of how the person in the video is feeling; the other was the affective measurement of the degree to which the viewer empathises with, or shares, the emotions shown in the video. Children with anti-social behaviour problems did particularly badly on the affective scale compared to children without these problems, and this seemed to link to the anti-social group's perception of social desirability.

## Evaluation

➕ Altruistic behaviour often depends on empathy, as was shown by Batson (1995) in a review of more than 25 studies.

➕ The findings are surprisingly positive given that most of the experiments have studied empathy and altruism towards strangers. As Batson (1995, p. 367) pointed out, "[empathic] feelings are more likely to be felt for those (a) who are friendly, kin, or similar to us in some way; (b) to whom we are emotionally attached; (c) for whom we feel responsible; or (d) whose perspective we adopt."

➖ It is hard to be sure that people offer help for altruistic reasons rather than simply to avoid the disapproval of others or the feelings of guilt associated with failing to help.

➖ Feelings of oneness may be more important than empathic concern in determining pro-social behaviour (Cialdini et al., 1997).

➖ Genuine concern is often outweighed by more selfish motives. Batson, O'Quinn, Fultz, Vanderplas, and Isen (1983) found that 86% of participants feeling empathic concern were willing to take Elaine's place when she received mild shocks, but this dropped to only 14% when Elaine received painful shocks.

➖ The experimental focus has been on short-term altruistic behaviour having only a modest effect on the participants. In real life, altruistic behaviour can involve providing almost non-stop care for an ageing relative for several years. It is not clear that the same processes are involved in the two cases.

➖ Individual differences are de-emphasised within the empathy–altruism hypothesis. For example, Oliner and Oliner (1988) studied heroic individuals who had risked their lives to rescue Jews in Nazi Europe, claiming to find evidence for an altruistic personality.

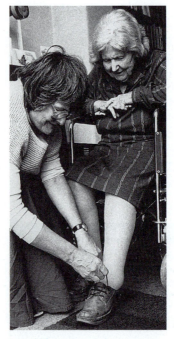

In real life as opposed to experimental situations, altruistic behaviour may involve many years of commitment rather than a brief impulse.

*How do you feel when you see other people in pain or distress?*

## Negative-state relief model

Cialdini, Schaller, Houlihan, Arps, Fultz, and Beaman (1987) put forward the negative-state relief model to explain why empathy leads to helping behaviour. According to this model, a person experiencing empathy for a victim usually feels sad as a result. They help the victim to reduce their own sadness. Thus, the negative-state relief model emphasises selfish reasons for engaging in helping behaviour. In contrast, the empathy–altruism hypothesis assumes the reasons can be unselfish.

It follows from the negative-state relief model that empathic concern should not lead to helping behaviour if the sadness usually found with empathy is not present. The model also includes the notion that helping is most likely when the rewards for helping are high and the costs low. Thus, people in an unpleasant mood are more likely to help than those in a neutral mood when helping is easy and very rewarding (e.g., it reduces their unpleasant mood).

The negative-state relief model was tested by Cialdini et al. (1987) using the same situation as Batson et al. (1981). The participants received a placebo drug having no actual effects. However, the experimenters claimed the drug would "fix" the participants' mood and prevent it being altered, a claim that may well not have been accepted by all of the participants! Cialdini et al. predicted that the participants would be less inclined to help the student receiving shocks if helping would not allow them to reduce their sad feelings. This prediction was supported: Participants feeling empathic concern were less likely to help if they had been given the drug.

Batson et al. (1989) set up a situation in which the predictions of the negative-state relief model and the empathy–altruism hypothesis would differ. In the key condition, participants in an empathic state were given the opportunity to help another person after being told they could anticipate a mood-enhancing experience even if they refused to help. According to the negative-state relief model, the fact that the participants' sadness would be removed anyway should reduce helping behaviour. In contrast, it follows from the empathy–altruism hypothesis that participants' high level of empathy should lead them to be helpful. The findings supported the prediction of the empathy–altruism hypothesis and disconfirmed that of the negative-state relief model.

Evidence that sadness does not *always* lead to helping behaviour was reported by Thompson, Cowan, and Rosenhan (1980). When they asked students to imagine the feelings that would be experienced by a friend who was dying, this led to an increase in helping behaviour. However, when they asked the students to imagine their own reactions to this situation, there was no increase in helping behaviour. This suggests that people can be so focused on their own emotional state that they fail to help others in need.

Events aimed at raising money for charity such as Live Aid in 1985, rely on high levels of empathic concern among those who are watching.

## Evaluation

- ⊕ Empathic concern sometimes leads to altruistic behaviour because altruistic behaviour reduces the helper's negative emotional state (e.g., sadness).
- ⊖ The negative-state relief model does not allow for the possibility that we might be motivated by unselfish motives, and is inconsistent with some of the evidence (e.g., Batson et al., 1989).
- ⊖ Bad moods are far more likely to increase helping behaviour in adults than in children (Franzoi, 1996). Thus, the model does not predict children's helping behaviour.
- ⊖ The model applies only to mild negative feelings. According to the model, intense negative feelings should not lead to helping behaviour.
- ⊖ It is hard to distinguish clearly between selfish and altruistic helping, and it is likely that much helping behaviour involves both forms of motivation.

## Cross-cultural differences

Most of the research discussed so far was carried out in the United States. It is dangerous to assume that what is true in one culture is true in other cultures. This danger is perhaps especially great with respect to altruism, because the United States is somewhat unusual in that the dominant approach to life in the United States is based on self-interest rather than on altruistic concern for others.

Cross-cultural research on pro-social or altruistic behaviour is discussed in Chapter 16. There is reasonable evidence that children in non-Western or collectivistic cultures behave more altruistically than do those brought up in Western or individualistic cultures. Eisenberg and Mussen (1989) reviewed several studies on cross-cultural differences in altruism, concluding that children in non-Western cultures are more co-operative, considerate, and kind than American children.

### Culture and childhood helping behaviour

Whiting and Whiting (1975) related childhood helping behaviour to background culture. Collectivistic cultures have a strong expectation, an important social norm, for altruism. This makes sense, as the culture is based on mutual support, with people being important because of what they can contribute to the group. The researchers found that in Kenya and Mexico, both collectivistic cultures, children are expected to take on family responsibilities such as helping siblings and doing chores. These children showed much greater helping behaviour than American children who are paid for doing chores and other help. The American culture is individualistic, i.e., it focuses on the individual as being important in their own right, with the norm that working for personal gain is worthy.

Further studies show that Israeli children who are brought up in Kibbutzim (collectivistic communities) show more helping behaviour than their peers who have been brought up by their families living in cities (more individualistic communities).

We need to be cautious in interpreting the above findings. As we saw earlier, Fijneman et al. (1996) found that those living in collectivistic cultures expect to receive more help from others than those living in individualistic cultures. The pro-social behaviour displayed by children in collectivist cultures may occur because they expect help in return rather than because their motives are entirely altruistic.

## Bystander intervention

A haunting image of our time is of someone being attacked violently in the middle of a city, with no-one helping them. This reluctance to help was shown in the case of Kitty Genovese. She was stabbed to death in New York as she returned home from work at three o'clock one morning in March 1964. Thirty-eight witnesses watched the murder from their apartments, but none of them intervened, and only one person called the police.

The police asked the witnesses why they had done nothing to help. According to a report in the *New York Times*:

> *The police said most persons had told them they had been afraid to call, but had given meaningless answers when asked what they had feared. "We can understand the reticence of people to become involved in an area of violence," Lieutenant Jacobs said, "but when they are in their homes, near phones, why should they be afraid to call the police?"*

### Diffusion of responsibility

John Darley and Bibb Latané (1968) tried to work out why Kitty Genovese was not helped by any of the numerous witnesses who saw her being attacked. According to them, a victim may be better placed when there is just one bystander rather than several. In such a situation, responsibility for helping the victim falls firmly on one person rather than being spread among many people. Thus, the witness or bystander has a sense of personal responsibility. If there are many observers of a crime or other incident, there is a **diffusion of responsibility**, with each person bearing only a small portion of the blame for not helping. Thus, there is less feeling of personal responsibility.

We also need to consider social norms or culturally determined expectations of behaviour. For example, there is the **norm of social responsibility**: We should help those who need help. Darley and Latané (1968) argued that this norm is more strongly activated when only one person observes the fate of a victim, rather than when there are several bystanders.

KEY TERMS
**Diffusion of responsibility:** the reduction in a sense of responsibility as the number of observers of an incident increases.
**Norm of social responsibility:** the cultural expectation that help should be given to those in need of help.

---

**CASE STUDY:** *The Kitty Genovese murder*

At approximately 3.20 in the morning on 13 March 1964, 28-year-old Kitty Genovese was returning to her home in a middle-class area of Queens, New York, from her job as a bar manager. She parked her car and started to walk to her second-floor apartment some 30 metres away. She got as far as a streetlight, when a man who was later identified as Winston Mosely grabbed her. She screamed. Lights went on in the nearby apartment building. Kitty yelled, "Oh my God, he stabbed me! Please help me!" A window opened in the apartment building and a man's voice shouted, "Let that girl alone!" Mosely looked up, shrugged, and walked off down the street. As Kitty Genovese struggled to get to her feet, the lights went off in the apartments. The attacker came back some minutes later and renewed the assault by stabbing her again. She again cried out, "I'm dying! I'm dying!" Once again the lights came on and windows opened in many of the nearby apartments. The assailant again left, got into his car and drove away. Kitty staggered to her feet as a city bus drove by. It was now 3.35 am. Mosely returned and found his victim in a doorway at the foot of the stairs. He then raped her and stabbed her for a third time—this time

fatally. It was 3.50 when the police received the first call. They responded quickly and were at the scene within two minutes, but Kitty Genovese was already dead.

The only person to call the police, a neighbour of Ms Genovese, revealed that he had phoned only after much thought and after making a call to a friend to ask advice. He said, "I didn't want to get involved." Later it emerged that there were 38 other witnesses to the events over the half-hour period. Many of Kitty's neighbours heard her screams and watched from the windows, but no-one came to her aid. The story shocked America and made front-page news across the country. The question people asked was why no-one had offered any help, or even called the police earlier when it might have helped. Urban and moral decay, apathy, and indifference were some of the many explanations offered. Two social psychologists, Bibb Latané and John Darley, were unsatisfied with these explanations and began a series of research studies to identify the situational factors that influence whether or not people come to the aid of others. They concluded that an individual is less likely to provide assistance the greater the number of other bystanders present.

Darley and Latané (1968) put their participants in separate rooms, and told them to put on headphones. They were asked to discuss their personal problems, speaking into a microphone, and hearing the contributions of others to the discussion over their headphones. They were led to think there were one, two, three, or six people involved in the discussion. In fact, however, all of the apparent contributions by other participants were tape recordings.

Each participant heard that one of the other people in the discussion was prone to seizures, especially when studying hard or taking examinations. Later on, they heard him say:

> *I—er—I—uh—I've got one of these—er—seizure—er—er—things coming on and—and—and I could really—er—use some help so if somebody would—er—er—help—er—er—help—er—uh—uh—uh [choking sounds] … I'm gonna die—er—er—I'm … gonna die—er—help—er—er—seizure—er … [choking sounds, silence].*

Of those who thought they were the only person to know that someone was having an epileptic fit, 100% left the room and reported the emergency. However, only 62% of participants responded if they thought there were five other bystanders. Those participants who thought they were the only bystander responded much more rapidly than those who thought there were five bystanders: 50% of them responded within 45 seconds of the onset of the fit, whereas none of those who believed there were five other bystanders did so.

There were two other interesting findings. First, the participants who believed that there were five other bystanders denied that this had influenced their behaviour. Thus, people are not fully aware of the factors determining whether or not they behave helpfully. Second, those participants not reporting the emergency were not apathetic or uncaring. Most of them had trembling hands and sweating palms, and they seemed more emotionally aroused than the participants who did report the emergency.

Several researchers have identified factors in addition to diffusion of responsibility determining whether or not a victim will be helped. We will consider some of these factors, and then discuss relevant theories (go straight to the theories if you want an overview right now!).

## Interpreting the situation

In real life, many situations are ambiguous. For example, someone collapsing in the street may have had a heart attack, or they may simply have had too much to drink. Not surprisingly, the chances of a bystander lending assistance to a victim are much greater if the situation is interpreted as a genuine emergency. Brickman, Rabinowitz, Karuza, Coates, Cohn, and Kidder (1982) carried out a study in which the participants heard a bookcase falling on another participant, followed by a scream. When someone else interpreted the situation as an emergency, the participant offered help more rapidly than when the other person said there was nothing to worry about.

In many incidents, the perceived relationship between those directly involved can have a major influence on the bystanders' behaviour. Shotland and Straw (1976) arranged for a man and a woman to stage a fight close to onlookers. In one condition, the woman screamed, "I don't know you." In a second condition, she screamed, "I don't know why I ever married you." When the onlookers thought the fight involved strangers, 65% of them intervened, against only 19% when they thought it involved a married couple. Thus, bystanders are reluctant to become involved in the personal lives of strangers. Kitty Genovese may have received no help because the bystanders assumed there was a close relationship between her and her male attacker. Indeed, a housewife who was among the bystanders said, "We thought it was a lovers' quarrel."

## Victim characteristics

Most bystanders are influenced by the victim's characteristics. Piliavin, Rodin, and Piliavin (1969) staged incidents in the New York subway, with a male victim staggering

*What factors influence whether or not you would help someone who was in difficulties?*

*Why might you be less likely to intervene in a domestic fight than in a confrontation between strangers?*

*What is it about some people that makes us more likely to help them than others?*

forwards and collapsing on the floor. He either carried a black cane and seemed sober, or he smelled of alcohol and carried a bottle of alcohol. Bystanders were much less likely to help when the victim was "drunk" than when he was "ill". Drunks are regarded as responsible for their own plight, and it could be unpleasant to help a smelly drunk who might vomit or become abusive.

## Bystander characteristics

Huston, Ruggiero, Conner, and Geis (1981) argued that bystanders with relevant skills or expertise will be most likely to help a victim. For example, suppose that a passenger on a plane collapses suddenly, and one of the stewardesses asks for help. It is reasonable to assume that a doctor will be more likely to offer his or her assistance than someone lacking any medical skills. Huston et al. found that those helping in dangerous emergencies had typically had training in relevant skills (e.g., life-saving, first aid, self-defence).

Eagly and Crowley (1986) reviewed the literature on gender differences in helping behaviour. Men are more likely than women to help when the situation involves danger, or when there is an audience. Men are more likely to help women than other men, especially when the women are attractive. In contrast, women are equally likely to help men and women.

Bystanders are most likely to help a victim who is similar to themselves (Hogg & Vaughan, 2002). Levine (2002) developed this idea in a study on bystander intervention when someone is exposed to physical violence. His key finding was that victims were more likely to be helped when they were described as belonging to the bystanders' ingroup than when they allegedly belonged to an outgroup.

Gaertner and Dovidio (1977) found that similarity between bystander and victim is not always important. They used a situation in which white participants heard a victim in the next room apparently being struck by a stack of falling chairs. When it was unclear whether there was an emergency (there were no screams from the victim), the white participants helped a white victim faster than a black one. The findings were different when the victim screamed, and so there was clearly an emergency. In that case, a black victim was helped as rapidly as a white victim. These findings indicate that the preference for helping those similar to ourselves can be eliminated if the situation is serious enough.

*To what extent does the amount of time you have influence whether or not you help someone?*

Bystanders take into account the activity in which they were involved when they came upon the emergency. Batson, Cochrane, Biederman, Blosser, Ryan, and Vogt (1978) sent their participants from one building to another to perform a task. On the way, they went past a male student who was slumped on the stairs coughing and groaning. Only 10% of those told that the task was important stopped to help the student compared to 80% of those told the task was unimportant.

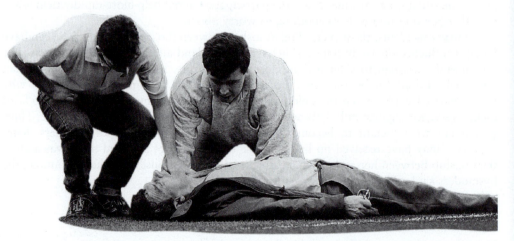

Bystanders who have some relevant skill to offer are more likely to get involved than those who don't know what to do.

### Late Samaritans

Darley and Batson's (1973) study assessed helping behaviour in students from a theological college—where they were studying to be ministers or priests.

The students had to give a presentation at a nearby building—half had to talk about the bible parable the Good Samaritan; the other half had to talk about the jobs the students enjoyed most. The students were also split up into three groups and were told one of the following:

● You are ahead of schedule and have plenty of time.
● You are right on schedule.
● You are late.

On their way to the talk, they passed a "victim", actually a stooge, who was collapsed in a doorway, coughing and groaning. The students were observed to see whether or not they stopped to help.

Darley and Batson found that the topic of the student's talk did not seem to influence helping. However, the perceived time pressure did. The results were as follows:

| Group condition | % helping |
| --- | --- |
| Ahead of schedule | 63 |
| Right on schedule | 45 |
| Late | 10 |

Bizarrely, several "late" condition students who were going to give a talk on the Good Samaritan actually stepped over the victim to get past.

## Decision model

How can we make theoretical sense of the various findings? Latané and Darley (1970) put forward a decision model. According to this model, bystanders lending assistance to a victim do so after working their way through a five-step sequence of decisions, producing a "yes" answer at each step. The complete decision-making sequence is as follows (relevant studies are shown in brackets):

*Step 1.* Is something the matter?
*Step 2.* Is the event or incident interpreted as one in which assistance is needed? (Brickman et al., 1982; Shotland & Straw, 1976)
*Step 3.* Should the bystander accept personal responsibility? (Darley & Latané, 1968; Piliavin et al., 1969)
*Step 4.* What kind of help should be provided by the bystander? (Huston et al., 1981)
*Step 5.* Should the help worked out at step 4 be carried out? (Batson et al., 1978)

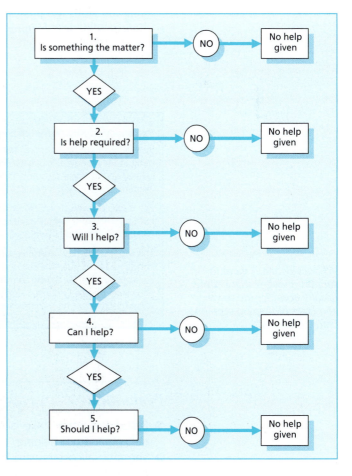

## Evaluation

● The experimental evidence supports the model's assumption that there are several reasons why bystanders do not provide assistance.
● The decision model provides a plausible account of why it is that bystanders so often fail to help a victim. If bystanders provide a "no" answer at any point in the decision sequence, then help will not be forthcoming.

- The model does not provide a detailed account of the processes involved in decision making. For example, we need to know more about the processes involved when "yes" decisions at steps 1, 2, and 3 are followed by a "no" decision at step 4 or 5.
- The decision model de-emphasises the influence of emotional factors on bystanders' behaviour. Bystanders who are anxious or terrified are unlikely to work carefully through the five decision-making stages contained in the model.

## Arousal/cost–reward model

Piliavin, Dovidio, Gaertner, and Clark (1981) put forward the arousal/cost–reward model. According to this model, there are five steps that bystanders go through before deciding whether or not to assist a victim:

1. Becoming aware of someone's need for help; this depends on attention.
2. Experience of arousal.
3. Interpreting cues and labelling the state of arousal they are experiencing.
4. Working out the rewards and costs associated with different actions.
5. Making a decision and acting on it.

The fourth step is the most important, and deserves more detailed consideration. Some of the major rewards and costs involved in helping and not helping are as follows (relevant studies are in brackets):

*What are the costs involved in deciding to intervene to help someone who is in trouble?*

- *Costs of helping*. Physical harm, delay in carrying out other activities (Batson et al., 1978; Piliavin et al., 1969).
- *Costs of not helping*. Ignoring personal responsibility, guilt, criticism from others, ignoring perceived similarity (Darley & Latané, 1969).
- *Rewards of helping*. Praise from victim, satisfaction from having been useful if relevant skills are possessed (Huston et al., 1981).
- *Rewards of not helping*. Able to continue with other activities as normal (Batson et al., 1978).

---

**Bystander apathy in the internet age**

Researchers in Israel (Barron & Yechiam, 2002) hypothesised that people would respond to a query much better if they thought they were being targeted as an individual, rather than as a set of people. They created an imaginary person, Sarah, on Yahoo who was enquiring about possible courses at a technical institute. Some of Sarah's emails were sent to individuals, and some to groups of five people.

The results showed that 50% of the sample did not reply at all if there were four others on the address list, but only 36% of the single recipients failed to reply. And almost 33% of single recipients sent back a very helpful response—with additional useful information—compared to 16% of the group sample.

*What evidence is there to support the view that people usually consider the rewards and costs of helping someone before taking action?*

This suggests that automatic emails to groups of people are not as successful in outcome as individual ones. This should hold true whether one is asking for a volunteer to help with an office birthday cake or a commercial advertiser trying to increase hits on a website. So the implication is that to be truly effective people need to be contacted singly. If they see they are part of a group they may feel that someone else will respond as required so they need not do anything. They will become virtual bystanders!

---

## Evaluation

- Bystanders often take account of the potential rewards and costs associated with helping and not helping.
- The arousal/cost–reward model provides a more complete account than the decision model of the processes involved in deciding whether or not to provide help.

- The arousal/cost–reward model implies that bystanders deliberately consider all the elements in the situation. In fact, bystanders often respond impulsively and without deliberation.
- Bystanders do *not* always need to experience arousal before helping a victim. For example, someone with much relevant experience (e.g., a doctor responding to someone having a heart attack) may provide efficient help without becoming aroused.

# AGGRESSION

This part of the chapter focuses on aggression, which is also covered from the developmental perspective in Chapter 16 (including a discussion of the effects of media violence). **Aggression** is:

> *any behaviour directed toward another individual that is carried out with the proximate (immediate) intent to cause harm. In addition, the perpetrator must believe that the behaviour will harm the target and that the target is motivated to avoid the behaviour. (Bushman & Anderson, 2001, p. 274)*

Note that the harm has to be *deliberate*. Someone who slips on the ice and crashes into someone by accident may cause harm, but should not be regarded as behaving aggressively. Note also that the victim must want to avoid harm. Whipping a masochist who derives sexual pleasure from the activity does not constitute aggressive behaviour.

*What would you like to be able to do to someone who had really annoyed or upset you?*

Many textbooks draw a distinction between hostile aggression and instrumental aggression. Hostile aggression involves impulsive behaviour driven by anger and intended to harm another person. An example occurred in 2001 when the British politician John Prescott punched a member of the public after something had been thrown at him. In contrast, instrumental aggression involves calculated behaviour, and harming the other person is used as a way of obtaining some goal (e.g., stealing money). It is typically assumed that hostile aggression is based on automatic processing, whereas instrumental aggression is based on controlled or deliberate processing (see Chapter 6).

In spite of the popularity of the distinction between hostile and instrumental aggression, there are good grounds for abandoning it. As Bushman and Anderson (2001) pointed out, it represents a gross over-simplification in two ways. First, most aggressive behaviour probably arises from a combination of automatic and controlled processes. Second, aggressive behaviour is typically based on multiple motives, and often involves instrumental motives as well as anger.

Deciding whether a particular piece of behaviour is aggressive depends on how that behaviour is interpreted. Such interpretations can be influenced by the perceiver's beliefs and knowledge. For example, Blumenthal, Kahn, Andrews, and Head (1972) studied the attitudes of American men towards police and student behaviour during student demonstrations. Students with negative attitudes towards the police judged the police's behaviour to be violent and aggressive, whereas the sit-ins and other actions of the students were regarded as non-violent. In contrast, men with positive attitudes towards the police did not regard their assaults on students or their use of firearms as violent. However, they condemned student sit-ins as violent acts deserving arrest.

The main goal of the aggression in this picture is to obtain a "reward" by stealing the bag, rather than to hurt someone. This is an example of instrumental aggression.

How do we decide whether someone is behaving aggressively? According to Ferguson and Rule (1983), there are three main criteria:

- Actual harm is caused to another person or to an object.
- Intention to harm.
- Norm violation, with the observed behaviour being illegitimate and against society's norms.

The norm of reciprocity is of particular importance in deciding whether an act is aggressive. According to the **norm of reciprocity**, if someone has done something to you, then you are justified in behaving in the same way to that person. Evidence that the norm of reciprocity applies to aggressive behaviour was reported by Brown and Tedeschi (1976). Someone who initiated a hostile act against another person was seen as aggressive and unfair. In contrast, someone who attacked another person after being provoked was regarded as behaving fairly and non-aggressively.

## Social learning theory

Bandura (e.g., 1973) put forward a social learning theory account of aggressive behaviour (see Chapter 16). It is assumed within the theory that much aggressive behaviour depends on observational learning or modelling. **Observational learning** involves watching the behaviour of other people and then imitating or copying it subsequently. More specifically, aggressive behaviour seen to be rewarded is imitated, whereas aggressive behaviour that is punished is typically not imitated.

There are numerous studies on children showing that they will often imitate aggressive behaviour they have observed (see Chapter 16). However, Bandura overestimated the extent to which children (and adults) imitate the behaviour of models. Social learning theory is limited, in that it does not take account of individual differences in the tendency to be aggressive, nor does it fully address the cognitive processes (e.g., interpretation of the situation) determining whether someone behaves aggressively or not. More generally, social learning theory ignores the role of biological factors in influencing levels of aggression (see Chapter 16).

## Frustration–aggression hypothesis

Think of occasions on which you have behaved aggressively. Many of them probably involved frustrating situations. Dollard, Doob, Miller, Mowrer, and Sears (1939) argued in their frustration–aggression hypothesis that there are close links between frustration and aggression. They assumed that frustration always causes aggression, and that aggression is always caused by frustration. However, there are many occasions on which it is dangerous or ill-advised to behave aggressively towards the source of the frustration (e.g., if he/she is your boss). Accordingly, Dollard et al. assumed that aggression is sometimes displaced from the source of the frustration on to someone else. For example, if some powerful person has frustrated you, you may behave aggressively towards your pet dog or cat.

Miller, Sears, Mowrer, Doob, and Dollard (1941) soon realised that the original frustration–aggression hypothesis was over-simplified. Accordingly, they changed the hypothesis to assert that aggression is the dominant response to frustration, but the precise behaviour produced is influenced by other factors in the situation.

### Evidence

Doob and Sears (1939) asked participants to imagine how they would feel in each of 16 frustrating situations. In one situation, the participants imagined they were waiting for a bus, but the bus driver went by without stopping. Most of the participants reported that they would feel angry in each of the frustrating situations. However, note that anger does not necessarily produce aggressive behaviour.

Pastore (1952) distinguished between justified and unjustified frustration. According to him, it is mainly *unjustified* frustration that produces anger and aggression. Doob and Sears (1939) obtained strong support for the frustration–aggression hypothesis because the situations they used involved unjustified frustration. Pastore produced different versions of the situations used by Doob and Sears using *justified* frustration. For example, the situation with the non-stopping bus was re-written to indicate that the bus was out of service. As predicted, justified frustration led to much lower levels of anger than did unjustified frustration.

*What makes you angry?*

There is more recent evidence supporting the frustration–aggression hypothesis. Catalano, Novaco, and McConnell (1997) carried out a study in San Francisco in which they looked at the relationship between job losses and violence. They found that small increases in job losses (a cause of frustration) was associated with an increase in violence (aggression).

The assumption that individuals will often displace their aggression on to someone other than the person responsible for their negative internal state or frustration has been tested many times. Marcus-Newhall, Pedersen, Carlson, and Miller (2000) carried out a meta-analysis of 82 studies on displaced aggression, and concluded that the evidence generally provided strong support for the existence of displaced aggression (see Chapter 22).

## Evaluation

➕ Frustration is a major factor causing aggressive behaviour.

➕ Aggression is often directed at someone other than the cause of frustration, i.e., displacement frequently occurs.

➖ The frustration–aggression hypothesis is over-simplified, even if it is accepted that frustration does not always lead to aggression.

➖ The frustration–aggression hypothesis ignores several important factors of relevance to aggressive behaviour, including personality, thoughts evoked by aspects of the situation, perceptions of the rewards and costs of behaving aggressively, and so on.

## Cue–arousal theory

According to Berkowitz (e.g., 1974), frustration produces a state of emotional arousal generally labelled as anger. This does *not* directly lead to aggressive behaviour. What is also important is the presence of aggressive cues (e.g., a gun or other weapon). Almost any stimulus can become an aggressive cue through a process of classical conditioning, in which that stimulus is associated with aggressive behaviour. This theoretical approach is known as cue–arousal theory, and represents an improvement on the earlier frustration–aggression hypothesis.

*Why do you think that frustration plays such a key role in aggression?*

## Evidence

Cue–arousal theory has received support from the **weapons effect**, an increase in aggression caused by the mere sight of a weapon (e.g., gun). The weapons effect was obtained by Berkowitz and LePage (1967). Male university students received electric shocks from another student, who was a confederate working for the experimenter. They were then given the chance to give electric shocks to the confederate. In one condition, a revolver and a shotgun were close to the shock machine. In another condition, nothing was placed nearby. The presence of the guns increased the average number of shocks given from 4.67 to 6.07. According to Berkowitz (1968, p. 22):

*Guns not only permit violence, they can stimulate it as well. The finger pulls the trigger, but the trigger may also be pulling the finger.*

**KEY TERM**

**Weapons effect:** an increase in aggression produced by the sight of a weapon.

*To what extent do you think that laboratory studies testing models of aggression have a great deal to say about violence in everyday life? How else might psychologists investigate the nature of aggression?*

Carlson, Marcus-Newhall, and Miller (1990) carried out a meta-analysis on 56 studies concerned with the effects of aggression-related cues on aggressive behaviour. As predicted by cue–arousal theory, such cues generally led to increased aggressive behaviour in negatively aroused individuals. However, aggression-related cues also produced aggression-related thoughts even in individuals who had not previously been frustrated, which seems contrary to the theory.

It is doubtful whether Berkowitz's interpretation of the weapons effect in terms of classical conditioning is correct. It may simply be the case that aggressive cues suggest that aggressive behaviour is acceptable in that situation.

## Evaluation

- ➕ Cue–arousal theory provides a more adequate account of aggressive behaviour than does the frustration–aggression hypothesis.
- ➕ Aggression-related cues help to determine aggressive behaviour.
- ➖ There is little evidence that the aggression-related cues are effective because of a prior process of classical conditioning.
- ➖ Cue–arousal theory de-emphasises the role of individual differences and biological factors in aggressive behaviour.
- ➖ Cue–arousal theory does not consider sufficiently individuals' cognitive processes in assessing the situation and deciding on the appropriate behaviour to perform.

## Cognitive-neoassociationistic approach

Berkowitz (1989) developed cue–arousal theory to produce a more general cognitive-neoassociationistic approach to aggression (see the diagram below). According to this approach, an aversive or unpleasant event (e.g., frustrating incident, environmental stressor) causes negative affect. This negative affect then activates an associative network within long-term memory. This produces effects on expressive motor patterns concerned with fight and flight, on emotions, and on cognitions.

Various predictions follow from this theoretical approach. First, aggressive behaviour can be triggered by numerous conditions provided that they produce a sufficiently high level of negative affect. This contrasts with the commonsensical view that anger is nearly always triggered by interpersonal disputes. Second, the emotion of anger can be produced by thoughts about aggression or hostility and by aggressive behaviour as well as by increased negative affect.

## Evidence

Support for the first prediction above was reported by Berkowitz, Cochran, and Embree (1981). Negative affect was created by requiring some of the participants to hold their hand in ice-cold water. These participants gave more bursts of unpleasant noise to another

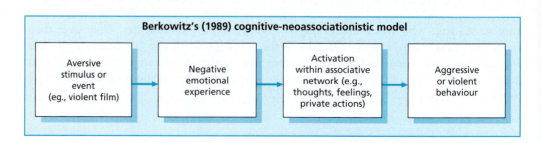

**Berkowitz's (1989) cognitive-neoassociationistic model**

Aversive stimulus or event (eg., violent film) → Negative emotional experience → Activation within associative network (e.g., thoughts, feelings, private actions) → Aggressive or violent behaviour

person who was being punished for poor performance than did other participants who held their hand in warm water.

Support for the second prediction above was obtained by Berkowitz and Heimer (1989). Their participants were told to hold their hand in either ice-cold water or luke-warm water, and at the same time to think of either punishment or some non-aggressive matter. Thinking about punishment and being exposed to ice-cold water both produced increased feelings of anger. They also led to increased aggression in the form of more bursts of unpleasant noise administered to another person.

The cognitive-neoassociationistic approach has similar strengths and weaknesses to cue–arousal theory. However, it is a more general and broader theory of aggression. It has the disadvantage that it is somewhat vaguer, and therefore more difficult to test.

## Negative affect escape model

Baron (1977) proposed a negative affect escape model. According to this model, as unpleasant stimuli (e.g., noise, heat) increase in intensity, they typically lead to increased aggressive behaviour. The reason is because aggressive behaviour reduces or eliminates the negative affect caused by the unpleasant stimulus. However, if the unpleasant stimuli become very intense, there is often *less* aggressive behaviour. What happens is that people try to escape the intense stimulus, or they simply become passive and fatigued.

### Evidence

Baron and Bell (1976) studied the effects of heat on aggression by seeing how willing participants were to give electric shocks to another person. Temperatures within the range 92–95 °F (33–35 °C) generally increased the level of aggression. However, extreme heat led to a reduced level of aggression towards another person who had provided a negative evaluation of the participant. In those conditions, the participants were very stressed. If they gave shocks to the other person, they would have had to deal with his angry reactions, and they felt unable to deal with the added stress.

Anderson (1989) considered the effects of temperature on various forms of aggressive behaviour (e.g., assault, rape, murder). All of these aggressive acts increased as the temperature rose, with no indication of any reduction in extreme heat. Anderson and Anderson (1996) found that violent crimes were more common in American cities that are mostly hot than in those that are not. It is hard to interpret these findings, because most of the hottest cities are in the southern states and most of the coolest cities are in the northern states. Thus, these findings may simply indicate that there is a "southern culture of violence". However, they discovered that violent crime rates are even more strongly linked to the warmth of a city than to its geographical location.

*Why would aggressive behaviour be linked to the temperature?*

### Evaluation

⊕ Most laboratory tests of the model support it, and data from real-life situations provide partial support.
⊕ Several unpleasant or aversive stimuli have been found to cause aggression.
⊖ It has proved harder to show reduced aggression with very intense unpleasant stimuli in the real world than in the laboratory. Perhaps it is easier to escape from unpleasant stimuli in the laboratory than in real life. Alternatively, intense provoking stimuli in real life may be more likely to produce high levels of negative affect and so trigger aggressive behaviour.
⊖ There are many causes of aggressive behaviour in addition to moderately intense stimuli, including psychologically threatening stimuli, biological factors, and certain types of personality.

## Excitation-transfer theory

Zillmann (e.g., 1988) developed excitation-transfer theory, according to which arousal caused by one stimulus can be transferred and added to the arousal produced by a second stimulus. What is important in determining the emotional reaction to the second stimulus is the *interpretation* of the transferred arousal. For example, suppose someone insults you on a very hot day. You might normally ignore the insult. However, because the hot weather has made you more aroused, you may become very aggressive. According to the theory, however, this should *only* happen if you attribute your aroused state to being insulted rather than to the temperature. The notion that the interpretation given to one's arousal level is important resembles the theoretical approach of Schachter and Singer (1962) in their two-factor theory of emotion (see Chapter 5).

### Evidence

Zillmann, Johnson, and Day's (1974) study provides an experimental example of excitation transfer—see Key Study.

Zillmann and Bryant (1984) considered the effects of watching several films of violent pornography. Such exposure led males and females to display higher levels of aggression against someone who irritated them, presumably because of the arousing nature of the films they had watched. Somewhat surprisingly, males and females recommended *more lenient* sentences for a rapist after exposure to violent pornography. According to Zillmann and Bryant, this may have occurred because watching violent pornography reduced the participants' concerns about sexual aggression by other people.

The finding that intense heat often leads to aggressive behaviour (see above) fits the excitation-transfer theory. Why is that? Although many people believe that heat lowers arousal, it actually increases it. Thus, the arousal experienced on hot days is likely to be misattributed to the situation in which people find themselves. In other words, there is excitation transfer.

## Zillmann et al.: Excitation-transfer theory

In a study by Zillmann, Johnson, and Day (1974), male participants were provoked by a confederate of the experimenter. Half the participants rested for 6 minutes and then pedalled on a cycling machine for 90 seconds, whereas the other half pedalled first and then rested. Immediately afterwards, all the participants chose the level of shock to be given to the person who had provoked them. Both groups were moderately aroused at that time, because the effects of pedalling on arousal last for several minutes.

What do you think happened? Zillmann et al. (1974) predicted that participants who had just finished cycling would attribute their level of arousal to the cycling, and so would not behave aggressively towards their provoker. In contrast, those who had just rested for 6 minutes would attribute their arousal to the provocation, and so would behave aggressively by delivering a strong electric shock. The results were in line with these predictions.

### KEY STUDY EVALUATION—Zillmann et al.

Like many social psychology experiments, Zillmann et al.'s study raises some ethical issues. If participants do not know the true nature of the study can they give informed consent to take part? Would it be possible to run the experiment if the participants knew of its true intention beforehand? Would those who behaved more aggressively and were prepared to give strong "shocks" have problems later dealing with this probably unwelcome self-knowledge?

### Discussion points

1. Do you think that excitation transfer happens often in everyday life?
2. Consider ways in which people's attributions of the cause of their arousal could be manipulated.

## Evaluation

● Unexplained arousal can lead to increased anger and aggression as predicted by excitation-transfer theory.
● The theory is rather limited. In real life, we generally know *why* we are aroused, and the theory does not apply to such situations.
● The theory exaggerates the role played by arousal in producing aggression.
● The theory does not provide a detailed account of the ways in which situations and arousal are interpreted.

# Biological factors

Human aggression clearly depends in part on biological factors. Some of the most convincing evidence was reported by Rhee and Waldman (2002). They carried out a meta-analysis of 51 twin and adoption studies investigating anti-social behaviour (e.g., anti-social personality disorder, aggressive behaviour, delinquency). They found that 41% of the variability in anti-social behaviour was due to genetic influences, 43% was due to non-shared environmental influences (influences differing among the children within a family), and 16% was due to shared environmental influences. The figures were very similar for males and females, and indicate that anti-social behaviour is fairly strongly influenced by genetic factors in both sexes.

Interesting evidence that sex hormones may influence aggressive behaviour was reported by van Goozen, Frijda, and van de Poll (1995). They studied transsexuals (male to female or female to male) who had received 3 months of treatment with sex hormones appropriate to their new sex. The female-to-male transsexuals had a particularly strong aggressive response to a videotape of an individual in an aversive and frustrating situation, having been told to imagine themselves in the same situation. In contrast, the male-to-female transsexuals had a very weak aggressive response.

More convincing evidence of the importance of sex hormones was provided by van Goozen et al. (1995). They studied transsexuals before and after 3 months of sex hormone treatment. Female-to-male transsexuals showed increased proneness to aggression after receiving male sex hormones. In contrast, male-to-female transsexuals deprived of male sex hormones had decreased proneness to anger and aggression.

> ### Cortisol and aggression
> McBurnett (2000) researched cortisol levels in saliva and violent behaviour in boys. He found a link between low levels of cortisol (a stress hormone) at age 7–12 years and a threefold increase in mean or combative acts to classmates. These anti-social behaviours also appeared earlier and were more persistent than in peers with higher or fluctuating cortisol levels. This indicates that problem aggression may have a biological source.

# Cross-cultural effects

Aggression and violence are frequent occurrences. There have been about 15,000 wars in the last 5600 years, which is almost 2.7 per year. However, there is evidence of cross-cultural differences in the level of aggression. For example, the United Nations in 1991 revealed information about murder rates in different countries. The countries with the worst records were Mexico, with a murder rate of about 20 per 100,000, and Brazil (15 per 100,000). At the other extreme, the murder rate was only about 1 per 100,000 people in the UK, Egypt, and Japan. Most European countries had low murder rates of about 2 per 100,000, which was about the same as China and Peru. However, the murder rate was 8 per 100,000 in the United States.

Murder rates around the world (UN, 1991)

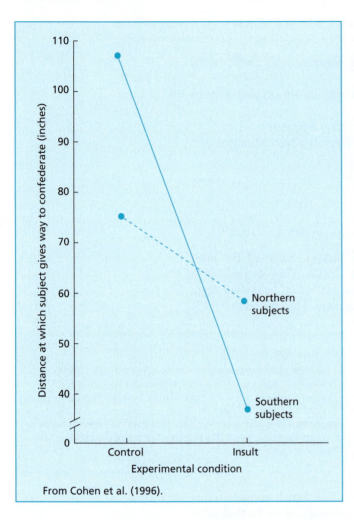

From Cohen et al. (1996).

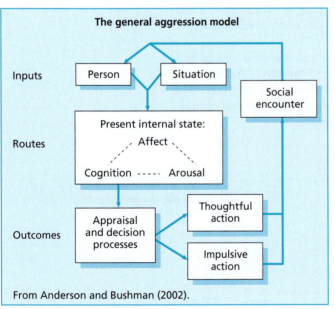

The general aggression model

From Anderson and Bushman (2002).

There are interesting cultural differences within some countries. Within the United States, there seem to be important differences between white males from the South and those from the North. More specifically, Cogan, Bhalla, Sefa-Dedeh, and Rothblum (1996) argued that the South has a "culture of honour", in which insults are regarded as an affront to a man's reputation. They arranged for male University of Michigan students who grew up in the North or the South to be insulted by a confederate working with the experimenter. This confederate bumped into the participant and called him an "asshole". As predicted, students from the South were much more affected by the insult and became more aggressive. For example, participants who had been insulted or not insulted were faced with a confederate who walked down a narrow hallway straight at them. Insulted students from the South allowed the confederate to get much closer to them than any other students before "chickening out" and giving way (see the figure on the left).

## General aggression model

Which theoretical approach to aggression is the most adequate? As we have seen, there is evidence that all of the key factors identified by the main theorists play some role in aggression. That led Anderson, Anderson, and Deuser (1996) and Anderson and Bushman (2002) to put forward a model including most of these factors. Their general aggression model is shown in the diagram below. As you can see, it basically consists of four stages:

*Stage 1.* At this stage, the key variables are situational cues (e.g., weapons present) and individual differences (e.g., aggressive personality). For example, Krueger et al. (2001) found that negative affectivity (a personality dimension involving anxiety and depression) correlated +.28 with anti-social or aggressive behaviour

*Stage 2.* What happens at stage 1 can cause a variety of effects at stage 2, including affect (e.g., hostile feelings), arousal (e.g., activation of the autonomic nervous system), and cognition (e.g., hostile thoughts). All of these effects are interconnected.

*Stage 3.* What happens at stage 2 leads to appraisal processes (e.g., interpretation of the situation, possible coping strategies, consequences of behaving aggressively).

*Stage 4.* Depending on the outcome of the appraisal processes at stage 3, the individual decides whether to behave aggressively or non-aggressively.

### Evidence

The general aggression model combines elements of several previous theories. As a result, many of the findings we have discussed so far (e.g., weapons effect) are consistent with the model's predictions. In addition, Dill, Anderson, and Deuser (1997) carried out a study to test some aspects of the model, especially those concerned with interpretation of the situation. They presented participants with a videotape of pairs of people arguing with each other. Those participants having an aggressive personality perceived more aggression and hostility in this interaction than did those with a non-aggressive personality. Individual differences in aggressive behaviour may well depend in part on differences in perception and interpretation of any given situation.

Anderson and Bushman (2001) carried out a meta-analysis of studies on violent video games, examining the effects on aggressive behaviour, aggressive cognitions or thoughts, aggressive affect or emotion, and physiological arousal. The situational cues provided by violent video games were associated with aggressive behaviour. The overall effect was of moderate size, and the magnitude of the effect was similar in males and females, and in children and adults.

According to the general aggression model, aggressive cognitions or thoughts play a central role in the development of the aggressive personality. As predicted, Anderson and Bushman (2001) found that exposure to violent video games reliably increased aggressive cognitions. They also found that exposure to violence produced aggressive affect or emotion and increased physiological arousal, both of which are predicted by the model. Anderson and Bushman (p. 358) concluded as follows: "Every theoretical prediction derived from prior research and from GAM [general aggression model] was supported by the meta-analysis of currently available research on violent video games."

## Evaluation

⊕ This model is more realistic than previous theories because it includes more relevant factors and processes.
⊕ Appraisal processes are probably of crucial importance in determining whether someone will behave aggressively.
⊕ There is evidence for an aggressive or anti-social personality (see Chapters 16 and 22; Krueger et al., 2001).
⊖ Negative affect, arousal, and negative cognitions all have complex effects on behaviour, and it is often hard to predict whether someone will behave aggressively.
⊖ Appraisal processes are generally assessed by self-report measures, but individuals may not have conscious awareness of all aspects of their appraisal of the situation and of their own coping strategies.
⊖ The general aggression model provides more of a general framework than a detailed theoretical account of the factors producing aggressive behaviour, and it de-emphasises biological factors.

# Alcohol and aggression

Much of the research we have considered so far has been concerned with relatively low levels of aggression produced under laboratory conditions. It is important to consider also aggression in the real world, which often happens in the context of alcohol or of close relationships and the family (see next section). It is well known that there is an association between alcohol consumption and physical aggression. This happens in part because alcohol can produce aggression, but also in part because many violent people drink a lot.

Several theories have been put forward to explain why alcohol can lead to aggressive behaviour. According to the anxiolysis-disinhibition model (e.g., Sayette, 1993), alcohol leads to aggression because it reduces anxiety. When people are sober, they are inhibited from behaving aggressively by anxieties about retaliation and the social disapproval of others.

Steele and Josephs (1990) proposed the inhibition conflict model. According to this model, sober individuals experience inhibition conflict. The essence of **inhibition conflict**

*Why should alcohol make people more aggressive?*

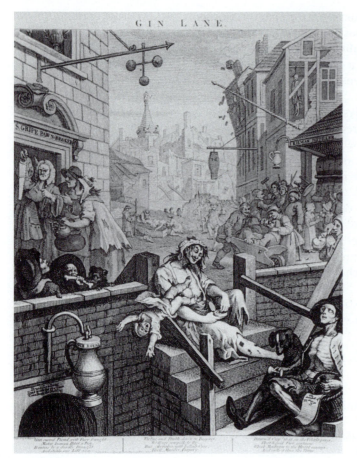

GIN LANE

An engraving from the 1750s entitled "Gin Lane" by William Hogarth (1697–1764) illustrates various problems caused by addiction to gin. Amongst other things we can see a woman dropping her baby, people fighting, and people pawning their goods.

is that there are cues (e.g., provocation) leading to aggressive behaviour, but this behaviour is inhibited by other cues (e.g., the presence of witnesses, social norms). Individuals who have consumed alcohol attend to a narrower range of cues, and are less likely to experience inhibition conflict. More specifically, they typically attend to the provoking situation or person, and ignore the inhibiting cues. As a result, they behave aggressively.

## Evidence

Ito, Miller, and Pollock (1996) carried out a meta-analysis of 49 studies on alcohol and aggression, and reported a moderate effect of alcohol on aggressive behaviour. Their findings provided some support for both models. We will start with the anxiolysis-disinhibition model, according to which alcohol reduces anxiety (shown by Gray, 1982), making people more aggressive. It follows from the model that alcohol should have more effect when there are strong anxiety-provoking cues in the situation than when there are not. As predicted, the tendency for intoxicated individuals to be more aggressive than sober ones was greatest in the presence of intense anxiety-provoking cues.

According to the inhibition conflict model, intoxicated people are more aggressive than sober individuals because they are less responsive to inhibition conflict. As predicted, alcohol led to increased aggression, especially in situations involving a high level of inhibition conflict. It is assumed within the theory that there will be little aggression when individuals have consumed low levels of alcohol and inhibition conflict is low. However, Ito et al. (1996) found increased aggression in those circumstances.

Zeichner, Pihl, Niaura, and Zacchia (1982) obtained evidence that was more consistent with the anxiolysis-disinhibition model than with the inhibition conflict model. Participants who had or had not consumed alcohol were told they could shock another person, but that person could retaliate by administering irritating noise to the participants. In the key condition, the participants had to write down after each trial the level of shock they had delivered and the level of noise they received back. The situation was arranged so that the level of noise increased in line with any increase in shock level.

What would be predicted by the two models? According to the inhibition conflict model, forcing intoxicated participants to attend to the negative consequences of their aggressive behaviour should make them focus on these inhibiting cues, and so reduce their level of aggression. According to the anxiolysis-disinhibition model, these inhibiting cues should not create anxiety in intoxicated participants, and so alcohol should produce the usual increase in aggressive behaviour. The findings supported this prediction rather than that of the inhibition conflict model.

## Evaluation

- ➕ Alcohol (especially in moderately large doses) reliably leads to increased aggression.
- ➕ The anxiolysis-disinhibition model provides a reasonable account of the effects of alcohol on aggression, and has received more experimental support than the inhibition conflict model.
- ➖ Alcohol probably produces more aggressive behaviour in laboratory studies than in the real world. As Ito et al. (1996, p. 77) pointed out, "Laboratory studies ... are specifically designed to facilitate aggression by creating situations in which participants feel

comfortable displaying it should they desire to do so. By contrast, most real-world settings contain many fewer aggression-instigating cues and many more inhibiting ones."

● The tendency to behave aggressively depends in part on personality (e.g., Krueger et al., 2001). However, individual differences are not considered systematically by the anxiolysis-disinhibition or inhibition conflict models.

## Aggression in relationships

Aggression in the real world often happens within close relationships and families. For example, Straus, Gelles, and Steinmetz (1980) found in a survey of over 2000 families in the United States that physical assault designed to injure the other person had occurred within 28% of married couples. In addition, over 70% of parents admitted that they had slapped and/or spanked their children, and 20% said they had hit their children with an object. As Gelles (1997, p. 1) concluded, "People are more likely to be killed, physically assaulted, hit, beat up, or spanked in their own homes by other family members than anywhere else, or by anyone else."

*What is it about family life that has led Gelles to conclude that you "are more likely to be killed … by other family members than … by anyone else"?*

Archer (2000) pointed out that there are two opposed views concerning aggression and violence between partners in a close relationship. According to family conflict researchers (e.g., Straus, 1990), aggression within relationships involves mutual combat. As a result, responsibility for aggressive behaviour is divided approximately equally between males and females. In contrast, many feminist theorists argue that violence within relationships typically involves male aggressors and female victims.

Why is there so much aggression within close relationships? Gelles (1997) argued that aggressive behaviour occurs when the rewards of aggression are perceived to be greater than the likely costs. The perceived costs of behaving aggressively or violently can be relatively low in some close relationships for the following reasons:

1. There is a relative lack of external social controls, because outsiders are reluctant to intervene or become involved.
2. There are power inequalities between men and women, with men having more power and greater physical strength.
3. Some men perceive aggressive behaviour positively as forming part of their image of being a man.

### Evidence

Archer (2000) carried out a meta-analysis of 82 studies concerned with physical aggression in heterosexual relationships. He concluded as follows:

> *When measures were based on specific acts, women were significantly more likely than men to have used physical aggression toward their partners and to have used it more frequently, although the effect size was very small … When measures were based on the physical consequences of aggression (visible injuries or injuries requiring medical treatment), men were more likely than women to have injured their partners, but again, effect sizes were relatively small (p. 664).*

Thus, women are slightly more likely than men to behave aggressively in a relationship, but men are more likely to inflict physical injury. Thus, there is some support for both family conflict and feminist theorists. However, the great majority of the studies in the meta-analysis were carried out in the United States, and the above findings may not generalise to other cultures.

It might be thought that most female aggression in relationships occurs as self-defence against physical aggression from the male partner. However, this is not supported by the evidence. Straus (1993) reported findings from a study of marriages in which there was physical aggression. The women admitted that they had initiated the aggression in 53% of the cases.

As we have seen, there are comparable levels of male aggression against female partners and of female aggression against male partners in Western cultures. However,

In what ways might cultural background be linked to domestic violence?

cross-cultural evidence suggests that men are much more likely to be physically aggressive to their female partners than vice versa in many non-Western cultures (see Archer, 2000, for a review). Why are there these cross-cultural differences? First, in most Western cultures, both sexes share the norm that physical aggression is worse when the aggressor is a man rather than a woman (e.g., Arias & Johnson, 1989). Second, the belief that men have the right to control the behaviour of their wives is much less prevalent in Western cultures than in some other, male-dominated cultures. Additional reasons were identified by Archer (p. 668):

> Aggression by men toward women ... is more common when female alliances are weak and where women lack the support of kin ... It is accentuated by stronger male alliances, where women are dependent on men for resources ..., and where there are pronounced inequalities between men, so that a few powerful men can control women's sexuality.

## FORMATION OF INTERPERSONAL RELATIONSHIPS

Numerous factors are involved in the formation of interpersonal relationships. There are several types of interpersonal relationships, ranging from romantic relationships to casual friendships in the workplace. However, our focus is mostly on four key factors determining our choice of friends and romantic partners: proximity, physical attractiveness, impression formation, and personality and attitude similarity. After that, we consider issues relating to mate selection and the maintenance of relationships.

### Proximity

Proximity or nearness influences our choice of friends and those with whom we develop a relationship. Festinger, Schachter, and Back (1950) studied married graduate students assigned randomly to flats in 17 different two-storey buildings. About two-thirds of their closest friends lived in the same building. Close friends living in the same building were twice as likely to be living on the same floor as the other floor.

The importance of proximity extends to romantic relationships leading to marriage. Bossard (1932) looked at 5000 marriage licences in Philadelphia, finding a clear tendency for those getting married to live close to each other. That may be less true nowadays, because people are generally more mobile than was the case in the 1930s.

Friendships arise and are maintained between people who live close to each other, and who enjoy similar leisure pursuits.

### Physical attractiveness

When meeting a stranger, we notice their physical appearance. This includes how they are dressed, whether they are clean or dirty, and often includes an assessment of their physical attractiveness. People tend to agree with each other about whether someone is physically attractive. Women whose faces resemble those of young children are often perceived as attractive. Thus, photographs of females with relatively large and widely separated eyes, a small nose, and a small chin are regarded as attractive. However, wide cheekbones and narrow cheeks are also seen as attractive (Cunningham, 1986), and these features are uncommon in young children.

Cunningham (1986) also studied physical attractiveness in males. Men having features such as a square jaw, small eyes, and thin lips were regarded as attractive by women. These features can be regarded as indicating maturity, as they are rarely found in children.

Average faces are regarded as attractive. Langlois, Roggman, and Musselman (1994) found that male and female computer-generated composites or "averaged" faces were perceived as more attractive than the individual faces forming the composite. Why is this? Langlois et al. found that averaged faces were regarded as more familiar than the individual faces, and argued that this sense of familiarity made the averaged faces seem attractive. Averaged faces are also more symmetrical than individual faces, and symmetry is associated with attractiveness (Grammer & Thornhill, 1994).

What features make you think that someone is really attractive?

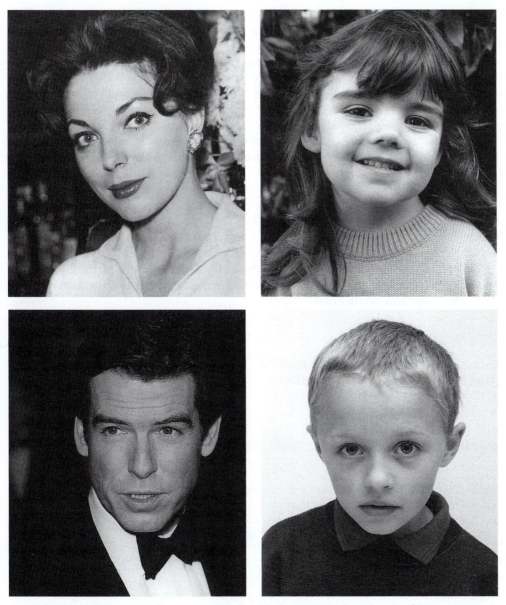

Joan Collins (top left) fits Cunningham's "attractive female" characteristics—note how her features are similar to the little girl's (top right). Pierce Brosnan (bottom left), however, looks very different from the little boy (bottom right).

Brigham (1971) found that males and females argued that physically attractive individuals are poised, sociable, interesting, independent, exciting, and sexually warm. Perhaps surprisingly, most of these assumptions are true. Langlois, Kalakanis, Rubenstein, Larson, Hallam, and Smoot (2000) carried out a meta-analysis, and found several significant differences between physically attractive and unattractive adults. Below in brackets are the percentages having each characteristic (attractive people first). Attractive individuals had more self-confidence (56% vs. 44%), better social skills (55% vs. 45%), better physical health (59% vs. 41%), more extraversion (56% vs. 44%), and more sexual experience (58% vs. 42%). Thus, beauty is more than skin deep!

Langlois et al. (2000) carried out further meta-analyses to assess the level of agreement in evaluating facial attractiveness both within and between cultures. They found that there was substantial agreement on the issue of who is attractive and unattractive within cultures. Perhaps surprisingly, there was a similarly high level of agreement in cross-cultural studies. However, the current standards of the dominant social group have some influence on ratings of attractiveness. In the North American culture, light skin is

*To what extent do you think that all cultures agree about what constitutes beauty and attractiveness?*

Grammer and Thornhill (1994) found that people find symmetrical faces attractive.

regarded as more attractive than dark skin by a majority of the population. Even African American college students express a preference for lighter skin tones (Bond & Cash, 1992).

Ratings of physical attractiveness are determined by other factors as well. One such factor was identified by the Country and Western singer Mickey Gilley, one of whose songs contains the following words: "Ain't it funny, ain't it strange/The way a man's opinions change/When he starts to face that lonely night", followed by "All the girls get prettier at closing time/They all get to look like movie stars." Psychologists found that Mickey Gilley was right: People in a bar on a Thursday evening rated members of the opposite sex as more physically attractive at midnight than at 10:30 pm (see Eysenck & Eysenck, 1981).

Stephan, Berscheid, and Walster (1971) identified another factor. Their male college students read either a sexually arousing article about a seduction scene or an unarousing article about the sex life of herring gulls. Then they rated the attractiveness of a pretty blonde girl. As you have probably guessed, the girl was rated as more attractive by the sexually aroused students than by the unaroused ones.

Anderson, Crawford, Nadeau, and Lindberg (1992) reported an interesting study on female body size preferences in 54 cultures categorised on the basis of the reliability of the food supply—see Key Study below.

## Matching hypothesis

Walster, Aronson, Abrahams, and Rottman (1966)—see Key Study on the next page— found that we are attracted to people who are at the same level of physical attractiveness

---

## Anderson et al.: Culture and physical attractiveness

Anderson et al. (1992) carried out a study on female body size preferences in 54 cultures. They divided these cultures into those with a very reliable food supply, those with a moderately reliable food supply, those with a moderately unreliable food supply, and those with a very unreliable food supply. Preferences for different female body sizes were divided into heavy body, moderate body, and slender body. The findings were as follows:

| | Food supply | | | |
| --- | --- | --- | --- | --- |
| Preference | Very unreliable | Moderately unreliable | Moderately reliable | Very reliable |
| Heavy body | 71% | 50% | 39% | 40% |
| Moderate body | 29% | 33% | 39% | 20% |
| Slender body | 0% | 17% | 22% | 40% |

### KEY STUDY EVALUATION—Anderson et al.

The research by Anderson et al. is important because it shows that there are considerable cultural differences in preferred female body size. However, we need to remember that this study is correlational in nature, and that we cannot establish causes from correlations. Thus, we cannot be sure that cultural differences in preferred female body size actually depend on the reliability of the food supply rather than on other ways in which cultures differ from each other.

In view of the obsessive focus on slimness in women in Western culture, it is surprising that heavy women are preferred to slender women in the great majority of the cultures studied by Anderson et al. (1992), especially those in which the food supply is moderately or very unreliable. Presumably these cultural differences occur because heavy women in cultures with unreliable food supplies are better equipped than slender women to survive food shortages, and to provide nourishment for their children. This factor is irrelevant in cultures having a very reliable food supply. In these cultures, heavy and slender women were regarded as equally attractive.

### Discussion points

1. Why are there such great cultural differences in preferred body shape for women?
2. Are eating disorders likely to become more common as a country becomes more affluent?

## Walster et al.: The matching hypothesis

Walster et al. (1966) organised a dance at which students were randomly allocated partners of the opposite sex. Half way through the dance, the students filled in a questionnaire giving their views about their partner. These views were compared with judges' ratings of the physical attractiveness of the students. The more physically attractive students were liked most by their partners. However, Walster et al. found 6 months later that partners were more likely to have dated if they were similar in physical attractiveness.

Walster et al. (1966) argued that we are initially attracted to those who are beautiful or handsome. However, we realise we are unlikely to be found attractive by someone much more physically attractive. Thus (perhaps with some reluctance!) we become attracted to those about as physically attractive as we are. This is known as the matching hypothesis, and it was tested by Walster and Walster (1969). They organised another dance. This time, however, the students had met each other beforehand. This may have led them to think more about the qualities they were looking for in a partner. As predicted by the matching hypothesis, students expressed the most liking for those at the same level of physical attractiveness.

### KEY STUDY EVALUATION—Walster et al.

Walster et al.'s matching hypothesis suggests that people are attracted to those of about the same level of physical attractiveness as themselves. This may indeed be the case in many situations, but it does not take account of many social factors that can also influence who we find attractive. Relationships often occur between people who have different levels of attractiveness but have got to know each other through working together or living nearby. Here mechanisms other than pure physical attractiveness are operating. In other situations, people who are generally considered very attractive may find that others think they are unapproachable. Some people may believe that a less attractive partner will be less likely to stray than a very attractive partner, and so have more confidence in the relationship.

### Discussion points

1. Does the matching hypothesis seem correct in your experience?
2. Why does physical attractiveness play such an important part in dating behaviour and in relationships?

as ourselves and termed this the **matching hypothesis**. Walster and Walster (1969) tested this hypothesis—see Key Study above.

Feingold (1988) carried out a meta-analysis of studies in which the physical attractiveness of relationship partners was assessed. The mean correlation was +.49 between physical attractiveness levels of the partners in romantic couples. This indicates that couples are generally fairly similar in physical attractiveness, and supports the matching hypothesis.

Detailed evidence that physical attractiveness influences behaviour was found by Garcia et al. (1991) in a study on male–female interaction during an initial encounter. The man's physical attractiveness was associated with the positive thoughts and feelings of both partners, as well as with the amount of smiling they did. The woman's physical attractiveness was strongly correlated with the partners' liking for each other, with their ratings of the quality of the interaction, and with the amount of talking during the interaction. Overall, the woman's level of attractiveness influenced the interaction more than did the man's.

The matching hypothesis predicts a match based on physical attractiveness. In fact, physical attractiveness can be matched with intelligence, as in the case of Marilyn Monroe and Arthur Miller.

## Impression formation

One factor determining whether we are attracted to someone else is the initial impression they make on us. Asch (1946) argued that we make use of an **implicit personality theory**, assuming that a person who has one particular personality trait will have various other, related traits. For example, suppose you know that a particular student is a generally anxious person. You might expect him/her to be fairly disorganised in his/her studying and to lack confidence in his/her abilities.

Asch (1946) also argued that key aspects of personality (central traits) influence the impression we form of others more than do other aspects of personality (peripheral traits). Finally, Asch claimed that our very first impressions are of crucial importance in

### KEY TERMS

**Matching hypothesis:** the notion that we are attracted to those who are about as physically attractive as we are.

**Implicit personality theory:** the assumption that we infer that someone who has a given personality trait will also possess other, related traits.

*How easy is it to over-ride our first impressions of someone?*

determining our overall view of someone else. In other words, information about another person that is presented first will have more influence on our impression of that person than will information presented subsequently. The term **primacy effect** is used to refer to this effect.

In one of his studies, Asch (1946) gave his participants a list of seven adjectives, which were said to describe an imaginary person called X. All the participants were given the following six adjectives: intelligent, skilful, industrious, determined, practical, and cautious. The seventh adjective was warm, cold, polite, or blunt. Then the participants had to select other adjectives that best described X.

The findings were clear-cut. The adjectives "warm" and "cold" were central traits, having marked effects on how all the other information about X was interpreted. For example, when X was warm, 91% of the participants thought he was generous, and 94% thought he was good-natured. In contrast, when X was cold, only 8% of the participants thought he was generous, and 17% thought he was good-natured. Thus, people believe that those who are warm have several other desirable characteristics, whereas those who are cold possess mostly undesirable characteristics.

One of the limitations with Asch's (1946) study was that it was very artificial. Kelley (1950) carried out a less artificial study in which students rated a guest lecturer who was described beforehand as being rather cold or very warm. The lecturer was rated much more positively on a wide range of dimensions (e.g., sociability, popularity, humour) when he was described as warm. The warm–cold manipulation also influenced the students' behaviour: They interacted more with him and asked more questions when he had been described as warm.

Asch (1946) studied the primacy effect by giving participants a mixture of positive and negative information about another person. There was a primacy effect: Those hearing the positive traits first formed a much more favourable impression than those hearing the negative traits first.

What is responsible for the primacy effect in impression formation? When someone feels they have formed an accurate impression of someone else on the basis of the initial information, they pay less attention to subsequent information. Belmore (1987) found that participants reading statements about another person spent less and less time on each successive statement. In addition, there are individual differences in the extent of the primacy effect. Kruglanski and Webster (1996) considered individuals high and low in **need for closure** (the desire to reduce ambiguity and uncertainty). Those high in need for closure had a larger primacy effect than the more open-minded individuals low in need for closure.

There are other central traits in addition to the warm–cold dimension. For example, Rosenberg, Nelson, and Vivekananthan (1968) claimed that two dimensions are of crucial importance in impression formation:

1. *Social evaluation.* The good end of this dimension has adjectives such as sociable, popular, and warm, and the bad end includes unsociable, cold, and irritable.
2. *Intellectual evaluation.* This dimension ranges from skilful and persistent (good end) to stupid and foolish (bad end).

There is inconsistent support for this proposal. For example, Vonk (1993) discovered that three dimensions seemed to be of central importance: evaluation (good–bad), potency (strong–weak), and social orientation (sociable–independent). Asch's warm–cold dimension formed an important part of the evaluation dimension, and there was no evidence supporting the notion of a separate intellectual dimension.

Personality theorists have often argued that the key dimensions in evaluating someone else's personality are rather different to those identified by social psychologists (see Chapter 13). For example, McCrae and Costa (1985) found evidence for five separate dimensions in personality ratings: openness, conscientiousness, extraversion, agreeableness, and neuroticism. The extraversion dimension has a substantial overlap with Vonk's (1996) social orientation, but otherwise the two sets of dimensions seem only modestly related to each other.

**KEY TERMS**

**Primacy effect:** the notion that our impressions of other people are heavily influenced by the first information about them that we encounter.

**Need for closure:** a dimension of individual differences, with high scorers being motivated to reduce ambiguity and uncertainty.

## Evaluation

⊕ As predicted by implicit personality theory, some traits are more important than others in impression formation.

⊕ There is a primacy effect in impression formation.

⊖ There are other important dimensions in addition to the warm–cold dimension emphasised by Asch. However, there is controversy as to the precise nature of these additional dimensions.

⊖ Asking people to form impressions of imaginary others from lists of adjectives is very artificial. It may involve different processes from those used in everyday life.

## Similarity

Do you think that friends or those romantically involved tend to be similar or dissimilar in personality? One view is that people who have similar personalities are most likely to become involved with each other ("Birds of a feather flock together"). Another view is that dissimilar people are most likely to become friends or to have a relationship ("Opposites attract"). Winch (1958) argued for the latter view. He claimed that married couples will be happy if they have complementary needs. For example, if a domineering person marries someone who is submissive, both of them can fulfil their needs.

*What are the advantages of having friends and partners who are similar to us?*

Winch (1958) found that married couples differing in personality were happier than those who were similar. However, most of the evidence indicates that people tend to be intimately involved with individuals like themselves. Burgess and Wallin (1953) obtained detailed information from 1000 engaged couples, including information about 42 personality characteristics. There was no evidence for the notion that opposites attract. There was significant within-couple similarity for 14 personality characteristics (e.g., feelings easily hurt, leader of social events), but the degree of similarity was not great.

Similarity of attitudes is also an important factor in attraction. For example, Byrne (1971) found that strangers holding similar attitudes to the participants were rated as more attractive than strangers holding dissimilar attitudes. The meaning of these findings was clarified by Rosenbaum (1986), who included a control condition in which no information about the stranger's attitudes was provided. The stranger with dissimilar attitudes was liked less than the control stranger, but the stranger with similar attitudes was liked no more than the control stranger. Thus, we dislike those whose attitudes differ from our own, but do not necessarily like those with similar attitudes.

Several researchers have replicated Rosenbaum's (1986) finding that dissimilarity of attitudes reduces liking. However, attitude similarity generally increases liking (e.g., Singh & Ho, 2000), even though the effects are smaller than those of dissimilarity on liking. Why does dissimilarity have more impact than similarity on liking? It is likely that we feel threatened and fear disagreements when we discover that another person has attitudes differing substantially from our own.

Brewer (1968) carried out a cross-cultural study on 30 tribal groups in East Africa. The extent to which any given tribe liked the members of another tribe was determined mostly by perceived similarity in attitudes. The second most important factor was the distance apart of the two tribes.

Sprecher (1998) studied the importance of similarity in opposite-sex friendships, same-sex friendships, and romantic relationships. Similarity of interest and leisure

Having similar leisure activities is an important aspect of same-sex friendships.

activities was very important in same-sex friendships, as was similarity of attitudes and values. However, these two types of similarity were less important in opposite-sex friendships and romantic relationships. Sprecher also found that similarity in background was relatively unimportant in all three types of relationship.

Why are we more attracted to those having similar attitudes? Part of the answer was provided by Condon and Crano (1988). They found that their participants were attracted to someone with similar attitudes because they inferred that that person would evaluate them positively. Thus, we like those who are similar to us, and this leads us to assume that those who are similar to us will like us.

In sum, various kinds of similarity (e.g., in attitudes, in personality) are important when it comes to establishing friendships and romantic relationships, and this seems to be true across cultures. Similarity is probably important because we expect to be liked by those who are similar to us. The negative effect of dissimilarity on liking is generally greater than the positive effect of similarity on liking, perhaps because we feel that dissimilar others will dislike us and be threatening.

## Mate selection

Probably the most important finding in the area of mate selection is that like mates with like. We tend to mate with those reasonably similar to us in physical attractiveness, attitudes, and personality. Buss (1985) considered historical evidence, concluding that this tendency for like to mate with like had remained essentially unchanged over the previous 50 years.

Buss (1989) studied 37 cultures around the world. Men in all these cultures preferred women younger than themselves, and women preferred men older than themselves in all cultures except Spain. Buss also found that the personal qualities of kindness and intelligence were regarded as important by both sexes in virtually every culture.

There are various reasons why men might prefer younger women, and women prefer older men. One explanation is provided by evolutionary psychology (a development of sociobiology), in which attempts are made to explain human social behaviour in evolutionary terms. According to evolutionary psychologists (e.g., Buss, 1989), what men and women find attractive in the opposite sex are those features maximising the probability of producing offspring and thus allowing their genes to carry over into the next generation. Younger women are preferred to older ones, because older women are less likely to be able to have children. In similar fashion, women prefer older men, because they are more likely to provide adequately for the needs of their offspring.

In Buss's (1989) study men preferred women younger than themselves and women preferred men older than they were. However, a relationship that is in the public eye seems to attract even more attention when the age gap is significant.

The approach offered by evolutionary psychology is inadequate (see also discussion in Chapter 3). Evolutionary psychologists do not explain *why* men and women in nearly all cultures regard kindness and intelligence as being more important than age. More generally, culture accounted for 14% of the variation in mate preferences in Buss's (1989) data, whereas gender accounted for only 2.4% of the variation (see Smith & Bond, 1998). Second, the factors determining the choice of marriage partner differ considerably across cultures. Evolutionary psychologists consistently under-estimate cultural factors when explaining social behaviour.

In spite of the limitations of the evolutionary psychology approach, it has been extended in interesting ways. Gangestad and Buss (1993) argued that physically attractive individuals are perceived as being more resistant to disease. This led them to predict that physical attractiveness would be valued more highly in cultures with a relatively great number of pathogens [agents causing disease]. They confirmed this prediction across 29 of the cultures studied by Buss (1989), and found it was true for men and for women. Gangestad (1993) argued that women may attach less importance than men to physical attractiveness because their relative lack of financial resources makes them dependent on the financial and other resources that men can provide. Thus, women from cultures providing them with good access to financial resources should attach more importance to male physical attractiveness than women denied reasonable financial resources. Gangestad obtained support for this hypothesis from Buss's cross-cultural data.

Feingold (1990) carried out various meta-analyses, finding that physical attractiveness is rated as more important to romantic attraction by men than it is by women. However, this gender difference was greater when based on self-report rather than behavioural data, suggesting that females may not be fully aware of the importance they attach to male physical attractiveness. For example, Sprecher (1989) found that women attributed the attraction they experienced to a man to his earning potential and expressiveness rather than his physical attractiveness, whereas men claimed to be most influenced by a woman's physical attractiveness. In fact, however, men and women were equally influenced by physical attractiveness when choosing a partner. In a thorough meta-analysis, Langlois et al. (2000) found that physical attractiveness was equally important for men and women.

Buss (1989) found in his cross-cultural study that men in nearly all cultures claim to be more influenced by physical attractiveness than do women. However, the effect was relatively small, with gender accounting for under 10% of the variance in the importance attached to physical attractiveness.

Feingold (1992b) carried out meta-analyses of studies (mostly American) that had focused on self-reports of the attributes that men and women desired in a potential mate. The largest gender differences were found with respect to status and ambition, with women rating these attributes as more important than did men. This provides modest support for the evolutionary psychology approach.

*To what extent are men and women looking for different things in their partners?*

## Maintenance of interpersonal relationships

We turn now to a brief consideration of factors involved in maintaining various kinds of interpersonal relationships (e.g., friendships) after they have been formed. We will start by returning to Sprecher's (1998) study on the determinants of initial attraction. Two factors of central importance in romantic relationships, same-sex friendships, and opposite-sex friendships were the desirability of the other's personality and his/her warmth and kindness. Other key factors for romantic relationships were reciprocal liking and similarity of attitudes and values. For opposite-sex friendships, reciprocal liking and similarity of social skills were important. For same-sex friendships, similarity of interest and leisure activities and proximity were important.

Argyle and Furnham (1983) obtained an understanding of similarities and differences among various types of relationships by asking their participants to rate nine different relationships in terms of their degree of satisfaction with them on 15 satisfaction scales. Analysis of the data produced three independent factors: material and instrumental help, social and emotional support, and common interests. The relationships highest and lowest on each of these factors were as follows:

*What can be done to maintain a relationship?*

| Factor | Highest scoring relationships | Lowest scoring relationships |
|---|---|---|
| Material and instrumental help | spouse<br>parent<br>same-sex friend | neighbour<br>work associate |
| Social and emotional support | spouse<br>same-sex friend<br>parent | neighbour<br>work superior<br>work associate |
| Common interests | spouse<br>same-sex friend<br>opposite-sex friend | neighbour<br>work associate<br>adolescent offspring |

The above findings indicate that we obtain the greatest satisfaction from those relationships (spouse, same-sex friend, opposite-sex friend) most important to us. Unimportant relationships (e.g., with neighbours or work associates) are not generally associated with high levels of satisfaction.

Argyle and Furnham (1983) also found that the spouse was the greatest source of conflict as well as of satisfaction. It seems reasonable to assume that marital satisfaction will be highest when the rewards greatly exceed the costs. In line with this, Howard and

Dawes (1976) found that a simple formula based on the frequency of a major reward (sexual intercourse) minus the frequency of a major cost (angry rows) was a good predictor of marital satisfaction.

Eshel, Sharabany, and Friedman (1998) asked Israeli adolescents between the ages of 17 and 19 to rate the actual and desired intimacy with their opposite-sex romantic partner and their same-sex best friend. Both actual and desired intimacy were greater for the romantic partner than for same-sex best friend. In addition, desired intimacy was greater than actual intimacy for both types of relationship. Thus, late adolescents expect and attain more intimacy in romantic relationships than in close friendships.

## Rules

Most interpersonal relationships are governed by unspoken rules. The rules applied to interpersonal relationships vary depending on the nature of the relationship. However, Argyle, Henderson, and Furnham (1985) found some general rules when their participants rated the importance of several rules in each of 22 relationships. The six most generally important rules (in descending order of importance) were as follows:

1. Respect the other person's privacy.
2. Do not discuss with someone else things said in confidence.
3. Look the other person in the eye during conversation.
4. Do not criticise the other person publicly.
5. Do not indulge in sexual activity with the other person.
6. Seek to repay all debts, favours, or compliments.

How do we know these rules are actually important? Argyle et al. (1985) studied broken friendships. As predicted, "the lapse of friendship was attributed in many cases to the breaking of certain rules, especially rules of rewardingness and rules about relations with third parties, e.g., not being jealous, and keeping confidences" (Argyle, 1988, pp. 233–234).

That's it, I cant live with you anymore.

There are interesting cultural differences in the importance attached to certain rules. For example, people in Hong Kong and Japan were more likely than those in Britain or Italy to support rules such as obeying superiors, preserving group harmony, and avoiding loss of face (Argyle, Henderson, Bond, Iizuka, & Contarello, 1986).

What functions are served by rules within interpersonal relationships? According to Argyle and Henderson (1984), some rules (known as regulatory rules) reduce conflict within relationships, because they indicate what is acceptable. There are also reward rules, which ensure that the rewards provided by each person are appropriate.

## Sex differences

Friendships between men are generally less intimate than those between women. Why is this the case? Reis, Senchak, and Solomon (1985) considered various explanations. First, men may define intimacy differently to women. This explanation was rejected, because men and women did not differ in their intimacy ratings of video fragments of people interacting.

Second, there may be no genuine difference in friendship intimacy, but men are less inclined to label their own behaviour as intimate. However, Reis et al. (1985) asked participants to indicate the level of intimacy revealed in actual conversation narratives, carefully edited so that it was totally unclear whether they came from a man or a woman. Male and female participants both perceived the narrative to be more intimate when it came from a woman.

Third, men may lack the social skills needed for same-sex intimacy. Reis et al. (1985) asked men and women to have an intimate conversation with their best friend. Men performed this task as well as women, indicating they have the necessary skills for intimate friendship. After rejecting all of the above explanations, Reis et al. concluded that women's role in society (involving caring for children) motivates them to develop intimate and nurturing relationships.

*How, if at all, do you think that men and women differ in their approach to relationships?*

## DEVELOPMENT OF CLOSE RELATIONSHIPS

What do we mean by a "close relationship"? According to Berscheid and Reis (1998, p. 199), most experts:

> *would require the interaction pattern to reveal that the partners frequently influence each other's behaviour (i.e., cognitive, affective, and conative [motivational]), that each person's influence on the other is diverse (e.g., not limited to certain kinds of behaviour in few situations), that the influence is strong, and, moreover, that all these properties have characterised the partners' interaction pattern for a considerable duration of time.*

It is hard to assess the development of close relationships scientifically. For example, we cannot easily study the process of falling in love under laboratory conditions! In practice, questionnaires are typically used to assess the processes involved in relationships, the level of satisfaction with relationships, and so on. Such questionnaires are open to social desirability bias (giving socially desirable but inaccurate answers to questions). For example, most married couples in the United Kingdom claim to be happily or very happily married. However, 40% of marriages end in divorce, suggesting that many married couples are less happily married than they admit.

The study of close relationships involves an emphasis on the interaction patterns between two people. As Berscheid and Reis (1998, p. 198) pointed out, "A relationship between two people is viewed as residing in neither one of the partners but, rather, in their interaction with each other." The factors determining such interactions are more numerous than those determining individuals' behaviour. For example, interaction patterns within a relationship depend on the characteristics of each partner, the extent to which these sets of characteristics are compatible or incompatible, and the situation in which the partners find themselves.

### Love

Our feelings for those with whom we develop close or romantic relationships typically include love. Evidence that love is important in newlyweds was reported by Huston, Caughlin, Houts, Smith, and George (2001). Married couples divorcing within 2 years of marriage were less in love with each other 2 months after marriage than were couples who divorced later or remained married.

It is important to distinguish between love and liking. Rubin (1970) did this with the Rubin Love Scale and the Rubin Liking Scale. The items on the love scale measure three main factors: (1) desire to help the other person, (2) dependent needs of the other person, and (3) feelings of exclusiveness and absorption. In contrast, the items on the liking scale measure respect for the other person's abilities, and similarity of the other person in terms of his/her attitudes and other characteristics.

*What do you think people mean when they say that they love someone? Is loving a parent the same as loving a spouse, a friend, or a child? How does loving someone differ from liking them?*

Dermer and Pyszczynski (1978) assessed the effects on men of having being exposed to sexually arousing material. This manipulation increased scores on the Love Scale but not on the Liking Scale with respect to a woman to whom they were attracted. Thus, sexual arousal increases love rather than liking.

Sternberg and Grajek (1984) found that liking and loving scores for a lover on Rubin's scales correlated +.72, and these scores correlated +.66 for best friend, +.73 for one's mother, and +.81 for one's father. These high correlations mean that Rubin's scales discriminate poorly between liking and loving.

The kind of lover you are may be related to the kind of attachment you had as an infant.

Which adults are most likely to fall in love and be emotionally intimate with others? According to attachment or pair-bonding theory (e.g., Bowlby, 1979; Hazan & Shaver, 1987, 1994; see Chapter 17), the answer lies in childhood. Children who formed an intense and secure affectional bond with their caregivers (e.g., mother) typically become adults capable of emotional intimacy. Klohnen and Bera (1998) tested this theory in a longitudinal study. Women identified as avoidantly attached (e.g., distrustful, self-reliant) or securely attached (e.g., trusting, emotionally open) were studied between the ages of 21 and 52. There were substantial differences between the two groups over the years. For example, by the age of 43, 95% of the securely attached women had been married, and only 24% of them had divorced. In contrast, only 72% of the avoidantly attached women had been married, and 50% of them had divorced.

The differences between the avoidantly and securely attached women seemed to have their origins in childhood. Avoidantly attached women were more likely to have suffered the early loss of a parent and to have experienced open conflict and an unpleasant atmosphere during childhood.

## Sternberg's triangular theory

Sternberg (1986) developed a triangular theory of love. According to this theory, love consists of three components: intimacy, passion, and decision/commitment. Sternberg (p. 120) defined them as follows:

*The intimacy component refers to feelings of closeness, connectedness, and bondedness in loving relationships ... The passionate component refers to the drives that lead to romance, physical attraction, sexual consummation, and related phenomena in loving relationships. The decision–commitment component refers to, in the short term, the decision that one loves someone else, and in the long term, the commitment to maintain that love.*

The relative importance of these three components differs between short-term and long-term relationships. The passion component is usually the most important in short-term relationships, with the decision/commitment component being the least important. In long-term relationships, however, the intimacy component is the most important, and the passion component is the least important.

Sternberg (1986) argued that there are several kinds of love, consisting of different combinations of the three components:

- *Liking or friendship*. This involves intimacy, but not passion or commitment.
- *Romantic love*. This involves intimacy and passion, but not commitment.
- *Companionate love*. This involves intimacy and commitment, but not passion.
- *Empty love*. This involves commitment, but not passion or intimacy.
- *Fatuous love*. This involves commitment and passion, but not intimacy.
- *Infatuated love*. This involves passion but not intimacy or commitment.
- *Consummate love*. This is the strongest form of love, since it involves all three components (commitment, passion, and intimacy).

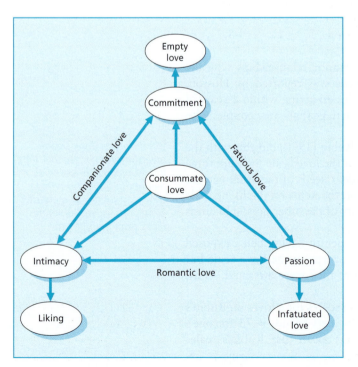

## Evidence

There is support for the notion that strong love does not have to involve sexual desire. Diamond (2003) presented evidence distinguishing between the sexual mating system (see Chapter 3) and the attachment or pair-bonding system discussed earlier. For example, Hatfield, Sprecher, Traupmann Pillemer, Greenberg, and Wexler (1988) asked young people between the ages of 4 and 18 to assess their feelings for an opposite-sexed boyfriend or girlfriend. The intensity of love feelings was similar at all ages, suggesting that sexual arousal and desire are not needed to produce intense feelings of love. Brain (1976) discussed passionate friendships in non-sexual relationships between heterosexual men in the Cameroon, Melanesia, Guatemala, and Samoa.

How adequate is Sternberg's triangular theory? Aron and Westbay (1996) reported good support for the theory in several studies. They asked participants to indicate the centrality of each of 68 words or phrases to the concept of love, and obtained three factors similar to those of Sternberg. The passion factor was most closely associated with euphoria, butterflies in the stomach, heart rate increases, gazing at the other, wonderful feelings, and sexual passion; intimacy was most closely associated with openness, feel free to talk about anything, supportive, honesty, and understanding; and the factor of commitment was associated with devotion, commitment, putting the other first, protectiveness, and loyalty.

Aron and Westbay (1996) also carried out a study in which the participants completed the Sternberg Triangular Love Scale either with respect to their current or most recent love relationship (concrete version) or with respect to what makes a relationship a love relationship (abstract version). Sternberg's three factors were obtained with both versions of the Triangular Love Scale. However, there were higher ratings for passion with actual relationships, but lower ratings on intimacy and decision/commitment. Aron and Westbay also found the three components of love are by no means independent of each other. With the concrete version of the Triangular Love Scale, passion correlated +.63 with intimacy, passion correlated +.62 with decision/commitment, and intimacy correlated +.72 with decision/commitment. All these correlations were somewhat lower with the abstract version of the questionnaire.

Aron and Westbay (1996) found that men and women responded in very similar ways to the concrete and abstract versions of the Triangular Love Scale except that women had slightly lower scores for intimacy. For both men and women, intimacy was the most important component in love, followed by commitment, with passion the least important.

> **Who do you love?**
>
> Who do we love and like the most? Sternberg and Grajek (1984) found that men generally love and like their lover more than their mother, father, sibling closest in age, or their best friend. Women also loved and liked their lover and best friend more than their mother, father, or sibling closest in age. However, women differed from men in that they loved their lover and their best friend of the same sex equally, but liked their best friend more than their lover.
>
> Sternberg and Grajek (1984) also found that the amount of love that someone has for one member of their family predicts the amount of love they have for the other members. For example, people who love their father very much typically have high levels of love for their mother and sibling closest in age. However, the amount of love someone has for their lover or best friend is *not* predictable from the amount of love they feel for members of their own family.

*Sternberg suggests that there is more than one type of love. How useful do you find his classification of love?*

## Evaluation

- ⊕ Love seems to consist of three factors resembling passion, intimacy, and decision/commitment.
- ⊕ Different types of love relationship can be described from the pattern across the three components of love identified by Sternberg.
- ⊖ The three components correlate fairly highly with each other, and so are not entirely separate.
- ⊖ Evidence about the components of love has been obtained from self-report questionnaires, which assess only those aspects of love that can be expressed in words and are accessible to conscious awareness.

## Self-disclosure

Altman and Taylor (1973) proposed a social penetration theory. According to this theory, the development of a relationship involves increasing levels of **self-disclosure**

**KEY TERM**

**Self-disclosure:** revealing personal or private information about oneself to someone else.

(revealing personal or intimate information about oneself to another person). Strangers initially follow the norm of self-disclosure, meaning they match the level of self-disclosure of the other person. According to the theory, high levels of self-disclosure often lead to greater attraction for the other person, and enhanced attraction leads to increased self-disclosure.

## Evidence

Self-disclosure is often associated with attraction. Collins and Miller (1994) obtained several findings in a meta-analysis of self-disclosure studies. First, individuals disclosing much intimate information about themselves are liked more than individuals who disclose little. Second, individuals disclose more personal information to those whom they already like than to those about whom they are more neutral. Third, individuals who disclose personal information to someone else tend to like that person more as a result.

On average, women disclose more personal and sensitive information about themselves to same-sex friends than men do.

It is often claimed that women have higher levels of self-disclosure in their various relationships than do men. The relevant evidence from 205 studies was reviewed by Dindia and Allen (1992). On average, women self-disclose more than men with their romantic partners of the opposite sex and with their same-sex friends. However, there was no difference between men and women in their self-disclosure levels to male friends. Most sex differences in self-disclosure are not large, but have remained relatively constant over several decades.

Research on self-disclosure has focused on the disclosure of factual information. However, the disclosure of self-relevant feelings may be more important in the development of a close relationship. This issue was addressed by Lin (1992), who asked participants to keep a detailed diary record of their social interaction over a 10-day period. Individuals who disclosed more factual information than most other participants also tended to disclose more about their personal emotions. However, further analysis revealed that relationship intimacy depended much more on the amount of emotional self-disclosure than on the amount of factual self-disclosure.

Cross-cultural research has indicated differences in self-disclosure across cultures. Gudykunst, Matsumoto, Toomey, and Nishida (1996b) found that people in individualistic cultures engage in more self-disclosure than those in collectivistic cultures (see Chapter 1). In addition, those in individualistic cultures tended to supply personal information, whereas those in collectivistic cultures supply information about group membership.

*Why might Americans be more likely to self-disclose than the Chinese?*

We must not exaggerate the importance of mutual self-disclosure in producing intimacy within a relationship. For example, Reis and Patrick (1996) argued in their intimacy model that self-disclosure will only lead to intimacy provided that the partner's response to an individual's disclosures makes him/her feel understood and respected. Support for this model was reported by Lin (1992), who measured perceived responsiveness (e.g., extent to which the partner responds appropriately to the individual's disclosures). Lin found that relationship intimacy was predicted better by perceived responsiveness than by the amount of self-disclosure.

## Evaluation

⊕ Increasing self-disclosure is one of the most important factors in the development of a close relationship.
⊕ Intimacy, which is a crucial aspect of love (Aron & Westbay, 1996), is typically associated with self-disclosure.

● Self-disclosure only has a major impact on relationship intimacy when accompanied by perceived responsiveness (Lin, 1992).
● The distinction between factual and emotional disclosure is important, but has often been ignored.

## Attributions

The partners within a relationship often try to understand each other's behaviour by attributing it to various causes (see Chapter 18). According to Fincham (e.g., Fincham & Hewstone, 2001), attributions for negative events or behaviour are of particular importance. We can distinguish between distress-maintaining attributions and relationship-enhancing attributions. Distress-maintaining attributions are those in which the partner's negative behaviour is attributed to his/her characteristics (e.g., personality), is assumed to be stable (i.e., likely to happen again), and is global (i.e., relevant to other areas of the marriage). In contrast, relationship-enhancing attributions are the opposite, with the partner being seen as personally responsible for positive but not for negative behaviour.

*Why is the way we interpret each other's behaviour so important in helping to maintain a relationship?*

Two main predictions follow from an attribution-theory perspective on relationships. First, distress-maintaining attributions should decrease marital satisfaction. Second, the attributions that spouses make should predict how they behave towards each other.

### Evidence

Bradbury and Fincham (1990) reviewed studies on the attributions made by married couples about each other's behaviour. Couples with poor marital quality were much more likely than those with good marital quality to attribute negative behaviour to global, stable, and personal characteristics of their partners. In contrast, they tended to attribute positive behaviour to specific and unstable causes.

The key issue is one of causality: Do negative attributions play a role in causing marital dissatisfaction or does marital dissatisfaction lead to negative attributions? This issue was addressed by Fincham and Bradbury (1993) in a 12-month longitudinal study with married couples. Attributions made at the start of the study predicted subsequent marital satisfaction, whereas level of marital satisfaction did not predict later attributions. These findings suggest that the causality is mostly from attributions to marital satisfaction.

The attributions made by married couples influence their behaviour towards each other. For example, Bradbury and Fincham (1992) found that wives who made distress-maintaining attributions were more likely than those who made relationship-enhancing attributions to behave negatively in response to negative behaviour from their husband. Perhaps this only means that couples with poor marital satisfaction have negative attributions and behave negatively towards each other. However, Bradbury and Fincham found that the relationship between negative attributions by wives and negative reactions to their husband's negative behaviour was still significant even when differences in marital satisfaction were statistically removed from the data.

## Evaluation

⊕ The attributions that spouses make about each other are associated with level of marital satisfaction and with their behaviour towards each other.

⊕ Negative attributions cause decreased marital satisfaction rather than vice versa.

⊖ Attribution theory is rather narrow in terms of the kinds of explanations it considers. As Planalp and Rivers (1996) pointed out, marriage partners typically explain their spouse's behaviour with reference to specific knowledge about him/her and the relationship rather than the abstract dimensions (e.g., stable–unstable) of attribution theory.

⊖ Information about attributions is nearly always obtained from self-report data. Such data are susceptible to deliberate distortion and ignore automatic processes of which the individual is unaware.

## Equity theory and beyond

Various theorists (e.g., Hatfield, Utne, & Traupmann, 1979) have proposed equity theory, according to which people expect to receive rewards from a relationship proportional to the rewards they provide for the other person. However, it is assumed within the theory that imbalance can be tolerated if the two people involved in a relationship accept the situation. Walster, Walster, and Berscheid (1978) expressed the main assumptions of equity theory as follows:

1. Individuals try to maximise the reward they receive and minimise the costs.
2. There is negotiation to produce fairness; for example, one partner may do the shopping every week to compensate for being away playing sport twice a week.
3. If the relationship is unfair or inequitable, it produces distress, especially in the disadvantaged person.
4. The disadvantaged person will try hard to make the relationship more equitable, particularly when it is very inequitable.

## Evidence

Hatfield et al. (1979) asked newlyweds to indicate the extent to which they felt that they were receiving more or less than they should in view of their contributions to the marriage. They were also asked to indicate their level of contentment, happiness, anger, and guilt. The under-benefited had the lowest level of overall satisfaction with their marriage, and tended to experience anger. The over-benefited came next (they tended to feel guilty), and those who perceived their marriage as equitable had the highest level of satisfaction. Men who were over-benefited were almost as satisfied as those in an equitable marriage, but over-benefited women were much less satisfied than women with equal benefit (Argyle, 1988).

The finding that those who perceive their marriages as equitable are happiest, and those who are under-benefited are least happy, was replicated by Buunk and Van Yperen (1991). However, these findings applied only to those individuals who were high in exchange orientation (i.e., expecting rewards given by one person in a relationship to be followed immediately by rewards given by the other person). Those low in exchange orientation had fairly high marriage satisfaction regardless of whether they were over-benefited, under-benefited, or receiving equal benefit.

Sharing domestic chores may be a result of negotiation in an equitable relationship, in which each partner feels the other takes their share of responsibilities.

Prins, Buunk, and Van Yperen (1993) found convincing evidence of the importance that women attach to equity. Married women in inequitable relationships were more likely than those in equitable ones to have been involved in extra-marital relationships. However, this was not found among married men.

*How valid do you think it is to see our friendships and relationships in terms of rewards and costs?*

## Evaluation

● Equity theory accounts for some of the satisfaction and dissatisfaction found in relationships, especially in individualistic cultures.
● Cultural differences are ignored within equity theory. For example, Gergen, Morse, and Gergen (1980) found that European students preferred equality in their relationships with an equal distribution of rewards, whereas American students favoured equity based on a constant ratio of rewards to inputs.
● Many happily married couples do not focus on equity. Murstein, MacDonald, and Cerreto (1977) found that marital adjustment was significantly poorer in those married couples who were concerned about equity than in those couples who were not.
● Cate, Lloyd, and Long (1988) found that satisfaction in romantic relationships depends on rewards (e.g., sexual satisfaction, love, status) more than on precise equity.

## Investment model

What determines an individual's commitment to his/her current relationship? Common sense might suggest that the crucial factor is the degree of attraction or love which the individual has towards his or her partner. No-one would dispute that attraction and love are important, but it is argued in the investment model (e.g., Rusbult, 1983; Rusbult, Martz, & Agnew, 1998) that there are other important factors. According to this model, three factors jointly determine an individual's level of commitment to a relationship:

● *Satisfaction.* This is based on the rewards and costs of the relationship, coupled with an evaluation of those rewards and costs relative to those which the individual feels he or she deserves.
● *Perceived quality of alternatives.* Individuals will be more committed to the present relationships if there are no other attractive options (e.g., an alternative partner, living alone with no commitments).
● *Investment size.* The more time, effort, money, personal sacrifices invested in the relationship, the greater will be the commitment.

*Why do people stay in relationships that don't necessarily make them happy?*

The investment model was developed by Wieselquist, Rusbult, Foster, and Agnew (1999), who pointed out that it is important that an individual's efforts are perceived accurately by the partner. They argued that commitment and trust in a relationship will be high when the following sequence occurs: "(a) dependence promotes strong commitment, (b) commitment promotes pro-relationship acts, (c) pro-relationship acts are perceived by the partner, (d) the perception of pro-relationship acts enhances the partner's trust, and (e) trust increases the partner's willingness to become dependent on the relationship" (p. 942).

## Evidence

Convincing support for the investment model was provided in a longitudinal study of heterosexual couples by Rusbult (1983). There were the predicted changes in commitment following changes in any of the three factors (satisfaction, quality of alternatives, investment). As predicted by the model, increases in rewards within the relationship were associated with increased commitment. The only finding that failed to support the model was that increased costs mostly failed to reduce either satisfaction or commitment.

*Why would women who have been in abusive relationships go back to their partners?*

Lund (1985) obtained good evidence for the importance of investment. Investment in the sense of time, effort, and resources was a good predictor of commitment to the relationship. Indeed, it was a better predictor than the rewards provided by the relationship.

Rusbult and Martz (1995) studied abused women who had sought safety in a women's shelter. Most experienced little satisfaction from the relationship, but many decided to return to the man who had abused them. It was not possible to predict which women would return to their partner on the basis of their feelings for him. What mattered was their level of investment in the relationship (e.g., joint children), coupled with poor alternatives (e.g., insufficient money to survive independently).

According to the investment model, individuals compare their current relationship with various alternatives. Rusbult, van Lange, Wildschut, Yovetich, and Verette (2000) developed this notion, arguing that people compare their relationship against the relationships of others. They found substantial evidence for the phenomenon of perceived superiority (regarding one's own relationship as better than those of other people). Perceived superiority increases couple well-being and helps couples to cope with problems and difficulties.

Rusbult et al. (2000) found that perceived superiority depends on commitment to the relationship: Couples with high levels of commitment had greater perceived superiority. Within married couples, the more committed partner generally showed more evidence of perceived superiority. Most importantly, the level of perceived superiority within married couples predicted their level of adjustment 20 months later, and also predicted whether the marriage would end.

Wieselquist et al. (1999) carried out two longitudinal studies, one on unmarried students in relationships and one on married couples. They obtained support for the six-stage sequence of developing trust and commitment described above.

What happens when commitment is low? Buunk and Bakker (1997) found that individuals low in commitment were more likely to have sex outside the relationship. In many cases, they had unprotected sex with one or more other people, and failed to take any steps to protect their partner from the risks caused by this behaviour.

## Evaluation

➕ Commitment to a relationship depends on the attractiveness of alternatives and amount of investment in the relationship as well as the satisfaction provided by the relationship.
➕ Perceived superiority is an important consequence of commitment, and helps to preserve relationships.
➖ The three factors determining commitment are not truly independent. For example, individuals very satisfied with a relationship are more likely to have a large investment in it.
➖ Most research has focused on short-term rather than on long-term relationships (Buunk, 2001).
➖ The investment model de-emphasises individual differences. For example, individuals distrustful of others because of childhood experiences are less likely than other people to commit themselves fully to a relationship (Shaver, Hazan, & Bradshaw, 1988).

## RELATIONSHIP STABILITY AND DISSOLUTION

This section is mostly devoted to the factors leading to the preservation or dissolution of marriages. However, the processes involved in the preservation and dissolution of premarital relationships are likely to be fairly similar, and we will start by considering such relationships. Relationships often break up because one of the partners has had an affair with someone else. Indeed, Harris (2002) found that an affair led to the end of the relationship in nearly 60% of the cases in which it was discovered. The effects of sexual and emotional infidelity on relationships are discussed in detail in Chapter 3.

According to Lee (1984), the break-up of premarital relationships generally occurs over a period of time rather than consisting of a single event. He argued that five stages are involved:

1. *Dissatisfaction*. One or both of the partners realise there are real problems within the relationship.
2. *Exposure*. The problems identified in the problem stage are brought out into the open.
3. *Negotiation*. There is much discussion about the issues raised during the exposure stage.
4. *Resolution attempts*. Both partners try to solve the problems discussed in the negotiation stage.
5. *Termination*. If the resolution attempts are unsuccessful, then the relationship ends.

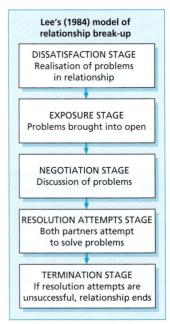

Lee's (1984) model of relationship break-up

DISSATISFACTION STAGE
Realisation of problems in relationship

EXPOSURE STAGE
Problems brought into open

NEGOTIATION STAGE
Discussion of problems

RESOLUTION ATTEMPTS STAGE
Both partners attempt to solve problems

TERMINATION STAGE
If resolution attempts are unsuccessful, relationship ends

Lee identified these five stages on the basis of a study of more than 100 premarital romantic break-ups. The exposure and negotiation stages tended to be the most intense and exhausting stages in the break-up. Those relationships that had been the strongest took the longest time to work through the five stages of dissolution. This makes sense: The more valuable a relationship has been, the harder it is worth fighting for its continuation.

We turn now to a consideration of what happens to marriages over time. Cross-sectional studies (e.g., Glenn & McLanahan, 1982) have indicated a U-shaped relationship between the length of the marriage and marital satisfaction. Marital satisfaction declines sharply with the birth of the first child, and only rises again when the last-born child leaves home. A limitation with these cross-sectional studies is that many of those questioned recalled their level of marital satisfaction at different points in their marriage, some of which might have occurred 30 years or more earlier. Obviously, what is recalled over such long periods of time might be inaccurate.

Longitudinal studies involve obtaining data during two or more time periods. They are generally more revealing than cross-sectional studies, because they provide information about *changes* over time. Vaillant and Vaillant (1993) reported a longitudinal study in which married couples indicated their level of marital satisfaction at several points over a 40-year period. The husbands' level of marital satisfaction remained fairly constant over the course of the marriage, whereas that of the wives showed a modest decline. The difference between the findings of Vaillant and Vaillant and those of most other researchers could be due to the fact that they did not ask their participants to recall feelings from the distant past. However, there was another important difference between their study and those of other researchers: Their male participants were all graduates from Harvard University, and thus on average very well off financially. Their affluence may have helped to prevent them from suffering some of the stresses of child rearing.

*What particular difficulties arise when trying to do research into relationships?*

The high divorce rate and extensive media coverage of marital problems have led many people to assume that marriage is a recipe for unhappiness and misery. In fact, most of the evidence suggests exactly the opposite (see, for example, Bradburn (1969) in the Key Study on the next page).

It is sometimes claimed that the advantages of marriage are greater for men than for women. We can test this by calculating for each sex the "happiness gap", which is the difference between the percentage of very happy married individuals and non-married individuals. Wood, Rhodes, and Whelan (1989) carried out a meta-analysis of 94 studies, and found that the happiness gap was almost identical for both sexes.

Why are married people relatively happy? As we saw earlier, Argyle and Furnham (1983) found three factors determining people's level of satisfaction with different kinds of relationships: material and instrumental help, social and emotional support, and common interests. Spouses were rated higher than individuals in any other kind of non-sexual relationship on all three factors, but especially on material and instrumental help.

Bradburn's (1969) findings need to be interpreted carefully. Divorced people may be less happy than married people mainly because they are divorced. It is also possible that those who are naturally unhappy and depressed are more likely to become divorced than those who are naturally happy and easy-going. There is some evidence that happy and well-adjusted people are more likely to marry and are also more likely to stay married (e.g., Mastekaasa, 1994). However, the effects are relatively weak, and can only account for some of the relationship between marriage and happiness.

# Bradburn: Marriage happiness

Bradburn (1969) in an American study found that 35% of married men and 38% of married women said they were "very happy". These figures were much higher than those for never-married men and women (18% for each sex). Of those who had been married, but were currently separated, divorced, or widowed, an even smaller percentage was "very happy". For example, only 7% of separated or widowed men said they were "very happy".

The conclusion that marriage is good for you was strengthened by Bradburn's (1969) findings of the percentages of people admitting they were "not too happy". Fewer than 10% of married people said they were "not too happy". This compares to a massive 40% of separated people, as well as over 30% of divorced people. Those who have never been married are less happy than married people. However, they are happier than those who have been married but are no longer in that state, with about 17% of them being "not too happy".

These findings need to be interpreted with care. Divorced people may be less happy than married people mainly because of the fact that they are divorced. However, it is also possible that those who are naturally unhappy and depressed are more likely to become divorced than those who are naturally happy and easy-going.

## KEY STUDY EVALUATION—Bradburn

Bradburn's study found that more married people claimed to be very happy compared to single people, 40% of whom said they were "not too happy". However, the study was carried out in 1969 in the United States, at a time when marriage was the norm, and couples who lived together outside marriage were regarded as slightly outrageous. The demand characteristics of being asked by a stranger about one's happiness at home may have affected married people's responses, as well as those of single people, who in 1969 were expected to aspire to being married.

## Discussion points

1. Why are married people generally happier than those who are not?
2. What are the limitations of self-report measures of happiness?

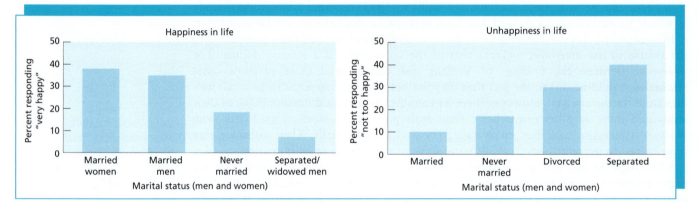

The results of Bradburn's (1969) study.

There are two additional points. First, many studies indicating that marriage is associated with high levels of happiness were carried out a long time ago. Marriage nowadays may have fewer beneficial effects than it used to have. However, the evidence generally does not support that view (Diener, Suh, Lucas, & Smith, 1999). Second, there has been a dramatic increase in the number of people cohabiting rather than marrying, and a major reason for this is because cohabitors perceive significant disadvantages in the state of marriage. For example, there is a common perception (which is sadly often correct) that married women often find themselves doing nearly all the housework as well as holding down a full-time job.

## Marriage success and failure

What determines which marriages or close relationships last and which do not? A common view is that newlyweds are blissfully happy and optimistic (cue violins), and it is the problems and difficulties occurring in the years after marriage which lead to divorce. This romantic view of the world was shattered by Huston, Niehuis, and Smith (2001b). They found that newlywed couples differed substantially in how much they loved each other. Those newlyweds deeply in love at the time of marriage were on average much happier than other newlyweds several years into the marriage. In addition, those who divorced within 7 years of marriage were much less in love and much less affectionate with each other as newlyweds than were those who divorced 7–13 years after marriage. Huston et al. incorporated these findings into their enduring-dynamics model. According to this model, much of what happens during the course of a marriage is predictable from a couple's closeness (or the lack thereof) during courtship and immediately after marriage.

Karney and Bradbury (1995, p.18) reviewed the evidence from numerous longitudinal studies concerned with factors associated with marriage quality or satisfaction and **marital stability** (whether it is continuing or has ended in separation or divorce). They came to the following conclusion:

*In general, positively valued variables—such as education, positive behaviour, and employment—predict positive marital outcomes (in terms of satisfaction and continuation of the marriage), whereas negatively valued variables—such as neuroticism, negative behaviour, and an unhappy childhood—predict negative marital outcomes.*

*What is it about some marriages that make them more successful than others?*

Karney and Bradbury found that most variables had similar effects on husbands and on wives. An important exception was employment. When the husband was employed, this was associated with greater marital satisfaction, but the opposite was the case when the wife was employed. However, most of the relevant studies were carried out over 20 years ago, and there is probably much less of a gender difference now that so many more women are in the workforce.

Duck (1992) used findings from longitudinal studies to identify several factors making marriages more fragile and liable to dissolution. First, marriages between people whose parents were themselves divorced are more likely to end in divorce. Second, marriages in which the partners are teenagers are less likely to last than marriages in which the partners are older. Potential explanations are that teenagers are more likely to be immature, they have not yet developed their adult personality, and they are less likely to have either a steady income or full-time employment.

Third, marriages in which the partners come from very different backgrounds in terms of culture, race, or religion are less stable than those in which the partners come from very similar backgrounds. One reason for this is that the partners may have very different expectations about marriage because of their differing backgrounds. Fourth, marriages between partners from the lower socio-economic groups and/or with lower educational levels are more likely to end in divorce. The partners in such marriages are often very young, which increases the probability of divorce. Fifth, marriages in which the partners have had numerous sexual partners beforehand are less stable. Those who have had numerous romantic relationships tend to find it harder to produce the long-term commitment needed to make marriage work.

**KEY TERM**
**Marital stability:** the status of a marriage (continuing vs. ended in separation or divorce).

The five factors identified by Duck (1992) tell only part of the story. There are successful and stable marriages in which the partners possess all the vulnerability factors, and there are partners having none of these factors who nevertheless have short-lived marriages. Some factors may be relatively complex. For example, consider the fact that couples with lower educational levels are more likely to divorce. What is important is not really the educational level itself, but rather the reduced prospects of such couples owning their own home and having reasonable full-time jobs following from the low level of education.

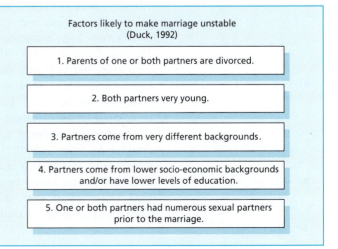

Factors likely to make marriage unstable
(Duck, 1992)

1. Parents of one or both partners are divorced.

2. Both partners very young.

3. Partners come from very different backgrounds.

4. Partners come from lower socio-economic backgrounds and/or have lower levels of education.

5. One or both partners had numerous sexual partners prior to the marriage.

The data from most longitudinal studies are limited. For example, 75% of the samples used in the longitudinal studies reviewed by Karney and Bradbury (1995) consisted mainly of middle-class white couples. In addition, there has been a very heavy reliance on self-report and interview data, both of which are susceptible to distortion (e.g., social desirability bias).

# Theories

Several theories have been put forward to explain the maintenance or dissolution of long-term relationships and marriages. Some of the main theoretical approaches will be discussed in this section.

## Cohesiveness model

Levinger (1976) put forward a cohesiveness model, in which he argued that the chances of a marriage surviving depend on three main factors:

1. The attractions of the relationships (e.g., emotional security, sexual satisfaction).
2. The barriers to leaving the marriage (e.g., social norms, financial pressures).
3. The presence of attractive alternatives (e.g., a more desirable partner).

Levinger (1999) added a fourth factor—barriers around alternative relationships. For example, a woman may be less likely to leave her husband in favour of another man if the other man is married and has a family. Divorce is most likely when the marriage has few attractions, there are only weak barriers to leaving the relationship, there are very attractive alternatives, and there are few barriers to pursuing attractive alternatives.

*What are some of the key factors that contribute to couples deciding to separate?*

Lewis and Spanier (1979) developed this approach. They regarded marital satisfaction and marital stability as separate dimensions. This led them to identify four types of marriage: satisfied and stable, satisfied but unstable, unsatisfied but stable, and unsatisfied and unstable. Unsatisfied but stable marriages are held together because there are considerable barriers to ending the marriage. In contrast, satisfied but unstable marriages typically end because the barriers to leaving the relationship are low and there are attractive alternatives.

## Evidence

As predicted by Levinger's cohesiveness model, there are typically only weak relationships between marital satisfaction and stability. In their review, Karney and Bradbury (1995) reported that the average correlation between wives' marital satisfaction and marital stability was +.33, and it was +.13 for husbands. Similar findings were reported by Attridge, Berscheid, and Simpson (1995) in a longitudinal study of 120 adult premarital relationships. They measured 13 variables generally thought to indicate relationship satisfaction (e.g., commitment, love, relationship closeness, self-disclosure, and positive emotional experiences). All 13 variables loaded on a single factor called the stability composite index. Scores on this factor did not predict very well whether couples would remain together or separate: "Even when using data from both partners on the stability composite index ... we were able to account for only about one-third of the variance in premarital romantic relationship stability" (p. 262).

Convincing support for the model comes from a longitudinal study of American couples by Udry (1981). Information was obtained from these couples about marital satisfaction, how much better or worse off they would be without their present spouse, and how easy it would be to replace their spouse with a comparable or superior alternative. Udry found that marital stability (or disruption) was predicted better by the availability of good marital alternatives than by marital satisfaction.

White and Booth (1991) interviewed married people, assessing their level of marital satisfaction, alternatives to the marriage relationship, and barriers to dissolving the marriage (e.g., home ownership, children). They then interviewed the same people 8 years later. Marriage stability was greater when there were few alternatives and several barriers, as well as when there was a high level of marital satisfaction at the start of the study. According to White and Booth (p. 19), "The rise in the divorce rate has occurred not because marriages are less happy, but because, in the presence of falling barriers and rising alternatives, the threshold of marital happiness necessary to prompt divorce is lower than it used to be."

## Evaluation

- ⊕ Levinger's social exchange theory helps to explain why marital dissatisfaction does not strongly predict subsequent divorce.
- ⊖ The theory does not explain the processes causing initially successful marriages to become unsuccessful.
- ⊖ The theory does not provide a detailed account of the various factors making a marriage attractive.

## Bank account model

Gottman (e.g., 1993, 1998) focused on the adaptive processes used by married couples when discussing issues, especially those causing conflict. He has consistently argued that we are much more likely to understand the processes involved in marriage via direct observation than via self-report questionnaire.

Gottman (1993) used videotape evidence from 79 couples who discussed events of the day, a problem area of disagreement, and a pleasant topic. Stable couples on average produced five times as many positive as negative comments, whereas unstable couples produced only 80% as many positive as negative comments.

The above distinction between stable and unstable couples proved to be important. Gottman (1993) found that 19% of unstable couples had divorced within 4 years of testing, compared to only 3% of stable couples. In unstable marriages, 52% of husbands and 48% of wives had seriously considered divorce during the 4-year period. In contrast, the figures in stable marriages were 18% and 33%, respectively.

Gottman (1998) reviewed observational studies on married couples in interaction, concluding there are seven consistent patterns distinguishing happy from unhappy couples. Unhappy couples show:

1. Lower ratios of positivity to negativity (Gottman, 1993).
2. Greater negative affect reciprocity: negative emotion expressed by one partner leading to negative emotion expressed by the other partner.
3. More criticism, contempt, and stonewalling.
4. More evidence of a pattern of the wife making demands and the husband withdrawing.
5. Less evidence of general positive feelings during times of conflict.
6. Negative and lasting attributions about the partner.
7. Increased physiological arousal.

Why is there so much less negativity in the interactions between husband and wife in happy couples than in unhappy ones? As we saw earlier, the partners in happy marriages attribute negative behaviour by their spouse to the situation rather than to his/her personality. As a result, they do not feel the need to respond negatively.

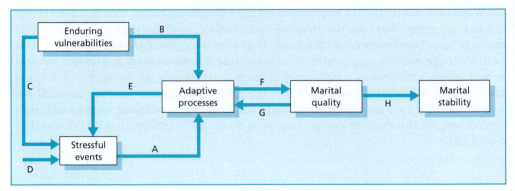

A vulnerability–stress–adaptation model of marriage. From Karney and Bradbury (1995).

## Vulnerability-stress-adaptation model

Karney and Bradbury (1995) proposed a vulnerability-stress-adaptation model of marriage (see the diagram above). According to this model, three major factors determine marital quality and stability or duration:

1. Enduring vulnerabilities. These include high neuroticism (a personality dimension concerned with anxiety and depression; see Chapter 13) and an unhappy childhood.
2. Stressful events. These include short- and long-lasting life events such as illness, unemployment, and poverty.
3. Adaptive processes. These include constructive and destructive coping strategies to resolve difficulties.

According to the model, adaptive processes have a *direct* impact on marital satisfaction. In contrast, enduring vulnerabilities and stressful events have an *indirect* impact via their effects on adaptive processes. For example, married people high on neuroticism or whose parents divorced tend to have relatively low marital satisfaction. According to the model, the reason why neuroticism and parental divorce are related negatively to marital satisfaction is because they lead individuals to use maladaptive processes (e.g., high ratio of negative to positive communications). Other aspects of the model are the assumptions that enduring vulnerabilities can play a role in creating stressful events, and that adaptive processes can create stressful conditions.

It is argued within the vulnerability-stress-adaptation model (Karney & Bradbury, 1995, p. 24) that marriages often disintegrate through the following vicious cycle:

*(a) stressful events challenge a couple's capacity to adapt, (b) which contributes to the perpetuation or worsening of those events, (c) which in turn further challenge and perhaps overwhelm their capacity to adapt. This vicious cycle is most likely to occur in couples having enduring vulnerabilities.*

## Evidence

Karney and Bradbury (1995) discussed 115 longitudinal studies on marital quality and stability in which almost 200 variables were considered. There is evidence for the involvement of the main factors of enduring vulnerabilities, stressful events, and adaptive processes in influencing marital satisfaction, and stability. We will start with enduring vulnerabilities. Neuroticism in both husbands and wives correlated about −.20 with marital satisfaction and stability, and there were similar findings with respect to an unhappy childhood for husbands and wives. Stress had a strong negative effect on marital satisfaction, and a smaller effect on marital stability. So far as adaptive processes are concerned, negative behaviour and maladaptive attributions were associated with low marital satisfaction, but had little effect on marital stability.

Of crucial importance is the assumption that there are several paths connecting the main factors in the model to each other. We will consider evidence relating to some of these paths. Support for path A (stressful events influence adaptive processes) was reported by Aubry, Tefft, and Kingsbury (1990), who found the stress caused by unemployment was associated with more negative and less constructive interactions with spouses. In addition, it was found in a diary study that negative marital interactions were more common on stressful days than on stress-free days (Halford, Gravestock, Lowe, & Scheldt, 1992). Evidence in favour of path B (enduring vulnerabilities influencing adaptive processes) is available in the finding that children brought up by parents who divorced have less adequate social skills than those brought up by parents who remained together (Franz, McClelland, & Weinberger, 1991).

Support for path C (enduring vulnerabilities helping to cause stressful events) was reported by Magnus, Diener, Fujita, and Pavot (1993). They found in a 4-year longitudinal study that neuroticism at the start of the study was associated with more negative life events assessed 4 years later. They concluded (p. 1046) that, "neuroticism predisposed people to experience more negative objective events".

Adaptive processes can create stressful conditions (path E). For example, clinically depressed individuals whose spouses were very critical were more likely to suffer relapses than were those with less critical spouses (Hooley, Orley, & Teasdale, 1986). With respect to path F (adaptive processes influencing marital satisfaction), we saw earlier in the chapter that attributions concerning the behaviour of one's spouse influence marital satisfaction (e.g., Fincham & Bradbury, 1993). With respect to path G (marital satisfaction influencing adaptive processes), wives having initially satisfied husbands became more affectionate during the first 2 years of marriage, and husbands having satisfied wives became less negative over the same time period (Huston & Vangelisti, 1991).

What about path H? As was discussed earlier, Karney and Bradbury (1995) found in their meta-analysis that there was a significant positive relationship between husbands' marital satisfaction and marital stability, and the same was the case for wives' marital satisfaction and marital stability.

## Evaluation

● Most factors associated with the maintenance or dissolution of marriages can be related directly to the three broad variables emphasised by the model.
● There is evidence for all of the paths among factors assumed to exist within the model.
● According to the model, marital quality and marital stability depend on complex interactions among several factors. However, little research has examined these complexities.
● The model does not provide a detailed account of constructive and destructive adaptive processes.
● The model exaggerates the role of marital satisfaction and de-emphasises factors external to the marriage (e.g., presence of attractive alternatives) in affecting marital stability.

*What particular problems do you see with the models designed to explain why long-term relationships break up? Can they be used across cultures?*

## Cultural differences

Most Western cultures are individualistic, whereas most Eastern cultures are collectivistic (see Chapter 1). Thus, it is expected in Western cultures that individuals will make their own decisions and take responsibility for their own lives. In Eastern cultures, in contrast, it is expected that individuals will regard themselves mainly as part of family and social groups, and that their decisions will be influenced strongly by their obligations to other people. This difference was summed up by Hsu (1981): "An American asks, 'How does my heart feel?'. A Chinese asks, 'What will other people say?'." As a result, those in

### The postmodern approach

Those who favour the postmodern approach (e.g., Wood & Duck, 1995) doubt the value of most research on interpersonal relationships. According to the postmodern approach, relationships need to be considered in terms of the context or environment in which they occur. There are various ways in which the available evidence can be interpreted, and it is hard or impossible to establish that one interpretation is preferable to any other.

### Social purpose

Lalljee (1981) put forward related ideas. According to him, we need to consider the underlying social purposes of the explanations that people provide for their behaviour. For example, when two people divorce, they typically explain the disintegration of their marriage in different terms. Each of them tends to suggest that it was the unreasonable behaviour of the other person that led to divorce. In view of people's need to justify their own behaviour to other people, it becomes very difficult to establish the truth. The postmodernists go further, and claim that there is no single "truth" that can be discovered. In a study carried out by Murray and Holmes (1993), it was shown that storytelling about one's relationship can easily be altered to accommodate awkward facts. This suggests that the truth is a flexible notion.

### Discourse analysis

Many postmodernists argue that progress can be made in understanding interpersonal relationships by making use of discourse analysis. Discourse analysis involves qualitative analysis of people's written or spoken communications; these are often taped under fairly natural conditions. An interesting example of discourse analysis is contained in the work of Gavey (1992). She studied the sexual behaviour of six women who had been forced to have sex. Here is part of what one of the women had to say:

> He kept saying, just, just let me do this or just let me do that and that will be all. And this could go on for an hour … So after maybe an hour of me saying "no", and him saying "oh, come on, come on", I'd finally think, "Oh my God … for a few hours' rest, peace and quiet, I may as well".

This example shows that discourse analysis can provide striking evidence about the nature of relationships. However, Gavey (1992) and others who have used discourse analysis have often obtained evidence from only a small number of participants. This raises the issue of whether the findings obtained can be generalised to larger populations. There are also issues concerning the validity of the procedure. For example, we might expect someone to describe their sexual experiences rather differently to their partner, to a close friend, to an acquaintance, and to a stranger.

*How might discourse analysis provide us with a deeper understanding of human relationships than experimental research?*

individualistic Western cultures tend to stress the personality of a potential spouse, whereas those in collectivistic Eastern cultures favour arranged marriages based on social status.

Collectivistic cultures are more traditional than individualistic ones. We might expect them to be less accepting of cohabiting couples, who might be less happy as a result. As predicted, cohabiting couples in collectivistic cultures have lower life satisfaction than married or single individuals; in contrast, cohabiting couples in individualistic cultures are happier and have higher life satisfaction than married or single people (Diener et al., 1999).

We must not exaggerate the differences between individualistic and collectivistic cultures. Even in societies in which arranged marriages are the norm, there is often some restricted element of choice of marriage partner. For example, De Munck (1996) studied marriage practices in a Sri Lankan Moslem community. There was an emphasis on arranged marriages, but romantic love was nevertheless accepted as a relevant factor in choice of marriage partner. In individualistic societies, parents often strive to influence the marriage choice of their children.

Evidence on love and marriage from India, Pakistan, Thailand, Mexico, Brazil, Hong Kong, the Phillipines, Australia, Japan, England, and the United States was reported by Levine, Sato, Hashimoto, and Verma (1995). There was a correlation of +.56 between a society's individualism and the perceived necessity of love for the establishment of a marriage. Thus, there was a fairly strong tendency for members of individualistic societies to regard love as more important in marriage than did members of collectivistic societies.

Levine et al. (1995) found a rather different pattern of results when the participants were asked whether, "If love has completely disappeared from a marriage … it is best to make a clean break and start new lives." The answers to this question did not differ between individualistic and collectivistic cultures.

*Why might it be argued that "marriages based on love" are more likely to break up than arranged marriages?*

In many non-Western cultures, arranged marriages are the norm. Evidence suggests that the average level of marital satisfaction is the same in both arranged marriages and those in which the partners have a free choice.

Are arranged marriages happier or less happy than love marriages? It seems that the average level of marital satisfaction is about the same. Yelsma and Athappily (1988) compared Indian arranged marriages with Indian and North American love marriages. In most respects, those in arranged marriages were at least as happy as those in love marriages. Gupta and Singh (1982) studied married couples in Jaipur, India. Those who had married for love were more in love than those in arranged marriages during the first 5 years of marriage. After that, however, those in arranged marriages became increasingly more in love than those in love marriages.

# SUMMARY

*Pro-social behaviour*

According to evolutionary psychologists, kin selection and reciprocal altruism are important factors underlying altruistic behaviour. According to Batson's empathy–altruism hypothesis, when we observe someone in distress, we are likely to respond with altruistic behaviour only if we experience empathic concern rather than personal distress. Most studies have focused only on short-term altruistic behaviour of little consequence. According to the negative-state relief model, we help victims to reduce our own feelings of sadness. Some evidence is inconsistent with this model, and it ignores the possibility that we might have unselfish motives for helping. Members of non-industrialised and collectivistic cultures are apparently more altruistic than those of industrialised and individualistic cultures. However, in both types of cultures individuals expect to give only a little more help than they receive. The reluctance of bystanders to intervene often occurs because of diffusion of responsibility. According to Darley and Latané's decision model, bystanders interpret the situation, decide whether they should accept responsibility, and then decide what kind of help they should provide. According to the arousal/cost–reward model, bystanders interpret their own state of arousal, and then assess the costs and rewards of helping.

*Aggression*

According to social learning theory, aggressive behaviour depends on observational learning. According to the frustration–aggression hypothesis, aggression is caused by frustration. This hypothesis is over-simplified. According to cue–arousal theory, aggression can be triggered by relevant environmental cues (e.g., weapons effect). According to the cognitive-neoassociationistic approach, aversive events cause negative affect, which then activates an associative network within long-term memory. According to the negative affect escape model, a moderately intense unpleasant stimulus can lead to aggressive behaviour designed to reduce the negative affect caused by the stimulus. According to excitation-transfer theory, arousal produced by one stimulus can be transferred and added to the arousal produced by a second stimulus. This can lead to increased aggression if the source of the arousal is misinterpreted. Such misinterpretations are probably rare in everyday life. According to the general affective aggression model, aggressive behaviour depends crucially on appraisal processes. This model is complex, and leads to few precise predictions. Alcohol leads to aggression because it reduces anxiety. Research on aggression within close relationships in Western cultures indicates that women are slightly more likely than men to behave aggressively, but men inflict more physical injuries than women. Male aggression greatly exceeds female aggression in cultures in which men have most of the power.

### Formation of interpersonal relationships

Proximity is one of the factors involved in the development of interpersonal relationships. Physical attractiveness is important in the development of a relationship, with relatively typical or symmetrical faces being favoured. Slim women are preferred in Western societies, but heavy women are preferred in societies in which the food supply is unreliable. Partners in a relationship tend to be of comparable levels of physical attractiveness. When we form an initial impression of someone, we are greatly influenced by central traits (e.g., warmth, intelligence), and by information presented first. We are attracted to those with similar personality and attitudes, because we infer that they will be likely to evaluate us positively. There are large cultural differences in mate preferences. However, men in most cultures prefer younger women, whereas women prefer older men. Physical attractiveness is a more important factor in mate preferences in cultures with numerous disease-causing agents. Women having access to financial and other resources emphasise physical attractiveness in mate preferences more than do women in other cultures.

### Development of close relationships

Love consists of the three components of intimacy, passion, and decision/commitment. There are different types of love depending on the relative involvement of these three components. Liking can be distinguished from love, and is characterised mainly by intimacy. Self-disclosure is positively associated with attraction and intimacy, because it indicates that we trust the other person and want them to know us. Women self-disclose more than men with their romantic partners. Emotional self-disclosure is more related to intimacy than is factual self-disclosure. Self-disclosure leads to intimacy only when one's partner is perceived to be responsive to such disclosure. Negative attributions about one's spouse increase negative behaviour towards him/her, and lead to reduced marital satisfaction. Equitable romantic relationships are generally happier than inequitable ones, but satisfaction in romantic relationships depends more on the rewards provided by the partner. Commitment to a relationship depends on satisfaction, perceived quality of alternatives, and investment size.

### Relationship stability and dissolution

Married individuals are happier than those who are not married, but marital satisfaction decreases over time. Factors associated with divorce include having parents who divorced, being teenagers at the time of marriage, and coming from different backgrounds. According to Levinger's cohesiveness model, marital stability depends on the attraction of the relationship, the barriers to leaving the marriage, the presence of attractive alternatives, and barriers around alternatives. As predicted, marital stability is only moderately associated with marital satisfaction. Marriages often end in divorce when there is a high ratio of negative to positive communications. According to Karney and Bradbury (1995), marital satisfaction and stability depend on enduring vulnerabilities, stressful events, and adaptive processes. The first two factors influence marital satisfaction via their effects on adaptive processes. This vulnerability-stress-adaptation model de-emphasises the role of factors external to the marriage (e.g., attractive alternatives). Love is more important for the establishment of a marriage in individualistic than in collectivistic cultures. Individuals in arranged marriages are as happy as those in love marriages.

## FURTHER READING

- Anderson, C.A., & Bushman, B.J. (2002). Human aggression. *Annual Review of Psychology*, *53*, 27–51. This chapter by two leading experts provides an overall framework for research on human aggression.
- Hewstone, M., & Stroebe, W. (2001). *Introduction to social psychology* (3rd ed.). Oxford, UK: Blackwell. There is good coverage of pro-social behaviour, aggressive behaviour, friendship, and close relationships in Chapters 9, 10, and 12 of this edited book.
- Hogg, M.A., & Vaughan, G.M. (2002). *Social psychology* (3rd ed.). New York: Prentice Hall. Introductory accounts of the topics covered in this chapter are given in Chapters 12, 13, and 14 of this textbook.

- **Obedience to authority**
  Milgram's obedience studies.

  *The theory and some replications*

- **Conformity**
  Research on conformity.

  *The desirability of conformity*
  *Sherif's autokinetic effect studies*
  *Asch's line-length and other studies;*
  *  cross-cultural studies*
  *Minority/majority and public/private*
  *  influence—Moscovici's studies*

- **Basic group characteristics**
  A discussion of the various
  characteristics of groups.

  *The cohesiveness of groups*
  *The formation of social norms*
  *Two life-cycle theories—group*
  *  socialisation theory*
  *The cognitive model*

- **Performance in groups**
  Group vs. individual performance.

  *Social facilitation—Zajonc's drive*
  *  theory and others*
  *Reduced performance in groups—*
  *  Latané et al.'s social loafing study;*
  *  social compensation*
  *The relative inaccuracy of group*
  *  judgements*

- **Group decision making**
  Several theories attempt to explain
  group polarisation.

  *Social comparison theory—aiming for*
  *  the highest positive regard*
  *Information theory—shared*
  *  persuasive facts from the majority*
  *Self-categorisation theory—ingroup vs.*
  *  outgroup*
  *Groupthink—the* Challenger *disaster*

- **Leadership**
  Leadership issues explored.

  *Personality traits—great man/person*
  *  theory*
  *The effectiveness of leadership styles:*
  *  democratic, autocratic, laissez-faire,*
  *  task, and socio-emotional*
  *Situational factors—Fiedler's*
  *  contingency model*
  *Bass' transactional and*
  *  transformational leadership styles*

- **Collective behaviour**
  How and why individual behaviour
  can change in a crowd.

  *Exploring crowd behaviour—riots;*
  *  football matches; demonstrations*
  *Anonymity in a crowd—*
  *  deindividuation*
  *Trigger factors for aggression—*
  *  emergent-norm theory*
  *The influence of group norms—social*
  *  identity model*

# Group processes

**20**

What we say (and how we behave) are heavily influenced by other people. They possess useful knowledge about the world, and it is often sensible to heed what they say. In addition, we want to be liked by other people, and to fit into society. As a result, we sometimes hide what we really think, and try to behave in ways that will meet with the approval of others. These issues relate to **social influence**, which "involves the exercise of social power by a person or group to change the attitudes or behaviour of others in a particular direction. Social power refers to the force available to the influence to motivate this change" (Franzoi, 1996, p. 258).

Social influence occurs when the behaviour of individuals is determined by the instructions given by those in a position of authority (e.g., police, doctors). We will start by considering obedience to authority. However, most social influence occurs within groups, and the rest of the chapter is concerned with groups, and their influence on the beliefs and behaviour of group members. What we do mean by a group? According to Brown (2000a, p. 3):

> *A group exists when two or more people define themselves as members of it and when its existence is recognised by at least one other [person or group].*

There are many kinds of group processes. These include conformity pressures, group cohesiveness, and group norms. The performance of groups often differs from that of individuals. Within groups, we need to consider the role of the leader, who is the person having the most influence on the group members. Finally, social or group influence influences the behaviour of individuals in crowds and mobs.

As you read this chapter, think about the individuals and groups you encounter every day. Do some of these individuals and groups have more influence than others over your behaviour? Why do you think this is the case? As we will see, one of the key findings in this area is that our behaviour is generally influenced much more by other people than we like to think.

## OBEDIENCE TO AUTHORITY

In nearly all societies, some people are given power and authority over others. In our society, for example, parents, teachers, and managers have varying degrees of authority. This does not cause any problems most of the time. If the doctor tells us to take some tablets three times a day, most of us accept that he/she is the expert and do as requested.

How far are most people willing to go in their obedience to authority? What happens if you are asked by a person in authority to do something you think is wrong? One of the lessons of history is that many people are willing to behave in ways totally inconsistent with moral principles when ordered to do so. For example, Adolf Eichmann was found guilty of ordering the deaths of millions of Jews during the Second World War. He denied any moral responsibility, claiming he had simply been carrying out other people's orders. The best-known research on obedience to authority was carried out by Stanley Milgram (1963, 1974), and is discussed in the Key Study on the next page.

**KEY TERM**

**Social influence:** the use of social power to produce changes in the attitudes or behaviour of others.

719

# Milgram: Obedience to authority

Milgram (1963, 1974) reported the findings from several studies carried out at Yale University. Pairs of participants were given the roles of teacher and learner for a simple learning test. In fact, the "learner" was always a confederate employed by Milgram to behave in certain ways. The "teacher" was told to give electric shocks to the "learner" every time the wrong answer was given, and to increase the shock intensity each time even though the learner had a heart condition. The apparatus was actually arranged so that the learner received no shocks, but the teacher did not know that. At 180 volts, the learner yelled, "I can't stand the pain", and by 270 volts the response had become an agonised scream. The maximum intensity of shocks was 450 volts, which was potentially fatal. If the teacher was unwilling to give the shocks, the experimenter urged him/her to continue.

Do you think you would have been willing to give the maximum (and potentially deadly) 450-volt shock? Milgram found that everyone he asked denied they personally would do any such thing. He also found that every single one out of 110 experts on human behaviour (e.g., psychiatrists) predicted that no-one would go on to the 450-volt stage. In fact, about 65% of Milgram's participants (there was no gender difference) gave the maximum shock using his standard procedure, which is hugely different from expert predictions!

One of the most striking cases of total obedience was that of Pasqual Gino, a 43-year-old water inspector. Towards the end of the experiment, he found himself thinking, "Good God, he's dead. Well, here we go, we'll finish him. And I just continued all the way through to 450 volts."

Milgram (e.g., 1974) carried out several variations on his basic experiment. He found two main ways in which obedience to authority could be reduced:

1. Increasing the obviousness of the learner's plight.
2. Reducing the authority or influence of the experimenter.

The impact of the first factor was studied by comparing obedience in four situations, differing in the extent to which the learner was made aware of the suffering he/she was inflicting (the percentage of totally obedient participants is shown in brackets):

* Touch-proximity. The participant had to force the learner's hand onto the shock plate (30%).
* Proximity. The learner was 1 metre away from the participant (40%).
* Voice feedback. The victim could be heard but not seen (62%).
* Remote feedback. The victim could not be heard or seen (66%).

*What criticisms have been levelled at Milgram's research, and do you think they are justified?*

Milgram (1974) reduced the authority of the experimenter by staging an experiment in a run-down office building rather than at Yale University. The percentage of totally obedient participants decreased from 65% at Yale University to 48% in the run-down office building. The experimenter's influence was reduced by having him give his orders by telephone rather than having him sitting close to the participant. This reduced obedience from 65% to 20.5%. This effect of distance may help to explain why it is less stressful to kill people by dropping bombs from a plane than by shooting them at close range. Finally, the authority of the experimenter was reduced by having him being apparently an ordinary member of the public rather than a white-coated scientist. This reduced the level of total obedience to 20%.

In a further study, Milgram (1974) made use of three teachers, two of whom were confederates working for the experimenter. In one condition, the two confederates were rebellious and refused to give severe shocks. In this situation, only 10% of the participants were fully obedient. The fact that two other people were willing to disobey the experimenter greatly reduced the influence of the experimenter over the participants. Finally, when two experimenters gave conflicting orders (one telling the teacher to continue and the other telling him/her to stop), not a single participant was fully obedient.

## Discussion points

1. Do most people simply obey authority in a rather mindless way?
2. What are the main factors determining whether or not there is obedience to authority?

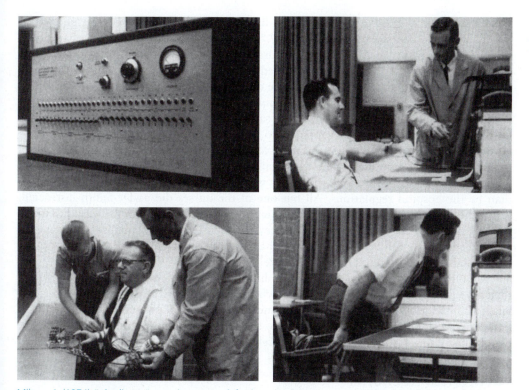

*How might society benefit if people were less obedient to authority?*

Milgram's (1974) "obedience" experiment. Top left: the "shock box"; top right: the experimenter demonstrating the shock box to the "teacher"; bottom left: wiring the "learner" up to the apparatus; bottom right: one of the "teachers" refusing to continue with the experiment.

## Evidence

Milgram's studies were carried out in the United States during the 1960s and 1970s, and it is important to know whether similar findings would be obtained in other cultures and at other times. The relevant cross-cultural evidence was discussed by Bond and Smith (1996). Unfortunately, key aspects of the procedure varied across cultures, making it hard to interpret the findings. However, the percentage of totally obedient participants was very high in several countries. It was 80% or higher in Italy, Spain, Germany, Austria, and Holland, in many cases several years after Milgram's studies. Thus, there was substantial obedience to authority in numerous cultures and over a period of several decades. However, nearly all the studies on obedience to authority have been carried out in advanced industrial countries, and it is unclear what would happen in non-industrialised countries.

The fact that about one-third of the participants failed to show complete obedience to authority in the Milgram studies suggests there may be important individual differences. However, it is unclear why some people are more obedient than others. According to van Avermaet (2001, p. 438):

> *In the Milgram situation, personality characteristics do not make a lot of difference: his analyses revealed only minor differences between men and women, between people holding different professions, or between those scoring differently on personality inventories.*

A rare exception to the generally non-significant findings was reported by Milgram (1974). Participants showing signs of independent behaviour tended to have low scores on the F (Fascism) Scale, which is a measure of authoritarian attitudes (see Chapter 21).

Milgram's research was carried out in a laboratory, and it would be useful to study obedience to authority in more realistic situations. Hofling, Brotzman, Dalrymple,

| Reducing obedience to authority was achieved by: | |
| --- | --- |
| **increasing the obviousness of the learner's plight …** | **reducing the authority or influence of the experimenter …** |
| | at Yale University    65% |
| victim not seen or heard    66% | at a run-down office    48% |
| | with experimenter sitting next to participant    65% |
| victim not seen but heard    62% | |
| | with experimenter giving orders via telephone    20.5% |
| victim one metre away    40% | |
| | with confederates of experimenter refusing to give shocks    10% |
| victim's hand placed on shock plate    30% | |

Graves, and Pierce (1966) carried out a real-life study in which 22 nurses were phoned up by someone who claimed to be "Dr Smith". The nurses were asked to check that a drug called Astroten was available. When the nurses did this, they saw on the bottle that the maximum dosage of this drug was supposed to be 10 mg. When they reported back to Dr Smith, he told them to give 20 mg of the drug to a patient.

There were two good reasons why the nurses should have refused to do as instructed. First, the dose was double the maximum safe dose. Second, the nurses did not know Dr Smith, and they were only supposed to take instructions from doctors they knew. However, the nurses' training had led them to obey instructions from doctors. There is a clear power structure in medical settings, with doctors in a more powerful position than nurses. As you probably guessed, the nurses were more influenced by the power structure than by the hospital regulations. All but one of the nurses did as Dr Smith instructed. When the nurses were asked what other nurses would have done in the circumstances, they all predicted they would not have obeyed the instructions. Thus, the pressures to show obedience to authority were greater than the nurses imagined.

Similar findings were reported more recently by Lesar, Briceland, and Stein (1997) in a study on medication errors in American hospitals. Their key finding was that nurses typically carried out doctors' orders even when they had good reasons for doubting the wisdom of those orders. However, Rank and Jacobsen (1977) found that only 11% of nurses obeyed a doctor's instruction to give too high a drug dose to patients when they had the chance to talk to other nurses beforehand.

*To what extent has Milgram's research demonstrated that obedience to authority is more dependent on situational factors than personality factors?*

## Theoretical accounts

Why were so many people obedient in the Milgram situation? Milgram (1974) argued that there are three main reasons:

1. Our experience has taught us that authorities are generally trustworthy and legitimate, and so obedience to authority is often appropriate. For example, it could be disastrous if those involved in carrying out an emergency operation refused to obey the orders of the surgeon in charge!
2. The orders given by the experimenter moved gradually from the reasonable to the unreasonable, and it was hard for the participants to notice when they began to be asked to behave unreasonably.
3. The participants were put into an "agentic" state, in which they became the instruments of an authority figure, and ceased to act according to their consciences. The attitude of those in the agentic state is as follows: "I am not responsible, because I was ordered to do it!" According to Milgram (1974), this tendency to adopt the agentic state, "is the fatal flaw nature has designed into us, and which in the long run gives our species only a modest chance for survival."

Milgram (1974) was probably too pessimistic. Most obedient participants experienced a strong conflict between the experimenter's demands and their own conscience. They seemed very tense and nervous, they perspired, they bit their lips, and they clenched and unclenched their fists. Such behaviour does *not* suggest they were in an agentic state.

Milgram and others have argued that there are links between his findings and the horrors of Nazi Germany. However, we must not exaggerate the similarities. In the first place, the values underlying Milgram's studies were the positive ones of understanding more about human learning and memory, in contrast to the values in Nazi Germany. Second, most participants in Milgram's studies had to be watched closely to ensure their obedience, which was not necessary in Nazi Germany. Third, most of Milgram's participants were in a state of great conflict and agitation. In contrast, those who carried out the atrocities in Nazi Germany often seemed unconcerned about moral issues.

Why was the actual behaviour of the participants in Milgram's studies so different from what most people would have expected? Part of the answer lies in the **fundamental attribution error** (see Chapter 18), which is the tendency to *under-estimate* the role of situational factors in determining the behaviour of others and to *over-estimate* the role of personal characteristics. When asked to decide how many people would show total

**KEY TERM**
**Fundamental attribution error:** the tendency to exaggerate the importance of other people's personality and other characteristics in determining their behaviour.

Unquestioning obedience to authority may have catastrophic consequences. The pictures show members of the Nazi Party (left) marching through Nuremberg during the Nazi Party congress in 1935, and (right) survivors of the Auschwitz concentration camp at the end of the war in 1945, following a decade of persecution, imprisonment, and genocide.

---

### CASE STUDY: *The My Lai massacre*

The My Lai massacre has become known as one of the most controversial incidents in the Vietnam War. On 14 December 1969 almost 400 Vietnamese villagers were killed in under 4 hours. The following transcript is from a CBS News interview with a soldier who took part in the massacre.

**Q.** How many people did you round up?
**A.** Well, there was about forty, fifty people that we gathered in the center of the village. And we placed them in there, and it was like a little island, right there in the center of the village, I'd say ... And ...
**Q.** What kind of people—men, women, children?
**A.** Men, women, children.
**Q.** Babies?
**A.** Babies. And we huddled them up. We made them squat down and Lieutenant Calley came over and said, "You know what to do with them, don't you?" And I said yes. So I took it for granted that he just wanted us to watch them. And he left, and came back about ten or fifteen minutes later and said, "How come you ain't killed them yet?" And I told him that I didn't think you wanted us to to kill them, that you just wanted us to guard them. He said, "No. I want them dead." So—

**Q.** He told this to all of you, or to you particularly?
**A.** Well, I was facing him. So, but the other three, four guys heard it and so he stepped back about ten, fifteen feet, and he started shooting them. And he told me to start shooting. So I started shooting, I poured about four clips into the group.
**Q.** You fired four clips from your ...
**A.** M-16.
**Q.** And that's about how many clips—I mean, how many—
**A.** I carried seventeen rounds to each clip.
**Q.** So you fired something like sixty-seven shots?
**A.** Right.
**Q.** And you killed how many? At that time?
**A.** Well, I fired them automatic, so you can't—You just spray the area on them and so you can't know how many you killed 'cause they were going fast. So I might have killed ten or fifteen of them.
**Q.** Men, women and children?
**A.** Men, women and children.
**Q.** And babies?
**A.** And babies.

---

obedience in Milgram's situation, we tend to think as follows: "Only a psychopath would give massive electric shocks to another person. There are very few psychopaths about, and so only a tiny percentage of people would be totally obedient." This line of reasoning focuses exclusively on the individual participant's characteristics. In contrast, the participants in Milgram's studies were influenced by situational factors such as the insistence of the experimenter that the participant continue to give shocks, the scientific expertise of the experimenter, and so on.

## Evaluation

⊕ A high level of obedience to authority has been found in several cultures over a long period of time.
⊕ Milgram's findings are regarded as being among the most unexpected in the history of psychology.

- ⊕ Milgram's findings are of direct relevance to many everyday situations (e.g., doctor and nurse, teacher and student).
- ⊖ It is not entirely clear how to explain the findings, and there are limitations in Milgram's notion of an agentic state.
- ⊖ The findings are less dramatic than is commonly assumed. As Jones (1998, p. 32) argued, "The degree of compliance [in the Milgram studies] could be readily understood once the extremely active role of the experimenter was fully detailed, something that was not at all clear in the earlier experimenter reports."
- ⊖ There are major ethical problems with Milgram's research. First, the participants did not give their informed consent. Second, they were not free to leave the experiment if they wanted to do so (the experimenter urged them to continue if they wanted to stop). Third, the participants were subjected to considerable conflict and distress. In spite of these serious problems, 84% of participants in Milgram's research reported they were glad to have taken part (Milgram, 1974).

> **KEY TERMS**
> **Conformity:** yielding publicly to group pressures.
> **Autokinetic effect:** the illusion that a stationary light in a dark room is moving about.

---

**Differences between obedience and conformity**

| OBEDIENCE | CONFORMITY |
|---|---|
| Occurs within a hierarchy. Actor feels the person above has the right to prescribe behaviour. Links one status to another. Emphasis is on power. | Regulates the behaviour among those of equal status. Emphasis is on acceptance. |
| Behaviour adopted differs from behaviour of authority figure. | Behaviour adopted is similar to that of peers. |
| Prescription for action is explicit. | Requirement of going along with the group is often implicit. |
| Participants embrace obedience as an explanation for their behaviour. | Participants deny conformity as an explanation for their behaviour. |

# CONFORMITY

**Conformity** can be defined as yielding to group pressures, something which nearly all of us do some of the time. Suppose, for example, you go with friends to see a film. You didn't think the film was very good, but all your friends thought it was absolutely brilliant. You might be tempted to conform by pretending to agree with their verdict on the film rather than being the odd one out.

Research on conformity differs in three ways from research on obedience. First, the participants can decide what to do rather than being ordered to behave in certain ways. Second, the participant is typically of equal status to the group members trying to influence him/her, whereas he/she is usually of lower status than the person issuing the orders in studies of obedience. Third, participants' behaviour in conformity studies is influenced mostly by the need for acceptance, whereas obedience is determined by social power.

## Is conformity undesirable?

As you read about the work on conformity, you may think that conformity to group pressures is undesirable. There are certainly cases in which that is true. For example, consider the case of Rodney King. He was a black man assaulted by four Los Angeles police officers. The assault was videotaped by a local resident, and shown in court to the jurors. The videotape seemed to show that Rodney King was a victim of police brutality, but the police officers were acquitted. Afterwards, one of the jurors, Virginia Loya, admitted that she had changed her vote from guilty to not guilty, because she felt under pressure to conform to the views of the other jury members. She did this while remaining unconvinced of their views. In her own words: "The tape was the big evidence to me. They [fellow jurors] couldn't see. To me, they were people who were blind and couldn't get their glasses clean."

However, conformity is *not* always undesirable. For example, suppose that all of your friends who are studying psychology have the same view on a topic in psychology, but it differs from your own. If they know more about the topic than you do, then you might be well advised to conform to their views rather than sticking to your own!

## Sherif

The first major study on conformity was carried out by Muzafer Sherif (1936), making use of the **autokinetic effect**. If we look at a stationary spot of light in a darkened room,

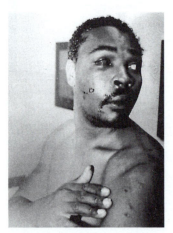

Group decisions can lead people to deny the evidence in front of their eyes. The picture shows Rodney King, victim of a videotaped beating by Los Angeles police officers in 1992. The four police officers involved were indicted a few weeks later.

very small movements of our eyes make the light appear to move. In Sherif's key condition, the participants were first of all tested one at a time, and then in small groups of three. They were asked to say how much the light seemed to move, and in what direction. Each participant rapidly developed his/her personal norm. When three individuals with very different personal norms were then put together into a group, they tended to make very similar judgements. The fact that a group norm rapidly replaced the personal norms of the group members indicates the existence of conformity.

Sherif (1936) also used a condition in which individuals started the experiment in groups of three, and were then tested on their own. Once again, a group norm tended to develop within the group. When the group members were then tested on their own, their judgements concerning the movement of the light continued to reflect group influence.

*Why do people prefer to explain their actions in terms of obeying orders rather than conforming to the group norm?*

## Evaluation

- Sherif (1936) used a very artificial situation, and it is not clear how relevant his findings are for everyday life.
- There was no "correct" answer in Sherif's situation. It is unsurprising that people rely on the judgements of others when they have no clear way of deciding what judgements to make.
- Conformity effects can be assessed more directly by arranging for all but one of the participants to give the same judgements, and then seeing what effect this has on the only genuine participant. This was done by Jacobs and Campbell (1961) using the autokinetic effect, and they found strong evidence of conformity.

## Asch-type conformity studies

Solomon Asch (1951, 1956) improved on the work of Sherif in his extremely influential research on conformity— see the Key Study on the next page.

It is sometimes argued that Asch only found strong conformity effects because he used a trivial task of no real importance to the participants. The issue of task importance was addressed by Baron, VanDello, and Brunsman (1996). The participants were given an eyewitness accuracy task, which was described as a pilot study (low importance) or as a way of establishing norms for a test to be used by the police (high importance). When the task was easy, there was less conformity with high-importance instructions than low-importance ones (see the diagram on the right). However, high-importance instructions led to *more* conformity than low-importance ones when the task was difficult. Thus, strong conformity effects can be found on important tasks provided that the participants do not have full confidence in their own beliefs.

Asch's studies on conformity are among the most famous in the whole of social psychology. However, there was nothing very social about them because Asch used groups of strangers! Suppose we introduced more social factors by making the participants perceive the other members of the group as belonging to one of their ingroups or to an outgroup. This was accomplished by Abrams, Wetherell, Cochrane, Hogg, and Turner (1990), who used first-year students of introductory psychology as participants. The confederates were introduced as first-year

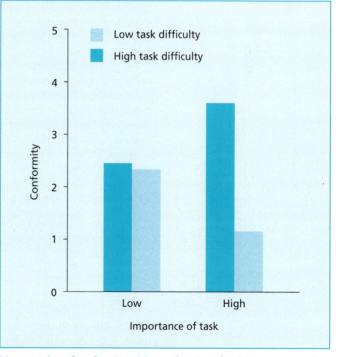

Mean number of conforming trials as a function of task importance and task difficulty (data from Baron et al., 1996).

# Asch: Conformity and group pressure

Asch (1951) set up a situation in which usually about seven people all sat looking at a display. They were given the task of saying out loud which one of three lines (A, B, or C) was the same length as a given stimulus line, with the experimenter working his way around the group members in turn. All but one of the participants were confederates of the experimenter, and had been told to give the same wrong answer on some of the trials. The one genuine participant was the last (or the last but one) to offer his/her opinion on each trial. The performance of participants exposed to such group pressure was compared to performance in a control condition with no confederates.

Asch's findings were dramatic. On the crucial trials on which the confederates all gave the same wrong answer, the genuine participants also gave the wrong answer on between 33% and 37% of these trials in different studies. This figure should be compared against an error rate of under 1% in the control condition. Thus, the correct answers were obvious, and it might have been expected that nearly all the participants would have given them. However, only about 25% of the participants exposed to the wrong judgements of the confederates avoided error during the course of the study, compared to 95% in the control condition.

Asch (1956) manipulated various aspects of the situation to understand more fully the factors underlying conformity behaviour. The conformity effect increased as the number of confederates went up from one to three, but there was no increase between three and sixteen confederates. However, a small increase in conformity as the number of confederates goes up above three has sometimes been found (see van Avermaet, 2001).

Another important factor is whether the genuine participant has a supporter in the form of a confederate giving the correct answer on all trials, and who gives his or her answer ahead of the genuine participant. Asch (1956) found that the presence of such a supporter reduced conformity to only 5% of the trials. More surprisingly, a confederate whose answers were even more incorrect than those of the other confederate also produced a substantial reduction in conformity. Thus, any kind of disagreement among other group members was sufficient to reduce conformity.

Asch's work raises ethical issues. His participants did not provide fully informed consent, because they were misled about key aspects of the experimental procedures (e.g., presence of confederates). In addition, they were put in a difficult and embarrassing position. Evidence that participants in Asch-type situations are highly emotional was obtained by Bogdonoff, Klein, Shaw, and Back (1961), who found that participants in the Asch situation had greatly increased levels of autonomic arousal. This finding also suggests that the participants were in a conflict situation, finding it hard to decide whether to report what they saw or to conform to the opinions of others.

## KEY STUDY EVALUATION—Asch

Asch is renowned for his work on conformity. In a situation where the correct answer was obvious people would agree with an incorrect answer on about 35% of trials. Only 25% of Asch's participants gave the correct answer on all the trials despite the incorrect answers of their fellow participants. The remaining 75% showed at least some tendency to conform to the confederates' views. More people conformed to the views of the confederate participants than gave a correct answer. However, the study took place in America in the 1950s before "doing your own thing" came to be regarded as socially acceptable. Also, Asch's participants were put in a difficult and embarrassing position, which may have led to greater levels of conformity due to the particular culture prevailing at the time. When participants had a supporter present, who gave the correct answer before the participant responded, conformity to the incorrect response dropped dramatically to 5% of trials. This suggests that social pressure and the feeling of being in a conflict situation may have been a major factor in the unexpectedly high level of conformity in the original study.

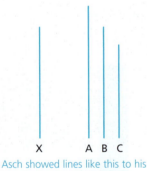

Asch showed lines like this to his participants. Which line do you think is the closest in height to line X? A, B, or C? Why do you think over 30% of participants answered A?

## Discussion points

1. Do Asch's findings apply outside the artificial situation he used in his studies?
2. Asch carried out his research in the United States. Why might the findings be different in other cultures?

students of psychology from a nearby university (ingroup) or as students of ancient history from the same university (outgroup). You would probably predict that the participants would be more influenced by the ingroup than by the outgroup. However, the size of the effect was dramatic: There was conformity on 58% of trials when the other group members belonged to an ingroup, but the figure dropped to only 8% when they belonged to an outgroup. Thus, conformity depends to a very large extent on the individual's perception of other group members as an ingroup or an outgroup.

In similar fashion, Abrams et al. (1990) suggested that Sherif's (1936) findings (discussed earlier) may have depended on the fact that his participants felt they belonged to a group. Accordingly, Abrams et al. carried out a study similar to those of Sherif with groups consisting of three genuine participants and three confederates. The confederates initially produced estimates of the amount of movement of the light 5 cm greater than those of the genuine participants. In the crucial condition, the genuine participants were made to feel they belonged to a different group to the confederates (they were given a different label and engaged in a prior task together). The key finding was as follows: "The impact of confederates on the formation of a norm decreases as their membership of a different category is made more salient [obvious] to subjects" (p. 97).

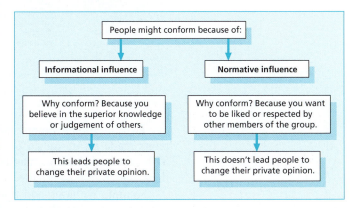

Deutsch and Gerard (1955) argued that people might conform in Asch-type studies because of informational influence or because of normative influence. **Informational influence** occurs when an individual conforms because of the superior knowledge or judgement of others. In contrast, **normative influence** occurs when an individual conforms because he/she wants to be liked or respected by other group members. This latter type of influence is probably of crucial importance in producing conformity effects.

Evidence of informational influence was obtained by Allen and Levine (1971). In one condition, the genuine participant had a single supporter who always gave the correct answer. When the informational value of the supporter's judgements was low because he had very poor vision, there was a much smaller reduction in conformity than when the supporter had normal vision.

Deutsch and Gerard (1955) reported evidence of the importance of normative influence. They increased the interdependence of group members by promising them all a reward in the form of tickets to a Broadway play if they made very few errors. This manipulation produced twice as much conformity as was found when no reward was offered for good group performance.

Abrams et al. (1990) argued that the distinction between informational and normative influence is of little value. According to them, *all* forms of effective influence within the Asch situation depend on other group members being regarded as members of the ingroup: "The basis of conformity is subjective uncertainty, and this uncertainty arises from comparison with in-group members" (p. 108). As we saw earlier, their findings provided strong support for this viewpoint.

## Cross-cultural studies

A possible limitation of Asch's research is that it was carried out in the United States in the late 1940s and early 1950s. Americans may differ from other people, and it is possible that people were more willing to conform in the days before it became fashionable to "do your own thing". Thus, the high levels of conformity found by Asch might reflect the particular culture in the United States shortly after the Second World War.

Perrin and Spencer (1980) tried to repeat Asch's study in England in the late 1970s. They found very little evidence of conformity, leading them to conclude that the Asch effect was "a child of its time". However, they used engineering students who had received training in accurate measurement. Smith and Bond (1998) considered numerous studies using Asch's task in the United States. They concluded that there had been a steady decline in conformity since the early 1950s.

There have been over 20 other cross-cultural studies of conformity using Asch's experimental design, the findings from which were summarised by Smith and Bond (1998). The participants gave the wrong answer on average on 31.2% of the trials across these studies, which is slightly lower than the figure reported by Asch. The highest figure was 58% wrong answers for Indian teachers in Fiji, and the lowest figure (apart from Perrin & Spencer, 1980) was 14% among Belgian students.

Smith and Bond (1998) concluded that conformity has declined since the 1950s when Asch carried out his studies.

**Key Terms**

**Informational influence:** this occurs when someone conforms because others in the group possess more knowledge.

**Normative influence:** this occurs when someone conforms so that others in the group will like or respect him/her.

*To what extent do you agree that Asch's research was "a child of its time"?*

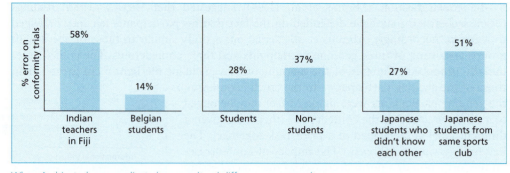

When Asch's study was replicated cross-cultural differences emerged.

Two additional points emerge from these conformity studies. First, student participants made errors on 26% of conformity trials, whereas non-students made errors on 37% of trials. Students may be more independent in their thinking than non-students, or their higher level of intelligence may make them more confident in their opinions.

Second, Williams and Sogon (1984) found that Japanese students made errors on 27% of trials when they did not know any of the other group members, but this increased to 51% when the group members all belonged to the same sports club. Thus, conformity can be much greater if we like and respect other group members. Asch's (1951, 1956) studies were limited because the students were mostly strangers to each other.

Are there differences between individualist and collectivist cultures (see Chapter 1)? Individualistic societies (e.g., Britain, the United States) emphasise the desirability of individuals being responsible for their own well-being and having a sense of personal identity. In contrast, collectivist cultures (e.g., China) emphasise group needs over those of individuals, and they also stress a sense of group identity. Smith and Bond (1998) analysed over 100 Asch-type studies in several countries. Conformity was greater among participants from collectivistic cultures in Asia, Africa, and elsewhere (37.1% of trials) than among participants from individualistic cultures in North America and Europe (25.3%). These findings can be explained in terms of the greater sense of personal responsibility in individualistic cultures.

Additional support for Bond and Smith's conclusions was reported by Kim and Markus (1999). They considered numerous magazine advertisements in an individualistic culture (the United States) and a collectivistic culture (Korea), arguing that advertisements reflect the beliefs and values of any given culture. They found that Korean advertisements emphasised conformity more than uniqueness, whereas the opposite was true for American advertisements (see the diagram on the left).

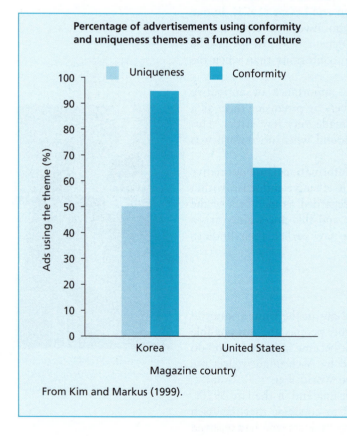

**Percentage of advertisements using conformity and uniqueness themes as a function of culture**

From Kim and Markus (1999).

## Evaluation

➕ Asch's findings have been very influential, because he found much conformity even in an unambiguous situation in which the correct answer was obvious.

➕ Asch identified key factors (e.g., number of confederates, presence vs. absence of a supporter) determining the amount of conformity observed.

➕ Asch's findings have been replicated in several countries and many years after his original research.

- Asch only considered conformity in a trivial situation, in which the participants' deeply held beliefs were not called into question. However, conformity effects are sometimes found with important tasks (Baron et al., 1996).
- Asch's situation was limited, in that he only assessed conformity among strangers. In fact, conformity effects can be much greater among friends (Williams & Sogon, 1984) or among those identified as members of an ingroup (Abrams et al., 1990).
- Asch did not really explain exactly *why* there are conformity effects, because he did not identify the underlying psychological processes.

## Minority influences on majorities

*Who are the great people of history who have managed to change the dominant world view?*

Asch was concerned with the influence of the majority on a minority (typically of one) within a group. However, social influences operate in both directions: Majorities influence minorities, but in turn minorities exert influence on majorities. The most developed theory in this area is that of Moscovici (1976, 1980), and so we will consider his approach.

What happens when a minority influences a majority? According to Moscovici's dual-process theory, disagreements from a minority of group members can cause the members of the majority to engage in a validation process in which they focus on the information contained in the arguments proposed by the minority. This often leads to **conversion**, in which there is more private than public influence, i.e., more effect on private beliefs than on public behaviour. This private influence can be subtle and indirect. It is difficult for a minority to influence the majority, and Moscovici (1980) argued that this happens most often when the members of the minority put forward a clear position, and maintain it consistently.

What happens when a majority influences a minority? Moscovici (1980) argued that members of the minority are subject to a comparison process, in which they focus on the differences between their views and those of the majority. This triggers the need for consensus, and often lead to **compliance**, in which there is public rather than private influence. Thus, there is a greater effect on public behaviour than on private beliefs. Compliance often occurs fairly rapidly and without much thought, whereas conversion is more time-consuming and occurs only after cognitive conflict and detailed thought.

An important real-life example of a minority influencing a majority was the suffragette movement in the early years of the 20th century. A relatively small group of suffragettes argued strongly for the initially unpopular view that women should be allowed to vote. The hard work of the suffragettes, combined with the justice of their case, finally led the majority to accept their point of view.

### Evidence

Moscovici, Lage, and Naffrenchoux (1969) found that minorities need to be consistent to influence majority judgements. Groups of six participants were presented with blue slides varying in intensity, and each individual had to say a simple colour. Two confederates of the experimenter said "Green" on every trial or on two-thirds of the trials. The percentage of "Green" responses given by the majority was 8% when the minority responded consistently. However, it was only 1% when the minority responded inconsistently.

Moscovici and Personnaz (1980, 1986) used the same basic method as Moscovici et al. (1969). Individual participants were exposed to a single confederate, who always said that obviously blue slides were green. The participants were told that most people (82%) would respond like the confederate, or that only a few people (18%) would do so. The participants called out the colour of each slide, and then wrote down privately the colour of the after-image. The participants did not know this, but the after-image is always the complementary colour (e.g., yellow when something blue has been presented). The after-image was reported as yellow when the participants were on their own or exposed to majority influence. The key finding was that the after-image shifted towards purple when the participants were exposed to minority influence, suggesting that they had "seen" a green slide. Thus, minority influence produced a subtle private effect. However, there have been several failures to replicate these findings (Hogg & Vaughan, 2002). Martin (1998) found that shifts in the after-image occurred mainly when participants attended closely to the blue slides. Thus, the findings of Moscovici and Personnaz (1980, 1986) may reflect attentional processes rather than minority influence *per se*.

Nemeth, Mayseless, Sherman, and Brown (1990) found that minorities can make group members engage in more thorough processing than majorities, as predicted by Moscovici's dual-process theory. The participants listened to word lists, and a majority or a minority consistently drew attention to words belonging to certain categories. There was then a recall test for the words presented. The words to which attention was drawn were much better recalled when a minority had drawn attention to them, presumably because they had been processed more systematically.

Wood, Lundgren, Ouellette, Busceme, and Blackstone (1994) reported various meta-analyses of studies testing Moscovici's theory. They identified three conformity effects:

1. *Public influence*, in which the individual's behaviour in front of the group is influenced by the views of others.
2. *Direct private influence*, in which there is a change in the individual's private opinions about the issue discussed by the group.
3. *Indirect private influence*, in which the individual's private opinions about related issues change.

As expected on Moscovici's theory, majorities in most studies had more public influence than minorities. In addition, minorities had more indirect private influence than majorities, especially when their opinions were consistent. However, majorities had more direct private influence than minorities. Wood et al. (1994, p. 335) concluded that their review, "provides clear evidence of the unique pattern of minority influence, distinct from the influence of majority sources".

David and Turner (1999) argued that minority influence will *only* be found when the minority is perceived as part of the ingroup rather than the outgroup. The participants were moderate feminists exposed to the minority views of extreme feminists. The participants were influenced by the minority when their fellow participants were said to be mostly anti-feminists, but not when they were said to be moderate feminists. Why was this? The extreme feminists were more likely to be perceived as part of the ingroup (feminists vs. non-feminists) when most of the participants were identified as anti-feminists. In contrast, the extreme feminists were relegated to an outgroup when most of the participants were identified as moderate feminists.

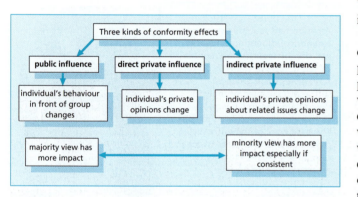

*What strategies can a minority group use to try to change the majority opinion?*

## Evaluation

● Minorities often influence majorities.
● The influence of minorities on majorities is mainly in the form of private agreement rather than public agreement, with the opposite pattern being found when majorities influence minorities.
● Moscovici probably exaggerated the differences between the ways in which majorities and minorities exert influence. As Smith and Mackie (2000, p. 371) concluded, "By and large, majorities and minorities achieve influence by pulling the same levers."
● The common finding that minorities are less influential than majorities on direct private measures is not easily explained by dual-process theory.
● Majorities typically differ from minorities in several ways (e.g., power, status). Any differences in the social influence exerted by majorities and minorities may depend on power or status rather than solely on their majority or minority position within the group (van Avermaet, 2001).

● Moscovici may have found strong evidence for minority influence because he used a fairly trivial task (e.g., colour naming). Minority influence is less with real social minorities and majorities dealing with important issues (Hogg & Vaughan, 2002).

# BASIC GROUP CHARACTERISTICS

Groups come in all kinds of shapes and sizes, and their goals can vary enormously (e.g., build a bridge, climb mountains, have fun). However, virtually all groups share certain key features. For example, every group has a level of cohesiveness that can vary between very low and very high, and its level of cohesion has various consequences for its functioning. Every group also possesses norms, which indicate the kinds of behaviour regarded as acceptable or desirable. Group members need to abide by most of these norms to be fully accepted by the other group members.

*Why do you belong to the groups that you do?*

Finally, there are systematic changes in the relationship between individuals and the group. For example, the individual's commitment to the group increases as he/she moves towards full membership of the group, but then decreases again as he/she experiences growing dissatisfaction with the group.

The three factors of group cohesiveness, social norms, and dynamic changes over time are all discussed below. Other features of groups are also mentioned from time to time.

## Group cohesiveness

As Brown (2000a) pointed out, the notion of group cohesiveness has been defined in various ways. It has been common to equate cohesiveness with the extent to which individual group members like each other (interpersonal attraction). However, this is limited, because it excludes group cohesiveness as it manifests itself within very large groups (e.g., a football crowd). It is preferable to define **group cohesiveness** in terms of "group members' attraction to the *idea* of the group, its consensual prototypical [ideal example] image and how that is reflected in typical member characteristics and behaviour" (p. 46).

Hogg and Hardie (1991) showed that the two meanings of group cohesiveness are quite different in a study on an Australian football team. Individuals' levels of cohesiveness in the sense of attraction to the team as a whole was related to group norms. However, cohesiveness in this sense was *not* related to measures of interpersonal attraction towards other team members.

What are the consequences of group cohesiveness? It has often been argued that the main consequence is that groups with high cohesiveness will perform better than those with low cohesion. Evidence relating to that prediction is discussed below.

Conforming to group norms is a part of group membership. At a football game, supporters are conforming to prescribed norms such as wearing certain clothes and singing certain songs.

## *Evidence*

Mullen and Copper (1994) carried out a meta-analysis of 49 studies. Overall, the average correlation between group cohesiveness and group performance was only about +.25, suggesting that group cohesiveness is not of great importance in determining performance. However, this was only an average figure. Mullen and Copper found that the association between cohesiveness and performance was greater in some types of groups (e.g., sports teams) than in others (e.g., laboratory groups). In addition, cohesiveness based on interpersonal attraction was more weakly related to group performance than was cohesiveness based on commitment to the task being performed by the group.

**KEY TERM**

**Group cohesiveness:** the extent to which the members of a group are attracted to the idea of the group.

Group cohesiveness seems to matter less in determining group performance than might have been imagined. Another finding reported by Mullen and Copper (1994) suggests that the effects of group cohesiveness may be even less than has been implied so far. The correlational evidence discussed above does not allow us to decide whether cohesiveness helps to determine performance, or whether performance helps to determine cohesiveness. In general, the evidence indicates that there are stronger effects of performance on cohesiveness than of cohesiveness on performance.

One reason for the variable effects of cohesiveness on performance is that cohesive groups typically have clearer and stronger norms than non-cohesive groups. Why does this produce variable effects? Seashore (1954) found that work performance was related to group norms. When there was a supportive management style, groups of workers typically set high-performance norms and had high productivity. However, when there was a hostile management style, groups of workers generally set low-performance norms and had low productivity.

It is important to distinguish between the effects of group cohesiveness on performance and on satisfaction. As Spector (2000, p. 277) pointed out, "Group cohesiveness … is related to job satisfaction within the group. Members of highly cohesive groups tend to be more satisfied than members of minimally cohesive groups." One reason may be because more social support is available in cohesive groups. This could help to explain the finding that members of cohesive groups cope better with stress than members of non-cohesive groups (Bowers, Weaver, & Morgan, 1996).

## Social norms

What do we mean by social norms? According to Smith and Mackie (2000, p. 594), **social norms** are "generally accepted ways of thinking, feeling, or behaving that people in a group agree and endorse as right and proper". Cialdini and Trost (1998) distinguished between descriptive norms, injunctive norms, and subjective norms. Descriptive norms "are derived from what other people *do* in any given situation. Watching others provides information about what is 'normal' in a novel or ambiguous situation" (p. 155). Injunctive norms "specify what 'should' be done and therefore the moral rules of the group. Injunctive norms motivate behaviour by promising social rewards or punishments for it" (p. 157). An individual's subjective norms consist of the injunctive norms held by people who are important to him/her to which he/she is willing to agree.

Several purposes are served by social norms. First, they can provide guidance as to appropriate behaviour, especially in ambiguous situations. Second, most group norms are related to the goals of the group, and make it easier for the group to attain its goals. Third, norms help to maintain (or even enhance) group identity.

*Why are group norms thought to be beneficial?*

### Evidence

A classic study on norm formation was reported by Newcomb (1961). This study was carried out at Bennington College, a small private institution in the United States. In this college, there was a great contrast between its predominantly liberal political ethos, and the extremely conservative, upper-middle-class families from which most of the students came. There was a presidential election shortly after the first-year students had arrived at Bennington College. Most of these students favoured the conservative Republican candidate to the more liberal Democratic candidate Roosevelt (62% vs. 29%, respectively), and very few favoured Socialist or Communist candidates (9%). In contrast, 54% of third- and fourth-year students favoured Roosevelt and 28% chose Socialist or Communist candidates, compared to only 18% favouring the Republican candidate. Thus, over time the liberal norms of Bennington College became more important to the students than the conservative norms endorsed by their parents. Newcomb, Koenig, Flacks, and Warwick (1967) found that, 25 years after leaving Bennington College, the ex-students were still more liberal in their political views than other groups of similar age and social class.

Another classic study on social norms was carried out by Sherif and Sherif (1964), who investigated gangs of adolescent boys in several American cities. Many of these gangs

**KEY TERM**

**Social norms:** rules and standards that are generally accepted by the members of a group or culture, and which influence their behaviour.

had rigid norms concerning insignia (e.g., badges), and the type of clothing regarded as appropriate for gang members. Presumably there was this emphasis on clothing because it provided a very important way of distinguishing one gang from another. In addition, most gangs had norms about sexual behaviour and about how to interact with outsiders such as parents and the police. Ordinary gang members were required to adhere to numerous strict social norms, but the leaders of most gangs had somewhat more freedom to behave as they wished.

The impact of norms on performance was studied by Marks, Mirvis, Hackett, and Grady (1986). They compared groups of American machine operators who were (or were not) allowed to set norms for their own work group. The productivity of those setting group norms increased by more than 20% over 2 years, whereas that of those not setting norms rose by only 4%. In addition, absenteeism was much lower among workers setting their own work norms.

Crips gang members in LA. Gang identity may be maintained by rigid norms concerning type of clothing, sexual behaviour, and how to interact with outsiders.

Some norms have great effects on behaviour. For example, there is the norm of social reciprocity, according to which we should return favours (see Chapter 19). You may have discovered the power of this norm if you have ever failed to buy a round of drinks when it was your turn! The norm of social commitment (we should honour our commitments) also has powerful effects. Moriarty (1975) carried out a study on a New York beach in which a confederate working with the researcher apparently stole his radio. When nearby sunbathers had previously agreed to keep an eye on it, 95% of them tried to stop the "thief". In contrast, only 20% tried to intervene when there was no prior social commitment.

There are clear cross-cultural differences with respect to many norms. Shweder, Mahapatra, and Miller (1990) asked Indian and American children and adults to place 39 norm-breaking actions in order of perceived seriousness. There was very little agreement between inhabitants of the two countries. For example, in the opinion of Indian children, here are two of the most serious norm-breaking actions: "The day after his father's death, the eldest son had a haircut and ate chicken"; "A widow in your community eats fish two or three times a week".

Argyle, Henderson, Bond, Iizuka, and Contarello (1986) considered various social norms or rules in Britain, Italy, Hong Kong, and Japan. They concluded that in the East, "there are more rules [than in the West] about obedience, avoiding loss of face, maintaining harmonious relationships in groups, and restraining emotional expression".

*How might culture influence group norms?*

## Dynamic changes over time

A key characteristic of most groups (but often overlooked) is that they undergo dynamic changes over time as some people join the group whereas others leave. There are various ways of conceptualising these changes. For example, Tuckman (1965) identified five successive stages:

1. *Forming*, in which group members get to know each other.
2. *Storming*, involving a certain amount of conflict.
3. *Norming*, a stage in which cohesiveness and common norms emerge.
4. *Performing*, a stage involving efficient and relatively stress-free working.
5. *Adjourning*, in which the group comes to an end.

A very influential approach was proposed by Moreland and Levine (1982). Their emphasis was on **group socialisation**, which is concerned with the relationships between a group and the members of that group (see the diagram overleaf). There are three key features of the theory. First, individuals' level of commitment to the group varies over time. Second, there are role transitions, in which the relationship between the individual

**KEY TERM**

**Group socialisation:** dynamic processes in which group members and groups influence each other.

*How do you feel when you join a new group?*

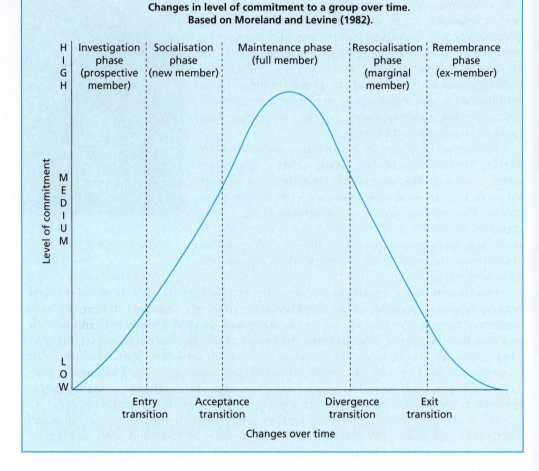

**Changes in level of commitment to a group over time.**
**Based on Moreland and Levine (1982).**

and the group changes. Third, and related to role transitions, there are five phases of group socialisation:

1. *Investigation phase.* Prospective group members assess whether they would like to join the group, and the group decides whether to accept them. After acceptance, there is the role transition of entry into the group.

2. *Socialisation phase.* The group teaches new members about its norms and goals, and new members try to change the group to suit them. If this phase is completed successfully, it leads to the role transition of group acceptance.

3. *Maintenance phase.* Members engage in role negotiation. Members unhappy with their role in the group may produce a partial split from the group, with this role transition known as divergence.

4. *Resocialisation phase.* Divergence is sometimes followed by attempts to bring the member back fully into the group. If such attempts fail, then exit is the following role transition.

5. *Remembrance phase.* After the member has left the group, there may be occasions on which happy memories of group membership are recalled.

*How do groups evolve over time?*

## Evidence

Eisenstat (1990) provided evidence in favour of Tuckman's (1965) five-stage theory. He studied the Ashland Corporation as they set up a new production line to make compressors. The newly established team had a successful forming stage, partly because the team members had frequent interactions. There were problems at the storming stage: The production workers needed training, but the trainers were heavily occupied with other tasks. As a result, the production workers felt neglected, whereas the trainers felt swamped. Norming occurred as the deadline for sending out the first compressors came close. According to one worker, "Then everyone gelled together ... Nobody said no, everybody said yes." The performing stage also went smoothly, with the compressors being rated as being of high quality. Finally, as the demand for the compressors declined, the adjourning stage was reached.

Some support for Moreland and Levine's (1982) notion that there are important differences between being a new member of a group and a more established member was reported by Moreland (1985). He set up five-person discussion groups, in which all members were actually new to the group. However, two members of each group (experimental participants) were told that the other three members of the group (control participants) had already met together on two previous occasions. The experimental participants were initially more anxious than the control participants. More importantly, they talked more to their fellow experimental participant than to what they perceived to be old members, and also agreed more with him/her than with the other old members.

The groups set up by Moreland (1985) met once a week for 3 weeks to discuss topical issues. What changes would we expect to find over time according to Moreland and Levine's (1982) theory? First, the experimental participants should have become more committed to the group. As predicted, their attitudes towards group membership became increasingly positive from the first to the third week. Second, the experimental participants should have gradually come to regard everyone as a full member of the group. As predicted, the distinction between new and old members became less relevant week by week. Third, and following on from the second point, the tendency for experimental participants to behave more favourably to the other experimental partici-pant than to the control participants should have diminished over time. As predicted, the deceived new members did not discriminate among other group members in the third session.

## Evaluation

- ⊕ There is support for the five stages identified by Tuckman (1965).
- ⊕ The relationship between group members and the groups to which they belong changes over time as predicted by group socialisation theory.
- ⊕ Prior to Moreland and Levine's (1982) theory, there had been a relative neglect of the notion that group members and groups systematically influence each other.
- ⊖ As Levine, Moreland, and Ryan (1998, p. 285) admitted, their model "is meant to apply primarily to small, autonomous [independent], voluntary groups, whose members interact on a regular basis, have affective ties with one another, share a common frame of reference, and are behaviourally interdependent."
- ⊖ Both theories we have discussed include stages (storming, socialisation phase, maintenance phase) in which tensions between individuals and the group may occur. Such tensions are more likely to occur in individualistic than in collectivistic cultures.

## PERFORMANCE IN GROUPS

The behaviour of individuals differs in many ways when in groups than when they are on their own. There is even evidence that an individual's behaviour is influenced by the presence of other people who remain passive and make no attempt to form a group with the individual. In this section, we consider some of the beneficial and detrimental effects other people can have on an individual's task performance. Finally, we discuss the issue of whether groups produce more accurate judgements than individuals.

*What evidence is there that working with a group enhances performance?*

# Social facilitation

*How does performing a task in front of others affect your behaviour?*

Imagine performing a task as rapidly as possible either on your own or in the presence of other people. Would the presence of others improve or impair your performance? It depends crucially on whether the task is simple or difficult. Performance on simple tasks is generally improved by the mere presence of others, even when they are passive and unresponsive. This effect is known as **social facilitation**. It is important to note that it occurs in the presence of others who do *not* in any real sense form a group. In contrast, the presence of others typically impairs performance on difficult tasks. Support for these conclusions was obtained by Bond and Titus (1983) in a meta-analysis of 241 studies. However, the magnitude of the social facilitation effect was generally small, with the mere presence of others accounting for only between 0.3% and 3% of the variation in performance. Nevertheless, social facilitation is a common phenomenon, and has been found in numerous species. For example, chickens and fish eat more (and pairs of rats have more sex) in the presence of members of the same species.

## Theory

The classic approach to social facilitation is Zajonc's (1965) drive theory. According to this theory, the presence of other people increases arousal and drive. Why does this happen? According to Zajonc, we need to be in a state of alertness in case they behave in unpredictable ways. Heightened arousal increases the probability that individuals will produce dominant or habitual responses when performing a task. This leads to improved performance on simple tasks, on which the correct responses are typically dominant. However, it leads to impaired performance on difficult or complex tasks, on which the correct responses are non-dominant.

Zajonc (1965) argued that the presence of others was naturally arousing. Other theorists have suggested additional reasons why individuals might be more aroused in the presence of others. Cottrell (1972) proposed an evaluation apprehension model based on the assumption that the presence of others causes arousal because of evaluation apprehension or concern. Baron (1986) put forward a distraction-conflict theory, according to which increased arousal or drive in the presence of others is produced by the distraction involved in attending to the other person as well as to the task.

Yet another arousal theory was put forward by Monteil and Huguet (1999). They based their theory on **Easterbrook's hypothesis**, which states that increased arousal leads to a narrowing of attention on to a few relevant cues. This narrowing of attention benefits performance on simple tasks, because they involve only a few cues. In contrast, narrowing of attention reduces performance on complex tasks, because such tasks involve numerous cues.

## Evidence

Zajonc's (1965) drive theory accounts for many of the findings. However, arousal increases in the presence of others for more reasons than he suggested. For example, evaluation apprehension is often an important factor. Aiello and Kolb (1995) considered what happened when workers' performance was monitored electronically, making them stressful and apprehensive about being evaluated. Highly skilled workers performed better when their performance was monitored than when it was not, whereas monitoring impaired the performance of relatively unskilled workers.

Evidence against the importance of **evaluation apprehension** was reported by Schmitt, Gilovich, Goore, and Joseph (1986) in a study in which the participants performed a simple and a hard task. They did these tasks while alone (individual condition), in the presence of a blindfolded confederate wearing a headset (mere presence condition), or while being closely observed by the experimenter (evaluation apprehension condition). The easy task was performed faster and the difficult task slower in the mere presence condition compared to the individual condition. There were only small differences between the mere presence and evaluation apprehension conditions, suggesting that social facilitation effects depend on mere presence.

**KEY TERMS**

**Social facilitation:** improved performance in the presence of others compared to when on one's own.

**Easterbrook's hypothesis:** the notion that increased arousal leads to a narrowing of attention to a small number of relevant cues.

**Evaluation apprehension:** concerns about being evaluated or judged by other people; sometimes assumed to produce increased arousal.

There is some support for Baron's (1986) distraction-conflict theory, in that several forms of distraction (e.g., flashing lights, noise, movement) have all been found to produce social facilitation effects (Baron, 1986). However, it is unclear whether the processes responsible for the effects of lights or noise on performance are the same as those responsible for the effects of the presence of others on performance.

The predictions from the theory of Monteil and Huguet (1999) are generally the same as those from Zajonc's drive theory. However, that is not always the case. Huguet, Galvaing, Monteil, and Dumas (1999) considered the impact of the presence of another person on the **Stroop effect**, in which the colours in which words are printed have to be named as rapidly as possible. Performance is slowed down when the words are themselves conflicting colour names (e.g., the word RED printed in green). This task involves only a few cues, and so Huguet et al. predicted that there would be a social facilitation effect. The opposite prediction follows from Zajonc's theory. Saying the word is the dominant or habitual response, and so the presence of another person should impair performance. In fact, the Stroop effect was smaller when another person was present, thus supporting Monteil and Huguet's theory.

There is a problem relating to all arousal-based theories. Measures of arousal (e.g., heart rate, galvanic skin response) often fail to indicate increased arousal in the presence of others (Bond & Titus, 1983). It can be argued that arousal in these theories is more a psychological than a physiological concept. However, if we follow that line of argument, then there is no independent evidence that arousal is actually increased by the mere presence of others.

*Why would being with other people lead to arousal, and how might arousal influence performance?*

## Evaluation

- ⊕ The mere presence of others typically produces social facilitation on easy tasks but impairs performance on difficult tasks.
- ⊕ It is likely that social facilitation effects often depend on increased arousal.
- ⊕ The cue-utilisation theory accounts for most of the data. It has the advantage over other theories that it focuses on the *mechanisms* (i.e., attentional processes) responsible for social facilitation effects.
- ⊖ There are various ways of defining easy and difficult tasks (e.g., use of dominant vs. non-dominant responses, reliance on a few vs. several cues), but very few attempts have been made to identify the key difference(s) between the two types of task.
- ⊖ It is not known exactly *why* the presence of others leads to increased arousal, although evaluation apprehension and distraction are often involved.
- ⊖ There is some validity associated with several theories, but the circumstances in which each theory is most applicable remain unclear.

## Social loafing

Suppose you are given the simple task of shouting as loudly as possible. Would you shout more or less loudly if you were on your own or in a group of people, all instructed to shout as loudly as possible? Latané, Williams, and Harkins (1979) provided a clear answer to this question. There was a reduction of 29% in the amount of noise produced per person in two-person groups compared to individuals on their own, and the reduction increased to 60% in six-person groups (see the diagram overleaf).

Latané et al. (1979) argued that there were two possible reasons for the reduction in performance within groups: (1) co-ordination loss, due to problems with synchronising the efforts of group members, and (2) **social loafing** (reduced motivation by individuals to perform a task well when in a group). They distinguished between these two possibilities by making use of pseudo-groups. In these pseudo-groups, individuals wore blindfolds and heard loud noise through headphones, and were led to believe that they were performing the task as members of a group. Individuals in pseudo-groups shouted significantly less

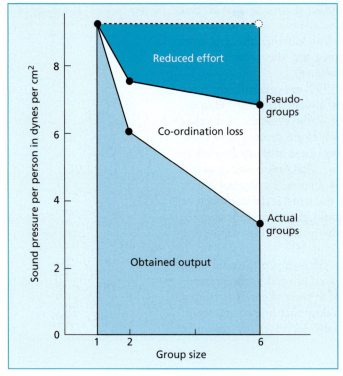

Intensity of sound produced per person when cheering in actual or perceived groups of 1, 2, and 6, as a result of reduced effort and faulty co-ordination of group efforts. From Latané et al., 1979.

*Why might social loafing be more prevalent in an individualistic culture than a collectivistic culture?*

loudly than when on their own (see the diagram on the left). This reduction in performance presumably reflected social loafing, since there was no need for individuals to co-ordinate their efforts.

Latané et al. (1979) also found that individuals in real groups performed significantly worse than individuals in pseudo-groups (see the diagram on the left). Presumably this was due to the co-ordination loss that occurred in real groups but not in pseudo-groups.

The phenomenon of social loafing is fairly general, having been found with tasks ranging from rope-pulling and swimming to generating ideas and rating poems for quality. For example, consider brainstorming groups in which the goal is to generate as many ideas as possible within a given period of time. When the number of ideas produced by such groups is compared against that produced by the same number of individuals working on their own, fewer ideas are generally produced in the brainstorming groups (see Stroebe & Diehl, 1994, for a review). This is due in part to social loafing. However, there is also production blocking, because only one member of the group can speak at any given time.

Karau and Williams (1993) found in a meta-analysis that there was evidence of social loafing in almost 80% out of a total of 78 studies. However, social loafing is more common in individualistic than in collectivistic societies (see Chapter 1), where the emphasis is more on benefiting the group than the individual. Earley (1993) used an office simulation task with trainee managers and managers from one individualistic society (the United States) and two collectivistic societies (China and Israel). There were three conditions: (1) working alone, (2) working in a group with others who were thought to be from the same region and to have shared interests, and (3) working in a group with others believed to be from a different region and not having shared interests. There was a consistent social loafing effect for the American managers, who worked harder on their own than in either of the groups. In contrast, the Chinese and Israeli managers worked harder when working with others believed to be similar to them than in either of the other two conditions. Thus, they showed **social compensation** (the opposite of social loafing) when they identified strongly with their group.

Social compensation has also been found in individualistic cultures in some circumstances. Plaks and Higgins (2000) argued that American students are motivated to ensure that the group performance is adequate. If they expect the other member of their group to perform poorly, this will motivate them to increase their effort. The participants were told that their scores and their partner's scores would be combined. Their performance was 30% better on a mathematics task when they thought their partner would be ineffective than when they thought the partner would be effective, and it was 14.5% better on a verbal task. The existence of social loafing or social compensation appears to depend on individuals' assessment of what is required to produce an adequate group or team performance.

Karau and Williams (1993) discovered in their meta-analysis that social loafing was reduced or eliminated when the task was important and/or the group members regarded the group as important. The impact of the second factor was shown by Worchel, Morales, Páez, and Deschamps (1998). All participants initially made paper chains individually, followed by performance of the same task in groups. When no other group was present, the usual social loafing effect was obtained. The remaining participants carried out the group task in the presence of another group, which was intended to increase ingroup identification. These participants performed better in the group situation than on their own (i.e., social compensation). Social compensation was especially great when all members of the ingroup wore coats of the same colour, presumably because this heightened a sense of identification with the ingroup.

## CASE STUDY: *Social loafing ("With a little help from my friends")*

Social loafing might also describe the lowered *quality* of effort, not just quantity of effort, in a collaborative task.

Jackson and Padgett (1982) analysed the Beatles' songs written by Lennon and McCartney pre- and post-1967. In that year it has been suggested that the band members' mutual relationships foundered somewhat. However, Lennon and McCartney continued to collaborate in writing some of their songs. The surprise finding was that post-1967 the songs they wrote independently were of a far higher standard, reaching higher in the pop charts, than those that were the result of collaboration. On the other hand, before 1967 the songs they wrote together were of an extremely high standard and were very successful.

One explanation of this change in the results of collaboration is that post-1967 one or other of the two musicians was exhibiting social loafing. As a result of the breakdown in their common relationship neither was prepared to contribute the quality of effort needed to produce songs comparable to those written in their earlier years.

Adapted from Jackson, J.M., & Padgett, V.R. (1982).

## Theory

Geen (1991) argued that there are three reasons why social loafing occurs. First, individuals in groups may expect others not to work very hard, thus justifying them in loafing. Second, when individuals in groups know their personal contribution cannot be identified, this reduces the concerns about being evaluated by others that they have when performing as individuals. Third, individuals in groups generally have no clear standard of performance that they are trying to achieve.

There is evidence supporting all three of Geen's (1991) explanations for social loafing (see Hogg & Vaughan, 2002). However, as Fielding and Hogg (2000) argued, what is most important is the extent to which individuals identify with the group. When steps are taken to increase social identity with the group (e.g., having similar co-members,

Sheer laziness or social loafing?

emphasising the importance of the group, enhancing ingroup identification), then social loafing is either much reduced or is even replaced with social compensation (e.g., Worchel et al., 1998). A social identity approach is also supported by cross-cultural differences, with much less evidence of social loafing in collectivistic cultures emphasising the importance of the group. Most studies have used groups of strangers carrying out meaningless tasks, and those are precisely the circumstances in which social loafing should be widespread.

## Evaluation

⊕ Social loafing has been obtained in dozens of studies.

⊕ It is of considerable practical importance to identify how individuals' motivation is influenced by working in a group with other people.

⊕ Several factors responsible for social loafing have been identified, including a lack of involvement with the group, a relative lack of concern about evaluation, and a lack of clear standards of performance.

⊖ Social loafing in everyday life may well be much less common than in the laboratory, because most of us do not spend much of our time engaging in meaningless group activities with several strangers.

⊖ With few exceptions (e.g., Fielding & Hogg, 2000), theories of social loafing have not attached enough significance to the role played by ingroup identification.

*Why is studying social loafing in laboratory studies problematic?*

# Group judgements

It is frequently assumed that judgements will typically be more accurate when made by groups rather than by individuals. This assumption is used to justify the extensive use of groups or teams within work organisations when important judgements or decisions need to be made. The assumption seems reasonable, given that the expertise and knowledge potentially available to groups is greater than that available to individuals working on their own.

Are groups generally more accurate than individuals? Gigone and Hastie (1997) reviewed studies in which small groups of between three and fifteen members provided quantity judgements on numerous tasks (e.g., estimating historical dates, prices of cars, course grades, and finishing order in horse races). All these tasks had clear answers, and so it was easy to compare the accuracy of groups and of individuals. Information on individual performance was usually obtained by asking the members of each group to provide judgements individually before becoming involved in group discussion. Group judgements are more variable than the mean of their members, with groups tending to make errors of greater magnitude. Group judgements increase inaccuracy nearly 20% over the means of the members' judgements.

Groups outperformed individuals in a few studies. For example, Henry (1993) studied three-member groups answering general knowledge questions such as the length of the Nile. Group accuracy was greater than the mean accuracy of its members on 82.2% of questions, and groups were more accurate than the most accurate individual member on 40.7% of the questions. However, there was not a general superiority of group judgements to those of individuals in most other studies, with the accuracy of group judgements generally being less than the mean judgements of their members.

Gigone and Hastie (1997) carried out various analyses to establish more precisely *why* group judgements are inferior to those of individuals. The conclusion they came to was as follows: "The group judgements increase

Large organisations often use teams of people to work on making important decisions, with the assumption that this increases the knowledge available, and the accuracy of judgements made. However, many studies have shown that this may not be the case.

*in*accuracy nearly 20.0% over the means of the members' judgements. The relative disadvantage of the groups comes out of their tendency to make more variable judgements" (Gigone & Hastie, 1997, p. 162).

# GROUP DECISION MAKING

How do you think decision making differs between individuals and groups? Many people think that groups will be more cautious, basing their decisions on a consensus of the views of all (or most) of the group members. In fact, however, many or most groups do *not* function in that way. More specifically, what often happens is **group polarisation**, which "occurs when the group's initial average position becomes more extreme following group interaction" (Smith & Mackie, 2000, p. 346).

Smith and Bond (1998) reported that group polarisation had been found in six countries other than the United States. However, they also noted that (for reasons which are unclear) group polarisation has not been found in studies carried out in Germany, Liberia, Taiwan, and Uganda. A point to which we will return is that the great majority of studies of group polarisation have used groups of a particular type, namely, groups without appointed leaders consisting of college or university students who do not know each other beforehand.

There is another important limitation of the research. As Brown (2000a, p. 199) pointed out, "Almost all the studies … were conducted in laboratory settings with ad hoc groups in which the decision-making task was a novel one and—even more importantly— in which the outcome was almost always hypothetical [imaginary]. The decisions seldom had any real consequences." Thus, it is unclear whether group polarisation is a phenomenon which applies to most real groups.

Several theories have been put forward to explain group polarisation. The main ones are discussed in turn below.

*Why might decisions made by groups be more extreme than those made by individuals?*

## Social comparison theory

According to Sanders and Baron (1977), individuals in a group want to present themselves in a favourable light, and want to be positively evaluated by the other group members. If individuals see other group members endorsing positions closer to some socially valued goal than their own, then they will change their position towards that goal to be regarded positively by the other group members.

A central prediction of social comparison theory is that there will be more group polarisation when a social value is made explicit in a social context. Baron and Roper (1976) tested this prediction in a study on the autokinetic effect: A stationary light viewed in an otherwise darkened room seems to move (discussed earlier in the chapter). Participants were told that large estimates of the amount of movement were a sign of high intelligence. The key finding was that groups in which the members heard others' estimates gave higher estimates themselves than did groups whose members responded in a private fashion.

Isenberg (1986) carried out a meta-analysis of 33 studies on group polarisation. Social comparison had a reasonably strong overall effect on group polarisation. However, the effects were much stronger when value- or emotion-laden issues were discussed than when factual issues were discussed.

## Information theory

A simple explanation of group polarisation was proposed by Burnstein and Vinokur (1973, 1977). According to them, group polarisation depends on the exchange of information among group members. In essence, the idea is that most of the information discussed within the group will favour the position already held by most of its members. The exposure to a range of convincing facts and arguments leads group members to move to more extreme positions than those which they adopted initially.

Burnstein and Vinokur (1973) set up a situation in which the predictions of information theory and social comparison theory differed. The participants were told that every member of their group would be instructed to argue for a point of view provided by the experimenter. In fact, the members of half of the groups were told to argue for their own point of view, whereas in the remaining groups the members argued against their own views. What predictions could we make? According to social comparison theory, there should not have been group polarisation in any of the groups. The reason is that the participants did not know the true views of any of the other group members, and so social comparisons were not possible. According to information theory, the information provided by other group members should have been more detailed and persuasive when they were arguing for their own point of view. Thus, there should have been more group polarisation in those groups arguing for what they believed than in those groups arguing against their beliefs. The results were consistent with the predictions of information theory, but not those of social comparison theory.

Some studies have been less favourable to information theory. For example, Zuber, Crott, and Werner (1992) presented some of their groups with a long list of the relevant arguments before the start of group discussion. It was predicted there would be more group polarisation when so much information was available to all of the group members. In fact, there was a comparable amount of group polarisation irrespective of whether the arguments were given to the participants beforehand, which is evidence against information theory.

The information discussed in groups is often biased in favour of information possessed by the majority. Stasser and Titus (1985) gave four members on a hypothetical personnel selection panel the task of discussing the relative merits of each of three candidates. The members of the panel were given information about the candidates beforehand, some of which was provided to all of them and some of which was given to only one of them. The key finding was that the group discussion focused mainly on information all of the panel members already shared, with non-shared information tending to be ignored. As a result, the panel generally failed to select the strongest candidate when information about him/her was not shared initially.

The tendency for groups to discuss shared rather than unshared information is general. Larson, Richards, Moneta, Holmbeck, and Duckett (1996) considered medical experts diagnosing medical cases. Shared information was more likely than unshared information to be introduced into the discussion, and it was generally discussed much earlier in the discussion.

*From the research into group decision making, why might we be concerned about committee decisions?*

The emphasis on shared information gives a clear advantage to majority opinion in the group. *Why* are individuals reluctant to discuss unshared information? Stewart and Stasser (1995) came up with a plausible answer to that question. They found that the validity of unshared information was often doubted because it could not be confirmed by other group members.

Information theory de-emphasises the importance of the *source* of any information made available to a group. Our opinions are influenced more by friends than by enemies and by experts than non-experts. The attitudes of group members changed more when they heard arguments from an ingroup than when they heard the same arguments from an outgroup (Mackie & Cooper, 1984; discussed later).

Isenberg (1986), in a meta-analysis discussed on the previous page, found that persuasive arguments had a powerful overall effect on group polarisation. However, such effects were much stronger when the groups were discussing factual issues rather than emotional or value-laden ones.

## Self-categorisation theory

An interesting approach to understanding group polarisation is provided by a development of social identity theory known as self-categorisation theory (e.g., Turner, 1987; see Chapter 21). The starting point for this theory is the assumption that the opinions of a group arise in a more general social context. More specifically, members of an ingroup often want to distinguish their group from other groups. They can do this by *differentiating* themselves from the views of an outgroup by adopting relatively extreme views themselves. What is especially important is the viewpoint best representing the combination of what the group itself has in common *and* what most clearly distinguishes it from an outgroup. This viewpoint is known as the prototype.

Evidence for the roles played by ingroups and outgroups was obtained by Mackie and Cooper (1984). Student participants listened to a tape on which the members of another group argued either that standardised tests for university entry should be retained or that such tests should be abandoned. The group on the tape was identified as an ingroup or an outgroup. As expected, an ingroup had much stronger effects than an outgroup in altering the views of the group listening to the tape, and thus in creating group polarisation. Changes in views among those listening to the tape produced by the outgroup tended to be in the *opposite* direction to the one advocated by that group, as predicted by the theory.

Several studies have provided more detailed support for self-categorisation theory. For example, Hogg et al. (1992) found that groups became more cautious than they had been previously after confrontation with a riskier outgroup. In contrast, they became riskier after confrontation with a more cautious outgroup. Self-categorisation theory is almost the only theory that provides an explanation for the effects of outgroup views on group polarisation.

## Evaluation

⊕ Group polarisation is an important phenomenon that has been obtained in several countries.

⊕ All three theoretical approaches discussed here explain some of the findings, i.e., each theoretical approach has identified some factors responsible for group polarisation.

⊖ Most studies are artificial and limited, being concerned with groups of strangers making decisions that have no real consequences.

⊖ The artificiality of most studies of group polarisation may be a serious problem. Semin and Glendon (1973) studied a committee in a British business organisation that made 28 job evaluations in a year, with all of the members of the committee making individual evaluations before group discussion. There was no evidence of group polarisation.

# Groupthink

The processes within groups leading to group polarisation can sometimes have very damaging consequences. This is especially the case when groups succumb to what Janis termed groupthink. According to Janis (1972, p. 8), groupthink is "the psychological drive for consensus at any cost that suppresses dissent and appraisal of alternatives in cohesive decision-making groups". He contrasted groupthink with vigilant decision making, in which there is critical appraisal and open discussion of the various options.

There are several clear examples of groupthink (e.g., the space shuttle *Challenger*). Several engineers had warned it could be dangerous to launch this space shuttle in cold temperatures. The reason was that the cold might cause the O-ring seals in the rocket boosters to fail, thereby producing a catastrophic explosion. On the morning of 28 January 1986, the temperature was below freezing. However, there was considerable public interest in the launch of *Challenger*, because it was to be the first time that an ordinary member of the public (a teacher called Christa McAuliffe) travelled in space. NASA decided to go ahead with it. The *Challenger* exploded 73 seconds after liftoff, killing all seven people on board, and the explosion was probably caused by failure of the O-ring seals.

What causes groupthink? According to Janis (1982), five features are typically present when groupthink occurs:

1. The group is very cohesive.
2. The group considers only a few options.

*What do you understand by the term groupthink?*

3. The group is insulated from information coming from outside the group.
4. There is much stress because of great time pressure.
5. The group is dominated by a very directive leader.

The above five factors can produce an illusion of group invulnerability, in which the members of the group are extremely confident of their decision-making ability. Group members often censor their own thoughts and even act as "mind guards" to prevent others from expressing ideas not fitting the group consensus. For example, consider the case of an engineer who opposed the launch of *Challenger*. He was persuaded to change his mind, "after being told to take off his engineering hat and put on one representing management".

## Evidence

Several very poor political decisions seem to be characterised by groupthink. For example, President Kennedy agreed to the Bay of Pigs invasion of Cuba after a series of meetings. This invasion was a disaster, and was only agreed to because accurate information about the potential dangers was minimised or suppressed at the meetings with the President. Tetlock, Peterson, McGuire, Chang, and Feld (1992) considered in detail eight of the cases used by Janis (1982) to support his theory. They agreed with Janis that groups showing groupthink typically had a strong leader and a high level of conformity. However, contrary to Janis's theory, groups showing groupthink were generally less (rather than more) cohesive than other groups. In addition, the evidence did not indicate that exposure to stressful circumstances contributed to the development of groupthink. Furthermore, there was more pessimism and less rigidity and conformity in the groupthink groups than was claimed by Janis (1982).

Tetlock et al. (1992) argued that the relationship between soundness of process (i.e., vigilance vs. groupthink) and success of outcome is much less strong than was implied by Janis (1982). They discussed cases (e.g., Iran hostage rescue attempt in early 1980) in which there was vigilant decision making, but the outcome was totally unsuccessful.

Kramer (1998) was also critical of the evidence assembled by Janis (1982), arguing that many of the faulty decisions were influenced at least as much by political considerations as by deficient group processes. For example, the *Challenger* disaster owed much to the fact that NASA was very keen to attract positive publicity to maintain its level of government funding. If NASA had decided not to proceed with the launch, there might have been negative publicity and accusations that it was incompetent. In similar fashion, the decision to invade Cuba was politically driven. At the start of the 1960s, there were very strong feelings against Communism. If the invasion of Communist-controlled Cuba had succeeded, it would have greatly boosted President Kennedy's popularity.

There is another major limitation with most of the cases used by Janis (1972). Much of the information about what had actually happened when events such as the launch of the *Challenger* or the Bay of Pigs invasion were discussed was based on the recollections of those involved. Many of them may have had deliberately distorted recollections, claiming for example to have been much more opposed to the decision than was actually the case.

Mullen, Anthony, Salas, and Driskell (1994) carried out a meta-analysis of studies focusing on groupthink.

---

### CASE STUDY: *Groupthink*

Conformity to group opinion has many important applications, such as in juries and in the management committees of large organisations. The way individuals behave in these groups is likely to matter a lot. Janis (1972) coined the term "groupthink" to describe how the thinking of people in these situations is often disastrously affected by conformity. Janis was describing the "Bay of Pigs" disaster to his teenage daughter and she challenged him, as a psychologist, to be able to explain why such experts could make such poor decisions. (The Bay of Pigs invasion took place in 1961. President Kennedy and a group of government advisers made a series of bad decisions that resulted in this extremely unsuccessful invasion of the Bay of Pigs in Cuba—disastrous because 1000 men from the invasion force were only released after a ransom payment of 53 million dollars' worth of food and medicine, and also because ultimately the invasion resulted in the Cuban missile crisis and a threat of nuclear war.) Janis suggested that there are a number of group factors that tend to increase conformity and result in bad decision-making.

- *Group factors*. People in groups want to be liked and therefore tend to do things to be accepted as one of the group.
- *Decisional stress*. A group feels under pressure to reach a decision. To reduce this sense of pressure they try to reach the decision quickly and with little argument.
- *Isolation*. Groups often work in isolation, which means there are no challenges to the way they are thinking.
- *Institutional factors*. Often people who are appointed to higher positions are those who tend to conform, following the principle that a good soldier makes a good commander.
- *Leadership*. The group is led by a strong leader who has clear ideas about what he/she wants the group to do.

As Janis predicted, high group cohesiveness reduced the quality of group decision making when the other factors producing groupthink were also present. However, high cohesiveness had little or no effect on group decision making when the other factors were absent.

Peterson, Owens, Tetlock, Fan, and Martorana (1998) studied top management teams at seven leading American companies during a time when the team was successful and during a time when it was unsuccessful. Symptoms of groupthink tended to be present during the unsuccessful time and symptoms of vigilant decision making were generally present during the successful time. However, as Peterson et al. (p. 272) concluded, "Successful groups showed some indicators of groupthink, whereas unsuccessful groups showed signs of vigilance." Thus, it is an over-simplification to categorise decision making as either groupthink or vigilant.

What can be done to reduce groupthink? Kroon et al. (1991) found that individuals within a group challenged its views when they thought they would be held personally accountable for their decisions. Postmes, Spears, and Cihangir (2001) argued that cohesiveness can be valuable, because it strengthens group norms. Cohesive groups with norms favouring critical and independent thinking performed much better than those with norms favouring maintaining consensus or agreement. Of key importance, group members were much more likely to share information with each other in groups with critical norms. Other suggestions are that independent experts or devil's advocates should be appointed to provide alternative points of view, and that the leader of the group should be non-directive, encouraging everyone to contribute their own views.

## Evaluation

- ➕ Groupthink is a genuine phenomenon, as has been demonstrated in several contexts.
- ➕ As Janis predicted, factors such as a strong leader and pressures towards conformity increase the likelihood that it will occur.
- ➖ Janis was incorrect in assuming that a high level of cohesiveness is needed for groupthink to occur, and exposure to threatening circumstances is less important than he claimed.
- ➖ The assumption that all decision making is characterised either by groupthink or by vigilance is over-simplified.
- ➖ Groupthink does not guarantee failure; neither does vigilant decision making guarantee success.
- ➖ As Brown (2000a, p. 215) pointed out, "Janis may have exaggerated the importance of social psychological processes at the expense of wider socio-political factors."

## LEADERSHIP

It is not easy to define leadership. It has been defined in terms of individual personality characteristics, types of behaviour, group processes, interaction patterns, and so on. However, a reasonable definition capturing the essence of **leaders** was suggested by Brown (2000a, p. 91):

> *What really characterises leaders is that they can influence others in the group more than they themselves are influenced.*

*To what extent do you think that anyone could become a great leader?*

### Great man (person) theory

What determines who fills the leadership role in a group? According to the great man (or person) theory of leadership, leaders possess certain personality or other characteristics distinguishing them from other people. Thus, for example, we might imagine that clever,

**KEY TERM**

**Leaders:** individuals within a group who exert most influence on group members.

Do leaders share any common characteristics?

dominant individuals would be most likely to find themselves in a leadership position, and would make more effective leaders than other people. However, a rapid consideration of well-known people in leadership positions suggests that they differ enormously in their personality traits. For example, Tony Blair, George Bush, and Nelson Mandela have very different personalities.

## Evidence

Mann (1959) considered studies looking at the personality traits of leaders. More than 70% of the relevant studies showed a positive relationship between perceived leadership status and intelligence, adjustment, extraversion, dominance, masculinity, and conservatism. However, most of the relationships were rather weak. Mann (p. 266) concluded that, "in no case is the median correlation between an aspect of personality … and performance higher than 0.25, and most of the median correlations are closer to 0.15. These correlations suggest that leaders only differ slightly from followers in personality."

Stogdill (1974) came to a similar conclusion in his review. He reported that leaders tend to be slightly more intelligent, self-confident, sociable, dominant, and achievement-oriented than their followers. However, these were all fairly small effects. Thus, it is not possible to predict with much accuracy who will become the leader of a group on the basis of the members' personality traits.

The great person theory of leadership is often dismissed out of hand nowadays. However, its deficiencies may have been exaggerated. Lord, de Vader, and Alliger (1986) pointed out that one of the reasons why correlations between personality measures and leadership are low is because of poor reliability of measurement. They carried out a meta-analysis of the studies discussed by Mann (1959), correcting for unreliability of measurement and other factors. The correlation between intelligence and leadership perception increased from +.25 to +.52, and that between masculinity–femininity and leadership perception went up from +.15 to +.34.

Lord et al. (1986) also considered studies published since Mann's (1959) review. When the data were corrected for unreliability, leadership perception correlated +.50 with intelligence, +.26 with extraversion, and +.24 with adjustment. As Lord et al. (p. 407) concluded, "personality traits are associated with leadership perception to a higher degree and more consistently than the popular literature indicates".

Are there consistent differences between men and women in leadership style? Eagly and Johnson (1990) reviewed over 150 studies of leadership in organisational settings, with the similarities in style between male and female leaders being much more obvious than the differences. For example, male and female leaders were equally task-oriented in their approaches. There were small gender differences, in that female leaders were more likely to include their followers or subordinates in decision making, and they were less likely than male leaders to be autocratic and domineering.

So far we have considered the issue of the personality characteristics of those perceived to have leadership status. A separate issue is to identify the personality characteristics of those who are *effective* leaders in terms of improving group performance. Heslin (1964) reviewed the literature, and found that intelligence was strongly related to group performance, with most correlations about +.60. In addition, adjustment was consistently related to group performance. Hogan, Curphy, and Hogan (1994) also reviewed research on this topic. They concluded that managerial performance can be predicted by various personal characteristics such as cognitive ability. Eagly, Karau, and Makhijani (1995) carried out a meta-analysis of studies comparing the effectiveness of male and female leaders. There were practically no overall differences in effectiveness. However, men performed slightly better than women in masculine leader roles, whereas women performed slightly better than men in feminine leader roles.

It seems likely that the characteristics of an effective leader depend on the goals and norms of the group in question rather than being fixed as is implied by the great person theory. For example, a more aggressive approach may be required to lead an adolescent gang than a group discussing flower arranging. Hains, Hogg, and Duck (1997) studied groups of college students meeting to discuss a social issue. In each group, a member was selected at random to be the leader. In those groups in which the members identified strongly with the group, leaders whose views were close to the average view in the group were rated as more effective leaders than leaders whose views differed from those of other group members. Thus, effective leaders need to embody the group norms to be effective, suggesting that the characteristics of effective leadership are much more flexible than is implied by the great person theory.

## Evaluation

⊕ There are predictable relationships between personality on the one hand and leadership perception and leadership performance on the other hand.

⊕ These relationships, while rarely strong, are of use in predicting who will achieve a leadership position and how effective a leader a given individual will be.

⊖ Only relatively few personality and ability characteristics (e.g., intelligence, adjustment, extraversion) are reasonably consistently related to leadership perception and performance.

⊖ The effectiveness of any given leadership style depends on the particular situation in which a group finds itself. However, the great person theory ignores the importance of the situation in determining who will become leader and their subsequent effectiveness.

⊖ The characteristics needed to be an effective leader vary depending on the norms of the group (Hains et al., 1997).

# Styles of leadership

A key issue in the study of leadership is to identify the main styles of leadership. A related issue is to try to work out which leadership styles are more and less effective. In this section, we will consider early attempts to address these issues, bearing in mind that there have been numerous other more recent attempts.

*How might leaders differ in their styles?*

## Democratic, autocratic, and laissez-faire leaders

Lewin, Lippitt, and White (1939) studied the effects of three styles of leadership (autocratic, democratic, laissez-faire) on 10-year-old boys in a model-making club. Autocratic leaders told the boys what to do, and with whom they were to work. They did not discuss issues with the boys or express an interest in their views. Democratic leaders allowed the boys to choose other boys with whom to work, and encouraged them to make their own decisions. The democratic leaders joined in many of the activities. Finally, laissez-faire leaders had little involvement in the running of the group. They left the boys free to do what they wanted, and did not encourage or criticise them.

There were three clubs and three adult leaders. The boys in any one club were exposed to only *one* leadership style, which was provided by each of the adult leaders in turn. In order to achieve this, the adult leaders adopted a different style of leadership with each club.

Democratic leaders were generally the most successful. The work was carried out well, there was good co-operation among the boys, the boys liked each other, and they carried on working when the leader left the room. Laissez-faire leadership was the least successful. The boys achieved little whether the leader was or was not in the room, they became

> **Leadership and group dynamics**
>
> George (1995) researched teams who worked for a major US retailer. She found that identifying individual performance and rewarding those whose efforts were good clearly reinforced the good work. Punishing individuals with a poor performance did not seem to deter those team members from repeating their lower efforts. Rewards and punishments which were unrelated to the quantity or quality of work were ineffective both in promoting good work and in deterring poor work. The message of this study is clearly that effective leadership rewards good work but does not reprimand poor workers.

discouraged when there were problems, and they behaved aggressively towards each other. Autocratic leadership led to the most productive work performance in that the most aircraft models were made. However, the boys were aggressive and tended to stop working when the leader left the room.

## Evaluation

⊕ The study by Lewin et al. (1939) was one of the first systematic attempts to study leadership styles.

⊕ The distinction between democratic and autocratic leadership styles has influenced several subsequent theories (see below).

⊖ The democratic style of leadership, regarded as the most acceptable style in America during the 1930s, might be less successful in other cultures.

⊖ Adults acting in an autocratic or laissez-faire way were less successful than those who acted democratically. Perhaps autocratic or laissez-faire leadership would be more effective if the leader were *naturally* autocratic or laissez-faire.

⊖ The democratic style of leadership was successful in the unthreatening context of a boys' club, even though not associated with the highest level of performance. However, a group faced by a sudden emergency requiring rapid decision making might be best served by autocratic leadership.

⊖ Lewin et al.'s (1939) findings are not applicable in other cultures. Meade (1985) found with adolescent boys that there was a strong preference for autocratic leadership in Hong Kong and in India.

## Task- and socio-emotional leaders

Bales (1950) introduced a very influential method for studying status differences within a group. He devised **interaction process analysis**, in which observers code the behaviour of group members into various categories. Interaction process analysis contains four general behavioural categories, with three sub-categories within each (sub-categories are shown in brackets):

- Positive socio-emotional behaviour (shows solidarity, shows tension release, agrees).
- Task behaviour (gives suggestion, gives opinion, gives orientation).
- Information exchange (asks for orientation, asks for opinion, asks for suggestion).
- Negative socio-emotional behaviour (disagrees, shows tension, shows antagonism).

Bales and Slater (1955) applied interaction process analysis to the behaviour of small groups. They found the members of any group varied considerably in the kinds of behaviour they tended to initiate and to receive. More specifically, there were usually two kinds of leader within a group: a task leader and a socio-emotional leader. The **task leader** initiated much of the task behaviour, disagreed with others, and showed antagonism, and received agreement, requests for orientation, opinions, and suggestions, and all types of negative socio-emotional behaviour. There are clear similarities between task leadership and the autocratic style identified by Lewin et al. (1939). In contrast, the **socio-emotional leader** initiated all types of positive socio-emotional behaviour, asked for orientation, opinions, and suggestions, showed tension, and received solidarity, tension release, orientation, suggestions, and opinions. The characteristics of the socio-emotional leader resemble those of the democratic style of leadership (Lewin et al., 1939).

Bales and Slater (1955) found that it was rare for the same person to be the task leader and the socio-emotional leader. Why is this so? One reason is that any individual is unlikely to possess the different qualities to fulfil both functions adequately. Another reason is that the task leader tends to arouse hostility in other members of the group, and it is hard for that person to provide effective socio-emotional leadership when exposed to so much negative socio-emotional behaviour.

Smith, Misumi, Tayeb, Peterson, and Bond (1989) considered leadership in the United States, Britain, Japan, and Hong Kong. They found that task-oriented and socio-emotional behaviour in leaders were both valued in all four countries. However, the appropriate ways of displaying each type of behaviour varied across cultures. For example, leaders in the work environment need to assess the performance of other workers. This is typically done face-to-face in Britain and the United States, but is more often done via co-workers in Hong Kong and Japan.

How useful do you think the distinction between task-leader and socio-emotional leader is?

## Evaluation

● Task-oriented leadership and socio-emotional leadership are valued in many cultures. There is also evidence from several countries (e.g., Finland, Japan, Hong Kong, and Sweden) that most groups have a task leader and a socio-emotional leader (Nystedt, 1996).
● The distinction between task and socio-emotional leadership is of crucial importance, and has influenced many theories of leadership (e.g., Fiedler, see below).
● Bales assumed that individuals high in task leadership would tend to be low in socio-emotional leadership, and vice versa. In fact, however, some individuals are high in both types of leadership (Sorrentino & Field, 1986).
● This approach emphasises the leader's behaviour. However, his/her effectiveness depends very much on the situation in which the group finds itself. For example, it may be important to have a task leader when decisions need to be made rapidly.

## Fiedler's contingency model

Many theorists have argued that it is important to study both the leader's personality or behaviour *and* the situation or situations in which leadership is exercised. According to this approach, the effectiveness of any particular leadership style is contingent on (i.e., depends on) the conditions in which the group finds itself. As a result, theories based on this approach are often described as contingency models. The most influential contingency model is the one proposed by Fiedler (1967, 1978), and that is the one we will consider in detail.

There are four basic components in Fiedler's contingency model. One refers to the personality of the leader, whereas the other three refer to characteristics of the situation in which the leader must lead. The leader's personality is assessed on the basis of the leader's liking for the least preferred co-worker. The least preferred co-worker (LPC) scale requires leaders to rate, on 18 scales (e.g., friendly–unfriendly, pleasant–unpleasant), the most difficult person with whom they have had to work. High scorers (high LPC) are those who evaluate their least preferred co-worker relatively favourably; they are said to adopt a relationship-oriented or considerate leadership style. In contrast, low scorers (low LPC) are said to be more task oriented.

There are three situational factors, which together determine the favourableness of the situation for the leader:

1. *Leader–member relations*. The relations between the leader and the other members of the group can vary from very good to very poor.
2. *Task structure*. The amount of structure in the task performed by the group can vary from high structure and goal clarity to low structure and goal clarity.
3. *Position power*. The power and authority of the leadership position are high if the leader can hire and fire, raise pay or status, and has support from the organisation, and are low if these factors are missing.

What situational factors should leaders consider if they want to be effective?

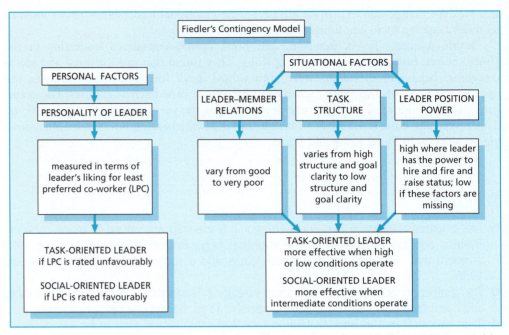

The personal and situational factors determining leaders' effectiveness according to Fiedler's contingency model.

If any given leadership situation is categorised as high or low on each of the three situational factors, we have eight possible combinations or levels of situation favourableness. The most favourable situation for a leader is one in which there are good leader–member relations, high task structure, and high position power, and the least favourable situation is one in which there are poor leader–member relations, a lack of task structure, and the leader has low position power. According to Fiedler, the most important of these situational factors is leader–member relations, and the least important is position power.

The key theoretical assumptions of Fiedler's contingency model are that task-oriented leaders (low LPC) will be more effective than relationship-oriented leaders (high LPC) when the situation is very favourable or very unfavourable for leaders, but the opposite will be the case when the situation is of intermediate favourableness. Why did Fiedler make these assumptions? When the situation is very favourable, the leader does not need to be unduly concerned about relationship issues, because the morale within the group is very high. When the situation is very unfavourable, feelings within the group probably cannot be improved much, and so it is most effective for the leader to focus on the task in hand. When the situation is of intermediate favourableness, a relationship-oriented leader can improve the morale of the group even though the task may be unclear and he/she has little power.

*Under what circumstances would you prefer to have a task-oriented leader rather than a social-oriented leader?*

### Evidence

Most studies provide some support for Fiedler's model. Fiedler and Potter (1983) summarised the findings from over 100 studies in which leadership effectiveness was assessed on the basis of group performance. Task-oriented (low LPC) leaders were generally more successful than relationship-oriented (high LPC) leaders when the situational favourableness was high or low, whereas the opposite was the case when the level of situational favourableness was moderate.

Schriesheim, Tepper, and Tetrault (1994) carried out a meta-analysis based on data from 1282 groups. Their findings were in broad agreement with those of Fiedler and

Potter (1983). Schriesheim et al. (p. 572) came to the following conclusion: "The findings presented here are encouraging and should be viewed as providing cautious support for the contingency model overall." However, small differences in the favourableness of the situation sometimes produced large differences in the effectiveness of task-oriented or relationship-oriented leaders, which is contrary to the theory.

Fiedler argued that the most important situational factor was leader–member relations, and the least important was position power. This approach is probably too rigid, since the relative importance of these factors probably varies from situation to situation. Singh, Bohra, and Dalal (1979) asked people to rate several situations for their favourableness to the leader. The relative importance of the three situational factors varied across situations. Contrary to the theory, it was found in each of four studies that position power was important; indeed, it was the most influential situational factor in two of the studies.

## *Evaluation*

- ➕ The effectiveness of leaders depends on the relationship between their personal characteristics and the particular situation in which they find themselves.
- ➕ Task-oriented leaders are most effective when the situation is very favourable or unfavourable, whereas relationship-oriented leaders are most effective when the situation is of intermediate favourableness.
- ➖ Fiedler assumed that individuals' leadership orientation as assessed by the least preferred co-worker scale remains relatively constant. However, the median test–retest reliability of the scale is only +.67 (Rice, 1978), meaning that leadership orientation often changes somewhat over time.
- ➖ It is over-simplified to claim that leaders are either task- or relationship-oriented. Some people are highly oriented in both ways, and those elected by their groups as leaders are often task- *and* relationship-oriented (Sorrentino & Field, 1986).
- ➖ Those obtaining average scores on the least preferred co-worker scale have been ignored in most studies. Kennedy (1982) found they were more effective leaders than the task- or relationship-oriented leaders in most situations. In addition, their performance was little affected by the situation, which is counter to Fiedler's emphasis on the interaction between leader and situation.
- ➖ There is some conceptual confusion within the contingency model. It is not very sensible to claim that leader–member relations are solely a function of the situation, since it is obvious that characteristics of the leader (e.g., warmth, agreeableness) will influence his/her relations with others within the group.
- ➖ Fiedler's contingency model is relatively uninformative about the dynamic processes over time that occur in groups. For example, what are the factors that determine the rise and fall of leaders?

## Transactional vs. transformational leadership

Several theorists have argued that the most effective leaders are those variously described as charismatic, inspirational, or transformational. The most influential theory here is probably that of Bass (1985), who distinguished between transactional leadership and transformational leadership. **Transactional leadership** involves various exchanges or bargains between leaders and followers, whereas **transformational leadership** involves providing one's followers with inspiration, and persuading them to rise above their own self-interests to achieve the leader's vision. Bass assumed that transactional leadership can be effective, but that transformational leaders are generally even more effective.

Avolio, Bass, and Jung (1999) clarified what is involved in transactional and transformational leadership. They reported findings based on 3786 participants who described their leader using the Multifactor Leadership Questionnaire. Six factors were identified:

1. *Charisma/inspirational*. Leader provides followers with a clear sense of purpose, and persuades them to identify with him/her.
2. *Intellectual stimulation*. Leader encourages followers to question conventional ways of solving problems.
3. *Individualised consideration*. Leader tries to understand the needs of his/her followers, and tries to get them to develop their potential.
4. *Contingent reward*. Leader makes it clear what he/she expects from followers, and how they will be rewarded if successful.
5. *Active management-by-exception*. Leader monitors the performance of followers, and helps to correct problems.
6. *Passive-avoidant leadership*. Leader becomes involved only when problems become serious.

The key finding reported by Avolio et al. (1999) was that factor analysis of the data produced two correlated factors of transformational leadership and transactional leadership. The factor of transformational leadership was based mainly on the charismatic/inspirational and intellectual stimulation factors, whereas the transactional factor was based on individualised consideration and contingent reward.

## Evidence

Several studies have shown that transactional and transformational leadership are both effective. Howell and Hall-Merenda (1999, p. 681) discussed several studies on transactional leadership, and concluded that, "The majority of research findings suggest that contingent reward leadership [an important aspect of transactional leadership] has a positive effect on individual follower performance." Yammarino, Spangler, and Bass (1993) carried out a longitudinal study of 193 graduates from the US Naval Academy. Measures of transformational leadership obtained at the start of the study predicted later performance appraisal.

Ross and Offermann (1997) studied American Air Force officers, each of whom led a squadron of about 120 cadets. Those officers scoring high on transformational leadership were typically self-confident, nurturant, and pragmatic. The cadets having transformational leaders were very satisfied with the leadership they provided. However, the same cadets did not perform any better than cadets having non-transformational leaders on measures of athletic, military, or academic performance.

Lowe, Kroeck, and Sivasubramiam (1996) carried out a meta-analysis of over 20 studies. Transformational leadership was generally superior to transactional leadership in producing effective performance in work groups. Moreover, this superiority of transformational leadership was obtained with groups as diverse as student leaders in laboratory studies, nursing supervisors, and German bank managers.

Kirkpatrick and Locke (1996) pointed out that most studies have been correlational in nature. Transformational leadership may correlate with follower performance because of the impact of the leader on his/her followers. However, it may also be the case that followers use their knowledge of the leader's success when deciding whether he/she is transformational. Kirkpatrick and Locke distinguished between these possibilities in an experimental study in which trained actors pretended to be transformational or non-transformational leaders. Group performance on a simulated production task was higher when the leader communicated a vision (e.g., instilling confidence in the followers, or raising expectations for high performance) and when he/she provided suggestions for

*What makes charismatic leaders successful?*

**CASE STUDY:** *The Heaven's Gate mass suicide*

The daily papers from 27 March 1997 were full of news that 39 people had committed suicide in a hilltop mansion in Rancho Santa Fe, California. As the story broke, it became apparent that the victims were members of a cult that called itself "Heaven's Gate". The Heaven's Gate cult emerged in the 1970s and was led by Marshall Applewhite and Bonnie Nettles. They were self-described "space age shepherds" who intended to lead a flock of humans to a higher level of existence.

Through the teachings of their charismatic leaders, who claimed to be extraterrestrial representatives of the "Kingdom Level Above Human", the cult members believed their bodies were mere vessels. By renouncing sex, drugs, alcohol, their birth names and all relationships with family and friends, disciples prepared to ascend to space, shedding their "containers", or bodies, and entering God's Kingdom. The cult members were led to believe that the appearance of comet Hale Bopp was a sign to move on to a more pure existence in outer space.

Investigations revealed that the mass suicide appeared to be a carefully orchestrated event. It took place over three days and involved three groups, proceeding in a calm, ritualistic fashion. Some members apparently assisted others and then went on to take their own dose of a fatal mixture. Lying on cots or mattresses with their arms at their sides, the victims each carried identification. Each of the members of the organisation gave a brief videotaped statement prior to their death. The essence of the statements was that they believed they were going to a better place.

Three things seem to be essential to the concept of a cult. Members think in terms of "us" and "them", with a total alienation from anyone perceived as "them". Intense, though often subtle, indoctrination techniques are used to recruit and hold members. The third ingredient is the presence of a charismatic cult leader who makes people want to follow his or her beliefs. Cultism usually involves some sort of belief that everything outside the cult is evil and threatening; inside the cult is the safe and special path to salvation through the cult leader and his or her teachings.

The cult leader must be extremely attractive to those who convert. He or she must satisfy the fundamental need to have someone to trust, depend on, and believe in totally. Charismatic leaders like Applewhite and Nettles gave purpose and meaning to the lives of their followers. Unquestioning devotion caused 38 Heaven's Gate cult members to voluntarily commit suicide. Marshall Applewhite was the 39th person to die in the mass suicide.

implementing the vision. These findings indicate that aspects of transformational leadership can have direct influence on group performance. However, leaders adopting a charismatic communication style (e.g., sounding dynamic and confident, making direct eye contact, animated facial expressions) were no more effective than those adopting a neutral or non-charismatic communication style.

Unfortunately, some transformational leaders have used their skills to produce tragic consequences. For example, Marshall Applewhite was a transformational leader who claimed that his Heaven's Gate group had reached a new stage of evolution in which they had no further need for their bodies. After they had discarded their bodies, they would go off in a spaceship travelling with the Hale-Bopp comet. On the basis of these claims, Marshall Applewhite persuaded nearly 40 members of his group to commit mass suicide in March 1997.

*Why do you think that research into leadership has largely ignored the role of followers?*

## Evaluation

⊕ Transactional and transformational leadership are both effective, with transformational leadership generally being more effective than transactional leadership.

⊕ Theories of transformational or charismatic leadership have focused on factors (e.g., vision for the future, instilling confidence in followers) ignored in other theories of leadership.

⊖ Theoretical approaches focusing on transformational or charismatic leadership may exaggerate the impact of the leader on the followers and minimise the impact of the followers on the leader.

⊖ According to Hogg and Vaughan (2002, p. 322), too much transformational leadership "may be dysfunctional, because it imbues the leader with excessive power and fragments the group through continual change. The limits of transformational leadership are not specified."

⊖ Transformational leaders can be dangerous if the achievement of their goals involves the destruction of group members or some other group.

# COLLECTIVE BEHAVIOUR

Individuals often behave differently when in a crowd than when on their own or with friends. For example, lynch mobs in the southern parts of the United States murdered about 2000 people (mostly blacks) during the first half of the twentieth century. Those involved in these atrocities would almost certainly not have behaved in that way if they had not been part of a highly emotional crowd.

Le Bon (1895) was a French journalist who put forward perhaps the first theory of crowd behaviour. According to him, a man who forms part of a crowd:

*descends several rungs in the ladder of civilisation, he is ... a creature acting by instinct ... [He can be] induced to commit acts contrary to his most obvious interest and best known habits. An individual in a crowd is a grain of sand amid other grains of sand.*

Do crowds always lead to negative behaviour?

Le Bon referred to the "law of mental unity" driving a crowd to behave like a mob. He also used the term social contagion to describe the way in which irrational and violent feelings and behaviour can spread rapidly through the members of a crowd.

Crowds do not always behave in senseless ways. Consider cases of fires in halls and other public buildings, in which several people die as everyone rushes to escape. This may seem like senseless and irrational behaviour. However, it would only make sense for each person to walk slowly to one of the exits if they could trust everyone else to do the same. As that trust is usually lacking, the most rational behaviour may well be to behave like everyone else, and try to be among the first out of the burning building.

Le Bon (1895) exaggerated the mindlessness of crowds. Part of the reason for the tendency to think that crowds are likely to behave badly is because those that are well behaved are typically ignored by the media. Thompson (cited in Postmes & Spears, 1998, p. 229), discussed food riots in England during the eighteenth century: "It is the restraint, rather than the disorder, which is remarkable; and there can be no doubt that the [collective] actions were supported by an overwhelming popular consensus."

## Crowd behaviour

Reicher (1984) studied a civil disturbance in the St Pauls area of Bristol, England, which involved the police and the mainly black community. There was considerable violence, with many people being seriously injured and several police cars destroyed. However, the behaviour of the crowd was much more controlled than might have been imagined. The crowd displayed violence towards the police, but did not attack or destroy local shops and houses. In addition, the actions of the crowd were confined to a small area lying at the heart of the community. If the members of the crowd had simply been intent on behaving violently, then the violence would have spread into the surrounding areas. Finally, those taking part denied that they had lost their identities during the process. Indeed, the opposite was closer to the truth, as they experienced an increased sense of pride in their community.

Reicher (1984) put forward a theory, according to which individuals in a crowd typically attend less than usual to themselves, focusing instead on the situation and the other members of the crowd to provide them with cues as to how to behave. This makes them responsive to group norms. These group norms will sometimes favour taking aggressive action, but very often will favour responsible behaviour. This theory was later developed into the social identity model of deindividuation effects by Reicher, Spears, and Postmes (1995), which is discussed below.

Further evidence that crowds typically share a social purpose was reported by Marsh, Rosser, and Harré (1978). They analysed the behaviour of football fans, and found evidence of long-lasting social structures and patterns of behaviour (e.g., ritualised aggression). Those fans showing the most ability to follow the rules and norms were very highly regarded and influential members of their group.

*Think of some examples where crowds are positive as well as negative.*

In spite of the stereotype of football fans as forming highly aggressive groups, Marsh et al. (1978) found that unrestrained fighting between rival fans happened very rarely. For example, football fans supporting the home team regarded it as their right to chase fans of the away team from the ground after the match, but the rival sets of fans usually kept their distance from each other. Football fans often use violent language and make threatening gestures, but these activities rarely turn into actual fighting.

Where does the physical violence come from at football matches? According to Marsh et al. (1978), most of it consists of isolated incidents involving individuals rather than arising from the violent intentions of a football crowd. However, Russell and Goldstein (1995) compared the male supporters of Utrecht football team with non-fans, finding that supporters scored significantly higher on a measure of psychopathic or anti-social tendencies.

Hundreds of thousands of fans attend football matches each week but only a tiny percentage show hooligan behaviour.

Waddington, Jones, and Critcher (1987) considered several major demonstrations. They argued that the police had a vital role to play in preventing crowd violence. The police should use as little force as possible, and should be accountable to the local community for their actions. In addition, there needs to be close co-operation between the police and the organisers of demonstrations, with both groups having been thoroughly trained in the skills of communicating with crowds. If feasible, the best method of preventing crowd violence is often to allow the crowd to police itself.

Waddington et al. (1987) discussed evidence supporting their view that crowd violence typically depends on the context in which the crowd finds itself, rather than on the characteristics of individuals in the crowd. They compared two public rallies held during the miners' strike in Britain in 1984, only one of which led to violence. In contrast to the peaceful rally, the violent one was controlled by the police rather than by the rally organisers. The violent rally had not been planned carefully with the police, and insufficient thought had been given to preventing large numbers of people being forced into a small area.

## Deindividuation

Le Bon (1895) argued that the anonymity of individuals in a crowd or mob plays an important part in removing normal social constraints, and producing violence. More recent theorists (e.g., Diener, 1980; Zimbardo, 1969) have accepted that part of Le Bon's theory. They have proposed accounts based on the notion of **deindividuation**, which is the loss of a sense of personal identity occurring in crowds and mobs. It is most likely to occur in conditions of high arousal, anonymity, and diffused responsibility (e.g., responsibility is spread among the members of the crowd).

According to Diener (1980), deindividuation is produced through decreased self-awareness, and leads to the following effects:

*Why do some people lose their sense of self in a crowd?*

- Poor monitoring of one's own behaviour.
- Reduced concern to have social approval of one's behaviour.
- Reduced constraints against behaving impulsively.
- Reduced capacity to think rationally.

### Evidence

Zimbardo (1970) reported a study on deindividuation. Female participants were told to give electric shocks to other women in a Milgram-type study (see earlier in chapter).

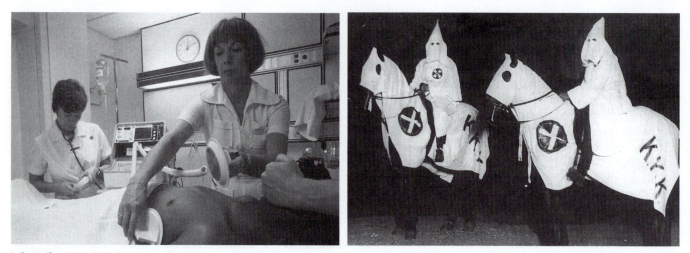

Left: Uniforms, such as those worn by nurses, increase an individual's sense of anonymity and make it more likely that they will conform to the role associated with the uniform. Right: Johnson and Downing (1979) pointed out the similarity between the clothes of Zimbardo's deindividuated participants and those of the Ku Klux Klan.

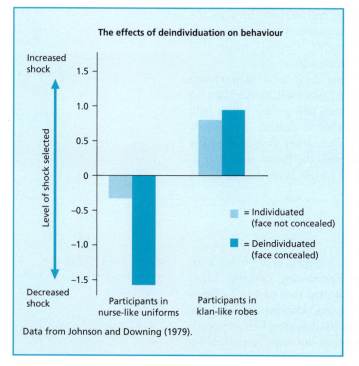

The effects of deindividuation on behaviour

Data from Johnson and Downing (1979).

Deindividuation was produced in half of the participants by having them wear laboratory coats and hoods covering their faces. In addition, the experimenter addressed them as a group rather than as individuals. The intensity of shocks given by the deindividuated participants was *twice* as great as that of participants who wore their own clothes and were treated as individuals.

Johnson and Downing (1979) pointed out that the clothing worn by the deindividuated participants in Zimbardo's (1970) study resembled that worn by the Ku Klux Klan (a secret organisation, which carried out many violent acts against American blacks). Deindividuated individuals who were dressed as nurses actually gave *fewer* electric shocks than did those who wore their own clothes. Thus, deindividuation sometimes has desirable rather than undesirable effects on behaviour.

Mann (1981) analysed newspaper accounts of crowds watching someone threatening suicide by jumping from a bridge, building, or other structure. Members of the crowd often jeered and encouraged the potential suicide to jump. This aggressive behaviour by the crowd was much more likely when those in the crowd were fairly anonymous (and thus deindividuated), either because the crowd was large or because the incident took place after dark.

## Evaluation

● Deindividuation can contribute towards groups and crowds behaving in an anti-social or aggressive way.
● Anonymity (a key part of deindividuation) often leads groups to behave badly, probably because it reduces the likelihood that individuals will be punished for acting anti-socially or illegally.

- Deindividuation does *not* always lead groups and crowds to behave badly; indeed, it can have the opposite effect (e.g., Johnson & Downing, 1979).
- Other theoretical developments (see below) provide a more adequate explanation of group behaviour than do accounts based on deindividuation.

*When might deindividuation lead people to act in a positive, rather than a negative way?*

## Emergent-norm theory

According to Zimbardo (1969) and Diener (1980), individuals in a crowd become deindividuated, and so less likely to conform to social norms or standards of behaviour. Turner and Killian (1972) favoured a very different approach. According to their emergent-norm theory, two factors need to be present for individuals in crowds to behave aggressively:

1. The crowd should develop a group norm favouring the use of aggression.
2. Individuals in the crowd should be identifiable, because this will increase the social pressures on them not to deviate from the group norm.

When these two factors are present, individuals in the crowd should conform to the new or emergent norm.

Let us consider an example of what is involved in emergent-norm theory. Suppose there is a confrontation between a group of demonstrators and the police. A new norm that people should defend themselves against the police may emerge, and this may lead to stone throwing. Individuals in the crowd who can be identified by others feel strong pressures to conform to the stone-throwing behaviour.

### Evidence

Mann, Newton, and Innes (1982) compared the deindividuation and emergent-norm approaches. Their participants observed two people having a discussion, and they could react to what they heard by pressing buttons to provide crowd noise. They were either anonymous or identifiable, and were given fake information indicating that the group norm was aggressive (loud noise) or non-aggressive (soft noise). According to deindividuation theory, individuals who were anonymous should have behaved more aggressively than those who were identifiable. That was exactly what Mann et al. found.

There was some support for the emergent-norm theory, because the participants were more aggressive when told there was an aggressive group norm rather than a non-aggressive norm. However, the prediction that the level of aggression should be greatest among identifiable participants exposed to the aggressive group norm was *not* supported. Overall, the findings provided more support for deindividuation theory than for emergent-norm theory. A problem for the emergent-norm theory is that it is not entirely clear *how* group norms generally emerge.

## Social identity model of deindividuation effects

Reicher et al. (1995) and Postmes and Spears (1998) put forward a social identity model of deindividuation effects (social identity theory is discussed in Chapter 21). This model combines aspects of deindividuation theory and emergent-norm theory. According to deindividuation theory, when individuals become deindividuated, their behaviour becomes uninhibited and freed from social constraints. According to Reicher et al.'s model, precisely the *opposite* is the case: When individuals in a group become deindividuated, their behaviour is strongly influenced by the prevailing group norms. This notion fits easily with the findings discussed earlier in the chapter showing powerful conformity effects in group situations.

Postmes and Spears (1998) emphasised three main assumptions of the social identity model of deindividuation effects:

1. Deindividuation leads *not* to a loss of self but only to a decreased focus on personal identity.
2. Deindividuation increases responsiveness to, or conformity with, situational group norms (what most people would regard as appropriate behaviour in any given situation). This can produce unusually controlled and restrained behaviour, or it can produce aggressive behaviour.
3. Deindividuation is neutral with respect to general social norms (which are standards of behaviour not taking account of the particular context).

According to the social identity model, anonymity (or its opposite, visibility) alters power relations between the ingroup and the outgroup (e.g., police). When individuals are anonymous so far as the outgroup is concerned, this reduces the ability of the outgroup to hold individuals accountable for their actions and encourages them to resist the outgroup and express group norms in their behaviour. When individuals are anonymous so far as their fellow ingroup members are concerned, this reduces their ability to support each other. As a result, there is a *reduced* likelihood that they will act in accordance with group norms and resist the outgroup.

## Evidence

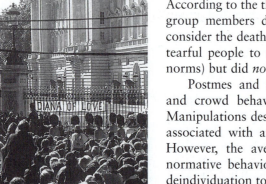

What norms appeared as the public waited to pay their respects to Diana, Princess of Wales?

According to the theory, deindividuation may or may not lead to anti-social behaviour by group members depending on the prevailing situational group norms. For example, consider the death of Princess Diana on 31 August 1997. This tragic event led crowds of tearful people to show their sadness and sense of loss (in line with situational group norms) but did *not* lead to any breaking of general social norms.

Postmes and Spears (1998) carried out a meta-analysis of 60 studies on group and crowd behaviour. There was only modest support for deindividuation theory. Manipulations designed to produce deindividuation (e.g., anonymity, large groups) were associated with anti-normative behaviour (behaviour breaking general social norms). However, the average correlation between deindividuation manipulations and anti-normative behaviour was only + .09, meaning there was a rather slight tendency for deindividuation to lead to behaviour opposed to general social norms.

Other analyses by Postmes and Spears (1998) undermined deindividuation theory even further. First, it is assumed within that theory that the reason *why* manipulations of anonymity lead to anti-social behaviour is because they reduce the individual's self-awareness. However, the evidence provided no support for this viewpoint. Second, there was strong evidence that manipulations designed to increase deindividuation *increased* adherence to situational group norms, whereas the prediction from deindividuation theory is that it should lead to *decreased* adherence to group norms.

The various findings of Postmes and Spears (1998) can readily be explained by the social identity model of deindividuation effects. According to that model, individuals in crowds typically adopt the social identity of the crowd and their behaviour is determined by situational group norms. That is precisely the central finding reported by Postmes and Spears (p. 253):

*The most striking result was that the deindividuation conditions of anonymity, larger groups, and reductions in self-awareness fostered adherence to situational norms. Thus, the factors that social psychologists have identified as playing a crucial role in the formation of collective behaviour appeared to lead to a specific form of social regulation rather than its breakdown.*

According to the social identity model, anonymity of individuals to the outgroup should *increase* adherence to group norms, whereas anonymity of individuals to the ingroup should often *reduce* adherence to group norms. The first prediction has been supported in several studies (e.g., Reicher et al., 1995). The second prediction was tested by Reicher, Levine, and Gordijn (1998). First-year psychology students responded to questionnaire statements about lying (e.g., "It is fine to give false excuses if one didn't prepare for a seminar"), having been told they would have to discuss the various issues with a member of the academic staff afterwards. Some students were visible to the other students (they were seated in a circle), whereas others sat in individual booths. As predicted, students who were anonymous to their fellow ingroup members were less likely to agree that lying was acceptable than were those visible to other students. Presumably visibility increased the students' perception of the power of their ingroup, and made them more willing to endorse statements contrary to the beliefs of the outgroup (academic staff).

## Evaluation

⊕ Deindividuation is important in increasing conformity behaviour by crowds, and its effects can be positive (e.g., after the death of Princess Diana) as well as negative.

⊕ The social identity model of deindividuation accounts for many of the phenomena of group and crowd behaviour (including the controlled aggression found by Reicher, 1984, in a study discussed earlier).

⊕ The assumption of the social identity model that deindividuation increases adherence to group norms has received much support.

⊕ The effects of anonymity on behaviour depend on how anonymity influences power relations between groups.

⊖ Members of a large group may experience exhilaration or great excitement, and the model has little to say about such emotional states.

⊖ It is hard to measure key concepts such as personal identity and social identity.

## S U M M A R Y

Milgram found that about 65% of his participants were willing to administer a potentially lethal electric shock to another person, whereas psychiatrists predicted that no-one would do so. There was less obedience to authority when the obviousness of the learner's plight was increased and/or the authority of the experimenter was reduced. High levels of obedience to authority are found in most countries. According to Milgram, individuals obeyed because the orders moved gradually from reasonable to unreasonable, and the individuals enter an "agentic" state. The extent of obedience to authority is underestimated in part because of the fundamental attribution error.

*Obedience to authority*

Asch found that people would respond in conformity with a group about 35% of the time even when the group's responses were clearly incorrect. The presence of a supporter markedly reduces conformity, but conformity is increased if the group members know and like each other. Conformity in the Asch situation has declined over time in the United States. It is greater in collectivistic cultures than in individualistic ones. Conformity in the Asch situation depends mostly on normative influence, but it can involve informational influence. According to Moscovici, majorities have public rather than private influence over minorities (compliance), whereas minorities have private rather than public influence over majorities (conversion). However, majorities generally have more direct private influence than minorities. Differences in the social influences exerted by majorities and by minorities may depend on power or status.

*Conformity*

Group cohesiveness is generally only moderately correlated with group performance, and this is due mostly to the effects of performance on cohesiveness. We can divide social

*Basic group characteristics*

norms into descriptive norms, injunctive norms, and subjective norms. Norms provide guidance as to the appropriate way to behave in ambiguous situations, and help to maintain group identity. Group norms can still affect individuals' behaviour many years after they have left a group. According to group socialisation theory, individuals go through five phases of group socialisation, with movement from one phase to the next marked by a role transition. In general, the individual's commitment to the group increases over the first three phases and then decreases over the last two.

### Performance in groups

Individuals generally perform simple tasks better in the presence of other people than when on their own, but the opposite is the case with difficult tasks. According to Zajonc's drive theory, the presence of others produces arousal, which leads to the production of dominant or habitual responses. Arousal can also be created by evaluation apprehension or distraction. Social loafing has often been found, but not when the task is important or the group members regard the group as important. Social loafing is less common in collectivistic societies than in individualistic ones. Group judgements are often less accurate than individual ones, in part because group judgements are more variable.

### Group decision making

According to social comparison theory, group polarisation occurs because individuals want to be positively evaluated by group members. According to information theory, group polarisation depends on the exchange of information among group members. According to social categorisation theory, members of a group want to differentiate themselves from other groups. There is some support for all three theories. Most group polarisation studies have used groups of strangers, and it is not clear that group polarisation is common in the work environment. According to Janis, groupthink typically

Collective behaviour: what do you do when your personal space is invaded?

occurs when a group is cohesive, insulated from outside information, under time pressure, and dominated by a directive leader. In fact, a high level of cohesiveness is *not* needed, and Janis de-emphasised socio-political factors.

According to the great man (or person) theory of leadership, leaders possess certain personality or other characteristics that distinguish them from other people. Leaders tend to be more intelligent, more extraverted, and more dominant than non-leaders. According to Fiedler's contingency model, the effectiveness of a leader depends on his/her personality in interaction with the favourableness of the situation (e.g., leader–member relations). As predicted, task-oriented leaders are more successful than relationship-oriented ones when the situation favourableness is high or low, whereas the opposite is the case with moderate situational favourableness. Transformational leadership is often more effective than transactional leadership, but transformational leaders can damage the group through continual change or through having misguided goals.

*Leadership*

Individuals in a crowd are very responsive to group norms, which can produce either aggressive or socially responsible behaviour. Crowd violence often depends on the social context rather than on the characteristics of individuals in the crowd. Deindividuation allegedly produces feelings of anonymity, reduces rational thinking, and leads to impulsive behaviour. According to the social identity model of deindividuation, when individuals in a group become deindividuated, they are more strongly influenced by group norms. In addition, anonymity influences power relations between groups, so that the effects of anonymity to the ingroup are often different from those of anonymity to the outgroup. There is good support for the main predictions of the social identity model.

*Collective behaviour*

# FURTHER READING

- Brown, R. (2000). *Group processes* (2nd ed.). Oxford, UK: Blackwell. Most of the topics dealt with in this chapter are discussed in a very accessible way in this textbook.
- Hewstone, M., & Stroebe, W. (2001). *Introduction to social psychology* (3rd ed.). Oxford, UK: Blackwell. Chapters 13 and 14 contain readable and up-to-date accounts of research on social influence and on group performance, respectively.
- Hogg, M.A., & Vaughan, G.M. (2002). *Social psychology* (3rd ed.). London: Prentice Hall. Several chapters in this book (especially 7, 8, and 9) provide clear accounts of key group processes.
- Smith, E.R., & Mackie, D.M. (2000). *Social psychology* (2nd ed.). Philadelphia, PA: Psychology Press. This introductory textbook covers group processes in a clear and readable way.

- ### Social identity theory
  Exploration of intergroup processes using social identities based on groups to which we belong.

  *Ingroup bias*
  *Turner's self-categorisation theory*
  *The minimal group paradigm*
  *The effect on self-esteem*

- ### Stereotypes
  Schemas that provide a way of perceiving the world.

  *Definitions of stereotypes; their accuracy*
  *Problems with measurement: social desirability bias; the Implicit Association Test*
  *Social and motivational functions: cognitive and social approaches*
  *Formation of stereotypes—outgroup homogeneity effect*
  *Maintenance—consistency, attention, priming, congruency, attributions*
  *The effect on behaviour*
  *Changing stereotypes*

- ### Prejudice and discrimination
  The effects of evaluation of a social group, and the actions directed at its members.

  *Distinction between prejudice and discrimination*
  *Allport's five stages of discrimination*
  *Racial bias; aversive racism*
  *Sexual bias; the "glass ceiling"*
  *Adorno et al.'s authoritarian personality: E-Scale, F-Scale*
  *Sherif's Robber's Cave study, and other studies of intergoup conflict*
  *Application of social identity theory*

- ### Reducing prejudice and discrimination
  A discussion of various methods.

  *Allport's intergroup contact hypothesis*
  *Other similar approaches: jigsaw classroom; desegregation*
  *Changing group identities: decategorisation, salient categorisation, and recategorisation*

# Intergroup processes

**21**

Everyday life is full of examples of interactions between groups. Some of these interactions are of major political and/or historical significance, as is the case with the numerous wars fought between different groups or countries. Other interactions are on a more minor scale (e.g., competitive team sports, work discussions between different groups). If we define "group" broadly, then we encounter members of other groups (and those we perceive to be our own group) nearly every day of our lives. As a result, the study of intergroup processes and behaviour is of vital importance.

How should we define intergroup processes or behaviour? Hogg and Vaughan (2002, p. 384) offered a reasonable definition: "Any perception, cognition or behaviour that is influenced by people's recognition that they and others are members of distinct social groups is intergroup behaviour." Social psychologists have devoted considerable attention to the problems which develop between groups. Accordingly, our coverage of intergroup processes includes sections on stereotypes and on prejudice and discrimination. Finally, we consider how prejudice and discrimination might be reduced or eliminated.

## SOCIAL IDENTITY THEORY

In recent years, there has been an increasing tendency to use social identity theory to explain many intergroup processes. It is a powerful and wide-ranging theory, and has also been used successfully to account for many processes occurring *within* groups (see Chapter 20).

Social identity theory was proposed by Henri Tajfel (e.g., 1978, 1981), and has since been developed and extended, notably by Tajfel and Turner (1986). According to this theory, we have a need to understand and to evaluate ourselves. This is achieved by thinking of ourselves as possessing a number of social identities. According to Tajfel (1981, p. 255), social identity is "that part of the individual's self-concept which derives from their knowledge of their membership of a social group (or groups), together with the value and emotional significance of that membership". We all have various social identities, based on the groups to which we belong and with which we identify. These social identities can include racial group, nationality, work group, social group, and so on. Thus, for example, an individual may identify herself as a student, as a member of a netball team, and as a Londoner, all at the same time.

Why is it important for people to possess various social identities? According to the theory, having a positive social identity enhances the individual's self-esteem. A major way of achieving a positive social identity is to draw favourable comparisons between a group to which one belongs (the ingroup) and some relevant outgroup: **ingroup bias** or favouritism. This kind of comparison between an ingroup and an outgroup is known as intergroup differentiation. According to Tajfel and Turner (1986), intergroup differentiation is especially likely to occur under the following conditions:

1. Individuals identify themselves with their ingroup.
2. The situation makes it easy to draw intergroup comparisons.
3. The outgroup is regarded as comparable to the ingroup, perhaps because it is broadly similar in nature.

According to social identity theory, intergroup differentiation typically occurs very rapidly and easily. Thus, we tend to identify ourselves as members of an ingroup that is

*How many different social identities do you think you have? Describe them.*

distinguished from an outgroup even when there are minimal differences between the groups. As we will see, this prediction has been tested using what is known as the minimal group paradigm. The notion that our social identities depend in part on contrasting ourselves with the members of other groups was expressed succinctly by Tajfel (1979, p. 188): "We are what we are because *they* are not what we are."

Social identity theory predicts the existence of ingroup bias or favouritism, in which one's own ingroup is compared favourably to some outgroup. According to the theory, ingroup bias is a very common phenomenon occurring almost whenever someone identifies with a particular group. In addition, social identity theory has been applied to several other areas within social psychology. For example, the relevance of the theory to group polarisation was discussed in Chapter 20. Later in this chapter, we will deal with applications of social identity theory to stereotyping and to reducing intergroup bias and prejudice.

Self-categorisation theory (e.g., Turner, 1985, 1999) represents a development of social identity theory. According to self-categorisation theory, the process of categorising oneself as a group member leads to social identity and phenomena such as ingroup favouritism. The self can be categorised at various levels. There is an important distinction between **personal identity** (involving self-definitions based on personal or idiosyncratic characteristics) and **social identity** (involving self-definitions based on membership of an ingroup). For example, a woman may mostly categorise herself in terms of her personal identity (e.g., friend of Susan, takes life seriously). However, if she is in a pub with a group of other women, she may categorise herself as a woman, which would lead her to emphasise her similarities to other women and her differences from men.

What determines whether an individual's personal identity or social identity is dominant at any given time? According to Turner (1999), four factors are involved:

1. The individual's past experience.
2. The individual's present expectations.
3. The individual's current motives, needs, and goals.
4. The fit between an individual's various identities and the current situation: The identity most appropriate to the current situation will be selected.

Members of the Elvis Presley Fan Club—a social identity?

What is the relationship between social identity theory and self-categorisation theory? The two theories are rather similar, and typically the same predictions flow from both of them (Cinnirella, personal comm.). However, self-categorisation theory has been applied to a wider range of phenomena in social psychology than social identity theory, which was originally designed mainly to account for intergroup processes. According to Turner (1999, p. 7), who had a central role in the development of both theories, "They are different theories, but they are allied and largely complementary, doing different jobs from the same broad social psychological perspective. It is for this reason that the term social identity is sometimes used (at a more inclusive level) to refer to both theories." We will follow this practice here.

**KEY TERMS**

**Personal identity:** an individual's sense of him/herself based on his/her idiosyncratic characteristics.
**Social identity:** an individual's sense of him/herself based on his/her group memberships.

## Evidence

According to social identity theory, we have a strong need to form social identities. As predicted, individuals form a social identity with amazing ease even with minimal groups scarcely deserving to be called groups at all. For example, Tajfel, Flament, Billig, and Bundy (1971) carried out a study using what has come to be known as the **minimal group paradigm,** in which 14- and 15-year-old boys estimated the number of dots seen in brief exposures. They were assigned at random to one of two minimal groups: the over-estimators or the under-estimators. After that, they awarded points (which could be exchanged for money) to other individuals identified as belonging to the same group or to the other group. Nearly all the boys showed ingroup bias by awarding more points to members of their own group than to members of the other group.

Tajfel et al.'s (1971) findings have been replicated numerous times in studies on minimal groups (see Brown, 2000b, for a review). There is also evidence of ingroup bias in real-world studies. Brown (1978) reported a study of factory workers, who were highly motivated to maintain the wage differentials between their department and others in the same factory. This remained the case, even when this would lead to a reduction in their own earnings.

According to social identity theory, ingroup bias occurs as a *direct* result of individuals identifying themselves with the ingroup. However, there are other ways of explaining the findings. Rabbie, Schot, and Visser (1989) argued in their ingroup reciprocity hypothesis that ingroup bias is due to self-interest. According to this hypothesis, individuals reward ingroup members more than outgroup members because they expect to be benefited in return by other ingroup members. They reported a study in which some participants would receive only what outgroup members gave them. These participants could *not* be benefited by other ingroup members, and so they showed outgroup favouritism rather than ingroup favouritism.

*Why do we invariably favour our ingroup over others?*

Additional evidence favouring the ingroup reciprocity hypothesis was reported by Gaertner and Insko (2000) using minimal groups. Some participants were told they would not receive any bonus money in contrast to the other ingroup members and most of the outgroup members. In those conditions, the participants showed no ingroup bias, presumably because other ingroup members could not benefit them in return. Thus, their thinking was along the lines, "If I can't have a bonus, then no-one will!"

Nearly all demonstrations of ingroup bias or favouritism in the minimal group paradigm have involved the allocation of positive outcomes (e.g., points, money). A natural prediction from social identity theory is that individuals should also show ingroup bias or favouritism when allocating *negative* outcomes. Thus, individuals should punish the outgroup more than the ingroup. In fact, most studies have *not* supported that prediction. For example, Mummendey et al. (1992) instructed participants to distribute different durations of an unpleasant, high-pitched tone to members of the ingroup and the outgroup. Contrary to prediction, there was no evidence at all of ingroup favouritism, with many participants simply equalising negative outcomes between the two groups.

The above finding is potentially important in two ways. First, it suggests that social identity theory may have rather limited explanatory power. Second, it suggests that social identity theory may lack relevance when explaining prejudice and discrimination. Allocating negative outcomes selectively to outgroups rather than to ingroups is precisely what is involved in prejudice and discrimination, and yet apparently ingroup favouritism does not produce such selective allocation of negative outcomes. These issues are considered further later in the chapter.

One explanation of this failure to find discrimination against outgroups when negative outcomes are involved was tested by Gardham and Brown (2001). They assumed that the participants would regard the experimenter's request to administer mild punishment to others as somewhat inappropriate. This might lead them to redefine the situation as one involving *all* the participants against the experimenter. In a sense, the distinction between an ingroup and an outgroup would be replaced by one large ingroup of participants ranged against the experimenter. In those circumstances, there would be no reason to expect ingroup favouritism.

**KEY TERM**

**Minimal group paradigm:** setting up essentially arbitrary groups in which the group members do not communicate with each other.

Strong negative emotions need to be created in order to make an ingroup justify its harmful behaviour towards an outgroup.

The above account may sound rather tortuous. However, Gardham and Brown (2000) obtained support for it in a study using the minimal group design. The typical bias effect was found when positive outcomes were distributed. However (in line with the previous findings of Mummendey et al., 1992), there was no evidence of ingroup bias when negative outcomes (bursts of unpleasant noise, removing small sums of money) were distributed. Of crucial importance, the participants in the groups distributing negative outcomes felt less identification with the ingroup than did those in the groups distributing positive outcomes. Thus, there was no ingroup bias in the negative-outcome groups because there was little sense of belonging to an ingroup in the first place.

There is another important reason for the lack of discrimination against outgroups in laboratory studies. Only weak emotions are aroused in most studies on ingroup bias, and it is likely that relatively strong negative emotions (e.g., hatred, disgust) need to be created to justify harm against an outgroup (Brewer, 2001). For example, Germans during the Second World War who identified most strongly with being German were more strongly opposed to the Jews than were Germans with less national ingroup identification (Goldhagen, 1996). Other examples of discrimination against outgroups associated with heightened emotion are discussed by Hewstone, Rubin, and Willis (2002).

A key prediction of social identity theory is that ingroup bias serves to increase an individual's self-esteem or positive distinctiveness. However, Turner (1999, p. 20) emphasised that self-esteem or positive distinctiveness can be boosted in various ways, and there are numerous factors determining whether ingroup bias occurs:

> *Ingroup bias ... is only one of several individual and group strategies which group members can pursue to achieve positive distinctiveness (others being individual mobility and social creativity). Factors relevant to determining whether ingroup bias is likely to occur include: (a) the degree of identification with a group ... ; (b) the salience of the relevant social identity in relation to which a specific comparative judgement is being made ... ; (c) the perceived social structure of the intergroup relationships; (d) the relevance of the comparative dimension to the intergroup status relationship; and/or (e) the relevance of the outgroup to the particular comparative judgement being made.*

*In what ways might belonging to a group raise your self-esteem?*

Much of the evidence supports the prediction that ingroup bias leads to increased self-esteem for its members. For example, Lemyre and Smith (1985) put their participants into groups at random. Some were then allowed to give rewards to members of either an ingroup or an outgroup, and thus show ingroup bias. The other participants had to give rewards *either* to one of two ingroups *or* to one of two outgroups, and so could not show ingroup bias. Those participants who could show ingroup bias had higher self-esteem than those unable to do so.

Abrams and Hogg (1988) proposed two ways in which self-esteem might be related to ingroup bias. First, as we have discussed, ingroup bias or favouritism increases self-esteem. Second, individuals who initially have low self-esteem will exhibit more ingroup bias, because they have a stronger motive to enhance their self-esteem.

Rubin and Hewstone (1998) reviewed research relevant to the above two predictions. They found that 9 out of 12 studies reported evidence supporting the first prediction. However, only 3 out of 19 studies provided support for the second prediction. For example, Crocker et al. (1987) found that individuals who were high in self-esteem identified more strongly with their ingroup than did those low in self-esteem. The conclusions of Rubin and Hewstone were confirmed in larger meta-analyses by Aberson, Healy, and Romero (2000).

According to social identity theory, members of high-status ingroups should have more self-esteem and thus less need to show ingroup bias. Mullen, Brown, and Smith (1992) carried out a meta-analysis of 42 studies on this issue. Members of groups accorded high status actually showed *more* ingroup bias than members of low-status groups, and this effect was larger under laboratory conditions than in naturalistic settings.

How would we expect individuals to react when they perform well on a task but their ingroup does not? According to social identity theory, one might expect that they would show a reduction in ingroup bias. Individuals identify with a group to enhance their self-esteem, but this is unlikely to happen when the group fails. In such circumstances, individuals might disengage somewhat from the ingroup, and so show less ingroup bias. Chen, Brockner, and Katz (1998) argued that the above line of reasoning may apply well in individualistic cultures, but seems less applicable to collectivistic cultures (see Chapter 1). People in collectivistic cultures attach more importance to the success of the group than to their own success. As Chen et al. (p. 1491) expressed it, "The belief that only when one's ingroup excels can the individual ever succeed is integral to socialisation processes in collectivistic cultures." Accordingly, Chen et al. predicted that individuals in collectivistic cultures who succeed while their ingroup fails would show *increased* (rather than decreased) ingroup bias (i.e., "I will support my group through thick and thin").

Chen et al. (1998) tested the above predictions in a study on students from China and the United States. The key condition was the one in which individual participants succeeded but their ingroup failed. The American students evaluated the outgroup more favourably than their ingroup in that condition (see diagram above). In contrast, as predicted, the Chinese evaluated the ingroup more favourably than the outgroup. As Chen et al. (p. 1500) concluded, "Ingroup favouritism may be governed by different psychological processes for people from varying cultural backgrounds."

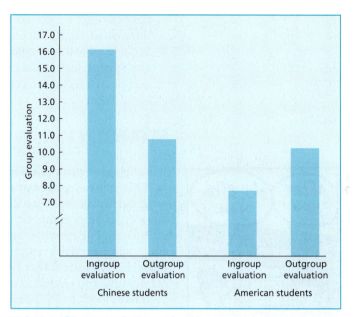

Evaluation of ingroup and outgroup by Chinese and American students following individual success but ingroup failure. Based on data in Chen et al. (1998).

*Why might collectivistic cultures show greater ingroup bias when the ingroup fails, but the individual succeeds?*

## Evaluation

- ⊕ The central assumption of social identity theory and self-categorisation theory that our self-concept depends importantly on the groups with which we identify has received considerable support.
- ⊕ Social identity theory has been applied successfully to numerous phenomena within social psychology, including ingroup bias, stereotyping, prejudice and prejudice reduction (see later in chapter), and group polarisation.
- ⊖ Social identity theory and self-categorisation theory are both rather complex. This can make it hard to work out what either theory would predict in a given situation.
- ⊖ The prediction that individuals low in self-esteem should exhibit more ingroup bias than those high in self-esteem has not been supported.
- ⊖ The notion that individuals are motivated to identify with various groups to achieve personal self-enhancement is less applicable to collectivistic cultures than to individualistic ones (e.g., Chen et al., 1998).
- ⊖ Social identity theory focuses on the conscious strategies which individuals use to enhance their social identity, and de-emphasises automatic processes relevant to social behaviour.
- ⊖ According to social identity theory, people very readily adopt social identities. However, there are (unknown) limits to this process. As Augoustinos and Walker (1995, p. 131)

pointed out, "People do not accept any social identity thrust upon them; they actively seek, avoid, resist, dispute and negotiate social identities."

● Social identity theory emphasises the cognitive processes underlying group identification and ingroup bias at the expense of emotional and motivational factors.

## STEREOTYPES

Many people have a stereotype of the English as intelligent, tolerant, and reserved.

It is important when discussing intergroup processes to consider stereotyping. A **stereotype** is, "A cognitive representation or impression of a social group that people form by associating particular characteristics and emotions with the group" (Smith & Mackie, 2000). Stereotypes are schemas or organised packets of knowledge relating to specific groups of individuals. For example, many people have a stereotype of the English as intelligent, tolerant, and reserved, even though I am sure you know many English people lacking all of those characteristics! That example is not entirely representative, because many stereotypes are negative and related to prejudice.

Fiske (1998, p. 357) defined stereotyping, prejudice, and discrimination: "Stereotyping is taken as the most cognitive component, prejudice as the most affective [emotional] component, and discrimination as the most behavioural component of category-based reactions—that is, reactions to people from groups perceived to differ significantly from one's own." However, note that some researchers define prejudice more broadly to cover the cognitive and emotional components.

It is often assumed that stereotypes are largely inaccurate. However, that is *not* always the case. For example, Triandis and Vassiliou (1967, p. 324) studied people from Greece and from the United States, and concluded as follows: "There is a 'kernel of truth' in most stereotypes *when they are elicited from people who have firsthand knowledge of the group being stereotyped.*" McCauley and Stitt (1978) asked various groups of Americans to estimate the percentage of adult Americans and the percentage of black Americans who had not completed high school, were born illegitimate, had been the victims of violent crime, and so on. There were differences in the estimates for most of the questions, thus showing the existence of stereotypes. McCauley and Stitt then compared the estimates against the relevant government statistics. In their answers to about half of the questions, the participants *underestimated* the actual differences between the two groups. Thus, stereotypes sometimes possess a kernel of truth.

There are three ways in which stereotypes can be inaccurate (Judd & Park, 1993). First, there is stereotypic inaccuracy, in which some attributes of a group are over-estimated or under-estimated. Second, there is valence inaccuracy, which is a consistent tendency to regard another group too positively or negatively. Third, there is dispersion inaccuracy: Group members are regarded as more or less variable than is actually the case. Judd and Park reviewed the literature, and found evidence that stereotypes of ingroups were consistently more accurate than stereotypes of outgroups with respect to all three forms of stereotypic inaccuracy. In general, outgroup stereotypes were much more likely to involve prejudice, exaggerated beliefs, and over-generalisation.

### Europe: The north–south divide

Linssen and Hagendoorn (1994) assessed national stereotypes among students in several European countries: England, France, Germany, Italy, the Netherlands, Denmark, and Belgium. The students were given the task of deciding the percentage of people in each of the seven countries possessing various characteristics. The findings showed a clear difference between the stereotypes of those living in the north and the south of Europe. The main differences were that the northern Europeans were perceived as more efficient than the southern Europeans, whereas the southern Europeans were seen as more emotional than inhabitants from northern Europe.

### KEY TERM

**Stereotype:** a simplified cognitive generalisation or categorisation (typically negative) about a group, generally based on easily identifiable characteristics (e.g., sex, ethnicity).

## Measurement issues

How can we assess stereotypical thinking? Katz and Braly (1933) carried out the first systematic study of stereotyping. They asked students to indicate which characteristics were typical of a series of groups (e.g., Germans, Black Africans, English). There was fairly good agreement that Germans were efficient and nationalistic, whereas black Africans were seen as happy-go-lucky and superstitious.

The above approach *forced* the participants to produce stereotypes, whether or not they actually thought in a stereotyped way. McCauley and Stitt (1978) used a preferable method in a study on stereotypes of Germans. They asked their participants questions such as, "What percentage of people in the world generally are efficient?", and "What percentage of Germans are efficient?" The average answer to the former question was 50%, whereas it was 63% to the latter one. Thus, most people do *not* think all Germans are efficient. The general feeling is that they are somewhat more efficient than other nationalities, a much less extreme form of stereotyping.

There are two major problems with traditional questionnaire measures. First, there is **social desirability bias**: Individuals with very negative stereotypes of other groups may feel it is socially desirable to pretend their stereotypes are less negative than is actually the case. Second, some aspects of an individual's stereotypes may not be accessible to conscious awareness. Thus, individuals may lack the ability to report accurately on their stereotypes when presented with a questionnaire.

Traditional questionnaire methods provide an assessment of *explicit* attitudes and stereotypes. However, it is also possible to assess *implicit* attitudes and stereotypes, which do not depend on conscious control and awareness. There are several ways of assessing implicit stereotypes. For example, we can study the apparently automatic activation of stereotypes below the level of conscious awareness. In one such study, Wittenbrink, Judd, and Park (1997) presented the word "black" or "white" so rapidly it could not be consciously perceived by the participants. However, Wittenbrink et al. assumed these words would nevertheless activate the stereotypes that the white participants had about white people and black people.

The above assumption was tested by using a lexical decision task very shortly after the presentation of the subliminal (below the conscious level) presentation of the word "black" or "white". On this task, the participants decided whether a string of letters formed a word. On some trials, a word relating to the stereotype of white people or black people was presented. For example, words such as "ignorant", "poor", and "lazy" form part of the negative stereotype of blacks held by whites in the United States, and "intelligent", "independent", and "ambitious" form part of their positive stereotype of whites. The key prediction was as follows: Any words on the lexical decision task forming part of the activated stereotype should be responded to *faster* than neutral words. As can be seen in the diagram overleaf, the word "black" activated negative aspects of the black stereotype, whereas the word "white" activated positive aspects of the white stereotype.

Wittenbrink et al. (1997) also addressed the issue of whether their *indirect* measure of stereotypical bias was related to a more *direct* measure (the Modern Racism Scale). In general, those most prejudiced on the indirect measure of stereotypical bias were also prejudiced on the direct or explicit measure.

Part of the stereotypical image of Italian matriarchs is that they are wonderful cooks.

**KEY TERM**

**Social desirability bias:** the tendency to provide socially desirable rather than truthful answers (e.g., to questionnaire items concerned with prejudice).

What characteristics do you think each of these people might possess?

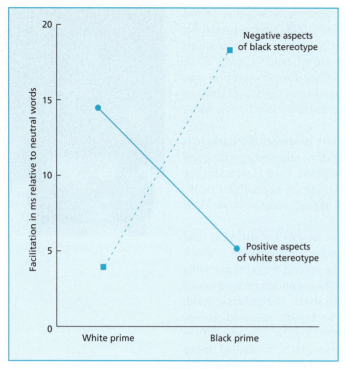

Facilitation effect (speeding up) as a function of prime (white vs. black) and word type (relevant to positive aspects of white stereotype or negative aspects of black stereotype). Based on data in Wittenbrink et al. (1997).

The Implicit Association Test (IAT) was devised by Greenwald, McGhee, and Schwartz (1998) to assess unconscious attitudes and stereotypes. We will consider the version of this test used by Cunningham, Preacher, and Banaji (2001). On some trials, the participants were presented with faces, and had to press one key for white faces and a second key for black faces. On other trials, they were presented with good (e.g., love, happy) and bad (e.g., poison, terrible) words, and had to press the same two keys to indicate whether each word was good or bad. In condition 1, white faces and good words were classified using one key and black faces and bad words were classified using the second key; in condition 2, white faces and bad words involved one key and black faces and good words the second key.

If the participants had no prejudice, there should be no difference in reaction time in the two conditions. However, Cunningham et al. (2001) found that reaction times were much faster in condition 1 than in condition 2 (613 ms vs. 744 ms). These findings suggest the existence of implicit pro-white and anti-black stereotypes.

How different are explicit and implicit stereotypes? Cunningham et al. (2001) found that three different measures of implicit racial stereotypes all correlated positively with scores on a measure of explicit racial stereotypes (the Modern Racism Scale). The mean correlation was +.35, revealing some tendency (but not a strong one) for individuals who have implicit racial stereotypes to have explicit ones as well. More strikingly, the participants showed more evidence of prejudice on the implicit measures than on the explicit measure, indicating that the implicit measures assess prejudice *not* revealed by questionnaires.

It has often been argued (e.g., Devine, 1989) that implicit stereotypes are typically activated automatically and without any conscious control. However, most of the evidence for automatic activation of stereotypes has come from research in which category labels (e.g., "black", "white") have been presented directly. It seems much less likely that there would be automatic activation of the white stereotype when you meet someone who is a lawyer, Italian, and young as well as being white (Macrae & Bodenhausen, 2000). More generally, it has proved very difficult in studies of stereotyping to show the existence of automatic processes in the sense of processes which are involuntary, unintentional, and effortless (see Chapter 6). In practice, stereotypical processing is more flexible and adaptable than is implied by the notion of automatic activation of stereotypes (Macrae & Bodenhausen, 2000).

## Why do we have stereotypes?

*How useful are stereotypes?*

Stereotypes provide a simple and economical way of perceiving the world (e.g., Macrae & Bodenhausen, 2000). Thus, for example, we can readily categorise someone we meet for the first time on the basis of their sex, age, clothing, and so on. However, stereotypes do *not* only fulfil the function of minimising the amount of information processing individuals need to carry out. Stereotypes also fulfil important social and motivational functions. They help us to achieve a sense of social identity by allowing us to distinguish ourselves clearly from the members of other groups (e.g., Oakes, Haslam, & Turner, 1994). These two theoretical approaches are considered in turn below.

### Cognitive approach

As we have seen, one view of stereotypes is that we use them because they reduce the amount of cognitive processing needed when we meet or think about other people.

How does this happen? Several theorists (e.g., Devine, 1989) have argued that relevant stereotypical information is activated automatically whenever a member of a given group is encountered. However, this creates problems, because most of the people we encounter can be categorised in several different ways (e.g., female; young; French; student), and so several stereotypes should be activated. Macrae and Bodenhausen (2000) suggested that what happens in such circumstances is as follows: All relevant stereotypes are activated, followed by a competition for mental dominance in which the nondominant stereotypes may be actively inhibited.

Stereotypes can help us achieve a sense of social identity.

## Evidence

Macrae, Milne, and Bodenhausen (1994) tested the notion of cognitive economy by asking their participants to perform two tasks at the same time. One task involved forming impressions of various imaginary people when given their names and personality traits. The other task involved listening to information presented on a tape followed by a test of comprehension. Half the participants were given the chance to use stereotypes by being told the job held by each of the imaginary people in the impression-formation task. The idea was that being told that someone was, for example, a used car salesperson or doctor would activate stereotypical information about the kind of person having that kind of job. The remaining participants were not given this stereotype-relevant information.

The key finding was that those participants able to use stereotypes performed better on both tasks. This suggests that using stereotypes saves precious cognitive resources, because stereotypes provide a convenient (if inaccurate) summary of a person or object.

Convincing evidence that relevant stereotypes can be inhibited was reported by Sinclair and Kunda (1999). According to them, we activate positive stereotypes and inhibit negative ones when motivated to think well of another person. In contrast, we activate negative stereotypes and inhibit positive ones when motivated to think badly about someone else.

Sinclair and Kunda (1999) tested the above predictions by giving white participants a measure of interpersonal skills followed by videotaped feedback of their performance. In the crucial conditions, this feedback (which was positive or negative) was provided by a black doctor. Control participants did not receive any feedback. After that, there was a test of stereotype activation. This was in the form of a lexical decision task on which the participants had to decide as rapidly as possible whether each string of letters formed a word. Some of the words were associated with the black stereotype (e.g., black, crime, jazz), whereas others were associated with the doctor stereotype (e.g., intelligent, educated, caring). It was assumed that fast responding indicated that the relevant stereotype was activated, and that unusually slow responding indicated that the relevant stereotype had been inhibited.

As shown in the figure on the right participants receiving positive feedback from a black doctor activated the

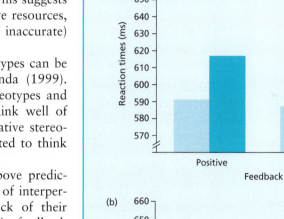

Speed of responding to black words (a) and to doctor words (b) as a function of feedback (positive or negative) received from a white doctor or a black doctor. From Sinclair and Kunda (1999).

doctor stereotype and inhibited the black stereotype. The opposite pattern was obtained from participants receiving negative feedback. As Sinclair and Kunda (1999, p. 903) concluded, "The same individual may be viewed through the lenses of different stereotypes by perceivers with different goals; the same Black doctor may be categorised and viewed as a doctor after delivering praise but as a Black person after delivering criticism."

## Evaluation

⊕ Stereotypes reduce the amount of cognitive processing that is required.
⊕ Cognitive processes can actively inhibit stereotypical information which is of little relevance in a given context.
⊖ As we will see shortly, stereotypes are much more *flexible* than is implied by the cognitive approach.
⊖ The nature of any given stereotype varies as a function of the particular social context in which it is used (see below).

## Social approach: Social identity theory

A purely cognitive approach to stereotypes is limited in various ways. According to Stroebe and Insko (1989, p. 4), "As applied to cognitive representations of social groups, the stereotype metaphor seemingly implies undesirable rigidity, permanence, and lack of variability from application to application." This contrasts strongly with the approach based on social identity theory:

> *Stereotyping reflects, and functions in the context of, changing intergroup relations ... Rather than focusing exclusively on the role which cognition plays in the aetiology [origins] of stereotypes, it [social identity theory] has re-emphasised the role which social factors play in shaping those cognitive processes and the interaction between the two.* (Haslam et al., 1992)

Turner (1999) pointed out that there are other important differences between social identity theory and most other theories in their approach to stereotyping. Most other theorists assume that stereotypes represent irrational and invalid prejudices. In contrast, it is claimed within social identity theory that it is inevitable (and even desirable) that individuals often categorise themselves and others on the basis of social identities (as members of groups) rather than personal identities (as individuals with idiosyncratic characteristics). According to Turner (p. 26):

> *It is no more a distortion to see people in terms of their social identity than in terms of their personal identity. Both are products of the same categorisation processes. It is not true that individual differences are real but that social similarities are fictions. It is not justifiable to assume that one level of categorisation is inherently more real than another.*

*Why do you think that some groups in society are more likely to be negatively stereotyped than others?*

## Evidence

Much evidence indicates that social context influences the nature of stereotypes as predicted by social identity theory. For example, Cinnirella (1998) carried out a study in which British students were assigned to one of three tasks:

1. Providing stereotype ratings of the British only.
2. Providing stereotype ratings of the Italians only.
3. Providing stereotype ratings of the British and of the Italians.

According to self-categorisation theory, the British stereotype should have been accentuated when it was compared against the Italian stereotype, because that provides clear differentiation between the groups. That prediction was confirmed, since some components of the British stereotype (reserved, industrious) were more pronounced in condition 3 than in condition 1. According to the theory, the Italian stereotype should have been less positive in condition 3 than in condition 2, because of the tendency to regard outgroups less favourably than ingroups. That prediction was also confirmed: The Italians were rated as less industrious, intelligent, and progressive when compared against the British than when considered on their own.

Haslam et al. (1992) found that stereotypes are flexible and influenced by social context. The stereotypes of Americans possessed by Australian students were assessed at the start and end of the Gulf War in 1991. The students did this either using Australia and Britain as the frame of reference (restricted range) or with Australia, Britain, Iraq, and the Soviet Union as the frame of reference (extended range). The favourability of the American stereotype changed as a function of the time of testing (start vs. end of conflict) and the frame of reference (see the figure on the right). When the frame of reference included only Australia and Britain, the students (who were predominantly anti-war) showed a reduction in stereotype favourableness over time. In contrast, when the frame of reference included a country (i.e., Iraq), with whom Australia was officially in conflict, the favourability of the American stereotype

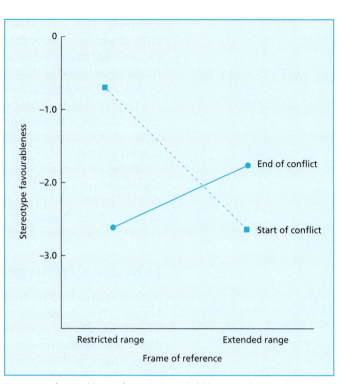

Stereotype favourableness for Americans held by Australian students as a function of time (start vs. end of 1991 Gulf War) and frame of reference (restricted range vs. extended range). Data from Haslam et al. (1992).

*increased* over time. This happened because America was regarded as an ingroup when compared against Iraq. These findings show that stereotypes can vary considerably as a function of the context (before vs. after war; frame of reference) in which they are elicited.

## Evaluation

⊕ As predicted by social identity theory, stereotypes are influenced by the immediate social context. Thus, they are flexible and not rigid as implied by the cognitive approach.

⊕ Evidence (e.g., from the minimal group paradigm) suggests strongly that perceiving oneself and others in terms of social identities and stereotypes is both natural and inevitable.

⊖ In spite of the variability across situations displayed by stereotypes, it is still entirely possible that most stereotypes possess a relatively unchanging central core of meaning (as suggested by cognitive theorists).

⊖ The precise nature of an individual's stereotypes in any given situation is very hard to predict, because it is assumed that they are determined jointly by several factors. In the words of Turner (1999, p. 26), "Like all perception, they [stereotypes] vary with the expectations, needs, values, and purposes of the perceiver."

## How are stereotypes formed?

A factor involved in the formation of stereotypes is known as the **outgroup homogeneity effect**, the tendency to perceive outgroup members as being very similar or homogeneous to each other (i.e., "They're all the same"). This effect was shown by Quattrone and Jones (1980). Students from Princeton University and from Rutgers University saw a videotape of a student allegedly from their own university or from the other university deciding whether to wait alone or with other participants while the experimenter fixed a piece of apparatus. They were then asked to estimate the percentage of other students from the same university as the videotaped student who would make the same choice. The participants tended to guess that nearly all of the students from the other university would make the same decision as the videotaped student. However, this was not the case when the student was from the same university as themselves.

Ostrom and Sedikides (1992) reviewed the evidence on the outgroup homogeneity effect. The effect was obtained fairly consistently, but was generally small in magnitude. However, the effect was relatively greater in natural groups than in artificial, laboratory-created groups.

Evidence that the outgroup homogeneity effect may be relevant to prejudice and discrimination was reported by Vanbeselaere (1991). The participants were led to believe that the members of the outgroup were either homogeneous or heterogeneous (dissimilar to each other). Ingroup members discriminated against homogeneous outgroups, but failed to do so against heterogeneous outgroups.

## How are stereotypes maintained?

*In what ways might stereotypes influence how we perceive other people?*

Various factors help to maintain stereotypes after they have been formed (Hilton & von Hippel, 1996). In general terms, information consistent with our stereotypes is attended to and stored away in memory, whereas information inconsistent with our stereotypes is often ignored and/or forgotten. Bodenhausen (1988) studied the negative stereotypes many Americans have about people of Spanish origin. In his first study, American participants pretended they were jurors at a trial. The defendant was described to some of them as Carlos Ramirez, a Spanish-sounding name. To others, he was described as Robert Johnson. The participants then read the evidence, and decided how likely it was the defendant was guilty. Those who knew him as Carlos Ramirez rated him as more guilty than those who knew him as Robert Johnson. Thus, stereotypes lead to biased processing of information.

In his second study, Bodenhausen (1988) tried to find out more about the processes involved. He argued that stereotypes might lead participants to *attend* only to information fitting their stereotype, or it might lead them to *distort* the information to make it support their stereotype. In order to prevent participants from attending selectively to stereotype-fitting information, Bodenhausen asked them to rate each item of evidence immediately in terms of whether it favoured or did not favour the defendant. Carlos Ramirez was no longer rated as more guilty than Robert Johnson. Thus, stereotypes make us *attend* to information fitting the stereotype, and cause us to disregard other items of information.

Another factor in maintaining stereotypes is known as priming: Seeing or hearing stereotypical information increases the tendency to think and behave in stereotype-consistent ways. For example, Rudman and Borgida (1995) asked men to watch television commercials in which women were portrayed as sexual objects. As a result, the men showed an increased tendency to respond to the next woman they met in a sexual way. They focused more on her appearance rather than on what she was saying, they were more likely to ask sexist questions, and they paid more attention to her body.

From what has been said so far, it might be imagined that most people would tend to remember information congruent or in line with their stereotypical views and to forget incongruent information. In fact, matters are actually more complicated. Stangor and McMillan (1992) carried out meta-analyses to establish which kind of information is better remembered. Among individuals having weak or moderate stereotypes, information *incongruent* with the stereotype was generally remembered better than congruent information. However, congruent information was better remembered than incongruent information for individuals having strong stereotypes. Thus, memory processes serve to maintain stereotypes only for those who already possess strong stereotypes.

Finally, stereotypes are also maintained by various attributional processes. When someone's behaviour is open to more than one explanation, the attributions made about that behaviour depend on whether the behaviour is consistent or inconsistent with the relevant stereotype. As we saw in Chapter 18, behaviour can be attributed to dispositional

Priming (seeing or hearing stereotyped information) maintains stereotypes.

or internal causes (e.g., personality) or to situational causes. Stereotype-consistent behaviour is more likely than stereotype-inconsistent behaviour to be attributed to dispositional causes (Jackson, Sullivan, & Hodge, 1993). When considering an ingroup, we are more inclined to use dispositional attributions to explain its positive behaviour than its negative behaviour (Hewstone & Jaspars, 1984); in contrast, with outgroups, we use dispositional attributions more often to explain its negative behaviour than its positive behaviour.

What do the above findings mean? When we attribute someone's behaviour to dispositional causes, we expect that behaviour to be repeated. On the other hand, behaviour attributed to situational causes will probably change when the situation changes. Thus, we expect stereotype-consistent behaviour to continue in the future, but this is not the case for stereotype-inconsistent behaviour.

Are we more likely to assume that this man is sleeping rough because of situational factors (he's been taken ill, forgotten his house keys) or dispositional factors (he can't keep a job, he's drunk and rowdy in accommodation, for example)?

## Stereotypes and behaviour

We currently know disappointingly little about the relationship between stereotypes and behaviour. As Fiske (2000, p. 312) pointed out, "The stereotyping literature needs a wake-up call … to get serious about predicting behaviour." Some evidence suggests that stereotypes are only weakly associated with negative behaviour or discrimination against members of other groups. For example, Dovidio, Brigham, Johnson, and Gaertner (1996) carried out a meta-analysis, in which it emerged that individual differences in stereotyping correlated on average only +16 with discrimination. Thus, there is a very weak association between stereotyping and discriminatory behaviour.

An amusing example of how stereotypes can influence behaviour was reported by Dijksterhuis and van Knippenberg (1998). There were three groups of participants. One group spent 5 minutes imagining a typical or stereotypical professor, listing the behaviour, lifestyle, and appearance appropriate to such a person. A second group did the same with respect to a typical or stereotypical secretary. A third or control group did not consider any stereotypes. After that, all participants answered questions from the game *Trivial Pursuit*. Participants who had

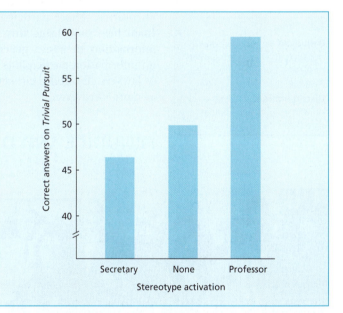

Performance on *Trivial Pursuit* as a function of stereotype activation (secretary, none, professor). Data from Dijksterhuis and van Knippenberg (1998).

focused on the stereotype of professors answered the most questions correctly, whereas those focusing on the secretary stereotype performed the worst (see the figure above). Thus, activation of the professor stereotype (in which intelligence and knowledge are key features) led participants to behave like a professor would. Now you know what to do to beat other people at *Trivial Pursuit*!

## How can we change stereotypes?

Most research has shown that it is remarkably difficult to produce long-lasting changes in someone's stereotypes. Why is this? One popular explanation is based on the subtyping model (e.g., Brewer, Dull, & Lui, 1981). According to this model, individuals violating the stereotype of their group are simply assigned to a separate subtype, and so are regarded as unrepresentative of the group. For example, suppose we have a stereotype that Germans

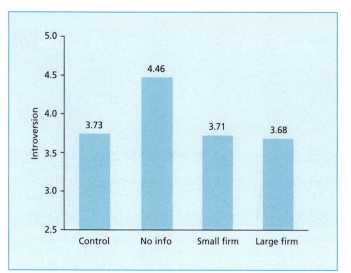

Beliefs about lawyers' introversion without specific information (control condition) or after reading about a specific lawyer called Steve (other conditions). From Kunda and Oleson (1995).

are efficient, but we meet an inefficient German professor. This may lead us to conclude that members of the subtype of German professors are inefficient, but all other Germans are efficient (Weber & Crocker, 1983).

Kunda and Oleson (1995) predicted that people will use almost any information about deviant (stereotype-breaking) individuals to justify subtyping them and thus regarding them as unrepresentative. They gave their participants a copy of an interview with an introverted lawyer called Steve. He was a deviant, because the stereotype of lawyers in the United States is that they are extraverted. In order to provide the participants with some (flimsy) grounds for subtyping Steve, some of them were told either that he worked for a small firm or for a large firm. Other participants were given no information about the size of firm for which Steve worked, and control participants did not read the interview. All groups of participants provided ratings of how introverted or extraverted lawyers are at the end of the experiment.

The findings are shown in the figure on the left. The ratings of the control group represent the standard stereotypical view that lawyers are not introverted. Those participants given the irrelevant information that Steve worked for a small firm or a large firm maintained their stereotypical view of lawyers, using that information to avoid generalising from Steve to lawyers in general. In contrast, the no-information participants who had no grounds for regarding Steve as unrepresentative of lawyers changed their stereotypical view of lawyers in the direction of perceiving them as more introverted.

# PREJUDICE AND DISCRIMINATION

Many people regard prejudice and discrimination as meaning the same thing. In fact, there is an important distinction between them. **Prejudice** is an attitude, whereas **discrimination** refers to behaviour or action. According to Smith and Mackie (2000, p. 156), prejudice is "the positive or negative evaluation of a social group and its members". It differs from stereotyping in that the emphasis with prejudice is more on emotional factors and less on cognitive ones. Discrimination involves negative actions (e.g., aggression) directed at the members of some group.

We saw in Chapter 18 that there is often a discrepancy between attitudes and behaviour. What often happens is that individuals have negative attitudes towards some other group (and are thus prejudiced), but this is not reflected in their behaviour (and so they show no discrimination). This was found in the study by LaPiere (1934; see Chapter 18), in which there was prejudice but not discrimination against Chinese people. Dovidio et al. (1996) carried out a meta-analysis, and found that prejudice correlated only +32 with discrimination, meaning that there is only a modest association between the two. There are generally greater social pressures to avoid discrimination (which is readily observable by others) than to avoid prejudice (which is less obvious to others).

Discrimination can take various forms. Allport (1954) argued that there are five stages of discrimination. In certain situations (e.g., Nazi Germany), the level of

Discrimination against specific groups is sometimes aided by distinguishing visual characteristics (skin colour, or style of dress, for example). Sometimes, however, minority group members are not clearly distinguishable from the majority and are forced to identify themselves. This was the case in Nazi Germany where Jews had to wear a Star of David on their clothing, making them a focus for racial hatred.

discrimination increases rapidly from the early stages to the later ones. Here are Allport's five stages:

1. *Anti-locution*. Verbal attacks are directed against some other group.
2. *Avoidance*. The other group is systematically avoided; this can involve steps to make it easier to identify group members (e.g., the Star of David worn by Jews in Nazi Germany).
3. *Discrimination*. The other group is deliberately treated less well than other groups in terms of civil rights, job opportunities, membership of clubs, and so on.
4. *Physical attack*. Members of the other group are attacked, and their property is destroyed.
5. *Extermination*. There are deliberate attempts to kill all members of the other group (e.g., the gas chambers built by the Nazis to murder the Jews).

We saw earlier in the chapter that there are various ways of assessing stereotypes related to prejudice. There is an important distinction between explicit stereotypes (of which the individual has full conscious awareness) and implicit stereotypes (found below the level of conscious awareness). In general, implicit stereotypes provide more evidence of prejudice than do explicit stereotypes.

Prejudice and discrimination have been found with respect to numerous groups within society. However, groups that are easily identified tend to be on the receiving end of the most prejudice and discrimination. This helps to explain why race, gender, and age are the "top three" categories used for purposes of stereotyping, prejudice, and discrimination (Fiske, 1998). In order to capture the flavour of research on prejudice and discrimination, we will focus mainly on racism, which is probably the most intensively studied form of prejudice. However, we will also consider sexism briefly.

In the early 1960s, during a period of high immigration from the West Indies to the UK, the MP Enoch Powell warned of the dangers of social unrest following the distortion of the labour market. His "rivers of blood" speech was taken by many as a call for repatriation of immigrants, and was quoted by both those for and those against immigration.

## Racism

**Racism** can be defined as prejudice and discrimination against others because of their race or their ethnicity. The evils of racism can be seen in the mass slaughter that took place in the twentieth century in several countries such as Germany, the former Yugoslavia, Rwanda, and South Africa. There is superficial evidence that racism is in decline in countries such as the United States and Britain. For example, numerous questionnaire studies have revealed a substantial reduction in racist attitudes (see Hogg & Vaughan, 2002). However, this reduction may be more apparent than real. Fiske (2002) argued that only about 10% of individuals in Western societies have overt and obvious racial biases. In addition, as many as 80% possess various subtle racial biases, which lead to "awkward social interactions, embarrassing slips of the tongue, unchecked assumptions, stereotypic judgements, and spontaneous neglect" (p. 124). We saw earlier in the chapter that there is more evidence of racial stereotyping when subtle, indirect measures are used rather than more direct ones (e.g., Wittenbrink et al., 1997).

Dovidio and Gaertner (1991) argued that large numbers of people exhibit what they called aversive racism. **Aversive racism** can be defined as "attitudes toward members of a racial group that incorporate both egalitarian [belief in equality] social values and negative emotions, causing one to avoid interaction with members of the group" (Franzoi, 1996, p. 405). The notion of ambivalent racism (McConahay, 1986) is similar. Individuals with ambivalent racism experience much conflict between their beliefs in equality and sympathy for those who are oppressed and their beliefs that individuals are responsible for what happens to them. As a result, many white Americans are willing to praise successful black Americans, but have poor opinions of black Americans who appear unwilling to work hard.

Swim, Aikin, Hall, & Hunter (1995) argued that there are three main ways in which modern racism expresses itself. First, modern racists deny there is prejudice and discrimination against minority groups. Second, they show annoyance and impatience at the fact that

*How does racism manifest itself in contemporary society?*

Perhaps the success of Martin Luther King's leadership in the civil rights movement was because he challenged role congruity by being both black and of an educated, higher socio-economic status than many of the people on whose behalf he campaigned.

minority groups demand equal treatment with the majority group. Third, they have feelings of resentment at the prospect of minority groups receiving positive action to assist them.

## Evidence

We can study racism by seeing whether a given ambiguous situation is interpreted differently depending on whether the central figure is, say, white or black. This was done by Duncan (1976), who asked white American students to watch a conversation between a black and a white man. When the white person gently shoved the black person, the behaviour was interpreted as violent by only 13% of the participants. In contrast, 73% of the participants interpreted the same behaviour as violent when it was the black man who did the shoving.

Pfeifer and Ogloff (1991) carried out a study in which white university students read a description of a rape case. The defendant in the case was either black or white. The key finding was that the black defendant was rated as more guilty than the white defendant. However, this effect disappeared when the participants were reminded that they should avoid prejudice.

Crosby, Bromley, and Saxe (1980) reviewed studies in which unobtrusive measures of prejudice and discrimination were obtained. Discrimination by whites against blacks occurred in 44% of the laboratory and field studies they considered, and was especially likely when the white participants did not come face-to-face with the black victims.

Racial bias influences even basic perceptual processes. Payne (2001) carried out a study in which a photograph of a male face (white or black) was presented briefly. The photograph of an object was then presented, and the task was to decide rapidly whether it was a handgun or a handtool. The white participants were more likely to identify a tool mistakenly as a gun when it was preceded by a black face than a white face, and this seemed to happen relatively automatically. Individuals high in explicit prejudice showed more racial bias than those low in explicit prejudice, whereas those who felt it was important not to experience or express prejudice showed relatively little racial bias.

## Sexism

**Sexism** involves prejudice against individuals purely on the basis of their sex. Probably the commonest sexist assumption is that women are more caring than men, but men are more assertive and competent. These assumptions have been found in many parts of the world, including Australia, Europe, North America, and South America (Deaux, 1985). Findings reported by Broverman, Broverman, Clarkson, Rosencrantz, and Vogel (1981) are more disturbing. They asked clinicians to identify the characteristics of the healthy adult, the healthy man, and the healthy woman. The characteristics of the healthy adult and the healthy man were very similar, including adjectives such as independent, decisive, and assertive. In contrast, the adjectives used to describe the healthy woman included adjectives such as dependent, submissive, and emotional.

Sexism is apparent in what is known as the "glass ceiling": Women in most Western societies are as highly qualified as men, but less than 10% of top positions (e.g., chief executives) are occupied by women. Eagly and Karau (2002) explained this state of affairs in their role congruity theory. According to this theory, women are thwarted in their attempts to achieve top positions because of the existence of two forms of prejudice:

1. Men typically evaluate women's potential for leadership less highly than that of men. The reason is that there are large discrepancies between the perceived qualities needed for leadership (e.g., decisive, action-oriented, courageous) and perceptions of the female gender role (e.g., helpful, sympathetic, nurturant).
2. Leadership behaviour that is decisive and action oriented and thus conforms to expectations is regarded more favourably when it is shown by a man than by a woman.

---

**Are women more caring?**

Sheridan and King's (1972) research asked men and women participants to give a real puppy real electric shocks whilst being able to see the puppy howl and yelp as they did so. Not all the men progressed to the maximum shock level but every woman participant did.

Does this mean women are less caring? Is the stereotype wrong? Or could it be that the women had been socialised into doing what men told them and being non-assertive? Are women blind followers and dependent, not suitable for leadership?

---

**KEY TERM**

**Sexism:** prejudice against individuals purely on the basis of whether they are male or female.

## Evidence

As a result of the above forms of prejudice, men and women in many countries express a preference for male rather than female bosses. For example, Simmons (2001) found a preference for male bosses in all 22 countries surveyed by Gallup in the mid-1990s. Further strong evidence of prejudice against women was reported by Davison and Burke (2000). They carried out a meta-analysis of studies in which participants rated the employability of fictitious job applicants when given a CV or completed application form. Half the participants received a CV with a male name attached to it and the other half received the same CV with a female name attached. Davison and Burke found that there was a clear tendency to prefer men to women for jobs rated as male sex-typed. The relevance of this finding is that most leadership positions are male sex-typed.

Even now, people in many countries express a preference for male rather than female bosses.

Additional support for role congruity theory comes from Eagly, Makhijani, and Konsky (1992) in a review of studies in which leadership behaviour was described and ascribed to a man or a woman. In their meta-analysis of 61 studies, there was a general tendency to rate this behaviour less highly when performed by a woman. Of most importance, the tendency to devalue women's leadership behaviour was much greater when the behaviour was stereotypically masculine (e.g., directive or autocratic).

According to role congruity theory, specific forms of prejudice against women hinder them in their efforts to achieve leadership roles. An alternative view is that there is a very general prejudice against women. However, women are often evaluated more favourably than men, and this has been found with both explicit and implicit measures of prejudice (Carpenter, 2001).

*To what extent do you think that sexism still limits women's aspirations and career prospects?*

## Evaluation

- ➕ The two forms of prejudice against women identified by role congruity theory exist and make it hard for women to become leaders.
- ➕ As predicted by role congruity theory, prejudice against female leaders is widespread, having been found cross-culturally and among women as well as men.
- ➕ Role congruity theory explains the data more adequately than an alternative theory based on the assumption that there is very general prejudice against women.
- ➖ The prejudicial effects obtained in most of the studies and meta-analyses accounted for only 1–5% of the variability in the data. As a result, it is not clear whether such effects can account fully for the "glass ceiling".

# Authoritarian personality

Adorno, Frenkel-Brunswik, Levinson, and Sanford (1950) argued that people with an authoritarian personality are most likely to be prejudiced. The **authoritarian personality** includes the following characteristics:

- Rigid beliefs in conventional values.
- General hostility towards other groups.
- Intolerance of ambiguity.
- Submissive attitudes towards authority figures.

Adorno et al. (1950) argued that childhood experiences are of crucial importance. Harsh treatment causes the child to have much hostility towards his or her parents. This hostility remains unconscious, because the child is unwilling to admit to it. This causes motivated forgetting, or what Freud called repression. The child seems to idealise his or

What do you understand by
the term "authoritarian"?

her parents, and in later life is submissive towards authority figures. However, repressed hostility is displaced on to nonthreatening minority groups in the form of prejudice. Prejudice is predicted to be shown by authoritarian adults to a wide range of other groups

## Evidence

Adorno et al. (1950) devised various questionnaires relating to their theory. One of these questionnaires was the Ethnocentrism Scale (E-Scale), ethnocentrism being the belief that one's ethnic group is superior to all others. The scale measures prejudice towards a number of minority groups including Blacks and Jews. However, the most important questionnaire was the **F (Fascism) Scale**, designed to measure the attitudes of the authoritarian personality (sample item: "Obedience and respect for authority are the most important virtues children should learn").

Adorno et al. (1950) found that high scorers on the F-Scale tended to be more prejudiced than low scorers (e.g., the F-Scale correlated +.75 with the Ethnocentrism Scale). As predicted by the theory, high scorers on the F-Scale reported being treated more harshly than nonauthoritarian individuals during childhood.

More evidence was reported by Milgram (1974). He found that most people are prepared to give very strong electric shocks to another person when ordered to do so by an authority figure (see Chapter 20). Those with an authoritarian personality are supposed to be submissive to authority, and, as predicted, gave stronger shocks than nonauthoritarians.

One of the main predictions of the theory is that authoritarian adults will show widespread prejudice against minority groups. This prediction was tested by Pettigrew and Meertens (1995) in a study on people living in France, the Netherlands, Britain, and Germany. They found in each country that those scoring high on ethnocentrism revealed considerable prejudice against a wide range of outgroups.

Altemeyer (1988) developed the ideas of Adorno et al. (1950), and produced his own questionnaire (the Right Wing Authoritarianism Scale). He obtained evidence suggesting that the roots of authoritarianism lie in adolescence rather than in early childhood. Adolescents whose parents are authoritarian imitate the behaviour of their parents, and are often rewarded for doing so. According to this view, the development of the authoritarian personality owes little or nothing to repressed hostility towards the parents.

Measures of the so-called authoritarian personality actually measure social attitudes and beliefs rather than personality. Personality changes relatively little over time (see Chapter 13), but individuals' scores on authoritarianism can vary considerably. For example, Altemeyer (1988) found that there were substantial increases in scores on the Right Wing Authoritarianism Scale when participants were shown scenarios concerning threatening social changes. Duckitt, Wagner, du Plessis, and Birum (2002) obtained evidence that a personality dimension of social conformity vs. autonomy (personal freedom) underlies authoritarian social attitudes.

Adorno et al. (1950) assumed that prejudice depends on individual personality. However, cultural norms are clearly more important. For example, Pettigrew (1958) considered prejudice in South Africa and in the United States. The levels of authoritarianism were equal in the two countries, but there was much more prejudice in South Africa than in the United States.

Major historical events can cause a substantial general increase in prejudice. A good example is the impact of the attack on the US fleet in Pearl Harbor on Americans' attitudes towards the Japanese. There was a large and immediate increase in prejudice against Japanese people among most of the population. Such increases are hard to explain in terms of the authoritarian personality. However, there is evidence that perceived social threat leads mildly authoritarian individuals to become more authoritarian in their attitudes (Doty, Peterson, & Winter, 1991).

### THE NINE PERSONALITY TRAITS OF THE AUTHORITARIAN PERSONALITY, FROM ADORNO ET AL.'S F-SCALE

| Traits | Description |
| --- | --- |
| Conventionalism | Very conventional, great dislike of change |
| Authoritarian–Submissive | Deferential to authority |
| Authoritarian–Aggressive | Very hostile to people who challenge authority |
| Anti-inception | Very intolerant of behaviour that is "Wrong" in any way |
| Superstition & stereotype | Believes in fate |
| Power & "toughness" | Has a dominating and bullying manner |
| Destructiveness & cynicism | Very hostile towards anyone with whom they disagree |
| Projectivity | Projects own unconscious impulses onto other people |
| Sex | Has an exaggerated interest in sexual behaviour that is not regarded as "normal" |

**KEY TERM**

**F (Fascism) Scale:** a test of tendencies towards fascism; high scorers are prejudiced, racist, and anti-Semitic.

## Evaluation

⊕ People differ in their level of prejudice, in part because of individual differences in authoritarian personality.

⊕ Childhood experiences influence whether someone develops an authoritarian personality.

⊖ Authoritarianism is not really a personality trait, because it varies from situation to situation.

⊖ Social and cultural factors are much more important than personality in determining widespread uniformity of prejudice.

⊖ All items on the F-Scale are worded so that agreement with them indicates an authoritarian attitude. Thus, those with an acquiescence response set (a tendency to agree to items regardless of meaning) seem to be authoritarian.

⊖ The finding of an association between certain childhood experiences and authoritarian personality does not show that the childhood experiences *caused* the authoritarian personality.

# Realistic group conflict

According to Sherif (1966), prejudice often results from intergroup conflict. Each group has its own interests and goals that it is trying to achieve. Sometimes two groups compete for the same goal, which creates realistic conflict. As a result, the members of each group tend to become prejudiced against the members of the other group. This is the central assumption of realistic conflict theory. In contrast, two groups will sometimes have the same interests and be pursuing the same goal. When that is the case, then the two groups will often co-operate with each other. This produces a situation in which there are friendly relationships between members of the two groups and an absence of prejudice.

People who feel strongly about a particular cause are sometimes likely to experience violent clashes with people who do not share the same values.

## Evidence

Realistic conflict theory developed from the well-known Robber's Cave study (Sherif, Harvey, White, Hood, & Sherif, 1961)—see Key Study overleaf.

Similar findings have been obtained in other cultures. Andreeva (1984) carried out a Russian study. Ingroup favouritism and prejudice towards the other group both increased while boys at Pioneer youth camps were engaged in competitive sports. Brewer and Campbell (1976) studied 30 tribes in Africa. Prejudice was greatest against tribes living nearby, presumably because such tribes were most likely to compete for valuable resources (e.g., water).

The notion that competition always leads to prejudice and intergroup conflict was rejected by Tyerman and Spencer (1983). They argued that competition mainly has dramatic effects when those involved are initially strangers, as was the case in the Sherif et al. (1961) and Andreeva (1984) studies. Tyerman and Spencer observed scouts who already knew each other well as they competed in groups against each other in their annual camp. Competition did not produce the negative effects obtained by Sherif et al.

Further evidence that the existence of perceived conflicts of interest does not necessarily produce strong prejudice was reported by Struch and Schwartz (1989). They studied levels of intergroup hostility and prejudice among various religious groups in Israel. Perceived conflicts of interest among these religious groups led to significantly more prejudice and aggression in those individuals who identified strongly with their religious ingroup than was the case in those individuals who identified less strongly. Thus, realistic conflict may need to be combined with strong ingroup identification to produce powerful negative attitudes and behaviour towards an outgroup.

*Why do you think that competition between groups sometimes leads to hostilities?*

## Evaluation

➕ Competition between two groups for the same goal can lead to prejudice.

➕ Realistic group conflict theory explains the large increases in prejudice which are found when countries are at war with each other (e.g., the Second World War).

➖ According to the theory, conflicts arise when group interests are threatened. However, group interests are defined very vaguely within the theory: "A real or imagined threat to the safety of the group, an economic interest, a political advantage, a military consideration, prestige, or a number of others" (Sherif, 1966, p. 15).

➖ Realistic conflict or competition between groups is not always *sufficient* to produce prejudice (e.g., Tyerman & Spencer, 1983). This is especially the case when individuals do not identify very strongly with their ingroup (e.g., Struch & Schwartz, 1989).

➖ Competition between groups is not *necessary* to produce prejudice. Millions of people have prejudiced attitudes towards people in other cultures whom they have never met, and with whom they are not in competition.

➖ Studies with the minimal group paradigm (discussed earlier in the chapter) reveal limitations in realistic conflict theory. These studies show the existence of intergroup rivalry in the complete absence of any objective conflict between the two groups.

## Social identity theory

Social identity theory (discussed earlier in the chapter) has been applied to prejudice and discrimination. According to the theory, individuals seek to distinguish or differentiate their ingroup as clearly as possible from outgroups. In order to boost their self-esteem, they typically regard their ingroup favourably in comparison with outgroups. As a result, members of outgroups may be exposed to prejudice and discrimination.

### Sherif et al.: The Robber's Cave study

In this study by Sherif et al. (1961) a total of 22 boys spent two weeks at a summer camp in the United States. They were put into two groups (called the Eagles and the Rattlers). These groups were told that whichever group did better in various sporting events and other competitions would receive a trophy, knives, and medals. As a result of this competition, a fight broke out between the members of the two groups, and the Rattlers' flag was burned.

Prejudice was shown by the fact that each group regarded its own members as friendly and courageous, whereas the members of the other group were regarded as smart-alecks and liars. When the boys were asked to say who their friends were, 93% of the choices were members of the same group, and only 7% were boys from the other group.

In order to reduce the conflict between the Rattlers and the Eagles, it was decided that the camp's drinking water should be turned off, with the two groups needing to combine forces to restore the supply. Several other situations were set up in which co-operation on a common goal was essential, including rescuing a truck that had got stuck, and pitching tents. As a result of pursuing these common goals the two groups developed much friendlier attitudes towards each other. When they were asked to name their friends at the camp, 30% of their choices after these co-operative activities were members of the other group. This was *four* times higher than before the groups started pursing common goals.

#### KEY STUDY EVALUATION—Sherif et al.

Sherif et al.'s study has been regarded as very important because it showed ordinary boys acting in different ways towards each other depending on the situation. Competition resulted in dislike and hostility, a common goal led to friendship and good feelings. It might be interesting to speculate about whether the results would have been different if all the participants had been girls. It has been argued that while they are growing up girls are rewarded for co-operation, whereas boys are rewarded for competitiveness. It could also be argued that the participants were not a representative group, in that they were not randomly selected especially for the study.

#### Discussion points

1. Why has the study by Sherif et al. been so influential?
2. How important is group conflict as a cause of prejudice?

Turner (1999) considered implications of the social identity approach to prejudice. He rejected the traditional view that prejudice and social conflict involving outgroups are irrational and reflect badly on individuals and on society generally. According to social identity theory, "We need to understand social conflict as psychologically meaningful, as an expression of how people define themselves socially ... It is a result of ordinary, adaptive and functional psychological processes in interplay with the realities of social life" (p. 19).

## Evidence

Some support for social identity theory was discussed in connection with realistic group conflict theory. Struch and Schwartz (1989) found that members of religious groups who had strong identification with their own religious group showed more prejudice and discrimination against other religious groups.

Doosje, Branscombe, Spears, and Manstead (1998) considered the attitudes of Dutch people towards Indonesia, which used to be a Dutch colony. Some of the participants had a high level of national identification with being Dutch, whereas others had only a low level. As predicted by social identity theory, those having the greatest ingroup bias (i.e., high level of national identification) felt less guilty about Dutch treatment of the Indonesians. They were also less willing to compensate the Indonesians than were those having little ingroup bias (i.e., low level of national identification).

Verkuyten, Drabbles, and van den Nieuwenhuijzen (1999) tested predictions of social identity theory in Dutch participants aged between 16 and 18. These participants indicated how strongly they identified themselves with the majority ingroup in Holland by the extent of their agreement with the following statement: "In many respects, I am like most of the Dutch." The participants' level of prejudice was assessed by asking them to indicate their emotional reactions to descriptions of situations involving ethnic minorities (e.g., "More and more Islamic people who have different views and habits have come to live in the Netherlands. Because of this there is an increasing danger that the Dutch norms and values are threatened." Individuals who identified themselves most strongly as Dutch revealed the greatest negative emotions towards ethnic minorities. Thus, group identification was related to prejudice as predicted by social identity theory.

*What do you understand by the term "national identification"? How would you describe your own national identity?*

## Evaluation

- ⊕ Prejudice is determined in part by strength of group identification.
- ⊕ Social identity theory helps to account for individual differences in prejudice.
- ⊖ Social identity theory provides a limited view of prejudice, in that it ignores important factors such as intergroup competition and conflict.
- ⊖ Social identity theory indicates *why* prejudice and social conflict exist, but does not make it clear in detail *how* they develop.

# REDUCING PREJUDICE AND DISCRIMINATION

Prejudice and discrimination are common in most cultures, and we must find suitable ways to reduce (and ideally eliminate) all forms of prejudice and discrimination. Some of the main approaches suggested by psychologists are discussed here.

*What strategies could be used to reduce prejudice between groups?*

## Intergroup contact hypothesis

An influential theory in this area was put forward by Allport (1954). According to his intergroup contact hypothesis, the most effective way of reducing prejudice is by intergroup contact. However, if such contact is to prove successful, four conditions have to be met:

1. The two groups have equal status within the situation in which the contact takes place.
2. The two groups are working towards common goals, and efforts to attain these common goals are based on intergroup co-operation.

*Why might intergroup contact reduce prejudice?*

3. Intergroup contact needs to occur with enough frequency and duration to permit the development of meaningful relationships between members of the different groups.
4. There should be social and institutional support for intergroup acceptance.

## Evidence

It might be thought that a key reason why intergroup contact has positive effects is because it allows individuals to acquire accurate information about the other group. There is some support for this point of view. Stephan and Stephan (1984) assessed the amount of knowledge that Anglo and Chicano high-school students had of the other group's cultural values and customs. Those individuals with the most cultural knowledge of the other group had more favourable attitudes about that group. This probably occurred in part because those who felt most positively towards the other group had taken the trouble to find out about its cultural values. However, more knowledge may often *not* reduce prejudice, because it can reveal that the other group has very different values and customs to one's own group (Brown, 2000a).

Sherif et al. (1961) used some of Allport's (1954) ideas (e.g., intergroup co-operation on common goals) in their field study discussed above. As described in the Key Study, when the experimenters replaced the competitive situation with a co-operative one in which the success of each group required the co-operation of the other one prejudice was much reduced.

Aronson and Osherow (1980) adopted a very similar approach to Sherif et al. (1961). The schools in Austin, Texas, had recently been desegregated, which led to concerns about the racial conflict which might result from having black and white children in the same classes. One class of black and white children was divided into small groups for a learning task (e.g., the life of Abraham Lincoln). Within each group, every child was made responsible for learning a different part of the information. Each member of the group then taught what she/he had learned to the other group members. After that, the children received a mark based on their overall knowledge of the topic. This approach was called the **jigsaw classroom**, because all the children made a contribution, just as all the pieces in a jigsaw puzzle are needed to complete it.

Having children work in groups helps reduce racial barriers.

The findings with the jigsaw classroom were promising. The children showed higher self-esteem, better school performance, more liking for their classmates, and some reduction in prejudice. However, these effects were small, probably because the jigsaw classroom was only used for 12 hours spread over 6 weeks.

Problems with the jigsaw classroom were identified by Rosenfield, Stephan, and Lucker (1981). Minority group members low in competence were blamed for slowing down the learning of the more competent students. This confirmed existing prejudiced attitudes rather than reducing them.

There is convincing evidence that co-operative learning environments can be effective in reducing prejudice and discrimination in ethnically mixed schools. Slavin (1983) discussed 14 studies in which the effects of a co-operative learning programme were compared against those of traditional teaching methods. In 11 of these studies, there were significantly more cross-ethnic friendships among children exposed to a co-operative learning programme. This conclusion was confirmed by Miller and Davidson-Podgorny (1987) in an analysis based on 25 studies.

A thorough test of the intergroup contact hypothesis was carried out at Wexler Middle School in Waterford in the United States (see Brown, 1986). A considerable amount of money was spent on the school to provide it with excellent facilities. It was decided that the number of black and white students should be similar, so that it would not be regarded as a black school or as a white school. Much was done to make all the students feel equal, with very little streaming on the basis of ability. Co-operation was encouraged by having the students work together to buy special equipment they could all use.

The results over the first 3 years were encouraging. There were many black–white friendships, but these friendships rarely extended to visiting each other's homes. There was a steady reduction in discrimination, with the behaviour of the black and white students towards each other being friendly. However, some stereotyped beliefs were still found. Black and white students agreed that black students were tougher and more assertive than white students, whereas white students were cleverer and worked harder than black students.

Other studies involving desegregation in schools have not worked well. Stephan (1987) reviewed studies on desegregation, and concluded that it often produces *increases* in white prejudice. In addition, contact between whites and blacks rarely has positive effects on the black students. One problem is that white and black students in desegregated schools often keep very much within their own group. According to Stephan desegregation is most likely to lead to reduced prejudice when the students are of equal status, there are co-operative, one-to-one interactions, members of the two groups have similar beliefs and values, and contact occurs in various situations and with several members of the other group. However, these requirements are not met in most desegregated schools.

---

**CASE STUDY: *New Era Schools Trust***

The New Era Schools Trust (or NEST) runs three boarding schools in South Africa, in Durban, Johannesburg, and Cape Town. The unique aim of all the NEST schools is not only to produce well-educated and personable young people, but also to eliminate any trace of racial prejudice in their students. To achieve this, all races are mixed together from the very first day at school, living and studying alongside each other in a way that is rare even in post-apartheid South Africa. The teachers are similarly multiracial, and there is an equal mix of boys and girls.

Not only are the different races regarded as equal in NEST schools, their cultures are also given equal value. Schools in South Africa have generally taken the view that African culture is irrelevant, and have taught exclusively from a white perspective. At NEST schools the pupils study Xhosa poets as well as Keats, and the lives of Zulu warriors as well as Napoleon. This sense of total equality permeates everything—there are no prefects or top-down discipline, no uniforms or corporal punishment, and everyone takes a hand in doing the chores.

NEST has found that more black parents than white parents wish their children to attend a NEST school. White children tend to have better access to well-equipped schools where they are not required to help clean the dormitories, whereas many black parents are keen for their children to leave the deprivation of the townships to receive their education. This imbalance is lessening, however, as white parents realise what good academic success the NEST schools are achieving. In 1992 their pass rate was 100%, when private white schools and white church schools averaged 90%.

(Based on an article by Prue Leith, *The Times*, May 1993.)

---

## Evaluation

⊕ The intergroup contact hypothesis identified several factors determining whether intergroup contact will reduce prejudice.

⊕ Most of the available evidence has provided general support for the intergroup contact hypothesis (Pettigrew, 1998). However, while it has proved reasonably easy to reduce prejudice towards individual members of another group, it is much harder to ensure that this reduction *generalises* to all members of the other group.

⊖ It is hard to interpret the finding that intergroup contact and prejudice are negatively correlated. As Pettigrew (1998, p. 80) pointed out, "Prejudiced people avoid intergroup contact, so the causal link between contact and prejudice is two-way."

⊖ The intergroup contact hypothesis has little to say about *how* or *why* contact reduces prejudice.

⊖ The contact hypothesis does not indicate how positive contact with members of an outgroup might *generalise* to other members of that outgroup.

---

## Decategorisation, salient categorisation, and recategorisation

Suppose someone who is prejudiced against an outgroup has positive social interactions with a member of that outgroup. Such interactions may well lead to liking for that individual. However, this will not necessarily generalise to produce reduced prejudice towards the outgroup as a whole. In this section, we will consider three theoretical attempts to understand how intergroup contact can lessen prejudice towards an entire outgroup. All these theoretical attempts have their origins in social identity theory (discussed earlier in the chapter), and it is recognised within each theory that individuals' group or social identities are important to them. In order to produce a generalised reduction in prejudice, it is necessary to change the salience or prominence of existing group identities. As we will see, however, there are differing views on how to achieve this goal.

*Why is it that liking one member of an outgroup doesn't necessarily generalise to the rest of the outgroup?*

The contact hypothesis did not indicate clearly *why* and *how* intergroup contact can reduce prejudice. The theoretical approaches that we are about to discuss all address these issues. More specifically, it is argued that intergroup contact can activate processes such as decategorisation, salient categorisation, and recategorisation, with these processes in turn leading to a significant reduction in prejudice.

## Decategorisation: The personalisation model

*What do you understand by the term "decategorisation"?*

Brewer and Miller (1984) argued that stereotyping and prejudice often develop when ingroup and outgroup identities become the focus of attention. They claimed that social contact will be most effective in reducing prejudice when the boundaries between conflicting groups become blurred or less rigid. In other words, there is a process of **decategorisation**. When this happens, members of each group are less likely to think of members of the other group in terms of categories or group membership. The key process in decategorisation is for people to treat the members of another group as individuals. This leads them to realise that their stereotype of the other group was over-simplified and incorrect.

## Evidence

Bettencourt, Brewer, Croak, and Miller (1992) reported findings consistent with decategorisation theory. The minimal group paradigm was used to set up groups of over-estimators and under-estimators on a dot-estimation task. After that, four-person teams were established, each consisting of two over-estimators and two under-estimators. The key manipulation occurred during a subsequent problem-solving task. Some groups were encouraged to get to know each other as individuals, whereas others groups were told to focus on the task itself. As predicted by decategorisation theory, participants in the personalised groups showed less ingroup bias than did those in the task-oriented groups.

A subsequent study by Bettencourt, Charlton, and Kernaham (1997) suggested that personalised contact does not always reduce ingroup bias. They replicated the findings of Bettencourt et al. (1992) with members of majority groups. However, members of minority groups actually showed *more* ingroup bias with personalised contact than with task orientation.

Hamburger (1994) reviewed studies on the effects of contact with other groups. The evidence indicated that people who had personalised contact with atypical outgroup members generally altered their group stereotype. This mostly took the form of recognising that the members of the other group were more variable than they had previously believed. It was less common for more major changes in stereotypes to result from personalised contact.

## Evaluation

⊕ Personalised contact with members of another group can reduce bias and prejudice, at least in some circumstances (e.g., Bettencourt et al., 1992, 1997).

⊖ Personalised contact with a member of an outgroup often fails to produce any generalised reduction in prejudice. There is a danger that the outgroup member will be regarded as "an exception to the rule", and thus the group stereotype does not change (e.g., Kunda & Oleson, 1995).

⊖ Most of the studies have used laboratory groups to which the members felt little attachment. As Brown (2000a, p. 355) pointed out, "This may have made it easy for the participants to shed these identities when encouraged to engage in 'personalised' interaction. In real intergroup contexts it may not be so simple to distract people's attention from their group memberships."

**KEY TERM**
**Decategorisation:** reducing or blurring the differences between groups.

## Salient categorisation: Distinct social identity model

Hewstone and Brown (1986) focused on the issue of how reduced prejudice might *generalise* from a given individual to his or her group. They argued that the individual must be seen as *representative* or typical of his or her group, and thus his/her group membership needs to be salient or obvious. Thus, salient categorisation is the key. These ideas form an important part of what is sometimes referred to as the distinct social identity model.

## Evidence

Wilder (1984) reported findings consistent with the above model. Students had a pleasant meeting with a student from a rival college. This led to reduced prejudice towards the rival college when the student was regarded as a typical member of that college (salient categorisation). In contrast, there was no reduction when he was regarded as atypical.

Van Oudenhouven, Groenewoud, and Hewstone (1996) tested the notion that it is important for the group membership of an outgroup member to be salient or obvious if prejudice is to be reduced. Dutch participants spent two hours interacting with a Turkish confederate in one of three conditions: (1) the experimenter never mentioned the confederate's ethnicity (low salience); (2) the experimenter only mentioned the confederate's ethnicity at the end of the 2-hour period (moderate salience); and (3) the confederate's ethnicity was emphasised throughout the session (high salience). The key finding was that attitudes towards Turks in general were more favourable in the moderate and high salience conditions than in the low salience condition.

Brown, Vivian, and Hewstone (1999) carried out a study in which British participants worked with a German confederate to obtain a substantial reward. The German either appeared to correspond fairly closely to the typical German stereotype or was clearly atypical. In addition, the participants were given false information about how homogeneous (similar) or heterogeneous (dissimilar) German people are with respect to several characteristics. It should have been easiest to generalise from the confederate to all Germans when the confederate was perceived as typical and the Germans were thought to be homogeneous. As predicted, the participants in that condition had the most favourable attitudes towards Germans.

*What roles do status, power, and economic difference have in creating prejudice?*

## Evaluation

⊕ Approaches to reducing prejudice based on salient categorisation can produce more generalisation from an individual to his/her group than is likely to occur with most other approaches.

⊖ People often have clear stereotypes of other groups. As a result, generalisation from individual group members to their group is only likely to occur when they are clearly typical of the relevant stereotype.

⊖ "If the co-operative interaction goes wrong, ... then structuring the interaction at the intergroup level could make matters worse ... there is a risk of reinforcing negative stereotypes of the outgroup precisely because those people are seen as typical of it" (Brown, 2000a, p. 353).

## Recategorisation: Common ingroup identity model

Another approach to reducing prejudice towards an entire outgroup is based on key assumptions of social identity theory. According to that theory, individuals show ingroup bias or favouritism, regarding their own group as superior to one or more outgroups. It should be possible to eliminate prejudice by a process of **recategorisation**, in which the ingroup and the outgroup are recategorised to form a single ingroup. In this, the outgroup members are re-defined as members of the ingroup. Precisely this was proposed by Gaertner, Dovidio, Anastasio, Bachman, and Rust (1993) in their common ingroup identity model.

## Evidence

Gaertner, Rust, Dovidio, Bachman, and Anastasio (1994) studied recategorisation in a multi-ethnic high school in the United States. They carried out a survey, part of which

**KEY TERM**

**Recategorisation:** the process of producing a new categorisation in which the ingroup and the outgroup form a single group.

consisted of items focusing on the perception that there was a single ingroup within the school (e.g, "Despite the different groups at school, there is frequently the sense that we are all just one group"). Those students who thought that the school consisted in part of one large ingroup tended to have the most positive attitudes towards other ethnic groups in the school.

Salient categorisation followed by recategorisation can be very effective (Dovidio, Gaertner, & Validzic, 1998). Two groups worked together on a task. These groups were either equal or unequal in status, and their area of expertise was either the same or different. There was the greatest amount of recategorisation of the two groups as a single ingroup when the two groups were equal in status and their expertise differed. As predicted, this was the *only* condition in which outgroup prejudice was eliminated. As Dovidio et al. p. 116) concluded, their findings strongly supported the view that, "more inclusive, one-group representations critically mediate the relationship between conditions of intergroup contact and the reduction of bias [prejudice]".

## Evaluation

- ⊕ Recategorisation is one of the factors responsible for the beneficial effects of intergroup contact on prejudice.
- ⊕ "It is not clear how the recategorisation strategy … will facilitate generalisation. To the extent that one is successful in dissolving subgroups in favour of a superordinate category, then the social benefits may not transfer to other subgroup members outside the immediate setting" (Brown, 2000a, p. 356).
- ⊖ Most of the support for the salient categorisation and recategorisation approaches has come from laboratory studies. Mullen, Anthony, Salas, and Driskell (1994) found in a meta-analysis that ingroup bias is typically greater in real-world conditions than in laboratory studies, which probably makes it harder to reduce prejudice.
- ⊖ Decategorisation, salient categorisation, and recategorisation all involve significant changes in perceptions of outgroup members. Such changes are very difficult to produce in the face of pre-existing strong and habitual prejudice, as is often the case in the real world.
- ⊖ "The fundamental limitation of both decategorisation and recategorisation models is that they threaten to deprive individuals of valued social identities in smaller, less inclusive groups" (Hewstone et al., 2002, p. 590). Thus, individuals may perceive any potential gains from decategorisation or recategorisation to be outweighed by the loss of their current social identity stemming from their current ingroup membership.
- ⊖ More research is needed to compare directly the usefulness of decategorisation, salient categorisation, and recategorisation in reducing prejudice.

## S U M M A R Y

*Social identity theory*

According to social identity theory, we possess various social identities based on the groups to which we belong. Social identities enhance self-esteem and produce ingroup bias. Ingroup bias has been found even with minimal groups; this may sometimes be due to self-interest rather than to group identification as claimed within social identity theory. Ingroup bias increases self-esteem, but individuals with low self-esteem do *not* show greater ingroup bias as predicted by the theory. Social identity theory is more applicable to individualistic than collectivistic cultures, and it addresses cognitive factors more effectively than emotional and motivational ones.

Stereotypes are often inaccurate, but this is less true for ingroups than for outgroups. Stereotypes can be assessed by indirect as well as by direct measures. Stereotypes provide an economical way of perceiving the world. According to self-categorisation theory, stereotypes are influenced by the immediate social context. The outgroup homogeneity effect is one of the factors associated with the formation of stereotypes. We attend more to information consistent with our stereotypes, and seeing or hearing stereotypical information increases stereotype-consistent behaviour. Information congruent with existing stereotypes is better remembered than incongruent information only among individuals having strong stereotypes. Stereotyping is only modestly related to negative behaviour or discrimination. It is hard to alter stereotypes because we tend to regard stereotype-deviant individuals as unrepresentative, and so assign them to a separate subtype.

*Stereotypes*

Prejudice correlates only moderately with discrimination, because there are greater social pressures to avoid discrimination. Overt racism is increasingly rare, but subtle forms of racism are still very prevalent. According to role congruity theory, it is difficult for women to achieve leadership positions because of two forms of prejudice (discrepancies between perceived qualities needed for leadership and the female gender role; less favourable perception of assertive leadership behaviour when exhibited by a woman). According to Adorno et al., harsh parental treatment in childhood can create an authoritarian personality and hostility that is later displaced on to minority groups. In fact, prejudice is generally determined more by social and cultural factors than by personality. According to Sherif et al., prejudice often results from realistic group conflict. However, intergroup rivalry can occur in the absence of group conflict, and group conflict produces little prejudice in individuals who do not identify very strongly with their own ingroup. As predicted by social identity theory, individuals identifying most strongly with their ingroup are most likely to show prejudice towards outgroups.

*Prejudice and discrimination*

According to the intergroup contact hypothesis, intergroup contact can reduce prejudice and discrimination when two groups have equal status, there is co-operation between the groups, meaningful relationships develop, and there is institutional support for intergroup acceptance. There is evidence for this hypothesis (e.g., from the jigsaw classroom), but how and why contact produces positive effects are not considered. It has been argued that salient categorisation is needed for reductions in prejudice to generalise from a given individual to his/her group. Another proposal is that ingroup bias can be reduced by recategorising the ingroup and outgroup to form a single ingroup. Laboratory studies support the notion that salient categorisation followed by recategorisation can reduce prejudice. However, ingroup bias is usually stronger in the real world than in the laboratory, making it harder to eliminate prejudice via recategorisation.

*Reducing prejudice and discrimination*

# FURTHER READING

- Brown, R. (2000a). *Group processes*. Oxford, UK: Blackwell. Chapters 6, 7, and 8 provide good introductory accounts of several intergroup phenomena.
- Brown, R. (2001). Intergroup relations. In M. Hewstone & W. Stroebe (Eds.), *Introduction to social psychology* (3rd ed.). Various relevant topics (including prejudice and discrimination) are discussed in this well-argued chapter.
- Hewstone, M., Rubin, M., & Willis, H. (2002). Intergroup bias. *Annual Review of Psychology, 53*, 575–604. This chapter contains a good account of various theoretical accounts of intergroup bias and conflict.
- Hogg, M.A., & Vaughan, G.M. (2002). *Social psychology* (3rd ed.). Harlow, UK: Prentice Hall. Chapters 10 and 11 of this book provide clear discussions of intergroup phenomena including prejudice.

# Abnormal Psychology

**VI**

W e live in an era in which huge numbers of people are trying to cope with serious psychological problems of one kind or another. As Comer (2001, p. 7) pointed out, in the United States,

> *"Up to 19 of every hundred adults have a significant anxiety disorder, 10 suffer from profound depression, 5 display a personality disorder ..., 1 has schizophrenia ... and 11 abuse alcohol or other drugs. Add to these figures as many as 600,000 suicide attempts, 500,000 rapes, and 3 million cases of child abuse each year, and it becomes apparent abnormal psychological functioning is a pervasive problem."*

The available evidence from numerous other countries suggests that such widespread incidence of serious psychological problems is not limited to the United States. Indeed, there are several countries (especially in the industrialised world) in which a similar pattern manifests itself (see Comer, 2001).

An important issue is whether the incidence of psychological problems is increasing as we lead lives which often seem to be becoming more and more stressful. The fact that it seems as if life nowadays is especially stressful does not, of course, prove that it is more stressful than it used to be. Perhaps what is more accurate is to argue that the nature of life's stressors has changed somewhat over the past century or so. As little as 100 years ago, life expectancy in the Western world was approximately 30 years less than it is now. As a result, young and middle-aged people in those days were probably much more worried and stressed about their physical health than is the case today.

One of the few studies to provide empirical evidence concerning changes over recent decades was that of Twenge (2000; see Chapter 13). In essence, she considered data from several studies on children or college students in which trait anxiety (a personality dimension relating to susceptibility to anxiety) had been assessed. Her key finding was that the mean score for trait anxiety of both children and college students has shown a considerable increase over the past 50 years. The significance of this finding was captured clearly in her dramatic conclusion: "The average American child in the 1980s reported more anxiety than child psychiatric patients in the 1950s" (Twenge, 2000, p. 1007). It would be valuable to have similar data with respect to other psychological characteristics (e.g., depression).

Many non-psychologists believe that psychology is mainly concerned with abnormality and mental disorder. Of course, that isn't the case. However, it is true that the psychological forms of treatment developed by psychologists have been hugely successful in alleviating human suffering all round the world, and that gives abnormal psychology a special importance. Indeed, if anyone doubts the value of psychology (do such people exist?), they might be convinced by thinking about the literally millions of individuals suffering from anxiety, depression, and other mental disorders whose lives have been permanently transformed for the better by therapy based on psychological principles.

The achievements of psychologists in the area of abnormal psychology can be seen clearly by considering what used to be the case. For many centuries, the treatment applied to those suffering from mental disorders was positively barbaric. It was believed that mental disorders were caused by demons or other supernatural forces. Popular "cures" for mental illness were based on the idea of making things as unpleasant as possible for the demon, and included immersing the patient in boiling hot water, flogging, starvation, and torture. It was often believed that these "cures" would persuade the demons to leave the patient's body, and thereby remove his/her disorder.

As is extremely well-known, Sigmund Freud (at the end of the nineteenth century) was the first psychologist to argue strongly that psychological approaches to treatment were needed. He also has the distinction of being the first psychologist to provide a detailed and systematic approach by developing psychoanalysis. As a result of these (and other) contributions, he is deservedly the most famous psychologist of all time

If we go back before the time of Sigmund Freud, it is worth mentioning the Austrian mystic and physician Franz Mesmer (1734–1815). He treated patients suffering from various complaints by sitting them around a tub containing magnetised iron filings with protruding iron rods. It was claimed that cures were produced by the "animal magnetism" generated by this bizarre arrangement. Subsequently, however, it became clear that the sleep-like or hypnotic state involved in the exercise (rather than any animal magnetism) was responsible for the cures that were achieved. The importance of Mesmer's work is that he showed (although he didn't realise it at the time!) that mental disorders could be cured by psychological techniques.

Chapters 22 and 23 are devoted to the key issues relating to mental disorders. These key issues can be expressed in the form of five questions. First, how can we best describe and categorise mental disorders? Second, what are the major psychological approaches that have been applied to mental disorders in recent decades? Third, what are the factors responsible for the development of the various mental disorders? Fourth, what are the main forms of psychological therapy that have been used to treat individuals with mental

Engraving of the treatment used to cure hysteria by the Dutch physician Hermann Boerhaave (1668–1738). Boerhaave (at centre) found that people suffering from hysteria (as seen here) could be calmed by making them frightened and so began threatening them with red-hot pokers.

disorders? Fifth, how can we assess the effectiveness of different forms of psychological therapy in producing beneficial changes in individuals suffering from mental disorders?

We can illustrate the above issues by considering a hypothetical individual, Matthew. Matthew is extremely shy, and dislikes most social occasions. Indeed, he is so frightened of possible humiliation when involved in a social event that he will often make feeble excuses to avoid them. He goes to see a clinical psychologist, because he is so concerned about his condition.

The successful treatment of Matthew's conditions involves several steps. First, we need to decide the precise nature of the problem. Thus, diagnosing his condition is important. Second, it may be useful to consider Matthew's condition within the context of the main models or theoretical approaches to abnormal psychology. Third, we need to combine our diagnosis of his condition with an appropriate model to appreciate the factors responsible for his problem. Fourth, we need to treat Matthew to eliminate his symptoms and prevent them from recurring. Fifth, we need to use various measures (e.g., assessing his mood state, ability to function in everyday life, and his general behaviour) to reassure ourselves that the treatment has been effective.

Chapter 22 deals with the various psychological problems and disorders that individuals can experience. This area is also known as **psychopathology**, which is "the field concerned with the nature and development of mental disorders" (Davison & Neale, 1998, p. G-19). More than 200 mental disorders have been identified, and most (but not all) of these disorders are found in virtually every country in the world. More specifically, Chapter 22 provides answers to the first three questions posed above. In other words, it is concerned with issues such as the diagnosis of mental disorders, identifying the main theoretical approaches to abnormality, and developing an understanding of the factors responsible for the main mental disorders.

The emphasis in Chapter 23 is very different from the one adopted in Chapter 22, because it is concerned with *practical* issues relating to the forms of therapy provided by clinical psychologists, psychiatrists, and others. It is over 100 years since Freud first proposed a systematic form of treatment for mental disorders, since when numerous other forms of treatment have been devised. Chapter 23 answers the fourth and fifth questions posed earlier. That is to say, there is a detailed discussion of the major forms of therapy associated with each of the main approaches to abnormality. After this has been accomplished there is an attempt to evaluate the effectiveness of these forms of treatment. As we will see, it is surprisingly difficult to come to definitive conclusions concerning the relative effectiveness of different forms of therapy. However, the good news is that all of the main types of treatment have been shown beyond any doubt to be at least moderately effective in the treatment of a wide range of mental disorders. There is also some evidence that certain forms of treatment are especially successful and effective when applied to specific mental disorders.

> **KEY TERM**
>
> **Psychopathology:** the study of the nature and development of mental disorders; an abnormal pattern of functioning.

# Approaches to abnormality

## WHAT IS ABNORMALITY?

### Statistical approach

There are several ways in which we might define "abnormality". One way is the statistical approach, according to which the abnormal is that which is statistically rare in the population. For example, consider trait anxiety (a personality dimension relating to the experience of anxiety) as assessed by Spielberger's (Spielberger, Gorsuch, & Lushene, 1970; Spielberger, Gorsuch, Lushene, Vagg, & Jacobs, 1983) State-Trait Anxiety Inventory. The mean score for trait anxiety is about 40, and only about one person in fifty obtains a score higher than 55. Thus, those scoring 55 or more are abnormal in that their scores deviate from those of the great majority of the population.

The statistical approach addresses part of what is meant by "abnormality" in the clinical context. However, it is not adequate. Many people whose scores on trait anxiety are unusually high nevertheless lead contented and fulfilled lives, and they are clearly *not* clinically abnormal. Very low scores on trait anxiety (25 or less) are also statistically abnormal. However, a low susceptibility to anxiety hardly indicates clinical abnormality.

The statistical approach takes no account of whether deviations from the average are desirable or undesirable. "Abnormality" refers to statistically rare behaviour. However, such behaviour must also be undesirable and damaging to the individual for it to be truly abnormal.

### Is mental illness a myth?

It has sometimes been argued that the entire notion of abnormality or mental disorder is merely a social construction used by society. In other words, mental illness is a myth. According to Szasz (1974, p. ix), "Strictly speaking ... disease or illness can affect only the body. Hence there can be no such thing as mental illness." The essence of Szasz's position was captured by Dammann (1997, p. 736): "Physical illness is something that one *has*, while mental illness is something one *does* ... even seemingly bizarre behaviour ... is really goal-directed and meaningful."

If mental illness or disorder does not exist, why do psychiatrists and clinical psychologists pretend that it does? According to Szasz (1974), society uses various labels to exclude those whose behaviour fails to conform to society's norms. The various categories of mental disorder are such labels, as are terms such as "criminal" and "prostitute".

Szasz's extreme views have not been generally accepted. Dammann (1997) pointed out that Szasz used the terms "disease" and "mental illness" in very narrow senses. He also argued that it is unreasonable to draw a sharp distinction between physical illness and mental conditions. For example, an outstanding sportswoman who breaks her leg obviously has a physical injury. However, she is also likely to experience psychological problems as a result.

What conclusions can we draw about the value of Szasz's contribution? According to Dammann (1997, p. 740), "It is clear that one's definition of illness will ... determine one's standing on the existence of mental illness. As there has yet to be a consensus on what constitutes illness, the debate ... appears to be more philosophical than scientific."

This palm tree differs from the norm.

## Evidence

Rosenhan (1973) carried out a famous (or notorious) study, which questioned the objective reality of mental illness (see the Key Study below).

Scheff (1966) identified other problems with the notion of abnormality or mental disorder. According to his **labelling theory**, someone acquiring the stigma (mark of social disgrace) of a psychiatric diagnosis or label will be treated as a mentally ill person. As a result, his/her behaviour may change to make the label more appropriate than it was initially. Thus, rather than the symptoms leading to the psychiatric label or diagnosis, the label may sometimes play a part in creating the symptoms.

## Rosenhan: A study of sane people in insane places

Eight normal people (five men and three women, all researchers) tried to gain admission to 12 different psychiatric hospitals. They all complained of hearing indistinct voices saying "empty", "hollow", and "thud". Even though this was the only symptom they reported, seven of them were diagnosed as suffering from **schizophrenia**, a very severe condition involving substantial distortions of thought, emotion, and behaviour.

After these normal individuals were admitted to psychiatric wards, they all said they felt fine, and that they no longer had any symptoms. However, it took an average of 19 days before they were discharged. For seven of them, the psychiatric classification at the time of discharge was "schizophrenia in remission", implying that the schizophrenia might recur.

Rosenhan (1973) was not content with finding that normal individuals can be classified as abnormal. He next decided to see whether abnormal individuals could be classified as normal. He told the staff at a psychiatric hospital that pseudo-patients (normal individuals pretending to have schizophrenic symptoms) would try to gain admittance. No pseudo-patients actually appeared, but 41 genuine patients were judged with great confidence to be pseudo-patients by at least one member of staff. Nineteen of these genuine patients were suspected of being frauds by one psychiatrist plus another member of staff. Rosenhan concluded, "It is clear that we cannot distinguish the sane from the insane in psychiatric hospitals."

There are various reasons for disagreeing with Rosenhan's (1973) conclusion. A convincing point was made by Kety (1974), who offered the following analogy:

*If I were to drink a quart of blood and, concealing what I had done, come to the emergency room of any hospital vomiting blood, the behaviour of the staff would be quite predictable. If they labelled and treated me as having a bleeding peptic ulcer, I doubt that I could argue convincingly that medical science does not know how to diagnose that condition.*

Psychiatrists cannot be blamed for not expecting completely normal people to try to gain admittance to a psychiatric hospital. Errors of diagnosis were made under the very unusual conditions of Rosenhan's study, but that does not mean that psychiatrists generally cannot distinguish between the normal and the abnormal.

Rosenhan's (1973) findings are less dramatic than they seem. The diagnosis "schizophrenia in remission" is used very rarely, and suggests that the psychiatrists were unconvinced that the patients had really suffered from schizophrenia. This is confirmed by the fact that these normal patients were released within a few days of admission.

### Discussion points

**1.** What do you think of Rosenhan's research?
**2.** Did Rosenhan show that psychiatrists cannot tell the difference between the sane and insane?

### KEY STUDY EVALUATION—Rosenhan

Rosenhan's research in the early 1970s exposed the imprecision of psychiatric diagnosis. Psychiatrists are often unable to verify patients' symptoms, and can only rely on observable behaviour. A number of observations can be made about Rosenhan's research. First, his findings demonstrate the lack of scientific evidence on which medical diagnoses can be made—a crucial issue when an individual's personal liberty may be at stake. Second, the use of somatic treatments such as drugs and ECT (electro-convulsive therapy) was the subject of much discussion in the 1960s and 1970s. Although Rosenhan's fake patients were not subjected to these treatments, the study underlined the need for caution when making decisions about appropriate types of therapy.

The main concerns about Rosenhan's research are ethical ones. In both studies, professionals were deliberately misled about the true status of patients. The deception of professionals whose job it is to treat people with mental disorders is no more ethically justified than the deception of patients or participants in a study. However, it is probable that a more open investigation, with the full knowledge and co-operation of the psychiatrists, would have failed to reveal anything of interest.

A further issue concerns the welfare of the genuine patients. During Rosenhan's second study, it would have been possible for a patient who was exhibiting normal behaviour, but in fact was suffering from a spasmodic mental disorder, to be mistakenly discharged from care.

### KEY TERMS

**Labelling theory:** the notion that attaching a psychiatric label to patients may cause them to be treated as someone who is mentally ill.

**Schizophrenia:** a very severe disorder characterised by hallucinations, delusions, lack of emotion, and very impaired social functioning.

Rosenhan (1973) also obtained evidence that how someone is treated is influenced by the label they have been given. Rosenhan's normal patients with a diagnosis of schizophrenia often approached a staff member in their psychiatric ward with a polite request for information. These requests were ignored 88% of the time by nurses and attendants, and 71% of the time by psychiatrists. This unresponsiveness by the psychiatric staff suggests that those labelled as schizophrenic have very low status. Such treatment could clearly increase the severity of the symptoms experienced by real patients.

Bean, Beiser, Zhang Wong, and Iacono (1996) found that negative labelling of schizophrenics by someone close to them is common, especially among older schizophrenics having a long period of deterioration before the onset of the disorder. However, problems highlighted by labelling theory may be less serious than Scheff (1966) and others have suggested. Gove and Fain (1973) considered patients 1 year after discharge from a mental hospital. Their descriptions of their current jobs, social relationships, and outside activities were similar to their descriptions of their lives before diagnosis and hospitalisation. Thus, the stigma of being diagnosed as suffering from a mental disorder need not have permanent effects on an individual's life, even though it undoubtedly does in some cases (Comer, 2001).

*Has Rosenhan satisfactorily shown that psychiatrists cannot tell the difference between the sane and the insane?*

## Abnormality and mental disorder

Concepts differ considerably in their precision. "Abnormality" or "mental disorder" is an imprecise concept. According to Lilienfeld and Marino (1999), the concept of "mental disorder" lacks a set of defining features. It has fuzzy boundaries, so that, "there is no ... set of criteria ... in nature that can be used to definitively distinguish all cases of disorder from all cases of non-disorder" (p. 400). This leads to the conclusion that, "the question of whether certain conditions are disorders or non-disorders has no true scientific answer" (p. 401).

Is there really no clear distinction between mental disorder or abnormality on the one hand and non-disorder or normality on the other hand? The answer seems to be, "Yes", in part because of the influence of social norms and values. Consider, for example, changing views about homosexuality as reflected in a major classificatory system known as the Diagnostic and Statistical Manual of Mental Disorders (DSM). In DSM-II, the second edition, which was published in 1968, homosexuality was classified as a mental disorder involving sexual deviation. In DSM-III, published in 1980, homosexuality was no longer categorised as a mental disorder. However, there was a new category of "ego-dystonic homosexuality", to be used only for homosexuals wishing to become heterosexual. In DSM-III-R (1987), the revised third edition, the category of ego-dystonic homosexuality had disappeared. However, there was a category of "sexual disorder not otherwise specified", with "persistent and marked distress about one's sexual orientation" being included. This remains the case in DSM-IV (American Psychiatric Association, 1994).

Homosexuality ceased to be categorised as a mental disorder in the 1980 edition of DSM.

## Seven features

In spite of the vagueness of the concept of "abnormality" or "mental disorder", we can identify some of the features often (but not invariably) associated with it. Various approaches have been adopted. However, we will focus on the one proposed by Rosenhan and Seligman (1989), who discussed seven features. The more of these features possessed by an individual, the greater the likelihood that he/she will be regarded as abnormal.

The seven main features of abnormality identified by Rosenhan and Seligman (1989) are as follows:

- *Suffering*. Most apparently abnormal individuals report that they are suffering, and so suffering is a key feature of abnormality. However, nearly all normal individuals grieve and suffer when a loved one dies. In addition, some abnormal individuals (e.g., psychopaths or those with anti-social personality disorder) treat other people very badly but do not suffer themselves.
- *Maladaptiveness*. Maladaptive behaviour is behaviour preventing an individual from achieving major life goals such as enjoying good relationships with other people or working effectively. Most abnormal behaviour is maladaptive. However, maladaptive

We all want to be mentally healthy, but should we all want to be totally "normal"?

behaviour can occur because of an absence of relevant knowledge or skills as well as because of abnormality.

- *Vivid and unconventional behaviour*. Vivid and unconventional behaviour is behaviour that is relatively unusual. The ways in which abnormal individuals behave in various situations differ substantially from how we would expect most people to behave. However, the same is true of non-conformists and eccentrics.

- *Unpredictability and loss of control*. Most people behave in a fairly predictable and controlled way. In contrast, the behaviour of abnormal individuals is often very variable and uncontrolled, and is inappropriate. However, the behaviour of most people is sometimes unpredictable and uncontrolled (e.g., after heavy drinking).

- *Irrationality and incomprehensibility*. A common feature of abnormal behaviour is that it is not clear why anyone would choose to behave in that way. Thus, the behaviour is irrational and incomprehensible. However, behaviour can seem incomprehensible simply because we do not know the reasons for it. For example, a migraine may cause someone to behave in ways that are incomprehensible to other people.

- *Observer discomfort*. Our social behaviour is governed by various unspoken rules of behaviour. These include maintaining reasonable eye contact and not standing too close to others. Those who see these rules being broken often experience discomfort. However, observer discomfort may reflect cultural differences rather than abnormality. For example, Arabs like to stand very close to other people, and this can disturb Europeans.

- *Violation of moral and ideal standards*. Behaviour may be judged to be abnormal when it violates moral standards, even when most people fail to maintain those standards. For example, some religious leaders claim that masturbation is wicked and abnormal, in spite of the fact that it is widespread.

*How would you distinguish between eccentric behaviour and abnormality?*

Rosenhan and Seligman (1989) defined "normality" as "simply the absence of abnormality" (p. 17). Thus, the fewer of the seven features of abnormality displayed by individuals in their everyday lives, the more they can be regarded as normal. Perhaps we should think in terms of *degrees* of normality and abnormality.

## Four Ds

Comer (2001) argued that most definitions of "abnormality" have certain features in common. More specifically, he claimed that there are four central features (known as the four Ds):

- *Deviance*. This involves thinking and behaving in ways not regarded as acceptable within a given society. According to Comer (2001, p. 3), "Behaviour, thoughts, and emotions are deemed abnormal when they violate a society's ideas about proper functioning. Each society establishes norms—explicit and implicit rules for proper conduct ... Behaviour, thoughts, and emotions that violate norms of psychological functioning are called abnormal."

- *Distress*. It is not sufficient for behaviour to be deviant for it to be regarded as abnormal. For example, Comer (2001) pointed out that there are people in Michigan called

Tunnelling may be considered an abnormal behaviour in our society, but it is acceptable to those involved in a road protest. This photo shows "Muppet Dave" emerging from a tunnel at a road protest camp in the UK.

the Ice Breakers, who go swimming in extremely cold lakes every weekend between November and February. This behaviour seems to violate society's norms, but it would not generally be regarded as abnormal. Why not? The key reason is that the Ice Breakers experience no distress as a result of their behaviour. Thus, deviant thoughts and behaviour need to cause distress to the individual and/or others to be considered abnormal.

*Abnormal behaviour...?*

- *Dysfunction.* According to Comer (2001, p. 4), "Abnormal behaviour tends to be dysfunctional; that is, it interferes with daily functioning. It so upsets, distracts, or confuses people that they cannot care for themselves properly, participate in ordinary social interactions, or work productively." Note that most people exhibit dysfunctional behaviour in this sense when bereaved, but the duration of such behaviour is less than in most cases of abnormality.
- *Danger.* Individuals whose behaviour poses a threat or danger to themselves or to others are generally regarded as abnormal. However, most individuals having a mental disorder do *not* pose a danger to anyone.

Comer (2001, p. 5) concluded that the four-D approach is an imprecise way of defining or identifying abnormality: "While we may agree to define psychological abnormalities as patterns of functioning that are deviant, distressful, dysfunctional, and sometimes dangerous, … these criteria are often vague and subjective. When is a pattern of behaviour deviant, distressful, dysfunctional, and dangerous enough to be considered abnormal? The question may be impossible to answer."

## Harmful dysfunction

As we have seen, several experts (e.g., Lilienfeld & Marino, 1995, 1999; Rosenhan & Seligman, 1989) have assumed that the concept of "disorder" or "mental disorder" is inevitably vague and arbitrary. According to Lilienfeld and Marino (1995, p. 411), "It is in principle impossible to explicitly define *mental disorder*, because *disorder* is a mental construction that lacks a clear point of demarcation [boundary] in the real world." In contrast, Wakefield (1992, 1999) argued that we can define "disorder" fairly precisely by assuming that its essence is what he calls "harmful dysfunction". More specifically, "A disorder exists when the failure of a person's internal mechanisms to perform their functions as designed by nature impinges harmfully on the person's well-being as defined by social values and meanings" (Wakefield, 1992, p. 373). He argued that this definition can be applied to physical disorders or illnesses as well as mental disorders.

We can see what he had in mind by considering two disorders discussed by Wakefield (1999). First, the heart's failure to pump blood qualifies as a physical disorder. There is a dysfunction, in that pumping is a natural function of the heart. This dysfunction is clearly harmful, in that a partial failure of the heart to pump blood can be fatal. Second, there is post-traumatic stress disorder, a mental disorder with extreme emotional reactions to a traumatic event months or even years afterwards. According to Wakefield (p. 390), dysfunction is present, because "fear and associated disruptions of functioning that continue at an intense, impairing level long after a threat is no longer present indicate a likely failure of coping mechanisms to perform their natural function". This dysfunction is harmful because the symptoms of post-traumatic stress disorder have adverse effects on the individual's well-being.

A claimed advantage of Wakefield's approach is that the notion of "harmful dysfunction" is equally applicable to physical and to mental disorders. However, it is easier to identify the functions of physical mechanisms than of psychological ones. As Wakefield (1992, p. 383) admitted, "Discovering what is natural or dysfunctional may be extraordinarily difficult … especially with respect to mental mechanisms, about which we are still in a great state of ignorance." In contrast, the value component seems more central to psychological disorders than to physical ones. We do not need to make complex value judgements to decide that physical disorders such as heart disease or diabetes are harmful, but value judgements are typically needed when deciding whether psychological symptoms are harmful.

*...Not when rescuing a cat!*

Another claimed advantage of Wakefield's approach to disorder is that it is more precise and scientific than other approaches. The argument is that dysfunction is clearly defined in terms of the failure of an internal mechanism to function as it was designed to do by evolutionary development. In practice, however, we cannot use this definition to decide when an individual's level of anxiety is so great that it is dysfunctional, or whether their personality is dysfunctional. In addition, as McNally (2001, p. 312) pointed out, "It seems neither feasible nor necessary to invoke evolutionary concepts to support a harmful dysfunction account. If harm arises from the failure of a psychological mechanism to perform its current causal role, affirming that the relevant function was naturally selected seems to add little to our understanding."

# CLASSIFICATION SYSTEMS

Results of medical tests provide more precise information than is available to psychiatrists and clinical psychologists.

Once abnormality has been agreed, the starting point in classifying mental disorders is to identify the individual's symptoms. However, the same (or very similar) symptoms are found in very different mental disorders. For example, anxiety is a major symptom in generalised anxiety disorder, obsessive-compulsive disorder, and the phobias. As a result, the emphasis in most classificatory systems is *not* on individual symptoms but on syndromes (sets of symptoms that are generally found together).

The symptom-syndrome approach to abnormality owes much to Emil Kraepelin (1856–1926). In medicine, it is usual to diagnose physical diseases on the basis of physical symptoms, and Kraepelin argued that the same approach is suitable for mental illness. He emphasised the use of physical or behavioural symptoms (e.g., insomnia, disorganised speech) rather than less precise symptoms such as poor social adjustment or misplaced drives.

Unfortunately, different individuals rarely present precisely the same symptoms. Thus, patients given the same psychiatric diagnosis (e.g., schizophrenia) differ in their sets of symptoms, possessing only some of the symptoms defining the diagnostic category. There is a grey area in which the fit between a patient's symptoms and those forming the syndrome of a diagnostic category is relatively poor.

Most of the major classificatory systems are based very much on Western assumptions about abnormality and mental disorder, and so represent a form of "psychiatric imperialism". However, it is very important to take account of cultural differences, an issue that is discussed a little later. There are several classificatory systems, but we will focus on the two most influential below.

## Diagnostic and Statistical Manual: DSM

The current version of the Diagnostic and Statistical Manual of Mental Disorders (DSM-IV), published in 1994, is the most widely used classificatory system. The first version of DSM was published in 1952, being replaced by DSM-II in 1968. The greatest problem with DSM-II was its poor reliability, in that two psychiatrists would often produce very different diagnoses of the same patient. Spitzer and Fleiss (1974) reviewed studies on the reliability of DSM-II. They concluded that reliability reached acceptable levels only with the broad categories of mental retardation, alcoholism, and organic brain syndrome.

A key reason why DSM-II was so unreliable was because many of its symptom definitions were vague. Attempts were made with DSM-III (1980) and DSM-III-R (1987) to offer more precise definitions. For example, DSM-II was vague about the length of time involved in a "major depressive episode". In contrast, DSM-III-R specified that five symptoms (including either depressed mood or loss of interest or pleasure) should be present over a 2-week period.

DSM-III and DSM-III-R were also an improvement over earlier versions of DSM in another important way. The two versions of DSM-III focus on diagnosing patients from their observable symptoms. In DSM-I and DSM-II, however, there was a strong emphasis on the supposed causes of mental disorders. Thus, there was a shift from a theoretically based approach to one that is more descriptive. That was desirable, because the theories used in the construction of DSM-I and DSM-II were seriously flawed.

There was another important change between DSM-II and DSM-III. In DSM-II, diagnosis consisted of a single category or label (e.g., schizophrenia). In contrast, DSM-III, DSM-III, and DSM-IV are all based on a multi-axial system with the patient evaluated on five different axes or scales.

*Why do you think it is so important to classify abnormal behaviour? Could classification cause any difficulties?*

## Axes and features of DSM

The first three axes or scales of DSM-IV are always used, whereas the last two are optional. Here are the axes:

**Axis 1:** *Clinical disorders.* This axis permits the patient's disorder to be diagnosed on the basis of symptom patterns.

**Axis 2:** *Personality disorders and mental retardation.* This axis identifies long-term patterns of impaired functioning stemming from personality disorders or mental retardation.

**Axis 3:** *General medical conditions.* This axis concerns any physical illness that might influence the patient's emotional state or ability to function effectively.

**Axis 4:** *Psychosocial and environmental problems.* This axis is concerned with any significant stressful events occurring within 12 months of the onset of the mental disorder.

**Axis 5:** *Global assessment of functioning.* This axis provides an overall measure of the patient's functioning at work and at leisure on a 100-point scale.

DSM-IV contains over 200 mental disorders arranged into various categories. The point to emphasise here is its wide-ranging nature. For example, DSM-IV covers disorders of infancy, childhood, and adolescence, sexual disorders, substance-related disorders (e.g., drugs), eating disorders, and cognitive impairment disorders, as well as anxiety disorders, depressive disorders, and schizophrenia and other disorders involving a partial or total loss of contact with reality.

Some more general features of DSM-IV should be mentioned before providing an overall evaluation of its usefulness. First, the disorders identified in DSM-IV are defined by descriptive and observable symptoms rather than by those features believed to cause each disorder. Second, each diagnostic category used in DSM-IV is based on prototypes (a set of features characteristic of a category). It is assumed that some symptoms are essential, but that others may or may not be present. For example, the diagnosis of generalised anxiety disorder requires the presence of excessive worry and anxiety. However, it requires in addition only three of the following symptoms: restlessness, being easily fatigued, difficulty concentrating, irritability, muscle tension, and sleep disturbance.

Third, DSM-IV was based in part on field trials, in which diagnostic issues were studied by means of research programmes. In spite of that, some controversial categories were included. Two such categories are dissociative amnesia (an inability to remember important personal events) and dissociative identity disorder (two or more separate identities or multiple personalities). Pope, Oliva, Hudson, Bodkin, and Gruber (1999, p. 321) surveyed 301 psychiatrists, and found that:

*Only about one-third of respondents replied that dissociative amnesia and dissociative identity disorder should be included without reservation in DSM-IV; a larger proportion replied that these categories should be included only as proposed diagnoses. Only about one-quarter of respondents felt that diagnoses of dissociative amnesia and dissociative identity disorder were supported by strong scientific validity.*

## Reliability and validity

Classificatory systems need to be reliable and valid. Reliability is high if different psychiatrists agree on patients' diagnoses; this is known as **inter-judge reliability**. **Validity** is concerned with the extent to which a classificatory system measures what it claims to measure. It is much harder to assess than reliability. Three kinds of validity are relevant to DSM-IV:

- *Aetiological validity.* This is high when the **aetiology** or cause of a disorder is the same for most patients suffering from it.
- *Descriptive validity.* The extent to which patients in the various diagnostic categories differ.
- *Predictive validity.* The extent to which the diagnostic categories allow us to predict the course and outcome of treatment.

Reliability and validity are not entirely independent. A classificatory system which is unreliable cannot be valid.

Fairly detailed evidence on the reliability of DSM-III-R is available. Inter-judge reliability for the major diagnostic categories in DSM-III-R was assessed by Williams et al. (1992). The reliability statistic they used was kappa, which measures the amount of agreement between raters in excess of chance expectations (kappas of about +.7 or above indicate high reliability).

- Bulimia nervosa: .86
- Alcohol abuse: .75
- Major depression: .64
- Panic disorder: .58

As can be seen, the reliability of DSM-III-R varies considerably from category to category, but was high for some diagnoses.

Nathan and Langenbucher (1999) compared the reliability of DSM-IV with previous versions, concluding there are:

*modest increments in the reliability of a few diagnostic categories (e.g., oppositional defiant disorder and conduct disorder in children and adolescence) but no real progress in addressing the substantial reliability problems of personality disorders, sleep disorders, disorders of childhood and adolescence, and some disorders within the schizophrenic spectrum (p. 82).*

There is little evidence on validity. The aetiological validity is probably fairly low for most categories of mental disorder, because the causes of any given disorder vary considerably from person to person (discussed later in this chapter). The descriptive validity of DSM-IV is reduced by **comorbidity** (the presence of two or more disorders in the same person). For example, up to two-thirds of patients with an anxiety disorder have also been diagnosed with one or more additional anxiety disorders (see Eysenck, 1997). Such extensive comorbidity blurs the distinctions among categories. The predictive validity of DSM-IV is unknown.

**KEY TERMS**

**Inter-judge reliability:** the extent to which different judges agree in their assessments (e.g., of diagnoses).

**Validity:** the extent to which a classificatory system measures what it claims to measure.

**Aetiology:** the factors causally responsible for the development of mental disorders.

**Comorbidity:** the presence of two or more disorders in a given individual at the same time.

# Cross-cultural differences

Are the same mental disorders found universally across the world's cultures or do they vary from one culture to another? It used to be assumed that there was universality, but this assumption is incorrect. This is important for the reasons proposed by Paniagua (2000, p. 139): "Inaccuracies in the assessment and diagnosis of psychopathological [abnormal] conditions with culturally diverse groups (i.e., overdiagnosis, underdiagnosis, and misdiagnosis) might result from a lack of understanding of the presence of cultural variants leading to symptoms resembling psychopathology [abnormality]." In other words, we will not understand the significance of individuals' symptoms in non-American cultures if we consider them only from the perspective of American-based systems (e.g., DSM).

In fact, there is a modest attempt in DSM-IV to take account of cultural factors. DSM-IV (p. 844) refers to **culture-bound syndromes**, which are "locality-specific patterns of aberrant [deviant] behaviour and troubling experience that may or may not be linked to a particular DSM-IV diagnostic category". Various culture-bound syndromes are described in an appendix. Here are three examples of such culture-specific disorders:

- *Ghost sickness.* The main symptom is an excessive focus on death and on those who have died (common in Native American tribes).
- *Koro.* This disorder involves extreme anxiety that the penis or nipples will recede into the body, and possibly cause death (south and east Asia).
- *Amok.* This disorder involves a period of time spent brooding, followed by a violent outburst; it is found mainly in men (originally identified in Malaysia).

Kleinman and Cohen (1997, p. 76) dismissed the appendix of DSM-IV as, "little more than a sop thrown to cultural psychiatrists and psychiatric anthropologists". This is fair comment when we consider the range of culture-bound syndromes around the world.

At present, it is unclear whether *all* of the proposed culture-bound syndromes are, in fact, specific to only one

In the UK, a person of African-Caribbean descent is more likely than a white person to be diagnosed with schizophrenia, and this is likely to be due to cultural bias.

### Some examples of culture-bound syndromes

| Country | Syndrome | Key features |
| --- | --- | --- |
| Caribbean | blacking out | Sudden fainting + hysterical blindness |
| China | pa-feng | Fear of wind |
| Greece | nevra | Emotional distress, stomach complaints, dizziness, and so on |
| Japan | taijin kyofusho | Extreme fear that one's body or body parts are offensive to other people |
| Latin America | mal de ojo | The "evil eye", responsible for behavioural problems and poor health |
| South Africa | amafufunyana | Violent behaviour caused by spirit possession |
| West Africa | brain fag | Problems in concentrating and thinking produced by excessive study (!) |

## CASE STUDY: *A culture-bound syndrome?—Hikikomori*

A condition attracting considerable concern in Japan over recent years is *Hikikomori*. There has been no official calculation of the number of cases, but some specialists have estimated that it may be affecting up to a million people. The condition affects mostly middle-class males in their late teens or early twenties who are otherwise healthy.

Sufferers withdraw completely from society, typically by locking themselves in their rooms, sometimes for up to 20 years. There have been some high-profile cases reported in the Japanese media where young men have left their homes and committed violent crimes, including murder. However, most of the sufferers are not violent and tend more towards depression and lethargy. Other symptoms can include insomnia, regressive behaviour, paranoia and aspects of agoraphobia and obsessive-compulsive disorder.

The Japanese government is of the opinion that *Hikikomori* is a social disorder rather than a mental disorder, and that it reflects the current economic downturn in the country. (In a similar way, *Karoshi*—death from overwork—was a symptom of Japan's huge economic success in the 1990s.)

**KEY TERM**

**Culture-bound syndromes:** patterns of disordered behaviour that are typically found in only certain cultures.

*How might cultural differences in mental disorders affect immigrants?*

or a small number of cultures. However, progress is being made. For example, Long and Zietkiewicz (1998) provided a fascinating account of the concept of "madness" within the South African context.

## Sex bias

A persistent criticism of DSM is that it is flawed by sex bias. It has been argued that male-biased assumptions about what should be regarded as abnormal have influenced the diagnostic categories incorporated in DSM. Some diagnoses (e.g., histrionic personality disorder, characterised by excessive emotionality) are said to represent distortions of stereotypical feminine traits, whereas other diagnoses (e.g., anti-social personality disorder) represent distortions of stereotypical masculine traits.

Evidence suggesting the existence of sex bias was reported by Ford and Widiger (1989). They presented therapists with written case studies of one patient with histrionic personality disorder and of another with anti-social personality disorder. Each patient was sometimes identified as male and sometimes as female, and the therapists had to decide on the appropriate diagnosis. Anti-social personality disorder was correctly diagnosed over 40% of the time when the patient was male, but under 20% of the time when the patient was female. In contrast, histrionic personality disorder was correctly diagnosed much more often when the patient was female: nearly 80% vs. just over 30%.

According to Funtowicz and Widiger (1999, p. 195), there would be sex bias in DSM-IV, "if the diagnostic thresholds for the PDs [personality disorders] that are said to occur more often in females ... are lower than the diagnostic thresholds for the PDs that are said to occur more often in males". They explored the issue of sex bias in DSM-IV. Clinical psychologists were asked to indicate the extent to which the criteria for the personality disorders listed in DSM-IV involve social dysfunction, occupational dysfunction, or subjective distress. Their conclusions were definite:

> *The results of this study failed to support a bias against women in the threshold for a diagnosis of PD [personality disorder]. There was no difference in the overall level of impairment suggested by the PD diagnostic criteria between the male-typed versus the female-typed PDs.*

The apparent reduction in sex bias over time may reflect greater awareness of the need to avoid it.

### Depression and sex bias

More women than men are diagnosed with and treated for depression/unipolar disorder in the UK. This could be because females are in some way more prone to depressive illness. On the other hand, because of differences in socialisation, women could feel less uncomfortable than men in admitting to emotions, feelings of negativity, or low mood, and might also therefore be more likely to seek help and treatment.

*What other explanations can you think of for the different rates of depression in men and women?*

## Evaluation

- ⊕ "There is no reason to believe that reliability [of DSM-IV] will be less than that of its predecessors, and there is reason to believe that validity will be greater" (Nathan & Langenbucher, 1999, p. 85).
- ⊕ DSM-IV itself seems to be free of sex bias, even though such bias may occur when therapists use it in practice.
- ⊖ DSM-IV takes some account of culture-bound syndromes, but much more needs to be done.
- ⊖ The reasonable reliability of DSM-IV may be less impressive than it sounds. High reliability can be achieved by using very precise (but arbitrary) criteria for each disorder. As the British psychologist David Pilgrim (2000, p. 303) pointed out, "DSM-IV insists on depressed mood and four other symptoms ... to diagnose major depression—but why four? Why not six or just one? ... how is this arbitrary decision making different from counting angels on pinheads?"
- ⊖ DSM-IV is a categorical classification, i.e., patients are assumed to have (or not have) a given mental disorder. This can be contrasted with a dimensional system, in which it is

assumed that individuals vary in the extent to which they possess various symptoms. Individuals have varying degrees of symptoms such as anxiety and depression, and so a dimensional approach may be superior.
- The substantial amount of comorbidity found when using DSM-IV may occur because its diagnostic categories are too narrow. Some patients may actually have a single mental disorder, but receive two or more diagnoses when DSM-IV is used.
- Pilgrim (2000) doubts the value of *all* diagnostic systems including DSM-IV. According to him, diagnosis is unhelpful in answering the central question, "How do we account for this person's actions and experience in this particular context" (p. 302). In other words, diagnoses are based on symptoms and ignore the personal and social context in which those symptoms occur.

## International Classification of Diseases (ICD)

The International Classification of Diseases was first produced by the World Health Organization in 1948 and covered both physical and mental illness. It is now in its tenth version (ICD-10) and there is a volume specifically for the classification of mental and behavioural disorders (WHO, 1992). ICD-10 is much used throughout Europe and other parts of the world. According to ICD-10, mental disorder implies, "the existence of a clinically recognisable set of symptoms or behaviour associated in most cases with distress and with interference with personal functions".

Eleven major categories of mental disorder are identified in ICD-10:

- Organic, including symptomatic, disorders.
- Schizophrenia, schizotypal, and delusional disorders.
- Mental and behavioural disorders due to psychoactive substance use.
- Mood (affective) disorders.
- Neurotic, stress-related, and somatoform disorders.
- Behavioural and emotional disorders with onset usually occurring in childhood and adolescence.
- Disorders of psychological development.
- Mental retardation.
- Disorders of adult personality and behaviour.
- Behavioural syndromes associated with physiological disturbances and physical factors.
- Unspecified mental disorder.

There are clear similarities between ICD-10 and DSM-IV. For example, there are close similarities between schizophrenia, schizotypal, and delusional disorders in ICD-10 and schizophrenia and other psychotic disorders in DSM-IV; between mental and behavioural disorders due to psychoactive substance use in ICD-10 and substance-related disorders in DSM-IV; and between mood (affective) disorders in ICD-10 and mood disorders in DSM-IV.

In spite of the similarities between ICD-10 and DSM-IV, there are some important differences. There are 16 major categories of mental disorder in DSM-IV compared to only 11 in ICD-10, mainly because the categories in ICD-10 tend to be more general. In addition, some of the major categories in DSM-IV (e.g., sexual and gender identity; eating disorders) are not represented directly in ICD-10.

### Evaluation

- ICD-10 has reasonable reliability, but there is little detailed information on its validity. According to Costello, Costello, and Holmes (1995), ICD-10 is more reliable than either ICD-9 or DSM-III-R. However, there are doubts whether it is more reliable than DSM-IV. The categories in DSM-IV tend to be more specific and the defining symptoms are more precise. In general terms, increased category specificity and symptom precision are associated with higher reliability.

● As with DSM-IV, the aetiological validity of ICD-10 is low. Its descriptive validity is also likely to be low, given the prevalence of comorbidity in diagnoses based on ICD-10.
● The usefulness of ICD-10 diagnoses as the basis for deciding on the appropriate treatment suggests that its predictive validity may be reasonable.

## MODELS OF ABNORMALITY

A **model** provides a framework or structure, and is put forward to provide a coherent overall account of some area. Several models of abnormality have been put forward over the years. These models are designed to explain *why* and *how* mental disorders occur. They have been very influential, because treatment for any given mental disorder is based in part on our understanding of the causes of that disorder. Each of the models of abnormality discussed here is also associated with certain kinds of therapy. These therapies, and their effectiveness, are discussed in Chapter 23.

The dominant model until fairly recently was the biological or biomedical model. According to this model, mental disorders are regarded as illnesses. Most psychiatrists accept the medical model, whereas most clinical psychologists favour psychological models. There are several psychologically based models of abnormality, but we will focus on the four most important ones here: the psychoanalytic, behavioural, cognitive, and humanistic models.

Why are there so many models of abnormality? Mental disorders are caused by numerous factors, and each model emphasises some factors at the expense of others. Each of the models is partially correct, and a full understanding of mental disorders requires us to combine information from all of them.

## Biological model

The biological model is sometimes called the biomedical model (Kendall & Hammen, 1998). According to Kendall and Hammen (p. 32), "The *biomedical model* suggests that the symptoms of psychological disorders are caused by biological factors … [it] identifies brain defects, infectious transmission, biochemical imbalances, and genetic predispositions as possible sources of psychological disorders."

According to the biological model, the causes of mental disorders resemble those of physical illnesses. One possible cause of abnormality is a germ or micro-organism producing disease. Another possible cause lies in genetic factors, which can be studied by looking at patterns of mental disorder within families or within twin pairs. For example, suppose we obtain information from numerous identical or monozygotic twin pairs and fraternal or dizygotic twin pairs in which at least one twin has a given mental disorder. If genetic factors play a role in the development of that disorder, then there should be more identical twin pairs than fraternal twin pairs in which both twins have the disorder. This is so because identical twins share 100% of their genes, whereas fraternal twins share only 50%.

A third possible cause of abnormality lies in the patient's biochemistry. For example, the brain contains dozens of **neurotransmitters**, which are chemicals involved in the transmission of electrical impulses between neurons. It has been argued that abnormal levels of various neurotransmitters are involved in disorders such as schizophrenia and major depression. A fourth possible cause lies in neuroanatomy, that is, the structure of the nervous system.

The biomedical model has had an enormous influence on the terms used to describe mental disorders and their treatment. In essence, advocates of this model (e.g., Szasz, 1974) assume that there are important similarities between mental illness and physical illness. As Maher (1966, p. 22) pointed out, deviant behaviour:

*is termed* pathological *and is classified on the basis of* symptoms, *classification being called* diagnosis. *Processes designed to change behaviour are called* therapies, *and are [sometimes] applied to patients in mental* hospitals. *If the deviant behaviour ceases, the patient is described as* cured.

*If two family members suffer from the same disorder, does this necessarily mean that it is genetic? What other factors might be responsible?*

What might we expect to find if mental illnesses resemble physical illness in key respects? First, the great majority of mental disorders should be found in virtually all cultures. In other words, there should be cultural universality for disorders, which we have seen is not the case. Second, the pattern of symptoms associated with any given mental disorder or illness should be very similar in different cultures.

## Evidence

Most of the evidence relating to the biological model is discussed later. However, a few examples showing the value of this model will be discussed here. Medical research showed that phenylketonuria (PKU), a form of mental retardation, is caused by a genetically determined enzyme deficiency. Treatment in the form of a special diet low in phenylalanine (an amino acid) is very effective in preventing the development of PKU.

There is also substantial evidence that genetic factors are important in the development of schizophrenia. If one identical twin has schizophrenia, then there is almost a 50% probability that the other twin also has schizophrenia (discussed more fully later). This figure should be compared against an incidence of only about 1% in the general population.

Three of the main neurotransmitters are dopamine, serotonin, and noradrenaline. Several theorists have argued that one of the factors involved in schizophrenia is an excessive amount of dopamine in the brain (see Chapter 23). Abnormal levels of noradrenaline and serotonin are found in patients suffering from major depression (Delgado & Moreno, 2000). However, abnormal levels of neurotransmitters may *not* cause these mental disorders, since the occurrence of these disorders may influence the production of neurotransmitters.

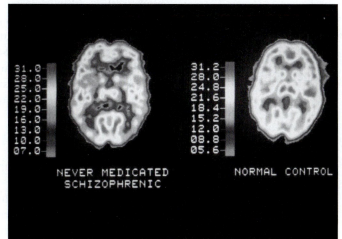

PET scans of schizophrenic (left) and normal brains (right). The darkest areas show levels of low activity.

It seems to follow from the biological model that most disorders would be found universally. However, several culture-bound syndromes (e.g., ghost sickness, koro, amok) have been identified in non-Western cultures. In addition, there are culture-bound syndromes found almost exclusively in Western cultures (e.g., anorexia nervosa, chronic fatigue syndrome).

The prediction from the biological model that the symptoms of any given disorder will be very similar in all cultures is hard to test. There is more cross-cultural evidence about schizophrenia than about any other mental disorder, and so we will consider that evidence. The World Health Organization (1981) considered the symptoms of schizophrenia in nine countries: England, China, India, Colombia, the United States, Denmark, the Soviet Union, Nigeria, and Czechoslovakia. Several symptoms were found in most of these countries. Some of the most common symptoms were as follows (the percentage of schizophrenics having each symptom is in brackets): lack of insight (97%), auditory hallucinations (74%), and verbal hallucinations (70%).

Other findings suggest that the symptoms of schizophrenia may vary across cultures. For example, the Inuit or Eskimos in Alaska have a concept of "being crazy". It resembles schizophrenia, but the Inuit concept also includes thinking one is an animal, drinking urine, killing dogs, and believing that a loved one was murdered by witchcraft (Eysenck, 2000). In sum, the central symptoms

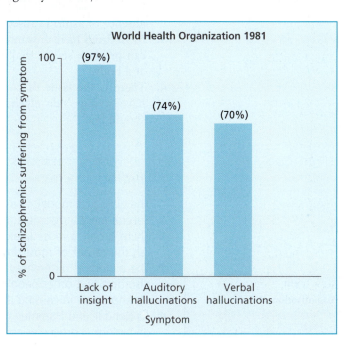

of schizophrenia are rather similar in most cultures, but some less central symptoms vary considerably across cultures.

Are the findings from schizophrenia representative of all mental disorders? There are reasons for doubt. Biological factors (e.g., genetic factors) are especially strong in the development of schizophrenia (see later), and there may more similarity of symptoms across different cultures for schizophrenia than for disorders having a small genetic component. Fortunately, we have reasonable cross-cultural evidence for depression. Sartorius, Jablensky, Gulbinat, and Ernberg (1983) carried out a cross-cultural study of the symptoms of depression in four countries (Canada, Iran, Japan, and Switzerland). Some of the main symptoms of depression (e.g., sad affect, loss of enjoyment) were found in depressed patients in all four countries. However, there were differences across countries in other symptoms such as sleep disturbance and hypochondriasis (abnormal anxiety about one's health).

There is clearer evidence for cross-cultural differences in depression when we consider **somatisation** (the experience of physical rather than psychological symptoms). Somatisation associated with depression is relatively rare in Western cultures, but is fairly common in some Asian cultures such as China (Zhang, 1995).

What can we conclude? Several of the symptoms of schizophrenia and depression are found across many cultures and countries as predicted by the biological model. However, other symptoms vary systematically from one country to another, and this variation is not expected on the biological model.

## Treatment implications

The biological model has clear implications for treatment. If mental disorders are basically diseases of the body, then treatment should involve *direct* manipulation of bodily processes (e.g., drugs). The basic logic is straightforward. If, for example, individuals with a given disorder have abnormally low levels of some neurotransmitter, then we could correct this by providing drugs containing the deficient chemical. Precisely this has been done with drug therapy for depression. Drugs such as Prozac are given to sufferers from depression to increase their low levels of serotonin.

We will consider four points about drug therapy:

*What are the ethical implications of drug therapy (e.g., for treating schizophrenia)?*

1. We do not always have a good understanding of *why* a given drug is effective in treating a particular disorder.
2. Discovering that increasing the level of a certain chemical reduces the symptoms of a mental disorder does not prove that a low level of that chemical caused the disorder. For example, the fact that aspirin often cures a headache does not prove that an absence of aspirin caused the headache.
3. Most drugs have unwanted side effects. For example, drugs used to treat schizophrenia can produce severe shaking, great restlessness, and peculiar contractions of the face and body.
4. There is the issue of compliance with treatment. Patients dislike taking drugs that have serious side effects, and such drugs are often not taken as and when they should be.

## Evaluation

- ⊕ The biological model is based on well-established sciences (e.g., medicine, biochemistry).
- ⊕ Several mental disorders (e.g., schizophrenia) are caused in part by genetic factors.
- ⊖ There is only a loose analogy between physical and mental illness. It is easier to establish the causes of most physical illnesses than mental ones.
- ⊖ The biological differences (e.g., in neurotransmitters) between individuals with mental disorders and other people may sometimes be by-products of the disorder rather than playing a role in causing it.
- ⊖ As Kendall and Hammen (1998, p. 40) pointed out, "A widespread and exclusive focus on biological processes could lead therapists to ignore or downplay the contributions of,

**KEY TERM**

**Somatisation:** the experience of physical symptoms rather than psychological ones.

say, personal learning histories, ongoing interpersonal conflicts, or cognitive misperceptions in the search for defective genes." Thus, the biological approach is narrow in scope.

Sigmund Freud, 1856–1939.

# Psychodynamic model

There are various psychodynamic approaches. The first (and most famous of these approaches) was psychoanalysis, proposed by the Austrian psychologist Sigmund Freud (1856–1939). However, as Westen (1998, p. 333) pointed out, "Psychodynamic theory and therapy have evolved considerably since 1939 when Freud's bearded countenance was last sighted in earnest." Several psychodynamic approaches appeared during the twentieth century, but we will focus later on the most important one—object relations theory. This theory has greatly influenced psychodynamic therapy. Westen asked 86 psychodynamic therapists to indicate the theoretical perspectives to which they subscribed. The most common response was object relations theory, followed by psychoanalysis.

## *Psychoanalysis*

Freud argued that the mind is divided into three parts. First, there is the **id**. This consists mainly of unconscious sexual and aggressive instincts, with the sexual instinct being called libido. Second, there is the **ego**, the rational and conscious part of the mind. It develops during the first 2 years of life. It works on the reality principle, taking account of what is going on in the environment. Third, there is the **superego**. This develops at the about the age of 5, when the child adopts many of the values of the same-sexed parent (the process of identification). It is partly conscious and partly unconscious. It consists of the conscience and the ego-ideal. The conscience is formed as a result of the child being punished, and it makes the child feel guilty after behaving badly. The ego-ideal is formed through the use of reward. It makes the child feel proud after behaving well.

Of key relevance to abnormal psychology is that the three parts of the mind are often in conflict. Conflicts occur most often between the id and the superego: The id wants immediate gratification, whereas the superego upholds moral standards. Conflicts cause the individual to experience anxiety, leading the ego to devote much time to resolving these conflicts. The ego defends itself by using various **defence mechanisms**, which are strategies designed to reduce anxiety. Some of the main defence mechanisms are as follows:

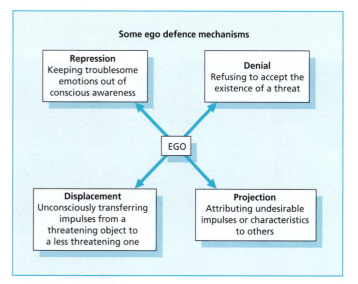

1. *Repression.* According to Freud (1915/1957, p. 86), "The essence of repression lies simply in the function of rejecting and keeping something out of consciousness." However, Freud extended the term "repression" to include conscious awareness of threatening thoughts in the absence of an emotional reaction.
2. *Displacement.* This involves the unconscious moving of impulses away from a threatening object and towards a less threatening object. For example, someone who has been made angry by their boss may go home and kick the cat.
3. *Projection.* This involves individuals attributing their undesirable characteristics to others. For example, someone who is very unfriendly may accuse other people of being unfriendly.
4. *Denial.* This involves simply refusing to accept the existence or reality of a threatening event. For example, patients with life-threatening diseases often deny that these diseases are affecting their lives (see Eysenck, 1998).

**KEY TERMS**

**Id:** the unconscious part of the mind concerned with sexual and aggressive instincts within Freudian theory.

**Ego:** the rational, conscious part of the mind within Freudian theory.

**Superego:** the part of the mind containing the conscience and ego-ideal in Freudian theory.

**Defence mechanisms:** strategies used by the ego to protect itself from threatening thoughts and feelings, especially anxiety created by the id.

## Evidence

We will start by considering the evidence for the main defence mechanisms. Some of the research on repression was discussed in Chapter 9. The most relevant studies on repression are those on clinical patients with recovered previously repressed memories of childhood abuse. Several of these studies (e.g., Andrews et al., 1999) support the notion of repression.

Another much-studied defence mechanism is displacement. Marcus-Newhall, Pedersen, Carlson, and Miller (2000) carried out a meta-analysis of 82 studies concerned with displaced aggression. They defined displaced aggression as aggressive behaviour directed towards someone not responsible for the provocation that the participants had experienced. The mean effect size was .54, indicating that displaced aggression is a moderately strong and replicable finding.

There was one major limitation of the studies analysed by Marcus-Newhall et al. (2000): The time interval between the provocation and the opportunity to show displaced aggression was typically only a few minutes. As Marcus-Newhall et al. (p. 684) pointed out, "If displaced aggression is to have explanatory value for aggressive actions seen in real-world settings, evidence of its occurrence with longer temporal intervals between an initial provocation and the subsequent display of displaced aggression will be needed."

Two of the key theoretical assumptions made by Freud were as follows:

- Adult mental disorders generally have their origins in childhood experiences.
- Personality development in childhood is relevant to later mental disorder.

Freud suggested that conflicts between parents and children during one stage of development could lead to fixation at that stage.

There is some support for both assumptions. So far as the first assumption is concerned, Kendler, Pedersen, Farahmand, and Persson (1996) studied adult female twins who had experienced parental loss through separation in childhood. These twins showed an above-average tendency to suffer from depression and alcoholism in adult life.

So far as the second assumption is concerned, Caspi, Moffitt, Newman, and Silva (1996) carried out a longitudinal study in which 3-year-olds were followed up 18 years later. Children who were inhibited at the age of 3 tended to be depressed at the age of 21, whereas those who were under-controlled and impulsive at 3 were more likely to have developed anti-social personality disorder by the time they reached 21. However, the links between childhood and subsequent adult mental disorder are often much less clear (Comer, 2001).

## Treatment implications

Freud argued in his theory of psychosexual development (see Chapter 13) that children pass through various psychosexual stages. If children experience excessive (or inadequate) gratification at any stage, then fixation occurs. **Fixation** involves the attachment of basic energy or libido to that stage of development. Later in life, adults who experience very stressful conditions are likely to show **regression**, in which their behaviour becomes less mature and like that displayed during the psychosexual stage at which they fixated as children.

So far as treatment is concerned, Freud emphasised the importance of **insight**, which involves a conscious understanding of the patient's underlying conflicts. These conflicts are unconscious, because various defence mechanisms have been used by the patient to prevent him/her from becoming aware of them. According to Freud, psychoanalysis can succeed only when the patient brings these conflicts into conscious awareness and resolves them.

In sum, Wachtel (1977, cited by Davison & Neale, 1998, p. 36) summarised the psychoanalytic model:

*The patient's neurosis is seen as deriving most essentially from his (sic) continuing and unsuccessful efforts to deal with internalised residues of his past which, by virtue of being isolated from his adaptive and integrated ego (i.e., conscious self), continue to make primitive demands wholly unresponsive to reality ... a fully successful treatment must create conditions whereby these anachronistic [from the past] inclinations can be experienced consciously and integrated into the ego, so that they can be controlled and modified.*

*What problems might arise as a result of attributing mental disorders to childhood experiences?*

## Object relations theory

Object relations theory was developed by theorists such as Bowlby (1969), Kohut (1977), and Mitchell (1988). One key assumption is that people are highly motivated to have successful relationships with other people. Another major assumption is that children's early interactions with others (especially their mother) have lasting effects on their subsequent interpersonal relationships. Some of the best-known research based on this theory concerns the possible long-term adverse effects of maternal deprivation (see Chapter 17).

Object relations therapists argue that it is crucially important for patients to consider the problems with relationships that they experienced as children, and then to work through those problems. Part of object relations therapy involves therapists trying to understand the nature of their clients' representations of people who are important to them. They also focus on developmental changes in such representations. In object relations therapy, the therapist experiences the client's "evoking style", which is his/her typical way of interacting with other people. This can enable the therapist to work out how other people are likely to react to the client, and this can facilitate the task of understanding the reasons why the client has poor or stressful interpersonal relationships.

## Evaluation

- ➕ The psychodynamic model proposed by Sigmund Freud was the first systematic model of abnormality focusing specifically on psychological factors as the cause of mental disorder and on psychological forms of treatment.
- ➕ Childhood traumatic experiences are sometimes a factor in the development of adult mental disorders.
- ➖ In the original psychoanalytic model, there was a relative lack of interest in the current problems faced by clients. This deficiency has been largely corrected in object relations theory.
- ➖ Freud over-emphasised sexual factors as the cause of mental disorders, and de-emphasised interpersonal and social factors. This limitation of psychoanalysis has also been addressed in object relations theory.
- ➖ The role of genetic factors in the development of mental disorders is downplayed within the psychodynamic model.
- ➖ Many of the key concepts used by Freud (e.g., id, ego, superego, fixation) are imprecise, which makes it hard to assess their usefulness.

## Behavioural model

The behavioural model of abnormality developed out of the behaviourist approach originally advanced by John Watson in the United States in the early part of the twentieth century. The behaviourists argued that psychology should be scientific, focusing on observable stimuli and responses. Their emphasis was on basic forms of learning, especially classical conditioning (learning by association) and operant conditioning (learning by reinforcement; see Chapter 8).

John Watson, 1878–1958.

Albert is shown the rat at the same time as he hears a loud noise.

Subsequent neo-behaviourists such as Bandura (1965) identified another basic form of learning known as observational learning or modelling. **Observational learning** or **modelling** occurs when an individual learns certain responses simply by observing someone else and then imitating their behaviour (see Chapter 8).

According to the behavioural model, individuals with mental disorders possess maladaptive forms of behaviour. These maladaptive forms of behaviour have been learned through classical conditioning, operant conditioning, or observational learning. The behavioural model differs from most others in that the focus is mainly on the client's behavioural symptoms. There is very little consideration of the client's internal thoughts and feelings, and the underlying cause of the client's disorder is not explored.

## Evidence

One clear advantage of the behavioural model over the psychodynamic model is that some of its assumptions can be (and have been) tested under laboratory conditions. Learning and performance can be greatly affected by classical conditioning, operant conditioning, and observational learning. We can even create some of the symptoms (e.g., anxiety) of mental disorders in the laboratory. For example, Watson and Rayner (1920) used

## Watson and Rayner: The classical conditioning of fear

According to the behavioural model, specific phobias may develop through classical conditioning. If a neutral stimulus (e.g., a furry rabbit) is presented at the same time as a frightening (unconditioned) stimulus (e.g., a very loud noise), then the two become paired so that eventually the neutral stimulus produces the same fear response as the frightening stimulus. This is what John Watson and Rosalie Rayner (1920) aimed to demonstrate in what has become a classic experiment in psychology. They wished to show that emotions could be classically conditioned in the same way as any response is conditioned.

Their participant was an 11-month-old boy called "Little Albert", an orphan living in a hospital. The nurses described him as a healthy boy, both emotionally and physically. At the start of the experiment Watson and Rayner established that such items as a white rat, a rabbit, and white cotton wool provoked no fear response. They were the neutral stimuli. The next phase of the experiment was to induce a fear response. Fear is an unconditioned response because no learning is required—fear is an innate reflex. Watson and Rayner put a steel bar 4 feet in length behind Albert and struck it with a hammer. Albert was startled and it made him cry.

Next, they gave him a white rat to play with and, as he reached out to touch it, they struck the bar to make him frightened. They repeated this three times, and did the same a week later. According to Watson and Rayner (1920, p. 161), "The instant the rat was shown the baby began to cry ... and began to crawl away so rapidly that he was caught with difficulty before he reached the edge of the mattress."

Watson and Rayner found that, now, the sight of any object that was white and furry, such as a white fur coat and a Father Christmas beard, provoked a fear response. This is called generalisation. Albert had learned to generalise his fear of the white rat to other similar objects. They intended to "recondition" Albert to eliminate these fearful reactions but he was taken away from the hospital before this could happen.

### KEY STUDY EVALUATION—Watson and Rayner

Not all research has found it possible to condition people to fear neutral stimuli by pairing them with unpleasant ones in the laboratory (Davison & Neale, 1996), and research into phobias has not found that all phobics have had prior traumatic experiences. For example, Menzies and Clarke (1993) carried out a study on child participants suffering from water phobia. Only 2% of them reported a direct conditioning experience involving water. DiNardo et al. (1988) found that about 50% of dog phobics had become very anxious during an encounter with a dog, which seems to support conditioning theory. However, they also found that about 50% of normal controls without dog phobia had also had an anxious encounter with a dog! Thus, these findings suggest that dog phobia does not depend on having had a frightening encounter with a dog.

Clearly there are ethical concerns in relation to this study, especially as Albert was never reconditioned. Watson and Rayner acknowledged these ethical issues from the outset. They said they conducted the research with hesitation, but decided that it was justifiable because children do experience fearful situations in day-to-day life and therefore they were not exposing Albert to anything out of the usual. They also did intend that he should be reconditioned.

## Discussion points

1. How convincing is the behavioural or conditioning account of specific phobias in the light of the evidence?
2. How could this experiment have been made more ethically acceptable?

### KEY TERMS

**Observational learning:** learning based on observing and imitating the actions of a model; also known as modelling.

**Modelling:** learning based on observing and imitating the actions of a model; also known as observational learning.

classical conditioning (pairing a loud noise with the presence of a white rat) to make a small boy called Little Albert frightened of rats (see Key Study opposite). However, it has proved hard to replicate their findings (e.g., Hallam & Rachman, 1976).

Fear reactions can be acquired via observational learning. Participants in a study by Bandura and Rosenthal (1966) observed a confederate of the experimenter responding to a buzzer by pretending to be in pain (e.g., twitching, shouting). After the participants had observed this reaction several times, they experienced a fear reaction whenever they heard the buzzer. However, there may be important differences between the laboratory and real life. As Comer (2001, p. 63) pointed out, "There is still no indisputable evidence that most people with psychological disorders are victims of improper conditioning."

*In what circumstances would you be most likely to learn by observing someone else's behaviour?*

## Treatment implications

According to the behavioural model, mental disorders occur because of maladaptive forms of learning based mainly on conditioning or observational learning. It is assumed that appropriate treatment for any mental disorder should involve further systematic conditioning or observational learning designed to eliminate the maladaptive forms of behaviour and to replace them with desirable forms of behaviour. Thus, the goal of therapy (known as **behaviour therapy**) is to change the client's behaviour rather than his or her inner thoughts. Note that the term "behaviour therapy" is sometimes applied *only* to treatment involving classical conditioning, with the term "behaviour modification" being used to refer to treatment involving operant conditioning.

We will consider two forms of therapy based on the behavioural model. First, there is systematic desensitisation. The essence of **systematic desensitisation** is that the fear response to phobic stimuli (e.g., spiders) is replaced by a different response (e.g., relaxation). This is an example of **counter-conditioning**, in which one response to a given stimulus is eliminated in favour of a different response.

In systematic desensitisation (Wolpe, 1958), patients are initially given special training in deep relaxation, until they can rapidly achieve muscle relaxation. After that, the patient and the therapist together construct a fear hierarchy, in which the patient's feared situations are ordered from the least to the most anxiety-provoking. Thus, for example, a spider phobic might regard one small, stationary spider five metres away as only modestly threatening, but a large, rapidly moving spider one metre away as highly threatening. The patient attains a state of deep relaxation, and then imagines the least threatening situation. The patient repeatedly imagines this situation until it fails to evoke any fear at all, indicating that counter-conditioning has been successful. The treatment involves working through all of the situations in the fear hierarchy, finishing up with the most fear-provoking one.

Second, there is **exposure**, in which the client is presented with a feared stimulus (see Chapter 23). This is essentially a development of systematic desensitisation, but with less emphasis on counter-conditioning. For example, someone with social anxiety or social phobia is exposed to progressively more threatening social situations. This is often accompanied by homework assignments, in which the clients force themselves to face certain social situations on their own (e.g., speaking in public). According to the behavioural model, the individual should become progressively less frightened of social events with repeated exposure to them. In essence, there is a process of **extinction**, in which the conditioned fear reaction to other people gradually decreases.

Behaviour therapy aims to replace maladaptive behaviour with adaptive and functional forms of behaviour. This goal is too narrow. Most clients have emotional and cognitive problems as well as behavioural ones. Therapy designed to change only behaviour will not necessarily reduce clients' emotional and cognitive concerns.

KEY TERMS
**Behaviour therapy:** a type of treatment based on conditioning and other learning principles; sometimes used more narrowly to refer to treatment based on classical conditioning only.
**Systematic desensitisation:** a form of treatment in which a fear response is replaced by a different response (e.g., relaxation).
**Counter-conditioning:** replacing one response to a given stimulus with a different response.
**Exposure:** a form of treatment in which clients are presented with the stimuli they fear.
**Extinction:** elimination of a conditioned response when the conditioned stimulus is not followed by the unconditioned stimulus or a response is not followed by a reward.

## Evaluation

● The basic concepts identified by the behavioural model (e.g., stimulus, response, reinforcement/reward) are easier to observe and to measure than the concepts emphasised in other models.

⊕ Conditioning experiences may play a role in the development of some mental disorders. However, this does *not* mean that conditioning is involved in the aetiology or causation of most mental disorders.

⊝ The behavioural model exaggerates the importance of environmental factors in causing disorders, and minimises genetic and other biological factors (see later in chapter).

⊝ The behavioural model emphasises behaviour rather than internal processes (e.g., thinking, feeling). That makes it more applicable to disorders with easily identifiable behavioural symptoms (e.g., the avoidance of phobic stimuli, such as spiders) shown by individuals with specific phobias than to disorders having few clear behavioural symptoms (e.g., generalised anxiety disorder).

⊝ It would be hard to show that specific conditioning experiences are causally linked to mental disorder. For example, to show that a patient's reinforcement history was responsible for his/her disorder, we would need to have detailed information about rewards or reinforcements received over a period of several years.

## Humanistic model

The humanistic approach was developed by Carl Rogers and Abraham Maslow in the 1950s. It focuses on personal responsibility, free will, and the striving towards personal growth and fulfilment. It was assumed that individuals have a need for **self-actualisation**, which involves individuals discovering and fulfilling their potential in all areas of functioning (see Chapter 3). The humanistic approach is an optimistic one, being based on the assumption that most people are naturally good, with the potential for personal growth in the right circumstances.

According to Rogers (1959), we all need to receive positive regard (e.g., affection) from the most important people in our lives. During the early years of life, it would typically be the parents who provide this positive regard. Of crucial importance, there are two main ways in which parents and others can provide this positive regard:

1. **Unconditional positive regard.** Affection is provided by important others regardless of the individual's behaviour.
2. **Conditions of worth.** Affection is only provided by important others when the individual behaves in accordance with their wishes (e.g., "We will only love you if you work hard at school.").

Rogers (1951, 1959) argued that children receiving unconditional positive regard develop a sense of self-worth, and are free to develop as they want. As a result, they are well placed to develop their potential. In contrast, children who acquire conditions of worth try to please other people rather than being true to their own needs and aspirations. They find themselves distorting or denying their thoughts and actions that are inconsistent with their conditions of worth. Eventually, they develop a distorted view of themselves, which prevents them from realising their potential and becoming self-actualised.

Rogers (1951, 1959) identified various ways in which clients use distorted thinking to defend themselves. One example is **rationalisation**, in which an individual distorts the interpretation of his/her own behaviour to make it consistent with his/her self-concept (e.g., "My behaviour looked bad, but it really wasn't my fault"). Another example is **fantasy**—an individual may fantasise about him/herself (e.g., "I am Napoleon"), and then deny or refuse to accept experiences disproving the fantasy (e.g., "I can't speak French").

### Evidence

Evidence relevant to the humanistic approach is discussed in Chapter 13. However, there have been few attempts to assess its value by scientific research, in part because Rogers did not believe that psychology should be a science. He favoured the use of

---

Maslow characterised Albert Einstein as a famous individual who demonstrated "self-actualisation".

Self-concept

Self-actualisation

Ideal self

*Can you think of any barriers that would prevent a person from attaining his or her "ideal self"? Are any of them related to "conditions of worth"?*

**phenomenology**, in which individuals report their conscious experiences in as pure and undistorted a way as possible. Rogers (1959) compared this approach against the scientific approach:

> *This personal, phenomenological type of study—especially when one reads all of the responses—is far more valuable than the traditional, "hard-head" empirical approach. This kind of study, often scorned by psychologists as being "merely self-reports", actually gives the deepest insight into what the experience has meant.*

## Treatment implications

What are the implications of humanistic ideas for therapy? According to Rogers (1967, p. 108), the following is of key importance:

> *Below the level of the problem situation about which the individual is complaining—behind the trouble with studies or wife or employer ... lies one central search ... at the bottom each person is asking "Who am I, really? How can I get in touch with this real self, underlying all my surface behaviour? How can I become myself?"*

Client-centred therapists aim to show unconditional positive regard, genuineness, and empathy for their clients.

Rogers (e.g., 1975) developed these ideas, arguing that severe problems can develop when there are discrepancies between an individual's self-concept and his/her experiences. These discrepancies can be reduced by the denials and distortions discussed above, but they prevent the individual from having a deep understanding of him/herself. Rogers developed **client-centred therapy** (now known as person-centred therapy). The main goals are to allow clients to develop a sense of personal agency and to become self-actualised by thinking about themselves in an honest and accepting way. These goals are achieved by the therapist consistently displaying three qualities:

1. *Unconditional positive regard.* The therapist is consistently supportive.
2. *Genuineness.* The therapist is spontaneous and open.
3. *Empathy.* The therapist has a good understanding of the client's feelings and concerns.

**KEY TERMS**

**Phenomenology:** a method involving the reporting of pure subjective experience; used by those who believe that our behaviour is determined by our subjective experience of the world.

**Client-centred therapy:** a type of treatment designed to permit the client to increase his/her self-esteem and achieve self-actualisation; now generally known as person-centred therapy.

You can see these qualities in operation in the following exchange taken from a therapy session with Rogers as the therapist and Mary Jane Tildon as the client (Rogers, 1947, pp. 138–139):

*Tildon:*  "I don't know what I'm looking for. It's just that I wonder if I'm going insane sometimes. I think I'm nuts."

*Rogers:*  "It just gives you concern that you're as far from normal as you feel you are."

*Tildon:*  "That's right. It's silly to tell me not to worry because I do worry. It's my life … well, I don't know how I can change my concept of myself because that's the way I feel."

*Rogers:*  "You feel very different from others and you don't see how you can fix that."

## Evaluation

● The humanistic model provided one of the first psychologically based alternatives to psychoanalysis.

● Client-centred or person-centred therapy gives power to clients and fosters independence and self-actualisation.

● Client-centred therapy has proved reasonably effective, but only with less severe problems (e.g., Greenberg, Elliott, & Lietaer, 1994).

● Rogers was one of the first therapists to make available detailed information about therapy sessions (e.g., tape recordings). As a result, Rogers can be credited with originating the field of psychotherapy research.

● The humanistic model emphasises the importance of individuals' conscious thoughts, and de-emphasises their non-conscious processes and behaviour.

● The humanistic model is limited because it ignores genetic factors influencing mental disorder, as well as the client's previous history.

● Rogers did not try to diagnose the specific mental disorder from which his clients were suffering. This limits the value of his approach.

## Cognitive model

The cognitive model of abnormality was developed mainly by Albert Ellis (1962) and by Aaron Beck (1967). This model is based in part on the psychodynamic model, especially the emphasis on the important role played by mental processes in the development and maintenance of mental disorder. However, as we will see, there are many major differences between the two models.

The central notion in the cognitive model is that individuals suffering from mental disorders have distorted and irrational thoughts and beliefs. The cognitive model is of potential relevance to numerous mental disorders, but has mainly been applied to depression and to the anxiety disorders. Warren and Zgourides (1991) discussed the kinds of distorted beliefs much more common among individuals with anxiety disorders than those not suffering from a mental disorder. Examples include, "I *must* perform well and/or win the approval of others, or else it's awful", and, "My life conditions *must* give me the things I want easily and with little frustration … or else life is unbearable."

*Can you think of any irrational thoughts that might occur in other mental disorders (e.g., OCD, phobias)?*

### Albert Ellis

Albert Ellis (1962) was one of the first therapists to advocate the cognitive model. He argued that anxiety and depression occur as the final stage in a three-point sequence (see the figure on the next page).

According to this A-B-C model, anxiety and depression do *not* occur as a direct result of unpleasant events, but are produced by the irrational thoughts triggered by unpleasant events. The interpretations produced at point B depend on the individual's belief system.

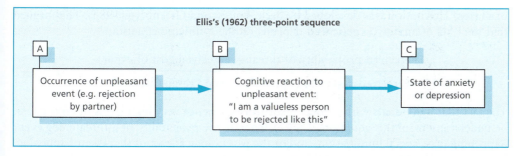

Ellis's (1962) three-point sequence

A — Occurrence of unpleasant event (e.g. rejection by partner)

B — Cognitive reaction to unpleasant event: "I am a valueless person to be rejected like this"

C — State of anxiety or depression

Ellis (1962) developed rational-emotive therapy as a way of removing irrational and self-defeating thoughts and replacing them with more rational and positive ones. As Ellis (1978) pointed out:

*If he [the client] wants to be minimally disturbable and maximally sane, he'd better substitute for all his absolutistic "It's terribles" two other words which he does not parrot or give lip-service to but which he incisively thinks through and accepts—namely, "Too bad!" or "Tough shit!"*

Thus, Ellis (1962) argued that individuals who are anxious or depressed should create a point D. This is a dispute belief system allowing them to interpret life's events in ways that do not cause them emotional distress.

## Aaron Beck

Aaron Beck developed and extended the cognitive model, focusing mainly on depression and on the anxiety disorders. Beck (1976) argued that many of the cognitive distortions of depressed patients centre around the **cognitive triad**. This consists of negative thoughts that depressed individuals have about themselves, about the world, and about the future. Depressed patients typically regard themselves as helpless, worthless, and inadequate. They interpret events in the world in an unrealistically negative and defeatist way, and they see the world as posing obstacles that cannot be handled. The final part of the cognitive triad involves depressed individuals seeing the future as totally hopeless, because their worthlessness will prevent any improvement occurring in their situation.

According to Beck, two maladaptive forms of thinking found in depressed patients are negative automatic thoughts and over-generalisation. **Negative automatic thoughts** (e.g., "I always make a mess of things") are triggered effortlessly when depressed individuals experience failure, and can maintain their depressed state. **Over-generalisation** involves drawing very general negative conclusions from specific evidence (e.g., failing to obtain one job is taken to mean that the depressed person will never find a job again).

What about the anxiety disorders? It is assumed that clients suffering from an anxiety disorder over-estimate the threateningness of certain external or internal stimuli. Thus, for example, spider phobics exaggerate the threat posed by spiders, and snake phobics exaggerate the threateningness

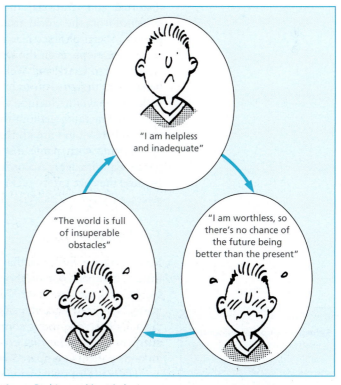

"I am helpless and inadequate"

"The world is full of insuperable obstacles"

"I am worthless, so there's no chance of the future being better than the present"

Aaron Beck's cognitive triad.

of snakes. This notion was developed by Beck, Emery, and Greenberg (1985). They argued that the level of anxiety experienced depends on the following equation:

$$\frac{\text{Perceived probability of threat} \times \text{Perceived cost of event}}{\text{Perceived ability to cope} \times \text{Perceived "rescue factors"}}$$

The fact that individuals with anxiety disorders experience very high levels of anxiety can be understood from this equation. They exaggerate the probability of a threatening event happening (e.g., social humiliation) and/or the psychological cost of that event happening. In addition, they minimise their ability to cope with such an event, and doubt whether rescue factors (e.g., help from other people) will be forthcoming.

Where do the distorted thoughts of patients with anxiety disorders or depression come from? According to Beck and Clark (1988, p. 24), "In psychopathological states, maladaptive idiosyncratic schemas dominate the information processing system ... The maladaptive schemas remain dormant *until triggered by appropriate environmental events* ... By possessing latent [hidden] maladaptive schemas, some individuals evidence a *cognitive vulnerability* for developing anxiety or depression."

There are various ideas contained in this theoretical statement by Beck and Clark (1988). First, some individuals possess cognitive vulnerability for anxiety or depression, because they have certain cognitive structures or schemas. Schemas are "functional structures of relatively enduring representations of prior knowledge and experience" (p. 24). The maladaptive schemas producing vulnerability for depression include, "negativity toward self, world and future as well as loss within the personal domain" (p. 26), whereas those producing vulnerability for anxiety include, "physical or psychological threat to one's personal domain and increased sense of vulnerability" (p. 26). Second, these maladaptive schemas remain latent or hidden most of the time. Third, certain environmental events (e.g., serious life events) cause the maladaptive schemas to become manifest, and this can lead the individual to become mentally disordered.

## Other developments

A key question raised by the cognitive model is the following: Why do patients maintain distorted and irrational thoughts and beliefs year after year in the face of contrary evidence from the world around them? We will answer this question with respect to social phobia. Social phobics fear they will experience catastrophe (e.g., public humiliation) in social situations, even though they have not actually experienced any such catastrophes. According to Clark and Wells (1995), they do so because they make use of **safety-seeking behaviours** designed to reduce the anxiety experienced in social situations. These safety-seeking behaviours include avoiding eye contact, talking very little, ignoring other people, and avoiding talking about themselves. Social phobics mistakenly believe that these safety-seeking behaviours are all that stands between them and social catastrophe.

Patients with panic disorder have catastrophic cognitions about fainting or being paralysed with fear. According to such patients, these catastrophes have not happened because they use safety-seeking behaviours such as holding on to people, distracting themselves, or trying to exercise during a panic attack (Salkovskis, Clark, & Gelder, 1996).

## Evidence

Much evidence indicates that anxious and depressed patients have irrational thoughts and distorted processing of threat-related information. For example, Newmark, Frerking, Cook, and Newmark (1973) found that 65% of anxious patients (but only 2% of normals) agreed with the statement, "It is essential that one be loved or approved of by virtually everyone in his community." The statement, "One must be perfectly competent, adequate, and achieving to consider oneself worthwhile", was agreed to by 80% of anxious patients compared with 25% of normals.

There is also convincing evidence that anxious and depressed patients exhibit various cognitive biases (see Beck & Clark, 1988; Eysenck, 1997, for reviews). Anxious patients exhibit an attentional bias: They are more likely than normals to attend to a threat-related stimulus rather than a neutral stimulus when both stimuli are presented together. Anxious and depressed patients both exhibit an interpretive bias: They tend to interpret ambiguous stimuli (e.g., "The two men watched as the chest was opened") in a threatening way. Finally, depressed patients show a memory bias: They recall more negative than positive information.

Why are these biases important? Attentional, interpretive, and memory biases help to maintain (or even worsen) the psychological state of those suffering from anxiety disorders or depression.

> **Common irrational beliefs**
> - I must be loved or liked by every significant person I meet
> - I must be perfect if I am worthwhile
> - The world will end if things are not as I want them to be
> - My unhappiness is not under my own control and I am powerless to change things
> - I should worry about bad things happening
> - It is better to put off dealing with anything unpleasant than to face it
> - I need a stronger person to depend on
> - My problems are the result of my past

## Treatment implications

Advocates of the cognitive model argue that individuals suffering from various mental disorders possess numerous negative thoughts, irrational forms of thinking, biased interpretations, and so on. This analysis led directly to the development of cognitive therapy. There are two central features of **cognitive therapy**:

- The therapist assists clients to recognise the dysfunctional thoughts helping to maintain their high level of anxiety and/or depression.
- The therapist uses various techniques to persuade clients to challenge their dysfunctional thoughts, and to replace them with more realistic and positive thoughts about themselves and about their lives.

Consider, for example, Ellis's rational-emotive therapy, in which clients are encouraged to ask themselves searching questions about their self-defeating beliefs (e.g., "Why is it essential to be liked by everybody?"). Clients are then taught more realistic beliefs (e.g., "No-one is liked by everybody, but most people like me"). The final step is to ensure that clients fully accept their new, rational beliefs.

*How could this approach be used to treat a person with anorexia?*

The primary goal of cognitive therapy is to allow clients to develop adaptive ways of thinking rather than their customary maladaptive ones. Critics of cognitive therapy have argued that this goal is too narrow. Such critics tend to ask questions such as the following: "Is it enough to change the cognitive habits of a person with a serious psychological dysfunction? Can such specific changes make a general and lasting difference in the way the person feels and behaves?" (Comer, 2001, p. 66).

There has been a rapid growth in **cognitive-behaviour therapy**, which combines cognitive therapy with attempts to change behaviour directly. For example, Beck (1976) recommended the use of homework assignments involving the client learning to behave in ways he/she finds difficult. An important ingredient in such homework is what is known as hypothesis testing. Individuals with social phobia may argue that talking to everyone in their office every day will make them look stupid, and lead to rejection. However, if they test this hypothesis, they typically find their fears were exaggerated. Disproving their hypotheses and expanding their social behaviour jointly assist in the process of recovery.

## Evaluation

- ⊕ Distorted and irrational beliefs are of central importance in anxiety disorders and depression.
- ⊕ Anxious and depressed patients possess various cognitive biases (e.g., attentional, interpretive, memory) that help to maintain their mental disorders.
- ⊕ Cognitive-behaviour therapy (with its joint emphasis on changing dysfunctional thoughts and inappropriate behaviour) combines the strengths of cognitive therapy and behaviour therapy.

> **KEY TERMS**
> **Cognitive therapy:** a type of treatment involving attempts to change or restructure the client's thoughts and beliefs.
> **Cognitive-behaviour therapy:** a combination of cognitive therapy with attempts to change behaviour directly.

- The cognitive model is not very explanatory: "That a depressed person has a negative schema tells us that the person thinks gloomy thoughts. But everyone knows that such a pattern of thinking is actually part of the diagnosis of depression" (Davison & Neale, 1998, p. 46).
- Distorted beliefs are prevalent in those with mental disorders. However, these beliefs may be merely a by-product of the disorder.
- Genetic factors are ignored, and little attention is paid to the role of social and interpersonal factors

## Overview

We have now considered five models in abnormal psychology. Each model is limited in two ways. First, only certain potential causes of mental disorder are emphasised. Second, the type of therapy associated with each model is mainly designed to achieve only certain therapeutic goals (e.g., changing behaviour, changing patterns of thinking). However, relatively few therapists nowadays are firmly committed to a single model or form of therapy. Thus, the models can be regarded as providing almost a caricature of the beliefs of currently practising therapists.

What approaches to abnormality have become more popular recently? There is growing support for **biopsychosocial theories**, according to which mental disorder results from the interaction of several factors (e.g., genetic, biochemical, behavioural, cognitive, and social). According to such theories, what is needed is to clarify the relative importance of each factor in producing mental disorders.

What is also needed is to explain *how* the various factors interact with each other. One possibility is that some main factors influence other factors, thereby increasing their intensity (e.g., Saudino, Pedersen, Lichtenstein, McClearn, & Plomin, 1997). For example, suppose Martin has a genetic tendency to develop an introverted personality. This may lead him to experience rejection in social situations, as a result of which his behaviour may change so as to avoid such rejections in future. Finally, the combined influence of these factors may mean that Martin develops social phobia, involving an extreme fear of social situations.

A willingness to adopt a more inclusive approach is clearly evident in the treatment offered by therapists. Prochaska and Norcross (1994) found that 38% of American therapists identified their theoretical orientation as eclectic, meaning they combined elements of various theoretical models. In contrast, 33% used only a psychodynamic approach, 5% used only behaviour therapy, 5% used only cognitive therapy, and 3% used client-centred therapy.

There is a final noteworthy development. As Kendall and Hammen (1998, p. 59) pointed out, "Historically, models of psychopathology have sought to explain all of human personality, pathology, and adjustment ... grand theories are now viewed as being so broad, and entailing so many mini-theories and sub-theories, that they can never be tested as a whole." We now have what Kendall and Hammen referred to as "micro-models", which are designed to provide a thorough account and explanation of *specific* disorders. Theorists proposing micro-models have set themselves more limited goals than past theorists, but these goals are more achievable.

## FACTORS CAUSING MENTAL DISORDERS

It is important to establish the causes of mental disorders, in part because such knowledge can help to reduce the incidence of such disorders in future. In this part of the chapter, we will focus on aetiology, which is the range of factors causally involved in the development of mental disorder.

The task of finding out *why* some people suffer from any given psychological disorder is very complex. However, we can start by distinguishing between one-dimensional and multi-dimensional causal models (Barlow & Durand, 1995). According to one-dimensional models, the origins of a psychological disorder can be traced to a single underlying cause. For example, it might be argued that severe depression is caused by a major loss (e.g., death of a loved one), or that schizophrenia is caused by genetic factors. One-dimensional models have been replaced by multi-dimensional models (e.g., biopsychosocial theories), in which it is recognised that abnormal behaviour is typically caused by several factors.

What factors play a part in producing psychological disorders? In general terms, we can distinguish between two categories of factors: genetic/biological factors and social/psychological factors. The biological model focuses on genetic/biological factors, whereas the behavioural, cognitive, humanistic, and psychodynamic models all focus on social/psychological factors. The main factors influencing the development of psychological disorders (with the category to which they belong) are as follows:

Death of a loved one rates as one of the most stressful events we experience, and may have long-term psychological repercussions, such as depression.

- *Genetic factors*. Twin studies, family studies, and adoption studies may indicate that some people are genetically more vulnerable than others to developing a disorder (genetic/biological factor).
- *Brain chemicals*. Individuals with unusually high or low levels of certain brain chemicals may be vulnerable to psychological disorders (genetic/biological factor).
- *Cultural factors*. Cultural values and expectations may be important in causing some disorders; for example, most Western cultures emphasise the desirability of thinness in women, and this may help to trigger eating disorders (social/psychological factor).
- *Social factors*. Individuals who experience severe life events (e.g., divorce, unemployment) may be at risk for various psychological disorders, as may those lacking social support or belonging to poorly functioning families. These adverse experiences may occur shortly before the onset of mental disorder. Alternatively, as Freud argued, events occurring in childhood may help to cause mental disorder in adulthood (social/ psychological factor).
- *Psychological factors*. Individuals having certain kinds of thoughts or beliefs, or who have learned particular inappropriate ways of behaving, may be vulnerable to mental disorders. For example, someone who exaggerates the threat of most situations may develop an anxiety disorder (social/psychological factor).

The factors identified above interact. For example, someone may have a very high or a very low level of a given brain chemical because of genetic factors or because he/she has recently experienced a severe life event. Another example concerns the impact of cultural expectations on eating disorders. This is clearly not the *only* factor causing eating disorders, because the overwhelming majority of women in Western societies do not suffer from eating disorders. Eating disorders occur in individuals exposed to cultural expectations of thinness *and* who are vulnerable (e.g., because of genetic factors).

The multi-dimensional approach to psychopathology is explicit in the **diathesis–stress model**, in which the occurrence of psychological disorders depends on two factors:

People living below the poverty line are more likely to have some mental disorders than those in comfortable financial circumstances.

1. *Diathesis*. A vulnerability or predisposition to disease or disorder. Diathesis used to be thought of as a genetic vulnerability. However, it is now regarded as "the aggregate of genetic and environmental risk factors that determine risk for developing a disease" (Faraone, Tsuang, & Tsuang, 1999).
2. *Stress*. Some severe or disturbing environmental event (e.g., divorce).

The key notion in this model is that both diathesis or vulnerability *and* stress are necessary for a psychological disorder to develop.

Some of the factors influencing the development of psychological disorders have large effects on only certain disorders, and will be discussed in the context of those disorders. Factors of general importance are discussed below.

**KEY TERM**

**Diathesis–stress model:** the view that mental disorders are caused jointly by a diathesis or vulnerability and a distressing event.

# Genetic factors

The best way of deciding whether genetic factors form part of the diathesis for any given mental disorder is by twin studies involving monozygotic or identical twins and dizygotic

Twin studies have been important in assessing the relative importance of genetic factors in mental disorders.

or fraternal twins. Twins are studied in which at least one twin has the disorder. If both twins have the disorder, they are concordant. The **concordance rate** is the likelihood that, if one twin has a disorder, the other twin also has it. For identical twins (who come from one fertilised egg), the extent of genetic similarity is 100%, compared to only 50% for fraternal twins (who come from two fertilised eggs). If genetic factors are important, the concordance rate will be higher for identical twins than for fraternal ones, and this should be the case even for twins brought up in separate families.

Information from twins can provide an estimate of the importance of genetic factors in the aetiology or causation of numerous disorders. What is done is to calculate what is known as heritability. **Heritability** is the ratio of genetically caused variation to total variation (a combination of genetic and environmental variation) within any given population (see Chapter 12 for further discussion).

There are some problems of interpretation with twin studies. For example, identical twins tend to experience more similar environments than fraternal twins, perhaps because they look more alike and so are treated more similarly. Higher concordance rates for identical twins than for fraternal ones could be partly due to their more similar environment rather than their greater genetic similarity. There are also potential problems with diagnosis. If it is known that one twin suffers from, say, generalised anxiety disorder, this may influence the diagnosis of the other twin. Accordingly, it is important that the assessment of the other twin is carried out "blind", i.e., by someone lacking that knowledge.

You might imagine that the heritability of any disorder would remain constant through the life cycle, but this is not the case. For example, Lyons et al. (1995) carried out a twin study of anti-social personality in juveniles and adults. Heritability was only 7% among juvenile twins, but it was 43% among adult twins. As Faraone et al. (1999, pp. 35–36) pointed out, estimates of the involvement of genes, "are snapshots of the changing landscape created by the confluence [merging] of genes and environment".

We can also assess the involvement of genetic factors in mental disorders by adoption studies. For example, adopted children whose biological parents had a given disorder can be compared with adopted children whose biological parents did not have the disorder. Alternatively, adopted people who are disordered or not disordered are identified. After that, the psychological status of the biological parents of these two groups is compared. If genetic factors are important, adopted individuals should tend to develop the same disorder as their biological parents, even though they were not brought up by those parents.

There are problems of interpretation with many adoption studies. Kendall and Hammen (1998, p. 152) identified the following issues:

*Adoption studies cannot eliminate the possibility that the prenatal environment influenced development of a disorder. Furthermore, it can be difficult to ensure that adopted children have not had contact with their biological relatives, that their adoptive parents do not have disorders themselves, and that their adoptive homes do not present other risk factors for the disorder.*

In addition, adoption can cause stress to both parents and children, and it is often hard to assess the biological parents accurately.

# Life events

The stress component within the diathesis–stress model often involves social factors such as life events (see Chapter 5). One of the best-known attempts to assess life events was the Social Readjustment Rating Scale developed by Holmes and Rahe (1967). Participants indicate which out of 43 life events have happened to them over a period of time (generally 6 or 12 months). These life events are assigned a value (out of 100) in terms of their severity. According to Holmes and Rahe, any change (whether desirable or undesirable) can be stressful. Thus, for example, they included marital reconciliation (45 life-change units), and gain of a new family member (30), among the 43 life events.

Those individuals experiencing events totalling more than 300 life-change units over a period of 1 year or so are more at risk than other people for a wide range of physical and mental illnesses (see Martin, 1989, for a review). These illnesses include heart attacks, diabetes, TB, asthma, anxiety, and depression. However, the correlations between life-change units and susceptibility to any particular illness or disorder are mostly rather low and rarely exceed +.30.

There are three limitations with the Social Readjustment Rating Scale and with most other life-event measures. First, it is often unclear whether life events have caused stress-related illness or disorder, or whether stress caused the life events. For example, stress may play an important part in producing life events such as marital separation, change in sleeping habits, or change in eating habits. In other words, many of the items directly ask about events relating to health and/or mental disorder.

Second, the impact of most life events varies from one person to another. For example, marital separation may be less stressful to someone who has already established an intimate relationship with someone else, and who long ago ceased to have any affection for his/her spouse. Brown and Harris (1978) addressed this issue by developing the Life Events and Difficulties Schedule (LEDS). The LEDS is based on a semi-structured interview approach to life events, involving detailed questioning about life events in order to understand the background context. The likely impact of any given event on the average person in that context is then assessed. This approach is superior to self-report approaches, but is much more time-consuming.

Unemployment may cause depression, affecting the person's belief in his or her abilities and future prospects. These unemployed men are waiting for work outside a factory gate in downtown Johannesburg.

Third, memory failures can reduce the usefulness of life-event measures. People often cannot remember minor life events from several months ago. Jenkins, Hurst, and Rose (1979) asked their participants to report the life events that had occurred during the same 6-month period

| LIFE EVENTS | | |
|---|---|---|
| Rank | Life Event | Stress value |
| 1 | Death of a spouse | 100 |
| 2 | Divorce | 73 |
| 3 | Marital separation | 65 |
| 13 | Sex difficulties | 39 |
| 23 | Son or daughter leaving | 29 |
| 38 | Change in sleeping habits | 16 |
| 41 | Vacation | 13 |

Adapted from T. Holmes, & R. Rahe (1967).

*Do you think that these life events are likely to have an equal impact in all cultures?*

on two occasions 9 months apart. The total scores were about 40% lower on the second occasion. With the LEDS structured interview approach, the interviewer asks several questions about the occurrence and dating of events. Brown and Harris (1982) found that there was much less forgetting when this approach was used.

## Psychological factors

Individuals with mental disorders (especially involving anxiety or depression) frequently have distorted and exaggerated views and beliefs about themselves and about the world. There are numerous measuring instruments to assess distorted ways of thinking. For example, the Dysfunctional Attitudes Scale (Weissman & Beck, 1978) assesses a range of dysfunctional attitudes (e.g., "People will probably think less of me if I make a mistake"; "My life is wasted unless I am a success"). Another example is the Attributional Style Questionnaire (Seligman, Abramson, Semmel, & von Baeyer, 1979), which assesses the tendency to attribute failure to long-lasting, global, personal deficiencies (e.g., an examination was failed because the individual lacks intelligence).

The main problem with most studies using such measures is that it is almost impossible to interpret the findings. Irrational ways of thinking may have influenced the development of a mental disorder, or the development of a mental disorder may have altered the individual's ways of thinking. It is generally not possible to decide between these two possible explanations.

Cultural factors are undoubtedly of importance in the development of many mental disorders. As we saw earlier in the chapter, there are several culture-bound syndromes which seem to be specific to one culture or to a small number of cultures. So far as Western cultures are concerned, the closest approximations to such culture-bound syndromes seem to be eating disorders such as anorexia nervosa and bulimia nervosa. These disorders have become much more common in Western countries, but are very rare in most other parts of the world. For example, Mumford, Whitehouse, and Choudry (1992) found that none out of 369 adolescent girls in Pakistan had anorexia and only one had bulimia. Clearer evidence that cultural factors are important comes in a study by Yates (1989). Women moving from cultures in which eating disorders were rare to cultures in which they were common had an increased risk of developing an eating disorder.

*Which of the models discussed earlier (cognitive, humanistic, psychodynamic, behavioural) are likely to account for this finding?*

## Research methods: Cross-sectional vs. longitudinal studies

Research on the factors responsible for mental disorders has typically involved **cross-sectional studies**, in which all of the information about individual patients is obtained at about the same time. Thus, we could study a group of patients suffering from depression, assessing the irrationality of their beliefs, the level of various neurotransmitters, and so on. We could also obtain the same measures from a control group of non-sufferers from depression. Suppose we find the depressed patients have more irrational beliefs and abnormal neurotransmitter levels. Could we conclude that the irrational beliefs and the abnormal neurotransmitter levels had played a part in causing the depression? The answer is, "No", because the depression may have led to the irrational beliefs and the abnormal neurotransmitter levels.

More useful information about the factors causing mental disorders can sometimes be obtained from **longitudinal studies**, in which a large group of individuals is investigated over a long period of time. For example, we could assess irrationality of thinking and neurotransmitter levels in a very large group of individuals whose everyday functioning was normal. These individuals would then be followed over a period of several months or years to see which individuals develop a depressive disorder. If those individuals with the most irrational beliefs at the outset of the study tended to develop a depressive disorder, this would suggest (but not prove) that irrational beliefs can be a risk factor for depression.

The main problem with longitudinal studies is that large numbers of participants are generally needed. Suppose that only about 1% of the population develop a given mental disorder. If we carry out a 1-year longitudinal study with a normal sample of 1000 individuals, only about 10 of them will have developed the mental disorder by the end of

**KEY TERMS**
**Cross-sectional studies:** studies in which various measures are obtained from one or more groups at a given point in time; see longitudinal studies.
**Longitudinal studies:** studies in which a group of individuals is investigated over a relatively long period of time.

the study. That is far too small a number on which to base any firm conclusions. Thus, we need to start with several thousand participants.

We can reduce the numbers of participants needed by focusing on individuals at high risk of developing the mental disorder of interest. For example, children whose father or mother suffers from schizophrenia are much more likely than other children to develop schizophrenia themselves. Parnas (1988) found that children whose parent had severe schizophrenia were most likely to develop a mental disorder and to commit crimes over the following several years.

Longitudinal studies have clear advantages over cross-sectional ones, but often fail to shed much light on causality. For example, consider the Parnas (1988) study we have just discussed. It seems probable that the children's problems did not produce schizophrenia in their parent. However, it is not clear whether the children with a severely schizophrenic parent were more at risk because of genetic factors or because of the adverse home environment.

## Summary

We have now discussed the main factors involved in the development of mental disorders. Some of the methods used by researchers have been analysed, and limitations with these methods identified. We turn now to evidence concerning the risk or causal factors for various mental disorders, including schizophrenia, depression, the anxiety disorders, eating disorders, and personality disorders.

## SCHIZOPHRENIA

Schizophrenia is a very serious condition. The term "schizophrenia" comes from two Greek words: *schizo* meaning "split", and *phren* meaning "mind". About 1% of the population in the United Kingdom suffer from schizophrenia during their lives, and the figure is similar elsewhere. The symptoms of schizophrenia vary somewhat, but typically include problems with attention, thinking, social relationships, motivation, and emotion. It is often characterised by delusions, hallucinations, lack of emotion, and very impaired social functioning.

According to DSM-IV, the criteria for schizophrenia include:

1. Two or more of the following symptoms: delusions, hallucinations, disorganised speech, grossly disorganised or catatonic (rigid) behaviour, and negative symptoms (lack of emotion, lack of motivation, speaking very little or uninformatively).
2. Continuous signs of disturbance over a period of at least 6 months.
3. Social and/or occupational dysfunction or poor functioning.

Schizophrenics generally have confused thinking, and often suffer from delusions. Many of these delusions involve what are known as "ideas of reference", in which the schizophrenic patient attaches great personal significance to external objects or events. Thus, for example, a schizophrenic seeing his neighbours talking may be convinced that they are plotting to kill him.

Schizophrenics often suffer from hallucinations. Delusions arise from mistaken interpretations of actual objects and events, but hallucinations occur without any external stimulus. Most schizophrenic hallucinations consist of voices, usually saying something of personal relevance to the patient. McGuigan (1966) suggested that

> **CASE STUDY: *A schizophrenic disorder***
>
> A young man of 19 (WG) was admitted to the psychiatric services on the grounds of a dramatic change in character. His parents described him as always being extremely shy with no close friends, but in the last few months he had gone from being an average-performing student to failing his studies and leaving college. Having excelled in non-team sports such as swimming and athletics, he was now taking no exercise at all. WG had seldom mentioned health matters, but now complained of problems with his head and chest. After being admitted, WG spent most of his time staring out of the window, and uncharacteristically not taking care over his appearance. Staff found it difficult to converse with him and he offered no information about himself, making an ordinary diagnostic interview impossible. WG would usually answer direct questions, but in a flat emotionless tone. Sometimes his answers were not even connected to the question, and staff would find themselves wondering what the conversation had been about. There were also occasions when there was a complete mismatch between WG's emotional expression and the words he spoke. For example, he giggled continuously when speaking about a serious illness that had left his mother bedridden. On one occasion, WG became very agitated and spoke of "electrical sensations" in his brain. At other times he spoke of being influenced by a force outside himself, which took the form of a voice urging him to commit acts of violence against his parents. He claimed that the voice repeated the command "You'll have to do it". (Adapted from Hofling, 1974.)

these auditory hallucinations occur because patients mistake their own inner speech for someone else's voice. He found that the patient's larynx was often active during the time that the auditory hallucination was being experienced. More recent studies have confirmed this explanation of auditory hallucinations (Frith, 1992).

Researchers have identified several risk factors involved in the development of schizophrenia. We will consider these risk factors with reference to the models discussed earlier in the chapter.

## Biological model

As expected on the biological model, genetic factors play a major role in the development of schizophrenia. Gottesman (1991) summarised the findings from about 40 twin studies. The concordance rate for a twin is 48% if he/she has a monozygotic or identical twin with schizophrenia, but is only 17% if he/she has a dizygotic or fraternal twin with schizophrenia. These figures suggest that the development of schizophrenia is much influenced by genetic factors. Indeed, as Faraone et al. (1999, p. 30) pointed out, "Having a schizophrenic co-twin is the most robust predictor of schizophrenia known to science." However, 50% of identical twins whose co-twin develops schizophrenia do *not* develop the disorder themselves, indicating that environmental factors also play a key role in the aetiology or causation of schizophrenia.

*Can you think of any environmental factors that might increase or decrease the chances of a person developing schizophrenia?*

Identical twins are generally treated more similarly than are fraternal twins (Loehlin & Nichols, 1976), and this might help to account for their higher level of concordance. However, there are two arguments against that view. First, identical twins elicit more similar treatment from their parents than do fraternal twins (Lytton, 1977). Thus, the greater concordance of identical twins may be a cause (rather than an effect) of their more similar parental treatment. Second, schizophrenia concordance rates for identical twins brought up apart resemble those for identical twins brought up together (Shields, 1962).

Among the most striking support for genetic factors was reported by Rosenthal (1963). He studied the Genain (dreadful genes) quadruplets, in which all four girls were identical to each other. Amazingly, all four of them developed schizophrenia.

Finally, Gottesman and Bertelsen (1989) found that their participants had a 17% chance of being schizophrenic if they had a parent with schizophrenia who was an identical twin. This finding could be due to either heredity or to environment. However, they also studied participants with a parent who did *not* have schizophrenia, but the parent had an identical twin having the disorder. These participants also had a 17% chance of being schizophrenic. Thus, what is of most importance is the genes that are handed on by the parents rather than the environment itself.

The notion that genetic factors are important in producing schizophrenia is supported by adoption studies. One approach is to look at adopted children, one of whose parents has schizophrenia. Tienari (1991) did this in Finland. He found 155 schizophrenic mothers who had given up their children for adoption, and they were compared against 155 adopted children *not* having a schizophrenic parent. Tienari found that 10.3% of

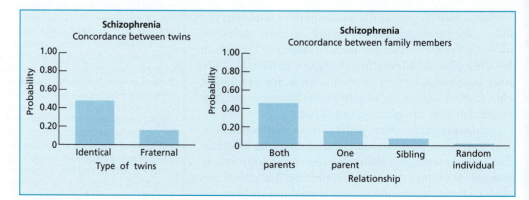

Research by Gottesman (1991) indicates that schizophrenia tends to run in families.

those with schizophrenic mothers had developed schizophrenia compared to only 1.1% of those without schizophrenic mothers.

Other evidence supporting the biological model comes from studies suggesting that the brains of schizophrenics may differ from those of normal individuals. For example, the ventricles (fluid-filled spaces in the brain) are often enlarged in schizophrenics (Andreasen, Swayze, Flaum, Yates, Arndt, & McChesney, 1990b). Such abnormalities may be present before the onset of schizophrenia, or may be produced as a consequence of schizophrenia. The former possibility was supported by Cannon, Mednick, Parnas, Schulsinger, Praestholm, and Vestergaard (1994), who found enlarged ventricles in children with schizophrenic mothers. Enlarged ventricles may reflect early brain damage, and this may influence the development of schizophrenia.

According to the dopamine hypothesis, schizophrenia may result in part from excess levels of the neurotransmitter dopamine (Seidman, 1983; see Chapter 2). There is support in the fact that neuroleptic drugs which block dopamine reduce the symptoms of schizophrenia (see Chapter 23). However, the evidence is rather inconsistent, and it is not entirely clear whether the heightened dopamine levels in schizophrenics occur before or after the onset of the disorder. If it occurs after, then clearly dopamine plays no part in causing schizophrenic symptoms.

## Psychodynamic model

Freud argued that conflicts and traumas influence the development of schizophrenia. These cause schizophrenics to regress or return to a state of primary narcissism (or great self-interest) occurring early in the oral stage. In this state, the ego or rational part of the mind has not separated from the id or sexual instinct. This is important, because the ego is involved in ego testing and responding appropriately to the external world. Schizophrenics have a loss of contact with reality, because their ego is no longer functioning properly.

This approach is limited for several reasons. First, it is unsupported by evidence. Second, adult schizophrenics do *not* resemble infants. Third, the psychodynamic approach ignores evidence showing the role of genetic factors in the development of schizophrenia.

## Behavioural model

According to the behavioural model, learning plays a key role in causing schizophrenia. Early experiences of punishment may lead children to retreat into a rewarding inner world. This causes others to label them as "odd" or "peculiar", and later on they may be diagnosed as suffering from "schizophrenia". According to Scheff's (1966) labelling theory, individuals labelled in this way may continue to act in ways that conform to the label (see earlier in this chapter). Their bizarre behaviour may be rewarded with attention and sympathy for behaving bizarrely; this is known as secondary gain.

Labelling theory is inadequate for various reasons. First, it does not explain where the symptoms of schizophrenia come from initially. Second, the behavioural approach ignores the genetic evidence. Third, it trivialises a very serious disorder, as is shown in the following anecdote. The schizophrenia expert Paul Meehl was giving a lecture, when a member of the audience argued in favour of labelling theory. Meehl states: "I was thinking of a patient … who kept his finger up his arse to 'keep his thoughts from running out', while with his other hand he tried to tear out his hair because it really 'belonged to his father'. And here was this man telling me that he was doing these things because someone had called him a schizophrenic"(Kimble, Robinson, & Moon, 1980, p. 453).

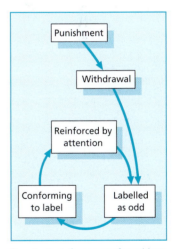

Constant reinforcement for odd or bizarre behaviour may cause a continuous cycle.

## Other factors

The cognitive and humanistic models have contributed little to our understanding of the origins of schizophrenia, and so will not be discussed. However, there are social factors de-emphasised by all the models considered in this chapter. Individuals belonging to the lower social classes are much more likely than those of the higher social classes to be diagnosed with schizophrenia (see Comer, 2001). We will consider three possible explanations here.

First, there may be a bias, with clinicians being more willing to diagnose schizophrenia when considering the symptoms of individuals from the lower social classes. Johnstone (1989) reviewed several studies showing that lower-class patients were more likely than middle-class patients to be given serious diagnoses (such as schizophrenia), even when there were few (if any) differences in symptoms.

Second, there is the social causation hypothesis, according to which members of the lowest classes in society experience more stressful lives than other people, because of poverty, poorer physical health, and so on. Stress is also likely through discrimination, because ethnic and racial minorities in many cultures often belong to the lower social classes. The high level of stress makes them more vulnerable than members of the middle class to schizophrenia. This hypothesis is reasonable, but there is little evidence providing direct support for it.

Third, there is the social drift hypothesis, according to which individuals who develop schizophrenia are likely to lose their jobs, and so their social status is reduced. Thus, schizophrenia causes reduced social status, rather than low social status causing schizophrenia. If so, schizophrenics should belong to a lower social class than their parents. Turner and Wagonfeld (1967) found this when comparing schizophrenics and their fathers. However, the fathers also tended to belong to the lower social classes themselves, as predicted by the social causation hypothesis.

Dohrenwend, Levar, Schwartz, Naveh, Link, Skodol et al. (1992) tested the social causation and social drift hypotheses. They compared two immigrant groups in Israel: (1) European Jews who had been settled in Israel for some time; and (2) more recent immigrants from North Africa and the Middle East. The latter group experienced much prejudice and discrimination, and so should have higher rates of schizophrenia according to the

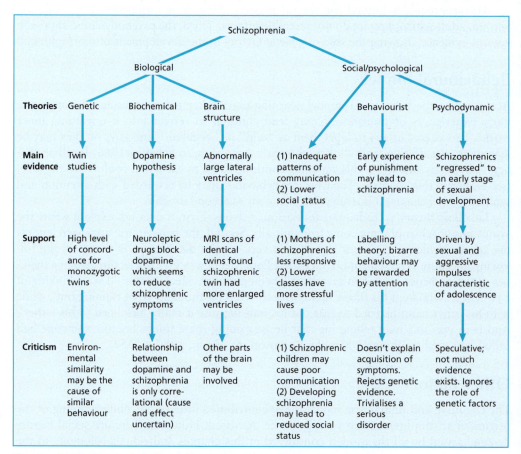

Theories of schizophrenia: strengths and weaknesses.

social causation hypothesis. In fact, the advantaged (former) group had a higher rate of schizophrenia, especially among those in the lowest social class. This fits the social drift hypothesis, if we assume that members of an advantaged group are likely to find themselves in the lowest social class because they have developed schizophrenia.

Stronger evidence that social factors influence the development of schizophrenia was reported by Brown and Birley (1968). They found that the onset of schizophrenia was often associated with negative or positive life events shortly beforehand. These findings suggest that many individuals who develop schizophrenia are vulnerable to sudden change or disruption in their lives.

Other social factors may be important. For example, the interactions within families can help to maintain the symptoms of schizophrenics who are trying to recover. What is important is the extent to which the family is high in **expressed emotion**, which involves criticism, hostility, and emotional over-involvement. Butzlaff and Hooley (1998) carried out a meta-analysis of 22 studies, and concluded that there is a significant relationship between high expressed emotion and schizophrenia relapse. Most of these studies were from Western countries, and it is not clear whether similar findings can be obtained in non-Western countries (Cheng, 2002). One issue here is that what counts as criticism, hostility, and emotional over-involvement varies considerably across cultures (Cheng, 2002).

*Can you think of any cultures that may differ in these respects?*

It is hard to establish causality in studies of expressed emotion. It is possible that expressed emotion within the family causes relapse. Alternatively, individuals in poor psychological shape may provoke expressed emotion from other members of the family. In fact, the causality probably operates in both directions.

## Conclusions

The development of schizophrenia depends strongly on genetic factors. However, the fact that the concordance rate is only about 50% for identical twins means that environmental factors must also be very important. It has proved hard to pinpoint these environmental factors. However, life events, poverty, discrimination, a critical and hostile family, and stress generally all probably contribute to the onset of schizophrenia.

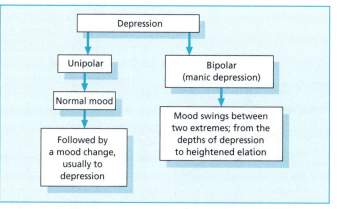

## DEPRESSION

There are various forms of depression. In DSM-IV, a distinction is drawn between **major depressive disorder** and bipolar disorder. The diagnosis of a major depressive episode requires that five of the following symptoms occur nearly every day for 2 weeks: sad, depressed mood; loss of interest and pleasure in usual activities; difficulties in sleeping; changes in activity level; weight loss or gain; loss of energy and tiredness; negative self-concept, self-blame, and self-reproach; problems with concentration; recurring thoughts of suicide or death. Patients with **bipolar disorder** experience both depression and mania (a mood state involving elation, talkativeness, and unjustified high self-esteem), and are thus prone to mood swings.

Bipolar disorder is relatively uncommon. For example, about 10% of men and 20% of women become clinically depressed at some time in their lives. Over 90% of them suffer from major depression rather than bipolar disorder.

We will shortly discuss the factors involved in producing major depressive disorder and bipolar disorder. As we will see, the relative importance of some of the factors differs between the two disorders.

## Biological model

According to the biological model, we might expect genetic factors to be involved in the development of depression. Bertelsen, Harvald, and Hauge (1977) carried out a twin study, and found a concordance (agreement) rate for major depressive disorder of 59% for identical twins and of 30% for fraternal twins. For bipolar disorder, the concordance rate was 80% for identical twins and 16% for fraternal twins. All of these figures are much higher than for randomly selected members of the population.

*Which model would predict that similar treatment would increase concordance in identical twins?*

The above findings suggest that genetic factors are involved, and that their involvement is greater for bipolar disorder than for major depressive disorder. Similar conclusions follow from more recent studies. McGuffin, Katz, Watkins, and Rutherford (1996) considered nearly 200 identical twin pairs, and found that the concordance rate for major depressive disorder was 46%, compared to 20% for fraternal twins. Craddock and Jones (1999) found with bipolar disorder that the concordance rate was 40% for identical twins, compared to between 5% and 10% for fraternal twins, siblings, and other close relatives. All of these figures are much lower than those reported by Bertelsen et al. (1977). Some of the difference in concordance rates between identical and fraternal twins may be due to greater similarity of treatment of identical twins.

Family studies also suggest the involvement of genetic factors. Gershon (1990) discussed numerous family studies in which depression was assessed in the first-degree relatives of patients with depression. For both major depressive disorder and bipolar disorder, the rates of depression were about two to three times those in the general population.

Additional evidence on genetic factors comes from adoption studies. Wender, Kety, Rosenthal, Schulsinger, Ortmann, and Lunde (1986) found that the biological relatives of adopted sufferers from major depression were eight times more likely than adoptive relatives to have had major depression themselves. In adopted children who later developed depression, their biological parents were eight times as likely as their adoptive parents to have suffered from clinical depression.

Preliminary attempts have been made to understand the genetic influences at work. For example, Berrettini (2000) linked bipolar disorder to genes on chromosomes 4, 6, 11, 12, 13, 15, 18, and 22.

Depressed patients may have abnormal levels of various neurotransmitters or other substances. Some evidence suggests that patients with major depressive disorder often have low levels of **noradrenaline** and **serotonin** (see Comer, 2001). However, the reality is more complex. For example, Rampello, Nicoletti, and Nicoletti, (2000) reported that patients with major depressive disorder have an imbalance in the activity of several neurotransmitters including noradrenaline, serotonin, dopamine, and acetylcholine. In addition, patients with major depressive disorder have high levels of the hormone cortisol, which is present in large amounts when individuals are stressed (Hedaya, 1996; see Chapter 5).

What about bipolar disorder? There are low levels of serotonin in the depressive *and* the manic phases of this disorder (Price, 1990). This seems surprising, but can be

---

### Depression and diet

Explanations of depression that are based on biological factors are generally related to endogenous depression, i.e., depression that is caused by internal factors. However, these internal conditions may in turn be influenced by what we eat. There is some evidence that what you eat may affect your mood and may, in extreme cases, lead to depression.

Tryptophan is a substance that is found in some foods, such as maize and other starchy foods. Delgado et al. (1990) found that acute tryptophan depletion (ATD) induces a temporary relapse in patients suffering from major depressive disorder. This is supported in a study by Smith et al. (1997) who found that women experienced depression when tryptophan was removed from their diets. In addition it has been suggested that serotonin may be involved in some cases of eating disorder, and that the reason why bulimics often eat a lot of starchy foods is in order to increase their levels of tryptophan and serotonin.

---

### KEY TERMS

**Noradrenaline:**
a neurotransmitter that is sometimes present in abnormal quantities in depression.

**Serotonin:** a neurotransmitter, low levels of which are claimed to be found in patients with major depressive disorder and bipolar disorder.

---

### CASE STUDY: *Manic behaviour in manic depression*

Robert B had been a successful dentist for 25 years, providing well for his wife and family. One morning he woke up with the idea that he was the best dental surgeon in the world, and that he should try to treat as many people as possible. As a result, he set about enlarging his practice from 2 chairs to 20, planning to treat patients simultaneously. He phoned builders and ordered the necessary equipment. After a day of feeling irritable that there had been delays, he decided to do the work himself and began to knock down the walls. When this proved difficult, he became frustrated and began to smash his X-ray equipment and washbasins. Robert B's family were unaware of his behaviour until patients began to phone his wife after being turned away from the dental surgery. When she mentioned the phone calls to him, Robert B "ranted and raved" at her for 15 minutes. She described her husband as looking "haggard, wild-eyed and run down" and his speech was "over-excited". After several days of this behaviour, Mrs B phoned her daughters and asked them to come over with their husbands to help. On the evening of their visit Robert B began to "brag about his sexual prowess and make aggressive advances towards his daughters". When one of his sons-in-law tried to intervene he was attacked with a chair. Robert B was admitted to hospital, and subsequently it was found that he had had a history of such behaviour.

**CASE STUDY: *Major (unipolar) depression***

Paul was a twenty-year-old college senior majoring in chemistry. He first came to the student psychiatric clinic complaining of headaches and a vague assortment of somatic problems. Throughout the interview, Paul seemed severely depressed and unable to work up enough energy to talk with the therapist. Even though he had maintained a B+ average, he felt like a failure.

His parents had always had high expectations for Paul, their eldest son, and had transmitted these feelings to him from his earliest childhood. His father, a successful thoracic surgeon, had his heart set on Paul's becoming a doctor. The parents saw academic success as very important, and Paul did exceptionally well in school. Although his teachers praised him for being an outstanding student, his parents seemed to take his successes for granted. In fact they often made statements such as "You can do better". When he failed at something, his parents would make it obvious to him that they not only were disappointed but felt disgraced as well. This pattern of punishment for failures without recognition of successes, combined with his parents' high expectations, led to the development in Paul of an extremely negative self-concept.

From Sue, Sue, and Sue (1994).

explained by the permissive amine theory (e.g., Mandell & Knapp, 1979). According to this theory, low levels of serotonin activity permit the activity of neurotransmitters such as noradrenaline to fluctuate and hence determine the precise symptoms experienced by the patient.

## Psychodynamic model

Freud argued that depression is like grief, occurring as a reaction to the loss of an important relationship. However, there is an important difference, because depressed people regard themselves as worthless. The depressed individual identifies with the lost person, so that repressed anger towards the lost person is directed inwards towards the self. This inner-directed anger reduces the individual's self-esteem, and makes him/her vulnerable to experiencing depression in the future.

Freud distinguished between actual losses (e.g., death of a loved one) and symbolic losses (e.g., loss of a job). Both kinds of loss can produce depression by causing the individual to re-experience childhood experiences relating to loss of affection from some significant person (e.g., parent).

What about bipolar disorder? According to Freud, the depressive phase occurs when the individual's superego or conscience is dominant. In contrast, the manic phase occurs when the individual's ego or rational mind asserts itself, and he/she feels in control.

In order to avoid loss from turning into depression, the individual needs to engage in a period of mourning work, during which he/she recalls memories of the lost one. This allows the individual to separate him/herself from the lost person, and so reduce the inner-directed anger. However, individuals who are very dependent on others for their sense of self-esteem may be unable to do this, and so remain extremely depressed.

As predicted by the psychodynamic approach, depression is associated with loss events. Finlay-Jones and Brown (1981) found that depressed patients experienced more stressful life events than normal controls in the year before onset of the depression, and most of these were loss events. However, the details of the psychodynamic approach are incorrect. Freud predicted that the repressed anger and hostility of depressed people would emerge in dreams, but Beck and Ward (1961) found no evidence of this. Freud also predicted that depressed people should express anger and hostility mainly towards themselves. In fact, they express considerable anger and hostility towards those close to them (Weissman, Klerman, & Paykel, 1971).

Finally, it follows from Freud's theory that individuals experiencing major loss early in their lives should be vulnerable to developing clinical depression in adult life. Childhood adversities and traumatic stresses have significant effects on depression starting before the age of 20 (Kessler, 1997). However, childhood adversities and stresses do *not* predict depression starting later in adulthood.

Marilyn Monroe suffered with unipolar depression. Famous people who suffered with bipolar depression include Sir Winston Churchill and Virginia Woolf.

## Behavioural + cognitive models

Seligman's (1975) theory and research on learned helplessness have been very influential. **Learned helplessness** refers to the passive behaviour shown when animals or humans perceive mistakenly that punishment is unavoidable. In his original studies, Seligman exposed dogs to unavoidable electric shocks. After that, they were put in a box with a barrier in the middle. The dogs were given shocks after a warning signal, but they could escape by jumping over the barrier into the other part of the box. However, most of them passively accepted the shocks, and did not learn to escape. Seligman described this as learned helplessness, and argued it was very similar to the behaviour of depressed people.

*How might the idea of "learned helplessness" be applied to "battered wife syndrome"?*

This learned helplessness theory was later turned into a cognitive theory by Abramson, Seligman, and Teasdale (1978; see below). A problem with the original theory was that it was intended to model the behaviour of patients with major depressive disorder. In fact, however, the symptoms of learned helplessness are more like those of patients with bipolar disorder during a depressive episode (Depue & Monroe, 1978).

Abramson et al. (1978) developed Seligman's (1975) learned helplessness theory by focusing on the thoughts of people experiencing learned helplessness. They argued that people respond to failure in various ways:

- Attributing the failure to an *internal* cause (themselves) or to an *external* cause (other people, circumstances).
- Attributing the failure to a *stable* cause (likely to continue in future) or to an *unstable* cause (might easily change in future).
- Attributing the failure to a *global* cause (applying to a wide range of situations) or to a *specific* cause (applying to only one situation).

Individuals suffering from depression see themselves as failures, and often attribute this to faults within themselves that cannot be changed.

People with learned helplessness attribute failure to internal, stable, and global causes. Thus, they have a negative attributional style: They feel personally responsible for failure, they think the factors causing that failure will persist, and they think those factors will influence most situations in future. As a result, it is no wonder that sufferers from learned helplessness are depressed.

The above cognitive theory was modified by Abramson, Metalsky, and Alloy (1989). They attached less importance than Abramson et al. (1978) to specific attributions, and more importance to the notion that depressed individuals develop a general sense of hopelessness.

Beck and Clark (1988) also argued that cognitive factors are important. They referred to depressive schemas consisting of organised information stored in long-term memory. According to their cognitive theory, "The schematic organisation of the clinically depressed individual is dominated by an overwhelming negativity. A negative cognitive trait is evident in the depressed person's view of the self, world, and future … As a result of these negative maladaptive schemas, the depressed person views himself [sic] as inadequate, deprived and worthless, the world as presenting insurmountable obstacles, and the future as utterly bleak and hopeless" (p. 26). The term cognitive triad is used to refer to the depressed person's dysfunctional attitudes about himself or herself, the world, and the future.

Depressed individuals have the kinds of negative thoughts described by Abramson et al. (1978) and by Beck and Clark (1988). Do these negative thoughts help to cause depression, or do they merely occur as a result of being depressed? Lewinsohn, Steimetz, Larsen, and Franklin (1981) carried out a prospective study in which negative attitudes and thoughts were assessed *before* any of the participants became depressed. Here are their conclusions:

*Future depressives did not subscribe to irrational beliefs, they did not have lower expectancies for positive outcomes or higher expectancies for negative outcomes, they did not attribute success experiences to external causes and failure experiences to internal causes ... People who are vulnerable to depression are not characterised by stable patterns of negative cognitions. (p. 218)*

However, reasonable evidence that dysfunctional attitudes are involved in the development of major depressive disorder was reported by Lewinsohn, Joiner, and Rohde (2001). They measured dysfunctional attitudes (e.g., "My life is wasted unless I am a success"; "I should be happy all the time") in adolescents not having a major depressive disorder at the outset of the study. One year later, Lewinsohn et al. assessed the negative life events experienced by the participants over the 12-month period, and also assessed whether they were suffering from major depressive disorder. Those who experienced many negative life events had an increased likelihood of developing a major depressive disorder *only* if they were initially high in dysfunctional attitudes (see the figure on the right). Since dysfunctional attitudes were assessed *before* the onset of major depressive disorder, dysfunctional attitudes seem to be a risk factor for developing that disorder when exposed to stressful life events.

Probability of developing Major Depressive Disorder (MDD) as a function of number of life events (high vs. low) and dysfunctional attitudes (low, medium, or high)

## Social factors

Patients suffering from major depression typically experience an above average number of stressful life events before the onset of depression. For example, Brown and Harris (1978) carried out an interview study on women in London. They found that 61% of the depressed women had experienced at least one very stressful life event in the 8 months before interview, compared with 19% of non-depressed women. However, many women manage to cope with major life events without becoming clinically depressed. Of those women who experienced a serious life event, 37% of those without an intimate friend became depressed, compared to only 10% of those who had a very close friend.

The findings of Brown and Harris (1978) have been replicated several times. Brown (1989) reviewed the various studies. On average, about 55% of depressed patients had at least one severe life event in the months before onset, compared to only about 17% of controls.

The probability of life events leading to depression depends in part on each individual's cognitions. This was shown in a study by Segal, Shaw, Vella, and Kratz (1992) on ex-patients who had recovered from depression. The patients were assessed for the presence of dysfunctional attitudes (e.g., believing that partial failure was as bad as total failure), and then followed up over 12 months. Those patients who experienced the greatest number of life events were most likely to relapse into depression. This happened most often when there was a match between the type of life event and the particular concerns of the patient. More specifically, life events involving problems with achievement triggered a relapse most often in patients who were very self-critical, and life events involving interpersonal problems triggered a relapse most often in patients who were dependent.

One limitation of most life-event studies is that the information is obtained retrospectively several months afterwards. As a result, there may be problems in remembering clearly what has happened. Another limitation is that the meaning of a life event depends on the context. For example, losing your job is very serious if you have a large family to support, but may be much less serious if you are nearing the normal retirement age and have a large pension. However, this limitation does not apply to the research of Brown and Harris (1978), because they took full account of the context in which the life events occurred.

# ANXIETY DISORDERS

Several anxiety disorders are included in DSM-IV. The main ones are as follows: panic disorder, panic disorder with agoraphobia, **generalised anxiety disorder**, social phobia, post-traumatic stress disorder, specific phobia, and obsessive-compulsive disorder. Many clients have two or more different anxiety disorders. Barlow, DiNardo, Vermilyea, Vermilyea, and Blanchard (1986) considered a sample of 108 patients presenting at their clinic. Across the entire sample, 66% were diagnosed with two or more anxiety disorders.

Panic disorder, post-traumatic stress disorder, social phobia, and specific phobia are discussed in detail below.

## Panic disorder

According to DSM-IV, the diagnosis of **panic disorder** is given to people who experience a number of unexpected panic attacks. One or more of these attacks needs to be followed by 1 month or more during which the individual has lasting concerns about one of more of the following: (1) having another panic attack; (2) changes in behaviour caused by the attack; or (3) the implications of the attack.

What is the definition of a panic attack? According to DSM-IV, a panic attack involves intense fear or discomfort, with four or more bodily symptoms suddenly appearing (e.g., palpitations, shortness of breath, accelerated heart rate, feeling of choking, nausea, sweating, chest pain, feeling dizzy, and fear of dying).

Many patients with panic disorder also suffer from agoraphobia. **Agoraphobia** is a condition in which the individual is frightened to leave the house, because he/she is very concerned about having a panic attack in a public place. In DSM-IV, the term panic disorder with agoraphobia describes such individuals.

### Biological model

Genetic factors are involved in the development of panic disorder. Kendler, Neale, Kessler, Heath, and Eaves (1993) carried out a twin study on panic disorder. Among identical twins, if one twin had panic disorder, then the other twin did as well in 24% of cases. Among fraternal twins, the other twin had panic disorder in only 11% of cases. Crowe, Noyes, Pauls, and Slyman (1983) found that panic disorder was present in nearly 25% of close relatives of clients with panic disorder. In contrast, panic disorder was found in only about 2% of the normal population. However, other research has been less clear-cut (see McNally, 1994).

**CASE STUDY: *Sarah—a case of agoraphobia***

Sarah, a woman in her mid-thirties, was shopping for bargains in a crowded department store during the January sales. Without warning and without knowing why, she suddenly felt anxious and dizzy. She worried that she was about to faint or have a heart attack. She dropped her shopping and rushed straight home. As she neared home, she noticed that her feelings of panic lessened.

A few days later she decided to go shopping again. On entering the store, she felt herself becoming increasingly anxious. After a few minutes she had become so anxious that a shop keeper asked her if she was OK and took her to a first aid room. Once there her feelings of panic became worse and she became particularly embarrassed at all the attention she was attracting.

After this she avoided going to the large store again. She even started to worry when going into smaller shops because she thought she might have Another panic attack, and this worry turned into intense anxiety. Eventually she stopped shopping altogether, asking her husband to do it for her.

Over the next few months, Sarah found that she had panic attacks in more and more places. The typical pattern was that she became progressively more anxious the further away from her house she got. She tried to avoid the places where she might have a panic attack, but as the months passed, she found that this restricted her activities. Some days she found it impossible to leave the house at all. She felt that her marriage was becoming strained and that her husband resented her dependence on him.

Clearly Sarah's behaviour was abnormal, in many of the ways described in the text. It was statistically infrequent and socially deviant. It interfered with her ability to function adequately, both from her own point of view and of her husband. She did not have many of the signs of mental healthiness.

Adapted from J.D. Stirling and J.S.E. Hellewell (1999).

Genetic factors influence individual differences in personality, and people who are high in anxiety sensitivity (i.e., very sensitive to certain bodily sensations) are vulnerable to developing panic disorder. Maller and Reiss (1992) found that individuals who were high in anxiety sensitivity in 1984 were five times as likely as those who were low to suffer from panic attacks in 1987.

## Cognitive model

According to the cognitive model (e.g., Clark, 1986), patients with panic disorder greatly exaggerate the threateningness of internal stimuli (e.g., fast heart rate). How did this happen in the first place? One possibility is that a history of respiratory disease (e.g., bronchitis) may sensitise individuals to their internal state, and lead them to exaggerate the significance of bodily symptoms. Verburg, Griez, Meijer, and Pols (1995) found that 43% of their panic disorder patients had suffered from at least one respiratory disease (e.g., bronchitis) during their lives compared to only 16% among patients with other anxiety disorders.

*Can we be sure that this exaggeration causes the panic disorder, rather than being an effect of it?*

## Social factors

Barrett (1979) found that panic patients reported significantly more undesirable life events in the 6 months before the onset of their anxiety disorder than did controls over the same period of time. In a study by Kleiner and Marshall (1987), 84% of patients having panic disorder with agoraphobia reported having experienced family problems in the months before they had their first panic attack.

# Post-traumatic stress disorder

**Post-traumatic stress disorder** (PTSD) first received official recognition in DSM-III (1980), although related notions such as "shell shock" and "combat fatigue" had been put forward much earlier. According to DSM-IV, there are three main categories of symptoms for PTSD:

1. *Re-experiencing the traumatic event:* The event is often recalled and nightmares about it are common. Stimuli triggering memories of the traumatic event cause intense emotional upset.
2. *Avoidance of stimuli associated with the event or alternatively reduced responsiveness to such stimuli:* The individual tries to avoid trauma-related stimuli or thoughts, and there is fluctuation between re-experiencing the traumatic event and a numbing of response to stimuli associated with the event.
3. *Increased arousal:* There are problems with sleep, difficulties with concentration, and an increased startle response.

Patients with PTSD may also suffer from anger, anxiety, depression, and guilt. In addition, there may be marital problems, headaches, suicidal thoughts, and explosive violence (Davison & Neale, 2001).

By definition, PTSD is triggered by a specific event such as war or a natural disaster (e.g., an earthquake). March (1991) reviewed evidence on the most common characteristics of events leading to PTSD. These events included physical injury, bereavement, participation in atrocities, exposure to grotesque death, and witnessing or hearing about death. As would be expected, the chances of developing PTSD are generally much greater if the traumatic event is life threatening than when it is not. Factors in addition to the traumatic event need to be taken into account. If numerous people are exposed to the same traumatic event (e.g., a sinking ship), what typically happens is that some develop PTSD, whereas others do not. We turn now to factors making some people more vulnerable than others to PTSD. For example, Bremner, Southwick, Johnson, Yehuda, and Charney, (1993) found that adults physically abused when they were children had an increased probability of developing PTSD as a result of their combat experiences in Vietnam.

**KEY TERM**

**Post-traumatic stress disorder:** a disorder triggered by a very distressing event, in which there is re-experiencing of the event, avoidance of stimuli associated with the event, and increased arousal.

## Biological model

The involvement of biological factors has been investigated in a few twin studies. Skre, Onstad, Torgersen, Lygren, and Kringlen (1993, p. 85) found greater concordance for PTSD in identical twins than in fraternal ones, and concluded that, "The results support the hypothesis of a genetic contribution in aetiology [causation] of ... PTSD." True et al. (1993) also found that the concordance rate was greater for identical than for fraternal twins. According to them (p. 257), "Genetic factors account for 13% to 30% of the variance in liability for symptoms in the re-experiencing cluster, 30% to 34% for symptoms in the avoidance cluster, and 28% to 32% for symptoms in the arousal cluster."

Foy et al. (1987) found that PTSD depends interactively on genetic factors and the severity of the traumatic event. A low level of combat exposure was much more likely to lead to PTSD in those having family members with other disorders, perhaps because of a genetic vulnerability. However, a high level of combat exposure led to PTSD in two-thirds of people regardless of whether family members had other disorders. These findings suggest that very traumatic events can cause PTSD in vulnerable *and* non-vulnerable individuals.

## Psychodynamic model

The onset of PTSD can occur months or even years after exposure to a traumatic event. Horowitz (1986) explained this delayed onset in a psychodynamic theory, according to which a traumatic event can make the individual feel overwhelmed, causing panic or exhaustion. These reactions are often so painful that the individual represses or deliberately suppresses thoughts of the traumatic event. This state of denial does not resolve matters, because the individual is unable to integrate information from the traumatic event into his/her sense of self.

Horowitz's (1986) psychodynamic approach provides a way of understanding the main symptoms of PTSD. However, the theory does not indicate *why* there are considerable individual differences in vulnerability to PTSD in the face of a traumatic event.

---

### CASE STUDY: *The Jupiter disaster*

On 21 October 1988, 391 British schoolchildren and 84 adults boarded the cruise liner *Jupiter* in the Greek port of Piraeus for the trip of a lifetime. Disaster struck within 15 minutes of the ship leaving harbour when a freight ship collided with the cruise liner, making a hole in the side of the ship. Within 40 minutes of the collision the ship had sunk in the Mediterranean Sea. Miraculously, only 4 people lost their lives in the disaster, with approximately 70 passengers and crew sustaining injuries. However, for the survivors of the disaster the ordeal of coming to terms with what had happened was the greatest challenge of all.

When the disaster occurred all on board were in danger of being drowned, electrocuted, or crushed to death. However, as most of the passengers were young teenagers who were used to being in a crowd and being guided by adults, the expected crushing, fighting, and trampling in terror did not happen. The teenagers had to play an active role in trying to contain the panic that was rising, and many were successful at calming and helping some of the younger children on the ship. It was partly due to their efforts to minimise panic and cope with the situation that the disaster claimed so few lives.

When the survivors returned to England they were encouraged to write about their experiences as part of their rehabilitation. These testimonies have provided psychologists with an insight into the disaster through the eyes of the victims, and the stories told reveal not only concern for their own well-being, but a deep anxiety for the others caught in the desperate plight. Chloe Warrington, aged 13, described her reaction when the impact occurred.

*Half-crying, half-laughing, we stood or sat nervously waiting. Inside I felt panic. A choke of screams in my throat emerged as*

*silence. The deck was now slanting. The wooden lines of the deck are embedded in my memory, as that is when I began to realise that what was happening was real. I felt not terror, not shock, just confusion; disbelief about what was happening. Questions floated in my mind to which I could find no answers.*

Another survivor, Carole Gardner, aged 14 at the time of the disaster remembers how as the ship slanted: "other people started sliding down into the chairs ... I felt the air being squeezed out of me by bodies on top of me. To my left was an elderly woman sitting above the chairs. She looked dazed, with blood pouring from her right temple. I wanted so much to help her, but I could not move."

Such testimonies made it apparent that the psychological impact of the disaster was overwhelming. Many of the children found that they suffered waves of total exhaustion, lack of sleep, difficulty concentrating, grief, and even guilt for surviving when others had perished. According to a recent report published by the Institute of Psychiatry, since the disaster in 1988 over half the survivors have been diagnosed as suffering from post-traumatic stress disorder (PTSD). The symptoms of PTSD include nightmares, flashbacks, depression, anxiety, guilt, excessive jumpiness, and constant thoughts of the trauma.

One of the survivors has committed suicide, and 15 of the 158 survivors interviewed by Institute psychologists said they had attempted to do likewise. Many are still haunted today by what happened to them in their early teens, but some have enrolled for counselling that has taught them various coping techniques to combat the psychological side-effects of living through such a frightening experience.

From Tester (1998).

*Can you think of any other factors (e.g., those related to cultural differences) that may help to prevent these people suffering from PTSD?*

PTSD can be triggered by a life-threatening event such as an earthquake. Here, survivors of the 1999 Turkish earthquake sit outside their destroyed apartment blocks.

## Behavioural model

According to the behavioural approach (e.g., Keane, Fairbank, Caddell, Zimmering, & Gender, 1985), classical conditioning at the time of the traumatic event causes the individual to acquire a conditioned fear to the neutral stimuli that were present. For example, a woman raped in a park may experience great fear when approaching that park in future. The fear produced when stimuli associated with the traumatic event are encountered or even thought about leads to avoidance learning. This avoidance reduces anxiety, and is thus rewarding or reinforcing.

The conditioning approach predicts the high level of anxiety produced by any stimuli associated with the traumatic event, and the avoidance of such stimuli by sufferers from PTSD. However, it does not provide a detailed account of *what* is happening. Moreover, it does not make clear *why* some individuals develop PTSD in response to a traumatic event, whereas others do not. Finally, it doesn't explain why some individuals develop PTSD rather than a specific phobia (see below).

## Social phobia

**Social phobia** involves extreme concern about one's own behaviour and the reactions of others. Social phobia can be either generalised or specific. The main diagnostic criteria for social phobia in DSM-IV include the following:

- Marked and persistent fear of one or more situations in which the individual will be exposed to unfamiliar people or to scrutiny.
- Exposure to the feared social situation nearly always produces considerable anxiety.
- The individual recognises that the fear experienced is excessive.
- The feared situations are either avoided or responded to with great anxiety.

**KEY TERM**

**Social phobia:** a disorder in which the individual has excessive fear of most situations, and will often avoid them.

Stage-fright: an example of fear when facing the scrutiny of others.

## CASE STUDY: *A Phobia*

A young student in his first year at university was referred to a therapist after seeking help at the student health centre. During initial interviews he spoke of feeling frightened and often panicking when heading for his classes. He claimed he felt comfortable in his room, but was unable to concentrate on his work or to face other people. He admitted to fears of catching syphilis and of going bald. These fears were so intense that at times he would compulsively scrub his hands, head, and genitals so hard that they would bleed. He was reluctant to touch door handles and would never use public toilets. The student admitted that he knew his fears were irrational, but felt that he would be in even more "mental anguish" if he did not take these precautions.

In later sessions with the therapist, the student's history revealed previous concerns about his sexual identity. As a child he harboured feelings of inferiority because he had not been as fast or as strong as his peers. These feelings were reinforced by his mother who had not encouraged him to play rough games in case he got hurt. At puberty the student had also worried that he might be sexually deficient. At a summer camp he had discovered that he was underdeveloped sexually compared to the other boys. He had even wondered if he was developing into a girl. Although he did in fact mature into a young man, he constantly worried about his masculine identity, even fantasising that he was a girl. The student admitted that at times his anxiety was so great that he considered suicide. (Adapted from Kleinmuntz, 1974.)

## KEY TERM

**Specific phobia:** a strong and irrational fear of a given object or situation.

---

• The phobic reactions interfere significantly with the individual's working or social life, or there is marked distress.

About 70% of sufferers with social phobia are female. It "tends to be more prevalent in people who are younger (aged 18–29 years), less educated, single, and of lower socio-economic class" (Barlow & Durand, 1995, p. 186).

### Biological model

Genetic factors are probably involved in the development of social phobia. Fyer, Mannuzza, Chapman, Liebowitz, and Klein (1993) discovered that 16% of the close relatives of social phobics developed the same disorder, against only 5% of the relatives of individuals without social phobia. Kendler, Karkowski, and Prescott (1999) carried out a twin study on 1708 female identical and fraternal twins. They argued that the heritability of various phobias had been under-estimated in the past, because unreliability of the assessment of phobias had been ignored. They took account of this unreliability, and concluded that the heritability of social phobia was .51, which is moderately high.

Personality (individual differences in which depend in part on genetic factors) may be involved in the development of social phobia. Stemberger, Turner, and Beidel (1995) found that most social phobics are extremely introverted. Comparisons indicate that social phobics are much more introverted than patients with other anxiety disorders (see Eysenck, 1997). Very introverted individuals tend to avoid social situations, and so introversion could be a risk factor for social phobia. However, the strong association between social phobia and introversion may have arisen in part because suffering from social phobia makes people more introverted.

### Social factors

Parental practices probably play a role in the development of social phobia. For example, Arrindell, Kwee, Methorst, van der Ende, Pol, and Moritz (1989) found that social phobics claimed that their parents were rejecting, lacking in emotional warmth, or over-protective. However, it is hard to interpret such findings. As Hudson and Rapee (2000, p. 115) pointed out, "Children born with anxious temperaments may influence the way parents respond to them. This is likely to occur in a context in which a parent is anxious and therefore more likely to overprotect."

There are other ways in which parents may influence the development of social phobia. Adult social phobics report that their parents over-emphasised the opinions of others, failed to stress the importance of family sociability, and tended to isolate their family from others (Bruch & Heimberg, 1994).

## Specific phobia

**Specific phobia** involves strong and irrational fear of some specific object or situation. Specific phobias include fear of spiders and fear of snakes, but there are hundreds of different specific phobias (e.g., claustrophobia or fear of enclosed spaces, fear of heights). According to DSM-IV, the main symptoms of specific phobia involve a marked and persistent fear of a specific object or situation, a recognition by the individual that his/her fear is excessive, the phobic stimulus is avoided or responded to with great anxiety, and the phobic reactions are distressed and/or disruptive of working or social life.

## Biological model

Genetic factors are involved in the origins or aetiology of several specific phobias. Fyer et al. (1990) found that 31% of close relatives of individuals with specific phobia also had a phobia. More striking findings were reported by Ost (1989) in a study on blood phobia. In 64% of the cases, these blood phobics had at least one close relative also suffering from blood phobia. Kendler et al. (1999) assessed heritability for several phobias in 1708 female twins. Heritability was .59 for blood-injury phobia, .47 for animal phobia, and .46 for situational phobia. Note that some of the tendency for specific phobias to run in families could well be due to the fact that members of the same family typically share many experiences. Thus, environmental factors may partly explain some findings discussed in this section.

| Specific phobias | |
| --- | --- |
| *Some of the more common specific phobias are:* | |
| Acrophobia | Fear of heights |
| Claustrophobia | Fear of enclosed spaces |
| Insectophobia | Fear of insects |
| Musophobia | Fear of mice |
| Orphidiophobia | Fear of snakes |
| Pediphobia | Fear of dogs |
| *Some more unusual phobias:* | |
| Batophobia | Fear of being close to high buildings |
| Catoptrophobia | Fear of mirrors |
| Dextrophobia | Fear of objects at the right side of the body |
| Genuphobia | Fear of knees |
| Helmintophobia | Fear of being infested with worms |
| Ichthyophobia | Fear of fish |
| Lachanophobia | Fear of vegetables |
| Mottephobia | Fear of moths |
| Nephophobia | Fear of clouds |
| Paraskavedekatriaphobia | Fear of Friday the 13th |
| Pogonophobia | Fear of beards |
| Sciophobia | Fear of shadows |
| Xanthophobia | Fear of the colour yellow |

## Psychodynamic model

According to Freud, phobias are a defence against the anxiety produced when the impulses of the id or sexual instinct are repressed or forced into the unconscious. This theory emerged from Freud's case study of Little Hans, who developed a phobia of horses. According to Freud, Little Hans was sexually attracted to his mother, but was very frightened that his father would punish him for this. Horses resembled his father in that their black muzzles and blinkers looked like his moustache and glasses, and so Little Hans transferred or displaced his fear of his father on to horses. On this account, Hans should have showed a phobic reaction every time he saw a horse. In fact, however, he *only* showed his phobia when he saw a horse pulling a cart at high speed. The horse phobia developed after Hans had seen a serious accident involving a horse and cart moving at high speed, which may have produced a conditioned fear response (see below).

There is practically no support for Freud's explanation of specific phobias. It is mentioned mainly because of its historical importance as the first systematic account of specific phobia.

## Behavioural model

According to the behavioural model, the development of a specific phobia involves classical conditioning. The conditioned stimulus is the phobic object and the unconditioned stimulus is some aversive event, and the conditioned and unconditioned responses are fear or anxiety. Some support for this view was reported by Watson and Rayner (1920), who studied an 11-month-old boy called Albert. He was a calm child, but the loud noise produced by a steel bar being struck made him cry. He became frightened of a rat when the sight of it was paired seven times with a loud noise. This involved classical conditioning.

After that, the fear produced by the previously neutral stimulus (i.e., the rat) was reduced by avoiding it. According to Jones (1925), "Albert not only became greatly disturbed at the sight of a rat, but this fear had spread to include a white rabbit, cotton wool,

*Does this study raise any ethical issues? Could they have been resolved?*

a fur coat and the experimenter's (white) hair." However, it has proved very difficult to replicate this classic study in laboratory experiments with children and adults (see Hallam & Rachman, 1976). Nevertheless, there is some support for the prediction that conditioning experiences help to cause specific phobias. For example, Barlow and Durand (1995) noted that nearly everyone they have treated for choking phobia has had some very unpleasant choking experience in the past.

Convincing support for the conditioning account would involve showing that phobic patients are much more likely than other people to have had a frightening experience with the phobic object. However, the crucial normal control group is often missing. Consider, for example, a study by DiNardo, Guzy, Jenkins, Bak, Tomasi, and Copland (1988). They found that 50% of dog phobics had become very anxious during an encounter with a dog, apparently supporting conditioning theory. However, 50% of normal controls *without* dog phobia had also had an anxious encounter with a dog! These findings suggest that dog phobia does *not* depend on having had a frightening encounter with a dog.

Keuthen (1980) reported that half of all phobics could not remember any highly unpleasant experiences relating to the phobic object. However, those favouring a conditioning account argue that phobics often forget conditioning experiences which happened many years previously. Menzies and Clarke (1993) reduced this problem in a study on children suffering from water phobia. Only 2% of them reported a direct conditioning experience involving water, and 56% said they had always been frightened of water, even on their first encounter with it.

If phobias develop because of accidental pairings of a neutral and a fearful or aversive stimulus, then people could become phobic to almost anything. In fact, many more people have phobias about spiders and snakes than about cars, even though we see cars much more often and they are considerably more dangerous. Seligman (1971) argued that the objects and situations forming the basis of most phobias were real sources of danger hundreds or thousands of years ago, and only those individuals who were sensitive to such objects and situations were favoured by evolution. Thus, there is a **preparedness** or biological predisposition to become anxious in the presence of certain stimuli rather than others.

## EATING DISORDERS

There are several eating disorders. The most common eating disorders in DSM-IV are anorexia nervosa and bulimia nervosa (discussed below). We might regard obesity as the most common eating disorder (S. Cave, personal communication). However (rightly or wrongly), it is *not* classified as an eating disorder in DSM-IV.

### Anorexia nervosa

What might be responsible for a) the original low rate of anorexia, and b) the recent increase of anorexia in African American women?

There are four DSM-IV criteria for **anorexia nervosa**:

- The individual has a bodyweight less than 85% of that expected.
- There is an intense fear of becoming fat in spite of being considerably underweight.
- The individual's thinking about his/her bodyweight is distorted, either by exaggerating its importance to self-evaluation or by minimising the dangers of being considerably underweight.
- In females, the absence of three or more consecutive menstrual cycles (amenorrhoea).

Over 90% of patients with anorexia nervosa are female, and the age of onset is typically between the ages of 14 and 18 (American Psychiatric Association, 2000). There has been an increase in the frequency of anorexia nervosa in Western societies in recent decades, with an incidence of about 0.5% in women (Cooper, 1994). Anorexia nervosa used to be very rare among African American women in the United States, but has shown signs of a marked increase (Hsu, 1990).

Most sufferers from anorexia nervosa recover over time. However, the near-starvation that anorexics impose on themselves can produce serious and even life-threatening physiological changes. These include lowered body temperature, reduced bone mineral density, low blood pressure, and slowed heart rate.

## Bulimia nervosa

According to DSM-IV, **bulimia nervosa** is defined by the following five criteria:

- Numerous episodes of binge eating, in which much more food is eaten within a 2-hour period than most people would eat, and the eater experiences a lack of control over his/her eating behaviour.
- Frequent inappropriate compensatory behaviour to prevent weight gain (e.g., self-induced vomiting, excessive exercise, going without meals).
- Binge eating and inappropriate compensatory behaviour occur at least twice a week over a 3-month period.
- The individual's self-evaluation depends excessively on his/her shape and weight.
- Binge eating and compensatory behaviour do not occur only during episodes of anorexia nervosa.

Binge eating is generally preceded by great tension, with the individual feeling powerless to control his/her compelling need to eat "forbidden" types of food. The binge eating itself reduces the tension, but leaves bulimics experiencing guilt, self-blame, and depression (American Psychiatric Association, 2000).

There has been a dramatic increase in sufferers from bulimia nervosa since the late 1970s. Garner and Fairburn (1988) reported figures from an eating disorder centre in Canada. The number of patients treated for bulimia nervosa increased from 15 in 1979 to over 140 in 1986. Over 95% of sufferers from bulimia nervosa are women, and the onset is generally between 15 and 21 years of age (American Psychiatric Association, 2000). Bulimia nervosa resembles anorexia nervosa in that both disorders are found much more in Western societies than elsewhere, and they occur more often in middle-class than working-class families.

The self-induced vomiting found in most bulimics produces various medical effects. It can damage the teeth by eroding dental enamel. It can also change the levels of sodium and potassium in bodily fluids, and these changes can be life threatening.

Even when sufferers from anorexia nervosa are significantly underweight, they continue to fear becoming fat.

### CASE STUDY: *An eating disorder*

At the age of 12, JC had weighed 115 pounds and had been teased by friends and family for being "podgy". At first JC had started to restrict her food intake by eating less at meal times, becoming selective about what she ate, and cutting out snacks between meals. Initially, JC's progressive weight loss was supported by her family and friends. However, as she began to lose pounds she would set herself new targets, ignoring feelings of hunger by focusing on each new target. In her first year of dieting JC's weight dropped from 115 pounds to 88 pounds. Her initial goal had been to lose 10 pounds. JC's periods stopped shortly after she started her regime, her appearance changed dramatically, and in the second year of her regime her weight loss was considered to be out of control. Her personality had also changed, and she was not the active, spontaneous, and cheerful girl she had been before dieting. Her girlfriends were less enthusiastic about coming over to her house, because JC would be stubborn and argumentative, designing strict programmes of activities for them to carry out.

JC's family had asked their GP for help. He had been alarmed at JC's appearance and designed a high calorific diet for her. However, JC believed that there was something inside her that would not let her gain weight. She would pretend to eat, often listing food she claimed to have eaten which had in fact been flushed down the toilet, or would not swallow food she put in her mouth. JC admitted that when she felt down over the past two years she would still feel driven to lose weight, and as a result would go on walks, run errands, or spend long periods of time keeping her room immaculate. (Adapted from Leon, 1984.)

## Anorexia nervosa vs. bulimia nervosa

There is some overlap between bulimia nervosa and anorexia nervosa, with many bulimic patients also having a history of anorexia. In addition, both disorders typically start during adolescence, and often follow a period of dieting by individuals who are very concerned about their weight, and who experience frequent feelings of anxiety and depression. Bulimics and anorexics have distorted views about their own appearance, and they exaggerate the importance of having an "ideal" body shape.

In spite of the similarities between anorexia nervosa and bulimia nervosa, there are several important differences. First, bulimia nervosa is far more common than anorexia nervosa. Second, nearly all patients with bulimia nervosa are within about 10% of their

### KEY TERM

**Bulimia nervosa:** an eating disorder in which there is binge eating and compensatory behaviour (e.g., self-induced vomiting) to prevent weight gain.

normal weight, whereas anorexic patients (by definition) are at least 15% below their normal weight. Third, bulimics are generally more concerned than anorexics about being attractive to other people, and are more involved with others. Fourth, bulimics are more likely than anorexics to have a history of mood swings, and to have poor control of their impulses (American Psychiatric Association, 2000).

## Biological model

Genetic factors play a part in the development of eating disorders. Relatives of patients with eating disorders are four or five times more likely than other members of society to suffer from an eating disorder (e.g., Strober & Humphrey, 1987). Holland, Sicotte, and Treasure (1988) studied anorexia in monozygotic (identical) and dizygotic (fraternal) twins. The concordance (agreement) rate for identical twins was 56%, compared to only 7% for dizygotic twins. Kendler et al. (1991) did a similar study on bulimia in 2163 female twins, finding a concordance rate of 23% for monozygotic twins compared to 9% for dizygotic twins.

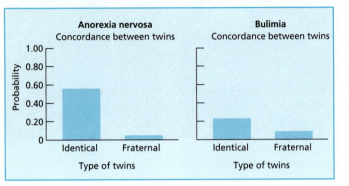

Holland et al. (1988) and Kendler et al. (1991) studied anorexia and bulimia in twins.

These findings suggest that genetic factors play a part in the development of eating disorders, especially anorexia nervosa. However, the family environment experienced by identical twins is more similar than that experienced by fraternal twins (Loehlin & Nichols, 1976). Thus, environmental factors may contribute towards the higher concordance rates for identical twins.

The recent dramatic increase in sufferers from eating disorders cannot be explained in genetic terms, because there have been no major genetic changes over the past 20–30 years. It is also very unlikely that the large differences in the incidence of eating disorders across cultures (Comer, 2001) can be accounted for by genetic factors.

The neurotransmitter serotonin may be involved in some cases of eating disorder. For example, Carrasco, Diaz-Marsa, Hollander, Cesar, and Saiz-Ruiz (2000) found that bulimics tended to have low serotonin activity. Bingeing on starchy foods containing carbohydrates can increase serotonin levels in the brain, and this may improve mood in individuals having low serotonin levels. However, patients with bulimia nervosa do not focus specifically on foods containing carbohydrates when they binge (Barlow & Durand, 1995). The finding that low serotonin levels are associated with eating disorder does not demonstrate that serotonin is important in their development. It could well be that the development of an eating disorder leads to a reduction in serotonin activity.

## Psychodynamic model

*Could this model explain a) the recent increase in anorexia in males, b) cases of anorexia in older women, and c) cultural variations in the rate of anorexia?*

There have been various psychodynamic approaches to anorexia nervosa (see Davison & Neale, 2001). The fact that the disorder is mostly found in adolescent girls suggests that anorexia might be due to fear of increasing sexual desires or to oral impregnation. Within that context, semi-starvation may reflect the desire to avoid becoming pregnant, because one of the symptoms of anorexia nervosa is the elimination of menstrual periods.

A somewhat different psychodynamic account is based on the notion that anorexia nervosa occurs in females having an unconscious desire to remain pre-pubescent. Their weight loss prevents them from developing the body shape associated with adult females, and thus allows them to preserve the illusion that they are still children.

Minuchin, Roseman, and Baker (1978) argued that the families of anorexics are characterised by **enmeshment**, meaning that none of the members of the family has a clear identity because everything is done together. Such families prevent children from becoming independent. A child growing up in an enmeshed family may rebel against its constraints by refusing to eat. Minuchin et al. (1978) also argued that enmeshed families find it hard to resolve conflicts. Parental conflicts are reduced by the need to attend to the symptoms of their anorexic child.

KEY TERM

**Enmeshment:** a situation in which none of the members of a family has a true sense of personal identity, because everything is done together.

**CASE STUDY: *Anorexics***

Hilde Bruch (1971) developed a theory of anorexia based on her experience in treating such patients. The cases below are adapted from her records.

**Case 1**

A 12-year-old girl from a prominent upper class family was seen when her mother consulted the psychiatrist about an older sister who was obese. The mother felt that she wanted to punish this daughter for being overweight, but spoke in glowing terms about her younger daughter who in every way was an ideal child. Her teachers would refer to her as the "best balanced" girl in the school, and relied on her helpfulness and kindness when another child was having difficulty making friends.

Later, when the anorexia developed, it became apparent to what extent the anxious and punitive behaviours of the mother had affected the way the younger daughter felt and thought about herself. She had become convinced that being fat was most shameful. As she began to put on weight in puberty, she felt horrified and that, if she was to retain respect, she would have to maintain her thinness. This led her to go on a starvation regime. At the same time she also began to realise that she didn't have to be an ideal daughter and do what others expected of her, but she could be the master of her own fate.

**Case 2**

A mother sought psychoanalytic treatment because she had become depressed. Her daughter was her one great satisfaction in life. The girl (aged 14) had always been a happy child who had no problems. She had had a governess, but the mother fed the daughter herself, making an especial effort to provide good food and tastefully present it.

Shortly after the mother had consulted the psychiatrist the daughter became anorexic, having started to get plump. When she visited the psychiatrist her version of childhood was the exact opposite of her mother's account. She remembered it as a time of constant misery and that she could never have what she wanted but always had to have exactly what her mother wanted. She knew her mother had talked about what she should be eating with their doctor, and this made her feel that every bite that went into her mouth was watched. The concern about her fatness was reinforced by her father's excessive attention to appearance. Theirs was a wealthy home and there were always lavish arrays of food. Her father showed his superiority by eating very little and making snide remarks about people who ate too much.

When the girl became plump at puberty she tried to outdo her father's haughty control. She felt she owed it to him to remain slim and aristocratic. Her life was dominated by trying to satisfy her father. She did well at school but was haunted by the fear of being found out to be stupid. She described her life as "I never deserved what they gave me" and that she was "worthless". Keeping her weight as low as possible was her only way of proving herself to be "deserving" and having "dignity".

Adapted from H. Bruch (1971).

---

It is hard to evaluate enmeshment theory. However, there are often high levels of parental conflict within the families of anorexics (Kalucy, Crisp, & Harding, 1977). Hsu (1990) reported that families with an anorexic child tend to deny or ignore conflicts and to blame other people for their problems. The problem is that these parental conflicts may be more a result of having an anorexic child than a cause of anorexia.

Family conflicts have also been identified in families with a child showing signs of bulimia as well as anorexia. Such families have more negative and fewer positive interactions than families with a normal adolescent (Humphrey, Apple, & Kirschenbaum, 1986). However, it is not clear whether the poor family interactions help to cause the disorder or are simply a reaction to it.

There is little support for the various psychodynamic accounts discussed, all of which seem to be based on the incorrect assumption that eating disorders only develop in adolescent females. Thus, they cannot explain eating disorders in males or in adults.

An alternative approach was taken by Bruch (e.g., 1991). She argued that individuals with eating disorders generally have ineffective parents who ignore the child's needs, and make inaccurate decisions as to whether he/she is hungry or tired. This makes the children confused and helpless, and causes them to rely heavily on other people to tell them when they are hungry. Bruch (1973) found that the mothers of anorexic children said that they had always anticipated their children's needs, and so their children had never experienced hunger. Anorexics and bulimics are very worried about how they are perceived by others, and also experience a general lack of control (Vitousek & Manke, 1994). Finally, patients with bulimia nervosa sometimes mistakenly believe that they are hungry when they become anxious (Rebert, Stanton, & Schwarz, 1991).

# Cognitive model

Patients with eating disorders have distorted views about themselves (e.g., their body shape and weight). Bulimics perceive their body size to be larger than do control individuals of the same size, and they also mistakenly believe that eating a small snack has a noticeable effect on their body size (McKenzie, Williamson, & Cubic, 1993). In patients with bulimia nervosa, the

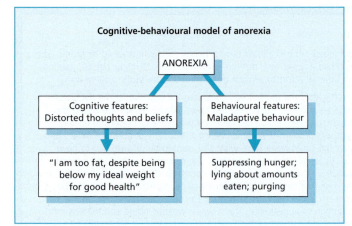

Cognitive-behavioural model of anorexia

ANOREXIA

Cognitive features: Distorted thoughts and beliefs

Behavioural features: Maladaptive behaviour

"I am too fat, despite being below my ideal weight for good health"

Suppressing hunger; lying about amounts eaten; purging

discrepancy between their *actual* bodyweight and their desired bodyweight is typically about the same as it is in healthy young women. However, the *perceived* discrepancy is much greater in bulimics (Cooper & Taylor, 1988): Bulimics are more likely to exaggerate their body size, and their desired body size is smaller than it is for healthy women.

It is hard to interpret the above findings, because we do not know whether the cognitive distortions shown by patients with eating disorders were present *before* the onset of the disorder. The cognitive distortions may be a by-product of the eating disorder, and so play no part in its development.

Another psychological factor of relevance to eating disorders is the personality characteristic of **perfectionism** (a strong desire to achieve excellence). Individuals high in perfectionism may strive to achieve an unrealistically slim body shape. The mothers of girls with disordered eating often have perfectionist tendencies (Pike & Rodin, 1991). These mothers were very keen that their daughters should be thin, they were likely to be dieting themselves, and they expressed low levels of satisfaction with their family. Steinhausen (1994) found that females with eating disorders showed signs of perfectionism, as well as of compliance and dependence. Low self-esteem is also often involved (Comer, 2001).

## Cultural factors

Eating disorders are considerably more common in Western than in non-Western societies (Cooper, 1994). For example, about one woman in 200 suffers from anorexia nervosa in Western Europe and the United States. In Hong Kong, in contrast, only one person out of more than 2000 Chinese people sampled had anorexia (Lee, 1994). Nasser (1986) compared Egyptian women studying in Cairo and in London. None of the women studying in Cairo developed an eating disorder, in contrast to 12% of those studying in London.

These cultural differences are most obviously explained by the pressures on young women within Western societies to have a thin body shape, pressures which have increased greatly in recent decades. The emphasis on slimness as desirable is illustrated by the finding that a majority of Miss America contestants are 15% or more below their expected bodyweight (Barlow & Durand, 1995). Being underweight by that amount is one of the criteria for anorexia nervosa!

Jaeger et al. (2002) studied women in 12 Western and non-Western countries. The most extreme body dissatisfaction was found in Mediterranean countries, followed in order by northern European countries, countries in the process of westernisation, and finally non-Western countries, which had the lowest levels of body dissatisfaction. It is of interest that there was a reasonably close relationship between a country's level of body dissatisfaction and its level of eating disorders.

Cogan, Bhalla, Sefa-Dedeh, and Rathblum (1996) compared the views of students in Ghana and in the United States: "Students in Ghana more often rated larger body sizes as ideal for both males and females, and also assumed that these larger sizes were held as ideal in society, than did U.S. students" (p. 98). In addition, thin females were rated by the American sample as being the happiest, whereas Ghanaians rated fat and thin males and females as equally happy.

**KEY TERM**

**Perfectionism:** a personality dimension on which high scorers believe they must achieve very high standards in everything they do.

Western fashions in body shapes have changed dramatically over recent decades: from the flat-chested "flapper" of the 1920s (left), through the curvaceous "hour-glass" figure of Diana Dors (centre) to the currently popular "waif-like" shape epitomised by the model Jodie Kidd (right).

The cultural pressures are greatest on adolescent girls for two reasons. First, they have reached the stage at which they want to appear attractive to boys. Second, most of the weight gain after puberty is in the form of fat tissue, which makes it harder for them to match the ideal shape.

Most of the distorted beliefs held by anorexic and bulimic patients (discussed above) are merely exaggerated versions of the beliefs held by society at large. Cooper (1994) argued that the self-worth of patients with eating disorders, "is seen as being evaluated largely in terms of their shape and weight: they view fatness as odious and reprehensible, they see slimness as attractive and desirable, and the maintenance of self-control is of prime importance. In addition, some attach extreme importance to weight loss … such beliefs are not radically different from views that are widely held."

Cultural factors cannot be the *only* reason for the occurrence of eating disorders. The great majority of young women exposed to cultural pressures towards slimness do *not* develop eating disorders. Only young women who are already vulnerable are likely to be greatly affected by such pressures.

In Cogan et al.'s (1996) study, Ghanaian students rated fat and thin people as being equally happy, whereas American students rated thin people as being the happiest.

## PERSONALITY DISORDERS

Comer (2001, p. 510), basing himself on DSM-IV, defined a **personality disorder** as "an enduring pattern of inner experience and behaviour that deviates markedly from the

> **KEY TERM**
>
> **Personality disorder:** an enduring pattern of inner experience and behaviour that is stable, long-lasting, and rigid, and that typically produces distress and/or impairment.

expectations of the individual's culture, with at least two of the following areas affected: cognition, affectivity, interpersonal functioning, impulse control." In addition, individuals with personality disorders exhibit a rigid and long-lasting pattern of inner experience and behaviour across different situations. In DSM-IV, the clinical disorders discussed so far (i.e., anxiety disorders, depression, schizophrenia) are all represented on axis I (see earlier). In contrast, personality disorders and mental retardation are represented on axis II. However, it is increasingly accepted that the distinction between axis I and axis II disorders is not clear-cut, and there is no attempt to draw a sharp distinction in DSM-IV. Axis II was retained in DSM-IV to remind clinicians to consider long-term personality abnormalities as well as the current symptoms of mental disorder. Note that any given individual can be given a diagnosis on *both* axes.

---

**DSM-IV identifies 10 personality disorders falling roughly into three clusters:**

*Odd/eccentric cluster*
- Paranoid: very suspicious of others and their motives
- Schizoid: emotionally cold and uninvolved
- Schizotypal: schizophrenia-like abnormalities of thought and behaviour

*Dramatic/erratic cluster*
- Anti-social: illegal behaviour, lack of remorse, deceitful, and impulsive
- Borderline: emotionally unstable, relationship problems
- Histrionic: attention seeking, overly emotional
- Narcissistic: great desire to be admired, lacking in empathy

*Anxious/fearful cluster*
- Avoidant: uncomfortable in social situations; very sensitive to negative evaluation
- Dependent: submissive and clinging behaviour; self-critical
- Obsessive-compulsive: preoccupied with control over self and others

---

## Issues of classification

Various difficulties are associated with attempts to categorise personality disorders. First, there is often unreliability of diagnosis. This problem has been reduced by the use of structured interviews. Loranger et al. (1994) reported a study in which structured interviews were used in 11 countries around the world. There was good agreement between clinicians on the appropriate diagnosis for all 10 personality disorders.

Second, and related to the first point, the symptoms of the various personality disorders overlap substantially. Relationship problems characterise all the personality disorders, and are central to the avoidant, borderline, dependent, schizoid, and schizotypal personality disorders. Feeling depressed and helpless are associated with every disorder except schizoid personality disorder, and being self-absorbed is a feature of all personality disorders except dependent personality disorder. As a result, misdiagnoses are common, and often lead clinicians to decide that a given individual is suffering from several personality disorders. For example, Oldham, Skodol, Kellman, Hyler, Rosnick, and Davies (1992) found that patients had an average of 3.4 personality disorders each.

Third, there is much overlap between the personality disorders on axis II of DSM-IV and mental disorders on axis I. For example, there are pronounced similarities between the symptoms of schizotypal personality disorder and schizophrenia, and between those of avoidant personality disorder and social phobia. Fabrega et al. (1992) considered over 2000 patients diagnosed as suffering from a personality disorder, and found that 79% of them also had one or more axis I mental disorder. Such findings shed doubt on the value of distinguishing personality disorders from other types of mental disorder.

Fourth, as MacLeod (1998, p. 558) pointed out, "Personality is ... the area of psychopathology where more than any other the influence of societal values can be clearly observed." Thus, many awkward individuals who do not conform fully to society's expectations are labelled as having a personality disorder.

*Looking at the personality disorders outlined above, are there any that you think could be misapplied to people from other cultures?*

## Personality dimensions

The various personality disorders are generally regarded as categories, implying there is a sharp boundary between individuals having (and not having) any given personality disorder. This assumption is almost certainly incorrect. As Frances et al. (1991, p. 408) pointed out, "Nature seems to abhor clear boundaries."

It probably makes more sense to relate the personality disorders to underlying personality dimensions. Widiger and Costa (1994) focused on the Big Five or five-factor model of personality (see Chapter 13). According to this model, the main personality dimensions are as follows: openness, conscientiousness, extraversion, agreeableness, neuroticism. Widiger and Costa made three key assumptions:

1. Patients with a personality disorder have extreme scores on one or more of these five dimensions.
2. The pattern of scores on the five dimensions varies across personality disorders.
3. There will be more comorbidity (the occurrence of two or more disorders in the same individual) for personality disorders associated with similar patterns of personality scores.

Widiger and Costa's (1994) findings provided support for all three assumptions. Patients with schizoid personality disorder and with avoidant personality disorder obtain very low scores on the extraversion dimension. They both score high on neuroticism, but those with avoidant personality disorder score higher than those with schizoid personality disorder. Very low scores on agreeableness are found in patients with borderline personality disorder, paranoid personality disorder, and anti-social personality disorder. It is thus not surprising that patients with one of these personality disorders often have one or both of the others.

## Evaluation

⊕ The dimensional approach explains comorbidity better than the categorical approach.
⊕ Personality research may potentially increase our understanding of the personality disorders. For example, individual differences in the Big Five personality factors all depend in part on genetic factors (Jang, Livesley, & Vernon, 1996; see Chapter 13), and the same may be true of the personality disorders.
⊖ We do not know why associations are found between personality and personality disorders. Particular personality patterns may make individuals vulnerable to certain personality disorders. However, it is also possible that developing a personality disorder produces changes in personality.

## Anti-social personality disorder

Much more research has been carried out on anti-social personality disorder than on any other personality disorder. According to DSM-IV criteria, patients with **anti-social personality disorder** had a conduct disorder (e.g., involving truancy, lying, and theft) starting before the age of 15. In addition, they possess at least three of the following symptoms:

1. Failure to conform to social norms relating to lawful behaviour.
2. Irritability and aggressiveness.
3. Consistent irresponsibility.
4. Impulsivity or failure to plan ahead.
5. Lack of remorse.
6. Deceitfulness.
7. Reckless disregard for the safety of self or others.

There are clear links between anti-social personality disorder and criminality. Between 40% and 75% of prisoners suffer from anti-social personality disorder (e.g., Widiger & Corbitt, 1995). Farrington (2000) reported findings from a British longitudinal study of men. Of 10-year-olds having a parent who had been convicted of crime, almost half had an anti-social personality at the age of 32. They were also very likely to have committed several crimes. There are also important differences between anti-social personality disorder and criminality. The former is a psychological concept, whereas the latter is a legal one. In addition, most individuals with anti-social personality disorder are not criminals.

**KEY TERM**
**Anti-social personality disorder:** a disorder involving aggressiveness, a failure to behave lawfully, deceitfulness, and a lack of remorse.

Below we discuss factors responsible for the development of anti-social personality disorder. Bear in mind that many of the studies have focused on the factors responsible for criminality, which are only of partial relevance.

## Biological model

Genetic factors play a role in the development of criminality, and probably also the anti-social personality. Gottesman and Goldsmith (1994) considered the amount of agreement in anti-social traits and criminal behaviour between monozygotic or identical twins, and between dizygotic or fraternal twins. On average, the similarity was more than twice as great for the identical twins as for the fraternal twins (51.5% vs. 23.1%, respectively).

Cloninger, Sigvardsson, Bohman, and von Knorring (1982) looked at criminal behaviour in men adopted as children. When neither the biological nor adoptive parents had criminal records, then only 3% of the men had become criminals. When the biological parents had a criminal record but the adoptive parents did not, 7% of the men were criminal. The figure was rather higher (12%) when the adoptive parents had a criminal record but the biological parents did not. Finally, 40% of the men had a criminal record when both their biological and adoptive parents had a history of criminality. Thus, genetic and environmental factors both contribute significantly to criminality, with the role of environment probably being stronger than that of heredity.

There have been various speculations concerning the physiological processes underlying anti-social personality disorder and criminality. For example, Virkkunen et al. (1994) argued that a low level of the neurotransmitter serotonin might be important. They found that violent criminals whose violence was impulsive had much lower levels of serotonin than did violent criminals whose violence was carefully planned. The relevance of this finding is that impulsiveness is a criterion for anti-social personality disorder.

## Psychodynamic model

According to advocates of the psychodynamic approach, the origins of anti-social personality disorder lie in a relative absence of parental love during the early years of life. Some children who have been deprived of early love become emotionally distant, and discover that they can only relate to other people through power and destructiveness. Bowlby's ideas on maternal deprivation are similar, and there is some support for these ideas (see Chapter 17).

*Does this finding support any other explanations for anti-social personality disorder?*

The evidence provides only inconsistent support for the psychodynamic perspective. However, adults with anti-social personality disorder have often had a difficult and stressful childhood. For example, they are more likely than most adults to have experienced family violence, parental divorce, and poverty (Marshall & Cooke, 1999). Farrington (2000) found several factors in childhood associated with anti-social personality later in life, including a convicted parent, a large family size, a young mother, and disrupted family. In general, poor parental discipline predicted adult anti-social personality and criminality.

## Behavioural model

Patterson (e.g., 1996; see Chapter 16) has argued that the rewards provided by parents can play a part in the development of children's anti-social behaviour. For example, when their child behaves aggressively, some parents respond by giving in to him/her to restore peace in the family. However, this has the effect of rewarding the child's aggressive behaviour, thus increasing the chances that he/she will behave aggressively in the future. Alternatively, some parents provide their children with little affection. This can lead the children to behave aggressively to attract their parents' attention.

Patterson (1996) discussed evidence from studies in which interaction patterns were studied in different types of families. As predicted, families in which there was a child with anti-social behaviour were much more likely to reward aggressive behaviour than was the case in more typical families.

## Psychological factors

Individuals with an anti-social personality disorder may experience less fear than other people in threatening circumstances. This low-fear hypothesis was expressed as follows by Lykken (1995, p. 134): "The fear of punishment and the coercive [restraining] voice of conscience both are, for some reason, weak or ineffectual."

The low-fear hypothesis was tested by Patrick, Bradley, and Lang (1993). The participants viewed pleasant slides (e.g., sunsets), neutral slides (e.g., hair dryer), and negative or frightening slides (e.g., an accident victim). Loud noise pips were presented unpredictably, and produced a startle reflex. Most people show the greatest startle reflex when viewing frightening slides and the smallest reflex when looking at pleasant slides. However, male prisoners high on a measure related to anti-social personality had a significantly *smaller* startle reflex with negative slides than with neutral ones, suggesting that they did not respond to the negative slides with fear.

# CONCLUSIONS

We have considered the factors that may be involved in causing a range of mental disorders. In this section of the chapter, we will first focus on general conclusions. Second, we will relate the evidence reviewed in this chapter to the five models of abnormality discussed earlier in the chapter.

## General conclusions

Below are general conclusions that follow from the evidence discussed in this chapter:

1. *All* of the disorders are multiply determined, meaning that biological, social, and psychological factors all contribute to their development.
2. Two or more factors typically interact to produce a given mental disorder. Thus, for example, an individual may develop major depressive disorder because he/she has a genetic vulnerability *and* experiences several life events *and* lacks strong social support.
3. There are large differences across patients having the same disorder in the relative importance of different factors. For example, genetic factors generally play some part in the development of bipolar disorder, but genetic factors are not always involved.
4. Cultural factors are more important in the development of bulimia nervosa and anorexia nervosa than most other disorders. Indeed, anorexia nervosa and bulimia nervosa hardly exist in many societies.
5. The notion that the values of society help to define what are regarded as mental disorders is probably most relevant to the personality disorders.

## Models of abnormality

Below, the main models of abnormality are evaluated in terms of the extent to which they identify correctly the factors responsible for mental disorders.

## Biological model

Much of the evidence supports the biological model. For example, twin, adoption, and family studies all indicate that genetic factors play a part in the development of most of the disorders we have considered. Note that we have little evidence about the involvement of genetic factors in the development of personality disorders.

Genetic factors seem to be especially important in the development of schizophrenia, bipolar disorder, major depressive disorder, and anorexia nervosa. Twin studies on the anxiety disorders have provided rather inconsistent findings, but the evidence is perhaps most convincing for social phobia and some specific phobias. The involvement of genetic factors is perhaps least clear in the case of bulimia nervosa.

It has proved hard to show that biochemical abnormalities are directly involved in the development of mental disorders. There are three main reasons. First, suppose that individuals with a particular mental disorder have abnormal levels of, say, a given neurotransmitter. This does not tell us whether the abnormal neurotransmitter levels helped to cause the disorder or whether the disorder caused the abnormal levels. Second, most chemicals in the body interact in very complex ways with each other, and it is difficult to understand these interactions. Third, some chemical abnormalities are not *specific* to a given disorder. For example, low levels of serotonin have been reported in patients with bipolar disorder, major depressive disorder, bulimia nervosa, and anti-social personality disorder. We do not know how serotonin abnormalities could be relevant to such diverse disorders.

## Psychodynamic model

The psychodynamic model has various strengths and weaknesses. On the positive side, there is support for some of its *general* assumptions. For example, it is assumed by psychodynamic theorists that unpleasant and traumatic experiences in childhood often increase the chances of adult mental disorder. We have seen that those who develop a depressive disorder before the age of 20 are unusually likely to have experienced childhood adversities. In addition, adults with social phobia tend to have parents who are rejecting or over-protective, and adults with anti-social personality disorder often had stressful childhoods (e.g., family violence).

On the negative side, most of the *specific* assumptions about the origins of given disorders have been disproved or lack empirical support. For example, the notion that schizophrenics have returned to an early part of the oral stage of development is incorrect. The same is true of the notion that patients with anorexia nervosa are trying to remain pre-pubescent or to avoid becoming pregnant.

## Behavioural model

There is little direct evidence that conditioning and observational learning are important in the development of most disorders. We rarely have detailed knowledge of patients' conditioning history, and so it is hard to link their current disorder to their conditioning experiences. The most convincing evidence that conditioning may be relevant relates to various specific phobias. Many individuals with specific phobia can remember specific unpleasant or aversive experiences with the phobic stimulus. However, conditioning theorists assume that the conditioned or neutral stimulus needs to be presented very shortly before the unconditioned or aversive stimulus for maximal conditioning to occur (see Chapter 8), and these conditions are often not met.

The behavioural model may also be relevant to post-traumatic stress disorder. The experience of a traumatic event may lead to conditioned fear for neutral stimuli that were present at the time. However, the behavioural model only provides an account of a few aspects of post-traumatic stress disorder.

The behavioural model may also be relevant to an understanding of the development of depression. Learned helplessness in animals may resemble depression in humans. However, cognitive factors may be more important in producing learned helplessness than originally suggested by advocates of the behavioural model.

Finally, the behavioural model may be relevant to anti-social personality disorder. Adolescents whose aggressive behaviour is rewarded are at greater risk of developing this disorder than are other adolescents.

In sum, the behavioural model may apply most to mental disorders in which there are very clear behavioural symptoms. For example, avoidance behaviour is a key symptom with phobias and with post-traumatic stress disorder. The behavioural model may be less relevant with mental disorders in which the key symptoms are internal (e.g., worries, emotional distress).

## Humanistic model

According to Rogers, a key reason why clients are anxious or depressed is because they have experienced insufficient unconditional self-regard during childhood. As a result, they find it hard to become self-actualised and realise their potential. Unfortunately, there is practically no research showing that these factors actually play a role in the development of mental disorders. Mental disorders vary considerably in the particular factors responsible for their development, and yet Rogers strongly implied that all forms of mental disorder are caused in the same way. If that were the case, it would be impossible to predict whether an individual who lacks unconditional self-worth and self-actualisation will develop schizophrenia, major depressive disorder, panic disorder, or anti-social personality disorder!

## Cognitive model

It remains unclear whether the factors (e.g., maladaptive schemas) emphasised within the cognitive model play an important role in the development of mental disorders. As Comer (2001, p. 65) pointed out, "Although disturbed cognitive processes are found in many forms of abnormality, their precise role has yet to be determined. The cognitions seen in psychologically troubled people could well be a result rather than a cause of their difficulties." In principle, we could clarify this causality issue by carrying out longitudinal studies to see whether individuals with distorted cognitions are more likely than those without to develop a mental disorder subsequently. Longitudinal studies suggest that distorted cognitive functioning plays a part in the development of major depressive disorder (Lewinsohn et al., 2001) and panic disorder (Maller & Reiss, 1992).

   Advocates of the cognitive model need to show that cognitive vulnerability in the form of maladaptive schemas and distorted cognitive functioning is involved in the development of mental disorders. As Clark (1989, p. 692) argued:

> *Support or disconfirmation of the vulnerability hypothesis will determine the fate of cognitive models. If cognitive mechanisms prove to be no more than symptoms of clinical states, then the explanatory value of these models is greatly restricted. If, on the other hand, cognitive mechanisms can be found which place individuals at risk for certain clinical disorders, then the theoretical and clinical value of these mechanisms is readily apparent.*

# SUMMARY

The statistical approach to abnormality is flawed. There is little support for the view that mental illness does not exist, and that diagnoses of mental disorder are used to exclude non-conformists. "Mental disorder" is a fuzzy concept lacking precise defining features. Features often associated with mental disorder are deviance, distress, dysfunction, and danger. A similar list of features was proposed by Rosenhan and Seligman (1989): suffering, maladaptiveness, vivid and unconventional behaviour, unpredictability and loss of control, irrationality and incomprehensibility, observer discomfort, and violation of moral and ideal standards. Wakefield (1999) argued that physical and mental disorder should be defined as harmful dysfunction. However, his assumption that we can discriminate clearly between natural functioning and dysfunction seems incorrect.

*What is abnormality?*

**Classification systems**

DSM-IV is the most-used system for classifying mental disorders. It consists of five axes: clinical disorders, personality disorders and mental retardation, general medical conditions, psychosocial and environmental problems, and global assessment. Disorders are identified by observable symptoms, and each diagnostic category is based on a prototype. DSM-IV has reasonable reliability, but low aetiological validity and descriptive validity. It is accepted within DSM-IV that there are culture-bound syndromes. DSM-IV appears to be free of sex bias.

**Models of abnormality**

According to the psychodynamic model, adult mental disorders develop because of unconscious conflicts originating in childhood. Therapy provides patients with insight into their repressed thoughts and feelings. According to the biological model, mental disorders may be caused by genetic factors and/or biochemical abnormalities; all disorders should be found universally, which is incorrect. Therapy based on the biological model typically involves drugs. According to the behavioural model, mental disorders develop because of maladaptive forms of learning. Therapy replaces maladaptive behaviour with desirable forms of behaviour by conditioning. In the humanistic model, mental disorders develop when individuals have distorted views of themselves. Therapy permits clients to think about themselves honestly and take control of their lives. According to the cognitive model, distorted and dysfunctional thoughts are of central importance in many mental disorders. Therapy persuades clients to replace their dysfunctional thoughts with more realistic and positive ones. All of the main models are limited, and biopsychosocial theories based on the assumption that mental disorders involve several interacting factors are preferable. "Micro-models" designed to account for specific disorders should be developed.

**Factors causing mental disorders**

The development of mental disorders is influenced by genetic factors, brain chemicals, cultural factors, social factors, and psychological factors. These factors typically interact with each other. According to the diathesis–stress model, mental disorders occur when there is a diathesis or vulnerability plus a severe or disturbing event. The role of genetic factors is assessed by twin or adoption studies. The stress component within the diathesis–stress model often involves life events. It is generally hard to know whether life events cause disorders or whether disorders help to produce life events.

**Schizophrenia**

Schizophrenia is a very serious disorder. Schizophrenics exhibit a wide range of symptoms (e.g., delusions, speaking very little, hallucinations, rigid behaviour). Twin and family studies indicate that genetic factors are important in developing schizophrenia, a conclusion that is confirmed by adoption studies. Social factors such as life events and expressed emotion within the family may play a part in the development of schizophrenia, as may the stressful environments faced by many members of the lowest social classes.

**Depression**

There are various forms of depression. Major depressive disorder is severe but often not very long lasting, whereas dysthymia is less severe but more long lasting. There is also bipolar disorder, in which depression alternates with mania. Twin and family studies indicate that genetic factors are involved in major depressive disorder and in bipolar disorder, possibly to a greater extent with bipolar disorder. It has been claimed that patients with major depressive disorder have low levels of noradrenaline and serotonin, but the reality is more complex. It has also been claimed that patients with bipolar disorder have low levels of serotonin in both the depressive and manic phases of their disorder. Learned helplessness may play a part in the development of depression, as may various depressive schemas. Serious life events have been linked to the onset of depression, especially in women without an intimate friend.

**Anxiety disorders**

There are several major anxiety disorders, including panic disorder, generalised anxiety disorder, post-traumatic stress disorder, social phobia, and specific phobia. Risk factors for panic disorder may include genetic factors, life events, and a previous occurrence of a respiratory disease. There is stronger evidence that genetic factors influence the development of generalised anxiety disorder, and its development is also affected by unexpected negative life events. The presence of a traumatic event is essential for the development of PTSD, but other factors are also involved. Twin studies have indicated that genetic factors play a role in the development of PTSD, and traumatic childhood experiences can increase the chances of developing PTSD in adulthood when exposed to different traumatic events. Genetic factors may be involved in the causation of social phobia, as may a high level of introversion. Lack of parental affection and over-protective parenting may be additional risk factors. Genetic factors contribute to many specific phobias. Conditioning experiences may sometimes play a part in the development of a specific phobia. However, it appears that humans are biologically predisposed to be sensitive to certain stimuli (e.g., snakes) rather than others (e.g., cars).

*Eating disorders*

Most patients with anorexia nervosa or bulimia nervosa are adolescent females. Both disorders have become much more common recently. The disorders differ in that bulimics are generally more involved with other people, and are more concerned about being attractive to others. Genetic factors play a part in the development of eating disorders, especially anorexia. Enmeshment or family conflicts may influence the development of anorexia. Individuals with a tendency towards perfectionism may be at risk of developing an eating disorder. Eating disorders are most common in Western societies, in which the cultural pressures for slimness are very strong.

*Personality disorders*

DSM-IV identified 10 personality disorders forming three clusters: odd/eccentric, dramatic/erratic, anxious/fearful. There is much overlapping of symptoms among the personality disorders, which makes diagnosis difficult. Individuals with one or more personality disorders generally also suffer from at least one mental disorder. It is reasonable to relate personality disorders to underlying personality dimensions. Genetic factors seem to be involved in anti-social personality disorder and criminality. Individuals with anti-social personality disorder have little fear of punishment, and they have often experienced family violence and parental divorce in childhood.

*Conclusions*

All mental disorders are multiply determined, with the relative importance of different factors varying across individuals. Genetic factors influence the development of most mental disorders, especially schizophrenia. Social factors are of particular importance with major depressive disorder, and cultural factors are of most significance with bulimia and anorexia. Cognitive distortions may play a part in the development of major depressive disorder and panic disorder, but it is typically unclear whether cognitive distortions help to cause mental disorders or whether the causality is in the opposite direction.

# FURTHER READING

- Champion, L., & Power, M. (2000). *Adult psychological problems: An introduction* (2nd ed.). This book, edited by two British clinical psychologists, provides good introductory accounts of numerous topics in abnormal psychology.
- Comer, R.J. (2001). *Abnormal psychology* (4th ed.). New York: Worth. Most of the most important issues are dealt with thoroughly and in an up-to-date way.
- Davison, G.C., & Neale, J.M. (2001). *Abnormal psychology* (8th ed.). New York: Wiley. This well-established textbook has readable accounts of the whole of abnormal psychology.
- Frude, N. (1998). *Understanding abnormal psychology*. Oxford, UK: Blackwell. The main topics and issues are discussed in a clear way in this British textbook.

- **Somatic therapy**
  The major forms of drug therapy for individuals with mental disorder.

  *MAOIs, TCAs, and SSRIs for depressive disorder, and ECT; lithium for bipolar disorder*
  *Benzodiazepines and tricyclics for anxiety disorders*
  *Neuroleptics and atypical anti-psychotic drugs for schizophrenia*

- **Psychodynamic therapy**
  Freud's ideas concerning neurosis, which he felt was based on unresolved conflicts.

  *Repression of thoughts and memories*
  *Treatment with psychoanalysis: hypnosis, regression, and free association*
  *Dream analysis*
  *Evidence of transference*

- **Behaviour therapy**
  The treatment of maladaptive learning with re-education through classical and operant conditioning.

  *Treatment of current problems and behaviour*
  *Exposure therapy for phobias*
  *Aversion therapy, to discourage behaviour such as alcoholism*
  *Token economies to reward behaviour*

- **Client-centred therapy**
  The humanistic approach to treating mental disorders.

  *Rogers' conditions for a positive client–therapist relationship*
  *Other studies*

- **Cognitive therapy and cognitive-behaviour therapy**
  Treatment founded on altering the stimulus–cognition response process.

  *Cognitive therapy focuses on current concerns and beliefs*
  *Basic assumptions*
  *Albert Ellis's rational-emotive theory*
  *Aaron Beck's cognitive triad, and hypothesis testing*
  *Safety-seeking behaviours*

- **Effectiveness of therapy**
  The measurement of efficacy and assessment of recovery.

  *The problems of measuring efficacy and assessing recovery*
  *Efficacy and effectiveness studies*
  *Meta-analyses of therapy effectiveness studies*
  *Common and specific factors*
  *The therapeutic alliance*
  *Minor differences among therapies*
  *New approaches, e.g., eclecticism*

- **Ethical issues in therapy**
  There are a number of important ethical issues.

  *Informed consent and its removal*
  *The confidentiality issue*
  *Choice and selection of therapeutic goals*
  *Relationships between therapists and clients*
  *Treatment variations*

# Therapeutic approaches  23

Individuals with mental disorders exhibit a wide range of symptoms. There may be problems associated with thinking and the mind (e.g., the hallucinations of the schizophrenic), with behaviour (e.g., the avoidance behaviour of the phobic), or with physiological and bodily processes (e.g., the highly activated physiological system of someone with post-traumatic stress disorder). However, note that thinking, behaviour, and physiological processes are all highly *interdependent*.

Therapeutic approaches to mental disorder could focus on producing changes in thinking, in behaviour, or in physiological functioning. At the risk of over-simplification, this is precisely what has happened. The psychodynamic approach was designed to change thinking, and the same is true of humanistic therapy and cognitive therapy. Behaviour therapy, as its name implies, emphasises the importance of changing behaviour. Drug therapy and other biologically-based forms of therapy focus on physiological and biochemical changes. Finally, cognitive-behaviour therapy falls somewhere between behaviour therapy and psychodynamic therapy, in that it attempts to produce changes in clients' thought processes *and* in their behaviour.

Many textbooks emphasise the differences among the major types of therapy rather than the similarities. What do major forms of therapy have in common? According to Brewin and Power (1999, p. 143), "A major vehicle for the success of any psychological therapy is its ability to transform the meanings that clients have attached to their symptoms, relationships, and life problems ... This common purpose of meaning transformation has, we believe, been obscured by the use of different terminologies [and] by different conceptualisations of meaning."

We can see the importance of changing clients' meanings if we consider a few of the major types of therapy. In psychoanalysis, the analyst tries to bring the client's previously unconscious impulses and memories into consciousness. This is followed by the analyst's attempts to persuade the client that these impulses and memories should be reinterpreted to reveal their hidden meaning and thus produce insight.

In humanistic therapy, the emphasis is on reducing discrepancies between the client's self-concept and his or her experiences. This is achieved in part by providing a positive atmosphere in which therapists can allow clients, "to recognise, own, and express

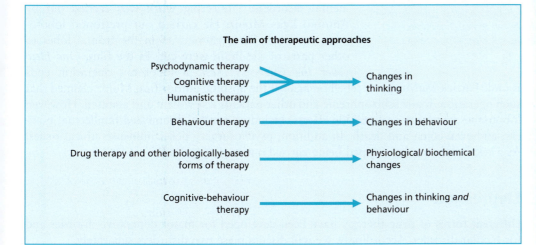

**The aim of therapeutic approaches**

Psychodynamic therapy
Cognitive therapy → Changes in thinking
Humanistic therapy

Behaviour therapy → Changes in behaviour

Drug therapy and other biologically-based forms of therapy → Physiological/ biochemical changes

Cognitive-behaviour therapy → Changes in thinking *and* behaviour

Avoid the treatment aetiology fallacy. Aspirin may cure headaches but lack of aspirin is not a *cause* of headaches.

feelings and personal meanings that have been hitherto disregarded" (Brewin & Power, 1999, p. 146).

In cognitive therapy, the central goal is to change the unduly negative interpretations or meanings which clients attach to themselves, to various stimuli, and to their current situation. For example, clients with panic disorder typically interpret their bodily sensations as indicating that they are likely to experience a heart attack, loss of control, or social humiliation (Clark, 1986). Cognitive therapy is designed to produce more realistic (and less threatening) interpretations.

What about behaviour therapy? As Brewin and Power (1999, p. 146) pointed out, "Behaviour therapy was relatively unconcerned with meaning … Psychopathology was regarded as the result of external events, and the individual's subjective interpretation of them was specifically excluded as a cause of emotions and behaviour. Thus, there was little point in talking to patients about the meaning of their symptoms."

It is important to avoid making the **treatment aetiology fallacy** (MacLeod, 1998). This is the mistaken notion that the success of a given form of treatment reveals the cause of the disorder. This fallacy is perhaps most common when explaining the effectiveness of drug therapy, but applies to all forms of therapy. For example, aspirin is an effective cure for headache, but no-one believes that a lack of aspirin is the cause of headaches.

In this chapter, we will be considering the main forms of therapy. We will also consider their appropriateness and effectiveness. Finally, we will discuss key ethical issues involved in therapy.

In the film *One Flew Over the Cuckoo's Nest*, Jack Nicholson played Randle Patrick McMurphy, who inspired and awakened his fellow patients, whilst falling out with the authorities. Eventually, the character is lobotomised and becomes calmer and easier to handle, but loses all his intellectual spark and energy.

## SOMATIC THERAPY

**Somatic therapy** is the term given to forms of treatment involving manipulations of the body. Somatic therapy (mostly involving the administration of drugs) is associated with the biological model (see Chapter 22). According to the biological model, mental disorders develop because of abnormalities in bodily functioning, especially within the brain, and drugs can often be used to reduce or eliminate these abnormalities.

Apart from drug therapy, two other main forms of biologically-based therapy are electroconvulsive therapy and psychosurgery. Electroconvulsive therapy is discussed below, but we will briefly consider psychosurgery here. **Psychosurgery** involves carrying out brain surgery to treat mental disorders. Pioneering work was carried out by Antonio Egas Moniz. He carried out prefrontal lobotomies, in which fibres running from the frontal lobes to other parts of the brain were cut. In the film, *One Flew Over the Cuckoo's Nest*, a lobotomy operation ends Randle Patrick McMurphy's rebellion against the hospital authorities. Moniz claimed that such operations made schizophrenic and other patients less violent and agitated. However, lobotomies have very serious side effects, including apathy, diminished intellectual powers, and even coma and death. In addition, psychosurgery poses immense ethical issues. As a result, lobotomies stopped being carried out many years ago.

### KEY TERMS

**Treatment aetiology fallacy:** the incorrect view that the success of a particular form of treatment for a disorder reveals the cause of that disorder.

**Somatic therapy:** forms of therapy involving manipulations of the body (e.g., drug treatment).

**Psychosurgery:** the use of brain surgery to treat mental disorders.

## Depression

Different forms of drug therapy have been developed for major depressive disorder and for bipolar disorder. Accordingly, we will discuss these two disorders separately.

## Major depressive disorder

There are three main types of anti-depressant drugs used in major depressive disorder: (1) monoamine oxidase inhibitors (MAOIs); (2) tricyclic anti-depressants (TCAs); and (3) selective serotonin re-uptake inhibitors (SSRIs). The MAOIs were developed during the 1950s, and the SSRIs were developed more recently.

The MAOIs block monoamine oxidase, and therefore help to prevent the destruction of noradrenaline. As a result, depressed patients taking MAOIs have increased noradrenaline activity, leading to a reduction in depressive symptoms. The MAOIs are reasonably effective in reducing depression. However, MAOIs produce various side effects. They block the production of monoamine oxidase in the liver, leading to the accumulation of tyramine. This is dangerous, because high levels of tyramine cause high levels of blood pressure. Accordingly, depressed patients taking MAOIs have to follow a careful diet, making sure to avoid foods (e.g., cheese, bananas) containing tyramine. Newer drugs (reversible inhibitors of monamine oxidase type A or RIMAs) create fewer problems.

The tricyclics appear to increase the activity of the neurotransmitters noradrenaline and serotonin, and are geneally effective in reducing the symptoms of depression. In a large-scale study (Elkin, 1994), a tricyclic (imipramine) was as effective as cognitive therapy and interpersonal psychotherapy in treating depression. However, there can be a fairly high relapse rate unless drug therapy is continued over a long period of time

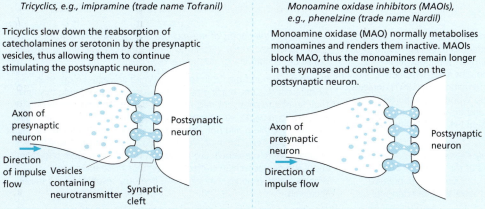

**The action of anti-depressants on the synapse**

Depressed individuals tend to have lower levels of monoamines, especially serotonin.

*Tricyclics, e.g., imipramine (trade name Tofranil)*

Tricyclics slow down the reabsorption of catecholamines or serotonin by the presynaptic vesicles, thus allowing them to continue stimulating the postsynaptic neuron.

Axon of presynaptic neuron

Postsynaptic neuron

Direction of impulse flow  Vesicles containing neurotransmitter  Synaptic cleft

*Monoamine oxidase inhibitors (MAOIs), e.g., phenelzine (trade name Nardil)*

Monoamine oxidase (MAO) normally metabolises monoamines and renders them inactive. MAOIs block MAO, thus the monoamines remain longer in the synapse and continue to act on the postsynaptic neuron.

Axon of presynaptic neuron

Postsynaptic neuron

Direction of impulse flow

(Franchini, Gasperini, Perez, Smeraldi, & Zanardi, 1997). The tricylics are less dangerous than the MAOIs, but they can impair driving to a dangerous extent.

The best known of the selective serotonin re-uptake inhibitors (SSRIs) is Prozac. These drugs are more selective in their functioning than the tricyclics, in that they increase serotonin activity without influencing other neurotransmitters such as noradrenaline. The SSRIs are about as effective as the tricyclics (Hirschfeld, 1999), but they possess some advantages. Depressed patients taking SSRIs are less likely to suffer from dry mouth and constipation than those taking tricyclics, and it is harder to overdose on SSRIs. However, SSRIs conflict with some other forms of medication.

## Electroconvulsive therapy

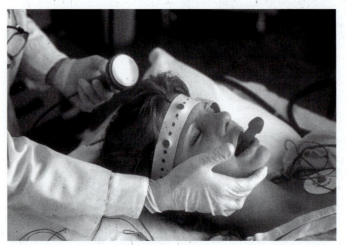

Electroconvulsive shock therapy has been found to be quite effective in cases of severe depression, though the reasons why it might be effective are uncertain.

Electroconvulsive therapy (ECT) is a form of treatment for major depressive disorder in which an electric current is passed through the head in order to create a convulsion. ECT used to produce broken bones, patient terror, and memory loss, but these problems have been almost eliminated in various ways. First, strong muscle relaxants are given to patients to prevent or minimise convulsions. Second, the current is generally only passed through the non-dominant brain hemisphere rather than through both hemispheres, reducing the danger of memory loss. Third, anaesthetics are used to put patients to sleep during ECT, thus reducing the chances of experiencing terror.

How effective is ECT? About 65% of patients with major depression benefit from ECT (Rey & Walter, 1997), and it has the advantage over drug therapy that beneficial effects typically occur more rapidly. This is especially useful in cases of severe depression in which attempts at suicide are possible.

There is still no detailed understanding of precisely why ECT is effective. It has numerous effects on the brain, and it is hard to establish *which* effects are the important ones in reducing the symptoms of depression.

## Bipolar disorder

The most commonly used drug for bipolar disorder is lithium. Various suggestions have been made as to the mechanism by which it has its effects. One idea is that lithium alters potassium and sodium ion activity in neurons, and hence transmission of nerve impulses. Lithium has beneficial effects in approximately 80% of patients (Prien & Potter, 1993), especially in reducing the symptoms associated with manic episodes. Discontinuation of lithium increases the chances that the symptoms of bipolar disorder will recur.

### CASE STUDY: *Virginia Woolf*

The author Virginia Woolf, who committed suicide in 1941 at the age of 59, was plagued by an intermittent form of depression. This affliction appears to have been bipolar depression, but was accompanied by extreme physical symptoms and psychotic delusions. In her biography of Woolf, Hermione Lee (1997) unravels the series of treatments administered to Woolf between 1895, when she experienced her first breakdown, and the 1930s. Later Woolf's husband Leonard made detailed notes on her breakdowns (Lee, 1997, pp. 178–179):

*In the manic stage she was extremely excited; the mind raced; she talked volubly and, at the height of the attack, incoherently; she had delusions and heard voices … During the depressive stage all her thoughts and emotions were the exact opposite …*

*she was in the depths of melancholia and despair; she scarcely spoke; refused to eat; refused to believe that she was ill and insisted that her condition was due to her own guilt.*

During the period from 1890 to 1930, Woolf consulted more than 12 different doctors, but the treatments barely altered during this time. They tended to consist of milk and meat diets to redress her weight loss; rest to alleviate her agitation; sleep and fresh air to help her regain her energy. Lithium had not yet been discovered as a treatment for manic depression. Instead, bromide, veronal, and chloral, most of which are sedatives, were prescribed. Lee points out that there is great uncertainty about the neuropsychiatric effects of some of these drugs, and Woolf's manic episodes may well have been the result of taking these chemicals.

Conversely, if lithium is taken after elimination of manic symptoms, this substantially reduces the chances of relapse (Viguera, Nonacs, Cohen, Tondo, Murray, & Baldessarini, 2000). Lithium produces various side effects (e.g., impaired co-ordination, tremors, and problems with digestion). In addition, 40% of patients fail to take the prescribed dosage of the drug (Basco & Rush, 1996).

*Some people (e.g., Van Gogh) have been found to be more creative during the manic phase of bipolar disorder. How might this affect their decision about whether or not to control the disorder using drug treatments?*

## Anxiety disorders

Patients with anxiety disorders (especially generalised anxiety disorder) are often given drugs to reduce anxiety. The most popular anti-anxiety drugs are the **benzodiazepines,** which include chlordiazepoxide (Librium) and diazepam (Valium). These drugs bind to receptor sites in the brain that generally receive the neurotransmitter GABA. What seems to happen is that the benzodiazepines increase the ability of GABA to bind to these sites, which enhances the ability of GABA to inhibit bodily arousal and anxiety.

The benzodiazepines are reasonably effective in the treatment of generalised anxiety disorder (Rickels, DeMartinis, & Aufdrembrinke, 2000), and have also been used to treat social phobia. However, social phobics often have symptoms of depression in addition to symptoms of anxiety. Gelernter et al. (1991) found that MAOIs (used to treat depression) were more effective than benzodiazepines in treating social phobia.

There are several unwanted effects of benzodiazepines:

1. Anxious symptoms often return when patients stop taking the drugs.
2. There are various side effects (e.g., lack of co-ordination, poor concentration, and memory loss).
3. There can be physical dependence, with patients finding it hard to manage without drugs.

Buspirone does not have the potentially dangerous sedative effects of the benzodiazepines. It acts differently to the benzodiazepines, namely, by stimulating serotonin receptors in the brain. Buspirone is as effective as the benzodiazepines in treating generalised anxiety disorder (Lader & Scotto, 1998), and it has the advantage of rarely leading to physical dependence.

Tricyclic drugs (most commonly used to treat major depression) have been used successfully to treat panic disorder. Barlow, Gorman, Shear, and Woods, (2000) compared drug therapy based on the tricyclic drug imipramine against cognitive-behaviour therapy. Both therapies were comparably effective in reducing the symptoms of panic disorder during treatment. However, drug therapy was less effective than cognitive-behaviour therapy at follow-up 6 months after treatment ended.

> **Benzodiazepines**
>
> Benzodiazepines are the most widely prescribed psychoactive drugs in the world, with annual worldwide sales of $21 billion (Gordon, 2001). It has been reported, for example, that in 2002 over 13 million prescriptions for benzodiazepines were written in the UK (Garfield, 2003) and that one in ten Canadians takes a benzodiazepine at least once a year (Gordon, 2001). The World Health Organization regards the excessive prescription of these drugs to be a global problem. Benzodiazepines are available under a variety of trade names such as Valium, Temazepam, Librium, and Rohypnol, the last of which has been implicated in date-rape cases, an obvious illegal as well as inappropriate use.

## Schizophrenia

It makes sense to distinguish between the positive and negative symptoms of schizophrenia (see Chapter 22). The positive symptoms include delusions and hallucinations, and the negative symptoms include lack of motivation, lack of emotion, and social withdrawal. Some drugs are more effective at reducing the positive symptoms than the negative ones. There are two main categories of drugs: (1) conventional or neuroleptic drugs, and (2) the newer atypical drugs.

### Neuroleptic drugs

**Neuroleptic drugs** (drugs reducing psychotic symptoms but producing some of the symptoms of neurological diseases) are conventional drugs often used in the treatment of schizophrenia. Common neuroleptic drugs include chlorpromazine (Thorazine), fluphenazine (Prolixin), and haloperidol (Haldol).

> **KEY TERMS**
>
> **Benzodiazepines:** drugs (e.g., Valium) that are used in order to reduce anxiety symptoms.
>
> **Neuroleptic drugs:** a range of drugs traditionally used to treat schizophrenia.

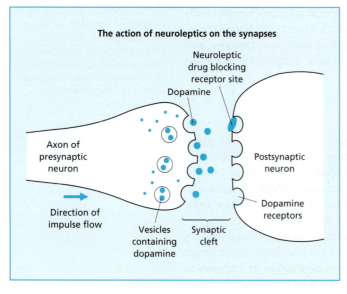

**The action of neuroleptics on the synapses**

Neuroleptic drug blocking receptor site

Dopamine

Axon of presynaptic neuron

Postsynaptic neuron

Dopamine receptors

Direction of impulse flow

Vesicles containing dopamine

Synaptic cleft

How do these drugs work? They block the activity of the neurotransmitter dopamine, particularly at the brain's dopamine D-2 receptors. Many schizophrenics seem to have excessive activity of dopamine (see Chapter 22). It is not clear how the neuroleptic drugs reduce the symptoms of schizophrenia. These drugs block dopamine receptors within 48 hours, but it takes several weeks of drug therapy before schizophrenic symptoms show substantial reduction.

The major neuroleptic drugs are of real value in treating schizophrenia. However, their effectiveness is greater in reducing positive symptoms than negative ones. According to Comer (2001, p. 457), these drugs "reduce schizophrenic symptoms in the majority of patients ... the drugs appear to be a more effective treatment for schizophrenia than any of the other approaches used alone."

Neuroleptic drugs produce some side effects. Windgassen (1992) found that 50% of schizophrenic patients taking neuroleptic drugs reported grogginess or sedation, 18% reported problems with concentration, and 16% had blurred vision. In addition, many schizophrenic patients

| Disorder | Drug/group of drugs | How they work | Drawbacks |
|---|---|---|---|
| Depression (major) | Monoamine oxidase inhibitors (MAOIs) | Block monoamine oxidase, helping to prevent the destruction of noradrenaline | A range of side effects |
| | Tricyclics (TCAs) | Increase activity of noradrenaline and serotonin | High relapse rate unless continued over long period |
| | Selective serotonin re-uptake inhibitors (SSRIs) (e.g., Prozac) | Increase serotonin activity | Conflict with some other forms of medication |
| Depression (bipolar) | Lithium | Anti-mania, but mechanism is imperfectly understood | Various side effects including impaired co-ordination, tremors, problems with digestion |
| Anxiety disorders | Benzodiazepines (e.g., Valium, Librium) | Enhance the ability of neurotransmitter GABA to inhibit bodily arousal and anxiety | Drowsiness, lethargy, impairments of long-term memory. Withdrawal symptoms and possible addiction |
| | Buspirone | Stimulates serotonin receptors in the brain | Does not appear to have sedative effect, but other side effects not yet established |
| Schizophrenia | Neuroleptic drugs (e.g., chlorpromazine, fluphenazine, haloperidol) | Block activity of dopamine | Some patients report grogginess, sedation, difficulty concentrating, dry mouth, blurred vision. Many develop symptoms closely resembling those of Parkinson's disease. Some develop tardive dyskinesia |
| | Atypical anti-psychotic drugs (e.g., clozapine, risperidone, olanzapine) | As neuroleptics, but with fewer side effects | Expensive. Clozapine may produce fatal blood disease in 1–2% of patients |

on neuroleptic drugs develop symptoms closely resembling those of Parkinson's disease (e.g., muscle rigidity, tremors, foot shuffling).

Most side effects occur within a few weeks of the start of drug therapy. However, more than 20% of patients who take neuroleptic drugs for over a year develop the symptoms of **tardive dyskinesia**. These symptoms include involuntary sucking and chewing, jerky movements of the limbs, and writhing movements of the mouth or face, and the effects can be permanent.

*What ethical issues are raised by a) the use of drugs that have such severe side effects, b) compulsory administration of such medication, and c) cultural differences in sensitivity to drugs?*

## Atypical anti-psychotic drugs

There is increasing usage of newer drugs in treating schizophrenia. These drugs include clozapine (trade name Clozaril), risperidone (Risperdal), and olanzapine (Zyprexa). They are called atypical anti-psychotic drugs to distinguish them from the earlier or conventional neuroleptic drugs.

The atypical anti-psychotic drugs have various advantages over the conventional drugs. First, atypical drugs benefit about 85% of schizophrenic patients, compared to about 65% of patients given conventional drugs (Awad & Voruganti, 1999). Second, the atypical drugs are of much more use in helping schizophrenic patients suffering mainly from negative symptoms (Remington & Kapur, 2000). Third, many side effects of the conventional drugs (especially tardive dyskinesia) are absent with the atypical drugs.

The atypical drugs can produce serious side effects. For example, schizophrenic patients who take clozapine have a 1–2% risk of developing agranulocytosis. This involves a substantial reduction in white blood cells, and the condition can be life threatening. However, olanzapine doesn't seem to cause agranulocytosis.

## Overall evaluation

✚ Drug therapy often produces rapid, beneficial effects in treating anxiety, depression, and schizophrenia.
✚ When one compares drug therapy against other forms of therapy, then drug therapy seems to be especially effective in reducing the symptoms of schizophrenia.
➖ Relapse is more common after drug therapy than after other types of therapy.
➖ The drop-out rate is often rather high when drug therapy is used.
➖ It has proved almost impossible to devise drugs with no unwanted side effects.

> **KEY TERMS**
>
> **Tardive dyskinesia:** some of the long-term effects of taking neuroleptic drugs, including writhing movements of the face, jerky limb movements, and involuntary chewing movements.
>
> **Repression:** the process of forcing very threatening thoughts and memories out of the conscious mind and into the unconscious.

# PSYCHODYNAMIC THERAPY

The first form of psychodynamic therapy was psychoanalysis, which was introduced by Sigmund Freud early in the twentieth century. Some of the principles of psychoanalysis were then developed in various ways by Freud's followers such as Carl Jung and Alfred Adler.

According to Freud, neuroses such as the anxiety disorders occur as a result of conflicts among the three parts of the mind: the ego (rational mind), the id (sexual and other instincts), and the superego (conscience). These conflicts (many of which go back to early childhood) cause the ego to use various defence mechanisms to protect itself (see Chapter 22). The key defence mechanism is repression. **Repression** consists of forcing painful, threatening, or unacceptable thoughts and memories out of consciousness into the unconscious mind. The repressed ideas concern impulses or memories that the client could not think about

Traditionally the psychoanalyst or psychodynamic therapist is out of sight of the client, who relaxes on a chair or couch. The analyst/therapist records and makes notes of what the client says and tries not to interrupt or make leading comments.

The Austrian psychiatrist Alfred Adler, 1870–1937. Influenced by Freud's ideas, he became interested in the study of mental disorders. Adler identified the cause of mental diseases in terms of an inferiority complex acquired during childhood.

without feeling intense anxiety. Repressed memories mostly refer to childhood, and to the conflicts between the instinctive (e.g., sexual) motives of the child and the restraints imposed by his or her parents. Repression serves the function of reducing the level of anxiety experienced by the client.

According to Freud, adults experiencing great personal problems tend to show regression. **Regression** involves going backwards through the stages of psychosexual development they went through in childhood (see Chapter 13). Children often fixate or spend an unusually long time at a given stage of psychosexual development if it is associated with conflicts or excessive gratification, and regression typically occurs back to a stage at which the person had previously fixated.

Freud argued that the way to cure neurosis was to allow the client to gain access to his/her repressed ideas and conflicts, and to encourage him/her to face up to whatever emerged from the unconscious. He insisted that the client should focus on the feelings associated with the repressed ideas, and should not simply regard them unemotionally. Freud used the term **insight** to refer to these processes. The ultimate goal of psychoanalysis is to provide the client with insight. There are great obstacles in the way, because the emergence of very painful memories into consciousness produces an extremely high level of anxiety. As a result, the attempt to uncover repressed ideas typically produces **resistance**, an unconscious refusal by the client to do his/her best to bring painful ideas into consciousness.

Freud (1917, p. 289) described some of the forms that resistance can take:

> *The patient attempts to escape by every possible means. First he says nothing comes into his head, then that so much comes into his head that he can't grasp any of it … At last he admits that he really cannot say something, he is ashamed to … So it goes on.*

Freud and the other psychoanalysts used various methods to uncover repressed ideas, and to permit the client to gain insight into his/her unresolved problems. The three main methods are as follows: hypnosis, free association, and dream analysis. The use of hypnosis came first in the history of psychoanalysis. Freud and Breuer (1895)

Freud asked his patients to lie on a couch during psychoanalysis. This is a photograph of his couch in his London house, which is now a museum.

## CASE STUDY: *Anna O*

Freud's theory was largely based on the observations he made during consultations with patients. He suggested that his work was similar to that of an archaeologist, who digs away layers of earth before uncovering what he or she was seeking. In a similar way, the psychoanalyst seeks to dig down to the unconscious and discover the key to the individual's personality dynamic.

*"Anna O was a girl of twenty-one, of a high degree of intelligence. Her illness first appeared while she was caring for her father whom she tenderly loved, during the severe illness which led to his death. The patient had a severe paralysis of both right extremities, disturbance of eye-movements, and intense nausea when she attempted to take nourishment, and at one time for several weeks a loss of the power to drink, in spite of tormenting thirst. She occasionally became confused or delirious and mumbled several words to herself. If these same words were later repeated to her, when she was in a hypnotic stage, she engaged in deeply sad, often poetically beautiful, day dreams, we might call them, which commonly took as their starting point the situation of a girl beside the sick-bed of her father. The patient jokingly called this treatment 'chimney sweeping'.*

*Dr Breuer [Freud's colleague] soon hit upon the fact that through such cleansing of the soul more could be accomplished than a temporary removal of the constantly recurring mental 'clouds'.*

*During one session, the patient recalled an occasion when she was with her governess, and how that lady's little dog, that she abhorred, had drunk out of a glass. Out of respect for the conventions the patient had remained silent, but now under hypnosis she gave energetic expression to her restrained anger, and then drank a large quantity of water without trouble, and woke from hypnosis with the glass at her lips. The symptom thereupon vanished permanently.*

*Permit me to dwell for a moment on this experience. No one had ever cured an hysterical symptom by such means before, or had come so near understanding its cause. This would be a pregnant discovery if the expectation could be confirmed that still other, perhaps the majority of symptoms, originated in this way and could be removed by the same method.*

*Such was indeed the case, almost all the symptoms originated in exactly this way, as we were to discover. The patient's illness originated at the time when she was caring for her sick father, and her symptoms could only be regarded as memory symbols of his sickness and death. While she was seated at her father's sick bed, she was careful to betray nothing of her anxiety and her painful depression to the patient. When, later, she reproduced the same scene before the physician, the emotion which she had suppressed on the occurrence of the scene burst out with especial strength, as though it has been pent up all along.*

*In her normal state she was entirely ignorant of the pathogenic scenes and of their connection with her symptoms. She had forgotten those scenes. When the patient was hypnotized, it was possible, after considerable difficulty, to recall those scenes to her memory, and by this means of recall the symptoms were removed."*

Adapted from Sigmund Freud (1910).

---

treated a young woman called Anna O, who suffered from several neurotic symptoms (e.g., paralysis, nervous coughs). Hypnosis uncovered a repressed memory of Anna hearing the sound of dance music coming from a nearby house while nursing her dying father, and her guilty feeling that she would rather be dancing. Her nervous coughing stopped after that repressed memory came to light.

Freud gradually lost interest in hypnosis, partly because many clients were hard or impossible to hypnotise. Another problem is that people under hypnosis become very suggestible (see Chapter 4). As a result, little reliance can be placed on the accuracy of what they claim to remember when hypnotised.

The method of **free association** is very simple. The client is encouraged to say the first thing that comes into his/her mind. It is hoped that fragments of repressed memories will emerge in the course of free association. However, free association loses some of its usefulness if the client shows resistance, and is reluctant to say what he/she is thinking. Nevertheless, the presence of resistance (e.g., excessively long pauses) suggests that the client is getting close to some important repressed idea, and that further probing by the therapist is needed.

According to Freud, the analysis of dreams provides "the via regia [royal road] to the unconscious". He argued that there is a censor in the mind, which keeps repressed material out of conscious awareness. This censor is less vigilant during sleep, and so repressed ideas from the unconscious are more likely to appear in dreams than in waking thought. These ideas usually emerge in disguised form because of their unacceptable nature. For example, the ideas may be altered by the process of condensation (combining various ideas into a smaller number) or by displacement (shifting emotion from the appropriate object to another one). The best-known examples of displacement involve sexual symbolism, such as someone dreaming about riding a horse rather than having sex.

Freud distinguished between the actual dream (the **manifest dream**) and the underlying repressed ideas (the **latent dream**; see Chapter 4). The unacceptability of the latent dream is changed into the more acceptable content of the manifest dream. Why do people dream? According to Freud, the main purpose is wish fulfilment: We dream about things

*Are there any types of mental disorder that you would consider difficult to treat using these methods? Why?*

**KEY TERMS**

**Free association:** a technique used in psychoanalysis, in which the patient says the first thing that comes into his/her mind.

**Manifest dream:** in Freud's theory, the surface or reported meaning of a dream.

**Latent dream:** in Freud's theory, the underlying or "true" meaning of a dream.

**Psychodynamic theory and dream analysis**

Freud hypothesised that in our dreams we realise those ideas, wishes, and needs that we have buried or repressed from our conscious mind as they are in some way unacceptable to us. Maybe they are socially unacceptable, or would for some other reason fill us with guilt or anxiety. Examples of this could be the inner conflicts between our id (primitive self), ego (socialised self), and superego (idealised self), or those between our libido (biological desires) and thanatos (turning away from pleasure), or others such as penis envy in females or Oedipal sexual desires for the opposite-sex parent. Dreams represent these thoughts and desires and their fulfilment in a form that does not threaten us or cause us pain (Freud, 1933).

Jung, a follower of Freud who later diverged to form his own psychodynamic theories, suggested that in our dreams we are able to access the store memories of all humanity, dating back to our primeval ancestry, He called this the collective unconscious. This could perhaps explain the dreams of inescapable pursuit or of falling as memories of highly emotionally charged events from other people in other times. He also believed that a main motivator or driving-force was not sex but the search for the spiritual and mystic. Maybe this combination of thoughts from the collective unconscious with desires for the awesome and wondrous could explain the apparently illogical narratives of dreams.

From Bentley, E. (2000).

we would like to see happen. Thus, dream analysis can uncover the neurotic client's basic motives.

Freud emphasised that clients should gain access not only to repressed events, but also to the accompanying feelings. This can be helped by **transference**, which involves the client transferring onto the therapist the powerful emotional reactions previously directed at his/her own parents (or other highly significant individuals). Freud (1912/1958) argued that we have a relationship template or pattern originating with our relationship with one or both parents. He wrote about this template, "which is constantly repeated—constantly repeated afresh—in the course of the person's life" (Freud, 1912/1958, p. 100). Transference provides "a kind of emotional reliving of the unresolved problems of the patient's childhood" (Gleitman, 1986, p. 696).

A crucial aspect of transference is that the therapist responds in a neutral way to the client's emotional outpourings. This allows the client freedom to express long-repressed anger or hostility to his/her parents. The neutrality of the therapist helps to make it clear to the client that his/her emotional outbursts stem from repressed memories rather than from the therapeutic situation.

## Evidence

Carl Gustav Jung (1875–1961), the Swiss psychiatrist. He was a disciple of Freud's for many years but broke away in 1912 because he rejected Freud's views that all disorders could be explained in terms of infantile sexuality.

Some of the evidence relating to Freud's theoretical ideas is dealt with in other chapters. For example, repression is discussed in Chapter 9, and Freud's dream theory in Chapter 4. Here we will consider other aspects of psychoanalysis.

There is no strong evidence of transference in the Freudian sense of sexual and other thoughts about the client's parents being transferred to the therapist. However, as Hinkley and Andersen (1996, p. 1279) pointed out, "At the heart of the clinical concept of *transference* is the notion that experiences with individuals who are personally important to the self might be retained in memory in some form and then re-experienced with a new person." Andersen has carried out several studies investigating this key aspect of transference (see Andersen & Miranda, 2000, for a review). Hinkley and Andersen (1996) presented participants with the description of a new person resembling someone who was very important to them. They indicated how they thought they would feel about themselves if they met this new person. Their reports indicated they would feel rather similar to the way they feel in the presence of the person who was very important to them.

Fried, Crits-Christoph, and Luborsky (1992) studied transference within psychodynamic therapy. They recorded what was said by patients about their interactions with the therapist and other important people in their lives (e.g., parents, spouse) during therapeutic sessions. There was some similarity between any given patient's views of other people and his/her views of the therapist. Fried et al. (1992, p. 328) concluded that, "patients have a relatively unique and pervasive relationship pattern, with a demonstrable parallel between the experience with the therapist and the experience with others". Thus, they obtained some evidence for transference within the therapeutic situation.

It is hard to test Freud's notion that insight is of crucial importance, because the concept is vague and poorly defined. For example, consider a study by Hoglend, Engelstad, Sorbye, Heyerdahl, and Amlo (1994). Psychiatrists rated the amount of insight shown by moderately disturbed outpatients, many with anxiety disorders or major depression. One key finding was that the psychiatrists showed poor agreement among themselves concerning patients' insight level. However, they also found that patients who

**KEY TERM**

**Transference:** the transfer of the patient's strong feelings concerning one or both parents onto the therapist.

had gained the most insight 2 years after the end of treatment showed the greatest beneficial changes 2 years later.

Other studies are generally less supportive of Freud's views on insight. Hoglend et al. (1994) reviewed nine previous studies. They concluded that only three had obtained moderately strong associations between level of insight early in treatment and the amount of recovery produced by treatment.

An early attempt to evaluate the effectiveness of psychoanalysis was reported by Eysenck (1952), who reviewed studies in which clients either received psychoanalysis or received no systematic treatment. The reported figures were striking: 72% of clients with no proper treatment recovered within 2 years (this is **spontaneous recovery**), compared to only 44% of those receiving psychoanalysis. These findings imply that psychoanalysis is actually bad for you!

Eysenck's (1952) findings cannot be accepted. He counted clients dropping out of psychoanalysis as clients for whom therapy had failed. If these clients are excluded, then the recovery rate was 66% for clients receiving psychoanalysis. Eysenck also regarded partially recovered clients as not having recovered at all, which makes little sense. Bergin (1971) considered the same information used by Eysenck, but used different criteria for recovery. According to his analyses, psychoanalysis produced an 83% success rate, whereas the spontaneous remission rate was only 30%.

Eysenck's (1952) figure for spontaneous recovery is also very dubious. Many of those allegedly showing spontaneous recovery received money from an insurance company while being treated, and so the insurance company had a strong vested interest in declaring them to be recovered. Most other studies have reported spontaneous recovery rates of only about 30–40% (Lambert & Bergin, 1994).

McNeilly and Howard (1991) reanalysed data from the studies used by Eysenck (1952). They found that about 50% of the treated patients showed some improvement within 8 weeks, compared to only 2% of the untreated patients.

Sloane, Staples, Cristol, Yorkston, and Whipple (1975) carried out a detailed study mainly on patients with anxiety disorders. Behaviour therapy and ego analysis (a form of psychodynamic therapy) both produced an 80% improvement rate, significantly greater than the 45% found in the waiting-list control group. However, the three groups did not differ at the 8-month follow-up, because the control patients had improved considerably. Thus, psychodynamic therapy in the form of ego analysis was as effective as behaviour therapy, and produced more rapid recovery than no treatment initially.

*Why might spontaneous recovery occur? What does this imply about the origins of mental disorder?*

## Evaluation

⊕ Psychoanalysis was the first systematic form of psychological treatment, and has proved moderately effective (see Lambert & Bergin, 1994).

⊕ Psychoanalysis has strongly influenced later forms of therapy (e.g., object relations therapy and cognitive therapy).

⊕ There is evidence for repression-like and transference-like processes.

⊖ "The concepts on which it [the psychodynamic model] are based are difficult to define and to research … Because processes such as id drives, ego defences, and fixation are abstract and supposedly operate at an unconscious level, there is no way of knowing for certain if they are occurring" (Comer, 2001, p. 59).

⊖ Freud argued that insight was needed to produce recovery. However, it could as reasonably be argued that recovery is needed to produce insight. It could also be argued that insight and recovery refer to rather similar (and overlapping) notions.

⊖ Freud argued that the evidence obtained from clients during therapy showed the value of his approach to treatment. However, there is a real danger of contamination in such evidence: What the client says may be influenced by what the therapist has said previously. In addition, the therapist may use his/her theoretical preconceptions to distort what the patient says.

**KEY TERM**

**Spontaneous recovery:** recovery from a mental disorder in the absence of any specific form of therapy.

## BEHAVIOUR THERAPY

Behaviour therapy developed during the late 1950s and 1960s, but its origins go back several decades before that. The underlying notions are that most forms of mental illness occur through maladaptive learning, and that the best treatment consists of appropriate new learning or re-education. Behaviour therapists believe that abnormal behaviour develops through conditioning (see Chapter 8), and it is through the use of the principles of conditioning that clients can recover. Thus, behaviour therapy is based on the assumption that classical and operant conditioning can change unwanted behaviour into a more desirable pattern of behaviour. Note that some experts limit the term "behaviour therapy" to treatment involving classical conditioning, and use the term "behaviour modification" to refer to treatment involving operant conditioning.

*If psychoanalysts are correct about the importance of unresolved conflicts, what may happen to individuals treated using behaviour therapy?*

Behaviour therapy has an emphasis on *current* problems and behaviour, and on attempts to remove any symptoms the client finds troublesome. This contrasts with psychoanalysis, where the focus on trying to uncover unresolved conflicts from childhood. Another distinguishing feature of behaviour therapy is that it is based on the scientific approach. As MacLeod (1998, p. 571) pointed out:

> *The behavioural model of disorders and behaviour was a direct application of behavioural principles from experimental psychology, and was closely related to laboratory-based studies of learning (conditioning) which were often carried out on rats. As such, behaviour therapy has been ... closely connected with scientific methodology.*

### Exposure

Among the most effective forms of behaviour therapy for the phobias is exposure. **Exposure therapy** involves putting the client in feared situations (e.g., social situations for social phobics), with the feared situations becoming gradually more intense over time.

Exposure therapy has proved effective with all types of phobia, including social phobia and agoraphobia. Indeed, it is sometimes described as the "gold standard" against which other forms of therapy should be compared. Its effectiveness in the treatment of social phobia was considered by Feske and Chambless (1995). They performed a meta-analysis of 15 studies in which cognitive-behaviour therapy and exposure therapy were compared: "The results ... indicate that exposure with and without cognitive modifications are equally effective in the treatment of social phobia."

It is often said that there is nothing new under the sun. Marks (1987) gave the following quotation from the philosopher John Locke's *Some Thoughts Concerning Education* (first published in 1693), in which Locke is advocating something very like exposure therapy:

> *If your child shrieks and runs away at the sight of a frog let another catch it and lay it down a good distance from him: at first accustom him to look upon it; when he can do that to come nearer to it and see it leap without emotion; then to touch it lightly when it is held fast in another's hand; and so on until he can come to handle it as confidently as a butterfly or a sparrow.*

**KEY TERM**

**Exposure therapy:** a form of therapy in which clients are exposed to stimuli or situations for which they have great fear.

What are the processes responsible for the effectiveness of exposure therapy? According to a traditional behaviourist account, phobic fears are acquired by classical conditioning, in which the conditioned or phobic stimulus (e.g., spider) is associated with a painful or aversive stimulus creating fear. In exposure therapy, the repeated presentation of the conditioned stimulus leads to extinction or habituation of the fear response.

However, the benefits of exposure therapy are explained differently by cognitive therapists (e.g., Salkovskis, 1996). They argue that exposure provides evidence that clients' fears have no objective basis, and this reduces clients' tendency to exaggerate the threat of phobic stimuli (see later in chapter).

*Evaluation*

➕ Exposure therapy is very effective in the treatment of several anxiety disorders (see Roth & Fonagy, 1996).

➖ It is not clear that exposure therapy is effective for the reasons proposed by behaviour therapists.

Flooding, or exposure, can be used to treat phobias. In the case of a spider phobic the client would be exposed to an extremely fear-provoking situation, such as being put in a room full of spiders—but not spiders as large as this one!

## Aversion therapy

In classical aversive conditioning, a neutral or positive stimulus is paired with an unpleasant or aversive stimulus (e.g., electric shock). This causes an aversive reaction (e.g., anxiety) to be produced in response to the neutral or positive stimulus. **Aversion therapy** is a form of treatment based on aversive conditioning. For example, an alcoholic is given aversive stimuli (e.g., shocks) while looking at or starting to drink alcohol. The intention is that alcohol will produce feelings of anxiety and so inhibit drinking.

Various types of aversive stimuli have been used to treat alcoholism. In addition to electric shocks, use has been made of emetic drugs causing vomiting and of drugs that impede breathing. Aversion therapy has sometimes been found to be moderately effective in the short term, but not in the long term (Comer, 2001).

*Evaluation*

➕ Aversion therapy has sometimes proved effective, especially over short periods of time.

➖ "Overall, there is little support for techniques using chemical or electrical aversion. Its use in service settings is made even more difficult to recommend given that there is (unsurprisingly) a high rate of attrition [dropping out from therapy]" (Roth & Fonagy, 1996, p. 226).

➖ There are serious ethical issues about a form of treatment which can cause high levels of discomfort and distress.

## Token economies

The **token economy** involves selective positive reinforcement or reward. It is used with institutionalised patients, who are given tokens (e.g., coloured counters) for behaving appropriately. These tokens can be used to obtain various privileges (e.g., obtaining cigarettes). Ayllon and Azrin (1968) carried out a classic study. Female schizophrenic patients who had been hospitalised for an average of 16 years were rewarded with plastic tokens for actions such as making their beds or combing their hair. The tokens were exchanged for pleasant activities (e.g., seeing a film). This token economy was very successful. The number of chores the patients performed each day increased from about five to over forty when this behaviour was rewarded with tokens.

Patterson has developed a form of treatment for children's anti-social behaviour based on rewarding desirable behaviour. As we saw in Chapter 22, Patterson (e.g., 1996) has found that children's anti-social behaviour often seems to develop because the child's aggressive behaviour is rewarded by getting its own way. Therapy involves rewarding the child's desirable behaviour and removing privileges (e.g., pocket money) when the child behaves badly. Patterson, Chamberlain, and Reid (1982) found that such changes in parents' behaviour were followed by substantial reductions in children's anti-social behaviour.

## Evaluation

⊕ Token economies have proved moderately effective with groups of patients (e.g., institutionalised schizophrenics) resistant to most forms of therapy. Programmes based on positive reinforcement of desirable behaviour are also effective in treating anti-social behaviour in children.

⊖ Token economies sometimes produce token (i.e., minimal) learning. They work because the environment is carefully structured so that only good behaviour is consistently rewarded. Patients find it hard to transfer what they have learned to the much less structured environment outside the institution.

⊖ Token economies are insufficient on their own. As Kendall and Hammen (1998, p. 74) pointed out, "Today, operant procedures [such as the token economy] are not used by themselves as a method of treatment. Rather, they are combined with many ... other forms of therapies."

## CLIENT-CENTRED THERAPY

The main approach to treatment of mental disorders stemming from the humanistic approach is client-centred or person-centred therapy, which was proposed by Carl Rogers (see Chapter 22). The essence of Rogers's approach was summarised by Kirschenbaum and Henderson (1990, p. xiv): "All individuals have within themselves the ability to guide their own lives in a manner that is both personally satisfying and socially constructive. In a particular type of helping relationship, we free the individuals to find their inner wisdom and confidence, and they will make increasingly healthier and more constructive choices."

Rogers (1957) discussed the conditions needed in therapy. He argued that there are six conditions, *all* of which have to be present in order for therapy to prove effective:

1. The therapist and the client are in psychological contact with each other.
2. The client is in a state of **incongruence**, meaning there are discrepancies between his/her self-concept and his/her experience, making him/her anxious or vulnerable.
3. The therapist behaves in a genuine fashion.
4. The therapist experiences unconditional positive regard for the client.
5. The therapist has a good empathic understanding of the client.
6. The therapist communicates his/her empathic understanding and unconditional positive regard to the client.

The above conditions can be applied to clients with any mental disorder. How is client-centred therapy influenced by the specific disorder from which the client suffers? In general terms, it hardly alters at all! Rogers did not believe in the value of categorising mental disorders, and argued that his six conditions are always all that is needed.

According to Rogers, there are three key characteristics that the therapist should display: genuineness, unconditional personal regard, and empathy. It follows that these characteristics should be associated with the success (or otherwise) of treatment. Orlinsky, Grave, and Parks (1994) reviewed the relevant literature. They found 32 studies in which the therapist's genuineness or congruence had been related to the outcome of therapy. In 11 of those studies, genuineness was positively related to outcome, and in 1 study it was negatively related. In the remaining 20 studies, there was no relationship between therapist genuineness and outcome.

Orlinsky et al. (1994) also considered the effects of therapist warmth or acceptance, qualities related to unconditional positive regard. They identified 50 studies, in 23 of

*Why did Rogers prefer the terms "facilitator" and "client" (or "person") to "therapist" and "patient"?*

which therapist warmth was positively related to client recovery. There was only one study in which therapist warmth was negatively related to outcome, and 26 studies in which there was no effect. Finally, Orlinsky et al. considered therapist empathy. Across 45 studies, there were 26 studies in which empathy was positively related to client recovery, and there were no effects in the remaining 19 studies.

Greenberg, Elliott, and Lietaer (1994) carried out a meta-analysis of studies on client-centred therapy, finding that the average client showed more improvement than 80% of individuals not receiving treatment. Grave, Caspar, and Ambuhl (1990) compared client-centred therapy with three forms of behaviour therapy in clients having mainly interpersonal problems. All four forms of treatment were moderately and comparably effective. The clients who did best with client-centred therapy had relatively high levels of social skills and assertiveness.

Client-centred therapists aim to create a comfortable atmosphere in which the client can share his or her experiences with the therapist.

## Evaluation

➕ Therapist empathy and unconditional positive regard assist in the treatment process, and therapist genuineness may also be of relevance.

➕ Client-centred therapy is reasonably effective with less severe disorders.

➖ Client-centred therapy is of little value in treating severe mental disorders (Rudolph, Langer, & Tausch, 1980; see Comer, 2001).

➖ Rogers's reluctance to accept that diagnosing mental disorders is important so that treatment can be tailored to the client's problems was unjustified.

➖ Rogers argued that the success of therapy does *not* depend on the specific factors unique to any given form of treatment. However, with severe disorders, the effectiveness of treatment depends *only* on specific factors and not on therapist empathy (Stevens, Hynan, & Allen, 2000).

## COGNITIVE THERAPY AND COGNITIVE-BEHAVIOUR THERAPY

Behaviour therapy originally focused on external stimuli and responses, and ignored cognitive processes (e.g., thoughts, beliefs) occurring between stimulus and response. This omission was dealt with in the early 1960s with the introduction of cognitive therapy. According to Beck and Weishaar (1989, p. 308), "Cognitive therapy consists of highly specific learning experiences designed to teach patients (1) to monitor their negative, automatic thoughts (cognitions); (2) to recognise the connections between cognitions, affect [emotion], and behaviour; (3) to examine the evidence for and against distorted automatic thoughts; (4) to substitute more reality-oriented interpretations for their biased cognitions; and (5) to learn to identify and alter the beliefs that predispose them to distort their experiences."

There are two important differences between cognitive therapy and psychodynamic therapy:

1. Cognitive therapists are mainly concerned with the patient's current concerns and beliefs, whereas psychodynamic therapists attach great significance to childhood events.

2. Cognitive therapists are much less interested in exploring the notion that crucial information is buried deep within the unconscious mind. According to Sacco and Beck (1985, p. 5), "The concept of unconscious processes is largely irrelevant to cognitive therapy."

Several cognitive therapists (including Aaron Beck) came to realise that restructuring a client's thoughts and beliefs is often not sufficient to produce full recovery. Many clients accepted that their previous thoughts were dysfunctional and replaced them with realistic thoughts. However, this did not always produce substantial behavioural changes. A social phobic might accept that there is much less to fear in social situations than they had previously believed, but they might still be reluctant to put themselves in difficult social situations. Such considerations led to the development of cognitive-behaviour therapy.

What is **cognitive-behaviour therapy?** As its name implies, cognitive-behaviour therapy involves elements of cognitive therapy and behaviour therapy. The basic notion is that the client needs to change his/her inappropriate behaviour *and* his/her dysfunctional thoughts. Note that there is no sharp dividing line between cognitive therapy and cognitive-behaviour therapy.

Kendall and Hammen (1998) argued that the four basic assumptions underlying cognitive-behaviour therapy are as follows:

1. Patients typically respond on the basis of their *interpretations* of themselves and the world around them rather than what is *actually* the case.
2. Thoughts, behaviours, and feelings are all interrelated, and all influence each other. Thus, it would be wrong to identify one of these factors (e.g., behaviour) as more important than the others.
3. In order for therapeutic interventions to be successful, they must clarify and change how people think about themselves and the world around them.
4. It is very desirable to change *both* the client's cognitive processes and his/her behaviour, because the benefits of therapy are likely to be greater than when only cognitive processes *or* behaviour are changed.

We can see what is involved in cognitive-behaviour therapy by considering a concrete example provided by Clark (1996). A 40-year-old man with panic disorder was very frightened he would have a heart attack or stroke whenever he suffered a panic attack. Accordingly, the patient tried to protect himself from this fate by distracting himself, by taking parecetamol, and by taking deep breaths. The therapist argued that there were two possible hypotheses: (1) There was something seriously wrong with the patient's heart; or (2) the central problem was the patient's *belief* he might have a heart attack. These hypotheses were tested by the therapist and patient alternately sprinting and jogging around a football pitch. In addition, the patient was given the homework of taking strenuous daily exercise without trying to control his breathing or distracting himself. The patient rapidly accepted that his problem centred on his own mistaken beliefs.

## Albert Ellis

Albert Ellis was one of the first therapists to put forward a version of cognitive therapy (see Chapter 22). He argued that anxiety and depression occur as the end points in a three-point sequence:

A. Occurrence of unpleasant event (e.g., rejection by partner).
B. Cognitive reaction to unpleasant event (e.g., "I am a valueless person to be rejected like this").
C. State of anxiety or depression.

According to the above A-B-C model, anxiety and depression do *not* occur as a direct result of unpleasant events, but are produced by the irrational thoughts following from the occurrence of unpleasant events. The interpretations produced at point B depend on the individual's belief system.

Ellis (1962) developed rational-emotive therapy as a way of removing irrational and self-defeating thoughts and replacing them with more rational and positive ones. He argued that individuals who are anxious or depressed should create a point D. This is a dispute belief system allowing them to interpret life's events in ways designed to reduce emotional distress.

Rational-emotive therapy starts with the therapist making patients aware of the self-defeating nature of their beliefs. Patients are then encouraged to question these beliefs vigorously to discover whether these beliefs are rational and logical. For example, clients may be told to ask themselves questions (e.g., "Why do I have to be liked by everybody?"). After that, patients are taught to replace these beliefs with more realistic ones (e.g., "It is impossible to be liked by everybody, but most people like me"). The crucial final step is for patients to have *full acceptance* of these new, rational beliefs.

Therapists using rational-emotive therapy are more argumentative than those using client-centred therapy. In addition, they show less concern for the sensitivities of their clients. Thus, the approach used by rational-emotive therapists may be unsuitable for those of a delicate disposition!

*Some non-Western cultures do not accept Western rational thought as the norm—for example, they may believe in the supernatural. How easy would it be to use this form of therapy with individuals from such a background?*

## Evaluation

⊕ Rational-emotive therapy is especially effective with clients who feel guilty because of their own perceived inadequacies and who impose high demands on themselves (Brandsma, Maultsby, & Welsh, 1978).

⊕ Rational-emotive therapy is more suitable for individuals suffering from anxiety or depression than for those with severe thought disorders (Barlow & Durand, 1995).

⊖ Some of the irrational beliefs which rational-emotive therapists seek to change are effective and adaptive (Arnkoff & Glass, 1982). For example, a belief such as, "It is essential for me to succeed academically", may help to lead to academic and career success.

⊖ "The procedures of RET [rational-emotive therapy] are put forth as appropriate treatment for a wide variety of disorders, … yet few of these procedures include specific prescriptions for tailoring therapeutic strategies to the target problems" (Kendall & Hammen, 1998, p. 77).

## Aaron Beck

Aaron Beck has focused mainly on depression and the anxiety disorders, and has moved from being a cognitive therapist to being a cognitive-behaviour therapist. As discussed in Chapter 22, Beck (1976) argued that many cognitive distortions of depressed patients involve the **cognitive triad**, consisting of negative thoughts about oneself, about the world, and about the future. Depressed patients generally perceive themselves to be helpless, worthless, and inadequate. They regard the world as posing insuperable obstacles, and the future as totally helpless, because their worthlessness makes it impossible for them to improve matters.

Beck, Emery, and Greenberg (1985) argued that individuals with an anxiety disorder over-estimate the likelihood of threat with respect to certain external or internal stimuli (e.g., snake phobics exaggerate the threateningness of snakes). An important part of cognitive therapy for the anxiety disorders involves correcting such overestimates.

These children are happy to touch this snake but a snake phobic, according to Beck, would over-estimate the danger the snake posed.

Beck (1976) argued that therapy should involve more than simply changing dysfunctional thoughts and replacing them with more appropriate and positive ones. He emphasised the use of homework assignments requiring clients to behave in certain ways they found difficult. A client suffering from social anxiety might be told to initiate conversations with everyone in his/her office over the following few days. A crucial ingredient in such homework assignments is hypothesis testing. Clients typically predict that carrying out their homework assignments will make them feel anxious or depressed, and so they are told to test these predictions. The clients' hypotheses are typically shown to be too pessimistic, and this speeds up the rate of recovery.

We will consider in more detail Beck's approach as it applies to depression. First, the therapist encourages the client to engage in increasing activities in order to elevate his/her mood. Second, the therapist instructs the client to recognise and record his/her negative automatic thoughts (unpleasant thoughts which spring to mind). After that, the therapist and client together challenge the validity of those thoughts. Third, the therapist persuades the client that most of these negative thoughts are too pessimistic, and are contributing to the client's depression. Attempts are made to change the thoughts to make them more realistic. Fourth, the therapist helps the client to change his/her underlying negative attitudes about him/herself (e.g., "I can never be successful") that played an important part in triggering the depression.

The usefulness of Beck's approach is considered later on in the overall evaluation of cognitive and cognitive-behaviour therapy.

## Other developments

Anxious patients often use **safety-seeking behaviours**, which are designed to reduce the level of anxiety (see Chapter 22). For example, social phobics may avoid eye contact and talk very little in social situations (Clark & Wells, 1995). These safety-seeking behaviours may reduce the value of exposure therapy (putting patients in feared situations) for social phobics. According to cognitive-behaviour therapists, exposure therapy is effective with social phobics because it allows them to disconfirm their unrealistically negative views about the dangers of social situations. It should be most effective if patients systematically avoid safety-seeking behaviours, which prevent proper disconfirmation of those negative views. In contrast, behaviour therapists attribute the success of exposure therapy to the extinction of conditioned fear responses. If that is so, it is not clear that the presence or absence of safety-seeking behaviours should influence the effectiveness of exposure therapy.

Morgan and Raffle (1999) instructed some social phobics receiving exposure therapy (e.g., giving talks in public) to avoid safety-seeking behaviours, whereas others were not

---

**CASE STUDY: *Social phobia***

Dinesh is a 25-year-old software engineer. He was an award-winning student at engineering college. After graduating he got a job and within a short span of time impressed his superiors with his quality of work.

In spite of his achievements, Dinesh faced social problems. In social situations he felt that everybody was watching him and that he might do something embarrassing. At official meetings, he was tense and did not express his views. The most difficult task was attending parties. He was extremely tense, at times trembling, giddy with fear that others might ridicule him. Then he began to stay away.

Dinesh was suffering from social phobia, the irrational fear of social situations. Sufferers are scared and anxious in social situations. The anxiety is because they feel that something awful will happen to them, for example, they may behave in an embarrassing way and others will ridicule them. This results in sweating, trembling, palpitations, and feeling giddy. Even though the individual is aware that such behaviour is silly, they are not able to overcome it. They start avoiding social situations and this results in difficulties in carrying out their work and personal activities. This deteriorated interaction with others and personal distress result in a lower level of functioning and low self-esteem.

For those afflicted with the disorder, both medical and non-medical treatments are available. In terms of medication, drugs like fluoxetine and recent arrivals like moclobemide are useful. But drugs take effect only after a few weeks, and do not provide a permanent cure.

Psychological treatment in the form of cognitive-behavioural therapy is useful. This aims at uncovering a person's automatic negative thoughts and cognitive schema, and helps them to understand and overcome these negative thoughts, in a gradual and systematic way. Relaxation therapy is also useful in helping an individual overcome basic anxiety.

Coming back to Dinesh, he was on medication and underwent cognitive-behavioural therapy. Gradually, he overcame his phobia. He is now attending parties and meetings, is able to travel, and feels good about himself.

Adapted from: Anandaram, T.S.J. (2001).

given these instructions. As predicted, those patients instructed to avoid safety-seeking behaviours showed more improvement from therapy.

In similar fashion, Salkovskis, Clark, Hackmann, Wells, and Gelder (1999) put patients suffering from panic disorder with agoraphobia in an exposure situation, during which they were instructed to use or avoid using safety-seeking behaviours (e.g., distracting themselves, holding on to people). Those patients who had avoided using safety-seeking behaviours showed a greater reduction in catastrophic beliefs and in anxiety.

## *Overall evaluation*

- ⊕ Cognitive therapy is effective in the treatment of anxiety disorders and depression.
- ⊕ Cognitive-behaviour therapy (as developed by Beck and others) is often more effective than cognitive therapy on its own (see Comer, 2001).
- ⊕ The effectiveness of exposure therapy is increased when patients avoid safety-seeking behaviours, as predicted by cognitive-behaviour therapists.
- ⊖ Cognitive therapy and cognitive-behaviour therapy are of only modest usefulness in treating very severe disorders (e.g., schizophrenia).
- ⊖ Beck and other cognitive-behaviour therapists are in danger of exaggerating the importance of cognitive processes and minimising that of physiological processes.
- ⊖ Clients sometimes develop more rational and less distorted ways of thinking about important issues without these changes altering their maladaptive behaviour.

## EFFECTIVENESS OF THERAPY

You might imagine that it would be easy to assess the effectiveness of therapy, and to decide whether one form of therapy is more or less effective than another. For example, we could carry out a study including three groups of clients:

- clients receiving therapy A.
- clients receiving therapy B.
- control clients who remain on a waiting list.

*What ethical issues does this pose?*

We could then compare the percentages of clients recovering in the three groups, which would indicate the relative effectiveness of therapies A and B. In fact, there are several problems in assessing therapeutic effectiveness, six of which are considered below.

First, there are numerous ways of assessing recovery, and therapists differ in what they regard as appropriate outcome measures. For example, a major goal of therapy for psychodynamic therapists is to resolve inner conflicts, whereas for behaviour therapists it is to produce desirable changes in overt behaviour. In terms of evaluating the effectiveness of therapy, note that some outcome measures are easier to change than others. Howard, Lueger, Maling, and Martinovitch (1993) proposed a phase model, according to which there are three successive phases of improvement during therapy:

1. Enhanced subjective well-being (e.g., the client feels better emotionally and psychologically). This often occurs very early in therapy.
2. Reduction of pathological symptoms (e.g., fewer phobic reactions or less worrying). This phase occurs *after* subjective well-being has improved.
3. Enhanced life function (e.g., developing an intimate relationship, finding a job). This is the last phase.

All three kinds of improvement are relevant to recovery. However, improvements at phase 1 are easier to produce via therapy than are improvements at phase 3.

Strupp (1996) pointed out that the effectiveness of any given form of therapy can be considered from three different perspectives: (1) The perspective of society (e.g., the individual's ability to function in society, the individual's adherence to social norms), (2) the client's own perspective, including his/her overall subjective well-being, (3) the therapist's perspective, which includes relating the client's thinking and behaviour to the theoretical framework underlying the therapy used by the therapist. The extent to which a client has recovered may vary considerably from one perspective to another.

Second, patients treated by different forms of therapy may vary in the severity of their symptoms. This is especially likely to be a significant factor when patients help to decide which therapy they will receive.

Third, the apparent effectiveness of any form of therapy depends on the skills and personal qualities of the therapist as well as on the content of the therapy itself. It is hard to establish the relative importance of those two factors in producing therapeutic effectiveness.

Fourth, therapy that is effective in producing recovery may not be effective in preventing relapse (return of symptoms). Thus, a follow-up several months after the conclusion of therapy is needed to see whether the short-term gains of therapy are preserved in the long term.

Fifth (and often neglected), most waiting-list clients are actively seeking ways of coping with their lives while awaiting therapy. Cross, Sheehan, and Khan (1980) found that most waiting-list clients obtained advice and guidance from other people. Surprisingly, clients receiving treatment sought outside help even more than waiting-list controls. Changes in treated and untreated client groups over time depend to an unknown extent on these non-therapist sources of assistance. Thus, a waiting-list control group is *not* the same as a no-treatment control group.

Sixth, there is perhaps the most crucial problem faced by researchers assessing the effectiveness of therapy. This problem arises because most researchers want to carry out studies conforming to the scientific requirements of good experimental design, which involves controlling as many aspects of therapy as possible. That has led to the widespread use of treatment manuals, which indicate in detail how a given form of therapy should be administered. It has also led to the use of relatively homogeneous (similar) groups of clients with the same DSM diagnosis. As a result, clients with more than one disorder are often excluded, because they would complicate the interpretation of the findings. In addition, the requirements of the scientific approach promote the use of a predetermined number of treatment sessions, and the random assignment of clients to different forms of therapy (which is hard to justify ethically).

Why is it problematical to carry out research on therapeutic effectiveness in a fully scientific way? According to Seligman (1995), scientifically-based research differs substantially from what typically happens in clinical practice, and so it is hard to know whether the findings obtained can be generalised to the normal therapeutic practice. Seligman distinguished between efficacy studies and effectiveness studies. **Efficacy studies** are scientific, well-controlled clinical trials focusing on the elimination of well-defined problems (e.g., social phobics' avoidance of social situations). In contrast, **effectiveness studies** deal with actual clinical practice with all of its scientific shortcomings, and the focus is on subjective measures of outcome (e.g., improved quality of life).

Should researchers carry out efficacy studies or effectiveness studies? Both kinds of studies are worthwhile. Efficacy studies have good internal validity, meaning that we can identify factors responsible for benefits to clients. However, they have low external validity, meaning that it is hard to *generalise* the findings to typical clinical practice. The strengths and weaknesses of effectiveness studies are exactly the opposite: They often have good external validity, but can lack internal validity. Our confidence in the effectiveness of any given form of therapy would clearly be greatest if it produced good outcomes in efficacy and effectiveness studies.

## Is therapy effective?

Much of the evidence on therapeutic effectiveness is in the form of meta-analyses. Each **meta-analysis** combines the findings from numerous studies to provide an overall estimate of the effectiveness of each form of treatment. This approach was first used systematically

---

**Individual cases**

The diagnosis and treatment of a person suffering from, for example, an eating disorder are likely to vary from one individual to another, depending on the person's symptoms, their severity, and the individual case history. The effectiveness of the treatment may therefore hinge on the extent of the therapist's knowledge and understanding of each individual case, rather than on a specific psychological approach to eating disorders.

---

**KEY TERMS**

**Efficacy studies:** assessments of therapeutic effectiveness based on well-controlled investigation of well-defined clinical problems.

**Effectiveness studies:** assessments of therapeutic effectiveness based on typical clinical practice.

**Meta-analysis:** combining the data from several studies to obtain an overall picture.

by Smith and Glass (1977) and discussed at greater length by Smith, Glass, and Miller (1980). They reviewed 475 diverse studies. Several different outcome measures were used in many of the studies, ranging from self-report measures to behavioural and physiological measures of various kinds. In all, there were 1776 outcome measures from the 475 studies.

Smith, Glass, and Miller (1980) concluded their review as follows: "Different types of psychotherapy (verbal or behavioural, psychodynamic, client-centred, or systematic desensitisation) do not produce different types or degrees of benefit." Their analyses indicated that on average clients receiving any systematic form of psychotherapy were better off than 80% of untreated controls in terms of recovery. Smith et al. reported that the effectiveness of therapy did not depend on its length. As behaviour therapy typically takes much less time than psychodynamic theory, that is an argument for preferring behaviour therapy.

Smith et al. (1980) reported two other important findings of note. First, some forms of therapy were especially effective with certain disorders. For example, cognitive therapy and cognitive-behaviour therapy were most effective with specific phobias, fear, and anxiety, whereas client-centred therapy worked best with patients having low self-esteem. Second, any form of therapy was more effective when provided by therapists who believed strongly in it.

The meta-analysis of Smith et al. (1980) has various limitations. First, they gave equal weight to all studies regardless of quality. Second, many of the studies included were of dubious relevance to therapy as it is typically carried out. For example, more than 50% of the patients receiving treatment across the 475 studies were students (Gross & McIlveen, 1996). Third, they deliberately reduced the size of the effects associated with behaviour therapy! They did this because they argued that the outcome measures used by behaviour therapists were less stringent than those used by other therapists.

Numerous meta-analyses followed the study by Smith et al. (1980). These meta-analyses have confirmed that every type of therapy is effective, and most have revealed no (or small) differences in the effectiveness of different forms of therapy. For example, Wampold, Mondin, Moody, Stich, Benson, and Ahn (1997) carried out a meta-analysis on studies in which two or more forms of therapy had been compared directly, and in which the same measures of improvement had been applied to patients receiving different forms of therapy. Their findings suggested that the beneficial effects of all forms of therapy are essentially the same. Wampold et al. (p. 211) concluded as follows:

*Why is it that researchers persist in attempts to find treatment differences, when they know that these effects are small in comparison to other effects, such as therapists' effects … or effects of treatment versus no-treatment comparisons?*

*If this is the case, what do you think should be the most important determinant of treatment choice (e.g., client preference, therapist preference, cost-effectiveness)?*

It can be argued that we should not take the findings from meta-analyses at face value, because many studies on therapeutic effectiveness are tightly controlled and unrepresentative of typical clinical practice. There is some evidence (e.g., Weisz, Chaiyasit, Weiss, Eastman, & Jackson, 1995) that treatment under normal clinical conditions is less effective than treatment in rigidly controlled clinical trials. However, Shadish, Matt, Navarro, and Phillips (2000, p. 512) obtained rather different findings. They focused on clinical representativeness, which "occurs when outcome studies use real clients and therapists in actual treatment settings and when treatment is not typically subjected to routine research standardisation procedures such as the use of manuals, treatment compliance checks, and special pretherapy training." Shadish et al. carried out a meta-analysis of studies in which therapy was carried out under clinically representative conditions. They found that such therapy was as effective as therapy that was not clinically representative.

Most outcome studies have focused on the clients' state at the end of therapy. However, we need to know whether the gains achieved in therapy are maintained thereafter. Most of the available evidence is encouraging. Nicholson and Berman (1983) considered 67 studies with a follow-up about 8 months after treatment ended. Therapeutic gains achieved by the end of therapy were maintained several months later. Lambert and Bergin (1994) concluded their review of follow-up studies as follows: "Long-term follow-up studies are no longer needed because treatment effects are usually maintained for at least several months."

## Why is therapy effective?

Most forms of therapy are of comparable effectiveness. Luborsky, Singer, and Luborsky (1975) called this the "dodo bird verdict". This is a reference to the dodo bird in *Alice in Wonderland*, who announced, "Everybody has won and all must have prizes." How can we explain the dodo bird effect? The most influential view (e.g., Lambert & Bergin, 1994) is that therapeutic success depends on common factors and specific factors. **Common factors** are aspects (e.g., therapist warmth, therapist empathy, therapeutic alliance between therapist and client) common to most forms of therapy. In contrast, **specific factors** are aspects of therapy specific or unique to one form of therapy. If the effectiveness of therapy depends mainly on common factors rather than specific ones (as some experts have suggested), this would account for the lack of difference in outcome across therapies.

Stevens et al. (2000) considered 80 outcome studies in which three types of groups were compared:

1. Specific therapy groups, for whom any benefits will depend on a combination of specific and common factors.
2. Common factor groups, who received general encouragement and support but no specific therapy; any benefits should depend only on common factors.
3. Waiting-list control groups, for whom no benefits were expected.

Stevens et al. (p. 283) concluded as follows:

> *The magnitude of specific treatment effects was roughly twice the size of common factor effects. The only exception to this pattern occurred when we examined severity of diagnosis. For the research participants with less severe disorders (and fewer sessions on the average), the magnitude of common factors and specific treatment effects was nearly identical. For the research participants with more severe disorders (and more sessions), only the specific treatment component was beneficial.*

There are three main sources of common factors within the therapeutic situation: the relationship between the therapist and client, therapist characteristics, and client characteristics. It is often assumed that therapy involves the therapist providing therapy to a passive client like a doctor provides patients with drugs. In fact, as Bergin (2000, p. 85) pointed out, the reality of therapy is very different: "We may say not only that 'therapy works' but that the 'therapist works' and the 'client works' … The patient is as much a cause as either the therapist or the technique. The collaborating interaction of these influences constitutes the change process."

An important aspect of the interactions between therapist and client (and an important common factor) is the **therapeutic alliance**. This incorporates the notion that the client is *actively* involved in the therapeutic process in co-operation with the therapist. An effective therapeutic alliance is a good predictor of treatment outcome (see Kopta, Lueger, Saunders, & Howard, 1999, for a review). For example, Krupnick et al. (1996) reported the findings from a large-scale study in which several treatments for depression were compared. The therapeutic alliance predicted the success of treatment with all forms of therapy.

The effectiveness of any form of therapy depends on various qualities of the therapist, and so therapist effectiveness is an important common factor. Crits-Christoph, Baranackie, Kurcias, Beck, Carroll, Perry et al. (1991) carried out a meta-analysis of therapist effects across several types of therapy. They found that the outcome of therapy depended more on therapist differences than on differences in the form of treatment.

What therapist characteristics are important? This issue was addressed by Lafferty, Beutler, and Crago (1991). The strongest finding was that the effective therapists had greater empathy or emotional understanding of their clients. In addition, effective therapists provided greater directiveness and support during therapy.

Najavits and Strupp (1994) considered the behaviour of effective and ineffective therapists during treatment. They distinguished between positive behaviours (e.g., warmth, understanding, helping) and negative behaviours (e.g., ignoring, rejecting, and attacking). The effective therapists showed more positive behaviours and fewer negative behaviours than did the ineffective therapists.

What characteristics of the client are important? The research on this issue has produced rather inconsistent findings (see Garfield, 1994, for a review). Of those offered therapy, a surprisingly large number (up to 40% in a few studies) refuse it. Clients of lower socio-economic status are more likely to refuse treatment (Garfield, 1994), even though they are less likely to be offered it in the first place. Socio-economic status also predicts continuing with treatment. For example, Berrigan and Garfield (1981) found there was a direct relationship between social class and continuation in psychotherapy, with clients from the higher social classes being most likely to continue. However, socio-economic status is generally unrelated to outcome in those who continue through to the end of therapy.

...warmth, acceptance and empathy on the part of the therapist.

The severity of the client's disturbance at the start of therapy is strongly related to outcome, with clients having the most severe disturbance generally having the worst outcomes. Steinmetz, Lewinsohn, and Antonuccio (1983) found in therapy for depression that the pretreatment depression score was the best predictor of outcome. As they concluded, "Participants at all levels of depression severity improved markedly, but those who were initially more depressed tended to maintain their relative ranking in posttreatment" (Steinmetz et al., 1983).

Psychodynamic therapy involves lengthy discussions of the client's past life. It seems likely that certain kinds of client would engage most productively in such discussions. Psychodynamic therapy seems to work best with clients who are young, attractive, verbally skilled, intelligent, and successful (Garfield, 1994). (If you take the first letters of young, attractive, and so on, you arrive at YAVIS, which may assist your memory for this list!)

*How might cultural factors influence the effectiveness of therapy?*

# Differences among therapies

The main finding from meta-analyses is that most types of therapy are approximately equal in their therapeutic effectiveness. However, it is still possible that there are minor differences among therapies. For example, Matt and Navarro (1997, p. 22) considered 63 meta-analyses in which different types of therapy had been compared (see Key Study on the next page). They found that about one-third of the meta-analyses they looked at did report differences in the effectiveness of various therapies, and, characteristically, concluded that behaviour and cognitive therapies were more effective than the psychodynamic and client-centered approach. However, Matt and Navarro argued that these differences in effectiveness were more apparent than real. Clients treated by behaviour or cognitive therapy often had less serious symptoms than those treated by psychodynamic or client-centred therapy. In addition, behaviour and cognitive therapists tended to use less stringent outcome measures than did psychodynamic and client-centred therapists.

Rosenhan and Seligman (1995) considered the issue of the most effective forms of therapy for various disorders. Some of their conclusions were as follows:

- *Anxieties, fears, phobias, and panic disorder:* Systematic desensitisation, cognitive therapy, and drugs are among the best forms of therapy.
- *Depression:* Cognitive therapy, electroconvulsive shock treatment, and drugs (e.g., Prozac) are all very effective.
- *Schizophrenia:* Drugs (e.g., neuroleptics) and family intervention (involving communication skills) are effective.

Prozac is an anti-depressant drug which inhibits the uptake of serotonin, a neurotransmitter chemical produced in the brain.

## Matt and Navarro: A review of the effects of therapy

Matt and Navarro (1997) considered evidence from 63 meta-analyses of the effects of therapy. Across the 28 analyses providing relevant data, the mean effect size was 0.67, meaning that 75% of patients improved more than untreated controls.

Matt and Navarro also addressed the issue of whether the effects of therapy are due to specific effects or to common effects (e.g., placebo effects). They did this by focusing on 10 meta-analyses in which three types of group were compared:

1. Specific therapy groups, for whom any benefits may depend on specific effects or common effects.
2. Placebo control groups (involving general encouragement but no specific therapy), for whom any benefits are likely to depend on common effects.
3. Waiting-list control groups, for whom no benefits are expected.

The evidence indicated that 57% of placebo control patients did better than the average waiting-list control patient, indicating that common or placebo effects did exist. However, 75% of the patients receiving specific therapy did better than the average placebo control patient, indicating that specific effects are almost four times more powerful than common or placebo effects.

Do different forms of therapy vary in their general effectiveness? Matt and Navarro (1997, p. 22) considered the relevant meta-analyses, and concluded as follows: "Approximately one-third of these meta-analyses report evidence of differential effectiveness of interventions. Typically, differences favoured behavioural and cognitive therapy approaches over psychodynamic and client-centred approaches." However, they accepted that it was hard to interpret such differences because there was no standardisation of disorder severity, outcome measures, and so on.

### KEY STUDY EVALUATIO—Matt and Navarro

A major criticism of Matt and Navarro's research concerns its lack of standardisation. The specific conditions of individual cases are vital in determining the effectiveness of therapy. Linked to this is the timescale used. Regression or relapse would indicate failure of therapy, but this is impossible to discover from Matt and Navarro's study. A much lengthier approach, capable of handling disparate sets of data, with a methodology using detailed case notes and follow-up research would be needed to address this problem.

Accuracy is difficult to determine in meta-analyses, and it would be of value to consider making more use of the case-study-centred approach. The inevitable cost and time implications militate against this more focused type of study. However, if psychologists wish to make any real impact on the effectiveness of therapy, it would make sense to involve clients' own testimonies as valid forms of data, rather than relying only on notes based on second-hand observation. This may not give such a tidy result, but might be an improvement in some ways on the sweeping generalisations that often result from meta-analyses.

### Discussion points

1. What are the strengths and weaknesses of meta-analyses as a way of discovering the effectiveness of therapy?
2. How impressed are you by the apparent effectiveness of most forms of therapy revealed by Matt and Navarro?

Roth and Fonagy (1996) analysed exhaustively the effectiveness of different forms of therapy (excluding drug therapy). For each disorder, they identified those forms of treatment that have been shown to be clearly effective, and those that are promising and/or currently have limited support:

| Disorder | Clearly effective | Promising/limited support |
|---|---|---|
| Depression | Cognitive-behaviour therapy | Psychodynamic therapy |
| Specific phobia | Exposure therapy | |
| Social phobia | Exposure therapy Cognitive therapy + exposure | |
| Panic disorder | Cognitive-behaviour therapy | |
| Generalised anxiety disorder | Cognitive-behaviour therapy | |
| Obsessive-compulsive disorder | Exposure therapy | Cognitive restructuring Rational-emotive therapy + exposure |

| Disorder | Clearly effective | Promising/limited support |
| --- | --- | --- |
| Post-traumatic stress disorder | Exposure + cognitive therapy | Psychodynamic therapy |
| Schizophrenia | Family intervention programme | Cognitive therapy for delusions |
| Personality disorders | Social skills training<br>Behaviour therapy | Psychodynamic therapy |

We have discussed most of the effective forms of therapy, but have not mentioned family intervention programmes for schizophrenia. As we saw in Chapter 22, schizophrenics are most likely to relapse when their families exhibit high levels of expressed emotion (hostility, criticism, emotional over-involvement). This led Falloon (e.g., Falloon, Boyd, McGill, Williamson, Razani, Moss et al., 1985) to develop an intervention programme, in which the families of schizophrenics were taught more constructive and non-demanding ways of interacting. They were also told to lower their expectations of the schizophrenic member of the family. This treatment greatly reduced the chances of major schizophrenic symptoms returning compared to standard treatment.

Falloon, Coverdale, Laidlaw, Merry, Kydd, and Morosini (1998) argued that it is very important to detect schizophrenic symptoms at an early stage. Early detection is followed by various attempts to improve the client's social functioning. These include family education (i.e., improving family interactions), carer-based stress management, and training in social skills for the schizophrenic client. In one study discussed by Falloon et al. the percentage of clients having severe symptoms after treatment was reduced from 54% with standard techniques to 14% with the techniques mentioned above. Use of similar techniques in a study in England reduced the incidence of schizophrenia from 7.4 cases per 100,000 to only 0.75.

Family therapy is not only effective in the treatment of schizophrenia. Family-based approaches have proved successful in the treatment of a wide range of child and adolescent problems (see Carr, 2000, for a review). In similar fashion, marital therapy has been found to be as effective as cognitive-behaviour therapy in the treatment of various adult disorders (Carr, 2000).

*What implications does this have for Care in the Community?*

In general terms, what emerges most clearly from Roth and Fonagy's (1996) analysis is the impressive effectiveness of cognitive-behaviour therapy in general and exposure in particular in the treatment of the anxiety disorders. However, they argued that no psychological form of treatment for bipolar disorder has been shown to be effective.

## Implications for the future

There are in general surprisingly small differences in effectiveness across several apparently very different forms of therapy. What are the implications of these findings for therapists? It could be argued that therapists should practice **eclecticism**, using techniques drawn from various types of therapy rather than a single therapeutic approach. As Kopta et al. (1999, p. 455) pointed out, "An increasingly popular view is that the long-term dominance of the major psychotherapies has ended and that integrationism and eclecticism is now the direction for technical advances in treatment."

The eclectic approach has been much used for many years already. Jensen, Bergin, and Greaves (1990) found that 68% out of 800 American therapists used an eclectic approach. Eclectic therapists varied in how many types of therapy they used, with four being the most common number. Unfortunately, very few studies have considered the effectiveness of eclectic approaches to treatment.

There has been controversy about how the eclectic approach should be used (e.g., Lazarus & Messer, 1991). Two problems which can arise with the eclectic approach will be raised here. First, some eclectic therapists simply choose techniques which they think are likely to be effective, but these choices are not driven by any clear rationale or theoretical understanding. Second, it may be hard to integrate most theoretical approaches to therapy, because they are basically incompatible. As Davison and Neale (1998, p. 553)

**KEY TERM**

**Eclecticism:** the use of a range of different forms of treatment by therapists.

noted, "The definition of a fact in psychoanalysis differs from the definition of a fact in behaviour therapy. Different standards of evidence prevail ... one cannot integrate two theories that do not share the same definition of reality."

## ETHICAL ISSUES IN THERAPY

There are important ethical issues relating to therapy. However, few people would go as far as Masson (1989). He was very concerned that the therapist is in a much more powerful position than the client, which led him to conclude that, "the very idea of psychotherapy is wrong. The structure of psychotherapy is such that no matter how kindly a person is, when that person becomes a therapist, he or she is engaged in acts that are bound to diminish the dignity, autonomy, and freedom of the person who comes for help" (p. 24).

Masson's attack on therapy is exaggerated. However, some significant issues need to be addressed, and are considered below:

1. Informed consent.
2. Confidentiality.
3. Choice of therapeutic goals.
4. Dual relationships.
5. Cultural and subcultural factors.

## Informed consent

It may seem obvious that therapy should only be carried out with the full informed consent of the client. To achieve that, the client should be fully informed about the various forms of treatment available, about the probability of success of each treatment, about any possible dangers or side effects, about the right to terminate treatment at any time, and about the likely cost of treatment. Evidence of the value of informed consent was reported by Devine and Fernald (1973). Snake phobics were shown four films of different forms of treatment. Those given their preferred form of treatment showed more recovery than those who were not.

There are strong ethical and practical reasons in favour of informed consent. In practice, however, there are several reasons why full informed consent is often not achieved.

First, the therapist may not have detailed information about the respective benefits and costs of different forms of treatment. In addition, some forms of treatment are very successful with some clients, but cause serious problems with others. Thus, the therapist may be unable to provide the client with enough information to make a clear decision.

Second, the client may find it hard to remember the information he/she has been given by the therapist. Irwin et al. (1985) engaged in detailed questioning of clients saying they understood the benefits and possible side effects of a form of treatment. About 75% of them were mistaken, because they had forgotten important information.

Third, many clients (e.g., young children, schizophrenics) are unable to provide full informed consent. So far as schizophrenics are concerned, there is evidence that they vary considerably in their ability to give informed consent (Davison & Neale, 2001). When clients are unable to give informed consent, a guardian or close relative typically provides it.

Fourth, clients may agree to a form of treatment because of their exaggerated respect for the expertise of the therapist, rather than because of relevant information about that treatment. This is especially likely to occur when the client has little or no prior knowledge of different forms of treatment.

Fifth, some clients may be unable to provide informed consent because of social and cultural pressures on them. For example, Silverstein (1972, p. 4) expressed clearly the difficulties that some homosexuals may have:

> *To suggest that a person comes voluntarily to change his sexual orientation is to ignore the powerful environmental stress ... that has been telling him for years that he should change ... to play in a playground and hear the words "faggot"*

*and "queer", to go ... to college and hear of "illness", and finally to the coun-
selling centre that promises to "cure", makes it hard [to live in] an environment
of freedom and voluntary choice.*

## Removal of informed consent

A key question regarding the issue of informed consent was posed by Barlow and Durand (1995, p. 675): "Are people with mental illness in need of help and protection from society, or is society in need of protection from them?" According to Barlow and Durand, the emphasis in the United States until about 1980 was on the rights and needs of the individual. Since then, however, there has been more emphasis on the needs of society, with individuals in the United States increasingly being required to have treatment and/or be committed to mental hospitals against their will. In other words, some patients are *not* allowed to give their informed consent to treatment.

In the United Kingdom, the key provisions are currently contained in the Mental Health Act for England and Wales (1983). As MacLeod (1998) pointed out, Section 2 of this Act allows for compulsory admission and detention of patients for up to 28 days if this is recommended by an approved social worker and two doctors. The grounds for such detention are as follows:

- The patient has a mental illness requiring treatment.
- Detention is needed for the patient's health and/or safety.
- Detention is needed for the protection of others.

Section 3 of the Mental Health Act of 1983 is concerned with renewable orders for compulsory treatment for up to 6 months, which can be obtained in the following circumstances:

- The patient is in need of treatment.
- The proposed treatment will probably be effective.
- The proposed treatment is necessary for the patient's health and/or safety, or to protect others.
- The proposed treatment can only be provided if the patient is detained.

Some of the criteria used in the various Sections of the Mental Health Act can be hard to use in practice. Account is supposed to be taken of the risks to the individual and to others if there is no detention. However, these risks are hard to assess with any precision. Mistakes will inevitably be made, with some patients being detained unnecessarily and others not being detained when they should have been.

*When, if ever, do you think that it is justifiable to treat mentally disordered individuals without their informed consent?*

## Confidentiality

Confidentiality is of basic importance in therapy. It is essential if the client is to trust the therapist, and so feel free to disclose intimate details. The law ensures confidentiality in most circumstances. For example, in the UK the Police and Criminal Evidence Act (1984) states that there must be an order signed by a judge before the authorities can consider gaining access to a client's confidential records.

MacLeod (1998) pointed out that absolute confidentiality is unusual. For example, cases are discussed with other therapists working in the same place (e.g., a National Health Service Trust). This is done to ensure that clients obtain the best possible treatment, and raises few concerns. However, sensitive information about a client is sometimes revealed to others *outside* the organisation for which the therapist works. Some examples are considered next.

Suppose it emerges during therapy that the client is thinking of killing someone. If the therapist believes this is

> **Confidentiality and anonymity**
> Anonymity is an important part of confidentiality. The discussion of case notes at a public lecture or in a published article or book must not involve identifying the client. A breach of this aspect of confidentiality could result in the client or client's relatives taking legal action against the therapist concerned. In situations like these, and with the permission of those involved, clients are usually identified by pseudonyms or initials only.

a serious threat, he/she is under an obligation to tell the relevant authorities. There are two sets of circumstances in which therapists in the United Kingdom have a legal obligation to disclose information about their clients to the relevant authorities. First, when the information is relevant to acts of terrorism. Second, when the information is of relevance to the welfare of children.

The situation is similar in the United States. The ethical position with respect to confidentiality was spelled out by the American Psychological Association (1991): "Psychologists disclose confidential information only as required by law, or where permitted by law, for a valid purpose such as: (1) to provide needed professional services to the patient or client, (2) to obtain appropriate professional consultations, (3) to protect the patient or client or others from harm, or (4) to obtain payment for services."

Ethical issues are raised by all these exceptions to the general rule of confidentiality. Wise (1978) surveyed therapists in California after legislation was passed requiring them to notify the authorities if their clients seemed to pose a danger to society. This led 20% of therapists to stop asking their clients about violence. This has the potential disadvantage that it might reduce therapeutic effectiveness.

Most clients initially expect that everything they disclose in therapy will remain confidential. Clients should be told before the outset of treatment that confidentiality does not extend to everything they might say. In addition, the kinds of information that therapists would have to disclose to others should be made clear.

## Choice of therapeutic goals

It is desirable that the client should set the goals for therapy. At the very least, he/she should be fully involved in selecting suitable goals. Alexander and Luborsky (1984) advocated a therapeutic alliance (discussed earlier), in which the therapist and the client co-operate in determining the goals of therapy and the ways of achieving them.

In practice, the client is sometimes not fully involved in setting therapeutic goals. For example, young children or severely disturbed patients such as schizophrenics cannot participate fully in the decision-making process. In such cases, a close relative should be consulted to ensure that the treatment goals are in the best interests of the client.

The dangers associated with certain therapeutic goals need to be spelled out clearly to patients. For example, psychodynamic therapy provides patients with insight into the childhood experiences underlying their current distress. However, such insight may involve bringing to light very disturbing memories (e.g., of physical or sexual abuse). There are also dangers if the retrieved memories are false (false memory syndrome). If the memories are false, then the parents of clients may be unjustly accused of having abused their children. Clients need to be aware of these potential dangers before accepting insight as a primary goal of therapy.

There are special problems in the case of therapy for couples or families. A form of therapy that benefits one individual may have negative effects on their partner or other family members. For example, an individual may benefit from becoming more assertive, but this may disrupt the communication patterns within the family.

Clients may be more influenced than they realise by the values and beliefs of their therapist. According to Halleck (1971, p. 19), "A model of psychiatric practice based on the contention that people should just be helped to learn to do the things they want to do seems uncomplicated and desirable. But it is an unobtainable model ... a psychiatrist cannot avoid communicating and at times imposing his own values upon his patients. The patient ... ends up wanting some of the things the psychiatrist thinks he should want."

## Dual relationships

Pope and Vetter (1992) asked therapists to identify ethical and other challenging issues they had had to deal with recently. Of the issues raised, 18% related to confidentiality, 17% to dual relationships, and 14% to payment. We will focus on dual relationships,

*To what extent can the different types of therapy be accused of encouraging conformity?*

i.e., the need for therapists not to have a personal relationship as well as a professional relationship with clients.

The most damaging form of personal relationship involves sexual intimacy. It is far more common between male therapists and female clients than between female therapists and male clients. It is totally unacceptable, because clients can be exploited by therapists with more status than they have. Sexual contact between therapist and client is explicitly forbidden by nearly all professional therapy organisations. The 1993 Ethical Standards of Psychologists strongly recommend that therapist should avoid a personal or sexual relationship with former clients. At the very least, they should not consider becoming romantically involved with any former client until at least 2 years after the end of treatment.

## Cultural and subcultural factors

Most therapists in Western societies are white and middle class. As a result, white, middle-class clients may benefit most from therapy. Sue, Fujino, Hu, Takeuchi, and Zane (1991) argued that therapy may be more effective when there is ethnic and language matching, i.e., the therapist and the client are from the same ethnic background and have the same native language.

The type of treatment given can be affected by clients' cultural background. Bond, DiCandia, and MacKinnon (1988) compared white and black American schizophrenic patients with similar symptoms. The white patients were less likely to be physically restrained. They were also less likely to receive high drug doses. There are various possible explanations of these findings, but they clearly raise ethical issues about the treatment of ethnic minorities.

## Sue et al.: Cultural responsiveness

Sue et al. (1991) examined community mental health services among black, Mexican, Asian, and white outpatient clinics in the United States. Using information obtained from client records they found that ethnic matching of therapist and client led to Asian Americans and Mexican Americans having lower dropout rates. However, there were no effects of ethnic matching for African Americans.

Sue et al. (1991) also found that language matching was associated with better treatment outcome for all non-English native speakers. This was presumably because communication is easier between people having the same native language. Sue et al. argued that treatment is most likely to be effective when therapists are sensitive to their clients' values and expectations. Some relevant considerations they identified were summarised by Davison and Neale (1998, p. 589):

> Asians respect structure and formality in interpersonal relationships, whereas a Western therapist is likely to favour informality and a less authoritarian attitude ... the acceptability of psychotherapy as a way to handle stress is likely to be much lower among Asian-Americans, who tend to see emotional distress as something to be handled on one's own ... Asian-Americans may consider some areas off-limits for discussion with a therapist, ... especially sex.

### Discussion points

1. How important is it for therapists to be sensitive to cultural differences?
2. Is ethnic matching needed in order that all clients have the best chance of benefiting from therapy?

### KEY STUDY EVALUATION—Sue et al.

The abilities of therapists to empathise in a non-judgemental fashion and to offer unconditional support to their clients would appear to be compromised by a significant difference in cultural background between client and therapist. Sue et al.'s research demonstrates that this is likely to be attributable to the predominance of white, middle-class therapists. The class element would appear to be more significant, as racial origin is not in itself a determinant of cultural values.

It seems obvious that for any therapist to be effective they must have the ability to communicate well with their client. This involves much more than the ability to converse in the same language. They must also have a thorough knowledge and understanding of their client's world-view, which includes an understanding of their cultural and class background.

One possible alternative to role preparation might be a provision for therapists to be counselled themselves by people from a variety of social and cultural backgrounds. As counselling is an important part of training in psychotherapy, this would be a good opportunity to develop the experience of new therapists, whatever their cultural background.

*Can you think of any other cultural or subcultural groups who may suffer from bias during the course of therapy?*

Sue et al. found that therapy sessions such as this might have greater effect if the therapist and client were from the same ethnic background.

Evidence of cultural bias was reported by Nazroo (1997), in a study based on over 8000 Caribbeans, Asians, and whites in the United Kingdom. The rate of psychoses such as schizophrenia among Caribbean men was no greater than among white men. However, they were *five* times as likely to be hospitalised. According to Nazroo, Caribbean men are assumed to be at higher risk of severe mental illness, and so are denied non-hospital options such as therapy.

Grant (1994) argued that special ethical issues are raised when white therapists treat black clients. The therapists may mistakenly believe there are "black problems", or that they understand how black people think. In either case, they may not respond to the particular problems and ways of thinking of the individual black patients.

How can we ensure that no group is disadvantaged? First, therapists must be sensitive to cultural issues, and must develop the skills to provide effective treatment of all ethnic groups. Second, the number of therapists from various minority ethnic groups should be increased. Third, there is **role preparation**, using brief discussions or audiotaped information to ensure that clients have realistic expectations about therapy before it starts. Lambert and Lambert (1984) found that role preparation improved attendance at therapy sessions. It also led to increased satisfaction with therapy, and to more favourable outcomes.

# SUMMARY

*Somatic therapy*

Major depressive disorder is often treated by drugs such as the tricyclics or SSRIs. In very severe cases, electroconvulsive therapy is used. Electroconvulsive therapy generally works rapidly, but we do not know *why* it is effective. Lithium is the drug most commonly used in the treatment of bipolar disorder. It benefits about 80% of patients. Benzodiazepines are often used to treat anxiety disorders. However, these drugs have various side effects, and there can be physical dependence. Neuroleptic drugs are used to treat schizophrenia; they are more effective at reducing the positive symptoms than the negative ones.

Atypical drugs are useful in treating schizophrenia, especially negative symptoms. Drug therapy is generally effective, but there are real dangers of relapse.

According to Freud, mental disorders develop when adults experience severe personal problems, and regress to an earlier psychosexual stage. Psychoanalysis aims to provide the individual with insight into repressed thoughts and feelings. Hypnosis, free association, and dream analysis have all been used to uncover repressed ideas. Transference of strong emotional feelings about the patient's parents onto the therapist ensures the patient's emotional involvement in therapy. Psychoanalysis has influenced object relations therapy and cognitive therapy. It may be that recovery is needed to produce insight rather than vice versa.

*Psychodynamic therapy*

Behaviour therapists assume that abnormal behaviour develops through maladaptive conditioning, and that conditioning can change unwanted behaviour into more desirable patterns. Exposure therapy is very effective in the treatment of all types of phobia, including social phobia and agoraphobia. However, its success may not be due simply to habituation of the fear response. Token economies are moderately effective in well-controlled environments, but the effects often fail to carry over into everyday life.

*Behaviour therapy*

Rogers developed client-centred therapy, arguing that therapist empathy, unconditional positive regard, and genuineness are all crucial to therapeutic success. All three therapist characteristics are important, especially empathy and unconditional positive regard. Client-centred therapy is effective with less severe disorders, but is of little use with more severe disorders. Rogers's refusal to accept the value of diagnosing mental disorders was ill-advised, and limits the value of client-centred therapy.

*Client-centred therapy*

Ellis developed rational-emotive therapy as a way of replacing irrational and self-defeating thoughts with rational and positive ones. The general procedures advocated by Ellis are not precisely tailored for specific disorders. According to Beck, anxious and depressed patients have unduly negative and threatening cognitions. These cognitions are maintained by safety-seeking behaviours. Cognitive therapy and cognitive-behaviour therapy involve disconfirming these cognitions by providing contrary evidence. Such disconfirmations account for the effectiveness of exposure therapy.

*Cognitive therapy and cognitive-behaviour therapy*

There are three successive phases of improvement during therapy: enhanced subjective well-being, reduction of pathological symptoms, and enhanced life function. Therapy effective in producing recovery may or may not prevent relapse. Efficacy studies have good internal validity but low external validity, whereas the opposite is the case with effectiveness studies. Most meta-analyses have reported that all the major forms of therapy are of roughly equal effectiveness. Therapeutic success depends on specific factors unique to that therapy plus common factors (e.g., the therapeutic alliance, therapist positivity and negativity, therapist's willingness to help clients). Cognitive-behaviour therapy (especially exposure therapy) is very effective in treating the anxiety disorders, whereas drug therapy is most effective for schizophrenia and bipolar disorder. There have been strong moves towards eclecticism.

*Effectiveness of therapy*

There are strong arguments in favour of informed consent, but many clients (e.g., young children, schizophrenics) cannot provide it. Patients posing a danger to society may receive compulsory treatment against their will. Confidentiality is desirable, but therapists must sometimes disclose information (e.g., to protect the client or other people from harm). The client should be fully involved in setting therapeutic goals, but they may be unduly influenced by the therapist's values and beliefs. Therapists must not have a personal as well as a professional relationship with their clients. Therapy is most effective when the therapist and client have the same ethnic background and native language. Therapists need to be sensitive to cultural issues, and should consider using role preparation.

*Ethical issues in therapy*

## FURTHER READING

- Comer, R.J. (2001). *Abnormal psychology* (4th ed.) New York: Worth. Issues relating to the effectiveness of the major forms of therapy are discussed in some detail in this textbook.
- MacLeod, A. (1998). Therapeutic interventions. In M.W. Eysenck (Ed.), *Psychology: An integrated approach*. Harlow, UK: Addison Wesley Longman. This chapter provides good introductory coverage of the main forms of therapy by a Scottish clinical psychologist.
- Shadish, W.R., Matt, G.E., Navarro, A.M., & Phillips, G. (2000). The effects of psychological therapies under clinically representative conditions: A meta-analysis. *Psychological Bulletin, 126*, 512–529. This article provides convincing evidence that all of the main forms of therapy are reasonably effective when carried out in the typical way.

# References

Aberson, C.L., Healy, M., & Romero, V. (2000). Ingroup bias and self-esteem: A meta-analysis. *Personality and Social Psychology Review, 4,* 157–173.

Abramov, I., & Gordon, J. (1994). Colour appearance: On seeing red, or yellow, or green, or blue. *Annual Review of Psychology, 45,* 451–485.

Abrams, D., & Hogg, M.A. (1988). Comments on the motivational status of self-esteem in social identity and intergroup discrimination. *European Journal of Social Psychology, 18,* 317–334.

Abrams, D., Wetherell, M., Cochrane, S., Hogg, M.A., & Turner, J.C. (1990). Knowing what to think by knowing who you are: Self-categorization and the nature of norm formation, conformity and group polarization. *British Journal of Social Psychology, 29,* 97–119.

Abramson, L.Y., Alloy, L.B., Hogan, M.E., Whitehouse, W.G., Donovan, P., Rose, D.T., Panzarella, C., & Raniere, D. (1999). Cognitive vulnerability to depression: Theory and evidence. *Journal of Cognitive Psychotherapy, 13,* 5–20.

Abramson, L.Y., Metalsky, G.I., & Alloy, L.B. (1989). Hopelessness depression: A theory-based subtype of depression. *Psychological Review, 96,* 358–372.

Abramson, L.Y., Seligman, M.E., & Teasdale, J. (1978). Learned helplessness in humans: Critique and reformulation. *Journal of Abnormal Psychology, 87,* 49–74.

Ackerman, P.L., Beier, M.E., & Boyle, M.O. (2002). Individual differences in working memory within a nomological network of cognitive and perceptual speed abilities. *Journal of Experimental Psychology: General, 131,* 567–589.

Adams, J.S. (1965). Inequity in social exchange. In L. Berkowitz (Ed.), *Advances in experimental social psychology.* New York: Academic Press.

Adolph, K.E. (2000). Specificity of learning: Why infants fall over a veritable cliff. *Psychological Science, 11,* 290–295.

Adorno, T.W., Frenkel-Brunswik, E., Levinson, D., & Sanford, R. (1950). *The authoritarian personality.* New York: Harper.

Aeschbach, D., Matthews, J.R., Postolache, T.T., Jackson, M.A., Giesen, H.A., & Wehr, T.A. (1997). Dynamics of the human EEG during prolonged wakefulness: Evidence for frequency–specific circadian and homeostatic influences. *Neuroscience Letters, 239,* 121–124.

Aggleton, J.P., & Brown, M.W. (1999). Episodic memory, amnesia, and the hippocampal-anterior thalamic axis. *Behavioral And Brain Sciences, 22,* 425–444; discussion 444–489.

Aglioti, S., Goodale, M.A., & DeSouza, J.F.X. (1995). Size-contrast illusions deceive the eye but not the hand. *Current Biology, 5,* 679–685.

Ahlskog, J.E., Randall, P.K., & Hoebel, B.G. (1975). Hypothalamic hyperphagia: Dissociation from hyperphagia following destruction of noradrenergic neurons. *Science, 190,* 399–401.

Aiello, J.R., & Kolb, K.J. (1995). Electronic performance monitoring and social context: Impact on productivity and stress. *Journal of Applied Psychology, 80,* 339–353.

Ainsworth, M.D.S. (1979). Attachment as related to mother–infant interaction. In J.G. Rosenblatt, R.A. Hinde, C. Beer, & M. Busnel (Eds.), *Advances in the study of behaviour, Vol. 9.* Orlando, FL: Academic Press.

Ainsworth, M.D.S. (1982). Infant–mother attachment. *American Psychologist, 34,* 932–937.

Ainsworth, M.D.S., & Bell, S.M. (1970). Attachment, exploration and separation: Illustrated by the behaviour of one-year-olds in a strange situation. *Child Development, 41,* 49–67.

Ainsworth, M.D.S., Bell, S.M., & Stayton, D.J. (1971). Individual differences in strange situation behaviour of one-year-olds.

In H.R. Schaffer (Ed.), *The origins of human social relations.* London: Academic Press.

Ainsworth, M.D.S., Blehar, M.C., Waters, E., & Wall, S. (1978). *Patterns of attachment: A psychological study of the strange situation.* Hillsdale, NJ: Lawrence Erlbaum Associates Inc.

Ajzen, I. (1985). From intentions to actions: A theory of planned behaviour. In J. Kuhl & J. Beckmann (Eds.), *Action-control: From cognition to behaviour.* Heidelberg, Germany: Springer-Verlag.

Ajzen, I. (1987). Attitudes, traits, and actions: Dispositional prediction of behavior in personality and social psychology. *Advances in Experimental Social Psychology, 20,* 1–63.

Ajzen, I. (1991). The theory of planned behaviour. *Organizational Behavior and Human Decision Processes, 50,* 179–211.

Akerstedt, T. (1977). Inversion of the sleep wakefulness pattern: Effects on circadian variations in psychophysiological activation. *Ergonomics, 20,* 459–474.

Alderfer, C.P. (1969). An empirical test of a new theory of human needs. *Organizational Behavior and Human Performance, 4,* 142–175.

Alexander, L., & Luborsky, L. (1984). Research on the helping alliance. In L. Greenberg & S. Pinsof (Eds.), *The psychotherapeutic process: A research handbook.* New York: Guilford Press.

Alibali, M.W. (1999). How children change their minds: Strategy change can be gradual or abrupt. *Developmental Psychology, 35,* 127–145.

Allen, B.P., & Lindsay, D.S. (1998). Amalgamations of memories: Intrusion of information from one event into reports of another. *Applied Cognitive Psychology, 12,* 277–285.

Allen, J.J.B., & Iacono, W.G. (2001). Assessing the validity of amnesia in dissociative identity disorder: A dilemma for the DSM and the courts. *Psychology, Public Policy, and Law, 7,* 311–344.

Allen, V.L., & Levine, J.M. (1971). Social support and conformity: The role of independent assessment of reality. *Journal of Experimental Social Psychology, 7,* 48–58.

Allison, T., & Cicchetti, D.V. (1976). Sleep in mammals: Ecological and constitutional correlates. *Science, 194,* 732–734.

Allport, D.A. (1989). Visual attention. In M.I. Posner (Ed.), *Foundations of cognitive science.* Cambridge, MA: MIT Press.

Allport, D.A., Antonis, B., & Reynolds, P. (1972). On the division of attention: A disproof of the single channel hypothesis. *Quarterly Journal of Experimental Psychology, 24,* 225–235.

Allport, G.W. (1935). Attitudes. In C.M. Murchison (Ed.), *Handbook of social psychology.* Worcester, MA: Clark University Press.

Allport, G.W. (1954). *The nature of prejudice.* Reading, MA: Addison-Wesley.

Allport, G.W., & Odbert, H.S. (1936).Trait-names: A psycho-lexical study. *Psychological Monographs, 47,* No. 211.

Allport, G.W., & Postman, L. (1947). *The psychology of rumour.* New York: Holt, Rinehart, & Winston.

Al-Rashid, R.A. (1971). Hypothalamic syndrome in acute childhood leukemia. *Clinical Pediatrics, 10,* 53–54.

Altamura, C., VanGastel, A., Pioli, R., Mannu, P., & Maes, M. (1999). Seasonal and circadian rhythms in suicide in Cagliari, Italy. *Journal of Affective Disorders, 53,* 77–85.

Altemeyer, B. (1988). *Enemies of freedom: Understanding right-wing authoritarianism.* San Francisco: Jossey-Bass.

Altenberg, B. (1990). Speech as linear composition. In G. Caie, K. Haastrup, A.L. Jakobsen, J.E. Nielsen, J. Sevaldsen, H. Sprecht, & A. Zetterstein (Eds.), *Proceedings from the fourth Nordic conference for English Studies.* Copenhagen, Denmark: Copenhagen University Press.

Altman, I., & Taylor, D.A. (1973). *Social penetration theory: The development of interpersonal relationships*. New York: Holt, Rinehart, & Winston.

Amelang, M., & Schmidt-Rathjens, C. (1992). Psychometric properties of modified Grossarth-Maticek and Eysenck Inventories. *Psychological Reports, 71*, 1251–1263.

Amelang, M., Schmidt-Rathjens, C., & Matthews, G. (1996). Personality, cancer and coronary heart disease: Further evidence on a controversial issue. *British Journal of Health Psychology, 1*, 191–205.

American Psychiatric Association. (1994). *Diagnostic and statistical manual of mental disorders* (4th ed.). Washington, DC: Author.

American Psychiatric Association. (2000). *DSM–IV text revision*. Washington, DC: Author.

American Psychological Association. (1991).Draft of APA ethics code. *APA Monitor, 22*, 30–35.

Ames, G.J., & Murray, F.B. (1982). When two wrongs make a right: Promoting cognitive change by social conflict. *Developmental Psychology, 18*, 894–897.

Amir, Y., & Sharon, I. (1987). Are social-psychological laws cross-culturally valid? *Journal of Cross-Cultural Psychology, 18*, 383–470.

Anand, B.K., & Brobeck, J.R. (1951). Hypothalamic control of food intake in rats and cats. *Yale Journal of Biological Medicine, 24*, 123–140.

Anandaram, T.S.J. (2001). Face your phobia. *The Hindu*, 2 September. www.hinduonnet.com/thehindu/

Andersen, S.M., & Miranda, R. (2000). Transference: How past relationships emerge in the present. *The Psychologist, 13*, 608–609.

Anderson, C.A. (1989). Temperature and aggression: Ubiquitous effects of heat on occurrence of human violence. *Psychological Bulletin, 106*, 74–96.

Anderson, C.A., & Anderson, K.B. (1996). Violent crime rate studies in philosophical context: A destructive testing approach to heat and southern culture of violence effects. *Journal of Personality and Social Psychology, 70*, 740–756.

Anderson, C.A., Anderson, K.B., & Deuser, W.E. (1996). A general framework for the study of affective aggression: Effects of weapons and extreme temperatures on accessibility of aggressive thoughts, affect, and attitudes. *Personality and Social Psychology Bulletin, 22*, 366–376.

Anderson, C.A., & Bushman, B.J. (2001). Effects of violent video games on aggressive behavior, aggressive cognition, aggressive affect, physiological arousal, and prosocial behavior: A meta-analytic review of the scientific literature. *Psychological Science, 12*, 353–359.

Anderson, C.A., & Bushman, B.J. (2002). Human aggression. *Annual Review of Psychology, 53*, 27–51.

Anderson, D.R., Huston, A.C., Schmitt, K.L., Linebarger, D.L., & Wright, J.C. (2001). Early childhood television viewing and adolescent behaviour: The recontact study. *Monographs of the Society for Research in Child Development, 66*, vii–147.

Anderson, J.L., Crawford, C.B., Nadeau, J., & Lindberg, T. (1992). Was the Duchess of Windsor right? A cross-cultural review of the socioecology of ideals of female body shape. *Ethology and Sociobiology, 13*, 197–227.

Anderson, J.R. (1983). *The architecture of cognition*. Harvard, MA: Harvard University Press.

Anderson, J.R. (1993). *Rules of the mind*. Hillsdale, NJ: Lawrence Erlbaum Associates Inc.

Anderson, J.R. (1996). ACT: A simple theory of complex cognition. *American Psychologist, 51*, 355–365.

Anderson, R.C., & Pichert, J.W. (1978). Recall of previously unrecallable information following a shift in perspective. *Journal of Verbal Learning and Verbal Behavior, 17*, 1–12.

Anderson, S.J., Holliday, I.E., Singh, K.D., & Harding, G.F.A. (1996). Localisation and functional analysis of human cortical area V5 using magneto-encephalography. *Proceedings of the Royal Society London, Series B, 263*, 423–431.

Andersson, B., Grant, R., & Larsson, S. (1956). Central control of heat loss mechanisms in the goat. *Acta Physiologica Scandinavica, 37*, 261–280.

Andrade, J. (Ed.). (2001). *Working memory in perspective*. Hove, UK: Psychology Press.

Andreasen, N.C., Ehrhardt, J.C., Swayze, V.W., Allinger, R.J., Yuh, W.T.C., Cohen, G., & Ziebell, S. (1990a). Magnetic resonance imaging of the brain in schizophrenia: The pathophysiologic significance of structural abnormalities. *Archives of General Psychiatry, 47*, 35–44.

Andreasen, N.C., Swayze, V.W., Flaum, M., Yates, W.R., Arndt, S., McChesney, C. (1990b). Ventricular enlargement in schizophrenia evaluated with computed tomographic scanning: Effects of gender, age, and stage of illness. *Archives of General Psychiatry, 47*, 1008–1015.

Andreeva, G. (1984). Cognitive processes in developing groups. In L.H. Strickland (Ed.), *Directions in Soviet social psychology*. New York: Springer.

Andrews, B., Brewin, C.R., Ochera, J., Morton, J., Bekerian, D.A., Davies, G.M., & Mollan, P. (1999). Characteristics, context and consequences of memory recovery among adults in therapy. *British Journal of Psychiatry, 175*, 141–146.

Andrisani, P.J., & Nestel, G. (1976). Internal–external control as a contributor to, and outcome of, work experience. *Journal of Applied Psychology, 61*, 156–165.

Annett, M. (1999). Handedness and lexical skills in undergraduates. *Cortex, 35*, 357–372.

Archer, J. (2000). Sex differences in aggression between heterosexual partners: A meta-analytic review. *Psychological Bulletin, 126*, 651–680.

Archer, J. (2001). Evolutionary social psychology. In M. Hewstone & W. Stroebe (Eds.), *Introduction to social psychology* (3rd ed.). Oxford, UK: Blackwell.

Argyle, M. (1988). Social relationships. In M. Hewstone, W. Stroebe, J.-P. Codol, & G.M. Stephenson (Eds.), *Introduction to social psychology*. Oxford, UK: Blackwell.

Argyle, M., & Furnham, A. (1983). Sources of satisfaction and conflict in long-term relationships. *Journal of Marriage and the Family, 45*, 481–493.

Argyle, M., & Henderson, M. (1984). The rules of friendship. *Journal of Social and Personal Relationships, 1*, 211–237.

Argyle, M., Henderson, M., Bond, M., Iizuka, Y., & Contarello, A. (1986). Cross-cultural variations in relationship rules. *International Journal of Psychology, 21*, 287–315.

Argyle, M., Henderson, M., & Furnham, A. (1985). The rules of social relationships. *British Journal of Social Psychology, 24*, 125–139.

Arias, I., & Johnson, P. (1989). Evaluations of physical aggression among intimate dyads. *Journal of Interpersonal Violence, 4*, 298–307.

Arkes, H.R., & Ayton, P. (1999). The sunk cost and Concorde effects: Are humans less rational than lower animals? *Psychological Bulletin, 125*, 591–600.

Armitage, C.J., & Conner, M. (2001). Efficacy of the theory of planned behaviour: A meta-analytic review. *British Journal of Social Psychology, 40*, 471–499.

Arnkoff, D.B., & Glass, C.R. (1982). Clinical cognitive constructs: Examination, evaluation, elaboration. In P.C.Kendall (Ed.), *Advances in cognitive–behavioural research and therapy, Vol. 1*. New York: Academic Press.

Arnold, J., Cooper, C.L., & Robertson, I.T. (1995). *Work psychology: Understanding human behaviour in the workplace* (2nd ed.). London: Pitman Publishing.

Aron, A., & Westbay, L. (1996). Dimensions of the prototype of love. *Journal of Personality and Social Psychology, 70*, 535–551.

Aronoff, J. (1967). *Psychological needs and cultural systems: A case study*. Princeton, NJ: Van Nostrand.

Aronson, E., & Mettee, D.R. (1968). Dishonest behaviour as a function of differential levels of induced self-esteem. *Journal of Personality and Soical Psychology, 9*, 121–127.

Aronson, E., & Osherow, N. (1980). Co-operation, prosocial behaviour, and academic performance: Experiments in the desegregated classroom. In L. Bickerman (Ed.), *Applied social psychology annual*. Beverly Hills, CA: Sage.

Arrindell, W.A., Kwee, M.G., Methorst, G.J., van der Ende, J., Pol, E., & Moritz, B.J. (1989). Perceived parental rearing styles of agoraphobic and socially phobic in-patients. *British Journal of Psychiatry, 155*, 526–535.

Arterberry, M., Yonas, A., & Bensen, A.S. (1989). Self-produced locomotion and the development of responsiveness to linear perspective and texture gradients. *Developmental Psychology, 25*, 976–982.

Asch, S.E. (1946). Forming impressions of personality. *Journal of Abnormal and Social Psychology, 41*, 258–290.

Asch, S.E. (1951). Effects of group pressure on the modification and distortion of judgements. In H. Guetzkow (Ed.), *Groups, leadership and men*. Pittsburgh, PA: Carnegie.

Asch, S.E. (1956). Studies of independence and conformity: A minority of one against a unanimous majority. *Psychological Monographs, 70* (Whole No. 416).

Aserinsky, E., & Kleitman, N. (1953). Regularly occurring periods of eye motility and concurrent phenomena during sleep. *Science, 118*, 273–274.

Ashton, H. (1997). Benzodiazepine dependency. In A. Baum, S. Newman, J. Weinman, R. West, & C. McManus (Eds.), *Cambridge handbook of psychology, health and medicine*. Cambridge, UK: Cambridge University Press.

Association for the Study of Dreams. (2001, July 15). Right-wingers have the scariest dreams. *Sunday Times*, p. 9.

Astington, J.W., & Jenkins, J.M. (1999). A longitudinal study of the relation between language and theory-of-mind development. *Developmental Psychology, 35*, 1311–1320.

Atkinson, J., & Braddick, O. (1981). *Acuity, contrast sensitivity, and accommodation in infancy*. New York: Academic Press.

Atkinson, R.C., & Shiffrin, R.M. (1968). Human memory: A proposed system and its control processes. In K.W. Spence & J.T. Spence (Eds.), *The psychology of learning and motivation, Vol. 2*. London: Academic Press.

Atkinson, R.L., Atkinson, R.C., Smith, E.E., & Bem, D.J. (1993). *Introduction to psychology* (11th ed.). New York: Harcourt Brace College Publishers.

Atkinson, R.L., Atkinson, R.C., Smith, E.E., Bem, D.J., & Nolen-Hoeksema, S. (1996). *Hilgard's introduction to psychology* (12th ed.). New York: Harcourt Brace.

Attridge, M., Berscheid, E., & Simpson, J.A. (1995). Predicting relationship stability from both partners versus one. *Journal of Personality and Social Psychology, 69*, 254–268.

Aubry, T., Tefft, B., & Kingsbury, N. (1990). Behavioural and psychological consequences of unemployment in blue-collar couples. *Journal of Community Psychology, 18*, 99–109.

Augoustinos, M., & Walker, I. (1995). *Social cognition: An integrated introduction*. London: Sage.

Avolio, B.J., Bass, B.M., & Jung, D.I. (1999). Re-examining the components of transformational and transactional leadership using the Multifactor Leadership Questionnaire. *Journal of Occupational and Organizational Psychology, 72*, 441–462.

Awad, A.G., & Voruganti, L.N. (1999). Quality of life and new antipsychotics in schizophrenia: Are patients better off? *International Journal of Social Psychiatry, 45*, 268–275.

Awh, E., & Pashler, H. (2000). Evidence for split attentional foci. *Journal of Experimental Psychology: Human Perception and Performance, 26*, 834–846

Axelrod, R. (1984). *The evolution of cooperation*. New York: Basic Books.

Axsom, D., & Cooper, J. (1985). Cognitive dissonance and psychotherapy: The role of effort justification in inducing weight loss. *Journal of Experimental Psychology, 53*, 30–40.

Ayllon, T., & Azrin, N.H. (1968). *The token economy: A motivational system for therapy and rehabilitation*. New York: Appleton-Century-Crofts.

Baars, B.J. (1997). Consciousness versus attention, perception, and working memory. *Consciousness and Cognition, 5*, 363–371.

Baars, B.J., & McGovern, K. (1996). Cognitive views of consciousness: What are the facts? How can we explain them? In M. Velmans (Ed.), *The science of consciousnessness: Psychological, neuropsychological, and clinical reviews*. London: Routledge.

Baars, B.J., Motley, M.T., & MacKay, D.G. (1975). Output editing for lexical status from artificially elicited slips of the tongue. *Journal of Verbal Learning and Verbal Behavior, 14*, 382–391.

Bachen, E., Cohen, S., & Marsland, A.L. (1997). Psychoimmunology. In A. Baum, S. Newman, J. Weinman, R. West, & C. McManus (Eds.), *Cambridge handbook of psychology, health, and medicine*. Cambridge, UK: Cambridge University Press.

Baddeley, A.D. (1982). Implications of neuropsychological evidence for theories of normal memory. *Philosophical Transactions of the Royal Society of London B: Biological Science, 25*, 298, 59–72.

Baddeley, A.D. (1986). *Working memory*. Oxford, UK: Oxford University Press.

Baddeley, A.D. (1990). *Human memory: Theory and practice*. Hove, UK: Psychology Press.

Baddeley, A.D. (1996). Exploring the central executive. *Quarterly Journal of Experimental Psychology, 49A*, 5–28.

Baddeley, A.D. (1997). *Human memory: Theory and practice* (Rev. ed.). Hove, UK: Psychology Press.

Baddeley, A.D., Gathercole, S., & Papagno, C. (1998). The phonological loop as a language learning device. *Psychological Review, 105*, 158–173.

Baddeley, A.D., & Hitch, G.J. (1974). Working memory. In G.H. Bower (Ed.), *The psychology of learning and motivation, Vol. 8*. London: Academic Press.

Baddeley, A.D., Thomson, N., & Buchanan, M. (1975). Word length and the structure of short-term memory. *Journal of Verbal Learning and Verbal Behavior, 14*, 575–589.

Baghdoyan, H.A., Spotts, J.L., & Snyder, S.G. (1993). Simultaneous pontine and basal forebrain microinjections of carbachol suppress REM sleep. *Journal of Neuroscience, 13*, 229–242.

Bagwell, C.L., Newcomb, A.F., & Bukowski, W.M. (1998). Preadolescent friendship and peer rejection as predictors of adult adjustment. *Child Development, 69*, 140–153.

Bailey, J.M., Dunne, M.P., & Martin, N.G. (2000). Genetic and environmental influences on sexual orientation and its correlates in an Australian twin sample. *Journal of Personality and Social Psychology, 78*, 524–536.

Bailey, J.M., & Pillard, R.C. (1991). A genetic study of male sexual orientation. *Archives of General Psychiatry, 48*, 1089–1096.

Bailey, J.M., Pillard, R.C., Neale, M.C., & Agyei, Y. (1993). Heritable factors influence sexual orientation in women. *Archives of General Psychiatry, 50*, 217–223.

Baillargeon, R. (1987). Object permanence in 31/2- and 4½-month-old infants. *Developmental Psychology, 23*, 655–664.

Baillargeon, R., & Graber, M. (1988). Evidence of location memory in 8-month-old infants in a nonsearch AB task. *Developmental Psychology, 24*, 502–511.

Bakeman, R., & Brownlee, J. (1980). The strategic use of parallel play: A sequential analysis. *Child Development, 51*, 873–878.

Bakermans-Kranenburg, M.J., van IJzendoorn, M.H., & Juffer, F. (2003). Less is more: Meta-analyses of sensitivity and attachment interventions in early childhood. *Psychological Bulletin, 129*, 195–215.

Balaz, M.A., Gutsin, P., Cacheiro, H., & Miller, R.R. (1982). Blocking as a retrieval failure: Reactivation of associations to a blocked stimulus. *Quarterly Journal of Experimental Psychology, 34B*, 99–113.

Bales, R.F. (1950). *Interaction process analysis: A method for the study of small groups*. Reading, MA: Addison-Wesley.

Bales, R.F., & Slater, P.E. (1955). Role differentiation in small decision-making groups. In T. Parsons & R.F. Bales (Eds.), *Family, socialisation and interaction process*. Glencoe, IL: Free Press.

Balota, D.A., Paul, S., & Spieler, D. (1999). Attentional control of lexical processing pathways during word recognition and reading. In S. Garrod & M.J. Pickering (Eds.), *Language processing*. Hove, UK: Psychology Press.

Baltesen, R. (2000). Maar het Baan-gevoel blijft. *FEM/DeWeek, 21*, 22–24.

Bandura, A. (1965). Influences of models' reinforcement contingencies on the acquisition of initiative responses. *Journal of Personality and Social Psychology, 1*, 589–593.

Bandura, A. (1973). *Aggression: A social learning analysis*. Englewood Cliffs, NJ: Prentice-Hall.

Bandura, A. (1977a). *Social learning theory*. Englewood Cliffs, NJ: Prentice-Hall.

Bandura, A. (1977b). Self-efficacy: Toward a unifying theory of behavioural change. *Psychological Review, 84*, 191–215.

Bandura, A. (1986). *Social foundations of thought and action: A social cognitive theory*. Englewood Cliffs, NJ: Prentice-Hall.

Bandura, A. (1999). Social cognitive theory of personality. In L.A. Pervin & O.P. John (Eds.), *Handbook of personality: Theory and research* (2nd ed.). New York: Guilford Press.

Bandura, A., & Rosenthal, T.L. (1966). Vicarious classical conditioning as a function of arousal level. *Journal of Personality and Social Psychology, 3*, 54–62.

Bandura, A., Ross, D., & Ross, S.A. (1963). Transmission of aggression through imitation of aggressive models. *Journal of Abnormal and Social Psychology, 66*, 3–11.

Banich, M.T. (1997). *Neuropsychology: The neural bases of mental function*. New York: Houghton Mifflin.

Banks, M.S., Aslin, R.N., & Letson, R.D. (1975). Sensitive periods for the development of human binocular vision. *Science, 190*, 675–677.

Banks, S.M., Salovey, P., Greener, S., Rothman, A.J., Moyer, A., Beuvais, J., & Epel, E. (1995). The effects of message framing on mammography utilisation. *Health Psychology, 14*, 178–184.

Barber, P. (2002). Critical analysis of psychological research: Rationale and design for a proposed course for the undergraduate psychology curriculum. *Psychology Learning and Teaching, 2*, 95–101.

Bard, P., & Mountcastle, V.B. (1948). Some forebrain mechanisms involved in the expression of rage with special reference to suppression of angry behaviour. *Association of Research into Nervous and Mental Disorders, 27*, 362–404.

Barglow, P., Vaughn, B.E., & Molitor, N. (1987). Effects of maternal employment on the quality of infant–mother attachment. *Child Development, 58*, 945–954.

Bar-Heim, Y., Sutton, B., Fox, N.A., & Marvin, R.S. (2000). Stability and change of attachment at 14, 24, and 58 months of age: Behaviour, representation, and life events. *Journal of Child Psychology and Psychiatry, 41*, 381–388.

Barkley, R.A., Ullman, D.G., Otto, L., & Brecht, J.M. (1977). The effects of sex typing and sex appropriateness of modelled behaviour on children's imitation. *Child Development, 48*, 721–725.

Barlow, D.H., Di Nardo, P.A., Vermilyea, B.B., Vermilyea, J.A., & Blanchard, E.B. (1986). Comorbidity and depression among the anxiety disorders: Issues in diagnosis and classification. *Journal of Nervous and Mental Disease, 174*, 63–72.

Barlow, D.H., & Durand, V.M. (1995). *Abnormal psychology: An integrative approach*. New York: Brooks/Cole.

Barlow, D.H., Gorman, J.M., Shear, M.K., & Woods, S.W. (2000). Cognitive-behavioral therapy, imipramine, or their combination for panic disorder: A randomized controlled trial. *Journal of the American Medical Association, 283*, 2529–2536.

Barnier, G. (1989). L'effet-tuteur dans des situations mettant en jeu des rapports spatiaux chez des enfants de 7–8 ans en interactions dyadiques avec des pairs de 6–7 ans. *European Journal of Psychology of Education, 4*, 385–399.

Baron, R.A. (1977). *Human aggression*. New York: Plenum.

Baron, R.A., & Bell, P.A. (1976). Aggression and heat: The influence of ambient temperature, negative affect, and a cooling drink on physical aggression. *Journal of Personality and Social Psychology, 33*, 245–255.

Baron, R.A., & Byrne, D. (1991). *Social psychology: Understanding human interaction* (6th ed.). Boston: Allyn & Bacon.

Baron, R.A., & Richardson, D.R. (1993). *Human aggression* (2nd ed.). New York: Plenum.

Baron, R.S. (1986). Distraction–conflict theory: Progress and problems. In L. Berkowitz (Ed.), *Advances in experimental social psychology* (Vol. 19). New York: Academic Press.

Baron, R.S., & Roper, G. (1976). Reaffirmation of social comparison views of choice shifts: Averaging and extremity effects in an autokinetic situation. *Journal of Personality and Social Psychology, 33*, 521–530.

Baron, R.S., VanDello, J., & Brunsman, B. (1996). The forgotten variable in conformity research: The impact of task importance on social influence. *Journal of Personality and Social Psychology, 71*, 915–927.

Baron-Cohen, S., Leslie, A.M., & Frith, U. (1985). Does the autistic child have a "theory of mind"? *Cognition, 21*, 37–46.

Barrett, J.E. (1979). The relationship of life events to the onset of neurotic disorders. In J.E. Barrett (Ed.), *Stress and mental disorder*. New York: Raven Press.

Barrett, P.T., & Kline, P. (1982). An item and radial parcel factor analysis of the 16PF questionnaire. *Personality and Individual Differences, 3*, 259–270.

Barrett, P.T., Petrides, K.V., Eysenck, S.B.G., & Eysenck, H.J. (1998). The Eysenck Personality Questionnaire: An examination of the factorial similarity of P, E, N, and L across 34 countries. *Personality and Individual Differences, 25*, 805–819.

Barrick, M.R., & Mount, M.K. (1991). The Big Five personality dimensions and job performance: A meta-analysis. *Personnel Psychology, 44*, 1–26.

Barron, G., & Yechiam, E. (2002). Private e-mail requests and the diffusion of responsibility. *Computers in Human Behaviour, 18*, 507–520; and *New Scientist* 20 July 2002, p. 9.

Barry, H., Bacon, M.K., & Child, I.L. (1957). A cross-cultural survey of some sex differences in socialisation. *Journal of Abnormal and Social Psychology, 55*, 327–332.

Barry, H., & Schlegel, A. (1984). Measurements of adolescent sexual behaviour in the standard sample of societies. *Ethnology, 23*, 315–329.

Bartlett, F.C. (1932). *Remembering: A study in experimental and social psychology*. Cambridge, UK: Cambridge University Press.

Basco, M.R., & Rush, A.J. (1996). *Cognitive-behavioral therapy for bipolar disorder*. New York: Guilford Press.

Bass, B.M. (1985). *Leadership and performance beyond expectations*. New York: Free Press.

Bates, E., Bretherton, I., & Snyder, L. (1988). *From first words to grammar: Individual differences and dissociable mechanisms*. Cambridge, UK: Cambridge University Press.

Bates, E., & Goodman, J.C. (1999). On the emergence of grammar from the lexicon. In B. MacWhinney (Ed.), *The emergence of language*. Mahwah, NJ: Lawrence Erlbaum Associates, Inc.

Bates, J.E., Maslin, C.A., & Frankel, K.A. (1985). Attachment security, mother–child interaction, and temperament as predictors of behaviour-problem ratings at age three years. In I. Bretherton & E. Waters (Eds.), *Growing points of attachment theory and research. Monographs of the Society for Research in Child Development, 50*.

Batson, C.D. (1987). Prosocial motivation: Is it ever truly altruistic? In L. Berkowitz (Ed.), *Advances in experimental social psychology, Vol. 20*. New York: Academic Press.

Batson, C.D. (1995). Prosocial motivation: Why do we help others? In A.Tesser (Ed.), *Advanced social psychology*. New York: McGraw-Hill.

Batson, C.D., Batson, J.G., Griffitt, C.A., Barrientos, S., Brandt, J.R., Sprengelmeyer, P., & Bayly, M.J. (1989). Negative-state relief and the empathy–altruism hypothesis. *Journal of Personality and Social Psychology, 56*, 922–933.

Batson, C.D., Cochrane, P.J., Biederman, M.F., Blosser, J.L., Ryan, M.J., & Vogt, B. (1978). Failure to help when in a hurry: Callousness or conflict? *Personality and Social Psychology Bulletin, 4*, 97–101.

Batson, C.D., Duncan, B.D., Ackerman, P., Buckley, T., & Birch, K. (1981). Is empathic emotion a source of altruistic motivation? *Journal of Personality and Social Psychology, 40*, 290–302.

Batson, C.D., Dyck, J.L., Brandt, J.R., Batson, J.G., Powell, A.L., McMaster, M.R., & Griffitt, C. (1988). Five studies testing new egotistic alternatives to the empathy–altruism hypothesis. *Journal of Personality and Social Psychology, 55*, 52–77.

Batson, C.D., O'Quinn, K., Fultz, J., Vanderplas, N., & Isen, A.M. (1983). Influence of self-reported distress and empathy on egoistic versus altruistic motivation to help. *Journal of Personality and Social Psychology, 45*, 706–718.

Battersby, W.S., Teuber, H.L., & Bender, M.B. (1953). Problem solving behaviour in men with frontal or occipital brain injuries. *Journal of Psychology, 35*, 329–351.

Bauer, P.J. (2002). Long-term recall memory: Behavioural and neuro-developmental changes in the first 2 years of life. *Current Directions in Psychological Science, 11*, 137–141.

Bauer, P.J., & Thal, D.J. (1990). Scripts or scraps: Reconsidering the development of sequential understanding. *Journal of Experimental Child Psychology, 50*, 287–304.

Bauer, R.M. & Verfaellie, M. (1988). Electrodermal recognition of familiar but not unfamiliar faces in prosopagnosia. *Brain and Cognition, 8*, 240–252.

Bauer, P.J., Wenner, J.A., Dropik, P.L., & Wewerka, S.S. (2000). Parameters of remembering and forgetting in the transition from infancy to early childhood. *Monographs of the Society for Research in Child Development, 65* (No. 263).

Baumeister, R.F. (1995). Self and identity: An introduction. In A. Tesser (Ed.), *Advances in social psychology*. New York: McGraw-Hill.

Baumeister, R.F. (1998). The self. In D.T. Gilbert, S.T. Fiske, & G. Lindzey (Eds.), *Handbook of social psychology, Vol. 1* (4th ed.). Boston: McGraw-Hill.

Baumeister, R.F. (2000). Gender differences in erotic plasticity: The female sex drive as socially flexible and responsive. *Psychological Bulletin, 126,* 347–374.

Baumeister, R.F., Smart, L., & Boden, J.M. (1996). Relation of threatened egotism to violence and aggression: The dark side of high self-esteem. *Psychological Review, 103,* 5–33.

Baumeister, R.F., & Sommer, K.L. (1997). What do men want? Gender differences and two spheres of belongingness: Comment on Cross and Madson (1997). *Psychological Bulletin, 122,* 38–44.

Baumrind, D. (1980). New directions in socialisation research. *American Psychologist, 35,* 639–652.

Baydar, N., & Brooks-Gunn, J. (1991). Effects of maternal employment and child-care arrangments on pre-schoolers' cognitive and behavioural outcomes. *Developmental Psychology, 27,* 932–945.

Baynes, K., & Gazzaniga, M. (2000). Consciousness, introspection, and the split-brain: The two minds/one body problem. In M.S. Gazzaniga (Ed.), *The new cognitive neurosciences.* Cambridge, MA: MIT Press.

Beach, C.M. (1990). The interpretation of prosodic patterns at points of syntactic structure ambiguity: Evidence for cue trading relations. *Journal of Memory and Language, 30,* 644–663.

Beales, S.A., & Parkin, A.J. (1984). Context and facial memory: The influence of different processing strategies. *Human Learning: Journal of Practical Research and Applications, 3,* 257–264.

Bean, G., Beiser, M., Zhang Wong, J., & Iacono, W. (1996). Negative labelling of individuals with first episode schizophrenia: The effects of premorbid functioning. *Schizophrenia Research, 22,* 111–118.

Beauducel, A., & Kersting, M. (2002). Fluid and crystallised intelligence and the Berlin Model of Intelligence Structure (BIS). *European Journal of Psychological Assessment, 18,* 97–112.

Beauvois, M.-F., & Dérouesné, J. (1979). Phonological alexia: Three dissociations. *Journal of Neurology, Neurosurgery and Psychiatry, 42,* 1115–1124.

Beauvois, M.-F., Dérouesné, J., & Bastard, V. (1980, June). *Auditory parallel to phonological alexia.* Paper presented at the third European conference of the International Neuropsychological Society, Chianciano, Italy.

Beck, A.T. (1967). *Depression: Clinical, experimental and theoretical aspects.* New York: Hoeber Medical Division, Harper & Row.

Beck, A.T. (1976). *Cognitive therapy of the emotional disorders.* New York: New American Library.

Beck, A.T., & Clark, D.A. (1988). Anxiety and depression: An information processing perspective. *Anxiety Research, 1,* 23–36.

Beck, A.T., Emery, G., & Greenberg, R. (1985). *Anxiety disorders and phobias: A cognitive perspective.* New York: Basic Books.

Beck, A.T., & Ward, C.H. (1961). Dreams of depressed patients: Characteristic themes in manifest content. *Archives of General Psychiatry, 5,* 462–467.

Beck, A.T., & Weishaar, M.E. (1989). Cognitive therapy. In R.J. Corsini & D. Wedding (Eds.), *Current psychotherapies.* Itacca, IL: Peacock.

Beck, I.L., & Carpenter, P.A. (1986). Cognitive approaches to understanding reading. *American Psychologist, 41,* 1088–1105.

Becker, J.M.T. (1977). A learning analysis of the development of peer-oriented behaviour in nine-month-old infants. *Developmental Psychology, 13,* 481–491.

Beckers, G., & Zeki, S. (1995). The consequences of inactivating areas V1 and V5 on visual motion perception. *Brain, 118,* 49–60.

Behrend, D.A., Harris, L.L., & Cartwright, K.B. (1992). Morphological cues to verb meaning: Verb inflections and the initial mapping of verb meanings. *Journal of Child Language, 22,* 89–106.

Behrmann, M., & Kimchi, R. (2003). What does visual agnosia tell us about perceptual organization and its relationship to object perception? *Journal of Experimental Psychology: Human Perception and Performance, 29,* 19–42.

Behrmann, M., Nelson, J., & Sekuler, E.B. (1998). Visual complexity in letter-by-letter reading: "Pure" alexia is not pure. *Neuropsychologia, 36,* 1115–1132.

Beidel, D.C., Turner, S.M., & Dancu, C.V. (1985). Physiological, cognitive and behavioural aspects of social anxiety. *Behaviour Research and Therapy, 23,* 109–117.

Bell, D. (2003, August 31). *BBCi news.* Retrieved from http://news.bbc.co.uk/go/pr/fr/-/1/hi/education/3195215.stm

Bell, V.A., & Johnson-Laird, P.N. (1998). A model theory of modal reasoning. *Cognitive Science, 22,* 25–51.

Belloc, N.B., & Breslow, L. (1972). Relationship of physical health status and health practices. *Preventative Medicine, 1,* 409.

Belmore, S.M. (1987). Determinants of attention during impression formation. *Journal of Experimental Psychology: Learning, Memory, and Cognition, 13,* 480–489.

Belsky, J. (1988). Infant day care and socio-emotional development: The United States. *Journal of Child Psychology and Psychiatry, 29,* 397–406.

Belsky, J., & Rovine, M. (1987). Temperament and attachment security in the Strange Situation: A rapprochement. *Child Development, 58,* 787–795.

Bem, D.J. (1972). Self-perception theory. *Advances in Experimental Social Psychology, 1,* 199–218.

Benenson, J.F., Apostolaris, N.H., & Parnass, J. (1997). Age and sex differences in dyadic and group interaction. *Developmental Psychology, 33,* 538–543.

Benenson, J.F., Morash, D., & Petrakos, H. (1998). Gender differences in emotional closeness between preschool children and their mothers. *Sex Roles, 38,* 975–985.

Benenson, J.F., Nicholson, C., Waite, A., Roy, R., & Simpson, A. (2001). The influence of group size on children's competitive behaviour. *Child Development, 72,* 921–928.

Benington, J.H., & Heller, H.C. (1995). Monoaminergic and cholinergic modulation of REM-sleep timing in rats. *Brain Research, 681,* 141–146.

Bentley, E. (2000). *Awareness: Biorhythms, sleep and dreaming.* London: Routledge.

Berenthal, B.I., Campos, J.J., & Barrett, K.C. (1984). Self-produced locomotion: An organiser of emotional, cognitive, and social development in infancy. In R.N. Emde & R.J. Harmon (Eds.), *Continuities and discontinuities in development.* New York: Plenum Press.

Bergeman, C.S., Plomin, R., McClearn, G.E., Pedersen, N.L., & Friberg, L.T. (1988). Genotype-environment interaction in personality development: Identical twins reared apart. *Psychology and Aging, 3,* 399–406.

Bergen, D.J., & Williams, J.E. (1991). Sex stereotypes in the United States revisited. *Sex Roles, 24,* 413–423.

Berger, R.J., & Phillips, N.H. (1995). Energy conservation and sleep. *Behavioural Brain Research, 69,* 65–73.

Berger, S.P., Hall, S., Mickalian, J.D., Reid, M.S., Crawford, C.A., Delucchi, K., Carr, K., & Hall, S. (1996). Haloperidol antagonism of cue-elicited cocaine craving. *The Lancet, 347,* 504–508.

Bergin, A.E. (1971). The evaluation of therapeutic outcomes. In A.E. Bergin & S.L. Garfield (Eds.), *Handbook of psychotherapy and behaviour change.* New York: Wiley.

Bergman, B.M., Rechtschaffen, A., Gilliland, M.A., and Quintans, J. (1996). Effect of extended sleep deprivation on tumor growth in rats. *American Journal of Physiology, 27,* 1460–1464.

Berk, L.E. (1994, November). Why children talk to themselves. *Scientific American,* 60–65.

Berko, J. (1958). The child's learning of English morphology. *Word, 14,* 150–177.

Berkowitz, L. (1968, September). Impulse, aggression and the gun. *Psychology Today,* pp. 18–22.

Berkowitz, L. (1974). Some determinants of impulsive aggression: The role of mediated associations with reinforcements of aggression. *Psychological Review, 81,* 165–176.

Berkowitz, L. (1989). Frustration–aggression hypothesis: Examination and reformulation. *Psychological Bulletin, 106,* 59–73.

Berkowitz, L., Cochran, S., & Embree, M. (1981). Physical pain and the goal of aversively stimulated aggression. *Journal of Personality and Social Psychology, 40,* 687–700.

Berkowitz, L., & Heimer, K. (1989). On the construction of the anger experience: Aversive events and negative priming in the formation of feelings. *Advances in Experimental Social Psychology, 22,* 1–37.

Berkowitz, L., & LePage, A. (1967). Weapons as aggression-eliciting stimuli. *Journal of Personality and Social Psychology, 7*, 202–207.

Berlin, B., & Kay, P. (1969). *Basic colour terms: Their universality and evolution.* Berkeley/Los Angeles: University of California Press.

Berlucchi, G., Maffei, L., Moruzzi, G., & Strata, P. (1964). EEG and behavioural effects elicited by cooling of medulla and pons. In A. Mosso, V. Adusso, & G. Moruzzi (Eds.), *Archives Italiennes de biologie, 102*, 373–392.

Bermond, B., Nieuwenhuyse, B., Fasotti, L., & Schwerman, J. (1991). Spinal cord lesions, peripheral feedback, and intensities of emotional feelings. *Cognition and Emotion, 5*, 201–220.

Berndt, R.S., Mitchum, C.C., & Haendiges, A.N. (1996). Comprehension of reversible sentences in "agrammatism": A meta-analysis. *Cognition, 58*, 289–308.

Berndt, T.J. (1989). Obtaining support from friends during childhood and adolescence. In D. Belle (Ed.), *Children's social networks and social supports.* New York: Wiley.

Berndt, T.J., Hawkins, J.A., & Jiao, Z. (1999). Influences of friends and friendships on adjustment to junior high school. *Merrill-Palmer Quarterly, 45*, 13–41.

Berndt, T.J., & Keefe, K. (1995). Friends' influence on adolescents' adjustment to school. *Child Development, 66*, 1312–1329.

Bernhardt, P.C. (1997). Influences of serotonin and testosterone in aggression and dominance: Convergence with social psychology. *Current Directions in Psychological Science, 6*, 44–48.

Bernstein, W.M., Stephan, W.G., & Davis, M.H. (1979). Explaining attributions for achievement: A path analytic approach. *Journal of Personality and Social Psychology, 37*, 1810–1821.

Berntsen, D. (1998). Voluntary and involuntary access to autobiographical memory. *Memory, 6*, 113–141.

Berrettini, W.H. (2000). Susceptibility loci for bipolar disorder: Overlap with inherited vulnerability to schizophrenia. *Biological Psychiatry, 47*, 245–251.

Berridge, K.C., Venier, I.L., & Robinson, T.E. (1989). Taste reactivity analysis of 6-hydroxydopamine-induced aphagia: Implications for arousal and anhedonia hypotheses of dopamine function. *Behavioral Neuroscience, 103*, 36–45.

Berrigan, L.P., & Garfield, S.L. (1981). Relationship of missed psychotherapy appointments to premature termination and social class. *British Journal of Clinical Psychology, 20*, 239–242.

Berry, D.T.R., & Webb, W.B. (1983). State measures and sleep stages. *Psychological Reports, 52*, 807–812.

Berry, J.W. (1969). On cross-cultural comparability. *International Journal of Psychology, 4*, 119–128.

Berry, J.W. (1974). Radical cultural relativism and the concept of intelligence. In J.W. Berry & P.R. Dasen (Eds.), *Culture and cognition: Readings in cross-cultural psychology.* London: Methuen.

Berscheid, E., & Reis, H.T. (1998). Attraction and close relationships. In D.T. Gilbert, S.T. Fiske, & G. Lindzey (Eds.), *The handbook of social psychology* (Vol. 2, 4th ed.). New York: McGraw-Hill.

Bertelsen, B., Harvald, B., & Hauge, M. (1977). A Danish twin study of manic-depressive disorders. *British Journal of Psychiatry, 130*, 330–351.

Bettencourt, B.A., Brewer, M.B., Croak, M.R., & Miller, N. (1992). Co-operation and the reduction of intergroup bias: The role of reward structure and social orientation. *Journal of Experimental Social Psychology, 28*, 301–309.

Bettencourt, B.A., Charlton, K., & Kernaham, C. (1997). Numerical representation of groups in co-operative settings: Social orientation effects on ingroup bias. *Journal of Experimental Social Psychology, 33*, 630–659.

Biassou, N., Obler, L.K., Nespoulous, J.-L., Dordain, M., & Haris, K.S. (1997). Dual processing of open- and closed-class words. *Brain and Language, 57*, 360–373.

Bickerton, D. (1984). The language bioprogram hypothesis. *Behavioural and Brain Sciences, 7*, 173–221.

Biederman, I. (1987). Recognition-by-components: A theory of human image understanding. *Psychological Review, 94*, 115–147.

Biederman, I. (1990). Higher-level vision. In D.N. Osherson, S. Kosslyn, & J. Hollerbach (Eds.), *An invitation to cognitive science: Visual cognition and action.* Cambridge, MA: MIT Press.

Biederman, I., Ju, G., & Clapper, J. (1985). *The perception of partial objects.* Unpublished manuscript, State University of New York at Buffalo.

Bierhoff, H.W. (1996). Prosocial behaviour. In M. Hewstone, W. Stroebe, & G. Stephenson (Eds.), *Introduction to social psychology* (2nd ed.). Oxford, UK: Blackwell.

Bierhoff, H.W. (1998). Prosocial behaviour. In D.T. Gilbert, S.T. Fiske, & G. Lindzey (Eds.), *The handbook of social psychology* (Vol. 2, 4th ed.). New York: McGraw-Hill.

Bierhoff, H.-W. (2001). Prosocial behaviour. In M. Hewstone & W. Stroebe (Eds.), *Introduction to social psychology* (3rd ed.). Oxford, UK: Blackwell.

Bierhoff, H.W., Klein, R., & Kramp, P. (1991). Evidence for the altruistic personality from data on accident research. *Journal of Personality, 59*, 263–280.

Billy, J.O.G., & Udry, J.R. (1985). Patterns of adolescent friendship and effects on sexual behaviour. *Social Psychology Quarterly, 48*, 27–41.

Binet, A., & Simon, T. (1905). Methodes nouvelles pour le diagnostic du niveau intellectual des anormaux. *L'Annee Psychologique, 11*, 191–244.

Birch, H.G. (1945). The relationship of previous experience to insightful problem solving. *Journal of Comparative Psychology, 38*, 267–283.

Bishop, D.V.M. (1997). *Uncommon understanding: Development and disorders of language comprehension in children.* Hove, UK: Psychology Press.

Bishop, E.G., Cherny, S.S., Corley, R., Plomin, R., DeFries, J.C., & Hewitt, J.K. (2003). Developmental genetic analysis of general cognitive ability from 1 to 12 years in a sample of adoptees, biological siblings, and twins. *Intelligence, 31*, 31–49.

Bisiach, E., & Geminiani, G. (1991). Anosognosia related to hemiplegia and hemianopia. In G.P. Prigatano & D.L. Schacter (Eds.), *Awareness of deficit after brain injury: Clinical and theoretical issues.* Oxford, UK: Oxford University Press.

Bjork, R.A., & Whitten, W.B. (1974). Recency-sensitive retrieval processes in long-term free recall. *Cognitive Psychology, 6*, 173–189.

Bjorkqvist, K., Lagerspetz, K.M.J., & Kaukiainen, A. (1992). Do girls manipulate and boys fight? Developmental trends regarding direct and indirect aggression. *Aggressive Behavior, 18*, 157–166.

Blades, M., & Banham, J. (1990). Children's memory in an environmental learning task. *Journal of Environmental Education and Information, 9*, 119–131.

Blake, M.J.F. (1967). Time of day effects on performance on a range of tasks. *Psychonomic Science, 9*, 349–350.

Blakemore, C., & Cooper, G.F. (1970). Development of the brain depends on the visual environment. *Nature, 228*, 477–478.

Blanchard, E.B. (1994). Behavioural medicine and health psychology. In A.E. Bergin & S.L. Garfield (Eds.), *Handbook of psychotherapy and behaviour change* (4th ed.). New York: Wiley.

Blandin, Y., & Proteau, L. (2000). On the cognitive basis of observational learning: Development of mechanisms for the detection and correction of errors. *Quarterly Journal of Experimental Psychology, 53A*, 846–867.

Blazer, D., Hughes, D.C., George, L.K. (1987). The epidemiology of depression in an elderly community population. *The Gerontologist, 27*, 281–287.

Blazer, D., Hughes, D.C., George, L.K., Swartz, M., & Boyer, R. (1991). Generalised anxiety disorder. In L.N. Robbins & D.A. Regier (Eds.), *Psychiatric disorders in America: The epidemiologic catchment area study.* New York: Maxwell Macmillan International.

Block, N. (1995a). How heritability misleads about race. *Cognition, 56*, 99–128.

Block, N. (1995b). On a confusion about a function of consciousness. *Behavioral and Brain Sciences, 18*, 227–287.

Bloj, M.G., Kersten, D., & Hurlbert, A.C. (1999). Perception of three-dimensional shape influences colour perception through mutual illumination. *Nature, 402*, 877–879.

Blumenthal, M., Kahn, R.L., Andrews, F.M., & Head, K.B. (1972). *Justifying violence: The attitudes of American men.* Ann Arbor, MI: Institute for Social Research.

Bodenhausen, G.V. (1988). Stereotypic biases in social decision making: Testing process models of stereotype use. *Journal of Personality and Social Psychology, 55*, 726–737.

Bodner, E., & Mikulincer, M. (1998). Learned helplessness and the occurrence of depressive-like and paranoid-like responses: The role of attentional focus. *Journal of Personality & Social Psychology, 74*, 1010–1023.

Bogdonoff, M.D., Klein, E.J., Shaw, D.M., & Back, K.W. (1961). The modifying effect of conforming behaviour upon lipid responses accompanying CNS arousal. *Clinical Research, 9*, 135.

Bogen, J.E. (1997). An example of access-consciousness without phenomenal consciousness? *Behavioral and Brain Sciences, 20*, 144.

Bohannon, J.N., & Warren-Leubecker, A. (1989). Theoretical approaches to language acquisition. In J.B. Gleason (Ed.), *The development of language*. Columbus, OH: Merrill.

Böhner, G. (2001). Attitudes. In M. Hewstone & W. Stroebe (Eds.), *Introduction to social psychology* (3rd ed.). Oxford, UK: Blackwell.

Boivin, D., Czeisler, C.A., Dijk, D.J., Duffy, J.F., Folkard, S., Minors, D., Totterdell, P., & Waterhouse, J. (1997). Complex interaction of the sleep–wake cycle and circadian phase modulates mood in healthy subjects. *Archives of General Psychiatry, 54*, 145–152.

Boland, J.E., & Blodgett, A. (2001). Understanding the constraints on syntactic generation: Lexical bias and discourse congruency effects on eye movements. *Journal of Memory and Language, 45*, 391–411.

Bolger, N., Foster, M., Vinokur, A.D., & Ng, R. (1996). Close relationships and adjustment to a life crisis: The case of breast cancer. *Journal of Personality and Social Psychology, 70*, 283–294.

Bolles, R.C. (1990). A functionalist approach to feeding. In E. Capaldi & T.L. Powley (Eds.), *Taste, experience and feeding*. Washington, DC: American Psychological Association.

Bonatti, L. (1994). Propositional reasoning by model? *Psychological Review, 101*, 725–733.

Bond, C.F., DiCandia, C.G., & MacKinnon, J.R. (1988). Responses to violence in a psychiatric setting: The role of the patient's race. *Personality and Social Psychology Bulletin, 14*, 448–458.

Bond, C.F., & Titus, L.J. (1983). Social facilitation: A meta-analysis of 241 studies. *Psychological Bulletin, 94*, 265–292.

Bond, R., & Smith, P.B. (1996). Culture and conformity: A meta-analysis of studies using Asch's line judgement task. *Psychological Bulletin, 119*, 111–137.

Bond, S., & Cash, T.F. (1992). Black beauty: Skin colour and body images among African-American college women. *Journal of Applied Social Psychology, 22*, 874–888.

Booth-Kewley, S., & Friedman, H.S. (1987). Psychological predictors of heart disease: A quantitative review. *Psychological Bulletin, 101*, 343–362.

Borkenau, P., Riemann, R., Angleitner, A., & Spinath, F.M. (2001). Genetic and environmental influences on observed personality: Evidence from the German Observational Study of Adult Twins. *Journal of Personality and Social Psychology, 80*, 655–668.

Bornstein, M.H., Toda, S., Azuma, H., Tamis-Lemonda, C., & Ogino, M. (1990). Mother and infant activity and interaction in Japan and in the United States: II. A comparative microanalysis of naturalistic exchanges focused on the organisation of infant attention. *International Journal of Behavioral Development, 13*, 289–308.

Bosma, H., Stansfeld, S.A., & Marmot, M.G. (1998). Job control, personal characteristics, and heart disease. *Journal of Occupational Health Psychology, 3*, 402–409.

Bossard, J. (1932). Residential propinquity as a factor in marriage selection. *American Journal of Sociology, 38*, 219–224.

Bouchard, T.J., Lykken, D.T., McGue, M., Segal, N.L., & Tellegen, A. (1990). Sources of human psychological differences: The Minnesota study of twins reared apart. *Science, 250*, 223–228.

Bouchard, T.J., & McGue, M. (1981). Familial studies of intelligence: A review. *Science, 212*, 1055–1059.

Boucher, J.D., & Carlson, G.E. (1980). Recognition of facial expression in three cultures. *Journal of Cross-Cultural Psychology, 11*, 263–280.

Bourke, P.A., Duncan, J., & Nimmo-Smith, I. (1996). A general factor involved in dual-task performance decrement. *Quarterly Journal of Experimental Psychology, 49A*, 525–545.

Bower, G.H., Black, J.B., & Turner, T.J. (1979). Scripts in memory for text. *Cognitive Psychology, 11*, 177–220.

Bower, T.G.R. (1979). *Human development*. San Francisco: W.H. Freeman.

Bower, T.G.R. (1982). *Development in infancy* (2nd ed.). San Francisco: W.H. Freeman.

Bowers, C.A., Weaver, J.L., & Morgan, B.B. (1996). Moderating the performance effects of stressors. In J.E. Driskell & E. Salas (Eds.), *Stress and human performance*. Mahwah, NJ: Lawrence Erlbaum Associates, Inc.

Bowers, K.S. (1983). *Hypnosis for the seriously curious*. New York: Norton.

Bowlby, J. (1946). *Forty-four juvenile thieves*. London: Bailliere, Tindall & Cox.

Bowlby, J. (1951). *Maternal care and mental health*. Geneva: World Health Organization.

Bowlby, J. (1953). *Child care and the growth of love*. Harmondsworth, UK: Penguin.

Bowlby, J. (1958). The nature of the child's tie to his mother. *International Journal of Psycho-Analysis, 39*, 350–373.

Bowlby, J. (1969). *Attachment and love: Vol. 1. Attachment*. London: Hogarth.

Bowlby, J. (1979). On knowing what you are not supposed to know and feeling what you are not supposed to feel. *Canadian Journal of Psychiatry, 24*, 403–408.

Bowlby, J. (1988). *A secure base: Clinical applications of attachment theory*. London: Routledge.

Bozarth, M.A., & Wise, R.A. (1985). Toxicity associated with long-term intravenous heroin and cocaine self-administration in the rat. *Journal of the American Medical Association, 254*, 81–83.

Brace, C.L. (1996). Review of *The Bell Curve*. *Current Anthropology, 37*, 5157–5161.

Bradbard, M.R., Martin, C.L., Endsley, R.C., & Halverson, C.F. (1986). Influence of sex stereotypes on children's exploration and memory: A competence versus performance distinction. *Developmental Psychology, 22*, 481–486.

Bradburn, T.N. (1969). *The structure of psychological well-being*. Chicago: Aldine.

Bradbury, T.N., & Fincham, F.D. (1990). Attributions in marriage: Review and critique. *Psychological Bulletin, 107*, 3–33.

Bradbury, T.N., & Fincham, F.D. (1992). Attributions and behavior in marital interaction. *Journal of Personality and Social Psychology, 63*, 613–628.

Braddick, O.J., & Atkinson, J. (1983). Some recent findings on the development of human binocularity: A review. *Behavioural Brain Research, 10*, 141–150.

Bradmetz, J. (1999). Precursors of formal thought: A longitudinal study. *British Journal of Developmental Psychology, 17*, 61–81.

Brain, R. (1976). *Friends and lovers*. New York: Basic Books.

Braine, M.D.S. (1978). On the relationship between the natural logic of reasoning and standard logic. *Psychological Review, 85*, 1–21.

Braine, M.D.S. (1994). Mental logic and how to discover it. In J. Macnamara & G.E. Reyes (Eds.), *The logical foundations of cognition*. Oxford: Oxford University Press.

Braine, M.D.S. (1998). Steps toward a mental predicate logic. In M.D.S. Braine & D.P. O'Brien (Eds.), *Mental logic*. Mahwah, NJ: Lawrence Erlbaum Associates Inc.

Braine, M.D.S., Reiser, B.J., & Rumain, B. (1984). Some empirical justification for a theory of natural propositional logic. In G.H. Bower (Ed.), *The psychology of learning and motivation, Vol. 18*. New York: Academic Press.

Brainerd, C.J. (1983). Modifiability of cognitive development. In S. Meadows (Ed.), *Developing thinking: Approaches to children's cognitive development*. London: Methuen.

Bramwell, D.I., & Hurlbert, A.C. (1996). Measurements of colour constancy by using a forced-choice matching technique. *Perception, 25*, 229–241.

Brandsma, J.M., Maultsby, M.C., & Welsh, R. (1978). Self-help techniques in the treatme t of alcoholism. Cited in G.T. Wilson

& K.D. O'Leary, *Principles of behaviour therapy*. Englewood Cliffs, NJ: Prentice-Hall.

Bransford, J.D. (1979). *Human cognition: Learning, understanding and remembering*. Belmont, CA: Wadsworth.

Bransford, J.D., Barclay, J.R., & Franks, J.J. (1972). Sentence memory: A constructive versus interpretive approach. *Cognitive Psychology, 3*, 193–209.

Bransford, J.D., Franks, J.J., Morris, C.D., & Stein, B.S. (1979). Some general constraints on learning and memory research. In L.S. Cermak & F.I.M.Craik (Eds.), *Levels of processing in human memory*. Hillsdale, NJ: Lawrence Erlbaum Associates, Inc.

Bransford, J.D., & Johnson, M.K. (1972). Contextual prerequisites for understanding: Some investigations of comprehension and recall. *Journal of Verbal Learning and Verbal Behavior, 11*, 717–726.

Braun, R., Balkin, T.J., Wesensten, N.J., Carson, R.E., Varga, M., Baldwin, P., Selbie, S., Belenky, M., & Hersovitch, P. (1997). Regional blood flow throughout the sleep–wake cycle: An $H_2$ $^{15}O$ PET study. *Brain, 120*, 1173–1197.

Bray, G.A. (1969). Effect of caloric restriction on energy expenditure in obese patients. *Lancet, ii*, 397.

Breland, K., & Breland, M. (1961). The misbehaviour of organisms. *American Psychologist, 61*, 681–684.

Bremer, J. (1959). *Asexualization: A follow-up study of 244 cases*. New York: Macmillan.

Bremner, J.D., Southwick, S.M., Johnson, D.R., & Yehuda, R., & Charney, D.S. (1993). Childhood physical abuse and combat-related posttraumatic stress disorder in Vietnam veterans. *American Journal of Psychiatry, 150*, 235–239.

Breslow, L., & Enstrom, J.E. (1980). Persistence of health habits and their relationship to mortality. *Preventative Medicine, 9*, 469–483.

Brewer, K.R., & Wann, D.L. (1998). Observational learning effectiveness as a function of model characteristics: Investigating the importance of social power. *Social Behavior and Personality, 26*, 1–10.

Brewer, M.B. (1968). Determinants of social distance among East African tribal groups. *Journal of Personality and Social Psychology, 10*, 279–289.

Brewer, M.B. (2001). The many faces of social identity: Implications for political psychology. *Political Psychology, 22*, 115–125.

Brewer, M.B., & Brown, R.J. (1998). Intergroup relations. In D.T. Gilbert, S.T. Fiske, & G. Lindzey (Eds), *The handbook of social psychology* (4th Ed.). Boston: McGraw-Hill.

Brewer, M.B., & Campbell, D.T. (1976). *Ethnocentrism and intergroup attitudes: East African evidence*. New York: Halstead Press.

Brewer, M.B., Dull, V., & Lui, L. (1981). Perceptions of the elderly: Stereotypes as prototypes. *Journal of Personality and Social Psychology, 41*, 656–670.

Brewer, M.B., & Miller, N. (1984). Beyond the contact hypothesis: Theoretical perspectives on desegregation. In N. Miller & M.B. Brewer (Eds.), *Groups in contact: The psychology of desegregation*. Orlando, FL: Academic Press.

Brewin, C.R. (1996). Theoretical foundations of cognitive-behaviour therapy for anxiety and depression. *Annual Review of Psychology, 47*, 33–57.

Brewin, C.R., & Power, M.J. (1999). Integrating psychological therapies: Processes of meaning transformation. *British Journal of Medical Psychology, 72*, 143–157.

Brickman, P., Rabinowitz, V.C., Karuza, J., Coates, D., Cohn, E., & Kidder, L. (1982). Models of helping and coping. *American Psychologist, 37*, 368–384.

Brigham, J.C. (1971). Ethnic stereotypes. *Psychological Bulletin, 76*, 15–38.

Brill, N.Q., & Christie, R.L. (1974). A theory of visual stability across saccadic eye movements. *Behavioral and Brain Sciences, 17*, 247–292.

Broadbent, D.E. (1958). *Perception and communication*. Oxford, UK: Pergamon.

Broadbent, D.E. (1982). Task combination and selective intake of information. *Acta Psychologica, 50*, 253–290.

Broder, A. (2000). Assessing the empirical validity of the "take-the-best" heuristic as a model of human probabilistic inference. *Journal of Experimental Psychology: Learning, Memory, and Cognition, 26*, 1332–1346.

Brody, G.H., & Shaffer, D.R. (1982). Contributions of parents and peers to children's moral socialisation. *Developmental Review, 2*, 31–75.

Bronfenbrenner, U. (1970). *Two worlds of childhood: US and USSR*. New York: Russell Sage Foundation.

Bronfenbrenner, U. (1979). *The ecology of human development: Experiments by nature and design*. Cambridge, MA: Cambridge University Press.

Brooks-Gunn, J., & Lewis, M. (1981). Infant social perception: Responses to pictures of parents and strangers. *Developmental Psychology, 17*, 647–649.

Broverman, I.K., Broverman, D.M., Clarkson, F.E., Rosencrantz, P.S., & Vogel, S.R. (1981). Sex role stereotypes and clinical judgements of mental health. In E. Howell & M. Bayes (Eds.), *Women and mental health*. New York: Basic Books.

Brown, G.W. (1989). Depression. In G.W. Brown & T.O. Harris (Eds.), *Life events and illness*. New York: Guilford Press.

Brown, G.W., & Birley, J.L.T. (1968). Crises and life changes and the onset of schizophrenia. *Journal of Health and Social Behavior, 9*, 203–214.

Brown, G.W., & Harris, T. (1978). *Social origins of depression*. London: Tavistock.

Brown, G.W., & Harris, T. (1982). Fall-off in the reporting of life events. *Social Psychiatry, 17*, 23.

Brown, J. (1991). Staying fit and staying well: Physical fitness as a moderator of life stress. *Journal of Personality and Social Psychology, 60*, 555–561.

Brown, N.R. (1995). Estimation strategies and the judgement of event frequency. *Journal of Experimental Psychology: Learning, Memory, & Cognition, 21*, 1539–1553.

Brown, R. (1973). *A first language: The early stages*. London: George Allen & Unwin.

Brown, R. (1978). Divided we fall: An analysis of relations between sections of a factory work-force. In H. Tajfel (Ed.), *Differentiation between social groups: Studies in the social psychology of intergroup relations*. London: Academic Press.

Brown, R. (1986). *Social psychology* (2nd ed.). New York: The Free Press.

Brown, R. (2000b). Social identity theory: Past achievements, current problems and future challenges. *European Journal of Social Psychology, 30*, 745–778.

Brown, R., & Kulik, J. (1977). Flashbulb memories. *Cognition, 5*, 73–99.

Brown, R., & McNeill, D. (1966). The "tip of the tongue" phenomenon. *Journal of Verbal Learning and Verbal Behavior, 5*, 325–337.

Brown, R.C., & Tedeschi, J.T. (1976). Determinants of perceived aggression. *Journal of Social Psychology, 100*, 77–87.

Brown, R.J. (2000a). *Group processes: Dynamics within and between groups* (2nd ed.). Oxford, UK: Blackwell.

Brown, R.J., Vivian, J., & Hewstone, M. (1999). Changing attitudes through intergroup contact: The effects of group membership salience. *European Journal of Social Psychology, 29*, 741–764.

Brownell, C.A., & Carriger, M.S. (1990). Changes in cooperation and self–other differentiation during the second year. *Child Development, 61*, 1164–1174.

Bruce, V. (1982). Changing faces: Visual and non-visual coding processes in face recognition. *British Journal of Psychology, 73*, 105–116.

Bruce, V., & Young, A.W. (1986). Understanding face recognition. *British Journal of Psychology, 77*, 305–327.

Bruch, H. (1971). Family transactions in eating disorders. *Comprehensive Psychiatry, 12*, 238–248.

Bruch, H. (1973). *Eating disorders: Obesity, anorexia and the person within*. New York: Basic Books.

Bruch, H. (1987). The changing picture of an illness: Anorexia nervosa. In D.P. Schwartz, J.L. Sacksteder, & Y. Akabane (Eds.), *Attachment and the therapeutic process: Essays in honour of Otto Allen Will Jr., M.D.* Madison, CT: International Universities Press.

Bruch, H. (1991). The sleeping beauty: Escape from change. In S.I. Greenspan & G.H. Pollock (Eds.), *The course of life: Vol. 4. Adolescence*. Madison, CT: International Universities Press.

Bruch, M.A., & Heimberg, R.G. (1994). Differences in perceptions of parental and personal between generalized and nongeneralized social phobics. *Journal of Anxiety Disorders, 8*, 155–168.

Bruck, M., & Ceci, S.J. (1999). The suggestibility of children's memory. *Annual Review of Psychology, 50*, 419–439.

Bruck, M., Ceci, S.J., & Hembrooke, H. (1997). Children's reports of pleasant and unpleasant events. In D. Read & S. Lindsay (Eds.), *Recollections of trauma: Scientific research and clinical practice*. New York: Plenum.

Bruno, N., & Cutting, J.E. (1988). Mini-modularity and the perception of layout. *Journal of Experimental Psychology: General, 117*, 161–170.

Bryant, P. (1998). Cognitive development. In M. Eysenck (Ed.), *Psychology: An integrated approach*. Harlow, UK: Addison Wesley Longman.

Bub, D., Cancelliere, A., & Kertesz, A. (1985). Whole-word and analytic translation of spelling to sound in a nonsemantic reader. In K.E. Patterson, J.C. Marshall, & M. Coltheart (Eds.), *Surface dyslexia: Neuropsychological and cognitive studies of phonological reading*. Hove, UK: Psychology Press.

Buehler, R., Griffin, D., & Ross, M. (1994). Exploring the "planning fallacy": Why people underestimate their task completion times. *Journal of Personality and Social Psychology, 67*, 366–381.

Bukowski, W.M., & Hoza, B. (1989). Popularity and friendship: Issues in theory, measurement, and outcome. In T. Berndt & G. Ladd (Eds.), *Peer relationships in child development*. New York: Wiley.

Bukowski, W.M., Hoza, B., & Boivin, M. (1994). Measuring friendship quality during pre- and early adolescence: The development and psychometric properties of the Friendship Qualities Scale. Journal of Social and Personal Relationships, 11, 471–484.

Bullock, M., & Lutkenhaus, P. (1990). Who am I? Self-understanding in toddlers. *Merrill-Palmer Quarterly, 36*, 217–238.

Bunker-Rohrbaugh, J. (1980). Women: *Psychology's puzzle*. Brighton: Harvester Press.

Burger, J.M. (1993). *Personality* (3rd ed.). Pacific Grove, CA: Brooks/Cole.

Burgess, P.W., & Shallice, T. (1996). Bizarre responses, rule detection and frontal lobe lesions. *Cortex, 32*, 241–259.

Burgess, R.L., & Wallin, P. (1953). Marital happiness of parents and their children's attitudes to them. *American Sociological Review, 18*, 424–431.

Burnstein, E., Crandall, C., & Kitayama, S. (1994). Some neo-Darwinian roles for altruism: Weighing cues for inclusive fitness as function of the biological importance of the decision. *Journal of Personality and Social Psychology, 67*, 773–789.

Burnstein, E., & Vinokur, A. (1973). Testing two classes of theories about group induced shifts in individual choice. *Journal of Experimental Social Psychology, 9*, 123–137.

Burnstein, E., & Vinokur, A. (1977). Persuasive argumentation and social comparison as determinants of attitude polarization. *Journal of Experimental and Social Psychology, 13*, 315–332.

Burt, C. (1955). The evidence for the concept of intelligence. *British Journal of Psychology, 25*, 158–177.

Burton, A.M., & Bruce, V. (1993). Naming faces and naming names: Exploring an interactive activation model of person recognition. *Memory, 1*, 457–480.

Bushman, B.J., & Anderson, C.A. (2001). Is it time to pull the plug on the hostile versus instrumental aggression dichotomy? *Psychological Review, 108*, 273–279.

Bushman, B.J., & Cooper, H.M. (1990). Effects of alcohol on human aggression: An integrative research review. *Psychological Bulletin, 107*, 341–354.

Bushnell, I.W.R. (1998). The origins of face perception. In F. Simion & G. Butterworth (Eds.), *The development of sensory, motor and cognitive capacities in early infancy*. Hove, UK: Psychology Press.

Bushnell, I.W.R., Sai, F., & Mullin, J.T. (1989). Neonatal recognition of the mother's face. *British Journal of Developmental Psychology, 7*, 3–13.

Buss, D.M. (1985). Human mate selection. *American Scientist, 73*, 47–51.

Buss, D.M. (1989). Sex differences in human mate preferences: Evolutionary hypotheses tested in 37 cultures. *Behavioral and Brain Sciences, 12*, 1–49.

Buss, D.M. (1999). *Evolutionary psychology: The new science of the mind*. Boston: Allyn & Bacon.

Buss, D.M., & Schmitt, D.P. (1993). Sexual strategies theory: An evolutionary perspective on human mating. *Psychological Review, 100*, 204–232.

Bussey, K., & Bandura, A. (1999). Social cognitive theory of gender development and differentiation. *Psychological Review, 106*, 676–713.

Butler, B.E. (1974). The limits of selective attention in tachistoscopic recognition. *Canadian Journal of Psychology, 28*, 199–213.

Butters, N., & Cermak, L.S. (1980). *Alcoholic Korsakoff's Syndrome: An information processing approach to amnesia*. New York: Academic Press.

Butterworth, G. (1977). Object disappearance and error in Piaget's stage 4 task. *Journal of Experimental Child Psychology, 23*, 391–401.

Butterworth, G.E., & Cicchetti, D. (1978). Visual calibration of posture in normal and Down's syndrome infants. *Perception, 5*, 155–160.

Butzlaff, R.L., & Hooley, J.M. (1998). Expressed emotion and psychiatric relapse: A meta-analysis. *Archives of General Psychiatry, 55*, 547–552.

Buunk, B.P. (2001). Affiliation, attraction and close relationships. In M. Hewstone & W. Stroebe (Eds.), *Introduction to social psychology* (3rd ed.). Oxford, UK: Blackwell.

Buunk, B.P., Angleitner, A., Oubaid, V., & Buss, D.M. (1996). Sex differences in jealousy in evolutionary and cultural perspective. *Psychological Science, 7*, 359–363.

Buunk, B.P., & Bakker, A.B. (1997). Commitment to the relationship, extradyadic sex, and AIDS prevention behavior. *Journal of Applied Social Psychology, 27*, 1241–1257.

Buunk, B.P., & VanYperen, N.W. (1991). Referential comparisons, relational comparisons and exchange orientation: Their relation to marital satisfaction. *Personality and Social Psychology Bulletin, 17*, 710–718.

Byrne, D. (1971). *The attraction paradigm*. New York: Academic Press.

Byrne, D.G., & Reinhart, M.I. (1989). Work characteristics, occupational achievement and the Type A behaviour pattern. *Journal of Occupational Psychology, 62*, 123–134.

Byrne, R.M.J. (1989). Suppressing valid inferences with conditionals. *Cognition, 31*, 61–63.

Cabanac, M., & Rabe, E.F. (1976). Influence of a monotonous food on body weight regulation in humans. *Physiology and Behavior, 17*, 675–678.

Cacioppo, J.T., & Petty, R.E. (1979). Attitudes and cognitive response: An electrophysiological approach. *Journal of Personality and Social Psychology, 37*, 2181–2199.

Cacioppo, J.T., Petty, R.E., Feinstein, J.A., Jarvis, W., & Blaire, G. (1996). Dispositional differences in cognitive motivation: The life and times of individuals varying in need for cognition. *Psychological Bulletin, 119*, 197–253.

Cahill, L., Babinsky, R., Markowitsch, H.J., & McGaugh, J.L. (1995). The amygdala and emotional memory. *Nature, 377*, 295–296.

Caillies, S., Denhiere, G., & Kintsch, W. (2002). The effect of prior knowledge on understanding from text: Evidence from primed recognition. *European Journal of Cognitive Psychology, 14*, 267–286.

Cairns, R. (1986). Predicting aggression in girls and boys. *Social Science, 71*, 16–21.

Calder, A.J., Young, A.W., Rowland, D., Perrett, D.I., Hodges, J., & Etcoff, N.L. (1996). Facial emotion recognition after bilateral amygdala damage: Differentially severe impairment of fear. *Cognitive Neuropsychology, 13*, 699–745.

Callahan, C.M., Tomlinson, C.A., & Plucker, J. (1997). *Project START using a multiple students intelligences model in identifying and promoting talent in high-risk students* [Tech. Rep.]. Storrs, CT: National Research Center for Gifted Talent, University of Connecticut.

Calvo, M.G. (2001). Working memory and inferences: Evidence from eye fixations during reading. *Memory, 9*, 365–381.

Cameron, C.M., & Gatewood, J.B. (2003). Seeking numinous experiences in the unremembered past (1). (Survey suggests Americans visit heritage sites for spiritual reasons.) *Ethnology, 42*, 55–72.

Campbell, F.A., & Ramey, C.T. (1994).Effects of early intervention on intellectual and academic achievement: A follow-up study of children from low-income families. *Child Development, 65*, 684–698.

Campbell, J.D. (1986). Similarity and uniqueness: The effects of attribute type, relevance, and individual differences in self-esteem and depression. *Journal of Personality and Social Psychology, 50*, 281–294.

Campbell, J.D., Chew, B., & Scratchley, L.S. (1991). Cognitive and emotional reactions to daily events: The effects of self-esteem and self-complexity. *Journal of Personality, 59*, 473–505.

Campbell, S.S., & Murphy, P.J. (1998). Extraocular circadian phototransduction in humans. *Science, 279*, 396–399.

Campbell, W.K., & Sedikides, C. (1999). Self-threat magnifies the self-serving bias: A meta-analytic integration. *Review of General Psychology, 3*, 23–43.

Campbell, W.K., Sedikides, C., Reeder, G.D., & Elliott, A.J. (2000). Among friends? An examination of friendship and the self-serving bias. *British Journal of Social Psychology, 39*, 229–239.

Campfield, L.A., Brandon, P., & Smith, F.J. (1985). On line continuous measurement of blood glucose and meal pattern in free-feeding rats: The role of glucose in meal initiation. *Brain Resolution Bulletin, 14*, 605–616.

Campfield, L.A., & Smith, F.J. (1990). Systemic factors in the control of food intake: Evidence for patterns as signals. In E.M. Stricker (Ed.), *Handbook of behavioural neurobiology: Vol. 10. Neurobiology of food and fluid intake*. New York: Plenum.

Campfield, L.A., Smith, F.J., Guisez, Y., Devos, R., & Burn, P. (1995). Recombinant mouse OB protein: Evidence for a peripheral signal linking adiposity and central neural networks. *Science, 269*, 546–549.

Campos, J.J., Bertenthal, B.I., & Kermoian, R. (1992). Early experience and emotional development: The emergence of wariness of heights. *Psychological Science, 3*, 61–64.

Canavan, A.G., Sprengelmeyer, R., Diener, H.C., & Hömberg, V. (1994). Conditional associative learning is impaired in cerebellar disease in humans. *Behavioral Neuroscience, 108*, 475–485.

Cannon, T.D., Mednick, S.A., Parnas, J., Schulsinger, F., Praestholm, J., & Vestergaard, A. (1994). Developmental brain abnormalities in the offspring of schizophrenic mothers: II. Structural brain characteristics of schizophrenia and schizotypal personality disorder. *Archives of General Psychiatry, 51*, 955–962.

Cannon, W.B. (1932). *The wisdom of the body* (2nd ed.). New York: Norton.

Caprara, G.V., Barbaranelli, C., & Pastorelli, C. (1998). *Comparative test of longitudinal predictiveness of personal self-efficacy and big five factors*. Paper presented at the European conference on Personality, University of Surrey, UK.

Capron, C., & Duyne, M. (1989). Assessment of effects of socio-economic status on IQ in a full cross-fostering study. *Nature, 340*, 552–554.

Cardwell, M., Clark, L., & Meldrum, C. (1996). *Psychology for A level*. London: Collins Educational.

Carey, D.P., Harvey, M., & Milner, A.D. (1996). Visuomotor sensitivity for shape and orientation in a patient with visual form agnosia. *Neuropsychologia, 34*, 329–338.

Carey, D.P., & Milner, A.D. (1994). Casting one's net too widely? *Behavioral and Brain Sciences, 17*, 65–66.

Carey, M.P., Kalra, D.L., Carey, K.B., Halperin, S., & Richard, C.S. (1993). Stress and unaided smoking cessation: A prospective investigation. *Journal of Consulting and Clinical Psychology, 61*, 831–838.

Carlezon, W.A., Jr., & Wise, R.A. (1996). Microinjections of phencyclidine (PCP) and related drugs into nucleus accumbens shell potentiate medial forebrain bundle brain stimulation reward. *Psychopharmacology (Berl.), 128*, 413–420.

Carlson, M., Marcus-Newhall, A., & Miller, N. (1990). Effects of situational aggression cues: A quantitative review. *Journal of Personality and Social Psychology, 58*, 622–633.

Carlson, N.R. (1994). *Physiology of behavior* (5th ed.). Boston: Allyn & Bacon.

Carpenter, G. (1975). Mother's face and the newborn. In R. Lewin (Ed.), *Child alive*. London: Temple Smith.

Carpenter, S.J. (2001). Implicit gender attitudes [Doctoral dissertation, Yale University, 2000]. *Dissertation Abstracts International, 61*, 5619.

Carr, A. (2000). *Family therapy: Concepts, process and practice*. Chichester, UK: Wiley.

Carrasco, J.L., Diaz-Marsa, M., Hollander, E., Cesar, J., & Saiz-Ruiz, J. (2000). Decreased platelet monoamine oxidase activity in female bulimia nervosa. *European Neuropsychopharmacology, 10*, 113–117.

Carroll, J.B. (1986). Factor analytic investigations of cognitive abilities. In S.E. Newstead, S.H. Irvine, & P.L. Dann (Eds.), *Human assessment: Cognition and motivation*. Dordrecht, The Netherlands: Nyhoff.

Carroll, J.B. (1993). *Human cognitive abilities: A survey of factor analytic studies*. New York: Cambridge University Press.

Cartwright, D.S. (1979). *Theories and models of personality*. Dubuque, IO: Brown Company.

Cartwright, S., & Cooper, C.L. (1997). *Managing workplace stress*. Thousand Oaks, CA: Sage.

Carver, C.S., Pozo, C., Harris, S.D., Noriega, V., Scheier, M., Robinson, D., Ketcham, A., Moffat, F.L., & Clark, K. (1993). How coping mediates the effect of optimism on distress: A study of women with early stage breast cancer. *Journal of Personality and Social Psychology, 65*, 375–390.

Carver, C.S., & Scheier, M.F. (2000). *Perspectives on personality* (4th ed.). Boston: Allyn & Bacon.

Cary, M., & Carlson, R.A. (1999). External support and the development of problem-solving routines. *Journal of Experimental Psychology: Learning, Memory, and Cognition, 25*, 1053–1070.

Case, R. (1974). Structures and strictures: Some functional limitations on the course of cognitive growth. *Cognitive Psychology, 6*, 544–573.

Case, R. (1985). *Intellectual development*. Orlando, FL: Academic Press.

Case, R. (1991). Stages in the development of the young child's first sense of self. *Developmental Review, 11*, 210–230.

Case, R. (1992). Neo-Piagetian theories of intellectual development. In H. Beilin & P.B. Pufall (Eds.), *Piaget's theory: Prospects and possibilities*. Hillsdale, NJ: Lawrence Erlbaum Associates, Inc.

Caspi, A., Moffitt, T.E., Newman, D.L., & Silva, P.A. (1996). Behavioral observations at age 3 years predict adult psychiatric disorders: Longitudinal evidence from a birth cohort. *Archives of General Psychiatry, 53*, 1033–1039.

Casscells, W., Schoenberger, A., & Graboys, T.B. (1978). Interpretation by physicians of clinical laboratory results. *New England Journal of Medicine, 299*, 999–1001.

Cassia, V.M., Simion, F., Milani, I., & Umiltà, C. (2002). Dominance of global visual properties at birth. *Journal of Experimental Psychology: General, 131*, 398–411.

Catalano, R., Novaco, R., & McConnell, W. (1997). A model of the net effect of job loss on violence. *Journal of Personality and Social Psychology, 72*, 1440–1447.

Cate, R., Lloyd, S. & Long, E. (1988). The role of rewards and fairness in developing premarital relationships. *Journal of Marriage and the Family, 50*, 443–452.

Cattell, R.B. (1946). *Description and measurement of personality*. Dubuque, IA: Brown Company Publishers.

Cattell, R.B. (1957). *Personality and motivation structure and measurement*. New York: World Book Company.

Cattell, R.B. (1963). Theory of fluid and crystallised intelligence: A critical experiment. *Journal of Educational Psychology, 54*, 1–22.

Cattell, R.B. (1971). *Abilities: Their structure, growth, and action*. Boston: Houghton-Mifflin.

Cavanagh, P., Tyler, C.W., & Favreau, O.E. (1984). Perceived velocity of moving chromatic gratings. *Journal of the Optical Society of America A, 1*, 893–899.

Ceci, S.J. (1995). Memory distortions in children. *Journal of the Neurological Sciences, 134*, 1–8.

Ceraso, J., & Provitera, A. (1971). Sources of error in syllogistic reasoning. *Cognitive Psychology, 2,* 400–410.

Cermak, L.S., Talbot, N., Chandler, K., & Wolbarst, L.R. (1985). The perceptual priming phenomenon in amnesia. *Neuropsychologia, 23,* 615–622.

Cha, J.-H., & Nam, K.D. (1985). A test of Kelley's cube theory of attribution: A cross-cultural replication of McArthur's study. *Korean Social Science Journal, 12,* 151–180.

Chaiken, S. (1987). The heuristic model of persuasion. In M.P. Zanna, J.M. Olson, & C.P. Herman (Eds.), *Social influence: The Ontario symposium, Vol. 5.* Hillsdale, NJ: Lawrence Erlbaum Associates, Inc.

Chaiken, S., & Eagly, A.H., (1983). Communication modality as a determinant of persuasion: The role of communicator salience. *Journal of Personality and Social Psychology, 45,* 241–256.

Chaiken, S., Giner-Sorolla, R., & Chen, S. (1996). Beyond accuracy: Defence and impression motives in heuristic and systematic information processing. In P.M. Gollwitzer & J.A. Bargh (Eds.), *The psychology of action: Linking cognition and motivation to behaviour.* New York: Guilford Press.

Chaiken, S., & Maheswaran, D. (1994). Heuristic processing can bias systematic processing: Effects of source credibility, argument ambiguity, and task importance on attitude judgement. *Journal of Personality and Social Psychology, 66,* 460–473.

Challis, B.H., & Brodbeck, D.R. (1992). Level of processing affects priming in word fragment completion. *Journal of Experimental Psychology: Human Perception and Performance, 11,* 317–328.

Challman, R.C. (1932). Factors influencing friendships among pre-school children. *Child Development, 3,* 146–158.

Chan, A. (1998). Musical memory. *New Scientist,* 14th November.

Channon, S., Shanks, D., Johnstone, T., Vakili, K., Chin, J., & Sinclair, E. (2002). Is implicit learning spared in amnesia? Rule abstraction and item familiarity in artificial grammar learning. *Neuropsychologia, 40,* 2185–2197.

Chapman, J.L., & Chapman, J.P. (1959). Atmosphere effect re-examined. *Journal of Experimental Psychology, 58,* 220–226.

Charlton, A. (1998, January 12). TV violence has little impact on children, study finds. *The Times,* p. 5.

Chase, W.G., & Simon, H.A. (1973). Perception in chess. *Cognitive Psychology, 4,* 55–81.

Chater, N. (2000). How smart can simple heuristics be? *Behavioral and Brain Sciences, 23,* 745–746.

Chater, N., & Oaksford, M. (1999). Information gain and decision-theoretic approaches to data selection: Response to Klauer (1999). *Psychological Review, 106,* 223–227.

Cheesman, J., & Merikle, P.M. (1984). Priming with and without awareness. *Perception and Psychophysics, 36,* 387–395.

Chen, C., Greenberger, E., Lester, J., Dong, Q., & Guo, M.-S. (1998b). A cross-cultural study of family and peer correlates of adolescent misconduct. *Developmental Psychology, 34,* 770–781.

Chen, D.Y., Deutsch, J.A., Gonzalez, M.F., & Gu, Y. (1993). The induction and suppression of c-fos expression in the rat brain by cholecystokinin and its antagonist L364,718. *Neuroscience Letters, 149,* 91–94.

Chen, J., Paredes, W., Li, J., Smith, D., Lowinson, J., & Gardner, E.L. (1990). Delta-9 tetrahydrocannabinol produces naloxone-blockable enhancement of presynaptic basal dopamine efflux in nucleus accumbens of conscious, freely-moving rats as measured by intracerebral microdialysis. *Psychopharmacology, 102,* 156–162.

Chen, X., Dong, Q., & Zhou, H. (1997). Authoritative and authoritarian parenting practices and social and school performance in Chinese children. *International Journal of Behavioral Development, 21,* 855–873.

Chen, Y.-R., Brockner, J., & Katz, T. (1998a). Toward an explanation of cultural differences in in-group favouritism: The role of individual versus collective primacy. *Journal of Personality and Social Psychology, 75,* 1490–1502.

Chen, Z. (2002). Analogical problem solving: A hierarchical analysis of procedural similarity. *Journal of Experimental Psychology: Learning, Memory, and Cognition, 28,* 81–98.

Cheng, A.T.A. (2002). Expressed emotion: A cross-culturally valid concept? *British Journal of Psychiatry, 181,* 466–467.

Cheng, P.W. (1985). Restructuring versus automaticity: Alternative accounts of skills acquisition. *Psychological Review, 92,* 414–423.

Cherlin, A.J., Furstenberg, F.F., Chase-Lonsdale, P.L., Kiernan, K.E., Robins, P.K., Morrison, D.R., & Teitler, J.O. (1991). Longitudinal studies of effects of divorce on children in Great Britain and the United States. *Science, 252,* 1386–1389.

Cherry, E.C. (1953). Some experiments on the recognition of speech with one and two ears. *Journal of the Acoustical Society of America, 25,* 975–979.

Cheung, F.M., & Leung, K. (1998). Indigenous personality measures: Chinese examples. *Journal of Cross-Cultural Psychology, 29,* 233–248.

Chi, M.T. (1978). Knowledge, structure and memory development. In R.S. Siegler (Ed.), *Children's thinking: What develops?* Hillsdale, NJ: Lawrence Erbaum Associates, Inc.

Child, I.L. (1968). Personality in culture. In E.F. Borgatta & W.W. Lambert (Eds.), *Handbook of personality theory and research.* Chicago: Rand McNally.

Childers, J.B., & Tomasello, M. (2002). Two-year-olds learn novel nouns, verbs, and conventional actions from massed or distributed exposures. *Developmental Psychology, 38,* 967–978.

Chodorow, N. (1978). *The reproduction of mothering.* Berkeley, CA: University of California Press.

Choi, I., Choi, K.W., & Cha, J.-H. (1992). *A cross-cultural replication of Festinger and Carlsmith (1959).* Unpublished manuscript, Seoul National University, Korea.

Choi, I., & Nisbett, R.E. (1998). Situational salience and cultural differences in the correspondence bias and actor–observer bias. *Personality and Social Psychology Bulletin, 24,* 949–960.

Choi, I., Nisbett, R.E., & Norenzayan, A. (1999). Causal attribution across cultures: Variation and universality. *Psychological Bulletin, 125,* 47–63.

Choi, I., Nisbett, R.E., & Smith, E.E. (1997). Culture, category salience, and inductive reasoning. *Cognition, 65,* 15–32.

Chomsky, N. (1965). *Aspects of the theory of syntax.* Cambridge, MA: MIT Press.

Chomsky, N. (1980). *Rules and representations.* New York: Columbia University Press.

Chomsky, N. (1986). *Knowledge of language: Its nature, origin, and use.* New York: Praeger.

Chorney, M.J., Chorney, K., Seese, N., Own, M.J., Daniels, J., McGuffin, P., Thompson, L.A., Detterman, D.K., Benbow, C.P., Lubinski, D., Eley, T.C., & Plomin, R. (1998). A quantitative trait locus (QTL) associated with cognitive ability in children. *Psychological Science, 9,* 159–166.

Church, A.T., & Katigbak, M.S. (2000). Trait psychology in the Philippines. *American Behavioral Science, 44,* 73–94.

Cialdini, R.B., Borden, R.J., Thorne, A., Walker, M.R., Freeman, S., & Sloan, L.R. (1976). Basking in reflected glory: Three (football) field studies. *Journal of Personality and Social Psychology, 34,* 366–375.

Cialdini, R.B., Brown, S.L., Lewis, B.P., Luce, C., & Neuberg, S.L. (1997). Reinterpreting the empathy–altruism relationship: When one into one equals oneness. *Journal of Personality and Social Psychology, 73,* 481–494.

Cialdini, R.B., Cacioppo, J.T., Bassett, R., & Miller, J.A. (1978). Low-balling procedure for producing compliance: Commitment then cost. *Journal of Personality and Social Psychology, 36,* 463–476.

Cialdini, R.B., Schaller, M., Houlihan, D., Arps, K., Fultz, J., & Beaman, A.L. (1987). Empathy-based helping: Is it selflessly or selfishly motivated? *Journal of Personality and Social Psychology, 52,* 749–758.

Cialdini, R.B., & Trost, M.R. (1998). Social influence: Social norms, conformity, and compliance. In D.T. Gilbert, S.T. Fiske, & G. Lindzey (Eds.), *The handbook of social psychology* (Vol. 2, 4th ed., pp. 151–192). New York: McGraw-Hill.

Cicerone, C.M., & Nerger, J.L. (1989). The relative number of long-wavelength-sensitive to middle-wavelength-sensitive cones in the human fovea centralis. *Vision Research, 29,* 115–128.

Cillessen, A.H.N., Van IJzendoorn, H.W., van Lieshout, C.F.M., & Hartup, W.W. (1992). Heterogeneity among peer-rejected boys: Subtypes and stabilities. *Child Development, 63,* 893–905.

Cinnirella, M. (1998). Manipulating stereotype ratings tasks: Understanding questionnaire context effects on measures of attitudes, social identity and stereotypes. *Journal of Community and Applied Social Psychology, 8*, 345–362.

Clancy, S.A., Schacter, D.L., McNally, R.J., & Pitman, R.K. (2000). False recognition in women reporting recovered memories of sexual abuse. *Psychological Science, 11*(1), 26–31. [Erratum, *Psychological Science* (2000), *11*(3), 265.]

Clancy, S.M., & Dollinger, S.J. (1993). Photographic depictions of the self: Gender and age differences in social connectedness. *Sex Roles, 29*, 477–495.

Claparède, E. (1911). Recognition et moitié. *Archives de Psychologie, 11*, 75–90.

Clark, D.A. (1989). Special review of Brewin's "Cognitive Foundations of Clinical Psychology". *Behaviour Research and Therapy, 27*, 691–693.

Clark, D.M. (1986). A cognitive approach to panic. *Behaviour Research and Therapy, 24*, 461–470.

Clark, D.M. (1996). Panic disorder: From theory to therapy. In P. Salkovskis (Ed.), *Frontiers of cognitive therapy*. New York: Guilford Press.

Clark, D.M., & Wells, A. (1995). A cognitive model of social phobia. In R.R.G. Heimberg, M. Liebowitz, D.A. Hope, & S. Scheier (Eds.), *Social phobia: Diagnosis, assessment and treatment*. New York: Guilford.

Clark, H.H., & Carlson, T.B. (1981). Context for comprehension. In J. Long & A. Baddeley (Eds.), *Attention and performance IX: Information processing*. Hillsdale, NJ: Lawrence Erlbaum Associates, Inc.

Clark, R.D., & Hatfield, E. (1989). Gender differences in receptivity to sexual offers. *Journal of Psychology and Human Sexuality, 2*, 39–55.

Clarke-Stewart, A. (1989). Infant day care: Maligned or malignant? *American Psychologist, 44*, 266–273.

Clarke-Stewart, K.A., VanderStoep, L.P., & Killian, G.A. (1979). Analysis and replication of mother–child relations at two years of age. *Child Development, 50*, 777–793.

Clifton, C., & Ferreira, F. (1987). Discourse structure and anaphora: Some experimental results. In M. Coltheart (Ed.), *Attention and performance XII: The psychology of reading*. Hove, UK: Psychology Press.

Cloninger, C.R. (1987). Neurogenetic adaptive mechanisms in alcoholism. *Science, 236*, 410–416.

Cloninger, C.R., Bohman, M., Sigvardsson, S., & von Knorring, A.-L. (1985). Psychopathology in adopted-out children of alcoholics: The Stockholm Adoption Study. *Recent Developments in Alcoholism, 3*, 37–51.

Cloninger, C.R., Sigvardsson, S., Bohman, M., & von Knorring, A.-L. (1982). Predisposition to petty criminality in Swedish adoptees: II. Cross-fostering analysis of gene–environment interaction. *Archives of General Psychiatry, 39*, 1242–1247.

Clough, P., & Sewell, D. (2000, March 1). In C. Brooke (Ed.), Why being idle puts us in a good mood. *Daily Mail*.

Coates, S., & Wolfe, S. (1997). Gender identity disorders in children. In P.F. Kernberg & J.R. Bemporad (Eds.), *Handbook of child and adolescent psychiatry, Vol. 2*. New York: Wiley.

Coe, W.C. (1989). Post-hypnotic amnesia: Theory and research. In N.P. Spanos & J.F. Chaves (Eds.), *Hypnosis: The cognitive-behavioural perspective*. Buffalo, NY: Prometheus.

Coenen, A. (2000). The divorce of REM sleep and dreaming. *Behavioral and Brain Sciences, 23*, 922–924.

Cogan, J.C., Bhalla, S.K., Sefa-Dedeh, A., & Rothblum, E.D. (1996). A comparison study of United States and African students on perceptions of obesity and thinness. *Journal of Cross-Cultural Psychology, 27*, 98–113.

Cohen, D., Nisbett, R.E., Bowdle, B.F., & Schwarz, N. (1996). Insult, aggression, and the southern culture of honour: An "experimental ethnography". *Journal of Personality and Social Psychology, 70*, 945–960.

Cohen, F., & Lazarus, R.S. (1973). Active coping processes, coping dispositions, and recovery from surgery. *Psychosomatic Medicine, 35*, 375–389.

Cohen, S., & Herbert, T.B. (1996). Health psychology: Psychological factors and physical disease from the perspective of human psychoneuroimmunology. *Annual Review of Psychology, 47*, 113–142.

Cohen, S., Tyrrell, D.A.J., & Smith, A.P. (1991). Psychological stress and susceptibility to the common cold. *New England Journal of Medicine, 325*, 606–612.

Cohen, S., & Williamson, G.M. (1991). Stress and infectious disease in humans. *Psychological Bulletin, 109*, 5–24.

Coie, J.D., Dodge, K.A., & Coppotelli, H. (1982). Dimensions and types of social status: A cross-age perspective. *Developmental Psychology, 18*, 557–570.

Colby, A., Kohlberg, L., Gibbs, J., & Lieberman, M. (1983). A longitudinal study of moral judgement. *Monographs of the Society for Research in Child Development, 48* (Nos. 1–2, Serial No. 200).

Cole, M., & Cole, S.R. (1993). *The development of children* (2nd ed.). New York: Scientific American Books.

Cole, M., & Cole, S.R. (2001). *The development of children* (4th ed.). New York: Worth.

Cole, M., Gay, J., Glick, J., & Sharp, D.W. (1971). *The cultural context of learning and thinking*. New York: Basic Books.

Collaer, M.L., & Hines, M. (1995). Human behavioural sex differences: A role for gonadal hormones during early development? *Psychological Bulletin, 118*, 55–107.

Collins, D.L., Baum, A., & Singer, J.E. (1983). Coping with chronic stress at Three Mile Island: Psychological and biochemical evidence. *Health Psychology, 2*, 149–166.

Collins, N.L., & Miller, L.C. (1994). Self–disclosure and liking: A meta–analytic review. *Psychological Bulletin, 116*, 457–475.

Coltheart, M. (1983). Ecological necessity of iconic memory. *Behavioral and Brain Sciences, 6*, 17–18.

Coltheart, M., Rastle, K., Perry, C., Ziegler, J., & Langdon, R. (2001). DRC: A dual route cascaded model of visual word recognition and reading aloud. *Psychological Review, 108*, 204–256.

Colvin, C.R., Block, J., & Funder, D.C. (1995). Overly positive self-evaluation and personality: Negative implications for mental health. *Journal of Personality and Social Psychology, 6*, 1152–1162.

Comer, R.J. (2001). *Abnormal psychology* (4th ed.). New York: Worth.

Comstock, G., & Paik, H. (1991). *Television and the American child*. San Diego: Academic Press.

Condon, J.W., & Crano, W.D. (1988). Inferred evaluation and the relation between attitude similarity and interpersonal attraction. *Journal of Personality and Social Psychology, 54*, 789–797.

Condry, J., & Condry, S. (1976). Sex differences: A study in the eye of the beholder. *Child Development, 47*, 812–819.

Condry, J.C., & Ross, D.F. (1985). The influence of gender label on adults' perceptions of aggression in children. *Child Development, 56*, 225–233.

Conley, J.J. (1984). The hierarchy of consistency: A review and model of longitudinal findings on adult individual differences in intelligence, personality and self-opinion. *Personality and Individual Differences, 5*, 11–25.

Conner, D.B., Knight, D.K., & Cross, D.R. (1997). Mothers' and fathers' scaffolding of their 2-year-olds during problem-solving and literary interactions. *British Journal of Developmental Psychology, 15*, 323–338.

Conner, M., & Armitage, C.J. (1998). Extending the theory of planned behaviour: A review and avenues for further research. *Journal of Applied Social Psychology, 28*, 1429–1464.

Connine, C.M., Blasko, P.J., & Titone, D. (1993). Do the beginnings of spoken words have a special status in auditory word recognition? *Journal of Memory and Language, 32*, 193–210.

Conrad, R. (1979). *The deaf school child: Language and cognitive functions*. London: Harper & Row.

Considine, R.V., Sinha, M.K., Heiman, M.L., Kriauciunas, A., Stephens, T.W., Nyce, M.R. et al. (1996). Serum immunoreactive-leptin concentrations in normal-weight and obese humans. *New England Journal of Medicine, 334*, 292.

Conway, A.R.A., Cowan, N., Bunting, M.F., Therriault, D.J., & Minkoff, S.R.B. (2002). A latent variable analysis of working memory capacity, short-term memory capacity, processing speed, and general fluid intelligence. *Intelligence, 30*, 163–183.

Conway, M.A. (1996). Autobiographical knowledge and autobiographical memories. In D.C. Rubin (Ed.), *Remembering our past: Studies in autobiographical memory*. Cambridge: Cambridge University Press.

Conway, M.A., Anderson, S.J., Larsen, S.F., Donnelly, C.M., McDaniel, M.A., McClelland, A.G.R., & Rawles, R.E. (1994). The formation of flashbulb memories. *Memory and Cognition, 22*, 326–343.

Conway, M.A., & Haque, S. (1999). Overshadowing the reminiscence bump: Memories of a struggle for independence. *Journal of Adult Development, 6*, 35–44.

Conway, M.A., & Pleydell-Pearce, C.W. (2000). The construction of autobiographical memories in the self-memory system. *Psychological Review, 107*, 261–288.

Conway, M.A., Pleydell-Pearce, C.W., & Whitecross, S.E. (2001). The neuroanatomy of autobiographical memory: A slow cortical potential study (SCP) of autobiographical memory retrieval. *Journal of Memory and Language, 45*, 493–524.

Conway, M.A. & Rubin, D.C. (1993). The structure of autobiographical memory. In A.F. Collins, S.E. Gathercole, M.A. Conway, & P.E. Morris (Eds.). *Theories of memory*. Hove, UK: Psychology Press.

Cook, M. (1993). *Personnel selection and productivity* (Rev. ed.). New York: Wiley.

Cook, M., & Mineka, S. (1989). Observational conditioning of fear to fear-relevant versus fear-irrelevant stimuli in rhesus monkeys. *Journal of Abnormal Psychology, 98*, 448–459.

Cooley, C.H. (1902). *Human nature and social order*. New York: Charles Scribner.

Cooper, C. (1998). *Individual differences*. London: Arnold.

Cooper, C. (2002). Individual differences (2nd Edition). London: Arnold.

Cooper, P.J. (1994). Eating disorders. In A.M. Colman (Ed.), *Companion encyclopaedia of psychology, Vol. 2*. London: Routledge.

Cooper, P.J., & Taylor, M.J. (1988). Body image disturbance in bulimia nervosa. *British Journal of Psychiatry, 153*, 32–36.

Cooper, R.M., & Zubek, J.P. (1958). Effects of enriched and restricted early environments on the learning ability of bright and dull rats. *Canadian Journal of Psychology, 12*, 159–164.

Cooper, S.J., & Dourish, C.T. (1990). Multiple cholecystokinin (CCK) receptors and CCK-monoamine interactions are instrumental in the control of feeding. *Physiology and Behavior, 48*, 849–857.

Coopersmith, S. (1967).*The antecedents of self-esteem*. San Francisco: W.H. Freeman.

Copeland, B.J. (1993). *Artificial intelligence: A philosophical introduction*. Oxford, UK: Blackwell.

Coren, S., & Girgus, J.S. (1972). Visual spatial illusions: Many explanations. *Science, 179*, 503–504.

Coslett, H.B. (1991). Read but not write "idea": Evidence for a third reading mechanism. *Brain and Language, 40*, 425–443.

Cosmides, L. (1989). The logic of social exchange: Has natural selection shaped how humans reason? Studies with the Wason selection task. *Cognition, 31*, 187–276.

Cosmides, L., & Tooby, J. (1992). Cognitive adaptations for social exchange. In J.H. Barkow Jerome, L. Cosmides, & J. Tooby (Eds.), *The adapted mind: Evolutionary psychology and the generation of culture* (pp. 163–228). New York: Oxford University Press.

Cosmides, L., & Tooby, J. (1996). Are humans good intuitive statisticians after all? Rethinking some conclusions from the literature on judgement under uncertainty. *Cognition, 58*, 1–73.

Costa, P.T., & McCrae, R.R. (1992). *NEO–PI–R, Professional manual*. Odessa, FL: Psychological Assessment Resources.

Costa, P.T., & Widiger, T.A. (1994). *Personality disorders and the five-factor model of personality*. Washington, DC: American Psychological Association.

Costanzo, P.R., Coie, J.D., Grumet, J., & Famill, D. (1973). A re-examination of the effects of intent and consequence on the quality of child rearing. *Child Development, 57*, 362–374.

Costello, T.W., Costello, J.T., & Holmes, D.A. (1995). *Abnormal psychology*. London: HarperCollins.

Cottrell, N. (1972). Social facilitation. In C. McClintock (Ed.), *Experimental social psychology*. New York: Holt, Rinehart, & Winston.

Council, J.R., & Kenny, D.A. (1992). Expert judgements of hypnosis from subjective state reports. *Journal of Abnormal Psychology, 101*, 657–662.

Cox, T. (1978). *Stress*. London: Macmillan Press.

Craddock, N., & Jones, I. (1999). Genetics of bipolar disorder. *Journal of Medical Genetics, 36*, 585–594.

Craik, F.I.M. (1973). A "levels of analysis" view of memory. In P. Pliner, L. Krames, & T.M. Alloway (Eds.), *Communication and affect: Language and thought*. London: Academic Press.

Craik, F.I.M. (2002). Levels of processing: Past, present ... and future? *Memory, 10*, 305–318.

Craik, F.I.M., & Lockhart, R.S. (1972). Levels of processing: A framework for memory research. *Journal of Verbal Learning and Verbal Behavior, 11*, 671–684.

Craik, F.I.M., & Tulving, E. (1975). Depth of processing and the retention of words in episodic memory. *Journal of Experimental Psychology: General, 104*, 268–294.

Craske, M.G., & Craig, K.D. (1984). Musical performance anxiety: The three-systems model and self-efficacy theory. *Behaviour Research and Therapy, 22*, 267–280.

Crick, N.R., & Dodge, K.A. (1994). A review and reformulation of social information-processing mechanisms in children's social adjustment. *Psychological Bulletin, 115*, 74–101.

Crick, N.R., & Ladd, G.W. (1990). Children's perceptions of the outcomes of aggressive strategies: Do the ends justify being mean? *Developmental Psychology, 26*, 612–620.

Critchley, H.D., & Rolls, E.T. (1996). Hunger and satiety modify the responses of olfactory and visual neurons in the primate orbitofrontal cortex. *Journal of Neurophysiology, 75*, 1673–1686.

Crits-Christoph, P., Baranackie, K., Kurcias, J.S., Beck, A.T., Carroll, K, Perry, K., Luborsky, L., McLellan, A.T., Woody, G., Thompson, L., Gallagher, D., & Zitrin, C. (1991). Meta-analysis of therapist effects in psychotherapy outcome studies. *Psychotherapy Research, 1*, 81–91.

Crocker, J., Thompson, L.L., McGraw, K.M., & Ingerman, C. (1987). Downward comparison, prejudice, and evaluations of others: Effects of self-esteem and threat. *Journal of Personality and Social Psychology, 52*, 907–916.

Cronbach, L.J. (1957). The two disciplines of scientific psychology. *American Psychologist, 12*, 671–684.

Crosby, F., Bromley, S., & Saxe, L. (1980). Recent unobtrusive studies of black and white discrimination and prejudice: A literature review. *Psychological Bulletin, 87*, 546–563.

Cross, D.G., Sheehan, P.W., & Khan, J.A. (1980). Alternative advice and counsel in psychotherapy. *Journal of Consulting and Clinical Psychology, 48*, 615–625.

Cross, S.E., & Madson, L. (1997). Models of the self: Self-construals and gender. *Psychological Bulletin, 122*, 5–37.

Crowe, R.R., Noyes, R., Pauls, D.L., & Slymen, D. (1983). A family study of panic disorder. *Archives of General Psychiatry, 40*, 1065–1069.

Crowe, R.R., Noyes, R., Wilson, A.F., Elston, R.C., & Ward, L.J. (1987). A linkage study of panic disorder. *Archives of General Psychiatry, 44*, 933–937.

Cumberbatch, G. (1990). *Television advertising and sex role stereotyping: A content analysis* [Working paper IV for the Broadcasting Standards Council]. Communications Research Group, Aston University, Birmingham, UK.

Cunningham, M.R. (1986). Measuring the physical in physical attractiveness: Quasi experiments on the sociobiology of female facial beauty. *Journal of Personality and Social Psychology, 50*, 925–935.

Cunningham, W.A., Preacher, K.J., & Banaji, M.R. (2001). Implicit attitude measures: Consistency, stability, and convergent validity. *Psychological Science, 12*, 163–170.

Curtis, A. (2000). *Psychology and health*. London: Routledge.

Curtiss, S. (1977). *Genie: A psycholinguistic study of a modern-day "wild child"*. London: Academic Press.

Curtiss, S. (1989). The independence and task-specificity of language. In M.H. Bornstein & J.S. Bruner (Eds.), *Interaction in human development*. Hillsdale, NJ: Lawrence Erlbaum Associates Inc.

Cutler, A., Mehler, J., Norris, D., & Segui, J. (1987). Phonemic identification and the lexicon. *Cognitive Psychology, 19*, 141–177.

Cutting, J.E. (1978). Generation of synthetic male and female walkers through manipulation of a biochemical invariant. *Perception, 7*, 393–405.

Cutting, J.E., Proffitt, D.R., & Kozlowski, L.T. (1978). A biomechanical invariant for gait perception. *Journal of Experimental Psychology: Human Perception and Performance, 4*, 357–372.

Cuvo, A.J. (1975). Developmental differences in rehearsal and free recall. *Journal of Experimental Child Psychology, 19*, 265–278.

Czeisler, C.A., Duffy, J.F., Shanahan, T.L., Brown, E.N., Mitchell, J.F., Rimmer, D.W., Ronda, J.M., Silva, E.J., Emens, J.S., Dijk, D.J., & Kronauer, R.E. (1999). Stability, precision, and near-24-hour period of the human circadian pacemaker. *Science, 284*, 2177–2181.

Czeisler, C.A., Kronauer, R.E., Allan, J.S., Duffy, J.F., Jewett, M.E., Brown, E.N., & Ronda, J.M. (1989). Bright light induction of strong (type 0) resetting of the human circadian pacemaker. *Science, 244*, 1328–1333.

Czeisler, C.A., Moore-Ede, M.C., & Coleman, R.M. (1982). Rotating shift work schedules that disrupt sleep are improved by applying circadian principles. *Science, 217*, 460–463.

Dalgleish, T. (1998). Emotion. In M.W. Eysenck (Ed.), *Psychology: An integrated approach*. Harlow, UK: Longman.

Dalton, K. (1964). *The premenstrual syndrome*. London: Heinemann.

Damasio, A.R. (1999). *The feeling of what happens: Body and emotion in the making of consciousness*. New York: Harcourt Brace.

Damasio, H., Grabowski, T., Frank, R., Galaburda, A.M., & Damasio, A.R. (1994). The return of Phineas Gage: The skull of a famous patient yields clues about the brain. *Science, 264*, 1102–1105.

Dammann, E.J. (1997). "The myth of mental illness": Continuing controversies and their implications for mental health professionals. *Clinical Psychology Review, 17*, 733–756.

Damon, W., & Hart, D. (1988). *Self-understanding in childhood and adolescence*. Cambridge, UK: Cambridge University Press.

Daneman, M., & Carpenter, P.A. (1980). Individual differences in working memory and reading. *Journal of Verbal Learning and Verbal Behavior, 19*, 450–466.

Daniels, D., & Plomin, R. (1985). Origins of individual differences in infant shyness. *Developmental Psychology, 21*, 118–121.

Darley, J.M., & Batson, C.D. (1973). From Jerusalem to Jericho: A study of situational and dispositional variables in helping behaviour. *Journal of Personality and Social Psychology, 27*, 100–108.

Darley, J.M., & Latané, B. (1968). Bystander intervention in emergencies: Diffusion of responsibility. *Journal of Personality and Social Psychology, 8*, 377–383.

Darling, N., & Steinberg, L. (1993). Parenting style as context: An integrative model. *Psychological Bulletin, 113*, 487–496.

Dartnall, H.J.A., Bowmaker, J.K., & Mollon, J.D. (1983). Human visual pigments: Microspectrophotometric results from the eyes of seven persons. *Proceedings of the Royal Society of London, Series B, 220*, 115–130.

Darwin, C. (1859). *The origin of species*. London: Macmillan.

Darwin, C.J., Turvey, M.T., & Crowder, R.G. (1972). An auditory analogue of the Sperling partial report procedure: Evidence for brief auditory storage. *Cognitive Psychology, 3*, 255–267.

David, B., & Turner, J.C. (1999). Studies in self-categorization and minority conversion: The in-group minority in intragroup and intergroup contexts. *British Journal of Social Psychology, 38*, 115–134.

Davidoff, J., & Warrington, E.K. (1999). Apperceptive agnosia: A deficit of perceptual categorisation of objects. In G.W. Humphreys (Ed.), *Case studies in the neuropsychology of vision*. Hove, UK: Psychology Press.

Davidson, D. (1994). Recognition and recall of irrelevant and interruptive atypical actions in script-based stories. *Journal of Memory & Language, 33*, 757–775.

Davidson, R. (1996). Act now, think later: Emotions. *New Scientist* (Suppl.).

Davies, D.R., & Parasuraman, R. (1982). *The psychology of vigilance*. London: Academic Press.

Davies, M., Stankov, L., & Roberts, R.D. (1998). Emotional intelligence: In search of an elusive construct. *Journal of Personality and Social Psychology, 75*, 989–1015.

Davis, J.D., Gallagher, R.J., Ladove, R.F., & Turausky, A.J. (1969). Inhibition of food intake by a humoral factor. *Journal of Comparative and Physiological Psychology, 67*, 407–414.

Davis, M. (2001). Tonight's the night. *New Scientist, 170*, 12.

Davis-Kean, P.E., & Sandler, H.M. (2001). A meta-analysis of measures of self-esteem for young children: A framework for future measures. *Child Development, 72*, 887–906.

Davison, G.C., & Neale, J.M. (1996). *Abnormal psychology* (Rev. 6th ed.). New York: Wiley.

Davison, G.C., & Neale, J.M. (1998). *Abnormal psychology* (7th ed.). New York: Wiley.

Davison, G.C., & Neale, J.M. (2001). *Abnormal psychology* (8th ed.). New York: Wiley.

Davison, H.K., & Burke, M.J. (2000). Sex discrimination in simulated employment contexts: A meta-analytic investigation. *Journal of Vocational Behavior, 56*, 225–248.

Dawes, R.M. (1988). *Rational choice in an uncertain world*. San Diego, CA: Harcourt Brace Jovanovich.

De Bleser, R. (1988). Localisation of aphasia: Science or fiction? In G. Denese, C. Semenza, & P. Bisiacchi (Eds.), *Perspectives on cognitive neuropsychology*. Hove, UK: Psychology Press.

De Boysson-Bardies, B., Sagart, L., & Durand, C. (1984). Discernible differences in the babbling of infants according to target language. *Journal of Child Language, 11*, 1–16.

De Castro, J.M., & de Castro, E.S. (1989). Spontaneous meal patterns of humans: Influence of the presence of other people. *American Journal of Clinical Nutrition, 50*, 237–247.

De Groot, A.D. (1965). *Thought and choice in chess*. The Hague, The Netherlands: Mouton.

De Groot, H.P., & Gwynn, M.I. (1989). Trance logic, duality, and hidden-observer responding. In N.P. Spanos & J.F. Chaves (Eds.), *Hypnosis: The cognitive-behavioural perspective*. Buffalo, NY: Prometheus.

De Haan, E.H.F., Young, A.W., & Newcombe, F. (1991). A dissociation between the sense of familiarity and access to semantic information concerning familiar people. *European Journal of Cognitive Psychology, 3*, 51–67.

De Knuif, P. (1945). *The male hormone*. New York: Harcourt Brace & Co.

De Munck, V.C. (1996). Love and marriage in a Sri Lankan Moslem community: Toward an evaluation of Dravidian marriage practices. *American Ethnologist, 23*, 698–716.

De Waal, F.B.M. (2002). Evolutionary psychology: The wheat and the chaff. *Current Directions in Psychological Science, 11*, 187–191.

De Wolff, M.S., & van IJzendoorn, M.H. (1997). Sensitivity and attachment: A meta-analysis on parental antecedents of infant attachment. *Child Development, 68*, 571–591.

Deater-Deckard, K. (2001). Annotation: Recent research examining the role of peer relationships in the development of psychopathology. *Journal of Child Psychology and Psychiatry, 42*, 565–579.

Deaux, K. (1985). Sex and gender. *Annual Review of Psychology, 36*, 49–81.

Deaux, K., & Wrightsman, L.S. (1988). *Social psychology* (5th ed.). Pacific Grove, CA: Brooks/Cole.

Debner, J.A., & Jacoby, L.L. (1994). Unconscious perception: Attention, awareness, and control. *Journal of Experimental Psychology: Learning, Memory, and Cognition, 20*, 304–317.

Dehaene, S., Naccache, L., Le Cle'H, G., Koechlin, E., Mueller, M., Dehaene-Lambertz, G., van de Moortele, P.-F., & Le Bihan, D. (1998). Imaging unconscious semantic priming. *Nature, 395*, 597–600.

Dekovic, M., & Janssens, J.M.A.M. (1992). Parents' child-rearing style and child's sociometric status. *Developmental Psychology, 28,* 925–932.

Delahanty, D.L., Dougall, A.L., Hawken, L., Trakowski, J.H., Schmitz, J.B., Jenkins, F.J., & Baum, A. (1996). Time course of natural killer cell activity and lymphocyte proliferation in healthy men. *Health Psychology, 15,* 48–55.

Delgado, P.L., Charney, D.S., Price, L.H., Aghajanian, G.K., Landis, H., & Heninger, G.R. (1990). Serotonin function and the mechanism of antidepressant action: Reversal of antidepressant induced remission by rapid depletion of plasma tryptophan. *Archives of General Psychiatry, 47,* 411–418.

Delgado, P.L., & Moreno, F.A. (2000). Role of norepinephrine in depression. *Journal of Clinical Psychiatry, 61* (Suppl. 1), 5–12.

Delk, J.L., & Fillenbaum, S. (1965). Differences in perceived colour as a function of characteristic colour. *American Journal of Psychology, 78,* 290–293.

Dell, G.S. (1986). A spreading-activation theory of retrieval in sentence production. *Psychological Review, 93,* 283–321.

Dell, G.S., Burger, L.K., & Svec, W.R. (1997). Language production and serial order: A functional analysis and a model. *Psychological Review, 104,* 123–147.

Dell, G.S., & O'Seaghdha, P.G. (1991). Mediated and convergent lexical priming in language production: A comment on Levelt et al. (1991). *Psychological Review, 98,* 604–614.

DeLucia, P.R., & Hochberg, J. (1991). Geometrical illusions in solid objects under ordinary viewing conditions. *Perception and Psychophysics, 50,* 547–554.

Dement, W.C. (1960). The effects of dream deprivation. *Science, 131,* 1705–1707.

Dement, W.C., Kleitman, N. (1957). The relation of eye movement during sleep to dream activity: An objective method for the study of dreaming. *Journal of Experimental Psychology, 53,* 339–346.

Dempster, F.N. (1996). Distributing and managing the conditions of encoding and practice. In E.L. Bjork & R.A. Bjork (Eds.), *Handbook of perception and cognition* (2nd ed.). New York: Academic Press.

Dennett, P. (2003, August 28). Children kept in cages. *Mid-Sussex Times,* p. 20.

Dennis, K.E., & Goldberg, A.P. (1996). Weight control self-efficacy types and transitions affect weight-loss outcomes in obese women. *Addictive Behaviors, 21,* 103–116.

Department of Health, Great Britain. (1992). *The health of the nation: A strategy for health in England.* London: HMSO.

Depue, R.A., & Monroe, S.M. (1978). Learned helplessness in the perspective of the depressive disorders: Conceptual and definitional issues. *Journal of Abnormal Psychology, 87,* 3–20.

Derakshan, N., & Eysenck, M.W. (1997). Interpretive biases for one's own behaviour in high-anxious individuals and repressors. *Journal of Personality and Social Psychology, 73,* 816–825.

Dermer, M., & Pyszczynski, T.A. (1978). Effects of erotica upon men's loving and liking responses for women they love. *Journal of Personality and Social Psychology, 36,* 1302–1309.

DeSteno, D., Bartlett, M.Y., Salovey, P., & Braverman, J. (2002). Sex differences in jealousy: Evolutionary mechanism or artifact of measurement? *Journal of Personality and Social Psychology, 83,* 1103–1116.

Detterman, D.K., Gabriel, L.T., & Ruthsatz, J.M. (1998). Absurd environmentalism. *Behavioral and Brain Sciences, 21,* 411–412.

Deutsch, J.A., & Deutsch, D. (1963). Attention: Some theoretical considerations. *Psychological Review, 70,* 80–90.

Deutsch, J.A., & Deutsch, D. (1967). Comments on "Selective attention: Perception or response?". *Quarterly Journal of Experimental Psychology, 19,* 362–363.

Deutsch, J.A., & Gonzalez, M.F. (1980). Gastric nutrient content signals satiety. *Behavioral and Neural Biology, 30,* 113–116.

Deutsch, M., & Gerard, H.B. (1955). A study of normative and informational influence upon individual judgement. *Journal of Abnormal and Social Psychology, 51,* 629–636.

DeValois, R.L., & DeValois, K.K. (1975). Neural coding of colour. In E.C. Carterette & M.P. Friedman (Eds.), *Handbook of perception, Vol. 5.* New York: Academic Press.

Devine, P.A., & Fernald, P.S. (1973). Outcome effects of receiving a preferred, randomly assigned or non-preferred therapy. *Journal of Consulting and Clinical Psychology, 41,* 104–107.

Devine, P.G. (1989). Stereotypes and prejudice: Their automatic and controlled components. *Journal of Personality and Social Psychology, 56,* 5–18.

DeVries, R. (2000). Vygotsky, Piaget, and education: A reciprocal assimilation of theories and educational practices. *New Ideas in Psychology, 18,* 187–213.

Di Tomaso, E., Beltramo, M., & Plomelli, D. (1996). Brain cannabinoids in chocolate. *Nature, 382,* 677–678.

Di Vesta, F.J. (1959). Effects of confidence and motivation on susceptibility to informational social influence. *Journal of Abnormal and Social Psychology, 59,* 204–209.

Diamond, M. (1982). Sexual identity, monozygotic twins reared in discordant sex roles and a BBC follow-up. *Archives of Sexual Behavior, 11,* 181–186.

Diamond, L.M. (2003). What does sexual orientation orient? A biobehavioural model distinguishing romantic love and sexual desire. *Psychological Review, 110,* 173–192.

Dick, F., Bates, E., Wulfeck, B., Utman, J.A., Dronkers, N., & Gernsbacher, M.A. (2001). Language deficits, localisation, and grammar: Evidence for a distributive model of language breakdown in aphasic patients and neurologically intact individuals. *Psychological Review, 108,* 759–788.

Dickens, W.T., & Flynn, J.R. (2001). Heritability estimates versus large environmental effects: The IQ paradox resolved. *Psychological Review, 108,* 346–369.

Dickinson, A., & Dawson, G.R. (1987). Pavlovian processes in the motivational control of instrumental performance. *Quarterly Journal of Experimental Psychology B, 39,* 201–213.

Diener, E. (1980). Deindividuation: The absence of self-awareness and self-regulation in group members. In P.B. Paulus (Ed.), *Psychology of group influence.* Hillsdale, NJ: Lawrence Erlbaum Associates, Inc.

Diener, E., Suh, E.M., Lucas, R.E., & Smith, H.E. (1999). Subjective well-being: Three decades of progress. *Psychological Bulletin, 125,* 276–302.

Dijksterhuis, A., & van Knippenberg, A. (1998). The relation between perception and behaviour, or how to win a game of trivial pursuit. *Journal of Personality and Social Psychology, 74,* 865–877.

Dill, K.E., Anderson, C.A., & Deuser, W.E. (1997a). Effects of aggressive personality on social expectations and social perception. *Journal of Research in Personality, 31,* 272–292.

Dill, K.E., Craig, A., & Deuser, W.E. (1997b). Effects of aggressive personality on social expectations and social perceptions. *Journal of Research in Personality, 31,* 272–292.

DiNardo, P.A., Guzy, L.T., Jenkins, J.A., Bak, R.M., Tomasi, S.F., & Copland, M. (1988). Aetiology and maintenance of dog fears. *Behaviour Research and Therapy, 26,* 241–244.

Dindia, K., & Allen, M. (1992). Sex differences in self-disclosure: A meta-analysis. *Psychological Bulletin, 112,* 106–124.

Dobzhansky, T. (1973). Nothing in biology makes sense except in the light of evolution. *American Biology Teacher, 35,* 125–129.

Dockrell, J., & Messer, D.J. (1999). *Children's language and communication difficulties: Understanding, identification, and intervention.* London: Cassell.

Dodge, K.A. (1997). Studies identify important variations in violent youth. *APA Monitor,* March.

Dodge, K.A., Pettit, G.S., McClaskey, C.L., & Brown, M.M. (1986). Social competence in children. *Monographs of the Society for Research in Child Development, 51,* No. 213.

Dodge, K.A., & Price, J.M. (1994). On the relation between social information processing and socially competent behaviour in early school-aged children. *Child Development, 65,* 1385–1397.

Dodson, C. S. & Reisberg, D. (1991). Indirect testing of eyewitness memory: The (non) effect of misinformation. *Bulletin of the Psychonomic Society, 29,* 333–336.

Doerr, K.H., Mitchell, T.R., Klastorin, T.D., & Brown, K.A. (1996). Impact of material flow policies and goals on job outcomes. *Journal of Applied Psychology, 75,* 142–152.

Dohrenwend, B.P., Levav, P.E., Schwartz, S., Naveh, G., Link, B.G., Skodol, A.E., & Stueve, A. (1992). Socioeconomic status and psychiatric disorders: The causation–selection issue. *Science, 255,* 946–952.

Doise, W. (1986). *Levels of explanation in social psychology*. Cambridge, UK: Cambridge University Press.

Doise, W., & Mugny, G. (1984). *The social development of the intellect*. Oxford, UK: Pergamon.

Doise, W., Rijsman, J.B., van Meel, J., Bressers, I., & Pinxten, L. (1981).Sociale markering en cognitieve ontwikkeling. *Pedagogische Studien, 58*, 241–248.

Doll, R., Peto, R., Wheatley, K., Gray, R., & Sutherland, I. (1994). Mortality in relation to smoking—40 years observations on male British doctors. *British Medical Journal, 309*, 901–911.

Dollard, J., Doob, L.W., Miller, N.E., Mowrer, O.H., & Sears, R.R. (1939).*Frustration and aggression*. New Haven, CT: Yale University Press.

Dollard, J., & Miller, N.E. (1950). *Personality and psychotherapy*. New York: McGraw-Hill.

Domhoff, G.W. (2000). Needed: A new theory. *Behavioral and Brain Sciences, 23*, 928–930.

Donahue, E.M., Robins, R.W., Roberts, B., & John, O.P. (1993). The divided self: Concurrent and longitudinal effects of psychological adjustment and self-concept differentiation. *Journal of Personality and Social Psychology, 64*, 834–846.

Doob, L.W., & Sears, R.R. (1939). Factors determining substitute behaviour and the overt expression of aggression. *Journal of Abnormal and Social Psychology, 34*, 293–313.

Doosje, B., Branscombe, N.R., Spears, R., & Manstead, A.S.R. (1998). Guilty by association: When one's group has a negative history. *Journal of Personality and Social Psychology, 75*, 872–886.

Dosher, B.A., & Corbett, A.T. (1982). Instrument inferences and verb schemata. *Memory and Cognition, 10*, 531–539.

Doty, R.M., Peterson, B.E., & Winter, D.G. (1991). Threat and authoritarianism in the United States, 1978–1987. *Journal of Personality and Social Psychology, 61*, 629–640.

Dovidio, J.F., Brigham, J.C., Johnson, B.T., & Gaertner, S. (1996). Stereotyping, prejudice, and discrimination: Another look. In C.N. Macrae, C. Stangor, & M. Hewstone (Eds.), *Stereotypes and stereotyping*. Guilford Press: New York.

Dovidio, J.F., & Gaertner, S.L. (1991). Changes in the expression and assessment of racial prejudice. In H.J. Knopke, R.J. Norrell, & R.W. Rogers (Eds.), *Opening doors: Perspectives on race relations in contemporary America*. Tuscaloosa, AL: University of Alabama Press.

Dovidio, J.F., Gaertner, S.L., & Validzic, A. (1998). Intergroup bias: Status, differentiation, and a common in-group identity. *Journal of Personality and Social Psychology, 75*, 109–120.

Draycott, S.G., & Kline, P. (1995). The Big Three or the Big Five—The EPQ-R vs. the NEO-PI: A research note, replication and elaboration. *Personality and Individual Differences, 18*, 801–804.

Dreifus, C. (1998). She talks to apes and, according to her, they talk back. *New York Times*, 14th April.

Drew, M.A., Colquhoun, W.P., & Long, M.A. (1958). Effect of small doses of alcohol on a task resembling driving. *British Medical Journal, 1*, 993–998.

Driscoll, M. (1998). Father forgive me. *The Sunday Times*. 29th March.

Driver, J. (2001). A selective review of selective attention research from the past century. *British Journal of Psychology, 92*, 53–78.

Drummond, S.P., Brown, G.G., Gillin, J.C., Stricker, J.L., Wong, E.C., & Buxton, R.B. (2000). Altered brain response to verbal learning following sleep deprivation. *Nature, 403*, 655–657.

Drury, J., & Reicher, S. (2000). Collective action and psychological change: The emergence of new social identities. *British Journal of Social Psychology, 39*, 579–604.

Duck, J.M., Hogg, M.A., & Terry, D.J. (1999). Social identity and perceptions of media persuasion: Are we always less influenced than others? *Journal of Applied Social Psychology, 29*, 1879–1899.

Duck, S. (1992). *Human relationships* (2nd ed.). London: Sage.

Duckitt, J., Wagner, C., du Plessis, I., & Birum, I. (2002). The psychological bases of ideology and prejudice: Testing a dual process model. *Journal of Personality and Social Psychology, 83*, 75–93.

Dunbar, R. (1993). Coevolution of neocortical size, group size and language in humans. *Behavioural and Brain Sciences, 16*, 681–735.

Duncan, J. (1979). Divided attention: The whole is more than the sum of its parts. *Journal of Experimental Psychology: Human Perception and Performance, 5*, 216–228.

Duncan, J., Seitz, R.J., Kolodny, J., Bor, D., Herzog, H., Ahmed, A., Newell, F.N., & Emslie, H. (2000). A neural basis for general intelligence. *Science, 289*, 457–460.

Duncan, S.L. (1976). Differential social perception and attribution of intergroup violence: Testing the lower limits of stereotyping of blacks. *Journal of Personality and Social Psychology, 34*, 590–598.

Duncker, K. (1945). On problem solving. *Psychological Monographs, 58* (Whole No. 270).

Dunn, J. (1987). The beginnings of moral understanding: Development in the second year. In J. Kagan & S. Lamb (Eds.), *The emergence of morality in young children*. Chicago: University of Chicago Press.

Dunn, J., & Plomin, R. (1990). *Separate lives: Why siblings are so different*. New York: Basic Books.

Dunne, M.P., Martin, N.G., Statham, D.J., Slutske, W.S., Dinwiddie, S.H., Bucholz, K.K., Madden, P.A.F., & Heath, A.C. (1997). Genetic and environmental contributions to variance in age at first sexual intercourse. *Psychological Science, 8*, 211–216.

Dunnett, S.B., Lane, D.M., & Winn, P. (1985). Ibotenic acid lesions of the lateral hypothalamus: Comparison with 6-hydroxydopamine-induced sensorimotor deficits. *Neuroscience, 14*, 509–518.

Durkin, K. (1995). *Developmental social psychology: From infancy to old age*. Oxford, UK: Blackwell.

Durrett, M.E., Otaki, M., & Richards, P. (1984). Attachment and the mother's perception of support for the father. *International Journal of Behavioral Development, 7*, 167–176.

Duval, T.S., & Silvia, P.J. (2002). Self-awareness, probability of improvement, and the self-serving bias. *Journal of Personality and Social Psychology, 82*, 49–61.

Dworetzsky, J.P. (1996). *Introduction to child development* (6th ed.). New York: West Publishing Co.

Dzewaltowski, D.A. (1989). Toward a model of exercise motivation. *Journal of Sport and Exercise Psychology, 32*, 11–28.

Eagly, A.H., & Carli, L. (1981). Sex of researchers and sex-typed communications as determinants of sex differences in influenceability: A meta-analysis of social influence studies. *Psychological Bulletin, 90*, 1–20.

Eagly, A.H., & Crowley, M. (1986). Gender and helping behaviour: A meta-analytic review of the social psychological literature. *Psychological Bulletin, 100*, 283–308.

Eagly, A.H., & Johnson, B.T. (1990). Gender and leadership style: A meta-analysis. *Psychological Bulletin, 108*, 233–256.

Eagly, A.H., & Karau, S.J. (2002). Role congruity theory of prejudice toward female leaders. *Psychological Review, 109*, 573–598.

Eagly, A.H., Karau, S.J., & Makhijani, M.G. (1995). Gender and the effectiveness of leaders: A meta-analysis. *Psychological Bulletin, 117*, 125–145.

Eagly, A.H., Makhijani, M.G., & Konsky, B.G. (1992). Gender and the evaluation of leaders: A meta-analysis. *Psychological Bulletin, 111*, 3–22.

Eagly, A.H., & Steffen, V.J. (1986). Gender and aggressive behaviour: A meta-analytic review of the social psychological literature. *Psychological Bulletin, 90*, 1–20.

Eames, D., Shorrocks, D., & Tomlinson, P. (1990). Naughty animals or naughty experimenters? Conservation accidents revisited with video-simulated commentary. *British Journal of Developmental Psychology, 8*, 25–37.

Earley, P.C. (1993). East meets West meets Mid-East: Further explorations of collectivistic and individualistic work groups. *Academy of Management Journal, 36*, 319–348.

Earley, P.C., Connolly, T., & Ekegren, G. (1989). Goals, strategy development and task performance: Some limits on the efficacy of goal-setting. *Journal of Applied Psychology, 74*, 24–33.

Early Child Care Research Network. (1999, October). In new day-care study results undersize need for quality. *APA Monitor*. Available from http://www.apa.org/monitor/oct99/toc.html

East, P., & Rook, K.S. (1992). Compensatory patterns of support among children's peer relationships: A test using school friends, nonschool friends, and siblings. *Developmental Psychology, 28*, 163–172.

Ebbinghaus, H. (1913). *Memory* (H. Ruyer & C.E. Bussenius, Trans.). New York: Teachers College, Columbia University. (Original work published 1885)

Eder, R. (1990). Uncovering young children's psychological selves: Individual and developmental differences. *Child Development, 61*, 849–863.

Edwards, C.P. (1993). Behavioural sex differences in children of diverse cultures: The cause of nurturance to infants. In M.E. Pereira & L.A. Fairbanks (Eds.), *Juvenile primates: Life history, development, and behaviour*. New York: Oxford University Press.

Egan, S.K., & Perry, D.G. (2001). Gender identity: A multidimensional analysis with implications for psychosocial adjustment. *Developmental Psychology, 37*, 451–463.

Eid, M., & Diener, E. (2001). Norms for experiencing emotions in different cultures: Inter- and intranational differences. *Journal of Personality and Social Psychology, 81*, 869–885.

Eisenberg, N. (1989). The development of prosocial values. In N. Eisenberg, J. Reyknowski, & E. Staub (Eds.), *Social and moral values: Individual and societal perspectives*. Hillsdale, NJ: Lawrence Erlbaum Associates, Inc.

Eisenberg, N. (2000). Emotion, regulation, and moral development. *Annual Review of Psychology, 51*, 665–697.

Eisenberg, N., & Fabes, R.A. (1992). Emotion regulation and the development of social competence. In M.S. Clark (Ed.), *Emotion and social behaviour: Vol. 14. Review of personality and social psychology*. Newbury Park, CA: Sage.

Eisenberg, N., Fabes, R.A., Guthrie, I.K., Murphy, B.C., Maszk, P., Holmgren, R., & Suh, K. (1996). The relations of regulation and emotionality to problem behaviour in elementary school children. *Development and Psychopathology, 8*, 141–162.

Eisenberg, N., Fabes, R.A., Shepard, S.A., Murphy, B.C., Guthrie, I.K., Jones, S., Friedman, J., Poulin, R., & Maszk, P. (1997). Contemporaneous and longitudinal prediction of children's social functioning from regulation and emotionality. *Child Development, 68*, 642–664.

Eisenberg, N., & Mussen, P.H. (1989). *The roots of prosocial behaviour in children*. Cambridge, UK: Cambridge University Press.

Eisenberg, N., Pidada, S., & Liew, J. (2001). The relations of regulation and negative emotionality to Indonesian children's social functioning. *Child Development, 72*, 1747–1763.

Eisenberg-Berg, N., & Hand, M. (1979). The relationship of preschoolers' reasoning about prosocial moral conflicts to prosocial behaviour. *Child Development, 50*, 356–363.

Eisenstat, R.A. (1990). Compressor team start-up. In J.R. Hackman (Ed.), *Groups that work (and those that don't)*. San Francisco: Jossey-Bass.

Ekman, P. (1993). Facial expression and emotion. *American Psychologist, 48*, 384–392.

Ekman, P., & Davidson, R.J. (1994). *The nature of emotion: Fundamental questions*. New York: Oxford University Press.

Ekman, P., & Friesen, W.V. (1971). Constants acrosss cultures in the face and emotion. *Journal of Personality and Social Psychology, 17*, 124–129.

Ekman, P., Friesen, W.V., & Ellsworth, P. (1972). *Emotion in the human face: Guidelines for research and an integration of findings*. New York: Pergamon.

Ekman, P., Friesen, W.V., O'Sullivan, M., Chan, A., Diacoyanni-Tarlatzis, I., Heider, K., Krause, R., LeCompte, W.A., Pitcairn, T., Ricci-Bitti, P.E., Scherer, K., & Tomita, M., & Tzavaras, A. (1987). Universals and cultural differences in the judgments of facial expressions of emotion. *Journal of Personality and Social Psychology, 53*, 712–717.

Elder, G.H. (1969). Appearance and education in marriage mobility. *American Sociological Review, 34*, 519–533.

Eley, T.C., Lichtenstein, P., & Stevenson, J. (1999). Sex differences in the aetiology of aggressive and non-aggressive antisocial behaviour: Results from two twin studies. *Child Development, 70*, 155–168.

Elicker, J., Englund, M., & Sroufe, L.A. (1992). Predicting peer competence and peer relationships in childhood from early parent–child relationships. In R.D. Parke & G.W. Ladd (Eds.), *Family–peer relationships: Modes of linkage*. Hillsdale, NJ: Lawrence Erlbaum Associates, Inc.

Elkin, I. (1994). The NIMH Treatment of Depression Collaborative Research Program: Where we began and where we are. In S. Garfield & A. Bergin (Eds.), *Handbook of psychotherapy and behavior change* (4th ed.). New York: John Wiley.

Elkind, D., & Schoenfeld, E. (1972). Identity and equivalence conservation at two age levels. *Developmental Psychology, 6*, 529–533.

Ellemers, N., Spears, R., & Doosje, B. (2002). Self and social identity. *Annual Review of Psychology, 53*, 161–186.

Ellis, A. (1962). *Reason and emotion in psychotherapy*. Secaucus, NJ: Prentice-Hall.

Ellis, A. (1978). The basic clinical theory of rational emotive therapy. In A. Ellis & R. Grieger (Eds.), *Handbook of rational emotive therapy*. New York: Springer.

Ellis, A.W. (1984). *Reading, writing, and dyslexia: A cognitive analysis*. London: Lawrence Erlbaum Associates Ltd.

Ellis, A.W. (1993). *Reading, writing, and dyslexia: A cognitive analysis* (2nd ed.). Hove, UK: Lawrence Erlbaum Associates Ltd.

Ellis, A.W., Miller, D., & Sin, G. (1983). Wernicke's aphasia and normal language processing: A case study in cognitive neuropsychology. *Cognition, 15*, 111–144.

Ellis, A.W., & Young, A.W. (1988). *Human cognitive neuropsychology*. Hove, UK: Lawrence Erlbaum Associates Ltd.

Ellis, R., & Humphreys, G. (1999). *Connectionist psychology: A text with readings*. Hove, UK: Psychology Press.

Ellis, S., & Gauvain, M. (1992). Social and cultural influences on children's collaborative interactions. In L.T. Winegar & J. Valsiner (Eds.), *Children's development within social context: Vol. 2. Research and methodology*. Hillsdale, NJ: Lawrence Erlbaum Associates, Inc.

Ember, C.R. (1978). Myths about hunter-gatherers. *Ethnology, 17*, 439–448.

Empson, J.A.C. (1989). *Sleep and dreaming*. London: Faber & Faber.

Endler, N.S., & Parker, J.D.A. (1990). Multidimensional assessment of coping: A critical evaluation. *Journal of Personality and Social Psychology, 58*, 844–854.

Engle, R.W. (2002). Working memory capacity as executive attention. *Current Directions in Psychological Science, 11*, 19–23.

Epping-Jordan, J.E., Compas, B.E., & Howell, D.C. (1994). Predictors of cancer progression in young adult men and women: Avoidance, intrusive thoughts, and psychological symptoms. *Health Psychology, 13*, 539–547.

Epstein, S. (1977). Traits are alive and well. In D. Magnusson & N.S. Endler (Eds.), *Perspectives in interactional psychology*. New York: Plenum.

Erel, O., Oberman, Y., & Yirmiya, N. (2000). Maternal versus nonmaternal care and seven domains of children's development. *Psychological Bulletin, 126*, 727–747.

Ericsson, K.A. (1996). *The road to excellence*. Mahwah, NJ: Lawrence Erlbaum Associates, Inc.

Ericsson, K.A., & Chase, W.G. (1982). Exceptional memory. *American Scientist, 70*, 607–615.

Ericsson, K.A., Krampe, R.T., & Tesch-Romer, C. (1993). The role of deliberate practice in the acquisition of expert performance. *Psychological Review, 100*, 363–406.

Ericsson, K.A., & Lehmann, A.C. (1996). Expert and exceptional performance: evidence of maximal adaptation to task constraints. *Annual Review of Psychology, 47*, 273–305.

Eriksen, C.W., & St. James, J.D. (1986). Visual attention within and around the field of focal attention: A zoom lens model. *Perception and Psychophysics, 40*, 225–240.

Erikson, E.H. (1950). *Childhood and society*. New York: Norton.

Erikson, E.H. (1968). *Identity: Youth and crisis*. New York: Norton.

Erikson, E.H. (1969). *Gandhi's truth: On the origin of militant nonviolence*. New York: W.W. Norton.

Eron, L.D. (1987). The development of aggressive behaviour from the perspective of a developing behaviourism. *American Psychologist, 42*, 435–442.

Eron, L.D., & Huesmann, L.R. (1984). The relation of prosocial behaviour to the development of aggression and psychopathology. *Aggressive Behavior, 10*, 201–211.

Eron, L.D., Huesmann, L.R., & Zelli, A. (1991). The role of parental variables in the learning of aggression. In D.J. Pepler & H.K. Rubin (Eds.), *The development and treatment of childhood aggression*. Hillsdale, NJ: Lawrence Erlbaum Associates, Inc.

Eshel, Y., Sharabany, R., & Friedman, U. (1998). Friends, lovers and spouses: intimacy in young adults. *British Journal of Social Psychology, 37*, 41–57.

Eslinger, P.J., & Damasio, A.R. (1985). Severe disturbance of higher cognition after bilateral frontal lobe ablation: Patient EVR. *Neurology, 35*, 1731–1741.

Essock-Vitale, S.M., & McGuire, M.T. (1985). Women's lives viewed from an evolutionary perspective: II. Patterns of helping. *Ethology and Sociobiology, 6*, 155–173.

Estes, W.K. (1944). An experimental study of punishment. *Psychological Monographs: General and Applied, 54* (No. 263).

Evans, J.St.B.T. (1989). *Bias in human reasoning*. Hove, UK: Psychology Press.

Evans, J.St.B.T. (2000). What could and could not be a strategy in reasoning. In W. Schaeken, G. de Vooght, A. Vandierendonck, & G. d'Ydewalle (Eds.), *Deductive reasoning and strategies*. Hove, UK: Lawrence Erlbaum Associates Ltd.

Evans, J.St.B.T., Clibbens, J., & Rood, B. (1995). Bias in conditional inference: Implications for mental models and mental logic. *Quarterly Journal of Experimental Psychology, 48A*, 644–670.

Evans, J.St.B.T., & Over, D.E. (1997). Are people rational? Yes, no, and sometimes. *The Psychologist, 10*, 403–406.

Evans, P. (1998). Stress and coping. In M. Pitts & K. Phillips (Eds.), *The psychology of health* (2nd ed.). London: Routledge.

Evans, P., Clow, A., & Hucklebridge, F. (1997). Stress and the immune system. *The Psychologist, 10*, 303–307.

Everson, C.A. (1993). Sustained sleep deprivation impairs host defense. *American Journal of Physiology, 265*, 1148–1154.

Everson, C.A., Bergmann, B.M., & Rechtschaffen, A. (1989). Sleep deprivation in the rat: III. Total sleep deprivation. *Sleep, 12*, 13–21.

Eysenck, H.J. (1944). Types of personality: A factorial study of 700 neurotic soldiers. *Journal of Mental Science, 90*, 851–861.

Eysenck, H.J. (1947). *Dimensions of personality*. London: Routledge & Kegan Paul.

Eysenck, H.J. (1952). The effects of psychotherapy: An evaluation. *Journal of Consulting Psychology, 16*, 319–324.

Eysenck, H.J. (1967). *The biological basis of personality*. Springfield, Ill.: C.C. Thomas.

Eysenck, H.J. (1971). *The IQ argument: Race, intelligence and education*. Oxford, UK: Library Press.

Eysenck, H.J. (1978). Superfactors P, E, and N in a comprehensive factor space. *Multivariate Behavioral Research, 13*, 475–482.

Eysenck, H.J. (1979). *The structure and measurement of intelligence*. Berlin: Springer.

Eysenck H.J. (1981). *The intelligence controversy: H.J. Eysenck vs. Leon Kamin*. New York: Wiley.

Eysenck, H.J. (1982). *Personality, genetics and behavior*. New York: Praeger.

Eysenck, H.J., & Eysenck, M.W. (1981). *Mindwatching*. London: Michael Joseph.

Eysenck, H.J., & Eysenck, M.W. (1985). *Personality and individual differences*. New York: Plenum.

Eysenck, M.W. (1982). *Attention and arousal: Cognition and performance*. Berlin, Germany: Springer.

Eysenck, M.W. (1984). *A handbook of cognitive psychology*. London: Lawrence Erlbaum Associates Ltd.

Eysenck, M.W. (1988). Individual differences, arousal, and monotonous work. In J.P. Leonard (Ed.), *Vigilance: Methods, models, and regulation*. Frankfurt, Germany: Peter Lang.

Eysenck, M.W. (1992). *Anxiety: The cognitive perspective*. Hove, UK: Lawrence Erlbaum Associates Ltd.

Eysenck, M.W. (1994a). *Individual differences: Normal and abnormal*. Hove, UK: Psychology Press.

Eysenck, M.W. (1994b). *Perspectives on psychology*. Hove, UK: Psychology Press.

Eysenck, M.W. (1997). *Anxiety and cognition: A unified theory*. Hove, UK: Psychology Press.

Eysenck, M.W. (1998). *Psychology: An integrated approach*. Harlow, UK: Addison Wesley Longman.

Eysenck, M.W. (2000). *Psychology: A student's handbook*. Hove, UK: Psychology Press.

Eysenck, M.W. (2001). *Principles of cognitive psychology* (2nd ed.). Hove, UK: Psychology Press.

Eysenck, M.W. (2002). *Simply psychology* (2nd ed.). Hove, UK: Psychology Press.

Eysenck, M.W., & Keane, M.T. (1995). *Cognitive psychology: A student's handbook* (3rd ed.). Hove, UK: Psychology Press.

Eysenck, M.W., & Keane, M.T. (2000). *Cognitive psychology: A student's handbook* (4th ed.). Hove, UK: Psychology Press.

Eysenck, M.W., MacLeod, C., & Mathews, A. (1987). Cognitive functioning and anxiety. *Psychological Research, 49*, 189–195.

Fabes, R.A., Fultz, J., Eisenberg, N., May-Plumlee, T., & Christopher, F.S. (1989). Effects of rewards on children's pro-social motivation: A socialization study. *Developmental Psychology, 25*, 509–515.

Fabrega, H., Ulrich, R., Pilkonis, P., & Mezzich, J. (1991). On the homogeneity of personality disorder clusters. *Comprehensive Psychiatry, 32*, 373–386.

Fabrega, H., Ulrich, R., Pilkonis, P., & Mezzich, J. (1992). Pure personality disorders in an intake psychiatric setting. *Journal of Personality Disorders, 6*, 153–161.

Fabricius, W.V., & Hagen, J.W. (1984). Use of causal attributions about recall performance to assess metamemory and predict strategic memory behaviour in young children. *Developmental Psychology, 20*, 975–987.

Fagot, B.I. (1985). Beyond the reinforcement principle: Another step toward understanding sex-role development. *Developmental Psychology, 21*, 1097–1104.

Fagot, B.I., & Leinbach, M.D. (1989). The young child's gender schema: Environmental input, internal organisation. *Child Development, 60*, 663–672.

Fahrenberg, J. (1992). Psychophysiology of neuroticism and anxiety. In A.Gale & M.W. Eysenck (Eds.), *Handbook of individual differences: Biological perspectives*. Chichester, UK: Wiley.

Falloon, I.R.H., Boyd, J.L., McGill, C.W., Williamson, M., Razani, J., Moss, H.B., Gilderman, A.M., & Simpson, G.M. (1985). Family management in the prevention of morbidity of schizophrenia. *Archives of General Psychiatry, 42*, 887–896.

Falloon, I.R.H., Coverdale, J.H., Laidlaw, T.M., Merry, S., Kydd, R.R., Morosini, P., & the OTP Collaborative Group. (1998). Early intervention for schizophrenic disorders. *British Journal of Psychiatry, 172*, 33–38.

Fantz, R.L. (1961). The origin of form perception. *Scientific American, 204*, 66–72.

Farah, M.J. (1990). Visual agnosia: *Disorders of object recognition and what they tell us about normal vision*. Cambridge, MA: MIT Press.

Farah, M.J. (1994). Specialisation within visual object recognition: Clues from prosopagnosia and alexia. In M.J. Farah & G. Ratcliff (Eds.), *The neuropsychology of high-level vision: Collected tutorial essays*. Hillsdale, NJ: Lawrence Erlbaum Associates, Inc.

Farah, M.J. (1999). Relations among the agnosias. In G.W. Humphreys (Ed.), *Case studies in the neuropsychology of vision*. Hove, UK: Psychology Press.

Faraone, S.V., Tsuang, M.T., & Tsuang, D.W. (1999). *Genetics of mental disorders: A guide for students, clinicians, and researchers*. New York: Guilford Press.

Farr, J.L. (1976). Task characteristics, reward contingency, and intrinsic motivation. *Organizational Behavior and Human Performance, 16*, 294–307.

Farrar, M.J. (1992). Negative evidence and grammatical morpheme acquisition. *Developmental Psychology, 28*, 90–98.

Farrington, D.P. (1995). The twelfth Jack Tizard Memorial Lecture: The development of offending and anti-social behaviour from childhood: Key findings from the Cambridge Study in Delinquent Development. *Journal of Child Psychology and Psychiatry and Allied Disciplines, 36*, 929–964.

Farrington, D.P. (2000). Psychosocial predictors of adult antisocial personality and adult convictions. *Behavioral Sciences and the Law, 18*, 605–622.

Fausel, D. (1995). Stress inoculation training for step-couples. *Marriage and Family Review, 21*, 135–157.

Fazio, R.H., & Zanna, M.P. (1981). Direct experience and attitude–behaviour consistency. In L. Berkowitz (Ed.)., *Advances in experimental social psychology, Vol. 14*. New York: Academic Press.

Fazio, R.H., Zanna, M.P., & Cooper, J. (1977). Dissonance versus self-perception: An integrative view of each theory's proper domain of application. *Journal of Experimental Social Psychology, 13*, 464–479.

Fein, S., Hilton, J.L., & Miller, D.T. (1990). Suspicion of ulterior motivation and the correspondence bias. *Journal of Personality and Social Psychology, 58*, 753–764.

Feingold, A. (1988). Matching for attractiveness in romantic partners and same-sex friends: A meta-analysis and theoretical critique. *Psychological Bulletin, 104*, 226–235.

Feingold, A. (1990). Gender differences in effects of physical attractiveness on romantic attraction: A comparison across five research paradigms. *Journal of Personality and Social Psychology, 59*, 981–993.

Feingold, A. (1992a). Gender differences in mate selection preferences: A test of the parental investment model. *Psychological Bulletin, 112*, 125–139.

Feingold, A. (1992b). Good-looking people are not what we think. *Psychological Bulletin, 111*, 304–341.

Feldman, S.S., Rosenthal, D.A., Mont-Reynaud, R., Lau, S., & Leung, K. (1991). Ain't misbehavin': Adolescent values and family environments as correlates of misconduct in Australia, Hong Kong, and the United States. *Journal of Research on Adolescence, 1*, 109–134.

Feldman Barrett, L., & Russell, J.A. (1998). Independence and bipolarity in the structure of affect. *Journal of Personality and Social Psychology, 74*, 967–984.

Fellner, C.H., & Marshall, J.R. (1981). Kidney donors revisited. In J.P. Rushton & R.M. Sorrentino (Eds.), *Altruism and helping behaviour*. Hillsdale, NJ: Lawrence Erlbaum Associates, Inc.

Fenson, L., Dale, P.S., Reznick, J.S., Bates, E., Thal, D.J., & Pethick, S.J. (1994). Variability in early communicative development. *Monographs of the Society for Research in Child Development, 59*, 173.

Fenzel, L.M. (2000). Prospective study of changes in global self-worth and strain during the transition to middle school. *Journal of Early Adolescence, 20*, 93–116.

Ferguson, T.J., & Rule, B.G. (1983). An attributional perspective on anger and aggression. In R. Green & E. Donnerstein (Eds.), *Aggression: Theoretical and empirical reviews: Vol. 1. Method and theory*. New York: Academic Press.

Ferreira, F., & Swets, B. (2002). How incremental is language production? Evidence from the production of utterances requiring the computation of arithmetic sums. *Journal of Memory and Language, 46*, 57–84.

Feske, U., & Chambless, D.L. (1995). Cognitive behavioural versus exposure only treatment for social phobia: A meta-analysis. *Behavioural Therapy, 26*, 695–720.

Festinger, L. (1957). *A theory of cognitive dissonance*. Stanford, CA: Stanford University Press.

Festinger, L., & Carlsmith, J.M. (1959). Cognitive consequences of forced compliance. *Journal of Abnormal and Social Psychology, 47*, 382–389.

Festinger, L., Schachter, S., & Back, K. (1950). *Social pressures in informal groups: A study of a housing community*. New York: Harper.

Fibiger, H.C., LePiane, F.G., Jakubovic, A., & Phillips, A.G. (1987). The role of dopamine in intracranial self-stimulation of the ventral tegmental area. *Journal of Neuroscience, 7*, 3888–3896.

Fiedler, F.E. (1967). *A theory of leader effectiveness*. New York: McGraw-Hill.

Fiedler, F.E. (1978). The contingency model and the dynamics of the leadership process. In L. Berkowitz (Ed.), *Advances in experimental social psychology, Vol. 12*. New York: Academic Press.

Fiedler, F.E., & Potter, E.H. (1983). Dynamics of leadership effectiveness. In H.H. Blumberg, A.P. Hare, V. Kent, & M. Davies (Eds.), *Small groups and social interaction, Vol. 1*. Chichester, UK: Wiley.

Fiedler, K. (1988). The dependence of conjunction fallacy on subtle linguistic factors. *Psychological Research, 50*, 123–129.

Fielding, K.S., & Hogg, M.A. (2000). Working hard to achieve self-defining goals: A social identity analysis. *Zeitschrift füuuml;r Sozialpsychologie, 4*, 191–203.

Fijneman, Y.A., Willemsen, M.E., & Poortinga, Y.H. (1996). Individualism_collectivism: An empirical study of a conceptual issue. *Journal of Cross-Cultural Psychology, 27*, 381–402.

Fincham, F.D., & Bradbury, T.N. (1993). Marital satisfaction, depression, and attributions: A longitudinal analysis. *Journal of Personality and Social Psychology, 64*, 442–452.

Fincham, F.D., & Hewstone, M. (2001). Attribution theory and research: From basic to applied. In M. Hewstone & W. Stroebe (Eds.), *Introduction to social psychology* (3rd ed.). Oxford, UK: Blackwell.

Finkel, D., Wille, D.E., & Matheny, A.P. (1999). *Behaviour genetic analysis of the relationship between attachment and temperament*. Paper presented at the biennial meeting of the Society for Research in Child Development, Albuquerque, NM.

Finlay-Jones, R.A., & Brown, G.W. (1981). Types of stressful life events and the onset of anxiety and depressive disorders. *Psychological Medicine, 11*, 803–815.

Fischhoff, B. (1977). Perceived informativeness of facts. *Journal of Experimental Psychology: Human Perception and Performance, 3*, 349–358.

Fischhoff, B., & Beyth, R. (1975). "I knew it would happen"— Remembered probabilities of once-future things. *Organizational Behaviour and Human Performance, 13*, 1–16.

Fischler, I., Rundus, D., & Atkinson, R.C. (1970). Effects of overt rehearsal procedures on free recall. *Psychonomic Science, 19*, 249–250.

Fishbein, M., & Ajzen, I. (1975). *Belief, attitude, intention and behaviour: An introduction to theory and research*. Reading, MA: Addison-Wesley.

Fishbein, M., & Coombs, F.S. (1974). Basis for decision: An attitudinal analysis of voting behavior. *Journal of Applied Social Psychology, 4*, 95–124.

Fiske, A.P. (2002). Using individualism and collectivism to compare cultures—A critique of the validity and measurement of the constructs: Comment on Oyserman et al. (2002). *Psychological Bulletin, 128*, 78–88.

Fiske, S.T. (1998). Stereotyping, prejudice, and discrimination. In D.T. Gilbert, S.T. Fiske, & G. Lindzey (Eds.), *The handbook of social psychology* (Vol. 2, 4th ed.). New York: McGraw-Hill.

Fiske, S.T. (2000). Stereotyping, prejudice, and discrimination at the seam between the centuries: Evolution, culture, mind, and brain. *European Journal of Social Psychology, 30*, 299–322.

Fiske, S.T. (2002). What we know now about bias and intergroup conflict, the problem of the century. *Current Directions in Psychological Science, 11*, 123–128.

Fitts, P.M. (1964). Perceptual-motor skill learning. In A.W. Melton (Ed.), *Categories of human learning*. New York: Academic Press.

Fitts, P.M., & Posner, M.I. (1967). *Human performance*. Belmont, CA: Brooks/Cole.

Fivush, R., Haden, C., & Reese, E. (1996). Remembering, recounting, and reminiscing: The development of autobiographical memory in social context. In D.C. Rubin (Ed.), *Remembering our past: Studies in autobiographical memory*. New York: Cambridge University Press.

Flavell, J.H. (1999). Cognitive development: Children's knowledge about the mind. *Annual Review of Psychology, 50*, 21–45.

Flavell, J.H., Beach, D.R., & Chinsky, J.M. (1966). Spontaneous verbal rehearsal in a memory task as a function of age. *Child Development, 37,* 283–299.

Flowerdew, J., & Tauroza, S. (1995). The effect of discourse markers on second language lecture comprehension. *Studies in Second Language Acquisition, 17,* 455–458.

Flynn, J.R. (1987). Massive IQ gains in 14 nations: What IQ tests really measure. *Psychological Bulletin, 101,* 271–291.

Flynn, J.R. (1994). IQ gains over time. In R.J. Sternberg (Ed.), *Encyclopedia of human intelligence.* New York: Macmillan.

Folkman, S., & Lazarus, R.S. (1985). If it changes it must be a process: Study of emotion and coping during three stages of a college examination. *Journal of Personality and Social Psychology, 48,* 150–170.

Folkman, S., Lazarus, R.S., Dunkel-Schetter, C., DeLongis, A., & Gruen, R.J. (1986). Dynamics of a stressful encounter: Cognitive appraisal, coping, and encounter outcomes. *Journal of Personality and Social Psychology, 50,* 992–1003.

Fonzi, A., Schneider, B.H., Tani, F., & Target, M. (1997). Predicting children's friendship status from their dyadic interaction in structured situations of potential conflict. *Child Development, 68,* 496–506.

Ford, M.E., & Tisak, M.S. (1983). A further search for social intelligence. *Journal of Educational Psychology, 75,* 196–206.

Ford, M.R., & Widiger, T.A. (1989). Sex bias in the diagnosis of histrionic and antisocial personality disorders. *Journal of Consulting and Clinical Psychology, 57,* 301–305.

Forgatch, M.S., & DeGarmo, D.S. (1999). Parenting through change: An effective prevention program for single mothers. *Journal of Consulting and Clinical Psychology, 67,* 711–724.

Forman, E.A., & Cazden, C.B. (1985). Exploring Vygotskian perspectives in education: The cognitive value of peer interaction. In J.V. Wertsch (Ed.), *Culture, communication, and cognition: Vygotskian perspectives.* Cambridge, UK: Cambridge University Press.

Forsterling, F. (1989). Models of covariation and causal attribution: How do they relate to the analysis of variance? *Journal of Personality and Social Psychology, 57,* 615–625.

Fortenberry, J.C., Brown, D.B., & Shevlin, L.T. (1986). Analysis of drug involvement in traffic fatalities in Alabama. *American Journal of Drug and Alcohol Abuse, 12,* 257–267.

Foulkes, D., & Vogel, G. (1965). Mental activity at sleep onset. *Journal of Abnormal Psychology, 70,* 231–243.

Fowles, D.C. (1987). Application of a behavioural theory of motivation to the concepts of anxiety and impulsivity. *Journal of Research in Personality, 21,* 417–435.

Fox Tree, J.E. (2000). Co-ordinating spontaneous talk. In L.R. Wheeldon (Ed.), *Aspects of language production.* Hove, UK: Psychology Press.

Fox, R., & McDaniel, C. (1982). The perception of biological motion by human infants. *Science, 218,* 486–487.

Foy, D.W., Resnick, H.S., Sipprelle, R.C., & Carroll, E.M. (1987). Premilitary, military, and postmilitary factors in the development of combat-related post-traumatic stress disorder. *The Behavior Therapist, 10,* 3–9.

Fraley, R.C., & Spieker, S.J. (2003). Are infant attachment patterns continuously or categorically distributed? A taxometric analysis of Strange Situation behaviour. *Developmental Psychology, 39,* 387–404.

Frances, A.J., First, M.B., Widiger, T.A., Miele, G.M., Tilly, S.M., Davis, W.W., & Pincus, H.A. (1991). An A to Z guide to DSM-IV conundrums. *Journal of Abnormal Psychology, 100,* 407–412.

Franchini, L., Gasperini, M., Perez, J., Smeraldi, E., & Zanardi, R. (1997). A double-blind study of long-term treatment with sertraline or fluvoxamine for prevention of highly recurrent unipolar depression. *Journal of Clinical Psychiatry, 58,* 104–107.

Frank, M.G., & Gilovich, T. (1989). Effect of memory perspective on retrospective causal attributions. *Journal of Personality and Social Psychology, 57,* 399–403.

Frankenhaeuser, M. (1975). Sympathetic-adreno medullary activity behavior and the psychosocial environment. In P.H. Venables & M.J. Christie (Eds.), *Research in psychophysiology.* New York: Wiley.

Frankenhaeuser, M. (1983). The sympathetic-adrenal and pituitary-adrenal response to challenges: Comparison between the sexes. In T.M. Dembroski, T.H. Schmidt, & G. Blumchez (Eds.), *Biobehavioural bases of coronary heart disease.* Basel, Switzerland: Karger.

Franklin, S., Turner, J., Ralph, M.A.L., Morris, J., & Bailey, P.J. (1996). A distinctive case of word meaning deafness? *Cognitive Neuropsychology, 13,* 1139–1162.

Franz, C., Weinberger, J., Kremen, W., & Jacobs, R. (1996). *Childhood antecedents of dysphoria in adults: A 36-year longitudinal study.* Unpublished manuscript, Williams College.

Franz, C.E., McClelland, D., & Weinberger, J. (1991). Childhood antecedents of conventional social accomplishment in midlife adults: A 36-year prospective study. *Journal of Personality and Social Psychology, 60,* 586–595.

Franzoi, S.L. (1996). *Social psychology.* Madison, WI: Brown & Benchmark.

Frazier, L., & Rayner, K. (1982). Making and correcting errors in the analysis of structurally ambiguous sentences. *Cognitive Psychology, 14,* 178–210.

Fredrickson, B.L. (1998). What good are positive emotions? *Review of General Psychology, 2,* 300–319.

Fredrickson, B.L., & Levenson, R.W. (1998). Positive emotions speed recovery from the cardiovascular sequelae of negative emotions. *Cognition and Emotion, 12,* 191–220.

Frensch, P.A., & Runger, D. (2003). Implicit learning. *Current Directions in Psychological Science, 12,* 13–18.

Freud, A., & Dann, S. (1951). An experiment in group upbringing. *Psychoanalytic Study of the Child, 6,* 127–168.

Freud, S. (1900). *The interpretation of dreams* (J. Strachey, Trans.). London: Allen & Unwin.

Freud, S. (1910). The origin and development of psychoanalysis. *American Journal of Psychology, 21,* 181–218.

Freud, S. (1915). Repression. In *Collected papers, Vol. IV.* London: Hogarth.

Freud, S. (1917). Introductory lectures on psychoanalysis. In J. Strachey (Ed.), *The complete psychological works, Vol. 16.* New York: Norton.

Freud, S. (1924). *A general introduction to psychoanalysis.* New York: Washington Square Press.

Freud, S. (1933). *New introductory lectures in psychoanalysis.* New York: Norton.

Freud, S. (1943). *A general introduction to psychoanalysis.* New York: Garden City.

Freud, S. (1950). The effects of cocaine on thought processes. In *Collected Papers, Vol. V.* London: Hogarth. (Original work published 1885)

Freud, S. (1957). Repression. In J. Strachey (Ed. & Trans.), *The standard edition of the complete psychological works of Sigmund Freud* (Vol. 14, pp. 146–158). London: Hogarth. (Original work published 1915)

Freud, S. (1958). The dynamics of transference. In J. Strachey (Ed. & Trans.), *The standard edition of the complete psychological works of Sigmund Freud* (Vol. 12, pp. 97–108). London: Hogarth Press. (Original work published 1912)

Freud, S., & Breuer, J. (1895). Studies on hysteria. In J. Strachey (Ed.), *The complete psychological works, Vol. 2.* New York: Norton.

Freud, S., & Breuer, J. (1895). Studies on hysteria. In J. Strachey (Ed.), *The complete psychological works, Vol. 2.* New York: Norton.

Fried, D., Crits-Christoph, P., & Luborsky, L. (1992). The first empirical demonstration of transference in psychotherapy. *Journal of Nervous and Mental Disease, 180,* 326–331.

Friedman, M., & Rosenman, R.H. (1959). Association of specific overt behaviour pattern with blood and cardiovascular findings. *Journal of the American Medical Association, 96,* 1286–1296.

Friedman, M.I., Tordoff, M.G., & Ramirez, I. (1986). Integrated metabolic control of food intake. *Brain Research Bulletin, 17,* 855–859.

Friedrich, L.K., & Stein, A.H. (1973). Aggressive and pro-social television programmes and the natural behaviour of pre-school children. *Monographs of the Society for Research in Child Development, 38,* 1–64.

Frijda, N.H. (1994). Universal antecedents exist, and are interesting. In P. Ekman & R.J. Davidson (Eds.), *The nature of emotion: Fundamental questions*. Oxford, UK: Oxford University Press.

Frijda, N.H., Kuipers, P., & ter Schure, E. (1989). Relations among emotion, appraisal, and emotional action readiness. *Journal of Personality and Social Psychology, 57*, 212–228.

Frith, C.D. (1992). *The cognitive neuropsychology of schizophrenia*. Hove, UK: Psychology Press.

Frith, C.D., Perry, R., & Lumer, E. (1999). The neural correlates of conscious experience: An experimental framework. *Trends in Cognitive Sciences, 3*, 105–114.

Fromkin, V.A. (1993). Speech production. In J.B. Gleason & N.B. Ratner (Eds.), *Psycholinguistics*. Orlando, FL: Harcourt Brace.

Frueh, T., & McGhee, P.E. (1975). Traditional sex-role development and the amount of time spent watching television. *Developmental Psychology, 11*, 109.

Fujii, T., Rukatsu, R., Watabe, S., Ohnura, A., Teramura, K., Kimura, I., Saso, S., & Kogure, K. (1990). Auditory sound agnosia without aphasia following a right temporal lobe lesion. *Cortex, 26*, 263–268.

Funder, D.C., & Ozer, D.J. (1983). Behaviour as a function of the situation. *Journal of Personality and Social Psychology, 44*, 107–112.

Funnell, E. (1983). Phonological processes in reading: New evidence from acquired dyslexia. *British Journal of Psychology, 74*, 159–180.

Funtowicz, M.N., & Widiger, T.A. (1999). Sex bias in the diagnosis of personality disorders: An evaluation of the DSM-IV criteria. *Journal of Abnormal Psychology, 108*, 195–201.

Furnham, A. (1981). Personality and activity preference. *British Journal of Social and Clinical Psychology, 20*, 57–68.

Fyer, A.J., Mannuzza, S., Chapman, T.F., Liebowitz, M.R., & Klein, D.F. (1993). A direct-interview family study of social phobia. *Archives of General Psychiatry, 50*, 286–293.

Fyer, A.J., Mannuzza, S., Gallops, M.S., Martin, L.Y., Aaronson, C., Gorman, J.M., Liebowitz, M.R., & Klein, D. (1990). Familial transmission of simple phobias and fears: A preliminary report. *Archives of General Psychiatry, 47*, 252–256.

Ffytche, D.H., Guy, C., & Zeki, S. (1995). The parallel visual motion inputs into areas V1 and V5 of the human cerebral cortex. *Brain, 118*, 1375–1394.

Gabrieli, J.D. (1998). Cognitive neuroscience of human memory. *Annual Review of Psychology, 49*, 87–115.

Gaertner, L., & Insko, C.A. (2000). Intergroup discrimination in the minimal group paradigm: Categorisation, reciprocation, or fear? *Journal of Personality and Social Psychology, 79*, 77–94.

Gaertner, S.L., & Dovidio, J.F. (1977). The subtlety of white racism, arousal, and helping behaviour. *Journal of Personality and Social Psychology, 35*, 691–707.

Gaertner, S.L., Dovidio, J.F., Anastasio, P.A., Bachman, B.A., & Rust, M.C. (1993). The common ingroup identity model: Recategorisation and the reduction of intergroup bias. In W. Stroebe & M. Hewstone (Eds.), *European Review of Social Psychology, Vol. 4*. London: Wiley.

Gaertner, S.L., Rust, M.C., Dovidio, J.F., Bachman, B.A., & Anastasio, P.A. (1994). The contact hypothesis: The role of a common ingroup identity on reducing intergroup bias. *Small Group Research, 25*, 224–249.

Gaffan, E.A., Hansel, M., & Smith, L. (1983). Does reward depletion influence spatial memory performance? *Learning and Motivation, 14*, 58–74.

Gale, A. (1983). Electroencephalographic studies of extraversion–introversion: A case study in the psychophysiology of individual differences. *Personality and Individual Differences, 4*, 371–380.

Gallup, G.G. (1979). Self-recognition in chimpanzees and man: A developmental and comparative perspective. In M. Lewis & L.A. Rosenblum (Eds.), *Genesis of behaviour: Vol. 2. The child and its family*. New York: Plenum.

Galton, F. (1869). *Hereditary genius: An inquiry into its laws and consequences*. London: Macmillan & Co.

Galton, F. (1883). *Inquiries into human faculty and its development*. London: Macmillan.

Gangestad, S.W. (1993). Sexual selection and physical attractiveness: Implications for mating dynamics. *Human Nature, 4*, 205–235.

Gangestad, S.W., & Buss, D.M. (1993). Pathogen prevalence and human mate preferences. *Ethology and Sociobiology, 14*, 89–96.

Ganster, D.C., Fox, M.L., & Dwyer, D.J. (2001). Explaining employees' health care costs: A prospective examination of stressful job demands, personal control, and physiological reactivity. *Journal of Applied Psychology, 86*, 954–964.

Ganster, D.C., Schaubroeck, J., Sime, W.E., & Mayes, B.T. (1991). The nomological validity of the Type A personality among employed adults. *Journal of Applied Psychology, 76*, 143–168.

Garcia, J., Ervin, F.R., & Koelling, R. (1966). Learning with prolonged delay of reinforcement. *Psychonomic Science, 5*, 121–122.

Garcia, J., & Koelling, R.A. (1966). Relation of cue to consequences in avoidance learning. *Psychonomic Science, 4*, 123–124.

Garcia, S., Stinson, L., Ickes, W., Bissonnette, V., & Briggs, S. (1991). Shyness and physical attractiveness in mixed sex dyads. *Journal of Personality and Social Psychology, 61*, 35–49.

Gardham, K., & Brown, R. (2001). Two forms of intergroup discrimination with positive and negative outcomes: explaining the positive–negative asymmetry effect. *British Journal of Social Psychology, 40*, 23–34.

Gardner, H. (1983). *Frames of mind: The theory of multiple intelligences*. New York: Basic Books.

Gardner, H. (1993). *Multiple intelligences: The theory in practice*. New York: Basic Books.

Gardner, H. (1998). Are there additional intelligences? The case for naturalist, spiritual, and existential intelligences. In J. Kane (Ed.), *Education, information, and transformation*. Englewood Cliffs, NJ: Prentice-Hall.

Gardner, H., Kornhaber, M.L., & Wake, W.K. (1996). *Intelligence: Multiple perspectives*. Orlando, FL: Harcourt Brace.

Gardner, R.A., & Gardner, B.T. (1969). Teaching sign language to a chimpanzee. *Science, 165*, 664–672.

Garfield, S. (2003, February 2). Unhappy anniversary. *The Observer*.

Garfield, S.L. (1994). Research on client variables in psychotherapy. In A.E. Bergin & S.L. Garfield (Eds.), *Handbook of psychotherapy and behavior change* (4th ed.). New York: Wiley.

Garner, D.M., & Fairburn, C.G. (1988). Relationship between anorexia nervosa and bulimia nervosa: Diagnostic implications. In D.M. Garner & P.E. Garfinkel (Eds.), *Diagnostic issues in anorexia nervosa and bulimia nervosa*. New York: Brunner/Mazel.

Garrett, M.F. (1975). The analysis of sentence production. In G.H. Bower (Ed.), *The psychology of learning and motivation, Vol. 9*. San Diego, CA: Academic Press.

Garrett, M.F. (1980). Levels of processing in sentence production. In B. Butterworth (Ed.), *Language production: Vol. 1. Speech and talk*. San Diego, CA: Academic Press.

Garrod, S., & Pickering, M.J. (1999). *Language processing*. Hove, UK: Psychology Press.

Gauld, A., & Stephenson, G.M. (1967). Some experiments relating to Bartlett's theory of remembering. *British Journal of Psychology, 58*, 39–50.

Gauthier, I., Behrmann, M., & Tarr, M.J. (1999). Can face recognition really be dissociated from object recognition? *Journal of Cognitive Neuroscience, 11*, 349–370.

Gavey, N. (1992). Technologies and effects of heterosexual coercion. *Feminism and psychology, 2*, 325–351.

Gazzaniga, M.S., Ivry, R.B., & Mangun, G.R. (1998). *Cognitive neuroscience: The biology of the mind*. New York: W.W. Norton.

Gazzaniga, M.S., & LeDoux, J.E. (1978). *The integrated mind*. New York: Plenum.

Geen, R.G. (1991). Social motivation. *Annual Review of Psychology, 42*, 377–399.

Geiselman, R.E., Fisher, R.P., MacKinnon, D.P., & Holland, H.L. (1985). Eyewitness memory enhancement in police interview: Cognitive retrieval mnemonics versus hypnosis. *Journal of Applied Psychology, 70*, 401–412.

Gelernter, C.S., Uhde, T.W., Cimbolic, P., Arnkoff, D.B., Vittone, B.J., Tancer, M.E., & Bartko, J.J. (1991). Cognitive-behavioral and pharmacological treatments of social phobia: A controlled study. *Archives of General Psychiatry, 48,* 938–945.

Gelfand, M.J., Triandis, H.C., & Chan, D.K.-S. (1996). Individualism versus collectivism or versus authoritarianism? *European Journal of Social Psychology, 26,* 397–410.

Gelles, R.J. (1997). *Intimate violence in families.* Thousand Oaks, CA: Sage.

Genta, M.L., Menesini, E., Fonzi, A., Costabile, A., & Smith, P.K. (1996). Bullies and victims in schools in central and southern Italy. *European Journal of Psychology of Education, 11,* 97–110.

Gentilucci, M., Chieffi, S., Daprati, E., Saetti, M.C., & Toni, I. (1996). Visual illusion and action. *Neuropsychologia, 34,* 369–376.

Gentner, D. (1982). Why nouns are learned before verbs: Linguistic relativity vs. natural partitioning. In S.A. Kuczaj (Ed.), *Language development: Vol. 2. Language, thought, and culture.* Hillsdale, NJ: Lawrence Erlbaum Associates, Inc.

George, J.M. (1995). Asymmetrical effects of rewards and punishments: the case of social loafing. *Journal of Occupational and Organizational Psychology, 68,* 327–338.

Georgopoulos, A.P. (1997). Voluntary movement: Computational principles and neural mechanisms. In M.D. Rugg (Ed.), *Cognitive neuroscience.* Hove, UK: Psychology Press.

Gergely, G., Bekkering, H., & Kiraly, I. (2002). Rational imitation in preverbal infants. *Nature, 415,* 755.

Gergen, K.J. (1978). Experimentation in social psychology: A reappraisal. *European Journal of Social Psychology, 26,* 309–320.

Gergen, K.J., Morse, S.J., & Gergen, M.M. (1980). Behaviour exchange in cross-cultural perspective. In H.C. Triandis & W.W. Lambert (Eds.), *Handbook of cross-cultural psychology: Vol. 5. Social psychology.* Boston: Allyn & Bacon.

Germain, A., Nielsen, T.A., Zadra, A., & Montplaisir, J. (2000). The prevalence of typical dream themes challenges the specificity of the threat simulation theory. *Behavioral and Brain Sciences, 23,* 940–941.

Gershoff, E.T. (2002). Corporal punishment by parents and associated child behaviours and experiences: A meta-analytic and theoretical review. *Psychological Bulletin, 128,* 539–579.

Gershon, E.S. (1990). Genetics. In F.K. Goodwin & K.R. Jamison (Eds.), *Manic-depressive illness.* Oxford, UK: Oxford University Press.

Gevirtz, R. (2000). Physiology of stress. In D. Kenney, J. Carlson, J. Sheppard, & F.J. McGuigan (Eds.), *Stress and health: Research and clinical applications.* Sydney, Australia: Harwood Academic Publishers.

Ghuman, P.A.S. (1982). An evaluation of Piaget's theory from a cross-cultural perspective. In S. Modgil & C. Modgil (Eds.), *Jean Piaget: Consensus and controversy.* New York: Holt, Rinehart, & Winston.

Gibbons, F.X., Eggleston, T.J., & Benthin, A.C. (1997). Cognitive reactions to smoking relapse: The reciprocal relation between dissonance and self-esteem. *Journal of Personality and Social Psychology, 72,* 184–195.

Gibbs, J., Young, R.C., & Smith, G.P. (1973). Cholecystokinin decreases food intake in rats. *Journal of Comparative and Physiological Psychology, 84,* 488–495.

Gibbs, W.W. (1996, August). Gaining on fat. *Scientific American,* pp. 70–76.

Gibson, E.J., & Walk, R.D. (1960). The "visual cliff". *Scientific American, 202* (April), 64–71.

Gibson, J.J. (1979). *The ecological approach to visual perception.* Boston: Houghton Mifflin.

Gick, M.L., & Holyoak, K.J. (1980). Analogical problem solving. *Cognitive Psychology, 12,* 306–355.

Giddens, A. (1982). *Profiles and critiques in social theory.* London: Macmillan.

Gigerenzer, G. (1996). On narrow norms and vague heuristics: A reply to Kahneman and Tversky (1996). *Psychological Review, 103,* 592–596.

Gigerenzer, G., & Hug, K. (1992). Domain-specific reasoning: Social contracts, cheating and perspective change. *Cognition, 43,* 127–171.

Gigerenzer, G., Todd, P.M., & the ABC Research Group (1999). *Simple heuristics that make us smart.* Oxford, UK: Oxford University Press.

Gigone, D., & Hastie, R. (1997). Proper analysis of the accuracy of group judgments. *Psychological Bulletin, 121,* 149–167.

Gilbert, A.N., Fridlund, A.J., & Sabini, J. (1987). Hedonic and social determinants of facial displays to odor. *Chemical Senses, 12,* 355–363.

Gilbert, D.T. (1995). Attribution and interpersonal perception. In A. Tesser (Ed.), *Advanced social psychology.* New York: McGraw-Hill.

Gilbert, D.T., & Malone, P.S. (1995). The correspondence bias. *Psychological Bulletin, 117,* 21–38.

Gilbert, D.T., Pelham, B.W., & Krull, D.S. (1988). On cognitive busyness: When person perceivers meet persons perceived. *Journal of Personality and Social Psychology, 54,* 733–740.

Gilhooly, K.J. (1996). *Thinking: Directed, undirected and creative* (3rd ed.). London: Academic Press.

Gilligan, C. (1977). In a different voice: Women's conception of the self and morality. *Harvard Education Review, 47,* 481–517.

Gilligan, C. (1982). *In a different voice: Psychological theory and women's development.* Cambridge, MA: Harvard University Press.

Gilligan, C., & Wiggins, G. (1987). The origins of morality in early childhood relationships. In J. Kagan & S. Lamb (Eds.), *The emergence of morality in young children.* Chicago: University of Chicago Press.

Glanzer, M., & Cunitz, A.R. (1966). Two storage mechanisms in free recall. *Journal of Verbal Learning and Verbal Behavior, 5,* 351–360.

Glascott Burriss, K. (2003). Motivation, stress, self-control ability, and self-control behavior of preschool children in China. *Childhood Education, 79,* 380.

Glaser, R., Rice, J., Speicher, C.E., Stout, J.C, & Kiecolt-Glaser, J. (1986). Stress depresses interferon production by leucocytes concomitant with a decrease in natural killer cell activity. *Behavioural Neuroscience, 100,* 675–678.

Glaser, W.R. (1992). Picture naming. *Cognition, 42,* 61–105.

Gleaves, D.H. (1996). The sociocognitive model of dissociative identity disorder: A reexamination of the evidence. *Psychological Bulletin, 120,* 42–59.

Gleaves, D.H., Hernandez, E., & Warner, M.S. (1999). Corroborating premorbid dissociative symptomatology in dissociative identity disorder. *Professional Psychology: Research and Practice, 30,* 341–345.

Gleitman, H. (1986). *Psychology* (2nd ed.). London: Norton.

Glenberg, A.M. (1987). Temporal context and recency. In D.S. Gorfein & R.R. Hoffman (Eds.), *Memory and learning: The Ebbinghaus centennial conference.* Hillsdale, NJ: Lawrence Erlbaum Associates, Inc.

Glenberg, A.M., Smith, S.M., & Green, C. (1977). Type 1 rehearsal: Maintenance and more. *Journal of Verbal Learning and Verbal Behavior, 16,* 339–352.

Glenn, N.D., & McLanahan, S. (1982). Children and marital happiness: A further specification of the relationship. *Journal of Marriage and the Family, 44,* 63–72.

Glover, S., & Dixon, P. (2001). Dynamic illusion effects in a reaching task: Evidence for separate visual representations in the planning and control of reaching. *Journal of Experimental Psychology: Human Perception and Performance, 27,* 560–572.

Glover, S., & Dixon, P. (2002a). Dynamic effects of the Ebbinghaus illusion in grasping: Support for a planning/control model of action. *Perception and Psychophysics, 64,* 266–278.

Glover, S., & Dixon, P. (2002b). Semantics affect the planning but not control of grasping. *Experimental Brain Research, 146,* 383–387.

Glushko, R.J. (1979). The organisation and activation of orthographic knowledge in reading aloud. *Journal of Experimental Psychology: Human Perception and Performance, 5,* 674–691.

Goa, K.L., & Ward, A. (1986). Buspirone: A preliminary review of its pharmacological properties and therapeutic efficacy as an anxiolytic. *Drugs, 32,* 114–129.

Gobet, F., & Simon, H.A. (1996). The roles of recognition processes and look-ahead search in time-constrained expert problem solving. *Psychological Science, 7*, 52–55.

Gobet, F., & Simon, H.A. (1998). Expert chess memory: Revisiting the chunking hypothesis. *Memory, 6*(3), 225–255.

Godden, D., & Baddeley, A. (1975). Context dependent memory in two natural environments: In land and under water. *British Journal of Psychology, 79*, 99–104.

Godden, D., & Baddeley, A. (1980). When does context influence recognition memory? *British Journal of Psychology, 71*, 99–104

Goldberg, L.R. (1990). An alternative "description of personality": The big–five factor structure. *Journal of Personality and Social Psychology, 59*, 1216–1229.

Goldfarb, W. (1947). Variations in adolescent adjustment of institutionally reared children. *American Journal of Orthopsychiatry, 17*, 499–557.

Goldhagen, D.J. (1996). *Hitler's willing executioners: Ordinary Germans and the Holocaust*. New York: Knopf.

Goldstein, D.G., & Gigerenzer, G. (2002). Models of ecological rationality: The recognition heuristic. *Psychological Review, 109*, 75–90.

Goldstein, D.G., & Gigerenzer, G. (2002). Models of ecological rationality: The recognition heuristic. *Psychological Review, 109*, 75–90.

Goldstein, E.B. (1996). *Sensation and perception* (4th ed.). New York: Brooks/Cole.

Goldstein, I. (2000). Oral phentolamine: An alpha-1, alpha-2 adrenergic antagonist for the treatment of erectile dysfunction. *International Journal of Impotence Research, 12*, 75–80.

Goldstein, J.S. (2001). *War and gender: How gender shapes the war system and vice versa*. Cambridge, UK: Cambridge University Press.

Goldwyn, E. (1979, May 24). The fight to be male. *Listener*, pp. 709–712.

Goleman, D. (1991, November 26). Doctors find comfort is a potent medicine. *The New York Times*.

Goleman, D. (1995). *Emotional intelligence*. New York: Bantam Books.

Gollwitzer, P.M. (1999). Implementation intentions. *American Psychologist, 54*, 493–503.

Gollwitzer, P.M., & Brandstatter, V. (1997). Implementation intentions and effective goal pursuit. *Journal of Personality and Social Psychology, 73*, 186–199.

Golombok, S., & Hines, M. (2002). Sex differences in social behaviour. In P.K. Smith & C.H. Hart (Eds.), *Blackwell handbook of childhood social development*. Oxford, UK: Blackwell.

Gomulicki, B.R. (1956). Recall as an abstractive process. *Acta Psychologica, 12*, 77–94.

Goodale, M.A., Milner, A.D., Jakobson, L.S., & Carey, D.P. (1991). A neurological dissociation between perceiving objects and grasping them. *Nature, 349*, 154–156.

Gooding, P.A., Mayes, A.R., & van Eijk R. (2000). A meta-analysis of indirect memory tests for novel material in organic amnesics. *Neuropsychologia, 38*, 666–676.

Goodkin, K., Blaney, T., Feaster, D., Fletcher, M., Baum, M.K., Mantero-Atienza, E., Klimas, N.G., Millon, C., Szapocznik, J., & Eisdorfer, C. (1992). Active coping style is associated with natural killer cell cytotoxicity in asymptomatic HIV-1 seropositive homosexual men. *Journal of Psychosomatic Research, 36*, 635–650.

Goodman, Y., & Goodman, K. (1990). Vygotsky in a whole language perspective. In L. Moll (Ed.), *Vygotsky and education*. Cambridge, UK: Cambridge University Press.

Goodnow, J.J., & Burns, A. (1985). *Home and school: A child's eye view*. Sydney, Australia: Allen & Unwin.

Gopnik, M. (1990). Feature blindness: A case study. *Language Acquisition, 1*, 139–164.

Gopnik, M. (1994a). Impairments of tense in a familial language disorder. *Journal of Neurolinguistics, 8*, 109–133.

Gopnik, M. (1994b). The perceptual processing hypothesis revisited. In J. Matthews (Ed.), *Linguistic aspects of familial language impairment*. Montreal, Canada: McGill University.

Gordon, A. (2001). Common questions about benzodiazepine risks. *Journal of Addiction and Mental Health, 4*, p.13.

Gordon, N.P. (1986). The prevalence and health impact of shiftwork. *American Journal of Public Health, 76*, 1225–1228.

Gorelick, D.A., & Balster, R.L. (1995). Phencyclidine (PCP). In F.E. Bloom & D.J. Kupfer (Eds.), *Psychopharmacology: The fourth generation of progress*. New York: Raven Press.

Gosling, S.D., & John, O.P. (1999). Personality dimensions in non-human animals: A cross-species review. *Current Directions in Psychological Science, 8*, 69–75.

Gossop, M. (1995). Factors affecting degree of dependence and other drug-related problems. In C.N. Stefanis & H. Hippius (Eds.), *Psychiatry in progress series: Vol. 2. Research in addiction: An update*. Kirkland, WA: Hogrefe & Huber.

Goswami, U. (1998). *Cognition in children*. Hove, UK: Psychology Press.

Gottesman, I.I. (1991). *Schizophrenia genesis: The origins of madness*. New York: W.H. Freeman.

Gottesman, I.I., & Bertelsen, A. (1989). Dual mating studies in psychiatry: Offspring of inpatients with examples from reactive (psychogenic) psychoses. *International Review of Psychiatry, 1*, 287–296.

Gottesman, I.I., & Goldsmith, H.H. (1994). Developmental psychopathology of antisocial behavior: Inserting genes into its ontogenesis and epigenesis. In C.A. Nelson (Ed.), *Threats to optimal development* (pp 69–104). Hillsdale, NJ: Lawrence Erlbaum Associates, Inc.

Gottfredson, L.S. (1997). Why *g* matters: The complexity of everyday life. *Intelligence, 24*, 79–132.

Gottfried, A.W. (1984). Home environment and early cognitive development: Integration, meta-analyses, and conclusions. In A.W. Gottfried (Ed.), *Home environment and early cognitive development: Longitudinal research*. Orlando, FL: Academic Press.

Gottman, J.M. (1993). The roles of conflict engagement, escalation, and avoidance in marital interaction: A longitudinal view of five types of couples. *Journal of Consulting and Clinical Psychology, 61*, 6–13.

Gottman, J.M. (1998). Psychology and the study of marital processes. *Annual Review of Psychology, 49*, 169–197.

Gough, H.G., Lazzari, R., & Fioravanti, M. (1978). Self versus ideal self: A comparison of five adjective check list indices. *Journal of Consulting and Clinical Psychology, 46*, 1085–1091.

Gove, W.R., & Fain, T. (1973). The stigma of mental hospitalisation: An attempt to evaluate its consequences. *Archives of General Psychiatry, 28*, 494–500.

Gove, W.R., & Fain, T. (1973). The stigma of mental hospitalisation. *Archives of General Psychiatry, 28*, 494–500.

Graesser, A.C., Millis, K.K., & Zwaan, R.A. (1997). Discourse comprehension. *Annual Review of Psychology, 48*, 163–189.

Graesser, A.C., Singer, M., & Trabasso, T. (1994). Constructing inferences during narrative text comprehension. *Psychological Review, 101*, 371–395.

Graf, P., & Schachter, D.L. (1985). Implicit and explicit memory for new associations in normal and amnesic subjects. *Journal of Experimental Psychology: Learning, Memory, and Cognition, 11*, 501–518.

Graf, P., Squire, L.R., & Mandler, G. (1984). The information that amnesic patients do not forget. *Journal of Experimental Psychology: Learning, Memory, and Cognition, 10*, 164–178.

Grafton, S., Hazeltine, E., & Ivry, R. (1995). Functional mapping of sequence learning in normal humans. *Journal of Cognitive Neuroscience, 7*, 497–510.

Graham, W.K., & Balloun, J. (1973). An empirical test of Maslow's need hierarchy theory. *Journal of Humanistic Psychology, 13*, 97–108.

Grammer, K., & Thornhill, R. (1994). Human (*Homo sapiens*) facial attractiveness and sexual selection: The role of symmetry and averageness. *Journal of Comparative Psychology, 108*, 233–242.

Grant, P. (1994). Psychotherapy and race. In P. Clarkson & M. Pokorny (Eds.), *The handbook of psychotherapy*. London: Routledge.

Grave, K., Caspar, F., & Ambuhl, H. (1990). Differentielle Psychotherapieforschung: Vier Therapieformen in Vergleich. *Zeitschrift fur Klinische Psychologie, 19*, 287–376.

Gravetter, F.J., & Forzano, L.-A.B. (2002). *Research methods for the behavioural sciences*. New York: Thomson/Wadsworth.

Gravetter, F.J., & Wallnau, L.B. (1998). *Essentials of statistics for the behavioural sciences*. New York: Thomson/Wadsworth.

Gray, J.A. (1982). *The neuropsychology of anxiety: An enquiry in to the functions of the septo-hippocampal system*. Oxford, UK: Clarendon Press.

Gray, J.A. (1994). Personality dimensions and emotion systems. In P. Ekman & R.J. Davidson (Eds.), *The nature of emotion: Fundamental questions*. Oxford, UK: Oxford University Press.

Gray, J.A., & Wedderburn, A.A. (1960). Grouping strategies with simultaneous stimuli. *Quarterly Journal of Experimental Psychology, 12*, 180–184.

Gray, P. (2002). *Psychology* (4th ed.). New York: Worth.

Green, D.P., Goldman, S.L., & Salovey, P. (1993). Measurement error masks bipolarity in affect ratings. *Journal of Personality and Social Psychology, 64*, 1029–1041.

Green, K.P., Kuhl, P.K., Meltzoff, A.N., & Stevens, E.B. (1991). Integrating speech information across talkers, gender, and sensory modality: Female faces and male voices in the McGurk effect. *Perception and Psychophysics, 50*, 524–536.

Green, M. (1995, October 14). In A. Coghlan, Dieting makes you forget. *New Scientist*.

Green, S. (1994). *Principles of biopsychology*, Hove, UK: Psychology Press.

Greenberg, J., & Ornstein, S. (1983). High status job title as compensation for underpayment: A test of equity theory. *Journal of Applied Psychology, 68*, 285–297.

Greenberg, J.H. (1963). Some universals of grammar with particular reference to the order of meaningful elements. In J.H. Greenberg (Ed.), *Universals of language*. Cambridge, MA: MIT Press.

Greenberg, L., Elliott, R., & Lietaer, G. (1994). Research on experiential psychotherapies. In A.E. Bergin & S.L. Garfield (Eds.), *Handbook of psychotherapy and behavior change* (4th ed., pp. 509–539). New York: Wiley.

Greenfield, P.M., & Lave, J. (1982). Cognitive aspects of informal education. In D.A. Wagner & H.W. Stevenson (Eds.), *Cultural perspectives on child development*. San Francisco: W.H. Freeman.

Greeno, J.G. (1974). Hobbits and orcs: Acquisition of a sequential concept. *Cognitive Psychology, 6*, 270–292.

Greenwald, A.G. (1992). New look 3: Unconscious cognition reclaimed. *The American Psychologist, 47*, 766–779.

Greenwald, A.G., McGhee, D.E., & Schwartz, J.L.K. (1998). Measuring individual differences in implicit cognition: The Implicit Association Test. *Journal of Personality and Social Psychology, 74*, 1464–1480.

Gregor, A.J., & McPherson, D.A. (1965). A study of susceptibility to geometrical illusion among cultural subgroups of Australian aborigines. *Psychology in Africa, 11*, 1–13.

Gregor, T. (1981). A content analysis of Mehinaku dreams. *Ethos, 9*, 353–390.

Gregory, R.L. (1970). *The intelligent eye*. New York: McGraw-Hill.

Gregory, R.L. (1972, June 23). Seeing as thinking. *Times Literary Supplement*.

Gregory, R.L. (1980). Perceptions as hypotheses. *Philosophical Transactions of the Royal Society of London, Series B, 290*, 181–197.

Grice, H.P. (1967). Logic and conversation. In P. Cole & J.L. Morgan (Eds.), *Studies in syntax, Vol. III*. New York: Seminar Press.

Grier, J.W., & Burk, T. (1992). *Biology of animal behaviour* (2nd ed.). Oxford, UK: W.C. Brown.

Griffiths, M.D. (2000). Cyberaffairs. *Psychology Review, 7*, 28–31.

Griggs, R.A., & Cox, J.R. (1982). The elusive thematic-material effect in Wason's selection task. *British Journal of Psychology, 73*, 407–420.

Grilo, C.M., & Pogue-Geile, M.F. (1991). The nature of environmental influences on weight and obesity: A behaviour genetic analysis. *Psychological Bulletin, 110*, 520–537.

Groeger, J.A. (1997). *Memory and remembering: Everyday memory in context*. Harlow, UK: Addison Wesley Longman.

Groos, G., & Hendricks, I. (1982). Circadian rhythms in electrical discharge of rat suprachiasmatic neurons recorded in vitro. *Neuroscience Letters, 34*, 283–288.

Gross, C.G. (1998). *Brain, vision, memory: Tales in the history of neuroscience*. Cambridge, MA: MIT Press.

Gross, C.G., & Graziano, M.S.A. (1995). Multiple representations of space in the brain. *The Neuroscientist, 1*, 43–50.

Gross, R. (1996). *Psychology: The science of mind and behaviour* (3rd ed.). London: Hodder & Stoughton.

Gross, R., & McIlveen, R. (1996). *Abnormal psychology*. London: Hodder & Stoughton.

Grossarth-Maticek, R., & Eysenck, H.J. (1995). Self-regulation and mortality from cancer, coronary heart disease, and other causes: A prospective study. *Personality and Individual Differences, 19*, 781–795.

Grossarth-Maticek, R., Eysenck, H.J., & Vetter, H. (1988). Personality type, smoking habit and their interaction as predictors of cancer and coronary heart disease. *Personality and Individual Differences, 9*, 479–495.

Grossman, K., Grossman, K.E., Spangler, S., Suess, G., & Unzner, L. (1985). Maternal sensitivity and newborn responses as related to quality of attachment in Northern Germany. In J. Bretherton & E. Waters (Eds.), Growing points of attachment theory. *Monographs of the Society for Research in Child Development, 50*, No. 209.

Grusec, J.E. (1988). *Social development: History, theory, and research*. New York: Springer.

Grusec, J.E., Davidov, M., & Lundell, L. (2002). Prosocial and helping behaviour. In P.K. Smith & C. Hart (Eds.), *Handbook of childhood social development*. Malden, MA: Blackwell.

Grusec, J.E., Saas-Kortsaak, P., & Simutis, Z.M. (1978). The role of example and moral exhortation in the training of altruism. *Child Development, 49*, 920–923.

Gruzelier, J.H. (1998). A working model of the neurophysiology of hypnosis: A review of evidence. *Contemporary Hypnosis, 15*, 3–21.

Gruzelier, J.H. (2002) http://www.med.ic.ac.uk/divisions/49/JohnModelofHypnoticRelaxation.htm

Gudykunst, W.B., Gao, G., & Franklyn-Stokes, A. (1996a). Self-monitoring and concern for social appropriateness in China and England. In J. Pandey, D. Sinha, & D.P.S. Bhawk (Eds.), *Asian contributions to cross-cultural psychology*. New Delhi, India: Sage.

Gudykunst, W.B., Matsumoto, Y., Toomey, T., & Nishida, T. (1996b). The influence of cultural individualism–collectivism, self construals and individual values on communication styles across cultures. *Human Communication Research, 22*, 510–543.

Gunther, H., Gfoerer, S., & Weiss, L. (1984). Inflection, frequency, and the word superiority effect. *Psychological Research, 46*, 261–281.

Gupta, U., & Singh, P. (1982). Exploratory studies in love and liking and types of marriages. *Indian Journal of Applied Psychology, 19*, 92–97.

Guthrie, E.R. (1952). *The psychology of learning* (Rev. ed.). Massachusetts: Harper Bros.

Haber, R.N. (1983). The impending demise of the icon: A critique of the concept of iconic storage in visual information processing. *Behavioral and Brain Sciences, 6*, 1–11.

Haber, R.N., & Levin, C.A. (2001). The independence of size perception and distance perception. *Perception and Psychophysics, 63*, 1140–1152.

Hadjikhani, N., & de Gelder, B. (2002). Neural basis of prosopagnosia: An fMRI study. *Human Brain Mapping, 16*, 176–182.

Haffenden, A.M., & Goodale, M.A. (1988). The effect of pictorial illusion on prehension and perception. *Journal of Cognitive Neuroscience, 10*, 122–136.

Haggbloom, S.J., Warnick, R., Warnick, J.E., Jones, V.K., Yarbrough, G.L., Russell T.M., Borecky, C.M., McGahhey, R., Powell, J.L., Beavers, J., & Monte, E. (2002). The 100 most eminent psychologists of the 20th century. *Review of General Psychology, 6*, 139–152.

Haimov, I., & Lavie, P. (1996). Melatonin—a soporific hormone. *Current Directions in Psychological Science, 5*, 106–111.

Hailman, J. (1992). The necessity of a "show-me" attitude in science. In J.W. Grier & T. Burk, *Biology of animal behaviour* (2nd Edn.). Dubuque, IO: W.C. Brown.

Hains, S.C., Hogg, M.A., & Duck, J.M. (1997). Self-categorisation and leadership: Effects of group prototypicality and leader stereotypicality. *Personality and Social Psychology Bulletin, 23*, 1087–1100.

Haith, M.M. (1980). *Rules that babies look by: The organisation of newborn visual activity*. Hillsdale, NJ: Lawrence Erlbaum Associates, Inc.

Hajek, P., & Belcher, M. (1991). Dreams of absent-minded transgression: An empirical study of a cognitive withdrawal symptom. *Journal of Abnormal Psychology, 100*, 487–491.

Halaas, J.L., Gajiwala, K.S., Maffei, M., Cohen, S.L., Chait, B.T., Rabinowitz, D., Lallone, R., Burley, S.K., & Friedman, J.M. (1995). Weight-reducing effects of the plasma protein encoded by the *obese* gene. *Science, 269*, 543–546.

Halford, W.K., Gravestock, F., Lowe, R., and Scheldt, S. (1992) Toward a behavioural ecology of stressful marital interactions. *Behavioural Assessment, 13*, 135–148.

Halgin, R.P., & Whitbourne, S.K. (1997). *Abnormal psychology: The human experience of psychological disorders*. Madison, WI: Brown & Benchmark.

Hall, C., & van de Castle, R. (1966). *The content analysis of dreams*. New York: Appleton-Century-Crofts.

Hall, C.S. (1966). *The meaning of dreams*. New York: McGraw-Hill.

Hallam, R., & Rachman, S. (1972). Theoretical problems of aversion therapy. *Behaviour Research and Therapy, 10*, 341–353.

Hallam, R.S., & Rachman, S. (1976). Current status of aversion therapy. In M. Hersen, R. Eisler, & P. Miller (Eds.), *Progress in behaviour modification, Vol. 2*. New York: Academic Press.

Halleck, S.L. (1971). *The politics of therapy*. New York: Science House.

Hamburger, Y. (1994). The contact hypothesis reconsidered: Effects of the atypical outgroup member on the outgroup stereotype. *Basic and Applied Social Psychology, 15*, 339–358.

Hamilton, L.W., & Timmons, C.R. (1995). Psycho-pharmacology. In D. Kimble & A. M. Colman (Eds.), *Biological aspects of behaviour*. London: Longman.

Hampson, P.J., & Morris, P.E. (1996). *Understanding cognition*. Oxford, UK: Blackwell.

Han, P.J., Feng, L.Y., & Kuo, P.T. (1972). Insulin sensitivity of pair-fed, hyperlipemic, obese hypothalamic rats. *American Journal of Physiology, 223*, 1206–1209.

Hardman, D., & Harries, C. (2002). How rational are we? *The Psychologist, 15*, 76–79.

Harley, K., & Reese, E. (1999). Origins of autobiographical memory. *Developmental Psychology, 35*, 1338–1348.

Harley, T. (2001). *The psychology of language: From data to theory* (2nd ed.). Hove, UK: Psychology Press.

Harlow, H. (1959). Love in infant monkeys. *Scientific American, 200*, 68–74.

Harm, M.W., & Seidenberg, M.S. (2001). Are there orthographic impairments in phonological dyslexia? *Cognitive Neuropsychology, 18*, 71–92.

Harris, C.R. (2002). Sexual and romantic jealousy in heterosexual and homosexual adults. *Psychological Science, 13*, 7–12.

Harris, E.L., Noyes, R., Crowe, R.R., & Chaudhry, D.R. (1983). Family study of agoraphobia: Report of a pilot study. *Archives of General Psychiatry, 40*, 1061–1064.

Harris, J.R. (1995). Where is the child's environment? A group socialisation theory of development. *Psychological Review, 102*, 458–489.

Harris, J.R. (2000). Socialisation, personality development, and the child's environments: Comment on Vandell (2000). *Developmental Psychology, 36*, 711–723.

Harris, M., & Butterworth, G. (2002). *Developmental psychology: A student's handbook*. Hove, UK: Psychology Press.

Harris, M., Jones, D., Brookes, S., & Grant, J. (1986). Relations between the non-verbal context of maternal speech and rate of language development. *British Journal of Developmental Psychology, 4*, 261–268.

Harris, P.L. (1992). From simulation to folk psychology: The case for development. *Mind and Language, 7*, 120–144.

Harris, P.L., German, T., & Mills, P. (1996). Children's use of counterfactual thinking in causal reasoning. *Cognition, 61*, 233–259.

Harris, T.O. (1997). Adult attachment processes and psychotherapy: A commentary on Bartholomew and Birtschnell. *British Journal of Medical Psychology, 70*, 281–290.

Harrison, L.J., & Ungerer, J.A. (2002). Maternal employment and infant–mother attachment security at 12 months postpartum. *Developmental Psychology, 38*, 758–773.

Harrison, Y., & Horne, J.A. (2000). The impact of sleep deprivation on decision making: A review. *Journal of Experimental Psychology: Applied, 6*, 236–249.

Hart, D., Fegley, S., Chan, Y.H., Mulvey, D., & Fischer, L. (1993). Judgements about personal identity in childhood and adolescence. *Social Development, 2*, 66–81.

Harter, S. (1982). The perceived competence scale for children. *Child Development, 53*, 87–97.

Harter, S. (1987). The determinants and mediational role of global self-worth in children. In N. Eisenberg (Ed.), *Contemporary topics in developmental psychology*. New York: Wiley.

Harter, S., & Monsour, A. (1992). Developmental analysis of conflict caused by opposing attributes in the adolescent self-portrait. *Developmental Psychology, 28*, 251–260.

Harter, S., & Pike, R. (1984). The pictorial scale of perceived competence and social acceptance for young children. *Child Development, 55*, 1969–1982.

Hartup, W.W. (1974). Aggression in childhood: Developmental perspectives. *American Psychologist, 29*, 337–341.

Hartup, W.W. (1996). The company they keep: Friendships and their developmental significance. *Child Development, 67*, 1–13.

Hartup, W.W., & Stevens, N. (1997). Friendships and adaptation in the life course. *Psychological Bulletin, 121*, 355–370.

Harvey, S.M. (1987). Female sexual behaviour: Fluctuations during the menstrual cycle. *Journal of Psychosomatic Research, 31*, 101–110.

Harwood, R.L., & Miller, J.G. (1991). Perceptions of attachment behaviour: A comparison of Anglo and Puerto Rican mothers. *Merrill-Palmer Quarterly, 37*, 583–599.

Haselager, G.J.T., Hartup, W.W., van Lieshout, C.F.M., & Riksen-Walraven, M. (1995). *Friendship similarity in middle childhood as a function of sex and sociometric status*. Unpublished manuscript, University of Nijmegen, The Netherlands.

Hashish, I., Finman, C., & Harvey, W. (1988). Reduction of postoperative pain and swelling by ultrasound: A placebo effect. *Pain, 83*, 303–311.

Haslam, S.A., Turner, J.C., Oakes, P.J., McGarty, C., & Hayes, B.K. (1992). Context-dependent variation in social stereotyping: 1. The effects of intergroup relations as mediated by social change and frame of reference. *European Journal of Social Psychology, 22*, 3–20.

Hatano, G., & Inagaki, K. (1986). Two courses of expertise. In H. Stevenson, H. Azuma, & K. Hatuka (Eds.), *Child development in Japan*. San Francisco: Freeman.

Hatfield, E., Sprecher, S., Traupmann Pillemer, J., Greenberg, D., & Wexler, P. (1988). Gender differences in what is desired in the sexual relationship. *Journal of Psychology and Human Sexuality, 1*, 39–52.

Hatfield, E., Utne, M.K., & Traupmann, J. (1979). Equity theory and intimate relationships. In R.L. Burgess & T.L. Huston (Eds.), *Exchange theory in developing relationships*. New York: Academic Press.

Hathaway, S.R., & McKinley, J.C. (1940). A multiphasic personality schedule (Minnesota): I. Construction of the schedule. *Journal of Psychology, 10*, 249–254.

Haxby, J.V., Horwitz, B., Ungerleider, L.G., Maisog, J.M., Pietrini, P., & Grady, C.L. (1994). The functional organisation of human extrastriate cortex: A PET-rCBF study of selective attention to faces and locations. *Journal of Neuroscience, 14*, 6336–6353.

Hay, D.F. (1994). Prosocial development. *Journal of Child Psychology and Psychiatry and Allied Disciplines, 35*, 29–71.

Hay, D.F., & Vespo, J.E. (1988). Social learning perspectives on the development of the mother–child relationship. In B. Birns & D.F. Hay (Eds.), *The different faces of motherhood.* New York: Plenum Press.

Hay, J.F., & Jacoby, L.L. (1996). Separating habit and recollection: Memory slips, process dissociations, and probability matching. *Journal of Experimental Psychology: Learning, Memory, and Cognition, 22*, 1323–1335.

Hayes, N. (1993). *Principles of social psychology.* Hove, UK: Psychology Press.

Hazan, C., & Shaver, P.R. (1987). Romantic love conceptualised as an attachment process. *Journal of Personality and Social Psychology, 52*, 511–524.

Hazan, C., & Shaver, P.R. (1994). Attachment as an organizational framework for research on close relationships. *Psychological Inquiry, 5*, 1–22.

Hearold, S. (1986). A synthesis of 1043 effects of television on social behaviour. In G. Comstock (Ed.), *Public communication and behaviour, Vol. 1.* Orlando, FL: Academic Press.

Heath, W.P., & Erickson, J.R. (1998). Memory for central and peripheral actions and props after various post-event presentations. *Legal and Criminal Psychology, 3*, 321–346.

Heather, N. (1976). *Radical perspectives in psychology.* London: Methuen.

Hebb, D.O. (1949). *The organisation of behaviour.* New York: Wiley.

Hedaya, R.J. (1996). *Understanding biological psychiatry.* New York: Norton.

Hedegaard, M. (1996). The zone of proximal development as basis for instruction. In H. Daniels (Ed.), *An introduction to Vygotsky.* London: Routledge.

Hedricks, C., Piccinino, L.J., Udry, J.R., & Chimbia, T.H. (1987). Peak coital rate coincides with onset of luteinising hormone surge. *Fertility and Sterility, 48*, 234–238.

Hegarty, M., Shah, P., & Miyake, A. (2000). Constraints on using the dual-task methodology to specify the degree of central executive involvement in cognitive tasks. *Memory and Cognition, 28*, 376–385.

Hegde, J., & van Essen, D.C. (2000). Selectivity for complex shapes in primate visual area V2. *Journal of Neuroscience, 20*, RC61.

Heider, E.R. (1972). Universals in colour naming and memory. *Journal of Experimental Psychology, 93*, 10–20.

Heider, F. (1958). *The psychology of interpersonal relations.* New York: Wiley.

Heine, S.J., & Lehman, D.R. (1997). The cultural construction of self-enhancement: An examination of group-serving biases. *Journal of Personality and Social Psychology, 72*, 1268–1283.

Heine, S.J., Lehman, D.R., Markus, H.R., & Kitayama, S. (1999). Is there a universal need for positive self-regard? *Psychological Review, 106*, 766–794.

Heisler, W.J. (1974). A performance correlate of personal control beliefs in an organisational context. *Journal of Applied Psychology, 59*, 504–506.

Hennigan, K.M., Del Rosario, M.L., Cook, T.D., & Calder, B.J. (1982). Impact of the introduction of television on crime in the United States: Empirical findings and theoretical implications. *Journal of Personality and Social Psychology, 42*, 461–477.

Henry, R.A. (1993). Group judgement accuracy: Reliability and validity of postdiscussion confidence judgements. *Organizational Behavior and Human Decision Processes, 56*, 11–27.

Henson, R.N.A., Burgess, N., & Frith, C.D. (2000). Recoding, storage, rehearsal and grouping in verbal short-term memory: An fMRI study. *Neuropsychologia, 38*, 426–440.

Herbert, T.B., & Cohen, S. (1993). Stress and immunity in humans: A meta-analytic review. *Psychosomatic Medicine, 55*, 364–379.

Hergenhahn, B.R., & Olson, M.H. (1999). *An introduction to theories of personality.* Upper Saddle River, NJ: Prentice Hall.

Herman, D., & Green, J. (1991). *Madness: A study guide.* London: BBC Education.

Herrnstein, R.J., & Murray, C.A. (1994). *The bell curve: Intelligence and class structure in American life.* New York: Free Press.

Heslin, R. (1964). Predicting group task effectiveness from member characteristics. *Psychological Bulletin, 62*, 248–256.

Hetherington, A.W., & Ranson, S.W. (1940). Hypothalamic lesions and adiposity in the rat. *Anatomical Record, 78*, 149–172.

Hetherington, E.M. (1979). Divorce, a child's perspective. *American Psychologist, 34*, 851–858.

Hetherington, E.M. (1988). Parents, children, and siblings six years after divorce. In R.A. Hinde & J. Stevenson-Hinde (Eds.), *Relationships within families: Mutual influences.* Oxford, UK: Clarendon Press.

Hetherington, E.M. (1989). Coping with family transitions: Winners, losers, and survivors. *Child Development, 60*, 1–14.

Hetherington, E.M. (1993). An overview of the Virginia longitudinal study of divorce and remarriage with a focus on early adolescence. *Journal of Family Psychology, 7*, 39–56.

Hetherington, E.M. (2002, January 27). In B. Summerskill and E. Vulliany, For the sake of the children … Divorce. *The Observer.*

Hetherington, E.M., Cox, M., & Cox, R. (1982). Effects of divorce on parents and children. In M. Lamb (Ed.), *Non-traditional families.* Hillsdale, NJ: Lawrence Erlbaum Associates, Inc.

Hetherington, E.M., & Stanley-Hagan, M. (1999). The adjustment of children with divorced parents: A risk and resiliency perspective. *Journal of Child Psychology and Psychiatry, 40*, 129–140.

Hewstone, M., & Jaspars, J. (1984). Social dimensions of attribution. In H. Tajfel (Ed.), *The social dimension: European developments in social psychology* (Vol. 2 pp. 379–404). Cambridge, UK: Cambridge University Press.

Hewstone, M., & Jaspars, J. (1987). Covariation and causal attribution: A logical model of the intuitive analysis of variance. *Journal of Personality and Social Psychology, 53*, 663–672.

Hewstone, M., Rubin, M., & Willis, H. (2002). Intergroup bias. *Annual Review of Psychology, 53*, 575–604.

Hewstone, M., & Stroebe, W. (2001). *Introduction to social psychology* (3rd ed.). Oxford, UK: Blackwell.

Hewstone, M.R.C., & Brown, R.J. (1986). Contact is not enough: An intergroup perspective on the contact hypothesis. In M.R.C. Hewstone & R.J. Brown (Eds.), *Contact and conflict in intergroup encounters.* Oxford, UK: Blackwell.

Heywood, C.A., Cowey, A., & Newcombe, F. (1994). On the role of parvocellular P and magnocellular M pathways in cerebral achromatopsia. *Brain, 117*, 245–254.

Hilgard, E.R. (1977). *Divided consciousness: Multiple controls in human thought and action.* New York: Wiley.

Hilgard, E.R. (1986). *Divided consciousness: Multiple controls in human thought and action* (Expanded ed.). New York: Wiley.

Hilgard, E.R., & Hilgard, J.R. (1983). *Hypnosis in the relief of pain.* Los Altos, CA: William Kaufmann.

Hill, J.O., & Peters, J.C. (1998). Environmental contributions to the obesity epidemic. *Science, 280*, 1371–1374.

Hilton, J.L., & von Hippel, W. (1996). Stereotypes. *Annual Review of Psychology, 47*, 237–271.

Hiniker, P.J. (1969). Chinese reactions to forced compliance: Dissonance reduction or national character. *Journal of Social Psychology, 77*, 157–176.

Hinkley, K., & Andersen, S.M. (1996). The working self-concept in transference: Significant–other activation and self change. *Journal of Personality and Social Psychology, 71*, 1279–1295.

Hirschberg, N. (1978). A correct treatment of traits. In H. London (Ed.), *Personality: A new look at metatheories.* New York: Macmillan.

Hirschfeld, R.M. (1999). Efficacy of SSRIs and newer antidepressants in severe depression: Comparison with TCAs. *Journal of Clinical Psychiatry, 60*, 326–335.

Hirsch-Pasek, K., & Golinkoff, R.M. (1996). *The origins of grammar: Evidence from early language comprehension.* Cambridge, MA: MIT Press.

Hirst, W., Spelke, E.S., Reaves, C.C., Caharack, G., & Neisser, U. (1980). Dividing attention without alternation or automaticity. *Journal of Experimental Psychology: General, 109*, 98–117.

Hobson, J.A. (1988). *The dreaming brain.* New York: Basic Books.

Hobson, J.A. (1994). Sleep and dreaming. In A.M. Colman (Ed.), *Companion encyclopedia of psychology, Vol. 1.* London: Routledge.

Hobson, J.A., & McCarley, R.W. (1977). The brain as a dream-state generator: An activation–synthesis hypothesis of the dream process. *American Journal of Psychiatry, 134,* 1335–1348.

Hobson, J.A., Pace-Schott, E.F., & Stickgold, R. (2000). Dreaming and the brain: Toward a cognitive neuroscience of conscious states. *Behavioral and Brain Sciences, 23,* 793–842.

Hocken, S. (1977). *Emma and I.* London: Gollancz.

Hockett, C.F. (1960). The origin of speech. *Scientific American, 203,* 89–96.

Hockey, G.R.J. (1983). Current issues and new directions. In R. Hockey (Ed.), *Stress and fatigue in human performance.* Chichester, UK: Wiley.

Hodges, J., & Tizard, B. (1989). Social and family relationships of ex-institutional adolescents. *Journal of Child Psychology and Psychiatry, 30,* 77–97.

Hoebel, B.G., & Hernandez, L. (1993). Basic neural mechanisms of feeding and weight regulation. In A.J. Stunkard & T.A. Wadden (Eds.), *Obesity: Theory and therapy* (2nd ed.). New York: Raven Press.

Hoebel, B.G., & Teitelbaum, P. (1966). Weight regulation in normal and hypothalamic hyperphagic rats. *Journal of Comparative and Physiological Psychology, 61,* 189–193.

Hoffman, C., Lau, I., & Johnson, D.R. (1986). The linguistic relativity of person cognition. *Journal of Personality and Social Psychology, 51,* 1097–1105.

Hoffman, H.S. (1996). *Amorous turkeys and addicted ducklings: A search for the causes of social attachment.* Boston, MA: Author's Cooperative.

Hoffman, M.L. (1970). Moral development. In P.H. Mussen (Ed.), *Carmichael's manual of child psychology, Vol. 2.* New York: Wiley.

Hoffman, M.L. (1975). Altruistic behaviour and the parent–child relationship. *Journal of Personality and Social Psychology, 31,* 937–943.

Hoffman, M.L. (1987). The contribution of empathy to justice and moral judgement. *Cognitive Psychology, 2,* 400–410.

Hoffman, M.L. (1988). Moral development. In M.H. Bornstein & M.E. Lamb (Eds.), *Developmental psychology: An advanced textbook.* Hillsdale, NJ: Lawrence Erlbaum Associates, Inc.

Hoffrage, U., Lindsey, S., Hertwig, R., & Gigerenzer, G. (2000). Communicating statistical information. *Science, 290,* 2261–2262.

Hofling, C.K. (1974). *Textbook of psychiatry for medical practice.* Philadelphia: Lippincott.

Hofling, K.C., Brotzman, E., Dalrymple, S., Graves, N., & Pierce, C.M. (1966).An experimental study in nurse–physician relationship. *Journal of Nervous and Mental Disorders, 143,* 171–180.

Hofstede, G. (1980). *Culture's consequences: International differences in work-related values.* Beverly Hills, CA: Sage.

Hofstede, G. (1983). Dimensions of national cultures in fifty countries and three regions. In J. Derogowski, S. Dzurawiece, & R. Annis (Eds.), *Explorations in cross-cultural psychology.* Lisse, The Netherlands: Swets & Zeitlinger.

Hogan, R., Curphy, G.J., & Hogan, J. (1994). What we know about leadership: Effectiveness and personality. *American Psychologist, 49,* 493–504.

Hogg, M.A. (2001). A social identity theory of leadership. *Personality and Social Psychology Review, 35,* 184–200.

Hogg, M.A., & Hardie, E.A. (1991). Social attraction, personal attraction and self-categorization: A field study. *Personality and Social Psychology Bulletin, 17,* 175–180.

Hogg, M.A., Turner, J.C., & Davidson, B. (1990). Polarised norms and social frames of reference: A test of the self-categorisation theory of group polarisation. *Basic and Applied Social Psychology, 11,* 77–100.

Hogg, M.A., & Vaughan, G.M. (2002). *Social psychology* (3rd ed.). New York: Prentice Hall.

Hoglend, P., Engelstad, V., Sorbye, O., Heyerdahl, O., & Amlo, S. (1994). The role of insight in exploratory psychodynamic psychotherapy. *British Journal of Medical Psychology, 67,* 305–317.

Hohmann, G.W. (1966). Some effects of spinal cord lesions on experienced emotional feelings. *Psychophysiology, 3,* 143–156.

Holding, D.H., & Reynolds, J.R. (1982). Recall or evaluation of chess positions as determinants of chess skill. *Memory and Cognition, 10,* 237–242.

Holender, D. (1986). Semantic activation without conscious identification in dichotic listening, parafoveal vision, and visual masking: A survey and appraisal. *Behavioral and Brain Sciences, 9,* 1–66.

Holland, A.J., Sicotte, N., & Treasure, J. (1988). Anorexia nervosa: Evidence for a genetic basis. *Journal of Psychosomatic Research, 32,* 561–572.

Hollis, K.L. (1997). Contemporary research on Pavlovian conditioning: A "new" functional analysis. *American Psychologist, 52,* 956–965.

Holloway, S. (1999, November 2). In N. Nuttall. Toys for the boys image scares off girls. *The Times.*

Holmberg, M.C. (1980). The development of social interchange patterns from 12 to 42 months. *Child Development, 51,* 448–456.

Holmes, T.H., & Rahe, R.H. (1967). The social readjustment rating scale. *Journal of Psychosomatic Research, 11,* 213–218.

Holroyd, K.A., & French, D.J. (1994). Recent developments in the psychological assessment and management of recurrent headache disorders. In A.J. Goreczyny (Ed.), *Handbook of health and rehabilitation psychology.* New York: Plenum Press.

Holroyd, K.A., Penzien, D., Hursey, K., Tobin, D., Rogen, L., Holm, J., Marcille, P., Hall, J., & Chila, A. (1984). Change mechanisms in EMG biofeedback training: Cognitive changes underlying improvements in tension headache. *Journal of Consulting and Clinical Psychology, 52,* 1039–1053.

Holway, A.F., & Boring, E.G. (1941). Determinants of apparent visual size with distance variant. *American Journal of Psychology, 54,* 21–37.

Hooley, J.M., Orley, J., & Teasdale, J.D. (1986). Levels of expressed emotion and relapse in depressed patients. *British Journal of Psychiatry, 148,* 642–647.

Horgan, D.D., & Morgan, D. (1990). Chess expertise in children. *Applied Cognitive Psychology, 4,* 109–128.

Horn, J.L. (1994). Fluid and crystallised intelligence, theory of. In R.J. Sternberg (Ed.), *Encyclopedia of human intelligence.* New York: Macmillan.

Horne, J. (1988). *Why we sleep? The functions of sleep in humans and other mammals.* Oxford, UK: Oxford University Press.

Horne, J. (2001). State of the art: Sleep. *The Psychologist, 14,* 302–306.

Horne, J., & Reyner, L. (1999). Vehicle accidents related to sleep: A review. *Occupational and Environmental Medicine, 56,* 289–294.

Horowitz, M.J. (1986). *Stress-response syndromes* (2nd ed.). Northvale, NJ: Jason Aronson.

Horton, W.S., & Keysar, B. (1996). When do speakers take into account common ground? *Cognition, 59,* 91–117.

House, J.S., Landis, K.R., & Umberson, D. (1988). Social relationships and health. *Science, 241,* 540–545.

Hovland, C., & Sears, R. (1940). Minor studies in aggression: VI. Correlation of lynchings with economic indices. *Journal of Personality, 9,* 301–310.

Hovland, C.I., & Weiss, W. (1951). The influence of source credibility on communication effectiveness. *Public Opinion Quarterly, 151,* 635–650.

Hovland, C.I., Lumsdaine, A.A., & Sheffield, R.D. (1949). *Experiments in mass communication.* Princeton, NJ: Princeton University Press.

Howard, D., & Orchard-Lisle, V. (1984). On the origin of semantic errors in naming: Evidence from the case of a global aphasic. *Cognitive Neuropsychology, 1,* 163–190.

Howard, D., Patterson, K.E., Wise, R.J.S., Brown, W.D., Friston, K., Weiller, C., & Frackowiak, R.S.J. (1992). The cortical localisation of the lexicons: Position emission tomography evidence. *Brain, 115,* 1769–1782.

Howard, D.V., & Howard, J.H. (1992). Adult age differences in the rate of learning serial patterns: Evidence from direct and indirect tests. *Psychology and Aging, 7,* 232–241.

Howard, J.W., & Dawes, R.M. (1976). Linear prediction of marital happiness. *Personality and Social Psychology Bulletin, 2,* 478–480.

Howard, K.I., Lueger, R.J., Maling, M.S., & Martinovich, Z. (1993). A phase model of psychotherapy outcome: Causal mediation of change. *Journal of Consulting and Clinical Psychology, 61*, 678–685.

Howe, C. (1980). Language learning from mothers' replies. *First Language, 1*, 83–97.

Howe, C., Tolmie, A., & Rodgers, C. (1992). The acquisition of conceptual knowledge in science by primary school children: Group interaction and the understanding of motion down an incline. *British Journal of Developmental Psychology, 10*, 113–130.

Howe, M. (1990).Useful word but obsolete construct. *The Psychologist, 3*, 498–499.

Howe, M.J.A. (1997). *IQ in question: The truth about intelligence.* Thousand Oaks, CA: Sage Publications.

Howe, M.J.A. (1999). *Genius explained.* Cambridge, UK: Cambridge University Press.

Howe, M.L., & Courage, M.L. (1997). The emergence and early development of autobiographical memory. *Psychological Review, 104*, 499–523.

Howell, J.M., & Hall-Merenda, K. (1999). The ties that bind: The impact of leader–member exchange, transformational and transactional leadership, and distance on predicting follower performance. *Journal of Applied Psychology, 84*, 680–694.

Howitt, D., & Owusu-Bempah, P. (1990). Racism in a British journal? *The Psychologist, 3*, 396–400.

Hsu, F. (1981). *Americans and Chinese: Passage to difference* (3rd ed.). Honolulu, AL: University Press of Honolulu.

Hsu, L.K. (1990). *Eating disorders.* New York: Guilford.

Hubel, D.H., & Wiesel, T.N. (1979). Brain mechanisms of vision. *Scientific American, 241*, 150–163.

Hüber-Weidman, H. (1976). *Sleep, sleep disturbances and sleep deprivation.* Cologne, Germany: Kiepenheuser & Witsch.

Hudson, J.L., & Rapee, R.M. (2000). The origins of social phobia. *Behavior Modification, 24*, 102–129.

Huesmann, L.R. (1996). Quoted in N. Seppa, Charlie's Angels made a negative, lasting impression. *APA Monitor*, April.

Huesmann, L.R., Lagerspetz, K., & Eron, L.D. (1984). Intervening variables in the TV violence–aggression relation: Evidence from two countries. *Developmental Psychology, 20*, 746–775.

Hughes, M. (1975). *Egocentrism in preschool children.* Unpublished PhD thesis, University of Edinburgh, UK.

Huguet, P., Galvaing, M.P., Monteil, J.M., & Dumas, F. (1999). Social presence effects in the Stroop task: Further evidence for an attentional view of social facilitation. *Journal of Personality and Social Psychology, 77*, 1011–1025.

Hulin, C.L., Henry, R.A., & Noon, S.L. (1990). Adding a dimension: Time as a factor in the generalisability of predictive relationships. *Psychological Bulletin, 107*, 328–340.

Hull, J.G., & Bond, C.F. (1986). Social and behavioural consequences of alcohol consumption and expectancy: A meta-analysis. *Psychological Bulletin, 99*, 347–360.

Hummel, J.E., & Holyoak, K.J. (1997). Distributed representations of structure: A theory of analogical access and mapping. *Psychological Review, 104*, 427–466.

Humphrey, L.L., Apple, R.F., & Kirschenbaum, D.S. (1986). Differentiating bulimic-anorexic from normal families using interpersonal and behavioural observational systems. *Journal of Consulting and Clinical Psychology, 54*, 190–195.

Humphreys, G.W. (1999a). Integrative agnosia. In G.W. Humphreys (Ed.), *Case studies in the neuropsychology of vision.* Hove, UK: Psychology Press.

Humphreys, G.W., & Bruce, V. (1989). *Visual cognition: Computational, experimental, and neuropsychological perspectives.* Hove, UK: Psychology Press.

Humphreys, G.W., & Riddoch, M.J. (1984). Routes to object constancy: Implications from neurological impairments of object constancy. *Quarterly Journal of Experimental Psychology, 36A*, 385–415.

Humphreys, G.W., & Riddoch, M.J. (1985). Author corrections to "Routes to object constancy". *Quarterly Journal of Experimental Psychology, 37A*, 493–495.

Humphreys, G.W., & Riddoch, M.J. (1987). *To see but not to see: A case study of visual agnosia.* Hove, UK: Psychology Press.

Humphreys, G.W., & Riddoch, M.J. (1993). Interactions between object and space systems revealed through neuropsychology. In D.E. Meyer & S.M. Kornblum (Eds.), *Attention and performance XIV: Synergies in experimental psychology, artificial intelligence, and cognitive neuroscience.* London: MIT Press.

Humphreys, G.W., Riddoch, M.J., Quinlan, P.T., Price, C.J., & Donnelly, N. (1992). Parallel pattern processing in visual agnosia. *Canadian Journal of Psychology, 46*, 377–416.

Humphreys, P.W. (1999b). Culture-bound syndromes. *Psychology Review, 6*, 14–18.

Hunt, E., & Agnoli, F. (1991). The Whorfian hypothesis: A cognitive psychological perspective. *Psychological Review, 98*, 377–389.

Hunter, J.E. (1986). Cognitive ability, cognitive aptitude, job knowledge, and job performance. *Journal of Vocational Behavior, 29*, 340–362.

Huseman, R.C., Hatfield, J.D., & Miles, E.W. (1987). A new perspective on equity theory: The equity sensitive construct. *Academy of Management Review, 12*, 222–234.

Huston, A.C. (1985). The development of sex typing: Themes from recent research. *Developmental Review, 5*, 1–17.

Huston, T.L., & Vangelisti, A.L. (1991). Socioemotional behavior and satisfaction in marital relationships: A longitudinal study. *Journal of Personality and Social Psychology, 61*, 721–733.

Huston, T.L., Caughlin, J.P., Houts, R.M., Smith, S.E., & George, L.J. (2001a). The connubial crucible: Newlywed years as predictors of marital delight, distress, and divorce. *Journal of Personality and Social Psychology, 80*, 237–252.

Huston, T.L., Niehuis, S., & Smith, S.E. (2001b). The early marital roots of conjugal distress and divorce. *Current Directions in Psychological Science, 10*, 116–119.

Huston, T.L., Ruggiero, M., Conner, R., & Geis, G. (1981). Bystander intervention into crime: A study based on naturally occurring episodes. *Social Psychology Quarterly, 44*, 14–23.

Hyde, J.S., & Durik, A.M. (2000). Gender differences in erotic plasticity—Evolutionary or sociocultural forces? Comment on Baumeister (2000). *Psychological Bulletin, 126*, 375–379.

Hyde, T.S., & Jenkins, J.J. (1973). Recall for words as a function of semantic, graphic, and syntactic orienting tasks. *Journal of Verbal Learning and Verbal Behavior, 12*, 471–480.

Imperato-McGinley, J., Guerro, L., Gautier, T., & Peterson, R.E. (1974). Steroid 5-reductase deficiency in man: An inherited form of male pseudohermaphroditism. *Science, 186*, 1213–1216.

Indefrey, P., & Levelt, W.J.M. (2000). The neural correlates of language production. In M. Gazzaniga (Ed.), *The new cognitive neurosciences* (2nd ed.). Cambridge, MA: MIT Press.

Inhelder, B., & Piaget, J. (1958). *The growth of logical thinking from childhood to adolescence.* London: Routledge & Kegan Paul.

Irwin, M., Lovitz, A., Marder, S.R., Mintz, J., Winslade, W.J., Van Putten, T., & Mills, M.J. (1985). Psychotic patients' understanding of informed consent. *American Journal of Psychiatry, 142*, 1351–1354.

Isawa, N. (1992). Postconventional reasoning and moral education in Japan. *Journal of Moral Education, 21*, 3–16.

Isenberg, D.J. (1986). Group polarization: A critical review and meta-analysis. *Journal of Personality and Social Psychology, 50*, 1141–1151.

Isozaki, M. (1994). Developmental change of self-evaluation maintenance process and childhood depression. *Japanese Journal of Psychology, 59*, 113–119.

Ito, T.A., Miller, N., & Pollock, V.E. (1996). Alcohol and aggression: A meta-analysis on the moderating effects of inhibitory cues, triggering events, and self-focused attention. *Psychological Bulletin, 120*, 60–82.

Ittelson, W.H. (1951). Size as a cue to distance: Static localisation. *American Journal of Psychology, 64*, 54–67.

Iverson, R.D., & Roy, P.K. (1994). A causal model of behavioural commitment: Evidence from a study of Australian blue-collar employees. *Journal of Management, 20*, 15–41.

Jackson, J.M., & Padgett, V.R. (1982). With a little help from my friend: Social loafing and the Lennon–McCartney songs.

*Personality and Social Psychology Bulletin,*
*8,* 672–677.

Jackson, L.A., Sullivan, L.A., & Hodge, C.N. (1993). Stereotype effects on attributions, predictions, and evaluations: No two social judgements are quite alike. *Journal of Personality and Social Psychology, 65,* 69–84.

Jackson, S.R., & Shaw, A. (2000). The Ponzo illusion affects grip-force but not grip-aperture scaling during prehension movements. *Journal of Experimental Psychology: Human Perception and Performance, 26,* 418–423.

Jacobs, K.C., & Campbell, D.T. (1961). The perpetuation of an arbitrary tradition through several generations of a laboratory microculture. *Journal of Abnormal and Social Psychology, 62,* 649–658.

Jacoby, L.L., Debner, J.A., & Hay, J.F. (2001). Proactive interference, accessibility bias, and process dissociations: Valid subjective reports of memory. *Journal of Experimental Psychology: Learning, Memory, and Cognition, 27,* 686–700.

Jaeger, B., Ruggiero, G.M., Gomez-Peretta, C., Lang, F., Mohammadkhani, P., Sahleen-Veasey, C., Schomer, H., & Lamprecht, F. (2002). Body dissatisfaction and its interrelations with other risk factors for bulimia nervosa in 12 countries. *Psychotherapy and Psychosomatics, 71,* 54–61.

Jaffee, S., & Hyde, J.S. (2000). Gender differences in moral orientation: A meta-analysis. *Psychological Bulletin, 126,* 703–726.

James, W. (1890). *Principles of psychology.* New York: Holt.

Jang, K.L., Livesley, W.J., & Vernon, P.A. (1996). Heritability of the Big Five personality dimensions and their facets: A twin study. *Journal of Personality, 64,* 577–591.

Janis, I. (1972). *Victims of groupthink: A psychological study of foreign-policy decisions and fiascos.* Boston: Houghton-Mifflin.

Janis, I. (1982). *Groupthink* (2nd ed.). Boston: Houghton Mifflin.

Jankowiak, J., & Albert, M.L. (1994). Lesion localisation in visual agnosia. In A. Kertesz (Ed.), *Localisation and neuroimaging in neuropsychology.* London: Academic Press.

Jenkins, C.D., Hurst, M.W., & Rose, R.M. (1979). Life changes: Do people really remember? *Archives of General Psychiatry, 36,* 379–384.

Jenkins, H.M., Barrera, F.J., Ireland, C., & Woodside, B. (1978). Signal-centred action patterns of dogs in appetitive classical conditioning. *Learning and Motivation, 9,* 272–296.

Jensen, A.R. (1969). How much can we boost IQ and scholastic achievement? *Harvard Educational Review, 39,* 1–123.

Jensen, A.R. (1998). *The g factor: The science of mental ability.* Westport, CT: Praeger Publishers/Greenwood Publishing Group.

Jensen, J., Bergin, A., & Greaves, D. (1990). The meaning of eclecticism: New survey and analysis of components. *Professional Psychology: Research and Practice, 21,* 124–130.

Jockin, V., McGue, M., & Lykken, D.T. (1996). Personality and divorce: A genetic analysis. *Journal of Personality and Social Psychology, 71,* 288–299.

Johansson, G. (1975). Visual motion perception. *Scientific American, 232,* 76–89.

John, O.P., & Srivastava, S. (1999). The Big Five trait taxonomy: History, measurement, and theoretical perspectives. In L.A. Pervin & O.P. John (Eds.), *Handbook of personality: Theory and research* (2nd ed.). New York: Guilford Press.

Johnson, J.S., & Newport, E.L. (1989). Critical period effects in second language learning: The influence of maturational state on the acquisition of English as a second language. *Cognitive Psychology, 21,* 60–99.

Johnson, M.H., Dziurawiec, S., Ellis, H., & Morton, J. (1991). Newborns' preferential tracking of face-like stimuli and its subsequent decline. *Cognition, 40,* 1–19.

Johnson, M.K., Hashtroudi, S., & Lindsay, D.S. (1993). Source monitoring. *Psychological Bulletin, 114,* 3–28.

Johnson, R.D., & Downing, L.L. (1979). Deindividuation and valence of cues: Effects on prosocial and antisocial behavior. *Journal of Personality and Social Psychology, 37,* 1532–1538.

Johnson-Laird, P.N. (1983). *Mental models.* Cambridge, UK: Cambridge University Press.

Johnson-Laird, P.N. (1999). Deductive reasoning. *Annual Review of Psychology, 50,* 109–135.

Johnson-Laird, P.N., & Byrne, R.M.J. (1991). *Deduction.* Hillsdale, NJ: Lawrence Erlbaum Associates Inc.

Johnson-Laird, P.N., & Goldvarg, Y. (1997). How to make the impossible seem possible. In *Proceedings of the 19th Annual Conference of the Cognitive Science Society.* Mahwah, NJ: Lawrence Erlbaum Associates Inc.

Johnson-Laird, P.N., Legrenzi, P., Girotto, V., Legrenzi, M.S., & Caverni, J.P. (1999). Naive probability: A mental model theory of extensional reasoning. *Psychological Review, 106,* 62–88.

Johnston, J., & Ettema, J.S. (1982). *Positive image: Breaking stereotypes with children's television.* Beverly Hills, CA: Sage.

Johnstone, L. (1989). *Users and abusers of psychiatry: A critical look at traditional psychiatric practice.* London: Routledge.

Jones, B. (1979). Elimination of paradoxical sleep by lesions of the pontine gigantocellular tegmental field in the cat. *Neuroscience Letters, 13,* 285–293.

Jones, E.E. (1998). Major developments in five decades of social psychology. In D.T. Gilbert, S.T. Fiske, & G. Lindzey (Eds.), *Handbook of social psychology* (Vol. 1, 4th ed., pp. 3–57). New York: McGraw-Hill.

Jones, E.E., & Davis, K.E. (1965). From acts to dispositions: The attribution process in person perception. In L. Berkowitz (Ed.), *Advances in Experimental Social Psychology, Vol. 2.* New York: Academic Press.

Jones, E.E., & Harris, V.A. (1967). The attribution of attitudes. *Journal of Experimental Social Psychology, 3,* 1–24.

Jones, E.E., & Nisbett, R.E. (1972). The actor and the observer: Divergent perceptions of the causes of behaviour. In E.E. Jones, D.E. Kanouse, H.H. Kelley, R.E. Nisbett, S. Vlins, & B. Weiner (Eds.), *Attribution: Perceiving the causes of behaviour.* Morristown, NJ: General Learning Press.

Jones, E.E., Rhodewalt, F., Berglas, S., & Skelton, J.A. (1981). Effects of strategic self-presentation on subsequent self-esteem. *Journal of Personality and Social Psychology, 41,* 407–421.

Jones, E.E., & Sigall, H. (1971). The bogus pipeline: A new paradigm for measuring affect and attitude. *Psychological Bulletin, 76,* 349–364.

Jones, M.C. (1925). A laboratory study of fear: The case of Peter. *Pedagogical Seminary, 31,* 308–315.

Jones, N.B. (1972). *Categories of child–child interaction: Ethological studies of child behaviour.* Cambridge, UK: Cambridge University Press.

Josephson, W.L. (1987). Television violence and children's aggression: Testing the priming, social script, and disinhibition predictions. *Journal of Personality and Social Psychology, 53,* 882–890.

Jouvet, M., & Renault, J. (1966). Insomnie persistante apres lesions des noyaux du raphe chez le chat. *Comptes Rendus du la Societe de Biologie (Paris), 160,* 1461–1465.

Judd, C.M., & Park, B. (1993). Definition and assessment of accuracy in social stereotypes. *Psychological Review, 100,* 109–128.

Judge, T.A., & Bono, J.E. (2001). Relationship of core self-evaluation traits—self-esteem, generalised self-efficacy, locus of control, and emotional stability—with job satisfaction and job performance: A meta-analysis. *Journal of Applied Psychology, 86,* 80–92.

Kagan, J. (1984). *The nature of the child.* New York: Basic Books.

Kagan, J., Kearsley, R.B., & Zelazo, P.R. (1980). *Infancy: Its place in human development.* Cambridge, MA.: Harvard University Press.

Kahneman, D. (1973). *Attention and effort.* Upper Saddle River, NJ: Prentice Hall, Inc.

Kahneman, D., & Henik, A. (1979). Perceptual organisation and attention. In M. Kubovy & J.R. Pomerantz (Eds.), *Perceptual organisation.* Hillsdale, NJ: Lawrence Erlbaum Associates, Inc.

Kahneman, D., & Tversky, A. (1973). On the psychology of prediction. *Psychological Review, 80,* 237–251.

Kahneman, D., & Tversky, A. (1979). Intuitive prediction: Biases and corrective procedures. *TIMS Studies in Management Science, 12,* 313–327.

Kahneman, D., & Tversky, A. (1984). Choices, values and frames. *American Psychologist, 39,* 341–350.

Kahneman, D., Tversky, B., Shapiro, D., & Crider, A. (1969). Pupillary, heart rate and skin resistance changes during a mental task. *Journal of Experimental* Psychology, 79, 164–167.

Kako, E. (1999). Elements of syntax in the systems of three language-trained animals. *Animal Learning and Behavior, 27,* 26–27.

Kalat, J.W. (1998). *Biological psychology* (6th ed.). Pacific Grove, CA: Brooks/Cole Publishing Co.

Kalat, J.W. (2000). *Biological psychology* (7th ed.). Belmont, CA: Wadsworth.

Kalucy, R.S., Crisp, A.H., & Harding, B. (1977). A study of 56 families with anorexia nervosa. *British Journal of Medical Psychology, 50,* 381–395.

Kamin, L. (1981). *The intelligence controversy: H.J. Eysenck vs. Leon Kamin.* New York: Wiley.

Kamin, L.J. (1969). Predictability, surprise, attention and conditioning. In R. Campbell & R. Church (Eds.), *Punishment and aversive behaviour.* New York: Appleton-Century-Crofts.

Kaneko, H., & Uchikawa, K. (1997). Perceived angular and linear size: The role of binocular disparity and visual surround. *Perception, 26,* 17–27.

Kanfer, R., & Ackerman, P.L. (1989). Motivation and cognitive abilities: An integrative/aptitude-treatment interaction approach to skill acquisition. *Journal of Applied Psychology, 74,* 657–690.

Kanizsa, G. (1976). Subjective contours. *Scientific American, 234,* 48–52.

Kanner, A.D., Coyne, J.C., Schaefer, C., & Lazarus, R.S. (1981). Comparison of two modes of stress measurement: Daily hassles and uplifts versus major life events. *Journal of Behavioural Medicine, 4,* 1–39.

Kanner, L. (1943). Autistic disturbances of affective contact. *Nervous Child, 2,* 217–250.

Kanwisher, N., McDermott, J., & Chun, M.M. (1997). The fusiform face area: A module in human extrastriate cortex specialised for face perception. *Journal of Neuroscience, 9,* 605–610.

Kaplan, G.A., & Simon, H.A. (1990). In search of insight. *Cognitive Psychology, 22,* 374–419.

Kaplan, M. (1983). A woman's view of DSM–III. *American Psychologist, 38,* 786–792.

Kapur, N. (1999). Syndromes of retrograde amnesia: A conceptual and empirical synthesis. *Psychological Bulletin, 125,* 800–825.

Karasek, R.A. (1979). Job demands, job decision latitude, and mental strain: Implications for job redesign. *Administrative Science Quarterly, 24,* 285–308.

Karau, S.J., & Williams, K.D. (1993). Social loafing: A meta-analytic review and theoretical integration. *Journal of Personality and Social Psychology, 65,* 681–706.

Karney, B.R., & Bradbury, T.N. (1995). The longitudinal course of marital quality and stability: A review of theory, method, and research. *Psychological Bulletin, 118,* 3–34.

Kashima, Y., & Kashima, E.S. (2003). Individualism, GNP, climate, and pronoun drop: Is individualism determined by affluence and climate, or does language use play a role? *Journal of Cross-Cultural Psychology, 34,* 125–134.

Kashima, Y., Siegal, M., Tanaka, K., & Kashima, E.S. (1992). Do people believe behaviours are consistent with attitudes? Towards a cultural psychology of attribution processes. *British Journal of Social Psychology, 31,* 111–124.

Kashima, Y., & Triandis, H.C. (1986). The self-serving bias in attributions as a coping strategy: A cross-cultural study. *Journal of Cross-Cultural Psychology, 17,* 83–97.

Katigbak, M.S., Church, A.T., Guanzon-Lapensa, M.A., Carlota, A.J., & del Pilar, G.H. (2002). Are indigenous personality dimensions culture specific? Philippine inventories and the Five-Factor model. *Journal of Personality and Social Psychology, 82,* 89–101.

Katz, D., & Braly, K.W. (1933). Racial stereotypes of one hundred college students. *Journal of Abnormal and Social Psychology, 28,* 280–290.

Katz, P., & Zigler, E. (1967). Self-image disparity: A developmental approach. *Journal of Personality and Social Psychology, 5,* 186–195.

Kay, J., & Ellis, A.W. (1987). A cognitive neuropsychological case study of anomia: Implications for psychological models of word retrieval. *Brain, 110,* 613–629.

Kay, J., & Marcel, T. (1981). One process not two in reading aloud: Lexical analogies do the work of nonlexical rules. *Quarterly Journal of Experimental Psychology, 39A,* 29–41.

Keane, M.T. (1987). On retrieving analogues when solving problems. *Quarterly Journal of Experimental Psychology, 39A,* 29–41.

Keane, T.M., Fairbank, J.A., Caddell, J.M., Zimmering, R.T., & Gender, M. (1985). A behavioural approach to assessing and treating posttraumatic stress disorder in Vietnam veterans. In C.R. Figley (Ed.), *Trauma and its wake: The study and treatment of post-traumatic stress disorder.* New York: Brunner/Mazel.

Keehn, R.J., Goldberg, I.D., & Beebe, G.W. (1974). Twenty-four-year mortality follow-up of army veterans with disability separations for psychoneurosis in 1944. *Psychosomatic Medicine, 36,* 27–46.

Keesey, R.E., & Boyle, P.C. (1973). Effects of quinine adulteration upon body weight of LH-lesioned and intact male rats. *Journal of Comparative and Physiological Psychology, 84,* 38–46.

Keiley, M.K., Bates, J.E., Dodge, K.A., & Pettit, G.S. (2000). A cross-domain growth analysis: Externalising and internalising behaviours during 8 years of childhood. *Journal of Abnormal Child Psychology, 28,* 161–179.

Keller, H., Scholmerich, A., & Eibl-Eibesfeldt, I. (1988). Communication patterns in adult–infant interactions in Western and non-Western cultures. *Journal of Cross-Cultural Psychology, 19,* 427–445.

Kelley, H.H. (1950). The warm–cold variable in first impressions of people. *Journal of Personality, 18,* 431–439.

Kelley, H.H. (1967). Attribution theory in social psychology. In D. Levine (Ed.), *Nebraska symposium on motivation, Vol. 15.* Lincoln, NE: University of Nebraska Press.

Kelley, H.H. (1973). The processes of causal attribution. *American Psychologist, 28,* 107–128.

Kellman, P.J. (1996) The origins of object perception. In R. Gelman & T.K.F. Au (Eds.), *Perceptual and cognitive development.* New York: Academic Press.

Kellman, P.J., & Spelke, E.S. (1983). Perception of partly occluded objects in infancy. *Cognitive Psychology, 15,* 483–524.

Kellogg, R.T. (1994). *The psychology of writing.* Oxford: Oxford University Press.

Keltner, D., & Gross, J.J. (1999). Functional accounts of emotions. *Cognition and Emotion, 13,* 467–480.

Kendall, P.C., & Hammen, C. (1998). *Abnormal psychology: Understanding human problems* (2nd ed.). New York: Houghton Mifflin.

Kendler, K.S. (1995). Adversity, stress and psychopathology: A psychiatric genetic perspective. *International Journal of Method in Psychiatric Research, 5,* 163–170.

Kendler, K.S., Karkowski, L.M., & Prescott, C.A. (1999). Fears and phobias: Reliability and heritability. *Psychological Medicine, 29,* 539–553.

Kendler, K.S., Maclean, C., Neale, M., Kessler, R., Heath, A., & Eaves, L. (1991). The genetic epidemiology of bulimia nervosa. *American Journal of Psychiatry, 148,* 1627–1637.

Kendler, K.S., Neale, M.C., Kessler, R.C., Heath, A.C., & Eaves, L.J. (1992). A population-based twin study of major depression in women: The impact of varying definitions of illness. *Archives of General Psychiatry, 49,* 257–266.

Kendler, K.S., Neale, M.C., Kessler, R.C., Heath, A.C., & Eaves, L.J. (1993). Panic disorder in women: A population-based twin study. *Psychological Medicine, 23,* 397–406.

Kendler, K.S., Neale, M.C., Prescott, C.A., Kessler, R.C., Heath, A.C., Corey, L.A., & Eaves, L.J. (1996). Childhood parental loss and alcoholism in women: A causal analysis using a twin-family design. *Psychological Medicine, 26,* 79–95.

Kendler, K.S., Pedersen, N.L., Farahmand, B.Y., & Persson, P.G. (1996). The treated incidence of psychotic and affective illness in twins compared with population expectation: A study in the Swedish Twin and Psychiatric Registries. *Psychological Medicine, 26,* 1135–1144.

Kenealy, P.M. (1997). Mood-state-dependent retrieval: The effects of induced mood on memory reconsidered. *Quarterly Journal of Experimental Psychology A, 50,* 290–317.

Kennedy, J. (1982). Middle LPC leaders and the contingency model of leader effectiveness. *Organizational Behavior and Human Performance, 30,* 1–14.

Kenrick, D.T. (2001). Evolutionary psychology, cognitive science, and dynamical systems: Building an integrative paradigm. *Current Directions in Psychological Science, 10*, 13–17.

Keppel, G., & Underwood, B. (1962). Proactive inhibition in short-term retention of single items. *Journal of Verbal Learning and Verbal Behaviour, 1*, 153–161.

Kessler, R.C. (1997). The effects of stressful life events on depression. *Annual Review of Psychology, 48*, 191–214.

Kettlewell, H.B.D. (1955). Selection experiments on industrial melanism in the Lepidoptera. Heredity, 9, 323–342.

Kety, S.S. (1974). From rationalisation to reason. *American Journal of Psychiatry, 131*, 957–963.

Keuthen, N. (1980). *Subjective probability estimation and somatic structures in phobic individuals.* Unpublished manuscript, State University of New York at Stony Brook.

Keysar, B., & Henly, A.S. (2002). Speakers' overestimation of their effectiveness. *Psychological Science, 13*, 207–212.

Kiecolt-Glaser, J.K., Garner, W., Speicher, C.E., Penn, G.M., Holliday, J., & Glaser, R. (1984). Psychosocial modifiers of immunocompetence in medical students. *Psychosomatic Medicine, 46*, 7–14.

Kiecolt-Glaser, J.K., Marucha, P.T., Atkinson, C., & Glaser, R. (2001). Hypnosis as a modulator of cellular immune dysregulation during acute stress. *Journal of Consulting and Clinical Psychology, 69*, 674–682.

Kiecolt-Glaser, R., Rice, J., Speicher, C.E., Stout, J.C., & Kiecolt-Glaser, J. (1986). Stress depresses interferon production by leucocytes concomitant with a decrease in natural killer cell activity. *Behavioural neuroscience, 100*, 675–678.

Kilpatrick, F.P., & Ittelson, W.H. (1953). The size–distance invariance hypothesis. *Psychological Review, 60*, 223–231.

Kim, H., & Markus, H.R. (1999). Uniqueness or deviance, harmony or conformity: A cultural analysis. *Journal of Personality and Social Psychology, 77*, 785–800.

Kimble, D.P., Robinson, T.S., & Moon, S. (1980). *Biological psychology.* New York: Holt, Reinhart, & Winston.

Kimble, D.P., Robinson, T.S., & Moon, S. (1992). Biological Psychology (2nd ed.). Orlando, FL: Harcourt Brace Jovanovich.

Kimchi, R. (1992). Primacy of wholistic processing and global/local paradigm: A critical review. *Psychological Bulletin, 112*, 24–38.

King, B.M., Smith, R.L., & Frohman, L.A. (1984). Hyper-insulinemia in rats with ventromedial hypothalamic lesions: Role of hyperphagia. *Behavioral Neuroscience, 98*, 152–155.

King, W.C., Jr., Miles, E.W., & Day, D.D. (1993). A test and refinement of the equity sensitivity construct. *Journal of Organizational Behavior, 14*, 301–317.

Kinnunen, T., Zamanky, H.S., & Block, M.L. (1995). Is the hypnotised subject lying? *Journal of Abnormal Psychology, 103*, 184–191.

Kintsch, W. (1988). The role of knowledge in discourse comprehension: A construction–integration model. *Psychological Review, 95*, 163–182.

Kintsch, W. (1994). The psychology of discourse processing. In M.A. Gernsbacher (Ed.), *Handbook of psycholinguistics.* London: Academic Press.

Kintsch, W., Welsch, D., Schmalhofer, F., & Zimny, S. (1990). Sentence memory: A theoretical analysis. *Journal of Memory and Language, 29*, 133–159.

Kirby, K.N. (1994). Probabilities and utilities of fictional outcomes in Wason's four-card selection task. *Cognition, 51*, 1–28.

Kirkpatrick, S.A., & Locke, E.A. (1996). Direct and indirect effects of three core charismatic leadership components on performance and attitudes. *Journal of Applied Psychology, 81*, 36–51.

Kirschenbaum, H., & Henderson, V.L. (Eds.). (1990). *The Carl Rogers Reader.* London: Constable.

Kisilevsky, B.S., Hains, S.M.J., Lee, K., Xie, X., Huang, H., Ye, H.H., & Wang, Z. (2003). Effects of experience on foetal voice recognition. *Psychological Science, 14*, 220–224.

Kitayama, S., Duffy, S., Kawamura, T., & Larsen, J.T. (2003). Perceiving an object and its context in different cultures: A cultural look at new look. *Psychological Science, 14*, 201–206.

Kitayama, S., Markus, H.R., Matsumoto, H., & Norasakkunkit, V. (1997). Individual and collective processes of self-esteem management: Self-enhancement in the United States and self-depreciation in Japan. *Journal of Personality and Social Psychology, 72*, 1245–1267.

Kitsantas, A. (2000). The role of self-regulation strategies and self-efficacy perceptions in successful weight loss maintenance. *Psychology and Health, 15*, 811–820.

Klaus, M.H., & Kennell, J.H. (1976). *Parent–infant bonding.* St. Louis, MO: Mosby.

Klayman, J., & Ha, Y.–W. (1987). Confirmation, disconfirmation and information in hypothesis testing. *Psychological Review, 94*, 211–228.

Klein, H.J., Wesson, M.J., Hollenbeck, J.R., & Alge, B.J. (1999). Goal commitment and the goal-setting process: Conceptual clarification and empirical synthesis. *Journal of Applied Psychology, 84*, 885–896.

Klein, K.E., Wegman, H.M., & Hunt, B.I. (1972). Desynchronisation of body temperature and performance circadian rhythm as a result of outgoing and homegoing transmeridian flights. *Aerospace Medicine, 43*, 119–132.

Kleiner, L., & Marshall, W.L. (1987). The role of interpersonal problems in the development of agoraphobia with panic attacks. *Journal of Anxiety Disorders, 1*, 313–323.

Kleinman, A., & Cohen, A. (1997, March). Psychiatry's global challenge. *Scientific American*, pp. 74–77.

Kleinmuntz, B. (1974). *Essentials of abnormal psychology.* New York: Harper & Row.

Kline, P. (1981). *Fact and fantasy in Freudian theory.* London: Methuen.

Kline, P., & Storey, R. (1977). A factor analytic study of the anal character. *British Journal of Social and Clinical Psychology, 16*, 317–328.

Klohnen, E.C., & Bera, S. (1998). Behavioural and experiential patterns of avoidantly and securely attached women across adulthood: A 31-year longitudinal perspective. *Journal of Personality and Social Psychology, 74*, 211–223.

Kluver, H., & Bucy, P.C. (1937). "Psychic blindness" and other symptoms following bilateral temporal lobectomy. *American Journal of Physiology, 119*, 352–353.

Kluver, H., & Bucy, P. (1939). Preliminary analysis of functions of the temporal lobes in monkeys. *Archives of Neurology and Psychiatry, 42*, 979–1000.

Knoblich, G., Ohlsson, S., Haider, H., & Rhenius, D. (1999). Constraint relaxation and chunk decomposition in insight problem solving. *Journal of Experimental Psychology: Learning, Memory, and Cognition, 25*, 1534–1555.

Knowlton, B.J., Ramus, S.J., & Squire, L.R. (1992). Intact artificial grammar learning in amnesia: Dissociation of classification learning and explicit memory for specific instances. *Psychological Science, 3*, 172–179.

Knox, J.V., Morgan, A.H., & Hilgard, E.R. (1974). Pain and suffering in ischemia: The paradox of hypnotically suggested anaesthesia as contradicted by reports from the "hidden-observer". *Archives of General Psychiatry, 30*, 840–847.

Kochanska, G., de Vet, K., Goldman, M., Murray, K., & Putnam, S.P. (1994). Maternal reports of conscience development and temperament in young children. *Child Development, 65*, 852–868.

Koedinger, K.R., & Anderson, J.R. (1990). Abstract planning and perceptual chunks: Elements of expertise in geometry. *Cognitive Science, 14*, 511–550.

Koehler, J.J. (1996). The base rate fallacy reconsidered: Descriptive, normative, and methodological challenges. *Behavioral and Brain Sciences, 19*, 1–53.

Koffka, K. (1935). *Principles of Gestalt psychology.* New York: Harcourt Brace.

Kohlberg, L. (1963). Development of children's orientations toward a moral order. *Vita Humana, 6*, 11–36.

Kohlberg, L. (1966). A cognitive-development analysis of children's sex-role concepts and attitudes. In E.E. Maccoby (Ed.),

*The development of sex differences*. Stanford, CA: Stanford University Press.

Kohlberg, L. (1975). The cognitive-developmental approach to moral education. *Phi Delta Kappan*, June, 670–677.

Kohlberg, L. (1976). Moral stages and moralization. In T. Likona (Ed.), *Moral development and behaviour*. New York: Holt, Rinehart, & Winston.

Kohlberg, L. (1981). *Essays on moral development: Vol. 1. The philosophy of moral development*. San Francisco: Harper & Row.

Kohler, I. (1962). Experiments with goggles. *Scientific American, 206*, 62–72.

Köhler, S., & Moscovitch, M. (1997). Unconscious visual processing in neuropsychological syndromes: A survey of the literature and evaluation of models of consciousness. In M.D. Rugg (Ed.), *Cognitive neuroscience*. Hove, UK: Psychology Press.

Köhler, W. (1925). *The mentality of apes*. New York: Harcourt Brace & World.

Kohut, H. (1977). *The restoration of the self*. Madison, CT: International Universities Press.

Kolb, B., & Whishaw, I.Q. (2001). *An introduction to brain and behaviour*. New York: Worth.

Koluchová, J. (1976). The further development of twins after severe and prolonged deprivation: A second report. *Journal of Child Psychology and Psychiatry, 17*, 181–188.

Koob, G.F., Markou, A., Weiss, F., & Schulteis, G. (1993). Opponent process and drug dependence: Neurobiological mechanisms. *Seminars in Neurosciences, 5*, 351–358.

Kopta, S.M., Lueger, R.J., Saunders, S.M., & Howard, K.I. (1999). Individual psychotherapy outcome and process research: Challenges leading to greater turmoil or a positive transition? *Annual Review of Psychology, 50*, 441–469.

Korchmaros, J.D., & Kenny, D.A. (2001). Emotional closeness as a mediator of the effect of genetic relatedness on altruism. *Psychological Science, 12*, 262–265.

Koriat, A., & Goldsmith, M. (1996). Monitoring and control processes in the strategic regulation of memory accuracy. *Psychological Review, 103*, 490–517.

Korsakoff, S.S. (1889). Uber eine besonderes Form psychischer Storung, kombiniert mit multiplen Neuritis. *Archiv für Psychiatrie und Nervenkrankheiten, 21*, 669–704.

Kosslyn, S.M., Thompson, W.L., Costantini-Ferrando, M.F., Alpert, N.M., & Spiegel, D. (2000). Hypnotic visual illusion alters colour processing in the brain. *American Journal of Psychiatry, 157*, 1279–1284.

Kowalski, R.M., & Leary, M.R. (1990). Strategic self-presentation and the avoidance of aversive events: Antecedents and consequences of self-enhancement and self-depreciation. *Journal of Experimental Social Psychology, 26*, 322–336.

Kraft, J.M., & Brainard, D.H. (1999). Mechanisms of colour constancy under nearly natural viewing. *Proceedings of the National Academy of Sciences, USA, 96*, 307–312.

Kramer, R.M. (1998). Revisiting the Bay of Pigs and Vietnam decisions 25 years later: How well has the groupthink hypothesis stood the test of time? *Organizational Behavior and Human Decision Processes, 73*, 236–271.

Kraus, S.J. (1995). Attitudes and the prediction of behaviour: A meta-analysis of the empirical literature. *Personality and Social Psychology Bulletin, 21*, 58–75.

Krebs, J.R., & Davies, N.B. (1993). *An introduction to behavioural ecology* (3rd ed.). Oxford, UK: Blackwell.

Krevans, J., & Gibbs, J.C. (1996). Parents' use of inductive discipline: Relations to children's empathy and prosocial behavior. *Child Development, 67*, 3263–3277.

Kroon, M.B.R., t'Hart, P., & van Kreveld, D. (1991). Managing group decision making processes: Individual versus collective accountability and groupthink. *International Journal of Conflict Management, 2*, 91–115.

Krueger, R.F., Hicks, B.M., & McGue, M. (2001). Altruism and anti-social behaviour: Independent tendencies, unique personality correlates, distinct aetiologies. *Psychological Science, 12*, 397–402.

Krugalanski, A.W., & Webster, D.M. (1996). Motivated closing of the mind: "Seizing" and "freezing". *Psychological Review, 103*, 263–283.

Krupnick, J.L., Sotsky, S.M., Simmens, S., Moyer, J., Elkin, I., Watkins, J., & Pilkonis, P.A. (1996). The role of the therapeutic alliance in psychotherapy and pharmacotherapy outcome: Findings in the National Institute of Mental Health Treatment of Depression Collaborative Research Program. *Journal of Consulting and Clinical Psychology, 64*, 532–539.

Kuhar, M.J., Ritz, M.C., & Boja, J.W. (1991). Cocaine and dopamine reward. *Trends in Neurosciences, 14*, 229–232.

Kuhlman, D.M., & Marshello, A.F. (1975). Individual differences in game motivation as moderators of preprogrammed strategic effects in prisoner's dilemma. *Journal of Personality and Social Psychology, 32*, 922–931.

Kuhn, D. (1995). Microgenetic study of change: What has it told us? *Psychological Science, 6*, 133–139.

Kuhn, T.S. (1962). *The structure of scientific revolutions*. Chicago: Chicago University Press.

Kuhn, T.S. (1977). *The essential tension: Selected studies in scientific tradition and change*. Chicago: Chicago University Press.

Kunda, Z., & Oleson, K.C. (1995). Maintaining stereotypes in the face of disconfirmation: Constructing grounds for subtyping deviants. *Journal of Personality and Social Psychology, 68*, 565–579.

Künnapas, T.M. (1968). Distance perception as a function of available visual cues. *Journal of Experimental Psychology, 77*, 523–529.

Kutnick, P.J., & Brees, P. (1982). The development of co-operation: Explorations in cognitive and moral competence and social authority. *British Journal of Educational Psychology, 52*, 361–365.

Kvavilashvili, L., & Ellis, J. (in press). Ecological validity and twenty years of real-life/laboratory controversy in memory research: A critical (and historical) review. *History and Philosophy of Psychology*.

La Freniere, P., Strayer, F.F., & Gauthier, R. (1984). The emergence of same-sex affiliative preferences among preschool peers: A developmental/aetiological perspective. *Child Development, 55*, 1958–1965.

LaBerge, D. (1983). Spatial extent of attention to letters and words. *Journal of Experimental Psychology: Human Perception and Performance, 9*, 371–379.

LaBerge, S., Greenleaf, W., & Kedzierski, B. (1983). Physiological responses to dreamed sexual activity during lucid REM sleep. *Psychophysiology, 20*, 454–455.

Lacey, J.I. (1967). Somatic response patterning and stress: Some revisions of the activation theory. In M.H. Appley & R. Trumbull (Eds.), *Psychological stress: Issues in research*. New York: Appleton-Century-Crofts.

Ladd, G.W. (1990). Having friends, keeping friends, making friends, and being liked by peers in the classroom: Predictors of children early school adjustment? *Child Development, 61*, 1081–1100.

Lader, M., & Scotto, J.C. (1998). A multicentre double-blind comparison of hydroxyzine, buspirone and placebo in patients with generalized anxiety disorder. *Psychopharmacology, 139*, 402–406.

Lafferty, P., Beutler, L.E., & Crago, M. (1989). Differences between more and less effective psychotherapists: A study of select therapist variables. *Journal of Consulting and Clinical Psychology, 57*, 76–80.

Laine, M., Salmelin, R., Helenius, P., & Marttila, R. (2000). Brain activation during reading in deep dyslexia: An MEG study. *Journal of Cognitive Neuroscience, 12*, 622–634.

Lalljee, M. (1981). Attribution theory and the analysis of explanations. In C. Antaki (Ed.), *The psychology of ordinary explanations of social behaviour*. London: Academic Press.

Lam, R.W., Tam, E.M., Shiah, I.S., Yatham, L.N., & Zis, A.P. (2000). Effects of light therapy on suicidal ideation in patients with winter depression. *Journal of Clinical Psychiatry, 61*, 30–32.

Lambert, M., & Bergin, A.E. (1994). The effectiveness of psychotherapy. In A.E. Bergin & S.L. Garfield (Eds.), *Handbook of psychotherapy and behavior change* (4th ed., pp. 143–189). New York: Wiley.

Lambert, R.G., & Lambert, M.J. (1984). The effects of role preparation for psychotherapy on immigrant clients seeking mental health services in Hawaii. *Journal of Community Psychology, 12,* 263–275.

Lambon Ralph, M.A., Sage, K., & Roberts, J. (2000). Classical anomia: A neuropsychological perspective on speech production. *Neuropsychologia, 38,* 186–202.

Lamont, A.M. (2001). Retrieved from www.le.ac.uk/pc/aml11/babies.html

Land, E.H. (1977). The retinex theory of colour vision. *Scientific American, 237,* 108–128.

Land, E.H. (1986). Recent advances in retinex theory. *Vision Research, 26,* 7–21.

Lang, P.J. (1971). The application of psychophysiological methods to the study of psychotherapy and behaviour modification. In A. Bergin & S. Garfield (Eds.), *Handbook of psychotherapy and behaviour change.* Chichester, UK: Wiley.

Lang, P.J. (1985). The cognitive psychophysiology of emotion: Fear and anxiety. In A.H. Tuma & J. Maser (Eds.), *Anxiety and the anxiety disorders.* Hillsdale, NJ: Lawrence Erlbaum Associates, Inc.

Langlois, J.H., Kalakanis, L., Rubenstein, A.J., Larson, A., Hallam, M., & Smoot, M. (2000). Maxims or myths of beauty? A meta-analytic and theoretical review. *Psychological Review, 126,* 390–423.

Langlois, J.H., Roggman, L.A., & Musselman, L. (1994). What is average and what is not average about attractive faces. *Psychological Science, 5,* 214–220.

LaPiere, R.T. (1934). Attitudes vs. actions. *Social Forces, 13,* 230–237.

Larivee, S., Normandeau, S., & Parent, S. (2000). The French connection: Some contributions of French-language research in the post-Piagetian era. *Child Development, 71,* 823.

Larsen, J.D., Baddeley, A., & Andrade, J. (2000). Phonological similarity and the irrelevant speech effect: Implications for models of short-term verbal memory. *Memory, 8,* 145–157.

Larson, R.W., Richards, M.H., Moneta, G., Holmbeck, G., & Duckett, E. (1996). Changes in adolescents' daily interactions with their families from ages 10 to 18: Disengagment and transformation. *Developmental Psychology, 32,* 744–754.

Larzelere, R.E. (2000). Child outcomes of nonabusive and customary physical punishment by parents: An updated literature review. *Clinical Child and Family Psychology Review, 3,* 199–221.

Lashley, K.S., Chow, K.L., & Semmes, J. (1951). An examination of the electrical field theory of cerebral integration. *Psychological Review, 58,* 123–136.

Lassiter, G.D. (2000). The relative contributions of recognition and search-evaluation processes to high-level chess performance: Comment on Gobet and Simon. *Psychological Science, 11,* 172–173.

Latané, B., & Darley, J.M. (1970). *The unresponsive bystander: Why doesn't he help?* Englewood Cliffs, NJ: Prentice-Hall.

Latané, B., Williams, K., & Harkins, S. (1979). Many hands make light the work: The causes and consequences of social loafing. *Journal of Personality and Social Psychology, 37,* 823–832.

Latham, G.P., & Yukl, G.A. (1975). Assigned versus participative goal setting with educated and uneducated woods workers. *Journal of Applied Psychology, 60,* 299–302.

Lau, J., Antman, E.M., Jimenez-Silva, J., Kuperlnik, B., Mostpeller, F., & Chalmers, T.C. (1992). Cumulative meta-analysis of therapeutic trials for myocardial infarction. *New England Journal of Medicine, 327,* 248–254.

Lavie, P. (2001). Sleep–wake as a biological rhythm. *Annual Review of Psychology, 52,* 277–303.

Lavin, J.H., Wittert, G., Sun, W.M., Horowitz, M., Morley, J.E., & Read, N.W. (1996). Appetite regulation by carbohydrate: Role of blood glucose and gastrointestinal hormones. *American Journal of Physiology—Endocrinology and Metabolism, 271,* 209–214.

Lazar, I., & Darlington, R. (1982). Lasting effects of early education: A report from the Consortium for Longitudinal Studies. *Monographs of the Society for Research in Child Development, 47.*

Lazarus, A.A., & Messer, S.B. (1991). Does chaos prevail? An exchange on technical eclecticism and assimilative integration. *Journal of Psychotherapy Integration, 1,* 143–158.

Lazarus, R.S. (1982). Thoughts on the relations between emotion and cognition. *American Psychologist, 37,* 1019–1024.

Lazarus, R.S. (1991). *Emotion and adaptation.* Oxford, UK: Oxford University Press.

Lazarus, R.S. (1993). Coping theory and research: Past, present, and future. *Psychosomatic Medicine, 55,* 234–247.

Lazarus, R.S., & Launier, R. (1978). Stress related transactions between person and environment. In L.A. Pervin & M. Lewis (Eds.), *Perspectives in interactional psychology.* New York: Plenum.

Le Bon, G. (1895). *The crowd.* London: Ernest Benn.

Le, A.D., Poulos, C.X., & Cappell, H. (1979). Conditioned tolerance to the hypothalamic effect of ethyl alcohol. *American Association for the Advancement of Science, 206,* 1109–1110.

Lea, W.A. (1973). An approach to syntactic recognition without phonemics. *IEEE Transactions on Audio and Electroacoustics, AU-21,* 249–258.

Leake, J. (1999). Scientists teach chimpanzees to speak English. *Sunday Times.*

LeDoux, J.E. (1992). Brain mechanisms of emotion and emotional learning. *Current Opinions in Neurobiology, 2,* 191–198.

LeDoux, J.E. (1996). *The emotional brain: The mysterious underpinnings of emotional life.* New York: Simon & Schuster.

Lee, D.N. (1980). Visuo-motor coordination in space–time. In G.E. Stelmach & J. Requin (Eds.), *Tutorials in motor behaviour.* Amsterdam: North-Holland.

Lee, H. (1997). *Virginia Woolf.* London: Vintage.

Lee, L. (1984). Sequences in separation: A framework for investigating endings of the personal (romantic) relationship. *Journal of Social and Personal Relationships, 1,* 49–74.

Lee, P.N. (1991). Personality and disease: A call for replication. *Psychological Inquiry, 2,* 242–247.

Lee, S. (1994). The heterogeneity of stealing behaviors in Chinese patients with anorexia nervosa in Hong Kong. *Journal of Nervous and Mental Disease, 182,* 304–307.

Lee, V.E., Brooks-Gunn, J., Schnur, E., & Liaw, F. (1990). Are Head Start effects sustained? A longitudinal follow-up comparison of disadvantaged children attending Head Start, no preschool, and other preschool programmes. *Child Development, 61,* 495–507.

Leibowitz, S.F., Hammer, N.J., & Chang, K. (1981). Hypothalamic paraventricular nucleus lesions produce overeating and obesity in the rat. *Physiology and Behavior, 27,* 1031–1040.

Lemerise, E.A., & Arsenio, W.F. (2000). An integrated model of emotion processes and cognition in social information processing. *Child Development, 71,* 107–118.

Lemyre, L., & Smith, P.M. (1985). Intergroup discrimination and self-esteem in the minimal group paradigm. *Journal of Personality and Social Psychology, 49,* 660–670.

Lenneberg, E.H. (1967). *The biological foundations of language.* New York: Wiley.

Lennie, P. (1998). Single units and visual cortical organisation. *Perception, 27,* 889–935.

Leon, G.R. (1984). *Case histories of deviant behaviour* (3rd ed.). Boston: Allyn & Bacon.

Lepage, M., Ghaffar, O., Nyberg, L., & Tulving, E. (2000). Prefrontal cortex and episodic memory retrieval mode. *Proceedings of the National Academy of Sciences, USA, 97,* 506–511.

Lesar, T.S., Briceland, L., & Stein, D.S. (1997). Factors related to errors in medication prescribing. *Journal of the American Medical Association, 277,* 312–317.

Leslie, A.M. (1987). Pretence and representation: The origins of "theory of mind". *Psychological Review, 94,* 412–426.

Leslie, A.M. (1994). ToMM, ToBY and Agency: Core architecture and domain specificity. In L.A. Hirschfeld & S.A. Gelman (Eds.), *Mapping the mind.* New York: Cambridge.

Leslie, A.M., & Thaiss, L. (1992). Domain specificity in conceptual development: Neuropsychological evidence from autism. *Cognition, 43,* 225–251.

LeVay, S. (1993). *The sexual brain.* Cambridge, MA: MIT Press.

Levelt, W.J.M. (1989). *Speaking: From intention to articulation.* Cambridge, MA: MIT Press.

Levelt, W.J.M., Roelofs, A., & Meyer, A.S. (1999a). A theory of lexical access in speech production. *Behavioral and Brain Sciences, 22*, 1–38.

Levelt, W.J.M., Roelofs, A., & Meyer, A.S. (1999b). Multiple perspectives on word production. *Behavioral and Brain Sciences, 22*, 61–75.

Levenson, R.W. (1999). The intrapersonal functions of emotions. *Cognition and Emotion, 13*, 481–504.

Levenson, R.W., & Ekman, P., & Friesen, W.V. (1990). Voluntary action generates emotion-specific autonomic nervous-system activity. *Psychophysiology, 27*, 363–384.

Leventhal, A.G., Thompson, K.G., Liu, D., Zhou, Y., & Ault, S.J. (1995). Concomitant sensitivity to orientation, direction, and colour of cells in layers 2, 3, and 4 of monkey striate cortex. *Journal of Neuroscience, 15*, 1808–1818.

Leventhal, H.R. (1970). Findings and theory in the study of fear communications. In L. Berkowitz (Ed.), *Advances in experimental social psychology, Vol. 5*. New York: Academic Press.

Leventhal, H.R., Singer, P., & Jones, S. (1965). Effects of fear and specificity of recommendations upon attitudes and behaviour. *Journal of Personality and Social Psychology, 2*, 20–29.

Levine, J., Warrenburg, S., Kerns, R., Schwartz, G., Delaney, R., Fontana, A., Gradman, A., Smith, S., Allen, S., & Cascione, R. (1987). The role of denial in recovery from coronary heart disease. *Psychosomatic Medicine, 49*, 109–117.

Levine, J.M., Moreland, R.L., & Ryan, C.S. (1998). Group socialization and intergroup relations. In C. Sedikides, J. Schopler, & C.A. Insko (Eds.), *Intergroup cognition and intergroup behavior* (pp. 283–308). Mahwah, NJ: Lawrence Erlbaum Associates, Inc.

Levine, M. (2002). *Walk on by?* [Relational Justice Bulletin]. Cambridge, UK: Relationships Foundation.

Levine, R., Sato, S., Hashimoto, T., & Verma, J. (1995). Love and marriage in eleven cultures. *Journal of Cross-Cultural Psychology, 26*, 554–571.

Levinger, G. (1976). A social psychological perspective on marital dissolution. *Journal of Social Issues, 32*, 21–47.

Levinger, G. (1999). Duty toward whom? Reconsidering attractions and barriers as determinants of commitment in a relationship. In J.M. Adams & W.H. Warren (Eds.), *Handbook of interpersonal commitment and relationship stability: Perspectives on individual differences*. Dordrecht, The Netherlands: Kluwer Academic Publishers.

Levinson, S.C., Kita, S., Haun, D.B.M., & Rasch, B.H. (2002). Returning the tables: Language affects spatial reasoning. *Cognition, 84*, 155–188.

Lewin, K., Lippitt, R., & White, R. (1939). Patterns of aggressive behaviour in experimentally created "social climates". *Journal of Social Psychology, 10*, 271–299.

Lewinsohn, P.M., Joiner, T.E., Jr., & Rohde, P. (2001). Evaluation of cognitive diathesis–stress models in predicting major depressive disorder in adolescents. *Journal of Abnormal Psychology, 110*, 203–215.

Lewinsohn, P.M., Steimetz, J.L., Larsen, D.W., & Franklin, J. (1981). Depression related cognitions: Antecedent or consequences? *Journal of Abnormal Psychology, 90*, 213–219.

Lewis, C., & Osborne, A. (1990). Three-year olds' problems with false belief: Conceptual deficit or linguistic artifact? *Child Development, 61*, 1514–1519.

Lewis, M. (1990). Social knowledge and social development. *Merrill-Palmer Quarterly, 36*, 93–116.

Lewis, M., & Brooks-Gunn, J. (1979). *Social cognition and the acquisition of self*. New York: Plenum.

Lewis, M., & Howland-Jones, J.M. (2000). *Handbook of emotions* (2nd ed.). New York: Guilford Press.

Lewis, M., Sullivan, M.W., Stanger, C., & Weiss, M. (1989). Self-development and self-conscious emotions. *Child Development, 60*, 146–156.

Lewis, R.A., & Spanier, G.B. (1979). Theorizing about the quality and stability of marriage. In W.R. Burr, R. Hill, F.I. Nye, & I.L. Reiss (Eds.), *Contemporary theories about the family* (Vol. 1, pp. 268–294). New York: Free Press.

Lewis, R.A., & Spanier, G.B. (1982). Marital quality, marital stability and social exchange. In F.I. Nye (Ed.), *Family relationships: Rewards and costs*. Beverly Hills, CA: Sage.

Leyens, J.-P., Camino, L., Parke, R.D., & Berkowitz, L. (1975). Effects of movie violence on aggression in a field setting as a function of group dominance and cohesion. *Journal of Personality and Social Psychology, 32*, 346–360.

Libet, B. (1989). Conscious subjective experience vs. unconscious mental functions: A theory of the cerebral processes involved. In R.M.J. Cotterill (Ed.), *Models of brain function*. Cambridge, UK: Cambridge University Press.

Libet, B. (1996). Neural processes in the production of conscious experience. In M. Velmans (Ed.), *The science of consciousness*. London: Routledge.

Lichtenstein, S., Slovic, P., Fischhoff, B., Layman, M., & Combs, B. (1978). Judged frequency of lethal events. *Journal of Experimental Psychology: Human Learning and Memory, 4*, 551–578.

Lichtman, S., Pisarska, K., Berman, E., Pestone, M., Dowling, H., Offenbacher, E., Weisel, H., Heshka, S., Matthews, D., & Heymsfield, S. (1992). Discrepancy between self-reported and actual caloric intake and exercise in obese subjects. *New England Journal of Medicine, 327*, 1947–1948.

Lied, T.R., & Pritchard, R.D. (1976). Relationships between personality variables and components of the expectancy–valence model. *Journal of Applied Psychology, 61*, 463–467.

Lief, H.I., & Fetkewicz, J.M. (1995). Retractors of false memories: The evolution of pseudomemories. *Journal of Psychiatry and Law, 23*, 411–435.

Light, P., Buckingham, N., & Robbins, A.H. (1979). The conservation task as an interactional setting. *British Journal of Educational Psychology, 49*, 304–310.

Light, P., Littleton, K., Messer, D., & Joiner, R. (1994). Social and communicative processes in computer-based problem solving. *European Journal of Psychology of Education, 9*, 93–109.

Lilienfeld, S.O., Lynn, S.J., Kirsch, I., Chaves, J.F., Sarbin, T.R., Ganaway, G.K., & Powell, R.A. (1999). Dissociative identity disorder and the sociocognitive model: Recalling the lessons of the past. *Psychological Bulletin, 125*, 507–523.

Lilienfeld, S.O., & Marino, L. (1995). Mental disorder as a Roschian concept: A critique of Wakefield's "harmful dysfunction" analysis. *Journal of Abnormal Psychology, 104*, 411–420.

Lilienfeld, S.O., & Marino, L. (1999). Essentialism revisited: Evolutionary theory and the concept of mental disorder. *Journal of Abnormal Psychology, 108*, 400–411.

Lin, Y.C. (1992). *The construction of the sense of intimacy from everyday interaction*. Unpublished PhD thesis, University of Rochester, New York.

Linssen, H., & Hagendorn, L. (1994). Social and geographical factors in the explanations of European nationality stereotypes. *British Journal of Social Psychology, 23*, 165–182.

Locke, E.A. (1968). Toward a theory of task motivation and incentives. *Organizational Behavior and Human Performance, 3*, 157–189.

Locke, E.A., & Henne, D. (1986). Work motivation theories. In C. Cooper & I. Robertson (Eds.), *International review of industrial and organizational psychology*. Chichester, UK: Wiley.

Locke, E.A., & Latham, G.P. (1990). *A theory of goal setting and task performance*. Englewood Cliffs, NJ: Prentice-Hall.

Locke, E.A., Bryan, J.F., & Kendlall, L.M. (1968). Goals and intention as mediators of the effects of monetary incentives on behaviour. *Journal of Applied Psychology, 52*, 104–121.

Locke, E.A., Shaw, K.N., Saari, L.M., & Latham, G.P. (1981). Goal setting and task performance: 1969–1980. *Psychological Bulletin, 90*, 125–152.

Lockhart, R.S., & Craik, F.I.M. (1990). Levels of processing: A retrospective commentary on a framework for memory research. *Canadian Journal of Psychology, 44*, 87–112.

Loehlin, J.C. (1985). Fitting heredity–environment models jointly to twin and adoption data from the California Psychological Inventory. *Behavior Genetics, 15*, 199–221.

Loehlin, J.C., McCrae, R.R., Costa, P.T., & John, O.P. (1998). Heritabilities of common and measure-specific components of the Big Five personality factors. *Journal of Research in Personality, 32*, 431–453.

Loehlin, J.C., & Nichols, R.C. (1976). *Heredity, environment and personality*. Austin, TX: University of Texas Press.

Loftus, E. (1979). *Eyewitness testimony*. Cambridge, MA: Harvard University Press.

Loftus, E.F. (1992). When a lie becomes memory's truth: Memory distortion after exposure to misinformation. *Current Directions in Psychological Science, 1*, 121–123.

Loftus, E.F., & Palmer, J.C. (1974). Reconstruction of automobile destruction: An example of the interaction between language and memory. *Journal of Verbal Learning and Verbal Behavior, 13*, 585–589.

Loftus, E.F., & Zanni, G. (1975). Eyewitness testimony: The influence of the wording of a question. *Bulletin of the Psychonomic Society, 5*, 86–88.

Loftus, E.F., Loftus, G.R., & Messo, J. (1987). Some facts about "weapons focus". *Law and Human Behavior, 11*, 55–62.

Logan, G.D. (1988). Toward an instance theory of automatisation. *Psychological Review, 95*, 492–527.

Logie, R.H. (1995). *Visuo-spatial working memory*. Hove, UK: Psychology Press.

Logie, R.H. (1999). State of the art: Working memory. *The Psychologist, 12*, 174–178.

Lohman, D.F. (2000). Complex information processing and intelligence. In R.J. Sternberg (Ed.), *Handbook of intelligence*. New York: Cambridge University Press.

Lohman, D.F. (2001). Fluid intelligence, inductive reasoning, and working memory: Where the theory of multiple intelligences falls short. In N. Colangelo & S.G. Assouline (Eds.), *Talent Development IV: Proceedings from the 1998 Henry B. and Jocelyn Wallace National Research Symposium on Talent Development*. Scottsdale, AZ: Great Potential Press.

Long, C., & Zietkiewicz, E. (1998, September). *Unsettling meanings of madness: Constructions of South African insanity*. Paper presented at the fourth annual Qualitative Methods conference, University of the Witwatersrand, Johannesburg, South Africa. Available on CD-Rom, *From Method to Madness: Five years of qualitative inquiry*. Johannesburg, South Africa: Loose Method Collective. Also available on http://criticalmethods.org/carol.htm

Long, N.C. (1996). Evolution of infectious disease: How evolutionary forces shape physiological responses to pathogens. *News in Physiological Sciences, 11*, 83–90.

Lopes, L.L. (1987). Between hope and fear: The psychology of risk. In L. Berkowitz (Ed.), *Advances in experimental social psychology, Vol. 20*. San Diego, CA: Academic Press.

Loranger, A.W., Sartorius, N., Andreoli, A., Berger, P., Buchheim, P., Channabasavanna, S.M., Coid, B., Dahl, A., Diekstra, R.F., Ferguson, B., et al. (1994). The International Personality Disorder Examination: The World Health Organization/Alcohol, Drug Abuse, and Mental Health Administration international pilot study of personality disorders. *Archives of General Psychiatry, 51*, 215–224.

Lord, R.G., de Vader, C.L., & Alliger, G.M. (1986). A meta-analysis of the relation between personality traits and leadership perception: An application of validity generalisation procedures. *Journal of Applied Psychology, 71*, 402–410.

Lourenço, O., & Machado, A. (1996). In defence of Piaget's theory: A reply to 10 common criticisms. *Psychological Review, 103*, 143–164.

Lovibond, P.F., & Shanks, D.R. (2002). The role of awareness in Pavlovian conditioning: Empirical evidence and theoretical implications. *Journal of Experimental Psychology: Animal Behavior Processes, 28*, 3–26.

Lowe, K.B., Kroeck, K.G., & Sivasubramiam, N. (1996). Effectiveness correlates of tranformational and transactional leadership: A meta-analytic review of the MLQ literature. *Leadership Quarterly, 7*, 385–425.

Lozoff, B. (1983). Birth and "bonding" in non-industrial societies. *Developmental Medicine and Child Neurology, 25*, 595–600.

Luborsky, L., Singer, B., & Luborsky, L. (1975). Comparative studies of psychotherapies: Is it true that "everywon has one and all must have prizes"? *Archives of General Psychiatry, 32*, 995–1008.

Lucas, M. (1999). Context effects in lexical access: A meta-analysis. *Memory and Cognition, 27*, 385–398.

Luchins, A.S. (1942). Mechanisation in problem solving: The effect of Einstellung. *Psychological Monographs, 54*, 248.

Luck, S.J. (1998). Neurophysiology of selective attention. In H. Pashler (Ed.), *Attention*. Hove, UK: Psychology Press.

Luckow, A., Reifman, A., & McIntosh, D.N. (1998). *Gender differences in caring: A meta-analysis*. Poster presented at 106th annual convention of the American Psychological Association, San Francisco.

Lueck, C.J., Zeki, S., Friston, K.J., Deiber, M.-P., Cope, P., Cunningham, V.J., Lammertsma, A.A., Kennard, C., & Frackowiak, R.S.J. (1989). The colour centre in the cerebral cortex of man. *Nature, 340*, 386–389.

Lugaressi, E., Medori, R., Montagna, P., Baruzzi, A., Cortelli, P., Lugaressi, A., Tinuper, A., Zucconi, M., & Gambetti, P. (1986). Fatal familial insomnia and dysautonomia in the selective degeneration of thalamic nuclei. *New England Journal of Medicine, 315*, 997–1003.

Lumsdaine, A., & Janis, I. (1953). Resistance to counterpropaganda produced by a one-sided versus a two-sided propaganda presentation. *Public Opinion Quarterly, 17*, 311–318.

Lund, M. (1985). The development of investment and commitment scales for predicting continuity of personal relationships. *Journal of Social and Personal Relationships, 2*, 3–23.

Lustig, C., & Hasher, L. (2001). Implicit memory is vulnerable to proactive interference. *Psychological Sciences, 12*, 408–412. OR Lustig, C., & Hasher, L. (2001). Implicit memory is not immune to interference. *Psychological Bulletin, 127*, 618–628.

Lykken, D.T. (1995). *The antisocial personalities*. Hillsdale, NJ: Lawrence Erlbaum Associates, Inc.

Lynam, D.R., & Widiger, T.A. (2001). Using the five-factor model to represent the DSM-IV personality disorders: An expert consensus approach. *Journal of Abnormal Psychology, 110*, 401–412.

Lyons, M.J., True, W.R., Eisen, S.A., Goldberg, J., Meyer, J.M., Faraone, S.V., Eaves, L.J., & Tsuang, M.T. (1995). Differential heritability of adult and juvenile antisocial traits. *Archives of General Psychiatry, 52*, 906–915.

Lytton, H. (1977). Do parents create, or respond to, differences in twins? *Developmental Psychology, 13*, 456–459.

Lytton, H., & Romney, D.M. (1991). Parents' differential socialisation of boys and girls: A meta-analysis. *Psychological Bulletin, 109*, 267–296.

Maccoby, E.E. (1998). *The two sexes: Growing up apart, coming together*. Cambridge, MA: Harvard University Press.

Maccoby, E.E. (2002). Gender and group process: A developmental perspective. *Current Directions in Psychological Science, 11*, 54–58.

Maccoby, E.E., & Martin, J.A. (1983). Socialisation in the context of the family: Parent–child interaction. In P.H. Mussen (Ed.), *Handbook of child psychology: Vol. 4. Socialisation, personality, and social development*. New York: Wiley.

MacDonald, C.D., & Cohen, R. (1995). Children's awareness of which peers like them and which peers dislike them. *Social Development, 4*, 182–193.

MacDonald, K., & Parke, R.D. (1984). Bridging the gap: Parent–child play interaction and peer interactive competence. *Child Development, 55*, 1265–1277.

MacDonald, M.C., Pearlmutter, N.J., & Seidenberg, M.S. (1994). Lexical nature of syntactic ambiguity resolution. *Psychological Review, 101*, 676–703.

MacDonald, S., Uesiliana, K., & Hayne, H. (2000). Cross-cultural and gender differences in childhood amnesia. *Memory, 8*, 365–376.

MacGregor, J.N., Ormerod, T.C., & Chronicle, E.P. (2001). Information processing and insight: A process model of performance on the nine-dot and related problems. *Journal of Experimental Psychology: Learning, Memory, & Cognition, 27*, 176–201.

MacKay, D. (1987). Divided brains—divided minds. In C. Blakemore & S. Greenfield (Eds.), *Mindwaves: Thoughts, identity and consciousness*. Oxford, UK: Blackwell.

Mackie, D.M., & Cooper, J. (1984). Group polarization: The effects of group membership. *Journal of Personality and Social Psychology, 46*, 575–585.

Mackintosh, N.J. (1986). The biology of intelligence? *British Journal of Psychology, 77,* 1–18.

Mackintosh, N.J. (1998). *IQ and human intelligence.* Oxford, UK: Oxford University Press.

MacLean, P.D. (1949). Psychosomatic disease and the "visceral brain": Recent developments bearing on the Papez theory of emotion. *Psychosomatic Medicine, 11,* 338–353.

MacLeod, A. (1998). Therapeutic interventions. In M.W. Eysenck (Ed.), *Psychology: An integrated approach.* Harlow, UK: Addison Wesley Longman.

Macrae, C.N., & Bodenhausen, G.V. (2000). Social cognition: Thinking categorically about others. *Annual Review of Psychology, 51,* 93–120.

Macrae, C.N., Milne, A.B., & Bodenhausen, G.V. (1994). Stereotypes as energy-saving devices: A peek inside the cognitive toolbox. *Journal of Personality and Social Psychology, 66,* 37–47.

Madison, P. (1956). Freud's repression concept: A survey and attempted clarification. *International Journal of Psychoanalysis, 37,* 75–81.

Maes, M., de Meyer, F., Thompson, P., Peeters, D., & Cosyns, P. (1994). Synchronized annual rhythms in violent suicide rate, ambient temperature and the light–dark span. *Acta Psychiatrica Scandinavica, 90,* 391–396.

Magnus, K., Diener, E., Fujita, F., & Pavot, W. (1993). Extraversion and neuroticism as predictors of objective life events: A longitudinal analysis. *Journal of Personality and Social Psychology, 65,* 1046–1053.

Magoun, H.W., Harrison, F., Brobeck, J.R., & Ranson, S.W. (1938). Activation of heat loss mechanisms by local heating of the brain. *Journal of Neurophysiology, 1,* 101–114.

Maher, B.A. (1966). *Principles of psychopathology: An experimental approach.* New York: McGraw-Hill.

Maher, L.M., Rothi, L.J.G., & Heilman, K.M. (1994). Lack of error awareness in an aphasic patient with relatively preserved auditory comprehension. *Brain and Language, 46,* 402–418.

Maier, N.R.F. (1931). Reasoning in humans: II. The solution of a problem and its appearance in consciousness. *Journal of Comparative Psychology, 12,* 181–194.

Main, M., & Solomon, J. (1986). Discovery of a disorganised disoriented attachment pattern. In T.B. Brazelton & M.W. Yogman (Eds.), *Affective development in infancy.* Borwood, NJ: Ablex.

Main, M., & Weston, D.R. (1981). The quality of the toddler's relationship to mother and father: Related to conflict behaviour and the readiness to establish new relationships. *Child Development, 52,* 932–940.

Main, M., Kaplan, N., & Cassidy, J. (1985). Security in infancy, childhood, and adulthood: A move to the level of representation. In I. Bretherton & E. Waters (Eds.), Growing points of attachment theory and research. *Monographs of the Society for Research in Child Development, 50.*

Maller, R.G., & Reiss, S. (1992). Anxiety sensitivity in 1984 and panic attacks in 1987. *Journal of Anxiety Disorders, 6,* 241–247.

Mandell, A.J., & Knapp, S. (1979). Asymmetry and mood, emergent properties of serotonin regulation: A proposed mechanism of action of lithium. *Archives of General Psychiatry, 36,* 909–916.

Mandler, G. (1997). Consciousness redux. In J.D. Cohen & J.W. Schooler (Eds.), *Scientific approaches to consciousness.* Hillsdale, NJ: Lawrence Erlbaum Associates, Inc.

Manetto, V., Medori, R., Cortelli, P., Montagna, P., Tinuper, P., Baruzzi, A., Rancurel, G., Hauw, J.J., Vanderhaeghen, J.J., & Mailleux, P. (1992). Fatal familial insomnia: Clinical and pathologic study of five new cases. *Neurology, 42,* 312–319.

Mann, L. (1981). The baiting crowd in episodes of threatened suicide. *Journal of Personality and Social Psychology, 41,* 703–709.

Mann, L., Newton, J.W., & Innes, J.M. (1982). A test between deindividuation and emergent norm theories of crowd aggression. *Journal of Personality and Social Psychology, 42,* 260–272.

Mann, R.D. (1959). A review of the relationships between personality and performance in small groups. *Psychological Bulletin, 56,* 241–270.

Manstead, A.S.R., & Semin, G.R. (2001). Methodology in social psychology: Tools to test theories. In M. Hewstone & W. Stroebe (Eds.), *Introduction to social psychology* (3rd ed.). Oxford, UK: Blackwell.

Maquet, P. (2000). Functional neuroimaging of normal human sleep by positron emission tomography. *Journal of Sleep Research, 9,* 207–231.

Maquet, P., Peters, J., Aerts, J., Delfiore, G., Degueldre, C., Luxen, A., & Franck, G. (1996). Functional neuroanatomy of human rapid-eye-movement sleep and dreaming. *Nature, 383,* 163–166.

Marañon, G. (1924). Contribution a l'étude de l'action emotive de l'adrenaline. *Révue Française d'Endocrinologie, 2,* 301–325.

Marcel, A.J. (1993). Slippage in the unity of consciousness. In *Ciba Foundation Symposium: No. 174. Experimental and theoretical studies of consciousness.* Chichester, UK: Wiley.

March, J.S. (1991). The nosology of posttraumatic stress disorder. *Journal of Anxiety Disorders, 4,* 61–81.

Marcus-Newhall, A., Pedersen, W.C., Carlson, M., & Miller, N. (2000). Displaced aggression is alive and well: A meta-analytic review. *Journal of Personality and Social Psychology, 78,* 670–689.

Marks, I.M. (1987). *Fears, phobias, and rituals.* Oxford, UK: Oxford University Press.

Marks, M.L., Mirvis, P.H., Hackett, E.J., & Grady, J.F. (1986). Employee participation in a quality circle programme: Impact on quality of work life, productivity, and absenteeism. *Journal of Applied Psychology, 71,* 61–69.

Markus, H. (1977). Self-schemata and processing information about the self. *Journal of Personality and Social Psychology, 35,* 63–78.

Markus, H., & Kitayama, S. (1991). Culture and the self: Implications for cognition, emotion and motivation. *Psychological Review, 98,* 224–253.

Markus, H., & Kunda, Z. (1986). Stability and malleability of the self-concept. *Journal of Personality and Social Psychology, 35,* 63–78.

Marmot, M.G., Bosma, H., Hemingway, H., Brunner, E., & Stansfeld, S. (1997). Contribution of job control and other risk factors to social variations in coronary heart disease incidence. *Lancet, 350,* 235–239.

Marr, D. (1982). *Vision: A computational investigation into the human representation and processing of visual information.* San Francisco: W.H. Freeman.

Marr, D., & Nishihara, K. (1978). Representation and recognition of the spatial organisation of three-dimensional shapes. *Philosophical Transactions of the Royal Society of London, Series B, 200,* 269–294.

Marsh, H.W. (1989). Age and sex effects in multiple dimensions of self-concept: A replication and extension. *Australian Journal of Psychology, 37,* 197–204.

Marsh, P., Rosser, E., & Harré, R. (1978). *The rules of disorder.* London: Routledge & Kegan Paul.

Marshall, G.D., & Zimbardo, P.G. (1979). Affective consequences of inadequately explained physiological arousal. *Journal of Personality and Social Psychology, 7,* 970–988.

Marshall, J., Robson, J., Pring, T., & Chiat, S. (1998). Why does monitoring fail in jargon aphasia? Comprehension, judgment, and therapy evidence. *Brain and Language, 63,* 79–109.

Marshall, J.C., & Newcombe, F. (1973). Patterns of paralexia: A psycholinguistic approach. *Journal of Psycholinguistic Research, 2,* 175–199.

Marshall, L.A., & Cooke, D.J. (1999). The childhood experiences of psychopaths: A retrospective study of familial and societal factors. *Journal of Personality Disorders, 13,* 211–225.

Marslen-Wilson, W.D. (1990). Activation, competition, and frequency in lexical access. In G.T.M. Altmann (Ed.), *Cognitive models of speech processing: Psycholinguistics and computational perspectives.* Cambridge, MA: MIT Press.

Marslen-Wilson, W.D., Moss, H.E., & van Halen, S. (1996). Perceptual distance and competition in lexical access. *Journal of*

*Experimental Psychology: Human Perception and Performance, 22*, 1376–1392.

Marslen-Wilson, W.D., & Tyler, L.K. (1980). The temporal structure of spoken language understanding. *Cognition, 8*, 1–71.

Marslen-Wilson, W.D., & Warren, P. (1994). Levels of perceptual representation and process in lexical access: Words, phonemes and features. *Psychological Review, 101*, 653–675.

Martin, C.L., & Fabes, R.A. (2001). The stability and consequences of young children's same-sex peer interactions. *Developmental Psychology, 37*, 431–446.

Martin, C.L., & Halverson, C.F. (1983). The effects of sex-typing schemas on young children's memory. *Child Development, 54*, 563–574.

Martin, C.L., & Halverson, C.F. (1987). The roles of cognition in sex role acquisition. In D.B. Carter (Ed.), *Current conceptions of sex roles and sex typing: Theory and research*. New York: Praeger.

Martin, C.L., Ruble, D.N., & Szkrybalo, J. (2002). Cognitive theories of early gender development. *Psychological Bulletin, 128*, 903–933.

Martin, R. (1998). Majority and minority influence using the afterimage paradigm: A series of attempted replications. *Journal of Experimental Social Psychology, 34*, 1–26.

Martin, R.A. (1989). Techniques for data acquisition and analysis in field investigations of stress. In R.W.J. Neufeld (Ed.), *Advances in the investigation of psychological stress*. New York: Wiley.

Martin, R.A., Kuiper, N.A., & Westra, H.A. (1989). Cognitive and affective components of the Type A behaviour pattern: Preliminary evidence for a self-worth contingency model. *Personality and Individual Differences, 10*, 771–784.

Maslow, A.H. (1954). *Motivation and personality*. New York: Harper.

Maslow, A.H. (1962). *Toward a psychology of being*. Princeton, NJ: Van Nostrand.

Maslow, A.H. (1968). *Toward a psychology of being* (2nd ed.). New York: Van Nostrand.

Maslow, A.H. (1970). *Toward a psychology of being* (3rd ed.). New York: Van Nostrand.

Mason, J.W. (1975). A historical view of the stress field. *Journal of Human Stress, 1*, 22–36.

Massaro, D.W. (1989). Testing between TRACE and the fuzzy logical model of speech perception. *Cognitive Psychology, 21*, 398–421.

Massaro, D.W. (1994). Psychological aspects of speech perception: Implications for research and theory. In M.A. Gernsbacher (Ed.), *Handbook of psycholinguistics*. San Diego: Academic Press.

Masson, J. (1989). *Against therapy*. Glasgow, UK: Collins.

Mastekaasa, A. (1994). Psychological well-being and marital dissolution: Selection effects? *Journal of Family Issues, 15*, 208–228.

Masters, J.C., Ford, M.E., Arend, R., Grotevant, H.D., & Clark, L.V. (1979). Modelling and labelling as integrated determinants of children's sex-typed imitative behaviour. *Child Development, 50*, 364–371.

Masters, R.S.W. (1992). Knowledge, nerves and know-how: The role of explicit versus implicit knowledge in the breakdown of a complex skill under pressure. *British Journal of Psychology, 83*, 343–358.

Masters, W.H., & Johnson, V.E. (1966). *Human sexual response*. Boston: Little, Brown.

Matheny, A.P. (1983). A longitudinal twin study of the stability of components from Bayley's Infant Behaviour Record. *Child Development, 54*, 356–360.

Mather, G., & Murdoch, L. (1994). Gender discrimination in biological motion displays based on dynamic cues. *Proceedings of the Royal Society of London, Series B, 258*, 273–279.

Mathes, E.W., Zevon, M.A., Roter, P.M., & Joerger, S.M. (1982). Peak experience tendencies: Scale development and theory testing. *Journal of Humanistic Psychology, 22*, 92–108.

Matlin, M.W., & Foley, H.J. (1997). *Sensation and perception* (4th ed.). Boston: Allyn & Bacon.

Matson, C.A., Wiater, M.F., Kuijper, J.L., & Weigle, D.S. (1997). Synergy between leptin and cholecystokinin (CCK) to control daily caloric intake. *Peptides, 18*, 1275–1278.

Matsuda, L.A., Lolait, S.J., Brownstein, M.J., Young, A.C., & Bonner, T.I. (1990). Structure of a cannabinoid receptor and functional expression of the cloned DNA. *Nature, 346*, 561–564.

Matt, G.E., & Navarro, A.M. (1997). What meta-analyses have and have not taught us about psychotherapy effects: A review and future directions. *Clinical Psychology Review, 17*, 1–32.

Matthews, G., Zeidner, M., & Roberts, R.D. (2002). *Emotional intelligence: Science and myth*. Cambridge, MA: MIT Press.

Matthews, K.A. (1988). Coronary heart disease and Type A behaviour: Update on and alternative to the Booth-Kewley and Friedman (1987) quantitative review. *Psychological Bulletin, 104*, 373–380.

Matthews, K.A., Glass, D.C., Rosenman, R.H., & Bortner, R.W. (1977). Competitive drive, Pattern A, and coronary heart disease: A further analysis of some data from the Western Collaborative Group. *Journal of Chronic Diseases, 30*, 489–498.

Maule, A.J., & Hodgkinson, G.P. (2002). Heuristics, biases and strategic decision making. *The Psychologist, 15*, 69–71.

Mayer, J. (1955). Regulation of energy intake and the body weight: The glucostatic theory and the lipostatic hypothesis. *Annals of the New York Academy of Sciences, 63*, 15–43.

Mayer, J.D., Caruso, D., & Salovey, P. (1999). Emotional initelligence meets traditional standards for an intelligence. *Intelligence, 27*, 267–298.

Mayer, R.E. (1990). Problem solving. In M.W. Eysenck (Ed.), *The Blackwell dictionary of cognitive psychology*. Oxford, UK: Blackwell.

Mayes, B.T., Sime, W.E., & Ganster, D.C. (1984). Convergent validity of Type A behaviour pattern scales and their ability to predict physiological responsiveness in a sample of female public employees. *Journal of Behavioural Medicine, 7*, 83–108.

McAdams, D.P. (1992). The five-factor model in personality: A critical appraisal. *Journal of Personality, 60*, 329–361.

McAndrew, F.T. (2002). New evolutionary perspectives on altruism: Multilevel selection and costly signalling theories. *Current Directions in Psychological Science, 11*, 79–82.

McArthur, L.A. (1972). The how and what of why: Some determinants and consequences of causal attributions. *Journal of Personality and Social Psychology, 22*, 171–193.

McArthur, L.Z., & Post, D.L. (1977). Figural emphasis and person perception. *Journal of Experimental Social Psychology, 13*, 520–535.

McBride, D. M., Dosher, B. A., & Gage, N. M. (2001). A comparison of forgetting for conscious and automatic memory processes in word fragment completion. *Journal of Memory and Language, 45*, 585–615.

McBride, D.M., & Dosher, B.A. (1999). Forgetting rates are comparable in conscious and automatic memory: A process-dissociation study. *Journal of Experimental Psychology: Learning, Memory and Cognition, 25*, 583–607.

McBride, P. (1994). *Study skills for success*. Cambridge, UK: Hobsons Publishing.

McBurnett, K. (2000, January 17). Violence hormone identified. *The Times*.

McCarthy, R., & Warrington, E.K. (1984). A two-route model of speech production. *Brain, 107*, 463–485.

McCartney, K., Harris, M.J., & Bernieri, F. (1990). Growing up and growing apart: A developmental meta-analysis of twin studies. *Psychological Bulletin, 107*, 226–237.

McCartney, K., Scarr, S., Phillips, D., & Grajek, S. (1985). Day care as intervention: Comparisons of varying quality programmes. *Journal of Applied Developmental Psychology, 6*, 247–260.

McCauley, C., & Stitt, C.L. (1978). An individual and quantitative measure of stereotypes. *Journal of Personality and Social Psychology, 36*, 929–940.

McClelland, J.L. (1991). Stochastic interactive processes and the effect of context on perception. *Cognitive Psychology, 23*, 1–44.

McClelland, J.L. (1993). Toward a theory of information processing in graded, random, and interactive networks. In D.E. Meyer & S.M. Kornblum (Eds.), *Attention and performance XIV: Synergies in experimental psychology, artificial intelligence, and cognitive neuroscience*. Cambridge, MA: MIT Press.

McClelland, J.L., & Elman, J.L. (1986). The TRACE model of speech perception. *Cognitive Psychology, 18*, 1–86.

McClelland, J.L., & Rumelhart, D.E. (1981). An interactive activation model of context effects in letter perception: Part 1. An account of basic findings. *Psychological Review, 88*, 375–407.

McConaghy, M.J. (1979). Gender permanence and the genital basis of gender: Stages in the development of constancy of gender identity. *Child Development, 50*, 1223–1226.

McConahay, J.B. (1986). Modern racism, ambivalence, and the Modern Racism Scale. In J.F. Dovidio & S.L. Gaertner (Eds.), *Prejudice, discrimination, and racism*. San Diego, CA: Academic Press.

McCrae, R.R., & Costa, P.T. (1985). Updating Norman's "adequate taxonomy": Intelligence and personality dimensions in natural language and in questionnaires. *Journal of Personality and Social Psychology, 49*, 710–721.

McCrae, R.R., & Costa, P.T. (1990). *Personality in adulthood*. New York: Guilford Press.

McCrae, R.R., & Costa, P.T. (1999). A five-factor theory of personality. In L.A. Pervin & O.P. John (Eds.), *Handbook of personality: Theory and research*. New York: Guilford Press.

McCrae, R.R., Costa, P.T., del Pilar, G.H., Rolland, J.P., & Parker, W.D. (1998). Cross-cultural assessment of the five factor model: The revised NEO personality inventory. *Journal of Cross-Cultural Psychology, 29*, 171–188.

McCrory, M.A., Fuss, P.J., McCallum, J.E., Yao, M., Vinken, A.G., Hays, N.P., & Roberts, S.B. (1999). Dietary variety within food groups: Association with energy intake and body fatness in men and women. *American Journal of Clinical Nutrition, 69*, 440–447.

McGarrigle, J., & Donaldson, M. (1974). Conservation accidents. *Cognition, 3*, 341–350.

McGinty, D.J., & Sterman, M.B (1968). Sleep suppression after basal forebrain lesions in the cat. *Science, 160*, 1253–1255.

McGlinchey-Berroth, R., Milber, W.P., Verfaellie, M., Alexander, M., & Kilduff, P.T. (1993). Semantic processing in the neglected visual field: Evidence from a lexical decision task. *Cognitive Neuropsychology, 10*, 79–108.

McGue, M., Brown, S., & Lykken, D.T. (1992). Personality stability and change in early adulthood: A behavioural genetic analysis. *Developmental Psychology, 29*, 96–109.

McGuffin, P., Katz, R., Watkins, S., & Rutherford, J. (1996). A hospital-based twin register of the heritability of DSM-IV unipolar depression. *Archives of General Psychiatry, 53*, 129–136.

McGuigan, F.J. (1966). Covert oral behaviour and auditory hallucinations. *Psychophysiology, 3*, 421–428.

McGuire, S., Neiderhiser, J., Reiss, D., Hetherington, E.M., & Plomin, R. (1994). Genetic and environmental influences on perceptions of self-worth and competence in adolescence: A study of twins, full siblings and step-siblings. *Child Development, 65*, 785–799.

McGuire, W.J. (1969). The nature of attitudes and attitude change. In G. Lindzey & E. Aronson (Eds.), *Handbook of social psychology, Vol. 3* (2nd ed.). Reading, MA: Addison-Wesley.

McGurk, H., & MacDonald, J. (1976). Hearing lips and seeing voices. *Nature, 264*, 746–748.

McIlveen, R. (1995). Hypnosis. *Psychology Review, 2*, 8–12.

McIlveen, R. (1996). Applications of hypnosis. *Psychology Review, 2*, 24–27.

McIlveen, R., & Gross, R. (1996). *Biopsychology*. London: Hodder & Stoughton.

McKenzie, S.J., Williamson, D.A., & Cubic, B.A. (1993). Stable and reactive body image disturbances in bulimia nervosa. *Behavior Therapy, 24*, 1958– 2220.

McKoon, G., & Ratcliff, R. (1986). Inferences about predictable events. *Journal of Experimental Psychology: Learning, Memory, and Cognition, 12*, 82–91.

McKoon, G., & Ratcliff, R. (1992). Inference during reading. *Psychological Review, 99*, 440–466.

McLeod, P. (1977). A dual-task response modality effect: Support for multiprocessor models of attention. *Quarterly Journal of Experimental Psychology, 29*, 651–667.

McNair, D.M., Lorr, M., & Droppelman, L.F. (1971). *Manual: Profile of mood states*. San Diego, CA: Educational and Industrial Testing Service.

McNally, R.J. (1981). Phobias and preparedness: Instructional reversal of electrodermal conditoning to fear-relevant stimuli. *Psychological Reports, 48*, 175–180.

McNally, R.J. (1994). *Panic disorder: A critical analysis*. New York: Guilford Press.

McNally, R.J. (2001). On Wakefield's harmful dysfunction analysis of mental disorder. *Behavioural Research Therapy, 39*, 309–314.

McNeal, E.T., & Cimbolic, P. (1986). Antidepressants and biochemical theories of depression. *Psychological Bulletin, 99*, 361–374.

McNeill, D. (1970). *The acquisition of language: The study of developmental psycholinguistics*. New York: Harper & Row.

McNeilly, C.L., & Howard, K.I. (1991). The effects of psychotherapy: A re-evaluation based on dosage. *Psychotherapy Research, 1*, 74–78.

Mead, G.H. (1934). *Mind, self, and society: From the standpoint of a social behaviourist*. Chicago: University of Chicago Press.

Meade, R.D. (1985). Experimental studies of authoritarian and democratic leadership in four cultures: American, Indian, Chinese and Chinese-American. *High School Journal, 68*, 293–295.

Meadows, S. (1986). *Understanding child development*. London: Routledge.

Meadows, S. (1994). Cognitive development. In A.M. Colman (Ed.), *Companion encyclopedia of psychology, Vol. 2*. London: Routledge.

Meddis, R. (1979). The evolution and function of sleep. In D.A. Oakley & H.C. Plotkin (Eds.), *Brain, behaviour and evolution*. London: Methuen.

Meddis, R., Pearson, A.J.D., & Langford, G. (1973). An extreme case of healthy insomnia. *Electroencephalography and Clinical Neurophysiology, 35*, 213–224.

Medori, R., Montagna, P., Tritschler, H.J., LeBlanc, A., Cortelli, P., Tinuper, P., Lugaresi, E., & Gambetti, P. (1992). Fatal familial insomnia: A second kindred with mutation of prion protein gene at codon 178. *Neurology, 42*, 669–670.

Mehler, J., Jusczyk, P.W., Dehaene-Lambertz, G., Dupoux, E., & Nazzi, T. (1994). Coping with linguistic diversity: The infant's viewpoint. In J.L. Morgan & K. Demuth (Eds.), *Signal to syntax: Bootstrapping from speech to grammar in early acquisition*. Mahwah, NJ: Lawrence Erlbaum Associates, Inc.

Meichenbaum, D. (1977). *Cognitive-behaviour modification: An integrative approach*. New York: Plenum Press.

Meichenbaum, D. (1985). *Stress inoculation training*. New York: Pergamon.

Meichenbaum, D. (1993). Stress inoculation training: A twenty-year update. In R.L. Woolfolk & P.M. Lehrer (Eds.), *Principles and practices of stress management*. New York: Guilford Press.

Mela, D.J., & Rogers, P.J. (1998). *Food, eating and obesity: The psychobiological basis of appetite and weight control*. London: Chapman & Hall.

Melhuish, E.C., Lloyd, E., Martin, S., & Mooney, A. (1990). Type of child care at 18 months: II. Relations with cognitive and language development. *Journal of Child Psychology and Psychiatry, 31*, 861–879.

Mellanby, J., Martin, M., & O'Doherty, J. (2000). Gender gap examined. *The Psychologist, 13*, 493.

Mellers, B.A., Schwartz, A., & Cooke, A.D.J. (1998). Judgement and decision making. *Annual Review of Psychology, 49*, 447–477.

Meltzoff, A.N. (1985). Immediate and deferred imitation in 14- and 24-month-old infants. *Child Development, 56*, 62–72.

Meltzoff, A.N. (1988). Infant imitation after a 1-week delay: Long-term memory for novel acts and multiple stimuli. *Developmental Psychology, 24*, 470–476.

Menzies, R.G., & Clarke, J.C. (1993). The aetiology of childhood water phobia. *Behaviour Research and Therapy, 31*, 499–501.

Merikle, P.M. (1980). Selection from visual persistence by perceptual groups and category membership. *Journal of Experimental Psychology: General, 109*, 279–295.

Merikle, P.M., Smilek, D., & Eastwood, J.D. (2001). Perception without awareness: Perspectives from cognitive psychology. *Cognition, 79*, 115–134.

Mesquita, B. (2001). Emotions in collectivist and individualist contexts. *Journal of Personality and Social Psychology, 80*, 68–74.

Messer, D. (2000). State of the art: Language acquisition. *The Psychologist, 13*, 138–143.

Metcalfe, J., & Weibe, D. (1987). Intuition in insight and noninsight problem solving. *Memory and Cognition, 15*, 238–246.

Mezzacappa, E.S., Katkin, E.S., & Palmer, S.N. (1999). Epinephrine, arousal, and emotion: A new look at two-factor theory. *Cognition and Emotion, 13*, 181–199.

Miceli, G., Silveri, M.C., Romani, C., & Caramazza, A. (1989). Variation in the pattern of omissions and substitutions of grammatical morphemes in the spontaneous speech of so-called agrammatic patients. *Brain and Language, 36*, 447–492.

Michalak, E.E., Wilkinson, C., Hood, K., & Dowrick, C. (2002). Seasonal and nonseasonal depression: How do they differ? Symptom profile, clinical and family history in a general population sample. *Journal of Affective Disorders, 69*, 185–192.

Mickelson, K., Kessler, R.C., & Shaver, P. (1997). Adult attachment in a nationally representative sample. *Journal of Personality and Social Psychology, 73*, 1092–1106.

Miles, D.R., & Carey, G. (1997). Genetic and environmental architecture of human aggression. *Journal of Personality and Social Psychology, 72*, 207–217.

Milgram, S. (1963). Behavioural study of obedience. *Journal of Abnormal and Social Psychology, 67*, 371–378.

Milgram, S. (1974). *Obedience to authority: An experimental view*. New York: Harper & Row.

Miller, G.A. (1956). The magic number seven, plus or minus two: Some limits on our capacity for processing information. *Psychological Review, 63*, 81–93.

Miller, G.A., & McNeill, D. (1969). Psycholinguistics. In G. Lindzey & E. Aronson (Eds.), *The handbook of social psychology, Vol. III*. Reading, MA: Addison-Wesley.

Miller, G.A., & Nicely, P. (1955). An analysis of perceptual confusions among some English consonants. *Journal of the Acoustical Society of America, 27*, 338–352.

Miller, H.G., Turner, C.F., & Moses, L.E. (1990). *AIDS: The second decade*. Washington, DC: National Academy.

Miller, J.G. (1984). Culture and the development of everyday social explanation. *Journal of Personality and Social Psychology, 46*, 961–978.

Miller, L.B., & Bizzell, R.P. (1983). Long-term effects of four preschool programs: Sixth, seventh, and eighth grades. *Child Development, 54*, 727–741.

Miller, M.A., & Rahe, R.H. (1997). Life changes: Scaling for the 1990s. *Journal of Psychosomatic Research, 43*, 279–292.

Miller, N., & Davidson-Podgorny, F. (1987). Theoretical models of intergroup relations and the use of co-operative teams as an intervention for desegregated settings. In C. Hendrick (Ed.), *Group process and intergroup relations: Review of personality and social psychology, Vol. 9*. Newbury Park, CA: Sage.

Miller, N.E., Sears, R.R., Mowrer, O.H., Doob, L.W., & Dollard, J. (1941). The frustration–aggression hypothesis. *Psychological Review, 48*, 337–342.

Miller, R.J., Hennessy, R.T., & Leibowitz, H.W. (1973). The effect of hypnotic ablation of the background on the magnitude of the Ponzo perspective illusion. *International Journal of Clinical and Experimental Hypnosis, 21*, 180–191.

Miller, R.R., Barnet, R.C., & Grahame, N.J. (1995). Assessment of the Rescorla–Wagner model. *Psychological Bulletin, 117*, 363–386.

Miller, T.Q., Turner, C.W., Tindale, R.S., Posavac, E.J., & Dugoni, B.L. (1991). Reasons for the trend toward null findings in research on Type A behaviour. *Psychological Bulletin, 110*, 469–485.

Miller-Johnson, S., Coie, J.D., Maumary-Gremaud, A., Lochman, J., & Terry, R. (1999). Relationship between childhood peer rejection and aggression and adolescent delinquency severity and type among African American Youth. *Journal of Emotional and Behavioral Disorders, 7*, 137–146.

Milner, A.D., & Goodale, M.A. (1995). *The visual brain in action* (Oxford Psychology series, no. 27). Oxford, UK: Oxford University Press.

Milner, A.D., & Goodale, M.A. (1998). The visual brain in action. *Psyche, 4*, 1–14.

Minuchin, S., Roseman, B.L., & Baker, L. (1978). *Psychosomatic families: Anorexia nervosa in context*. Cambridge, MA: Harvard University Press.

Mirenowicz, J., & Schultz, W. (1996). Preferential activation of midbrain dopamine neurons by appetitive rather than aversive stimuli. *Nature, 379*, 449–451.

Mischel, W. (1968). *Personality and assessment*. London: Wiley.

Mishkin, M., & Ungerleider, L.G. (1982). Contribution of striate inputs to the visuospatial functions of parieto-preoccipital cortex in monkeys. *Behavioral Brain Research, 6*, 57–77.

Mitchell, S. (1988). *Relational concepts in psychoanalysis*. Cambridge, MA: Harvard University Press.

Mitroff, I.I. (1974). *The subjective side of science*. Amsterdam: Elsevier.

Mlicki, P.P., & Ellemers, N. (1996). Being different or being better? National stereotypes and identifications of Polish and Dutch students. *European Journal of Social Psychology, 26*, 97–114.

Molfese, D.L. (1977). Infant cerebral asymmetry. In S.J. Segalowitz & F.A. Gruber (Eds.), *Human behaviour and the developing brain*. New York: Guilford Press.

Money, J., & Ehrhardt, A.A. (1972). *Man and woman, boy and girl*. Baltimore: John Hopkins University Press.

Monk, T. (2001, December 1). *In space, no one gets to sleep*. Retrieved from www.newscientist.com

Monk, T.H., & Folkard, S. (1983). Circadian rhythms and shiftwork. In R. Hockey (Ed.), *Stress and fatigue in human performance*. Chichester, UK: Wiley.

Monnier, J., Hobfoll, S.E., & Stone, B.K. (1996). Coping resources and social context. In W. Battmann & S. Dutke (Eds.), *Processes of the molar regulation of behavior*. Lengerich, Germany: Pabst Science Publishers.

Montangero, J. (2000). A more general evolutionary hypothesis about dream function. *Behavioral and Brain Sciences, 23*, 972–973.

Monteil, J.-M., & Huguet, P. (1999). *Social context and cognitive performance*. Hove, UK: Psychology Press.

Moore, B.R. (1973). The form of the auto-shaped response with food or water reinforcers. *Journal of the Experimental Analysis of Behavior, 20*, 163–181.

Moore, C., & Frye, D. (1986). The effect of the experimenter's intention on the child's understanding of conservation. *Cognition, 22*, 283–298.

Moore-Ede, M., Sulzman, F., & Fuller, C. (1982). *The clocks that time us: Physiology of the circadian timing system*. Cambridge, MA: Harvard University Press.

Moray, N. (1959). Attention in dichotic listening: Affective cues and the influence of instructions. *Quarterly Journal of Experimental Psychology, 11*, 56–60.

Moreland, R.L. (1985). Social categorisation and the assimilation of "new" group members. *Journal of Personality and Social Psychology, 48*, 1173–1190.

Moreland, R.L., & Levine, J.M. (1982). Socialisation in small groups: Temporal changes in individual–group relations. In L. Berkowitz (Ed.), *Advances in Experimental Social Psychology* (Vol. 15, pp. 137–192). New York: Academic Press.

Morgan, C.D., & Murray, H.A. (1935). A method of investigating fantasies: The thematic apperception test. *Archives of Neurological Psychiatry, 34*, 289–306.

Morgan, H., & Raffle, C. (1999). Does reducing safety behaviours improve treatment response in patients with social phobia? *Australian and New Zealand Journal of Psychiatry, 33*, 503–510.

Moriarty, T. (1975). Crime, commitment, and the responsive bystander: Two field experiments. *Journal of Personality and Social Psychology, 31*, 370–376.

Morley, J.E., Levine, A.S., Gosnell, B.A., Mitchell, J.E., Krahn, D.D., & Nizielski, S.E. (1985). Peptides and feeding. *Peptides, 6*, 181–192.

Morris, C.D., Bransford, J.D., & Franks, J.J. (1977). Levels of processing versus transfer appropriate processing. *Journal of Verbal Learning and Verbal Behavior, 16*, 519–533.

Morris, N.M., Udry, J.R., Khan-Dawood, F., & Dawood, M.Y. (1987). Marital sex frequency and midcycle female testosterone. *Archives of Sexual Behavior, 16*, 27–37.

Morris, P.E. (1979). Strategies for learning and recall. In M.M. Gruneberg & P.E. Morris (Eds.), *Applied problems in memory*. London: Academic Press.

Morrison, A.R., Sanford, L.D., Ball, W.A., Mann, G.L., & Ross, R.J. (1995). Stimulus-elicited behavior in rapid eye movement sleep without atonia. *Behavioral Neuroscience, 109*, 972–979.

Morsella, E., & Miozzo, M. (2002). Evidence for a cascade model of lexical access in speech production. *Journal of Experimental Psychology: Learning, Memory, and Cognition, 28*, 555–563.

Morton, J., & Johnson, M.H. (1991). CONSPEC and CONLEARN: A two-process theory of infant face recognition. *Psychological Review, 98*, 164–181.

Moruzzi, G., & Magoun, H.W. (1949). Brain stem reticular formation and activation of the EEG. *Electroencephalography and Clinical Neurophysiology, 1*, 455–473.

Moscovici, S. (1976). *Social influence and social change*. London: Academic Press.

Moscovici, S. (1980). Toward a theory of conversion behaviour. In L. Berkowitz (Ed.), *Advances in experimental social psychology, Vol. 13*. New York: Academic Press.

Moscovici, S., Lage, E., & Naffrenchoux, M. (1969). Influence of a consistent minority on the responses of a majority in a colour perception task. *Sociometry, 32*, 365–380.

Moscovici, S., & Personnaz, B. (1980). Studies in social influence: V. Minority influence and conversion behaviour in a perceptual task. *Journal of Experimental Social Psychology, 16*, 270–282.

Moscovici, S., & Personnaz, B. (1986). Studies on latent influence by the spectorometer method: 1. The impact on psychologisation in the case of conversion by a minority or a majority. *European Journal of Social Psychology, 16*, 345–360.

Moscovitch, M., Winocur, G., & Behrmann, M. (1997). What is special about face recognition? Nineteen experiments on a person with visual object agnosia and dyslexia but normal face recognition. *Journal of Cognitive Neuroscience, 9*, 555–604.

Moscovitz, S. (1983). *Love despite hate: Child survivors of the Holocaust and their adult lives*. New York: Schocken.

Moskowitz, H., Hulbert, S., & McGlothin, W.H. (1976). Marijuana: Effects on simulated driving performance. *Accident Analysis and Prevention, 8*, 45–50.

Moss, E. (1992). The socioaffective context of joint cognitive activity. In L.T. Winegar & J. Valsiner (Eds.), *Children's development within social context: Vol. 2. Research and methodology*. Hillsdale, NJ: Lawrence Erlbaum Associates, Inc.

Mowrer, O.H. (1947). On the dual nature of learning: A re-interpretation of "conditioning" and "problem-solving". *Harvard Educational Review, 17*, 102–148.

Mueller, E., & Lucas, T. (1975). A developmental analysis of peer interaction among toddlers. In M. Lewis & L. Rosenblum (Eds.), *Friendship and peer relations*. New York: Wiley.

Muir, D., & Field, J. (1979). Newborn infants orient to sounds. *Child Development, 50*, 431–436.

Mukhametov, L.M. (1984). Sleep in marine mammals. In A. Borbely & J.L. Valatx (Eds.), *Sleep mechanisms* [Experimental Brain Research Suppl. 8]. Berlin, Germany: Springer-Verlag.

Mullen, B., Anthony, T., Salas, E., & Driskell, J. E. (1994). Group cohesiveness and quality of decision making: An integration of tests of the groupthink hypothesis. *Small Group Research, 25*, 189–204.

Mullen, B., Brown, R., & Smith, C. (1992). Ingroup bias as a function of salience, relevance and status: An integration. *European Journal of Social Psychology, 22*, 103–122.

Mullen, B., & Copper, C. (1994). The relation between group cohesiveness and performance: An integration. *Psychological Bulletin, 115*, 210–227.

Mumford, D.B., Whitehouse, A.M., & Choudry, I.Y. (1992). Survey of eating disorders in English-medium schools in Lahore, Pakistan. *International Journal of Eating Disorders, 11*, 173–184.

Mumme, R.L. (1992). Do helpers increase reproductive success: an experimental analysis in the Florida scrub jay. *Behavioural Ecology and Sociobiology, 31*, 319–328.

Mummendey, A., Simon, B., Dietze, C., Grunert, M., Haeger, G., Kessler, S., Lettgen, S., & Schaferhoff, S. (1992). Categorisation is not enough: Intergroup discrimination in negative outcome allocations. *Journal of Experimental Social Psychology, 28*, 125–144.

Munroe, R.H., Shimmin, H.S., & Munroe, R.L. (1984). Gender understanding and sex-role preferences in four cultures. *Developmental Psychology, 20*, 673–682.

Murphy, G., & Kovach, J.K. (1972). *Historical introduction to modern psychology*. London: Routledge & Kegan Paul.

Murphy, S., & Zajonc, R. (1996). An unconscious subjective emotional response. In D. Concar (Ed.), Act now, think later: Emotions. *New Scientist* (Suppl.).

Murphy, S.T., & Zajonc, R.B. (1993). Affect, cognition, and awareness: Affective priming with optimal and suboptimal stimulus exposures. *Journal of Personality and Social Psychology, 64*, 723–739.

Murray, S.L., & Holmes, J.G. (1993). Seeing virtues in faults: Negativity and the transformation of interpersonal narratives in close relationships. *Journal of Personality and Social Psychology, 65*, 707–722.

Murstein, B.I., MacDonald, M.G., & Cerreto, M. (1977). A theory and investigation of the effects of exchange-orientation on marriage and friendship. *Journal of Marriage and the Family, 39*, 543–548.

Mussen, P.H., & Rutherford, E. (1963). Parent–child relations and parental personality in relation to young children's sex-role preferences. *Child Development, 34*, 589–607.

Muter, P. (1978). Recognition failure of recallable words in semantic memory. *Memory and Cognition, 6*, 9–12.

Mynatt, C.R., Doherty, M.E., & Tweney, R.D. (1977). Confirmation bias in a simulated research environment: An experimental study of scientific inference. *Quarterly Journal of Experimental Psychology, 29*, 85–95.

Myrtek, M. (1995). Type A behaviour pattern, personality factors, disease, and physiological reactivity: A meta-analytic update. *Personality and Individual Differences, 18*, 491–502.

Nader, K. (1996). Children's traumatic dreams. In D. Barrett (Ed.), *Trauma and dreams*. Cambridge, MA: Harvard University Press.

Nairne, J.S., Whiteman, H.L., & Kelley, M.R. (1999). Short-term forgetting of order under conditions of reduced interference. *Quarterly Journal of Experimental Psychology, 52A*, 241–251.

Naito, M. (1990). Repetition priming in children and adults: Age-related dissociation between implicit and explicit memory. *Journal of Experimental Child Psychology, 23*, 237–251.

Naito, T., Lin, W.Y., & Gielen, U.P. (2001). Moral development in East Asian societies: A selective review of the cross-cultural literature. *Psychologia: An International Journal of the Orient, 44*, 148–160.

Naitoh, P. (1975). Sleep stage deprivation and total sleep loss: Effects on sleep behaviour. *Psychophysiology, 12*, 141–146.

Najavits, L.M., & Strupp, H.H. (1994). Differences in the effectiveness of psychodynamic therapists: A process–outcome study. *Psychotherapy, 31*, 114–123.

Nash, A. (1988). Ontogeny, phylogeny, and relationships. In S. Duck (Ed.), *Handbook of personal relationships: Research and interventions*. Chichester, UK: Wiley.

Nasser, M. (1986). Eating disorders: The cultural dimension. *Social Psychiatry and Psychiatric Epidemiology, 23*, 184–187.

Nathan, P.E., & Langenbucher, J.W. (1999). Psychopathology: Description and classification. *Annual Review of Psychology, 50*, 79–107.

National Commission on Marijuana and Drug Abuse. (1972). *Marijuana: A signal of misunderstanding*. New York: New American Library.

National Institute of Child Health and Human Development (NICHD) Early Child Care Research Network. (1997a). Familial factors associated with characteristics of non-maternal care for infants. *Journal of Marriage and the Family, 59,* 389–408.

National Institute of Child Health and Human Development (NICHD) Early Child Care Research Network. (1997b). The effects of infant child care on infant–mother attachment security: Results of the NICHD study of early child care. *Child Development, 68,* 860–879.

National Institute of Child Health and Human Development (NICHD) Early Child Care Research Network. (2003). Does quality of child care affect child outcomes at age 4½? *Developmental Psychology, 39,* 451–469.

Nazroo, J. (1997, September). Research scotches racial myth. *The Independent,* p. 2.

Neisser, U. (1982). *Memory observed.* San Francisco, CA: Freeman.

Neisser, U. (1996). *Intelligence: Knowns and unknowns* [Report]. Washington DC: Board of Scientific Affairs (BSA) of the American Psychological Association.

Nelson, K. (1973). Structure and strategy in learning to talk. *Monographs of the Society for Research in Child Development, 38*(Serial no. 149).

Nemeth, C., Mayseless, O., Sherman, J., & Brown, Y. (1990). Exposure to dissent and recall of information. *Journal of Personality and Social Psychology, 58,* 429–437.

Newcomb, A.F., & Bagwell, C.L. (1995). Children's friendship relations: A meta-analytic review. *Psychological Bulletin, 117,* 306–347.

Newcomb, T.M. (1961). *The acquaintance process.* New York: Holt, Rinehart, & Winston.

Newcomb, T.M., Koenig, K., Flacks, R., & Warwick, D. (1967). *Persistence and change: Bennington College and its students after 25 years.* New York: John Wiley & Sons.

Newell, A., & Simon, H.A. (1972). *Human problem solving.* Englewood Cliffs, NJ: Prentice-Hall.

Newell, K.M., & van Emmerik, R.E.A. (1989). The acquisition of co-ordination: Preliminary analysis of learning to write. *Human Movement Science, 8,* 17–32.

Newmark, C.S., Frerking, R.A., Cook, L., & Newmark, L. (1973). Endorsement of Ellis' irrational beliefs as a function of psychopathology. *Journal of Clinical Psychology, 29,* 300–302.

Newstead, S.E. (2000). What is an ecologically rational heuristic? *Behavioral and Brain Sciences, 23,* 759–760.

Newton, J.T.O., Spence, S.H., & Schotte, D. (1995). Cognitive-behavioural therapy versus EMG biofeedback in the treatment of chronic low back pain. *Behaviour Research and Therapy, 33,* 691–697.

Nicholson, R.A., & Berman, J.S. (1983). Is follow-up necessary in evaluating psychotherapy? *Psychological Bulletin, 93,* 261–278.

Nielsen, T.A. (1999). Mentation during sleep. The NREM/REM distinction. In R. Lydic & H.A. Baghdoyan (Eds.), *Handbook of behavioral state control: Cellular and molecular mechanisms.* Boca Raton, FL: CRC Press.

Nisbett, R.E. (1972). Hunger, obesity and the ventromedial hypothalamus. *Psychological Review, 79,* 433–453.

Nisbett, R.E., Caputo, C., Legant, P., & Maracek, J. (1973). Behaviour as seen by the actor and as seen by the observer. *Journal of Personality and Social Psychology, 27,* 154–164.

Nisbett, R.E., & Ross, L. (1980). *Human inference: Strategies and shortcomings of social judgment.* Englewood Cliffs, NJ: Prentice Hall.

Nisbett, R.E., & Wilson, T.D. (1977). Telling more than we can know: Verbal reports on mental processes. *Psychological Review, 84,* 231–259.

Norenzayan, A., Choi, I., & Nisbett, R.E. (1999). Eastern and Western perceptions of causality for social behaviour: Lay theories about personalities and situations. In D.A. Prentice & D.T. Miller (Eds.), *Cultural divides: Understanding and overcoming group conflict.* New York: Russell Sage Foundation.

Norman, D.A., & Bobrow, D.G. (1975). On data-limited and resource-limited processes. *Cognitive Psychology, 7,* 44–64.

Norman, D.A., & Shallice, T. (1986). Attention to action: Willed and automatic control of behaviour. In R.J. Davidson, G.E. Schwartz, & D. Shapiro (Eds.), *The design of everyday things.* New York: Doubleday.

Norman, P., & Smith, L. (1995). The theory of planned behaviour and exercise: An investigation into the role of prior behaviour: Behavioural intentions and attitude variability. *European Journal of Social Psychology, 25,* 403–415.

Norman, W.T. (1963). Toward an adequate taxonomy of personality attributes: Replicated factor structure in peer nomination personality ratings. *Journal of Abnormal and Social Psychology, 66,* 574–583.

Nunes, T. (1994). Street intelligence. In R.J. Sternberg (Ed.), *Encyclopedia of human intelligence.* New York: Macmillan.

Nunn, C. (2000, November 15). Programmed for monogamy. *The Scotsman,* p. 5.

Nyberg, L. (2002). Levels of processing: A view from functional brain imaging. *Memory, 10,* 345–348.

Nystedt, L. (1996). *Who should rule? Does personality matter?* [Rep. No. 812]. Stockholm, Sweden: Department of Psychology, Stockholm University, Sweden.

O'Brien, D.P., Braine, M.D.S., & Yang, Y. (1994). Propositional reasoning by mental models? Simple to refute in principle and practice. *Psychological Review, 101,* 711–724.

O'Brien-Malone, A., & Mayberry, M. (1998). Implicit learning. In K. Kirsner, C. Speelman, M. Mayberry, A. O'Brien-Malone, & C. MacLeod (Eds.), *Implicit and explicit mental processes.* Mahwah, NJ: Lawrence Erlbaum Associates, Inc.

O'Connor, T.G., Caspi, A., DeFries, J.C., & Plomin, R. (2000a). Are associations between parental divorce and children's adjustment genetically mediated? An adoption study. *Developmental Psychology, 36,* 429–437.

O'Connor, T.G., & Croft, C.M. (2001). A twin study of attachment in pre-school children. *Child Development, 72,* 1501–1511.

O'Connor, T.G., Deater-Deckard, K., Fulker, D., Rutter, M., & Plomin, R. (1998). Genotype–environment correlations in late childhood and early adolescence: Antisocial behavioural problems and coercive parenting. *Developmental Psychology, 34,* 970–981.

O'Connor, T.G., Rutter, M., Beckett, C., Keaveney, L., Kreppner, J.M., and the English and Romanian Adoptees Study Team. (2000b). *Child Development, 71,* 376–390.

O'Connor, T.G., Thorpe, K., Dunn, J., & Golding, J. (1999). Parental divorce and adjustment in adulthood: Findings from a community sample. *Journal of Child Psychology and Psychiatry, 40,* 777–789.

O'Craven, K., Downing, P., & Kanwisher, N. (1999). fMRI evidence for objects as the units of attentional selection. *Nature, 401,* 584–587.

O'Malley, P.M., & Bachman, J.G. (1983). Self-esteem: Change and stability between ages 13 and 23. *Developmental Psychology, 19,* 257–268.

O'Neill, D.K. (1996). Two-year-old children's sensitivity to parent's knowledge state when making requests. *Child Development, 67,* 659–677.

Oakes, P.J., Haslam, S.A., & Turner, J.C. (1994). *Stereotyping and social reality.* Malden, MA: Blackwell.

Oakhill, J., Garnham, A., & Johnson-Laird, P.N. (1990). Belief bias effects in syllogistic reasoning. In K.J. Gilhooly, R.H. Logie, & G. Erdos (Eds.), *Lines of thinking, Vol. 1.* New York: Wiley.

Oaksford, M. (1997). Thinking and the rational analysis of human reasoning. *The Psychologist, 10,* 257–260.

Oatley, K., & Johnson-Laird, P.N. (1987). Towards a cognitive theory of emotions. *Cognition and Emotion, 1,* 29–50.

Ochs, E., & Schieffelin, B. (1995). The impact of language socialisation on grammatical development. In P. Fletcher & B. Macwhinney (Eds.), *The handbook of child language.* Oxford, UK: Blackwell.

Ogden, J. (1996). *Health psychology: A textbook.* Buckingham, UK: Open University Press.

Ohlsson, S. (1992). Information processing explanations of insight and related phenomena. In M.T. Keane & K.J. Gilhooly (Eds.),

*Advances in the psychology of thinking*. London: Harvester Wheatsheaf.

Ohlsson, S. (1996). Learning from performance errors. *Psychological Review, 103*, 241–262.

Ohman, A., & Soares, J.J.F. (1994). "Unconscious anxiety": Phobic responses to masked stimuli. *Journal of Abnormal Psychology, 103*, 231–240.

Okada, S., Hanada, M., Hattori, H., & Shoyama, T. (1963). A case of pure word deafness. *Studia Phonologica, 3*, 58–65.

Oldham, J.M., Skodol, A.E., Kellman, H.D., Hyler, S.E., Rosnick, L., & Davies, M. (1992). Diagnosis of DSM-III-R personality disorders by two structured interviews: Patterns of comorbidity. *American Journal of Psychiatry, 149*(2), 213–220.

Olds, J., & Milner, P. (1954). Positive reinforcement produced by electrical stimulation of septal area and other regions of rat brain. *Journal of Comparative and Physiological Psychology, 47*, 419–427.

Olds, M.E., & Olds, J. (1963). Pharmacological patterns in subcortical reinforcement behavior. *International Journal of Neuropharmacology, 64*, 309–325.

Oliner, S.P., & Oliner, P.M. (1988). *The altruistic personality: Rescuers of Jews in Nazi Europe*. New York: The Free Press.

Oliver, M.B., & Hyde, J.S. (1993). Gender differences in sexuality: A meta-analysis. *Psychological Bulletin, 114*, 29–51.

Olson, D.R. (1980). *The social foundation of language and thought*. New York: W.W. Norton.

Olweus, D. (1980). Familial and temperamental determinants of aggressive behaviour in adolescent boys: A causal analysis. *Developmental Psychology, 16*, 644–660.

Olweus, D. (1985). Aggression and hormones: Behavioural relationships with testosterone and adrenalin. In D. Olweus, J. Block, & M. Radke-Yarrow (Ed.), *The development of antisocial and prosocial behaviour: Research, theories and issues*. New York: Academic Press.

Olweus, D., & Endresen, I.M. (1998). The importance of sex-of-stimulus object: Trends and sex differences in empathic responsiveness. *Social Development, 3*, 370–388.

Ones, D.S., Viswesvaran, C., & Reiss, A.D. (1996). Role of social desirability in personality testing for personnel selection: The red herring. *Journal of Applied Psychology, 81*, 660–679.

Orlinsky, D.E., Grave, K., & Parks, B.K. (1994). Process and outcome in psychotherapy—Noch Einmal. In A.E. Bergin & S.L. Garfield (Eds.), *Handbook of psychotherapy and behavior change* (4th ed., pp. 270–376). New York: Wiley.

Orne, M.T. (1959). The nature of hypnosis: Artifact and essence. *Journal of Abnormal and Social Psychology, 58*, 277–299.

Ornstein, P.A., & Haden, C.A. (2001). *Memory development or the development of memory? Current Directions in Psychological Science, 10*, 202–205.

Ost, L.G. (1989). *Blood phobia: A specific phobia subtype in DSM-IV*. Paper requested by the Simple Phobia subcommittee of the DSM-IV Anxiety Disorders Work Group.

Osterman, K., Bjorkqvist, K., Lagerspetz, K., Landau, S., Fraczek, A., & Pastorelli, C. (1997). Sex differences in styles of conflict resolution: A developmental and cross-cultural study with data from Finland, Israel, Italy, and Poland. In D. Fry & K. Bjorkqvist (Eds.), *Cultural variations in conflict resolution*. Mahwah, NJ: Lawrence Erlbaum Associates, Inc.

Ostrom, T.M., & Sedikides, C. (1992). Outgroup homogeneity effect in natural and minimal groups. *Psychological Bulletin, 112*, 536–552.

Oswald, I. (1980). *Sleep* (4th ed.). Harmondsworth, UK: Penguin Books.

Ouellette, J.A., & Wood, W. (1998). Habit and intention in everyday life: The multiple processes by which past behaviour predicts future behaviour. *Psychological Review, 124*, 54–74.

Owusu-Bempah, P., & Howitt, D. (1994). Racism and the psychological textbook. *The Psychologist, 7*, 163–166.

Oyserman, D., Coon, H.M., & Kemmelmeier, M. (2002). Rethinking individualism and collectivism: Evaluation of theoretical assumptions and meta-analyses. *Psychological Bulletin, 128*, 3–72.

Palincsar, A.S., & Brown, A.L. (1984). Reciprocal teaching of comprehension-fostering and comprehension-monitoring activities. *Cognition and Instruction, 1*, 117–175.

Palinkas, L., Reed, H.L., Reedy, K.R., van Do, N., Case, H.S., & Finney, N.S. (2001). Circannual pattern of hypothalamic-pituitary-thyroid (HPT) function and mood during extended antarctic residence. *Psychoneuroendocrinology, 26*, 421–431.

Palmer, S.E. (1975). The effects of contextual scenes on the identification of objects. *Memory and Cognition, 3*, 519–526.

Palmer, S.E. (2002). Perceptual grouping: It's later than you think. *Current Directions in Psychological Science, 11*, 101–106.

Panda, S., Hogenesch, J.B., & Kay, S.A. (2002). Circadian rhythms from flies to human. *Nature, 417*, 329–335.

Paniagua, F.A. (2000). Culture-bound syndromes, cultural variations, and psychopathology. In J. Cuellar & F.A. Paniagua (Eds.), *Handbook of multicultural mental health: Assessment and treatment of diverse populations*. New York: Academic Press.

Panksepp, J. (1985). Mood changes. In P. Vinken, G. Bruyn, & H. Klawans (Eds.), *Handbook of clinical neurology, Vol. 45*. Amsterdam: Elsevier.

Panksepp, J. (1994). The basic of basic emotion. In P. Ekman & R.J. Davidson (Eds.), *The nature of emotion: Fundamental questions*. Oxford, UK: Oxford University Press.

Panksepp, J. (2000). Emotions as natural kinds within the mammalian brain. In M. Lewis & J.M. Howland-Jones (Eds.), *Handbook of emotions* (2nd ed.). New York: Guilford Press.

Papagno, C., Valentine, T., & Baddeley, A.D. (1991). Phonological short-term memory and foreign-language learning. *Journal of Memory and Language, 30*, 331–347.

Papez, J.W. (1937). A proposed mechanism of emotion. *Archives of Neurology and Psychiatry, 38*, 725–743.

Parkin, A.J. (1996). *Explorations in cognitive neuropsychology*. Oxford, UK: Blackwell.

Parkin, A.J. (2001). The structure and mechanisms of memory. In B. Rapp (Ed.), *The handbook of cognitive neuropsychology: What deficits reveal about the human mind*. Philadelphia, PA: Psychology Press.

Parkinson, B. (1994). Emotion. In A.M. Colman (Ed.), *Companion encyclopedia of psychology, Vol. 2*. London: Routledge.

Parkinson, B., & Manstead, A.S.R. (1992). Appraisal as a cause of emotion. In M.S. Clark (Ed.), *Review of personality and social psychology, Vol. 13*. New York: Sage.

Parnas, J. (1988). Assortative mating in schizophrenia: Results from the Copenhagen High-Risk Study. *Psychiatry, 51*, 58–64.

Parten, M. (1932). Social participation among preschool children. *Journal of Abnormal and Social Psychology, 27*, 243–269.

Pascalis, O., de Schonen, S., Morton, J., Deruelle, C., & Fabre-Grenet, M. (1995). Mother's face recognition by neonates: A replication and an extension. *Infant Behavior and Development, 18*, 79–85.

Pascual-Leone, J. (1984). Attentional, dialectic, and mental effort. In M.L. Commons, F.A. Richards, & C. Armon (Eds.), *Beyond formal operations*. New York: Plenum.

Pascual-Leone, J. (2000). Is the French connection neo-Piagetian? Not nearly enough! *Child Development, 71*, 843.

Pashler, H. (1998). *Attention*. Hove, UK: Psychology Press.

Pashler, H., Johnston, J.C., & Ruthruff, E. (2001). Attention and performance. *Annual Review of Psychology, 52*, 629–651.

Pastore, N. (1952). The role of arbitrariness in the frustration–aggression hypothesis. *Journal of Abnormal and Social Psychology, 47*, 728–731.

Patrick, C.J., Bradley, M.M., & Lang, P.J. (1993). Emotion in the criminal psychopath: Startle reflex modulation. *Journal of Abnormal Psychology, 102*, 82–92.

Patterson, D.R., & Jensen, M.P. (2003). Hypnosis and clinical pain. *Psychological Bulletin, 129*, 495–521.

Patterson, G.R. (1982). *Coercive family processes*. Eugene, OR: Castilia Press.

Patterson, G.R. (1996). Some characteristics of a developmental theory for early onset delinquency. In M.F. Lenzenweger & J.J. Haugaard (Eds.), *Frontiers of developmental psychopathology*. Oxford, UK: Oxford University Press.

Patterson, G.R., Chamberlain, P., & Reid, J.B. (1982). A comparative evaluation of a parent training program. *Behavior Therapy, 13*, 638–650.

Patterson, G.R., DeBaryshe, B.D., & Ramsey, E. (1989). A developmental perspective on antisocial behaviour. *American Psychologist, 44*, 329–335.

Patterson, G.R., Reid, J.B., & Dishion, T.J. (1992). *Antisocial boys.* Eugene, OR: Castalia Press.

Pattie, F.A. (1937). The genuineness of hypnotically produced anaesthesia of the skin. *American Journal of Psychology, 49*, 435–443.

Paulhus, D.L., Trapnell, P.D., & Chen, D. (1999). Birth order effects on personality and achievement within families. *Psychological Science, 10*, 482–488.

Paunonen, S.V. (2003). Big Five factors of personality and replicated predictions of behaviour. *Journal of Personality and Social Psychology, 84*, 411–424.

Payne, B.K. (2001). Prejudice and perception: The role of automatic and controlled processes in misperceiving a weapon. *Journal of Personality and Social Psychology, 81*, 181–192.

Peaker, G.F. (1971). *The Plowden children four years later.* Oxford, UK: National Foundation for Educational Research.

Pears, R., & Bryant, P. (1990). Transitive inferences by young children about spatial position. *British Journal of Psychology, 81*, 497–510.

Pecoraro, N., Timberlake, W., & Tinsley, M. (1999). Incentive downshifts evoke search behavior in rats (*Rattus norvegicus*). *Journal of Experimental Psychology: Animal Behavior Processes, 25*, 153–167.

Pedersen, N.L., Plomin, R., McClearn, G.E., & Friberg, I. (1988). Neuroticism, extraversion, and related traits in adult twins reared apart and reared together. *Journal of Personality and Social Psychology, 55*, 950–957.

Pederson, E., Danziger, E., Wilkins, D., Levinson, S., Kita, S., & Senft, G. (1998). Semantic typology and spatial conceptualisation. *Language, 74*, 557–589.

Pengelley, E.T., & Fisher, K.C. (1957). Onset and cessation of hibernation under constant temperature and light in the golden-mantled ground squirrel, *Citellus lateralis. Nature, 180*, 1371–1372.

Peper, C.E., Bootsma, R.J., Mestre, D.R., & Bekker, F.C. (1994). Catching balls: How to get the hand to the right place at the right time. *Journal of Experimental Psychology: Human Perception and Performance, 20*, 591–612.

Perenin, M.-T., & Vighetto, A. (1988). Optic ataxia: A specific disruption in visuomotor mechanisms. 1. Different aspects of the deficit in reaching for objects. *Brain, 111*, 643–674.

Perfect, T.J., & Hollins, T.S. (1996). Predictive feeling of knowing judgements and postdictive confidence judgements in eyewitness memory and general knowledge. *Applied Cognitive Psychology, 10*, 371–382.

Perner, J., Leekam, S., & Wimmer, H. (1987). Three-year olds' difficulty with false belief: The case for a conceptual deficit. *British Journal of Developmental Psychology, 5*, 127–137.

Perner, J., & Wimmer, H. (1985). "John thinks that Mary thinks that ... ": Attribution of second-order beliefs by 5- to 10-year-old children. *Journal of Experimental Child Psychology, 39*, 437–471.

Perrin, S., & Spencer, C. (1980). The Asch effect: A child of its time. *Bulletin of the British Psychological Society, 33*, 405–406.

Perrin, S., & Spencer, C. (1981). The Asch effect and cultural factors: Further observations and evidence. *Bulletin of the British Psychological Society, 34*, 385–386.

Perry, D.G., & Bussey, K. (1979). The social learning theory of sex differences: Imitation is alive and well. *Journal of Personality and Social Psychology, 37*, 1699–1712.

Pervin, L.A. (1993). *Personality: Theory and research* (6th ed.). Chichester, UK: Wiley.

Pervin, L.A., & John, O.P. (1997). *Personality: Theory and research* (7th ed.). New York: Wiley.

Pervin, L.A., & John, O.P. (Eds.). (1999). *Handbook of personality* (2nd ed.). New York: Guilford Press.

Peterson, C., Seligman, M.E., & Vailliant, G.E. (1988). Pessimistic explanatory style is a risk factor for physical illness: A thirty-five year longitudinal study. *Journal of Personality and Social Psychology, 55*, 23–27.

Peterson, L.R., & Peterson, M.J. (1959). Short-term retention of individual verbal items. *Journal of Experimental Psychology, 58*, 193–198.

Peterson, M.S., Kramer, A.F., Wang, R.F., Irwin, D.E., & McCarley, J.S. (2001). Visual search has memory. *Psychological Science, 12*, 287–292.

Peterson, R.S., Owens, P.D., Tetlock, P.E., Fan, E.T., & Martorana, P. (1998). Group dynamics in top management teams: Groupthink, vigilance, and alternative models of organizational failure and success. *Organizational Behavior and Human Decision Processes, 73*, 272–305.

Pettigrew, T.F. (1958). Personality and sociocultural factors in intergroup attitudes: A cross-national comparison. *Journal of Conflict Resolution, 2*, 29–42.

Pettigrew, T.F. (1998). Intergroup contact theory. *Annual Review of Psychology, 49*, 65–85.

Pettigrew, T.F., & Meertens, R.W. (1995). Subtle and blatant prejudice in Western Europe. *European Journal of Social Psychology, 25*, 57–75.

Pettit, G.S., Bates, J.E., Dodge, K.A., & Meece, D.W. (1999). The impact of after-school peer contact on early adolescent externalising problems is moderated by parental monitoring, perceived neighbourhood safety, and prior adjustment. *Child Development, 70*, 768–778.

Petty, R.E. (1995). Attitude change. In A. Tesser (Ed.), *Advanced social psychology.* New York: McGraw-Hill.

Petty, R.E., & Cacioppo, J.T. (1981). *Attitudes and persuasion: Classic and contemporary approaches.* Dubuque, IA: W.C. Brown.

Petty, R.E., Cacioppo, J.T., & Goldman, R. (1981). Personal involvement as a determinant of argument-based persuasion. *Journal of Personality and Social Psychology, 41*, 847–855.

Petty, R.E., & Wegener, D.T. (1998). Attitude change: Multiple roles for persuasion variable. In D.T. Gilbert, S.T. Fiske, & G. Lindzey (Eds.), *The handbook of social psychology* (4th ed., pp. 323–390). Boston: McGraw-Hill.

Pfeifer, J.E., & Ogloff, J.R.P. (1991). Ambiguity and guilt determinations: A modern racism perspective. *Journal of Applied Social Psychology, 21*, 1713–1725.

Phelps, J.A., Davis, J.O., & Schartz, K.M. (1997). Nature, nurture, and twin research strategies. *Current Directions in Psychological Science, 6*, 117–121.

Piaget, J. (1932). *The moral judgement of the child.* Harmondsworth, UK: Penguin.

Piaget, J. (1967). *The child's conception of the world.* Totowa, NJ: Littlefield, Adams.

Piaget, J. (1972). Intellectual evolution from adolescence to adulthood. *Human Development, 15*, 1–12.

Piaget, J., & Szeminska, A. (1952). *The child's conception of number.* London: Routledge & Kegan Paul.

Pickering, M.J., & Traxler, M.J. (1998). Plausibility and recovery from garden paths: An eye-tracking study. *Journal of Experimental Psychology: Learning, Memory, and Cognition, 24*, 940–961.

Pierrel, R., & Sherman, J.G. (1963). Train your pet the Barnabus way. *Brown Alumni Monthly*, February, 8–14.

Pike, K.M., & Rodin, J. (1991). Mothers, daughters, and disordered eating. *Journal of Abnormal Psychology, 100*, 198–204.

Pilcher, J.J., Nadler, E., & Busch, C. (2002). Effects of hot and cold temperature on performance: A meta-analytic review. *Ergonomics, 45*, 682–698.

Pilgrim, D. (2000). Psychiatric diagnosis: More questions than answers. *The Psychologist, 13*, 302–305.

Piliavin, I.M., Rodin, J., & Piliavin, J.A. (1969). Good samaritarianism: An underground phenomenon? *Journal of Personality and Social Psychology, 13*, 289–299.

Piliavin, J.A., Dovidio, J.F., Gaertner, S.L., & Clark, R.D. (1981). *Emergency intervention.* New York: Academic Press.

Pillemer, D., Goldsmith, L.R., Panter, A.T., & White, S.H. (1988). Very long-term memories of the first year in college. *Journal of Experimental Psychology: Learning, Memory, and Cognition, 14*, 709–715.

Pilleri, G. (1979). The blind Indus dolphin, *Platanista indi. Endeavour, 3*, 48–56.

Pinel, J.P.J. (1997). *Biopsychology* (3rd ed.). Boston: Allyn & Bacon.

Pinel, J.P.J., Assanand, S., & Lehman, D.R. (2000). Hunger, eating, and ill health. *American Psychologist, 55*, 1105–1116.

Pinker, S. (1984). *Language learnability and language development.* Cambridge, MA: Harvard University Press.

Pinker, S. (1989). Learnability and cognition: *The acquisition of argument structure.* Cambridge, MA: MIT Press.

Pinker, S. (1994). *The language instinct.* Harmondsworth, UK: Allen Lane.

Pinker, S. (1997). *How the mind works.* New York: Norton.

Pisella, L., Grea, H., Tilikete, C., Vighetto, A., Desmurget, M., Rode, G., Boisson, D., & Rossetti, Y. (2000). An "automatic pilot" for the hand in human posterior parietal cortex: Toward reinterpreting optic ataxia. *Nature Neuroscience, 3*, 729–736.

Pi-Sunyer, X., Kissileff, H.R., Thornton, J., & Smith, G.P. (1982). C-terminal octapeptide of cholecystokinin decreases food intake in obese men. *Physiology and Behavior, 29*, 627–630.

Pitts, M., & Phillips, K. (1998). *The psychology of health: An introduction* (2nd ed.). London: Routledge.

Plaks, J.E., & Higgins, E.T. (2000). Pragmatic use of stereotyping in teamwork: Social loafing and compensation as a function of inferred partner–situation fit. *Journal of Personality and Social Psychology, 79*, 962–974.

Planalp, S., & Rivers, M. (1996). Changes in knowledge of close relationships. In G. Fletcher & J. Fitness (Eds.), *Knowledge structures in close relationships: A social psychological approach* (pp. 299–324). Mahwah, NJ: Lawrence Erlbaum Associates, Inc.

Plaut, D.C., McClelland, J.L., Seidenberg, M.S., & Patterson, K. (1996). Understanding normal and impaired word reading: Computational principles in quasi-regular domains. *Psychological Review, 103*, 56–115.

Plomin, R. (1988). The nature and nurture of cognitive abilities. In R.J. Sternberg (Ed.), *Advances in the psychology of human intelligence, Vol. 4.* Hillsdale, NJ: Lawrence Erlbaum Associates, Inc.

Plomin, R. (1990). The role of inheritance in behaviour. *Science, 248*, 183–188.

Plomin, R. (1999). Genetics and general cognitive ability. *Nature, 402*, C25–C29.

Plomin, R., Corley, R., DeFries, J.C., & Fulker, D. (1990). Individual differences in television viewing in early childhood: Nature as well as nurture. *Psychological Science, 1*, 371–377.

Plomin, R., DeFries, J.C., & McClearn, G.E. (1997). *Behavioural genetics: A primer* (3rd ed.). New York: Freeman.

Poldrack, R.A., & Gabrieli, J.D. (2001). Characterizing the neural mechanisms of skill learning and repetition priming: Evidence from mirror reading. *Brain, 124*, 67–82.

Poole, D.A., & Lindsay, D.S. (1996). *Effects of parents' suggestions, interviewing techniques, and age on young children's event reports.* Paper presented at NATO Advanced Study Institute, Port de Bourgenay, France.

Pope, H.G., Oliva, P.S., Hudson, J.I., Bodkin, J.A., & Gruber, A.J. (1999). Attitudes towards DSM–IV dissociative disorders diagnoses among board-certified American psychiatrists. *American Journal of Psychiatry, 156*, 321–323.

Pope, K.S., & Vetter, V.A. (1992). Ethical dilemmas encountered by members of the American Psychological Association. *American Psychologist, 47*, 397–411.

Popper, K.R. (1969). *Conjectures and refutations.* London: Routledge & Kegan Paul.

Popper, K.R. (1972). *Objective knowledge.* Oxford, UK: Oxford University Press.

Postmes, T., & Spears, R. (1998). Deindividuation and anti-normative behaviour: A meta-analysis. *Psychological Bulletin, 123*, 238–259.

Postmes, T., Spears, R., & Cihangir, S. (2001). Quality of decision making and group norms. *Journal of Personality and Social Psychology, 80*, 918–930.

Povinelli, D.J., Landau, K.R., & Perilloux, H.K. (1996). Self-recognition in young children using delayed versus live feedback: Evidence of a developmental asynchrony. *Child Development, 67*, 1540–1554.

Power, M.J., & Dalgleish, T. (1997). *Cognition and emotion: From order to disorder.* Hove, UK: Psychology Press.

Pratkanis, A.R., & Aronson, E. (1992). *Age of propaganda: The everyday use and abuse of persuasion.* New York: W.H. Freeman.

Preuss, T.M., Qi, H., & Kaas, J.H. (1999). Distinctive compartmental organisation of human primary visual cortex. *Proceedings of the National Academy of Science, 96*, 11601–11606.

Price, D.D., & Barrell, J.J. (2000). Mechanisms of analgesia produced by hypnosis and placebo suggestions. In E.A. Mayer & C.B. Saper (Eds.), *Progress in brain research, Vol. 122.* New York: Elsevier Science.

Price, L.H. (1990). Serotonin reuptake inhibitors in depression and anxiety: An overview. *Annuals of Clinical Psychiatry, 2*, 165–172.

Price, T.S., Eley, T.C., Dale, P.S., Stevenson, J., Saudino, K., & Plomin, R. (2000). Genetic and environmental covariation between verbal and nonverbal cognitive development in infancy. *Child Development, 71*, 948.

Price-Williams, D., Gordon, W., & Ramirez, M. (1969). Skill and conservation: A study of pottery-making children. *Developmental Psychology, 1*, 769.

Prien, R.F., & Potter, W.Z. (1993). Maintenance treatment for mood disorders. In D.L. Dunner (Ed.), *Current psychiatric therapy.* Philadelphia: Saunders.

Prins, K.S., Buunk, B.P., & van Yperen, N.W. (1993). Equity, normative disapproval and extramarital relationships. *Journal of Social and Personal Relationships, 10*, 39–53.

Probhakaran, V., Smith, J.A.L., Desmond, J.E., Glover, G., & Gabrieli, J.D.E. (1997). Neural substrates of fluid reasoning: An fMRI study of neocortical activation during performance of the Raven's Progressive Matrices Test. *Cognitive Psychology, 33*, 43–63.

Prochaska, J.O., & Norcross, J.C. (1994). *Systems of psychotherapy: A transtheoretical analysis* (3rd ed.). Pacific Grove, CA: Brooks/Cole.

Protopapas, A. (1999). Connectionist modeling of speech perception. *Psychological Bulletin, 125*, 410–436.

Putnam, B. (1979). Hypnosis and distortions in eyewitness memory. *International Journal of Clinical and Experimental Hypnosis, 27*, 437–448.

Putnam, F.W. (1984). The psychophysiologic investigation of multiple personality disorder. *Psychiatric Clinics of North America, 7*, 31–40.

Quattrone, G.A., & Jones, E.E. (1980). The perception of variability within ingroups and outgroups. *Journal of Personality and Social Psychology, 38*, 141–152.

Quigley-Fernandez, B., & Tedeschi, J.T. (1978). The bogus pipeline as lie detector: Two validity studies. *Journal of Personality and Social Psychology, 36*, 247–256.

Quinlan, J., & Quinlan, J. (1977). *Karen Ann: The Quinlans tell their story.* Toronto: Doubleday.

Quinlan, P.T., & Wilton, R.N. (1998). Grouping by proximity or similarity? Competition between the Gestalt principles in vision. *Perception, 27*, 417–430.

Quinn, J.G., & McConnell, J. (1996a). Irrelevant pictures in visual working memory. *Quarterly Journal of Experimental Psychology, 49A*, 200–215.

Quinn, J.G., & McConnell, J. (1996b). Indications of the functional distinction between the components of visual working memory. *Psychologische Beitrage, 38*, 355–367.

Rabain-Jamin, J. (1989). Culture and early social interactions. The example of mother–infant object play in African and native French families. *European Journal of Psychology of Education, 4*, 295–305.

Rabbie, J.M., Schot, J.C., & Visser, L. (1989). Social identity theory: A conceptual and empirical critique from the perspective of a behavioural interaction model. *European Journal of Social Psychology, 19*, 171–202.

Radvansky, G.A., & Copeland, D.E. (2001). Working memory and situation model updating. *Memory and Cognition, 29*, 1073–1080.

Rafal, R., Smith, J., Krantz, J., Cohen, A., & Brennan, C. (1990). Extrageniculate vision in hemianopic humans: Saccade inhibition by signals in the blind field. *Science, 250*, 118–121.

Rahe, R.H. (1968). Life crisis and health change. In P.R. May & J.R. Wittenborn (Eds.), *Psychotropic drug response: advances in prediction*. Oxford, UK: C.C. Thomas.

Rainville, P., Hofbauer, R.K., Bushnell, M.C., Duncan, G.H., & Price, D.D. (2001). Hypnosis modulates activity in brain structures involved in the regulation of consciousness. *Journal of Cognitive Neuroscience, 14*, 887–901.

Ralph, M.R., Foster, R.G., Davis, F.C., & Menaker, M. (1990). Transplanted suprachiasmatic nucleus determines circadian period. *Science, 247*, 975–978.

Ramey, C.T., Bryant, D.M., & Suarez, T.M. (1985).Preschool compensatory education and the modifiability of intelligence: A critical review. In D.K. Detterman (Ed.), *Current topics in human intelligence: Vol. 1. Research methodology*. Norwood, NJ: Ablex.

Rampello, L., Nicoletti, F., & Nicoletti, F. (2000). Dopamine and depression: Therapeutic implications. *CNS Drugs, 13*, 35–45.

Randich, A., & LoLordo, V.M. (1979). Associative and non-associative theories of the UCS pre-exposure phenomenon: Implications for Pavlovian conditioning. *Psychological Bulletin, 86*, 523–548.

Rank, S.G., & Jacobsen, C.K. (1977). Hospital nurses' compliance with medication overdose orders: A failure to replicate. *Journal of Health and Social Behaviour, 18*, 188–193.

Raven, J. (1980). *Parents, teachers and children: A study of an educational home visiting scheme*. London: Hodder & Stoughton.

Ravizza, K. (1977). Peak experiences in sport. *Journal of Humanistic Psychology, 17*, 35–40.

Rayner, K., Inhoff, A.W., Morrison, R.E., Slowiaczek, M.L., & Bertera, J.H. (1981). Masking of foveal and parafoveal vision during eye fixations in reading. *Journal of Experimental Psychology: Human Perception and Performance, 18*, 163–172.

Rayner, K., & Sereno, S.C. (1994).Eye movements in reading: Psycholinguistic studies. In M.A. Gernsbacher (Ed.), *Handbook of psycholinguistics*. New York: Academic Press.

Raynor, H.A., & Epstein, L.H. (2001). Dietary variety, energy regulation, and obesity. *Psychological Bulletin, 127*, 325–341.

Raz, A., & Shapiro, T. (2002). Hypnosis and neuroscience: A cross talk between clinical and cognitive research. *Archives of General Psychiatry, 59*, 85–90.

Reason, J.T. (1979). Actions not as planned: The price of automatisation. In G. Underwood & R. Stevens (Eds.), *Aspects of consciousness: Vol. 1. Psychological issues*. London: Academic Press.

Reason, J.T. (1992). Cognitive underspecification: Its variety and consequences. In B.J. Baars (Ed.), *Experimental slips and human error: Exploring the architecture of volition*. New York: Plenum Press.

Reber, A.S. (1993). *Implicit learning and tacit knowledge: An essay on the cognitive unconscious*. Oxford, UK: Oxford University Press.

Reber, A.S. (1997). How to differentiate implicit and explicit modes of acquisition. In J.D. Cohen & J.W. Schooler (Eds.), *Scientific approaches to consciousness*. Hillsdale, NJ: Lawrence Erlbaum Associates, Inc.

Reber, A.S., Walkenfeld, F.F., & Hernstadt, R. (1991). Implicit and explicit learning: Individual differences and IQ. *Journal of Experimental Psychology: Learning, Memory, and Cognition, 17*, 888–896.

Rebert, W.M., Stanton, A.L., & Schwarz, R.M. (1991). Influence of personality attributes and daily moods on bulimic eating patterns. *Addictive Behaviors, 16*, 497–505.

*Rechov Sumsum/Shara'a Simsim* research symposium. (1999). Israel Education Television, Al-Quds University Institute of Modern Media and Children's Television Workshop: New York.

Rechtschaffen, A., Gilliland, M., Bergmann, B., & Winter, J. (1983). Physiological correlates of prolonged sleep deprivation in rats. *Science, 221*, 182–184.

Redelmeier, D., Koehler, D.J., Liberman, V., & Tversky, A. (1995). Probability judgement in medicine: Discounting unspecified alternatives. *Medical Decision Making, 15*, 227–230.

Reed, J.M., & Squire, L.R. (1998). Retrograde amnesia for facts and events: findings from four new cases. *Journal of Neuroscience, 18*, 3943–3954.

Reicher, G.M. (1969). Perceptual recognition as a function of meaningfulness of stimulus material. *Journal of Experimental Psychology, 81*, 274–280.

Reicher, S., Levine, R.M., & Gordijn, E. (1998). More on deindividuation, power relations between groups and the expression of social identity: Three studies on the effects of visibility to the in-group. *British Journal of Social Psychology, 37*, 15–40.

Reicher, S., Spears, R., & Postmes, T. (1995). A social identity model of deindividuation phenomena. In W. Stroebe & M. Hewstone (Eds.), *European review of social psychology, Vol. 6*. Chichester, UK: Wiley.

Reicher, S.D. (1984). The St. Pauls' riot: An explanation of the limits of crowd action in terms of a social identity model. *European Journal of Social Psychology, 14*, 1–21.

Reicher, S.D., Spears, R., & Postmes, T. (1995). A social identity model of deindividuation phenomena. *European Review of Social Psychology, 6*, 161–198.

Redelmeier, D., Koehler, D.J., Liberman, V., & Tversky, A. (1995). Probability judgement in medicine: Discounting unspecified alternatives. *Medical Decision Making, 15*, 227–230.

Reichle, E.D., Pollatsek, A., Fisher, D.L., & Rayner, K. (1998). Toward a model of eye movement control in reading. *Psychological Review, 105*, 125–157.

Reinberg, R. (1967). *Eclairement et cycle menstruel de la femme* [Rapport au Colloque International du CRNS, la photorégulation de la reproduction chez les oiseaux et les mammifères]. Montpelier, France.

Reis, H.T. & Patrick, B.C. (1996). Attachment and intimacy: Component processes. In E.T. Higgins & A.W. Kruglanski (Eds.), *Social psychology: Handbook of basic principles* (pp. 523–563). New York: Guilford Press.

Reis, H.T., Senchak, M., & Solomon, B. (1985). Sex differences in the intimacy of social interaction: Further examination of potential explanations. *Journal of Personality and Social Psychology, 48*, 1204–1217.

Remington, G., & Kapur, S. (2000). Atypical antipsychotics: Are some more atypical than others? *Psychopharmacology, 148*, 3–15.

Renegar, K.B., Crouse, D., Floyd, R.A., & Krueger, J. (2000). Progression of influenza viral infection through the murine respiratory tract: The protective role of sleep deprivation. *Sleep, 23*, 859–863.

Rescorla, R.A., & Wagner, A.R. (1972). A theory of Pavlovian conditioning: Variations in the effectiveness of reinforcement and nonreinforcement. In A.H. Black & W.F. Prokasy (Eds.), *Classical conditioning: II. Current research and theory*. New York: Appleton-Century-Crofts.

Revonsuo, A. (2000). The reinterpretation of dreams: An evolutionary hypothesis of the function of dreaming. *Behavioral and Brain Sciences, 23*, 877–901.

Rey, J.M., & Tennant, C. (2002). Cannabis and mental health: More evidence establishes clear link between use of cannabis and psychiatric illness. *British Medical Journal, 325*, 1183.

Rey, J.M., & Walter, G. (1997). Half a century of ECT use in young people. *American Journal of Psychiatry, 154*, 595–602.

Rhee, S.H., & Waldman, I.D. (2002). Genetic and environmental influences on antisocial behaviour: A meta-analysis of twin and adoption studies. *Psychological Bulletin, 128*, 490–529.

Rice, R.W. (1978). Construct validity of the least preferred co-worker score. *Psychological Bulletin, 85*, 1199–1237.

Richards, F.A., & Armon, C. (Eds.), *Beyond formal operations*. New York: Plenum.

Rickels, K., DeMartinis, N., & Aufdrembrinke, B. (2000). A double-blind, placebo-controlled trial of abecarnil and diazepam in the treatment of patients with generalised anxiety disorder. *Journal of Clinical Psychopharmacology, 20*, 12–18.

Rickels, K., Schweizer, E., Case, W.G., & Greenblatt, D.J. (1990). Long-term therapeutic use of benzodiazepines: Effects of abrupt discontinuation. *Archives of General Psychiatry, 47*, 899–907.

Ridley, M. (1996). *Evolution* (2nd ed.). Cambridge, MA: Blackwell Science.

Riggio, R.E. (2000). *Introduction to industrial/organisational psychology* (3rd ed.). Upper Saddle River, NJ: Prentice Hall.

Riggs, K.J., Peterson, D.M., Robinson, E.J., & Mitchell, P. (1998). Are errors in false belief tasks symptomatic of a broader difficulty with counterfactuality? *Cognitive Development, 13*, 73–90.

Ritov, I., & Baron, J. (1990). Reluctance to vaccinate: Omission bias and ambiguity. *Journal of Behavioral Decision Making, 3*, 263–277.

Ritter, S., & Taylor, J.S. (1990). Vagal sensory neurons are required for lipoprivic but not glucoprivic feeding in rats. *American Journal of Physiology, 258*, R1395–R1401.

Rivera, S.M., Wakeley, A., & Langer, J. (1999). The drawbridge phenomenon: Representational reasoning or perceptual preference? *Developmental Psychology, 35*, 427–435.

Robarchek, C., & Robarchek, C.J. (1992). Cultures of war and peace: A comparative study of the Waorani and Semai. In J. Silverberg & J.P. Gray (Eds.), *Aggression and peacefulness in humans and other primates*. New York: Oxford University Press.

Robbins, T.W., Anderson, E.J., Barker, D.R., Bradley, A.C., Fearnyhough, C., Henson, R., Hudson, S.R., & Baddeley, A. (1996). Working memory in chess. *Memory and Cognition, 24*, 83–93.

Roberson, D., Davies, I., & Davidoff, J. (2000). Colour categories are not universal: Replications and new evidence from a stone-age culture. *Journal of Experimental Psychology: General, 129*, 369–398.

Roberts, R.D., Zeidner, M., & Matthews, G. (2001). Does emotional intelligence meet traditional standards for an intelligence? Some new data and conclusions. *Emotion, 1*, 196–231.

Roberts, W.W., & Mooney, R.D. (1974). Brain areas controlling thermoregulatory grooming, prone extension, locomotion, and tail vasodilation in rats. *Journal of Comparative Physiological Psychology, 86*, 470–480.

Robertson, I.H., Manly, T., Andrade, J., Baddeley, B.T., & Yiend, J. (1997). "Oops!" Performance correlates of everyday attentional failures in traumatic brain injured and normal subjects. *Neuropsychologia, 35*, 747–758.

Robertson, J., & Bowlby, J. (1952). Responses of young children to separation from their mothers. *Courier Centre International de l'Enfance, 2*, 131–142.

Robertson, J.J., & Robertson, J. (1971). Young children in brief separation. *Psychoanalytic Study of the Child, 26*, 264–315.

Robertson, S.I. (2001). *Problem solving*. Hove, UK: Psychology Press.

Robins, R.W., Spranca, M.D., & Mendelsohn, G.A. (1996). The actor–observer effect revisited: Effects of individual differences and repeated social interactions on actor and observer attributions. *Journal of Personality and Social Psychology, 71*, 375–389.

Robinson, J.L., Zahn-Waxler, C., & Emde, R.N. (1994). Patterns of development in early empathic behaviour: Environmental and child constitutional influences. *Social Development, 3*, 125–145.

Robinson, T.E., & Berridge, K.C. (1993). The neural basis of drug craving: An incentive-sensitisation theory of addiction. *Brain Research Reviews, 18*, 247–291.

Rock, I., & Palmer, S. (1990, December). The legacy of Gestalt psychology. *Scientific American*, pp. 48–61.

Roelofs, A. (2000). WEAVER++ and other computational models of lemma retrieval and word-form encoding. In L. Wheeldon (Ed.), *Aspects of language production*. Hove, UK: Psychology Press.

Rogers, B.J., & Collett, T.S. (1989). The appearance of surfaces specified by motion parallax and binocular disparity. *Quarterly Journal of Experimental Psychology, 41A*, 697–717.

Rogers, C.R. (1947). The case of Mary Jane Tilden. In W.U. Snyder (Ed.), *Casebook of non-directive counseling*. Cambridge, MA: Houghton Mifflin.

Rogers, C.R. (1951). *Client-centred therapy*. Boston: Houghton Mifflin.

Rogers, C.R. (1957). The necessary and sufficient conditions of therapeutic personality change. *Journal of Consulting Psychology, 21*, 95–103.

Rogers, C.R. (1959). A theory of therapy, personality, and interpersonal relationships as developed in the client-centred framework. In S. Koch (Ed.), *Psychology: A study of a science*. New York: McGraw-Hill.

Rogers, C.R. (1967). *On becoming a person*. London: Constable.

Rogers, C.R. (1975). Client-centered psychotherapy. In A.M. Freedman, H.I. Kaplan, & B.J. Sadock (Eds.), *Comprehensive textbook of psychiatry, Vol. II*. Baltimore: Williams & Wilkins.

Rogers, L. (2001, May 6). Cannabis-like molecules in their brains, which trigger hunger pangs: Medical notes. *Sunday Times*, p. 33.

Rogers, R.W. (1983). Cognitive and physiological processes in fear appeals and attitude change: A revised theory of protection motivation. In J.T. Cacioppo & R.E. Petty (Eds.), *Social psycho-physiology: A sourcebook*. New York: Guilford Press.

Rogers, R.W., & Prentice-Dunn, S. (1997). Protection motivation theory. In D. Gochman (Ed.), *Handbook of health behaviour research, Vol. 1*. New York: Plenum.

Rogoff, B. (1990). *Apprenticeship in thinking: Cognitive development in social context*. Oxford, UK: Oxford University Press.

Rohner, R.P. (1975). Parental acceptance–rejection and personality development: A universalist approach to behavioural science. In R.W. Brislin, S. Bochner, & W.J. Lonner (Eds.), *Cross-cultural perspectives on learning*. New York: Sage.

Rohner, R.P. (1986). *The warmth dimension: Foundations of parental acceptance–rejection theory*. Beverly Hills, CA: Sage.

Rohner, R.P., & Pettengill, S.M. (1985). Perceived parental acceptance–rejection and parental control among Korean adolescents. *Child Development, 56*, 524–528.

Rohner, R.P., & Rohner, E.C. (1981). Parental acceptance–rejection and parental control: Cross-cultural codes. *Ethnology, 20*, 245–260.

Rolls, B.J., Rolls, E.T., & Rowe, E.A. (1982). The influence of variety on human food selection and intake. In L.M. Barker (Ed.), *The psychobiology of human food selection*. Westport, CT: AVI.

Rolls, B.J., Rowe, E.A., & Rolls, E.T. (1982). How flavour and appearance affect human feeding. *Proceedings of the Nutrition Society, 41*, 109–117.

Rolls, B.J., van Duijvenvoorde, P.M., & Rolls, E.T. (1984). Pleasantness changes and food intake in a varied four-course meal. *Appetite, 5*, 337–348.

Rolls, E.T. (1981). Central nervous mechanisms related to feeding and appetite. *British Medical Bulletin, 37*, 131–134.

Rolls, E.T., & Rolls, J.H. (1997). Olfactory sensory-specific satiety in humans. *Physiology and Behavior, 61*, 461–473.

Rolls, E.T., & Tovée, M.J. (1995). Sparseness of the neuronal representation of stimuli in the primate temporal visual cortex. *Journal of Neurophysiology, 73*, 713–726.

Ronningstam, E., & Gunderson, J.G. (1990). Identifying criteria for narcissistic personality disorder. *American Journal of Psychiatry, 147*, 918–922.

Rortvedt, A.K., & Miltenberger, R.G. (1994). Analysis of a high-probability instructional sequence and time-out in the treatment of child noncompliance. *Journal of Applied Behavior Analysis, 27*, 327–330.

Rose, G.A., & Williams, R.T. (1961). The psychobiology of meals. *British Journal of Nutrition, 15*, 1–9.

Rosenbaum, D.A., Carlson, R.A., & Gilmore, R.O. (2001). Acquisition of intellectual and perceptual-motor skills. *Annual Review of Psychology, 52*, 453–470.

Rosenbaum, M.E. (1986). The repulsion hypothesis: On the non-development of relationships. *Journal of Personality and Social Psychology, 51*, 1156–1166.

Rosenberg, S., Nelson, C., & Vivekananthan, P.S. (1968). A multidimensional approach to the structure of personality impressions. *Journal of Personality and Social Psychology, 9,* 283–294.

Rosenfield, D., Stephan, W.G., & Lucker, G.W. (1981). Attraction to competent and incompetent members of cooperative and competitive groups. *Journal of Applied Social Psychology, 11,* 416–433.

Rosenhan, D.L. (1973). On being sane in insane places. *Science, 179,* 250–258.

Rosenhan, D.L., & Seligman, M.E.P. (1989). *Abnormal psychology* (2nd ed.). New York: Norton.

Rosenhan, D.L., & Seligman, M.E.P. (1995). *Abnormal psychology* (3rd ed.). New York: Norton.

Rosenman, R.H., Brand, R.J., Jenkins, C.D., Friedman, M., Straus, R. & Wurm, M. (1975). Coronary heart disease in the Western Collaborative Group Study: Final follow-up experience of 8½ years. *Journal of the American Medical Association, 22,* 872–877.

Rosenthal, D. (1963). *The Genain quadruplets: A case study and theoretical analysis of heredity and environment in schizophrenia.* New York: Basic Books.

Rosenthal, R. (1966). *Experimenter effects in behavioural research.* New York: Appleton-Century-Crofts.

Rosenzweig, M.R. (1992). Psychological science around the world. *American Psychologist, 47,* 718–722.

Rosenzweig, M.R., Breedlove, S.M., & Leiman, A.L. (2002). *Biological psychology: An introduction to behavioural, cognitive, and clinical neuroscience* (3rd ed.). Sunderland, MA: Sinauer Associates.

Rosenzweig, M.R., Leiman, A.L., & Breedlove, S.M. (1999). *Biological psychology: An introduction to behavioural, cognitive, and clinical neuroscience* (2nd ed.). Sunderland, MA: Sinauer Associates.

Ross, C.A., Miller, S.D., Reagor, P., Bjornson, L., Fraser, G., & Anderson, G. (1990). Structured interview data on 102 cases of multiple personality disorder from four centres. *American Journal of Psychiatry, 147,* 596–601.

Ross, S.M., & Offermann, L.R. (1997). Transformational leaders: Measurement of personality attributes and work group performance. *Personality and Social Psychology Bulletin, 23,* 1078–1086.

Roth, A., & Fonagy, P. (1996). *What works for whom? A critical review of psychotherapy research.* New York: Guilford Press.

Rothbaum, F., Weisz, T., Pott, M., Miyake, K., & Morelli, G., (2000). Attachment and culture: Security in the United States and Japan. *American Psychologist, 55,* 1093–1104.

Rothman, A.J., & Salovey, P. (1997). Shaping perceptions to motivate healthy behaviour: The role of message framing. *Psychological Bulletin, 121,* 3–19.

Rotter, J.B. (1966). Generalized expectancies for internal versus external control of reinforcement. *Psychological Monographs, 80,* 1–28.

Roy, P., Rutter, M., & Pickles, A. (2000). Institutional care: Risk from family background or pattern of rearing? *Journal of Child Psychology and Psychiatry, 41,* 139–149.

Rubin, D.C. (2000). The distribution of early childhood memories. *Memory, 8,* 265–269.

Rubin, D.C., Rahhal, T.A., & Poon, L.W. (1998). Things learned in early adulthood are remembered best. *Memory and Cognition, 26,* 3–19.

Rubin, D.C., & Wenzel, A.E. (1996). One hundred years of forgetting: A quantitative description of retention. *Psychological Bulletin, 103,* 734–760.

Rubin, D.C., Wetzler, S.E., & Nebes, R.D. (1986). Autobiographical memory across the lifespan. In D.C. Rubin (Ed.), *Autobiographical memory.* Cambridge, UK: Cambridge University Press.

Rubin, K.H., Bukowski, W., & Parker, J.G. (1998b). Peer interactions, relationships, and groups. In W. Damon (Ed.), *Handbook of child psychology: Vol. 3. Social emotional and personality development* (5th ed.). New York: Wiley.

Rubin, M., & Hewstone, M. (1998). Social Identity Theory's self-esteem hypothesis: A review and some suggestions for clarification. *Review of Personality and Social Psychology, 2,* 40–62.

Rubin, Z. (1970). Measurement of romantic love. *Journal of Personality and Social Psychology, 16,* 265–273.

Ruble, D.N. (1987). The acquisition of self-knowledge: A self-socialisation perspective. In N. Eisenberg (Ed.), *Contemporary topics in developmental psychology.* New York: Wiley.

Ruble, D.N., Balaban, T., & Cooper, J. (1981). Gender constancy and the effects of sex-typed televised toy commercials. *Child Development, 52,* 667–673.

Ruble, D.N., Boggiano, A.K., Feldman, N.S., & Loebl, J.H. (1980). A developmental analysis of the role of social comparison in self-evaluation. *Developmental Psychology, 16,* 105–115.

Rudge, P., & Warrington, E.K. (1991). Selective impairment of memory and visual perception in splenial tumours. *Brain, 114,* 349–360.

Rudman, L.A., & Borgida, E. (1995). The afterglow of construct accessibility: The behavioural consequences of priming men to view women as sexual objects. *Journal of Experimental Social Psychology, 31,* 493–517.

Rudolph, J., Langer, I., & Tausch, R. (1980). Demonstrations of the psychic results and conditions of person-centred individual psychotherapy. *Zeitschrift für Klinische Forschung und Praxis, 9,* 23–33.

Rumelhart, D.E., & Ortony, A. (1977). The representation of knowledge in memory. In R.C. Anderson, R.J. Spiro, & W.E. Montague (Eds.), *Schooling and the acquisition of knowledge.* Hillsdale, NJ: Lawrence Erlbaum Associates, Inc.

Rumiati, R.I., Humphreys, G.W., Riddoch, M.J., & Bateman, A. (1994). Visual object agnosia without prosopagnosia or alexia: Evidence for hierarchical theories of visual recognition. *Visual Cognition, 1,* 181–225.

Rundus, D., & Atkinson, R.C. (1970).Rehearsal processes in free recall, a procedure for direct observation. *Journal of Verbal Learning and Verbal Behavior, 9,* 99–105.

Runeson, S., & Frykholm, G. (1983). Kinematic specifications of dynamics as an informational basis for person-and-action perception: Expectation, gender recognition, and deceptive intention. *Journal of Experimental Psychology: General, 112,* 585–615.

Rusak, B. (1977). Involvement of the primary optic tracts in mediation of light efferents on hamster circadian rhythms. *Journal of Comparative Physiology, 118,* 165–172.

Rusak, B., Robertson, H.A., Wisden, W., & Hunt, S.P. (1990). Light pulses that shift rhythms induce gene expression in the suprachiasmatic nucleus. *Science, 248,* 1237–1240.

Rusbult, C. (1983). A longitudinal test of the investment model: The development (and deterioration) of satisfaction and commitment in heterosexual involvements. *Journal of Personality and Social Psychology, 45,* 101–117.

Rusbult, C.E., & Martz, J.M. (1995). Remaining in an abusive relationship: An investment model analysis of nonvoluntary dependence. *Personality and Social Psychology Bulletin, 21,* 558–571.

Rusbult, C.E., Martz, J.M., & Agnew, C.R. (1998). The investment model scale: Measuring commitment level, satisfaction level, quality of alternatives, and investment size. *Personal Relationships, 5,* 357–391.

Rusbult, C.E., van Lange, P.A.M., Wildschut, T., Yovetich, N.A., & Verette, J. (2000). Perceived superiority in close relationships: Why it exists and persists. *Journal of Personality and Social Psychology, 79,* 521–545.

Rushton, J.P. (1975). Generosity in children: Immediate and long-term effects of modelling, preaching, and moral judgement. *Journal of Personality and Social Psychology, 31,* 459–466.

Russek, M. (1971). Hepatic receptors and the neurophysiological mechanisms controlling feeding behaviour. In S. Ehrenpreis (Ed.), *Neurosciences Research, Vol. 4.* New York: Academic Press.

Russell, G.W., & Goldstein, J.H. (1995).Personality differences between Dutch football fans and non-fans. *Social Behavior and Personality, 23,* 199–204.

Russell, J.A., & Carroll, J.M. (1999). On the bipolarity of positive and negative affect. *Psychological Bulletin, 125,* 3–30.

Russell, J.A., & Feldman Barrett, L. (1999). Core affect, prototypical emotional episodes, and other things called *emotion*: Dissecting the elephant. *Journal of Personality and Social Psychology, 76,* 805–819.

Russo, R., Nichelli, P., Gibertoni, M., & Cornia, C. (1995). Developmental trends in implicit and explicit memory: A picture completion study. *Journal of Experimental Child Psychology, 59,* 566–578.

Rutter, M. (1981). *Maternal deprivation re-assessed* (2nd ed.). Harmondsworth, UK: Penguin.

Rutter, M., and the English and Romanian Adoptees (ERA) Team. (1998). Developmental catch-up and deficit following adoption after severe global early privation. *Journal of Child Psychology and Psychiatry, 39,* 465–476.

Ryan, J.D., Althoff, R.R., Whitlow, S., & Cohen, N.J. (2000). Amnesia is a deficit in relational memory. *Psychological Science, 11,* 454–461.

Rymer, R. (1993). *Genie: Escape from a silent childhood.* London: Michael Joseph.

Sabey, B.E., & Codling, P.J. (1975). Alcohol and road accidents in Great Britain. In S. Israelstam & S. Lambert (Eds.), *Alcohol, drugs and traffic safety.* Ontario: Liquor Control Board.

Sacco, W.P., & Beck, A.T. (1985). Cognitive therapy for depression. In E.E. Beckham & W.R. Leber (Eds.), *Handbook of depression: Treatment, assessment and research.* Homewood, IL: Dorsey Press.

Saffran, E.M., Marin, O.S.M., & Yeni-Komshian, G.H. (1976). An analysis of speech perception in word deafness. *Brain and Language, 3,* 209–228.

Saffran, E.M., Schwartz, M.F., & Marin, O.S.M. (1980a). Evidence from aphasia: Isolating the components of a production model. In B. Butterworth (Ed.), *Language production, Vol. 1.* London: Academic Press.

Saffran, E.M., Schwartz, M.F., & Marin, O.S.M. (1980b). The word order problem in agrammatism: II. Production. *Brain and Language, 10,* 249–262.

Saffran, J.R., Aslin, R.N., & Newport, E.L. (1996a). Statistical learning by 8-month-old infants. *Science, 274,* 1926–1928.

Saffran, J.R., Newport, E.L., & Aslin, R.N. (1996b). Word segmentation: The role of distributional cues. *Journal of Memory and Language, 35,* 606–621.

Sagi, A., & Lewkowicz, K.S. (1987). A cross-cultural evaluation of attachment research. In L.W.C. Tavecchio & M.H. van IJzendoorn (Eds.), *Attachment in social networks: Contributions to the Bowlby–Ainsworth attachment theory.* Amsterdam: North-Holland.

Sagi, A., van IJzendoorn, M.H., & Koren-Karie, N. (1991). Primary appraisal of the Strange Situation: A cross-cultural analysis of the pre-separation episodes. *Developmental Psychology, 27,* 587–596.

Sagotsky, G., Wood-Schneider, M., & Konop, M. (1981). Learning to co-operate: Effects of modelling and direct instructions. *Child Development, 52,* 1037–1042.

Salkovskis, P.M. (1996). The cognitive approach to anxiety: Threat beliefs, safety-seeking behaviour, and the special case of health anxiety and obsessions. In P.M. Salkovskis (Ed.), *Frontiers of cognitive therapy.* New York: Guilford.

Salkovskis, P.M., Clark, D.M., & Gelder, M.G. (1996). Cognition-behaviour links in the persistence of panic. *Behavioural Research Therapy, 34,* 453–458.

Salkovskis, P.M., Clark, D.M., Hackmann, A., Wells, A., & Gelder, M.G. (1999). An experimental investigation of the role of safety-seeking behaviours in the maintenance of panic disorder with agoraphobia. *Behaviour Research and Therapy, 37,* 559–574.

Salomon, G., & Globerson, T. (1989). When groups do not function the way they ought to. *International Journal of Educational Research, 13,* 89–99.

Salovey, P., & Mayer, J.D. (1990). Emotional intelligence. *Imagination, Cognition and Personality, 9,* 185–211.

Sameroff, A.J., Seifer, R., Baldwin, A., & Baldwin, C. (1993). Stability of intelligence from preschool to adolescence: The influence of social and family risk factors. *Child Development, 64,* 80–97.

Sameroff, A.J., Seifer, R., Barocas, R., Zax, M., & Greenspan, S. (1987). Intelligence quotient scores of 4-year-old children: Social-environmental risk factors. *Paediatrics, 79,* 343–350.

Samson, H.H., Hodge, C.W., Tolliver, G.A., & Haraguchi, M. (1993). Effect of dopamine agonists and antagonists on ethanol-reinforced behavior: The involvement of the nucleus accumbens. *Brain Research Bulletin, 30,* 133–141.

Samuel, A.G. (1981). Phonemic restoration: Insights from a new methodology. *Journal of Experimental Psychology: General, 110,* 474–494.

Samuel, A.G. (1990). Using perceptual–restoration effects to explore the architecture of perception. In G.T.M. Altmann (Ed.), *Cognitive models of speech processing.* Cambridge, MA: MIT Press.

Samuel, A.G. (1997). Lexical activation produces potent phonemic percepts. *Cognitive Psychology, 32,* 97–127.

Sanders, G.S., & Baron, R.S. (1977). Is social comparison irrelevant for producing choice shifts? *Journal of Experimental Social Psychology, 13,* 303–314.

Sanocki, T., Bowyer, K.W., Heath, M.D., & Sarkar, S. (1998). Are edges sufficient for object recognition? *Journal of Experimental Psychology: Human Perception and Performance, 24,* 340–349.

Santrock, J.W. (1975). Moral structure: The interrelations of moral behaviour, moral judgement, and moral affect. *Journal of Genetic Psychology, 127,* 201–213.

Sapolsky, R.M. (1992). Neuroendocrinology of the stress-response. In J.B. Becker, S.M. Breedlove, & D. Crews (Eds.), *Behavioral endocrinology.* Cambridge, MA: MIT Press.

Sarason, I.G., Smith, R.E., & Diener, E. (1975). Personality research: Components of variance attributable to the person and the situation. *Journal of Personality and Social Psychology, 32,* 199–204.

Sarbin, T.R., & Slayle, R.W. (1972). Hypnosis and psychophysiological outcomes. In E. Fromm & R.E. Shor (Eds.), *Hypnosis: Research, developments and perspectives.* Chicago: Aldine–Atherton.

Sartorius, N., Jablensky, A., Gulbinat, W., & Ernberg, G. (1983). *Depressive disorders in different cultures.* Geneva: World Health Organisation.

Satinoff, E. (1978). Neural organization and evolution of thermal regulation in mammals. *Science, 201,* 16–22.

Saudino, K.J., Pedersen, N.L., Lichtenstein, P., McClearn, G.E., & Plomin, R. (1997). Can personality explain genetic influences on life events? *Journal of Personality and Social Psychology, 72,* 196–206.

Savage-Rumbaugh, E.S., McDonald, K., Sevcik, R.A., Hopkins, W.D., & Rupert, E. (1986). Spontaneous symbol acquisition and communicative use by pygmy chimpanzees (*Pan paniscus*). *Journal of Experimental Psychology: General, 115,* 211–235.

Savage-Rumbaugh, E.S., Murphy, J., Sevcik, R.A., Brakke, K.E., Williams, S.L., & Rumbaugh, D.M. (1993). Language comprehension in ape and child. *Monographs of the Society for Research in Child Development, 58* (Whole Nos. 3–4).

Savelsbergh, G.J.P., Pijpers, J.R., & van Santvoord, A.A.M. (1993). The visual guidance of catching. *Experimental Brain Research, 93,* 148–156.

Saville, P., & Blinkhorn, S. (1981). Reliability, homogeneity and the construct validity of Cattell's 16PF. *Personality and Individual Differences, 2,* 325–333.

Sawatari, A., & Callaway, E.M. (1996). Convergence of magno- and parvocellular pathways in layer 4B of macaque primary visual cortex. *Nature, 380,* 442–446.

Saxton, M. (1997). The contrast theory of negative input. *Journal of Child Language, 24,* 139–161.

Sayette, M.A. (1993). An appraisal–disruption model of alcohol's effect on stress responses in social drinkers. *Psychological Bulletin, 114,* 459–476.

Scarr, S. (1997). Why child care has little impact on most children's development. *Current Directions in Psychological Science, 6,* 143–148.

Scarr, S., & Weinberg, R.A. (1983). The Minnesota adoption studies: Genetic differences and malleability. *Child Development, 54,* 260–267.

Schachter, S. (1959). The psychology of affiliation: *Experimental studies of the sources of gregariousness*. Stanford, CA: Stanford University Press.

Schachter, S., & Singer, J.E. (1962). Cognitive, social, and physiological determinants of an emotional state. *Psychological Review, 69*, 379–399.

Schachter, S., & Wheeler, L. (1962). Epinephrine, chlorpromazine and amusement. *Journal of Abnormal and Social Psychology, 65*, 121–128.

Schacter, D.L. (1987). Implicit memory: History and current status. *Journal of Experimental Psychology: Learning, Memory, and Cognition, 13*, 501–518.

Schacter, D.L., Savage, C.R., Alpert, N.M., Rauch, S.L., & Albert, M.S. (1996). The role of hippocampus and frontal cortex in age-related memory changes: A PET study. *Neuroreport, 7*, 1165–1169.

Schacter, D.L., Wagner, A.D., & Buckner, R.L. (2000). Memory systems of 1999. In E. Tulving & F.I.M. Craik (Eds.) *Handbook of memory*. New York: Oxford University Press.

Schaefer, C., Coyne, J.C., & Lazarus, R.S. (1981). The health-related functions of social support. *Journal of Behavioral Medicine, 4*, 381–406.

Schaffer, H.R. (1996). *Social development*. Oxford, UK: Blackwell.

Schaffer, H.R., & Emerson, P.E. (1964). The development of social attachments in infancy. *Monographs of the Society for Research on Child Development, 29*.

Schaie, K.W. (1996). *Intellectual development in adulthood: The Seattle Longitudinal Study*. Cambridge, UK: Cambridge University Press.

Schank, R.C., & Abelson, R.P. (1977). *Scripts, plans, goals and understanding*. Hillsdale, NJ: Lawrence Erlbaum Associates, Inc.

Scheerer, M. (1963). Problem-solving. *Scientific American, 208*, 118–128.

Scheff, T.J. (1966). *Being mentally ill: A sociological theory*. Chicago: Aldine.

Scheper-Hughes, N. (1992). *Death without weeping: The violence of everyday life in Brazil*. Berkeley, CA: University of California Press.

Schermerhorn, J.R., Hunt, J.G., & Osborn, R.N. (2000). *Organizational behaviour* (7th ed.). New York: Wiley.

Schieffelin, B.B. (1990). *The give and take of everyday life: Language socialisation of Kaluli children*. Cambridge, UK: Cambridge University Press.

Schieffelin, B.B. (1990). *The give and take of everyday life: Language socialisation of Kaluli children*. Cambridge, UK: Cambridge University Press.

Schiff, B.B., & Lamon, M. (1994). Inducing emotion by unilateral contraction of face muscles. *Cortex, 30*, 247–254.

Schiffman, H.R. (1967). Size estimations of familiar objects under informative and reduced conditions of viewing. *American Journal of Psychology, 80*, 229–235.

Schlegel, A., & Barry, H. (1986). The cultural consequences of female contribution to subsistence. *American Anthropologist, 88*, 142–150.

Schlenker, B.R., Dlugolecki, D.W., & Doherty, K. (1994). The impact of self-presentations on self-appraisals and behaviour: The roles of commitment and biased scanning. *Personality and Social Psychology Bulletin, 20*, 20–33.

Schliefer, S.J., Keller, S.E., Camerino, M., Thornton, J.C., & Stein, M. (1983). Suppression of lymphocyte stimulation following bereavement. *Journal of the American Medical Association, 250*, 374–377.

Schmidt, R.A., & Lee, T.D. (1999). *Motor control and learning—a behavioural emphasis* (3rd ed.). Champaign, IL: Human Kinetics.

Schmitt, B.H., Gilovich, T., Goore, N., & Joseph, L. (1986). Mere presence and social facilitation: One more time. *Journal of Experimental Social Psychology, 22*, 242–248.

Schneider, W. (1986). The role of conceptual knowledge and metamemory in the development of organisational processes in memory. *Journal of Experimental Child Psychology, 42*, 218–236.

Schneider, W., Gruber, H., Gold, A., & Opwis, K. (1993). Chess expertise and memory for chess positions in children and adults. *Journal of Experimental Child Psychology, 56*, 328–349.

Schneider, W., & Pressley, M. (1989). *Memory development between two and twenty*. New York: Springer.

Schneider, W., & Pressley, M. (1997). *Memory development between two and twenty* (2nd ed.). New York: Springer.

Schneider, W., & Shiffrin, R.M. (1977). Controlled and automatic human information processing: I. Detection, search and attention. *Psychological Review, 84*, 1–66.

Schooler, J.W., Ohlsson, S., & Brooks, K. (1993). Thoughts beyond words: When language overshadows insight. *Journal of Experimental Psychology: General, 122*, 166–183.

Schriesheim, C.A., Tepper, B.J., & Tetrault, L.A. (1994). Least preferred co-worker score, situational control, and leadership effectiveness: A meta-analysis of contingency model performance predictions. *Journal of Applied Psychology, 79*, 561–573.

Schumacher, E.H., Seymour, T.L., Glass, J.M., Fencsik, D.E., Lauber, E.J., Kieras, D.E., & Meyer, D.E. (2001). Virtually perfect sharing in dual-task performance: Uncorking the central cognitive bottleneck. *Psychological Science, 12*, 101–108.

Schwartz, M.F., Saffran, E.M., & Marin, O.S.M. (1980). Fractioning the reading process in dementia: Evidence for word-specific print-to-sound associations. In M. Coltheart, K.E. Patterson, & J.C. Marshall (Eds.), *Deep dyslexia*. London: Routledge & Kegan Paul.

Schwartz, S.H. (1977).Normative influences on altruism. In L. Berkowitz (Ed.), *Advances in experimental social psychology, Vol. 10*. New York: Academic Press.

Schweinhart, L.J., & Weikart, D.P. (1985).Evidence that good early childhood programs work. *Phi Delta Kappa, 66*, 545–551.

Sclafini, A., Springer, D., & Kluge, L. (1976). Effects of quinine adulteration on the food intake and body weight of obese and non-obese hypothalamic hyperphagic rats. *Physiology and Behavior, 16*, 631–640.

Scott, S.K., Young, A.W., Calder, A.J., Hellawell, D.J., Aggleton, J.P., & Johnson, M. (1997). Impaired auditory recognition of fear and anger following bilateral amygdala lesions. *Nature, 385*, 254–257.

Searcy, J.H., & Bartlett, J.C. (1996). Inversion and processing of component and spatial-relational information in faces. *Journal of Experimental Psychology: Human Perception and Performance, 22*, 904–915.

Searle, L.V. (1949). The organisation of hereditary maze-brightness and maze-dullness. *Genetic Psychology Monographs, 39*, 279–325.

Seashore, S.E. (1954). *Group cohesiveness in the industrial work group*. Ann Arbor, MI: Institute for Social Research, University of Michigan.

Segal, S.J., & Fusella, V. (1970). Influence of imaged pictures and sounds on detection of visual and auditory signals. *Journal of Experimental Psychology, 83*, 458–464.

Segal, Z.V., Shaw, B.F., Vella, D.D., & Kratz, R. (1992). Cognitive and life stress predictors of relapse in remitted unipolar depressed patients: Test of the congruency hypothesis. *Journal of Abnormal Psychology, 101*, 26–36.

Segall, M.H., Campbell, D.T., & Herskovits, M.J. (1963). Cultural differences in the perception of geometrical illusions. *Science, 139*, 769–771.

Seidenberg, M.S., & Petitto, L.A. (1987). Communication, symbolic communication, and language: Comment on Savage-Rumbaugh, McDonald, Sevcik, Hopkis, and Rupert (1986). *Journal of Experimental Psychology: General, 116*, 279–287.

Seidman, L.J. (1983). Schizophrenia and brain dysfunction: An integration of recent neurodiagnostic findings. *Psychological Bulletin, 94*, 195–238.

Seifer, R., Schiller, M., Sameroff, A.J., Resnick, S., & Riordan, K. (1996). Attachment, maternal sensitivity, and infant temperament during the first year of life. *Developmental Psychology, 32*, 12–25.

Sekuler, R., & Blake, R. (2002). *Perception* (4th ed.). New York: McGraw-Hill.

Selfe, L. (1983). *Normal and anomalous representational drawing ability in children*. London: Academic Press.

Seligman, M.E. (1995). The effectiveness of psychotherapy: The Consumer Reports study. *American Psychology, 50*, 965–974.

Seligman, M.E.P. (1971). Phobias and preparedness. *Behavior Therapy, 2*, 307–320.

Seligman, M.E.P. (1975). *Helplessness: On depression, development and death*. San Francisco: W.H. Freeman.

Seligman, M.E.P., Abramson, L.Y., Semmel, A., & von Baeyer, C. (1979). Depressive attributional style. *Journal of Abnormal Psychology, 88*, 242–247.

Sellen, A.J., & Norman, D.A. (1992). The psychology of slips. In B.J. Baars (Ed.), *Experimental slips and human error: Exploring the architecture of volition*. New York: Plenum Press.

Selman, R.L. (1980). *The growth of interpersonal understanding*. New York: Academic Press.

Selye, H. (1950). *Stress*. Montreal, Canada: Acta.

Selye, H. (1956). *The stress of life*. New York: McGraw-Hill.

Semin, G.R., & Glendon, A.I. (1973). Polarisation and the established group. *British Journal of Social and Clinical Psychology, 12*, 113–121.

Serbin, L.A., Powlishta, K.K., & Gulko, J. (1993). The development of sex-typing in middle childhood. *Monographs of Society for Research in Child Development, 58*, 1–74.

Sereno, S.C., Rayner, K., & Posner M.I. (1998). Establishing a time-line of word recognition: Evidence from eye movements and event-related potentials. *Neuroreport, 9*, 2195–2200.

Sergent, J., & Poncet, M. (1990). From covert to overt recognition of faces in a prosopagnosic patient. *Brain, 113*, 989–1004.

Serpell, R. (1982). Measures of perception, skills, and intelligence. In W.W. Hartup (Ed.), *Review of child development research*. Chicago: University of Chicago Press.

Servan-Schreiber, D., & Perlstein, W.M. (1998). Selective limbic activation and its relevance to emotional disorders. *Cognition and Emotion, 12*, 331–352.

Shadish, W.R., Matt, G.E., Navarro, A.M., & Phillips, G. (2000). The effects of psychological therapies under clinically representative conditions: A meta-analysis. *Psychological Bulletin, 126*, 512–529.

Shaffer, D.R. (1993). *Developmental psychology: Childhood and adolescence* (3rd ed.). Pacific Grove, CA: Brooks/Cole.

Shaffer, D.R. (2000). *Social and personality development* (4th ed.). Belmont, CA: Wadsworth.

Shaffer, L.H. (1975). Multiple attention in continuous verbal tasks. In P.M.A. Rabbitt & S. Dornic (Eds.), *Attention and performance V: Information processing*. London: Academic Press.

Shafir, E., & LeBoeuf, R.A. (2002). Rationality. *Annual Review of Psychology, 53*, 491–517.

Shafir, E., Simonson, I., & Tversky, A. (1993). Reason-based choice. *Cognition, 49*, 11–36.

Shah, P., & Miyake, A. (1996). The separability of working memory resources for spatial thinking and language processing: An individual difference approach. *Journal of Experimental Psychology: General, 125*, 4–27.

Shallice, T., & Burgess, P. (1993). Supervisory control of action and thought selection. In A. Baddeley & L. Weiskrantz (Eds.), *Attention: Selection, awareness and control*. Oxford, UK: Clarendon Press.

Shallice, T., & Burgess, P. (1996). The domain of supervisory processes and temporal organisation of behaviour. *Philosophical Transactions of the Royal Society of London B, 351*, 1405–1412.

Shallice, T., & Warrington, E.K. (1970). Independent functioning of verbal memory stores: A neuropsychological study. *Quarterly Journal of Experimental Psychology, 22*, 261–273.

Shallice, T., & Warrington, E.K. (1974). The dissociation between long-term retention of meaningful sounds and verbal material. *Neuropsychologia, 12*, 553–555.

Shafir, E., & LeBoeuf, R.A. (2002). Rationality. *Annual Review of Psychology, 53*, 491–517.

Shafir, E., Simonson, I., & Tversky, A. (1993). Reason-based choice. *Cognition, 49*, 11–36.

Shanks, D.R., & St. John, M.F. (1994). Characteristics of dissociable human learning systems. *Behavioral and Brain Sciences, 17*, 367–394.

Shapiro, C.M., Bortz, R., Mitchell, D., Bartel, P., & Jooste, P. (1981). Slow-wave sleep: A recovery period after exercise. *Science, 214*, 1253–1254.

Shatz, M., & Gelman, R. (1973). The development of communication skills: Modifications in the speech of young children as a function of the listener. *Monographs of the Society for Research in Child Development, 38*.

Shaver, P., Hazan, C., & Bradshaw, D. (1988). Love as attachment: The integration of three behavioural systems. In R.J. Sternberg & M. Barnes (Eds.), *The psychology of love*. New Haven, CT: Yale University Press.

Shavitt, S. (1989). Operationising functional theories of attitude. In A.R. Pratkanis, S.J. Breckler, & A.G. Greenwald (Eds.), *Attitude structure and function*. Hillsdale, NJ: Lawrence Erlbaum Associates, Inc.

Shaw, G. (1997, October 12). In Norton, C. Early music lessons boost brain power. *Sunday Times*.

Shea, C.H., Wulf, G., Whitacre, C.A., & Park, J.-H. (2001). Surfing the implicit wave. *Quarterly Journal of Experimental Psychology, 54A*, 841–862.

Shea, J.D.C. (1981). Changes in interpersonal distances and categories of play behaviour in the early weeks of preschool. *Developmental Psychology, 17*, 417–425.

Shekelle, R.B., Raynor, W.J., Jr., Ostfeld, A.M., Garron, D.C., Bieliauskas, L.A., Liu, S.C., Maliza, C., & Paul, O. (1981). Psychological depression and 17-year risk of death from cancer. *Psychosomatic Medicine, 43*, 117–125.

Sheridan, C.L., & King, K.G. (1972). Obedience to authority with an authentic victim. In *Proceedings of the 80th annual convention of the American Psychological Association, 7*, 165–166.

Sherif, M. (1936). *The psychology of social norms*. New York: Harper & Row.

Sherif, M. (1966). *Group conflict and co-operation: Their social psychology*. London: Routledge & Kegan Paul.

Sherif, M., Harvey, O.J., White, B.J., Hood, W.R., & Sherif, C.W. (1961). *Intergroup conflict and co-operation: The robber's cave experiment*. Norman, OK: University of Oklahoma.

Sherif, M., & Sherif, C.W. (1964). *Reference groups: Exploration into conformity and deviation of adolescents*. New York: Harper & Row.

Sherwin, B.B. (1985). Changes in sexual behaviour as a function of plasma sex steroid levels in post-menopausal women. *Maturitas, 7*, 225–233.

Sherwin, B.B. (1988). A comparative analysis of the role of androgen in human male and female sexual behaviour: Behavioural specificity, critical thresholds, and sensitivity. *Psychobiology, 16*, 416–425.

Sherwin, B.B., Gelfand, M.M., & Brender, W. (1985). Androgen enhances sexual motivation in females: A prospective, crossover study of sex steroid administration in the surgical menopause. *Psychosomatic Medicine, 47*, 339–351.

Shields, J. (1962). *Monozygotic twins*. Oxford, UK: Oxford University Press.

Shiffrin, R.M., & Schneider, W. (1977). Controlled and automatic human information processing: II. Perceptual learning, automatic attending, and a general theory. *Psychological Review, 84*, 127–190.

Shifren, J.L., Braunstein, G.D., Simon, J.A., Casson, P.R., Buster, J.E., Redmond, G.P., Burki, R.E., Ginsburg, E.S., Rosen, R.C., Leiblum, S.R., Caramelli, K.E., Mazer, N.A., Jones, K.P., & Daugherty, C.A. (2000). Transdermal testosterone treatment in women with impaired sexual function after oophorectomy. *New England Journal of Medicine, 343*, 682–688.

Shipp, S., de Jong, B.M., Zihl, J., Frackowiak, R.S.J., & Zeki, S. (1994). The brain activity related to residual activity in a patient with bilateral lesions of V5. *Brain, 117*, 1023–1038.

Shochat, T., Luboshitzky, R., & Lavie, P. (1997). Nocturnal melatonin onset is phase locked to the primary sleep gate. *American Journal of Physiology, 273*, R364–R370.

Shotland, R.L., & Straw, M.K. (1976). Bystander response to an assault: When a man attacks a woman. *Journal of Personality and Social Psychology, 34*, 990–999.

Shrauger, J.S. (1975). Responses to evaluation as a function of initial self-perceptions. *Psychological Bulletin, 82,* 581–596.

Shweder, R.A. (1990). Cultural psychology: What is it? In J.W. Stigler, R.A. Shweder, & G. Herdt (Eds.), *Cultural psychology.* Cambridge, UK: Cambridge University Press.

Shweder, R.A. (1994). "You're not sick, you're just in love": Emotion as an interpretative system. In P. Ekman & R.J. Davidson (Eds.), *The nature of emotion: Fundamental questions.* Oxford, UK: Oxford University Press.

Shweder, R.A., Mahapatra, M., & Miller, J.G. (1990). Culture and moral development. In J. Stigler, R.A. Shweder, & G. Herdt (Eds.), *Cultural psychology: Essays in comparative human development* (pp. 130–204). New York: Cambridge University Press.

Siegel, J.M. (1994). Brainsteam mechanisms generating REM sleep. In M.H. Kryger, T. Roth, & W.C. Dement (Eds.), *Principles and practice of sleep medicine* (2nd ed.). Philadelphia: Saunders.

Siegler, R.S. (1976). Three aspects of cognitive development. *Cognitive Psychology, 8,* 481–520.

Siegler, R.S. (1998). *Children's thinking* (3rd ed.). Upper Saddle River, NJ: Prentice Hall.

Siegler, R.S., & Chen, Z. (1998). Developmental differences in rule learning: A microgenetic analysis. *Cognitive Psychology, 36,* 273–310.

Siegler, R.S., & Chen, Z. (2002). Development of rules and strategies: Balancing the old and the new. *Journal of Child Psychology, 81,* 446–457.

Siegler, R.S., & Jenkins, E.A. (1989). *How children discover new strategies.* Hillsdale, NJ: Lawrence Erlbaum Associates, Inc.

Siegler, R.S., & Stern, E. (1998). A microgenetic analysis of conscious and unconscious strategy discoveries. *Journal of Experimental Psychology: General, 127,* 377–397.

Siegler, R.S., & Svetina, M. (2002). A microgenetic/cross-sectional study of matrix completion: Comparing short-term and long-term change. *Child Development, 73,* 793–809.

Silverstein, C. (1972). *Behaviour modification and the gay community.* Paper presented at the annual convention of the Association for Advancement of Behaviour Therapy, New York.

Simion, F., Valenza, E., Macchi Cassia, V., Turati, C., & Umiltà, C. (2002). Newborns' preference for up–down asymmetrical configurations. *Developmental Science, 5,* 427–434.

Simon, H.A. (1955). A behavioural model of rational choice. *Quarterly Journal of Economics, 69,* 99–118.

Simmons, R.G., Burgeson, R., & Careton-Ford, S. (1987). The impact of cumulative change in early adolescence. *Child Development, 58,* 1220–1234.

Simmons, W.W. (2001). *When it comes to choosing a boss, Americans still prefer me.* Retrieved from http://www.gallup.com/poll/releases/pr010111.asp

Simon, H.A. (1974). How big is a chunk? *Science, 183,* 482–488.

Simon, H.A. (1990). Invariants of human behaviour. *Annual Review of Psychology, 41,* 1–19.

Simon, H.A., & Reed, S.K. (1976). Modelling strategy shifts on a problem solving task. *Cognitive Psychology, 8,* 86–97.

Simonson, I, & Staw, B.M. (1992). Deescalation strategies: A comparison of techniques for reducing commitment to losing courses of action. *Journal of Applied Psychology, 77,* 419–426.

Sinclair, L., & Kunda, Z. (1999). Reactions to a black professional: Motivated inhibition and activation of conflicting stereotypes. *Journal of Personality and Social Psychology, 77,* 885–904.

Sing, L. (1994). The Diagnostic Interview Schedule and anorexia nervosa in Hong Kong. *Archives of General Psychiatry, 51,* 251–252.

Singer, J.F., & Kolligan, J.J. (1987). Developments in the study of private experience. *Annual Review of Psychology, 38,* 533–574.

Singer, M. (1994). Discourse inference processes. In M.A. Gernsbacher (Ed.), *Handbook of psycholinguistics.* San Diego: Academic Press.

Singh, R., & Ho, S.Y. (2000). Attitudes and interaction: A new test of the attraction, repulsion, and similarity–dissimilarity asymmetry hypotheses. *British Journal of Social Psychology, 39,* 197–211.

Singh, R., Bohra, K.A., & Dalal, A.K. (1979). Favourableness of leadership situations studies with information integration theory. *European Journal of Social Psychology, 9,* 253–264.

Siqueland, E.R., & DeLucia, C.A. (1969). Visual reinforcement of non-nutritive sucking in human infants. *Science, 165,* 1144–1146.

Skinner, B.F. (1938). *The behaviour of organisms.* New York: Appleton-Century-Crofts.

Skinner, B.F. (1948). *Walden two.* New York: Macmillan.

Skinner, B.F. (1953). *Science and human behavior.* New York: Macmillan.

Skinner, B.F. (1957). *Verbal behavior.* New York: Appleton-Century-Crofts.

Skre, I., Onstad, S., Torgersen, S., Lygren, S., & Kringlen, E. (1993). A twin study of DSM-III-R anxiety disorders. *Acta Psychiatrica Scandinavica, 88,* 85–92.

Skuse, D. (1984). Extreme deprivation in early childhood: II. Theoretical issues and a comparative review. *Journal of Child Psychology and Psychiatry, 25,* 543–572.

Slaby, R.G., & Frey, K.S. (1975). Development of gender constancy and selective attention to same-sex models. *Child Development, 46,* 849–856.

Slamecka, N.J. (1966). Differentiation versus unlearning of verbal associations. *Journal of Experimental Psychology, 71,* 822–828.

Slater, A. (1998). The competent infant: Innate organisation and early learning in infant visual perception. In A. Slater (Ed.), *Perceptual development: Visual, auditory and speech perception in infancy.* Hove, UK: Psychology Press.

Slater, A., & Morison, V. (1985). Shape constancy and slant perception at birth. *Perception, 14,* 337–344.

Slater, A., Brown, E., & Badenoch, M. (1997). Intermodal perception at birth: Newborn infants' memory for arbitrary auditory–visual pairings. *Early Development and Parenting, 6,* 99–104.

Slater, A., Mattock, A., & Brown, E. (1990). Newborn infants' responses to retinal and real size. *Journal of Experimental Child Psychology, 49,* 314–322.

Slater, A.M. (1990). Perceptual development. In M.W. Eysenck (Ed.), *The Blackwell dictionary of cognitive psychology.* Oxford, UK: Blackwell.

Slavin, R.E. (1983). When does cooperative learning increase student achievement? *Psychological Bulletin, 94,* 429–445.

Sloane, R.B., Staples, F.R., Cristol, A.H., Yorkston, N.J., & Whipple, K. (1975). *Psychotherapy versus behaviour therapy.* Cambridge, MA: Harvard University Press.

Sloboda, J.A., Davidson, J.W., Howe, M.J.A., & Moore, D.G. (1996). The role of practice in the development of performing musicians. *British Journal of Psychology, 87,* 287–309.

Sloman, A. (1997). *What sorts of machine can love? Architectural requirements for human-like agents both natural and artificial.* Retrieved from http://www.sbc.org.uk/literate.htm

Sloman, A., & Logan, B. (1998, April). *Architectures for human-like agents.* Paper presented at the European conference on Cognitive Modelling, Nottingham, UK.

Slovic, P., & Fischhoff, B. (1977). On the psychology of experimental surprises. *Journal of Experimental Psychology: Human Perception and Performance, 3,* 544–551.

Smetana, J.G., & Adler, N.E. (1980). Fishbein's value X expectancy model: An examination of some assumptions. *Personality and Social Psychology Bulletin, 6,* 89–96.

Smith, C.A., & Lazarus, R.S. (1993). Appraisal components, core relational themes, and the emotions. *Cognition and Emotion, 7,* 233–269.

Smith, E.E., & Jonides, J. (1997). Working memory: A view from neuroimaging. *Cognitive Psychology, 33,* 5–42.

Smith, E.R., & Mackie, D.M. (2000). *Social psychology* (2nd ed.). Philadelphia, PA: Psychology Press.

Smith, J., & Campfield, L.A. (1993). Meal initiation occurs after experimental induction of transient declines in blood glucose. *American Journal of Physiology—Regulatory, Integrative and Comparative Physiology, 265,* 1423–1429.

Smith, K.A., Clifford, E.M., Hockney, R.A., & Clark, D.M. (1997). Effect of tryptophan depletion on mood in male and female volunteers: A pilot study. *Human Psychopharmacology, Clinical and Experimental, 12,* 111–117.

Smith, M. (2000). Conceptual structures in language production. In L. Wheeldon (Ed.), *Aspects of language production.* Hove, UK: Psychology Press.

Smith, M.L., & Glass, G.V. (1977). Meta-analysis of psychotherapy outcome measures. *American Psychologist, 32,* 752–760.

Smith, M.L., Glass, G.V., & Miller, T.I. (1980). *The benefits of psychotherapy.* Baltimore: John Hopkins Press.

Smith, P.B., & Bond, M.H. (1998). *Social psychology across cultures* (2nd ed.). New York: Harvester Wheatsheaf.

Smith, P.B., Misumi, J., Tayeb, M., Peterson, M., & Bond, M. (1989). On the generality of leadership style measures across cultures. *Journal of Occupational Psychology, 62,* 97–109.

Smith, P.B., & Schwartz, S.H. (1997). Values. In J.W. Berry, M.H. Segall, & C. Kagitcibasi (Eds.), *Handbook of cross-cultural psychology* (2nd ed., Vol. 3). Boston: Allyn & Bacon.

Smith, P.K. (1983). Human sociobiology. In J. Nicholson & B. Foss (Eds.), *Psychology survey, No. 4.* Leicester: British Psychological Society.

Smith, P.K., Cowie, H., & Blades, M. (1998). *Understanding children's development* (3rd ed.). Oxford, UK: Blackwell.

Smith, P.K., Cowie, H., & Blades, M. (2003). *Understanding children's development* (4th ed.). Oxford, UK: Blackwell.

Smith, S.S., O'Hara, B.F., Persico, A.M., Gorelick, D.A., Newlin, D.B., Vlahov, D., Solomon, L., Pickens, R., & Uhl, G.R. (1992). Genetic vulnerability to drug abuse. The D2 dopamine receptor Taq I B1 restriction fragment length polymorphism appears more frequently in polysubstance abusers. *Archives of General Psychiatry, 49,* 723–727.

Snarey, J.R. (1985). Cross-cultural universality of social-moral development: A critical review of Kohlbergian research. *Psychological Bulletin, 97,* 202–232.

Solms, M. (1997). *The neuropsychology of dreams.* Mahwah, NJ: Lawrence Erlbaum Associates, Inc.

Solms, M. (2000a). Dreaming and REM sleep are controlled by different brain mechanisms. *Behavioral and Brain Sciences, 23,* 843–850.

Solms, M. (2000b). Freudian dream theory today. *The Psychologist, 13,* 618–619.

Solomon, R.L., & Wynne, L.C. (1953). Traumatic avoidance learning: Acquisition in normal dogs. *Psychological Monographs, 67,* 1–19.

Solso, R.L. (1994). *Cognition and the visual arts.* Cambridge, MA: MIT Press

Sorrentino, R.M., & Field, N. (1986). Emergent leadership over time: The functional value of positive motivation. *Journal of Personality and Social Psychology, 50,* 1091–1099.

Spangler, G. (1990). Mother, child, and situational correlates of toddlers' social competence. *Infant Behavior and Development, 13,* 405–419.

Spanos, N.P. (1982). A social psychological approach to hypnotic behaviour. In G. Weary & H.L. Mirels (Eds.), *Integrations of clinical and social psychology.* New York: Oxford University Press.

Spanos, N.P. (1989). Experimental research on hypnotic analgesia. In N.P. Spanos & J.F. Cahves (Eds.), *Hypnosis: The cognitive-behavioural perspective.* Buffalo, NY: Prometheus.

Spanos, N.P., Perlini, A.H., Patrick, L., Bell, S., & Gwynn, M.I. (1990). The role of compliance in hypnotic and nonhypnotic analgesia. *Journal of Research in Personality, 24,* 433–453.

Spearman, C. (1923). *The nature of intelligence and the principles of cognition.* London: Macmillan.

Speareman, C. (1927). *The abilities of man.* New York: Macmillan.

Spector, P. (1982). Behavior in organizations as a function of employees' locus of control. *Psychological Bulletin, 91,* 482–497.

Spector, P.E. (1988). Development of a work locus of control scale. *Journal of Occupational Psychology, 61,* 335–340.

Spector, P.E. (2000). *Industrial and organizational psychology: Reasearch and practice* (2nd ed.). New York: John Wiley & Sons.

Spector, P.E. (2002). Employee control and occupational stress. *Current Directions in Psychological Science, 11,* 133–136.

Spector, P.E., Dwyer, D.J., & Jex, S.M. (1988). The relationship of job stressors to affective, health, and performance outcomes: A comparison of multiple data sources. *Journal of Applied Psychology, 73,* 11–19.

Speisman, J.C., Lazarus, R.S., Mordkoff, A., & Davison, L. (1964). Experimental reduction of stress based on ego-defence theory. *Journal of Abnormal and Social Psychology, 68,* 367–380.

Spelke, E.S., Breinlinger, K., Jacobson, K., & Phillips, A. (1993). Gestalt relations and object perception: A developmental study. *Vision Research, 22,* 531–544.

Spelke, E.S., Hirst, W.C., & Neisser, U. (1976). Skills of divided attention. *Cognition, 4,* 215–230.

Spence, S., Shapiro, D., & Zaidel, E. (1996). The role of the right hemisphere in the physiological and cognitive processing of emotional stimuli. *Psychophysiology, 33,* 112–122.

Sperling, G. (1960). The information available in brief visual presentations. *Psychological Monographs, 74* (Whole No. 498), 1–29.

Spielberger, C.D., Gorsuch, R., & Lushene, R. (1970). *The State–Trait Anxiety Inventory (STAI) Test Manual Form X.* Palo Alto, CA: Consulting Psychologists Press.

Spielberger, C.D., Gorsuch, R.L., Lushene, R., Vagg, P.R., & Jacobs, G.A. (1983). *Manual for the State–Trait Anxiety Inventory (Form Y).* Palo Alto, CA: Consulting Psychologists Press.

Spiers, H.J., Maguire, E.A., & Burgess, N. (2001). Hippocampal amnesia. *Neurocase, 7,* 357–382.

Spinoza, B. (1677). *On the improvement of the understanding, the ethics, correspondence* (R.H.M. Elwes, Trans.). New York: Dover Publications. (Original work published 1955)

Spitz, R.A. (1945). Hospitalism: An inquiry into the genesis of psychiatric conditions in early childhood. *Psychoanalytic Study of the Child, 1,* 113–117.

Spitzer, R.L., & Fleiss, J.L. (1974). A re-analysis of the reliability of psychiatric diagnosis. *British Journal of Psychiatry, 125,* 341–347.

Sporer, S.L., Penrod, S., Read, D., & Cutler, B. (1995). Choosing, confidence and accuracy: A meta-analysis of the confidence–accuracy relation in eyewitness identification studies. *Psychological Bulletin, 118,* 315–327.

Sprafkin, J.N., Liebert, R.M., & Poulos, R.W. (1975). Effects of a pro-social televised example on children's helping. *Journal of Experimental Child Psychology, 20,* 119–126.

Sprecher, S. (1989). The importance to males and females of physical attractiveness, earning potential and expressiveness in initial attraction. *Sex Roles, 21,* 591–607.

Sprecher, S. (1998). Insider's perspectives on reasons for attraction to a close other. *Social Psychology Quarterly, 61,* 287–300.

Stajkovic, A.D., & Luthans, F. (1998). Self-efficacy and work-related performance: A meta-analysis. *Psychological Bulletin, 124,* 240–261.

Stams, G.-J.J.M., Juffer, F., & van IJzendoorn, M.H. (2002). Maternal sensitivity, infant attachment, and temperament in early childhood predict adjustment in middle childhood: The case of adopted children and their biologically unrelated parents. *Developmental Psychology, 38,* 806–821.

Stangor, C., & McMillan, D. (1992). Memory for expectancy-congruent and expectancy-incongruent information: A review of the social and social developmental literatures. *Psychological Bulletin, 111,* 42–61.

Stanislaw, H., & Rice, F.J. (1988). Correlation between sexual desire and mentstrual cycle characteristics. *Archives of Sexual Behavior, 17,* 499–508.

Stanley, B.G., Kyrkouli, S.E., Lampert, S., & Leibowitz, S.F. (1986). Neuropeptide Y chronically injected into the hypothalamus: A powerful neurochemical inducer of hyperphagia and obesity. *Peptides, 7,* 1189–1192.

Stanovich, K.E., & West, R.F. (1998). Individual differences in framing and conjunction effects. *Thinking and Reasoning, 4,* 289–317.

Stanovich, K.E., & West, R.F. (2000). Individual differences in reasoning: Implications for the rationality debate? *Behavioral and Brain Sciences, 23,* 645–726.

Stasser, G., & Titus, W. (1985). Pooling of unshared information in group decision making: Biased information sampling during discussion. *Journal of Personality and Social Psychology, 48,* 1467–1478.

Steblay, N.M. (1987). Helping behaviour in rural and urban environments: A meta-analysis. *Psychological Bulletin, 102,* 346–356.

Steel, P., & Ones, D.S. (2002). Personality and happiness: A national-level analysis. *Journal of Personality and Social Psychology, 83,* 767–781.

Steele, C.M., & Josephs, R.A. (1990). Alcohol myopia: Its prized and dangerous effects. *American Psychologist, 45,* 921–933.

Stein, J.A., Newcomb, M.D., & Bentler, P.M. (1992). The effect of agency and communality on self-esteem: Gender differences in longitudinal data. *Sex Roles, 26,* 465–481.

Steinberg, M.D., & Dodge, K.A. (1983). Attributional bias in aggressive adolescent boys and girls. *Journal of Social and Clinical Psychology, 1,* 312–321.

Steinhausen, H.C. (1994).Anorexia and bulimia nervosa. In M. Rutter, E. Taylor, & L. Hersov (Eds.), *Child and adolescent psychiatry.* Oxford, UK: Blackwell.

Steinmetz, J.L., Lewinsohn, P.M., & Antonuccio, D.O. (1983). Prediction of individual outcome in a group intervention for depression. *Journal of Consulting and Clinical Psychology, 51,* 331–337.

Stemberger, J.P. (1982). The nature of segments in the lexicon: Evidence from speech errors. *Lingua, 56,* 235–259.

Stemberger, R.T., Turner, S.M., & Beidel, D.C. (1995). Social phobia: An analysis of possible developmental factors. *Journal of Abnormal Psychology, 104,* 526–531.

Stephan, F. (1992). Resetting of a circadian clock by food pulses. *Physiology and Behavior, 52,* 997–1008.

Stephan, F.K., & Nunez, A.A. (1977). Elimination of circadian rhythms in drinking, activity, sleep, and temperature by isolation of the suprachiasmatic nuclei. *Behavioral Biology, 20,* 1–61.

Stephan, W., Berscheid, E., & Walster, E. (1971). Sexual arousal and heterosexual perception. *Journal of Personality and Social Psychology, 20,* 93–101.

Stephan, W.G. (1987). The contact hypothesis in intergroup relations. In C. Hendrick (Ed.), *Review of personality and social psychology: Vol. 9. Group processes in intergroup relations.* Newbury Park, CA: Sage.

Stephan, W.G., & Stephan, C.W. (1984). The role of ignorance in intergroup relations. In N. Miller & M.B. Brewer (Eds.), *Groups in contact: The psychology of desegregation.* New York: Academic Press.

Stephens, T.W., Basinski, M., Bristow, P.K., Bue-Valleskey, J.M., Burgett, S.G., Craft, L., Hale, J., Hoffman, J., Hsiung, H.M., Kriauciunas, A., MacKellar, W., Rosteck, P.R., Jr., Schoner, B., Smith, D., Tinsley, F.C., Zhang, W.-Y., & Heiman, M. (1995). The role of neuropeptide Y in the antiobesity action of the *obese* gene product. *Nature, 377,* 530–532.

Steptoe, A. (1997). Stress management. In A. Baum, S. Newman, J. Weinman, R. West, & C. McManus (Eds.), *Cambridge handbook of psychology, health, and medicine.* Cambridge, UK: Cambridge University Press.

Steptoe, A., & Vogele, C. (1986). Are stress responses influenced by cognitive appraisal? An experimental comparison on coping strategies. *British Journal of Psychology, 77,* 243–255.

Steptoe, A., & Wardle, J. (1992). Cognitive predictions of health behaviour in contrasting regions of Europe. *British Journal of Clinical Psychology, 31,* 485–502.

Sterman, M.B., & Clemente, C.D. (1962). Forebrain inhibitory mechanisms: Sleep patterns induced by basal forebrain stimulation in the behaving cat. *Experimental Neurology, 6,* 103–117.

Stern, K., & McClintock, M.K. (1998). Regulation of ovulation by human pheromones. *Nature, 392,* 177–179.

Sternberg, R.J. (1985). *Beyond IQ: A triarchic theory of human intelligence.* Cambridge, UK: Cambridge University Press.

Sternberg, R.J. (1986). A triangular theory of love. *Psychological Review, 93,* 119–135.

Sternberg, R.J. (1994). Intelligence and cognitive styles. In A.M. Colman (Ed.), *Companion encyclopedia of psychology, Vol. 1.* London: Routledge.

Sternberg, R.J. (1995). *In search of the human mind.* Orlando, FL: Harcourt Brace College Publishers.

Sternberg, R.J. (1997). *Successful intelligence.* New York: Plenum.

Sternberg, R.J. (2003, April). The other three Rs: Part two, reasoning. *APA Monitor.*

Sternberg, R.J., & Ben-Zeev, T. (2001). *Complex cognition: The psychology of human thought.* Oxford, UK: Oxford University Press.

Sternberg, R.J., Conway, B.E., Ketron, J.L., & Bernstein, M. (1981). People's conceptions of intelligence. *Journal of Personality and Social Psychology, 41,* 37–55.

Sternberg, R.J., & Detterman, D.K. (1986). *What is intelligence? Contemporary viewpoints on its nature and definition.* Norwood, NJ: Ablex.

Sternberg, R.J., & Grajek, S. (1984). The nature of love. *Journal of Personality and Social Psychology, 47,* 312–329.

Sternberg, R.J., Grigorenko, E.L., Ngorosho, D., Tantufuye, E., Mbise, A., Nokes, C., Jukes, M., & Bundy, D.A. (2002). Assessing intellectual potential in rural Tanzanian school children. *Intelligence, 30,* 141–162.

Sternberg, R.J., & Kaufman, J.C. (1998). Human abilities. *Annual Review of Psychology, 49,* 479–502.

Sternberg, R.J., & Weil, E.M. (1980). An aptitude X strategy interaction in linear syllogistic reasoning. *Journal of Educational Psychology, 72,* 226–239.

Stevens, R. (1989). *Freud and psychoanalysis.* Milton Keynes: Open University Press.

Stevens, S., Hynan, M.T., & Allen, M. (2000). A meta-analysis of common factor and specific treatment effects across the outcome domains of the phase model of psychotherapy. *Clinical Psychology: Science and Practice, 7,* 273–290.

Stevenson, M.R., & Black, K.N. (1988). Paternal absence and sex-role development: A meta-analysis. *Child Development, 59,* 793–814.

Stewart, D.D., & Stasser, G. (1995). Expert role assignment and information sampling during collective recall and decision making. *Journal of Personality and Social Psychology, 69,* 619–628.

Stigler, J.W., Lee, S.Y., & Stevenson, H.W. (1987). Mathematics classrooms in Japan, Taiwan, and the United States. *Child Development, 60,* 521–538.

Stirling, J.D., & Hellewell, J.S.E. (1999). *Psychopathology.* London: Routledge.

Stogdill, R.M. (1974). *Handbook of leadership: A survey of theory and research.* New York: Free Press.

Stone, A.A., Reed, B.R., & Neale, J.M. (1987). Changes in daily life event frequency precede episodes of physical symptoms. *Journal of Human Stress, 13,* 70–74.

Storms, M.D. (1973). Videotape and the attribution process: Reversing actors' and observers' points of view. *Journal of Personality and Social Psychology, 27,* 165–175.

Strack, F., Martin, L.L., & Stepper, S. (1988). Inhibiting and facilitating conditions of facial expressions: A non-obtrusive test of the facial feedback hypothesis. *Journal of Personality and Social Psychology, 54,* 768–776.

Strassberg, Z., & Dodge, K.A. (1987). *Focus of social attention among children varying in peer status.* Paper presented at the annual meeting of the Association for the Advancement of Behaviour Therapy, Boston.

Straus, M.A. (1990). The Conflict Tactics Scales and its critics: An evaluation and new data on validity and reliability. In M.A. Straus & R.J. Gelles (Eds.), *Physical violence in American societies: Risk factors and adaptations to violence in 8,145 families.* New Brunswick, NJ: Transaction Publications.

Straus, M.A. (1993). Physical assault by wives: A major social problem. In R.J. Gelles & D.R. Loseke (Eds.), *Current controversies on family violence* (pp. 67–87). Newbury Park, CA: Sage.

Straus, M.A., Gelles, R.J., & Steinmetz, S.K. (1980). *Behind closed doors: Violence in the American family.* New York: Doubleday.

Strayer, J., & Cohen, D. (1988). In N. Eisenberg and J. Strayer (Eds.), *Empathy and its development. Cambridge studies in social and emotional development*. New York: Cambridge University Press.

Strayer, D.L., & Johnston, W.A. (2001). Driven to distraction: Dual-task studies of simulated driving and conversing on a cellular telephone. *Psychological Science, 12*, 462–466.

Strober, M., & Humphrey, L.L. (1987). Familial contributions to the aetiology and course of anorexia nervosa and bulimia. *Journal of Consulting and Clinical Psychology, 55*, 654–659.

Stroebe, W., & Diehl, M. (1994). Why groups are less effective than their members: On productivity losses in idea-generating groups. *European Review of Social Psychology, 5*, 271–303.

Stroebe, W., & Insko, C.A. (1989). Stereotype, prejudice, and discrimination: Changing conceptions in theory and research. In D. Bar-Tal, C.F. Graummann, A.W. Kruglanski, & W. Stroebe (Eds.), *Stereotyping and prejudice: Changing conceptions*. New York: Springer-Verlag.

Stroop, J.R. (1935). Studies of interference in serial verbal reactions. *Journal of Experimental Psychology, 18*, 643–662.

Struch, N., & Schwartz, S.H. (1989). Intergroup aggression: Its predictors and distinctness from ingroup bias. *Journal of Personality and Social Psychology, 56*, 364–373.

Strupp, H.H. (1996). The tripartite model and the Consumer Reports study. *American Psychologist, 51*, 1017–1024.

Stryker, S. (1995). "In the begging there is society": Lessons from a sociological social psychology. In C. McGarty & S.A. Haslam (Eds.), *The message of social psychology*. Oxford, UK: Blackwell.

Stryker, S. (1997). "In the beginning there is society": Lessons from a sociological social psychology. In C. McGarty, S. Haslam, & S. Alexander (Eds.), *The message of social psychology: Perspectives on mind in society*. Malden, MA: Blackwell.

Stunkard, A.J., Sorensen, T.I.A., Hanis, C., Teasdale, T.W., Chakraborty, R., Schull, W.J., & Schulsinger, F. (1986). An adoption study of human obesity. *New England Journal of Medicine, 314*, 193–198.

Sturges, J.W., & Rogers, R.W. (1996). Preventive health psychology from a developmental perspective: An extension of protection motivation theory. *Health Psychology, 15*, 158–166.

Styles, E.A. (1997). *The psychology of attention*. Hove, UK: Psychology Press.

Sue, S., Fujino, D.C., Hu, L., Takeuchi, D.T., & Zane, N.S.W. (1991). Community mental health services for ethnic minority groups: A test of the cultural responsiveness hypothesis. *Journal of Consulting and Clinical Psychology, 59*, 533–540.

Sue, D., Sue, D., & Sue, S. (1994). *Understanding abnormal behaviour*. Boston, MA: Houghton Mifflin.

Sugase Y., Yamane, S., Ueno, S., & Kawano, K. (1999). Global and fine information coded by single neurons in the temporal visual cortex. *Nature, 400*, 869–873.

Suh, E., Diener, E., Oishi, S., & Triandis, H.C. (1998). The shifting basis of life satisfaction judgements across cultures: Emotions versus norms. *Journal of Personality and Social Psychology, 74*, 482–493.

Suinn, R.M., Osborne, D., & Winfree, P. (1962). The self concept and accuracy of recall of inconsistent self-related information. *Journal of Clinical Psychology, 18*, 473–474.

Sulin, R.A., & Dooling, D.J. (1974). Intrusion of a thematic idea in retention of prose. *Journal of Experimental Psychology, 103*, 255–262.

Sullivan, L. (1976). Selective attention and secondary message analysis: A reconsideration of Broadbent's filter model of selective attention. *Quarterly Journal of Experimental Psychology, 28*, 167–178.

Sussman, H.M., Hoemeke, K.A., & Ahmed, F.S. (1993). A cross-linguistic investigation of locus equations as a phonetic descriptor for place of articulation. *Journal of the Acoustical Society of America, 94*, 1256–1268.

Swann, W.B. (1987). Identity negotiation: Where two roads meet. *Journal of Personality and Social Psychology, 53*, 1038–1051.

Swanson, H.L. (1999). What develops in working memory? A life span perspective. *Developmental Psychology, 35*, 986–1000.

Swim, J.K., Aikin, K.J., Hall, W.S., & Hunter, B.A. (1995). Sexism and racism: Old-fashioned and modern prejudices. *Journal of Personality and Social Psychology, 68*, 199–214.

Symington, T., Currie, A.R., Curran, R.S., & Davidson, J. (1955). The reaction of the adrenal cortex in conditions of stress. *Ciba Foundations Colloquia on Endocrinology, 20*, 156–164.

Szasz, T.S. (1962). *The myth of mental illness: Foundations of a theory of personal conduct*. New York: Hoeber-Harper.

Szasz, T.S. (1974). *The age of madness: The history of involuntary hospitalisation*. New York: Jason Aronson.

Tache, J., Selye, H., & Day, S. (1979). *Cancer, stress, and death*. New York: Plenum Press.

Tager-Flusberg, H. (1999). Language development in atypical children. In M. Barrett (Ed.), *The development of language*. Hove, UK: Psychology Press.

Tajfel, H. (1969). Social and cultural factors in perception. In G. Lindzey & E. Aronson (Eds.), *Handbook of social psychology, Vol. 3*. Reading, MA: Addison-Wesley.

Tajfel, H. (1978). Intergroup behaviour: Vol. 1. Individualistic perspectives. In H. Tajfel & C. Fraser (Eds.), *Introducing social psychology*. Harmondsworth, UK: Penguin.

Tajfel, H. (1979). Individuals and groups in social psychology. *British Journal of Psychology, 18*, 187–190.

Tajfel, H. (1981). *Human groups and social categories: Studies in social psychology*. Cambridge, UK: Cambridge University Press.

Tajfel, H., Flament, C., Billig, M.G., & Bundy, R.P. (1971). Social categorisation and intergroup behaviour. *European Journal of Social Psychology, 1*, 149–178.

Tajfel, H., & Turner, J.C. (1986). The social identity theory of intergroup behaviour. In S. Worchel & W.G. Austin (Eds.), *Psychology of intergroup relations*. Chicago: Nelson-Hall.

Takahashi, K. (1990). Are the key assumptions of the "strange situation" procedure universal? A view from Japanese research. *Human Development, 33*, 23–30.

Takahashi, Y. (1979). Growth hormone secretion related to the sleep and waking rhythm. In R. Doncker-Colin, M. Shkurovich, & M.B. Sterman (Eds.), *The functions of sleep*. New York: Academic Press.

Tanenhaus, M.K., Spivey-Knowlton, M.J., Eberhard, K.M., & Sedivy, J.C. (1995). Integration of visual and linguistic information in spoken language comprehension. *Science, 268*, 1632–1634.

Tarr, M.J., & Bülthoff, H.H. (1995). Is human object recognition better described by geon structural descriptions or by multiple views? Comment on Biederman and Gerhardstein (1993). *Journal of Experimental Psychology: Human Perception and Performance, 21*, 1494–1505.

Tarr, M.J., & Bülthoff, H.H. (1998). Image-based object recognition in man, monkey and machine. *Cognition, 67*, 1–20.

Tarr, M.J., Williams, P., Hayward, W.G., & Gauthier, I. (1998). Three-dimensional object recognition is viewpoint-dependent. *Nature Neuroscience, 1*, 195–206.

Taubes, G. (1998). As obesity rates rise, experts struggle to explain why. *Science, 280*, 1367–1368.

Taylor, A., Sluckin, W., Davies, D.R., Reason, J.T., Thomson, R., & Colman, A.M. (1982). *Introducing psychology* (2nd ed.). Harmondsworth, UK: Penguin.

Taylor, S.E., Klein, L.C., Greendale, G., Seeman, T.E. (1999). Oxytocin and HPA response to acute stress in women with or without HRT. Cited in Taylor et al. (2000)—article in *Psychological Review*.

Taylor, M.S., Locke, F.A., Lee, C., & Gist, M. (1984). Type A behavior and faculty research productivity: What are the mechanisms? *Organizational Behavior and Human Performance, 34*, 402–418.

Taylor, S.E., Klein, L.C., Lewis, B.P., Gruenewald, T.L., Gurung, R.A.R., & Updegraff, J.A. (2000). Biobehavioural responses to stress in females: Tend-and-befriend, not fight-or-flight. *Psychological Review, 107*, 411–429.

Teasdale, J.D. (1999). Multi-level theories of cognition–emotion relations. In T. Dalgleish & M.J. Power (Eds.), *Handbook of cognition and emotion*. Chichester, UK: Wiley.

Teitelbaum, P. (1957). Random and food-directed activity in hyperphagic and normal rats. *Journal of Comparative and Physiological Psychology, 50*, 486–490.

Teitelbaum, P., & Stellar, E. (1954). Recovery from the failure to eat produced by hypothalamic lesions. *Science, 120*, 894–895.

Tellegen, A., Watson, D., & Clark, L.A. (1999). On the dimensional and hierarchical structure of affect. *Psychological Science, 10*, 297–303.

Teller, D.Y. (1997). First glances: the vision of infants. The Friedenwald lecture. *Investigative Ophthalmology and Visual Science, 38*, 2183–2203.

Terman, M. (1988). On the question of mechanism in phototherapy for seasonal affective disorder: Considerations of clinical efficacy and epidemiology. *Journal of Biological Rhythms, 3*, 155–172.

Terrace, H.S. (1989). *Nim*. New York: Alfred Knopf.

Terrace, H.S., Petitto, L.A., Sanders, D.J., & Bever, T.G. (1979). On the grammatical capacities of apes. In K. Nelson (Ed.), *Children's language, Vol. 2*. New York: Gardner Press.

Terrace, H.S., Petitto, L.A., Sanders, R.J., & Bever, T.G. (1979). Can an ape create a sentence? *Science, 206*, 891–902.

Tesser, A. (1988). Toward a self-evaluation maintenance model of social behaviour. In L. Berkowitz (Ed.), *Advances in Experimental Social Psychology, Vol. 21*. San Diego, CA: Academic Press.

Tesser, A., Campbell, J., & Smith, M. (1984). Friendship choice and performance: Self-evaluation maintenance in children. *Journal of Personality and Social Psychology, 46*, 561–574.

Tester, N. (1998, October 10). Forty minutes that changed everything. *The Independent Magazine*.

Tetlock, P.E. (2002). Social functionalist frameworks for judgment and choice: Intuitive politicians, theologians, and prosecutors. *Psychological Review, 109*, 451–471.

Tetlock, P.E., Peterson, R.S., McGuire, C., Chang, S., & Feld, P. (1992). Assessing political group dynamics: A test of the groupthink model. *Journal of Personality and Social Psychology, 63*, 403–425.

Teuting, P., Rosen, S., & Hirschfeld, R. (1981). *Special report on depression research*. NIMH–DHHS Publication No. 81–1085: Washington, DC.

Thomas, J.C. (1974). An analysis of behaviour in the hobbits–orcs problem. *Cognitive Psychology, 6*, 257–269.

Thomas, M., Sing, H., Belenky, G., Holcomb, H., Mayberg, H., Dannals, R., Wagner, H., Thorne, D., Popp, K., Rowland, L., Welsh, A., Balwinski, S., & Redmond, D. (2000). Neural basis of alertness and cognitive performance impairments during sleepiness. I. Effects of 24h of sleep deprivation on waking human regional brain activity. *Journal of Sleep Research, 9*, 335–352.

Thompson, W.C., Clarke-Stewart, K.A., & Lepore, S. (1997). What did the janitor do? Suggestive interviewing and the accuracy of children's accounts. *Law and Human Behavior, 21*, 405–426.

Thompson, W.C., Cowan, C.L., & Rosenhan, D.L. (1980). Focus of attention mediates the impact of negative affect on altruism. *Journal of Personality and Social Psychology, 38*, 291–300.

Thomson, R. (1968). *The Pelican history of psychology*. Harmondsworth, UK: Penguin.

Thorndike, E.L. (1898). Animal intelligence: An experimental study of the associative processes in animals. *The Psychological Review Monograph Supplements, 2*, No. 4 (Whole No. 8).

Thorndike, R.L. (1987). Stability of factor loadings. *Personality and Individual Differences, 8*, 585–586.

Thurstone, L.L. (1938). *Primary mental abilities*. Chicago, IL: University of Chicago Press.

Tice, D.M. (1992). Self-presentation and self-concept change: The looking glass self as magnifying glass. *Journal of Personality and Social Psychology, 63*, 435–451.

Tice, D.M., Butler, J.L., Muraven, M.B., & Stillwell, A.M. (1995). When modesty prevails: Differential favourability of self-presentation to friends and strangers. *Journal of Personality and Social Psychology, 69*, 1120–1138.

Tieger, T. (1980). On the biological basis of sex differences in aggression. *Child Development, 51*, 943–963.

Tienari, P. (1991). Interaction between genetic vulnerability and family environment: The Finnish adoptive family study of schizophrenia. *Acta Psychiatrica Scandinavica, 84*, 460–465.

Tizard, B. (1977). *Adoption: A second chance*. London: Open Books.

Tizard, B. (1986). *The care of young children*. London: Institute of Education.

Tizard, B., Cooperman, A., & Tizard, J. (1972). Environmental effects on language development: A study of young children in long-stay residential nurseries. *Child Development, 43*, 337–358.

Tizard, B., & Hodges, J. (1978). The effect of early institutional rearing on the development of eight-year-old children. *Journal of Child Psychology and Psychiatry, 19*, 99–118.

Tobin, J.J., Wu, D.Y.H., & Davidson, D.H. (1989). *Preschool in three cultures: Japan, China, and the United States*. New Haven, CT: Yale University Press.

Todd, P.M., & Gigerenzer, G. (2000). Précis of "Simple heuristics that make us smart". *Behavioral and Brain Sciences, 23*, 727–780.

Tolman, E.C. (1959). Principles of purposive behaviour. In S. Koch (Ed.), *Psychology: A study of a science: Vol. 2. General systematic formulations, learning, and special processes*. New York: McGraw-Hill.

Tolman, E.C., & Honzik, C.H. (1930). Introduction and removal of reward and maze learning in rats. *University of California Publications in Psychology, 4*, 257–275.

Tomarken, A.J., Davidson, R.J., Wheeler, R.E., & Dass, R.C. (1992). Individual differences in anterior brain asymmetry and fundamental dimensions of emotion. *Journal of Personality and Social Psychology, 62*, 676–677.

Tomarken, A.J., Mineka, S., & Cook, M. (1989). Fear-relevant selective associations and covariation bias. *Journal of Abnormal Psychology, 98*, 381–394.

Tomasello, M. (1992). *First verbs: A case study of early grammatical development*. Cambridge, UK: Cambridge University Press.

Tomasello, M., Akhtar, N., Dodson, K., & Rekau, L. (1997). Differential productivity in young children's use of nouns and verbs. *Journal of Child Language, 24*, 373–387.

Tomasello, M., & Brooks, P.J. (1999). Early syntactic development: A construction grammar approach. In M. Barrett (Ed.), *The development of language*. Hove, UK: Psychology Press.

Tomasello, M., & Farrar, M.J. (1986). Object permanence and relational words: A lexical training study. *Journal of Child Language, 13*, 495–505.

Tomlinson-Keasey, C., Eisert, D.C., Kahle, L.R., Hardy-Brown, K., & Keasey, B. (1979). The structure of concrete-operational thought. *Child Development, 57*, 1454–1463.

Tomlinson-Keasey, C., & Keasey, C.B. (1974). The mediating role of cognitive development in moral judgement. *Child Development, 45*, 291–298.

Tourangeau, R., Smith, T.W., & Rasinski, K.A. (1997). Motivation to report sensitive behaviors on surveys: Evidence from a bogus pipeline experiment. *Journal of Applied Social Psychology, 27*, 209–222.

Treisman, A.M. (1960). Contextual cues in selective listening. *Quarterly Journal of Experimental Psychology, 12*, 242–248.

Treisman, A.M. (1964). Verbal cues, language, and meaning in selective attention. *American Journal of Psychology, 77*, 206–219.

Treisman, A.M. (1988). Features and objects: The fourteenth Bartlett memorial lecture. *Quarterly Journal of Experimental Psychology, 40A*, 201–237.

Treisman, A.M. (1992). Spreading suppression or feature integration? A reply to Duncan and Humphreys (1992). *Journal of Experimental Psychology: Human Perception and Performance, 18*, 589–593.

Treisman, A.M., & Davies, A. (1973). Divided attention to ear and eye. In S. Kornblum (Ed.), *Attention and performance IV: Information processing*. London: Academic Press.

Treisman, A.M., & Geffen, G. (1967). Selective attention: Perception or response? *Quarterly Journal of Experimental Psychology, 19*, 1–18.

Treisman, A.M., & Gelade, G. (1980). A feature integration theory of attention. *Cognitive Psychology, 12*, 97–136.

Treisman, A.M., & Riley, J.G.A. (1969). Is selective attention selective perception or selective response: A further test. *Journal of Experimental Psychology, 79*, 27–34.

Treisman, A.M., & Sato, S. (1990). Conjunction search revisited. *Journal of Experimental Psychology: Human Perception and Performance, 16*, 459–478.

Treisman, A.M., & Schmidt, H. (1982). Illusory conjunctions in the perception of objects. *Cognitive Psychology, 14*, 107–141.

Tremblay-Leveau, H., & Nadel, J. (1996). Exclusion in triads: Can it serve "metacommunicative" knowledge in 11 and 24 months children? *British Journal of Developmental Psychology, 14*, 145–158.

Tresilian, J.R. (1995). Perceptual and cognitive processes in time-to-contact estimation: Analysis of prediction–motion and relative judgement tasks. *Perception and Psychophysics, 57*, 231–245.

Trevarthen, C. (1980). Development of interpersonal and cooperative understanding in infants. In D. Olson (Ed.), *The social foundations of language and thought: Essays in honor of J.S. Bruner*. New York: W.W. Norton.

Triandis, H.C. (1993). The contingency model in cross-cultural perspective. In M.M. Chemers & R. Ayman (Eds.), *Leadership theory and research: Perspectives and directions*. San Diego, CA: Academic Press.

Triandis, H.C. (1994). *Culture and social behaviour*. New York: McGraw-Hill.

Triandis, H.C., Carnevale, P., Gelfand, M., Robert, C., Wasti, A., Probst, T.M., Kashima, E.S., Dragonas, T., Chan, D., Chen, X.P., Kim, U., Kim, K., de Dreu, C., van de Vliert, E., Iwao, S., Ohbuchi, K., & Schmitz, P. (2001). Culture, personality and deception in intercultural management negotiations. *International Journal of Cross-Cultural Management, 1*, 73–90.

Triandis, H.C., McCusker, C., Betancourt, H., Iwao, S., Leung, K., Salazar, J.M., Setiadi, B., Sinha, J.B.P., Touzard, H., Wang, D., & Zaleski, S. (1993). An etic–emic analysis of individualism and collectivism. *Journal of Cross-Cultural Psychology, 24*, 366–384.

Triandis, H.C., McCusker, C., & Hui, C.H. (1990). Multimethod probes of individualism and collectivism. *Journal of Personality and Social Psychology, 59*, 1006–1020.

Triandis, H.C., & Suh, E.M. (2002). Cultural influences on personality. *Annual Review of Psychology, 53*, 133–160.

Triandis, H.C., & Vassiliou, V. (1967). A comparative analysis of subjective culture. In H.C. Triandis (Ed.), *The analysis of subjective culture*. New York: Wiley.

Trivers, R.L. (1971). The evolution of reciprocal altruism. *Quarterly Review of Biology, 46*, 35–57.

Trivers, R.L. (1972). Parental investment and sexual selection. In B. Campbell (Ed.), *Sexual selection and the descent of man, 1871–1971*. Chicago: Aldine.

Trope, Y., & Gaunt, R. (2000). Processing alternative explanations of behaviour: Correction or integration? *Journal of Personality and Social Psychology, 79*, 344–354.

True, M.M., Pisani, L., & Oumar, F. (2001). Infant–mother attachment among the Dogon of Mali. *Child Development, 72*, 1451–1466.

True, W.R., Rice, J., Eisen, S.A., Heath, A.C., Goldberg, J., Lyons, M.J., & Nowak, J. (1993). A twin study of genetic and environmental contributions to liability for posttraumatic stress symptoms. *Archives of General Psychiatry, 50*, 257–264.

Tryon, R.C. (1940). Genetic differences in maze learning ability in rats. *Yearbook of the National Society for the Study of Education, 39*, 111–119.

Tuckman, J. (1965). College students' judgment of the passage of time over the life span. *Journal of Genetic Psychology, 107*, 43–48.

Tulving, E. (1972). Episodic and semantic memory. In E. Tulving & W. Donaldson (Eds.), *Organisation of memory*. Hillsdale, NJ: Lawrence Erlbaum Associates, Inc.

Tulving, E. (1974). Cue-dependent forgetting. *American Scientist, 62*, 74–82.

Tulving, E. (1979). Relation between encoding specificity and levels of processing. In L.S. Cermak & F.I.M. Craik (Eds.), *Levels of processing in human memory*. Hillsdale, NJ: Lawrence Erlbaum Associates, Inc.

Tulving, E. (2002). Episodic memory: From mind to brain. *Annual Review of Psychology, 53*, 1–25.

Tulving, E., & Psotka, J. (1971). Retroactive inhibition in free recall: Inaccessibility of information available in the memory store. *Journal of Experimental Psychology, 87*, 1–8.

Tulving, E., Schachter, D.L., & Stark, H.A. (1982). Priming effects in word-fragment completion are independent of recognition memory. *Journal of Experimental Psychology: Learning, Memory, and Cognition, 17*, 595–617.

Tulving, E., & Thomson, D.M. (1973). Encoding specificity and retrieval processes in episodic memory. *Psychological Review, 8*, 352–373.

Turati, C., Simion, F., Milani, I., & Umiltà, C. (2002). Newborns' preference for faces: What is crucial? *Developmental Psychology, 38*, 875–882.

Turiel, E. (1998). The development of morality. In N. Eisenberg (Ed.), *Handbook of child psychology: Vol. 3. Social, emotional, and personality development*. New York: Wiley.

Turner, J.C. (1985). Social categorisation and the self-concept: A social cognitive theory of group behaviour. In E.J. Lawler (Ed.), *Advances in group processes: Theory and research, Vol. 2*. Greenwich, CT: JAI Press.

Turner, J.C. (1987). *Rediscovering the social group: A self-categorisation theory*. Oxford, UK: Blackwell.

Turner, J.C. (1999). Some current issues in research on social identity and self-categorisation theories. In N. Ellemers, R. Spears, & B. Doosje (Eds.), *Social identity*. Oxford, UK: Blackwell.

Turner, J.C., Hogg, M.A., Oakes, P.J., Reicher, S.D., & Wetherell, M.S. (1987). *Rediscovering the social group: A self-categorization theory*. Oxford, UK: Blackwell.

Turner, J.C., & Oakes, P.J. (1997). The social structured mind. In C. McGarty & S. Alexander (Eds.), *The message of social psychology: Perspectives on mind in society*. Malden, MA: Blackwell.

Turner, R.A., Altemus, M., Enos, T., Cooper, B., & McGuinness, T. (1999). Preliminary research on plasma oxytocin in normal cycling women: Investigating emotion and interpersonal distress. *Psychiatry, 62*, 97–113.

Turner, R.H., & Killian, L.M. (1972). *Collective behaviour* (2nd ed.). Englewood Cliffs, NJ: Prentice-Hall.

Turner, R.J., & Wagonfeld, M.O. (1967). Occupational mobility and schizophrenia. *American Sociological Review, 32*, 104–113.

Tversky, A., & Kahneman, D. (1973). Availability: A heuristic for judging frequency and probability. *Cognitive Psychology, 5*, 207–232.

Tversky, A., & Kahneman, D. (1980). Causal schemas in judgements under uncertainty. In M. Fishbein (Ed.), *Progress in social psychology*. Hillsdale, NJ: Lawrence Erlbaum Associates, Inc.

Tversky, A., & Kahneman, D. (1981). The framing of decisions and the psychology of choice. *Science, 211*, 453–458.

Tversky, A., & Kahneman, D. (1983). Extensional versus intuitive reasoning: The conjunction fallacy in probability judgement. *Psychological Review, 90*, 293–315.

Tversky, A., & Koehler, D.J. (1994). Support theory: A nonextensional representation of subjective probability. *Psychological Review, 101*, 547–567.

Tversky, A., & Shafir, E. (1992). The disjunction effect in choice under uncertainty. *Psychological Science, 3*, 305–309.

Tweney, R.D., Doherty, M.E., Worner, W.J., Pliske, D.B., Mynatt, C.R., Gross, K.A., & Arkelin, D.L. (1980). Strategies for rule discovery in an inference task. *Quarterly Journal of Experimental Psychology, 32*, 109–123.

Twenge, J.M. (2000). The age of anxiety? Birth cohort change in anxiety and neuroticism, 1952–1993. *Journal of Personality and Social Psychology, 79*, 1007–1021.

Tyerman, A., & Spencer, C. (1983). A critical test of the Sherifs' Robbers' Cave experiment: Intergroup competition and co-operation between groups of well-acquainted individuals. *Small Group Behaviour, 14*, 515–531.

Tyrell, J.B., & Baxter, J.D. (1981). Glucocorticoid therapy. In P. Felig, J.D. Baxter, A.E. Broadus, & L.A. Frohman (Eds.), *Endocrinology and metabolism*. New York: McGraw-Hill.

Uchino, B.N., Cacioppo, J.T., & Kiecolt-Glaser, K.G. (1996). The relationships between social support and physiological processes: A review with emphasis on underlying mechanisms and implications for health. *Psychological Bulletin, 119*, 488–531.

Uchino, B.N., Uno, D., & Holt-Lunstad, J. (1999). Social support, physiological processes, and health. *Current Directions in Psychological Science, 8*, 145–148.

Udry, J.R. (1981). Maritial alternatives and marital disruption. *Journal of Marriage and the Family, 43*, 889–898.

Underwood, B.J. (1957) Interference and forgetting. *Psychological Review, 64*, 49–60.

Underwood, B.J., & Postman, L. (1960). Extra-experimental sources of interference in forgetting. *Psychological Review, 67*, 73–95.

Underwood, G. (1974). Moray vs. the rest: The effect of extended shadowing practice. *Quarterly Journal of Experimental Psychology, 26*, 368–372.

Uvnäs-Moberg, K. (1996). Neuroendocrinology of the mother–child interaction. *Trends in Endocrinology and Metabolism, 7*, 126–131.

Vandello, J.A., & Cohen, D. (1999). Patterns of individualism and collectivism across the United States. *Journal of Personality and Social Psychology, 77*, 279–292.

Vaillant, C.O., & Vaillant, G.E. (1993). Is the U-curve of marital satisfaction an illusion? A 40-year study of marriage. *Journal of Marriage and the Family, 55*, 230–239.

Vaina, L.M. (1998). Complex motion perception and its deficits. *Current Opinion in Neurobiology, 8*, 494–502.

Valdois, S., Carbonnel, S., David, D., Rousset, S., & Pellat, J. (1995). Confrontation of PDP models and dual-route models through the analysis of a case of deep dysphasia. *Cognitive Neuropsychology, 12*, 681–724.

Valentine, E.R. (1982). *Conceptual issues in psychology*. London: Routledge.

Valentine, E.R. (1992). *Conceptual issues in psychology* (2nd ed.). London: Routledge.

Valentine, T., Bredart, S., Lawson, R., & Ward, G. (1991). What's in a name? Access to information from people's names. *European Journal of Cognitive Psychology, 3*, 147–176.

VanLehn, K. (1996). *Cognitive skill acquisition*. Annual Review of Psychology, 47, 513–539.

Van Avermaet, E. (2001). Social influence in small groups. In M. Hewstone & W. Stroebe (Eds.), *Introduction to social psychology* (3rd ed., pp. 403–443). Oxford, UK: Blackwell.

Van den Putte, B. (1993). *On the theory of reasoning action*. Unpublished doctoral dissertation, University of Amsterdam, The Netherlands.

Van Essen, D., & DeYoe, E.A. (1995). Concurrent processing in the primate visual cortex. In M.S. Gazzaniga (Ed.), *The cognitive neurosciences*. Cambridge, MA: MIT Press.

Van Goozen, S.H.-M., Cohen-Kettenis, P.T., Gooren, L.J.G., Frijda, N.H., & van de Poll, N.E. (1995a). Gender differences in behaviour: Activating effects of cross-sex hormones. *Psychoneuroendocrinology, 20*, 343–363.

Van Goozen, S.H.-M., Frijda, N.H., & van de Poll, N.E. (1995b). Anger and aggression during role-playing: Gender differences between hormonally treated male and female transsexuals and controls. *Aggressive Behavior, 21*, 257–273.

Van Goozen, S.H.-M., Wiegant, V., Endert, E., Helmond, F., & van de Poll, N. (1997). Psychoendocrinological assessment of the menstrual cycle: The relationship between hormones, sexuality, and mood. *Archives of Sex Behavior, 26*, 359–382.

Van IJzendoorn, M.H., & de Wolff, M.S. (1997). In search of the absent father—Meta-analyses of infant–father attachment: A rejoinder to our discussants. *Child Development, 68*, 604–609.

Van IJzendoorn, M.H., & Kroonenberg, P.M. (1988). Cross-cultural patterns of attachment: A meta-analysis of the Strange Situation. *Child Development, 59*, 147–156.

Van Marken-Lichenbelt, W.D., Westerterp-Plantenga, M.S., & van Hoydonck, P. (2001). Individual variation in the relation between body temperature and energy expenditure in response to elevated ambient temperature. *Physiology and Behavior, 73*, 235–242.

Van Oudenhouven, J.P., Groenewoud, J.T., & Hewstone, M. (1996). Co-operation, ethnic salience and generalisation of inter-ethnic attitudes. *European Journal of Social Psychology, 26*, 649–662.

Van Selst, M.V., Ruthruff, E., & Johnston, J.C. (1999). Can practice eliminate the Psychological Refractory Period effect? *Journal of Experimental Psychology: Human Perception and Performance, 25*, 1268–1283.

Van Zoren, J.G., & Stricker, E.M. (1977). Effects of preoptic, lateral hypothalamic, or dopamine-depleting lesions on behavioural thermoregulation in rats exposed to the cold. *Journal of Comparative and Physiological Psychology, 91*, 989–999.

Vanbeselaere, N. (1991). The impact of in-group and out-group homogeneity/heterogeneity upon intergroup relations. *Basic and Applied Social Psychology, 12*, 291–301.

Vance, E.B., & Wagner, N.D. (1976). Written descriptions of orgasm: A study of sex differences. *Archives of Sexual Behavior, 5*, 87–98.

Vandell, D.L. (2000). Parents, peer groups, and other socialising influences. *Developmental Psychology, 36*, 699–710.

Vandell, D.L., & Mueller, E.C. (1980). Peer play and friendships during the first two years. In H.C. Foot, A.J. Chapman, & J.R. Smith (Eds.), *Friendship and social relations in children*. Chichester, UK: Wiley.

Vandell, D.L., & Wilson, K.S. (1987). Infants' interactions with mother, sibling, and peer: Contrasts and relations between interaction systems. *Child Development, 59*, 1286–1292.

VanLehn, K. (1996). Cognitive skill acquisition. *Annual Review of Psychology, 47*, 513–539.

Vanrie, J., Béatse, E., Wagemans, J., Sunaert, S., & van Hecke, P. (2002). Mental rotation versus invariant features in object perception from different viewpoints: An fMRI study. *Neuropsychologia, 40*, 917–930.

Vargha-Khadem, F., Gadian, D.G., & Mishkin, M. (2001). Dissociations in cognitive memory: The syndrome of developmental amnesia. *Philosophical Transactions of the Royal Society of London, Series B: Biological Science, 356*, 1435–1440.

Vargha-Khadem, F., Gadian, D.G., Watkins, K.E., Connelly, A., van Paesschen, W., & Mishkin, M. (1997). Differential effects of early hippocampal pathology on episodic and semantic memory. *Science, 277*, 376–380.

Vecera, S.P., & Farah, M.J. (1997). Is visual image segmentation a bottom-up or an interactive process? *Perception and Psychophysics, 59*, 1280–1296.

Velmans, M. (1996a). *The science of consciousness*. London: Routledge.

Velmans, M. (1996b). An introduction to the science of consciousness. In M. Velmans (Ed.), *The science of consciousness*. London: Routledge.

Velmans, M. (2000). *Understanding consciousness*. London: Routledge.

Veniegas, R., & Conley, T. (2000). Biological research on women's sexual orientations: Evaluating the scientific evidence. *Journal of Social Issues, 56*, 267.

Verburg, K., Griez, E., Meijer, J. & Pols, H. (1995). Respiratory disorders as a possible predisposing factor for panic disorder. *Journal of Affective Disorders, 33*, 129–134.

Verkuyten, M., Drabbles, M., & van den Nieuwenhuijzen, K. (1999). Self-categorisation and emotional reactions to ethnic minorities. *European Journal of Social Psychology, 29*, 605–619.

Vernon, P.E. (1971). *The structure of human abilities*. London: Methuen.

Victor, R., Mainardi, J.A., & Shapiro, D. (1978). Effects of biofeedback and voluntary control procedures on heart rate and perception of pain during the cold pressor test. *Psychosomatic Medicine, 40*, 216–225.

Viguera, A.C., Nonacs, R., Cohen, L.S., Tondo, L., Murray, A., & Baldessarini, R.J. (2000). Risk of recurrence of bipolar disorder in pregnant and nonpregnant women after discontinuing lithium maintenance. *American Journal of Psychiatry, 157*, 179–184.

Viguera, A.C., Nonacs, R., Cohen, L.S., Tondo, L., Murray, A., & Baldessarini, R.J. (2000). Risk of recurrence of bipolar disorder in pregnant and nonpregnant women after discontinuing lithium maintenance. *American Journal of Psychiatry, 157*, 179–184.

Virkkunen, M., Rawlings, R., Tokola, R., Poland, R.E., Guidotti, A., Nemeroff, C., Bissette, G., Kalogeras, K., Karonen, S.L., & Linnoila, M. (1994). CSF biochemistries, glucose metabolism, and diurnal activity in alcoholic, violent offenders, fire setters, and healthy volunteers. *Archives of General Psychiatry, 51*, 20–27.

Vitousek, K., & Manke, F. (1994). Personality variables and disorders in anorexia nervosa and bulimia nervosa. *Journal of Abnormal Psychology, 103*, 137–147.

Vogel, G.W. (2000). Critique of current dream theories. *Behavioral and Brain Sciences, 23*, 1014.

von Neumann, J., & Morgenstern, O. (1947). *Theory of games and economic behaviour* (2nd Rev. ed.). Princeton, NJ: Princeton University Press.

Von Wright, J.M., Anderson, K., & Stenman, U. (1975). Generalisation of conditioned GSRs in dichotic listening. In P.M.A. Rabbitt & S. Dornič (Eds.), *Attention and performance V: Information processing*. New York: Academic Press.

Vonk, R. (1993). Individual differences and universal dimensions in Implicit Personality Theory. *British Journal of Social Psychology, 32*, 209–226.

Vonk, R. (1996). Negativity and potency effects in impression formation. *European Journal of Social Psychology, 26*, 851–865.

Vuchinich, S., Hetherington, E.M., Vuchinich, R.A., & Clingempeel, W.G. (1991). Parent–child interaction and gender differences in early adolescents' adaptation to stepfamilies. *Developmental Psychology, 27*, 618–626.

Vygotsky, L.S. (1962). *Thought and language*. Cambridge, MA: MIT Press.

Vygotsky, L.S. (1976). Play and its role in the mental development of the child. In J.S. Bruner, A. Jolly, & K. Sylva (Eds.), *Play*. Harmondsworth, UK: Penguin.

Vygotsky, L.S. (1978). *Mind in society: The development of higher psychological processes*. Cambridge, MA: MIT Press.

Vygotsky, L.S. (1981). The genesis of higher mental functions. In J.V. Wertsch (Ed.), *The concept of activity in Soviet psychology*. Armonk, NY: Sharpe, Inc. (Original work published 1930)

Vygotsky, L.S. (1987). Thinking and speech. In *The collected works of L.S. Vygotsky: Vol 1. Problems of general psychology* (N. Minick, Trans.). New York: Plenum Press. (Original work published 1934)

Waddington, D., Jones, K., & Critcher, C. (1987). Flashpoints of public disorder. In G. Gaskell & R. Benewick (Eds.), *The crowd in contemporary Britain*. London: Sage.

Wade, A.R., Brewer, A.A., Rieger, J.W., & Wandell, B.A. (2002). Functional measurements of human ventral occipital cortex: Retinotopy and colour. *Philosophical Transactions of the Royal Society of London, Series B, 357*, 963–973.

Wade, N. (1997, June 24). Dainty worm tells secrets on the human genetic code. *New York Times*.

Wade, N.J., & Swanston, M.T. (2001). *Visual perception* (2nd ed.). Hove, UK: Psychology Press.

Wagenaar, W.A. (1986). My memory: A study of autobiographical memory over six years. *Cognitive psychology, 18*, 225–252.

Wagenaar, W.A. (1994). Is memory self-serving? In U. Neisser & R. Fivish. *The remembering self* (pp. 191–204). Cambridge, UK: Cambridge University Press.

Wagner, H.L., MacDonald, C.J., & Manstead, A.S.R. (1986). Communication of individual emotions by spontaneous facial expressions. *Journal of Personality and Social Psychology, 50*, 737–743.

Wagstaff, G.F. (1977). An experimental study of compliance and post-hypnotic amnesia. *British Journal of Social and Clinical Psychology, 16*, 225–228.

Wagstaff, G.F. (1991). Compliance, belief and semantics in hypnosis: A non-state sociocognitive perspective. In S.J. Lynn & J.W. Rhue (Eds.), *Theories of hypnosis: Current models and perspectives*. New York: Guilford.

Wagstaff, G.F. (1994). Hypnosis. In A.M. Colman (Ed.), *Companion encyclopaedia of psychology, Vol. 2*. London: Routledge.

Wakefield, J.C. (1992). The concept of mental disorder: On the boundary between biological facts and social values. *American Psychologist, 47*, 373–377.

Wakefield, J.C. (1999). Evolutionary versus prototype analyses of the concept of disorder. *Journal of Abnormal Psychology, 108*, 374–399.

Walker, L.J., Gustafson, P., & Hennig, K.H. (2001). The consolidation/transition model in moral reasoning development. *Developmental Psychology, 37*, 187–197

Wallace, A.R. (1858). On the tendency of varieties to depart indefinitely from the original type. *Journal of the Proceedings of the Linnean Society (Zoology), 3*, 53–62.

Wallen, K. (2001). Sex and context: Hormones and primate sexual motivation. *Hormones and Behavior, 40*, 339–357.

Wallerstein, J.S. (1987). Children of divorce: Report of a ten-year follow-up of early latency-age children. *American Journal of Orthopsychiatry, 57*, 199–211.

Walster, E., Aronson, V., Abrahams, D., & Rottman, L. (1966). The importance of physical attractiveness in dating behaviour. *Journal of Personality and Social Psychology, 4*, 508–516.

Walster, E., & Walster, G.W. (1969). *A new look at love*. Reading, MA: Addison Wesley.

Walster, E., Walster, G.W., & Berscheid, E. (1978). *Equity: Theory and research*. Boston: Allyn & Bacon.

Walters, J., & Gardner, H. (1986). The crystallizing experience: Discovering an intellectual gift. In R.J. Sternberg & J.E. Davidson (Eds.), *Conceptions of giftedness*. New York: Cambridge University Press.

Walton, G.E., Bower, N.J.A., & Bower, T.G.R. (1992). Recognition of familiar faces by newborns. *Infant Behaviour and Development, 15*, 265–269.

Waltz, J.A., Knowlton, B.J., Holyoak, K.J., Boone, K.B., Mishkin, F.S., Santos, M. de M., Thomas, C.R., & Miller, B.L. (1999). A system for relational reasoning in human prefrontal cortex. *Psychological Science, 10*, 119–125.

Wampold, B.E., Mondin, G.W., Moody, M., Stich, F., Benson, K., & Ahn, H. (1997). A meta-analysis of outcome studies comparing bona fide psychotherapies: Empirically, "All must have prizes". *Psychological Bulletin, 122*, 203–215.

Wang, X.T. (1996). Domain-specific rationality in human choices: Violations of utility axioms and social contexts. *Cognition, 60*, 31–63.

Wann, J.P. (1996). Anticipating arrival: Is the tau margin a specious theory? *Journal of Experimental Psychology: Human Perception and Performance, 22*, 1031–1048.

Wann, J.P., & Rushton, S.K. (1995). Grasping the impossible: Stereoscopic virtual balls. In B.G. Bardy, R.J. Bootsma, & Y. Guiard (Eds.), *Studies in perception and action, Vol. III*. Hillsdale, NJ: Lawrence Erlbaum Associates, Inc.

Wanous, J.P., & Zwany, A. (1977). A cross-sectional test of need hierarchy theory. *Organizational Behavior and Human Performance, 18*, 78–97.

Warr, P.B. (1964). The relative importance of proactive interference and degree of learning in retention of paired associate items. *British Journal of Psychology, 55*, 19–30.

Warr, P. (1996). *Psychology at work* (3rd ed.). Harmondsworth, UK: Penguin.

Warren, R., & Zgourides, G.D. (1991). *Anxiety disorders: A rational-emotive perspective*. New York: Pergamon Press.

Warren, R.M., & Warren, R.P. (1970). Auditory illusions and confusions. *Scientific American, 223*, 30–36.

Warrington, E.K., & James, M. (1988). Visual apperceptive agnosia: A clinico-anatomical study of three cases. *Cortex, 24*, 13–32.

Warrington, E.K., & Taylor, A.M. (1978). Two categorical stages of object recognition. *Perception, 7*, 695–705.

Wartner, U.G., Grossmann, K., Fremmer-Bombik, E., & Suess, G. (1994). Attachment patterns at age 6 in south Germany: Predictability from infancy and implications for pre-school behaviour. *Child Development, 65*, 1014–1027.

Wason, P.C. (1960). On the failure to eliminate hypotheses in a conceptual task. *Quarterly Journal of Experimental Psychology, 12*, 129–140.

Wason, P.C. (1968). Reasoning about a rule. *Quarterly Journal of Experimental Psychology, 20*, 273–281.

Wason, P.C., & Shapiro, D. (1971). Natural and contrived experience in reasoning problems. *Quarterly Journal of Experimental Psychology, 23*, 63–71.

Waters, E., Wippman, J., & Sroufe, L.A. (1979). Attachment, positive affect, and competence in the peer group: Two studies in construct validation. *Child Development, 50*, 821–829.

Watson, D., & Clark, L.A. (1984). Negative affectivity: The disposition to experience aversive emotional states. *Psychological Bulletin, 96*, 465–490.

Watson, D., & Clark, L.A. (1992). Affects separable and inseparable: On the hierarchical arrangement of the negative affects. *Journal of Personality and Social Psychology, 62*, 489–505.

Watson, D., & Clark, L.A. (1994). *The PANAS–X: Manual for the Positive and Negative Affect Schedule—expanded form.* Unpublished manuscript, University of Iowa, Iowa City.

Watson, D., & Pennebaker, J.W. (1989). Health complaints, stress, and distress: Exploring the central role of negative affectivity. *Psychological Review, 96*, 234–254.

Watson, D., & Tellegen, A. (1985). Toward a consensual structure of mood. *Psychological Bulletin, 98*, 219–235.

Watson, D., Wiese, D., Vaidya, J., & Tellegen, A. (1999). The two general activation systems of affect: Structural findings, evolutionary considerations, and psychobiological evidence. *Journal of Personality and Social Psychology, 76*, 82–88.

Watson, J. (1930). *Behaviorism* (Rev. ed.). New York: Norton.

Watson, J.B. (1913). Psychology as the behaviourist views it. *Psychological Review, 20*, 158–177.

Watson, J.B., & Rayner, R. (1920). Conditioned emotional reactions. *Journal of Experimental Psychology, 3*, 1–14.

Webb, W.B. (1968). *Sleep: An experimental approach.* New York: Macmillan.

Weber, R., & Crocker, J. (1983). Cognitive processes in the revision of stereotypic beliefs. *Journal of Personality and Social Psychology, 45*, 961–977.

Wechsler, D. (1981). The psychometric tradition: Developing the Wechsler Adult Intelligence Scale. *Contemporary Educational Psychology, 6*, 82–85.

Weinberger, D.A., Schwartz, G.E., & Davidson, J.R. (1979). Low-anxious, high-anxious, and repressive coping styles: Psychometric patterns and behavioural and physiological responses to stress. *Journal of Abnormal Psychology, 88*, 369–380.

Weingarten, H.P., & Kulikovsky, O.T. (1989). Taste-to-postingestive consequence conditioning: Is the rise in sham feeding with repeated experience a learning phenomenon? *Physiology and Behavior, 45*, 471–476.

Weir, W. (1984, October 15). Another look at subliminal "facts". *Advertising Age*, p. 46.

Weisberg, R.W., & Suls, J. (1973). An information-processing model of Duncker's candle problem. *Cognitive Psychology, 4*, 255–276.

Weiskrantz, L. (1986). *Blindsight: A case study and its implications.* Oxford, UK: Oxford University Press.

Weiskrantz, L. (2002). Prime-sight and blindsight. *Consciousness and Cognition, 11*, 568–581.

Weiskrantz, L., Barbur, J.L., & Sahraie, A. (1995). Parameters affecting conscious versus unconscious visual discrimination with damage to the visual cortex V1. *Proceedings of the National Academy of Sciences, USA, 92*, 6122–6126.

Weiskrantz, L., Warrington, E.K., Sanders, M.D., & Marshall, J. (1974). Visual capacity in the hemianopic field following a restricted occipital ablation. *Brain, 97*, 709–728.

Weisner, T.S., & Gallimore, R. (1977). My brother's keeper: Child and sibling caretaking. *Current Anthropology, 18*, 169–190.

Weissman, A.N., & Beck, A.T. (1978). *Development and validation of the Dysfunctional Attitude Scale.* Paper presented at the annual meeting of the Association for the Advancement of Behaviour Therapy, Chicago, IL.

Weissman, M.M., Klerman, G.L., & Paykel, E.S. (1971). Clinical evaluation of hostility in depression. *American Journal of Psychiatry, 39*, 1397–1403.

Weisstein, N., & Wong, E. (1986). Figure–ground organisation and the spatial and temporal responses of the visual system. In E.C. Schwab & H.C. Nusbaum (Eds.), *Pattern recognition by humans and machines, Vol. 2.* New York: Academic Press.

Weisz, J.R., Chaiyasit, W., Weiss, B., Eastman, K., & Jackson, E. (1995). A multimethod study of problem behaviour among Thai and American children in school: Teacher reports versus direct observations. *Child Development, 66*, 402–415.

Weizman, Z.O., & Snow, C.E. (2001). Lexical input as related to children's vocabulary acquisition: Effects of sophisticated exposure and support for meaning. *Developmental Psychology, 37*, 265–279.

Welford, A.T. (1952). The psychological refractory period and the timing of high-speed performance. *British Journal of Psychology, 43*, 2–19.

Weller, A., & Weller, L. (1993). Human menstrual synchrony: A critical assessment. *Neuroscience and Biobehavioral Reviews, 17*, 427–439.

Wellman, H.M., Cross, D., & Watson, J. (2001). Meta-analysis of theory-of-mind development: The truth about false belief. *Child Development, 72*, 655–684.

Wellman, H.M., & Gelman, S.A. (1987). Children's understanding of the nonobvious. In R.J. Sternberg (Ed.), *Advances in the psychology of human intelligence, Vol. 4.* Hillsdale, NJ: Lawrence Erlbaum Associates, Inc.

Wells, C.G. (1981). *Learning through interaction: The study of language development.* Cambridge, UK: Cambridge University Press.

Wells, G.L. (1993). What do we know about eyewitness identification? *American Psychologist, 48*, 553–571.

Wender, P.H., Kety, S.S., Rosenthal, D., Schulsinger, F., Ortmann, J., & Lunde, I. (1986). Psychiatric disorders in the biological and adoptive families of adopted individuals with affective disorders. *Archives of General Psychiatry, 43*, 923–929.

Wertsch, J.V., McNamee, G.D., Mclane, J.B., & Budwig, N.A. (1980). The adult–child dyad as a problem-solving system. *Child Development, 51*, 1215–1221.

Weisner, T.S., & Gallimore, R. (1977). My brother's keeper: Child and sibling caretaking. *Current Anthropology, 18*, 169–190.

West, D.B., Fey, D., & Woods, S.C. (1984). Cholecystokinin persistently suppresses meal size but not food intake in free-feeding rats. *American Journal of Physiology—Regulatory Integrative and Comparative Physiology, 246*, 776–787.

Westen, D. (1996). *Psychology: Mind, brain, and culture.* New York: Wiley.

Westen, D. (1998). The scientific legacy of Sigmund Freud: Toward a psychodynamically informed psychological science. *Psychological Bulletin, 124*, 333–371.

Westen, D., & Gabbard, G.O. (1999). Psychoanalytic approaches to personality. In L.A. Pervin & O.P. John (Eds), *Handbook of personality: Theory and research.* New York: Guilford Press.

Weston, D.R., & Main, M. (1981). The quality of the toddler's relationship to mother and to father: Related to conflict behaviour and the readiness to establish new relationships. *Child Development, 52*, 932–940.

Wever, R. (1979). *Circadian rhythms system of man: Results of experiments under temporal isolation.* New York: Springer.

Wharton, C. M., Grafman, J., Flitman, S. K., Hansen, E. K., Brauner, J., Marks, A., & Honda, M. (1998). The neuroanatomy of analogical reasoning. In K.J. Holyoak, D. Gentner, & B. Kekinar (Eds.), *Analogy 98.* Sofia, Bulgaria: New University of Bulgaria.

Wheatstone, C. (1838). Contributions to the physiology of vision: Part I. On some remarkable and hitherto unobserved phenomena of binocular vision. *Philosophical Transactions of the Royal Society of London, 128*, 371–394.

Wheeler, M.A., Stuss, D.T., & Tulving, E. (1997). Toward a theory of episodic memory: the frontal lobes and autonoetic consciousness. *Psychological Bulletin, 121*, 331–354.

Wheldall, K., & Poborca, B. (1980). Conservation without conversation: An alternative, non-verbal paradigm for assessing conservation of liquid quantity. *British Journal of Psychology, 71*, 117–134.

White, L.E., & Hain, R.F. (1959). Anorexia in association with a destructive lesion of the hypothalamus. *Archives of Pathology, 43*, 443–471.

White, L.K., & Booth, A. (1991). Divorce over the life course: The role of marital happiness. *Journal of Family Issues, 12*, 5–21.

Whitehouse, W.G., Dinges, D.F., Orne, E.C., Keller, S.E., Bates, B.L., Bauer, N.K., Morahan, P., Haput, B.A., Carlin, M.M.,

Bloom, P.B., Zaugg, L., & Orne, M.T. (1996). Psychosocial and immune effects of self-hypnosis training for stress management throughout the first semester of medical school. *Psychosomatic Medicine, 58,* 249–263.

Whiting, B.B., & Whiting, J.W.M. (1975). *Children of six cultures: A psychocultural analysis.* Cambridge, MA: Harvard University Press.

Whorf, B.L. (1956). *Language, thought, and reality: Selected writings of Benjamin Lee Whorf.* New York: Wiley.

Whyte, M.K. (1978). *The status of women in preindustrial societies.* Princeton, NJ: Princeton University Press.

Wickelgren, I. (1998). Obesity: how big a problem? *Science, 280,* 1364–1367.

Wickens, A. (2000). *Foundations of biopsychology.* Harlow, UK: Prentice-Hall.

Wickens, C.D. (1984). Processing resources in attention. In R. Parasuraman & D.R. Davies (Eds.), *Varieties of attention.* London: Academic Press.

Wickens, C.D. (1992). *Engineering psychology and human performance* (2nd ed.). New York: HarperCollins.

Wicker, A.W. (1969). Attitudes versus actions: The relationship of verbal and overt behavioural responses to attitude objects. *Journal of Social Issues, 25,* 41–78.

Wicklund, R.A., & Gollwitzer, P.M. (1982). *Symbolic self-completion.* Hillsdale, NJ: Lawrence Erlbaum Associates, Inc.

Widiger, T.A., & Corbitt, E.M. (1995). Are personality disorders well-classified in DSM–IV? In W.J. Lively (Ed.), *The DSM–IV personality disorders* (pp. 103–134). New York: Guilford.

Widiger, T.A., & Costa, P.T., Jr. (1994). Personality and personality disorders. *Journal of Abnormal Psychology, 103,* 78–91.

Widiger, T.A., Verheul, R., & van den Brink, W. (1999). Personality and psychopathology. In L.A. Pervin & O.P. John (Eds.), *Handbook of personality: Theory and research* (2nd ed.). New York: Guilford Press.

Wiegman, O., & van Schie, E.G. (1998). Video game playing and its relations with aggressive and prosocial behaviour. *British Journal of Social Psychology, 37,* 367–378.

Wieselquist, J., Rusbult, C.E., Foster, C.A., & Agnew, C.R. (1999). Commitment, pro-relationship behaviour, and trust in close relationships. *Journal of Personality and Social Psychology, 77,* 942–966.

Wilder, D.A. (1984). Intergroup contact: The typical member and the exception to the rule. *Journal of Experimental Social Psychology, 20,* 177–194.

Wilkinson, R.T. (1969). Sleep deprivation: Performance tests for partial and selective sleep deprivation. In L.A. Abt & J.R. Reiss (Eds.), *Progress in clinical psychology.* New York: Grune & Stratton.

Willerman, L. (1979). *The psychology of individual and group differences.* San Francisco: W.H. Freeman.

Williams, J.B.W., Gibbon, M., First, M.B., Spitzer, R.L., Davies, M., Borus, J., Howes, M.J., Kane, J., Harrison, G.P.Jr., Rounsaville, B., & Wittchen, H.U. (1992). The Structured Clinical Interview for DSM–III–R (SCID): II. Multisite test–retest reliability. *Archives of General Psychiatry, 49,* 630–636.

Williams, J.E., & Best, D.L. (1990). *Measuring sex stereotypes: A multination study.* Newbury Park, CA: Sage.

Williams, J.M.G., Watts, F.N., MacLeod, C., & Mathews, A. (1997). *Cognitive psychology and emotional disorders* (2nd ed.). Chichester, UK: Wiley.

Williams, R.L. (1972). *The BITCH Test (Black Intelligence Test of Cultural Homogeneity).* St. Louis, MI: Washington University.

Williams, T.M. (Ed.). (1986). *The impact of television: A national experiment in three communities.* New York: Academic Press.

Williams, T.P., & Sogon, S. (1984). Group composition and conforming behaviour in Japanese students. *Japanese Psychological Research, 26,* 231–234.

Willingham, D.B., & Goedert-Eschmann, K. (1999). The relation between implicit and explicit learning: Evidence for parallel development. *Psychological Science, 10,* 531–534.

Wills, S., & Mackintosh, N.J. (1998). Peak shift on an artificial dimension. *Quarterly Journal of Experimental Psychology B, 32,* 1–32.

Wills, T.A. (1985). Supportive function of interpersonal relationships. In S. Cohen & S.L. Syme (Eds.), *Social support and health.* Orlando, FL: Academic Press.

Wilson, B.A., & Wearing, D. (1995). Prisoner of consciousness: A state of just awakening following herpes simplex encephalitis. In R. Campbell & M. Conway (Eds.), *Broken memories.* Oxford, UK: Blackwell.

Wilson, E.O. (1975). *Sociobiology: The new synthesis.* Cambridge, MA: Harvard University Press.

Wilson, G.T., & O'Leary, K.D. (1978). *Principles of behaviour therapy.* Englewood Cliffs, NJ: Prentice-Hall.

Wilson, S.R., & Spencer, R.C. (1990). Intense personal experiences: Subjective interpretations, and after-effects. *Journal of Clinical Psychology, 46,* 565–573.

Wimmer, H., & Perner, J. (1983). Beliefs about beliefs: Representation and the constraining function of wrong beliefs in young children's understanding of deception. *Cognition, 13,* 103–128.

Winch, R.F. (1958). *Mate selections: A study of complementary needs.* New York: Harper.

Windgassen, K. (1992). Treatment with neuroleptics: The patient's perspective. *Acta Psychiatrica Scandinavica, 86,* 405–410.

Winner, E. (1998). Talent: Don't confuse necessity with sufficiency, or science with policy. *Behavioral and Brain Sciences, 21,* 430–431.

Winningham, R.G., Hyman, I.E., & Dinnel, D.L. (2000). Flashbulb memories? The effects of when the initial memory report was obtained. *Memory, 8,* 209–216.

Winter, D.G., & Barenbaum, N.B. (1999). History of modern personality theory and research. In L.A. Pervin & O.P. John (Eds.), *Handbook of personality: Theory and research* (2nd ed.). New York: Guilford Press.

Wirz-Justice, A., Graw, P., Krauchi, K., Sarrafzadeh, A., English, J., Arendt, J., & Sand, L. (1996). "Natural" light treatment of seasonal affective disorder. *Journal of Affective Disorders, 37,* 109–120.

Wise, R.A. (1996). Addictive drugs and brain stimulation reward. *Annual Review of Neuroscience, 19,* 319–340.

Wise, R.A., & Bozarth, M.A. (1984). Brain reward circuitry: Four circuit elements "wired" in apparent series. *Brain Research Bulletin, 12,* 203–208.

Wise, T. (1978). Where the public peril begins: A survey of psychotherapists to determine the effects of Tarasoff. *Stanford Law Review, 31,* 165–190.

Wittenbrink, B., Judd, C.M., & Park, B. (1997). Evidence for racial prejudice at the implicit level and its relationship with questionnaire measures. *Journal of Personality and Social Psychology, 72,* 262–274.

Wittgenstein, L. (1953). *Philosophical investigations.* New York: Macmillan.

Woike, B., Gershkovich, I., Piorkowski, R., & Polo, M. (1999). The role of motives in the content and structure of autobiographical memory. *Journal of Personality and Social Psychology, 76,* 600–612.

Wojciulik, E., Kanwisher, N., & Driver, J. (1998). Modulation of activity in the fusiform face area by covert attention: An fMRI study. *Journal of Neurophysiology, 79,* 1574–1579.

Woldorff, M.G., Gallen, C.C., Hampson, S.A., Hillyard, S.A., Pantev, C., Sobel, D., & Bloom, F.E. (1993). Modulation of early sensory processing in human auditory cortex during auditory selective attention. *Proceedings of the National Academy of Sciences, 90,* 8722–8726.

Wolfe, J.M. (1998). Visual search. In H. Pashler (Ed.), *Attention.* Hove, UK: Psychology Press.

Wolpe, J. (1958). *Psychotherapy by reciprocal inhibition.* New York: Pergamon Press.

Wood, D. (1998). *How children think and learn* (2nd ed.). Oxford, UK: Blackwell.

Wood, D.J., Bruner, J.S., & Ross, G. (1976). The role of tutoring in problem solving. *Journal of Child Psychology and Psychiatry, 17,* 89–100.

Wood, J.T., & Duck, S. (Eds.). (1995). *Understanding relationships: Off the beaten track*. Thousand Oaks, CA: Sage.

Wood, R.E., Mento, A.J., & Locke, E.A. (1987). Task complexity as a moderator of goal effects: A meta-analysis. *Journal of Applied Psychology, 72*, 416–425.

Wood, W., & Eagly, A.H. (2002). A cross-cultural analysis of the behaviour of women and men: Implications for the origins of sex differences. *Psychological Bulletin, 128*, 699–727.

Wood, W., & Kallgren, C.A. (1988). Communicator attributes and persuasion: Recipients' access to attitude-relevant information in memory. *Personality and Social Psychology Bulletin, 14*, 172–182.

Wood, W., Lundgren, S., Ouellette, J.A., Busceme, S., & Blackstone, T. (1994). Minority influence: A meta-analytic review of social influence processes. *Psychological Bulletin, 115*, 323–345.

Wood, W., Rhodes, N., & Whelan, M. (1989). Sex differences in positive well-being: A consideration of emotional style and marital status. *Psychological Bulletin, 106*, 249–264.

Wood, W., Wong, F.Y., & Chachere, J.G. (1991). Effects of media violence on viewers' aggression in unconstrained social interaction. *Psychological Bulletin, 109*, 371–383.

Woods, K.A., Camacho-Hubner, C., Savage, M.O., & Clark, A.J.L. (1996). Intrauterine growth retardation and postnatal growth failure associated with deletion of the insulin-like growth factor I gene. *New England Journal of Medicine, 335*, 1363–1367.

Woods, S.C., Lotter, E.C., McKay, L.D., & Porte, D. (1979). Chronic intracerebroventricular infusion of insulin reduces food intake and body weight of baboons. *Nature, 282*, 503–505.

Woods, S.C., Seeley, R.J., Porte, D., Jr., & Schwartz, M.W. (1998). Signals that regulate food intake and energy homeostasis. *Science, 280*, 1378–1383.

Woodworth, R.S., & Sells, S.B. (1935). An atmosphere effect in formal syllogistic reasoning. *Journal of Experimental Psychology, 18*, 451–460.

Worchel, S., Morales, J.F., Páez, D., & Deschamps, J.-C. (1998). *Social identity: International perspectives*. London: Sage Publications.

Worchel, S., Rothgerber, H., Day, E.A., Hart, D., & Butemeyer, J. (1998). Social identity and individual productivity within groups. *British Journal of Social Psychology, 37*, 389–413.

World Health Organization (1992). *The ICD-10 Classification of Mental and Behavioural Disorders*. Geneva: WHO.

Wright, D.B., Gaskell, G.D., & O'Muircheartaigh, C.A. (1998). Flashbulb memory assumptions: Using national surveys to explore cognitive phenomena. *British Journal of Psychology, 89*, 103–122.

Wynn, V.E., & Logie, R.H. (1998). The veracity of long-term memories: Did Bartlett get it right? *Applied Cognitive Psychology, 12*, 1–20.

Yammarino, F.J., Spangler, W.D., & Bass, B.M. (1993). Transformational leadership and performance: A longitudinal investigation. *Leadership Quarterly, 4*, 81–102.

Yang, S., & Sternberg, R.J. (1997). Conceptions of intelligence in ancient Chinese philosophy. *Journal of Theoretical and Philosophical Psychology, 17*, 101–119.

Yaniv, I., & Meyer, D.E. (1987). Activation and metacognition of inaccessible information: Potential bases for incubation effects in problem solving. *Journal of Experimental Psychology: Learning, Memory and Cognition, 13*, 187–205.

Yates, A. (1989). Current perspectives on the eating disorders: I. History, psychological and biological aspects. *Journal of the American Academy of Child and Adolescent Psychiatry, 28*, 813–828.

Yearta, S., Maitlis, S., Briner, R.B. (1995). An exploratory study of goal setting in theory and practice: A motivational technique that works? *Journal of Occupational and Organisational Psychology, 68*, 237–252.

Yeates, K.O., MacPhee, D., Campbell, F.A., & Ramey, C.T. (1983). Maternal IQ and home environment as determinants of early childhood intellectual competence: A developmental analysis. *Developmental Psychology, 19*, 731–739.

Yelsma, P., & Athappily, K. (1988). Marital satisfaction and communication practices: Comparisons among Indian and American couples. *Journal of Comparative Family Studies, 19*, 37–54.

Yerkes, R.M., & Morgulis, S. (1909). The method of Pavlov in animal psychology. *Psychological Bulletin, 6*, 257–273.

Young, A.W. (1996). Dissociable aspects of consciousness. In M. Velmans (Ed.), *The science of consciousness*. London: Routledge.

Young, A.W., Hay, D.C., & Ellis, A.W. (1985). The faces that launched a thousand slips: Everyday difficulties and errors in recognising people. *British Journal of Psychology, 76*, 495–523.

Young, A.W., McWeeny, K.H., Hay, D.C., & Ellis, A.W. (1986a). Matching familiar and unfamiliar faces on identity and expression. *Psychological Research, 48*, 63–68.

Young, A.W., McWeeny, K.H., Hay, D.C., & Ellis, A.W. (1986b). Naming and categorisation latencies for faces and written names. *Quarterly Journal of Experimental Psychology, 38A*, 297–318.

Young, A.W., Newcombe, F., de Haan, E.H.F., Small, M., & Hay, D.C. (1993). Face perception after brain injury: Selective impairments affecting identity and expression. *Brain, 116*, 941–959.

Young, W.C., Goy, R.W., & Phoenix, C.H. (1964). Hormones and sexual behaviour. *Science, 143*, 212–219.

Yuille, J.C., & Cutshall, J.L. (1986). A case study of eyewitness memory of a crime. *Journal of Applied Psychology, 71*, 291–301.

Yussen, S.R., & Levy, V.M. (1975). Developmental changes in predicting one's own span of short-term memory. *Journal of Experimental Child Psychology, 19*, 502–508.

Zadra, A.L. (1996). Recurrent dreams: Their relation to life events. In D. Barrett (Ed.), *Trauma and dreams*. London: Harvard University Press.

Zahn-Waxler, C., Radke-Yarrow, M., & King, R.A. (1979). Child rearing and children's prosocial initiations toward victims of distress. *Child Development, 50*, 319–330.

Zahn-Waxler, C., Robinson, J., & Emde, R.N. (1992). The development of empathy in twins. *Developmental Psychology, 28*, 1038–1047.

Zaitchik, D. (1990). When representations conflict with reality: The preschoolers' problem with false beliefs and "false" photographs. *Cognition, 35*, 41–68.

Zajonc, R.B. (1965). Social facilitation. *Science, 149*, 269–274.

Zajonc, R.B. (1980). Feeling and thinking: Preferences need no inferences. *American Psychologist, 35*, 151–175.

Zajonc, R.B. (1984). On the primacy of affect. *American Psychologist, 39*, 117–123.

Zanna, M.P., & Cooper, J. (1974). Dissonance and the pill: An attribution approach to studying the arousal properties of dissonance. *Journal of Personality and Social Psychology, 29*, 703–709.

Zarbatany, L., Hartmann, D.P., & Gelfand, D.M. (1985). Why does children's generosity increase with age: Susceptibility to experimenter influence or altruism? *Child Development, 56*, 746–756.

Zbrodoff, N.J. (1995). Why is 9 + 7 harder than 2 + 3? Strength and interference as explanations of the problem-size effect. *Memory and Cognition, 23*, 689–700.

Zeichner, A., Pihl, R.O., Niaura, R., & Zacchia, C. (1982). Attentional processes in alcohol-mediated aggression. *Journal of Studies on Alcohol, 43*, 714–724.

Zeier, H., Brauchli, P., & Joller-Jemelka, H.I. (1996). Effects of work demands on immunoglobin A and cortisol in air-traffic controllers. *Biological Psychology, 42*, 413–423.

Zeki, S. (1992). The visual image in mind and brain. *Scientific American, 267*, 43–50.

Zeki, S. (1993). *A vision of the brain*. Oxford, UK: Blackwell.

Zhang, D. (1995). Depression and culture—A Chinese perspective. *Canadian Journal of Counselling, 29*, 227–233.

Zihl, J., von Cramon, D., & Mai, N. (1983). Selective disturbance of movement vision after bilateral brain damage. *Brain, 106*, 313–340.

Zihl, J., von Cramon, D., Mai, N., & Schmid, C. (1991). Disturbance of movement vision after bilateral posterior brain damage: Further evidence and follow up observations. *Brain, 114*, 2235–2252.

Zillmann, D. (1988). Cognition–excitation interdependencies in aggressive behaviour. *Aggressive Behavior, 14*, 51–64.

Zillmann, D., & Bryant, J. (1984). Effects of massive exposure to pornography. In N.M. Malamuth & E. Donnerstein (Eds.), *Pornography and sexual aggression* (pp. 115–138). New York: Academic Press.

Zillmann, D., Johnson, R.C., & Day, K.D. (1974). Attribution of apparent arousal and proficiency of recovery from sympathetic activation affecting excitation transfer to aggressive behaviour. *Journal of Experimental Social Psychology, 10*, 503–515.

Zimbardo, P. (1969). The human choice: Individuation, reason, and order versus deindividuation, impulse, and chaos. In W.J. Arnold & D. Levine (Eds.), *Nebraska Symposium on Motivation, 17*. Lincoln, NE: University of Nebraska Press.

Zimbardo, P. (1970). The human choice: Individuation, reason, and order versus deindividuation, impulse, and chaos. In W.J. Arnold & D. Levine (Eds.), *Nebraska Symposium on Motivation, 17* (pp. 237–307). Lincoln, NE: University of Nebraska Press.

Zimbardo, P., McDermott, M., Jansz, J., & Metaal, N. (1995). *Psychology: A European text*. London: HarperCollins.

Zuber, J.A, Crott, H.W., & Werner, H. (1992). Choice shift and group polarization: An analysis of the status of arguments and social decision schemes. *Journal of Personality and Social Psychology, 62*, 50–61.

Zubin, J., Eron, L.D., & Shumer, F. (1965). *An experimental approach to projective techniques*. New York: Wiley.

Zuckerman, M. (1989). Personality in the third dimension: A psychobiological approach. *Personality and Individual Differences, 10*, 391–418.

Zwaan, R.A. (1994). Effects of genre expectations on text comprehension. *Journal of Experimental Psychology: Learning, Memory and Cognition, 20*, 920–933.

Zwaan, R.A., Langston, M.C., & Graesser, A.C. (1995a). The construction of situation models in narrative comprehension: An event-indexing model. *Psychological Science, 6*, 292–297.

Zwaan, R.A., Magliano, J.P., & Graesser, A.C. (1995b). Dimensions of situation-model construction in narrative comprehension. *Journal of Experimental Psychology: Learning, Memory, and Cognition, 21*, 386–397.

Zwaan, R.A., & van Oostendorp, U. (1993). Do readers construct spatial representations in naturalistic story comprehension? *Discourse Processes, 16*, 125–143.

Zwitserlood, P. (1989). The locus of the effects of sentential-semantic context in spoken-word processing. *Cognition, 32*, 25–64.

# Author index

# Subject index

# Illustration credits

## Chapter 1

Page 4: popperfoto.com. Page 5 (top): popperfoto.com. Page 5 (bottom): Bettman/CORBIS. Page 6 (top): Photofusion/David Montford. Page 6 (bottom): Photofusion/Steve Eason. Page 7 (top): Bettman/CORBIS. Page 7 (bottom): CORBIS. Page 9: Science Photo Library. Page 11: Hulton-Deutsch Collection/CORBIS. Page 12: TRIP/T. Morse. Page 14 (top): Peter Johnson/CORBIS. Page 14 (bottom): Royalty-free/CORBIS. Page 17 (top): Royalty-free/CORBIS. Page 17 (bottom): Stephanie Maze/CORBIS.

## PART I

### Chapter 2

Page 28: John Bavosi/Science Photo Library. Page 30: CORBIS. Page 31: Jeanne White/Science Photo Library. Page 32 (top): Heather Angel/Natural Visions. Page 32 (bottom): A. Barrington Brown/Science Photo Library. Page 33: Bettmann/CORBIS. Page 34: Roger Harris/Science Photo Library. Page 36: From Kenrick, D.T. (2001). Evolutionary psychology, cognitive science, and dynamical systems: Building an integrative paradigm. *Current Directions in Psychological Science, 10*, 13–17. Copyright © 2001 American Psychological Association. Page 39: John Bavosi/Science Photo Library. Page 41: Mehau Kulyk/Science Photo Library. Page 51: popperfoto.com. Page 52: Chris Lisle/CORBIS. Page 53: popperfoto.com. Page 57: From Wise, R.A. (1996). Addictive drugs and brain stimulation reward. *Annual Review of Neuroscience, 19*, 319–340. With permission from the Annual Review of Neuroscience, Volume 19 ©1996 by Annual Reviews annualreviews.org.

### Chapter 3

Page 64: Tim De Waele/Isosport/CORBIS. Page 67: TRIP/J. Greenberg. Page 69: Jean-Loup Charmet/Science Photo Library. Page 71 (left): Bettmann/CORBIS. Page 71 (right): Adrian Arbib/CORBIS. Page 72: Photofusion/Mark Campbell. Page 73: Photofusion/Bob Watkins. Page 74 (top): Tim De Waele/Isosport/CORBIS. Page 74 (bottom): Science Photo Library. Page 75: Catherine Pouedras/Eurelios/Science Photo Library. Page 80: Patrik Giardino/CORBIS. Page 83: Francis Leroy, Biocosmos/Science Photo Library. Page 87: Peter Chadwick/Science Photo Library. Page 89: Bettmann/CORBIS. Page 93: Will & Deni McIntyre/CORBIS. Page 94: Bettmann/CORBIS. Page 97: Reprinted from Klein, H.J., Wesson, M.J., Hollenbeck, J.R., & Alge, B.J. (1999). Goal commitment and the goal-setting process: Conceptual clarification and empirical synthesis. *Journal of Applied Psychology, 84*, 885–896. Copyright © American Psychological Association. Page 100: James Leynse/CORBIS.

### Chapter 4

Page 102: BSIP, Laurent/LAE. HOP AMER/Science Photo Library. Page 105: George Bernard/Science Photo Library. Page 109: popperfoto.com. Page 115: Annebicque Bernard/CORBIS. Page 117: Photofusion/Gina Glover. Page 120: Bettmann/CORBIS. Page 123: Photofusion/Sarah Saunders. Page 125: Michael & Patricia Fogden/CORBIS. Page 126: Jim Wileman/Caters News Agency. Page 127: BSIP, Laurent/LAE. HOP AMER/Science Photo Library.

Page 132: Hulton-Deutsch Collection/CORBIS. Page 134 (top): Richard T. Nowitz/Science Photo Library. Page 134 (bottom): Photographed and supplied by Bipinchandra J. Mistry.

### Chapter 5

Page 142: John Springer Collection/CORBIS. Page 145: John Springer Collection/CORBIS. Page 147: Photographed by Tom Hunt, supplied by Bipinchandra J. Mistry. Page 169: Photofusion/Peter Olive. Page 173: S.H.E. Kaufman & J.R. Goleck/Science Photo Library. Page 179: Popperfoto/Reuters. Page 181: Science Photo Library. Page 182 (top): popperfoto.com. Page 182 (bottom): Photographed and supplied by Bipinchandra J. Mistry. Page 183: Royalty-free/CORBIS. Page 184: Sean Sprague/Panos Pictures.

## PART II

### Chapter 6

Page 192: TRIP/G. Howe. Page 194: Tom and Dee Ann McCarthy/CORBIS. Page 201: Photofusion/Louis Quail. Page 207 (top): Reprinted from Kahneman, D. (1973). *Attention and effort*. New Jersey: Prentice-Hall. Reprinted with permission from Pearson Education. Page 209: Reprinted from Wickens, C.D. (1984). Processing resources in attention. In R. Parasuraman and D.R. Davies (Eds.), *Varieties of attention*. New York: Academic Press. With permission from Elsevier. Page 216: TRIP/G. Howe.

### Chapter 7

Page 218: Royalty-free/CORBIS. Page 222: Wellcome Dept. of Cognitive Neurology/Science Photo Library. Page 228 (top): Reproduced from Kitayama, S., Duffy, S., Kawamura, T., & Larsen, J.T. (2003). Perceiving an object and its context in different cultures: A cultural look at new look. *Psychological Science, 14*, 201–206. Reprinted with permission from Blackwell Publishing. Page 228 (bottom): TRIP/P. Babb. Page 240: popperfoto.com. Page 242: popperfoto.com. Page 247: Photographed and supplied by Bipinchandra J. Mistry.

### Chapter 8

Page 260: Will & Deni McIntyre/Science Photo Library. Page 263: Bettmann/CORBIS. Page 265 (top): Royalty-free/CORBIS. Page 265 (bottom): Reprinted from Lovibond, P.F., & Shanks, D.R. (2002). The role of awareness in Pavlovian conditioning: Empirical evidence and theoretical implications. *Journal of Experimental Psychology: Animal Behavior Processes, 28*, 3–26. Copyright © 2002 American Psychological Association. Page 266: Archives of the History of American Psychology/University of Akron. Page 267: From Hilgard's *Introduction to Psychology* 13th ed. by Atkinson. Copyright © 2000. Reprinted with permission of Wadsworth, a division of Thomson Learning: thomsonrights.com. Page 267 (bottom): popperfoto.com. Page 268: popperfoto.com. Page 271: Will & Deni McIntyre/Science Photo Library. Page 275: Reproduced by kind permission of Professor Albert Bandura. Page 281: Royalty-free/CORBIS. Page 283: Royalty-free/CORBIS. Page 284: Jacques M. Chenet/CORBIS. Page 285: From Anderson (1983, 1993). Reprinted by permission of the author.

### Chapter 9

Page 290: Royalty-free/CORBIS. Page 292: Royalty-free/CORBIS. Page 307: Royalty-free/

CORBIS. Page 309: VinMag Archive. Page 317 (bottom): Reproduced from Ryan et al. (2000) with permission from Blackwell Publishing. Page 323: Popperfoto/ Reuters. Page 324: TRIP/S. Grant. Page 325: Adapted from E.F. Loftus and J.C. Palmer (1974). Reconstruction of automobile destruction: An example of the interaction between language and memory. *Journal of Verbal Learning and Verbal Behavior, 13*, 585–589. Page 328: TRIP/Foto Werbung.

### Chapter 10

Page 334: Jason Hawkes/CORBIS. Page 336 (top): Jason Hawkes/CORBIS. Page 336 (bottom): Royalty-free/CORBIS. Page 340 (top): Reproduced with permission from Knoblich, G., Ohlsson, S., Haider, H., & Rhenius, D. (1999). Constraint relaxation and chunk decomposition in insight problem solving. *Journal of Experimental Psychology: Learning, Memory, and Cognition, 25*, 1534–1555. Copyright © 1999 American Psychological Association. Page 345 (top): Reprinted with permission from Hoffrage, U., Lindsey, S., Hertwig, R., & Gigerenzer, G. (2000). Communicating statistical information. *Science, 290*, 2261–2262. Copyright © 2000 AAAS. Page 348: Royalty-free/CORBIS. Page 350: Reproduced with permission from Kahneman, D., & Tversky, A. (1984). Choices, values, and frames. *American Psychologist, 39*, 341–350. Copyright © 1984 American Psychological Association. Page 353: Simon Fraser/Science Photo Library. Page 365: Roger Ressmeyer/CORBIS. Page 370: George Disario/CORBIS.

### Chapter 11

Page 372: popperfoto.com. Page 374: Royalty-free/CORBIS. Page 383: Reproduced with permission from Coldheart, M., et al. (2001). DRC: A dual route cascaded model of visual word recognition and reading aloud. *Psychological Review, 108*, 204–256. © 2001 American Psychological Association. Page 395: Christie's Images/CORBIS. Page 400: popperfoto.com. Page 403: Szenes Jason/CORBIS. Page 404: Montreal Neuro. Institute/ McGill University/ CNRI/ Science Photo Library.

## PART III

### Chapter 12

Page 418: Image 100/Royalty-Free/CORBIS. Page 420: Bettman/CORBIS. Page 426 (bottom): popperfoto.com. Page 430: Photofusion/Crispin Hughes. Page 432: Adapted from A.J. Sameroff, R. Seifer, A. Baldwin, and C. Baldwin (1993). Stability of intelligence from preschool to adolescence: The influence of social and family risk factors. *Child Development, 64*, 80–97. Page 433: Popperfoto/Reuters. Page 434: Brooklyn Production/CORBIS. Page 435: Image 100/Royalty-Free/CORBIS. Page 438 (left): Bettman/CORBIS. Page 438 (centre): popperfoto.com. Page 438 (right): TRIP/Dinodia. Page 442: Laura Dwight/CORBIS.

### Chapter 13

Page 444: L. Clarke/CORBIS. Page 446: Bettman/CORBIS. Page 447: Image 100/Royalty-Free/CORBIS. Page 448: Bettman/CORBIS. Page 451 (top): Bettman/CORBIS. Page 451 (bottom): Roger Ressmeyer/CORBIS. Page 455: Photographed and supplied by Bipinchandra J. Mistry. Page 456: popperfoto.com.

## PART IV

### Chapter 14

Page 486: Laura Dwight/CORBIS. Page 489: Bettman/CORBIS. Page 490 (top): Photograph by David Linton, in *Scientific American*. Reproduced with permission. Page 490 (bottom): Reproduced with permission from Turati, C., Simion, F., Milani, I., & Umiltà, C. (2002). Newborns' preference for faces: What is crucial? *Developmental Psychology, 38*, 875–882. Page 493 (top): Reprinted with permission from Blakemore, C., & Cooper, G.F. (1970). Development of the brain depends on the visual environment. *Nature, 228*, 477–478. Copyright © 1970 Macmillan Magazines Limited. Page 493 (bottom): Reproduced from Spelke, E.S., Breinlinger, K., Jacobson, K., & Phillips, A. (1993). Gestalt relations and object perception: A developmental study. *Vision Research, 22*, 531–544. With permission from Elsevier. Page 497: popperfoto.com. Page 498: Laura Dwight/CORBIS. Page 501: Photos by C. Trevarthen, reproduced with permission. From Trevarthen, C. (1980). Development of interpersonal cooperative understanding in infants. In D. Olson (Ed.), *The social foundations of language and thought: Essays in honor of J.S. Bruner*. New York: W.W. Norton. Page 512: Reproduced with permission from Savage-Rumbaugh, E.S., & Lewin, R. (1994). *Kanzi: At the brink of the human mind*. New York: Wiley. Copyright © 1994, reprinted by permission of John Wiley and Sons, Inc. Page 515: movie.it. Page 517: From Selfe, L. (1977). An autistic child with exceptional drawing ability. In G.E. Butterworth (Ed.), *The child's representation of the world*. New York: Plenum Press. Reproduced with permission from Kluwer Academic Publishers. Page 518: Lupe Cunha Photographer and Picture Library.

### Chapter 15

Page 520: Photofusion/Bob Watkins. Page 522 (bottom): popperfoto.com. Page 523 (top): Image 100/Royalty-free/CORBIS. Page 523 (bottom): Photos by Peter Willatts. Reproduced with permission. Page 535 (top): Photofusion/Christa Stadtler. Page 537: popperfoto.com. Page 538: Photofusion/Bob Watkins. Page 539: Lupe Cunha Photographer and Picture Library. Page 540: Photofusion/Ewa Ohlsson. Page 543: Reprinted from Siegler, R.S. (1976). Three aspects of cognitive development. *Cognitive Psychology, 8*, 481–520. With permission from Elsevier.

### Chapter 16

Page 548: popperfoto.com. Page 550: Photos by Donna Bierschwale, courtesy of the University of Southwestern Louisiana. Reproduced with permission. Page 552: Reproduced from Hart, D., Fegley, S., Chan, Y.H., Mulvey, D., & Fischer, L. (1993). Judgements about personal identity in childhood and adolescence. *Social Development, 2*, 66–81. With permission from Blackwell Publishing. Page 557: popperfoto.com. Page 558 (left): Photofusion/Helen Stone. Page 558 (right): Photofusion/David Montford. Page 563: TRIP/H. Rogers. Page 564: Photofusion/Crispin Hughes. Page 566: TRIP/H. Rogers. Page 568: Photofusion/Gina Glover. Page 569: CRDPHOTO/CORBIS. Page 572 (top): Nick Kelsh/CORBIS. Page 572 (bottom): Patrik Giardino/CORBIS. Page 573: movie.it. Page 575 (top): TRIP/H. Rogers. Page 575 (bottom): Image 100/Royalty-Free/CORBIS. Page 576: Reproduced by kind permission of Professor Albert Bandura. Page 578: Left Lane Productions/CORBIS.

### Chapter 17

Page 592: Jose Luis Pelaez, Inc./CORBIS. Page 595 (top): Reproduced with kind permission of Harlow Primate Laboratory, University of Wisconsin. Page 595 (bottom): Science Photo Library. Page 600 (top): Photograph by Martin Argles. Copyright © The Guardian. Page 600 (bottom): Royalty-Free/CORBIS. Page 604 (top): Popperfoto/Reuters. Page 604 (bottom): Peter Turnley/CORBIS. Page 608: Bob Krist/CORBIS. Page 609: Christa Stadtler/Photofusion. Page 610: Heldur Netocny/Panos Pictures. Page 612: Jose Luis Pelaez, Inc./CORBIS. Page 615: popperfoto.com. Page 620: Gaetano/CORBIS. Page 623: Gaetano/CORBIS.

## PART V

### Chapter 18

Page 632: Gisele Wulfsohn/Panos Pictures. Page 634: TRIP/H. Rogers. Page 636: Royalty-free/CORBIS. Page 637: Tom Grill/CORBIS. Page 638: Photofusion. Page 640: Brooklyn Production/CORBIS. Page 648: movie.it. Page 659: Orban Thierry/Corbis Sygma. Page 663 (top): Vince Streano/CORBIS. Page 663 (bottom): William Gottlieb/CORBIS.

### Chapter 19

Page 666: National Library of Medicine/Science Photo Library. Page 668: TRIP/H. Rogers. Page 672: Photofusion/Vicky White. Page 673: popperfoto.com. Page 676: popperfoto.com. Page 679: Photographed by Tom Hunt, supplied by Bipinchandra J. Mistry. Page 686 (top): Reproduced with permission from Cohen, D., Nisbett, R.E., Bowdle, B.F., & Schwarz, N. (1996). Insult, aggression, and the southern culture of honour: An "experimental ethnography". *Journal of Personality and Social Psychology, 70*, 945–960. Page 686 (bottom): With permission, from the *Annual Review of Psychology*, Volume 53 © 2002 by Annual Reviews annualreviews.org. Page 688: National Library of Medicine/Science Photo Library. Page 690: TRIP/S. Grant. Page 691 (top left): popperfoto.com. Page 691 (top right): Photofusion/David Montford. Page 691 (bottom left): popperfoto.com. Page 691 (bottom right): Photofusion/Janis Austin. Page 692: TRIP/M. Clement. Page 693: popperfoto.com. Page 695: TRIP/G. Kufner. Page 696: popperfoto.com. Page 700: Photofusion/Pete Jones. Page 702: TRIP/Picturesque Inc. Page 704: Damian Lovegrove/Science Photo Library. Page 715: Photofusion/Sarah Wyld.

### Chapter 20

Page 718: popperfoto.com. Page 721: From the film Obedience. Copyright © 1965 by Stanley Milgram and distributed by Penn State Media Sales. Permission granted by Alexandra Milgram. Page 723 (left): popperfoto.com. Page 723 (right): Popperfoto/Reuters. Page 724: Popperfoto/Reuters. Page 727: TRIP/Chris Parker. Page 728 (bottom): Reproduced with permission from Kim, H., & Markus, H.R. (1999). Deviance or uniqueness, harmony or conformity? A cultural analysis. *Journal of Personality and Social Psychology, 77*, 785–800. Page 729: Hulton Getty. Page 731: popperfoto.com. Page 733: Daniel Lainé/CORBIS. Page 738: Reproduced with permission from Latané, B., Williams, K.D., & Harkins, S.G. (1979). Many hands make light the work: The causes and consequences of social loafing. *Journal of Personality and Social Psychology, 37*, 822–832. Page 739: popperfoto.com. Page 740: Photofusion/Crispin Hughes. Page 746 (top): Photofusion/Steve Eason. Page 746

(middle): Popperfoto/Reuters. Page 746 (bottom): TRIP/S. Harris. Page 754: popperfoto.com. Page 755: popperfoto.com. Page 756 (left): TRIP/S.Grant. Page 756 (right): popperfoto.com. Page 758: TRIP. Page 760: popperfoto.com.

### Chapter 21

Page 762: Popperfoto/Reuters. Page 764: Mark Cator/Impact. Page 766: popperfoto.com. Page 769 (top): TRIP/H. Rogers. Page 769 (left): Bruce Parton/Panos Pictures. Page 769 (second from left): Photofusion/Bonaventura. Page 769 (second from right): Börje Tobiasson/Panos Pictures. Page 769 (right): Sean Sprague/Panos Pictures. Page 771 (top): TRIP/M. Bourdillon. Page 771 (bottom): Adapted with permission from Sinclair, L., & Kunda, Z. (1999). Reactions to a black professional: Motivated inhibition and activation of conflicting stereotypes. *Journal of Personality and Social Psychology, 77*, 885–904. Page 774: popperfoto.com. Page 775: Photofusion/John Southworth. Page 776 (top): Reproduced with permission from Kunda, Z., & Oleson, K.C. (1995). Maintaining stereotypes in the face of disconfirmation: Constructing grounds for subtyping deviants. *Journal of Personality and Social Psychology, 68*, 565–579. Page 776 (bottom): popperfoto.com. Page 777: popperfoto.com. Page 778: popperfoto.com. Page 779: popperfoto.com. Page 781: Popperfoto/Reuters. Page 784: Photofusion/Emily Barney.

## PART VI

Page 792: Science Photo Library

### Chapter 22

Page 797: Popperfoto/Reuters. Page 798: Photofusion/Mark Campbell. Page 803: Photofusion/Louis Quail. Page 807: Dr Monty Buchsbaum, Peter Arnold Inc/Science Photo Library. Page 809: Archives of the History of American Psychology/The University of Akron. Reproduced with permission. Page 810: Photofusion/Bob Watkins. Page 811: Archives of the History of American Psychology/The University of Akron. Reproduced with permission. Page 812: Reproduced with permission of Benjamin Harris, University of New Hampshire. Page 814: popperfoto.com. Page 815: John Greim/Science Photo Library. Page 821 (top): popperfoto.com. Page 821 (bottom): Photofusion/Liza Hamlyn. Page 822: Photofusion/Linda Sole. Page 823: Popperfoto/Reuters. Page 831: popperfoto.com. Page 832: Photofusion/Lisa Woollett. Page 833: Adapted with permission from Lewinsohn, P.M., Joiner, T.E., & Rohde, P. (2001). Evaluation of cognitive diathesis-stress models in predicting major depressive disorder in adolescents. *Journal of Abnormal Psychology, 110*, 203–215. Page 837: Popperfoto/Reuters. Page 841: Sally and Richard Greenhill. Page 845 (top left): popperfoto.com. Page 845 (top centre): popperfoto.com. Page 845 (top right): Popperfoto/Reuters. Page 845 (bottom): TRIP/J. Highet.

### Chapter 23

Page 854: National Library of Medicine/Science Photo Library. Page 856: movie.it. Page 857: National Library of Medicine/Science Photo Library. Page 858: Science Photo Library. Page 861: BSIP Laurent/Pioffet/Science Photo Library. Page 862 (top): BSIP Laurent/Pioffet/Science Photo Library. Page 862 (bottom): popperfoto.com. Page 864: BSIP Laurent/Pioffet/Science Photo Library. Page 867: TRIP/T. Long. Page 869: TRIP/S. Grant. Page 871: Photofusion/Bob Watkins. Page 877: BSIP Laurent/Pioffet/Science Photo Library. Page 884: Photofusion/Helen Stone.